HANDBOOK OF PATTERN RECOGNITION & COMPUTER VISION

HANDBOOK OF PATTERN RECOGNITION & COMPUTER VISION

edited by

C H Chen
Electrical and Computer Engineering Department,
University of Massachusetts Dartmouth, N. Dartmouth, MA, USA

L F Pau
Digital Equipment Corporation, Sophia Antipolis, Valbonne, France

P S P Wang
College of Computer Science, Northeastern University, Boston, MA, USA

World Scientific
Singapore • New Jersey • London • Hong Kong

Published by

World Scientific Publishing Co. Pte. Ltd.

P O Box 128, Farrer Road, Singapore 9128

USA office: Suite 1B, 1060 Main Street, River Edge, NJ 07661

UK office: 57 Shelton Street, Covent Garden, London WC2H 9HE

First published 1993
First reprint 1995

HANDBOOK OF PATTERN RECOGNITION AND COMPUTER VISION

ISBN 981-02-1136-8
ISBN 981-02-2276-9 (pbk)

Printed in Singapore by Uto-Print

*Dedicated to the memory of
Professor King Sun Fu*

PREFACE

The area of pattern recognition and computer vision, after over 35 years of continued development, has now reached its maturity. The theories, techniques and algorithms are mostly well developed. There are a number of applications which are still being explored. New approaches motivated by applications and new computer architectures available are still being studied. Also the recently renewed and intensive efforts on neural networks have had great and positive impact on pattern recognition and computer vision development. Pattern recognition and computer vision will definitely play a very major role in advanced automation as we enter the 21st century.

Amid all of these activities now going on, this new ***Handbook of Pattern Recognition and Computer Vision*** is much needed to cover what has been well developed in theory, techniques and algorithms and the major applications of pattern recognition and computer vision as well as the new hardware/architecture aspects of computer vision and the related development in pattern recognition. The previous *Handbook of Pattern Recognition and Image Processing*, edited by T. Y. Young and the late K. S. Fu (Academic Press, 1986) was well received. The progress in pattern recognition and computer vision has been particularly significant in the recent past. We believe this new handbook that reflects more recent developments especially in computer vision will serve well the increasingly larger community of readers in the area. As students and friends of Prof. Fu, we remember well his vigorous efforts to broaden the frontiers of pattern recognition and computer vision in both theories and applications, to build it as an interdisciplinary area, and to lay down the foundation of intelligent and automated systems based on pattern recognition and computer vision. The book, in keeping up with his vision for the area, provides an extensive coverage of major research progress since the publication of Young and Fu's book.

The book is organized into five parts. Part 1 presents a thorough coverage of the basic methods in pattern recognition including clustering techniques, statistical pattern recognition, neural network computing, feature selection, and syntactic, structural and grammatical pattern recognition. Part 2 presents comprehensively the basic methods in computer vision including texture image analysis and model based segmentation, color and geometrical tools, 3-D motion analysis, mathematical morphology, and parallel thinning algorithms. Part 3 presents several major pattern recognition applications in nondestructive evaluation, geophysical signal interpretation, economics and business, underwater signals, character recognition and document understanding, biomedical image recognition and medical image understanding. Part 4 focuses on unique applications in inspection and robotics with topics on computer vision in the food processing industry, context modeling and position estimation for robots, and related issues. Part 5, on the other hand, examines the broader system aspects, including designing computer vision systems, optical pattern recognition, spatial knowledge representation, neural network architecture for image segmentation, architectures for computer vision and image information systems. More than 85 per cent of the chapters are original and unpublished work while the remaining reprint chapters provide complementary coverage.

There is no doubt that a single volume handbook like this cannot examine every aspect of pattern recognition and computer vision, nor can it present the contributions of all leading researchers. However, we believe the book has captured both the scope and depth of progress in this highly dynamic and multidisciplinary area. In preparing the book, we are most fortunate to bring together all contributors who are among the leaders in the area. We would like to take this opportunity to express our deep gratitude to their unselfish and timely efforts to share their expertise with the readers. We also like to thank Dr. K. K. Phua and Ms. Jennifer Gan of World Scientific Publishing for their help and encouragement throughout the preparation of this volume.

C. H. Chen
L. F. Pau
P. S. P. Wang

September 1992

CONTENTS

PART 3. RECOGNITION APPLICATIONS

PART 4. INSPECTION AND ROBOTICS APPLICATIONS

PART 5. ARCHITECTURES AND TECHNOLOGY

PART 1

BASIC METHODS IN PATTERN RECOGNITION

Handbook of Pattern Recognition and Computer Vision, pp. 3–32
Eds. C. H. Chen, L. F. Pau and P. S. P. Wang
© 1993 World Scientific Publishing Company

CHAPTER 1.1

CLUSTER ANALYSIS AND RELATED ISSUES

RICHARD C. DUBES

Department of Computer Science, Michigan State University,
East Lansing, MI 48824-1027, USA
Internet:dubes@cps.msu.edu

This chapter explains how cluster analysis organizes information in applications such as Computer Vision and Pattern Recognition. Information is represented as points in multidimensional feature spaces where each coordinate represents a measurement. Some tools from exploratory data analysis are discussed, with an emphasis on linear projections derived from the covariance matrix. Two types of clustering are reviewed — hierarchical and partitional. Hierarchical clustering leads to nested partitions of the data. SAHN algorithms for hierarchical clustering are defined and some of the common characteristics are explained. Partitional clustering arranges data in separate clusters, as with the K-Means algorithm. The chapter ends with a discussion of validation that centers on external and internal tests of validity and tests for the number of clusters. A bibliography is provided for further reading.

Keywords: Proximity, exploratory data analysis, projection, hierarchies, dendrograms, K-means, cluster validity, algorithms.

1. Introduction

Organizing information is an essential part of any learning task. Cluster analysis is the formal study of methods and algorithms for objectively organizing numerical data. One finds cluster analysis in the literature of almost all disciplines, including engineering, statistics, psychology, sociology, biology, astronomy, business, medicine, archeology, psychiatry, geography, anthropology, economics, and computer science, to name a few. No single definition of "cluster" is universally accepted. Cluster analysis includes the process of "looking" at data, known as *exploratory data analysis*, which is a tool for igniting creativity and suggesting alternative models for the data. This chapter views cluster analysis as the initial step in organizing numerical data so as to abstract the essence of the data and describe the data as simply as possible. The discussion is informal and omits mathematical proofs. Computational issues are mentioned only briefly.

Cluster analysis is sometimes called "unsupervised learning" because only actual observations affect the data organization. By contrast, pattern recognition uses *a priori* labels to "learn" the parameters of models for the categories, or pattern classes, present in the data. A pattern recognition algorithm seeks to define a good

3

decision rule for labeling patterns of unknown origin, based on information gleaned from labeled patterns. The algorithms of cluster analysis make no decisions but fit various structures, such as partitions and hierarchies, to the data. Although the literature in several fields of application carry papers on clustering, the only journal exclusively devoted to the methodology of clustering is the *Journal of Classification*, published by the Classification Society of North America since 1984. Some general books on the topic are [1,2,3,4,5].

One application, image segmentation, will help explain the context of this chapter. Each pixel, or each small sub-image, is characterized by a set of numbers [6]. Candidates for the numbers are co-occurrence features, gray-level intensities, measures of fractal dimension, estimates of Markov random field-parameters, and other indices popular in the computer vision community. Cluster analysis labels each pixel or sub-image so that regions from the same underlying class, such as land-use category in remote sensing, have the same label and regions from different classes have different labels. The organization is done in the feature space, in which each axis represents one of the measurements. One must develop faith in the clustering algorithm and must formally validate the results. The cluster labels are then transferred to the image for interpretation.

This chapter will concentrate on the process of assigning the cluster labels, and not on the choice of features. Figure 1 is an overview of the most important aspects of a typical cluster analysis. Once data have been gathered and some type of exploratory data analysis has been applied to evaluate the data representation, one can apply *clustering tendency* algorithms to ensure that the data are not random. This avoids the embarrassment and futility of imposing sophisticated procedures for analyzing data that contain no clusters [4].

This chapter covers two types of clustering: hierarchical clustering creates a complete hierarchy, or nested sequence of partitions; partitional clustering creates one partition of the data. Omitted due to lack of space are treatments of fuzzy clustering [7,8], conceptual clustering [9,10], and any mention of neural nets [11]. The validation step, in which one applies statistical tests to ensure that the structure recovered from the clustering algorithm is "real" in some sense, is the most difficult step of the entire process. The interpretation of the results requires experience and interaction with the expert in the field of application. The entire process, or any part of it, may need to be repeated until one is satisfied with the result. All this effort should reveal the underlying structure of the data so that sharper and more definitive studies can be planned.

2. Data

The procedures and algorithms of cluster analysis are geared towards the type and scale of the data, so this section begins by reviewing some basic definitions about data in Section 2.1 and about normalization in Section 2.2. The most important

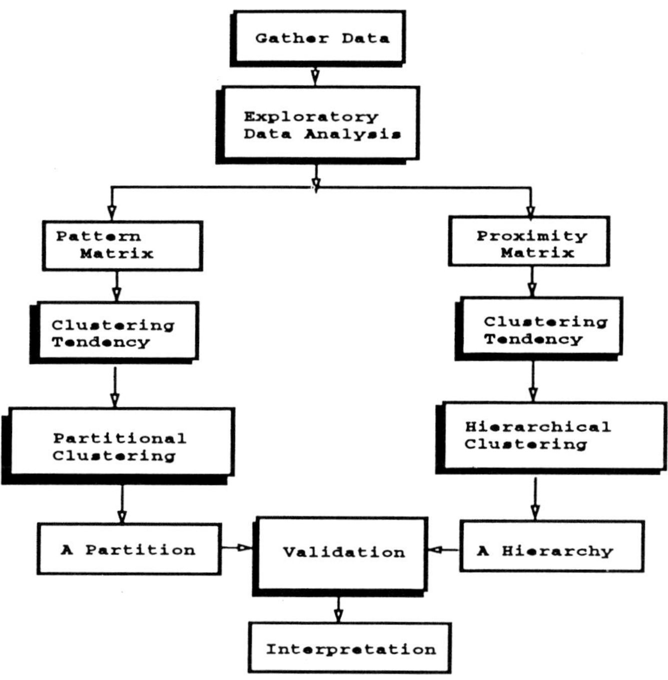

Fig. 1. Methodology of cluster analysis.

characteristic of a set of data is its dimensionality, which is briefly explained in Section 2.3.

2.1. *Representing Numerical Information*

2.1.1. *Scale and type*

Data occur in several types and scales. The simplest unit of data is a number. Vectors and matrices are built from numbers, but all numbers should be on the same scale and have the same type. The *scale* of a number refers to its relative significance. Usually recognized are *nominal, ordinal, interval,* and *ratio* scales. A number on a nominal scale is simply a numerical tag, such as "1" for "Ford", "2" for "Chevy", and "3" for "Toyota". Numbers on an ordinal scale have significance only in their relative positions. Numbers on nominal and ordinal scales are sometimes called *qualitative,* whereas numbers on the interval and ratio scales are called *quantitative.* The gap between numbers has significance when the numbers are on an interval scale. If, for example, a person were asked to state his preference for soda on a scale of "1" to "10" with "10" being most preferred, then responses 1,5,9 and 1,2,9 would have different meanings on an interval scale, but not on an ordinal scale.

The most important data scale in engineering work is the *ratio* scale, which is the interval scale with a natural zero. Data from sensors, and numbers which can be placed on the real line are examples. For example, distance is measured on a ratio scale. Doubling the distance between two towns means using twice as much gas to get between them, whatever the unit of distance. Temperature, on the other hand, is an interval measurement because its significance depends on the unit. Measuring in degrees Kelvin is a ratio-scale measurement, while temperature in degrees Celsius is an interval-scale measurement.

Data *type* refers to degree of quantization. The three types recognized here are *binary*, or two-valued, *discrete*, or multi-valued, and *continuous*, or data taken from the mathematical real line. Binary data, also called dichotomous data, are for situations where the possible responses are ("yes", "no"), or ("on", "off"). A discrete type has a small number of values, where "small" depends on the situation. Since instruments have finite resolution, all data measured in the real, as opposed to the mathematical, world are discrete. Calculus ordinarily requires that data be continuous. Thus, we often assume data are continuous and ignore the unpleasant reality.

2.1.2. *Patterns and proximity*

Whatever the scale and type, data are collected in one of two basic formats, called a *pattern matrix* and a *proximity matrix*. A pattern matrix represents each object under examination as a set of measurements. Each measurement is called a *feature* and a *pattern* is a set of feature values measured on an object. The set of d measurements form the feature space, each feature corresponding to one orthogonal axis. A pattern matrix is thus an $n \times d$ matrix, where n is the number of patterns and d is the number of features. The notation for the jth feature of pattern i will be x_{ij} and the ith pattern itself will be denoted by the column vector $\mathbf{x}_i$. Letting superscript T denote matrix transpose,

$$\mathbf{x}_i = [x_{i1}\, x_{i2} \cdots x_{id}]^T \, .$$

We require $n \gg d$ and think of the patterns as a swarm of n points floating in a d-dimensional space. The transpose of the $n \times d$ pattern matrix $\mathbf{X}$ is written as:

$$\mathbf{X}^T = [\mathbf{x}_1\, \mathbf{x}_2 \cdots \mathbf{x}_n] \, .$$

A pattern matrix, called the *speaker data*, that consists of 40 rows (patterns) and 5 columns (features) will be used to demonstrate several procedures. A listing is given in Table 1. Each pattern represents a spoken phrase and each feature represents a measurement taken on the spectrum derived from the phrase. There are eight categories, one for each person involved in the study. Eight male speakers spoke the same phrase five times; patterns 1–5 are from speaker number 1, patterns 6–10 from speaker number 2, and so forth. The category labels are on a nominal scale

Table 1. Speaker data.

Category	Pattern	Features				
1	1	107.0000	18.0000	87.0000	94.6500	89.0000
1	2	105.5000	15.0000	90.0000	96.4750	91.0000
1	3	106.5000	13.0000	88.0000	94.9500	93.0000
1	4	102.5000	13.0000	85.0000	91.1250	90.0000
1	5	106.0000	17.0000	85.0000	93.1250	87.0000
2	6	118.0000	17.0000	97.0000	103.3000	100.0000
2	7	116.5000	13.0000	97.0000	103.3500	103.0000
2	8	123.0000	16.0000	100.0000	105.7250	104.0000
2	9	119.0000	15.0000	98.0000	103.5000	104.0000
2	10	122.0000	16.0000	101.0000	105.1750	104.0000
3	11	103.5000	10.0000	78.0000	83.9000	81.0000
3	12	104.0000	12.0000	81.0000	86.9750	81.0000
3	13	104.5000	10.0000	77.0000	84.5250	91.0000
3	14	104.5000	11.0000	78.0000	86.3000	83.0000
3	15	100.0000	11.0000	79.0000	87.0000	84.0000
4	16	109.0000	16.0000	82.0000	91.6000	87.0000
4	17	113.0000	22.0000	85.0000	94.0250	90.0000
4	18	111.0000	16.0000	85.0000	92.6750	90.0000
4	19	113.0000	15.0000	78.0000	94.3250	100.0000
4	20	112.0000	20.0000	84.0000	93.5500	90.0000
5	21	122.5000	30.0000	87.0000	89.6500	93.0000
5	22	119.0000	28.0000	81.0000	87.0750	90.0000
5	23	122.5000	24.0000	87.0000	92.1750	97.0000
5	24	125.5000	32.0000	87.0000	94.3000	90.0000
5	25	119.0000	23.0000	83.0000	89.7000	96.0000
6	26	95.5000	23.0000	72.0000	78.9000	74.0000
6	27	94.0000	15.0000	76.0000	79.0250	78.0000
6	28	103.0000	24.0000	77.0000	82.7500	78.0000
6	29	106.5000	28.0000	76.0000	84.2750	78.0000
6	30	102.5000	19.0000	75.0000	79.9750	84.0000
7	31	111.0000	25.0000	77.0000	86.7750	82.0000
7	32	110.0000	26.0000	78.0000	89.7500	78.0000
7	33	109.0000	22.0000	78.0000	87.5250	84.0000
7	34	109.0000	23.0000	78.0000	89.3250	83.0000
7	35	110.5000	22.0000	81.0000	88.7750	82.0000
8	36	107.0000	16.0000	79.0000	87.3250	81.0000
8	37	107.0000	16.0000	77.0000	86.3500	81.0000
8	38	105.0000	20.0000	78.0000	87.6500	80.0000
8	39	111.0000	18.0000	80.0000	87.5000	84.0000
8	40	110.0000	15.0000	85.0000	86.2000	88.0000

while the features are on a ratio scale since all have natural zeros. The features are assumed to be continuous.

A *proximity matrix* is a square, symmetric matrix. Its rows and columns both correspond to patterns, or to features. The (i, j) entry contains an index of proximity that denotes the degree of closeness or alikeness between the objects corresponding to row i and column j. If the proximity matrix is a *dissimilarity* matrix, then the larger the entry (i, j), the less items i and j resemble one another, as when Euclidean distance measures the proximity between two patterns. In a *similarity* matrix, a large value indicates a close resemblance between the two objects, as when a correlation coefficient measures the proximity between two features.

2.1.3. *Indices of proximity*

Clustering algorithms require that an index of proximity be established between all pairs of items. Anderberg [1] defines several such measures of proximity. This chapter covers only the case when proximities are computed from a pattern matrix. An index of dissimilarity $d(q, r)$ between patterns x_q and x_r is a real-valued function satisfying the following for all q and r.

$$d(q, r) = d(r, q) \tag{2.1}$$

$$d(q, r) \geq 0 \tag{2.2}$$

$$d(q, q) = d(r, r) = 0 \tag{2.3}$$

An index of similarity satisfies the first two conditions, but replaces the third with

$$d(q, q) \geq \max_r \{d(q, r)\} \, .$$

The most common index of dissimilarity in engineering work is the Minkowski metric (2.4).

$$d(q, r) = \left(\sum_{j=1}^{d} |x_{qj} - x_{rj}|^m \right)^{(1/m)} \tag{2.4}$$

See [12] for a full discussion of this and related indices of dissimilarity. Common parameter values are $m = 2$, or Euclidean distance, $m = 1$, or Manhattan distance, also called taxicab and city-block distance, and $m \to \infty$, or "sup" distance. The Euclidean distance must be carefully separated from the *squared* Euclidean distance. The Minkowski metric is for continuous data on a ratio scale and is itself on a ratio scale. The Minkowski metric satisfies the *triangle inequality*.

$$d(q, r) \leq d(q, s) + d(s, r) \text{ for all } (q, r, s) \tag{2.5}$$

A common index of similarity between features u and v is the sample correlation coefficient.

$$r_{uv} = \frac{\sum_{i=1}^{n} x_{iu} x_{iv} - n m_u m_v}{n s_u s_v} \tag{2.6}$$

The sample means, m_u and m_v, and the sample standard deviations, s_u and s_v, are defined in (2.7). The sample correlation coefficient indicates the degree of linear dependence between two features, with a value of 0 indicating linear independence. The absolute value measures the degree of resemblance between two features since negative and positive correlations with the same magnitude have the same interpretation.

A number of indices of proximity for binary data, such as the simple matching coefficient and the Jaccard coefficient, have been proposed [1,4] but are not discussed here.

2.2. *Normalization and Standardization*

A pattern matrix is normalized to equalize the contributions of the features to a projection or a clustering. Milligan and Cooper [13] noted that some normalizations that appeal to our intuition may affect performance in unexpected ways. In this section, a "∗" superscript will denote the raw, or un-normalized, data, as in x_{ij}^*. Throughout the remainder of the chapter, the context must make clear which normalization has been applied.

One common normalization is to move the origin of the feature space to the grand mean vector, which is the vector of sample means for the d features. The sample mean m_j, and the sample standard variance s_j^2, for feature j are:

$$m_j = \frac{1}{n} \sum_{i=1}^{n} x_{ij}^* \qquad s_j^2 = \frac{1}{n-1} \sum_{i=1}^{n} (x_{ij}^* - m_j)^2 \, . \tag{2.7}$$

The origin is shifted to the grand mean vector by defining, for all $i = 1, 2, \ldots, n$ and $j = 1, 2, \ldots, d$:

$$x_{ij} = x_{ij}^* - m_j \, . \tag{2.8}$$

This shifting of the origin does not affect Euclidean distance and merely simplifies equations. The *z-score* normalization divides each feature by its standard deviation s_j in (2.9).

$$x_{ij} = \frac{x_{ij}^* - m_j}{s_j} \, . \tag{2.9}$$

This normalization stretches or squeezes each of the coordinate axes to equalize the spreads along all axes. A third normalization, called a *range* method, reduces all features to the range [0,1] by subtracting the smallest value in each column and dividing by the range of each column.

$$x_{ij} = \frac{x_{ij}^* - \min\{x_{ij}\}}{\max\{x_{ij}\} - \min\{x_{ij}\}}$$

The min and max are taken over the jth column of the pattern matrix. Miligan and Cooper [13] found that the range normalization outperformed the z-score normalization when extracting the structure of the data.

2.3. *Dimensionality*

The dimensionality of data refers to the number of independent parameters required to describe the data. These parameters for each pattern are often taken to be the feature values on the d coordinate axes. However, data can sometimes be projected to fewer than d dimensions, as discussed in Sections 3.1 and 3.2. The number of dimensions in the target space is called the *intrinsic* dimensionality [14,15] since it represents the dimensionality suggested by the data themselves and provides a parsimonious characterization of the data. Dimensionality has taken on new importance with the emergence of fractal geometry as a cross-disciplinary field of study [16]. The true dimensionality of the data, whether fractional or integer, may become an important characteristic of the data in exploratory data analysis. The estimation of fractal dimensionality [17] is beyond the scope of this paper.

3. Exploratory Data Analysis

Cluster analysis includes a variety of heuristic procedures for getting to know data. Whereas clustering algorithms strive to be objective and quantitative, exploratory data analysis is purposefully subjective. The goal is to use whatever tools are available to look at the data, with emphasis on graphs, charts, projections, and any graphical representation that assists the visual system and nudges intuition. Everitt [18] describes several techniques that go beyond simple graphing of functions. Recent advances in graphical computer displays have made the techniques of exploratory data analysis widely available. Two that I have found useful are the **S** program [19] originally developed at AT&T and the MacSpin program for the Macintosh.[a] A few standard techniques are explained in this section to indicate the flavor of exploratory data analysis.

3.1. *Linear Projections*

Why represent d-dimensional data in two or three dimensions? One reason is to be able to see the data. A second reason is to simplify the data by eliminating redundancy and isolating the important characteristics of the data. The process of representing data in a new space is sometimes called *ordination*. No two- or three-dimensional representation can fully capture the intricacies and complexity of, say, ten-dimensional data. A linear projection does little "violence" to the data since relative distances are preserved and certain geometrical characteristics are maintained. Several schemes for representing data have been proposed [20], including discriminant analysis [4].

The transformation discussed here has been called the *principal component*, the *Karhunen-Loeve*, and, simply, the *eigenvector* transformation. It is based on the eigenvalues and eigenvectors of the $d \times d$ sample covariance matrix $\mathbf{R}$ computed

---

[a]The **S** software is available from Statistical Sciences, Inc., 1700 Westlake, Seattle, WA 98109, USA. The MacSpin program is marketed by Abacus Concepts.

from the given $n \times d$ pattern matrix, $\mathbf{X}$.

$$\mathbf{R} = \frac{1}{n-1}\mathbf{X}^T\mathbf{X} = \frac{1}{n-1}\sum_{i=1}^{n}\mathbf{x}_i\mathbf{x}_i^T \tag{3.1}$$

Equation (3.1) assumes that either (2.8) or (2.9) has been applied to the raw data. If (2.8) has been applied, $\mathbf{R}$ is a *covariance* matrix whose diagonal entries are the variances of the columns in $\mathbf{X}$. If (2.9) has been applied, $\mathbf{R}$ is a *correlation* matrix meaning that all diagonal entries are unity and off-diagonal entries are correlation coefficients between -1 and 1.

Most linear algebra texts show that the eigenvalues of $\mathbf{R}$ are solutions for the scalar λ to the determinant equation (3.2).

$$|\mathbf{R} - \lambda\mathbf{I}| = \mathbf{O} \tag{3.2}$$

Here, $\mathbf{I}$ is a unit matrix of order $d \times d$ and $\mathbf{O}$ is a vector of zeros. If $\mathbf{R}$ has full rank of d, and we denote its (necessarily real and non-negative) eigenvalues by $\lambda_1 \geq \lambda_2 \geq \cdots \geq \lambda_d$, then the eigenvectors $\mathbf{c}_1$, $\mathbf{c}_2$, $\ldots$, $\mathbf{c}_d$ are orthonormal (column) vectors satisfying, for each j from 1 to d:

$$(\mathbf{R} - \lambda_j)\mathbf{c}_j = \mathbf{O} \tag{3.3}$$
$$\mathbf{c}_j^T\mathbf{c}_k = 0 \text{ if } j \neq k \tag{3.4}$$
$$= 1 \text{ if } j = k\,. \tag{3.5}$$

Eigenvectors are not unique.

The eigenvector transformation from d to $m \leq d$ dimensions is defined by a coefficient matrix whose rows are eigenvectors corresponding to the m largest eigenvalues of $\mathbf{R}$. If $\mathbf{x}_i$ is a pattern in the original d-dimensional space, its image $\mathbf{y}_i$ is the m-vector defined in (3.6).

$$\mathbf{y}_i = \begin{bmatrix} \mathbf{c}_1^T \\ \mathbf{c}_2^T \\ \vdots \\ \mathbf{c}_m^T \end{bmatrix} \mathbf{x}_i \tag{3.6}$$

If the rank of $\mathbf{R}$ is full and $m = d$, then (3.6) rotates the coordinate axes and decorrelates the features. That is, the covariance matrix computed from the new vectors $\{\mathbf{y}_i\}$ is a diagonal matrix whose diagonal entries are the eigenvalues λ_1, λ_2, $\ldots$, λ_d. Thus, the eigenvalues of $\mathbf{R}$ can be interpreted as sample variances in the rotated space.

The d-dimensional patterns can be projected to two or three dimensions for viewing by setting m to 2 or 3 in (3.6). Why the top rows? A reasonable criterion for projecting data is square-error, meaning that the target space saves as much of the variance as possible. The total variance is the sum of the diagonal elements of $\mathbf{R}$.

$$\text{trace}(\mathbf{R}) = \sum_{j=1}^{d} r_{jj} = \sum_{j=1}^{d} \lambda_j$$

Since the eigenvalues are ordered by size, it makes sense to save eigenvectors corresponding to the largest eigenvalues. Tou and Heydorn [21] phrase this problem nicely and prove these facts.

Figure 2 shows the eigenvector transformation for the speaker data both with pattern numbers and with category labels. Some clustering of the patterns is suggested, especially in Fig. 2(b).

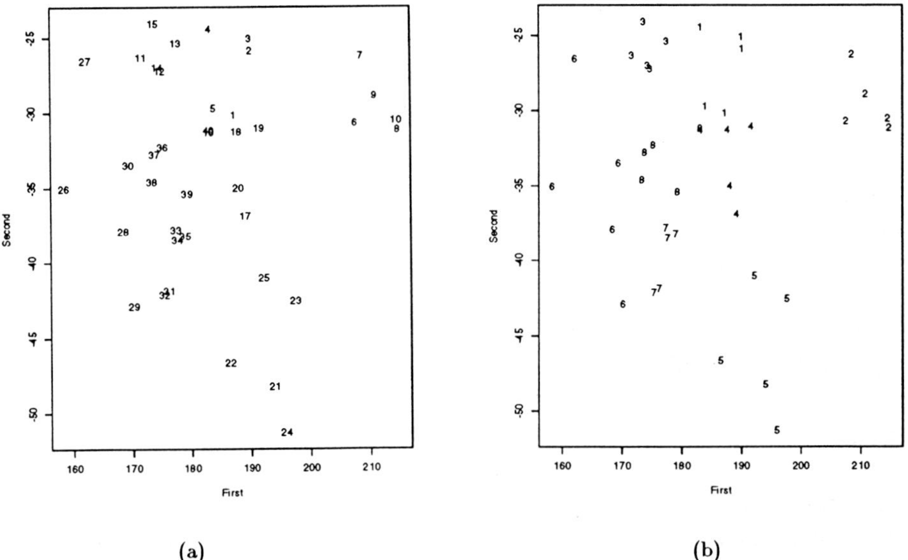

(a)   (b)

Fig. 2. Eigenvector projections of speaker data; (a) pattern labels; (b) category labels.

3.2. *Nonlinear Projections*

Nonlinear projections share the goals of linear projections but the details differ. The projection introduced by Sammon [22] illustrates these differences. Sammon's projection begins with an $n \times n$ dissimilarity matrix whose entries are Euclidean distances between all pairs of patterns in the d-dimensional feature space. A set of n points is scattered randomly in a portion of the two-dimensional target space, with each point representing one pattern. Given such a *configuration* of n points, the following *stress* criterion can be computed.

$$E = \frac{1}{\Sigma\Sigma d(q,\,r)} \Sigma\Sigma \frac{[d(q,\,r) - D(q,\,r)]^2}{d(q,\,r)} \tag{3.7}$$

Here, $d(q, r)$ is the Euclidean distance between patterns q and r in the d-dimensional feature space and $D(q, r)$ is the Euclidean distance between the points representing patterns q and r in the two-dimensional target space. The sums are over all pairs of patterns $1 \leq q \leq r \leq n$. Stress is a function of the $2n$ coordinates of the points in the target space. The idea is to move the points around so as to minimize E. The configuration at which E is minimum is taken to be the Sammon projection. A configuration for which $D(q, r) = d(q, r)$ for all q and r would be ideal, but it is seldom possible to match all d-dimensional distances in two dimensions.

The stress function resembles the criterion function in multidimensional scaling [23]. However, multidimensional scaling begins with ordinal data and Sammon's method begins with ratio data. Since E uses the difference between two distances, one must have ratio-scale dissimilarities between all pairs of patterns. The denominators normalize the stress. The term $d(r, q)$ in the sum on the right weights small distances more heavily than large ones and tends to preserve local structure. The multiplier on the left, which is fixed throughout the minimization procedure, tends to make E insensitive to changes in scale and sample size.

Several algorithms exist for minimizing functions of many variables. Sammon [22] proposed a gradient descent algorithm. Simulated annealing has also been tried [24] but the results were disappointing. Whatever the minimization technique, one encounters the usual problems of stopping at local, rather than global, minima and of dependence on the starting configuration. Any minimization should be run several times and the one achieving the smallest stress should be retained. Our implementation requires that the user supply the maximum number of iterations allowed in the gradient descent algorithm and a "magic factor", which influences the internal stopping criterion.

An advantage of a nonlinear projection over a linear projection is its greater flexibility and ability to "see" complex structures. A disadvantage is that a nonlinear method can distort the data unduly and paint a misleading picture. In addition, extra points cannot be easily located in the target space of a nonlinear projection whereas the entire feature space can be projected to two dimensions with (3.6).

Figure 3 pictures the speaker data with Sammon's projection. The gradient descent algorithm was run ten times and the best of the ten runs is exhibited. The stress values for the ten runs ranged from 0.02512 to 0.0009157. The algorithm always stopped because it had achieved a minimum, not because it had reached the maximum number of iterations. Figures 2 and 3 agree on the structure of the data and provide evidence for the conclusion that the clustering by category is real, and not an artifact of an algorithm. One can try to name the variables on the Sammon plot in Fig. 3 from characteristics of the pattern, but no conclusions about correlation between these new variables can be drawn. The last step in the Sammon projection is to apply the eigenvector rotation to decorrelate the variables.

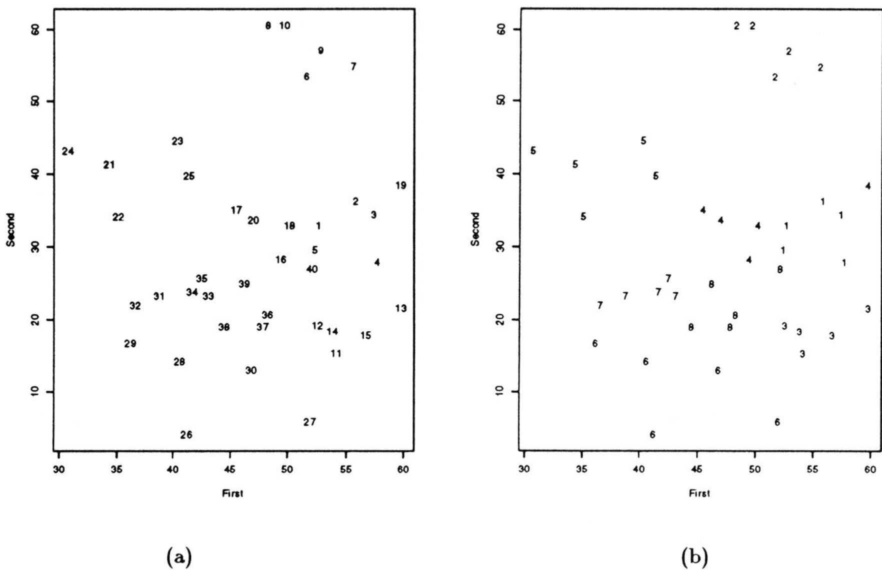

(a)   (b)

Fig. 3. Sammon projection of speaker data; (a) pattern labels; (b) category labels.

3.3. *Graphical Procedures*

Everyone has their favorite graphical representation of data. A few possibilities are mentioned in this section. Both the columns (features) and the rows (patterns) of the pattern matrix can be depicted by graphical methods. *Box* plots and *histograms* provide quick looks at the distribution of a feature. Figure 4(a) shows box plots for the first three features of the speaker data. Each box identifies the 25th and 75th percentiles of the data. The horizontal line inside the box is at the median value. The dashed vertical lines are drawn from the minimum value to the 25th percentile and from the 75th percentile to the maximum. A star is drawn to signal that an outlier has occurred according to a particular criterion. Figure 4b gives histograms for the same three features. The number of bins is about $\sqrt{n}$, or 7 in this case. The ordinate is the number of feature values in each bin. Box plots are best for quick comparisons among features. Differences in ranges and locations are obvious at a glance. The fact that feature 3 has a larger right tail than left is also obvious. Histograms provide more detailed information and exhibit the modes in multi-modal data.

Graphical representations of the patterns can also be useful. Figure 5 exhibits Chernoff faces [25] for the first 20 patterns from the speaker data. Each face depicts one row in the pattern matrix by associating one characteristic of the face with each feature. Feature 1 is proportional to the area of the face, feature 2, to the shape

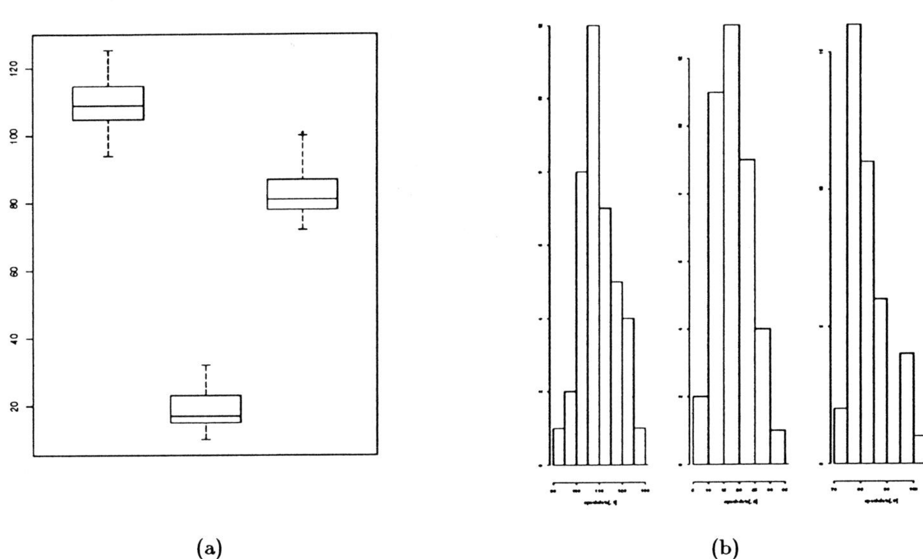

(a)   (b)

Fig. 4. Graphical views of the first three features of the speaker data. (a) Box plots; (b) histograms.

Fig. 5. Chernoff faces of the speaker data.

of the face, feature 3, to the length of the nose, feature 4, to the location of the mouth, and feature 5 is related to the curve of the smile. The faces are arranged in Fig. 5 so that each column contains faces from a different category. Associations among the patterns can be recognized by mentally clustering the faces. Outliers can sometimes be quickly identified. For example, pattern 19 in Fig. 15 might be considered different from other faces. All features were normalized to fall between 0 and 1 before the faces were drawn.

4. Hierarchical Clustering

Clustering data means grouping either patterns or features such that items in the same group are more alike than are items in different groups. The objective is to abstract the essence of the data by isolating groups, or clusters, which explain the data. A hierarchical clustering is a sequence of nested groupings. In some biological applications, the hierarchical structure itself is fitted to the data. In many engineering problems, one searches the hierarchy for a single significant grouping. This section explains the basic mathematical structure for describing hierarchical clustering and presents some standard clustering algorithms. For more complete treatments, see [1,4,2,26] and Chapter 5 of [27].

4.1. *Hierarchies and Dendrograms*

A hierarchical clustering method is a mathematical procedure for creating a sequence of nested partitions from a proximity matrix, assumed to be a dissimilarity matrix for patterns. Let $\mathcal{X}$ denote the set of n patterns. A *partition* $C = \{C_1, C_2, \ldots, C_m\}$ of $\mathcal{X}$ is a set of disjoint, non-empty subsets of $\mathcal{X}$ which, taken together, constitutes $\mathcal{X}$. That is, if $i \neq j$,

$$C_i \cap C_j = \Phi; \quad C_1 \cup C_2 \cup \cdots \cup C_m = \mathcal{X}. \tag{4.1}$$

where "$\cap$" denotes set intersection, "$\cup$" denotes set union and "Φ" denotes the empty set. Each set C_i is called a component of the partition.

A *clustering* is a partition of $\mathcal{X}$; its components are formally called *clusters*. A *hierarchical clustering* is a sequence of nested partitions starting with the trivial clustering in which each pattern is in a unique cluster and ending with the trivial clustering in which all patterns are in the same cluster. Partition $\mathcal{B}$ is nested into partition $\mathcal{C}$ if every component of $\mathcal{B}$ is a subset of a component of $\mathcal{C}$, so $\mathcal{C}$ is formed by merging components of $\mathcal{B}$.

A *dendrogram* is a binary tree that depicts a hierarchical clustering. Each node in the tree represents a cluster. Cutting the dendrogram horizontally creates a clustering. A dendrogram represents n clusterings of n patterns, including the two trivial clusterings. Figure 6 is a simple dendrogram for five patterns. The five pattern labels can be permuted in several ways without altering the information in the dendrogram. Murtagh [28] enumerated several types of dendrograms. Dendrograms can simply picture the clusterings, as in Fig. 6, or can have a scale showing the level of dissimilarity at which each clustering is formed.

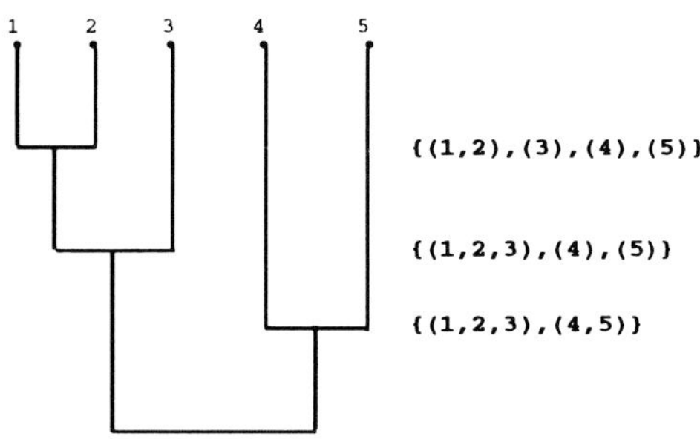

Fig. 6. Dendrogram for five patterns.

4.2. *Recovered Structure and Ultrametricity*

A hierarchical clustering method tries to fit a dendrogram to the given dissimilarity matrix. The dendrogram imposes a measure of dissimilarity called the *cophenetic* dissimilarity on the patterns as follows. Let $\{C_0, C_1, \ldots, C_{n-1}\}$ be the sequence of partitions in a dendrogram where C_0 is the trivial clustering that puts each pattern in its own cluster and C_{n-1} places all patterns in the same cluster. The clusters in the mth clustering are denoted $\{C_{m1}, C_{m2}, \cdots, C_{m(n-m)}\}$. A *level* function $L(m)$ is defined on the partitions as the dissimilarity level at which clustering m first forms. Specific level functions are defined by each clustering method. The *cophenetic dissimilarity* d_C between patterns $\mathbf{x}_q$ and $\mathbf{x}_r$ is defined in (4.2).

$$d_C(q, r) = L(k_{q,r}) \tag{4.2}$$

where

$$k_{q,r} = \min[m : (\mathbf{x}_q, \mathbf{x}_r) \in C_{mt}, \text{ some } t].$$

The cophenetic dissimilarity is a dissimilarity index in the sense of (2.1). However, it also satisfies the *ultrametric inequality.*

$$d_C(q, r) \leq \max\{d_C(q, t), d_C(t, r)\} \text{ for all } (q, r, t) \tag{4.3}$$

The nesting of partitions to form the hierarchy and the monotonicity of the level function ensure that (4.3) is satisfied. This inequality is stricter than the triangle inequality (2.5). For the distances between patterns in a feature space to satisfy the ultrametric inequality, for example, all triples of patterns must form isosceles triangles with the one side being shorter than the two sides of equal length. This demands that many ties in proximity occur at just the right places.

4.3. *Hierarchical Clustering Algorithms*

A hierarchical clustering *algorithm* is a process for constructing a sequence of partitions from a proximity matrix. A particular clustering method can be implemented by several algorithms. Some hierarchical clustering algorithms for constructing dendrograms by hand are based on graph theory [4]. This section is limited to a class of algorithms commonly known as "SAHN" (Sequential, Agglomerative, Hierarchical, Nonoverlapping) algorithms.

A SAHN algorithm begins with an $n \times n$ dissimilarity matrix $[d(q, r)]$ between patterns. All SAHN algorithms are appropriate when the dissimilarities are on a ratio scale, as with distances in a feature space. In addition to a sequence of clusterings, a SAHN algorithm creates a level function. The algorithm begins with $L(0) = 0$ and each pattern in a unique cluster. A cluster is denoted (s).

SAHN Algorithm for Hierarchical Clustering

1. Set the sequence number of the clustering: $m = 0$.
   Repeat the following steps until $m = n$.
2. Find the pair of clusters $[(s), (t)]$ for which

$$d[(s), (t)] = \min\{d[(q), (r)]\} \tag{4.4}$$

   where the minimum is taken over all pairs of clusters.
3. Increment m by 1. Merge clusters (s) and (t) into a single cluster to define clustering m. Define the level of this clustering as:

$$L(m) = d[(s), (t)]. \tag{4.5}$$

4. Update the dissimilarity matrix by deleting the rows and columns corresponding to clusters (s) and (t) and adding a row and column for the newly formed cluster (s, t). The dissimilarity between this new cluster and an existing cluster, cluster (k), depends on the clustering method being employed and is given by (4.6).

$$d[(k), (s, t)] = \alpha_s d[(k), (s)] + \alpha_t d[(k), (t)] + \beta d[(k), (s)] + \gamma \, | \, d[(k), (s)]$$

$$-d[(k), (t)]| \tag{4.6}$$

where the coefficients are given in Fig. 7 and n_s refers to the number of patterns in cluster (s).

4.4. *Characteristics of Hierarchies and Algorithms*

Day [29] explains the computational complexities of hierarchical and partitional clustering algorithms. Some comments on practical aspects of hierarchical clustering are given below without justification. The primary application of hierarchical clustering in engineering work is to create a representative sequence of clusterings while searching for a single "good" clustering. It is seldom the case that data are hierarchically related on more than a few levels.

Clustering method	α_s	α_t	β	γ
Single-link	$1/2$	$1/2$	0	$-1/2$
Complete-link	$1/2$	$1/2$	0	$1/2$
UPGMA	$\dfrac{n_s}{n_s + n_t}$	$\dfrac{n_s}{n_s + n_t}$	0	0
WPGMA	$1/2$	$1/2$	0	0
UPGMC	$\dfrac{n_s}{n_s + n_t}$	$\dfrac{n_s}{n_s + n_t}$	$\dfrac{-n_s n_t}{(n_s + n_t)^2}$	0
WPGMC	$1/2$	$1/2$	$-1/4$	0
Ward's	$\dfrac{n_s + n_k}{n_s + n_t + n_k}$	$\dfrac{n_t + n_k}{n_s + n_t + n_k}$	$\dfrac{-n_k}{n_s + n_t + n_k}$	0
Flexible	α	α	$1 - 2\alpha$	0

Fig. 7. Coefficients for SAHN hierarchical clustering algorithms.

The single-link method is also called the *connectedness* method, the *minimum* method, and the *nearest neighbor* method. The updating equation uses the minimum of the two dissimilarities. Single-link clusters can be "straggly" since the smallest of the pairwise dissimilarities between two clusters determines when the clusters join. Other algorithms for the single-link method involve the minimum spanning tree [30] and graph theory [31]. By contrast, the complete-link method is also called the *completeness* method and the *maximum* method. The updating equation translates into taking the maximum of the dissimilarities between pairs of patterns in different clusters. Complete-link clusters often form in small clumps because the largest of the pairwise distances determines when two clusters are merged. Figure 8 shows the complete-link dendrogram for the speaker data.

The visual impact of the dendrograms is obvious. It should also be clear why dendrograms are not very useful for more than 200 patterns. The scale on the left is on the same scale as the dissimilarity matrix. The patterns were normalized by (2.9). Some of the clusters in Fig. 8 can be identified in Figs. 2 and 3. With the single-link and complete-link methods, hierarchies merge only at dissimilarities that occur in the given dissimilarity matrix. Other clustering methods do not have this property.

Ward's method [32] is also called the *minimum square error* method because it merges, at each level, the two clusters which will minimize the square error from among all mergers of pairs of *existing* clusters. Ward's method does not create the clustering which minimizes square error among all clusterings with that number of clusters, however. Two characteristics of Ward's method should be noted. First, it minimizes square error as described above only when the dissimilarity index is the *squared* Euclidean distance. Second, the scale on the dendogram is not the same as the dissimilarity scale between patterns. Hierarchies can merge at levels several hundred times the largest dissimilarity between patterns. The visual effect on dendrograms is to accentuate the "lifetime" of individual clusters.

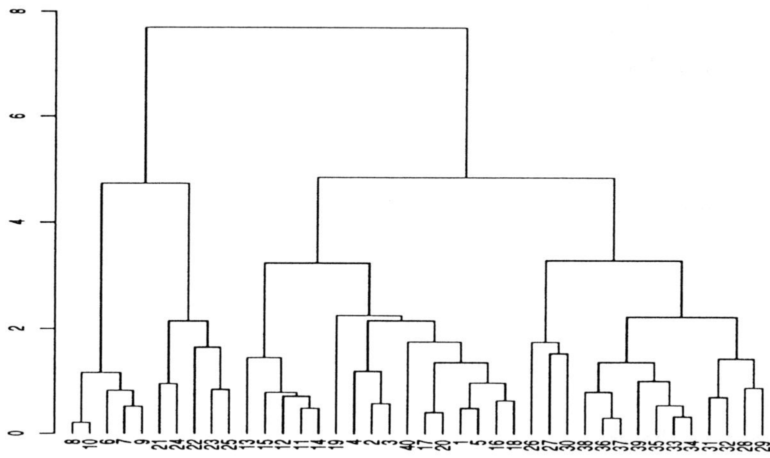

Fig. 8. Complete-link dendrogram for speaker data.

The acronym "PGM" refers to "pair group method" since clusters are merged in pairs. The prefixes "U" and "W" refer to "unweighted" and "weighted" methods, repectively. A weighted method treats all clusters the same in (4.6), so patterns in small clusters achieve more individual importance than do patterns in large clusters. An unweighted method takes the size of the clusters into account, so the patterns are treated equally. The suffixes "A" and "C" refer to "arithmetic averages" and "centroids", respectively. Thus, the full name for the UPGMA method is "unweighted pair group method using arithmetic averages", sometimes called the *group average* method. The UPGMC and WPGMC methods have direct geometric interpretations with patterns in a feature space [27]. The UPGMA and WPGMA methods have no simple geometric interpretation.

An implicit assumption underlying this entire discussion is that no two entries in any of the matrices encountered in matrix updating are the same. Ties in dissimilarity can produce unexpected and baffling dendrograms for all methods except the single-link method. Jardine and Sibson [33] show that the single-link method is the only method having a continuity property, whereby dendrograms merge smoothly as dissimilarities approach one another. Unfortunately, the single-link method has performed much worse that other methods in extracting the true structure of the data. If the dissimilarity matrix contains ties, either break the ties or use the single-link method.

A clustering method is *monotone* if, when merging clusters (s) and (t) into cluster (s, t), then for all clusters (k) distinct from (s) and (t),

$$d[(k), (s, t)] \geq d[(s), (t)].$$

Monotonicity permits dendrograms to be drawn as binary trees, as in Figures 6 and 8. The cophenetic dissimilarity is satisfied only for monotone clustering methods. Without monotonicity, *crossovers* or *reversals* can occur in which two clusters merge at a level lower than the level at which one of the two clusters was formed. This counter-intuitive phenomenon has nothing to do with the data, but is a characteristic of the clustering method. Interpreting a non-monotone dendrogram is extremely difficult. A simple condition for monotonicity, proved by Milligan [34], is that the coefficients in (4.6) satisfy (4.7).

$$\alpha_s + \alpha_t + \beta \geq 1 \text{ and } \gamma \geq 1. \tag{4.7}$$

Which clustering method is best? No clear answers exits, even though several comparative studies have been conducted [35]. If the input dissimilarity matrix satisfies the ultrametric inequality then the single-link and complete-link dendrograms will be exactly the same. This is usually taken to mean that the data are organized in a perfect hierarchy. The degree to which the two dendrograms resemble one another is an indication of how appropriate a hierarchical structure is for the data. Defining a quantitative measure of similarity between dendrograms is a very difficult task.

5. Partitional Clustering

A dendrogram displays n clusterings, or partitions, of n patterns, but how do we find a single good clustering of the data? A partitional clustering method handles a large number of patterns and applies an objective criterion in an attempt to achieve the "best" clustering. A solution to the clustering problem is easy to state. Select a criterion and evaluate it for all clusterings, saving the optimal result. This solution is impractical for two main reasons. First, the number of possible clusterings is astronomical [4]. For example, there are about 11,259,666,000 clusterings of 19 objects into 4 clusters. Evaluating a criterion for all clusterings is out of the question.

Even if one could enumerate all clusterings, the choice of a single criterion function raises severe difficulties. Clusters of patterns in d dimensions can have a variety of shapes, from spherical to line-like [36]. No single criterion can search for shapes simultaneously. Before choosing a clustering criterion, one must determine what is meant by "cluster" in the application at hand. One general definition is that a cluster is a set of patterns whose inter-pattern distances are smaller than inter-pattern distances for patterns not in the same cluster. This idea of "cluster" leads to accepting the square-error criterion stated below. One can also reasonably decide that a cluster is a region of high density in the feature space, surrounded by regions of low density. Square-error is not the only criterion. However, square-error is relatively easy to compute, makes good intuitive sense, and the clusters can be interpreted as hyperspheres in the feature space.

Given n patterns $\{\mathbf{x}_1, \mathbf{x}_2, \ldots, \mathbf{x}_n\}$ in the d-dimensional feature space, define an indicator function as follows. Let $z_{ik} = 1$ if pattern $\mathbf{x}_i$ is a member of the kth cluster and 0 if not. Every pattern must belong to one cluster and the clusters are labeled sequentially. The *center* of the kth cluster is the centroid of the patterns belonging to the cluster.

$$\mathbf{m}_k = \frac{1}{n_k} \sum_{i=1}^{n} z_{ik} \mathbf{x}_i \tag{5.1}$$

Here, $n_k = \Sigma_{i=1}^{n} z_{ik}$ is the number of patterns in cluster k. The *square-error* e_k^2 for cluster k is the sum of the squared Euclidean distances between patterns in cluster k and $\mathbf{m}_k$.

$$e_k^2 = \sum_{i=1}^{n} z_{ik} (\mathbf{x}_i - \mathbf{m}_k)^T (\mathbf{x}_i - \mathbf{m}_k) \tag{5.2}$$

The square-error for the entire clustering is the sum of the square-errors for the individual clusters.

$$E_K^2 = \sum_{k=1}^{K} e_k^2 \tag{5.3}$$

The clustering problem can be stated as the problem of minimizing E_K^2, for K fixed, by selecting the binary weights $\{z_{ik}\}$ in such a way that each row of the $n \times K$ matrix of weights has exactly one "1" in each row and at least one "1" in each column. That is, each pattern can belong to only one cluster and no cluster can be empty. In fuzzy clustering [7] z_{ik} is taken to be the *degree of belonging* for pattern i in cluster k and z_{ik} in (5.2) is replaced by z_{ik}^q where q is chosen empirically, and is usually 2.

One can approach this optimization in many ways, including simulated annealing [24]. Gordon and Henderson [37] translate the constrained optimization problem into an unconstrained problem to simplify the solution. The computational demands of formal minimization techniques have encouraged the development of simple, heuristic algorithms [1,4]. The most popular of these is the *K-means* method.

K-Means Algorithm for Partitional Clustering

1. Select an initial clustering of the n patterns with K clusters and initialize the cluster centers.
   Repeat until the clustering stablizes:
2. Assign cluster labels to all patterns by finding the closest cluster centers.
3. Compute cluster centers for all clusters with (5.1).
   Repeat Steps 2 and 3 until no cluster labels change.
4. Apply heuristic splitting and lumping criteria.
   End the repeat.
5. Compute statistics of the final clustering.

The clustering with the smallest square-error is retained as the solution. Although the convergence of the algorithm can be proven [38] no assurances that the solution is optimal can ever be given. It is easy to propose data that will defeat the algorithm [4]. One hopes that running the algorithm several times for different starting configurations leads to a reasonable solution. The problem of choosing the number of clusters and of formally validating the results is discussed in Section 6.

Steps 2 and 3 constitute a *K-means pass.* An alternative is to recompute the cluster centers after each cluster label is changed. Step 4 changes the number of clusters by merging small clusters, removing outliers, or splitting large clusters. Criteria for these operations are chosen heuristically. The initial partition can be chosen in several ways [1]. For example, one can choose k patterns at random as seed points. One can also choose k patterns that are reasonably separated from one another as seed points. In any event, the algorithm should be run with different seed points to seek the best clustering.

Any program for implementing a partitional clustering method involves several parameters. The primary ones are K and any parameters associated with splitting clusters, lumping clusters, and identifying outliers. An exception is the CLUSTER program [4] which creates a sequence of clusterings and uses no parameters. Only experience can dictate selection of these parameters. The manner in which the data are normalized must also be considered. Normalization (2.9) can reduce the effects of spreads in the individual variables and equalize the contributions of all variables to Euclidean distance.

The results of any partitional clustering algorithm is a set of tables of numbers showing the cluster centers, the square-errors for the individual clusters, the covariance matrices for the clusters, and various statistics which try to quantify the characteristics of the clustering [4]. Clustering algorithms are often run to see if patterns are clustered according to some *a priori* category information and a cluster-by-category table is displayed to see if the clusters correspond to categories in any way. The cluster centers can be taken as a sampling of the original data and one can represent the data by projecting the cluster centers to two dimensions.

Figure 9 shows the cluster-by-category table from the CLUSTER program with the speaker data, after normalizing by (2.9). Also shown are the square-errors for all clusters. Comparing the table entries to Fig. 2, 3, and 8 may justify some of the entries in the table. For example, categories 1, 2, 3, and 5 are in unique clusters. However, cluster 3 has a much larger square-error than clusters 1, 2, and 5. This suggests that clusters 1, 2, and 5 have smaller dispersions than cluster 3.

6. Validation and Interpretation

Validation refers to the objective assessment of a clustering structure so as to determine whether a structure is meaningful. The structures under consideration are hierarchies, clusterings, and individual clusters. The sense of validity explained here calls a structure *valid* if it is unusual under the circumstances of the study. That is, a structure is valid if it cannot reasonably be assumed to have occurred by chance or to be an artifact of a clustering algorithm. Validation is accomplished by carefully applying statistical methods and testing hypotheses.

	Category								
Cluster	1	2	3	4	5	6	7	8	e_k^2
1	0	0	0	0	0	3	0	0	274.1
2	0	5	0	0	0	0	0	0	139.5
3	0	0	0	0	5	0	0	0	441.4
4	0	0	5	0	0	0	0	0	177.4
5	5	0	0	0	0	0	0	0	192.4
6	0	0	0	0	0	2	5	1	438.3
7	0	0	0	4	0	0	0	0	296.9
8	0	0	0	1	0	0	0	4	221.5

Fig. 9. Clusters by category for speaker data.

6.1. *An Attitude Towards Validation*

One might argue that a structure is "valid" if it makes sense or is useful or can be interpreted or provides new insight. The list of ways to justify a result is endless. This section considers only objective measures of validity that can be tested statistically. Formal testing may not be required in every application. One might use experience and judgement to interpret a clustering structure or use clustering in an exploratory manner.

In addition to the three types of structure (hierarchy, clustering, cluster), three types of validation studies called external, internal, and relative can be defined [4]. An index must be chosen to reflect the sense of validity being examined, with the structure and type of study in mind. An *external* assessment of validity objectively compares the recovered structure to an *a priori* structure and tries to quantify the match between the two. For example, one might test how closely cluster labels match category labels. An *internal* examination of validity uses no *a priori* information but tries to determine if the structure is intrinsically appropriate for the data. For example, one might try to determine if a cluster derived from the single-link method is unusually compact or isolated, as compared to other single-link clusters of the same size in random data. A *relative* test compares two structures and measures their relative merit. For example, one might compare a 4-cluster clustering to a 5-cluster clustering without using any *a priori* information. Several indices have been proposed for this purpose and some are explained in Section 6.4. The paradigm for testing the validity of a clustering structure is summarized below.

Validity Paradigm

1. Identify the clustering structure (hierarchy, clustering, cluster) and the type of validation (external, internal, relative).
2. Select an index.
3. Select an hypothesis of "no structure".
4. Obtain (by theory or simulation) the *baseline* distribution of the index under the "no structure" hypothesis.
5. Compute the index for the structure being tested.
6. Formally test the hypothesis of "no structure" by determining whether the observed index is "unusual".

Establishing the baseline distribution might require extensive statistical sampling such as Monte Carlo estimation or bootstrapping. Although the same index can apply to all three types of tests, the circumstances of the application are very different.

External tests of validity are generally much easier to apply than internal tests because hypotheses of randomness are easier to propose and baseline distributions are easier to derive than for internal tests. One example of an external test is the Bailey profile [39,4] which measures the validity of an individual cluster that is defined before the analysis begins. The natural indices of validity for an individual cluster are simple measures of compactness and isolation derived from graph theory. Bailey profiles are restricted to ordinal data and use the hypergeometric distribution to derive baseline distributions. Baseline distributions of compactness and isolation indices cannot be derived when the cluster is obtained by applying a clustering method because the cluster depends on the method itself, among other things. Even though data are purely random, a diligent clustering method might uncover an unusual cluster. An internal test of validity should recognize such clusters as being artifacts. Three validation problems of practical interest are discussed in this section.

6.2. *External Tests of Validity for a Partition*

Suppose two partitions of n patterns are to be compared. One is from category information, obtained before the analysis is begun. The other is obtained from some clustering method. How well does the clustering match the categories? The labels themselves are not important, so renaming categories or clusters cannot affect the degree of match. Hubert and Arabie [40] studied the Rand index as a means for assessing the match between two such clusterings.

Let a denote the number of pairs of objects that are in the same cluster in both clusterings and let d denote the number of pairs in different groups. There are

$n(n - 1)/2$ pairs of objects to check. The Rand index [41] measures the degree of match.

$$R = (a + d) \setminus \binom{n}{2}$$

Other statistics have been suggested for this purpose but they are linear functions of one another [4]. A clustering is termed "valid" if $\mathbf{R}$ is unusually high, as measured with respect to some baseline distribution. To make $\mathbf{R}$ less sensitive to problem parameters. Hubert and Arabie [40] corrected it for chance. The hypergeometric distribution was applied to find $\varepsilon(R)$, the expected value of $\mathbf{R}$ under the baseline distribution. The maximum possible value of $\mathbf{R}$ is 1, so the corrected Rand index is:

$$R' = \frac{R - \varepsilon(R)}{1 - \varepsilon(R)} \, .$$

Detailed formulas are given elsewhere [40,4].

Using the Rand index, corrected or not, in a test for external validity requries that a baseline distribution be developed. The variance of R' is known when one of the partitions is assumed to be assigned at random. However, the full baseline distribution of R' is required to formally test this hypothesis of randomness.

6.3. *Internal Tests of Validity for a Partition*

The paradigm for external tests of validity is the same as for internal tests. The hypothesis of randomness and the baseline distributions differ. This has led to some confusion in the literature. For example, the distribution of certain F-statistics and χ^2 statistics are listed in standard books on multivariable statistics. These distributions assume that the groups have been chosen without reference to the data, as when one assigns *a priori* category labels. These distributions are not applicable to the internal validation of clusterings found by sifting through the data. Using them can create misleading results [35]. Milligan [42] compared the performances of 30 internal indices of validity.

Three primary difficulties arise in obtaining the baseline distribution needed for an internal test of validity. The first difficulty lies in choosing a hypothesis of "no structure" or "randomness". To create purely random data, one must choose the region of space in which the random data are to be generated. To be fair, this region must match the characteristics of the data. The second difficulty is the necessity to match all the data parameters. This implies that one must estimate the baseline distribution anew in every application, usually by Monte Carlo sampling. Bock [43] has derived asymptotic distributions for some indices, but it is seldom clear when the assumptions of the derivation are satisfied.

The third difficulty is a bit subtle. It is not fair to compare a clustering obtained from a clustering algorithm to just any clustering of random data. One should compare it to the *best* clustering of random data. That is, before calling a result valid, one should be reasonably certain that the same result could not be obtained from any random data, not simply that the result could not be obtained from some random data. Engelman and Hartigan [44] demonstrated this point in estimating the distribution of the ratio of between to within scatter for one-dimensional data. Given a set of random data (from a normal distribution), they found the ratio for the best separation of the data into two clusters. They published the percentage points for the distribution of the best value of the ratio. However, the result is only applicable to one-dimensional data. The methodology cannot be extended to more than one dimension easily because the number of clusterings to be examined increases exponentially with dimension. These difficulties may explain why more internal validation is not performed.

6.4. *Relative Tests of Validity — How Many Clusters?*

The problem of determining the "true" number of clusters has been called the fundamental problem of cluster validity [45,46]. This question is particularly important in image segmentation, where the number of categories, such as land-use categories, is not know in advance. The question "How many clusters are there in the data?" can be asked in at least three meaningful ways.

- Do the data contain the number of clusters I expect? This clearly calls for an external test of validation and one might use the procedures of Section 6.2.

- Is it unusual to find this many clusters with data of this sort? This somewhat vague statement can best be answered with an internal criterion, as in Section 6.3. The basis for comparison must be defined and a baseline distribution must be derived — two difficult tasks.

- Which of a few clusterings is best? This is more difficult to answer than the first question, but is more specific than the second. The question implies that several clusterings, such as those derived by cutting a dendrogram at several levels, or running a partitional clustering algorithm several times, be considered as candidates. The number of clusters in the best of these clustering is taken to be the "correct" number.

This section considers the third question by examining a sequence of clusters as the number of clusters changes monotonically. For example, one might seek a *stopping rule* for choosing the best level for cutting a dendrogram. What is a good index? One possibility is to pick the clustering that minimizes square-error (5.3). Square-error is a strong function of the dimensionality, the number of patterns, and the number of clusters [4]. As the number of clusters increases, the square-error has a tendency to decrease whether or not one clustering is better than another. Milligan and Cooper [47] compared 30 indices as stopping rules by applying each to a wide variety of data and ranking them according to the one which found the correct answer most frequently. The correct answer was known because they generated their own data. Any index that performed well should, logically, be trusted with real data. Dubes [48] made more detailed comparisons of two other indices. Zhang and Modestino [49] integrate formal estimation of the number of clusters into image segmentation.

Three representative indices are defined below; n is the number of patterns, K is the number of clusters in the clustering being evaluated, and E_K^2 is the square-error of the clustering (5.3). To estimate the number of clusters, plot the chosen index as K varies and look for either a peak, a valley, or a knee in the curve, depending on the index. Two underlying assumptions are that the data are not random and at least two clusters exist.

- The Calinski–Harabasz index, $CH(k)$ was the best of the 30 indices tested by Milligan and Cooper [13].

$$CH(K) = \frac{n-K}{K-1}\left[\frac{E_1^2}{E_K^2} - 1\right]$$

  The index will always be positive and will be zero for $K = 0$. Its upper bound depends on problem parameters. The value of K that maximizes $CH(K)$ is chosen to estimate K. This index normalizes the square-error and tends to depend less on problem parameters than does the square-error itself.

- The C index is a normalized form of the Γ statistic [50] proposed to measure the correlation between spatial observations and time. Let $c(q, r)$ be 1 if patterns $\mathbf{x}_q$ and $\mathbf{x}_r$ are in the same cluster and 0 if not. Let $d(q, r)$ denote the dissimilarity, or Euclidean distance, between the two patterns. The "raw" Γ statistic is:

$$\Gamma = \sum_{q=1}^{n-1} \sum_{r=q+1}^{n} d(q, r)c(q, r).$$

  The dissimilarities need not be distances. Let a_K be the number of *pairs* of patterns in which both patterns are in the same cluster. Define the following two statistics as the smallest and largest possible values of Γ for a clustering of the kind being examined.

$$\min(\Gamma) = \text{sum of } a_K \text{ smallest dissimilarities}$$
$$\max(\Gamma) = \text{sum of } a_K \text{ largest dissimilarities}$$

  The C index is defined as:

$$C(K) = \frac{\Gamma - \min(\Gamma)}{\max(\Gamma) - \min(\Gamma)}.$$

  The range of the C index is limited to $[0, 1]$. The value of K that minimizes $C(K)$ estimates the number of clusters.

- The Goodman–Kruskal γ statistic [51,4] measures the rank correlation between Euclidean distances $d(q, r)$ and function $f(q, r)$ for the clustering being evaluated, where $f(q, r) = 1 - c(q, r)$ is 1 if $\mathbf{x}_q$ and $\mathbf{x}_r$ are in different clusters and 0, if in the same cluster. In standard notation, $S(+)$ denotes the number of concordant quartets and $S(-)$, the number of discordant quartets. This requires some explanation. A "quartet" is two pairs of numbers. One is a pair of dissimilarities, say $[d(q, r), d(s, t)]$, and the other is the corresponding pair of indicator values, $[f(q, r), f(s, t)]$. A quartet is *concordant* either if $d(q, r) < d(s, t)$ and $f(q, r) < f(s, t)$ or if $d(q, r) > d(s, t)$ and $f(q, r) > f(s, t)$. A quartet is *discordant* either if $d(q, r) < d(s, t)$ and $f(q, r) > f(s, t)$ or if $d(q, r) > d(s, t)$ and $f(q, r) < f(s, t)$. If either pair is tied, the quartet is neither concordant nor discordant. Then,

$$\gamma(K) = \frac{S(+) - S(-)}{S(+) + S(-)}.$$

This index is limited to the range $[-1, 1]$. The value of K then maximizes $\gamma(K)$ estimates of the number of clusters.

Studies [13] have shown that some indices proposed in the literature perform very poorly, while some perform very well. It is impossible to claim optimality for any of them, because the characteristics of the data can affect performance in unknown ways.

7. Final Comments

Cluster analysis is a valuable tool for organizing, summarizing, and exploring multivariate data. Among the problems that appear in applications are the choice of a clustering criterion that recognizes only clusters of interest, and the choice of a clustering algorithm. Validating the results objectively is the most difficult problem of all. Notwithstanding these real problems, cluster analysis has proved enlightening, especially when invoked by a careful practioner who is aware of inherent limitations and has the proper computer tools.

Acknowledgements

I acknowledge the support of the National Science Foundation, most recently through grant IRI-8901513 and grant CDA-8806599.

References

[1] M. R. Anderberg, *Cluster Analysis for Applications* (Academic Press, New York, NY, 1973).

[2] A. D. Gordon, *Classification* (Chapman and Hall, London, 1981).

[3] J. A. Hartigan, *Clustering Algorithms* (John Wiley & Sons, New York, NY, 1975).

[4] A. K. Jain and R. C. Dubes, *Algorithms for Clustering Data* (Prentice-Hall, Engelwood Cliffs, NJ, 1988).

[5] L. Legendre and P. Legendre, *Numerical Ecology* (Elsevier Scientific, Amsterdam, 1983).

[6] J. M. Jolion, P. Meer and S. Bataouche, Robust clustering with applications in computer vision, *IEEE Trans. Pattern Anal. Mach. Intell.* **13** (1991) 791–802.

[7] J. C. Bezdek, *Pattern Recognition with Fuzzy Objective Function Algorithms* (Plenum Press, New York, NY, 1981).

[8] X. L. Xie and G. Beni, A validity measure for fuzzy clustering, *IEEE Trans. Pattern Anal. Mach. Intell.* **13** (1991) 841–847.

[9] R. S. Michalski and R. E. Stepp, Automated construction of classifications: Conceptual clustering versus numerical taxonomy, *IEEE Trans. Pattern Anal. Mach. Intell.* **5** (1983) 396–410.

[10] G. Matthews and J. Hearne, Clustering without a metric, *IEEE Trans. Pattern Anal. Mach. Intell.* **13** (1991) 175–184.

[11] Institute of Electrical and Electronics Engineers, *Special Issue of Proceedings on Neural Networks, I: Theory and Modeling*, Sept. 1990.

[12] J. C. Gower and P. Legendre, Metric and Euclidean properties of dissimilarity coefficients, *J. Classification* **3** (1986) 5–48.

[13] G. W. Milligan and M. C. Cooper, A study of standardization of variables in cluster analysis, *J. Classification* **5** (1988) 181–204.

[14] K. Pettis, T. Bailey, A. K. Jain and R. Dubes, An intrinsic dimensionality estimator from near-neighbour information, *IEEE Trans. Pattern Anal. Mach. Intell.* **1** (1979) 25–37.

[15] N. Wyse, R. Dubes and A. K. Jain, A critical evaluation of intrinsic dimensionality algorithms, in E. S. Gelsema and L. N. Kanal (eds.), *Pattern Recognition in Practice* (North-Holland Amsterdam, 1980) p. 415–425.

[16] K. Falconer, *Fractal Geometry* (John Wiley & Sons, New York, NY, 1990).

[17] J. Theiler, Estimating fractal dimension, *J. Opt. Soc. Am. A* **7** (1990) 1055–1073.

[18] B. S. Everitt, *Graphical Techniques for Multivariate Data* (Elsevier North-Holland, New York, NY, 1978).

[19] R. A. Becker, J. M. Chambers and A. R. Wilke, *The New S Language* (Wadsworth & Brooks/Cole, Pacific Grove, CA, 1988).

[20] T. Okada and S. Tomita, An optimal orthonormal system for discriminant analysis, *Pattern Recogn.* **18** (1985) 139–144.

[21] J. T. Tou and R. P. Heydorn, Some approaches to optimum feature extraction, in J. T. Tou (ed.), *Computer and Information Sciences II* (Academic Press, New York, NY, 1967) 57–89.

[22] J. W. Sammon, A nonlinear mapping for data structure analysis, *IEEE Trans. Comput.* **18** (1969) 401–409.

[23] J. B. Kruskal, Multidimensional scaling and other methods for discovering structure, in K. Enslein, A. Ralston, and H. S. Wilf (eds.), *Statistical Methods for Digital Computers* (John Wiley & Sons, New York, NY, 1977) 296–339.

[24] R. W. Klein and R. C. Dubes, Experiments in projection and clustering by simulated annealing, *Pattern Recogn.* **22** (1989) 213–220.

[25] H. Chernoff, The use of faces to represent points in k-dimensional space graphically, *J. Am. Stat. Assoc.* **68** (1973) 361–368.

[26] A. D. Gordon, Hierarchical classification, in P. Arabie and L. Hubert (eds.), *Clustering and Classification* (World Scientific, Singapore, 1992).

[27] P. H. A. Sneath and R. R. Sokal, *Numerical Taxonomy* (W. H. Freeman and Company, San Francisco, CA, 1973).

[28] F. Murtagh, Counting dendrograms: A survey, *Disc. Appl. Math.* **7** (1984) 191–199.

[29] W. H. E. Day, Complexity theory: An introduction for practitioners of classification, in P. Arabie and L. Hubert (eds.), *Clustering and Classification* (World Scientific, Singapore, 1992).

[30] J. C. Gower and G. J. S. Ross, Minimum spanning trees and single-linkage cluster analysis, *Appl. Stat.* **18** (1969) 54–64.

[31] L. J. Hubert, Some applications of graph theory to clustering, *Psychometrika* **39** (1974) 283–309.

[32] J. H. Ward, Hierarchical grouping to optimize an objective function, *J. Am. Stat. Assoc.* **58** (1963) 236–244.

[33] N. Jardine and R. Sibson, *Mathematical Taxonomy* (John Wiley & Sons, New York, NY, 1971).

[34] G. W. Milligan, Ultrametric hierarchical clustering algorithms, *Psychometrika* **44** (1979) 343–346.

[35] G. W. Milligan, A review of Monte Carlo tests of cluster analysis, *Multivar. Behav. Res.* **16** (1981) 379–407.

[36] C. T. Zahn, Graph-theoretical methods for detecting and describing gestalt clusters, *IEEE Trans. Comput.* **20** (1971) 68–86.

[37] A. D. Gordon and J. T. Henderson, Algorithm for Euclidean sum of squares classification, *Biometrics* **33** (1977) 355–362.

[38] S. Z. Selim and M. A. Ismail, K-means type algorithms: A generalized convergence theorem and characterization of local optimality, *IEEE Trans. Pattern Anal. Mach. Intell.* **6** (1984) 81–87.

[39] T. A. Bailey and R. C. Dubes, Cluster validity profiles, *Pattern Recogn.* **15** (1982) 61–83.

[40] L. J. Hubert and P. Arabie, Comparing partitions, *J. Classification* **2** (1985) 193–218.

[41] W. M. Rand, Objective criteria for the evaluation of clustering methods, *J. Am. Stat. Assoc.* **66** (1971) 846–850.

[42] G. W. Milligan, A Monte Carlo study of 30 internal criterion measures for cluster-analysis, *Psychometrika* **46** (1981) 187–195.

[43] H. H. Bock, On some significance tests in cluster analysis, *J. Classification* **2** (1985) 77–108.

[44] L. Engelman and J. A. Hartigan, Percentage points of a test for clusters, *J. Am. Stat. Assoc.* **64** (1969) 1647–1648.

[45] R. O. Duda and P. E. Hart, *Pattern Classification and Scene Analysis* (John Wiley & Sons, New York, NY, 1973).

[46] B. S. Everitt, Unresolved problems in cluster analysis, *Biometrics* **35** (1979) 169-181.

[47] G. W. Milligan and M. C. Cooper, An examination of procedures for determining the number of clusters in a data set, *Psychometrika* **50** (1985) 159–179.

[48] R. C. Dubes, How many clusters are best? — An experiment, *Pattern Recogn.* **20** (1987) 645–663.

[49] J. Zhang and J. W. Modestino, A model-fitting approach to cluster validation with application to stochastic model-based image segmentation, *IEEE Trans. Pattern Anal. Mach. Intell.* **12** (1990) 1007–1009.

[50] L. J. Hubert and J. Schultz, Quadratic assignment as a general data-analysis strategy, *British J. Math. Stat. Psychol.* **29** (1976) 190–241.

[51] L. A. Goodman and W. H. Kruskal, Measures of association for cross-classifications, *J. Am. Stat. Assoc.* **49** (1954) 732–764.

Handbook of Pattern Recognition and Computer Vision, pp. 33–60
Eds. C. H. Chen, L. F. Pau and P. S. P. Wang

CHAPTER 1.2

STATISTICAL PATTERN RECOGNITION

KEINOSUKE FUKUNAGA

School of Electrical Engineering, Purdue University
West Lafayette, IN 47907, USA

In the introductory Section 1, the problems of statistical pattern recognition are defined, and a flow chart is presented to show how a classifier ought to be designed. In Section 2, the theoretically optimal (Bayes) classifier and its variations are introduced. The discussion is extended to show how the resulting classification (Bayes) error can be computed for some limited cases. Also, the upper and lower bounds of the Bayes error are shown. Section 3 discusses how a classifier is designed in practice. Linear, quadratic and piecewise classifiers are included. These are based on the expected vectors and covariance matrices of underlying probability distributions. In practice, these vectors and matrices are not given, and must be estimated from an available set of samples. Consequently, the designed classifier variates and the classification error becomes a random variable. Section 4 discusses how the number of available samples affects the classification performance, and also how to allocate the samples into design and test. In Section 5, nonparametric techniques are presented. They are needed in the estimation of the Bayes error and the structure analysis of data, where a mathematical formula such as Gaussianness cannot be applied. Both the Parzen and k nearest neighbor approaches are discussed. Feature extraction and clustering are discussed in other chapters.

Keywords: Statistical pattern recognition, classifier, probability of error, hypothesis tests, effect of sample size, nonparametric.

1. Introduction

The purpose of statistical pattern recognition is to determine to which category or class a given sample belongs. Through observation and measurement processes, we obtain a set of numbers which make up the measurement vector. The vector is a random vector and its density function depends on its class.

The design of a classifier consists of two parts. One is to collect data samples from various classes and to find the boundaries which separate the classes. This process is called *classifier design, training,* or *learning.* The other is to *test* the designed classifier by feeding the samples whose class identities are known.

Figure 1 shows a flow chart of how a classifier is designed [1]. After data is gathered, samples are normalized and registered. Normalization and registration are very important processes for a successful classifier design. However, different data require different normalization and registration, and it is difficult to discuss

33

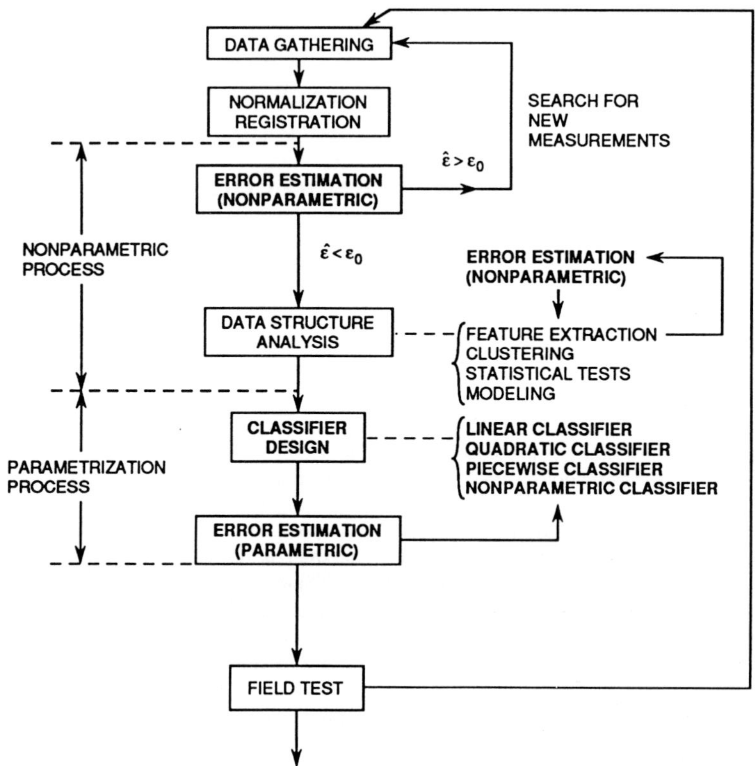

Fig. 1. Process of designing a classifier. (From [1], reprinted with permission.)

these subjects in a generalized way. Therefore, these subjects are not included in this chapter.

After normalization and registration, the class separability of the data is measured. This is done by estimating the *Bayes error*, the overlap among different class densities, in the measurement space. Since it is not appropriate at this stage to assume a mathematical form for the data structure, the estimation procedure must be *nonparametric*. If the Bayes error is larger than the final classifier error we wish to achieve (denoted by ε_0), it means the data does not carry enough classification information to meet the specification. Selecting features and designing a classifier in the later stages merely increase the classification error. Therefore, we must go back to data gathering and seek better measurements.

Only when the estimate of the Bayes error is less than ε_0, may we proceed to the next stage of data structure analysis in which we study the characteristics of the data. All kinds of data analysis techniques are used here. They include feature extraction, clustering, statistical tests, modeling, and so on. Note that each time a feature set is chosen, the Bayes error in the feature space is estimated and compared with the one in the measurement space. The difference between them indicates how much classification information is lost in the feature selection process.

Once the structure of the data is thoroughly understood, the data dictate which classifier must be adopted. Our choice is normally either a linear, quadratic, or piecewise classifier, and rarely a nonparametric classifier. Nonparametric techniques are required in off-line analyses to carry out many important operations such as the estimation of the Bayes error and data structure analysis. However, they are often too complex for any on-line operation.

After a classifier is designed, the classifier must be evaluated. The resulting error is compared with the Bayes error in the feature space. The difference between these two errors indicates how much the error is increased by adopting the classifier. If the difference is unacceptably high, we must re-evaluate the design of the classifier.

At last, the classifier is tested in the field. If the classifier does not perform as was expected, the database used for designing the classifier is different from the test data in the field. Therefore, we must expand the database and design a new classifier.

In this chapter, only the boldfaced portions of Fig. 1 will be discussed briefly. More details are found in [1]. Clustering and feature extraction are discussed in other chapters. Also, unless otherwise stated, only the two-class problem is discussed in this chapter, although the results for a more general multi-class problem are listed whenever available.

The notations, which are frequently used in this chapter, are summarized as follows:

Notation	
n	Dimensionality
L	Number of classes
N	Number of total samples
N_i	Number of class i samples
ω_i	Class i
P_i	*A priori* probability of ω_i
$X = [x_1 x_2 \ldots x_n]^T$	Vector
$\mathbf{X} = [\mathbf{x}_1 \mathbf{x}_2 \ldots \mathbf{x}_n]^T$	Random vector
$p_i(X) = p(x_1, x_2, \ldots, x_n)$	Conditional density function of ω_i
$p(X) = \sum_{i=1}^{L} P_i p_i(X)$	Density function
$q_i(X) = P_i p_i(X)/p(X)$	*A posteriori* probability of ω_i given X
$M_i = \mathrm{E}\{\mathbf{X}|\omega_i\}$	Expected vector of ω_i
$M = \mathrm{E}\{\mathbf{X}\} = \sum_{i=1}^{L} P_i M_i$	Expected vector
$\Sigma_i = \mathrm{E}\{(\mathbf{X} - M_i)(\mathbf{X} - M_i)^T|\omega_i\}$	Covariance matrix of ω_i
$\Sigma = \mathrm{E}\{\mathbf{X} - M)(\mathbf{X} - M)^T\}$	
$\quad = \sum_{i=1}^{L}\{P_i \Sigma_i + P_i(M_i - M)(M_i - M)^T\}$	Covariance matrix

2. The Bayes Classification

In this section, the classification algorithms and the resulting errors are presented, based on the assumption that $p_i(X)$ and P_i are known. The classification algorithms are also known as *hypothesis tests*.

2.1. *Likelihood Ratio Classifier*

The probability of the classification error can be minimized by classifying X into either ω_1 or ω_2, depending on whether $q_1(X) > q_2(X)$ or $q_1(X) < q_2(X)$ is satisfied. That is,

$$q_1(X) \underset{\omega_2}{\overset{\omega_1}{\gtrless}} q_2(X) \qquad \text{(Bayes classifier)}. \tag{2.1}$$

The resulting risk at X is

$$r^*(X) = \min[q_1(X),\, q_2(X)] \qquad \text{(Bayes risk)}. \tag{2.2}$$

The overall error is obtained by taking the expectation of (2.2) over $\mathbf{X}$:

$$\varepsilon^* = \mathrm{E}\{r^*(\mathbf{X})\} = P_1 \int_{\Gamma_2} p_1(X)dX + P_2 \int_{\Gamma_1} p_2(X)dX \qquad \text{(Bayes error)} \tag{2.3}$$

where $\varepsilon_1 = \int_{\Gamma_2} p_1(X)dX$ and $\varepsilon_2 = \int_{\Gamma_1} p_2(X)dX$ are called the ω_1 and ω_2 errors, respectively. Γ_i is the region where X is classified to ω_i.

For the multiclass problem,

$$q_k(X) = \max_i q_i(X) \to X \in \omega_k \tag{2.4}$$

$$\varepsilon^* = \mathrm{E}\left\{1 - \max_i q_i(\mathbf{X})\right\}. \tag{2.5}$$

A more convenient form of the Bayes classifier is obtained by applying the Bayes theorem, $q_i(X) = P_i p_i(X)/p(X)$, and taking negative logarithm:

$$h(X) = -\ln[p_1(X)/p_2(X)] \underset{\omega_2}{\overset{\omega_1}{\gtrless}} \ln[P_1/P_2] \tag{2.6}$$

The $h(X)$ combined with a threshold is called the *likelihood ratio classifier*.

When $\mathbf{X}$ is distributed Gaussianly with M_i and Σ_i for ω_i,

$$-\ln p_i(X) = \frac{1}{2}(X - M_i)^T \Sigma_i^{-1}(X - M_i) + \frac{1}{2}\ln|\Sigma_i| + \left(\frac{n}{2}\right)\ln 2\pi. \tag{2.7}$$

The threshold of the classifier could be changed according to various requirements as follows:

Bayes classifier for minimum cost. Let c_{ij} be the cost of classifying a ω_i sample into ω_j. The expected cost of classifying X into ω_i is

$$c_i(X) = \sum_{j=1}^{L} c_{ji} q_j(X). \tag{2.8}$$

The classification rule and the resulting cost are

$$c_k(X) = \min_i \, c_i(X) \rightarrow X \in \omega_k \tag{2.9}$$

$$c^* = \mathrm{E}\left\{\min_i \, c_i(\mathbf{X})\right\}. \tag{2.10}$$

For the two-class problem,

$$h(X) = -\ln[p_1(X)/p_2(X)] \underset{\omega_2}{\overset{\omega_1}{\lessgtr}} \ln[(c_{12} - c_{11})P_1/(c_{21} - c_{22})P_2]. \tag{2.11}$$

This is a likelihood ratio classifier with a new threshold.

Neyman–Pearson test. Let ε_1 and ε_2 be the error probabilities from ω_1 and ω_2, as shown in (2.3). The likelihood ratio classifier minimizes ε_1 subject to ε_2 being equal to a given constant, say, ε_0. The threshold value must be selected to satisfy $\varepsilon_2 = \varepsilon_0$ and is normally determined empirically. A plot of ε_1 vs. ε_2 for the likelihood ratio classifier with varying threshold is called the *operating characteristics* and is used frequently as a visual aid to see how two errors are traded by changing the threshold. In the Neyman–Pearson test, $\varepsilon_2 = \varepsilon_0$ is the operating point and the corresponding threshold value is chosen. When ω_2 represents a target to be identified against the other class (ω_1), ε_1, ε_2, and $1 - \varepsilon_2$ are called the *false alarm*, the *leakage*, and the *detection probability*, respectively.

Minimax test. We can make the expected cost invariant even when P_i varies unexpectedly after the classifier has been implemented. This is done by selecting the threshold of the likelihood ratio classifier to satisfy

$$(c_{11} - c_{22}) + (c_{12} - c_{11})\varepsilon_1 - (c_{21} - c_{22})\varepsilon_2 = 0. \tag{2.12}$$

Particularly, when $c_{11} = c_{22}$ and $c_{12} - c_{11} = c_{21} - c_{22}$, the threshold is chosen to satisfy $\varepsilon_1 = \varepsilon_2$. This classifier eliminates the possibility of having an unexpected large error due to the unexpected variation of P_i.

In all of these three cases, the likelihood ratio classifier is commonly used, and only the threshold varies. This may be interpreted as replacing the true P_i's of (2.6) by artificial P_i's. Therefore, theoretically, all these cases may be treated as the Bayes classifier, assigning the different meaning to P_i for each application.

Some other subjects related to hypothesis tests are as follows.

Independent measurement set. When $\mathbf{X}$ consists of statistically independent measurement sets as $\mathbf{X}^T = [\mathbf{X}_1^T \mathbf{X}_2^T \cdots \mathbf{X}_M^T]$, the Bayes classifier becomes

$$-\ln[p_1(X)/p_2(X)] = \sum_{i=1}^{M} -\ln[p_1(X_i)/p_2(X_i)] \underset{\omega_2}{\overset{\omega_1}{\lessgtr}} \ln[P_1/P_2] \tag{2.13}$$

This suggests how to combine, for classification, seemingly unrelated information such as radar and infrared signatures.

One-class classifier. When one clearly defined class is classified against all other (sometimes not well-defined) possibilities, the boundary may be determined from the knowledge of one class only. A typical example is a hyperspherical boundary around a Gaussian distribution with $M = 0$ and $\Sigma = I$. This technique could work when the dimensionality of the data, n, is very low (such as 1 or 2). However, as n increases, the error of this technique increases significantly. The mapping from the original n-dimensional space to a one-dimensional distance space destroys valuable classification information which existed in the original space. For an example with $n = 64$, the error increases from 0.1% to 8.4%.

Reject. When X falls in the region where the Bayes risk $r^*(X)$ is high, we may decide not to classify the sample. This concept is called *reject*. The *reject region* $\Gamma_r(t)$ and the resulting *probability of rejection $R(t)$* are specified by the threshold t as

$$\Gamma_r(t) = \{X : r^*(X) > t\} \tag{2.14}$$

$$R(t) = \Pr\{r^*(\mathbf{X}) > t\} = 1 - \Pr\{r^*(\mathbf{X}) \le t\}. \tag{2.15}$$

Note that $\Pr\{r^*(\mathbf{X}) \le t\}$ is the distribution function of a random variable $r^*(\mathbf{X})$. The probability of error with reject is the integration of $r^*(X)p(X)$ in $\bar{\Gamma}_r$, outside Γ_r, and thus depends on t. The error may be evaluated directly from the reject probability as

$$\varepsilon(t) = -\int_0^t \xi \, dR(\xi). \tag{2.16}$$

The error decreases as the reject probability increases, and vice versa. A plot of $\varepsilon(t)$ vs. $R(t)$ is called the *error-reject curve*, and is used as a visual aid to see how $\varepsilon(t)$ and $R(t)$ are traded by changing the threshold t. With the largest possible $t = 1 - 1/L$ for the L-class problem, $R(1 - 1/L) = 0$ and $\varepsilon(1 - 1/L)$ is equal to the Bayes error, ε^*.

Model validation. The distribution function of the random variable $r^*(\mathbf{X})$ is a simple and good parameter to characterize the classification environment, determining both $\varepsilon(t)$ and $R(t)$. Thus, when samples are drawn and a mathematical model is assumed, two distribution functions of $r^*(\mathbf{X})$ may be obtained: one empirically from the samples and the other theoretically from the model. The comparison of these two distribution functions could be used to test the validity of the mathematical model.

2.2. *The Bayes Error*

The Bayes error of (2.3) is generally hard to compute, except for the following two cases.

(1) *Gaussian* $\mathbf{X}$ *with* $\Sigma_1 = \Sigma_2 = \Sigma$. For this case, the Bayes classifier becomes a linear function of X as

$$h(X) = (M_2 - M_1)^T \Sigma^{-1} X + \frac{1}{2}(M_1^T \Sigma^{-1} M_1 - M_2^T \Sigma^{-1} M_2) \lessgtr t. \tag{2.17}$$

Since $\mathbf{X}$ is Gaussianly distributed, $h(\mathbf{X})$ is also a Gaussian random variable. Therefore,

$$\varepsilon_1 = \int_{(t-m_1)/\sigma_1}^{+\infty} \frac{1}{\sqrt{2\pi}} e^{-\xi^2/2} d\xi \quad \text{and} \quad \varepsilon_2 = \int_{-\infty}^{(t-m_2)/\sigma_2} \frac{1}{\sqrt{2\pi}} e^{-\xi^2/2} d\xi \tag{2.18}$$

where

$$m_1 = E\{h(\mathbf{X})|\omega_1\} = -\frac{1}{2}(M_2 - M_1)^T \Sigma^{-1}(M_2 - M_1) \tag{2.19}$$

$$m_2 = E\{h(\mathbf{X})|\omega_2\} = +\frac{1}{2}(M_2 - M_1)^T \Sigma^{-1}(M_2 - M_1) \tag{2.20}$$

$$\sigma_i^2 = \text{Var}\{h(\mathbf{X})|\omega_i\} = (M_2 - M_1)^T \Sigma^{-1}(M_2 - M_1) \quad (i = 1, 2). \tag{2.21}$$

(2) *Gaussian* $\mathbf{X}$ *with* $\Sigma_1 \neq \Sigma_2$. The Bayes classifier for this case is

$$h(X) = \frac{1}{2}(X - M_1)^T \Sigma_1^{-1}(X - M_1) - \frac{1}{2}(X - M_2)^T \Sigma_2^{-1}(X - M_2)$$

$$+ \frac{1}{2}\ln(|\Sigma_1|/|\Sigma_2|) \lessgtr t. \tag{2.22}$$

The distribution of $h(\mathbf{X})$ is no longer Gaussian, but the errors for a general $h(X)$ can be expressed as follows:

$$\varepsilon_1 = \int_{h(X)>t} p_1(X)dX = \frac{1}{2} + \frac{1}{2\pi}\int\int \frac{e^{j\omega[h(X)-t]}}{j\omega} p_1(X)d\omega\, dX \tag{2.23}$$

$$\varepsilon_2 = \int_{h(X)<t} p_2(X)dX = \frac{1}{2} - \frac{1}{2\pi}\int\int \frac{e^{j\omega[h(X)-t]}}{j\omega} p_2(X)d\omega\, dX \tag{2.24}$$

where the unspecified integral regions are the entire domain for X and $[-\infty, +\infty]$ for ω. Particularly, when $h(X)$ is the quadratic function of (2.22) and $p_i(X)$'s are Gaussian, we can integrate (2.23) and (2.24) explicitly with respect to X to obtain

$$\varepsilon_1 = \frac{1}{2} + \frac{1}{\pi}\int_0^\infty \frac{\prod_{i=1}^n |\phi_{1i}(\omega)|}{\omega} \sin\left\{\left[\sum_{i=1}^n \angle\phi_{1i}(\omega)\right] - \omega t\right\} d\omega \tag{2.25}$$

$$\varepsilon_2 = \frac{1}{2} - \frac{1}{\pi}\int_0^\infty \frac{\prod_{i=1}^n |\phi_{2i}(\omega)|}{\omega} \sin\left\{\left[\sum_{i=1}^n \angle\phi_{2i}(\omega)\right] - \omega t\right\} d\omega \tag{2.26}$$

where

$$|\phi_{ji}(\omega)| = (1 + \omega^2 a_{ji})^{-1/4} \exp\left[\frac{1}{2}(-b_{ji}^2\omega^2)/(1 + \omega^2 a_{ji}^2)\right] \tag{2.27}$$

$$\angle\phi_{ji}(\omega) = \frac{1}{2}\tan^{-1}(a_{ji}\omega) - \frac{1}{2}\omega[c_{ji} + (a_{ji}b_{ji}^2\omega^2)/(1 + \omega^2 a_{ji}^2)] \tag{2.28}$$

$$a_{1i} = 1 - \frac{1}{\lambda_i}, \quad b_{1i} = \frac{d_{2i} - d_{1i}}{\lambda_i}, \quad c_{1i} = \frac{b_{1i}^2}{1 - a_{1i}} + \ln\lambda_i \tag{2.29}$$

$$a_{2i} = \lambda_i - 1, \quad b_{2i} = \sqrt{\lambda_i}(d_{2i} - d_{1i}), \quad c_{2i} = \frac{-b_{2i}^2}{1 + a_{2i}} + \ln\lambda_i. \tag{2.30}$$

The λ's are the diagonal components of Λ which are obtained by simultaneously diagonalizing Σ_1 and Σ_2 as

$$A^T \Sigma_1 A = I \quad \text{and} \quad A^T \Sigma_2 A = \Lambda \tag{2.31}$$

and the $(d_{2i} - d_{1i})$ is the ith component of the vector $A^T(M_2 - M_1)$. Equations (2.25) and (2.26) must be integrated numerically, but they are one-dimensional integrations.

Upper and lower bounds. The computation of the Bayes error is very complex unless $h(X)$ is linear. Furthermore, since a numerical integration is involved, the Bayes error cannot be expressed explicitly. An alternative is to use the *upper* and *lower bounds* of the Bayes error as a measure of class separability. Some of popular bounds are listed as follows:

$$E\{q_1(\mathbf{X})q_2(\mathbf{X})\} : \qquad \text{2 nearest-neighbor error} \tag{2.32}$$

$$E\{\min[q_1(\mathbf{X}), q_2(\mathbf{X})]\} : \qquad \text{Bayes error} \tag{2.33}$$

$$2E\{q_1(\mathbf{X})q_2(\mathbf{X})\} : \qquad \text{Nearest-neighbor error} \tag{2.34}$$

$$-\tfrac{1}{2\ln 2}\, E\{q_1(\mathbf{X})\ln q_1(\mathbf{X}) + q_2(\mathbf{X})\ln q_2(\mathbf{X})\} : \qquad \text{Equivocation} \tag{2.35}$$

$$E\{\sqrt{q_1(\mathbf{X})q_2(\mathbf{X})}\} : \qquad \text{Bhattacharyya bound} \tag{2.36}$$

The inequalities $(2.32) \leq (2.33) \leq (2.34) \leq (2.35) \leq (2.36)$ hold regardless of the distributions.

One of the popular bounds is the *Bhattacharyya bound*, which has an explicit expression for *Gaussian distributions*:

$$E\{\sqrt{q_1(\mathbf{X})q_2(\mathbf{X})}\} = \sqrt{P_1 P_2}\, e^{-\mu} \tag{2.37}$$

$$\mu = \frac{1}{8}(M_1 - M_2)^T \left[\frac{\Sigma_1 + \Sigma_2}{2}\right]^{-1}(M_1 - M_2) + \frac{1}{2}\ln \frac{|(\Sigma_1 + \Sigma_2)/2|}{\sqrt{|\Sigma_1|}\sqrt{|\Sigma_2|}} . \tag{2.38}$$

The first term of (2.38) indicates the class separability due to the mean difference, and the second term gives that due to the covariance difference.

When the distributions are non-Gaussian, (2.37) with (2.38) is no longer guaranteed to bound the Bayes error. Still, in order to use (2.38) as an effective class separability measure, one may transform each variable to a Gaussian-like one. For example, *power transforms, $y_i = x_i^\nu$ $(i = 1, \ldots, n)$*, may be used for causal distributions. Such a variable transformation is useful not only for measuring the class separability, but also for designing a better classifier. Designing the Bayes classifier for Gaussian distributions, even with additional variable transformations, is often easier than designing the Bayes classifier for non-Gaussian distributions.

Scatter measures. The bounds discussed above are valid only for two class problems. There exist no well accepted extensions of the above bounds to multiclass. *Scatter measures*, introduced here as an alternative, are intuitively derived, simple, but not directly related to the Bayes error. They are for multiclasses. Let us define for L-class:

$$S_b = \sum_{i=1}^{L} P_i(M_i - M)(M_i - M)^T \quad \text{Between-class scatter matrix} \quad (2.39)$$

$$S_w = \sum_{i=1}^{L} P_i\Sigma_i \quad \text{Within-class scatter matrix} \quad (2.40)$$

$$S_m = \mathrm{E}\{(\mathbf{X} - M)(\mathbf{X} - M)^T\} = S_b + S_w \quad \text{Mixture scatter matrix} \quad (2.41)$$

The class separability can be measured by the combinations of these matrices:

$$\mathrm{tr}S_w^{-1}S_b, \quad \mathrm{tr}\, S_m^{-1}S_w, \quad \ln|S_m^{-1}S_w| \quad \text{etc.} \quad (2.42)$$

where trace and log-determinant are for converting a matrix to a number. The first and second ones are often used for feature extraction and clustering respectively. All combinations, $S_w^{-1}S_b$, $S_m^{-1}S_w$, $S_m^{-1}S_b$ etc., share the same eigenvectors, and their eigenvalues are well related. The first one of (2.42) measures class separability based on the scatter of class means, normalized by S_w, and the others are the variations. Therefore, the scatter measures can be applied only for the cases where classes are separated mainly by mean-difference. There are no measures available for multiclasses mainly separated by covariance-difference.

3. Classifier Design

Once the structure of data is studied thoroughly, it is easy to select a proper classifier for the data. This section presents how several typical classifiers can be designed.

3.1. *Linear Classifiers*

The Bayes classifier becomes linear for the following two cases.

(1) *Gaussian* $\mathbf{X}$ *with* $\Sigma_1 = \Sigma_2 = \Sigma$: For this case, the Bayes classifier is expressed by (2.17), which is linear. In particular, when $\Sigma = I$,

$$h(X) = (M_2 - M_1)^T X + \frac{1}{2}(M_1^T M_1 - M_2^T M_2) \lessgtr t. \quad (3.1)$$

This classifier is also known as the *distance classifier* in which $(X - M_1)^T(X - M_1) \underset{\omega_2}{\overset{\omega_1}{\lessgtr}} (X - M_2)^T(X - M_2)$, or the *correlation classifier* in which $M_1^T X \underset{\omega_2}{\overset{\omega_1}{\gtrless}} M_2^T X$ with an energy constant condition $M_1^T M_1 = M_2^T M_2$. In both cases, $P_1 = P_2$ and thus $t = 0$ is assumed. When $\Sigma \neq I$, the distance or correlation classifier may still be applied, but only after $\mathbf{X}$ is linearly transformed to $\mathbf{Y} = A^T \mathbf{X}$ in order to make $\Sigma_Y = A^T \Sigma A = I$.

(2) *Binary independent* $\mathbf{x}_i$'*s*: For independent $\mathbf{x}_j$'s taking either $+1$ or -1,

$$p_i(X) = \prod_{j=1}^{n} w_{ij}^{(1+x_j)/2}(1 - w_{ij})^{(1-x_j)/2}[\delta(x_j - 1) + \delta(x_j + 1)] \quad (3.2)$$

where $w_{ij} = \Pr\{x_j = +1|\omega_i\}$. Substituting (3.2) into (2.6),

$$h(X) = -\frac{1}{2}\left\{\sum_{j=1}^{n}\left[\ln\frac{w_{1j}(1-w_{2j})}{w_{2j}(1-w_{1j})}\right]x_j + \sum_{j=1}^{n}\left[\ln\frac{w_{1j}(1-w_{1j})}{w_{2j}(1-w_{2j})}\right]\right\}. \qquad (3.3)$$

For Gaussian $\mathbf{X}$ with $\Sigma_1 \neq \Sigma_2$ and more general non-Gaussian $\mathbf{X}$, a linear classifier is not the best one. However, because of its simplicity and robustness, a linear classifier is frequently adopted. The design procedure is as follows.

$$h(X) = V^T X \underset{\omega_2}{\overset{\omega_1}{\gtrless}} t. \qquad (3.4)$$

Equation (3.4) indicates that $\mathbf{X}$ is linearly mapped down to a variable $\mathbf{h}$ and the distributions of $\mathbf{h}$ for ω_1 and ω_2 are separated by a threshold t. Thus, the optimum V is found by minimizing the probability of error in the h-space. Because of complexity in the error computation, simpler criteria such as $f(m_1, m_2, \sigma_1^2, \sigma_2^2)$ are often used, where $m_i = \mathrm{E}\{h(\mathbf{X})|\omega_i\} = V^T M_i$ and $\sigma_i^2 = \mathrm{Var}\{h(\mathbf{X})|\omega_i\} = V^T\Sigma_i V$. The typical examples are

$$f = \frac{(m_1 - m_2)^2}{\sigma_1^2 + \sigma_2^2} \qquad \text{Fisher's criterion} \qquad (3.5)$$

$$f = \frac{P_1(m_1 - m_0)^2 + P_2(m_2 - m_0)^2}{P_1\sigma_1^2 + P_2\sigma_2^2} \qquad \left(\frac{\text{between class scatter}}{\text{within class scatter}}\right) \qquad (3.6)$$

where $m_0 = P_1 m_1 + P_2 m_2$ is the mixture mean. These criteria measure the class separability of the distributions of $\mathbf{h}$. The solution of $\partial f/\partial V = 0$ is

$$V \propto [s\Sigma_1 + (1-s)\Sigma_2]^{-1}(M_2 - M_1) \qquad (3.7)$$

where

$$s = \frac{\partial f/\partial\sigma_1^2}{\partial f/\partial\sigma_1^2 + \partial f/\partial\sigma_2^2}. \qquad (3.8)$$

That is, the optimum V always takes the form of (3.7) regardless of the functional form of f. The effect of f is observed only in the averaging coefficient of covariance matrices, s. For example, $s = 0.5$ for (3.5) and $s = P_1$ for (3.6).

V can be found even without specifying f. Since the form of V is known as in (3.7), we change s from 0 to 1 with a certain increment, say, 0.1, compute the empirical distribution functions of $\mathbf{h} = V^T\mathbf{X}$ for ω_1 and ω_2 from the given data set, select the value of the threshold, and count the number of misclassified samples. The optimum s is the one which gives the smallest error in this operation.

The Bhattacharyya bound of (2.38) gives a simple test to decide whether or not a linear classifier is appropriate. When the first term of (2.38) is dominant, the classifiability comes mainly from the mean difference. Therefore, a linear classifier is a proper choice. However, if the second term is significant, the covariance difference plays an important role, and a quadratic classifier is called for.

3.2. *Quadratic Classifiers*

For Gaussian $\mathbf{X}$, the Bayes classifier becomes quadratic, as shown in (2.7) or (2.22). In practice, the quadratic classifier of (2.22) is widely adopted in many applications, even without checking the Gaussianness of $\mathbf{X}$, and with much success. Probably, this is the classifier everyone may try first, even before conducting data structure analysis.

However, it is not known how to design the optimum quadratic classifier for non-Gaussian distributions, as the linear classifier was designed. The optimization of $f(m_1, m_2, \sigma_1^2, \sigma_2^2)$ for $\mathbf{h} = \mathbf{X}^T Q \mathbf{X} + V^T \mathbf{X}$ with respect to a matrix Q and a vector V is too complex. If quadratic terms $\mathbf{x}_j \mathbf{x}_k$'s are treated as new variables $\mathbf{y}_i$, $\mathbf{h} = \Sigma\Sigma q_{jk}\mathbf{x}_j\mathbf{x}_k + \Sigma\nu_i\mathbf{x}_i$ becomes a linear equation as $\mathbf{h} = \Sigma a_i\mathbf{y}_i + \Sigma\nu_i\mathbf{x}_i$. However, for high-dimensional cases, the number of $\mathbf{y}_i$'s becomes prohibitively large.

Two-dimensional display. One of the procedures used to improve the performance of the quadratic classifier is to plot $\mathbf{X}$ in a two-dimensional display where $d_i^2(X) = (X - M_i)^T \Sigma_i^{-1} (X - M_i)$ for $i = 1, 2$ are used as the x and y axes. If $\mathbf{X}$ is Gaussian, the Bayes classifier becomes a $45°$ line with a proper y-crossing point. When the distribution is not perfectly Gaussian, we can observe in the display that the $45°$ line is not the best boundary to minimize the number of misclassified samples. Then, visually we can find a better line to classify samples by changing the slope and the y-crossing point of the line. It corresponds to adjusting α and β of the following quadratic classifier:

$$d_2^2(X) \underset{\omega_2}{\overset{\omega_1}{\gtrless}} \alpha d_1^2(X) + \beta. \tag{3.9}$$

Once samples are plotted and examined, the boundary in the display need not be restricted to a line. Any curve could be drawn. This flexibility is the advantage of seeing the data on the display.

Fourier transform. When a *stationary* random process is time-sampled, the coefficients of the *discrete Fourier transform* are uncorrelated, and its covariance matrix becomes diagonal. Thus, the quadratic classifier of the Fourier coefficients $\mathbf{y}_i$ is reduced to $\mathbf{h} = \Sigma_{i=1}^n (q_i|\mathbf{y}_i|^2 + v_i\mathbf{y}_i) + v_0$. This is the Bayes classifier, if $\mathbf{y}_i$'s are Gaussian.

Approximation of covariance matrices. If we can assume a structure for a covariance matrix, we can simplify the design of a quadratic classifier. In addition, the classifier becomes less sensitive to the parameter variation due to the estimation process by using a finite number of design samples. This will be discussed in the next section.

One of the possible structures is the *toeplitz form* for the correlation matrix, allowing each variable to have its distinct variance. In this case, parameters must be selected to assure that the toeplitz matrix be positive-definite. In particular, when the correlation coefficient between the ith and jth variables, γ_{ij}, is approximated by $\rho^{|i-j|}$ (ρ: a constant), the entire correlation matrix is characterized by one parameter, ρ, and its determinant and inverse matrix may be expressed explicitly.

3.3. *Piecewise Classifiers*

For the *multiclass problem*, the boundary must have a piecewise structure as follows.

Piecewise quadratic classifiers. If **X** is Gaussian, the classifier becomes, from (2.7), piecewise quadratic:

$$\min_i[\frac{1}{2}(X - M_i)^T\Sigma_i^{-1}(X - M_i) + \frac{1}{2}\ln|\Sigma_i| - \ln P_i]. \qquad (3.10)$$

The first term of (3.10) is widely used even for non-Gaussian distributions. However, it must be noted that the normalized distance of X from each class mean, M_i, must be adjusted by two constant terms, $\frac{1}{2}\ln|\Sigma_i|$ and $\ln P_i$.

Piecewise linear classifiers. When Σ_i's are similar, the quadratic term $X^T\Sigma_i^{-1}X$ is eliminated from (3.10) to get a piecewise linear classifier:

$$\min_i[-M_i^T\Sigma_i^{-1}X + \frac{1}{2}M_i^T\Sigma_i^{-1}M_i + \frac{1}{2}\ln|\Sigma_i| - \ln P_i]. \qquad (3.11)$$

Or, replacing Σ_i by the averaged covariance, $\Sigma = (\Sigma_1 + \cdots + \Sigma_L)/L$,

$$\min_i[-M_i^T\Sigma^{-1}X + \frac{1}{2}M_i^T\Sigma^{-1}M_i - \ln P_i]. \qquad (3.12)$$

Another possibility is to design the optimal linear classifier for each pair of classes. In this case, $L(L-1)/2$ classifiers must be designed, instead of L in (3.11) or (3.12).

Clustering. In some applications, each class distribution would be handled better by dividing it into several clusters. For example, take the signatures of a target viewed from the front and side. Since they are so different, it may be more appropriate to separate them into several clusters rather than to treat all of them as one class.

Considering each cluster as a class, we can form a new multiclass problem with a significantly increased number of classes. However, the details of designing such a classifier depend very much on how clusters are defined and obtained and how many classes are generated. Therefore, although important, the subject is not discussed in this chapter.

k nearest neighbor (kNN). The *kNN* classifier forms a piecewise linear boundary, although it is very complex and data dependent. The simpler boundary could be obtained by merging samples into a smaller number of representatives and then applying the *kNN* classifier to these representatives.

3.4. *Sequential Classifiers*

When m consecutive observation vectors, $X_1, \ldots, X_m$, are known as coming from the same class, we can use this additional information to reduce the classification error. That is, the number of variables is extended from n for one vector to $m \times n$ for m vectors. Thus, we can form a new random vector with $m \times n$ components and design a classifier in the $(m \times n)$-dimensional space. However, when these vectors are *statistically independent*, a simpler formula could be adopted:

$$-\ln[p_1(X_1, \ldots, X_m)/p_2(X_1, \ldots, X_m)] = \sum_{i=1}^{m} \{-\ln[p_1(X_i)/p_2(X_i)]\} \underset{\omega_2}{\overset{\omega_1}{\lessgtr}} t. \quad (3.13)$$

That is, the likelihood ratio classifier is applied to the incoming sample X_i, and the output is accumulated. Rewriting the left-hand side of the inequality as

$$\mathbf{s} = \frac{1}{m} \sum_{i=1}^{m} h(\mathbf{X}_i) \quad (3.14)$$

the expected values and variances of $\mathbf{s}$ and $\mathbf{h} = h(\mathbf{X})$ are related by

$$E\{\mathbf{s}|\omega_i\} = E\{\mathbf{h}|\omega_i\} \quad \text{and} \quad \text{Var}\{\mathbf{s}|\omega_i\} = \frac{1}{m} \text{Var}\{\mathbf{h}|\omega_i\}. \quad (3.15)$$

Thus, we can reduce the variances of $\mathbf{s}$ by increasing m, while maintaining the expected values of $\mathbf{s}$. Furthermore, the density function of $\mathbf{s}$ becomes close to a Gaussian by the central limit theorem.

Two important properties of the sequential classifier emerge from the above discussion. One is that we can make the error as small as we like by increasing m. The other is that the error is determined by a small number of parameters, $E\{\mathbf{h}|\omega_i\}$, $\text{Var}\{\mathbf{h}|\omega_i\}$, and m, and is little affected by the higher-order moments of $\mathbf{h}$.

In practice, the true $p_i(X)$'s are never known, and $h(X) = -\ln[p_1(X)/p_2(X)]$ must be replaced by some function $\hat{h}(X)$. A desired property for $\hat{h}(X)$ is

$$E\{\hat{h}(\mathbf{X})|\omega_1\} \leq 0 \quad \text{and} \quad E\{\hat{h}(\mathbf{X})|\omega_2\} \geq 0. \quad (3.16)$$

regardless of the distribution of $\mathbf{X}$. As long as (3.16) is satisfied, the random variable $\hat{h}(\mathbf{X})$ carries classification information, however small, regardless of the distribution of $\mathbf{X}$. The classifiable information can be enhanced as much as we like by increasing m in the sequential operations. Two $\hat{h}(X)$'s are known to satisfy (3.16) for all distributions of $\mathbf{X}$, whose expected vectors and covariance matrices are M_1 and Σ_1 for ω_1 and M_2 and Σ_2 for ω_2:

$$\hat{h}(X) = (M_2 - M_1)^T \Sigma^{-1} X + \frac{1}{2}(M_1^T \Sigma^{-1} M_1 - M_2^T \Sigma^{-1} M_2) \quad (3.17)$$

$$\hat{h}(X) = \frac{1}{2}(X - M_1)^T \Sigma_1^{-1}(X - M_1) - \frac{1}{2}(X - M_2)^T \Sigma_2^{-1}(X - M_2)$$

$$+ \frac{1}{2}\ln(|\Sigma_1|/|\Sigma_2|). \quad (3.18)$$

Any positive-definite matrix Σ in (3.17) satisfies (3.16). But, the averaged covariance matrix such as the one in (3.7) would be a better Σ to achieve the same performance with a smaller m. Equation (3.17) could be used, if the first term is dominant in the Bhattacharyya bound (2.38), but (3.18) is more appropriate otherwise. Note that these equations are the same as (2.17) and (2.22), respectively.

One of the most important aspects in classifier design is to make the classifier *robust*. That is, the performance of the classifier must be maintained, even if the distribution of test samples becomes somewhat different from the one used for design. The sequential technique can compensate the degradation of the performance of $h(X_i) \lessgtr t$ by increasing m.

4. Estimation of Classification Errors

So far, we have discussed the design of parametric classifiers, assuming that M_i and Σ_i are given. In practice, these parameters are estimated by using a finite number of available samples, and the estimates are random variables. Consequently, the classifier designed with these estimates variates, and its performance is also random. Therefore, it is important to know how the sample size affects classifier design and performance.

4.1. *Effect of Sample Size on Estimation*

General formula. First let us consider the problem of estimating $f = f(y_1, \ldots, y_q)$ by $\hat{f} = f(\hat{y}_1, \ldots, \hat{y}_q)$, where f is a given function, the y_i's are the true parameter values, and $\hat{y}_i$'s are their estimates. When the deviation of $\hat{y}_i$ from y_i is small, $\hat{\mathbf{f}}$ may be expanded by a Taylor series as follows:

$$\hat{\mathbf{f}} \cong f + \sum_{i=1}^{q} \frac{\partial f}{\partial y_i} \Delta \mathbf{y}_i + \frac{1}{2} \sum_{i=1}^{q} \sum_{j=1}^{q} \frac{\partial^2 f}{\partial y_i \partial y_j} \Delta \mathbf{y}_i \Delta \mathbf{y}_j \tag{4.1}$$

where $\Delta \mathbf{y}_i = \hat{\mathbf{y}}_i - y_i$. If the estimates are *unbiased*,

$$\mathrm{E}\{\hat{\mathbf{f}}\} \cong f + \frac{1}{2} \sum_{i=1}^{q} \sum_{j=1}^{q} \frac{\partial^2 f}{\partial y_i \partial y_j} \, \mathrm{E}\{\Delta \mathbf{y}_i \Delta \mathbf{y}_j\} \tag{4.2}$$

$$\mathrm{Var}\{\hat{\mathbf{f}}\} \cong \sum_{i=1}^{q} \sum_{j=1}^{q} \frac{\partial f}{\partial y_i} \frac{\partial f}{\partial y_j} \, \mathrm{E}\{\Delta \mathbf{y}_i \Delta \mathbf{y}_j\} . \tag{4.3}$$

In most parametric cases, the y_i's are the components of M_r and Σ_r ($r = 1, 2$), and $Y^T = [y_1 \cdots y_q]$ can be expressed as

$$Y^T = [m_1^{(1)}, \ldots, m_n^{(1)}, m_1^{(2)}, \ldots, m_n^{(2)}, c_{11}^{(1)}, \ldots, c_{nn}^{(1)}, c_{11}^{(2)}, \ldots, c_{nn}^{(2)}] \tag{4.4}$$

where $m_i^{(r)}$ and $c_{ij}^{(r)}$ ($i \leq j$) are the components of M_r and Σ_r respectively. Their unbiased estimates are obtained by the *sample mean* and *sample covariance matrix* as

$$\hat{\mathbf{M}}_r = \frac{1}{N_r} \sum_{i=1}^{N_r} \mathbf{X}_i^{(r)} \quad \text{and} \quad \hat{\Sigma}_r = \frac{1}{N_r - 1} \sum_{i=1}^{N_r} (\mathbf{X}_i^{(r)} - \hat{\mathbf{M}}_r)(\mathbf{X}_i^{(r)} - \hat{\mathbf{M}}_r)^T \quad (4.5)$$

where $\mathbf{X}_i^{(r)}$ is the ith sample from ω_r. When $\mathbf{X}_i^{(r)}$'s are drawn from Gaussian distributions, $E\{\Delta y_i \Delta y_j\}$ for the y_i's of (4.4) are known, and (4.2) and (4.3) become

$$E\{\Delta f\} \cong \frac{1}{2N} \sum_{r=1}^{2} \left[\sum_{i=1}^{n} \frac{\partial^2 f}{\partial m_i^{(r)2}} \lambda_i^{(r)} + \sum_{i=1}^{n} \frac{\partial^2 f}{\partial c_{ii}^{(r)2}} 2\lambda_i^{(r)2} + \sum_{i=1}^{n} \sum_{j=1}^{i-1} \frac{\partial^2 f}{\partial c_{ij}^{(r)2}} \lambda_i^{(r)} \lambda_j^{(r)} \right]$$
$$(4.6)$$

$$\text{Var}\{\hat{\mathbf{f}}\} \cong \frac{1}{N} \sum_{r=1}^{2} \left[\sum_{i=1}^{n} \left(\frac{\partial f}{\partial m_i^{(r)}} \right)^2 \lambda_i^{(r)} + \sum_{i=1}^{n} \left(\frac{\partial f}{\partial c_{ii}^{(r)}} \right)^2 2\lambda_i^{(r)2} \right.$$
$$\left. + \sum_{i=1}^{n} \sum_{j=1}^{i-1} \left(\frac{\partial f}{\partial c_{ij}^{(r)}} \right)^2 \lambda_i^{(r)} \lambda_j^{(r)} \right] \qquad (4.7)$$

where both Σ_1 and Σ_2 are assumed to be diagonal with $\lambda_i^{(r)}$ ($r = 1, 2$) as their diagonal components. Without loss of generality, any two covariance matrices can be simultaneously diagonalized. Also, $N_1 = N_2 = N$ is assumed for simplicity. Note that both the bias of (4.6) and the variance of (4.7) are proportional to $1/N$. The other terms are determined by the underlying distributions. This is true even when $\mathbf{X}_i^{(r)}$'s are drawn from non-Gaussian distributions.

Estimation procedure of $\mathbf{f}$. Equation (4.6) can be rewritten as

$$E\{\hat{\mathbf{f}}\} \cong f + \frac{\nu}{N}. \qquad (4.8)$$

This equation suggests the following procedure to estimate f:

(1) Change N to $N_1, \ldots, N_\ell$. For each N_i, compute $\hat{\mathbf{M}}_r$ and $\hat{\Sigma}_r$ and subsequently $\hat{\mathbf{f}}$. Repeat this τ times independently, and approximate $E\{\hat{\mathbf{f}}\}$ by the sample mean of the τ results.

(2) Plot the empirical points of $E\{\hat{\mathbf{f}}\}$ vs. $1/N$. Then, find the line best fitted to these points. The slope of the line is ν, and the y-crossing point is the estimate of f.

Bhattacharyya distance. The Bhattacharyya distance of (2.38) is a function of M_r and Σ_r. Thus, the bias of (4.6) can be further reduced by computing the partial derivatives of this function. Treating the first and second terms separately,

$$E\{\Delta\mu_1\} \cong \frac{1}{4N} \left[n + \sum_{i=1}^{n} \sum_{j=1}^{n} \frac{m_j^2(1 + \lambda_i\lambda_j)}{(1 + \lambda_j)^2(1 + \lambda_i)} + \sum_{i=1}^{n} \frac{m_i^2(1 + \lambda_i^2)}{(1 + \lambda_i)^3} \right] \qquad (4.9)$$

$$E\{\Delta\mu_2\} \cong \frac{1}{4N} \left[n(n+1) - \sum_{i=1}^{n} \sum_{j=1}^{n} \frac{1 + \lambda_i\lambda_j}{(1 + \lambda_i)(1 + \lambda_j)} - \sum_{i=1}^{n} \frac{1 + \lambda_i^2}{(1 + \lambda_i)^2} \right] \qquad (4.10)$$

where $M_1 = 0$, $M_2 = [m_1 \ldots m_n]^T$, $\lambda_i^{(1)} = 1$ $(\Lambda_1 = I)$ and $\lambda_i^{(2)} = \lambda_i$ $(\Lambda_2 = \Lambda)$ are used without losing generality. For example, when $m_i = 0$ and $\lambda_i = 1$, $\mathrm{E}\{\Delta\mu_1\} \cong n/(4N)$ and $\mathrm{E}\{\Delta\mu_2\} \cong n(n+1)/(8N)$. This is the case where the Bhattacharyya distance is measured between two sample sets generated from the same Gaussian distribution. Although $\mu_1 = \mu_2 = 0$ for $N = \infty$, a finite N creates the biases. Note that $\mathrm{E}\{\Delta\mu_1\}$ is proportional to $1/k$ $(k = N/n$: ratio of sample size and dimensionality) while $\mathrm{E}\{\Delta\mu_2\}$ depends on $(n+1)/k$. In order to maintain the same amount of bias $(\mathrm{E}\{\Delta\mu\} = \mathrm{E}\{\Delta\mu_1\} + \mathrm{E}\{\Delta\mu_2\})$, a larger k must be chosen as n increases. For example, to meet $\mathrm{E}\{\Delta\mu\} \leq 0.223$, k must be larger than 6.2 and 39.6 for $n = 8$ and 64 respectively. The variances of (4.7) also can be computed similarly.

4.2. *Estimation of Classification Errors*

The classification errors of (2.23) and (2.24) are the members of the family of functions presented in (4.1) and (4.4), when $h(X)$ and $p_r(X)$ are functions of M_r and Σ_r. However, in this case, the randomness comes from two sources: the finite design-sample set to make $\hat{h}(X)$ random and the finite test-sample set to make $\hat{p}_i(X)$ random. Since these two affect the error differently, we need to discuss their effects separately.

Effect of test samples. When a finite number of samples is available for testing a given classifier, an *error-counting* procedure is the only feasible possibility in practice. That is, each sample is tested by the classifier and the number of misclassified samples is counted. Then,

$$\mathrm{E}_t\{\hat{\varepsilon}_r\} = \varepsilon_r \quad \text{and} \quad \mathrm{Var}_t\{\hat{\varepsilon}_r\} = \frac{\varepsilon_r(1 - \varepsilon_r)}{\mathcal{N}_r} \quad (r = 1, 2) \tag{4.11}$$

where E_t and Var_t indicate that the expectations are taken with respect to test samples, and $\mathcal{N}_r$ is the number of test samples from ω_r. This is an unbiased estimate. Furthermore, (4.11) is valid regardless of functional forms for $h(X)$ and $p_r(X)$.

Effect of design samples. When a finite number of design samples is used to compute $\hat{M}_r$, $\hat{\Sigma}_r$ and then $\hat{h}(X)$, $\mathrm{E}_d\{\hat{\varepsilon}_r\}$ and $\mathrm{Var}_d\{\hat{\varepsilon}_r\}$ can be obtained through (2.23) and (2.24) for given test distributions, $p_r(X)$, where E_d and Var_d indicate the expectations with respect to design samples. The resulting bias is

$$\mathrm{E}_d\{\hat{\varepsilon}\} \cong \varepsilon + \frac{\nu}{N} \tag{4.12}$$

where $\varepsilon = P_1\varepsilon_1 + P_2\varepsilon_2$, and ν is determined by the underlying distributions of design samples, given test distributions and the functional form of $h(X)$. The number of design samples is denoted by N $(= N_1 = N_2)$ and distinguished from the test sample size $\mathcal{N}$. Although ν is a complicated function and can be computed explicitly only for simple special cases, ν can be obtained empirically by the estimation procedure of (4.8).

When $h(X)$ is the quadratic classifier of (2.22) with $\Sigma_1 = \Sigma_2 = I$ and $P_1 = P_2$, ν becomes

$$\nu_q \cong \frac{1}{4\sqrt{2\pi M^T M}} e^{-M^T M/8} \left[n^2 + \left(1 + \frac{M^T M}{2} \right) n + \left(\frac{(M^T M)^2}{16} - \frac{M^T M}{2-1} - 1 \right) \right] \tag{4.13}$$

where $M = M_2 - M_1$.

On the other hand, when $h(X)$ is the linear classifier of (2.17) with $\Sigma_1 = \Sigma_2 = I$ and $P_1 = P_2$, ν becomes

$$\nu_\ell = \frac{1}{4\sqrt{2\pi M^T M}} e^{-M^T M/8} \left[\left(1 + \frac{M^T M}{4} \right) n - 1 \right] . \tag{4.14}$$

When $\Sigma_1 = \Sigma_2$, the quadratic $h(X)$ of (2.22) becomes the same as the linear $h(X)$ of (2.17). However, when the estimated covariance matrices, $\hat{\Sigma}_1 \neq \hat{\Sigma}_2$, are used, $\hat{h}(X)$ of (2.22) differs from that of (2.17). As a result, $\mathrm{E}\{\Delta\varepsilon\}$ for the quadratic classifier is proportional to n^2/N while $\mathrm{E}\{\Delta\varepsilon\}$ for the linear classifier tends to n/N when n gets large. This implies that many more samples are needed to properly design a quadratic classifier than a linear classifier.

More generally, (4.6) suggests that the bias could be proportional to n^2 because of the double summation of the last term. This is due to the fact that n^2 correlations are estimated. This number could be significantly reduced, if we assume a structure of the covariance matrix and estimate a smaller number of parameters.

As for $\mathrm{Var}_d\{\hat{\varepsilon}\}$, we have

$$\mathrm{Var}_d\{\hat{\varepsilon}\} \propto \begin{cases} \dfrac{1}{N^2} & \text{for the Bayes classifier} \\[2mm] \dfrac{1}{N} & \text{otherwise} \end{cases} . \tag{4.15}$$

Effect of independent design and test samples. When both design and test samples are finite and they are independent, the bias and variance of $\hat{\varepsilon}$ are

$$\mathrm{E}\{\hat{\varepsilon}\} \cong \mathrm{E}_d\{\hat{\varepsilon}\} \tag{4.16}$$

$$\mathrm{Var}\{\hat{\varepsilon}\} \cong \sum_{r=1}^{2} P_r^2 \frac{\mathrm{E}_d\{\hat{\varepsilon}_r\}[1 - \mathrm{E}_d\{\hat{\varepsilon}_r\}]}{N_r} + \mathrm{Var}_d\{\hat{\varepsilon}\} \tag{4.17}$$

where E and Var indicate that the expectations are taken with respect to both design and test samples. Note that $\mathrm{Var}_t\{\hat{\varepsilon}_r\}$ of (4.11) is obtained from the first term of (4.17) by replacing $\mathrm{E}_d\{\hat{\varepsilon}_r\}$ by ε_r. Since $\mathrm{E}_d\{\hat{\varepsilon}_r\} \cong \varepsilon_r + \nu_r/N_r$ we can conclude as follows:

(1) the bias of the classification error comes entirely from the finite design set, and

(2) the variance comes predominantly from the finite test set.

4.3. *Holdout, Leave-One-Out, and Resubstitution Methods*

When only one set of samples is available and the performance of the specified classifier is to be estimated, we need to decide how to divide the samples into two groups, design and test.

Upper and lower bounds of the Bayes error. In general, the classification error is a function of two sets of data, the design set $\mathcal{P}_D$ and the test set $\mathcal{P}_T$, and may be expressed as $\varepsilon(\mathcal{P}_D, \mathcal{P}_T)$ where ε is an operator to compute the Bayes error. We assume that both $\mathcal{P}_D$ and $\mathcal{P}_T$ are drawn from the same set of underlying distributions $\mathcal{P} = \{p_1(X), p_2(X)\}$. If $\mathcal{P}$ is used for design, the resulting classifier is the Bayes which produces the Bayes error by testing $\mathcal{P}$. That is, the Bayes error is expressed by $\varepsilon(\mathcal{P}, \mathcal{P})$. Letting $\hat{\mathcal{P}}_1$ and $\hat{\mathcal{P}}_2$ be two different sets of samples independently drawn from $\mathcal{P}$, $\varepsilon(\mathcal{P}, \mathcal{P})$ can be bounded as

$$\mathrm{E}_{\hat{\mathcal{P}}_1}\{\varepsilon(\hat{\mathcal{P}}_1, \hat{\mathcal{P}}_1)\} \leq \varepsilon(\mathcal{P}, \mathcal{P}) \leq \mathrm{E}_{\hat{\mathcal{P}}_2}\{\varepsilon(\hat{\mathcal{P}}_1, \hat{\mathcal{P}}_2)\}. \tag{4.18}$$

The rightmost term indicates that, as long as design and test sample sets are independent, the resulting error is larger than the Bayes in expectation with respect to test samples. The leftmost term suggests that, if the same set is used for both design and test, the resulting error is smaller than the Bayes in expectation. These procedures are called the *holdout (H)* and *resubstitute (R) methods* respectively.

The *H* method works well, if many data sets can be generated by a computer. However, in practice, with only one set of data, we need to divide the available data into two independent groups. This reduces the number of samples available for each of design and test. Also, it must be assured that the distributions of design and test samples are close. Another problem is how to allocate samples to design and test. This is normally done by balancing the bias due to the design sample size and the variance due to the test sample size.

The *leave-one-out (L) method* alleviates the above difficulties of the *H* method. In this method, one sample is excluded, the classifier is designed on the remaining $N-1$ samples, and the excluded sample is tested by the classifier. This is repeated N times to test all N samples. The number of misclassified samples is counted to obtain the estimate of the error. Since each test sample is excluded from the design sample set, the design and test sets are independent. Also, since all N samples are tested and $N-1$ samples are used for design, the available samples are more effectively utilized. Furthermore, we do not need to worry about dissimilarity between the design and test distributions. Although the *L* method requires N classifiers (one for each sample), these classifiers may be computed with little extra computer time as the perturbations from the classifier designed from N samples. This will be shown for the quadratic classifier next and for nonparametric cases later.

R and L methods for the quadratic classifiers. In the *R* method, all available samples, $X_i^{(r)}$ ($r = 1, 2$; $i = 1, \ldots, N_r$), are used to compute $\hat{\mathbf{M}}_r$ and $\hat{\Sigma}_r$ of (4.5).

Then, the same samples are tested as to whether or not the following inequality is satisfied:

$$h_R(X_k) = \frac{1}{2}(X_k - \hat{M}_1)^T \hat{\Sigma}_1^{-1}(X_k - \hat{M}_1) - \frac{1}{2}(X_k - \hat{M}_2)^T \hat{\Sigma}_2^{-1}(X_k - \hat{M}_2)$$

$$+ \frac{1}{2}\ln(|\hat{\Sigma}_1|/|\hat{\Sigma}_2|) \underset{\omega_2}{\overset{\omega_1}{\lessgtr}} t$$

$$\text{for testing } X_k \in \{X_1^{(1)}, \ldots, X_{N_1}^{(1)}, X_1^{(2)}, \ldots, X_{N_2}^{(2)}\}. \tag{4.19}$$

Then, the number of misclassified samples is counted. This error is supposed to be smaller than the true error of the classifier.

On the other hand, in the L method, $X_k^{(1)} \in \omega_1$ is excluded from the computations of $\hat{M}_1$ and $\hat{\Sigma}_1$, and the modified $\hat{M}_1$ and $\hat{\Sigma}_1$ are used in (4.19) to test $X_k^{(1)}$. Similarly, $\hat{M}_2$ and $\hat{\Sigma}_2$ are modified for testing $X_k^{(2)} \in \omega_2$. The resulting quadratic equation $h_L(X_k)$ becomes

$$h_L(X_k) = h_R(X_k) + \begin{cases} +g(N_1, d_1^2(X_k)) & \text{for } X_k \in \omega_1 \\ -g(N_2, d_2^2(X_k)) & \text{for } X_k \in \omega_2 \end{cases} \tag{4.20}$$

where

$$g(N_r, d_r^2(X_k)) = \frac{1}{2}\frac{(N_r^2 - 3N_r + 1)d_r^2(X_k)/(N_r - 1) + N_r d_r^4(X_k)}{(N_r - 1)^2 - N_r d_r^2(X_k)}$$

$$+ \frac{1}{2}\ln\left[1 - \frac{N_r}{(N_r - 1)^2}d_r^2(X_k)\right] + \frac{n}{2}\ln\frac{N_r - 1}{N_r - 2} > 0 \tag{4.21}$$

and

$$d_r^2(X_k) = (X_k - \hat{M}_r)^T \hat{\Sigma}_r^{-1}(X_k - \hat{M}_r). \tag{4.22}$$

Equation (4.20) indicates that, for $X_k \in \omega_1$, $h_L(X_k)$ is larger than $h_R(X_k)$, and the chance of X_k being misclassified is increased. The same is true for $X_k \in \omega_2$. Therefore, the L error is always larger than the R error.

When the R method is used to count the error, $h_R(X_k)$ and $d_r^2(X_k)$ $(r = 1, 2)$ must be computed for all $(N_1 + N_2)X_k$'s. The L method requires an additional computation of (4.21) for each k. However, since (4.21) is a scalar function, the computation time for this part is negligibly small. Thus, when $h_R(X_k)$ is computed and tested for each X_k, $h_L(X_k)$ is also computed and tested at the same time with little additional computer time.

5. Nonparametric Procedures

As Fig. 1 shows, nonparametric procedures are necessary for *error estimation* in both measurement and feature spaces and *data structure analysis* before a para-

metric structure of the data is determined. Nonparametric procedures are based on
the estimation of a density function without assuming any mathematical form.

5.1. *Estimation of a Density Function*

There are two approaches for density estimation: one is the *Parzen* approach
and the other is the *k-nearest neighbor (NN)* approach. They have similar statistical
properties with minor differences.

Parzen density estimate. When N samples $\mathbf{X}_1, \ldots, \mathbf{X}_N$, are given, but no mathematical form can be assumed for the density function, the value of the density
function at X may be estimated by

$$\hat{\mathbf{p}}(X) = \frac{1}{N} \sum_{i=1}^{N} \kappa(X - \mathbf{X}_i) \tag{5.1}$$

where $\kappa(\cdot)$ is called a *kernel function*. In practice, selection of the kernel function is
limited to either Gaussian or uniform particularly in a high-dimensional space. A
more general form for $\kappa(\cdot)$ is

$$\kappa(X) = \frac{m\Gamma\left(\dfrac{n}{2}\right)\Gamma^{n/2}\left(\dfrac{n+2}{2m}\right)}{(n\pi)^{n/2}\Gamma^{n/2+1}\left(\dfrac{n}{2m}\right)} \cdot \frac{1}{r^n |A|^{1/2}} \exp\left[-\left\{\frac{\Gamma\left(\dfrac{n+2}{2m}\right)}{n\Gamma\left(\dfrac{n}{2m}\right)} X^T (r^2 A)^{-1} X\right\}^m\right]$$

$$\tag{5.2}$$

where $\Gamma(\cdot)$ is the gamma function. When $m = 1$ and ∞, $\kappa(\cdot)$ of (5.2) are reduced
to the Gaussian and uniform kernels respectively. The matrix A, which is called
a *metric*, determines the shape of the hyperellipsoid, and r controls its size (both
in the uniform case). Otherwise coefficients are selected to satisfy two conditions:
$\int \kappa(X)dX = 1$ (which is required to satisfy $\int \hat{\mathbf{p}}(X)dX = 1$) and $\int XX^T \kappa(X)dX =
r^2 A$ (the covariance matrix of $\kappa(X)$).

The bias and variance of (5.1) are

$$\mathrm{E}\{\hat{\mathbf{p}}(X)\} \cong p(X)\left[1 + \frac{1}{2}\mathrm{tr}\left\{\frac{\nabla^2 p(X)}{p(X)} A\right\} r^2\right] \tag{5.3}$$

$$\mathrm{Var}\{\hat{\mathbf{p}}(X)\} \cong \frac{wp(X)}{N} \text{ with } w = \int \kappa^2(X)dX . \tag{5.4}$$

The control parameters of the Parzen density estimate are m, r, A and N and their
optimal choices could be found by minimizing $\mathrm{E}\{[\hat{\mathbf{p}}(X) - p(X)]^2\}$ which is $(\text{Bias})^2 +$
Var. However, the optimal selection of parameters for density estimation does not
coincide with the one for classification.

kNN density estimate. In this approach, the kth *NN* sample of X is found, and the
distance d_k (or the corresponding volume v_k) is measured, where $d_k^2 = (X_{kNN} -$

$X)^T A^{-1}(X_{kNN} - X)$, $v_k = c|A|^{1/2} d_k^n$, A is a metric, and c is a constant. Then, the density estimate at X is

$$\hat{\mathbf{p}}(X) = \frac{k-1}{N \mathbf{v}_k(X)} \, . \tag{5.5}$$

where $\mathbf{v}_k$ is a random variable and the function of X. Defining u as the probability of a sample falling within v_k, the density function of $\mathbf{u}$ is known as

$$p_u(u) = \frac{N!}{(k-1)!(N-k)!} \, u^{k-1}(1-u)^{N-k} \quad 0 \le u \le 1 \, . \tag{5.6}$$

Since $u \cong v_k p(X)$ for a small v_k, the density function of $\mathbf{v}_k$ can be computed from (5.6). Thus, the bias and variance of the kNN density estimate are also obtained, resulting in

$$E\{\hat{\mathbf{p}}(X)\} \cong p(X) \left[1 + \frac{1}{2} \operatorname{tr}\left\{ \frac{\nabla^2 p(X)}{p(X)} A \right\} \left(\frac{k-1}{N \, c|A|^{1/2} p(X)} \right)^{2/n} \right] \tag{5.7}$$

$$\operatorname{Var}\{\hat{\mathbf{p}}(X)\} \cong \frac{p^2(X)}{k-2} \, . \tag{5.8}$$

The term $(\cdot)^{2/n}$ of (5.7) is d_k^2 by (5.5). Also, Var $\{\hat{\mathbf{p}}(X)\}$ of (5.4) becomes $p^2(X)/k$ for a uniform kernel in which w is $1/v$. That is, the biases and variances of the Parzen and kNN density estimates are very similar. The kNN density estimate could be considered as the Parzen one with a uniform kernel whose kernel size is adjusted by $p(X)$. The control parameters of the kNN density estimate are k, A and N, and their optimal choices are found by minimizing $E\{\hat{\mathbf{p}}(X) - p(X)]^2\}$.

Moments of the kNN distance. Since the density function of $\mathbf{v}_k$ is known, the moments of $\mathbf{d}_k$ can be computed, resulting in

$$E\{\mathbf{d}_k^m\} \cong \frac{\Gamma^{m/n}(1+n/2)}{pi^{m/2}|A|^{m/2n}} \cdot \frac{\Gamma(k+m/n)}{\Gamma(k)} \cdot \frac{\Gamma(N+1)}{\Gamma(N+1+m/n)} \int p^{-m/n}(X)dX \tag{5.9}$$

where the integrals for some distributions with the covariance matrix Σ are

$$\text{Gauss:} \quad (2\pi)^{m/2}|\Sigma|^{m/2n}(1-m/n)^{-n/2} \tag{5.10}$$

$$\text{Uniform:} \quad (2\pi)^{m/2}|\Sigma|^{m/2n}\Gamma^{-m/n}(1+n/2)(1+n/2)^{m/2} \, . \tag{5.11}$$

When m/n is small in a high-dimensional space, and A is selected as $A = \Sigma$, $E\{\mathbf{d}_k^m\}$ is determined predominantly by n and m. The effects of k and N are minimal as $\Gamma(k+m/n) \cong \Gamma(k)$ and $\Gamma(N+1+m/n) \cong \Gamma(N+1)$. Also, $E\{\mathbf{d}_k^m|X\}$ is computed by (5.9) without taking the integration, but is little affected by $p(X)$ because of a small m/n in power. The variance of $\mathbf{d}_k$ is very small and all $\mathbf{d}_k$'s are close to the expected value.

Estimation of the local dimensionality. The ratio of two averaged kNN distances depends only on k and n, but not on N and $p(X)$ as follows:

$$\frac{E\{\mathbf{d}_{k+1}\}}{E\{\mathbf{d}_k\}} = \frac{E\{\mathbf{d}_{k+1}|X\}}{E\{\mathbf{d}_k|X\}} = 1 + \frac{1}{kn} \, . \tag{5.12}$$

The n computed from $\mathbf{d}_k$'s and $\mathbf{d}_{k+1}$'s by (5.12) depends only on neighboring information, and thus indicates the *local dimensionality* (or *intrinsic dimensionality*). Generally, the dimensionality plays a dominant role in determining the statistical properties of any nonparametric estimation. For example, $E\{\mathbf{d}_k^m\}$ of (5.9) with $A = \Sigma$ is predominantly determined by n and m. However, it must be kept in mind that the n of (5.9) means the local dimensionality but not the global one.

Very large number of classes. When the number of classes is very large as in the hundreds, we may consider class expected vectors M_i $(i = 1, \ldots, L)$ as random vectors drawn from a distribution, $p(M)$. The classification error between a pair of classes, ω_i and ω_j, is determined by the distance between M_i and M_j and the amounts of noises around these M's. The overall error depends on how many neighboring classes contribute the error. On the other hand, the previous discussion indicates that, in a high-dimensional space, the kNN distance is not affected by k, L and $p(M)$. That is, each class is surrounded by many other neighboring classes with almost equal distances. Thus, almost-equal pairwise errors are added up to form the total error which could become large. Classification of a very large number of classes must be handled with special care. It is not enough to confirm that each pair of classes can be classified with a reasonably small error.

5.2. *Classification*

Parzen classifier. Substituting the Parzen density estimates into the likelihood ratio classifier of (2.6),

$$
\hat{h}(X) = - \ln \frac{\hat{p}_1(X)}{\hat{p}_2(X)} = - \ln \frac{\dfrac{1}{N_1} \sum_{i=1}^{N_1} \kappa_1(X - X_i^{(1)})}{\dfrac{1}{N_2} \sum_{i=1}^{N_2} \kappa_2(X - X_i^{(2)})} \underset{\omega_2}{\overset{\omega_1}{\gtrless}} t . \tag{5.13}
$$

This is called the *Parzen classifier* and can be used to classify X, when a set of samples $\{X_1^{(1)}, \ldots, X_{N_1}^{(1)}, X_1^{(2)}, \ldots, X_{N_2}^{(2)}\}$ is given. Each class may have a distinct kernel function.

In order to find the upper and lower bounds of the Bayes error, we may adopt the resubstitution (R) and leave-one-out (L) methods for the Parzen classifier. In the R method, the same samples, $X_i^{(r)}$ $(r = 1, 2; \; i = 1, \ldots, N_r)$, are tested by (5.13), and the number of misclassified samples is counted. On the other hand, when $X_\ell^{(1)}$ is tested in the L method, $X_\ell^{(1)}$ is excluded to form the Parzen density estimate of ω_1. Therefore, the numerator of (5.13) must be replaced by

$$
\hat{p}_{1L}(X_\ell^{(1)}) = \frac{1}{N_1 - 1} \left[\sum_{i=1}^{N_1} \kappa_1(X_\ell^{(1)} - X_i^{(1)}) - \kappa_1(X_\ell^{(1)} - X_\ell^{(1)}) \right] . \tag{5.14}
$$

The denominator stays the same as $\hat{p}_2(X_\ell^{(1)})$. Again, $X_\ell^{(1)}$ $(\ell = 1, \ldots, N_1)$ are tested and the number of misclassified samples is counted. Note that the amount subtracted in (5.14), $\kappa_1(0)$, does not depend on ℓ. When an ω_2 sample is tested, the denominator of (5.13) is modified in the same way. It can be proved that $\hat{p}_{1L}(X_\ell^{(1)}) \leq \hat{p}_1(X_\ell^{(1)})$ if $\kappa(X) \leq \kappa(0)$ which is satisfied for the kernel functions of (5.2). Therefore, the tested sample has more of a chance to be misclassified in the L method than in the R method. Also, note that the L density estimate of (5.14) can be obtained from the R density estimate by simple scalar operations — subtracting $\kappa_1(0)$ and dividing by $N_1 - 1$. Therefore, the computation time needed to obtain both the L and R density estimates is almost the same as that needed for the R density estimate alone.

kNN classifier. Using the *kNN* density estimates of (5.5), the likelihood ratio classifier becomes

$$\hat{h}(X) = -\ln \frac{\hat{p}_1(X)}{\hat{p}_2(X)} = -n \ln \frac{d_{k_2}^{(2)}(X)}{d_{k_1}^{(1)}(X)} - \ln \frac{(k_1 - 1)N_2|A_2|^{1/2}}{(k_2 - 1)N_1|A_1|^{1/2}} \underset{\omega_2}{\overset{\omega_1}{\gtrless}} t \qquad (5.15)$$

where $v_{k_r}^{(r)} = c|A_r|^{1/2}d_{k_r}^{(r)n}$ and $d_{k_r}^{(r)2}(X) = (X_{k_rNN}^{(r)} - X)^T A^{-1}(X_{k_rNN}^{(r)} - X)$. That is, in order to test X, the k_1NN from ω_1, $X_{k_1NN}^{(1)}$, and the k_2NN from ω_2, $X_{k_2NN}^{(2)}$, are found, the distances from X to these neighbors, $d_{k_1}^{(1)}$ and $d_{k_2}^{(2)}$, are measured, and $d_{k_1}^{(1)}$ and $d_{k_2}^{(2)}$ are inserted into (5.15) to test whether the left hand side is smaller or larger than t. For simplicity, $k_1 = k_2 = k$ is used in this chapter. Normally, the class covariance matrix is used for A_r and therefore $A_1 \neq A_2$.

The R and L methods of the *kNN* classifier are used to bound the Bayes error. In the R method, all samples are included in the list of design samples from which the *kNN* of the test sample is found, and the same samples are tested. When $X_\ell^{(1)}$ is tested, $X_\ell^{(1)}$ itself is the closest sample in the list. Therefore, $d_{k-1}^{(1)}(X_\ell^{(1)})$ is inserted into the denominator of (5.15) while $d_k^{(2)}(X_\ell^{(1)})$ is inserted into the numerator. On the other hand, when $X_\ell^{(1)}$ is tested in the L method, $X_\ell^{(1)}$ must be excluded from the list of design samples. Therefore, $d_k^{(1)}(X_\ell^{(1)})$ and $d_k^{(2)}(X_\ell^{(1)})$ are compared. Since $d_{k-1}^{(1)}(X_\ell^{(1)}) \leq d_k^{(1)}(X_\ell^{(1)})$, $X_\ell^{(1)}$ has more of a chance to be misclassified in the L method than in the R method. Also, note that in order to find the *kNN*, the distances to all samples are computed and compared. When $d_k^{(1)}(X_\ell^{(1)})$ is obtained, $d_{k-1}^{(1)}(X_\ell^{(1)})$ is also available. This means that the computation time needed to get both the L and R results is practically the same as the time needed for the R method alone. Similarly, for testing a ω_2 sample, $X_\ell^{(2)}$, $d_{k-1}^{(2)}(X_\ell^{(2)})$ and $d_k^{(2)}(X_\ell^{(2)})$ are compared with $d_k^{(1)}(X_\ell^{(2)})$ in the R and L method respectively.

Voting kNN classifier. Instead of selecting *kNN* from each class separately and comparing the distances, the *kNN*'s of a test sample are selected from the mixture of classes, and the number of neighbors from each class k_i, among the *kNN* is counted. The test sample is then classified to the class represented by a majority of the kNN's. That is,

$$k_r = \max\{k_1, \ldots, k_L\} \quad \rightarrow \quad X \in \omega_r \quad \left(\sum_{i=1}^{L} k_i = k\right). \tag{5.16}$$

In order to avoid confusion between these two kNN procedures, we will call (5.16) the *voting kNN* procedure and (5.15) the *volumetric kNN* procedure.

For the voting kNN procedure, it is common practice to use the same metric to measure the distances to samples from all classes, although each class could use its own metric. Since the k_i's are integers and a ranking procedure is used, it is hard to find a component of (5.16) analogous with the threshold of (5.15).

It can be shown that, with $t = 0$ in (5.15), the volumetric kNN and voting $(2k-1)NN$ procedures give identical classification results for the two-class problem using the same metric for both classes. For example, let k and $(2k-1)$ be 3 and 5 respectively. In the voting $5NN$ procedure, a test sample is classified to ω_1, if 3, 4, or 5 of the $5NN$'s belong to ω_1. This is equivalent to saying that the third NN from ω_1 is closer to the test sample than the third NN from ω_2.

In the voting kNN classification for the two-class problem, k must be odd. Otherwise, $k_1 = k_2$ could occur and we cannot decide which class the test sample is classified to. This problem may be alleviated by introducing the concept of *rejection*. That is, when $k_1 = k_2$ occurs, the test sample is rejected, and not counted as misclassified one. As a result, the classification error becomes smaller than even the Bayes error. This happens because some of the to-be-misclassified samples are rejected and not counted as the error.

The *asymptotic* $(N_r = \infty)$ performance of the voting kNN is known. For the two-class problem, the *risk* of the voting kNN classification given X, $r_k(X)$, is

$$r_{2k-1}(X) = \sum_{i=1}^{k} \frac{1}{i} \binom{2i-2}{i-1} \xi^i(X) + \frac{1}{2}\binom{2k}{k} \xi^k(X) \tag{5.17}$$

$$r_{2k}(X) = \sum_{i=1}^{k} \frac{1}{i} \binom{2i-2}{i-1} \xi^i(X) \tag{5.18}$$

where $\xi(X) = q_1(X)q_2(X)$. On the other hand, the *Bayes risk* given X is

$$r^*(X) = \min[q_1(X), q_2(X)] = \frac{1}{2} - \frac{1}{2}\sqrt{1 - 4\xi(X)}$$

$$= \sum_{i=1}^{\infty} \frac{1}{i} \binom{2i-2}{i-1} \xi^i(X). \tag{5.19}$$

Using (5.17)–(5.19), it is not difficult to prove that these conditional risks satisfy the following inequalities

$$\frac{1}{2} r^* \leq r_2 \leq r_4 \leq \cdots \leq r^* \leq \cdots \leq r_3 \leq r_1 \leq 2r^*. \tag{5.20}$$

Taking the expectation of these risks with respect to $\mathbf{X}$, the corresponding errors can be obtained. Therefore, these errors also satisfy the inequalities of (5.20). Thus,

$$\frac{1}{2}\varepsilon^* \leq \varepsilon_{2NN} \leq \varepsilon_{4NN} \leq \cdots \leq \varepsilon^* \leq \cdots \leq \varepsilon_{3NN} \leq \varepsilon_{NN} \leq 2\varepsilon^* \qquad (5.21)$$

where

$$\varepsilon^* = \mathrm{E}\{r^*(\mathbf{X})\} \quad \text{and} \quad \varepsilon_{kNN} = \mathrm{E}\{r_k(\mathbf{X})\}\,.$$

Equation (5.21) indicates that asymptotically ($N_r = \infty$) the Bayes error is bounded by the voting kNN errors; the upper bounds for odd k's and the lower bounds for even k's.

5.3. *Selection of Parameters*

As is seen in Fig. 1, one of the major objectives of nonparametric classification is to estimate the Bayes error. This is done by finding the upper and lower bounds, using the L and R methods. However, normally nonparametric estimates are heavily biased unless the parameters are carefully chosen, and the results might not bound the Bayes error. Simply increasing the sample size is not the way to reduce the biases. The required number of samples could be astronomical particularly in a high-dimensional space.

Bias of the voting kNN classification. The asymptotic kNN error is obtained by assuming $q_r(X_{\ell NN}) = q_r(X)$ where $X_{\ell NN}$ is the ℓNN of X. However, as (5.9) suggests, $X_{\ell NN}$ and X are not close in a high dimensional space. Using a better approximation, $q_r(X_{\ell NN}) \cong q_r(X) + \nabla^T q_r(X)(X_{\ell NN} - X) + \frac{1}{2}\mathrm{tr}\{\nabla^2 q_r(X)(X_{\ell NN} - X)(X_{\ell NN} - X)^T\}$, we can compute the simplest case, the bias of the NN error, for a finite sample size, resulting in

$$\mathrm{E}\{\hat{\varepsilon}_{NN}\} \cong \varepsilon_{NN} + \beta_1 \mathrm{E}_X\{|A|^{-1/n}\mathrm{tr}\{AB_1(X)\}\} \qquad (5.22)$$

where ε_{NN} is the asymptotic NN error, A is the metric, $B_1(X)$ is a matrix determined by the underlying distributions, and β_1 is a constant related to N and n as follows:

$$\beta_1 = \frac{\Gamma^{2/n}(1+n/2)\Gamma(1+2/n)}{n\pi} \cdot \frac{\Gamma(N+1)}{\Gamma(N+1+2/n)} \cong c_1(n)N^{-2/n}\,. \qquad (5.23)$$

For given distributions (given $B_1(X)$ and n), the bias is controlled by N and A. However, the reduction of β_1 in (5.23) by increasing N is very slow for a large n. For example, for $n = 64$, $N^{-2/n}$ is 0.81, 0.65 and 0.52 for $N = 10^3$, 10^6 and 10^9 respectively. The optimal A should be obtained by minimizing $\mathrm{E}_X\{\cdot\}$ of (5.22) for the global metric and $|A|^{-1/n}\mathrm{tr}\{AB_1(X)\}$ for the local metric. However, since $B_1(X)$ is too complex to compute in practice, we do not know how to select A.

The above result can be extended to the $2NN$ error as

$$\mathrm{E}\{\hat{\varepsilon}_{2NN}\} \cong \varepsilon_{2NN} + \beta_2 \mathrm{E}_X\{[|A|^{-1/n}\,\mathrm{tr}\{AB_2(X)\}]^2\} \tag{5.24}$$

$$\beta_2 = \left[\frac{\Gamma^{2/n}(1+n/2)}{n\pi}\right]^2 \frac{(1+4/n)\Gamma(1+4/n)}{(1+2/n)} \cdot \frac{\Gamma(N+1)}{\Gamma(N+1+4/n)} \cong c_2(n)N^{-4/n} \tag{5.25}$$

where $B_2(X)$ is another matrix determined by the underlying distributions. In (5.25), β_2 is proportional to $N^{-4/n}$ while β_1 is to $N^{-2/n}$. That is, as N increases, the $2NN$ error converges to its asymptotic value more quickly than the NN error – as if n were half as large. Also, note that β_2 is significantly smaller than β_1, because $\Gamma^{2/n}/n\pi$ (0.071 for $n = 64$) is squared. Since their asymptotic errors are related by $\varepsilon_{NN} = 2\varepsilon_{2NN}$ from (5.17) and (5.18), a better estimate of ε_{NN} could be obtained by estimating ε_{2NN} first and doubling it.

Parzen classifiers. In the L method, design and test samples are independent, and the bias of the classification error comes from the finite design samples. In this case, $h(X)$ in (2.23) and (2.24) is replaced by $\hat{\mathbf{h}}(X)$ of (5.13) in which the bias and variance of $\hat{p}_r(X)$ are given in (5.3) and (5.4). Therefore, we can express the bias of the error of the Parzen classifier in terms of r and N as

$$\mathrm{E}\{\Delta\hat{\varepsilon}\} \cong a_1 r^2 + a_2 r^4 + a_3 \frac{r^{-n}}{N} \tag{5.26}$$

where a_1, a_2 and a_3 are determined by the underlying distributions, the metrics A_1 and A_2 for ω_1 and ω_2, the parameter to control the shape of the kernel m, and the threshold t in (5.13). Recall in (5.3) and (5.4) that the bias of the Parzen density estimate is a function of $\nabla^2 p(X)$, A and r^2 while the variance is a function of $p(X)$, N and w (which is a function of r, A and m).

The $a_1 r^2$ and $a_2 r^4$ terms indicate how biases in the density estimates influence the performance of the classifier, while the $a_3 r^{-n}/N$ term reflects the role of the variance of the density estimates. For small values of r, the variance term dominates (5.26), and the observed error rates are significantly above the Bayes error. As r grows, however, the variance term decreases while the $a_1 r^2$ and $a_2 r^4$ terms play an increasingly significant role. Thus, for a typical plot of the observed error rate versus r, $\hat{\varepsilon}$ decreases for small values of r until a minimum point is reached, and then increases as the bias terms of the density estimates become more significant.

The r^{-n} in the third term of (5.26) for a small r and a large n is astronomically large (for example, $r^{-n} = 1.8 \times 10^{19}$ for $r = 0.5$ and $n = 64$). It is futile to attempt to bring down this term by selecting a large N and reducing a_3. The optimal r can be obtained by taking the derivative of (5.26) with respect to r and equating it to zero. The more practical solution is to compute the L and R errors for the various values of r, plot the curves, and find the optimal r.

As r increases, the biases of both L and R errors increase, and they do not bound the Bayes error. In order to reduce this bias, we must make a_1 and a_2 of (5.26) small by selecting parameters, t, A_1, A_2 and m.

(1) *Selection of the decision threshold t.* Changing t is a very effective way to reduce a_1 and a_2. Since a_1 and a_2 are very complicated functions, it is more practical to find the optimal value for t experimentally. The different optimal value for t must be computed for each selection of r. Although better but more complex procedures are available, a simple procedure to determine t is presented as follows:

For each value of r, find the value of t which minimizes the R error, and then use this value of t to find the L error. Since the selection of t is isolated from the actual values of the L estimate of the likelihood ratio, using this method helps to maintain the independence of the test operation from the design one.

(2) *Selection of metrics, A_1 and A_2.* Minimization of a_1 and a_2 with respect to A_1 and A_2 does not give any easy answer. Also, since A_1 and A_2 are $n \times n$ matrices, empirical try-and-error cannot be applied easily. An intuitive selection, which is normally used, is $A_r = \Sigma_r$. But, this is far from the optimal solution. Another alternative is $A_i = \Sigma_i - \gamma_i (X - M_i)(X - M_i)^T$ with a constant γ_i, the properties of which have not been studied extensively.

Even if $A_1 = \Sigma_r$ is a good selection of the metric, the estimation of Σ_r needs special care. That is, if the same sample set is used for both estimating Σ_r and computing the L and R errors, both L and R errors are severely and optimistically biased, and often they do not bound the Bayes error. In order to avoid this optimistic bias, we must use two independent sample sets, one for each of the above two operations. A better but more complex procedure is to exclude $X_\ell^{(r)}$ from estimating Σ_r, when $X_\ell^{(r)}$ is tested by the L and R classifiers.

(3) *Selection of m.* As m increases, the L error curve is little affected. But, the R curve steadily rises closer to the Bayes error line until $m = 4$, and then stops to improve. It means that (1) both Gaussian and uniform kernels give the similar L errors, (2) the uniform kernel is better to compute the R error than the Gaussian kernel, and (3) the uniform-like kernels are obtained by selecting $m = 4$.

kNN classifiers. The parameters of the *kNN* classifier, k, t, A_1 and A_2, are chosen in the same way as the ones of the Parzen classifier. That is, k and t are determined empirically. We do not know how to select A_1 and A_2. Samples to compute the L and R errors must be independent from samples to estimate the metrics.

References

[1] K. Fukunaga, *Introduction to Statistical Pattern Recognition*, Second Ed. (Academic Press, San Diego, CA, 1990).

[2] R. O. Duda and P. E. Hart, *Pattern Classification and Scene Analysis* (Wiley, New York, 1973).

[3] P. R. Devijver and J. Kittler, *Pattern Recognition: A Statistical Approach* (Prentice-Hall, Englewood Cliffs, New Jersey, 1982).

[4] A. K. Agrawala (ed.), *Machine Recognition of Patterns* (IEEE Press, New York, 1977).

[5] P. R. Krishnaiah and L. N. Kanal (eds.), *Handbook of Statistics 2: Classification, Pattern Recognition and Reduction of Dimensionality* (North-Holland Publ., Amsterdam, 1982).

[6] T. Y. Young and K. S. Fu (eds.), *Handbook of Pattern Recognition and Image Processing* (Academic Press, San Diego, 1986).

[7] B. V. Dasarathy (ed.), *Nearest Neighbor (NN) Norms: NN Pattern Classification Techniques* (IEEE Computer Society Press, Los Alamitos, CA, 1991).

Handbook of Pattern Recognition and Computer Vision, pp. 61–123
Eds. C. H. Chen, L. F. Pau and P. S. P. Wang
© 1993 World Scientific Publishing Company

$\boxed{\text{CHAPTER 1.3}}$

LARGE-SCALE FEATURE SELECTION

JACK SKLANSKY and WOJCIECH SIEDLECKI

Department of Electrical and Computer Engineering
University of California, Irvine, California 92717, USA

One of the most difficult and important problems in the design of automatic pattern classifiers is the selection of the measured parameters or descriptors upon which the classifier bases its determination of the classes of the observed objects. These parameters or descriptors are often referred to as *features*. We refer to the process of choosing these features from an initial set of candidates as *feature selection*.

When the initial set contains 20 or more features and the selected subset contains ten or fewer features, the problem of selecting a best or near-best subset can be quite difficult because we must search a large—often astronomically large—space of subsets of candidate features, and determine a figure of merit for an optimum or near-optimum classifier operating on each subset in this space. We refer to such problems as *large-scale feature selection*.

Large-scale feature selection may be viewed as a paradigm for a common form of intelligent behavior: the process of distinguishing phenomena that are relevant from those that are irrelevant to the occurrence of classes of events. For example, determining those factors in a person's environment that are relevant to his or her risk to various diseases is generally a difficult task requiring high intelligence.

Below we present three papers which report on successive stages of our investigation of large-scale feature selection at the University of California.

The first paper, "On automatic feature selection," presents an overview of the research on automatic feature selection, including simulated annealing and our early ideas on genetic algorithms.

The second paper, "A note on genetic algorithms for large-scale feature selection," shows how a penalty function transforms a constrained optimization problem (e.g. finding the smallest subset of features yielding an acceptably small probability of misclassification) into an unconstrained optimization, thereby facilitating the use of conventional genetic algorithms for large-scale feature selection. This approach, for an initial set of 24 features, produced genetic algorithms having a computational advantage of two orders of magnitude over a branch-and-bound search.

61

The third paper, "Constrained genetic optimization via dynamic reward-penalty balancing and its use in pattern recognition," describes the use of a dynamically adjusted penalty coefficient as a means of restricting the search of a genetic algorithm almost completely to the feasible region of the search space, even in situations where the feasible region is disjoint (i.e. consists of several components which are not connected to each other). With this modification we found that our genetic algorithm outperformed sequential search, finding smaller acceptable subsets in shorter times. For large-scale selection problems, the time complexity of branch-and-bound search grows exponentially, while our genetic search grows quadratically.

The research reported in these papers was supported by the U.S. Army Research Office under Contract DAAG29-84-K-0208.

ON AUTOMATIC FEATURE SELECTION

WOJCIECH SIEDLECKI and JACK SKLANSKY

Pattern Recognition Project, Department of Electrical Engineering
University of California, Irvine, Irvine, CA 92717, U.S.A.

We review recent research on methods for selecting features for multidimensional pattern classification. These methods include nonmonotonicity-tolerant branch-and-bound search and beam search. We describe the potential benefits of Monte Carlo approaches such as simulated annealing and genetic algorithms. We compare these methods to facilitate the planning of future research on feature selection.

Keywords: Feature selection, pattern classifier, search, decision rule, discrimination.

Introduction

Over the last twenty-five years, extensive research has taken place on the development of efficient and reliable methods for the selection of features in the design of pattern classifiers, where the features constitute the inputs to the classifier. The quality of this design depends on the relevancy, discriminatory power and ease of computation of various features.

Selecting features is an extremely difficult task, charged both with theoretical and computational problems. An effective mathematical theory for feature selection seems achievable only for a narrow specialization of the problem: linear transformations for reducing the dimensionality of the feature space, with the assumption that data are drawn from normal distributions [1–4]. The theoretical problems are usually associated with two closely related questions:

(a) "What does it mean that a feature is good or irrelevant?"
(b) "What criteria should be used to evaluate features?"

From the standpoint of Bayesian decision rules there are no bad features. One cannot improve the performance (usually understood as an error committed by the classifier) of a Bayes classifier by eliminating a feature (this property is called *monotonicity*). However, in practice the assumptions in the design of Bayes classifiers are almost never valid. As a consequence, it is possible to improve the performance of a nonideal classifier by deleting a feature (this phenomenon will be discussed later).

Reprinted from *International Journal of Pattern Recognition and Artificial Intelligence*, Vol. 2, No. 2 (1988) 197–220. © World Scientific Publishing Co.

Moreover, for a given amount of data, reducing the number of features increases the accuracy of estimates of the classifier's performance. These two facts have tremendous consequences for computational problems associated with feature selection and have led in the past to other methods for evaluating features [5–7]. These methods do not estimate the misclassification rate (i.e. the "error rate") of a classifier associated with a given set of features, but rather tend to estimate the Bayes error for this set of features. The criteria used by these methods (for instance Bhattacharyya distance or Vajda's entropy) satisfy the monotonicity property, which permits the use of efficient computational techniques. However, some evidence [8] indicates that they do not induce over an arbitrary set of features the same preference order as would be obtained by comparing the errors of the Bayes classifier. Thus, it seems that the only promising and legitimate way of evaluating features must be through the error rate of the classifier being designed (this also satisfies our intuitive understanding of the design policy, although it has some theoretical drawbacks [5,9]).

Unfortunately, none of the forms of classifiers realizable in practice by known techniques — except for the linear classifier when optimized to certain criteria — exhibits the monotonicity property. This fact is important when we realize that the problem of feature selection is essentially equivalent to searching a directed graph (in which the root node corresponds to the set of all features) and could be solved by artificial intelligence or "AI" (e.g. *branch and bound* [6]) techniques. Moreover, the total number of all possible subsets of an n-element set of features totals around 2^n and, therefore, even for small n (say, 10) any brute force method leads to a computational impracticality (especially when the evaluation of the classifier's error is costly).

In this paper we present an overview of our research on methods for automatic feature selection carried out at the Pattern Recognition Project of the University of California, Irvine over the last six years (1981–1987) [10,11]. This research has produced a group of suboptimal but efficient and robust methods. This group includes:

(1) AI methods utilizing the idea of *approximate monotonicity* [10].
(2) Other AI methods for graph searching.
(3) Monte Carlo optimization methods for combinatorial problems.

Our current research is focused on two Monte Carlo combinatorial optimization methods which have attracted much recent interest: genetic algorithms and simulated annealing. We are also investigating new means of controlling the complexity of the branch and bound algorithm.

1. The Past: A Historical Note

The pioneering work in the area of feature selection is associated with the names of Sebestyen [12], Lewis [13] and Marill and Green [14], who made their contributions in the early sixties. Since at that time the theoretical framework for evaluating the error rate of classifiers was also in its preliminary stage of development, the original approaches to feature selection were based on probabilistic measures of class separability and on entropies. In some cases (e.g. [13]) the independence of features was assumed and the features were selected on the basis of their individual merits. However, even such a simplified model did not guarantee the optimality of a selected feature subset (for instance, two independent features don't have to be the two best, as was pointed out by Cover [15]).

The question of the trade-off between the optimality and efficiency of algorithms for NP-problems (feature selection, by definition, seems to qualify as an NP-problem) was recognized early, and the mainstream of research on feature selection was thus directed toward suboptimal search methods. The invention of sequential backward selection (SBS) in 1963 [14] gave rise to a family of suboptimal stepwise forward and backward methods. The research in this direction was concluded by introducing the generalization of these algorithms proposed by Kittler in 1978 [16]. Another approach to feature selection based on the concept of dynamic programming was proposed by Chang [17], but this approach is burdened by numerous restrictive requirements (e.g. the monotonicity condition and statistical independence of features) and, therefore, has not been heavily pursued by other researchers.

The potential of any suboptimal search algorithm to select the worst possible set of features was indicated by Cover and Campenhout [18]. A breakthrough came in 1977 with the introduction of the *branch and bound algorithm*. This method, proposed by Narendra and Fukunaga [6], guaranteed the selection of an optimal feature subset if *the monotonicity condition* is satisfied. The monotonicity condition requires that a criterion function J used to evaluate feature subsets change (in our case: grow) monotonically over a sequence of nested feature subsets $\{F_1, \ldots, F_k\}$, that is

$$F_1 \subset F_2 \subset \cdots \subset F_k \quad \Rightarrow \quad J(F_1) \geq J(F_2) \geq \cdots \geq J(F_k). \tag{1}$$

Based on this concept Narendra and Fukunaga showed how to determine the subsets of features which *cannot* be considered optimal. Roughly speaking the branch and bound procedure searches in an optimally organized way the feature selection lattice, illustrated in Fig. 1. (In the lattice each node represents a feature subset, and each link represents a subset inclusion. The subsets are coded as bit-strings, i.e. as sequences of zeros and ones. The integer 1 indicates that a feature is present in a subset, and 0 indicates that the feature does not belong to it. In Fig. 1 the numbers inside the nodes denote the observed error rates, expressed as percentages, of a hypothetical classifier.

Since the kind of graph generated in the feature selection problem (each node represents a subset of features) has finite depth, the depth first search technique appeared very effective in this case and has resulted in a very efficient enumeration scheme.

When no restrictions on examining nodes (feature subsets) in the graph are assumed, the branch and bound leads to exhaustive search. However, if each node

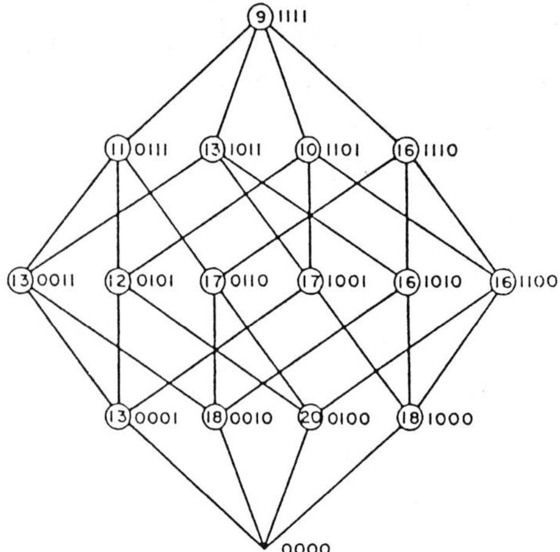

Fig. 1. An example of a feature selection lattice. The numbers in circles are error percentages.

is evaluated with the aid of a criterion function J_1 and an upper limit is set for the acceptable values of J_1 — thereby making some feature subsets *infeasible* — then the algorithm backtracks whenever an infeasible node is discovered. If the criterion function is monotonic with respect to feature subset inclusion (1), no feasible node is omitted as a result of early backtracking and, therefore, the gained savings in the search time do not violate the optimality of the selected subset.

Among all examined and, therefore, feasible subsets of features one can look for the best group of features according to a second criterion J_2. If J_2 is also monotonic with respect to a sequence of nested feature subsets, but in the direction opposite to that of J_1, then J_1 and J_2 can be interchanged, yielding a search for a feasible node among the best nodes, which is equivalent to a backward branch and bound scheme in which one takes the empty set of features as a start node.

All the considerations regarding the branch and bound procedure as applied to optimal feature selection are valid only for monotonic evaluation functions. Narendra and Fukunaga originally proposed to use probabilistic separability measures as criterion functions. This approach, however, has a number of disadvantages:

(a) Feature selection is done based on finite samples and should refer to any particular classifier's performance rather than to intrinsic discriminant properties of the data. Furthermore, because of the sampling process, these discriminant properties cannot be reliably uncovered.

(b) To use any of these criteria one has to estimate them based on the sample, which introduces some error and can turn a monotonic criterion into a nonmonotonic one.

(c) As some evidence indicates [8], even in an asymptotic case (i.e. when the number of data points grows to infinity) certain criteria in the class of probabilistic separability measures may yield results which are nonoptimal in the sense of the Bayes risk.

While the second disadvantage can prevent the search procedure from finding an optimal solution, the first and the third ones are more dangerous when a selected subset of features is to be used to build a practical classifier.

As many authors have pointed out, the only remaining alternative is to use the error rate of a classifier as a design criterion. Unfortunately, due to the phenomena similar in origin to those mentioned in the second of the above disadvantages, the error rate of a classifier (if it is not a Bayes classifier) does not satisfy the monotonicity condition. Such a case can be observed in the feature selection lattice shown in Fig. 1. The error rate along the path (1111)–(1101)–(1001)–(0001) has a monotonicity defect at the node (1001). The lack of monotonicity in the classifier's error rate made it useless for the branch and bound procedure. In 1985 Foroutan and Sklansky [10] introduced the concept of *approximate monotonicity* and demonstrated that a locally trained piecewise linear classifier yields error rate functions that are only mildly nonmonotonic. Consequently, they successfully used a modified branch and bound with the classifier's error rate to search for the optimal feature subset. Although the supporting tests were done only for one data set the idea of approximate monotonicity constitutes another breakthrough in understanding and applying methods for optimal feature selection for certain classifiers.

An excellent overview of major classical feature selection methods is presented in the book by Devijver and Kittler [40].

2. The Present: Approximate Monotonicity and AI View of the Graph Search Problem

The concept of approximate monotonicity opened a new chapter in the research on optimal feature selection. It allows the use of branch and bound to obtain with high confidence an optimal subset of features even though the monotonicity condition is to some extent violated in some cases. Below we discuss two ways of coping with the negative effects of the lack of monotonicity in the error rate on the optimal branch and bound search procedure. Also we present other approaches to searching the feature selection lattice, originating from artificial intelligence (AI).

2.1. *The Branch and Bound Procedure for Nonmonotonic Criteria*

In their work Foroutan and Sklansky [10] used a tolerance Δ imposed on the assumed threshold for branch and bound search: If the specified upper limit of the error rate for a subset of features to be considered feasible is $e_{\max}$, then a subset of features F is assumed to be

(a) feasible if the associated error rate $e(F)$ is less than or equal to $e_{\max}$,
(b) conditionally feasible if $e_{\max} < e(F) \le e_{\max}(1 + \Delta)$, and
(c) infeasible if $e(F) > e_{\max}(1 + \Delta)$.

In this procedure both feasible and conditionally feasible nodes are visited, but the best subset of features is chosen only from the set of feasible nodes. In Fig. 2 a feature subset (00110101) is found to be conditionally feasible, and search is continued. This allows the branch and bound algorithm to search for feasible feature subsets behind a conditionally feasible subset. In experiments described in [10], despite the lack of strict monotonicity, a procedure using the error tolerance was able to find an optimal subset of features with over 90% in computational savings compared with exhaustive search.

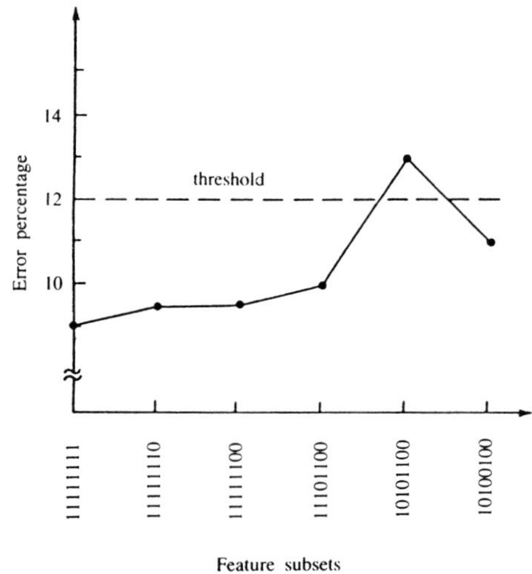

Fig. 2. Illustration of a nonmonotonic behavior of the error rate.

Another way of avoiding the negative effects of using an estimated and, consequently, nonmonotonic error rate of a classifier is to estimate the expected value of the error rate for an examined subset of features. Assuming that departures from monotonicity are caused by errors in estimating the error rate, and that the classifier's true error rate should increase monotonically over a sequence of nested feature subsets (1), we can try to estimate the general trend of error rate variation in a specific classifier. We consider the error rate a function of nested feature subsets, which corresponds to a path in the feature selection graph. Since the observed error rate may not be monotonic, we may observe that along this path it rises and falls even though the expected error rate does not decrease. As a result, it might happen that the current node is infeasible based on its observed error rate, but that it ought to be feasible because the expected error associated with a classifier trained on an infinite sample is below the threshold of acceptability. In Fig. 3. the feature subset (00110101) would be considered infeasible based on the observed error rate associated with it. However, as one can notice the trend along this path (in this case we use linear prediction) indicates that the value of the expected error rate associated with this subset should be less than the presumed threshold and, therefore, the subset is treated as if it were feasible.

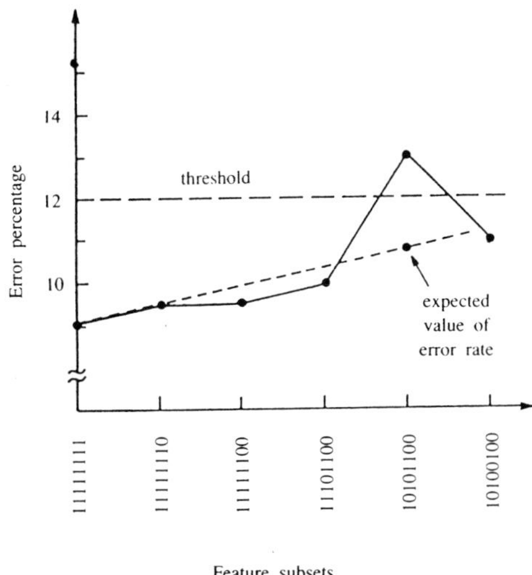

Fig. 3. The trend tracking technique smooths nonmonotonicities of the observed error rate.

Thus, if we analyze the trend of changes of the observed error rate over a sequence of nested feature subsets and, based on this information, we use the approximation of the expected error rate rather than the currently observed error rate, we may successfully use the branch and bound algorithm to search for the optimal subset of features.

The strategy of enumeration in the branch and bound method is another important factor influencing the efficiency and optimality of the feature selection process. When the monotonicity condition is satisfied it does not matter in which order we will examine the descendants of the current node — we will always find the optimum solution and the number of visited nodes in the feature selection lattice will be about the same in each case. In this case one usually takes the node with the highest error rate as the next current node, for it increases the chance for finding the next infeasible node and consequently for pruning some part of the lattice below it. However, when the monotonicity condition is not satisfied, by using this strategy we could prune a part of the lattice including feasible nodes and, which is likely, the best node. Such a case is observed in the feature selection lattice depicted in Fig. 1. Here, if the threshold is set to 15% the optimal node (0001) will be pruned due to the fact that it is a subset of the set (1001), which is infeasible. On the other hand, if we select a subset with the lowest error as the next node in the lattice this subset (0001) will be discovered in the sequence (1101)–(0101)–(0001). Hence, the strategy of choosing the node with the lowest error rate is more likely to avoid local nonmonotonicities and to continue searching those parts of the feature selection lattice that would be skipped by using the traditional strategy.

An important question in feature selection with the aid of branch and bound is how to choose the threshold that defines the feasibility of subsets of features. We can assume that we do not want a big degradation of the classifier's performance and, therefore, we set the threshold at a low level. However, we don't know what price we will pay for selecting an optimal subset of features. In other words, we do not know in advance if the cost of removing one feature from the selected optimal subset would only minimally increase the value of the error rate or whether by adding one feature we can significantly improve the classifier's performance. This might be important, since by properly setting the threshold we could avoid an examination of a significant number of nodes in the feature selection lattice.

A way to predict the best value of the threshold would be to use a sequential forward or backward method to look for the best path in the feature selection lattice, where the best path is a path along which the error rate increases as slowly as possible. By doing this we can scan the feature selection lattice and obtain an estimate of the minimum achievable error rate as a function of the number of removed features. This function is illustrated in Fig. 4. It enables us to choose a threshold on the error rate corresponding to a specified number of features. Or, on the other hand, we can estimate the size of the optimal feature subset corresponding to a specified threshold.

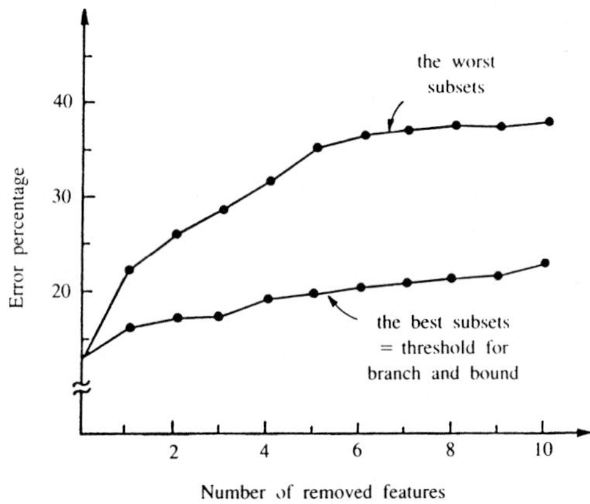

Fig. 4. Selecting the feasibility threshold for branch and bound.

Unfortunately, both forward and backward selection can easily be derailed. For instance, the forward selection algorithm can add two features which are subsequently the best ones but they are bad if used together. This could be to some extent avoided if the sequential forward and backward methods are used at the same time. We call this method a *bidirectional search*. Its concept originates from the MEA (i.e. *means-ends-analysis* method used for problem solving in AI).

In the bidirectional search we conduct the search for the best path from two end nodes (that is, the node representing the full set of features and the node associated with the empty set) at the same time. The feature selection lattice is examined in a DFS (*depth first search*) fashion, in two directions:

(a) from the full set node toward the empty set node and
(b) from the empty set node toward the full set node.

The search is conducted simultaneously from both terminal nodes and concludes in the middle of the lattice, resulting in a path that goes from the top to the bottom of the feature selection lattice. The path is determined by a local comparison of values of the criterion J associated with the feature subset evaluation. At every step, in the forward as well as in the backward search, for the current feature subset all its successor nodes (its subsets in the forward direction and supersets in the backward direction) are evaluated and the most promising ones are selected. If there is a conflict, then the second best successors are selected. A conflict arises if at a given step the same feature is selected in both directions, that is, is chosen to be both added and discarded. This corresponds to the situation in the sequential forward selection algorithm mentioned above: a feature is considered good by the forward selection method but the backward selection algorithm indicates that it also could be removed with no harm. In other words, the conflict suggests that the information obtained from the two methods is contradictory and should be disregarded. If this conflict were not resolved, it would be impossible to conclude both searches in the same place in the feature selection lattice, for no path connecting the two current nodes contains both nodes determined by adding and removing the same feature at the same time.

An example illustrating the bidirectional search procedure is given in Fig. 5. This comparison was made for the feature selection lattice obtained from a piecewise linear classifier trained on a synthetic data set with known properties. The analysis of the lattice suggests that the error rate is nonmonotonic (in fact the data contained six deliberately inserted irrelevant features). As one can see, the resulting error rates along the path selected by the bidirectional search seem to follow closely the minimum error rates obtained from exhaustive analysis. This encourages the use of the bidirectional search algorithm to predict the value of threshold for efficient branch and bound search. Moreover, the bidirectional search is insensitive to the monotonicity of the error rate function.

2.2. *Other AI Methods in Feature Selection*

Both branch and bound and MEA are commonly recognized as techniques developed by AI researchers. While the branch and bound algorithm can supply the optimum solution, provided that some conditions are satisfied, the other AI techniques are typically heuristic in that they generally do not guarantee that the optimal solution will be found. However, when the original dimensionality d of feature space is large (say $d > 15$) then the optimality must be given up because

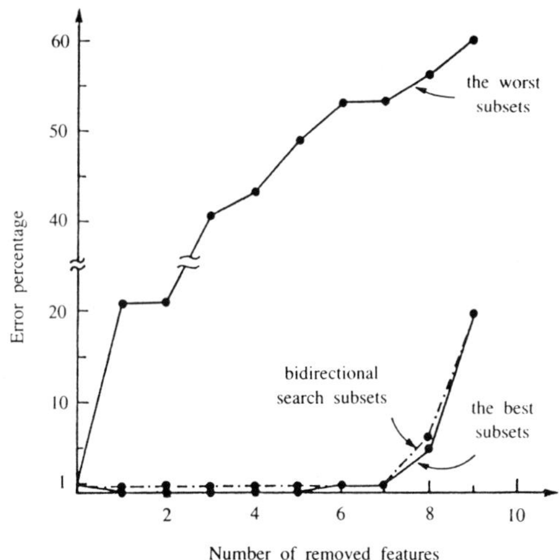

Fig. 5. Bidirectional search versus the best feature subsets.

the complexity of the problem impedes the use of the branch and bound technique (for a discussion of limitations encountered in branch and bound refer to Section 3.1). Of course, one could enumerate the nodes in the feature selection lattice backward, that is starting from the node associated with the empty set. However, if the selected threshold allows the algorithm to visit nodes too deep in the lattice, this solution would be as useless as the original version of the branch and bound enumeration scheme. In such a case we have to look for substitute solutions, which are most likely nonoptimal.

The branch and bound technique in its application to searching the feature selection lattice is nothing but a method of enumerating nodes in this graph. Its advantage over other possible enumeration schemes is such that no node is examined more than once and, therefore, by forcing the algorithm to backtrack earlier than at the terminal node corresponding to the empty set, we can eliminate those parts of the lattice which for some reason (in our case the nodes with excessive error rates) are of no interest to us, thereby increasing the efficiency of the search.

Other known AI techniques do not have this property. They guarantee the optimum solution in feature selection only if they are allowed to do exhaustive search. The following are a few examples:

(a) depth-first search, which, if terminated without backtracking, turns out to be sequential forward or backward selection,

(b) breadth-first search, which has no equivalent in feature selection literature, and

(c) best-first search, which also has no equivalent.

In best-first search one expands the top node and builds from its descendants a queue according to decreasing values of the so-called *heuristic evaluation function* associated with them. Next, the first node in the queue is expanded and the queue updated. This process is repeated until a *goal node* is detected. In the feature selection problem we do not explicitly look for a goal node, because we are unable to detect whether a given node is a goal or not. Instead, we are interested in searching some part of the feature selection lattice, which should contain the node that is optimal with regard to some assumed criterion.

The heuristic evaluation function is another unknown in the definition of the best-first search method. For instance, one could assume that the observed error rate of a classifier is this function.

The major disadvantage of the best-first search algorithm is its space complexity (i.e. the size of the computer memory required to execute an algorithm), which in the worst case, when all nodes from the middle level in the lattice have to be placed in the queue, equals

$$\binom{d}{\lfloor d/2 \rfloor} \leq 2^{d-2} \tag{2}$$

where d is the total number of features. This number is prohibitive even for d as small as 20, so the full queue cannot be stored in the computer's memory. However, we can restrict the length of the queue to a specified maximum. This revision of the best-first search procedure is referred to as the *beam search* technique.

The limitation of the size of the queue has two consequences. First, the space complexity is much less and can be arbitrarily set. Second, some nodes and, as a result, some parts of the feature selection lattice are never visited, which significantly improves the efficiency of the beam search compared to the exhaustive search scheme pursued by the best-first search algorithm. The second observation suggests also that the beam search procedure may not find the optimal solution (unless all feasible nodes are stored in the queue and the error rate has the monotonicity property).

Recently we have conducted experiments with a version of the beam search procedure which incorporates into the heuristic evaluation function not only the error rate associated with the current node but also uses a prediction scheme to speed up the search process. Its algorithm contains the same elements as the original beam search. First the top node is expanded and the priority queue built according to increasing values of the error rate associated with each descendant. Next, from a few levels ahead some assumed number of nodes is drawn at random from the lattice. If there is a node with the error rate lower than the error rate of the first node in the queue, then as the current node we choose the best node in the queue from which there is a path toward the node on the lower level. Otherwise, we select the first node in the queue as the best node. Finally, we expand the best node and the process of generating goal nodes (these nodes are drawn only from levels below the level at which the current best node is placed) and selecting of the next best node is repeated. The natural stop condition is satisfied if all prospective nodes are infeasible with regard to a given threshold.

The drawback to this method is that, for a high dimensionality of the feature space, the number of nodes checked may become very large, and the stop condition may not be reached soon enough. This could be resolved in one of the following ways:

(a) by setting an upper bound to the number of nodes checked,
(b) by making the stop condition user interactive or
(c) by using the two options given above.

We have tested this algorithm on the data used for the bidirectional search. The results are very encouraging: for each data set this method performed as well as the branch and bound algorithm, but the number of examined nodes was much less. However, we emphasize that the beam search algorithm is suboptimal, and for this reason it is not competitive with branch and bound wherever the latter method can be used. On the other hand, its usefulness can be appreciated in feature selection problems in which the dimensionality of the feature space prohibits the use of the branch and bound enumeration scheme.

Another interesting aspect of the beam search technique is that it can be viewed as a generalization of the popular sequential selection methods: If the length of the queue is set equal to one and we start searching from the node associated with the full set of features, then beam search is equivalent to sequential backward selection.

3. The Future

In this section we sketch several directions of research on optimal feature selection. Some of these directions are already under study at our Pattern Recognition Project.

3.1. *Branch and Bound and Large-Scale Feature Selection*

The introduction of the branch and bound search scheme to feature selection opened a way to optimal feature selection. As we indicated in the previous section, only methods that are potentially capable of examining all nodes in the feature selection lattice can be optimal. Branch and bound offers both efficiency and optimality under certain conditions. By introducing the idea of approximate monotonicity, Foroutan and Sklansky relaxed the monotonicity requirement to achieve suboptimal results. Their method, based on classifier error comparison, retained the efficiency of the original algorithm of Narendra and Fukunaga while providing results close to optimum.

Tremendous savings in the number of nodes to be examined, expressed by percentages as high as 99.9, is achieved in branch and bound by pruning nodes that are considered infeasible. The infeasibility is determined by comparing the classifier's error rate with the fixed threshold, selected by the user in advance. As we suggested in the previous section, guidance on the value of the threshold can be obtained by sampling the feature selection lattice along some path. By observing the changes in the error rate along this path the user may decide what value of the threshold might be reasonable, considering both the degradation of classifier performance and the desired size of the optimal feature subset.

However, the trade-off between the "want" and "can" in the feature selection lattice is ambiguous and does not give any guarantee of finishing a larger task (containing, say, 30 features) in a reasonable time. In fact, whatever the fixed value of the threshold is, we still may face an unexpected overhead in the number of nodes that must be visited. This is illustrated by our recent experience on an image processing research project, in which we attempted to select six or seven features out of a 30-element set. We ran our feature selection program on a VAX11/780 for two weeks and then we decided to abort it because the remaining computing time could not be estimated with satisfactory confidence. Next we used the best eighteen-feature subset as the root node of a new lattice which was then searched to yield the selected six-feature subset.

The critical nature of this problem can be appreciated by trying to estimate the number of nodes that are left for examination after deleting a number of nodes only on the second level from the top of the feature selection lattice. For a set initially consisting of 30 features the number of active nodes is expressed by the formula 2^{30-s}, where s is the number of nodes pruned on the second level. For example, if we delete 10 features on the first level (which is a quite impressive result for the first step in *optimal* feature selection) then we have an astonishing number of nodes — over a *million* — left for examination. This number, however, is only 0.1 % of the total number of subsets of a 30-element set. Even if we accept the assumption that additional nodes will be pruned on subsequent levels, those 20 active features means that 190 and up to 1140 subsets will have to be examined on the second and third level from the top, respectively. In many large-scale classification problems these numbers may be already prohibitive.

Therefore, it is clear that we need a version of the branch and bound algorithm that would be very aggressive at the beginning of the selection process and less aggressive at its end. This aim can be achieved only if such a method adjusts the value of the feasibility threshold according to the estimates of the number of nodes left for examination.

3.2. *Monte Carlo Approach to Feature Selection*

Recently there have been surprising successes in solving NP-complete problems in computer science using two classes of techniques that simulate natural processes in metallurgy and biology. These two classes of techniques, *simulated annealing* and *genetic algorithms*, are based on the assumption that large domains of data are organized and evolve in a manner akin to processes occurring in nature.

3.2.1. *Simulated annealing*

In simulated annealing the analogy is drawn between the solution space of a combinatorial optimization problem and the atoms or molecules of a system tending to cool to an optimal equilibrium. In much the same way as the atoms perturb their orientations, the coordinates of the current solution point in parameter space are varied, pulling it to a (locally) optimal solution.

Annealing, in its original formulation, is concerned with the behavior of thermal systems in low temperature equilibrium. The behavior of such thermal systems is determined by the displacements of atoms over time. Since the number of atoms is of order 10^{23} per cm^3, only the most probable behavior of the system in thermal equilibrium at a given temperature is observed in experiments. Some of the fundamental questions in statistical mechanics, which deals with thermal systems in a macro scale, concern what happens to the system in the limit of low temperature: for example, whether the system remains fluid or solidifies, and if it solidifies, whether the atoms in the system create crystalline or glassy structure. Ground states and configurations close to them in energy are extremely rare among all the possible configurations of a macroscopic body, yet they dominate its properties at low temperatures because as the temperature of the system is lowered, the system, ruled by the Boltzmann distribution, collapses into one of the lowest energy states.

In practical contexts, low temperature is not a sufficient condition for finding ground states of matter. Experiments which determine the low temperature state of a material are done by careful annealing, first melting the substance, then lowering its temperature slowly, and spending a long time at temperatures in the vicinity of the freezing point. If such a procedure, called the *cooling schedule*, is not exactly followed, and the substance is allowed to get out of equilibrium, the resulting material will have a glassy structure (overcooled fluid) with only metastable, locally optimal structures, or if it crystallizes, then the structure of the crystal will exhibit many defects.

Metropolis *et al.* [19], in the earliest days of scientific computing, introduced a simple algorithm which can be used to analyze the behavior of a collection of atoms (or molecules) in equilibrium at a given temperature. Through the use of random variates and a probabilistic model, they successfully simulated the behavior of thermal systems. Their model always accepts a change in the system that corresponds to a decrease in internal thermal energy of the system (i.e. kinetic energy of atoms). A random variate is used to determine whether to accept a change in the system that corresponds to an increase in the thermal energy. Although the exact nature of the random variate's distribution is dependent on the system being simulated, most applications used a variant of the Boltzmann distribution, $e^{-\Delta E/k_B T}$. Here ΔE is the change of the energy of the system from the previous to the current state, k_B is Boltzmann's constant, and T is the temperature of the system.

Kirkpatrick *et al.* first realized that simulated annealing can be used to solve NP-hard combinatorial optimization problems. The simulated annealing algorithm introduced in [20] transforms an optimization problem in a problem-specific manner into an annealing problem. The simulated annealing model assumes without loss of generality that the objective function is to be minimized. The correspondents in the simulated annealing transformation are the internal energy of the system with the objective (criterion) function, atomic positions with problem parameters, and a stable low temperature equilibrium state with a near-optimal solution. Unfortunately, neither the concept of the temperature of the system nor the Boltzmann constant has correspondents in combinatorial optimization. The intuition behind the probabilistic acceptance of solutions that represent a decrease in solution quality is an attempt to avoid local optima that are far from being globally optimal.

A high level algorithmic description of the simulated annealing technique is given below.

---

1. Pick an annealing schedule $[T_0, n_0], \ldots, [T_m, n_m]$. Usually $T_{i+1} = r * T_i$, $0 < r < 1$. Set initial solution x.
2. **For** $i \leftarrow 0$ **to** m **do**
   2a. $y = transform(x),\ \Delta J = J(y) - J(x)$
   2b. Accept move with the probability $P = \exp(-\Delta J/T_i)$
   2c. **If** move not accepted **then** $n_i \leftarrow n_i - 1$
   2d. **If** $n_i = 0$ **then** system is *frozen*, break the loop and decrease the temperature. Otherwise replace x by y and go to 2a.

Research in simulated annealing has been divided into two areas: applications and the analysis of its performance. In the first group we can find a wide range of problems successfully solved with the aid of this method, beginning from the traveling salesman problem and ending at computer vision problems (e.g. [21–25]). The research on the performance of the simulated annealing was focused on the optimality of the method, its expected time complexity and possible improvements (c.f. [26–31]).

It was pointed out by Kirkpatrick *et al.* [20] that simulated annealing is a general recipe for Monte Carlo combinatorial optimization, and that each new optimization task should create its own problem-dependent version of this technique. In fact, the *transform(x)* operator determines how the annealing scheme will work. For example, if the *transform(x)* is independent of x, then the annealing scheme turns out to be Monte Carlo scanning, and the final solution is just the best solution of all solutions generated at random during the execution of the algorithm. Hence simulated annealing is a general skeleton in which each new application introduces its own problem-specific contents.

In our case suppose first that we have an unconstrained optimization problem in which the objective is to minimize the function $J(f)$, where f is a feature vector or bit string representing a feature subset (zeros denote deleted features). Let $P_J = \exp(-\Delta J/T)$. According to the paradigm used in simulated annealing, a new state (here a new feature vector f_{i+1}) is accepted with the probability

$$P_i = P_J(f_{i+1}) = \min[1, \exp(-\Delta J/T)] \tag{3}$$

where $\Delta J = J(f_{i+1}) - J(f_i)$ is the difference between the values of J after and before the i-th step. The acceptance of the i-th step is determined in the following way:

First, the probability of acceptance P_i is calculated. Next, a random number R is drawn from a uniform distribution and compared with P_i. If $R < P_i$ then the step is accepted. Otherwise the i-th step is rejected.

In the case of the constrained optimization problem assume additional constraint functions, C_j, $j = 1, \ldots, m$. The acceptance of the i-th step (that is the feature subset obtained at this step) can be assessed in two different ways. First, we can assume that the new state is accepted if it is sufficiently probable (according to (3)) and no constraint is violated. On the other hand, we can assume that the constraints can be violated with some probability. This assumption is important if the area of feasibility, that is the part of the solution space where all the constraints are satisfied, consists of several disconnected parts. Such situation seems to be very likely, particularly in feature selection, if the error rate (which does not have the monotonicity property) is one of the constraints. In this case the probability of accepting a violated constraint can be defined as follows:

$$P_{C_j}(f_{i+1}) = \min[1, \exp(-C_j/T)] \quad j = 1, \ldots, m \tag{4}$$

Note that, by definition, a constraint is satisfied if $C_j(f_{i+1}) \leq 0$. The procedure to determine whether the i-th step is to be accepted or not is the same as for an unconstrained problem, except that now we have to generate additional m random numbers and compare them with the probabilities of constraint violation acceptance.

There is also possibly another simplified rule for determining whether violated constraints are acceptable. In this case we calculate a single acceptance probability for all constraints

$$P_C(f_{i+1}) = \min\left[1, \exp\left(-\sum_{j=1}^{m} C_j/T\right)\right]. \tag{5}$$

And finally, we can compute a total acceptance probability for both the criterion J and constraints C_j

$$P_{J\&C}(f_{i+1}) = \min\left[1, \exp\left(-\left\{\Delta J + \gamma \sum_{j=1}^{m} C_j\right\}/T\right)\right], \tag{6}$$

where γ is a constant. This last approach resembles the classical penalty function method used to solve constrained optimization problems. It is also equivalent to the formulation (3) which uses a single criterion function and a single acceptance threshold.

At the time this paper was prepared no test of simulated annealing for feature selection was carried out. The authors plan to carry out and report such tests in the near future.

3.2.2. *Genetic algorithms*

Though research in genetic algorithms by the Artificial Intelligence community predates (c.f. [32], 1975) research in simulated annealing, it is only very recently that this technique has received wide-spread attention [33–38]. Like the simulated annealing approach, the genetic algorithm approach is a paradigm for examining a state-space to obtain good solutions. However, while simulated annealing attempts to produce a quality solution through nondeterministic hill-climbing, a genetic algorithm is a parallel test-and-go technique, in which a predefined number of possible solutions is modified, tested and stored at the same time. The name *genetic* arises from the way the possible solutions are interpreted, represented and transformed.

In a genetic algorithm a solution, which is usually represented by a finite sequence of numbers (i.e. a point in the state-space), is called a *chromosome*. The algorithm manipulates a set of chromosomes, the *population*, in a manner resembling the mechanics of natural evolution. In this mechanics the chromosomes are allowed to *mate* or *crossover*, and *mutate*. The mating of two chromosomes produces an offspring chromosome which is a synthesis of its parents. A mutation of a chromosome produces a near identical copy with some components of the chromosome altered. An exponential growth of the system of chromosomes is achieved by introducing the *score function*, which is basically the function to be optimized, and by limiting the size of the population. In other words, each chromosome is evaluated and only a predefined number of the best ones survives to the next cycle of reproduction. The population of chromosomes is evolved through a number of such cycles called the *generations*. Despite the limited size of the population, it is capable of fast adaptation which results in rapid optimization of the score function.

A high-level algorithmic description of the basic method is given below. Though many variations of this basic method exist, our description captures its primary characteristics.

---

1. Construct an initial population set $Population = \{x_i\}_{i=1,\dots,n}$
2. **For** $i \leftarrow 1$ **to** *Number_of_generations* **do**
   2a. *Offspring* $\leftarrow \emptyset$
   2b. **For** $j \leftarrow 1$ **to** n **do**
       For $k \leftarrow 1$ **to** *weight* $(J(x_j))$ **do**
       Offspring $\leftarrow$ *Offspring* $\cup$ *mutate*(x_j)
   2c. **For** $j \leftarrow 1$ **to** $n-1$ **do**
       For $k \leftarrow j+1$ **to** n **do**
       If $J(x_j) >$ *fitness(Population)* **and**
       If $J(x_k) >$ *fitness(Population)* **then**
           Offspring $\leftarrow$ *Offspring* $\cup$ *crossover* (x_j, x_k)
   2d. *Population* $\leftarrow n$ best from *Population* $\cup$ *Offspring*

As in the simulated annealing algorithm the proper choice of operators (*crossover* and *mutate*), as well as the evaluation functions (*weight* and *fitness*) is the key to the creation of an efficient application-oriented version of the genetic algorithm.

In the original biological model the crossover operator refers to the exchange of information between chromosomes. In particular if a chromosome is represented by a binary string (as in feature selection), crossover can be implemented by randomly choosing a point, called the *crossover point*, in which two chromosomes exchange their parts to create two new chromosomes. For instance two strings, 00101101 and 10111001, if cut in the middle, will produce two new chromosomes: 00101001 and 10111101.

When the crossover operator provides new solution points for further evaluation, it serves two complementary search functions. First, it creates new structures (e.g. the substring $\#\#1111\#\#$, where $\#$ means "don't care"), which were not present in parent chromosomes. These structures, when evaluated and accepted, create a new track toward the optimal solution. Second, this operator retains old structures within new solution points (for instance, $0010\#\#\#\#$), which, if accepted within the newly created solution, makes the presence of this structure in the population stronger. As a result, this structure has greater chance to survive and proliferate within the future solutions.

Mutation is a secondary search operator which increases the variability of the population and prevents premature convergence to a poor local minimum. In our examples involving bit strings a mutant can be created by changing at random one or more bits in the structure.

This original framework which uses bit strings is a ready-to-use formulation suitable for feature selection. Whether the definition of the crossover operator can lead to efficient optimization schemes still remains in the realm of speculation.

3.3. *A Comparison of Search Techniques*

So far we have presented a wide variety of methods that were, are or could be used for near-optimal selection of features. Although the introduction of these methods span the last twenty five years, surprisingly, there are substantial similarities among them. Below we present a series of statements that tie these methods in similarity groups.

(1) The *sequential backward selection* method is equivalent to the *depth-first search* technique with no backtracking.

(2) *Beam search* with a queue length of one is equivalent to *sequential backward selection*.

(3) The second method of Chang based on *dynamic programming* is a form of Stearn's (r, s)-*search* algorithm [39].

(4) *Simulated annealing* is a randomized version of the (r, s)-*search* algorithm.

(5) *Genetic algorithms* are randomized versions of *beam search* if the influence of *crossover* is predominant.

(6) *Genetic algorithms* are randomized versions of the multiple (r, s)-*search* technique if the influence of *mutate* is predominant.

Another way of comparing these methods is through the visualization of typical search paths in the feature selection lattice explored by them. These paths are illustrated schematically in Fig. 6.

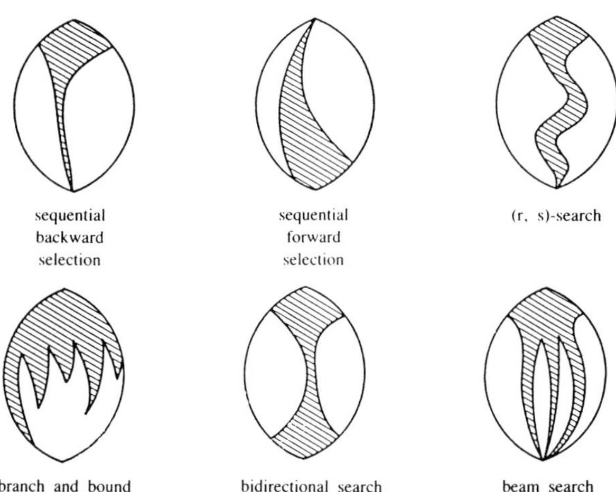

Fig. 6. Shaded areas mark the parts of the feature selection lattices visited by the search procedures.

3.4. *Other Problems to be Resolved*

The techniques for feature selection discussed so far assumed a search for the best subset of features among a number of feasible subsets. Such a statement of the problem presents several difficulties:

(a) The search problem is NP hard. Consequently, for even moderate numbers of features (say between 15 and 30) the problem must be solved with the aid of suboptimal methods. These methods, by definition, do not ensure that the selected subset is optimal.

(b) Given a selected optimal subset of features we are still unable to determine the usefulness of a particular feature (called sometimes its *discriminatory power*).

(c) If a feature selection process uses a criterion function involving an error rate of a classifier, then it must be recognized as a process in which this classifier is optimized and, therefore, trained. Hence, the only error rate that can be computed for this classifier is an apparent error rate, which is known to be very biased.

It is very likely that a panaceum for all these problems does not exist, although we can try to solve each of them independently. For instance, instead of selecting a subset of features we can evaluate a discriminatory power of each feature. A potentially promising approach is based on the concept of classifiers optimized with regard to the use of available features [11]. In this approach we define a classifier as a function $F: X \times P \to \Omega$, where X is a feature space, P is a set of parameters of the classifier and Ω is a set of class labels (decisions). We assume that our classifier is trainable with respect to a criterion function $J: P \to \Re$, where $\Re$ is a set of real numbers, that is, we can find a parameter vector $p^* \in P$ such that $J(p^*)$ is a minimum. In this notation a classifier $F(., p^*)$ is assumed to be an optimally trained classifier. Now suppose we discard the i-th feature, that is for any two feature vectors

$$x = [x_1, \ldots, x_i, \ldots, x_d]^T, \ x' = [x_1, \ldots, x_i', \ldots, x_d]^T \quad \text{and} \quad x_i \neq x_i'$$
$$\text{but } F(x, p) = F(x', p) \, . \tag{7}$$

We call a classifier a *scalable classifier* if the effect described above can be accomplished by imposing a certain value to the parameter vector p. In fact, many known classifiers, including linear, piecewise linear and quadratic ones are scalable classifiers. Other types of classifiers like k-NN rule or classifiers based on density function estimation, which involve the use of distance functions, can be transformed to satisfy the definition of scalable classifiers.

In the Appendix we have shown that if a classifier is a scalable classifier then its error rate satisfies the monotonicity condition provided that we use an optimum training procedure to minimize the error rate of the classifier. This theorem can be rephrased for a linear classifier into the following form: if a linear classifier is trained with the aid of a procedure that guarantees a minimum resubstitution error rate then this error rate is monotonic over a sequence of nested feature subsets. With some additional assumptions a similar theorem was proven for piecewise linear classifiers [10].

If we optimally train a scalable classifier, we receive a vector of optimal parameters, p^*. Some of these parameters are responsible for amplifying or reducing the influence of each feature (for instance, weights in linear classifiers). Hence, by comparing these parameters we can deduce the discriminatory power of each feature (assuming that all features are statistically equivalent, that is, they have the same mean and variance).

The following approach can be called a *fuzzy* treatment of the feature selection problem:

> *Given a scalable classifier, train it optimally over a set of statistically equivalent features and compare parameters associated with the various features. These parameters can be viewed as values of a fuzzy membership function computed for the associated features, where the membership is in the class of features with high discriminatory power.*

Unfortunately, there are no known optimal training procedures for finite samples of correctly labeled data using the classifier's error rate as a criterion of optimality.

The fuzzy treatment may overcome the first two of the three difficulties described at the beginning of this section. However, the third difficulty — the biasedness of an error rate of a classifier built for a selected optimal subset of features — would remain unresolved. To deal with that difficulty we could try to use a form of cross-validation for feature selection. Given a finite sample we divide it into two parts: the training set and the test set. Next, we design a classifier and perform feature selection for this classifier based on its observed error rate. Finally, we compute a new error estimate for the classifier whose design is based on the selected subset of features. This procedure is repeated a number of times, and each time we divide the data set into two subsets in a different way. At the end of the process we take a mean of all estimated final error rates. This estimator is known as a *rotation error* estimator, and is less biased than the resubstitution error estimator. However, this solution has one significant drawback: it requires that the feature selection process be repeated a number of times, which further increases the already discouraging computational complexity of the problem.

5. Summary and Concluding Remarks

In this paper we gave an overview of combinatorial feature selection methods. We divided our discussion into three parts, each part referring to a distinct era in the development of these methods. First we described the methods that belong to an arsenal of classical algorithms for searching the feature selection lattice. Next, we described methods that were developed in the last five years. In this era we placed branch and bound methods based on the concept of approximate monotonicity (including two ways of defining the *infeasible* nodes and the bidirectional search algorithm as a tool for setting the feasibility threshold) and the beam search algorithm. The third part, concerned with current and future research, received our greatest attention. We described the limitations of the methods developed so far, indicating their infeasibility for large-scale problems. (We consider a 20-element selection problem to be in the large scale domain; this is about the limiting size of problems that could be handled with the aid of the branch and bound algorithm.)

We pointed out the need for a variable infeasibility threshold for branch and bound. In particular we showed that the classical version of branch and bound, as used by Foroutan and Sklansky, is not capable of handling problems involving more than 20 features even though the savings incurred by pruning nodes are expected to exceed 99.9% of the total number of feature subsets. To handle large-scale problems we proposed the use of simulated annealing and genetic algorithms. Both methods, which have gained much attention in the recent years for their spectacular efficiency in such classical NP-hard problems as the *traveling salesman* or *min-cut partitioning*, seem to be extremely well suited to feature selection tasks. Research on the application of these algorithms to efficient and close to optimal feature selection is currently being conducted by the authors of this paper. In this research a major concern is the validation of the results obtained from Monte Carlo simulations.

Finally, we compared several classical search methods as well as several we have devised. By analyzing search paths typical to each method we pointed out major differences and similarities among the methods.

Although this paper does not offer an ultimate solution to the feature selection problem, we believe our discussion provides improved insights into this difficult and challenging research area.

Postscript

When this paper was submitted for publication no practical experiments with genetic algorithms for feature selection had been as yet carried out. However, when the paper was returned from the reviewers several such tests had been completed by the authors. These tests indicated that indeed genetic algorithms are a powerful new technique for optimal feature selection, insensitive to the nonmonotonicity of subset inclusion. The authors plan to report on this subject in the near future.

Acknowledgements

This research was supported by the U.S. Army Research Office Grant via Research Contract No. DAAG29-84-K-0208. Some of the reported research was carried out in collaboration with Dr. Iman Foroutan of the Hughes Aircraft Company's Microelectronic Circuits Division, Mr. S. Richard F. Sims of the U.S. Army, and Mr. Roger Crump of Applied Research, Inc.

References

[1] J. Kittler, On the discriminant vector method of feature selection, *IEEE Trans. Comput.* **26** (1977) 604–606.

[2] H. P. Decell, P. L. Odell and W. A. Coberly, Linear dimension reduction and Bayes classification, *Pattern Recogn.* **15** (1979) 51–54.

[3] D. M. Young, A formulation and comparison of two linear feature selection techniques applicable to statistical classification, *Pattern Recogn.* **17** (1984) 331–337.

[4] S. D. Morgera and L. Datta, Toward a fundamental theory of optimal feature selection: Part I, *IEEE Trans. Pattern Anal. Mach. Intell.* **6** (1984) 601–616.

[5] M. Ben-Bassat, Use of distance measures, information measures and error bounds in feature evaluation, in P. R. Krishnaiah and L. N. Kanal (eds.), *Handbook of Statistics, Vol. 2* (North-Holland, 1982).

[6] P. M. Narendra and K. Fukunaga, A branch and bound algorithm for feature subset selection, *IEEE Trans. Comput.* **26** (1977) 917–922.

[7] K. S. Fu, Recent developments in pattern recognition, *IEEE Trans. Comput.* **29** (1977) 845–854.

[8] M. Ben-Bassat, f-entropies, probability of error, and feature selection, *Inf. Control* **39** (1978) 227–242.

[9] M. Ben-Bassat, On the sensitivity of the probability of error rule for feature selection, *IEEE Trans. Pattern Anal. Mach. Intell.* **2** (1980) 57–60.

[10] I. Foroutan and J. Sklansky, Feature selection for automatic classification of non-Gaussian data, *IEEE Trans. Syst. Man Cybern.* **17** (1987) 187–198.

[11] W. Siedlecki and J. Sklansky, Towards optimal feature selection: past, present and future in *Trans. of the 4th Army Conf. on Applied Mathematics and Computing*, Cornell University, Ithaca, NY, 1986, 721–729.

[12] G. Sebestyen, *Decision Making Processes in Pattern Recognition*, New York, 1962.

[13] P. M. Lewis, The characteristic selection problem in recognition systems, *IEEE Trans. Inf. Theory* **8** (1962) 171–178.

[14] T. Marill and D. M. Green, On the effectiveness of receptors in recognition systems, *IEEE Trans. Inf. Theory* **9** (1963) 11–17.

[15] T. M. Cover, The best two independent measurements are not the two best, *IEEE Trans. Syst. Man Cybern.* **4** (1974) 116–117.

[16] J. Kittler, Une généralisation de quelques algorithmes sous-optimaux de recherche d'ensembles d'attributs, *Proc. Congrès Reconnaissance des Formes et Traitement des Images*, Paris, 1978.

[17] C. Y. Chang, Dynamic programming as applied to feature selection in pattern recognition systems, *IEEE Trans. Syst. Man Cybern.* **3** (1973) 166–171.

[18] T. M. Cover and J. M. Van Campenhout, On the possible orderings in the measurement selection problem, *IEEE Trans. Syst. Man Cybern.* **7** (1977) 657–661.

[19] N. Metropolis, A. Rosenbluth, M. Rosenbluth, A. Teller and E. Teller, Equation of state calculation by fast computing machines, *J. Chem. Phys.* **21** (1953) 1087–1092.

[20] S. Kirkpatrick, C. D. Gelatt and M. P. Vecchi, Optimization by simulated annealing, IBM Research Report RC 9355 (# 41093), 1982.

[21] W. E. Smith, H. H. Barret and R. G. Paxman, Reconstruction of objects from coded images by simulated annealing, *Opt. Lett.* **8** (1983) 199–201.

[22] S. Kirkpatrick, C. D. Gelatt and M. P. Vecchi, Optimization by simulated annealing, *Science* **220** (1983) 671–680.

[23] M. P. Vecchi and S. Kirkpatrick, Global wiring by simulated annealing, *IEEE Trans. Computer-Aided Design* **2** (1983) 215–222.

[24] E. Bonomi and J. Lutton, The N-city traveling salesperson problem: statistical mechanics and the Metropolis algorithm, *SIAM Rev.* **26** (1984) 551–568.

[25] D. H. Ballard, G. E. Hinton and T. J. Sejnowski, Parallel visual computation, *Nature* **306** (1984) 21–26.

[26] S. R. White, Concepts of scale in simulated annealing, *Int. Conf. on Computer Design: VLSI in Computers Proc.*, Port Chester, NY, 1984, 646–651.

[27] F. Romeo, A. Sangiovanni-Vincentelli and S. Sechen, Research on simulated annealing at Berkeley, *Int. Conf. on Computer Design: VLSI in Computers Proc.*, Port Chester, NY, 1984, 652–657.

[28] J. W. Greene and K. J. Supowit, Simulated annealing without rejected moves, *Int. Conf. on Computer Design: VLSI in Computers Proc.*, Port Chester, NY, 1984, 658–663.

[29] S. Kirkpatrick, Optimization by simulated annealing: quantitative studies, *J. Stat. Phys.* **34** (1984) 975–986.

[30] S. Nahar, S. Sahni and E. Shragowitz, Experiments with simulated annealing, *22nd ACM/IEEE Design Automation Conf.*, Las Vegas, NV, 1985, 748–752.

[31] F. Romeo and A. Sangiovanni-Vincentelli, Probabilistic hill climbing algorithms: properties and applications, *1985 Chapel Hill Conf. on VLSI*, 1985, 393–418.

[32] J. H. Holland, *Adaptation in Natural and Artificial Systems*, Univ. Michigan, Ann Arbor, 1975.

[33] J. J. Grefenstette, Optimization of control parameters for genetic algorithms, *IEEE Trans. Syst. Man Cybern.* **16** (1986) 122–128.

[34] D. E. Goldberg, Optimal initial population size for binary-coded genetic algorithms, TCGA Report No. 85001, University of Alabama, 1985.

[35] C. L. Bridges and David E. Goldberg, An analysis of reproduction and crossover in a binary-coded genetic algorithm, in *Proc. Second Int. Conf. on Genetic Algorithms*, Cambridge, 1987, 9–13.

[36] J. E. Baker, Reducing bias and inefficiency in the selection algorithm, in *Proc. Second Int. Conf. on Genetic Algorithms*, Cambridge, 1987, 14–21.

[37] D. J. Sirag and P. T. Weisser, Toward a unified thermodynamic genetic operator, in *Proc. Second Int. Conf. on Genetic Algorithms*, Cambridge, 1987, 116–122.

[38] J. P. Cohoon, S. U. Hedge, W. N. Martin and D. Richards, Punctuated equilibria: a parallel genetic algorithm, in *Proc. Second Int. Conf. on Genetic Algorithms*, Cambridge, 1987, 148–154.

[39] S. D. Stearns, On selecting features for pattern classifiers, in *Proc. Third Int. Conf. on Pattern Recognition*, Coronado, CA, 1976, 71–75.

[40] P. A. Devijver and J. Kittler, *Pattern Recognition: A Statistical Approach* (Prentice-Hall, London, 1982).

Appendix. Monotonicity of Scalable Classifiers

Let X be a d-dimensional feature space, P be a m-dimensional parameter space and Ω be a set of class (decision) labels. The function $F: X \times P \rightarrow \Omega$ is called a *trainable classifier*, if there exists a function $J: P \rightarrow \Re^+$, where $\Re^+$ is a set of positive real numbers. The function J is a criterion according to which the classifier is trained in the parameter space P, that is, there exists a parameter vector $p^* \in P$ such that $J(p^*)$ is a minimum.

We call a classifier a *scalable classifier* if for a certain value of the parameter p

$$x = [x_1, \ldots, x_i, \ldots, x_d]^T, \ x' = [x_1, \ldots, x_i', \ldots, x_d]^T \quad \text{and} \quad x_i \neq x_i'$$
$$\text{but } F(x, p) = F(x', p). \tag{A-1}$$

This condition is equivalent to stating that for some p the classifier disregards the i th feature.

Theorem. If F is a scalable classifier and there exists a perfect training procedure (that is, $J(p^*)$ is a global minimum) then the minima of J grow monotonically over a sequence of nested subsets of features.

Proof. To prove the theorem we will show that the minimum of the criterion J after the i-th feature is being discarded, $J(p_i^*)$, is no less than the minimum of J for all features, $J(p^*)$. Let $P^{(i)}$ be a subset of P containing all p satisfying (A–1).

Then clearly

$$J(p^*) = \min_{p \in P} J(p) \leqslant \min_{p \in P^{(i)}} J(p) = J(p_i^*)$$

which results from the fact that we are using a perfect training procedure which is capable of finding global minima and, therefore, $J(p^*)$ is a global minimum.

Corollary. Let the resubstitution error be a training criterion. Let the training procedure be capable of finding the minimum error rate for a classifier for each set of features. Then, according to our theorem, the resubstitution error will satisfy the monotonicity condition.

CHAPTER 1.3.2

A NOTE ON GENETIC ALGORITHMS FOR LARGE-SCALE FEATURE SELECTION

W. SIEDLECKI and J. SKLANSKY

University of California, Irvine, Irvine, CA 92717, USA

We introduce the use of genetic algorithms (GA) for the selection of features in the design of automatic pattern classifiers. Our preliminary results suggest that GA is a powerful means of reducing the time for finding near-optimal subsets of features from large sets.

Keywords: Feature selection, genetic algorithms, classifier, search, multidimensional data.

1. Introduction

We introduce a form of genetic algorithm (GA) for selecting a small subset from an initially large set of coordinates of the feature space in the design of a pattern classifier. Reducing the dimensionality of the feature space not only decreases the cost and time of feature extraction in the operation of the classifier, but it also raises the credibility of the estimated performance of the classifier. Our initial experiments indicate that GA is a powerful tool for feature selection when the dimensionality of the initial feature set is large — specifically, greater than 20.

There are two versions of the problem of feature selection in the design of pattern classifiers, each version addressing a specific objective and leading to a distinct type of optimization. In one version the objective is to find a subset that yields the lowest error rate of a classifier. This version of the problem leads to unconstrained combinatorial optimization in which the error rate is the search criterion. In the second version of the problem we seek the smallest subset of features for which the error rate (or perhaps some other measure of performance) is below a given threshold. This version leads to a constrained combinatorial optimization task, in which the error rate serves as a constraint and the number of features is the primary search criterion.

In the search for subsets of features each subset can be coded as a d-element bit string or binary-valued vector (d is the initial number of features), $a = \{\alpha_1, \ldots, \alpha_d\}$,

Reprinted with permission from *Pattern Recognition Letters*, Vol. 10 (1989) 335–347. ©1989, Elsevier Science Publishers B.V. (North-Holland).

where α_i assumes value 0 if the i-th feature is excluded from the subset and 1 if it is present in the subset. We refer to a as a *feature selection vector* and α_i is a *feature selection variable*. Thus the search space for the feature selection problem is a space of d-element bit strings.

The search space can be conveniently represented in the form of a lattice (an example of the 4-dimensional lattice is shown in Fig. 1). In the lattice, which is an undirected graph, nodes correspond to points in the search space, and every pair of nodes is connected by a link if and only if the set of features represented by one of the linked nodes is an immediate subset (or superset) of the set represented by the other node. The top node in the lattice represents the full set of features and the bottom node corresponds to the empty set. The nodes in the lattice are grouped in levels: all nodes at the same level have the same number of features. By convention, the empty set node is placed at level 0, and the full set node occupies level d.

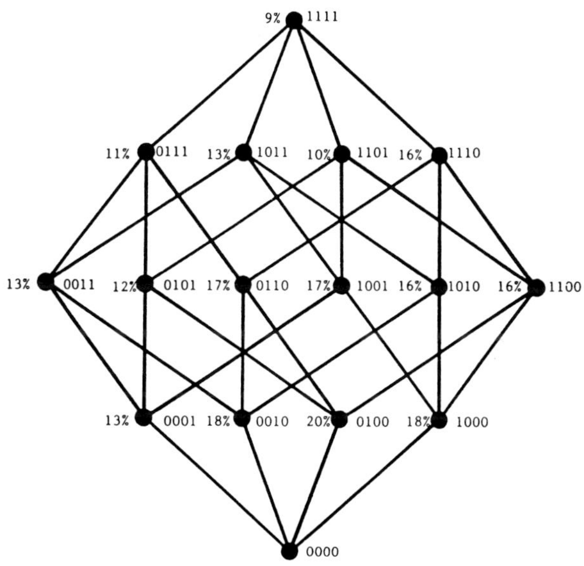

Fig. 1. A 4-dimensional feature selection lattice.

We say that a function $e(\cdot)$ has the *monotonicity property*, or is *monotonic*, if for every pair of linked nodes in the lattice, a and b, the following is true:

$$\text{if } l(a) < l(b) \text{ then } e(a) > e(b), \tag{1.1}$$

where $l(\cdot)$ is the level function,

$$l(a) = \sum_{i=1}^{n} \alpha_i. \tag{1.2}$$

The research on feature selection dates back to the early sixties (for an overview and biographical notes see [1] or later [2]). The most recent advances in this area are attributed to Narendra and Fukunaga [3], who introduced and tested the use of branch and bound, and Foroutan and Sklansky [4], who introduced the concept of *approximate monotonicity* and studied the use of branch and bound for selecting features for piecewise linear classifiers. In both cases the branch and bound method was used to minimize the number of features provided that a certain additional constraint was satisfied. The constraint induces backtracking in the branch and bound algorithm and, consequently, limits the size of the search space (which in our case is the *feature selection lattice*) to a *feasible region*.

Narendra and Fukunaga used probabilistic separability measures as the constraint while Foroutan and Sklansky used the error rate of the piecewise linear classifier. Although the branch and bound technique was reported to achieve about a 99% reduction over exhaustive search [4], it suffers from two major problems. The first problem becomes evident when we realize that in order for the branch and bound algorithm to find the optimal solution, it has to search the entire feasible region. If the constraint criterion does not have the monotonicity property, branch and bound is likely to prune a feasible part of the search space. In the worst case the feasible region may be even disconnected, i.e., it may consist of several parts separated by the infeasible area, and then the ordinary branch and bound procedure has no means to access and explore all disconnected feasible parts of the feature selection lattice. This problem was addressed by Foroutan and Sklansky in [4] and to some extent was overcome in the case of the error rates of piecewise linear classifiers, which were demonstrated to be only slightly nonmonotonic with respect to subset inclusion so that certain modifications to the backtracking rule in branch and bound would enable (with a certain likelihood) the algorithm to explore the entire feasible region.

The second major problem in the use of branch and bound for feature selection is that this algorithm performs an exhaustive search in the feasible region. The size of this region may have different values, depending on the value of the threshold selected by the user, but generally is uncontrollable and grows at the same rate as the size of the entire search space, i.e., as 2^d, where d is the initial number of features. While search by branch and bound in up to 20-dimensional feature space is still feasible it becomes rapidly impractical as this dimensionality is approached and exceeded.

Since the evaluation of the discriminatory power of a subset of features requires an estimate of the error rate of a classifier optimized for that subset, the complexity of the combinatorial search encountered in feature selection is amplified by the time required for designing the optimum classifier and estimating its error rate. We refer to such complex evaluation problems as *large-scale feature selection*. For such cases we need further search time reductions of two or more orders of magnitude. Toward this end we developed a feature selection procedure based on the concepts of genetic algorithms. Preliminary tests on this procedure, reported here, suggest that this might be a way to achieve the desired reductions in search time.

2. The Concept of Genetic Algorithms (GA)

Although research in genetic algorithms has a twenty-year history it has been just recently that theoretical advances and several spectacular successes in practical application attracted more attention to this field and caused its rapid growth. (For details on genetic algorithms the reader is encouraged to refer to the classical book by Holland [5] or to the recent book by Goldberg [6].)

The ordinary genetic algorithm is an optimization procedure working in binary search spaces, i.e., the search spaces consisting of binary strings, but after some coding it can be also applied to continuous search spaces. Unlike classical hill-climbers it does not evaluate and improve a single solution but, instead, it analyzes and modifies a *population* (that is, a set) of solutions at the same time. The power of this intrinsic parallelism of genetic search is amplified by the mechanics of population modification, allowing the genetic algorithms to attack successfully even NP-hard problems (see [5] for more details).

In the genetic algorithm a solution, i.e., a point in the search space, is represented by a finite sequence of 0's and 1's, called a *chromosome*. (In the application of GA to feature selection, each chromosome represents a subset of features, the k-th bit denoting the presence or absence of the k-th feature.) The algorithm manipulates a finite set of chromosomes, the *population*, in a manner resembling the mechanism of natural evolution. In this mechanism, the chromosomes are allowed to *mate* or *crossover*, and to *mutate*. The mating of two chromosomes produces a pair of offspring chromosomes which are syntheses of their parents. A mutation of a chromosome produces a near identical copy with some components of the chromosome altered.

The optimization process is carried out in cycles called *generations*. During each generation a set of new chromosomes or bit strings $\{a_i\}$ is created through crossover, mutated and evaluated. Since the population size is finite, only a predefined number of the (best) chromosomes survives to the next cycle of reproduction. Despite its limited size, the population is capable of fast adaptation which results in rapid optimization of the criterion function (*score*).

A high-level algorithmic description of the basic method is given below. Though many variations of this basic method exist, our description captures its primary characteristics.

---

1. Construct an initial population set $\Pi = \{a_i\}_{i=1,\ldots,n}$
2. **For** $i \leftarrow 1$ **to** *Number_of_generations* **do**
   (a) Initialize mating set $M \leftarrow \emptyset$ and offspring O.
   (b) **For** $j \leftarrow 1$ **to** n **do**
           Add $f(a_i)/\bar{f}$ copies of a_i to M.
   (c) **For** $j \leftarrow 1$ **to** $n/2$ **do**
           Select a pair a_j and a_k from M and do $O = O \cup crossover(a_j, a_k)$
           with probability P_c.
   (d) **For** $i \leftarrow 1$ **to** n **do**
           For $j \leftarrow 1$ **to** d **do**
               Switch the j-th bit in $a_i \in O$ with probability P_m.
   (e) Update the population $\Pi \leftarrow Combine(\Pi, O)$.

In the above algorithm f is the so-called *fitness* function and

$$\bar{f} = \sum_{i=1}^{n} f(a_i)/n.$$

In the form of genetic algorithms that were originally designed for modeling biological evolution, the crossover operator, $crossover(\cdot,\cdot)$, implements exchanges of information among chromosomes. In particular, if a chromosome is represented by a binary string (as in feature selection), crossover can be implemented by randomly choosing a point, called the *crossover point*, at which two chromosomes exchange their parts to create two new chromosomes. For instance, given two strings, 00100101 and 10111010, the crossover operator can cut them in the middle and, as a result, $crossover(00100101, 10111010)$ will produce two new chromosomes: 00101010 and 10110101.

When the crossover operator provides new solution points for further evaluation, it serves two complementary search functions. First, it creates new structures (e.g., the substring ##1111##, where # means 'don't care'), which were not present in parent chromosomes. These structures, when evaluated and accepted, create a new track toward the optimal solution. Second, this operator retains old structures within new solution points (for instance, 0010####), which, if accepted within the newly created solution, makes the presence of this structure in the population stronger. As a result, this structure has greater chance to survive and proliferate within the future solutions.

Mutation is a secondary search operator which increases the variability of the population. In our examples involving bit strings a mutant can be created by changing at random one or more bits in the structure.

The new population is created by combining the old population and the offspring, which is symbolically denoted as $\Pi \leftarrow Combine(\Pi, O)$. There are a number of possible implementations of this procedure, ranging from more radical, like $\Pi \leftarrow O$, to less restrictive, like "select n best chromosomes from Π and O." The *fitness* function is another key element in the efficient application-oriented version of the genetic algorithm. The execution and performance of genetic search is also determined by a number of parameters, some of them specific for distinct implementations of genetic algorithms. However, the *population size, crossover rate* and *mutation rate* are common for all implementations. The crossover rate is the probability of accepting an eligible pair of chromosomes for crossover. The mutation rate is the probability of switching bits in the chromosomes. The crossover rate usually assumes high values, close or equal to one, while the mutation rate is typically small (1 to 15%).

3. Applying GA to Feature Selection

In our research on the use of genetic algorithms in feature selection we followed the formulation of the search problem utilized by Narendra and Fukunaga [3], and later by Foroutan and Sklansky [4] in their work on the branch and bound procedure. This approach assumes that we seek the smallest or the least costly subset of features for which the classifier's performance does not deteriorate below a certain specified level. When the error of a classifier is used to measure the performance, a subset is defined as *feasible* if the classifier's error rate is below the so-called *feasibility threshold*. We search for the smallest subset of features among all feasible subsets.

In this form feature selection is a constrained optimization problem, not readily handled by genetic algorithms. To make the constrained optimization suitable for genetic search we introduce the following *penalty function*:

$$p(e) = \frac{\exp((e - t)/m) - 1}{\exp(1) - 1}, \tag{3.1}$$

where e is the error rate, t is the feasibility threshold and m is a scale factor (referred to as the 'tolerance margin'). Note that the penalty function is monotonic with respect to e. If $e < t$ then $p(e)$ is negative and, as e approaches zero, $p(e)$ slowly approaches its minimal value:

$$p(0) = \frac{\exp(-t/m) - 1}{\exp(1) - 1} > -\frac{1}{\exp(1) - 1}. \tag{3.2}$$

Note also that $p(t) = 0$ and $p(t + m) = 1$. For greater values of the error rate the penalty function quickly rises toward infinity. We add this penalty function to the number of features in the evaluated subset to produce the score $J(a)$:

$$J(a) = l(a) + p(e(a)), \tag{3.3}$$

where $a = (\alpha_1, \ldots, \alpha_d)$ is a bit string representing a feature subset; α_i is a binary number set to 0 if the i-th feature is not present in the subset and set to 1 if it is included in the subset; and $l(a)$ is the level in the lattice occupied by a, defined in (1.2). Note that $l(a)$ represents approximately the cost of extracting features (assuming that the costs of extracting the individual features are equal).

Recall the properties of the penalty function defined in (3.1) and note the following:

(a) Feature subsets (i.e., chromosomes in the terminology of GA) for which the error rate is below the feasibility threshold receive a small reward (i.e., a negative penalty).

(b) Feature subsets at the same level are validated according to the error rates associated with them: the ones with the lower error rates are better adapted (adaptation is measured by the score (3.3)).

(c) Feature subsets for which the error rate is above the threshold t but below $t + m$ receive a small penalty (between 0 and 1), which makes them about as well adapted as the subsets at one level higher. As a result, it is possible that a subset at level k will be considered better than a subset at level $k + 1$.

(d) Feature subsets for which the error rate exceeds $t + m$ receive a relatively high penalty (over 1) and cannot compete with subsets at the next higher level in the feature selection lattice.

Based on these properties of the score function (3.3) we anticipated that the genetic algorithm that would use it to validate the population of chromosomes should rapidly converge to the feasibility/infeasibility border in the feature selection lattice, and thereafter to operate in the vicinity of this border. In the next section we describe experiments which confirmed this anticipated behavior of our genetic algorithm.

Going back to the definition of the ordinary genetic algorithm given in Section 2, we need to define the fitness function and the $Combine(\cdot,\cdot)$ operator. Let $\Pi = \{a_1, \ldots, a_n\}$ denote a population of feature selection vectors. Thus each feature selection vector represents a chromosome. Since in our case we look for a minimum of the score (3.3), we define the fitness function as

$$f(a_i) = (1 + \varepsilon) \max_{a_j \in \Pi} J(a_j) - J(a_i), \tag{3.4}$$

where ε is a small positive constant which assures that $\min f(a_i) > 0$, i.e., even the least fit chromosome is given a chance to reproduce. The $Combine(\cdot,\cdot)$ operator selects the best n chromosomes from $\Pi \cup O$.

4. Experimental Study

The intent of the experiments reported here was first to evaluate GA as a tool for feature selection in competition with classical procedures for small scale problems, and then to evaluate it for large scale problems. By 'small scale problems' we refer to cases where the feature selection task can be handled in a reasonable time by exhaustive search or by a branch and bound search, as in the Foroutan–Sklansky formulation. In practice the initial number of features, d, in small scale problems never exceeds 20. We refer to feature selection problems in which the initial number of features exceeds 20 as *large scale*.

In an ideal experimental situation it would be desirable to test our feature selection procedure on a group of real data sets derived from various applications (e.g., medical, industrial or military), because that would give the results of such testing credibility and statistical validity. However, for practical reasons any extensive testing involving real data is prohibitive. Therefore, we followed the following path in our experiments:

(a) First, we compared sequential search, branch and bound and our procedure on simulated data of moderate dimensionality. Where possible, we included exhaustive search in these tests. The speedups obtained by replacing the training of a classifier and the estimation of its error rate by a simulation of the error rate were in the range of 10^3 to 10^4.

(b) Next, to verify the results obtained on the simulated data we performed limited tests on real data.

4.1. *Experiments on Simulated Data*

To simulate the conditions encountered by feature selection procedures in practice we replaced the true error rate function with a model of the classifier's error rate. Building adequate approximations of the error rates of some types of classifiers is possible, but in practice it does not lead to substantial savings in the computation time. For instance, there is an analytic formula for the error rate for the optimal classifier for two Gaussian distributions in the feature space with equal covariance matrices. However, the computation or approximation of this formula requires inverting the common covariance matrix, which yields the time complexity of $O(d^3)$. Not only is this complexity too high for our purposes, but the assumed form of class distributions in the feature space is so restrictive that the error rate function is hardly representative of any real application.

To resolve this dilemma we modeled the error rate as a function of the feature selection vector, accounting for various interactions among the features and various defects of the classifier training procedures — but without assuming any forms of underlying distributions in the data.

Let $a = (\alpha_1, \ldots, \alpha_d)$ denote a chromosome or feature selection vector representing a feature subset in a d-dimensional space. Recall that in this vector $\alpha_i = 0$ means that the i-th feature is not included in the subset and $\alpha_i = 1$ means that the i-th feature belongs to the subset. Let $\tilde{\alpha}_i$ denote $1 - \alpha_i$.

The error rate function can be represented as

$$e(a) = \sum_{j=1}^{2^d} m_j(a)e_j, \qquad (4.1)$$

where

$$m_j(a) = \begin{cases} 1 & \text{if } j = \text{bin}(a), \\ 0 & \text{otherwise} \end{cases} \qquad (4.2)$$

and bin(a) is a function that transforms the binary vector a into a corresponding decimal equivalent (e.g., bin(011) = 3). But this form merely provides a means for expressing the error rate as a function. It does not reflect various phenomena observed in the behavior of error rate function encountered in practice. Consequently, instead of the above formulation we have built our error rate model around the k-degree algebraic form

$$e = e_0 + \sum_{i_1,\ldots,i_k} w_{i_1,\ldots,i_k} \tilde{\alpha}_{i_1} \ldots \tilde{\alpha}_{i_k} \tag{4.3}$$

where e_0 is a constant and $w_{i_1,\ldots,i_k}$ are constants. For $k = 1$ this definition reduces to a linear form

$$e = e_0 + W^T \tilde{a}, \quad \text{where} \quad W = [w_1, \ldots, w_d]^T. \tag{4.4}$$

For $k = 2$, Eq. (4.3) becomes a quadratic form

$$e = e_0 + \tilde{a}^T W \tilde{a}, \quad W = [w_{ij}], \quad i,j = 1,\ldots,d. \tag{4.5}$$

By Eq. (4.3) a constant $w_{i_1,\ldots,i_k}$ is added to the base error rate e_0 if the features corresponding to $\alpha_{i_1} \cdots \alpha_{i_k}$ are not included in the current feature subset. Since Bayes theory states that the error rate function should increase when features are dropped (this effect is known as the *monotonicity property* of the *Bayes classifier*), the constants $w_{i_1,\ldots,i_k}$ should be nonnegative. In that sense these constants represent the penalty for dropping the information contained in features. Hence we call these constants *penalty factors.*

In practice classifiers do not behave exactly as their Bayesian models. Training procedures used to construct the classifiers are sensitive to various anomalies in the data. The data itself may be underrepresented — which may result from a small sample size, unfavorable size/dimensionality ratio or both. These properties of the data affect the chances for the success or failure by the training procedures to construct the optimal classifier for the given data. Consequently, when a feature or a group of features is dropped from the data, the error rate of a classifier trained on the remaining features may *decrease*. In our error rate model we simulate several possible causes of deviations from strict monotonicity in real classifiers. We discuss these simulated deviations below.

We allow a certain fraction of the penalty factors $w_{i_1,\ldots,i_k}$ to be negative. These negative constants represent the improvements in the performance of a training procedure when noise-inducing features are removed. Such an effect occurs often in the k-NN rule, which requires comparisons of distances to perform classification. If a feature with low discriminatory power has much larger variance than other features with inherently high discriminatory power, it is very likely to suppress the influence of the otherwise strong features on the overall classification results. When this irrelevant feature is dropped, the features with high discriminatory power can be more fully utilized by the k-NN procedure and yield smaller error rates. The negative penalty factors occur with a probability which we call the *defect probability*.

Beside strictly data-dependent effects we also observe in practice *training defects*. This class of defects covers situations when the training procedure does not produce the best classifier for the data. An example here would be any iterative procedure (e.g., the *window training procedure* [9]), where the error rate varies stochastically and for which the stopping rule is inaccurate. The error in estimating the error rate based on the evaluation of the trained classifier on the test data also varies stochastically. We simulate these training defects by imposing an extra variance on the error rate obtained from (4.5):

$$e = e_0 + \sum_{i_1,\ldots,i_k} w_{i_1,\ldots,i_k} \bar{\alpha}_{i_1} \cdots \bar{\alpha}_{i_k} + \varepsilon, \tag{4.6}$$

where ε has a normal distribution $N(0, \varepsilon_0)$. We call the constant ε_0 the *estimation error level*.

Additionally we include a number of local defects associated with specific subsets of features that are significantly larger than those generated by (4.5). Those additional defects are determined by indicating their absolute value and the combinations of features for which they occur. Thus our full representation of the error rate is as follows:

$$e = e_0 + \sum_{i_1,\ldots,i_k} w_{i_1,\ldots,i_k} \tilde{\alpha}_{i_1} \ldots \tilde{\alpha}_{i_k} + \varepsilon + \sum_{j=1}^{s} v_j \hat{\alpha}_{i_1} \ldots \hat{\alpha}_{i_d}, \tag{4.7}$$

where $\hat{\alpha}_i$ can stand for α_i, $\tilde{\alpha}_i$ or a 'don't care' case. Note that while the first sum consists of k-element binary feature code multiplications, the second one may use even all features to determine defects. Those features that are marked as 'don't care' are dropped from the products. Thus the products describing the local defects may have a varying number of features involved.

We implemented and tested the error rate model described above. In particular we generated a quadratic-type error function for 24 features. Beside the GA we tested three other procedures: exhaustive search, (p, q)-search introduced by Stearns [7] as a generalization of sequential search techniques, and the branch and bound as modified by Foroutan and Sklansky [4]. Our objective was to find the smallest (i.e., containing the smallest number of elements) subset of features for which the error rate does not exceed a given threshold. Below we describe the results of our test on these four algorithms.

Exhaustive search

The results of the exhaustive search of the 2^{24}-node feature selection lattice are given in Table 1. In this table we list minimum and maximum errors for each level in the feature selection lattice and feature subsets (the rightmost column)

Table 1. Exhaustive search results.

Level	Min. error	Max. error	Best subset (min. error)
1	0.349	0.400	000000000000000000010000
2	0.320	0.397	001010000000000000000000
3	0.297	0.386	001010000000000000010000
4	0.273	0.370	011000000001100000000000
5	0.248	0.354	011001000000110000000000
6	0.228	0.347	011001000000110000010000
7	0.211	0.338	011001000000110000010100
8	0.195	0.326	011001000000110000010110
9	0.182	0.314	011001000000110100010110
10	0.169	0.302	011001000000110110010110
11	0.158	0.290	011001000000110110011110
12	0.148	0.279	011001000000110110111110
13	0.139	0.269	011001111000110010010111
14	0.130	0.259	011001011100110011010111
15	0.122	0.250	011001011100110011110111
16	0.116	0.241	011001011100110111110111
17	0.111	0.235	011001011100110111111111
18	0.113	0.229	010001111110110111111111
19	0.109	0.224	011011111101100111111111
20	0.106	0.218	011011111101101111111111
21	0.106	0.214	011011101111111111111111
22	0.108	0.208	011011111111111111111111
23	0.113	0.168	101111111111111111111111
24	0.124	0.124	111111111111111111111111

corresponding to the minimum errors. It took 95,214 seconds (approximately 26 hours) of CPU time on a MicroVAX II to complete the search. Note that any additional feature would increase this more than twofold (the number of nodes would double and the time needed to compute a single error rate value would increase slightly).

Branch and bound

Recall that the threshold t, used to induce backtracking in branch and bound, determines the size of the feasible region and that if the constraint criterion (e.g., the error rate) has the monotonicity property, branch and bound performs exhaustive search in the feasible region. The Foroutan–Sklansky modified branch and bound (BB) algorithm, which allows for certain departures from strict monotonicity, requires additionally that we set the tolerance margin m (see [4]). Effectively, the size of the feasible region is determined by $t + m$. To avoid an excessively large feasible region we chose the threshold $t = 12.5\%$ and $m = 1\%$. From Table 1 we see that the feasible region would contain no more than

$$n_f = \sum_{i=14}^{24} \binom{24}{i} \approx 7 \cdot 10^6$$

nodes, since exhaustive search found a 14-element feature subset with an error rate of 13.0% and no subset at the level 13 had an error rate smaller than 13.9%. Recall that the level in the lattice at which a node is placed is equivalent to the number of features the corresponding subset contains.

The Foroutan–Sklansky modified branch and bound algorithm did not find a feasible subset at the level 15 in the feature selection lattice. After executing 134,122 criterion function evaluations, which yields 99.2% savings over exhaustive search, it completed its search. The results of branch and bound search are given in Table 2. In this table we show only the levels that were visited by the branch and bound procedure. The rightmost column, titled 'Excess error,' contains the amount by which the error rate obtained from branch and bound exceeds the minimal achievable error rate at the same level. Note that the branch and bound algorithm found optimal subsets only at the levels 20, 23 and 24.

Table 2. The Foroutan–Sklansky BB-search.

Level	Min. error	Best subset (min. error)	Excess error
14	0.142	001011000001100111111111	0.012
15	0.132	011001110100110110111110	0.010
16	$\rightarrow$ 0.124	111101100010110110111110	0.008
17	0.119	111001001111100111111101	0.008
18	0.114	111001001111110110111111	0.001
19	0.110	111001001111110111111111	0.001
20	0.106	011011111101110111111111	0.000
21	0.114	101111111111110111111110	0.008
22	0.113	101111111111110111111111	0.005
23	0.113	101111111111111111111111	0.000
24	0.124	111111111111111111111111	0.000

As we see from Table 2, the best subset satisfying the error-rate constraint was located at the level 16 (marked by an arrow). The best subset found by branch and bound at the level 15 has an error rate of 13.2 %, which is 1% higher than the minimal achievable error at this level. While the one-percent difference between the error rate corresponding to the optimal subset and the error rate of the best subset actually detected by branch and bound at the level 15 may not seem significant in practice (as the estimated error rates are always corrupted by the imperfect estimation process itself), it nevertheless signals a deeper problem in the actual performance of this procedure. Apart from the already huge number of visited nodes, the Foroutan–Sklansky modification of branch and bound still did not deal adequately with the nonmonotonicities in the feature selection lattice despite the fact that $t + m$ should have forced it to search all subsets at the level 14 and 15.

(p, q)-search

The (p, q)-search procedure also failed to find the optimal solution. We tested several settings for p and q (e.g., (2,1), (1,0), (0,1), (3,2), etc.) but for none of them was the excess error rate less than 1 %. The results of (1,0)-search, which is equivalent to sequential backward selection, are given in Table 3(a). The results of (2,1)-search are shown in Table 3(b). The number of criterion function evaluations was 301 for (1,0)-search and 433 for (2,1)-search.

Table 3(a). Sequential backward selection — (1,0)-search.

Level	Min. error	Best subset (min. error)	Excess error
1	0.371	001000000000000000000000	0.022
2	0.325	001001000000000000000000	0.005
3	0.311	001001000000100000000000	0.014
4	0.281	001001100000100000000000	0.008
5	0.267	001001110000100000000000	0.019
6	0.252	101001110000100000000000	0.024
7	0.241	101001110010100000000000	0.030
8	0.234	101001110011100000000000	0.039
9	0.208	101001110111100000000000	0.026
10	0.195	101001110111110000000000	0.026
11	0.192	101001111111110000000000	0.034
12	0.187	101011111111110000000000	0.029
13	0.164	101111111111110000000000	0.025
14	0.153	101111111111110000000100	0.023
15	0.143	101111111111110000010100	0.021
16	0.135	101111111111110000010110	0.019
17	0.128	101111111111110000110110	0.017
18	→0.123	101111111111110000111110	0.010
19	0.118	101111111111110100111110	0.009
20	0.116	101111111111110110111110	0.010
21	0.114	101111111111110111111110	0.008
22	0.113	101111111111110111111111	0.005
23	0.113	101111111111111111111111	0.000
24	0.124	111111111111111111111111	0.000

Genetic search

The margin used by the penalty function was set to $m = 1\%$ as in the branch and bound procedure. Although when these tests were conducted we did not know any theoretical justification for assigning any particular value to m, this value seemed

Table 3(b). The Stearns algorithm — (2,1)-search.

Level	Min. error	Best subset (min. error)	Excess error
1	0.349	000000000000000000010000	0.000
2	0.325	001001000000000000000000	0.005
3	0.302	001001000000000000010000	0.005
4	0.281	001001100000100000000000	0.008
5	0.260	001001100000100000010000	0.012
6	0.252	101001110000100000000000	0.024
7	0.234	101001110000100000010000	0.023
8	0.234	101001110011100000000000	0.039
9	0.208	101001110111100000000000	0.026
10	0.195	101001110111110000000000	0.026
11	0.181	101001110111110000010000	0.023
12	0.187	101011111111110000000000	0.039
13	0.164	101111111111110000000000	0.025
14	0.153	101111111111110000000100	0.023
15	0.143	101111111111110000010100	0.021
16	0.135	101111111111110000010110	0.019
17	0.128	101111111111110000110110	0.017
18	→ 0.123	101111111111110000111110	0.010
19	0.118	101111111111110100111110	0.009
20	0.116	101111111111110110111110	0.010
21	0.114	101111111111110111111110	0.008
22	0.113	101111111111110111111111	0.005
23	0.113	101111111111111111111111	0.000
24	0.124	111111111111111111111111	0.000

to work properly on a wide range of tests. In addition we tested other values of the threshold and did not see any significant correlation between t and m.

The genetic algorithm implemented to satisfy the specification given in the previous section executed a moderate number of criterion function evaluations (1000 to 3000) before it found the optimal (!) solution. We tested a broad range of values of parameters (*crossover rate, mutation rate* and *population size*) that control the performance of the genetic algorithm. For almost all cases the optimal solution was found in the first 1000 to 3000 criterion function evaluations. Each test consisted of 25 runs of genetic search for the same parameter setting but for different initial populations. To suppress the dependency of the results on the initial population, the results of these runs were averaged and also standard deviations were calculated. Each of the runs performed up to 3000 error evaluations (that is, it visited up to 3000 nodes). The results of these comparative tests are presented in Table 4. In this table the population size is listed in the first column and the mutation rate in the next column. The crossover rate for all listed tests was equal to 1.0. The following six columns list the error rates (columns titled E14, E15 and E16) and their standard deviations (V14, V15, V16) for the levels of interest, that is, 14, 15 and 16. As

Table 4. Genetic algorithm: an overview.

n	mutation rate	E14	V14	E15	V15	E16	V16
10	0.10	0.135	0.004	0.127	0.004	0.121	0.004
10	0.15	0.134	0.004	0.126	0.004	0.120	0.004
10	0.20	0.134	0.004	0.126	0.004	0.121	0.004
14	0.10	0.134	0.004	0.127	0.004	0.120	0.004
14	0.15	0.134	0.004	0.126	0.004	0.119	0.004
14	0.20	0.133	0.004	0.126	0.004	0.120	0.004
20	0.05	0.134	0.004	0.127	0.004	0.120	0.004
20	0.10	0.135	0.004	0.127	0.004	0.120	0.004
20	0.15	0.133	0.004	0.126	0.004	0.120	0.004
20	0.20	0.134	0.004	0.127	0.004	0.120	0.004
30	0.05	0.135	0.004	0.128	0.004	0.121	0.004
30	0.10	0.133	0.004	0.125	0.004	0.119	0.004
30	0.15	0.133	0.004	0.126	0.004	0.120	0.004
30	0.20	0.134	0.004	0.127	0.004	0.121	0.004
40	0.05	0.134	0.004	0.127	0.004	0.120	0.004
40	0.10	0.134	0.004	0.127	0.004	0.121	0.004
40	0.15	0.134	0.004	0.127	0.004	0.120	0.004
40	0.20	0.135	0.004	0.127	0.004	0.122	0.004
50	0.05	0.135	0.004	0.128	0.004	0.121	0.004
50	0.10	0.135	0.004	0.127	0.004	0.121	0.004
50	0.15	0.135	0.004	0.127	0.004	0.122	0.004
50	0.20	0.135	0.003	0.127	0.003	0.122	0.004
76	0.05	0.136	0.004	0.128	0.004	0.121	0.004
76	0.10	0.135	0.004	0.128	0.004	0.122	0.004
76	0.15	0.137	0.004	0.128	0.004	0.122	0.003
76	0.20	0.137	0.004	0.129	0.004	0.123	0.004

Minimal achievable errors at these levels

0.130	0.122	0.116

we see, the error obtained by the best performing search procedures does not exceed the minimal error rate by more than 0.4 %. The corresponding standard deviations are equal to 0.4 %, which implies that in several cases the optimum feature subsets were found by our genetic algorithm.

As an example, the result of search based on a 10-element population, with the crossover rate equal to 100% and mutation rate equal to 15 % is presented in Table 5. Note that the excess error at the optimal level, marked by an arrow, is only 0.1 %.

As we mentioned before, we expected the genetic algorithm to concentrate on searching the boundary between the feasible and infeasible nodes in the feature selection lattice. This effect is confirmed in Table 5. The second column in this table lists the number of nodes (feature subsets) visited at each level. We see here that most of the visited nodes are at levels 13 to 16.

Table 5. GA: an example run.

Level	Visited nodes	Min. error	Best subset (min. error)	Excess error
8	1	0.226	001001001100110110000000	0.031
9	12	0.192	011000001000100111010100	0.010
10	52	0.177	011001010000110100110100	0.008
11	169	0.163	011001010000110110010110	0.005
12	349	0.149	011001111000110000110110	0.001
13	551	0.139	011001011100110011010110	0.000
14	702	0.131	011001011100110110110110	0.001
15	624	→ 0.123	011001011100110110110111	0.001
16	422	0.116	011001011100110111110111	0.000
17	208	0.119	111101000110110111111110	0.008
18	89	0.124	111111100111110110011101	0.011
19	34	0.119	111001111100110111111111	0.010
20	7	0.115	111111100111111011111110	0.009
21	6	0.116	111111110101111011111111	0.010
22	4	0.126	111111111111111111001111	0.018

4.2. *Experiments on Real Data*

In order to verify the power of our genetic feature selection procedure we devised a 5-NN classifier trained on digitized infrared imagery of real scenes. This data was provided by the U.S. Army. It consisted of 150 30-dimensional feature vectors, each vector belonging to one of two classes. The purpose of this experiment was to compare our method with sequential methods, particularly with the Stearns (p, q)-search procedure, which at this dimensionality of the problem is the only algorithm able to give solutions in reasonable time. The k-NN rule is known to react strongly to undersampling (i.e., the situation when the training set is small)[1] and the scaling problem (i.e., the problem of scaling features). To avoid the latter we scaled all features to a unit standard deviation. The influence of undersampling manifests itself in significant nonmonotonicity of its error rate function. This effect is even stronger if the parameter k (the number of neighbors checked for classification) is fixed. Consequently, we expected that the resulting error rate function would be ill-behaved and would present difficulties to search algorithms.

Our procedure in this experiment was as follows. First, we ran sequential backward selection, which is equivalent to (1,0)-search in Stearns' notation. It is important to note here that sequential algorithms produce a path through all the levels of the feature selection lattice. The error rates along this path can be drawn versus the levels in the lattice (see Fig. 2). Based on the observation of the path through the feature selection lattice found by backward selection we chose the threshold $t = 0.145$ for our genetic feature selector. By selecting $t = 0.145$ we intended to

---

[1]For discussions of undersampling and related phenomena we refer the reader to [1] and [8].

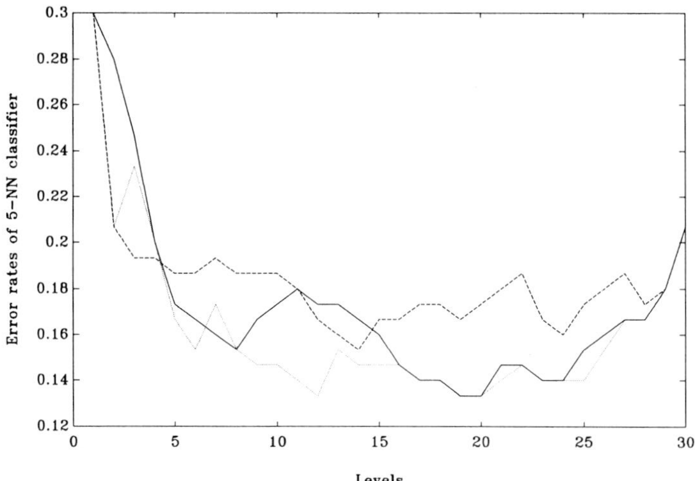

Fig. 2. Paths obtained from sequential procedures: the solid line denotes (1,0)-search (sequential backward selection), the dashed line denotes (0,1)-search (sequential forward selection), and the dotted line denotes (2,1)-search.

reduce the size of the feasible region, hereby making it more difficult for the genetic algorithm to find. In particular, according to the result obtained from backward selection the feasible region was placed between levels 17 and 20, and also at levels 23 and 24.

Our next step was to execute the genetic algorithm. Based on the results of simulations with the aid of the modeled error rate functions described in the previous section we chose the population size equal to 40, the mutation rate equal to 0.1 and we began search at level 2, creating the initial population with the aid of a random number generator. We ran our genetic algorithm 9 times. In each run the genetic algorithm was terminated when the number of tested subsets exceeded 2000.

Our final tests were done with the aid of the Stearns (2,1)-search algorithm and sequential forward selection (i.e., (0,1)-search in Stearns'-notation). The number of nodes (feature subsets) tested was 465 by forward and backward selection, and 1395 by (2,1)-search.

In Fig. 2 we summarize the results obtained from sequential search procedures. In this figure the solid line corresponds to the path obtained from (1,0)-search, the dashed line comes from (0,1)-search and the dotted line denotes (2,1)-search. As expected the (2,1)-search procedure provided the best results (the lowest error rates) for all levels except 3, 4 and 7. The (1,0)-search algorithm found the best feasible subset consisting of 17 features. The (2,1)-search algorithm found a smaller feasible subset, consisting of 11 features. The (0,1)-search algorithm did not find a feasible subset at all.

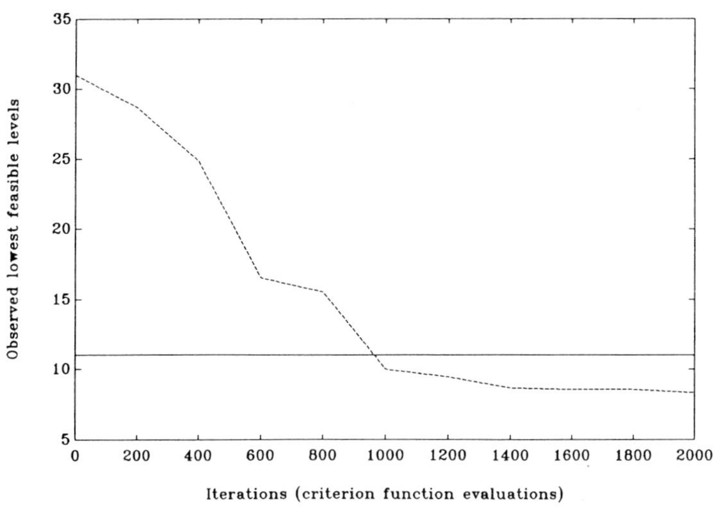

Fig. 3. An averaged convergence curve of genetic search for 5-NN rule.

An average of 9 runs of our procedure starting with different initial populations is presented in Fig. 3. In this figure we plot the observed lowest feasible level versus the number of executed iterations. The solid line denotes the lowest feasible level, equal to 11, found by (2,1)-search. The dashed line denotes the progress of genetic search. As we see from the figure, the genetic feature selection procedure found a feasible subset at the level 11 after approximately 1000 iterations. This compares favorably with the number of iterations executed by (2,1)-search. On average, the lowest feasible level detected by our method was equal approximately to 8. In one run the genetic algorithm found a node with error rate 0.133 at the level 7, that is, it reduced the size of the best feasible subset of features by four features.

5. Concluding Remarks

In this communication we discussed the use of genetic algorithms for selecting features for statistical pattern classifiers when the initial number of features exceeds 20. In our formulation, which follows the formalism used earlier by Narendra and Fukunaga [3] and later by Foroutan and Sklansky [4], the feature selection problem is a constrained optimization problem. In accordance with this formulation we adapted the ordinary genetic algorithm to the problem of feature selection by incorporating a penalty function into the criterion function or 'score.'

Our feature selection procedure based on the modified genetic algorithm was subject to numerous experiments described in detail in Section 4. We showed, on both real and modeled error rate functions, that our feature selection procedure outperforms all other nonexhaustive methods, in particular sequential search and branch and bound. In particular, on the 24-dimensional feature selection lattice with modeled error rate our method exhibited better results than branch and bound while yielding computational savings of two orders of magnitude over branch and bound. On 30-dimensional real data the genetic algorithm also outperformed sequential search (branch and bound was not tested because of its prohibitive time complexity), finding smaller feature subsets after exploring similar number of nodes. This advantage is more prominent when the dimensionality of the initial feature space is large, since the sequential procedures have quadratic time complexity and genetic search exhibits slightly more than linear increase of time complexity.

The success of the feature selection procedure based on the genetic algorithm can be attributed to the following facts:

(a) Branch and bound performs exhaustive search in the feasible region.

(b) Sequential search performs locally exhaustive search by testing all connected subsets on its way through the lattice. There is also no theoretical indication for what values of p and q the (p, q)-search procedure is going to yield the best results, so that multiple runs are needed.

(c) In contrast, the genetic algorithm performs directed scanning of the lattice and searches only the most promising parts of the lattice. Since during genetic search a set of candidate solutions is processed at the same time, the genetic algorithm is more likely to find the optimal solution than any other method that modifies and evaluates a single solution at a time. This inherent parallelism of the genetic algorithm results also in a very high efficiency of search, which, in terms of the number of visited nodes, rivals that of sequential search.

Acknowledgements

We are indebted to Richard Sims of the U.S. Army Missile Command for discussions and comments on the use of genetic algorithms for the design of classifiers. The research reported here was supported by the U.S. Army Research Office under Contract DAAG29-84-K-0208.

References

[1] P. A. Devijver and J. Kittler, *Pattern Recognition: A Statistical Approach*, Prentice-Hall, London, 1982.

[2] W. Siedlecki and J. Sklansky, On automatic feature selection, *Int. J. Pattern Recognition and Artificial Intelligence* **2** (1988) 197–220.

[3] P. M. Narendra and K. Fukunaga, A branch and bound algorithm for feature subset selection, *IEEE Trans. Computers* **26** (1977) 917–922.

[4] I. Foroutan and J. Sklansky, Feature selection for automatic classification of non-Gaussian data, *IEEE Trans. Syst. Man Cybern.* **17** (1987) 187–198.

[5] J. H. Holland, *Adaptation in Natural and Artificial Systems*, University of Michigan Press, Ann Arbor, MI, 1975.

[6] D. E. Goldberg, *Genetic Algorithms in Search, Optimization and Machine Learning*, Addison-Wesley, Reading, MA, 1989.

[7] S. D. Stearns, On selecting features for pattern classifiers, *Proc. of the Third Int. Conf. on Pattern Recognition*, Coronado, CA, 1976, 71–75.

[8] A. K. Jain and R. Chandrasekaran, Dimensionality and sample size considerations in pattern recognition practice, in P. R. Krishnaiah and L. N. Kanal (eds.), *Handbook of Statistics*, Vol. 2 (*Classification, Pattern Recognition and Reduction of Dimensionality*), North-Holland, New York, 1982.

[9] J. Sklansky and G. N. Wassel, *Pattern Classifiers and Trainable Machines*, Springer-Verlag, New York, 1981.

CHAPTER 1.3.3

CONSTRAINED GENETIC OPTIMIZATION VIA DYNAMIC REWARD-PENALTY BALANCING AND ITS USE IN PATTERN RECOGNITION

W. SIEDLECKI and J. SKLANSKY

Department of Electrical Engineering, University of California, Irvine, California 92717, USA

In this report we discuss a constrained optimization problem which is frequently encountered in the design of statistical pattern classifiers. We describe a modification of the ordinary genetic algorithm that enables it to perform sustained search for the optimal solution in the most promising parts of the search space.

1. Introduction

Let S be a metric space consisting of d-element bit strings, $x = (\chi_1, \ldots, \chi_d) \in S$, $\chi_i \in \{0, 1\}$, with the Hamming distance, $H(., .)$, serving as the metric. We say that an area A in S is connected if for any two points $x, y \in A$ there is a path $x_1, \ldots, x_k$ such that $H(x_i, x_{i+1}) = 1$, $i = 1, \ldots, k - 1$ and $x_1 = x$, $x_k = y$.

Consider the following constrained optimization problem:

$$\min J(x) \ \text{ for } \ x : e(x) \leq t \,, \tag{1-1}$$

where J is a real valued function that has only one minimum and only one maximum in S and the sets of points for which the function J reaches minimum and maximum are connected. Let x_{max} be a point of maximum of J and x_{min} be a point of minimum of J. Suppose that $H(x_{max}, x_{min}) = d$, and that the objective function J decreases along any d-step path between the point of maximum and the point of minimum. Among the functions that satisfy these conditions there are, for instance, linear and quadratic criteria. In the problem (1-1) the constraint criterion $e(x)$ is a real valued function and t is a user-defined constant.

The search space for problem (1-1) can be conveniently presented in the form of a lattice (an example of the four-dimensional lattice is shown in Fig. 1.1). In the lattice, which is an undirected graph, nodes correspond to points in the space S, and every two nodes are connected by a link if their Hamming distance is equal to

108

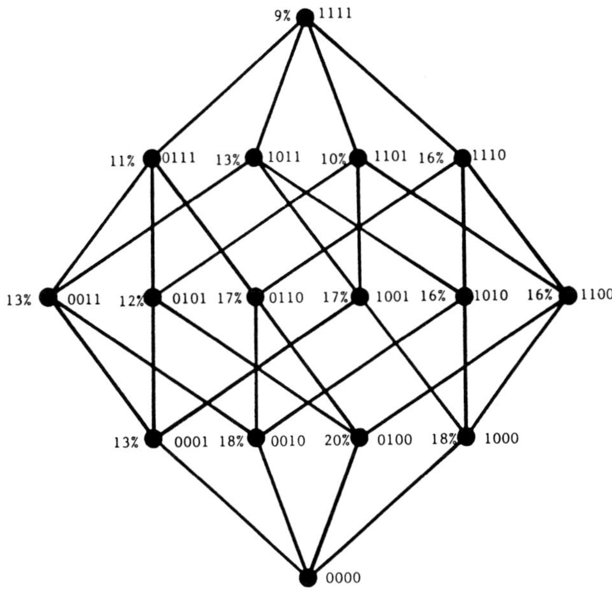

Fig. 1.1. A 4-dimensional search lattice.

one. The orientation of the lattice is determined by the function J in such a way that it reaches its maximum at the top node and its minimum at the bottom node.

The nodes in the lattice are grouped in levels: all nodes at the same level have the same Hamming distance from the bottom node x_{min}. By convention we will say that the bottom node is placed at the level 0, while the top node occupies the level d.

We say that the function $e(.)$ has the *monotonicity* property if for every two nodes in the lattice, x and y, the following is true:

$$\text{if } H(x,y) = 1 \text{ and } H(x, x_{min}) < H(y, x_{min})$$
$$\text{then } e(x) \geq e(y). \tag{1-2}$$

Should we assume monotonicity, the problem might be treated by *branch and bound*. However, even branch and bound would be of limited use on more than 20-dimensional spaces. The reason for this is that the size of the feasible region is usually unpredictable and grows as fast as the size of the whole search space. The branch and bound algorithm, which performs exhaustive search of the feasible region, becomes therefore impractical. In addition, the monotonicity of the function $e(.)$ is not guaranteed in the practical problem that we describe in Section 3, so the branch and bound algorithm has one more reason to fail. Other methods, like *sequential search procedure* discussed briefly in Section 3, also do not guarantee satisfactory solutions.

The important aspect of the problem (1–1) is that the constrained minima of the objective function always occur at the bottom (in the sense of the direction defined in the search lattice) boundary of the *feasible region* in the search space, i.e. the part of the search space where the constraint is satisfied). Since we do not want to assume any additional properties of the constraint function $e(.)$ (including its monotonicity), the feasible region may be in particular disconnected, that is, composed of several isolated pieces, and, in addition, some isolated parts of the feasible region may contain very few points.

Recently we have focused our attention on the possibility of using genetic algorithms to solve problem (1–1). While the basic architecture of genetic algorithms does not exclude their applicability to constrained search (which was demonstrated by Goldberg [1]), it is not well matched to it. In [2] Goldberg suggests a penalty function approach in which the objective function is replaced by the compound objective function:

$$J_s(x) = J(x) + \alpha \cdot \Phi(e(x) - t) , \qquad (1\text{–}3)$$

where α is a positive constant penalty coefficient and $\Phi(.)$ is a non-negative penalty function. While this approach should work properly in situations where the minimum is expected inside the feasible region, it is likely to fail when the minimum occurs at the boundary of the feasible region. The reason for this phenomenon is simple: the search will always end inside the infeasible part of the feature space where the value of the original objective function J balances the penalty for constraint violation. Certainly, we could observe the progress of genetic search and periodically adjust the value of the penalty coefficient when the search stagnates too far from the feasible part of the space, but such a solution is neither elegant nor convenient.

In the next section we propose a simple tracking technique that analyzes the position of the population before reproduction and balances the penalty with the value of the objective function to achieve a desired placement of the new population in the search space. The procedure is completely automatic and does not increase the time complexity of the genetic algorithm.

In the third section we present an example of the constrained optimization problem (1-1) encountered in statistical pattern recognition. We present the results of tests on real data that confirm the usefulness of our procedure.

2. Balancing the Penalties and Rewards

Let the following be a skeleton of the genetic algorithm used as a basis for our considerations:

> 1. Construct an initial population set $\Pi = \{x_1, \ldots, x_n\}$.
> 2. *For $l \leftarrow 1$ to Number_of_generations* **do**
>   2a Initialize mating set $M \leftarrow \emptyset$ and offspring $O \leftarrow \emptyset$.
>   2b **For $i \leftarrow 1$ to n do**
>   Add an expected number of $f(x_i)/\bar{f}$ copies of x_i to M.
>   2c **For $i \leftarrow 1$ to $n/2$ do**
>   Select a pair x_j and x_k from M and do $O = O \cup crossover(x_j, x_k)$
>   with probability P_c.
>   2d **For $i \leftarrow 1$ to n do**
>   **For $j \leftarrow 1$ to d do**
>   Switch the j-th bit in $x_i \in O$ with probability P_m.
>   2e Update the population $\Pi \leftarrow Combine(\Pi, O)$.

In this algorithm

$$\bar{f} = \sum_{i=1}^{n} f(x_i)/n \; . \tag{2-1}$$

and $f(.)$ is the so called *fitness* function, defined in our case as

$$f(x_i) = \max_{j=1,\ldots,n} J_s(x_j) - J_s(x_i) \; . \tag{2-2}$$

The crossover and mutation operators are implemented in their classical versions. The operator $Combine(\cdot, \cdot)$ will be discussed later.

As we have already pointed out, the important property of our optimization problem (1-1) is that the constrained minima of the objective function always occur at the boundary of the feasible region. While searching for the feasible region can be done by the plain genetic algorithm (just by minimizing the function $e(.)$ until the constraint is satisfied), the optimization around the feasibility boundary has to incorporate the policy of the "carrot and stick." First of all, we would like to encourage the genetic algorithm to search for isolated parts of the feasible region. On the other hand, we do not want the algorithm to end up wandering in the infeasible part of the search space.

The search process executed by the genetic algorithm proceeds through periodic modification and evaluation of the population of solutions. In order to force the genetic algorithm to explore the infeasible region below the feasible one, and at a given distance from it, we need to control the placement of the population of solutions in the space. Let $L(x)$ be a level of the node x in the lattice and let $P_o(l)$ be a distribution of levels in the current population, defined as follows:

$$P_o(l) = \frac{\sum_{L(x_i)=l} 1}{n} \; . \tag{2-3}$$

Let l_{min} and l_{max} denote the minimum and maximum levels in the current population, respectively. In terms of the search lattice our requirements are met if the distribution of levels in the population approximates a desired shape. For instance, this desired distribution can be Gaussian-like with fixed variance σ_l, but with the mean m_l, depending on whether feasible nodes are present in the current population or not. An example of a possible rule could be as follows:

(a) if one or more feasible nodes are present in the population then $m_l = l_o - \Delta l$, where l_o is the lowest level occupied by a feasible node and Δl is a desired depth of exploration, and

(b) if no feasible node is present in the population then $m_l = (l_{min} + 4l_{max})/5$.

$$(2\text{-}4)$$

The only place in the algorithm in which we can influence the placement of the population in the space without compromising the principles of genetic search is the reproduction stage, when the mating set is created.[a] Certainly, the crossover and mutation will partially ruin the effect of our efforts toward this aim, but if we keep repeating this process every generation the net effect will be to our benefit.

Consider now the distribution of levels in the mating set, i.e. the new population after the reproduction stage. The probability of being copied from the current population to the mating set is for a single individual equal to

$$P(x_i \in M) = \frac{f(x_i)}{\sum_{j=1}^{n} f(x_j)}. \tag{2-5}$$

The corresponding expected distribution of levels in the mating set will then be

$$P(l, \alpha) = \sum_{L(x_i)=l} P(x_i \in M) = \frac{\sum_{L(x_i)=l} f(x_i)}{\sum_{j=1}^{n} f(x_j)}, \tag{2-6}$$

where the penalty coefficient α was included because the compound criterion $J_s(.)$ depends on it. Hence the distribution of levels also depends on the value of the penalty coefficient, and, consequently on the balance between the original optimization criterion $J(.)$ and the penalty function $\Phi(.)$. It seems, therefore, plausible that by changing the value of the penalty coefficient we can adjust the shape of the level distribution in the mating set. The following two lemmas show that such adjustment is indeed possible.

Lemma 1. Let x_i and x_j be two points such that

$$J_s(x_i) > J_s(x_j) \quad \text{and} \quad e(x_j) > e(x_i) \tag{2-7}$$

for a given penalty coefficient $\alpha_1 > 0$. If the penalty function Φ is monotonically growing on $\Re$, then there exists another penalty coefficient $\alpha_2 > 0$, for which $J_s(x_i) < J_s(x_j)$.

---

[a]Actually the selection stage (Step 2e) is the other feasible place, but we do not investigate this possibility in this report.

Proof. The condition (2–7) is equivalent to

$$J(x_i) - J(x_j) > \alpha_1 \left(\Phi[e(x_j) - t] - \Phi[e(x_i) - t] \right) > 0 \ . \tag{2–8}$$

The second inequality holds because the penalty function Φ is monotonically growing and $e(x_j) - t > e(x_i) - t$. It is then trivial that if

$$\alpha_2 > \frac{J(x_i) - J(x_j)}{\Phi[e(x_j) - t] - \Phi[e(x_i) - t]} \tag{2–9}$$

then $J_s(x_i) < J_s(x_j)$. $\qquad\square$

We say that the solution x_i is *dominated* by the solution x_j if

$$J(x_i) > J(x_j) \quad \text{and} \quad e(x_i) > e(x_j). \tag{2–10}$$

Lemma 2. If the solution x_i is dominated by the solution x_j then $J_s(x_i) > J_s(x_j)$ for all values of the penalty coefficient α.

Proof. Assuming conditions (2–10) and recalling that the penalty function is monotonically increasing we conclude that the inequality

$$J(x_i) - J(x_j) > \alpha \left(\Phi[e(x_j) - t] - \Phi[e(x_i) - t] \right) \tag{2–11}$$

always holds because the left side is positive and the right side remains negative for all positive values of α. $\qquad\square$

According to Lemma 1, by adjusting the penalty coefficient we can change the fitness-based ordering of the solutions in the population, provided that the solutions are not in the relation of *dominance*. On the other hand, Lemma 2 says that dominating solutions are never reordered. It is also interesting to notice that both lemmas hold even if one or both solutions are feasible.

Although, the desired penalty coefficient usually cannot be found from an analytic formula, there still exists a fairly simple way of approximating it. Let $P_o(l)$ be a desired distribution of levels represented in the mating set after reproduction. Let, similarly, $P(l, \alpha)$ be a probability distribution of levels represented in the mating set after reproduction with penalty function-induced preference, with a given penalty coefficient α. This distribution can be calculated directly from the data available in the genetic algorithm, that is, levels, $L(x_i)$, and fitness values $f(x_i)$, which can be computed in any valid way (e.g., via formula (2–2)). Given these two distributions we can measure the *impact function*,

$$\Delta P(l, \alpha) = P(l, \alpha) - P_o(l), \tag{2–12}$$

of the penalty coefficient α on the reproduction process. To measure a total impact of the penalty coefficient α on the change of level distribution during the reproduction process we introduce the following *impact index*:

$$\sigma(\alpha) = \frac{l_{max} - l_{min}}{|l_{max} - l_{min}|} \sum_{l=1}^{d} \Delta P(l, \alpha)^2, \tag{2–13}$$

where l_{min} and l_{max} are levels such that

$$\Delta P(l_{min}, \alpha) = \min_l \Delta P(l, \alpha),$$
$$\Delta P(l_{max}, \alpha) = \max_l \Delta P(l, \alpha). \tag{2-14}$$

Hence, the impact index is positive if higher levels are emphasized and negative if lower levels are emphasized.

Recall from the previous section that there is only one value of the penalty coefficient α for which the preference between two nondominated solutions may change. Similarly, since the impact index is a compounded effect of all these preference changes taking place in the population when the penalty coefficient changes its value, $\sigma(\alpha) = 0$ will indicate the switch from the dominance of lower levels over higher levels and vice versa. Therefore, by observing values of the impact index over a range of values of α we can infer its switch-imposing value.

To demonstrate the effect of shifting the emphasis on certain levels in the population caused by changes of the penalty coefficient, we devised a simple numerical example. This example is prepared by a computer program that first generates a set of pairs $(L(x_i), e(x_i))$, that is levels and constraint values, according to a normal distribution rotated slightly in a negative angle direction to avoid introducing dominance chains in the hypothetical population. Assuming a certain feasibility threshold t and a penalty function, we can calculate both the impact function $\Delta P(l, \alpha)$ and the impact index, $\sigma(\alpha)$, over a wide range of values of α. Figures 2.1, 2.2 and 2.3 depict how both functions change depending on α. The impact function is presented in the form of a mesh. The horizontal coordinates are l and α, while the vertical coordinate represents $\Delta P(l, \alpha)$. In Figures 2.1 and 2.4 the south-east axis corresponds to α and the south-west axis corresponds to l. Figures 2.2 and 2.5 provide transposed views of the drawings in Figures 2.1 and 2.4, respectively.

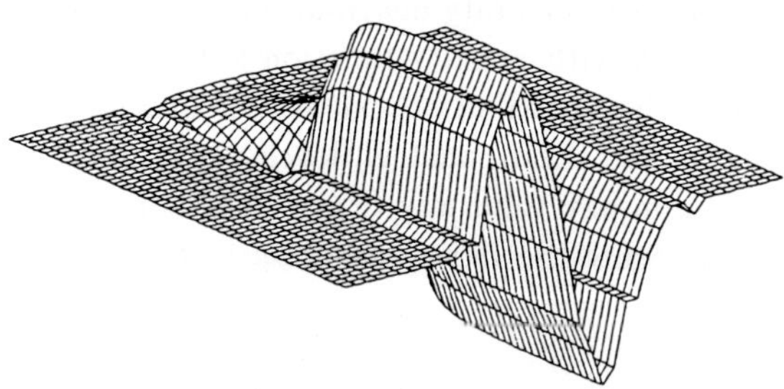

Fig. 2.1. The impact function for the $\Phi(z) = (e^z - 1)/(e - 1)$ penalty function.

Based on the discussions conducted so far we can add missing elements in the definition of our genetic algorithm for constrained optimization presented at the

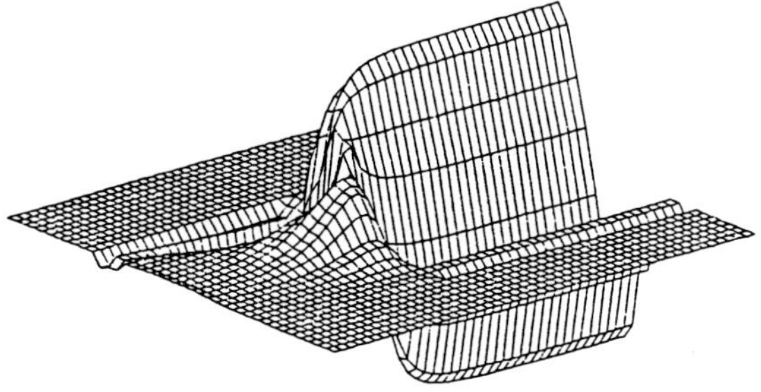

Fig. 2.2. Another view of Figure 2.1.

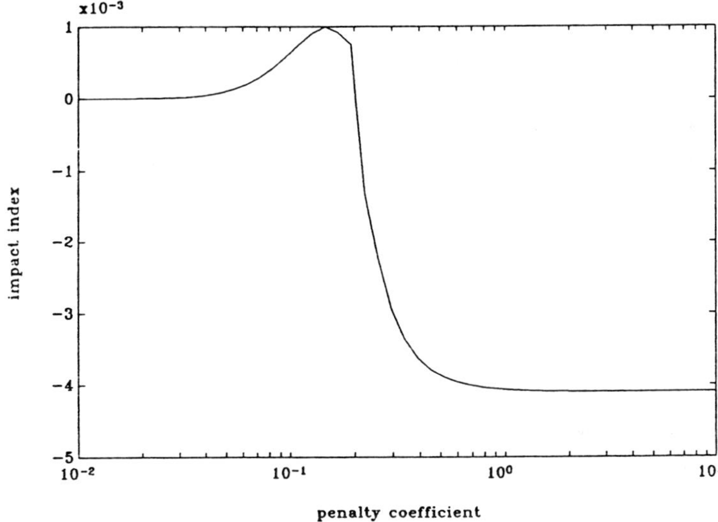

Fig. 2.3. The impact index for the $\Phi(z) = (e^z - 1)/(e - 1)$ penalty function.

beginning of this section. In order to adjust the shape of the population in subsequent generations we use a simple tracking procedure. For a range of values of the penalty coefficient we compute impact indices. These indices are computed for the impact function (2–12). In our particular implementation we use a Gaussian-like distribution with both tails truncated, and then standardized (to assure a unit sum of all probabilities $P_o(l)$) over the range of levels in the current population as the desired distribution, $P_o(l)$. The mean of this distribution is determined according to the formula (2–4). Next, given the overview of the impact index for a range of values of the penalty coefficient we select such a penalty coefficient that the corresponding impact index reaches minimum. (In this case the impact index is not given a sign because it is just a measure of fitting the current level distribution to a desired level distribution.)

Considering all these suggestions the reproduction procedure should include the following steps:

1. Define the desired level distribution $P_o(l)$ according to the search context.
2. Analyze the values of $\sigma(\alpha)$, searching for $\min \sigma(\alpha)$ within a given interval.
3. Calculate probabilities of reproduction for the best-fit penalty coefficient and perform reproduction.

We should note here that in certain situations the function $\sigma(\alpha)$ may turn out flat within the observed range. In such a case we just accept the previous value of α.

To assure proper realization of the reproduction probabilities we use the stochastic universal sampling (SUS) procedure devised by Baker [3]. As far as the operator $Combine(\cdot,\cdot)$ is concerned, we found that selecting n best solutions from both the current population and the offspring yields the best results.

To complete our definition we need to indicate the initialization point. As it turned out from practical tests the bottom levels of the lattice are the best place to begin search. The reason for this is that all nodes there are infeasible so the genetic algorithm can make its own choices as where to search for feasible nodes. Starting from the top of the lattice would cause quite an opposite effect: a few feasible solutions might severely dominate the population and, as a result, lead to premature convergence.

In order to establish whether our algorithm for adjusting the penalty factor makes the genetic algorithm more efficient in solving the constrained optimization problem we compared our method with the fixed penalty factor procedure. The primary criterion function J was defined as

$$J(x) = \sum_{j=1}^{d} \chi_j \tag{2-15}$$

and the constraint criterion e was defined as

$$e(x) = \sum_{\substack{i=1 \\ j=1}}^{n} w_{ij}\chi_i\chi_j + \sum_{k=1}^{s} v_k \tilde{\chi}_1 \cdot \ldots \cdot \tilde{\chi}_d + \varepsilon \tag{2-16}$$

where $x = (\chi_1, \ldots, \chi_d)$, $\varepsilon \sim N(\mu, \sigma)$, and $\tilde{\chi}_i$ may be equal to χ_i, $1 - \chi_i$ or #, the "don't care" operator. The function J satisfies the conditions stated in Section 1. If $w_{ij} < 0$ then $e(x)$ is nonmonotonic. The second term in (2-16) introduces additional defects to the regular shape of the constraint function and the third term adds noise to it, increasing the probability of the feasible region being disconnected even further. In our particular case, the function e assumed values between 0 and 1 for x in the search space.

The optimization problem consisting of these two functions and the threshold $t = 0.115$ was subject to multiple test runs with the use of a genetic algorithm with the fixed and variable penalty factor, with different initial populations. In our algorithm we used the following penalty function

$$p(z) = \begin{cases} z^2 & \text{for } z \geq 0, \\ -z^2 & \text{for } z < 0 \end{cases} \qquad (2\text{--}17)$$

and the procedure for adjusting the penalty factor in our version of the genetic algorithm was identical with the one suggested in (2–4). The fixed penalty factor algorithm used a similar penalty function, except that it did not assign rewards (negative penalties) for satisfying constraints.

The algorithm with the variable penalty factor was run 40 times, with the initial value of $\alpha = 10^4$. The algorithm with the fixed penalty factor was run 40 times for each of the following values of α: $25\cdot10^2$, 10^4, $4\cdot10^4$, $16\cdot10^4$ and $64\cdot10^4$. The results of this experiment are summarized in Table 1. The numbers in the second column are the average number of criterion function evaluations before optimum level was reached by a particular algorithm. The third column contains standard deviations corresponding to these average values.

Table 1. Performance of Search Procedures.

Penalty factor	Ave. number of evaluations	Standard deviation
64.10^4	3730	2865
16.10^4	3330	2824
4.10^4	3280	2754
1.10^4	3345	2631
$0.25.10^4$	3626	2605
variable	2836	2011

As we note, there seem to be a preference among the genetic algorithms with the fixed penalty factor. On average, the best performance was observed for $\alpha = 4 \cdot 10^4$. Our procedure exhibited a slightly better performance than the fixed factor algorithm. Also the standard deviation, which was smaller in this case than for fixed penalty factor algorithms, suggests that our procedure was more consistent in finding the global minimum.

In Figure 2.7 we compare observed probabilities of reaching the global optimum by tested algorithms. The plotted lines denote the differences between these probabilities for each fixed penalty factor algorithm and for the variable penalty factor method. As we see, our procedure performs similarly in the initial stage of the search (typically first 2000 iterations), usually spent by the algorithms on looking for a feasible region, but exhibits much better results in the latter stage when the algorithms search for the minimum value of the objective function in the feasible area.

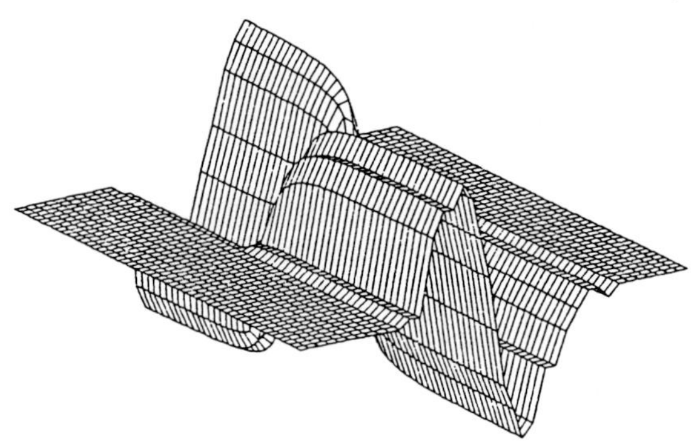

Fig. 2.4. The net impact function for the $\Phi(z) = z^2$ penalty function.

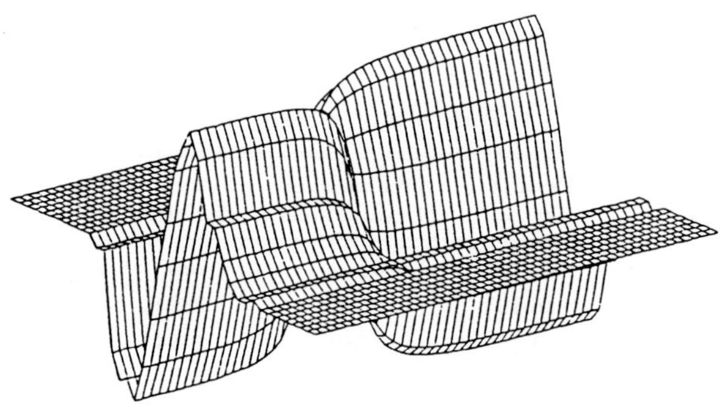

Fig. 2.5. Another view of Figure 2.4.

3. Constrained Genetic Search in Feature Selection

This optimization problem introduced in Section 1 is encountered in statistical pattern recognition. The string $x = (\chi_1, \ldots, \chi_d)$ is a binary coding of a subset of *features* (i.e. measurements) used by a pattern classifier to assign class labels to objects. If $\chi_i = 1$ then the i-th feature is included in the subset and it is excluded otherwise. The criterion function J is a cost of extracting features and usually it is defined as

$$J(x) = \sum_{j=1}^{d} \chi_j. \tag{3-1}$$

The constraint function $e(x)$ is the error rate of a classifier trained for the data that incorporate features coded by x.

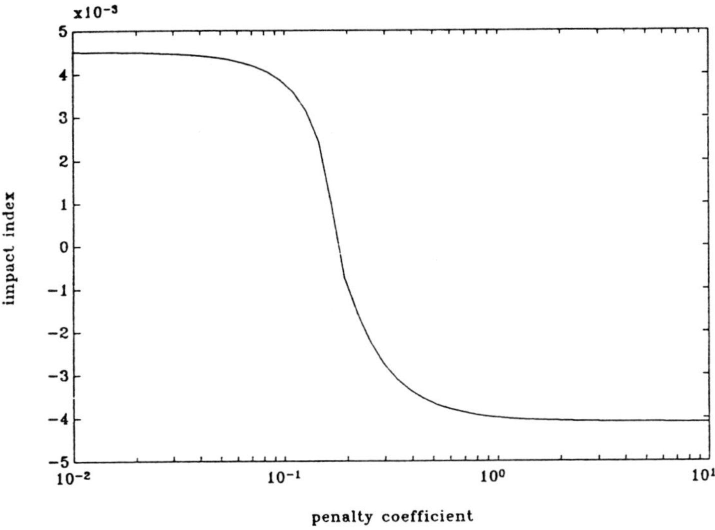

Fig. 2.6. The impact index for the $\Phi(z) = z^2$ penalty function.

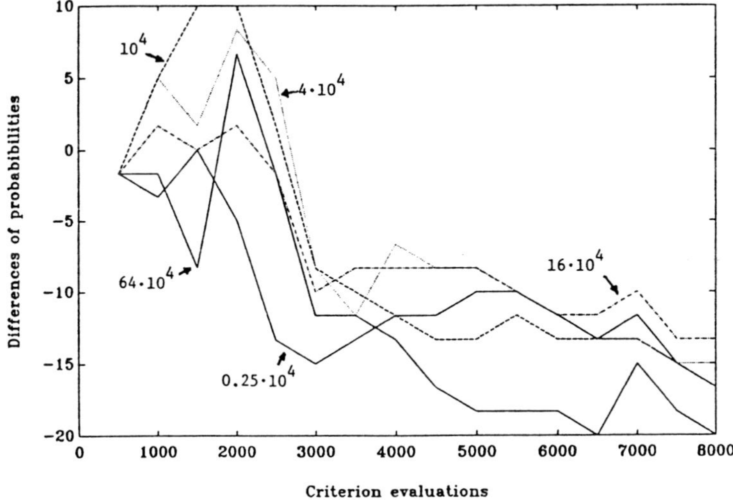

Fig. 2.7. Differences between the probabilities (%) of reaching the global minimum after a given number of criterion function evaluations for the genetic algorithm with varoius penalty factors (pointed by arrows) and the same probablilities for our genetic algorithm with the variable penalty factor.

The research on feature selection dates back to the early sixties (for an overview and biographical notes see [4] or later [5]). The most recent advances in this area are attributed to Narendra and Fukunaga [6], who introduced and tested the use of branch and bound, and Foroutan and Sklansky [7], who modified branch and bound to combat the lack of the monotonicity property in the classifier's error rate and tried it on piecewise linear classifiers. Although the branch and bound technique achieves about a 99% reduction over exhaustive search in many practical applications, it is prohibitively inefficient for more than 20-dimensional problems. Since the evaluation of the discriminatory power of a subset of features requires an estimate of the error rate of a classifier optimized for that subset, the complexity of the combinatorial search encountered in feature selection is amplified by the time needed to design the optimum classifier and estimate its error rate.

In order to verify the power of our genetic feature selection procedure we devised a 5-NN classifier (for the definition and properties of the *k-nearest neighbor classifier* see [4]) trained on real infrared imagery data provided by the U.S. Army. The data set consisted of 150 feature vectors belonging to one of two classes. Each vector contained 30 features. The purpose of this experiment was to compare our method with sequential methods, particularly with the Stearns (p, q)-search procedure [8], which at this dimensionality of the problem is the only algorithm able to give solutions in reasonable time. The (p, q)-search procedure is a sequential procedure that picks the next node in the feature selection lattice on the basis of its corresponding value of the error rate. First, it performs p steps downward, selecting the best nodes and then makes q steps up, again selecting the best nodes. The (p, q)-search algorithm does not make a direct use of the threshold t as it moves through the entire lattice from the top node down (when $p > q$) or from the bottom node up (when $p < q$). As a result, it provides a list of the best nodes at all levels and then it is up to the user which node satisfies the constraint and, in consequence, is considered optimal.

The k-NN rule is known to react strongly to undersampling (i.e. the situation when the training set is small)[b] and the scaling problem (i.e. the problem of scaling features). To avoid the latter we scaled all features to a unit standard deviation. The influence of undersampling manifests itself in significant nonmonotonicity of its error rate function. This effect is even stronger if the parameter k (the number of neighbors checked for classification) is fixed. Consequently, we expected that the resulting error rate function would be ill-behaved and would present difficulties to the search algorithms.

Our procedure in this experiment was as follows. First, we ran *sequential backward selection*, which is identical with (1,0)-search in Stearns' notation. Based on the observation of the path through the feature selection lattice found by backward selection we chose the threshold $t = 0.145$ for our genetic feature selector. By selecting $t = 0.145$ we intended to reduce the size of the feasible region to make it more difficult for the genetic algorithm to find. In particular, according to the result obtained from backward selection the feasible region was placed between levels 17 and 20, and also levels 23 and 24.

---

[b]For discussion of undersampling and related phenomena the reader may refer to [4] or [9].

The next step was to execute our genetic algorithm. Following the results of
simulations with the aid of the modeled error rate functions [10] we chose a population size equal to 40, a mutation rate equal to 0.1 and we began search at level
2, creating the initial population with the aid of a random number generator. We
ran our genetic algorithm 9 times. In each run the genetic algorithm was allowed
to test no more (with the precision to one generation) than 2000 feature subsets.

Our final tests were done with the aid of the Stearns (2,1)-search algorithm and
sequential forward selection (i.e. (0,1)-search in Stearns' notation). The number
of nodes (feature subsets) tested was 465 by forward and backward selection, and
1395 by (2,1)-search.

In Fig. 3.1 we summarize the results obtained from sequential search procedures.
In this figure the solid line corresponds to the path obtained from (1,0)-search,
the dashed line comes from (0,1)-search and the dotted line denotes (2,1)-search.
As expected the (2,1)-search procedure provided the best results (the lowest error
rates) for all levels except 3, 4 and 7. The (1,0)-search algorithm found the best
feasible subset consisting of 17 features. The (2,1)-search algorithm found a smaller
feasible subset, consisting of 11 features. The (0,1)-search algorithm did not find a
feasible subset at all.

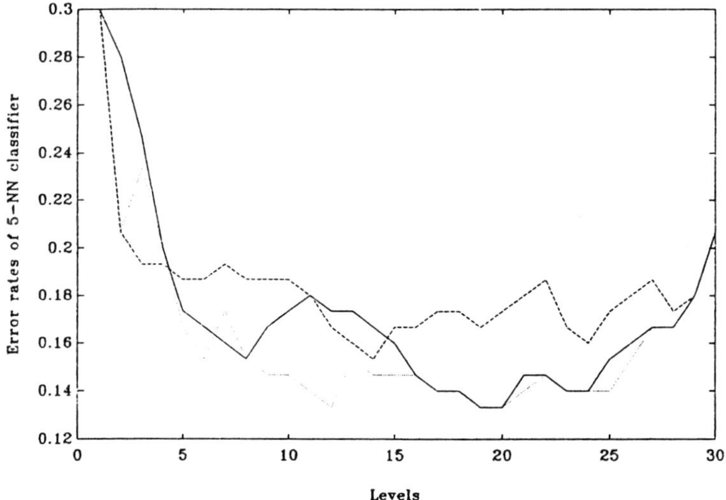

Fig. 3.1. Paths obtained from sequential procedures: the solid line denotes (1, 0)-search (sequential
backward selection), the dashed line denotes (0, 1)-search (sequential forward selection), and the
dotted line denotes (2, 1)-search.

An average of nine runs of our genetic algorithm starting with different initial
populations is presented in Figure 3.2. In this figure we plot the observed lowest
feasible level versus the number of executed iterations. The solid line denotes the
lowest feasible level, equal to 11, found by (2,1)-search. The dashed line denotes the
progress of genetic search. As we see from the figure, the genetic feature selection

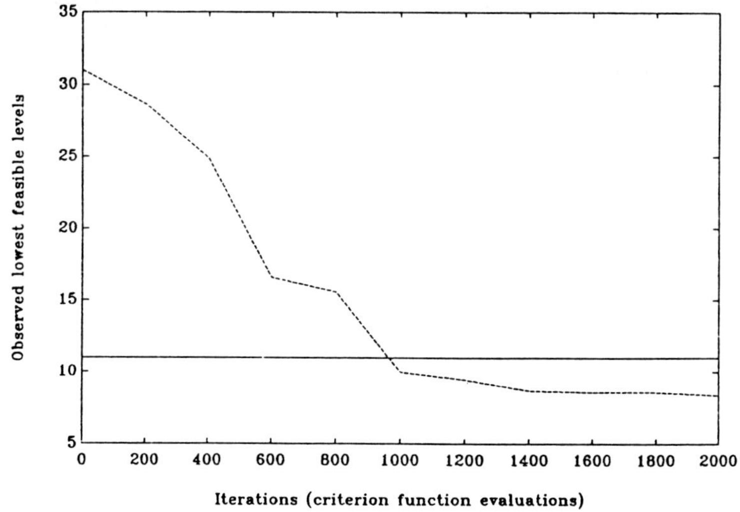

Fig. 3.2. An averaged convergence curve of genetic search for 5-NN rule.

procedure found a feasible subset at the level 11 after approximately 1000 iterations. This compares favorably with the number of iterations executed by (2,1)-search. On average, the lowest feasible level detected by our method was equal approximately to 8. In one run the genetic algorithm found a node with error rate 0.133 at the level 7, that is, it reduced the size of the best feasible subset of features by four features.

4. Concluding Remarks

In this paper we approached the problem of constrained genetic optimization for the case where the criterion to be optimized introduces a uniform orientation in the search space (1–1). An important feature of such an optimization problem is that the minima are expected to occur on the boundary of the feasible region.

In Section 2 we developed a rationale for modifying the ordinary genetic algorithm to conduct efficient search in the feasible part of the search space. We compared our algorithm with the algorithm using the penalty function approach with the fixed penalty factor. We showed that the genetic algorithm with a variable or dynamically adjusted penalty coefficient outperforms the fixed penalty factor algorithm. Considering the fact that the optimal fixed penalty factor is application dependent and has to be determined empirically, our procedure seems to bring clear advantages.

As a practical example of our constrained optimization problem we presented a task of selecting features for statistical pattern classifiers, in particular when the initial number of features exceeds 20. Our feature selection procedure based on the modified genetic algorithm was subjected to experiments described in detail in Section 3. We showed that our feature selection procedure outperformed sequential search (branch and bound was not tested because of its prohibitive time complexity), finding smaller feature subsets after exploring similar number of nodes. This advantage becomes more prominent when the dimension of the problem grows since the sequential procedures have quadratic time complexity and genetic search exhibits slightly more than linear increase of time complexity.

The success of the feature selection procedure based on the genetic algorithm can be attributed to the fact that while branch and bound or sequential procedures perform globally or locally exhaustive search, the genetic algorithm is a self-directing optimization procedure. In addition, because of its inherent non-deterministic behavior it is capable of searching the entire feasible region in the feature selection lattice, even if this region consists of several isolated parts.

Acknowledgements

The research reported here was supported by the U.S. Army Research Office under Contract DAAG29-84-K-0208. We are indebted to Mr. Richard Sims of the U.S. Army Missile Command for providing the infrared imagery data used in the tests described in Section 3.

References

[1] D. E. Goldberg, "Genetic algorithms in pipeline optimization," *Journal of Computing in Civil Engineering*, Vol. 1, pp. 128-141, 1987.

[2] D. E. Goldberg, *Genetic Algorithms in Search, Optimization and Machine Learning*, Addison-Wesley, 1989.

[3] J. E. Baker, "Reducing bias and inefficiency in the selection algorithm," *Proceedings of the Second Int. Conf. on Genetic Algorithms*, Lawrence Erlbaum Associates, Publishers, Hillsdale, 1987, pp. 14–21.

[4] P. A. Devijver and J. Kittler, *Pattern Recognition: A Statistical Approach*, Prentice-Hall, London, 1982.

[5] W. Siedlecki and J. Sklansky, "On automatic feature selection," *Int. Journal of Pattern Recognition and Artificial Intelligence*, Vol. 2, pp. 197–220, 1988.

[6] P. M. Narendra and K. Fukunaga, "A branch and bound algorithm for feature subset selection," *IEEE Trans. Computers*, Vol C-26, pp. 917–922, 1977.

[7] I. Foroutan and J. Sklansky, "Feature selection for automatic classification of non-Gaussian data," *IEEE Trans. Systems, Man and Cybernetics*, Vol. SMC-17, pp. 187–198, 1987.

[8] S. D. Stearns, "On selecting features for pattern classifiers," *Proceedings of the Third Int. Conf. on Pattern Recognition*, Coronado, CA, 1976, pp. 71-75.

[9] A. K. Jain and R. Chandrasekaran, "Dimensionality and sample size considerations in pattern recognition practice," in P. R. Krishnaiah and L. N. Kanal (eds.), *Handbook of Statistics*, Vol. 2 (*Classification, Pattern Recognition and Reduction of Dimensionality*), North-Holland, New York, 1982.

[10] W. Siedlecki, *Feature Selection for Large Scale Problems*, Ph.D. Dissertation, Department of Electrical Engineering, University of California, Irvine, 1988.

Handbook of Pattern Recognition and Computer Vision, pp. 125–162
Eds. C. H. Chen, L. F. Pau and P. S. P. Wang

CHAPTER 1.4

NEURAL NET COMPUTING FOR PATTERN RECOGNITION

YOH-HAN PAO

Electrical Engineering and Computer Science, Case Western Reserve University
10900 Euclid, Cleveland, Ohio 44106-7221, USA

In this chapter we discuss Artificial Neural Net computing from the viewpoint of
its being an enabling methodology for pattern recognition research and practice. The
four functionalities of clustering, learning functional mappings, classification through
associative recall, and optimization are discussed in a comparative manner relative to
other practices in pattern recognition and also relative to each other. In addition to
references, two bibliographies, one for books and the other for journals, are provided as
guides for further reading.

Keywords: Neural net computing, ART, Hopfield net, optimization, functional mapping, supervised learning, Boltzmann machine, simulated annealing, functional-link net,
associative memory.

1. Introduction

In this chapter, we address Artificial Neural Net (ANN) computing from the
perspective of its being a tool for implementing pattern recognition algorithmic
practices. The primary context of our discussion is that of pattern recognition, but
the topic of specific interest is how neural net computing can be used for attaining
pattern-based information processing objectives, especially those which have been
established over the years to be of central interest and importance to the pattern
recognition research and practitioner communities.

Researchers in information processing have long recognized the strikingly different information processing propensities of serial digital computers and of biological
systems. The former rely on speed and accuracy and on ability to execute vast
amounts of detailed programmed instructions precisely. But they are, nevertheless,
easily overwhelmed by algorithmic tasks, which are of exponential or greater complexity. Unfortunately most real-world perception/cognition tasks, if approached in
a direct manner, are of such a nature.

In contrast, the nature of biological systems is that of distributed parallel processing systems, made up of large numbers of interconnected elemental processors of
rather slow processing speed. In addition, information processing seems to depend
on the ability to discern what is cogent and relevant, and to focus on that while

125

sustaining a minimal degree of maintenance on other matters. Situations, circumstances, and events seem to be evaluated on the basis of the "pattern-ness" of things and on similarities between patterns, and on associations between patterns. This is in marked contrast to the operational strategies of the high-speed, general-purpose, serial-digital computers.

At the risk of overstating the case, it almost seems that in approaching the performance of a task, serial-digital computer algorithms tend to search all of the system space to find a reasonably good path from start state to goal state. We know such approaches are doomed to failure because of the combinatorial explosion in the number of paths to be tried.

In contrast to the systematic, frontal-attack approach, biological systems seem to rely more on experience and education so that any good path or even a segment of a good path is remembered, and that knowledge is transmitted through generations, either genetically or through education. In this latter mode of information processing, individual operations are of limited significance but patterns, both spatial and temporal, are of central importance. The significance of patterns is established by associations between a pattern (or a set of patterns) and other patterns (or sets of patterns). Accordingly, the formation of such associations and the activation of such linkages are matters of critical importance.

One of the practical objectives of pattern recognition researchers has always been the ability to design and implement machine systems, which are able to perform perception tasks competently to degrees of proficiency comparable to that of biological systems. To date it cannot be said that progress in that respect has been as substantial as desired or as expected.

If we try to identify reasons for this relative lack of success, we might include the following. It would seem that detailed studies of information processing architectures and procedures in actual biological neuronal studies are so difficult that progress comes at a very slow pace, indeed. Therefore guidance from that source, though much valued, is limited. In addition, tragically, one of the few initial attempts at artificial neural net computing was so thoroughly discredited at its onset that no academic research in that topic could be sustained for the past decades, until recently. For example, pattern recognition texts have always taught the Widrow–Hoff algorithm [1] as a procedure for learning a linear discriminant but never with any suggestion that it might also be considered to be a representation of a net capable of learning functional mappings. These matters and others contributed to the absence of a coherent body of commonly-shared knowledge of adaptive and associative pattern-based, information processing practice, even when it was clear that such knowledge and activity were critical to further progress in pattern recognition research.

The most recent resurgence in artificial neural net computing is due to initiatives from the cognitive psychology sciences and from researchers interested in biological information processing matters.

It is a huge and high risk jump to go from well-accepted, highly professional psychological or biological studies to the dubious practice of postulating some drastically simplified "neuronal" computational models and to try to establish some relevancy between the two types of endeavors. However, at any rate, as is well known, such initiatives were carried out over the past decade and have stimulated a powerful resurgence of interest and activity in artificial net computing [2].

Of primary significance to us, is the outcome *that regardless of whether the artificial neural net computing paradigm models biology or not, it is of intrinsic value to information processing researchers* especially pattern recognition researchers who are interested in the "pattern-ness" of matters and in the rapid distributed parallel processing of associated nets of such patterns [2].

Currently there is not only interest in basic matters in artificial neural net computing, but also extensive activity in the application of this technology to practical tasks, with reports of considerable success.

This chapter is primarily in the nature of an annotated guide to the knowledge which comprises the core of the state-of-the-art in this field at this time. The guide is, therefore, selective rather than comprehensive, and the notation reflects our personal biases and viewpoints, as indeed must be the case for the annotation to be meaningful.

The organization of our presentation of materials is described in Section 2. The topical matters themselves are discussed in subsequent sections. These rather sparse schematic discussions are stressed in a section on comments and bibliographic remarks and by a list of titles for further reading.

2. Organization of Chapter

In a manner consonant with accepted practice, we divide the architectures and algorithms of artificial neural net computing into four parts characterized by the headings of unsupervised learning, supervised learning, associative memory, and optimization. In addition we list a fifth area, which addresses systems level issues.

In Table 1 we list for each such topical area some typical architectures, algorithms, and functionalities supported by the algorithms and corresponding activities and results in traditional pattern recognition research.

We believe that Table 1 indicates that neural net computing does indeed address issues of interest to pattern recognition and might indeed provide effective means for realizing the computational objectives of pattern recognition.

There are aspects of artificial neural net computing which have been well discussed in literature and even in books. There is no need for us to repeat such discussions in this brief chapter. For accepted background material, we refer the reader to the referenced works and also to the additional bibliographies.

In the following sections, we discuss each of these areas.

Table 1. Neural net computing and pattern recognition.

ANN Computing Area	Representation Algorithms	Functionality	Traditional Pattern Recognition Issues	Comments
Unsupervised Learning	• ART 1 & 2 • LVQ • Topologically correct mapping	• Disconcerning regularities in data • Classification	• Data reduction • Forming clusters • K-means and ISODATA • Classification	New concepts: • Max nets • Vigilance factor • Topologically correct • Modifying clusters • Neural net computing does not deal with feature extraction
Supervised Learning	• Generalized delta rule/back propagation-of-error • Functional-link net	Learning a functional mapping from a set of examples	Non-parametric estimation (usually limited to estimation of density distribution functions)	This area is of great importance but underdeveloped in traditional pattern recognition
Associative Memory	• Hopfield net • ART 1, 2 or 3	• Restoration of corrupted patterns • Associative recall • Classification	Distributed matrix associative memories	Undeveloped in pattern recognition
Optimization	• Hopfield and Tank approach	Optimal activation to complex problems gradient search	No direct correspondence	Underdeveloped in pattern recognition
System Level Issues	• Pao and Hafez algorithm for concept formation	• Inductive learning • Feature extraction • Concept formation	• Feature extraction • Learning discriminant • Associative memory	

3. Unsupervised Learning

We can distinguish between three types of unsupervised learning represented by the algorithms of the types of ART [3–5], LVQ [6], and topologically correct mapping [7,8].

To some this area of neural net computing contributes the least to pattern recognition, because in a sense nothing significantly new is added to the principal functionality of cluster formation. Indeed, it might be argued that existing methods, such as the K-means [9] algorithm or the ISODATA [10] algorithm, can do just as well if not better than the corresponding neural net algorithms. However to others it is exactly this close correspondence which is satisfying and stimulating.

Currently in neural computing, clustering is established on the basis of some *metric* defined in the actual pattern space in question. This means that we establish a rule for calculating the "distance" between two patterns, and decide whether they should be considered sufficiently similar to be grouped within one and the same cluster or whether they should be in different clusters. This is illustrated in Fig. 1(a) for some geometric but not necessarily isotropic metric.

If the metric is isotropic, meaning that the rule for calculating distances is the same regardless of the direction in which we look from any one pattern, then the result is a partitioning of pattern space into distinctive nonoverlapping hyperspherical regions or clusters, as shown in Fig. 1(b), for a Euclidean distance metric, in two dimensions.

Even in such a straightforward simple procedure, we can introduce variety by specifying different cluster radius thresholds for different regions of the pattern space. That can and in general does result in the need for special procedures for resolving conflict and for ensuring convergence.

To date no neural net algorithm provides the capability of shaping clusters of the form shown in Fig. 1(c) in a meaningful and adaptive manner.

3.1. *ART*

The well-accepted ART algorithms might seem to differ from the above Euclidean distance approach but actually deviate from it only slightly, being exactly the Euclidean distance approach if all of the vectors are of the same length.

As shown in Fig. 2, in the ART algorithm each input pattern vector $\mathbf{x}$ is projected on each and all of the prototype vectors $\mathbf{b}_j$, and the cluster (prototype) node with the largest projection sum $y_j = \sum b_{ji} x_i$ is identified with the use of the MAXNET.

The proposition that the input vector $\mathbf{x}$ belongs to cluster j is then checked by forming the vigilance factor $\sum_i t_{ji} x_i$. If that exceeds a threshold value (say) ρ, then the vector $\mathbf{x}$ is accepted as an additional new member of that jth cluster, and the values b_j are updated. The top down vigilance factor components are updated also.

The ART algorithms are well explained in the literature [3–5], but we advocate and practice a slightly modified version of these especially in so far as updating is concerned [11].

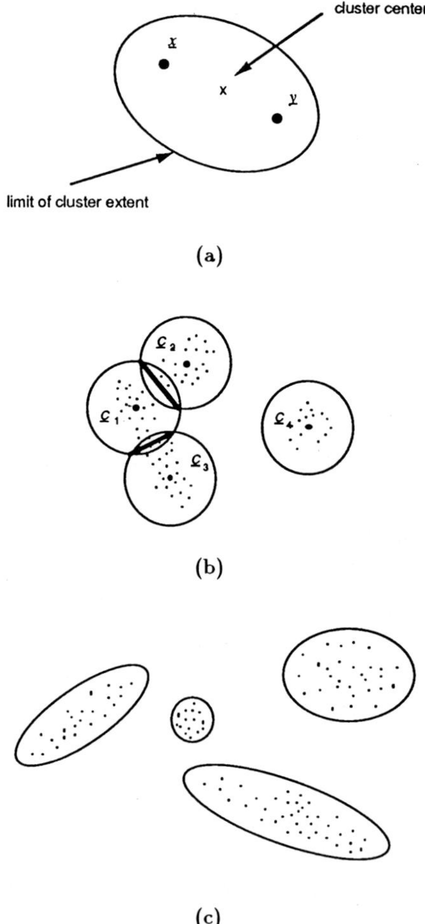

Fig. 1. Formation of clusters in unsupervised learning: (a) essentials of a cluster, (b) formation of distinctive non-overlapping clusters, and (c) more general cluster formation.

The projection procedure is adequate as long as both the **b** vectors and the input vectors are all of the same length. Under such circumstances, the scalar product of the two vectors **b** and **x** do, indeed, provide a measure of the similarity. Also we note that the square of the Euclidean distance between the $\mathbf{b}_j$ vector and **x** vector is

$$d^2(\mathbf{b}_j, \mathbf{x}) = (\mathbf{b}_j - \mathbf{x})^t(\mathbf{b}_j - \mathbf{x})$$
$$= \mathbf{b}_j^t\mathbf{b}_j - 2\mathbf{b}_j^t\mathbf{x} + \mathbf{x}^t\mathbf{x}. \tag{3.1}$$

Clearly the larger the value of $(\mathbf{b}_j\mathbf{x})$, the smaller the Euclidean distance between $\mathbf{b}_j$ and **x** or, in other words, the more similar they are. Also clearly all the previous remarks are also valid for the case of binary valued features as in ART 1.

In general, however, we advocate the practice described in Box 1, which is compatible with standard pattern recognition practice and with ART 2.

Box 1

1. Activate all output nodes j, $j = 1, 2, \ldots, J$.
2. Initialize weights $b_{ji} = \varepsilon_{ji}$ where ε_{ji} are random numbers $(-1 < \varepsilon_{ji} < 1)$.
3. Input pattern $\{x_i\}$ $i = 1, \ldots, N$.
4. Calculate the square of the Euclidean distance $ED^2_{ji} = \sum_1 (b_{ji} - y_i)^2$.
5. Determine that j for which $ED^2_{ji} < ED^2_{ki}$ for all $k = 1, 2, \ldots, J$; $K \neq j$.
6. Assign pattern $\{x_i\}$ as belonging to node j if ED^2_{ji} also is equal to or less than ED^2_{ji} (limit), where ED^2_{ji} (limit) is a more or less arbitrary chosen limiting radius beyond which patterns are not considered to be of that cluster.
7. Update $b_{ji}(n+1) = \dfrac{n}{n+1} \, b_{ji}(n) + \dfrac{1}{n+1} \, x_i$ ($n = 0$ at initialization). Therefore, after the input of the first pattern $b_{ji}(1) = x_i$.
8. Input the next pattern, determine to which unsupervised learning node it belongs, and update corresponding $\{b_{ji}\}$.

We note that the cluster centers, the $\mathbf{b}_j$ vectors, are only slightly perturbed by the inclusion of a new member, especially if the cluster already contains a number of members. The updating of $\mathbf{b}_j$ is weighted so that

$$\mathbf{b}_j(n + 1) = \frac{n}{n+1} \mathbf{b}_j(n) + \frac{1}{n+1} \mathbf{x} \tag{3.2}$$

when the jth cluster with n members in the cluster adds an additional member $\mathbf{x}$ to the cluster.

The top-down vigilance vector $\mathbf{t}_j$ is then taken to be equal to $\mathbf{b}_j$ and is updated in the same manner.

There are different ways of exercising this algorithm depending on whether one should activate all cluster prototype nodes initially or activate additional ones only as needed. In contrast to concerns which might dominate if we were endeavoring to build models of the brain, in artificial neural net computing it would seem that the latter practice, that of activating each additional new prototype cluster as needed, is more reasonable and usually convergence to stable cluster centers occurs in a straightforward manner.

Also in the case of artificial neural net computing, there may be circumstances where determination of maximum similarly might be carried out more simply than with use of the MAXNET [12].

This type of algorithm corresponds closely to the K-means and ISODATA algorithms, and more to the former than to the latter. Our interest in the ART type of algorithm lies in the suggested net architecture and in the fact that the procedure corresponds to that of the K-means algorithm.

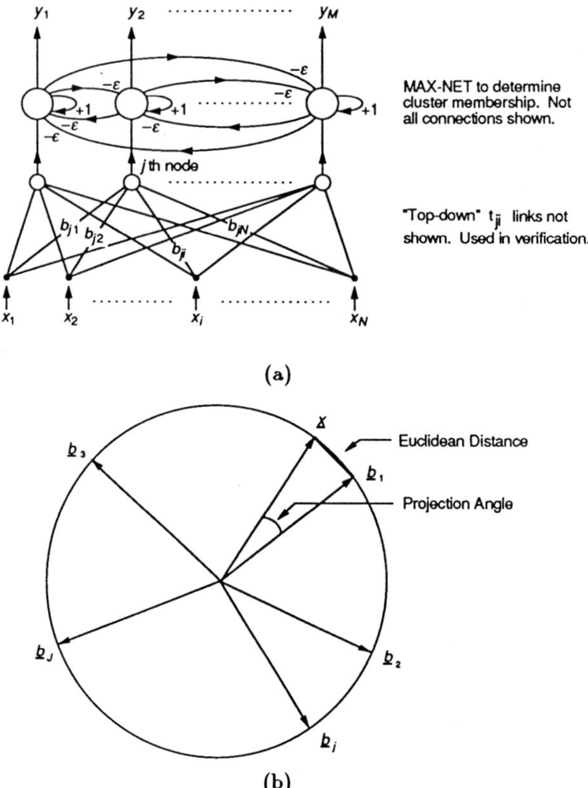

Fig. 2.   Some aspects of the ART algorithm.   (a) Schematic illustration of the ART net, (b) two-dimensional illustration of the equivalence of the projection and distance measures when all pattern vectors are of the same length.

The ART algorithm has been extended to hierarchical ART structures [5] in work which addresses systems issues in the use of such algorithms. What is a little disappointing is the lack of opportunity to shape the clusters and to merge or split them as in the case of ISODATA, as illustrated in Fig. 1(c).

3.2. *Learning Vector Quantization*

The Learning Vector Quantization (LVQ) algorithm builds [6] on the ART type of algorithm and mixes supervised learning with cluster formation. In a manner similar to that of the Widrow-Hoff [1] algorithm of pattern recognition, it refines the structure of a cluster by examining the class membership of each of the members in turn. The assumption is that nearly all of the cluster members belong to one and the same class. Now as each member is examined in turn, the cluster prototype is modified to move closer to the current member under consideration or away from it depending on whether that member is or is not a member of the majority class.

That is

$$\mathbf{m}(n+1) = \mathbf{m}(n) + \alpha(\mathbf{x} - \mathbf{m}(n)) \quad \text{if } \mathbf{x} \text{ is of the class of the cluster} \qquad (3.3)$$

or

$$\mathbf{m}(n+1) = \mathbf{m}(n) - \alpha(\mathbf{x} - m(n)) \quad \text{if } \mathbf{x} \text{ is not of that class} \qquad (3.4)$$

where n is the number of cluster members already checked, and $\mathbf{m}$ is the vector denoting the cluster center. The parameter α is a fractional quantity which decreases with n so that there is convergence.

This situation is depicted schematically in Fig. 3.

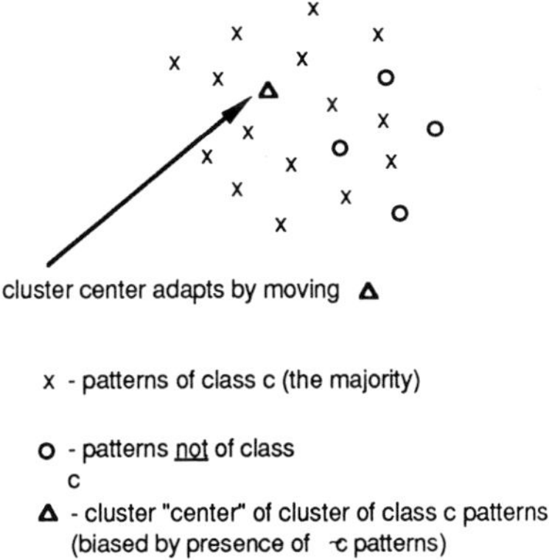

Fig. 3. The Learning Vector Quantization (LVQ) algorithm incorporating supervised classification into the cluster procedures.

3.3. *Topologically-Correct Mapping*

The topologically correct mapping approach to clustering allows us to investigate relationships between the following matters:

- patterns defined in an N-dimensional positional space X,
- a process (or metric) defined on X and on the patterns described in X,
- nodes (or neurons) located spatially in an M-dimensional positional space Y, and
- an interactional process (or metric) defined for the neurons described in Y.

These entities are described in Fig. 4 where we show pattern vectors $\{\mathbf{x}\}$ defined in pattern space X. The *ordering process* we impose on top of the patterns in that space is not limited to a determination of the inter-pattern Euclidean distance, but can be quite general indeed. Given the patterns in X and the ordering process, we ask how the consequences of that ordering might be reflected in another space. In particular, for instance, for an array of fixed position neurons in space Y with

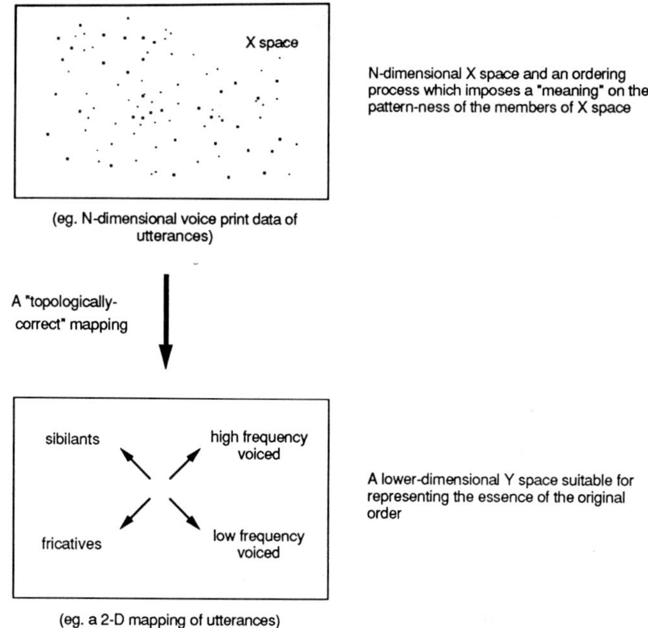

Fig. 4. Schematic illustration of a hypothetical instance of a useful topologically correct mapping.

on-center off-surround interneuron interactions, how might the original X-space ordering process influence the correspondences between the pattern vectors in X-space and their representation neurons in Y-space?

The illustrations given by Kohonen [7,8] are for one- and two-dimensional Y-spaces, the "exhibit" space, so to speak. Although the illustrations are striking and may provide insight for understanding how biological neuronal spatial structures are achieved in nature, our feeling is that in a sense those examples are perhaps too obvious. For example, in the two-dimensional case, the "process" or "metric" ordering the random vectors is determination of the inter-pattern Euclidean distance, and the underlying factor governing the positions of the representative neurons in Y-space is also the Euclidean distance. Under such circumstances, it is not surprising that a good "topologically correct" mapping should have been achieved. This is not to say that demonstration of such a mapping is insignificant, but rather that we are not quite clear what other possibilities are implied. The one-dimensional acoustic signal spectral ordering example is slightly more intriguing, but it can be understood in about the same manner as a mapping from a one-dimensional (spectral) space to another one-dimensional (positional) space with corresponding Euclidean distance type of metrics in both cases. The finite Q filter banks are interesting but tend to obscure the situation slightly. However the intrinsic measure in both spaces is still that of inter-frequency distance. That and the additional requirement that neighboring neurons should resonate to about the same frequency suffices to establish a monotonic spectral ordering in neuron positional space.

Despite our attempts to rationalize our ready acceptance of the results of those illustrations, it is true that very little has been said about the theory of such mapping processes and work remains.

In our fanciful illustration exhibited in Fig. 4, we suggest that in speech processing some weighting of formant-time values of utterances together with an inter-neuron interaction in display space might result in a *meaningful* topologically correct mapping, in which the underlying order, always present, is now made manifest. Such mappings might provide some model of how biological systems organize themselves, but also would be interesting for neural net computing and pattern recognition purposes.

4. Supervised Learning

In neural net computing, the notion of "supervised learning" corresponds to the inductive learning of a functional mapping from R^n to R^m, given a set of examples of instances of that mapping. In other words, if we know that the vectors $\mathbf{x}_i$ map into vectors y_i for $i = 1, 2, 3, \ldots, I$, can we construct a network computational structure which will accurately map all other $\mathbf{x}$ vectors in the N-dimensional X-space into the corresponding correct image $\mathbf{y}$ vectors in the M-dimensional Y-space? This situation is illustrated schematically in Fig. 5.

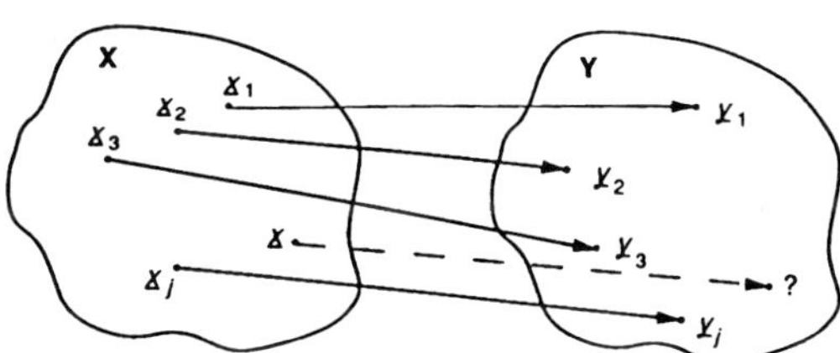

Fig. 5.   The concept of learning a functional mapping from observation of examples of such mappings.

This type of activity corresponds most closely to the pattern recognition task of learning a discriminant function for the purposes of classification. It is interesting to note that the task of quantitative estimation is not addressed in pattern recognition except for estimation of density distribution functions, and even there the nature of the task is closer to synthesizing an analytical representation of known (measurable) densities rather than the inductive learning of functional mapping identified only through a set of examples.

In this section, we comment on the backpropagation-of-error algorithm, briefly and schematically, because it is well known and the details of the algorithm have been widely disseminated [2].

In so far as learning procedures are concerned, we describe briefly two others in the following, these being the Boltzmann machine (with simulated annealing) [13] and the other being the functional-link net approach [11,14].

4.1. *Backpropagation-of-Error Learning Algorithm*

The feedforward net is illustrated schematically in Fig. 6, for a functional mapping of $R^n \rightarrow R$. The input to such a net is a vector in N-dimensional space and the output is a single real number. It is assumed that there is a functional mapping $y = f(\mathbf{x})$, instances of which are known $\{y_p = f(\mathbf{x}_p)\}$, and the learning task consists of determining the values of the weights $\{A_{ji}\}$ and $\{\beta_j\}$ and the thresholds $\{b_j\}$ so that the mean of the squares of the error, $\sum_p (\hat{f}(\mathbf{x}_p - f(\mathbf{x}_p))^2$, is minimized. There is no loss of generality in omitting a nonlinear transform at the single output node. In the general case, there would be more than a single output and there could be more than one hidden layer. The weights and thresholds are determined on the basis of minimizing the overall system error averaged over all the training sets. That is, the quantity $\sum_k \sum_p (\hat{O}_k(\mathbf{x}_p) - O_k(\mathbf{x}_p))^2$ is minimized where $O_k(\mathbf{x}_p)$ is the desired (or target) output at the kth node for the pth pattern, and $\hat{O}_k(\mathbf{x}_p)$ is the actual computed value of the kth output for the same pattern.

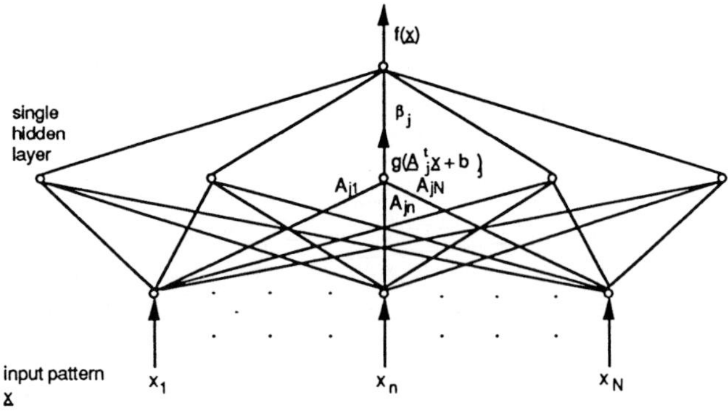

Fig. 6. A feedforward neural net with hidden layer and no intra-layer node interactions, used with the backpropagation-of-error algorithm. Shown for $R^n \rightarrow R$.

In the learning process, the weights β_j (or β_{kj} in the multi-output case) are readily learned because we have a direct measure of the error $(\hat{O}_k(\mathbf{x}_p) - O_k(\mathbf{x}_p))$, at each and all outputs, for all of the training set patterns. However, for the hidden nodes, there is no direct measure of the relevant error ascribable to a particular hidden node and so the output pattern *error has to be propagated backwards* and interpreted appropriately to serve as a measure of guidance for improving the values of the weights leading into the hidden-layer node.

Although the overall learning procedure of the backpropagation-of-error algorithm is that of gradient search in weight space and that protocol is rapidly adhered to in all cases, there are, nevertheless, many variations on the adaptation scheme, primarily on how to improve the rate of convergence to the point of least error.

There exist a number of papers which prove that a multilayer feedforward net can serve as a universal approximator, *from a computational point of view*, of quite general functional mappings. In other words, provided the spaces X and Y are measurable spaces and the known function is well behaved, then a net of the type shown in Fig. 6 can, indeed, reproduce the *known* mapping [15–17] and even the derivatives of the functional mapping [18]. Furthermore, even nets with only a single hidden layer can serve as a universal approximator provided the activation functions are of an appropriately constrained form. The multilayer feedforward net depicted in Fig. 6 has linear links and nonlinear activation functions at the nodes. The theoretical proofs of the adequacy of this computational model assure us that the known mapping *as made evident* by the act of examples $\{\mathbf{x}_i \rightarrow \mathbf{y}_i\}$ can, indeed, be computed by that type of net.

However in pattern recognition and in applications of pattern recognition, interest in supervised learning goes beyond the question of whether known instances of mappings can be duplicated or not. In fact, the primary interest is whether the net can *inductively learn* a representation of the *presumed functional mapping*, which is valid for samples of $\mathbf{x}$ not included in the training set. In other words, as in other cases of pattern recognition, the interest is in whether the learned mapping is valid for the test set (of $\mathbf{x}$ vectors) also. *The critical issue is the validity of the generalization.*

From a signal processing point of view, the generalized delta rule (GDR) multilayer feedforward net is a complex system. If we want to represent the functionality of such a net in terms of a transfer function, we would find that perhaps the best we could do would be to give instances of the effective small-signal transfer function at different signal regions. Even then there remain questions of the efficiency of learning and the quality of the learning achieved with use of different learning procedures. We will discuss these latter issues again briefly in the following in the context of the functional-link net.

4.2. *The Boltzmann Machine and Simulated Annealing*

An alternate approach to learning an optimal set of weight and threshold values is to "generate and test". In this alternate approach [13,19,20], different states in weight space can be generated statistically and each new proposed state is evaluated as being accepted or not, depending on whether the LMS error is decreased or whether the increase in the magnitude of the LMS error is within a tolerable amount.

In the simulated annealing approach to matters, we evaluate the change in the magnitude of error $\Delta\varepsilon = \varepsilon(n+1) - \varepsilon(n)$ as we generate the $(n+1)$th state. We also generate a random number ρ in the interval [1,0].

If $\Delta\varepsilon < 0$ then we accept the new set of weights as a better set and go on to generate yet another (hopefully) even better set. In this way we let the system migrate to an optimum state in weight space.

However if $\Delta\varepsilon > 0$, we do not necessarily reject the new state. Instead, we compare $\exp(-\Delta\varepsilon/c)$ with the random number ρ.

If $\exp(-\Delta\varepsilon/c) > \rho$, we accept the new set of weights even though there is an increase in error.

However if $\exp(-\Delta\varepsilon/c) \leq \rho$, we reject the new state and go on to generate another trial state.

In simulated annealing the "temperature" parameter c, at first, is taken to be quite large so that $\Delta\varepsilon/c$ is liable to be quite small, and $\exp(-\Delta\varepsilon/c)$ large, and the state of the system can wander quite a bit in weight space. As $c \to 0$ large increases in error becomes less and less tolerated and the overall effect is to cause the state of the system to search for and to diffuse toward regions of lower and lower error. If and when carried out well, the simulated annealing procedure allows the system to explore, at first, wide regions of weight space and to avoid being trapped in narrow local minima.

Use of the expression $(\exp -\Delta\varepsilon/c)$ is inspired by an analogy to the Boltzmann distribution of energy states in a classic (nonquantum-mechanic) system in thermodynamic equilibrium at some temperature. The gradual lowering of the "temperature" parameter corresponds to annealing, hence the term "simulated" annealing. It is amusing to note that in practice we often have simulated quenching working quite well also [20].

The term Boltzmann machine generally refers to network structures other than the feedforward net, but does not exclude the feedforward architecture. Indeed, it is used frequently for nets which have bidirectional excitatory and inhibitive internode interactions [13]. The procedure we have just described can also be considered to be an instance of the "generate and test" approach to learning in contrast to the gradient search approach.

In practice, use of the Boltzmann machine comprises two separate tasks, one being the choice of an appropriate structure and the other the learning of the values of the weights. To illustrate this and other points we have made, we discuss briefly the task of training a Boltzmann machine digit recognizer [11].

The numerical digits are represented in terms of the segments of a seven-segment display as shown in Fig. 7 and the input/output relationships of the Boltzmann machine are shown in Fig. 8.

For this case no "hidden" nodes are needed, and the structure of the machine is that shown in Fig. 9. An important point is that there are extensive intra-layer node-to-node interactions.

However it is not always true that "hidden" nodes can be avoided.

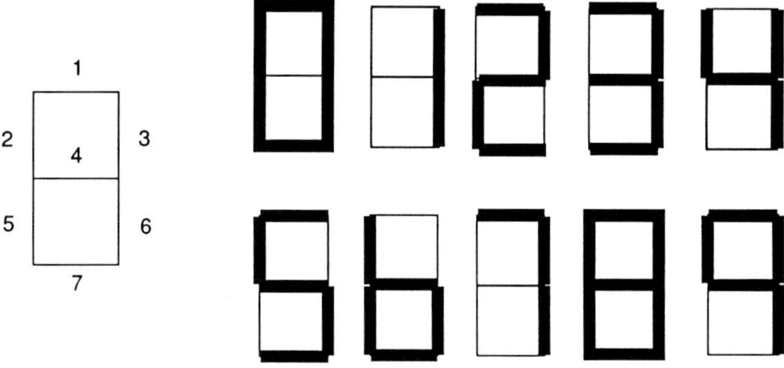

Fig. 7. A seven-segment display format for numerical digits [11].

digit	input	output
0	1 1 1 0 1 1 1	1 0 0 0 0 0 0 0 0 0
1	0 0 1 0 0 1 0	0 1 0 0 0 0 0 0 0 0
2	1 0 1 1 1 0 1	0 0 1 0 0 0 0 0 0 0
3	1 0 1 1 0 1 1	0 0 0 1 0 0 0 0 0 0
4	0 1 1 1 0 1 0	0 0 0 0 1 0 0 0 0 0
5	1 1 0 1 0 1 1	0 0 0 0 0 1 0 0 0 0
6	0 1 0 1 1 1 1	0 0 0 0 0 0 1 0 0 0
7	1 0 1 0 0 1 0	0 0 0 0 0 0 0 1 0 0
8	1 1 1 1 1 1 1	0 0 0 0 0 0 0 0 1 0
9	1 1 1 1 0 1 0	0 0 0 0 0 0 0 0 0 1

Fig. 8. Input/output relationship for a Boltzmann machine classification net [11].

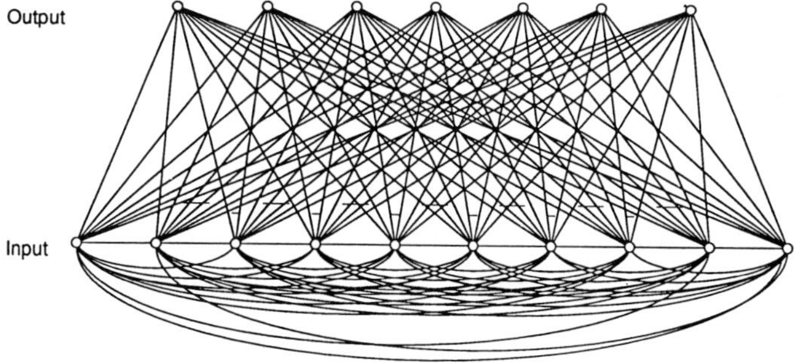

Fig. 9. Structure of digit recognition Boltzmann machine [11].

4.3. *The Functional-Link Net*

Experience with the backpropagation-of-error algorithm indicates that the algorithm is often slow and does not extrapolate well to high dimensions or to large training sets. However users often find that ease of learning can be greatly enhanced by appropriate "preprocessing". It is because of that type of experience that we initially advocated a functional-link net approach to supervised learning. Instead of using a multilayer feedforward net with backpropagation of error, we advocated enhancing the input vector with functional-links $g_j(\mathbf{x})$ to yield a description of the input in an extended pattern space, with additional dimensions [11,14]. The functions $g(\mathbf{x})$ are functions of the entire input pattern vector $\mathbf{x}$ and not just functions of any one component x_i.

In one version of that approach, the one which approaches the back-propagation-of-error algorithm the closest, our approach consists in simply claiming that the first layer weights A_{ji} and thresholds b_j in the feedforward net of Fig. 6 need not be learned. Subject to rather general and easily satisfied constraints, only the output weights β_j need to be learned. This is easily demonstrated.

For illustration purposes we consider a functional mapping $R \to R$. Namely, both the input and output spaces are one-dimensional. There is no loss of generality. We choose the one-dimensional case because of the ease of displaying results graphically. In other words we assume that there is a mapping $y = f(x)$. Given instances $\{y_i = f(x)\}$, can we learn the functional mapping sufficiently well so that we can interpolate and extrapolate to values of x not encountered in the training set? This is a question of utmost importance and interest. Both the BP net and the functional-link net are illustrated in Fig. 10 for this case.

Let there be J hidden-layer nodes in a BP net.

Then the value of the output is

$$y = f(x) = \sum \beta_j g(A_j x + b_j) \tag{4.1}$$

where $g()$ is the activation function.

Let there be N training set patterns so that the entire set of N simultaneous equations to be solved can be written as

$$\mathbf{G}\,\beta = \mathbf{f} \tag{4.2}$$

or

$$\sum_j g_{nj}\beta_j = f_n \quad \text{for} \quad n = 1, 2, 3, \dots, N \tag{4.3}$$

Equation 4.1 can be expressed in component form as follows:

$$
\begin{vmatrix}
g_1(x_1) & g_2(x_1) & g_3(x_1) & \cdots & g_j(x_1) & \cdots & g_J(x_1) \\
g_1(x_2) & g_2(x_2) & g_3(x_2) & \cdots & g_j(x_2) & \cdots & g_J(x_2) \\
g_1(x_3) & g_2(x_3) & g_3(x_3) & \cdots & g_j(x_3) & \cdots & g_J(x_3) \\
\vdots & \vdots & \vdots & & \vdots & & \vdots \\
\vdots & \vdots & \vdots & & \vdots & & \vdots \\
g_1(x_n) & g_2(x_n) & g_3(x_n) & \cdots & g_j(x_n) & \cdots & g_J(x_n) \\
\vdots & \vdots & \vdots & & \vdots & & \vdots \\
g_1(x_N) & g_2(x_N) & g_3(x_N) & \cdots & g_j(x_N) & \cdots & g_J(x_N)
\end{vmatrix}
\begin{vmatrix}
\beta_1 \\ \beta_2 \\ \beta_3 \\ \vdots \\ \beta_j \\ \vdots \\ \beta_J
\end{vmatrix}
=
\begin{vmatrix}
f(x_1) \\ f(x_2) \\ f(x_3) \\ \vdots \\ f(x_n)j \\ \vdots \\ f(x_N)
\end{vmatrix}
\tag{4.4}
$$

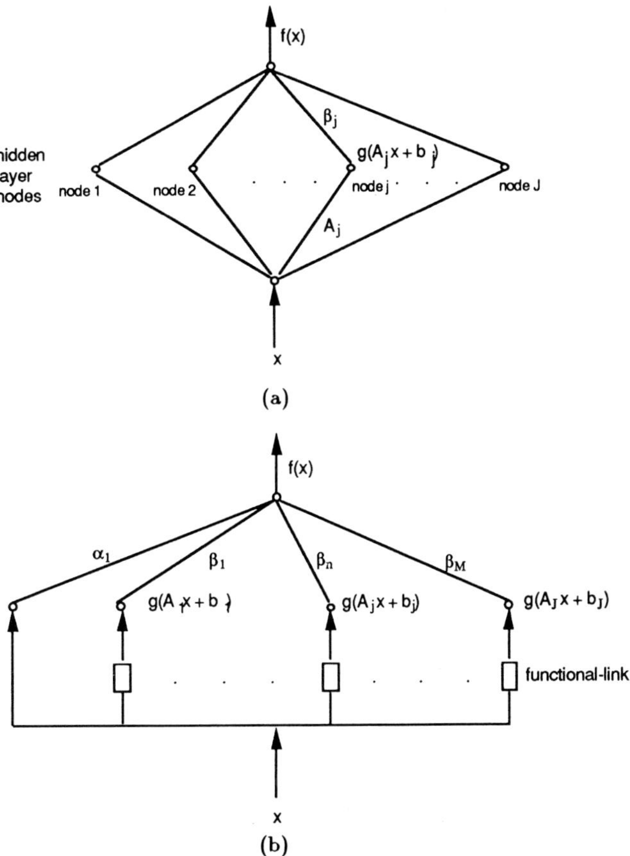

Fig. 10. Comparison of backpropagation of functional-link nets.

where $g_j(x_n) \equiv g_{nj} = g(A_j x_n + b_j)$ and x_n is the value of the input for the nth training set pattern.

It is clear the nature of the solutions of Eq. (4.4) depends critically on the rank of the G matrix, and the values of the individual components are to some extent immaterial.

That is, instead of the feedforward net of Fig. 10(a), we advocate the net illustrated in Fig. 10(b) in which the initial input x is enhanced in dimensions and has the additional components $g_j(A_j x + b_j)$.

If G is exactly of the correct rank, then a unique solution exists. If there are too many constraints, then there is only an LMS solution or possibly a degenerate set of such solutions. If there is an insufficient number of constraining equations, then there may be an infinite number of solutions for the weights $\{\beta_j\}$. The point we make is that the weights A_j (and thresholds b_j) can be randomly generated with no loss of generality.

For a mapping $R^n \to R$, *the input is a vector rather than a scalar*, but the argument remains the same. The equations to be solved are then

$$y_n = f(\mathbf{x}_n) = \sum \beta_j g(\mathbf{A}_j^t \mathbf{x}_n + b_j) \, . \tag{4.5}$$

Our point is that the vectors $\mathbf{A}_j$ and thresholds b_j may be generated randomly and only the weights β_j need to be learned.

The function $g_j()$ is a function of the entire input pattern vector $\mathbf{x}$ and not just a function of any one component x_i. The function $g()$ is not *learned* but is a "hardwired" functional transform of the input vector constituting a preprocessing set, so to speak.

In view of these findings, we advocate regarding a supervised learning net to be essentially a linear net with the input augmented with extra (non-linear) nodes.

A large set of experiences indicate that our view is correct and that there are very large improvements in the fidelity of representation. The rate of learning can be achieved with use of the random vector version of the functional-link net. *However there is a very important precaution to be observed.* The range of the amplitude of the "random" vectors $\mathbf{A}_j$ need to be scaled so that the functional outputs $g(\mathbf{A}_j \mathbf{x} + b_j)$ are not all saturated, nor are all so small so that the additional components are linearly dependent. In general this precaution is not difficult to deal with. A normalizing scaling of the *range* of the input vectors and of the norms of random vectors would be sufficient.

The situation is changed significantly if we insist that both the derivative of the function $f(\mathbf{x})$ as well as the function itself be approximated well. Under such circumstances the vectors $\mathbf{A}_j$ and thresholds b_j do indeed need to be learned and the two sets of equations to be satisfied are

$$\sum_j \beta_j \, g(\mathbf{A}_j^t \mathbf{x}_n + b_j) = f(\mathbf{x}_n) \tag{4.6}$$

and

$$\sum \beta_j \, A_{ji} g_i'(\mathbf{A}_j^t \mathbf{x}_n + b_j) = f_i'(\mathbf{x}_n) \tag{4.7}$$

where

$$g_i'() = \frac{\partial}{\partial x_i} \, g(\mathbf{A}_j^t \mathbf{x}_n + b_j) \tag{4.8}$$

representing differentiation with respect to the ith component of the vector x and

$$f_i'(\mathbf{x}_n) = \frac{\partial}{\partial x_i} \, f(\mathbf{x}_n) \, . \tag{4.9}$$

It is difficult to solve Eqs. (4.6) and (4.7) simultaneously for a set of $\{\beta_j\}$, $\{A_{ji}\}$, and $\{b_j\}$ values which will approximate the derivative as well as the functions. But good mappings can be learned, nevertheless, by retreating to our simple functional-link net approach and taking sets of points *near* each training set input vector so that in essence something is learned about how the functions varies in different directions.

The result of the use of this "random vector" version of the functional-link net approach is that we can achieve the learning of rather complex functional mappings in moderate lengths of time. The nets used are linear nets with the input augmented with extra non-linear functional transforms of the input vector.

We present and discuss some experimental results in the following subsection. These results are suggestive, but we refrain from generalizing too optimistically on the basis of these partial findings.

4.4. *Experimental Results in Support of the Functional-Link Net*

For rather straightforward *training* tasks, the "random vector" functional-link net outperforms the BP algorithm, principally, in terms of the rapidity with which learning is achieved.

However we are also concerned about the ability to *inductively* learn a mapping of which we know a few instances. To explore the interpolation and extrapolation capabilities of such nets, we revert initially to the one-dimensional case and consider the task of learning a function $y = f(x)$ where both x and y are scalar quantities.

Of course sometimes correct interpolation cannot be achieved because not enough information was available in the first place.

Given the training set of Fig. 11, there is simply no way for either the BP net or the functional-link net to guess what nature had in mind. Actually, in practice, both nets learned the smooth function $f_2(x)$.

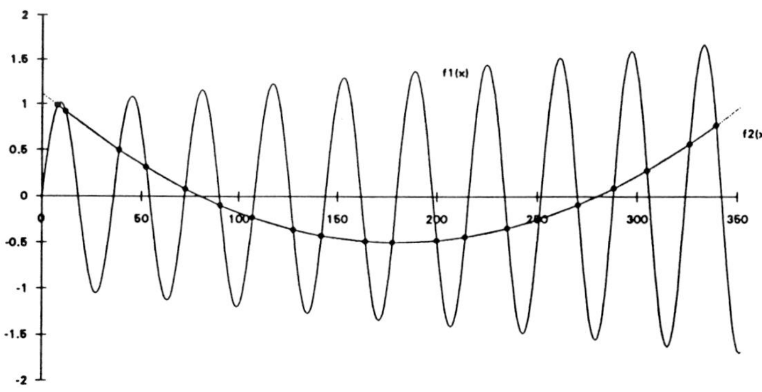

Fig. 11. An ambiguous training set of patterns for $R \rightarrow R$ mapping.

However we might add a few (non-random) instances of the function to provide further information as shown in Fig. 12, in which case both the functional-link net and the backpropagation net interpolated well, but in different ways. The BP net

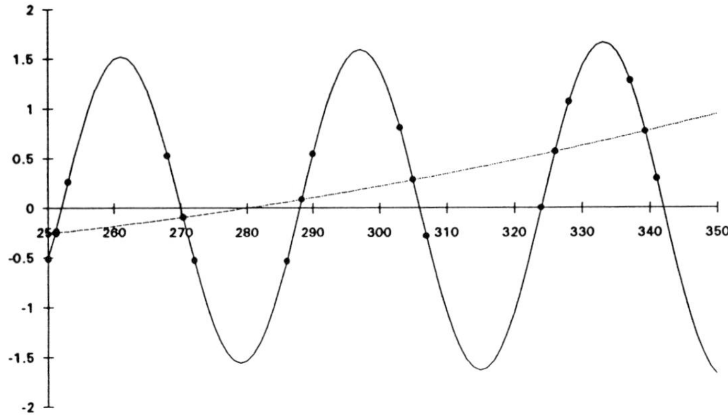

Fig. 12. An augmented training set.

took a very long time and a large number of iterations. The functional-link net used a large number of augmentations, but learned rapidly in about 10^{-3} of the time required by the BP net. These matters are illustrated in Figs. 13 and 14.

To explore comparable circumstances for higher dimensions, we also considered a two-input and two-output learning task. This can be visualized as learning two surfaces in a three-dimensional space. In every instance the input is a pair of coordinates (x, y) and the outputs are $f_1(x, y)$, and $f_2(x, y)$ representing the upper and lower surfaces of a bounded region.

The net configurations are depicted in Fig. 15 and the surfaces to be learned are shown in Figs. 16 and 17.

Given a reasonably uniform and representative sampling of the two surfaces, both the BP net and functional-link net do learn the two surfaces and interpolate reasonably well. However the functional-link net again learns much more rapidly. The interpolation achieved by the BP net and the FLN net for the upper surface are shown in Figs. 18 and 19, respectively. The BP net and the FLN net for the lower (and smoother surface) that are achieved are shown in Figs. 20 and 21, respectively. To the eye, the FLN results look more irregular, but actually the estimated results are more accurate. Again, the FLN net is faster by a factor of about 10^3.

We mention, in passing, that in the case of the BP net the hidden layer nodes serve both outputs. The hidden layer nodes are therefore constrained. There are advantages and disadvantages. One disadvantage is that any change in the input/output relationships at any single output will have widespread and severe repercussions throughout the entire net. One advantage is that such severe interactions might indeed force the hidden layer to take on the form of a *meaningful* internal representation. But that would be attained only by paying a high price in the form of the difficulty of learning!

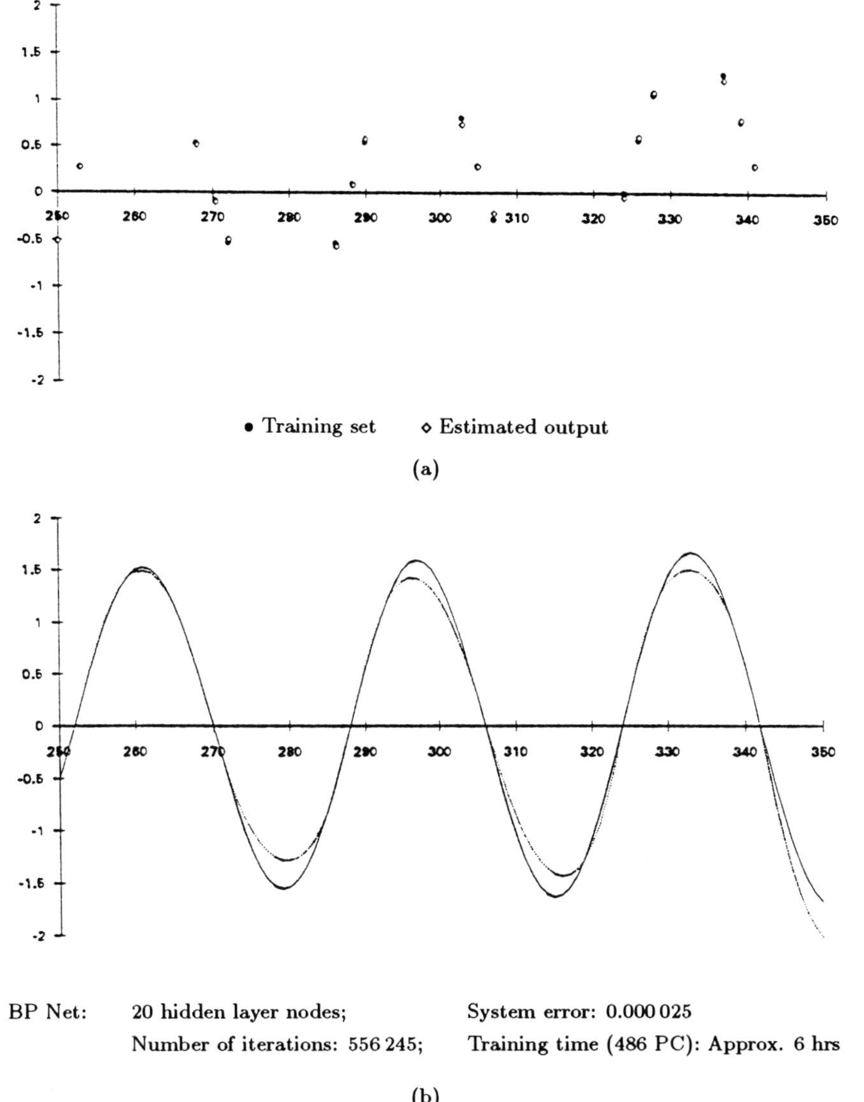

BP Net: 20 hidden layer nodes;   System error: 0.000 025
            Number of iterations: 556 245; Training time (486 PC): Approx. 6 hrs

(b)

Fig. 13. Demonstration of interpolation achieved with a BP net for $R \to R$ mapping.

In contrast, in the case of the functional-link net, each output would be served by its own net and learning is rapidly achieved. However this does not mean that interactions between components of the components of the input vector are neglected.

5. Associative Memories

The term associative memories is used in different ways within neural net computing practice, as well as vis-à-vis pattern recognition.

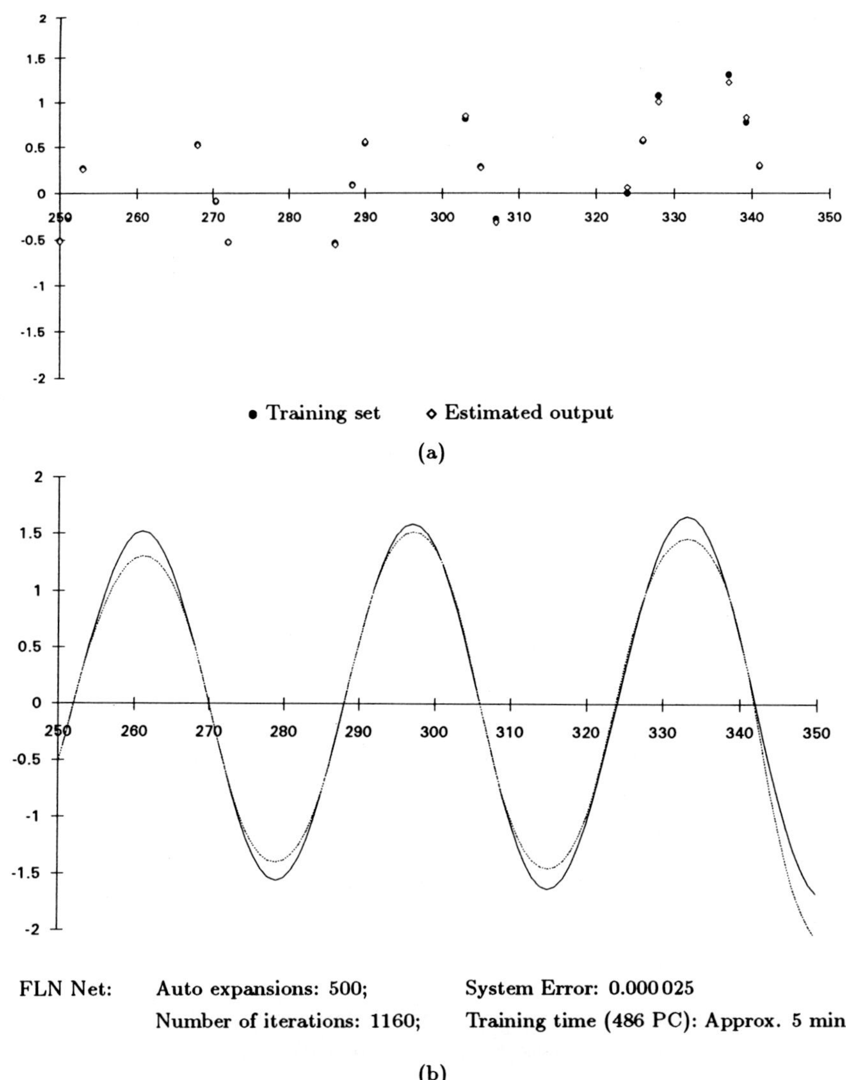

FLN Net: Auto expansions: 500;   System Error: 0.000 025
             Number of iterations: 1160;   Training time (486 PC): Approx. 5 min

(b)

Fig. 14. Demonstration of interpolation achieved with a FLN net for $R \to R$ mapping.

For example, the matrix associative memory was studied by Nakano [21], Kohonen [22], Willshaw [23], Pao [24], and others primarily as models of distributed content-addressable memories, which were forgiving of errors or distortion in the cue and also forgiving of local damage to the memory.

Hopfield [25] accentuated the perspective of viewing such distributed content-addressable devices as nets. In the Hopfield net, there is no learning *per se*, just memorization, and the net computes a more nearly correct output pattern in response to a possibly distorted input pattern. These nets are fully and widely described in literature.

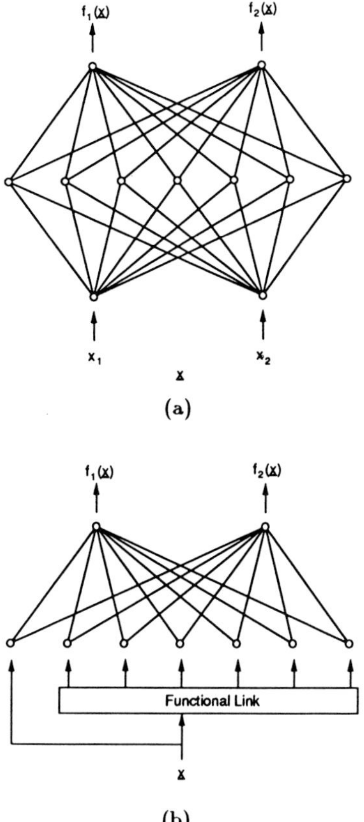

Fig. 15. Illustration of a two-input/two-output net. (a) The BP net configuration and (b) the FLN configuration.

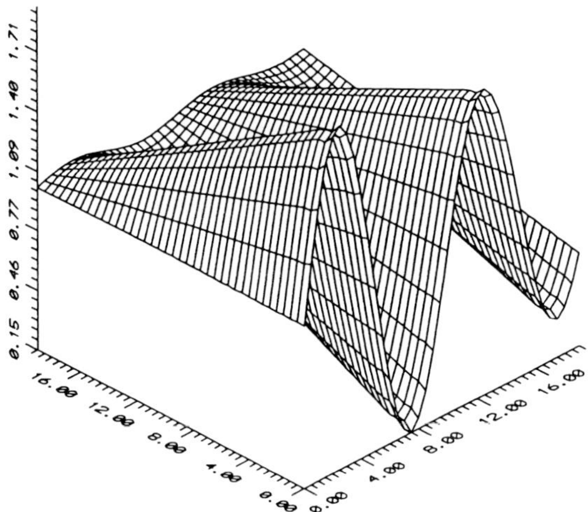

Fig. 16. Output 1 of the two-output net.

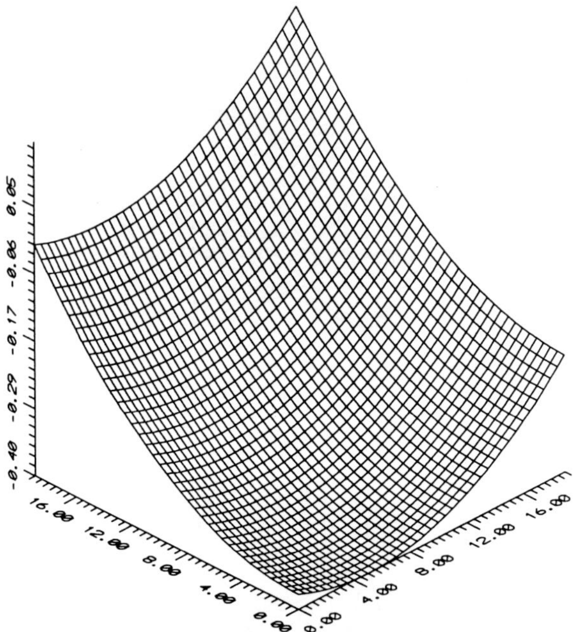

Fig. 17. Output 2 of the two-output net.

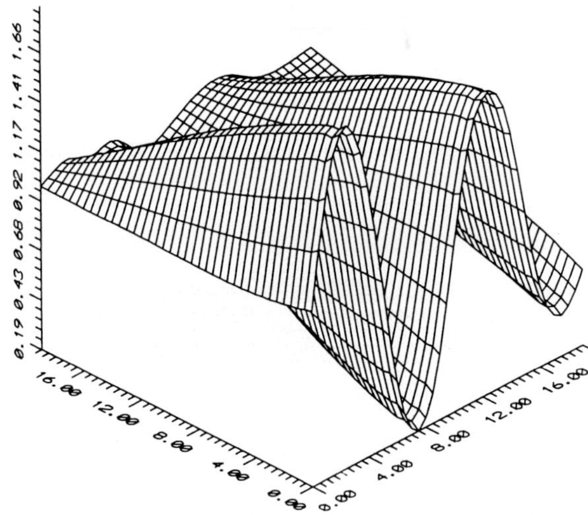

Fig. 18. 2-D mapping learned with a BP net: the upper surface $f_1(\mathbf{x})$.

In a series of papers, Kosko [26] explored the question of whether bidirectional associative memories could be synthesized with the memory still in distributed matrix form, but with a nonlinear transformation at each end so that

$$\mathbf{M}S(\mathbf{y}) = \mathbf{x} \tag{5.1}$$

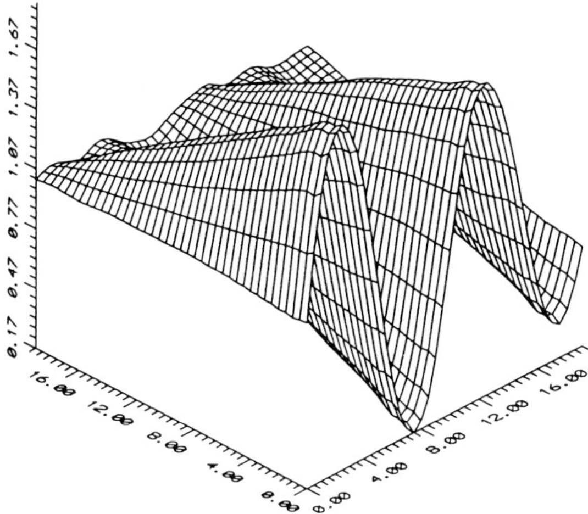

Fig. 19. 2-D mapping learned with an FL net: the upper surface $f_1(\mathbf{x})$.

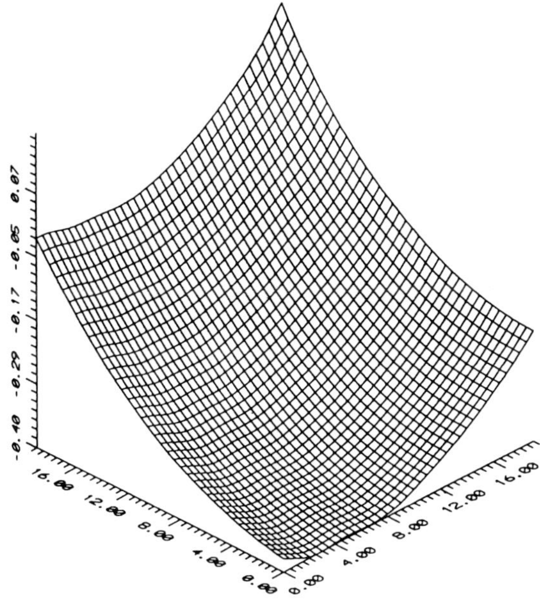

Fig. 20. The surface $f_2(\mathbf{x})$ as learned with a BP net.

and

$$\mathbf{M}^t S(\mathbf{x}) = \mathbf{y}. \tag{5.2}$$

Such memories can indeed be achieved, but often only with great difficulty. They are, nevertheless, noteworthy because they are not limited to being auto-associative memories.

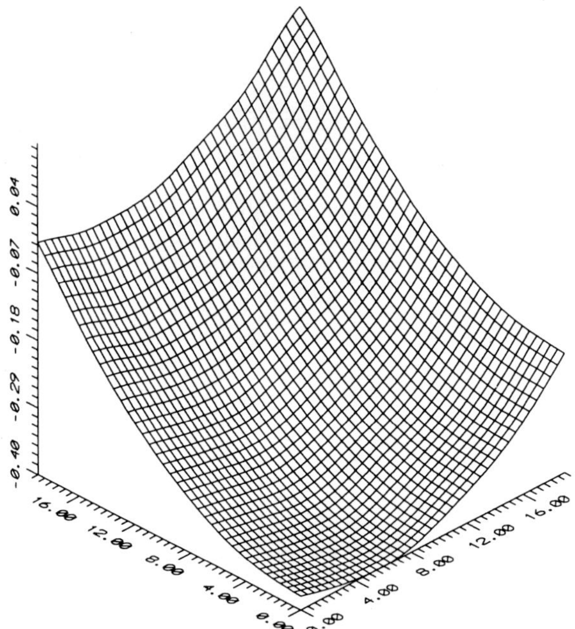

Fig. 21. The surface $f_2(\mathbf{x})$ as learned with an FL net.

In contrast to such associative memories, we also have nets such as ART 1, ART 2 and ART 3 [3–5], which are also considered to be associative memories. These are probably closer in spirit to the associative memory models such as ACT [27] and ACT* [28], models devised by psychologists in attempts to mirror the workings of human memory.

As far as pattern recognition is concerned, a memory such as the Hopfield net might be considered to be an excellent pattern recognizer capable of accepting partial or distorted cue patterns and returning a fully restored correct pattern. But, in practice, such fully connected nets are inefficient with the need for N^2 links for an N neuron net and with low storage capacity.

6. Optimization

In pattern recognition research, interest in the topic of optimization manifests itself somewhat indirectly in the search for optimal values of decision functions, usually for classification purposes. This type of interest is different from the optimization concerns in systems or controls research where a typical task is to find that system state or control path for which an appropriately defined objective function has an optimal value, subject to certain constraints on the system.

Despite this large difference in the degree and mode of involvement, we discuss briefly a widely known but somewhat controversial approach to optimization, which is part of neural net computing practice.

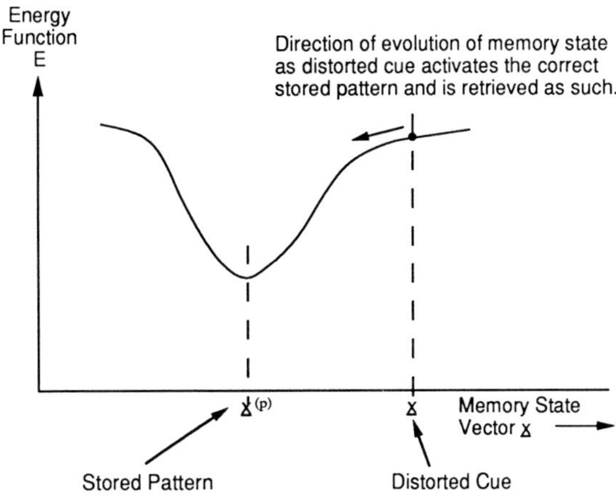

Fig. 22. Associative recall as optimization.

We start by going back to the Hopfield net auto-associative memory. For that memory, storage of a pattern may be likened to the creation of a (local) minimum in an energy function as indicated schematically in Fig. 22. In associative retrieval the Hopfield net is activated by an input which might be a distorted version of the stored pattern. The algorithm of the net is such that the system evolves to that state (that pattern) which corresponds to the energy function being at the (local) minimum. In this manner retrieval with the Hopfield associative memory is equivalent to a set of optimization tasks.

We know, from Hopfield and Tank [29], that given any initial state **v** the system evolves to the state corresponding to a minimum in the energy, if we let the system update itself iteratively in accordances with the equation

$$\frac{du_i}{dt} = -\eta \frac{\partial E}{\partial v_i} \tag{6.1}$$

where u_i is the input to the ith neuron and $v_i = g(u_i)$ is the output of the ith neuron.

For such a system, we have for the temporal evolution of the energy

$$\frac{dE}{dt} = \frac{\partial E}{\partial V_i} \frac{\partial u_i}{\partial v_i} \frac{du_i}{dt} = -\frac{1}{\eta} \left(\frac{du_i}{dt} \right)^2 g(u_i). \tag{6.2}$$

And we see that E, indeed, evolves to a minimum if $g(u_i)$, the neuron activation function, is a nondecreasing function of u_i.

Hopfield and Tank suggested that the well-studied Traveling Salesman Problem (TSP) be encoded in the following manner. As illustrated in Fig. 23, a five city/five day planning task would be represented by the values of a set of 25 neurons. A

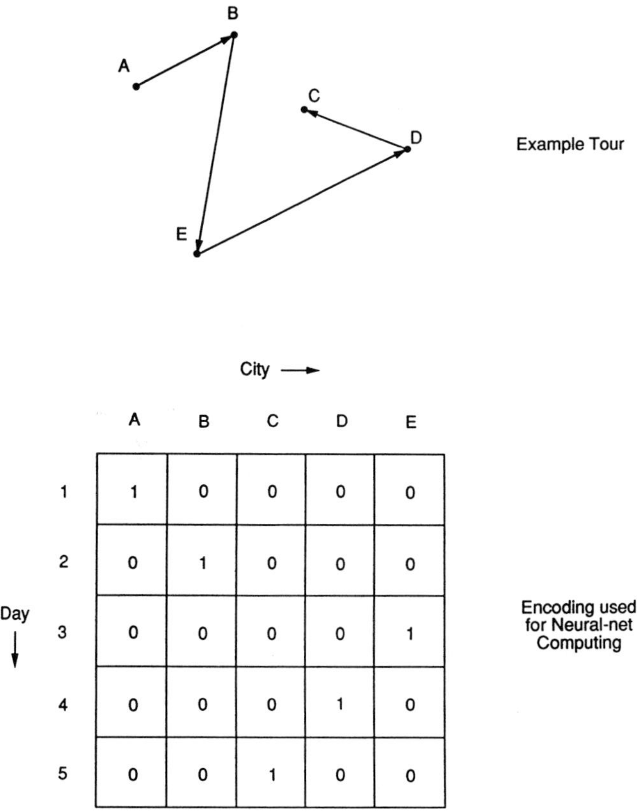

Fig. 23. Encoding the TSP Problem for neural net computing.

neuron would represent a specific city visited on a specific day and that neuron would have an output value of 1 if that combination were part of the salesman's tour and it would have a value of 0 if it were not.

Hopfield and Tank synthesized an energy function in analytical form, which represented not only the length of the salesman's path, but also imposed penalties for nonvalid solutions, such as a city being visited twice or the salesman being at two different places at the same time.

In their approach, although the ultimate acceptable values for the neuron outputs were restricted to 1 or 0, they were treated as continuous variables in the processing. In this manner, *a combinatorial optimization problem was converted into a gradient search task* for neural net computing. In our opinion this constitutes both the strength and the weakness of this approach.

A gradient search approach is advantageous because it obviates the necessity for devising some algorithm for generating new trial states. However the advantage is real only if one can be reasonably assured of a smooth descent into the minimum state or into one of the sets of acceptable minima.

The hypothetical advantage is more than offset by the real difficulties if there is a tremendous number of spurious local minima in the energy function so that the search procedure almost immediately comes to a halt in the nearest spurious local minimum.

We believe that imposition of constraints in the energy function results in the creation of very large numbers of such minima.

Some researchers, nevertheless, have employed this methodology to good effect for subclasses of optimization tasks. Takefuji [30], for example, has used "hill-climbing" terms in the energy function to eject the system state out of a local minimum if the state is not one which is acceptable as a solution. Other innovations, such as "maximum neuron", have also been helpful for certain other circumstances. In other words Takefuji and his collaborators found that the neural net version of gradient search for optimization is viable if certain acceptability conditions are known for the solution. These should not be incorporated into the energy function but can be used to activate "hill-climbing" terms if one or more of the validation conditions are not satisfied.

7. Representation, Feature Extraction and Concepts

In our opinion the most valuable aspect of neural net computing lies in none of the above four computational capabilities. It is rather in the promises of its being a useful (perhaps even the *correct*) tool for research in a very *murky* area of information processing research. This is an area which is only dimly perceived by many, denied by others, and partitioned and vehemently defended in isolated parts by yet others, but, nevertheless, tantalizing and beguiling to almost all.

We speak of some underlying mysteries of human behavior, perhaps ultimately attributable to the nature of our "hardware", in this case the left and right halves of the brain, with different functionalities and propensities and not overly communicative with each other.

In human behavior we have the dichotomy of perception and action on the one hand and language and reason on the other.

In some human cultures, the importance of an internal "knowing" is elevated above all other considerations. Thus, one behaves well not necessarily through elaborate reasoning, but because we "know" that it is the correct behavior. One aims an arrow most accurately when one almost feels that no deliberate aiming is being done. In such behavior, perception and action are everything, and all matters can proceed smoothly and rapidly in an easy flow.

To the modern day information processing researcher, it is interesting and entertaining to go back into the history of philosophy and psychology to see that other human cultures have glorified the "pure light of reason". Language and reason are then supreme. There is even the hypothesis that humans are rational beings and always act to optimize attainment of their goals [28].

Most of us will admit that, in practice, our cultures and our behavior comprise admixtures of both aspects of behavior and both are important. The perception and action channel allows us to carry out intricate actions appropriately and rapidly in response to rapidly changing external conditions with no time for explicit cognitive deliberations. Thus, we can ride bicycles even on highly uneven roadways. Incidentally we note that some bears can also be trained to ride bicycles, but they do not articulate their skill at all, as far as we can tell. However humans can articulate some aspects of the bike-riding skill in language and help teach other humans that skill through use of the language and reasoning channel as well.

Interactions between the two channels are, indeed, of great importance and value. One demonstration of the value and effectiveness of such interaction is provided by the example of an athletics' coach being able to produce significant improvements in the performance of a star athelete even though the performance capabilities of the coach himself may be substantially below that of the athlete.

In another instance it is found that improvements in foundry practice are obtained when experiences are carefully documented and the information shared with the foundry shop community through the language and symbols channel.

It seems to us that one bottleneck to communications between the channels lies in the discovery and articulation of *concepts*. This same matter is also encountered under the guises of feature extraction, knowledge representation and so on.

We believe that the perception and action channel draws a veil over its workings, so as to speak, and in that mode of information processing, both for humans and in algorithms, uniqueness in representation or in feature selection might not be critical. To use an analogy, it is as if matrix operations proceed equally well in general representations as in eigenfunction representation. To pursue the analogy, matters are very different when one wants to describe matters in terms of concepts expressible in terms of linguistic symbols. In artificial intelligence, researchers do strive to learn concepts and there is success when concepts are "learned" in the sense of being inferred from other sets of concepts. However the bridge between the linguistic symbolic world and that of perception is weak.

These matters are very important not only because the subject matter is so interesting, but also because there may be the opportunity to fashion computer aids in ways to compensate for inadequacies due to the idiosyncrasies of human physiology.

We believe that neural net computing provides a tool for capturing and manipulating the "pattern-ness" of things and also for encoding and articulating such matters into the linguistic symbol world. Some work by Pao and Hafez [31] address these matters.

Hinton, McClelland, Rumelhart, Touretsky and others [32,33] have addressed the relationships between distributed associative processing and linguistic symbolic, logic-based, and information processing. But the emphasis has been to ask how the same type of rule-based processing, entirely with linguistic symbols on both the antecedent and consequent sides of the scale, might be carried out in a "connectionist" representation.

We believe what is just as interesting, perhaps more so, is to investigate what can be achieved if the distributed coarse-coding connectionist scheme is used as an interface between the pattern-ness of things and the extracted linguistic symbolic entities.

In terms of human behavior, we would be striving to understand how we learn how to dance a fast waltz not only by example but also aided by spoken instructions. Or in a related matter, how do we "internalize" perceptual experiential knowledge so that we can verbalize that information and reason with it.

Finally, it can be said that it is not that neural net computing is relevant to pattern recognition and to computer vision. It is rather that neural net computing might turn out to be an essential tool for unifying our pieces of knowledge in the fragmented bastions of research endeavor known presently as artificial intelligence, pattern recognition, fuzzy logic, computer vision, and so on.

References

[1] R. O. Duda and P. E. Hart, *Pattern Classification and Scene Analysis* (John Wiley, NY, 1973).

[2] D. E. Rumelhart and J. L. McClelland, *Parallel Distributed Processing: Explorations in the Microstructure of Cognition*, Vols. 1 & 2 (MIT Press, Cambridge, MA, 1986).

[3] G. A. Carpenter and S. Grossberg, A massively parallel architecture for a self-organizing neural pattern recognition machine, *Comput. Vision Graph. Image Process.* **37** (1987) 54–115.

[4] G. A. Carpenter and S. Grossberg, ART2: Self-organization of stable category recognition codes for analog input patterns, *Appl. Opt.* **26** (1987) 4919–4930.

[5] G. A. Carpenter and S. Grossberg, ART3: Hierarchical search using chemical transmitters in self-organizing pattern recognition architectures, *Neural Networks* **3** (1990) 129–152.

[6] T. Kohonen, An introduction to neural computing, *Neural Networks* **1** (1988) 3–16.

[7] T. Kohonen, Self-organized formation of topologically correct feature maps, *Biol. Cybern.* **43** (1988) 59–69.

[8] T. Kohonen, Clustering, taxonomy, and topological maps of patterns, in *Proc. Sixth Int. Conf. on Pattern Recognition*, Silver Spring, MD (IEEE Computer Society Press, 1982) 114–128.

[9] C. H. Chen, *Statistical Pattern Recognition* (Hayden, Washington, DC, 1973).

[10] G. H. Ball and D. J. Hall, ISODATA, an interative method of multivariant data analysis and pattern classification, in *Proc. IEEE Int. Communication Conf.*, Philadelphia, PA, Jun. 1966.

[11] Y. H. Pao, *Adaptive Pattern Recognition and Neural Networks* (Addison-Wesley, Reading, MA, 1988).

[12] R. P. Lippman, B. Gold and M. L. Malpass, A comparison of Hamming and Hopfield neural nets for pattern classification, MIT Lincoln Laboratory Technical Report, TR-769, Massachusetts Institute of Technology, Cambridge, MA, 1987.

[13] E. Aarts and J. Korst, *Simulated Annealing and Boltzmann Machines* (John Wiley, New York, 1989).

[14] Y. H. Pao and Y. Takefuji, Functional-link net computing, *IEEE Computer* **3** (1992) 76–79.

[15] G. Cybenko, Approximation by superpositions of a sigmoidal function, *Mathematics of Control, Signal, and Systems* **2** (1989) 303–314.

[16] M. Hornik, M. Stinchcombe and H. White, Multilayer feedforward networks are universal approximators, *Neural Networks* **2** (1989) 359–366.

[17] K. Funahashi, On the approximate realization of continuous mappings by neural networks, *Neural Networks* **2** (1989) 183–192.

[18] K. Hornik, M. Stinchcombe and H. White, Universal approximation of an unknown mapping and its derivatives using multilayer feedforward networks, *Neural Networks* **3** (1990) 551–560.

[19] G. E. Hinton and T. J. Sejnowski, Analyzing cooperative computation, in *Proc. Fifth Annual Conf. of the Cognitive Science Society*, Rochester, NY, May 1983.

[20] D. S. Touretzky and G. E. Hinton, Pattern matching and variable binding in a stochastic neural network, in L. Davis (ed.), *Genetic Algorithm and Simulated Annealing* (Morgan Kaufmann, Inc., Los Altos, CA, 1987).

[21] K. Nakano, Associatron – A model of associative memory, *IEEE Trans. Syst. Man Cybern.* **2** (1972) 380–388.

[22] T. Kohonen, *Associative Memory: A System-Theoretical Approach* (Springer-Verlag, New York, 1977).

[23] D. J. Willshaw, Model of distributed associative memory, unpublished doctoral dissertation, Department of Machine Intelligence, University of Edinburgh, Edinburgh, 1971.

[24] Y. H. Pao and G. P. Hartoch, Fast memory access by similarity measure, in J. Hayes, D. Michie and Y. H. Pao (eds.), *Machine Intelligence 10* (Wiley, New York, 1982).

[25] J. J. Hopfield, Neural networks and physical systems with emergent collective computational abilities, in *Proc. Nat. Acad. Sci.* **74** (1982) 2554–2558.

[26] B. Kosko, *Neural Networks and Fuzzy Systems* (Prentice-Hall, Englewood Cliffs, NJ, 1992).

[27] J. R. Anderson and G. H. Bower, *Human Associate Memory* (V. H. Winston, Washington, DC, 1973) (distributed by the Halsted Press, Division of Wiley, NY).

[28] J. J. Hopfield and D. W. Tank, Neural computation of decisions in optimization problems, *Biol. Cybern.* **52** (1985) 144–152.

[29] Y. Takefuji, *Neural Network Parallel Computing* (Kluwer Academic, Boston, MA, 1992).

[30] J. R. Anderson, *The Adaptive Character of Thought* (Lawrence Erlbaum Associates, Hillsdale, NJ, 1990).

[31] Y. H. Pao and W. Hafez, Analog computational models of concept formation, *International Journal of Analog Integrated Devices and Signal Processing*, Special Neural-Net Issue on Analog VLSI Neural Networks **2** (1992) 3–10.

[32] G. E. Hinton, J. M. McClelland and D. E. Rumelhart, Distributed Representations, in D. E. Rumelhart and J. M. McClelland (eds.), *Parallel Distributed Processing: Explorations in the Microstructure of Cognition*, Vol. 1 (Bradford Books, Cambridge, MA, 1986).

[33] D. S. Touretzky, BoltzCONS: Reconciling connectionism with the recursive nature of stacks and trees, in *Proc. Eighth Annual Conf. of the Cognitive Science Society*, Amherst, MA, Aug. 1986.

Appendix A

A list of texts, monographs and edited volumes which might contain detailed information of interest to readers:

Adaptive Pattern Recognition and Neural Networks. AUTHOR: Pao, Yoh-Han. PUBLISHER: Reading, MA: Addison-Wesley, 1989. ISN/OTHER No.: 0201125846.o

Advanced Neural Computers. EDITOR: Rolf Eckmiller. PUBLISHER: Amsterdam; New York: North-Holland, 1990. ISN/OTHER No.: 0444884009 (U.S.)

Analog VLSI: Implementation of Neural Systems. EDITORS: Carver Mead and Mohammed Ismail. PUBLISHER: Boston: Kluwer Academic Publishers, 1989. SERIES: The Kluwer international series in engineering and computer science; SECS 80. ISN/OTHER No. 0792390407

Artificial Neural Networks for Computer Vision. AUTHORS: Yi-Tong Zhou and Rama Chellappa. PUBLISHER: New York: Springer-Verlag, 1992. SERIES: Research ISN/OTHER No.: 0387976833 (New York), 3540976833 (Berlin)

Artificial Neural Networks: Theoretical Concepts. AUTHOR: V. Vemuri. PUBLISHER: Washington, D.C.: IEEE Computer Society Press, 1988. SERIES: Neural networks. Computer Society Press technology series. ISN/OTHER No.: 0818608552

Artificial Neural Systems: Foundations, Paradigms, Applications, and Implementations. AUTHOR: Patrick K. Simpson. PUBLISHER: New York: Pergamon Press, 1990. SERIES: Neural networks, research and applications. ISN/OTHER No.: 0080378951, 0080378943 (pbk.)

Code Recognition and Set Selection with Neural Networks. AUTHOR: Clark Jeffries. PUBLISHER: Boston: Birkhauser, 1991. SERIES: Mathematical modeling (Boston, MA); no. 7. ISN/OTHER No.: 0817635858 (acid-free paper), 3764335858 (acid-free paper)

Cognizers: Neural Networks and Machines That Think. AUTHOR: R. Collin Johnson and Chappell Brown; illustrated by Lisa Metzger. PUBLISHER: New York: Wiley, 1988. SERIES: Wiley science editions. ISN/OTHER No.: 0471611611

Cognitive Psychology: A Neural-Network Approach. AUTHOR: Colin Martindale. PUBLISHER: Pacific Grove, CA: Brooks/Cole Pub. Co., 1991. ISN/OTHER No.: 23654900, 0534141307

Common LISP Modules: Artificial Intelligence in the Era of Neural Networks and Chaos Theory. AUTHOR: Mark Watson. PUBLISHER: New York: Springer-Verlag, 1991. ISN/OTHER No.: 0387976140, 3540976140

Competitively Inhibited Neural Networks for Adaptive Parameter Estimation. AUTHOR: Michael Lemmon; foreword by B. V. K. Vijaya Kumar. PUBLISHER: Boston: Kluwer Academic, 1991. SERIES: The Kluwer international series in engineering and computer science; SECS 111. Knowledge representation, learning, and expert systems. ISN/OTHER No.: 0792390865

Computer Systems that Learn: Classification and Prediction Methods from Statistics, Neural Nets, Machine Learning, and Expert Systems. AUTHORS: Sholom M. Weiss and Casimir Kulikowski. PUBLISHER: San Mateo, CA: M. Kaufmann Publishers, 1990. ISN/OTHER No.: 1558600655

Connectionist Modeling and Brain Function: The Developing Interface. EDITORS: Stephen Jose Hanson and Carl R. Olson. PUBLISHER: Cambridge, MA: MIT Press, 1990. SERIES: Neural network modeling and connectionism. ISN/OTHER No.: 0262081938

DARPA Neural Network Study: October 1987–February 1988. AUTHOR: DARPA Neural Network Study (U.S.). PUBLISHER: Fairfax, VA: AFCEA International Press, 1988. LC Card Number: 88031655//r90 ISBN No.: 0-916159-17-5

Exploring the Geometry of Nature: Computer Modeling of Chaos, Fractals, Cellular Automata, and Neural Networks. AUTHOR: Ed Rietman. PUBLISHER: Blue Ridge Summit, PA: Windcrest, 1989. SERIES: The advanced programming technology series. ISN/OTHER No.: 0830691375, 0830631372 (pbk.)

Hebbian Neural Network Simulation: Computer Program Documentation. AUTHORS: Robert G. Day and Lee J. White. PUBLISHER: Columbus, OH: Computer and Information Science Research Center, Ohio State University, 1969. SERIES: Ohio State University, Columbus, Computer and Information Science Research Center, Technical report series; OSU-CISRC-TR-69-19

Introduction to Artificial Neural Systems. AUTHOR: Jacek M. Zurada. PUBLISHER: St. Paul, New York, Los Angeles, San Francisco: West Publishing Company, 1992. ISN/OTHER No.: ISBN 0-314-93391-3

An Introduction to Fuzzy Logic Applications in Intelligent Systems. EDITORS: Ronald R. Yager and Lotfi A. Zadeh. PUBLISHER: Boston: Kluwer Academic, 1992. SERIES: The Kluwer International series in engineering and computer science; SECS 165. ISN/OTHER No.: 0792391918

An Introduction to Neural Computing. AUTHOR: Igor Aleksander and Helen Morton. PUBLISHER: London: Chapman and Hall, 1990. ISN/OTHER No.: GB90-14110, 0412377802 (pbk)

Introduction to Neural Networks. AUTHORS: Jeannette Stanley and Evan Bak. EDITOR: Sylvia Luedeking. PUBLISHER: Sierra Madre, CA 91024: California Science Software, 1988

The Metaphorical Brain 2: Neural Networks and Beyond. AUTHOR: Michael A. Arbib. PUBLISHER: New York: Wiley, 1989. ISN/OTHER No.: 0471098531

Modeling Brain Function: The World of Attractor Neural Networks. AUTHOR: Daniel J. Amit. PUBLISHER: New York: Cambridge University Press, 1989. ISN/OTHER No.: 0521361001

Models of Neural Networks. EDITORS: E. Domany, J. L. van Hemmen and K. Schulten. PUBLISHER: Berlin, New York: Springer-Verlag, 1991. SERIES: Physics of neural networks. ISBN 0387511091

Nested Neural Networks [microform]. AUTHOR: Yoram Baram. PUBLISHER: Moffett Field, CA.: National Aeronautics and Space Administration, Ames Research Center (Springfield, VA: For sale by the National Technical Information Service, 1988). SERIES: NASA technical memorandum; 101032. ISN/OTHER No.: N 88-30373 NASA., 0830-d (MF), GOV DOC No.: NAS 1.15:101032

Neural and Automata Networks: Dynamical Behavior and Applications. AUTHOR: Eric Goles Servet Martinez. PUBLISHER: Dordrecht, Boston: Kluwer Academic 1990. SERIES: Mathematics and its applications (Kluwer Academic Publishers); Vol. 58. ISN/OTHER No.: 0792306325 (alk. paper)

Neural and Intelligent Systems Integration: Fifth and Sixth Generation Integrated Reasoning Information Systems. AUTHORS: Branko Soucek and the IRIS Group. PUB-

LISHER: New York: Wiley, 1991. SERIES: Sixth-generation computer technology series. ISN/OTHER No.: 0471536768

Neural and Massively Parallel Computers: The Sixth Generation. AUTHORS: Branko Soucek and Marina Soucek. PUBLISHER: New York: Wiley, 1988. ISN/OTHER No.: 0471635332

Neural Computation and Self-Organizing Maps: An Introduction. AUTHORS: Helge Ritter, Thomas Martinez and Klaus Schulten. PUBLISHER: Addison-Wesley Publishing Co., 1992. ISN/OTHER No.: ISBN 0-201-55443-7 (hbk.), 0-201-55442-9 (pbk.)

Neural Computers. EDITORS: Rolf Eckmiller and Christoph v.d. Malsburg. CONFERENCE: NATO Advanced Research Workshop on Neural Computers (1987: Neuss, Germany) PUBLISHER: Berlin, New York: Springer-Verlag, 1989. SERIES: NATO ASI Series (Advanced Science Institute Series) F, Computer and systems sciences; vol. 41. ISN/OTHER No.: 0387508929 (U.S.)

Neural Computing: An Introduction. AUTHORS: R. Beale and T. Jackson. PUBLISHER: Bristol: Hilger, 1990. ISN/OTHER No.: GB90-35434, 0852742622

Neural Computing: Theory and Practice. AUTHOR: Philip D. Wasserman. PUBLISHER: New York: Van Nostrand Reinhold, 1989. ISN/OTHER No.: 0442207433

Neural Dynamics of Adaptive Sensory-motor Control. AUTHORS: Stephen Grossberg and Michael Kuperstein. EDITION: Expanded ed. PUBLISHER: New York: Pergamon Press, 1989. SERIES: Neural networks, research and applications. ISN/OTHER No.: 008036828X, 0080368271 (pbk.)

Neural Models and Algorithms for Digital Testing. AUTHORS: Srimat T. Chakradhar, Vishwani D. Agrawal and Michael L. Bushnell. PUBLISHER: Boston: Kluwer Academic Publishers, 1991. SERIES: The Kluwer international series in engineering and computer science; SECS 140. VLSI, computer architecture, and digital signal processing. ISN/OTHER No.: 0792391659 (acid-free paper)

Neural Network Application to Aircraft Control System Design [microform]. AUTHORS: Terry Troudet, Sanjay Garg and Walker C. Merrill. PUBLISHER: Washington, DC: National Aeronautics and Space Administration; [Springfield, VA: For sale by the National Technical Information Service, 1991]. SERIES: NASA technical memorandum; 105151. ISN/OTHER No.: N 91-27167 NASA. 0830-D (MF), GOV DOC No.: NAS 1.15:105151

Neural Networks Architectures: An Introduction. AUTHOR: Judith E. Dayhoff. PUBLISHER: New York: Van Nostrand Reinhold, 1990. ISN/OTHER No.: 0442207441

Neural Network Design and the Complexity of Learning. AUTHOR: J. Stephen Judd. PUBLISHER: Cambridge, MA: MIT Press, 1990. SERIES: Neural network modeling and connectionism. ISN/OTHER No.: 0262100452

Neural Network Models in Artificial Intelligence. AUTHOR: Matthew Zeidenberg. PUBLISHER: New York: Ellis Horwood, 1990. SERIES: Ellis Horwood series in artificial intelligence. ISN/OTHER No.: 0136121853, 0745806007

Neural Network Parallel Computing. AUTHOR: Yoshiyasu Takefuji. PUBLISHER: Boston: Kluwer Academic publishers, 1992. The Kluwer international series in engineering and computer science; SECS 0164. ISN/OTHER No.: 079239190X (acid-free paper)

Neural Networks: An Introduction. AUTHOR: B. Muller and J. Reinhardt. EDITION: Corr. 2nd print. PUBLISHER: Berlin, New York: Springer-Verlag, 1991. SERIES: Physics of neural networks. ISN/OTHER No.: 3540523804 (Berlin: alk. paper), 0387523804 (New York: alk. paper)

Neural Networks and Natural Intelligence. EDITOR: Stephen Grossberg. PUBLISHER: Cambridge: MIT Press, 1988. ISN/OTHER No.: 026207107X

Neural Networks and Speech Processing. AUTHORS: David P. Morgan and Christopher L. Scofield; foreword by Leon N. Cooper. PUBLISHER: Boston: Kluwer Academic publishers, 1991. SERIES: The Kluwer international series in engineering and computer science. VLSI, computer architecture, and digital signal processing. ISN/OTHER No.: 0792391446 (alk. paper)

Neural Networks: Concepts, Applications, and Implementations. EDITORS: Paolo Antognetti and Veljko Milutinovic. PUBLISHER: Englewood Cliffs, NJ: Prentice Hall, 1991. SERIES: Prentice Hall advanced reference series. Engineering. ISN/OTHER No.: 0136125166 (Vol. 1), 0136127630 (Vol. 2)

Neural Networks for Computing, Snowbird, UT, 1986. EDITOR: John S. Denker. PUBLISHER: New York: American Institute of Physics, 1986. AIP conference proceedings; no. 151. ISN/OTHER No.: 088318351X

Neural Networks for Control. EDITORS: W. Thomas Miller, III, Richard S. Sutton and Paul J. Werbos. PUBLISHER: Cambridge, MA: MIT Press, 1990. SERIES: Neural network modeling and connectionism. ISN/OTHER No.: 0262132613

Neural Networks for Perception. EDITOR: Harry Wechsler. PUBLISHER: Boston: Academic Press, 1992. ISN/OTHER No.: 0127412514 (Vol. 1: acid-free paper), 0127412522 (Vol. 2: acid-free paper)

Neural Networks: Theoretical Foundations and Analysis. EDITOR: Clifford Lau. PUBLISHER: New York: IEEE Press, 1992. ISN/OTHER No.: 0879422807

Neural Networks: Theory and Applications. EDITORS: Richard J. Mammone and Yehoshua Y. Zeevi. PUBLISHER: Boston: Academic Press, 1991. ISN/OTHER No.: 0124670504 (alk. paper)

Neurale Netvaerk. In English: *Neural Networks: Computers with Intuition.* AUTHORS: Soren Brunak and Benny Lautrup. PUBLISHER: Singapore: World Scientific Pub. Co., 1988. ISN/OTHER No.: 9971509385, 9971509393 (pbk.)

NeuralSource: The Bibliographic Guide to Artificial Neural Network. AUTHORS: Philip D. Wasserman and Roberta M. Oetzel. PUBLISHER: New York: Van Nostrand Reinhold, 1990. ISN/OTHER No.: 0442237766

Neurocomputing. AUTHOR: Robert Hecht-Nielsen. PUBLISHER: Reading, MA: Addison-Wesley, 1990. ISN/OTHER No.: 0201093553

Neurocomputing: Foundations of Research. EDITORS: James A. Anderson and Edward Rosenfeld. PUBLISHER: Cambridge, MA: MIT Press, 1988. ISN/OTHER No.: 0262010976

New Developments in Neural Computing: Proceedings of a meeting on neural computing sponsored by the Institute of Physics and the London Mathematical Society held in London, 19–21 April 1989. EDITORS: J. G. Taylor and C. L. T. Mannion. PUBLISHER: Bristol [England], New York: A. Hilger, 1989. ISN/OTHER No.: 0852741936

Orthogonal Patterns in Binary Neural Networks [microform]. AUTHOR: Yoram Baram. PUBLISHER: Moffett Field, CA: National Aeronautics and Space Administration, Ames Research Center; (Springfield, VA: For sale by the National Technical Information Service, 1988). SERIES: NASA technical memorandum; 100060. ISN/OTHER No.: A-88068., 0830-D (MF), GOV DOC No.: NAS 1.15: 10060

Pattern Recognition by Self-Organizing Neural Networks. EDITORS: Gail A. Carpenter and Stephen Grossberg. PUBLISHER: Cambridge, MA: MIT Press, 1991. ISN/OTHER No.: 0262031760

The Perception of Multiple Objects: A Connectionist Approach. AUTHOR: Michael C. Mozer. PUBLISHER: Cambridge, MA: MIT Press, 1991. SERIES: Neural network modeling and connectionism. ISN/OTHER No.: 0262132702 (hc)

Physical Models of Neural Networks. AUTHOR: Tamas Geszti. PUBLISHER: Singapore: World Scientific, 1990. ISN/OTHER No.: 9810200129

A Real Time Neural Net Estimator of Fatigue Life [microform]. AUTHOR: T. Troudet and W. Merrill. PUBLISHER: Washington, DC: National Aeronautics and Space Administration; [Springfield, VA: For sale by the National Technical Information Service, 1990]. SERIES: NASA technical memorandum; 103117. ISN/OTHER No.: N 90-21564 NASA., 0830-D (MF), GOV DOC No.: NAS 1.15:103117

Recursive Neural Networks for Associative Memory. AUTHORS: Yves Kamp and Martin Hasler. PUBLISHER: Chichester, New York: John Wiley and Sons, 1990. SERIES: Wiley-Interscience series in systems and optimization. ISN/OTHER No.: 0471928666

Simulation Tests of the Optimization Method of Hopfield and Tank Using Neural Networks [microform]. AUTHOR: Russell A. Paielli. PUBLISHER: Moffett Field, CA: National Aeronautics and Space Administration, Ames Research Center; [Springfield, VA: For sale by the National Technical Information Service, 1988]. SERIES: NASA technical memorandum; 101047. ISN/OTHER No.: A-88275

Structure Level Adaptation for Artificial Neural Networks. AUTHOR: Tsu-Chang Lee; foreword by Joseph W. Goodman. PUBLISHER: Boston: Kluwer Academic publishers, 1991. SERIES: The Kluwer international series in engineering and computer science; SECS 133. Knowledge representation, learning, and expert systems. ISN/OTHER No.: 0792391519

VLSI Design of Neural Networks. EDITOR: Ulrich Ramacher. PUBLISHER: Boston: Kluwer Academic Publishers, 1991. ISN/OTHER No.: 0792391276

Appendix B

A list of names of journals wholly or partially devoted to publishing neural net computing articles:

Advances in Connectionist and Neural Computation Theory. Frequency: Irregular. PUBLISHER: Ablex Publishing Corp., 355 Chestnut St., Norwood, NJ 07648. Tel: (201) 767-8450. EDITOR: John Barnden.

Biological Cybernetics. Frequency: monthly. PUBLISHER: Springer-Verlag, Heidelberger Platz 3, D–1000 Berlin 33, Germany (also in New York). Tel: 030-8207-1. EDITOR: W. Reichardt.

IEEE Transactions on Neural Networks. Frequency: Bi-monthly. PUBLISHER: IEEE, Inc., 345 E. 47th St., New York, NY 10017-2394. Tel: (212) 705-7366. Subscriptions to 445 Hoes Lane, Box 1331, Piscataway, NJ 08855-1331. Tel: (908) 562-3948. EDITOR: Herbert Rauch.

IEEE Transactions on Pattern Analysis and Machine Intelligence. Frequency: monthly. PUBLISHER: IEEE, Inc., 345 E. 47th St., New York, NY 10017-2394. Tel: (212) 705-7366. Subscriptions to 445 Hoes Lane, Box 1331, Piscataway, NJ 08855-1331. Tel: (908) 562-3948. EDITOR: Anil K. Jain.

International Journal of Neural Networks. Frequency: quarterly. PUBLISHER: Learned Information, Inc., 143 Old Marlton Pike, Medford, NJ 08055. Tel: (609) 654-6266. EDITOR: Kamal Karna and Ian Croall.

Journal of Parallel and Distributed Computing. Frequency: monthly. PUBLISHER: Academic Press, Inc., JOURNAL Division, 1250 Sixth Ave., San Diego, CA 92101. Tel: (619) 230-1840. EDITOR: Kai Hwang and Howard Siegel.

Neural Computation. Frequency: quarterly. PUBLISHER: MIT Press, 55 Hayward St., Cambridge, MA 02142. Tel: (617) 253-2889. EDITOR: Terence Sejnowski, Salk Institute, Box 85800, San Diego, CA 92138.

Neural Network Review. Frequency: quarterly. PUBLISHER: Lawrence Erlbaum Associates, Inc., 365, Broadway, Hillsdale, NJ 07642. Tel: (201) 666-4110. EDITOR: Craig Will.

Neural Networks. Frequency: Bi-monthly. PUBLISHER: Pergamon Press, Inc., JOURNALs Division, Maxwell House, Fairview Park, NY 10523. Tel: (914) 592-0770.

Neurocomputing. Frequency: Bi-monthly. PUBLISHER: North Holland (Subsidiary of Elsevier Science Publishers B. V.), P.O. Box 211, 1000 AE Amsterdam, Netherlands. EDITOR: V. David Sanchez.

Pattern Recognition. Frequency: monthly. PUBLISHER: Pergamon Press, Inc., JOURNALs Division, Maxwell House, Fairview Park, NY 10523. Tel: (914) 592-0770. EDITOR: Robert Ledley.

Progress in Neural Networks. Frequency: annual. PUBLISHER: Ablex Publishing Corp., 355 Chestnut St., Norwood, NJ 07648. Tel: (201) 767-8450. EDITOR: Omid Omidvar.

Handbook of Pattern Recognition and Computer Vision, pp. 163–209
Eds. C. H. Chen, L. F. Pau and P. S. P. Wang
© 1993 World Scientific Publishing Company

CHAPTER 1.5

STRUCTURAL AND SYNTACTIC PATTERN RECOGNITION

HORST BUNKE

Institut für Informatik und angewandte Mathematik, Universität Bern, Länggassstrasse 51
CH-3012 Bern, Switzerland

Structural and syntactic pattern recognition is based on symbolic data structures
like strings, trees, graphs, or arrays for pattern representation. These data structures
allow the description of relations between elementary pattern components and provide
means for hierarchical models showing how complex patterns are built up from simpler
parts. The recognition of an unknown pattern is accomplished by comparing its symbolic
representation with a number of predefined object models. In the structural approach,
the comparison is made by a symbolic match that computes a measure of similarity
between the unknown input and a number of prototype models. In syntactic pattern
recognition, a parser or error correcting parser checks an unknown input whether it is in
accordance with the rules of a grammar that describes all members of a pattern class.
This chapter reviews basic concepts and algorithms applied in structural and syntactic
pattern recognition. It introduces several grammar models, hidden Markov models, and
gives detailed algorithms for string matching, graph matching, grammatical parsing and
error correcting parsing. Also it discusses advanced topics and applications.

Keywords: symbolic pattern representation, formal grammars, string matching, graph
matching, Markov models, syntactic parsing, error correcting parsing.

1. Introduction

The term structural and syntactic pattern recognition (sspr) was coined at the
end of the 1960's and the beginning of the 1970's. The fundamental idea in sspr
is the use of symbolic data structures like strings, trees, graphs, or arrays for pattern representation instead of vectors of numbers that are used in the statistical
approach. Symbolic data structures allow the explicit description of relations between elementary pattern components. These relations may be of spatial, temporal,
conceptual, etc. nature. Moreover, symbolic data structures facilitate hierarchical
pattern models that describe how a pattern or subpattern is built up from simpler
parts. In sspr, the recognition of an unknown pattern is usually accomplished by
comparing its symbolic representation with a number of predefined object models.
These object models may be given in terms of structural prototypes or grammars,
and the process of comparison is based on symbolic matching or syntactic parsing.
No matter which particular alternative is selected, sspr seems to be the method
of choice if the patterns under consideration are characterized by complex struc-

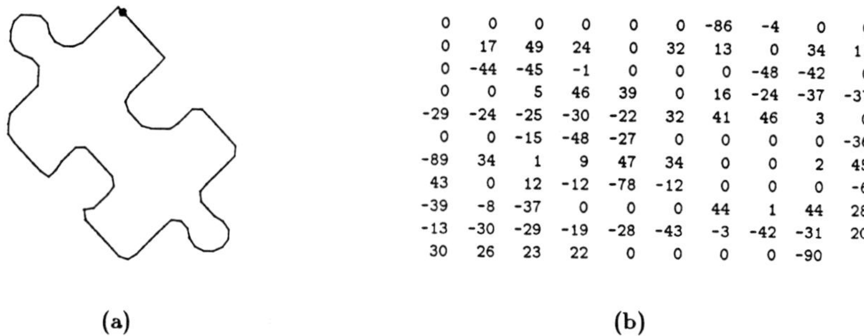

0	0	0	0	0	0	-86	-4	0	0
0	17	49	24	0	32	13	0	34	11
0	-44	-45	-1	0	0	0	-48	-42	0
0	0	5	46	39	0	16	-24	-37	-37
-29	-24	-25	-30	-22	32	41	46	3	0
0	0	-15	-48	-27	0	0	0	0	-36
-89	34	1	9	47	34	0	0	2	45
43	0	12	-12	-78	-12	0	0	0	-6
-39	-8	-37	0	0	0	44	1	44	28
-13	-30	-29	-19	-28	-43	-3	-42	-31	20
30	26	23	22	0	0	0	0	-90	

(a)   (b)

Fig. 1. (a) Polygonal contour approximation; (b) string representation (see text).

tural relationships rather than the statistical distribution of a fixed set of pattern features.

Today, the borders of sspr are not clearly defined. The discipline has evolved and interacted with a number of other areas in pattern recognition and artificial intelligence. Many of its basic algorithms, like string matching, graph matching, hidden Markov models, or syntactic parsing exist in numerous different versions and are used as fundamental techniques in a wide variety of applications, like speech understanding, character recognition, document analysis, dynamic scene interpretation, or 3-D object recognition.

The aim of this chapter is twofold. First, it provides, in all necessary detail, some of the fundamental algorithms used in sspr. Secondly, it discusses more advanced and recent developments and gives pointers to the literature. Some general textbooks on sspr are [21,37,44,72]. An edited volume covering early applications of sspr is [36]. Recent progress in the field has been reported in the special issue [20] and a series of workshop proceedings [34,74,5,7,11]. Further work which has been published in major journals and conference proceedings will be referenced throughout the text.

2. Symbolic Pattern Representation

In the structural and syntactic approach, symbolic data structures are used for the representation of the patterns under study. These patterns are usually divided into two sets. First, there is the sample set of patterns that are used for system design. These patterns are also called model or prototype patterns. Secondly, there are the unknown patterns to be recognized in the actual application phase of a pattern recognition system. Typically, the same kind of data structures is used for the unknown patterns and the samples. In this section, we introduce the most important data structures for symbolic pattern representation.

Words of symbols, or *strings*, are the most fundamental data structure for pattern representation. The individual symbols in a string usually represent atomic pattern components. An example is shown in Fig. 1. In Fig. 1(a) the contour of a 2-D shape is approximated by a polygon using line segments of fixed length. If we start at the position that is marked by a dot and record the change in direction between two consecutive line segments in clockwise order, then we obtain the sequence of numbers shown in Fig. 1(b). If we consider only discrete values, say integers from the interval $[-180,180]$, then the sequence in Fig. 1(b) can be interpreted as a string of symbols.

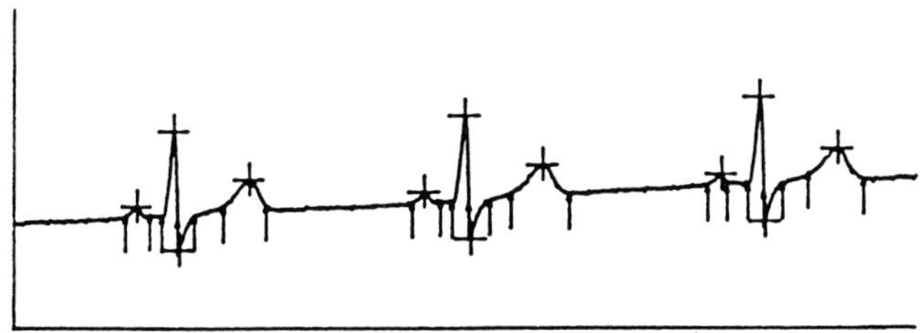

Fig. 2. An ECG pattern.

Another example is the string representation of the ECG in Fig. 2. (This example is taken, with some slight simplifications, from [89].) The curve in Fig. 2 has been segmented. Positive and negative peaks are marked by "+" and arrows indicate the borders between adjacent primitive elements. If we represent a positive peak by +, a negative peak by −, and a straight or parabolic curve segment by 0, then the ECG in Fig. 2 can be symbolically described by the string

$$0 + 0 + -0 + 0 + 0 + -0 + 0 + 0 + -0 + 0 \qquad (2.1)$$

A representation like in Fig. 1(b) or (2.1) can be very useful for recognizing the type of the object in Fig. 1(a), or for analyzing the ECG in Fig. 2 as to whether it is normal or abnormal. More powerful string representations include the use of attributes or relational symbols. Relational symbols do not have a direct physical manifestation but they represent relations between different pattern primitives. An example is the PDL formalism that will be discussed in greater detail in Section 6.4 [87].

Strings are a one-dimensional formalism but many patterns are inherently two- or more-dimensional. For this reason, more general data structures for pattern representation have been proposed. The most powerful class of symbolic structures for more-dimensional representation is graphs. A *graph* consists of a set of nodes and a set of edges. If a pattern is given in terms of a graph, then the nodes usually represent simpler subpatterns and the edges indicate relations between those subpatterns. The relations may be of spatial, temporal, or any other type.

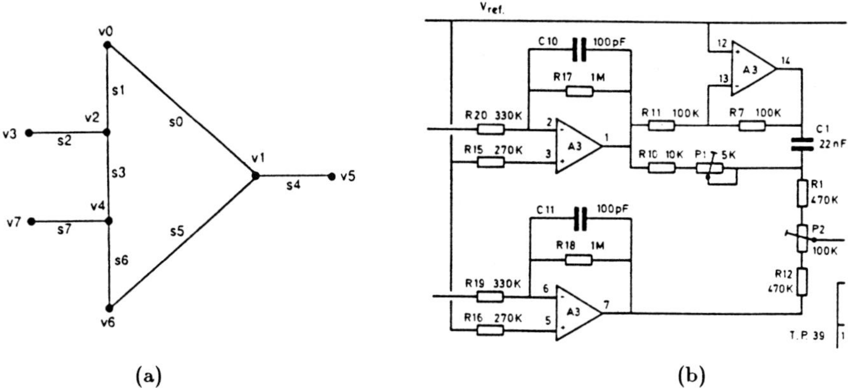

Fig. 3. (a) A graph representation of an amplifier; (b) a circuit diagram.

An example of pattern representation by means of graphs is shown in Fig. 3. (This example is taken from [65].) The graph in Fig. 3(a) represents an amplifier that may occur in a circuit diagram like in Fig. 3(b). The nodes in the graph represent vertices in the diagram, and there is an edge between two nodes in the graph if there exists a line connecting the two corresponding vertices in the drawing. Note that a representation like in Fig. 3(a) is invariant under translation, rotation, and scaling. It may be very useful for the recognition of the individual elements in a circuit diagram and for the inference of a logical description of a circuit diagram. For more details see [65].

For another example of symbolic image representation by means of graphs look at Fig. 4. In Fig. 4(a) the gray-level image of a three-dimensional scene is given. Figure 4(b) shows the needle map of the same scene. The needle map consists of vectors of unit length that are perpendicular to the three-dimensional surfaces of the objects in the scene. Figure 4(c) shows the result of segmenting the needle map into surface patches that are uniform in their curvature characteristics. This segmentation result can be symbolically represented by means of a region adjacency graph. In such a graph we have nodes, which represent surface patches, and edges, which indicate if two surface patches are adjacent to each other. The nodes of the graph in Fig. 4(c) are numbered from 1 to 6. There are two different types of edges in this example. Solid edges represent strong and dashed edges weak neighborhood relations. A neighborhood relation is strong (weak) if there is a long (short) common boundary between two adjacent surface patches. A graph representation like in Fig. 4(c) is very useful for deriving a symbolic scene interpretation. For more details see [57].

An important subclass of graphs is trees. A *tree* has three different classes of nodes, namely root, interior, and leave. There is exactly one root. It is defined by having only outgoing and no incoming edges. Each interior node has exactly one incoming and at least one outgoing edge. Leaves have exactly one incoming and no outgoing edge. Trees are intermediate between strings and graphs. In

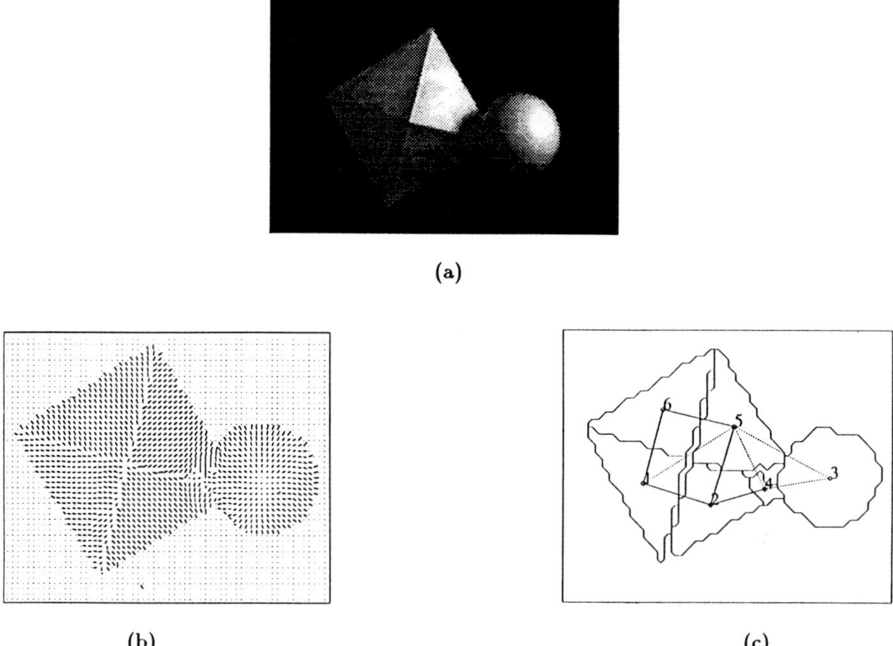

(a)

(b)   (c)

Fig. 4. (a) The gray-level image of a scene; (b) the needle diagram of (a); (c) the region adjacency graph of the scene after segmentation.

fact, each string constsiting of n symbols can be interpreted as a tree with one root, one leave, and $n - 2$ intermediate nodes. On the other hand, each tree is by defintion a graph that fulfills certain restrictions. Trees are interesting for pattern recognition applications as they are representationally more powerful than strings but algorithmically less expensive than graphs. Application examples of pattern representation by means of trees can be found in [79,80,91].

An *array* is a special type of graph where the nodes and edges are arranged in a regular form. Particular examples of arrays are rectangular arrays with 4- or 8-neighborhood, or hexagonal arrays. This type of data structure is particularly useful for low level pattern representation. Examples of array representations can be found in [109] and Chapter 1.6 by P. S. P. Wang in this volume.

3. String Matching

In this section, we consider methods for the comparison of two sequences of symbols and their application to pattern recognition. We start with some preliminary definitions and the basic algorithm for string distance computation in Section 3.1. Then we discuss the kind of pattern recognition problems string distance is useful for. Finally, various modifications and generalizations of the basic algorithm and some concrete applications of string distance will be presented in Section 3.3.

3.1. *Preliminary Definitions and the Basic Algorithm*

An *alphabet* T is a finite set of symbols. A *word*, or *string*, x over T is a sequence of symbols $x = x_1 \ldots x_n$ where $x_i \in T$; $i = 1, \ldots, n$. The *empty word* ϵ is the sequence with no symbols. The *length* of a word, denoted by $|x|$, is equal to the number of symbols contained in it. Thus $|\epsilon| = 0$. The set of all words over an alphabet is denoted by T^*. For example, if $T = \{a, b\}$, then $T^* = \{\epsilon, a, b, aa, ab, ba, bb, aaa, aab, \ldots\}$. The set of all words over an alphabet excluding the empty word is denoted by T^+, i.e. $T^+ = T^* - \{\epsilon\}$. We write a^n for $aa \ldots a$ (n consecutive occurrences of symbol a). The *concatenation* of two words $x = x_1 \ldots x_n$ and $y = y_1 \ldots y_m$ is given by $xy = x_1 \ldots x_n y_1 \ldots y_m$. Notice that $x\epsilon = \epsilon x = x$ and $(xy)z = x(yz)$ for any $x, y, z \in T^*$. Concatenation can be extended to sets of words X and Y by defining $XY = \{xy | x \in X, y \in Y\}$. For example, if $X = \{01, 10\}$ and $Y = \{00, 11\}$, then $XY = \{0100, 0111, 1000, 1011\}$.

Let T be an alphabet of symbols and $x = x_1 \ldots x_n \in T^*$, $y = y_1 \ldots y_m \in T^*$; $n, m \geq 0$. The distance between x and y is defined in terms of elementary *edit operations* which are required in order to transform x into y. In this section, we consider three different types of edit operations:

(a) *substitution* of a symbol $a \in T$ in x by a symbol $b \in T$ in y, $a \neq b$,
(b) *insertion* of a symbol $a \in T$ in y,
(c) *deletion* of a symbol $a \in T$ in x.

Symbolically, we write $a \to b$ for a substitution, $\epsilon \to a$ for an insertion and $a \to \epsilon$ for a deletion. Obviously, any given word x can be transformed into any other sequence of symbols y by repeated application of these edit operations.

Given two strings x and y, there is usually more than one sequence of edit operations transforming x into y. The edit operations are used for modelling variations which may change an ideal prototype string into its actual, noisy version. Depending on the particular application, certain distortions, i.e. edit operations, may be more likely than others. In order to take account of this observation, costs of edit operations are introduced. We define small costs for distortions that occur frequently and high costs for unfrequent distortions. Symbolically, we write $c(a \to b)$ for the cost of the substitution $a \to b$, $c(\epsilon \to a)$ for the cost of the insertion $\epsilon \to a$ and $c(a \to \epsilon)$ for the cost of the deletion $a \to \epsilon$. All costs are assumed to be real numbers greater than or equal to zero. Let $s = e_1, e_2, \ldots, e_k$ be a sequence of edit operations transforming string x into string y. The cost $c(s)$ of this sequence is defined as

$$c(s) = \sum_{i=1}^{k} c(e_i).$$

```
input:
x = x₁ ... xₙ ∈ T*, y = y₁ ... yₘ ∈ T*, cost (a → b); a, b ∈ T ∪ {ε}; (a, b) ≠ (ε, ε)
output:
d(x, y)
method:
begin
   D(0, 0) := 0;
   for i = 1 to n do D(i, 0) := D(i − 1, 0) + c(x(i) → ε);
   for j = 1 to m do D(0, j) := D(0, j − 1) + c(ε → y(j));
   for i = 1 to n do
      for j = 1 to m do
         begin
         m₁ := D(i − 1, j − 1) + c(x(i) → y(j));
         m₂ := D(i − 1, j) + c(x(i) → ε);
         m₃ := D(i, j − 1) + c(ε → y(j));
         D(i, j) = min(m₁, m₂, m₃);
         if m₁ = D(i, j) then set pointer from (i, j) to (i − 1, j − 1);
         if m₂ = D(i, j) then set pointer from (i, j) to (i − 1, j);
         if m₃ = D(i, j) then set pointer from (i, j) to (i, j − 1);
         end;
   d(x, y) := D(n, m);
end
```

Fig. 5. Algorithm for the computation of $d(x, y)$.

Given two strings x and y, we define the *distance* $d(x, y)$ between x and y by

$$d(x, y) = min\{c(s) | s \text{ is a sequence of edit operations transforming } x \text{ into } y\}.$$

According to this definition, the distance between x and y is the cost of the minimum cost sequence of edit operations that transforms x into y. Intuitively, it is not obvious how the minimum in the equation above can be found efficiently since there may be many sequences of edit operations which transform x into y. A solution to the problem is provided by the algorithm in Fig. 5. This algorithm computes the elements of the $(n + 1) \times (m + 1)$ matrix $D(i, j)$ row by row from left to right. The first row and first column of $D(i, j)$ are separately computed in an initial phase. The symbols x_i and y_j in x and y are denoted by $x(i)$ and $y(j)$, respectively; $i = 1, \ldots, n$; $j = 1, \ldots, m$. The basic idea is to find a minimum cost path from $D(0, 0)$ to $D(n, m)$. This path corresponds to the minimum cost sequence of edit operations for transforming x into y. In each element $D(i, j)$ of the path, the minimum accumulative costs are stored transforming $x' = x_1 \ldots x_i$ into $y' = y_1 \ldots y_j$, i.e. $D(i, j) = d(x', y')$. Hence, the lower right corner of the matrix, $D(n, m)$, holds the value $d(x, y)$. For any path element $D(i, j)$ there exist three potential predecessors, namely, $D(i, j − 1), D(i − 1, j − 1)$, and $D(i − 1, j)$. Going from $D(i − 1, j − 1)$ to $D(i, j)$ corresponds to a substitution of x_i by y_j, while a step from $D(i, j − 1)$ to $D(i, j)$ represents the insertion of y_j, and a step from

$D(i-1,j)$ to $D(i,j)$ the deletion of x_i. The pointers can be used in order to find, in a backward trace starting at $D(n,m)$ and proceeding to $D(0,0)$, the actual sequence of edit operations. Hence, the algorithm in Fig. 5 gives not only the distance $d(x,y)$ but also the way in which the symbols of x correspond with the symbols of y.

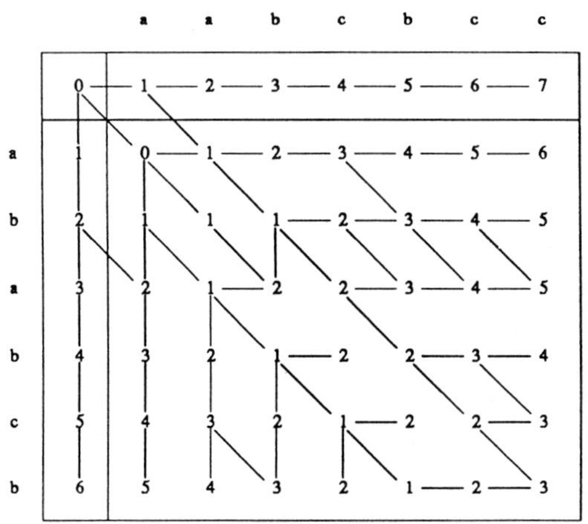

Fig. 6. An example of string distance computation.

As an example, consider the strings $x = ababcb$ and $y = aabcbcc$ and costs $c(a \to b) = c(\epsilon \to a) = c(a \to \epsilon) = 1, c(a \to a) = 0$ for any $a, b \in T; a \neq b$. The corresponding matrix $D(i,j)$ is shown in Fig. 6. The distance is $d(x,y) = 3$. There are three different paths which can be traced back from $D(n,m)$ to $D(0,0)$ since $D(n,m)$ and other matrix elements have more than one pointer. All these paths are equivalent in the sense that they represent a sequence of edit operations with minimum cost.

It is obvious from Fig. 5 that the computational complexity of the string distance computation is $O(nm)$ with respect to both time and space. The algorithm in Fig. 5 is also known as the *Levenshtein distance*, or *weighted Levenshtein distance* and has been reported in a number of papers [83,106].

3.2. *Pattern Recognition using String Distance*

In the application of string distance to pattern recognition, a pattern is represented by a sequence of symbols. Usually, the symbols correspond to primitive pattern components that are extracted in a preprocessing and feature detection phase. For examples of pattern representation by means of strings see Section 2.

One of the most frequent applications of string distance to pattern recognition is *nearest-neighbor classification* (NN-classification). In NN-classification we have two sets of prototypical strings $P = \{p_1, p_2, \ldots, p_N\}$, $N \geq 1$, $Q = \{q_1, q_2, \ldots, q_M\}$, $M \geq 1$, representing two different pattern classes. Given an unknown pattern represented by a string x, we assume that x is a noisy version of one of the prototype patterns and assign x to class P if the prototype that is most similar to x is from P. Otherwise, x is assigned to Q. Formally, the decision rule is

$$x \in \begin{cases} P & \text{if } min\{d(x,y)|y \in P \cup Q\} = d(x,p) \wedge p \in P \\ Q & \text{otherwise} \end{cases}$$

NN-classification can be generalized in a number of ways, for example, by considering more than two classes, introducing a threshold for rejection, or using k nearest neighbors, where $k > 1$. For more details, see [10].

The decision rule given above is easy to implement but it may take a long time on a sequential computer to calculate $d(x,y)$ for each prototype $y \in P \cup Q$. There are a number of ways to speed up the computation, either by reducing the number of prototypes or by avoiding the exhaustive search through the complete set of prototypes. For more details and references see [10].

A useful feature of the string distance computation algorithm according to Fig. 5 is that it not only gives a global measure of similarity between two strings but also allows to reconstruct all local deformations, i.e. all symbol substitutions, insertions, and deletions that are required to transform an ideal prototype into its noisy version that has been observed. In this way, not only the classification of an unknown pattern can be accomplished but also a qualitative description of an unknown input with respect to a reference pattern from the set of prototypes is achieved.

Another interesting pattern recognition problem to which string distance can be applied is unsupervised string *clustering*. Given a set $P = \{z_1, \ldots, z_N\}$ of (unclassified) strings, we want to divide P into subsets of similar strings. Formally, the goal is to find a partition of P into subsets $P_1, \ldots, P_M$ such that $P_i \cap P_j = \emptyset$ if $i \neq j$, and $\bigcup_{i=1}^{M} P_i = P$. Furthermore, it is required that the average distance between two strings within one subset is minimized while maximizing the average distance between strings belonging to different subsets. Basically, using the string distance measure introduced in Section 3.1, any of the numeric clustering techniques known from the literature can be applied to this problem. For more details on clustering see Chapter 1.1 by R. C. Dubes in this volume.

3.3. *Modifications of the Basic Algorithm and Further Comments*

Improving the time and space complexity of the algorithm given in Fig. 5 has been a subject of intensive research for many years. If only the edit distance between x and y but not the sequence of edit operations is required then it is sufficient to keep only two rows of the matrix $D(i,j)$, namely the row corresponding to the actual symbol of the string x and its predecessor. This results in a reduction of the space complexity to $O(min(n,m))$ [53]. An algorithm that runs in $O(nm/min(m,\log n))$ time has been described in [71]. It is based on the idea of splitting the matrix $D(i,j)$ into submatrices and precomputing all operations to be performed on these submatrices. Although the method is asymptotically quite fast, it may not be as efficient as the algorithm given in Fig. 5 for short strings. Another algorithm with a time and space complexity of $O(d \cdot min(n, m))$, where $d = d(x, y)$, has been given in [100]. Note that the complexity is dependent on the actual distance of the two strings under consideration. Hence, this algorithm may be the method of choice if it can be expected that the strings to be compared are similar. For the special cost function $c(a \to b) = 2, c(a \to \epsilon) = c(\epsilon \to a) = 1$, for any $a, b \in T, a \neq b$, the problem of string distance computation is equivalent to finding the longest common subsequence of two strings. There exist algorithms which solve this problem in $O(n \log n)$ time [56]. Relationships between substring and subsequence computation have been discussed in [26].

Motivated by either theoretical considerations or special applications, a large number of different versions of string matching methods have been developed. Some of them will be discussed below. The representational power of strings can be enhanced if a vector of attributes is added to each symbol. A string distance measure that takes such attributes into account has been proposed in [38]. For applications like the processing of human speech where strings represent sound waves sampled at certain time intervals, it is desirable to allow the stretching, or expansion, of one single symbol into k consecutive occurrences or, conversely, the compression of k consecutive identical symbols into one symbol without any cost. This problem is often referred to as elastic matching, or warping [1]. For other applications it may be desirable to consider the substitution, insertion, or deletion of a complete sequence of symbols rather than a single symbol as one basic edit operation [61]. Context dependent costs have been studied in [92]. In a recent paper, an algorithm for computing the edit distance of run-length coded strings has been given [15]. In most of these modified versions of string matching, only minor changes of the basic algorithm described in Fig. 5 are required. More references can be found in [2].

An open problem in string matching is the proper adjustment of the costs of the elementary edit operations. The distance of any two strings depends critically on these costs. Changing the edit costs only slightly may result in a drastic change in recognition performance. A novel approach to the adjustment of edit costs has been proposed in [14]. The idea is to consider the edit costs as parameters and to compute, in the training phase, string distances as a function of these parameters. Then, given some optimization criterion, for example, the minimization of the re-classification error, certain intervals of the parameters, i.e. edit costs, can be found where the optimization criterion does not change. Hence, the search for the optimal combination of edit costs can be restricted to one representative value from each interval and the blind combinatorial exploration of all possible combinations of edit costs can be avoided.

An application of string matching is the recognition of 2-D shapes [13,28,42,45, 69,99]. A particular subproblem in 2-D shape analysis is the matching of cyclic strings [48,68]. Other applications of string matching include character recognition [39], bar code reading [108], and human chromosome analysis [46]. Further references covering applications of string matching in speech recognition, molecular biology and other fields can be found in [83].

4. Graph Matching

Strings are a useful class of data structures as they allow the efficient implementation of many operations. On the other hand, they are limited in their representational power because they are intrinsically one-dimensional. To overcome this problem, graphs have been used as a more general method of pattern representation. In this section we introduce similarity measures on graphs and procedures for their computation. Two basic algorithms for subgraph isomorphism and error tolerant graph matching will be given in Sections 4.1 and 4.2, respectively. Further issues and applications will be discussed in Section 4.3. All concepts, like NN-classification or clustering, which have been discussed in Section 3.2 for the case of strings, can be applied to graphs if we use graph distance instead of string distance.

4.1. *Graph and Subgraph Isomorphism Detection*

A *directed graph* $g = (V, E)$ is a pair where V is a finite set of nodes and $E \subseteq V \times V$ is a finite set of edges. There is a directed edge from node x to node y if $(x, y) \in E$. A graph $g_1 = (V_1, E_1)$ is a *subgraph* of a graph $g_2 = (V_2, E_2)$, symbolically $g_1 \subseteq g_2$, if $V_1 \subseteq V_2$ and $E_1 \subseteq E_2$. Two graphs are *isomorphic* if they are, informally speaking, structurally identical. Formally, a *graph isomorphism* between $g_1 = (V_1, E_1)$ and $g_2 = (V_2, E_2)$ is a bijective mapping $f : V_1 \rightarrow V_2$ such that $(f(x), f(y)) \in E_2 \Leftrightarrow (x, y) \in E_1$. There is a *subgraph isomorphism* between g_1 and g_2 if there exists a subgraph $g_2' \subseteq g_2$ that is isomorphic to g_1. An example is shown in Fig. 7. The graph g_2 is isomorphic to g_3 and there is a subgraph isomorphism between g_1 and both g_2 and g_3.

In pattern recognition, we usually attach labels to the nodes and edges of a graph. The concepts of graph and subgraph isomorphism can be generalized to labeled graphs in a straightforward way by requiring that labels of corresponding nodes and edges be identical.

There are applications in pattern recognition where we have a model, or prototype pattern, represented by a graph g_1 and some observed data represented by a graph g_2, and where we want to find out whether the observed data is, or contains, an instance of the model. Formally, we want to know if there is a graph or subgraph isomorphism between g_1 and g_2. The algorithm given in Fig. 8 finds a subgraph isomorphism between two graphs g_1 and g_2 if there exists one. If g_1 and g_2 are isomorphic to each other then this algorithm will find, as a special case, an isomorphism between g_1 and g_2. Initially, we call this algorithm by **subgraph-isomorphism** $(g_1, g_2, \emptyset)$. It constructs a search tree in a depth-first manner.[a] As an example, the tree con-

---

[a]The nodes of this search tree must not be confused with the nodes of the two graphs g_1 and g_2 to be checked for subgraph isomorphism!

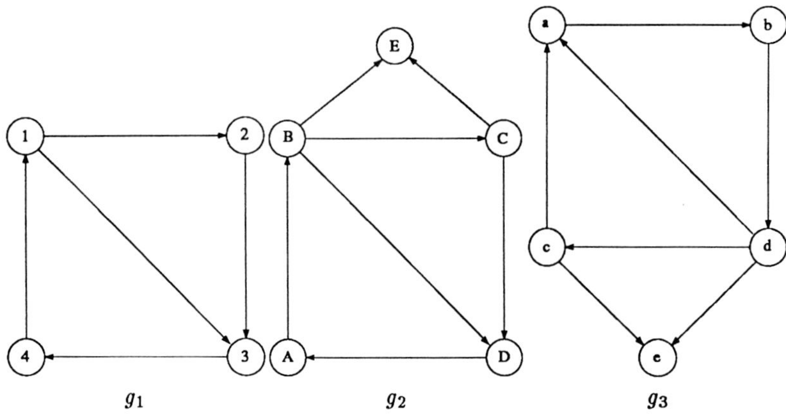

Fig. 7. An example: g_2 and g_3 are isomorphic to each other; g_1 is a subgraph of both g_2 and g_3.

```
subgraph-isomorphism (g1, g2, f)
parameters: two graphs g1 = (V1, E1) and g2 = (V2, E2);
            a partial mapping f : V1 → V2.
method:
begin
x := first element from V1;
for each element y from V2 do
    begin
    f' = f ∪ {x ↦ y};
    if for each (x, z) ∈ E1, where z is in the domain of f,
    (y, f(z)) is in E2 and
    for each (z, x) ∈ E1, where z is in the domain of f,
    (f(z), y) is in E2 then
        begin
        construct g1' from g1 by removing x,
        and g2' from g2 by removing y;
        if g1' is empty then output (f')
        else subgraph-isomorphism (g1', g2', f')
        end
    end
end
```

Fig. 8. An algorithm for subgraph isomorphism detection.

structed for the two graphs g_1 and g_2 in Fig. 7 is shown in Fig. 9. The subgraph isomorphism that is found in this example is $f = \{1 \mapsto B, 2 \mapsto C, 3 \mapsto D, 4 \mapsto A\}$.

Let $|V_1| = N_1$ and $|V_2| = N_2$. Then the algorithm given in Fig. 8 has to consider, in the worst case, $N_2(N_2 - 1) \cdot \ldots \cdot (N_2 - N_1 + 1)$ different nodes in the

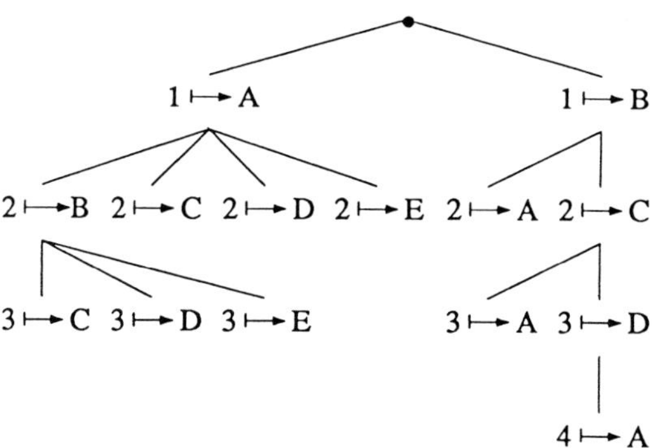

Fig. 9. The search tree constructed by the algorithm in Fig. 8 for g_1 and g_2 from Fig. 7.

search tree, resulting in a computational time complexity of $O(N_2^{N_1})$. There are some useful heuristics that can be used to speed up the algorithm in the average case. One of these heuristics was introduced by Ullman [101]. It aims at pruning the search tree. Ullman's rule says that, if $f(x) = y$, then any node $x' \in V_1$ with $(x, x') \in E_1$ or $(x', x) \in E_1$ can be mapped only to a node $y' \in V_2$ with $(y, y') \in E_2$ or $(y', y) \in E_2$, respectively. This simple rule can be utilized in the following forward checking procedure. We augment the algorithm given in Fig. 8 by a future error table $FET(x, y)$ where we provide one row for each node $x \in V_1$ and one column for each node $y \in V_2$. $FET(x, y)$ is a binary array where $FET(x, y) = 1$ means that x is eligible for being mapped to y, based on the partial mapping f constructed up to the actual state of the search. $FET(x, y) = 0$ if x cannot be mapped to y. Initially we set $FET(x, y) = 1$ if the in- or out-degree of x is not greater than the in- or out-degree of y, respectively. In the outer **for**-loop in the algorithm in Fig. 8 we consider only nodes $y \in V_2$ with $FET(x, y) = 1$. If the mapping f is augmented by $x \mapsto y$ then we update the future error table. First, we delete all 1's in the x-row except for the y-column, and delete all 1's in the y-column except for the x-row. This corresponds to the constraint that after assigning x to y, these nodes are no longer eligible for any other assignment. Secondly, we consider each future node x' from g_1, i.e. each node that is not yet in the domain of f. For each $y' \in V_2$ such that $FET(x', y') = 1$ we set $FET(x', y') = 0$ if Ullman's rule is violated. As soon as we encounter a row in the future error table that consists entirely of 0's, we backtrack one step, i.e. we return to the outer **for**-loop and continue with the next element from V_2.

An example of this forward checking procedure is given in Fig. 10. As one can easily verify, the left part of the tree in Fig. 9 is completely pruned as initially $FET(1, A) = 0$. Similarly, the assignments $2 \mapsto A$ and $3 \mapsto A$ in the right part of the tree are never tried. In summary, only four nodes in the search tree have to be explored with forward checking as opposed to 14 nodes without forward checking.

$FET(x, y)$ initially:

	A	B	C	D	E
1		1	1		
2	1	1	1	1	
3				1	
4	1	1	1	1	

$FET(x, y)$ after update at $1 \mapsto B$:

	A	B	C	D	E
1		1			
2			1	1	
3				1	
4	1				

$FET(x, y)$ after update at $2 \mapsto C$:

	A	B	C	D	E
1		1			
2			1		
3				1	
4	1				

search tree:

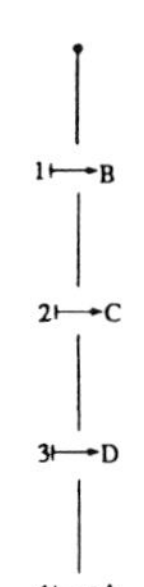

Fig. 10. Pruning the search tree by forward checking.

In the general case, a further pruning of the search tree can be achieved if we reorder the nodes of g_1 such that those nodes which have the fewest 1's in their future error table — ideally only one — are selected first.

For an arbitrary pair of graphs g_1 and g_2, we have to explore the full search tree consisting of $N_2(N_2 - 1) \cdot \ldots \cdot (N_2 - N_1 + 1)$ nodes in the worst case. There is evidence that no faster algorithm exists as subgraph isomorphism belongs to the class of NP-complete problems [41]. In many practical cases, however, a great reduction of the average computation time can be expected by forward checking or similar heuristics.

4.2. *Error Tolerant Graph Matching*

As patterns are usually distorted, the concepts of graph and subgraph isomorphism are limited in their applicability. As a generalization, error tolerant graph matching will be introduced in this section. First, we define a formal measure of graph distance. Then an algorithm for calculating this distance measure will be given. Throughout this section, we will consider graphs with labeled nodes and edges.

Let $g_1 = (V_1, E_1)$ and $g_2 = (V_2, E_2)$ be two graphs. An error tolerant match between g_1 and g_2 maps the nodes and edges of g_1 to g_2 such that g_2 is interpreted as a distorted version of g_1. Conceptually, this is similar to string matching as it was discussed in Section 3. Formally, an *error tolerant graph match* is a bijective function $f : \overline{V_1} \to \overline{V_2}$ where $\overline{V_1} \subseteq V_1$ and $\overline{V_2} \subseteq V_2$. For each node $n \in V_1 - \overline{V_1}$ we write $f(n) = \lambda$, and for each node $m \in V_2 - \overline{V_2}$ we write $f(\lambda) = m$. The intuitive meaning of this notation is that any node $k \in \overline{V_1}$ is substituted by $f(k) \in \overline{V_2}$, while any $n \in V_1$ with $f(n) = \lambda$ is deleted, and any $m \in V_2$ with $f(\lambda) = m$ is inserted.

Notice that the function f not only represents an explicit mapping betwen the nodes of g_1 and g_2, but also implicitly defines a mapping between the edges. If there is an edge $(n, m) \in E_1$ and $(f(n), f(m)) \in E_2$, then we say that (n, m) is substituted by the edge $(f(n), f(m))$. If there is an edge $(n, m) \in E_1$ but no edge $(f(n), f(m)) \in E_2$ then (n, m) is deleted, and if there is an edge $(n', m') \in E_2$ but no $n, m \in V_1$ with $(n, m) \in E_1$, $f(n) = n'$, and $f(m) = m'$ then (n', m') is inserted. Notice that both edge insertion and edge deletion may have several causes. For example, if (n, m) is deleted then this may be due to the fact that there exist nodes $f(n) \in V_2$ and $f(m) \in V_2$ but no edge $(f(n), f(m)) \in E_2$. Alternatively, it may be due to the fact that $f(n) = \lambda$ or $f(m) = \lambda$.

Substitutions, insertions, and deletions of both nodes and edges are the elementary transformations that change the graph representation of an ideal pattern into what will be actually observed. We define an individual cost for each such elementary transformation. Similarly to the string case, a cost is a non-negative real number that represents the likelihood of the corresponding elementary graph transformation. If a transformation is very likely to occur then its cost should be close to zero and, conversely, unlikely transformations should have high costs. We denote the cost for deleting (inserting) a node with label a by $DELNODE(a)$ $(INSNODE(a))$. The cost for substituting a node with label a by a node with label b are given by $SUBNODE(a, b)$. Similarly $SUBEDGE(a, b)$ is the cost for substituting an edge with label a by an edge with label b. Defining costs for edge deletion and insertion needs some additional considerations as these transformations are dependent on the nodes to which the considered edge is incident. When a node is deleted then all the edges originating or terminating in that node are deleted, too. Similarly, when we insert a node, then we usually insert also some edges in order to connect the new node with the rest of the graph. As a consequence, we distinguish between the cost of edge deletion or insertion without affecting any of the nodes to which the edge is incident, and the cost of edge deletion or insertion in case one or both of these nodes are deleted or inserted, too. Formally, $DELEDGE(a)$ $(INSEDGE(a))$ is the cost of deleting (inserting) an edge with label a if none of the nodes at the origin or the end of the edge is affected, and $DELNODE^+(a)$ $(INSNODE^+(a))$ is the corresponding cost if at least one of the nodes, to which the edge is incident, is also deleted (inserted). Given a set of particular distortion costs, we define the cost of an error tolerant graph match f, $cost(f)$, as the sum of the costs of the individual error transformations resulting from f. An example is shown in Fig. 11, where the labels for nodes and edges are $\{A, B\}$ and $\{X, Y\}$, respectively. Assume our error tolerant graph match is $f(1) = 3$, $f(2) = 4$, $f(\lambda) = 5$. Furthermore, assume

$$SUBNODE(A,B) = SUBNODE(B,A) = 1,$$
$$INSNODE(B) = 2, \ INSNODE(A) = 1,$$
$$DELNODE(A) = DELNODE(B) = 2,$$
$$SUBEDGE(X,Y) = SUBEDGE(Y,X) = 1,$$
$$DELEDGE(X) = DELEDGE(Y) = DELEDGE^+(X) =$$
$$\qquad DELEDGE^+(Y) = 1,$$
$$INSEDGE(X) = INSEDGE(Y) = INSEDGE^+(X) = INSEDGE^+(Y) = 1.$$
Then
$$cost(f) = SUBNODE(A,B) + SUBNODE(B,A) + SUBEDGE(X,Y)+$$
$$INSNODE(B) + 2 \cdot INSEDGE^+(Y) = 7.$$

Given g_1 and g_2 there are many different error tolerant graph matches, each having a different cost, in general. We define the *distance* of g_1 and g_2, $d(g_1, g_2)$, as the cost of the minimum cost error tolerant graph match between g_1 and g_2. That is,

$$d(g_1, g_2) = min\{cost(f)|f \text{ is an error tolerant graph match between } g_1 \text{ and } g_2\}.$$

One can easily see that $d(g_1, g_2) = 0$ if there exists a graph isomorphism between g_1 and g_2, provided that $SUBNODE(A,A) = SUBEDGE(A,A) = 0$ for all node and edge labels A. If also the cost of any insertion operation is equal to zero, then $d(g_1, g_2) = 0$ if there is a subgraph isomorphism between g_1 and g_2.

Given g_1 and g_2 and a set of elementary graph transformation costs, the actual computation of $d(g_1, g_2)$ can be done by a tree search procedure. A state in the search tree corresponds to a partial match that maps a subset of the nodes of g_1 to a subset of the nodes in g_2. Initially, we start with an empty mapping at the root of the search tree. Expanding a state corresponds to adding a pair of nodes, the first one from V_1 and the second one from $V_2 \cup \{\lambda\}$, to the partial mapping constructed so far. A final state in the search tree is a match that maps all elements of V_1 to $V_2 \cup \{\lambda\}$.

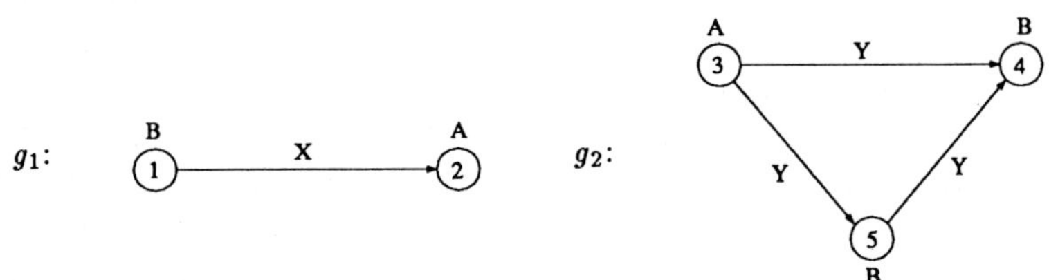

Fig. 11. An example of an error tolerant graph match (see text).

The complete search tree of the example in Fig. 11 is shown in Fig. 12. As we are eventually interested in the mapping with minimum cost, each state in the search tree gets assigned the cost of the partial mapping it represents. Hence, the

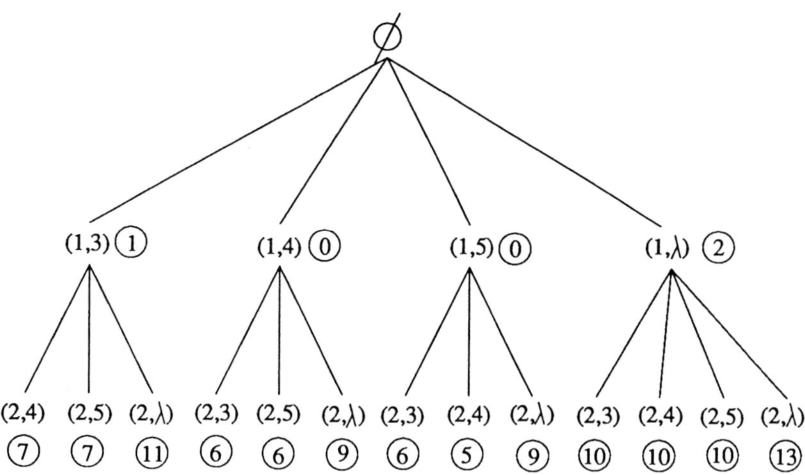

Fig. 12. The search tree for the computation of the distance between g_1 and g_2 in Fig. 11. The numbers in circles represent the cost of a state under the elementary transformation costs given in the text.

goal state to be found by the tree search procedure is the final state with minimum cost among all final states. From Fig. 12 we conclude that the minimum cost error tolerant match of g_1 and g_2 is given by the mapping $f(1) = 5$, $f(2) = 4$, $f(\lambda) = 3$. Its cost is 5 and, therefore, $d(g_1, g_2) = 5$. In Fig. 12 the full search tree for finding the minimum cost error tolerant graph match between g_1 and g_2 is shown. The construction of such a tree needs exponential time. Using a best first search procedure with heuristic information it is possible to find, in the average case, the minimum cost leave node without exploring the full search tree. For more details see [12].

4.3. Further Comments on Graph Matching

The idea of structural similarity, or distance, is not only applicable to strings and graphs, but also to trees. An overview of algorithms for tree matching can be found in [79]. As an important result, the time complexity of tree matching is only polynomial, as opposed to exponential of graph matching. An extension of graphs is called relational structures [85]. In a relational structure there may be any number of n-ary relations between the nodes. This allows more flexibility in modeling the patterns of a particular problem domain. Graphs are a special case of relational structures for $n = 2$. All algorithms for graph matching presented in the previous sections can be easily extended to relational structures. In many applications it is useful to augment a graph or a relational structure by attributes. Formally, we add an attribute vector $(x_1, x_2, \ldots, x_n) \in I\!\!R^n$ to each node and each edge. The number of attributes and the meaning of each individual attribute may be dependent on the particular node or edge label. It is straightforward to include attributes in the algorithm for graph matching discussed in the previous section. Another interesting generalization of graphs is random graphs [112]. A random graph is a graph with randomly varying node and edge attribute values. This concept allows the incorporation of statistical knowledge into the structural representation of patterns.

The algorithms for graph matching introduced in Sections 4.1 and 4.2 are based on tree search with exponential time complexity. Although heuristics for pruning the search tree can be used to speed up the computation, graph matching can become computationally intractable if large graphs are involved. One potential solution to overcome this problem is the application of stochastic optimization procedures to graph matching. In [52], simulated annealing has been proposed. As a great advantage, the time complexity of simulated annealing does not exponentially grow with the size of the underlying graphs. As a disadvantage, however, the procedure is not guaranteed to converge to the correct solution and there are a number of parameters the proper setting of which may critically influence the performance of the method. Another stochastic optimization procedure for graph matching has been described in [63]. Also the application of relaxation to graph matching has been proposed in the literature [23,60]. An iterative, suboptimal procedure avoiding the combinatorial testing of all possible assignments has been proposed in [102].

A new type of matching procedure for subgraph isomorphism based on the RETE algorithm has been described in [16]. The RETE matching algorithm was originally developed in the context of forward chaining production systems. Its basic idea is to compile the left-hand side conditions of a set of production rules into a network such that the changes that occur to the database of a rule-based system during runtime can be efficiently determined. It was shown in [16] that this idea can be applied to graph matching in a straightforward way. The new matching procedure is potentially more efficient than tree search based graph maching in the case of dynamically changing patterns.

Applications of graph matching include character recognition [64,66,112], schematic drawing analysis [63,65], 2-D shape analysis [12,49], stereo matching [51,52], scene interpretation of 3-D objects [43,60,86,113,114], dynamic scene analysis [16,22], machine learning [54], muscle tissue analysis [82], and chip inspection [107].

5. Hidden Markov Models

If the number of prototypes is large then the string matching procedure that was discussed in Section 3 may be computationally costly. Particularly, if some strings vary only slightly, it may be not economical to store them all as prototypes and to match them all against the unknown input. Hidden Markov models (HMMs) provide a solution to this problem. In this approach, one representative model for a class is generated from all its prototypes. Consequently, there is only one match per class to be done for an unknown input pattern. The variations that may exist between the different samples within a class are captured in terms of stochastic information, i.e. probability distributions. In Section 5.1, we introduce the basic theory of HMMs. Our notation will be similar to that used in [77]. Some extensions and application examples are presented in Section 5.2.

5.1. *Basic Theory of HMMs*

A *hidden Markov model* is a 5-tuple $M = (Q, V, A, B, \pi)$ where

$$
\begin{aligned}
Q &= \{q_1, \ldots, q_N\} \text{ is a finite set of states;} \\
V &= \{v_1, \ldots, v_M\} \text{ is a finite set of observation symbols;} \\
A &= (a_{ij}) \text{ is a matrix of state transition probabilities, i.e.} \\
  &\quad a_{ij} = prob(q_j \text{ at time } t+1 | q_i \text{ at time } t); \; i, j = 1, \ldots, N; \\
B &= (b_{jk}) \text{ is a matrix of observation symbol probabilities for} \\
  &\quad \text{each state } q_j \text{ and each symbol } v_k, \text{ i.e.} \\
  &\quad b_{jk} = prob(v_k \text{ at time } t | q_j \text{ at time } t); \\
\pi &= (\pi_i) \text{ is a vector of initial state probabilities, i.e.} \\
  &\quad \pi_i = prob(q_i \text{ at time } t = 1).
\end{aligned}
$$

A HMM can be interpreted as a formal device that generates a sequence $x = x_1 \ldots x_n \in V^+$ of observation symbols according to the following algorithm:

```
begin
choose an initial state q_{i_1} according to π;
t = 1;
repeat
    begin
    choose x_t = v_k according to b_{i_t k};
    choose the next state, q_{i_{t+1}}, according to a_{i_t i_{t+1}};
    end
until t > n
end
```

The HMM goes through a sequence of states $q_{i_1} q_{i_2} \cdots q_{i_n}$ and produces one observation symbol in each state. Intuitively, it is assumed that only the sequence $x = x_1 \cdots x_n$ of symbols can be externally observed. The states are hidden. The choice of the initial state, the transitions from one state to the next, and the selection of the observation symbol in a state are random processes. Given a HMM M, an observation sequence $x = x_1 \cdots x_n \in V^+$ is generated with a certain probability $prob(x|M)$. In the application of HMMs to pattern recognition problems, the observation sequence is identical with the unknown input pattern. If there are K different pattern classes and each class i is represented by one HMM M_i, $i = 1, \ldots, K$, then we are interested in finding that HMM M^* that maximizes the probability of the observation sequence, i.e.

$$
prob(x|M^*) = max\{prob(x|M_i)|i = 1, \ldots, K\}. \tag{5.1}
$$

If the *a priori* probabilities of the different classes, $prob(M_i)$, are available, then we maximize $prob(x|M_i) \cdot prob(M_i)$ instead of $prob(x|M_i)$.

Given a HMM M and an observation sequence $x = x_1 \cdots x_n = v_{k_1} \cdots v_{k_n}$ there is a naive procedure for the computation of $prob(x|M)$. Consider a sequence of states $q = q_{i_1} \cdots q_{i_n}$. Obviously,

$$prob(x|q, M) = b_{i_1 k_1} b_{i_2 k_2} \cdots b_{i_n k_n}, \quad \text{and} \tag{5.2}$$

$$prob(q|M) = \pi_{i_1} a_{i_1 i_2} a_{i_2 i_3} \cdots a_{i_{n-1} i_n}. \tag{5.3}$$

It follows from Bayes' theorem that

$$prob(x, q|M) = prob(x|q, M) \cdot prob(q|M). \tag{5.4}$$

Now the desired probability can be easily obtained by summing over all possible sequences of states:

$$prob(x|M) = \sum_{q \in Q^n} prob(x, q|M). \tag{5.5}$$

The problem with the implementation of Eq. (5.5) is the enumeration of all possible sequences of states, which has a time complexity of $O(N^m)$. Fortunately, there is a more efficient procedure that requires only $O(nN^2)$ time. Consider

$$\alpha_t(i) = prob(x_1 \cdots x_t, q_i \text{ at time } t|M), \tag{5.6}$$

which is the probability of being in state q_i at time t and having observed the partial string $x_1 \cdots x_t = v_{k_1} \cdots v_{k_t}$, given M. Obviously, $\alpha_t(i)$ can be inductively defined:

$$\alpha_1(i) = \pi_i b_{i k_1}, i = 1, \ldots, N \tag{5.7}$$

$$\alpha_{t+1}(j) = \left[\sum_{i=1}^{N} \alpha_t(i) a_{ij} \right] b_{j k_{t+1}}; t = 1, \ldots, n-1; j = 1, \ldots, N. \tag{5.8}$$

From (5.7) and (5.8), we finally get

$$prob(x|M) = \sum_{i=1}^{N} \alpha_n(i). \tag{5.9}$$

The procedure given by Eqs. (5.7) to (5.9) is known as forward algorithm. There is a similar algorithm, known as backward procedure, where we start with the last observation symbol x_n and work backwards to x_1 in order to compute $prob(x|M)$. Also a combination of the forward and backward procedure can be used for the computation of $prob(x|M)$, see [77].

Formula (5.9) is the basis for the implementation of the decision rule given in (5.1). If we are not only interested in the classification of an unknown pattern but also in its interpretation in the sense that we want to know which symbol corresponds with which state of the model, then we need to uncover the sequence of states that accounts for the given input pattern, i.e. the observation sequence. There are two well known approaches to solving this problem. First, one can select the states $q_{i_1}, \ldots, q_{i_n}$ that are individually most likely. This maximizes the expected number of correct individual states. The drawback of this approach is that it neglects any global constraints. For example, there may be forbidden transitions, i.e. $a_{ij} = 0$, for some pairs of states q_i and q_j. Such forbidden transitions are not taken into account if we individually maximize the likelihood of states. The second solution to the problem is to find the single best path, i.e. the state sequence $q = q_{j_1}, \ldots, q_{j_n}$ that maximizes $prob(x, q|M)$. This state sequence can be found by the Viterbi algorithm given in Fig. 13. This algorithm is similar to the forward algorithm based on (5.7) and (5.8).

The algorithm in Fig. 13 calculates two matrices $D(k, l)$ and $P(k, l)$. In each matrix there is one row for each state and one column for each observed symbol. $D(k, l)$ holds $prob(x', q'|M)$ where $q' = q_{j_1} \cdots q_{j_l}$ is the best state sequence for the partial observation $x' = x_1 \cdots x_l, k = 1, \ldots, N; l = 1, \ldots, n$. The matrices are computed one column after the other. The maximum element in the last column of

---

input: a HMM M and an observation sequence $x_1 \cdots x_n = v_{k_1} \cdots v_{k_n}$
output: a state sequence $q = q_{j_1} \cdots q_{j_n}$ that maximizes $prob(x, q \mid M)$
      and $p^* = max\{prob(x, q \mid M) \mid q \in Q^n\}$.
method:
begin /*initialization*/
for $i = 1$ to N do
begin
$D(i, 1) = \pi_i b_{ik_1}$;
$P(i, 1) = 0$
end
/*main loop*/
for $j = 2$ to n do
   for $i = 1$ to N do
      begin
      $D(i, j) = max\{D(l, j - 1)a_{li}b_{ik_j} \mid l = 1, \ldots, N\}$;
      $P(i, j) = argmax\{D(l, j - 1)a_{lj} \mid l = 1, \ldots, N\}$
      end
/*termination*/
$p^* = max\{D(i, n) \mid i = 1, \ldots, N\}$;
/*best state sequence*/
$j_n = argmax\{D(i, n) \mid i = 1, \ldots, N\}$;
for $l = n - 1$ down to 1 do
   $j_l = P(j_{l+1}, l + 1)$
end

Fig. 13. The Viterbi algorithm for finding the best state sequence.

$D(k,l)$ corresponds to the desired maximum value of $prob(x,q|M)$. Each element in $P(k,l)$ is a pointer to the previous column. Tracing back these pointers gives the desired best state sequence.

One important aspect in the application of HMMs to problems in pattern recognition is the inference of the probabilities $A, B,$ and π, given a set of samples from the same class. The classical approach to inferring these probabilities is the reestimation procedure by Baum–Welch. This procedure starts with some initial values for $A, B,$ and π and iteratively updates the probability distributions. It can be shown that the updated values $A', B',$ and π' increase $prob(x|M)$. This means that $prob(x|M') \geq prob(x|M)$, or in other words, the probability of x being generated by the given model M is increased in each iteration step until the procedure converges. The details of the inference procedure are given in [77,78].

5.2. *Further Comments on Markov Models*

In the application of HMMs the observed symbols usually represent primitive pattern components, similar to string matching as it was discussed in Section 3. The states of a model correspond to certain states in the recognition process of an unknown pattern. The availability of training procedures is a great advantage of HMMs. Despite this learning capability, there remain some problems for the designer of a pattern recognition system based on HMMs. For example, one has to define the observation symbols, i.e. the pattern primitives, and the number and meaning of states.

A generalized inference algorithm for HMMs has been described in ref. [97]. This inference procedure is applicable if the number of states and their reachability are not known *a priori*. The inference is a data-driven procedure that processes a finite number of sample strings sequentially using dynamic programming. It creates an HMM, called *Markov network*, with a unique starting and a unique absorbing state. The reachability of a node in the network is left-to-right, i.e. if $i < j$ then $a_{ji} = 0$. The output of each state is deterministic, i.e. there is exactly one symbol v_k for each state q_j such that $b_{jk} = 1$ and $b_{jl} = 0, l \neq k$. In the inference of the network, a single path is created for the first sample string. Then each additional sample is incorporated into the network via a string-to-network alignment which maximizes the probability of the sample as a network realization. The string-to-network alignment procedure is an extension of the string-to-string matching algorithm described in Section 3. The concept of forced landmark Markov networks has been introduced in [46].

Numerous applications of HMMs to speech understanding have been published in the literature. For more details see [77,78]. An application to character recognition has been reported in [62]. The recognition of two-dimensional shapes by means of HMMs has been described in [50,70]. Extensions of the basic HMM into two dimensions and applications to image analysis have been proposed in [25,27]. A hybrid approach combining Markov networks with concepts from statistical pattern recognition and its application to human chromosome analysis has been described in [47].

6. Formal Grammars for Pattern Class Representation

In string or graph matching, the symbolic representation of an unknown input pattern is compared to a finite number of prototype patterns. This procedure is computationally inexpensive in the sense that no particular learning or inference procedure for the generation of models is required. Instead, the symbolic representations of the prototypes in their "pure" form are used as models, or reference patterns. On the other hand, the comparison of an unknown pattern with all prototypes may be time consuming. If formal grammars are used for pattern class representation, this exhaustive comparison can be avoided. A formal grammar is a condensed representation of a potentially large set of prototype patterns. In a grammar, common substructures that occur repetitively within the same or within different prototypes, are represented only once. Besides, grammars are inherently capable of dealing with recursive pattern substructures. Essentially, a grammar is a set of rules that describe how the patterns of one or more classes can be built up, or generated, from simpler subpatterns. In the recognition process, it is checked if an unknown pattern can be generated by the rules of a given grammar. The term syntactic pattern recognition usually refers to the application of formal grammar for pattern class representation.

In this section, we first present basic definitions. Then we show how the concepts from formal language theory can be applied to pattern recognition problems. Two important generalizations of the basic grammar model, attributed grammars and higher-dimensional grammars, are introduced in Sections 6.3 and 6.4, respectively. Further extensions of the basic model and applications will be discussed in Section 6.5.

6.1. *Basic Definitions*

A *formal grammar* is a four-tuple $G = (N, T, P, S)$ where

> N is a finite set of *nonterminal symbols*,
> T is a finite set of *terminal symbols*,
> P is a finite set of *productions*, or *rewriting rules*, and
> $S \in N$ is the *initial* or *starting symbol*.

It is required that $N \cap T = \emptyset$; the union of N and T is called the *vocabulary* $V = N \cup T$. Each production $p \in P$ is of the form $\alpha \rightarrow \beta$ where α and β are called the *left-hand* and *right-hand side*, respectively, with $\alpha \in V^{+}$ and $\beta \in V^{*}$.

The most important part of a grammar is the set of productions. The intuitive meaning of a production $\alpha \rightarrow \beta$ is to replace the occurrence of the left-hand side in a word by the right-hand side, obtaining a new word thus. This idea can be formally captured as described below. Let G be a grammar and $\alpha \rightarrow \beta$ a production in P. Any word $v = x\alpha y$ with $x, y \in V^{*}$ can be *derived* into the word $w = x\beta y$. We write $v \to w$, and $v \overset{*}{\to} w$ if there exist words $v = v_0, v_1, \ldots, v_n = w$ such that $v_i \to v_{i+1}; i = 0, 1, \ldots, n-1$.

The *language* generated by a grammar G is given by

$$L(G) = \{x | x \in T^*, S \overset{*}{\to} x\}.$$

Thus in the derivation of an element $x \in L(G)$ we start with the initial symbol S and successively apply rules until a word is obtained which contains only symbols from the terminal alphabet.

Example 6.1. Consider the grammar $G = (N, T, P, S)$ where $N = \{S, A, B\}, T = \{a, b, c\}$, $P = \{S \to cAb, A \to aBa, B \to aBa, B \to cb\}$. This grammar generates the language

$$L(G) = \{ca^n cba^n b | n \geq 1\}.$$

For example, for the generation of the word *caacbaab*, i.e. $n = 2$, the following sequence of replacement steps are applied:

$$S \to cAb \to caBab \to caaBaab \to caacbaab.$$ $\square$

From this example we conclude that the language generated by a grammar is an infinite set of words in general, although all components of a grammar are finite.

A grammar is called *context-sensitive* if all its productions are of the form $xAy \to xzy$ where $x, y \in V^*; A \in N; z \in V^+$. This means that the nonterminal symbol A can be replaced by the non-empty string z only if it has x as left and y as right context. A grammar is called *context-free* if all its productions are of the form $A \to z$ where $A \in N; z \in V^+$. This means that any rule in a context-free grammar describes the replacement of a single nonterminal symbol A by a non-empty word z. This replacement is independent of the context of A. A grammar is called *regular* if any production is of the form $A \to aB$, or $A \to a$ where $A, B \in N; a \in T$. Obviously, regular grammars are a special case of context-free grammars where the right-hand side of each production fulfills additional constraints. A grammar is called *unrestricted* if none of the above restrictions applies. A language is of type i if it is generated by a grammar of type i. Apparently, the grammar in Example 6.1 is context-free and context-sensitive but not regular.

Let $G = (N, T, P, S)$ be a context-free grammar. A *derivation tree* is a tree where

(1) each node is labeled with a symbol $z \in V$ such that
   - each leaf is labeled with a symbol $a \in T$,
   - each non-leaf is labeled with a symbol $A \in N$,
   - the root is labeled with the initial symbol S;
(2) if there exists a node with label $A \in N$ such that its successor nodes
   are labeled with $x_1, \ldots, x_n \in V$ then there exists a production
   $A \to x_1 \cdots x_n$ in P.

We will use derivation trees for the representation of the derivation steps applied to generate a word $x \in L(G)$. Since context-free grammars play the most important role in syntactic pattern recognition, we will limit our considerations to this type of grammar.

Example 6.2. Consider the grammar in Example 6.1 and the word *caacbaab*. Its derivation tree is given in Fig. 14.   □

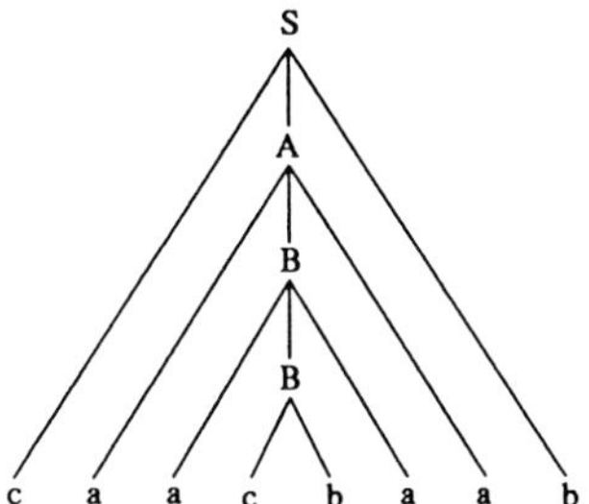

Fig. 14. An example of a derivation tree.

It can be easily seen that, for any grammar G and any word $x \in T^*$, there exists a derivation tree if and only if $x \in L(G)$. Hence, the task is to decide if $x \in L(G)$ is equivalent to the construction of a derivation tree. This problem is also called *parsing*. Detailed parsing algorithms will be presented in Section 7. More details about formal grammars and languages can be found in textbooks on formal language theory, for example [55].

6.2. *Formal Grammars for Pattern Recognition*

In the application of formal grammars to pattern recognition problems, the terminals of a grammar correspond to primitive, or elementary, pattern constituents which can be directly extracted from an input pattern by means of suitable preprocessing and segmentation methods. The set of grammar nonterminals corresponds to subpatterns of greater complexity, which are hierarchically built up from primitive elements. The process of constructing complex (sub)patterns from simpler parts is modeled by the productions of the grammar. Finally, the language generated by the grammar represents a whole class of patterns.

In order to illustrate these ideas consider the grammar in Example 6.1. Assume that the terminal symbols represent line segments of fixed length according to Fig. 15. A class of arrow-like shapes is shown in Fig. 16. Each shape can be represented by a string of terminal symbols if we follow the boundary of the pattern in a clockwise direction. We assume the starting point to be at the middle of the tail, as indicated by the small circles in Fig. 16. So the class of patterns in Fig. 16 can be represented by the set of words

$$\{cacbab, caacbaab, caaacbaaab, \ldots\}$$

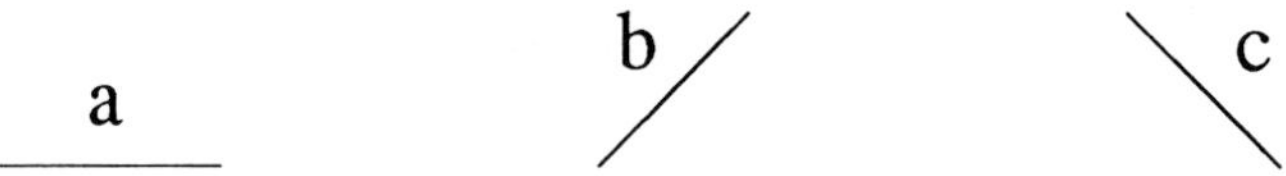

Fig. 15. Line segments as primitives for contour representation.

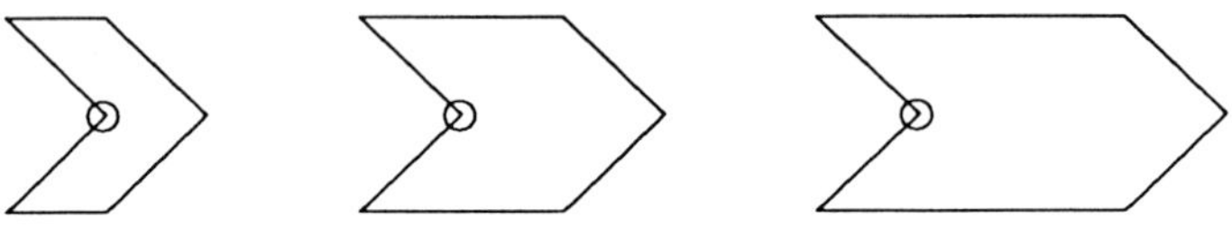

Fig. 16. Sample patterns of a class.

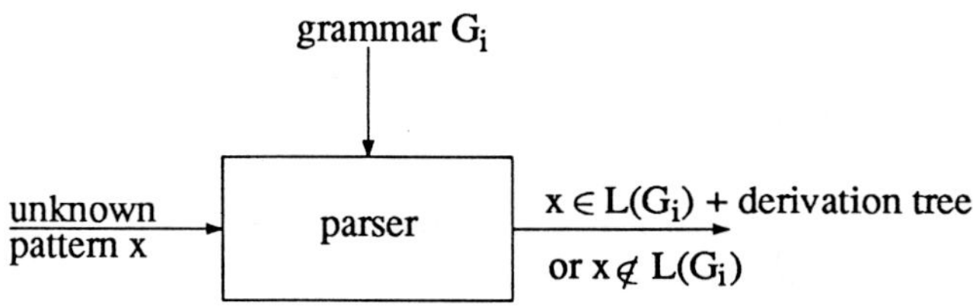

Fig. 17. Basic schema of syntactic pattern recognition.

which is identical to $L(G)$. The problem of classifying an unknown pattern x into one out of N classes can be solved by constructing a grammar G_i for each pattern class and parsing x according to each $G_i; i = 1, \ldots, N$. A graphical illustration is given in Fig. 17. If $x \in L(G_i)$ then it is decided that x belongs to class i. If there does not exist any G_i with $x \in L(G_i)$, then x is rejected. It is very important to notice that we get, as a byproduct of parsing, the derivation tree of x according to G_i if $x \in L(G_i)$. This derivation tree provides insight into how x is hierarchically composed of simpler subpatterns or pattern primitives. Hence, the syntactic approach can be used not only for classification, but also for deriving a hierarchical symbolic interpretation of the input patterns according to the underlying grammar.

6.3. *Attributed Grammars*

The rules of a formal grammar are a suitable tool for modeling structural properties of patterns, particularly for describing how a complex pattern is hierarchically composed of simpler constituents. However, there are deficiencies in adequately representing quantitative information such as the length and orientation of lines, textural parameters of regions, or 3-D surface orientation. A solution to this problem is provided by attributed grammars. The idea is to augment each grammar symbol $Y \in V$ by a vector of attribute values $m(Y) = (x_1, \ldots, x_k)$ where an *attribute* α is a function $\alpha : Y \to D_Y$ mapping a symbol $Y \in V$ into a domain D_Y of numerical values. We note that $x_1, \ldots, x_k \in D_Y$. An attribute vector can be interpreted as a numerical feature vector in the sense of statistical pattern recognition.

In considering a context-free production $A \to B_1 \cdots B_m$ with $A \in N, B_i \in V$ there is usually a relationship between the attributes of the symbols in the left-hand side and those in the right-hand side. Two cases must be distinguished. First, the attributes in the left-hand side can be dependent on those in the right-hand side (synthesized attributes), i.e. $\alpha(A) = f(\alpha(B_1), \ldots, \alpha(B_m))$, or the attributes in the right-hand side can be dependent on those in the left-hand side (inherited attributes), i.e. $\alpha(B_i) = g_i(\alpha(A)), i = 1, \ldots, m$.

Example 6.3. Suppose we have to take into account the length of the contour of the patterns in Fig. 16. This can be easily achieved by introducing the length l as an attribute for each grammar symbol. For the case of synthesized attributes, the productions of the grammar in Example 6.1 can be augmented by the following functions:

$$
\begin{aligned}
l(S) &= l(c) + l(A) + l(b), &\quad \text{for} \quad & S \to cAb, \\
l(A) &= 2l(a) + l(B), &\quad \text{for} \quad & A \to aBa, \\
l(B) &= 2l(a) + l(B), &\quad \text{for} \quad & B \to aBa, \\
l(B) &= l(c) + l(b), &\quad \text{for} \quad & B \to cb.
\end{aligned}
$$
$\hfill \square$

As one can observe from this example, the expressive power of grammar productions can be greatly enhanced by the use of attributes. As a matter of fact, attributed grammar has been preferred over the basic model introduced in Section 6.1 in almost any syntactic pattern recognition application.

6.4. *Two-Dimensional Grammar Models*

String grammars are very restricted if two- or even higher-dimensional patterns are to be described. There are several possible extensions leading to more effective representations of higher-dimensional patterns. Among the first of these extensions was the *picture description language* (PDL) [87]. In PDL, it is assumed that each primitive part of a pattern has exactly two points, called *tail* and *head*, where it can be linked to other primitives. Formally, we can represent each primitive by a directed and labeled edge of a graph. In the picture description language, there are four ways of joining a pair of primitives. These four binary operations are denoted by $+, -, \times$, and $*$. Additionally there are two unary operators. The four binary operations and their geometric interpretation are shown in Fig. 18. Each entity resulting from the linking of two primitives has a tail and a head, too, as shown in Fig. 18. So we can extend the four binary operations $+, -, \times$, and $*$ to higher level structures, i.e. we can use more complex PDL expressions as arguments of the operators. An example is shown in Fig. 19. In this example the unary operator $\sim$ is used, which reverses the tail and head of a primitive, or a more complex expression.

It can be shown that any directed graph with labeled edges can be represented by a PDL expression. Consequently, there exists a PDL expression for any pattern which can be represented by a graph of primitive elements. In the application of PDL to pattern recognition, a whole pattern class is represented by a grammar that generates a set of PDL expressions. Recognition of an unknown pattern is accomplished by first converting it to its symbolic PDL representation, and then by parsing it according to the underlying grammar.

Operator	Meaning	Geometric interpretation
$a + b$	head (a) linked to tail (b) head $(a + b) =$ head (b) tail $(a + b) =$ tail (a)	
$a - b$	head (a) linked to head (b) head $(a - b) =$ head (b) tail $(a - b) =$ tail (a)	
$a \times b$	tail (a) linked to tail (b) head $(a \times b) =$ head (b) tail $(a \times b) =$ tail (a)	
$a * b$	tail (a) linked to tail (c) and head (a) linked to head (c) head $(a * c) =$ head (c) tail $(a * c) =$ tail (a)	

Fig. 18. The four binary PDL operators.

Example 6.4. A grammar generating PDL expressions is
$$G = (N, T, P, S) \text{ with}$$
$$N = \{S, A, HOUSE, TRIANGLE\}$$
$$T = \{a, b, c, d, (,), |, -, \times, *, \sim\}$$
$$P : S \rightarrow A, S \rightarrow HOUSE,$$
$$A \rightarrow b + ((TRIANGLE) + c),$$
$$HOUSE \rightarrow (d + (a + (\sim d))) * (TRIANGLE),$$
$$TRIANGLE \rightarrow (b + c) * a.$$

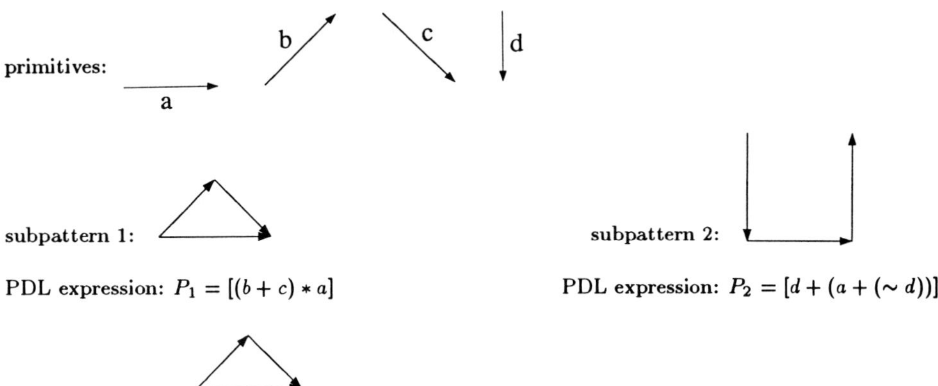

PDL expression: $P_1 = [(b + c) * a]$

PDL expression: $P_2 = [d + (a + (\sim d))]$

PDL expression $P = P_1 * P_2 = [(b + c) * a] * [d + (a + (\sim d))]$

Fig. 19. An example of a PDL expression and its corresponding pattern.

Obviously,

$$L(G) = \{b + (((b + c) * a) + c), (d + (a + (\sim d))) * ((b + c) * a)\}.$$

If we interpret the terminals a, b, c, and d according to Fig. 19, then this language represents the letter "A" and the pattern shown in Fig. 19. □

The main drawback of PDL is its limitation to only two concatenation points of subexpressions. This limitation is overcome by *plex structures* [33]. Such a structure consists of a list of primitive elements, a list of internal, and a list of external connections. In contrast with PDL, a primitive element in a plex structure may have any number of concatenation points. A *plex grammar* consists of nonterminals, terminals, a starting symbol, and a set of productions. The language generated by a plex grammar is the set of all terminal plex structures that can be derived from the starting symbol by means of productions. The application of plex grammars to pattern recognition is very similar to PDL. That is, a class of patterns is represented by means of a plex grammar. Any unknown pattern to be recognized is first converted to a symbolic representation in terms of a plex structure. Then this symbolic representation is parsed according to the underlying grammar.

In PDL and plex grammar, the generalization of string grammar into more dimensions is accomplished by introducing special relational symbols. A completely different approach is the use of a representational formalism that is inherently more-dimensional. Graphs are a universal data structure for the representation of two- or more-dimensional entities. If we use graphs instead of strings as fundamental data structures of a grammar, then we obtain a *graph grammar* [8,76]. Conceptually, a graph grammar is very similar to a string grammar. It consists of a set of nonterminal node and edge labels, a set of terminal node and edge labels, a starting graph, and a set of productions. The only major difference is the form of the productions. A production of a graph grammar consists of a left-hand and a right-hand side. Both the left-hand and right-hand side are graphs. In a context-free graph grammar, the left-hand side of each production is a graph consisting of a single node. The language generated by a graph grammar is the set of all graphs with terminal node and edge labels that can be derived from the starting graph by means of productions.

The application of a production of a grammar consists of replacing an occurrence of the left-hand side by the right-hand side. Usually, the occurrence of the left-hand side, which is to be replaced, is embedded via a number of edges in a host graph. After the replacement of the left-hand side by the right-hand side, this embedding is lost. In order to specify the embedding of the right-hand side after its insertion in the host graph, an embedding transformation is given for each production in addition to the left- and right-hand side.

Example 6.5. The productions of a graph grammar are given in Fig. 20. The only nonterminal node label is n and the only terminal node label is t. There are no edge labels in this example. The starting graph is a single node labeled with n.

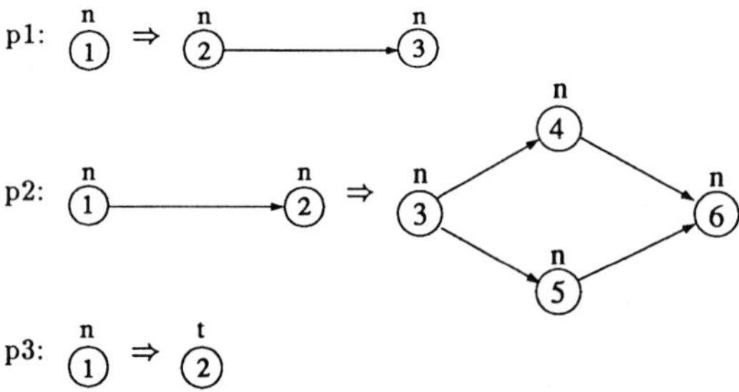

Fig. 20. Productions of a graph grammar. (The numbers inside the circles are node identifiers; node labels are n and t. The symbol $\Rightarrow$ is used instead of $\rightarrow$ to separate the left- and right-hand side of a production.)

The first production splits a node into a sequence of two nodes. The embedding of this production is such that any edge entering node 1 in the left-hand side is transformed into an edge entering node 2 in the right-hand side. Moreover, any edge leaving node 1 in the left-hand side is transformed into an edge leaving node 3 in the right-hand side. Production 2 generates two parallel nodes. Its embedding is such that any edge entering node 1 in the left-hand side is transformed into an edge entering node 3 in the right-hand side, and any edge leaving node 2 is transformed into an edge leaving node 6. Production 3 replaces the nonterminal label n by

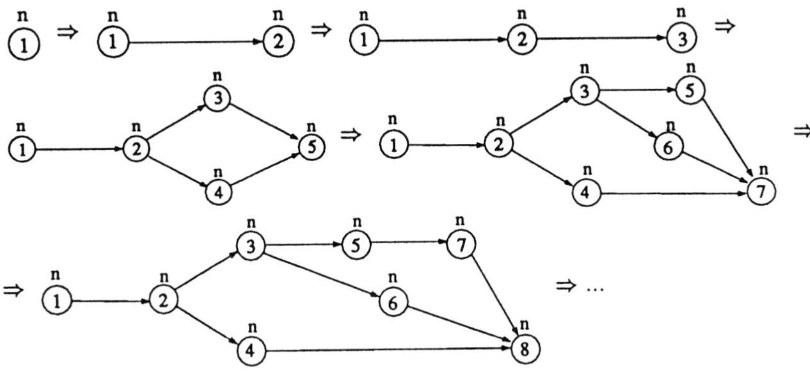

Fig. 21. A sequence of derivation steps using the productions given in Fig. 20.

the terminal label t and leaves everything else unchanged. Obviously, the language generated by this graph grammar is the set of all serial/parallel networks with one source and one sink node. An example of a sequence of derivation steps is shown in Fig. 21.   □

It can be concluded from Example 6.5 that graph grammars are a means for describing 2-D problems in a compact way, and at a problem-oriented level. Hence, it may be very convenient for the designer of a syntactic pattern recognition system to apply graph grammars. On the other hand, parsing of graph grammars is difficult and has a high computational complexity. One special case of graph grammars is *tree grammars* [37]. They provide a good balance between representational power and computational complexity. It is important to note that there exist normal forms of tree grammars that are parsable in linear time. Another special case of graph grammars is *array grammars*. More details on this type of grammar can be found in Chapter 1.6 by P. S. P. Wang in this volume and in [109].

6.5. *Further Comments*

There are applications where different pattern classes overlap each other. For example, in character recognition consider the classes "O" (capital letter O), "o" (small letter o), and 0 (digit zero). They can be distinguished only if some contextual information is taken into account. In terms of the syntactic recognition schema shown in Fig. 17, such an ambiguity means that there are elements x which are generated by different grammars. In such a situation the application of a *stochastic grammar* may be very meaningful [37]. A stochastic grammar G is characterized by the fact that for each element $x \in L(G)$ there is an associated number, $p(x|G)$, which tells us the probability that x is generated by G. If the *a priori* probability of G, $p(G)$, is known, then the following decision rule can be directly derived from

Bayes' theorem:

If $x \in L(G_i)$ and $x \in L(G_j)$ then decide

$$x \in \begin{cases} \text{class } i, & \text{if } p(G_i)p(x|G_i) > p(G_j)p(x|G_j) \\ \text{class } j, & \text{otherwise} \end{cases} .$$

The probability $p(x|G)$ is obtained by parsing x according to G, i.e. by finding the productions of G that are required to generate x, and multiplying their probabilities. A serious drawback of this approach is the requirement that a probability for each production must be known. The inference of these probabilities may be a difficult problem in a practical application. A theoretical study of the probability generating functions of stochastic context-free grammars has been described in [96].

An approach to dealing with ambiguities that is complementary to stochastic grammars has been proposed in [19]. Sometimes the main source of ambiguity lies not in the productions but in the classification of the terminals. In such a situation it may be useful to allow several interpretations for the same pattern primitive. That is, one observed primitive pattern is labeled with several terminal symbols. Depending on the degree of match between an ideal instance of a terminal and the pattern primitive actually observed, a measure of certainty is attached to each terminal symbol. In [19] a recognition procedure has been introduced that disambiguates the given input, i.e. it finds that interpretation that maximizes the global certainty and is compatible with the underlying grammar. Applications of this approach are noisy waveform analysis, extraction of distorted edges from images, and the interpretation of heart volume curves [17].

Many applications of syntactic pattern recognition have been reported in the literature. Earlier work has been described in [36,37]. More recent applications include character recognition [84,90,91,110,111,115], recognition of music notation [32], recognition of mathematical formulas [24], document analysis [104,105], line drawing interpretation [8,29,58,75], ECG-analysis [84,89], speech recognition [40, 103], 3-D object recognition [80], and DNA-sequence analysis [84]. For an overview of industrial applications see [6].

7. Syntactic Parsing

Given a grammar G describing our patterns of interest and a symbolic representation x of an unknown pattern, the problem of syntactic pattern recognition turns into parsing x according to G. Parsing means nothing else but deciding whether $x \in L(G)$ or not, and reconstructing the derivation tree of x according to G if $x \in L(G)$. A graphical representation of this recognition schema is shown in Fig. 17.

As context-free grammars play the most important role in practical applications, we restrict our considerations to this type of grammar in this section. It is known from the theory of formal languages that the parsing of context-free languages is a non-deterministic problem. In other words, the only parsing algorithms that run in linear time and space are for a subclass of context-free grammars. This subclass properly includes the class of regular languages. For a context-free grammar without any restrictions, parsing requires polynomial time and space. Note that for unrestricted grammars, the parsing problem is not even fully decidable. That is, there exists no general parsing algorithm working for any unrestricted grammar that is guaranteed to terminate in finite time for any input. Only if $x \in L(G)$, the algorithm will always terminate with the correct result. But the parser may enter an infinite loop if $x \notin L(G)$.

Existing parsing algorithms can be roughly classified into bottom-up and top-down methods. Bottom-up parsing algorithms attempt to reconstruct the derivation tree of an input string from bottom to top, i.e. from the leaves to the root, while top-down parsers proceed in the opposite direction. Of course, there exist hybrid approaches combining top-down with bottom-up parsing. In Subsection 7.1 we introduce Earley's algorithm, a well known top-down parser which has been widely applied in pattern recognition. There are numerous extensions and modifications of this algorithm. One important generalization that is able to deal with distorted strings is introduced in Subsection 7.2. Further extensions and other parsing algorithms are briefly discussed in Subsection 7.3.

7.1. *Earley's Parser*

This algorithm has originally published in [30]. A pseudocode description is given in Fig. 22. The algorithm takes as input a string $x_1 \cdots x_n$ of terminal symbols and a context-free grammar $G = (N, T, P, S)$. It generates lists $L(0), L(1), \ldots, L(n)$. That is, there is one list for each input symbol and one additional list $L(0)$. Initially all these lists are empty. A list item is of the form $(A \rightarrow \alpha \bullet \beta, j)$ where

(a) $A \rightarrow \alpha\beta$ is a production; $A \in N; \alpha, \beta \in V^*$.
(b) α is the first part of the right-hand side. It has already been recognized in the input string at the time the list item is generated.
(c) j is a pointer to list $L(j)$ or, equivalently, to input position j. The part of the input corresponding to α starts at position $j + 1$.

It follows from the algorithm that always $j \leq i$ if $(A \rightarrow \alpha \bullet \beta, j)$ is in $L(i)$. Furthermore, if $(A \rightarrow \alpha \bullet \beta, j)$ is in $L(i)$, then $\alpha \xrightarrow{*} x_{j+1} x_{j+2} \cdots x_i$. Substituting S for A, ϵ for β, 0 for j, and n for i, we observe that if $(S \rightarrow \alpha\bullet, 0)$ is in $L(n)$ then $S \xrightarrow{*} x_1 \cdots x_n$ or, equivalently, $x \in L(G)$. This means that for deciding whether $x \in L(G)$ or not, we sequentially generate all lists $L(0), L(1), \ldots, L(n)$. If a list item $(S \rightarrow \alpha\bullet, 0)$ is contained in $L(n)$, then we conclude that $x \in L(G)$. If no such item exists in $L(n)$, then $x \notin L(G)$. The time and space complexity of Earley's parser are $O(n^3)$ and $O(n^2)$, respectively. There exist algorithms for reconstructing one or all possible derivation trees from $L(0), L(1), \ldots, L(n)$ if $x \in L(G)$ [30].

---

input: $x = x_1 \ldots x_n \in T^*$ and a context-free grammar $G = (N, T, P, S)$
output: $L(0), L(1), \ldots, L(n)$
method:
begin
/* initialization: construction of $L(0)$ */
for each production $S \to \alpha$ in P add $(S \to \bullet\alpha, 0)$ to $L(0); \alpha \in V^+$;
repeat
   for each item $(A \to \bullet B\beta, 0)$ in $L(0)$ and for each production $B \to \gamma$ in P
   add $(B \to \bullet\gamma, 0)$ to $L(0); A, B \in N; \beta \in V^*; \gamma \in V^+$
until no new item can be added to $L(0)$;
/* main loop: construction of $L(1), \ldots, L(n)$ */
for $i = 1$ **to** n **do**
   begin
   /* subroutine scanner */
   for each item $(A \to \alpha \bullet a\beta, j)$ in $L(i-1)$ where $a = x_i$
   add $(A \to \alpha a \bullet \beta, j)$ to $L(i); A \in N; a \in T; \alpha, \beta \in V^*$;
   repeat
      /* subroutine completer */
      for each item $(B \to \gamma\bullet, j)$ in $L(i)$ and each item $(A \to \alpha \bullet B\beta, k)$ in $L(j)$
      add $(A \to \alpha B \bullet \beta, k)$ to $L(i); A, B \in N; \alpha, \beta \in V^*; \gamma \in V^+$;
      /* subroutine predictor */
      for each item $(A \to \alpha \bullet B\beta, j)$ in $L(i)$ and each production $B \to \gamma$ in P
      add $(B \to \bullet\gamma, i)$ to $L(i); A, B \in N; \alpha, \beta \in V^*; \gamma \in V^+$;
   until no new item can be added to $L(i)$
   end
end

Fig. 22. Earley's parsing algorithm.

Example 7.1. Consider the grammar in Example 6.1 and the input string $x = cacbab$. The parser constructs the following list items:

$L(0)$:	(1)	$(S \to \bullet cAb, 0)$	/* initialization	*/
$L(1)$:	(2)	$(S \to c \bullet Ab, 0)$	/* scanner from (1)	*/
	(3)	$(A \to \bullet aBa, 1)$	/* predictor from (2)	*/
$L(2)$:	(4)	$(A \to a \bullet Ba, 1)$	/* scanner from (3)	*/
	(5)	$(B \to \bullet aBa, 2)$	/* predictor from (4)	*/
	(6)	$(B \to \bullet cb, 2)$	/*predictor from (5)	*/
$L(3)$:	(7)	$(B \to c \bullet b, 2)$	/* scanner from (6)	*/
$L(4)$:	(8)	$(B \to cb\bullet, 2)$	/* scanner from (7)	*/
	(9)	$(A \to aB \bullet a, 1)$	/* completer from (8,4)	*/
$L(5)$:	(10)	$(A \to aBa\bullet, 1)$	/* scanner from (9)	*/
	(11)	$(S \to cA \bullet b, 0)$	/* completer from (10,2)	*/
$L(6)$:	(12)	$(S \to cAb\bullet, 0)$	/* scanner from (11)	*/

As item (12) in $L(6)$ is of the required form, we conclude that $x \in L(G)$.

7.2. *Error Correcting Parsing*

The recognition method which is based on the parsing algorithm introduced in the last section cannot be used if the patterns under consideration are distorted. Even in the case of a slight distortion, say, only one symbol has been changed, the parser will reject the input. To overcome this problem, error correcting parsing can be applied. The theoretical foundation of error correcting parsing is the string distance $d(x, y)$ introduced in Section 3.1. This distance measure can be generalized to the distance $d(x, L(G))$ between a string x and a language $L(G)$. For the computation of this generalized distance, an extension of Earley's parser can be used.

Let $G_1, \ldots, G_N$ be a set of grammars, representing one pattern class each. Given x, a distorted version of an unknown pattern, we compute N different distances $d(x, L(G_1)), \ldots, d(x, L(G_N))$ and decide for class i if $d(x, L(G_i))$ is the minimum of all $d(x, L(G_j)); j = 1, \ldots, N$. A threshold Θ can be defined such that x is assigned to the class i only if $d(x, L(G_i)) \leq \Theta$. Otherwise x is rejected. Next, we develop the procedure for the computation of $d(x, L(G))$.

In error correcting parsing the same set of error transformations as in Section 3.1 are used, namely the substitution, insertion, and deletion of terminal grammar symbols. For the purpose of simplification, we assume the cost of any of these transformations equal to one. Let G be a context-free grammar. Then we define

$$d(x, L(G)) = min\{d(x, y) | y \in L(G)\}. \tag{7.1}$$

Clearly, if $x \in L(G)$ then $d(x, L(G)) = 0$. Although Eq. (7.1) is conceptually simple, it is not obvious how $d(x, L(G))$ can be actually computed as $L(G)$ may be infinite. For the actual computation of $d(x, L(G))$ we first introduce the *covering grammar* of a grammar. Let $G = (N, T, P, S)$ be a context-free grammar. Its covering grammar $G' = (N', T', P', S')$ is obtained by the following steps:

1. $N' = N \cup \{S'\} \cup \{E_a | a \in T\}$.
   S' is the (new) starting symbol of the covering grammar. Each E_a is a new non-terminal that is a representative for the terminal a of the original grammar G.
2. P' is obtained by means of Steps (2.1) and (2.2):
   (2.1) For each production $p \in P$ of the form $A \rightarrow \alpha_0 a_1 \alpha_1 a_2 \cdots a_m \alpha_m$; $m \geq 0; \alpha_j \in N^*; a_i \in T$ add the production $A \rightarrow \alpha_0 E_{a_1} \alpha_1 E_{a_2} \cdots E_{a_m} \alpha_m$ to P'. This means simply the replacement of each terminal a by its corresponding nonterminal E_a, in each production.
   (2.2) For each symbol $a \in T$ we add the following productions to P':
   a) $E_a \rightarrow a$
   b) $E_a \rightarrow b$ for all $b \in T, b \neq a$
   c) $E_a \rightarrow \epsilon$
   d) $E_a \rightarrow bE_a$ for all $b \in T$, including $b = a$
   e) $S' \rightarrow S'a$
   f) $S' \rightarrow S$

By means of the productions in P' we are able to simulate any sequence of error transformations that may affect a terminal in the original grammar G. The productions under a) correspond to the case where no error has occurred. Cases b) and c) represent a substitution and a deletion, respectively. Insertions at the beginning and in the middle of a word are simulated under d), while e) and f) cover insertions at the end. The productions b)– e) are called *error productions*. Obviously, the covering grammar G' always generates T^*, i.e. $L(G') = T^*$, independently of the original grammar G. Hence, G' is certainly powerful enough to simulate any sequence of error transformations that may affect a word from $L(G)$.

The error correcting version of Earley's parser was originally published in [3]. A pseudocode description is given in Fig. 23. The input and output of the algorithm are the same as in the original version of Earley's parser. The list items in $L(i), i = 0, 1, \ldots, n$ are of the form $(A \rightarrow \alpha \bullet \beta, j, t)$ where A, α, β and j have the same meaning as before and t gives the minimum number of error transformations needed to derive α into $x_{j+1}x_{j+2} \cdots x_i$. The operation "add $(A \rightarrow \alpha \bullet \beta, j, t)$ to $L(i)$" is defined as follows:

if there is no item $(A \rightarrow \alpha \bullet \beta, j, \_\_)$ in $L(i)$
   then add $(A \rightarrow \alpha \bullet \beta, j, t)$ to $L(i)$
   else /* there is an item $(A \rightarrow \alpha \bullet \beta, j, t')$ in $L(i)$ */
      if $t' > t$
      then replace $(A \rightarrow \alpha \bullet \beta, j, t')$ by $(A \rightarrow \alpha \bullet \beta, j, t)$

If there exist items $(A \rightarrow \alpha \bullet \beta, j, t)$ and $(A \rightarrow \alpha \bullet \beta, j, t')$ in $L(i)$ that differ only in the number of error transformations, then two different derivations have been found by the parser. In such a case only the alternative with fewer error transformations is kept.

It can be shown that if $(A \rightarrow \alpha \bullet \beta, j, t)$ is in $L(i)$, then $\alpha \xrightarrow{*} a_{j+1}a_{j+2} \cdots a_i$ with t error productions and there exists no other such derivation with fewer error productions. It follows that $d(x, L(G)) = t$ if there is an item $(S \rightarrow \alpha \bullet, 0, t)$ in $L(n)$. This means that in the application of the error correcting parser we generate $L(0), L(1), \ldots, L(n)$ and look for an item $(S \rightarrow \alpha \bullet, 0, t)$ in $L(n)$. The existence of such an item is guaranteed and we know that $d(x, L(G)) = t$. The time and space complexity of the algorithm are $O(n^3)$ and $O(n^2)$, respectively. Similarly to the original version, the derivation tree of an input string x with respect to the covering grammar G' can be reconstructed from the lists $L(0), L(1), \ldots, L(n)$ [3]. This derivation tree will contain all error productions that are necessary to generate x. If the error productions are deleted, we obtain the corrected version of x, i.e. the string $y \in L(G)$ that satisfies Eq. (7.1). Hence, error correcting parsers are useful not only for the classification of distorted patterns, but also for the explicit correction of errors and for the structural interpretation of distorted input strings.

---

input: $x = x_1 \cdots x_n \in T^*$ and the covering grammar $G' = (N', T', P', S')$ of a context-free grammar.

output: $L(0), L(1), \ldots, L(n)$

method:

begin

/* initialization: construction of $L(0)$ */

for each production $S' \to \alpha$ in P' add $(S' \to \bullet\alpha, 0, 0)$ to $L(0)$; $\alpha \in V'^*$;

repeat

    /* subroutine predictor for $L(0)$ */

    for each item $(A \to \bullet B\beta, 0, t)$ in $L(0)$ and for each production $B \to \gamma$ in P' add $(B \to \bullet\gamma, 0, 0)$ to $L(0)$; $A, B \in N'; \beta, \gamma \in V'^*$;

    /*subroutine completer for $L(0)$ */

    for each item $(B \to \gamma\bullet, 0, t)$ and $(A \to \alpha \bullet B\gamma, 0, t')$ in $L(0)$ add $(A \to \alpha B \bullet \gamma, 0, t'')$ to $L(0)$, where

$$t'' = \begin{cases} t + t' + 1, & \text{if } B \to \gamma \text{ is an error production} \\ t + t', & \text{otherwise} \end{cases}$$

    $A, B \in N'; \alpha, \beta, \gamma \in V'^*$;

until no new item can be added to $L(0)$;

/* main loop: construction of $L(1), \ldots, L(n)$ */

for $i = 1$ to n **do**

    begin

    /* subroutine scanner */

    for each item $(A \to \alpha \bullet a\beta, j, t)$ in $L(i-1)$ where $a = x_i$ add $(A \to \alpha a \bullet \beta, j, t)$ to $L(i)$; $A \in N'; a \in T'; \alpha, \beta \in V'^*$;

    repeat

        /* subroutine completer */

        for each item $(B \to \gamma\bullet, j, t)$ in $L(i)$ and each item $(A \to \alpha \bullet B\beta, k, t')$ in $L(j)$ add $(A \to \alpha B \bullet \beta, k, t'')$ to $L(i)$, where

$$t'' = \begin{cases} t + t' + 1, & \text{if } B \to \gamma \text{ is an error production} \\ t + t', & \text{otherwise} \end{cases}$$

        $A, B \in N'; \alpha, \beta, \gamma \in V'^*$;

        /* subroutine predictor */

        for each item $(A \to \alpha \bullet B\beta, j, t)$ in $L(i)$ and each production $B \to \gamma$ in P' add $(B \to \bullet\gamma, j, 0)$ to $L(i)$; $A, B \in N'; \alpha, \beta, \gamma \in V'^*$;

    until no new item can be added to $L(i)$

    end

end

Fig. 23. Error correcting parsing algorithm.

Example 7.2. Consider the grammar $G = (N, T, P, S)$ where $N = \{S\}$, $T = \{a\}$ and $P = \{S \to aSa, S \to a\}$. This grammar generates the language

$$L(G) = \{a^n | n \geq 1, n \text{ is odd}\}.$$

The covering grammar $G' = (N', T, P', S')$ is given by

$N' = \{S, S', A\}$ (we write A instead of E_a),
P': $S \rightarrow ASA$, $S \rightarrow A$
  $A \rightarrow a$, $A \rightarrow \epsilon$, $A \rightarrow aA$,
  $S' \rightarrow S'a$, $S' \rightarrow S$.

Let the input string be $x = a$. Then the parser will produce the following lists:

$L(0)$:	$L(1)$:
$(S' \rightarrow \bullet S'a, 0, 0)$	$(A \rightarrow a\bullet, 0, 0)$
$(S' \rightarrow \bullet S, 0, 0)$	$(A \rightarrow a \bullet A, 0, 0)$
$(S \rightarrow \bullet ASA, 0, 0)$	$(S' \rightarrow S'a\bullet, 0, 1)$
$(S \rightarrow \bullet A, 0, 0)$	$(S \rightarrow A \bullet SA, 0, 0)$
$(A \rightarrow \bullet a, 0, 0)$	$(S \rightarrow A\bullet, 0, 0)$
$(A \rightarrow \bullet, 0, 0)$	$(S \rightarrow ASA\bullet, 0, 2)$
$(A \rightarrow \bullet aA, 0, 0)$	$(S' \rightarrow S' \bullet a, 0, 2)$
$(S \rightarrow A \bullet SA, 0, 1)$	$(S' \rightarrow S\bullet, 0, 0)$
$(S \rightarrow A\bullet, 0, 1)$	$\vdots$
$(S' \rightarrow S\bullet, 0, 1)$	$\vdots$
$(S \rightarrow AS \bullet A, 0, 2)$	and further items
$(S' \rightarrow S' \bullet a, 0, 1)$	$\vdots$

It follows from item $(S' \rightarrow S\bullet, 0, 0)$ in $L(1)$ that $a \in L(G)$. Furthermore, it can be concluded from $(S' \rightarrow S\bullet, 0, 1)$ in $L(0)$ that the empty string ϵ is not an element of $L(G)$, but $d(\epsilon, L(G)) = 1$. Clearly, it requires one insertion to change ϵ into a which is the most similar element in $L(G)$. $\qquad \square$

7.3. *Further Comments on Parsing*

Many syntactic pattern recognition applications are based on Earley's parser. Either the algorithm has been applied in its original or its error correcting version, or some modifications have been made to specifically tailor it to the particular problem at hand. Due to its flexibility and broad applicability, Earley's algorithm is perhaps the most important parsing method in pattern recognition. From a theoretical point of view, however, Earley's algorithm is just one example of a parser for context-free grammars among many others. Another algorithm, which is simpler and easier to implement, is that by CYK [4]. However, this algorithm requires the underlying grammar in a special form. Another method of syntactic analysis is direct parsing [94]. This method has a time complexity that is exponential in the length of the input string. Nevertheless, there are practical cases where a direct parser works faster than the algorithm by Earley and CYK. More parsers are described in [4].

The error correcting parser introduced in Section 7.2 is a straightforward extension of Earley's algorithm. Although the theoretical time and space complexity of the original algorithm and its error correcting version are the same, error correcting parsing will take more time in practical applications as it has to deal with the covering grammar which is larger than the original grammar. For an example, see the grammar in Example 7.2. A faster algorithm for error correcting parsing has been described in [67]. The theoretical time and space complexity is the same as for the parser described in Section 7.2, but the algorithm uses the original grammar instead of the covering grammar. All substitution, deletion, and insertion errors are directly incorporated into the list operations performed by the scanner and completer. This may result in a speedup over the parser presented in Section 7.2. More error correcting parsing methods are referenced in [93].

A problem that is closely related with parsing is *syntax directed translation*. Informally speaking, a syntax directed translation schema is a pair of grammars the rules of which are locked together to allow simultaneous derivation of a string and its translation. In pattern recognition applications, the rules of the first grammar are used in order to parse an unknown input x. Once the derivation of x has been reconstructed, the corresponding rules of the second grammar are applied to generate the translation of x. This method can be applied to error correction [95], the generation of symbolic interpretations of input patterns, or for image sequence analysis [31].

Many parsing algorithms for more-dimensional grammar models have been published in the literature. A recursive decent parser for PDL has been introduced in [87]. An extension of Earley's parser for plex grammars has been proposed in [18]. The parsing of tree grammars by means of tree automata including error correcting capabilities have been described in [37]. The parsing of graph grammars is a difficult problem if the underlying grammar is unrestricted. Parsing algorithms for special types of graph grammars have been reported in [35,59,81,88].

8. Additional Remarks

One important problem in syntactic pattern recognition is *grammatical inference*. It is the task of inferring a grammar from a sample set of patterns. Note that the inference problem does not exist in structural prototype matching if the samples are directly used as prototypes. In many practical situations, grammatical inference is done by hand in a trial and error fashion. But this procedure, which is mainly guided by intuition and experience, is somewhat unsatisfactory. A number of algorithms for automatically inferring a grammar from samples have been published in the literature. They can be categorized according to the type of grammar that is to be inferred. For example, there are inference algorithms for regular, context-free, tree, graph, array grammars, and others. For a comprehensive overview and a discussion of grammatical inference see [73].

Work on grammatical inference is theoretically very interesting and stimulating. But for real applications, most inference algorithms are limited for a number of reasons. First, grammatical inference is an ill-posed problem. Given a finite set of sample patterns, there are infinitely many grammars generating languages that contain the sample set as a subset. Therefore, one needs additional constraints for making a choice among the grammars that provide a potential solution. However, formal criteria for such constraints are difficult to find. Secondly, "pure" formal grammars, like regular or context-free grammars, are often not powerful enough to cope with real applications. Therefore additional heuristics have to be added to a grammar. However, such heuristics are beyond the scope of most inference algorithms. Thirdly, the design of a syntactic pattern recognition system requires not only the construction of a grammar but also the choice of pattern primitives and the selection of a grammar model, like string, tree or graph grammar with regular or context-free productions. Therefore, even if useful grammatical inference procedures were available, these tasks would still remain to be solved by means of intuition and experience. The situation in grammatical inference is similar to symbolic expert systems where, due to the lack of learning algorithms that are applicable to real world problems, the knowledge base of a system is usually designed by hand. Nevertheless, many successful applications of symbolic expert systems have been reported in recent years. Therefore, it can be argued that the lack of practical grammatical inference procedures is not a principal obstacle in the successful application of syntactic pattern recognition techniques.

Prototype matching, Markov models and grammatical parsing, which have been studied in this chapter, are just three classes of methods in pattern recognition. There are other classes of methods based on statistical decision theory, neural networks, or artifical intelligence, for example. Each category of methods has its strength and its limitations. In order to overcome these limitations, different approaches are combined sometimes. This results in a *hybrid method.* Typically, hybrid methods are able to achieve an effect which each method is individually incapable of. Examples of hybrid approaches are stochastic grammars, combining statistical decision theory and syntactic methods, or attributed grammars, integrating numerical feature vectors into symbolic data structures for pattern recognition. As other examples, consider prototype matching and error correcting parsing. If the costs of the basic error transformations are an inverse measure of distortion likelihood, then these methods can be understood as statistical decision procedures [98]. A comprehensive review and detailed discussion of hybrid methods can be found in [9].

9. Summary and Conclusion

The fundamental idea in syntactic and structural pattern recognition is the use of symbolic data structures like strings, trees, graphs, or arrays for pattern representation. These data structures allow the explicit description of relations between elementary pattern components and facilitate hierarchical models that represent how patterns or subpatterns are built up from simpler parts. Structural and syntactic models are particularly useful if the number of features, or primitive components, and their relations may vary from one individual pattern of a class to another.

In the syntactic and structural approach, the recognition of an unknown pattern is usually accomplished by comparing its symbolic representation with predefined object models. There are two principal ways for performing this comparison. In symbolic matching, a number of object prototypes are stored and the unknown pattern is directly matched with each of these prototypes. As a result of the matching process, we get a similarity measure between the unknown pattern and each prototype. This similarity measure may be used for nearest-neighbor classification. Additionally, symbolic matching yields a correspondence between the elementary parts and relations of the unknown input pattern and each prototype. This correspondence can be understood as an interpretation of the unknown input in terms of the prototype. A great advantage of structural matching is the fact that there is no need for grammatical inference. This makes the method applicable even if there are very few structural prototypes available. One of the problems in structural matching is the computational cost, which may be high in case of many prototypes. If graphs are used as data structures for pattern representation, then the exponential nature of the graph matching algorithms may be another hard problem.

In the syntactic approach, a grammar is used for the representation of predefined object models. The grammar is a compact representation of a potentially large set of object models in the sense that repetitive substructures occurring in one or in different models are represented only once. The comparison on an unknown input with a grammar is done by a parser. The parser checks if the unknown input string can be generated by the grammar and reconstructs the derivation tree. This derivation tree can be used as a hierarchical description of the input pattern. In order to deal with distortions, error correcting parsers have to be applied. Syntactic pattern recognition is based on well developed concepts from formal language theory. This theory provides many useful results about power, limitations, and computational complexity of recognition procedures. However, for many real world applications, the "pure" concepts from formal language theory need to be augmented by additional heuristics. Unfortunately, these heuristics do not fit any longer into the classical theory of formal languages. The inference of a grammar from a set of sample patterns is a problem that requires special attention as general procedures for practical problems are not available.

In the design of a structural and syntactic pattern recognition system, one has to make many decisions. One of these decisions concerns the data structures used for pattern representation. On the one end, there are strings as the cheapest but weakest solution with regard to algorithmic complexity and representational power, respectively. On the other end, there are graphs as the most expensive but most powerful solution. Another decision concerns the general approach, i.e. the use of a Markov model, or prototypes in conjunction with a symbolic matcher, or a grammar together with a parser. It has been shown in [9] that prototypes and grammars are theoretically equivalent for finite sample sets. That is, a grammar–parser combination can be simulated by a prototype–matcher combination and vice versa, in case of a finite sample set.

Despite this equivalence for finite sample sets one method can be superior to the other for a specific application. Generally, if the number of prototype patterns is small it is usually not possible to derive a grammar, or there is no need for a condensed class representation by means of a grammar. Instead, a direct representation by means of prototypes is preferable. On the other hand, if a large number of sample patterns is involved, pattern recognition and pattern class representation is perhaps more efficient if a grammar or a Markov model is used. One has to notice, however, that pattern class representation by means of a grammar or a Markov model makes sense only if there are common substructures in the patterns. For a practical application, the *existence* of common substructures among different patterns is not sufficient. Instead, such substructures must be *explicitly known* to the system designer. If this knowledge is not available, grammatical inference or the construction of a Markov model will not succeed and a prototype matching approach has to be adopted.

According to the experience made in pattern recognition during the past thirty years, *the* optimal class of algorithms does not exist. Therefore, structural and syntactic pattern recognition can give a contribution to only a limited number of problems. However, a synergetic effect can be expected from the combination of structural and syntactic methods with statistical, neural network, or artificial intelligence based approaches. Also, recent advances in computer technology, including parallel architectures, provide a promising basis for future progress in the field.

Acknowledgement

The author wants to thank U. Meier, P. Graber and B.T. Messmer who helped in typing and formatting the manuscript. Further thanks are due to G. Kaufmann and X.-Y. Jiang who provided some of the graphical illustrations. Figure 2 has been reprinted from [21], page 513, and Fig. 3 has been reprinted from [65], pages 2 and 7, with the permission of World Scientific Publ. Co. and the authors.

References

[1] K. Abe and N. Sugita, Distances between strings of symbols — review and remarks, *Proc. 6th ICPR*, Munich, 1982, 172–174.

[2] A. V. Aho, Algorithms for finding patterns in strings, in J. van Leeuwen (ed.), *Handbook of Theoretical Computer Science* (Elsevier Science Publishers B.V., 1990) 255–300.

[3] A. V. Aho and T. G. Peterson, A minimum distance error-correcting parser for context-free languages, *SIAM J. Comput.* 1 (1972) 305–312.

[4] A. V. Aho and J. D. Ullman, *The Theory of Parsing, Translation, and Compiling, Vol. 1: Parsing* (Prentice-Hall, Englewood Cliffs, NJ, 1972).

[5] H. Baird (ed.), *Pre-proceedings SSPR 90, IAPR Workshop on Syntactic and Structural Pattern Recognition*, Murray Hill, 1990.

[6] H. S. Baird, Industrial applications, in [21], 369–380.

[7] H. Baird, H. Bunke and K. Yamamoto (eds.), *Structured Document Image Analysis* (Springer Verlag, 1992).

[8] H. Bunke, Attributed programmed graph grammars and their application to schematic diagram interpretation, *IEEE Trans. Pattern Anal. Mach. Intell.* 4 (1982) 574–582.

[9] H. Bunke, Hybrid pattern recognition methods, in [21], 307–347.

[10] H. Bunke, String matching for structural pattern recognition, in [21], 119–145.

[11] H. Bunke (ed.), *Advances in Structural and Syntactic Pattern Recognition, Proc. SSPR 92* (World Scientific, 1992).

[12] H. Bunke and G. Allermann, Inexact graph matching for structural pattern recognition, *Pattern Recogn. Lett.* 1 (1983) 245–253.

[13] H. Bunke and U. Buehler, 2-D invariant shape recognition using string matching, *Proc. ICARCV '92, Second Int. Conf. on Automation, Robotics and Computer Vision*, Singapore, 1992.

[14] H. Bunke and J. Csirik, Inference of edit costs using parametric string matching, *Proc. 11th ICPR*, The Hague, 1992, Vol. 2, 549–552.

[15] H. Bunke and J. Csirik, Edit distance of run-length coded strings, *Proc. ACM Symp. on Applied Computing*, Kansas City, 1992.

[16] H. Bunke, T. Glauser and T.-H. Tran, Efficient matching of dynamically changing graphs, *Proc 7th Scandinavian Conference on Image Analysis*, Aalborg, 1991, 282–290. Extended version in P. Johanson and S. Olsen (eds.), *Theory and Applications of Image Analysis — Selected Papers from the 7th Scandinavian Conference on Image Analysis* (World Scientific, 1992) 110–124.

[17] H. Bunke, K. Grebner and G. Sagerer, Syntactic analysis of noisy input strings with an application to the analysis of heart-volume curves, *Proc. 7th ICPR*, Montreal, 1984, 1145–1147.

[18] H. Bunke and B. Haller, Syntactic analysis of context-free plex languages for pattern recognition, in [5], 57–77; also in [7].

[19] H. Bunke and D. Pasche, Parsing multivalued strings and its application to image and waveform recognition, in [74], 1–15.

[20] H. Bunke and A. Sanfeliu (eds.), *Advances in Syntactic Pattern Recognition, Special Issue of Pattern Recognition* **19**, 4 (1986).

[21] H. Bunke and A. Sanfeliu (eds.), *Syntactic and Structural Pattern Recognition – Theory and Applications* (World Scientific, 1990).

[22] J.-C. Cheng and H.-S. Don, A graph matching approach to 3-D point correspondences, *Int. J. Pattern Recogn. Artif. Intell.* 5 (1991) 399–412.

[23] J. K. Cheng and T. S. Huang, Image recognition by matching relational structures, *IEEE Proc. PRIP*, Dallas, 1981, 542–547.

[24] P. Chou, Recognition of equations using a two-dimensional stochastic context-free grammar, *Proc. SPIE, Visual Communications and Image Processing IV*, Philadelphia, 1989, 852–863.

[25] G. R. Cross and A. K. Jain, Markov random field texture models, *IEEE Trans. Pattern Anal. Mach. Intell.* 5 (1983) 24–39.

[26] J. Csirik and H. Bunke, Longest k-distance substrings of two strings, *Proc. 9th ICPR*, Rome, 1988, 69–71.

[27] P. A. Devijver and M. M. Dekesel, Learning the parameters of a hidden Markov random field image model: A simple example, in P. A. Devijver and J. Kittler (eds.), *Pattern Recognition Theory and Applications* (Springer Verlag, 1987) 141–163.

[28] I. Dinstein, G. M. Landau and G. Guy, Parallel (PRAM EREW) algorithms for contour-based 2D shape recognition, *Pattern Recogn.* **24** (1991) 929–942.

[29] D. Dori, A syntactic/geometric approach to recognition of dimensions in engineering machine drawings, *Comput. Vision Graph. Image Process.* **47** (1989) 271–291.

[30] J. Earley, An efficient context-free parsing algorithm, *Commun. ACM* **13** (1970) 94–102.

[31] T. I. Fan and K. S. Fu, A syntactic approach to time-varying image analysis, *Comput. Graph. Image Process.* **11** (1979) 138–149.

[32] H. Fahmy, A graph-grammar approach to high-level music recognition, TR 91-318, Queens University, Kingston, Ontario, 1991.

[33] T. Feder, Plex languages, *Inf. Sci.* **3** (1971) 225–241.

[34] G. Ferrate, T. Pavlidis, A. Sanfeliu and H. Bunke (eds.), *Syntactic and Structural Pattern Recognition* (Springer Verlag, 1988).

[35] M. Flasinski, Characteristics of edNLC-graph grammars for scene analysis, *Pattern Recogn.* **21** (1988) 623–630.

[36] K. S. Fu (ed.), *Syntactic Pattern Recognition, Applications* (Springer Verlag, 1977).

[37] K. S. Fu, *Syntactic Pattern Recognition and Applications* (Prentice Hall, Englewood Cliffs, NJ, 1982).

[38] K. S. Fu, A step towards unification of syntactic and statistical pattern recognition, *IEEE Trans. Pattern Anal. Mach. Intell.* **5** (1983) 200–205.

[39] K. S. Fu and S. Y. Lu, A clustering procedure for syntactic patterns, *IEEE Trans. Syst. Man Cybern.* **7** (1977) 734–742.

[40] P. Garcia, E. Segarra, E. Vidal and I. Galiano, On the use of the morphic generator grammatical inference (MGG) methodology in automatic speech recognition, *Int. J. Pattern Recogn. Artif. Intell.* **4** (1990) 667–685.

[41] M. R. Garey and D. S. Johnson, *Computers and Intractability: A Guide to the Theory of NP-Completeness* (W. H. Freeman, San Francisco, CA, 1979).

[42] T. Glauser and H. Bunke, Edge length ratios: an affine invariant shape representation for recognition with occlusions, *Proc. 11th ICPR*, The Hague, 1992, Vol. 1, 437–440.

[43] E. Gmuer and H. Bunke, 3-D object recognition based on subgraph matching in polynomial time, in [74], 131–147.

[44] R. C. Gonzalez and M. G. Thomason, *Syntactic Pattern Recognition* (Addison Wesley, Reading, MA, 1978).

[45] J. W. Gorman, O. R. Mitchell and F. Kuhl, Partial shape recognition using dynamic programming, *IEEE Trans. Pattern Anal. Mach. Intell.* **10** (1988) 257–266.

[46] J. Gregor and E. Granum, String segmentation and classification by forced landmark Markov networks, *Int. J. Pattern Recogn. Artif. Intell.* **5** (1991) 413–423.

[47] J. Gregor and M. G. Thomason, A hybrid pattern recognition approach applied to Chromosomal Band Structures, submitted for publication.

[48] J. Gregor and M. G. Thomason, Dynamic programming alignment of sequences representing cyclic patterns, to appear in *IEEE Trans. Pattern Anal. Mach. Intell.*

[49] P. M. Griffin and B. L. Denermayer, A methodology for pattern matching of complex objects, *Pattern Recogn.* **23** (1990) 245–254.

[50] Y. He and A. Kundu, 2-D shape classification using hidden Markov model, *IEEE Trans. Pattern Anal. Mach. Intell.* **13** (1991) 1172–1184.

[51] L. Herault, R. Horaud, F. Veillon and J.-J. Niez, Symbolic image matching by simulated annealing, *Proc. British Machine Vision Conference*, Oxford, 1990, 319–324.

[52] R. Horaud and T. Skordas, Structural matching for stereo vision, *Proc. 9th ICPR*, Rome, 1988, 439–445.

[53] D. S. Hirschberg, A linear space algorithm for computing maximal common subseqences, *Commun. ACM* **18**, 6 (1975) 341–343.

[54] L. B. Holder, D. J. Cook and H. Bunke, Fuzzy substructure discovery, *Proc. Conference on Machine Learning*, Scotland, 1992.

[55] J. E. Hopcroft and J. D. Ullmann, *Introduction to Automata Theory, Languages, and Computation* (Addison Wesley, Reading, MA, 1979).

[56] J. W. Hunt and T. G. Szymanski, A fast algorithm for computing longest common subsequences, *Commun. ACM* **20**, 5 (1977) 350–353.

[57] X.-Y. Jiang and H. Bunke, Recognition of overlapping convex objects using interpretation tree search and EGI matching, in *Applications of Digital Image Processing XII*, A. Tescher (ed.), *SPIE Proc.*, Vol. 1153, 1989, 611–620.

[58] S. H. Joseph, An entity extractor for images of engineering drawings, in [74], 217–228.

[59] M. Kaul, Computing the minimum error distance of graphs in $O(n^3)$ time with precedence graph grammars, in [34], 69–83.

[60] W. Y. Kim and A. C. Kak, 3-D object recognition using bipartite matching embedded in discrete relaxation, *IEEE Trans. Pattern Anal. Mach. Intell.* **13** (1991) 224–251.

[61] J. B. Kruskal and D. Sankoff, An anthology of algorithms and concepts for sequence comparison, in [83], 265–310.

[62] A. Kundu, Y. He and P. Bahl, Recognition of handwritten words: First and second order hidden Markov model based approach, *Pattern Recogn.* **22**, 3 (1989) 283–297.

[63] P. Kuner and B. Ueberreiter, Pattern recognition by graph matching — combinatorial versus continuous optimization, *Int. J. Pattern Recogn. Artif. Intell.* **2** (1988) 527–542.

[64] S. Lee and J.-H. Kim, Attribute stroke graph matching for seal imprint verification, *Pattern Recogn. Lett.* **9** (1989) 137–145.

[65] S.-W. Lee, J. H. Kim and F. C. A. Groen, Translation-, rotation- and scale-invariant recognition of hand-drawn symbols in schematic diagrams, *Int. J. Pattern Recogn. Artif. Intell.* **4** (1990) 1–25.

[66] S.-W. Lu, Y. Reng and C. Y. Suen, Hierarchical attributed graph representation and recognition of handwritten Chinese characters, *Pattern Recogn.* **24** (1991) 617–632.

[67] G. Lyon, Syntax-directed least-errors analysis for context-free languages: A practical approach, *Commun. ACM* **17** (1974) 3–14.

[68] M. Maes, On a cyclic string-to-string correction problem, *Inf. Process Lett.* **35** (1990) 73–78.

[69] M. Maes, Polygonal shape recognition using string matching techniques, *Pattern Recogn.* **24**, 5 (1991) 433–440.

[70] W. D. Mao and S. Y. Kung, An object recognition system using stochastic knowledge source and VLSI parallel architecture, *Proc. 10th ICPR*, Atlantic City, 1990, 832–836.

[71] W. J. Masek and M. S. Paterson, A faster algorithm for computing string-edit distances, *J. Comput. Syst. Sci.* **20**, 1 (1980) 18–31.

[72] L. Miclet, *Structural Methods in Pattern Recognition* (North-Oxford Academic, 1986).

[73] L. Miclet, Grammatical inference, in [21], 237–290.

[74] R. Mohr, T. Pavlidis and A. Sanfeliu (eds.), *Structural Pattern Analysis* (World Scientific, 1990).

[75] R. Mohr, A general purpose line drawing analysis system, in [21], 479–497.

[76] M. Nagl, A tutorial and bibliographical survey on graph grammars, in *Graph Grammars and Their Application to Computer Science and Biology*, Lecture Notes in Computer Science 73 (Springer Verlag, New York, 1979) 70–126.

[77] L. R. Rabiner and B. H. Juang, An introduction to hidden Markov models, *IEEE ASSP Mag.*, Jan. (1986) 4–16.

[78] L. R. Rabiner, A tutorial on hidden Markov models and selected applications in speech recognition, *Proc. IEEE* **77** (1989) 257–286.

[79] A. Sanfeliu, Matching tree structures, in [21], 145–178.

[80] A. Sanfeliu, Matching complex structures: The cyclic tree representation scheme, in [74], 67–93.

[81] A. Sanfeliu and K. S. Fu, Tree-graph grammars for pattern recognition, in H. Ehrig, M. Nagl and G. Rozenberg (eds.), *Graph Grammars and Their Applications to Computer Science* (Springer Verlag, Berlin, 1982) 349–368.

[82] A. Sanfeliu, K. S. Fu and J. Prewitt, An application of a graph distance measure to the classification of muscle tissue patterns, *Int. J. Pattern Recogn. Artif. Intell.* **1** (1987) 17–42.

[83] D. Sankoff and J. R. Kruskal, *Time Warps, String Edits, and Macromolecules: The Theory and Practice of Sequence Comparison* (Addison Wesley, Reading, MA, 1983).

[84] D. B. Searls and S. A. Liebowitz, Logic grammars as a vehicle for syntactic pattern recognition, in [5], 402–422.

[85] L. G. Shapiro and R. M. Haralick, Matching relational structures using discrete relaxation, in [21], 179–195.

[86] L. G. Shapiro and H. Lu, Accumulator-based inexact matching using relational summaries, *Mach. Vision Appl.* **3** (1990) 143–158.

[87] A. C. Shaw, Parsing of graph-representable pictures, *J. ACM* **17** (1969) 453–487.

[88] Q. Y. Shi and K. S. Fu, Parsing and translation of (attributed) expansive graph languages for scene analysis, *IEEE Trans. Pattern Anal. Mach. Intell.* **5** (1983) 472–484.

[89] E. Skordalakis, ECG analysis, in [21], 499–522.

[90] L. Stringa, A new set of constraint-free character recognition grammars, *IEEE Trans. Pattern Anal. Mach. Intell.* **12** (1990) 1210–1217.

[91] J. W. Tai and Y. J. Liu, Chinese character recognition, in [21], 415–451.

[92] E. Tanaka, A string correction method based on the context-dependent similarity, in [34], 3–17.

[93] E. Tanaka, Parsing and error-correcting parsing for string grammars, in [21], 55–83.

[94] E. Tanaka, M. Ikeda and K. Ezure, Direct parsing, in [20], 315–323.

[95] M. G. Thomason, Stochastic SDTS for correction of errors in context-free languages, *IEEE Trans. Comput.* **24** (1975) 1211–1216.

[96] M. G. Thomason, Generating functions for stochastic context-free grammars, *Int. J. Pattern Recogn. Artif. Intell.* **4** (1990) 553–572.

[97] M. G. Thomason and E. Granum, Dynamic Programming inference of Markov networks from finite sets of sample strings, *IEEE Trans. Pattern Anal. Mach. Intell.* **8** (1986) 491–501.

[98] W.-H. Tsai, Combining statistical and structural methods, in [21], 349–366.

[99] Y.-T. Tsay and W.-H. Tsai, Model-guided attributed string matching by split-and-merge for shape recognition, *Int. J. Pattern Recogn. Artif. Intell.* **3** (1989) 159–179.

[100] E. Ukkonen, Algorithms for approximate string matching, *Inf. Control* **64** (1985) 100–118.

[101] J. R. Ullman, An algorithm for subgraph isomorphism, *J. ACM* **23** (1976) 31–42.

[102] S. Umeyama, An eigen decomposition approach to weighted graph matching problems, *IEEE Trans. Pattern Anal. Mach. Intell.* **10** (1988) 695–703.

[103] E. Vidal, P. Garcia and E. Segarra, Inductive learning of finite-state transducers for the interpretation of unidimensional objects, in [74], 17–35.

[104] M. Viswanathan and M. D. Krishnamoorthy, A syntactic approach to document segmentation, in [74], 197–215.

[105] M. Viswanathan, Analysis of scanned documents — a syntactic approach, in [5], 450–459.

[106] R. A. Wagner and M. J. Fischer, The string-to-string correction problem, *J. ACM* **21** (1974) 168–173.

[107] J.-R. Wang and J.-G. Li, Double subgraph isomorphism method for matching LSI chip images, *Proc. 9th ICPR*, Rome, 1988, 945–947.

[108] Y. P. Wang and T. Pavlidis, Optimal correspondence of string subsequences, *IEEE Trans. Pattern Anal. Mach. Intell.* **12** (1990) 1080–1087.

[109] P. S. P. Wang (ed.), Special Issue on Array Grammars, Patterns and Recognizers, *Int. J. Pattern Recogn. Artif. Intell.* **3**, 3 & 4 (1989).

[110] P. S. P. Wang (ed.), Special Issue on Character and Handwriting Recognition: Expanding Frontiers, *Int. J. Pattern Recogn. Artif. Intell.* **5**, 1 & 2 (1991).

[111] G. Wolberg, A syntactic omni-font character recognition system, *Int. J. Pattern Recogn. Artif. Intell.* **1** (1987) 303–322.

[112] A. K. C. Wong, J. Constant and M. L. You, Random graphs, in [21], 197–234.

[113] A. K. C. Wong, S.-W. Lu and M. Rioux, Recognition and shape synthesis of 3-D objects based on attributed hypergraph, *IEEE Trans. Pattern Anal. Mach. Intell.* **11** (1989) 279–290.

[114] E. K. Wong, Three-dimensional object recognition by attributed graphs, in [21], 381–414.

[115] M. Zhao, Two-dimensional extended attribute grammar method for the recognition of hand-printed Chinese characters, *Pattern Recogn.* **23** (1990) 685–696.

Handbook of Pattern Recognition and Computer Vision, pp. 211–231
Eds. C. H. Chen, L. F. Pau and P. S. P. Wang

CHAPTER 1.6

A FORMAL PARALLEL MODEL FOR THREE-DIMENSIONAL OBJECT PATTERN REPRESENTATION

P. S. P. WANG

College of Computer Science, Northeastern University, Boston, MA 02115, USA

A new model for three-dimensional object pattern representation is introduced. It uses parallel techniques and significantly reduces the time required for dealing with three-dimensional image analysis problems. The fundamental properties, the concept of finite representations, the tools of three-dimensional feature extraction and segmentation are investigated and several interesting examples are illustrated. In addition to its importance in theoretical study, the model can also be applied to three-dimensional object recognition, image processing, and computer vision in industries, and the military and medical fields.

Keywords: Computer vision, image processing, 3-D array grammars, universal array grammars, parallel derivation and generation, object pattern representation.

1. Introduction

Three-dimensional vision and image processing problems have attracted wide attention among pattern recognition researchers. Because of its complexity and the large number of pixels involved in a 3-D image, sequential methods normally take too much time and are not very practical. One way to overcome such difficulty is to use "parallel processing", i.e. to handle several pixels at the same time (simultaneously) rather than one at a time. As mentioned in [12,13] by Rosenfeld, pictorial patterns often consist of subpatterns of simple(r) types that are combined in particular ways. The subpatterns in turn may consist of still simpler sub-subpatterns, and so on. This method of describing patterns in terms of subpatterns, sub-subpatterns, etc. is analogous to describing sentences in terms of clauses, phrases, etc. Since one can determine the syntactic structure of a sentence by parsing it in accordance with grammatical rules, this suggests that it should be possible to determine the structure of a pictorial pattern by "parsing" it in accordance with the rules of a "picture grammar".

Ever since such an idea was first raised by Minsky [10], there have been many syntactic and structural methods developed for solving scene analysis, image understanding, and pattern recognition problems [5,13]. But most of them are sequential and are limited to two-dimensional space only. Today, in dealing with more and

211

more complicated problems, there is a need to establish a more general model for higher-dimensional images and patterns.

In this chapter, we introduce such a formal model known as "array grammar", which has several advantages over others. It is a powerful pattern generative model generalized from Chomsky's phrase structure grammar [3]; it is sufficiently flexible to be extended to higher dimensions [6,18]; it has been shown to be more accurate than some other methods for clustering analysis [22]; it can be highly parallel and as powerful as tessellation or cellular automata [6,7]; and it can provide a sequential/parallel model that serves as a compromise between a purely sequential model, which takes too much time for large arrays, and a purely parallel one, which normally requires too much hardware for large digital patterns [20]. Besides, it provides a good setting to get inside and in-depth views of multi-dimensional parallel computation, automata, and language theory [11,14,15].

Part of this research was motivated by the work done at MIT [8,9,10] and a preliminary version of the idea was presented at the SPIE Conference on Intelligent Robotics and Computer Vision [2].

2. Preliminaries, Notations, Definitions and Examples

Let us take a look at the two objects in Fig. 1. From what we see, how do we describe them and what are the differences (and similarities) between the two objects? One probable answer is, "Both are wire-like objects, but Fig. 1(a) has

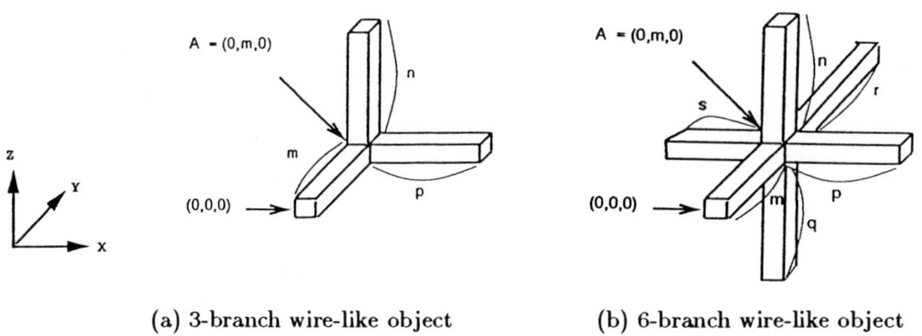

(a) 3-branch wire-like object   (b) 6-branch wire-like object

Fig. 1. Two multi-branch wire-like objects.

three branches while Fig. 1(b) has six, and they are of various lengths." More specifically, if we look at these objects from location (0,0,0), then (a) has a line segment stretching m units along the y direction, reaching location A, then from A it stretches p units in the x direction, and n units in the z direction. Likewise, object (b) can be perceived, understood, described, analyzed, memorized, and recognized in a similar way. This is from the human point of view. But what about the point of view of the computer? What is a mechanical way of describing an object like in Fig. 1 and can the computer understand it? This involves a very important concept in pattern recognition, known as *pattern representation*. Here we propose a structural approach using *universal array grammar* for three-dimensional objects representation.

We adapt the basic definitions and notations of array grammars from earlier work in the literature [2,18,24]. The concept of three-dimensional (3-D) array grammars will be introduced, which can be considered as an extension or generalization of their two-dimensional (2-D) counterparts. It also retains the basic properties of array grammars, i.e. all productions (generating, rewriting, or derivation rules) are isometric, i.e. both sides of each rule are geometrically identical. This is to avoid the shearing effect [18].

Definition 2.1. A 3-D array grammar is $G = (V_n, V_t, P, S, \#)$,

where V_n: set of nonterminals,

$\quad$ V_t: terminals,

$\quad$ $S \in V_n$: start symbol,

$\quad$ $\# \notin V_n \cup V_t$: blank symbol,

$\quad$ P: $\alpha \longrightarrow \beta$, $\alpha(x, y, z) \longrightarrow \beta\,(x, y, z)$.

During the derivation process, the locations of each nonterminal that should be applied (replaced) simultaneously (in parallel) are specified (by their (x, y, z) coordinates).

Definition 2.2. Parallel derivation. When a rule is applied, it is applied to all nonterminals of the α simultaneously (under specifications).

Let $\Longrightarrow$ be a binary relation between two sentential arrays (arrays that are connected and derivable from the initial sentential array with a singleton S surrounded by an infinite number of blank symbols in the 3-D cartesian space) α and β .

We say $\alpha \Longrightarrow \beta$ if α produces (generates, derives) β. Let $\stackrel{*}{\Longrightarrow}$ be a transitive and reflexive closure of $\Longrightarrow$. Then the language (pattern) generated by G is denoted as follows:

$$L(G) = \{ R \mid S \stackrel{*}{\Longrightarrow} R \in V_t^{++} \text{ according to the coordinates specified and are connected (according to the six-neighborhood)} \} .$$

The six direction vectors of 3-D space and the basic 3-D six neighborhood are shown in Fig. 2.

Example 2.1.

$G_u = (V_n, V_t, P, S, \#)$, where $V_n = \{S\}, V_t = \{*\}$ and

P: (1) $S \longrightarrow S\ S$

$\qquad \# \qquad S$

$\quad$ (2) $S \longrightarrow S$

$\quad$ (3) $\#S \longrightarrow S\ S$

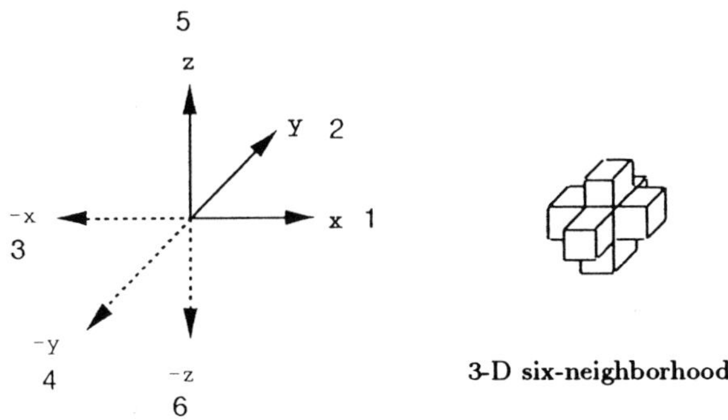

Fig. 2. 3-D space and six-neighborhood.

$$S \qquad S$$

(4) $\# \longrightarrow S$

(5) $Sa\# \longrightarrow Sa\,S$

[where a means the left symbol is above the right symbol]
(along z-axis)

(6) $Sb\# \longrightarrow Sb\,S$

[where b means the left symbol is below the right symbol]
(along z-axis)

(7) $S \longrightarrow *$

Without loss of generality, let us assume at the beginning that S is at $(0,0,0)$ (surrounded by an infinite number of $\#$'s). Notice that the neighborhood of $(0,0,0)$ is

$$\{(0,0,0),(1,0,0),(0,1,0),(0,0,1),(-1,0,0),(0,-1,0),(0,0,-1)\}\,.$$

In general, the neighborhood of $(i,\,j,\,k)$ is

$$\{(i,j,k),(i+1,j,k),(i,j+1,k),(i,j,k+1),(i-1,j,k),(i,j-1,k),(i,j,k-1)\}\,.$$

Consider $*$ as a unit cube where $* = $.

G_u works as a "universal 3-D array grammar" extended from 2-D universal array grammar introduced in [24]. In conventional syntactic pattern recognition, each pattern is characterized by a grammar. When the number of classes under consideration is very large, the grammar becomes very big, involving many grammar symbols and production rules evolved from combining all classes of patterns, each represented by its individual grammar. Therefore parsing a given input pattern is very time consuming. This in turn makes classification, clustering and recognition very difficult, if not impossible.

The 3-D universal array grammar introduced in this paper can overcome such difficulty. Each 3-D object can be represented by a 1-D string (parsing sequence).

Patterns of similar properties or characteristics are represented by the same or similar parsing sequence, as illustrated by the following examples.

Example 2.2. Consider the objects in Fig. 1. The parsing sequence of Fig. 1(a) is:

$$2^m A 1^p A 5^n 7 \,.$$

Since every sequence is terminated by the rule 7, from now on, we will omit '7' without loss of generality, and combining the two A's, make a more compact representation for Fig. 1(a) as:

$$2^m A (1^p 5^n) \,.$$

Similarly the parsing sequence of Fig. 1(b) is:

$$2^m A (1^p 2^r 3^s 5^n 6^q) \,.$$

3. Finite Representation of Infinite Class of Objects

The formulas shown in Section 2 actually illustrate the concept of *finite representation* of objects. For instance, in Example 2.2, the last formula represents an infinite class of wire-like line drawing objects with six branches (arms) of various lengths denoted by variables m, n, p, q, r and s along $-y$, z, x, $-z$, y and $-x$ axis respectively. When $m = p = r = s = n = q$, i.e. $2^m A (1^m 2^m 3^m 5^m 6^m)$, it represents a proper *infinite* subclass of six-branch wire-like objects whose six arms are all of equal length.

This idea can be used for describing many interesting real 3-D objects. Here are some more examples.

Example 3.1. A track hurdle is shown in Fig. 3, together with its digitized 3-D object as a 3-D array.

Its pattern representation is:

$$2^m A \; 1^p \{A, B\} 5^{n+q}(x \geq 0, \, m, \, n + q \geq z \geq n) 1^p B 4^m \,.$$

Notice that this is a *finite representation*, which actually characterizes an *infinite* class of objects sharing some common patterns (structural shapes) with various side lengths, e.g. they can have the same base width denoted by the variable p, but different heights denoted by the variable n, and vice versa. Also notice that all locations A, B, C, D are relative coordinates from $(0, 0, 0)$ and can be easily computed, e.g. A is reached after stretching m units along the y-axis (2), therefore A is $(0, m, 0)$ etc. Figure 4 shows three different values of n, representing three different types of track hurdles. Also notice that this finite representation is better and simpler than a grammar, which is very difficult to find and will involve too many nonterminal symbols and rewriting rules for patterns sensitive to the "lengths" even in 2-D cases [3,21,25].

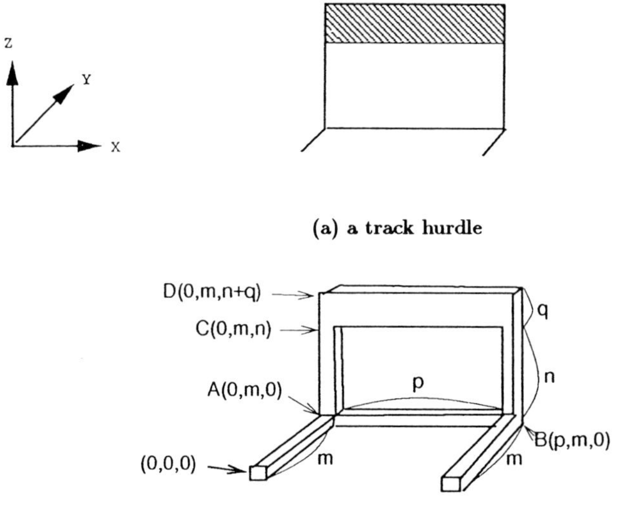

(a) a track hurdle

(b) the digitized array object of (a)

Fig. 3. A track hurdle and its digitized 3-D array object version.

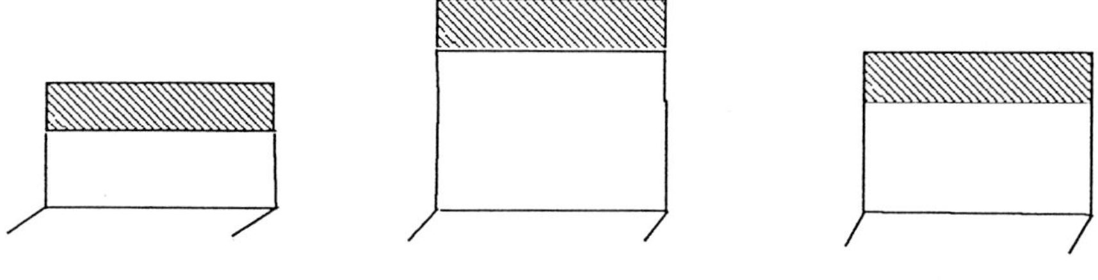

(a) 200 m dash low hurdle   (b) 110 m dash high hurdle   (c) 400 m dash middle hurdle

Fig. 4. Three types of track hurdles in different height values from Fig. 3.

Example 3.2. Several illustrations of n-tooth rakes are shown in Figs. 5 and 6. The original three-tooth rake (x, y, z) cartesian coordinates are shown as follows (for $m = 9$, $p = 4$, $n = 3$):

$$\{(0,0,0),(0,1,0),(0,2,0),(0,3,0),(0,4,0),(0,5,0),(0,6,0),(0,7,0),(0,8,0),$$
$$(0,9,0),(1,9,0),(2,9,0),(3,9,0),(4,9,0),(-1,9,0),(-2,9,0),(-3,9,0),(-4,9,0),$$
$$(4,9,1),(4,9,2),(4,9,3),(0,9,1),(0,9,2),(0,9,3),(-4,9,1),(-4,9,2),(-4,9,3)\}$$

Notice that in contrast to the cartesian coordinates, its string pattern representation,

$$2^9 A(1^4 3^4)\{A, B, C\}5^3 ,$$

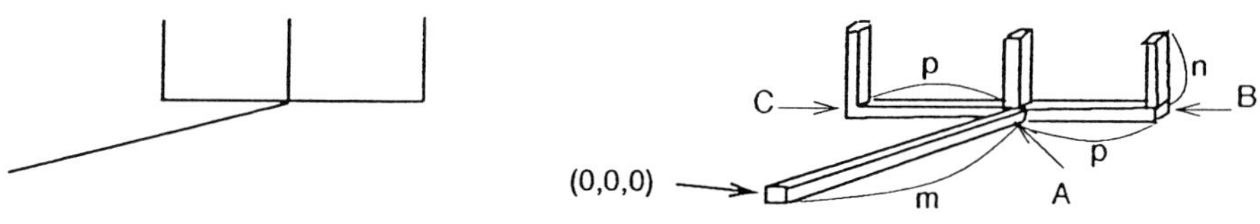

(a) three-tooth rake   (b) the 3-D array object of (a)

Fig. 5. A three-tooth rake and its 3-D array object.

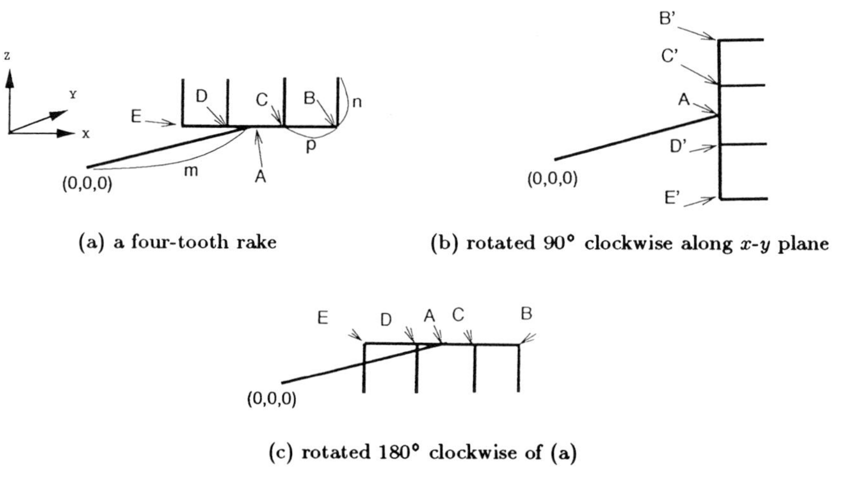

(a) a four-tooth rake   (b) rotated 90° clockwise along *x-y* plane

(c) rotated 180° clockwise of (a)

Fig. 6. A four-tooth rake and its rotations.

is a better way to describe the object, and is easier to understand, manipulate and be compared with other objects. Its structural similarities and differences are clearly reflected from the pattern representation when compared with other objects including its variations and rotations as shown in Figs. 6(a), (b) and (c), whose string representations are as follows:

$$(a)\colon 2^m A(1^{1.5p} 3^{1.5p})\{B, C, D, E\}5^n ,$$
$$(b)\colon 2^m A(5^{1.5p} 6^{1.5p})\{B', C', D', E'\}1^n ,$$
$$(c)\colon 2^m A(1^{1.5p} 3^{1.5p})\{B, C, D, E\}6^n .$$

4. Parallelism in 3-D UAG

This *finite representation* not only works for wire-like line-drawing objects, but also for other interesting non-wire-like objects. In fact, its property and advantage of *parallelism* will be even more obvious for describing these non-wire-like objects.

Example 4.1. Figure 7 shows a solid $5 * 5 * 5$ cube, whose derivation process is illustrated as follows:

$$S \# \overset{1}{\Rightarrow} S S \# \overset{1}{\Rightarrow} S S S \# \overset{1}{\Rightarrow} S S S S \# \overset{1}{\Rightarrow} \#\#\#\#\#$$
$$\phantom{S \# \overset{1}{\Rightarrow} S S \# \overset{1}{\Rightarrow} S S S \# \overset{1}{\Rightarrow} S S S S \# \overset{1}{\Rightarrow}} S\,S\,S\,S\,S$$

$$\overset{2}{\Rightarrow} \begin{matrix} S\,S\,S\,S\,S \\ S\,S\,S\,S\,S \end{matrix} \overset{2}{\Rightarrow} \begin{matrix} S\,S\,S\,S\,S \\ S\,S\,S\,S\,S \\ S\,S\,S\,S\,S \end{matrix} \overset{2}{\Rightarrow} \begin{matrix} S\,S\,S\,S\,S \\ S\,S\,S\,S\,S \\ S\,S\,S\,S\,S \\ S\,S\,S\,S\,S \end{matrix} \overset{2}{\Rightarrow} \begin{matrix} S\,S\,S\,S\,S \\ S\,S\,S\,S\,S \\ S\,S\,S\,S\,S \\ S\,S\,S\,S\,S \\ S\,S\,S\,S\,S \end{matrix}$$

$$\overset{5}{\Rightarrow} \overset{5}{\Rightarrow} \overset{5}{\Rightarrow} \overset{5}{\Rightarrow} \overset{7}{\Rightarrow} \; 5 * 5 * 5 \text{ cube (solid)}$$

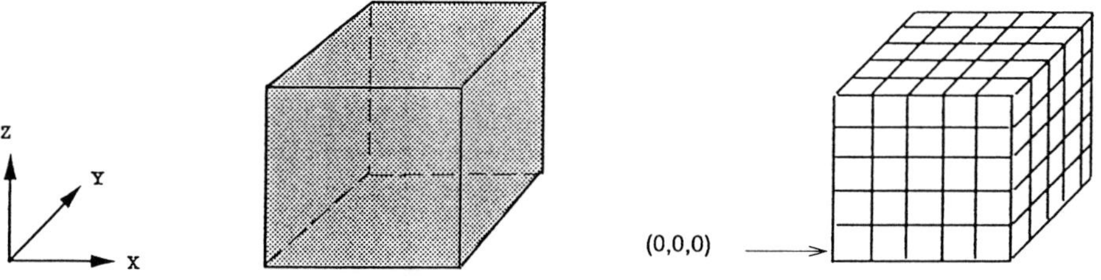

Fig. 7. A $5 * 5 * 5$ solid cube.

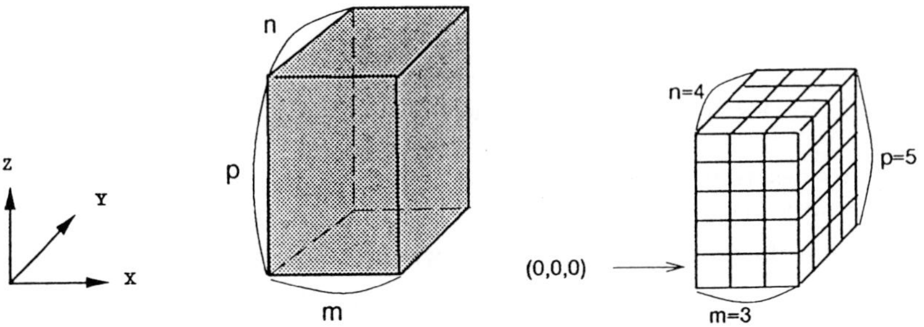

Fig. 8. A $3 * 4 * 5$ solid brick.

Note that if no positions (locations) are specified during the derivation process, by default, all locations wherever applicable are applied in parallel (simultaneously). Therefore, the derivation sequence is: 1 1 1 1 2 2 2 2 5 5 5 5 7 or $1^4 2^4 5^4 7$. In general the derivation sequence $1^{n-1} 2^{n-1} 5^{n-1} 7$ is for an $n \times n \times n$ solid cube, where $n \geq 1$. Notice that a solid cube is a special case of the following solid brick objects.

Example 4.2.

$$S \overset{1^2}{\Longrightarrow} \overset{2^3}{\Longrightarrow} \overset{5^4}{\Longrightarrow} \overset{7}{\Longrightarrow} 3*4*5 \text{ brick (solid)}$$

In general the $m*n*p$ solid brick sequence is $1^{m-1}2^{n-1}5^{p-1}7$, where $m,n,p \geq 1$. Notice that in dealing with three-dimensional patterns by the conventional sequential methods, it normally takes $O(n*m*p)$ *or* $O(n^3)$ cubic time, whereas here it only takes $O(n+m+p)$ *or* $O(n)$ linear time.

Here we also point out a concept which is very important and fundamental to the formation of *geometric objects* as shown in Fig. 9.

The trajectory of a moving dot forms a line, i.e.

$$. \Rightarrow \ldots\ldots\ldots \Rightarrow \text{\_\_\_\_\_\_\_\_\_\_\_\_\_\_\_}$$

The trajectory of a moving line segment forms a plane (area), i.e.

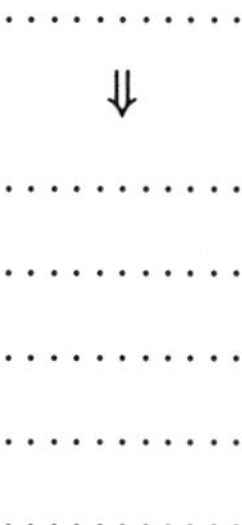

The trajectory of a moving plane forms a volume, i.e.

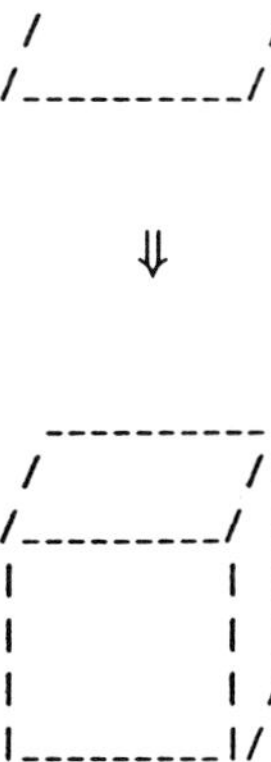

Fig. 9. Geometric object formation.

This also serves as a simulation of what one may perceive, that a *line, area, or volume* is from the very basic geometric unit of a dot(.). Such a concept can be extended to more complicated objects such as a pyramid and stair-like objects as illustrated in Examples 4.4 and 4.5.

Example 4.3.

$$S \overset{1^{n-1}}{\Longrightarrow} \overset{2^{p-1}}{\Longrightarrow} \{(0 \le x \le n-1, y = 0, z > 0),\ (0 \le x \le n-1, y = p-1, z > 0),$$
$$(x = 0, 0 \le y \le p-1, z > 0),\ (x = n-1, 0 \le y \le p-1, z > 0)\}$$
$$\overset{5^{m-1}}{\Longrightarrow} \overset{7}{\Longrightarrow} n^*p^*m \text{ hollow (up) brick}$$

or $1^{n-1}\ 2^{p-1}\ C\ 5^{m-1}\ 7$, where C is the set of cells defined above within the brackets {}.

An $n \times p \times m$ hollow(up) brick is shown in Fig. 10. It is interesting to compare the figures in Examples 4.1–4.6 with the object figures in [4,8,16,17,19], which are typical 3-D illustrations used for analyzing 3-D objects .

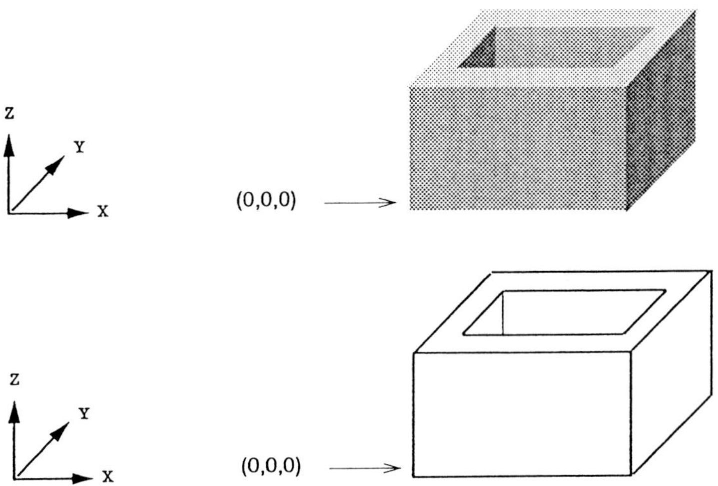

Fig. 10. An upward hollow brick realized from a real 3-D object image in different gray levels.

Example 4.4. The pyramid is an interesting object, which has been widely used by many computer vision and pattern recognition researchers as a challenging test data for image description, understanding, representation, and recognition [8,9,12]. Here we show how a pyramid can be *structurally* represented by a 3-D UAG. Without loss of generality, a $5 * 5 * 3$ pyramid is shown in Fig. 11 and its parsing sequence (representation) is shown as follows:

$$S \xRightarrow{1^4} \xRightarrow{2^4} \; S\,S\,S\,S\,S \xRightarrow{5}$$
$$S\,S\,S\,S\,S \qquad \{(1 \le x \le 3, 1 \le y \le 3, z = 0)\} = C_1$$
$$S\,S\,S\,S\,S$$
$$S\,S\,S\,S\,S$$
$$S\,S\,S\,S\,S$$
$$\xRightarrow{5} \; (2,2,1) = C_2$$
$$\xRightarrow{7} \; 5 * 5 * 3 \text{ pyramid}$$

or the parsing sequence is

$$1^4 \; 2^4 \; C_1 \; 5 \; C_2 \; 5 \; 7$$

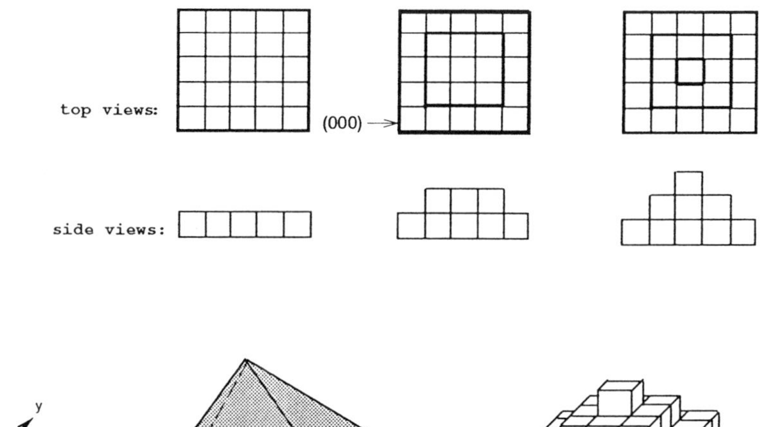

Fig. 11. A $5 * 5 * 3$ solid pyramid.

Example 4.5. Figure 12 shows a stair, which can also be considered as an approximation of Fig. 12(b). Its string representation is

$$1^n \; 2^m \; 5^k \; (x, y \ge k, z)5^k \; (x, y \ge 2k, z)5^k \; (x, y \ge 3k, z)5^k \; (x, y \ge 4k, z)5^k \,.$$

Example 4.6. Compare the two stairs in Fig. 13, which cannot be properly distinguished by the method in [8], but can be clearly distinguished by 3-D UAG from their respective representations as follows:

$$\text{(a): } 1^n \; 2^m \; 5^k \; (x, y \ge k, z)5^k \; (x, y \ge 2k, z)5^{4k}$$
$$\text{(b): } 1^n \; 2^m \; 5^{2k} \; (x, y \ge k, z)5^{2k} \; (x, y \ge 2k, z)5^{2k} \,.$$

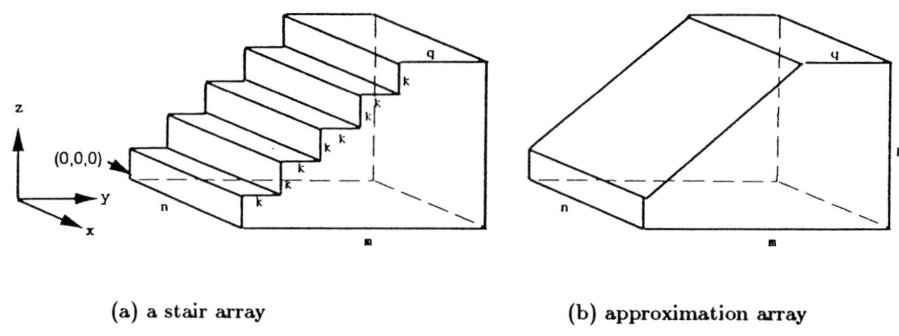

(a) a stair array   (b) approximation array

Fig. 12. A stair and its approximation arrays.

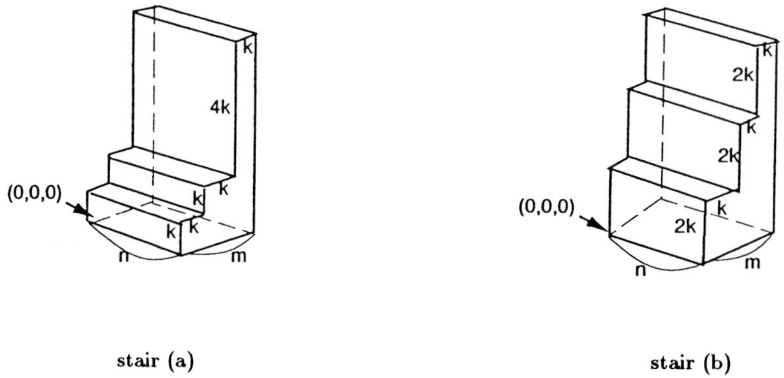

stair (a)   stair (b)

Fig. 13. Two similar but different objects (stairs) that cannot be distinguished by Marill's method in [8].

5. 26-Neighborhood UAG and from Pixels to Object Features

So far, the 3-D UAG uses the six-neighborhood, which can handle changes of $n*90°$ only. In this section, this restriction is lifted by expanding the six-neighborhood to a 26-neighborhood. In this case, a 3-D UAG using 26-neighborhood is defined in Example 5.1, using two-point normal form [3].

Example 5.1.

$G_u = (V_n,\ V_t,\ P,\ S,\ \#)$, where $V_n = \{S\}$, $V_t = \{*\}$ as defined in Section 2, and rewriting rules in P are in the following form:

$P:\ (v)\ (S,\ SS,\ v)$ where v in $\{1, 2, \ldots, 6, a, b \ldots, n, p, q \ldots, u\}$, and each of these 26 symbols is a neighbor as defined as a vector in Fig. 14. (Note that we exclude the letter "o" (oh) to avoid confusion with the original location $(0,0,0)$).

or $(S,\ *,\ -)$ for a terminal rule.

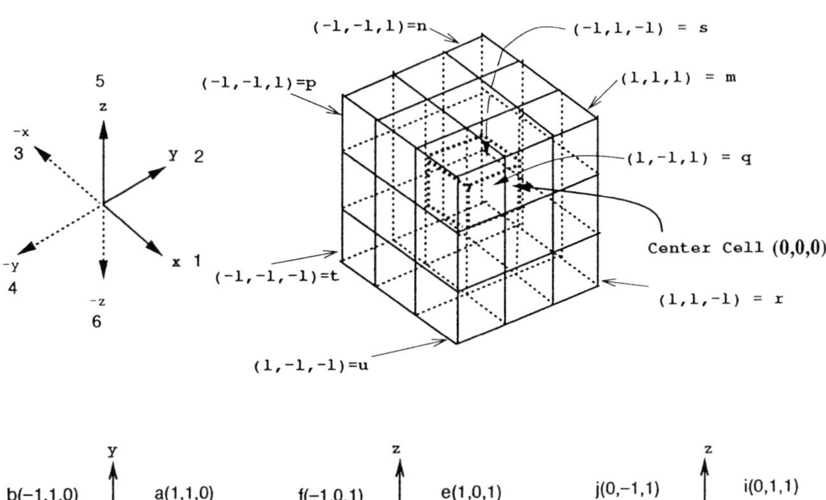

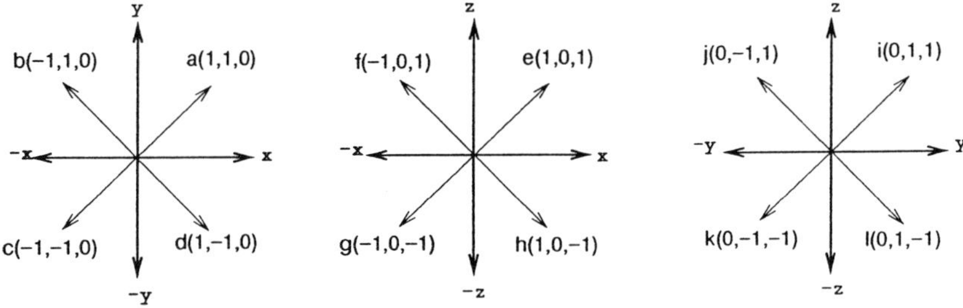

Fig. 14. 3-D space with its center cell and 2-D-neighborhood, each denoted by an alphanumeral ranging from 1 to 6, and a to u (excluding "oh").

Notice that there are 27 rules including the terminal rule. Again, since every array sentence must terminate by the terminal rule, in the parsing sequence, the last digit indicating the terminal rule can be omitted, without loss of generality.

Example 5.2. A standing up coat rack is shown in Fig. 15. Its string representation is

$$2^m A(1^m 2^m 3^m 5^{n+q+r})B(e^p f^p)C(i^p j^p),$$

where $A = (0, m, 0)$, $B = (0, m, n)$ and $C = (0, m, n+q)$.

A more complicated example combining both wire-like and solid volume objects is illustrated in the following example.

Example 5.3. Two types of overhead projectors are shown in Fig. 16, with their back, side and bird's-eye views. Their string pattern representations are:

(a): $1^m\, 2^n\, 5^p\, A^{r+q}\, Bm^{\sqrt{3}s}C(1^u 2^v 5)(x, y \geq i, z)5, i = 1, \ldots, w-1$

(b): $1^m\, 2^n\, 5^p\, A^{r+q}\, Bi^{\sqrt{2}s}1^s C(1^u 2^v 5)(x, y \geq i, z)5, i = 1, \ldots, w-1$

where A, B and C are computed and shown in Fig. 16.

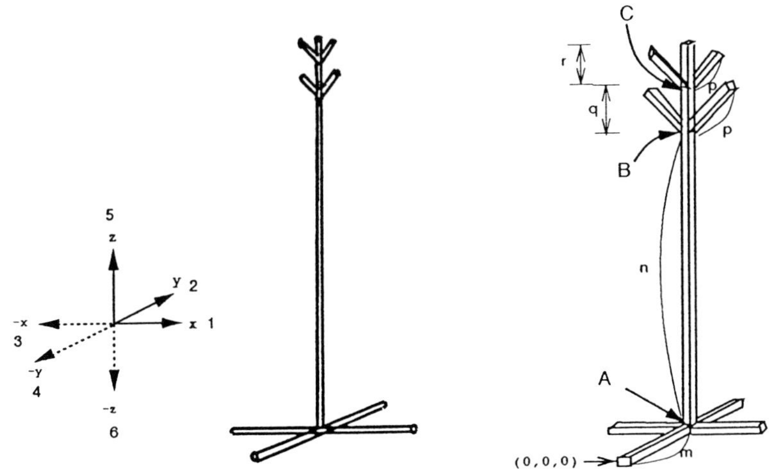

Fig. 15. A standing up coat rack and its digitized 3-D array object.

Again this example demonstrates two structurally similar but distinguishable objects, which are reflected from their respective string pattern representations. In fact, its representation also shows a *segmentation* of the object into four major portions (feature extraction) shown by four different shadings in Fig. 16, where the key difference between the two objects is indicated by the darkest black region (neck of the overhead projector).

6. Approximating Distorted, Noisy and Curved Objects

Distorted and noisy objects, can be approximated by straight line segments according to probabilistic distribution and thresholding, very much similar to those methods for 2-D line drawings [5,22]. Objects whose line drawing have arbitrary angles θ, rather than a multiple of 45°, can be approximated by x and $y = \tan \theta$ line segments along a particular plane.

Example 6.1. In Fig. 17, (i) is a noisy line segment along the x-axis in the x–y plane, whose representation is $1^m a^1 d^1 1^n d^1 a^1 1^p$. If m, n, $p \gg 1$, then this representation can be approximated as 1^{m+n+p}. Figure 17 (ii) with an arbitrary angle θ can be approximated by a sequence of line segments in the x–y plane by $1^x 2^{x \tan \theta}$.

Curved objects can be approximated by line segments along the quantized planes tangent to the quantized 45°'s, as shown in Example 6.2.

Example 6.2. Figure 18 shows a type of glass and the different angles of its views. Its string pattern presentation is

$$1^t 2^t 3^t 4^t a^t b^t c^t d^t 5^u B(e^v f^v i^v j^v m^v n^v p^v q^v) C 5^w \,,$$

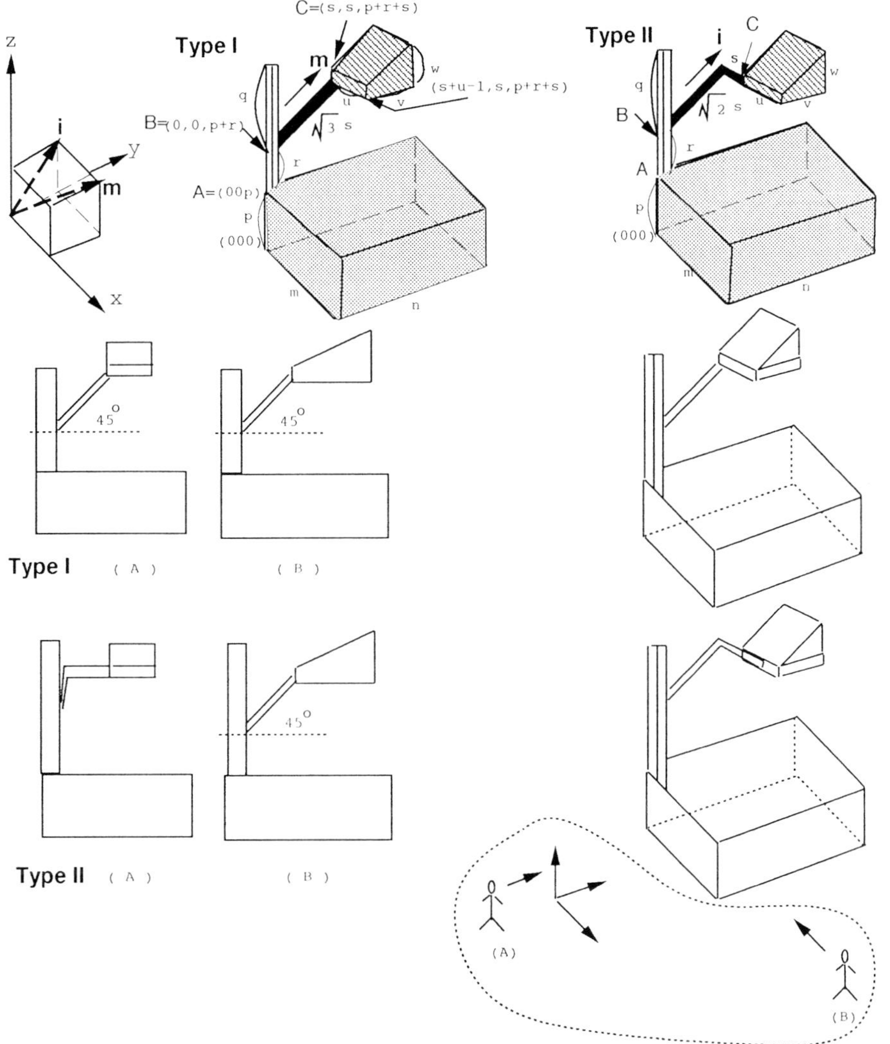

Fig. 16. Two types of overhead projectors I and II, and their different views.

where C is a circle described by $x^2 + y^2 = r^2$ at $z = u + \frac{\sqrt{2}}{2}v$, i.e. $C = (\pm x,$ $\pm\sqrt{r^2 - x^2},\ u + \frac{\sqrt{2}}{2}v)$, where $x \le r$.

Example 6.3. More examples of curved objects are illustrated in Fig. 19. Their respective pattern representations are as follows:

(a) $1^t 2^t 3^t 4^t a^t b^t c^t d^t 5^u B(1^{\frac{r}{2}} 2^{\frac{r}{2}} 3^{\frac{r}{2}} 4^{\frac{r}{2}} a^{\frac{r}{2}} b^{\frac{r}{2}} c^{\frac{r}{2}} d^{\frac{r}{2}}) C(e^{\frac{\sqrt{2}}{2}r} f^{\frac{\sqrt{2}}{2}r} i^{\frac{\sqrt{2}}{2}r} j^{\frac{\sqrt{2}}{2}r} m^{\frac{\sqrt{2}}{2}r} n^{\frac{\sqrt{2}}{2}r} p^{\frac{\sqrt{2}}{2}r}$ $q^{\frac{\sqrt{2}}{2}r}) D 5^{\frac{r}{2}}$,

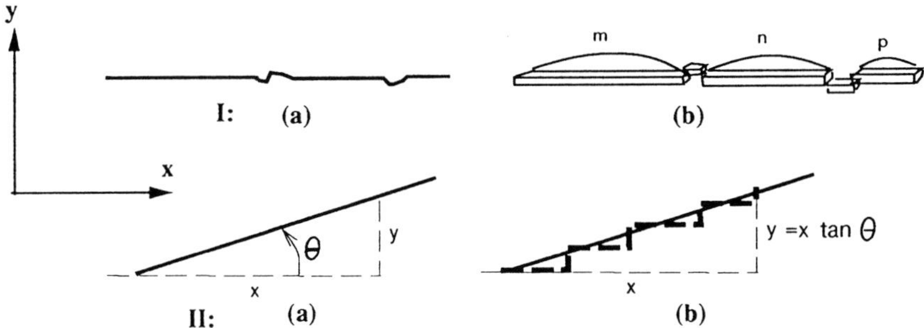

Fig. 17. Noisy line segments, with arbitrary angle θ and their digitized arrays.

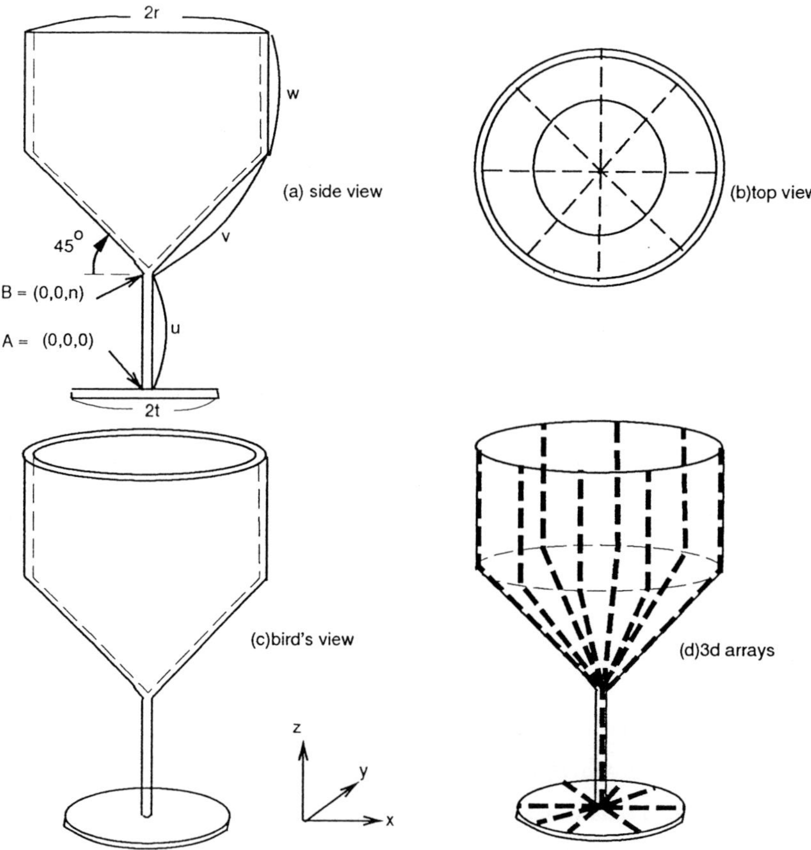

Fig. 18. A glass and its 3-D arrays.

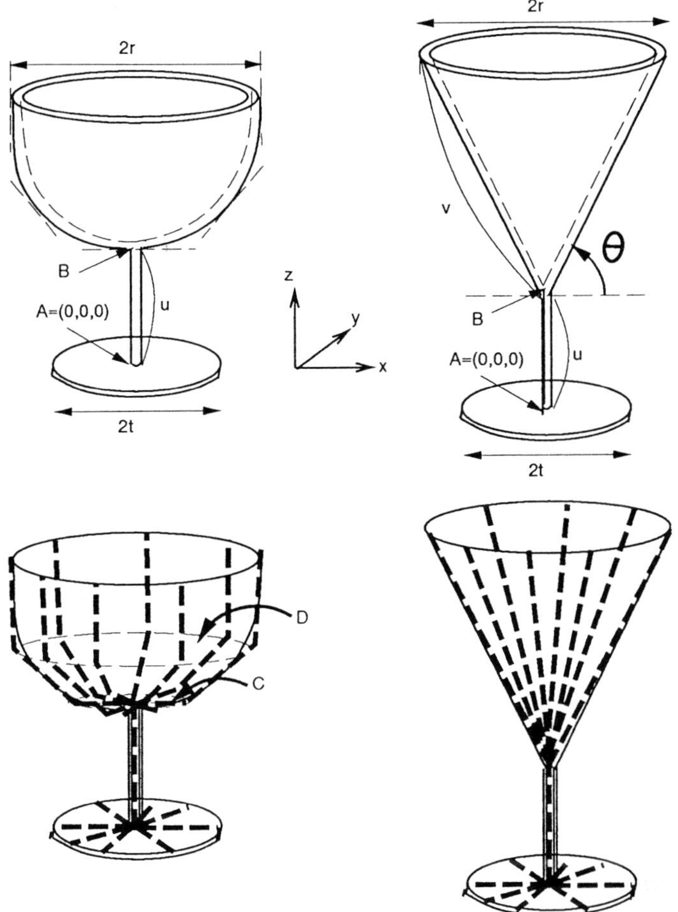

Fig. 19. More illustrations of curved objects and their 3-D arrays.

where C and D are two circles indicated in the figure, i.e. $C = (\pm x, \pm \frac{\sqrt{r^2 - 4x^2}}{2}, u)$, where $x \le \frac{r}{2}$, and $D = (\pm x, \pm \sqrt{r^2 - x^2}, u + \frac{r}{2})$, where $x \le r$, $C = (\pm x, \pm \sqrt{r^2 - x^2}, \frac{\sqrt{2}}{2} v)$, where $x \le r$;

$$\text{(b)} \quad 1^t 2^t 3^t 4^t a^t b^t c^t d^t 5^u B (1^x 5^y 2^x 5^y 3^x 5^y 4^x 5^y a^x 5^y b^x 5^y c^x 5^y d^x 5^y)^w \,,$$

where $y = x \tan \theta$ and $w = \frac{v \cos \theta}{x}$.

Notice that the three different types of glasses shown in Figs. 18 and 19 have structural similarities and differences, which are reflected from their respective string pattern representations via 3-D UAG shown in Examples 6.2 and 6.3.

7. Discussions and Future Research

We have introduced a formal model known as "3-D universal array grammar" (3-D UAG) for three-dimensional object representation. It is parallel, and simple to manipulate by computers, including orientations (along the x-, y- and z-axis), shift, enlargement, elongations and reductions. This model is basically extended from 2-D universal array grammar (2-D UAG) [23]. But the difference here is not just the dimensionality. The types of production rules are different and it is parallel. The 2-D UAG in [23] uses regular (type 3) rules while here the 3-D UAG G_u uses "context-free" (type 2) rules. Please note that here by "context-free" we mean to borrow the terminology from Chomsky [3,25]. Because of its dimensions and the use of blanks (#) in the context, it is still more or less sensitive to the # symbols. Nevertheless it is interesting to see that 3-D UAG G_u is more powerful (in terms of generative capability) than 2-D UAG, in that the following "multi-branch wire-like" patterns shown in Fig. 20 (i) (symbolizing a digitized Chinese character meaning "center" or " central") can be generated by G_u but not by any 2-D UAG even in two-dimensional space [3].

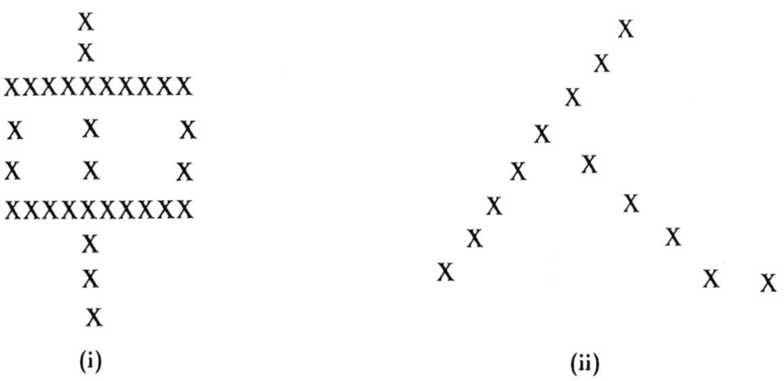

(i)   (ii)

Fig. 20. (i) Multi-branch wire-like pattern symbolizing a digitized Chinese character "center", and (ii) diagonal pattern symbolizing a Chinese character "human" or "man".

Further, neither G_u nor 2-D UAG can generate any "diagonal" patterns shown in Fig. 20 (ii) (symbolizing a Chinese digitized character meaning "human" or "man"). This is because the limitation of "6-neighborhood". But with "26-neighborhood" introduced in Section 5 of this article, it can. Therefore there is a certain hierarchy in the patterns depending not only on their production rules but also on neighborhood definitions. It would be interesting to investigate such a three-dimensional pattern hierarchy, whose 2-D array counterpart has been investigated in [21]. It is also interesting to explore multi-dimensional arrays in other spaces such as hexagonal space using 60 and 120 degrees (rather than 90 degrees) as illustrated in 2-D space [1].

The idea introduced in this paper cannot only generate many interesting 3-D objects, but can also be used for 3-D object learning, understanding, and description. For example, according to the sequence of rules (universal array grammar), Fig. 8 can be described and understood as a 3-D object with 12 sides, forming six *perpendicular* rectangle surface areas, i.e. a brick. When all sides are of equal length, it is a cube, i.e. a cube is a brick (with all six surfaces *perpendicular* to each other) with all sides of equal length. Indeed, when one *learns, understands, describes, memorizes*, and *recognizes* a cube, these are the key characteristics all reflected by our representation :

$$1^{n-1}2^{n-1}5^{n-1}\,.$$

From the theory in *The Society of Mind* [9], the idea of which was reiterated in [26], this can be considered as a small *agent* that can recognize all sizes of cubes. Another small agent is able to recognize bricks. These two small agents are very much alike in nature, and probably reside in one's *brain* (memory) very close to each other. Translating to pattern recognition terms, their string pattern representations occupy nearby or neighboring addresses in the dictionary. There are also many other small agents, each recognizing an *infinite* subclass of objects sharing some common properties characterized by its representation, and so on. Altogether, we have a society that can recognize (describe, understand, memorize, and interpret) any object that has been *taught* through training via a 3-D UAG.

For future research, more can be done, including: (1) 3-D objects clustering, need alignment, dictionary construction, matching, (2) from pixels to 3-D object feature extraction, segmentation, scene analysis, understanding, description, representation, and recognition, and (3) thinning (skeletonization) 3-D digitized arrays. For example, there are some more interesting applications to the real world, e.g. satellite launching environment such as the one shown in Fig. 21 that can be described by 3-D UAG.

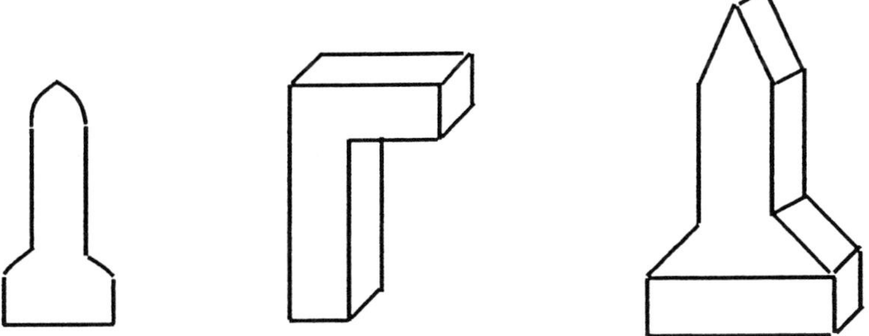

Fig. 21. Some illustrations of 3-D objects from a shuttle launching station.

It is the author's hope that this ground work can also pave the way for further studies of the 3-D formal model for object pattern recognition and to stimulate research in 3-D object clustering analysis involving noisy and distorted patterns.

Acknowledgement

Part of this work was done when the author was visiting the LIPN Labs of University of Paris VII and XIII. The author is grateful to Profs. M. Nivat and A. Saoudi for providing an excellent environment for research and for the financial support.

References

[1] K. Aizawa and A. Nakamura, Grammars on the hexagonal array, in P. S. P. Wang (ed.), *Array Grammars, Patterns and Recognizers* (World Scientific, 1989) 191–200.

[2] L. Baird and P. S. P. Wang, 3-D object recognition using gradient descent and the universal 3-D array grammar, *SPIE Vol. 1607 Intelligent Robots and Computer Vision*, 1992, 711–719.

[3] C. Cook and P. S. P. Wang, A chomsky hierarchy of isotonic array grammars and languages, *Comput. Graph. Image Process.* **8** (1978) 144–152.

[4] S. Edelman, H. Bulthoff and D. Weinshall, Stimulus Familiarity Determines Recognition Strategy for Novel 3-D, MIT AI Lab. Memo 1138, Jul. 1989.

[5] K. S. Fu, *Syntactic Pattern Recognition and Applications* (Prentice-Hall, Englewood Cliffs, NJ, 1982).

[6] W. I. Grosky and P. S. P. Wang, The relation between uniformly structured tessellation automata and parallel array grammars, in *Proc. IEEE ISUSAL 75*, Tokyo, Japan (1975) 97–102.

[7] K. Inoue, I. Sakuramoto, M. Sakamoto and I. Itsanami, 2-D automata operating in parallel, in *Proc. Int. Colloquium on Parallel Image Processing*, Paris, 1991, 239–262.

[8] T. Marill, Emulating the human interpretation of line-drawings as 3-D objects, *Int. J. Comput. Vision* **6**, 2 (1991) 147–161. A preliminary version of this paper also appeared as a technical report: Recognizing Three-Dimensional Objects Without the Use of Models, MIT AI Lab. Memo 1157, Sept. 1989.

[9] M. L. Minsky, *The Society of Mind* (Heinemann, London, 1986).

[10] M. L. Minsky, Steps toward artificial intelligence, in *Proc. IRE 49*, 1961, 8–30.

[11] M. Nivat, A. Saoudi and V. R. Dare, Parallel generation of finite images, in P. S. P. Wang (ed.), *Array Grammars Patterns and Recognizers* (World Scientific, 1989) 1–16.

[12] A. Rosenfeld, *Picture Languages: Formal Models for Picture Recognition* (Academic Press, New York, 1979).

[13] A. Rosenfeld, Preface, in P. S. P. Wang (ed.), *Array Grammars, Patterns and Recognizers* (World Scientific, 1989).

[14] A. Rosenfeld, Coordinate grammars revisited: generalized isometric grammars, in P. S. P. Wang (ed.), *Array Grammars, Patterns and Recognizers* (World Scientific, 1989) 157–166.

[15] A. Saoudi, M. Nivat and P. S. P. Wang (eds.), *Parallel Image Processing* (World Scientific, 1992).

[16] R. N. Shepard and J. Metzler, Mental rotation of 3-D objects, *Science* **171** (1971) 701–703.

[17] R. N. Shepard and J. Metzler, Mental rotation: Effects of dimensionality of objects and type of task, *J. Exp. Psychol.: Human Perception and Performance* **14** (1988) 3–11.

[18] R. Siromoney, Array language and Lindenmayer systems – A survey, in G. Rozenberg and A. Salomaa (eds.), *The Book of L* (Springer Verlag, 1986).

[19] S. Ullman, An Approach to Object Recognition: Aligning Pictorial Descriptions, MIT AI Lab. Memo 931, Dec. 1986.

[20] P. S. P. Wang, Finite-turn repetitive checking automata and sequential/parallel matrix languages, *IEEE Trans. Comput.* **30** (1981) 366–370.

[21] P. S. P. Wang, Hierarchical structures and complexities of isometric patterns, *IEEE Trans. Pattern Anal. Mach. Intell.* **5**, 1 (1983) 92–99.

[22] P. S. P. Wang, An application of array grammars to clustering analysis for syntactic patterns, *Pattern Recogn.* **17**, 4 (1984) 441–451.

[23] P. S. P. Wang, On-line Chinese character recognition by array grammars, in *Proc. 6th IGC Int. Conference on Electronic Image '88* (1988) 209–214.

[24] P. S. P. Wang (ed.), *Array Grammars, Patterns and Recognizers* (World Scientific, 1989).

[25] Y. Yamamoto, K. Morita and K. Sugata, Context-sensitivity of 2-D regular array grammars, in P. S. P. Wang (ed.), *Array Grammars, Patterns and Recognizers* (World Scientific, 1989) 17–41.

[26] P. Winston with S. Shellard (eds.), *Artificial Intelligence at MIT — Expanding Frontiers* (MIT Press, 1990).

PART 2

BASIC METHODS IN COMPUTER VISION

Handbook of Pattern Recognition and Computer Vision, pp. 235–276
Eds. C. H. Chen, L. F. Pau and P. S. P. Wang
© 1993 World Scientific Publishing Company

CHAPTER 2.1

TEXTURE ANALYSIS

MIHRAN TUCERYAN

European Computer Industry Research Center (ECRC)
Arabellastr. 17, D-8000 München 81, Germany
Email: mihran@ecrc.de

and

ANIL K. JAIN

Computer Science Department, Michigan State University
East Lansing, MI 48824-1027, USA
Internet: jain@cps.msu.edu

This chapter reviews and discusses various aspects of texture analysis. The concentration is on the various methods of extracting textural features from images. The geometric, random field, fractal, and signal processing models of texture are presented. The major classes of texture processing problems such as segmentation, classification, and shape from texture are discussed. The possible application areas of texture such as automated inspection, document processing, and remote sensing are summarized. A bibliography is provided at the end for further reading.

Keywords: Texture, segmentation, classification, shape, signal processing, fractals, random fields, Gabor filters, wavelet transform, gray level dependency matrix.

1. Introduction

In many machine vision and image processing algorithms, simplifying assumptions are made about the uniformity of intensities in local image regions. However, images of real objects often do not exhibit regions of uniform intensities. For example, the image of a wooden surface is not uniform but contains variations of intensities which form certain repeated patterns called *visual texture*. The patterns can be the result of physical surface properties such as roughness or oriented strands which often have a tactile quality, or they could be the result of reflectance differences such as the color on a surface.

We recognize texture when we see it but it is very difficult to define. This difficulty is demonstrated by the number of different texture definitions attempted by vision researchers. Coggins [1] has compiled a catalogue of texture definitions in the computer vision literature and we give some examples here.

- "We may regard texture as what constitutes a macroscopic region. Its structure is simply attributed to the repetitive patterns in which elements or primitives are arranged according to a placement rule." [2]

235

- "A region in an image has a constant texture if a set of local statistics or other local properties of the picture function are constant, slowly varying, or approximately periodic." [3]
- "The image texture we consider is nonfigurative and cellular... An image texture is described by the number and types of its (tonal) primitives and the spatial organization or layout of its (tonal) primitives... A fundamental characteristic of texture: it cannot be analyzed without a frame of reference of tonal primitive being stated or implied. For any smooth gray-tone surface, there exists a scale such that when the surface is examined, it has no texture. Then as resolution increases, it takes on a fine texture and then a coarse texture." [4]
- "Texture is defined for our purposes as an attribute of a field having no components that appear enumerable. The phase relations between the components are thus not apparent. Nor should the field contain an obvious gradient. The intent of this definition is to direct attention of the observer to the global properties of the display — i.e. its overall "coarseness," "bumpiness," or "fineness." Physically, nonenumerable (aperiodic) patterns are generated by stochastic as opposed to deterministic processes. Perceptually, however, the set of all patterns without obvious enumerable components will include many deterministic (and even periodic) textures." [5]
- "Texture is an apparently paradoxical notion. On the one hand, it is commonly used in the early processing of visual information, especially for practical classification purposes. On the other hand, no one has succeeded in producing a commonly accepted definition of texture. The resolution of this paradox, we feel, will depend on a richer, more developed model for early visual information processing, a central aspect of which will be representational systems at many different levels of abstraction. These levels will most probably include actual intensities at the bottom and will progress through edge and orientation descriptors to surface, and perhaps volumetric descriptors. Given these multilevel structures, it seems clear that they should be included in the definition of, and in the computation of, texture descriptors." [6]
- "The notion of texture appears to depend upon three ingredients: (i) some local 'order' is repeated over a region which is large in comparison to the order's size, (ii) the order consists in the nonrandom arrangement of elementary parts, and (iii) the parts are roughly uniform entities having approximately the same dimensions everywhere within the textured region." [7]

This collection of definitions demonstrates that the "definition" of texture is formulated by different people depending upon the particular application and that there is no generally agreed upon definition. Some are perceptually motivated, and others are driven completely by the application in which the definition will be used.

Image texture, defined as a function of the spatial variation in pixel intensities (gray values), is useful in a variety of applications and has been a subject of intense study by many researchers. One immediate application of image texture is the recognition of image regions using texture properties. For example, in Fig. 1(a), we

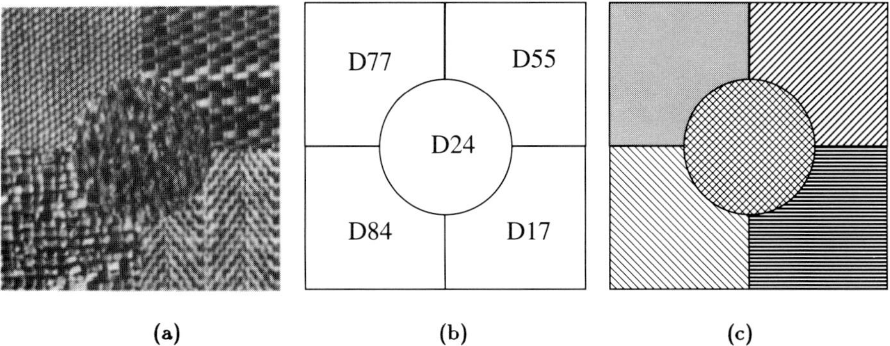

(a)   (b)   (c)

Fig. 1. (a) An image consisting of five different textured regions: cotton canvas (D77), straw matting (D55), raffia (D84), herringbone weave (D17), and pressed calf leather (D24) [8]. (b) The goal of texture classification is to label each textured region with the proper category label: the identities of the five texture regions present in (a). (c) The goal of texture segmentation is to separate the regions in the image which have different textures and identify the boundaries between them. The texture categories themselves need not be recognized. In this example, the five texture categories in (a) are identified as separate textures by the use of generic category labels (represented by the different fill patterns).

can identify the five different textures and their identities as cotton canvas, straw matting, raffia, herringbone weave, and pressed calf leather. Texture is the most important visual cue in identifying these types of homogeneous regions. This is called *texture classification*. The goal of texture classification then is to produce a classification map of the input image where each uniform textured region is identified with the texture class it belongs to as shown in Fig. 1(b). We could also find the texture boundaries even if we could not classify these textured surfaces. This is then the second type of problem that texture analysis research attempts to solve – *texture segmentation*. The goal of texture segmentation is to obtain the boundary map shown in Fig. 1(c). *Texture synthesis* is often used for image compression applications. It is also important in computer graphics where the goal is to render object surfaces which are as realistic looking as possible. Figure 2 shows a set of synthetically generated texture images using Markov random field and fractal models [9]. The *shape from texture* problem is one instance of a general class of vision problems known as "shape from X". This was first formally pointed out in the perception literature by Gibson [10]. The goal is to extract three-dimensional shape information from various cues such as shading, stereo, and texture. The texture features (texture elements) are distorted due to the imaging process and the perspective projection which provide information about surface orientation and shape. An example of shape from texture is given in Fig. 3.

2. Motivation

Texture analysis is an important and useful area of study in machine vision. Most natural surfaces exhibit texture and a successful vision system must be able to

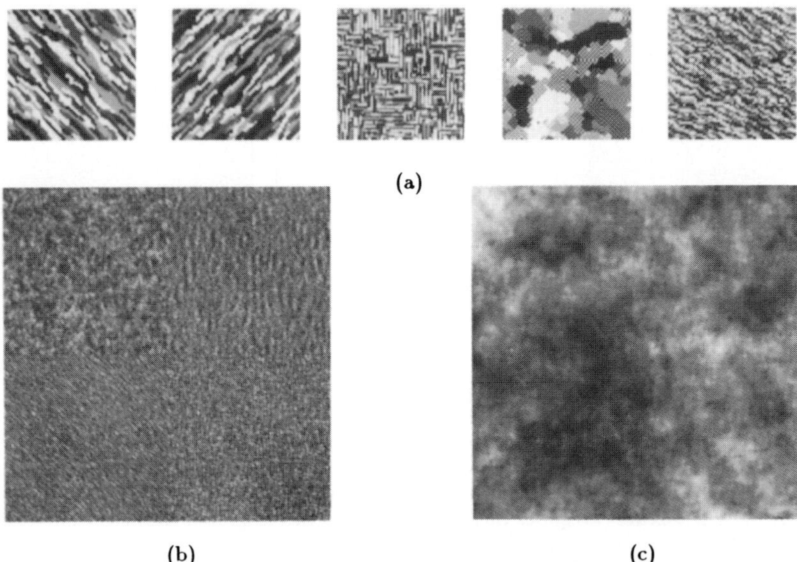

(a)

(b)   (c)

Fig. 2. A set of example textures generated synthetically using only a small number of parameters. (a) Textures generated by discrete Markov random field models. (b) Four textures (in each of the four quadrants) generated by Gaussian Markov random field models. (c) Texture generated by fractal model.

Fig. 3. We can extract the orientation of the surface from the variations of texture (defined by the bricks) in this image.

deal with the textured world surrounding it. This section will review the importance of texture perception from two viewpoints — from the viewpoint of human vision or psychophysics and from the viewpoint of practical machine vision applications.

2.1. *Psychophysics*

The detection of a tiger among the foliage is a perceptual task that carries life and death consequences for someone trying to survive in the forest. The success of the tiger in camouflaging itself is a failure of the visual system observing it. The failure is in not being able to separate figure from ground. Figure–ground separation is an issue which is of intense interest to psychophysicists. The figure–ground separation can be based on various cues such as brightness, form, color, texture, etc. In the example of the tiger in the forest, texture plays a major role. The camouflage is successful because the visual system of the observer is unable to discriminate (or segment) the two textures of the foliage and the tiger skin. What are the visual processes that allow one to separate figure from ground using the texture cue? This question is the basic motivation among psychologists for studying texture perception.

Another reason why it is important to study the psychophysics of texture perception is that the performance of various texture algorithms is evaluated against the performance of the human visual system doing the same task. For example, consider the texture pair in Fig. 4(a), first described by Julesz [11]. The image consists of two regions each of which is made up of different texture tokens. Close scrutiny of the texture image will indicate this fact to the human observer. The immediate perception of the image, however, does not result in the perception of two different textured regions; instead only one uniformly textured region is perceived. Julesz says that such a texture pair is not "effortlessly discriminable" or "preattentively discriminable." Such synthetic textures help us form hypotheses about what image properties are important in human texture perception. In addition, this example raises the question of how to evaluate the performance of computer algorithms that analyze textured images. For example, suppose we have an algorithm that can discriminate the texture pair in Fig. 4(a). Is this algorithm "correct?" The answer, of course, depends on the goal of the algorithm. If it is a very special purpose algorithm that should detect such scrutably different regions, then it is performing correctly. On the other hand, if it is to be a computational model of how the human visual system processes texture, then it is performing incorrectly.

Julesz has studied texture perception extensively in the context of texture discrimination [11,12,13]. The question he posed was "When is a texture pair discriminable, given that they had the same brightness, contrast, and color?" Julesz concentrated on the spatial statistics of the image gray levels that are inherent in the definition of texture by keeping other illumination-related properties the same.

To discuss Julesz's pioneering work, we need to define the concepts of first- and second-order spatial statistics.

(i) *First-order statistics* measure the likelihood of observing a gray value at a randomly-chosen location in the image. First-order statistics can be computed from the histogram of pixel intensities in the image. These depend only on individual pixel values and not on the interaction or co-occurrence of neigh-

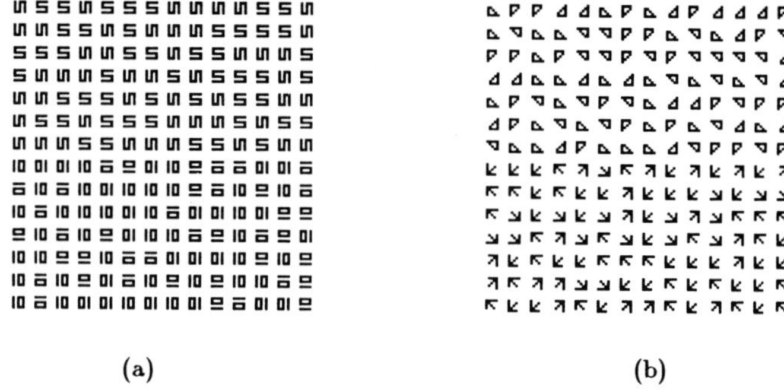

(a)   (b)

Fig. 4. Texture pairs with identical second-order statistics. The bottom halves of the images consist of texture tokens that are different from the ones in the top half. (a) Humans cannot perceive the two regions without careful scrutiny. (b) The two different regions are immediately discriminable by humans.

boring pixel values. The average intensity in an image is an example of the first-order statistic.

(ii) *Second-order statistics* are defined as the likelihood of observing a pair of gray values occurring at the endpoints of a dipole (or needle) of random length placed in the image at a random location and orientation. These are properties of pairs of pixel values.

Julesz conjectured that two textures are not preattentively discriminable if their second-order statistics are identical. This is demonstrated by the example in Fig. 4(a). This image consists of a pair of textured regions whose second-order statistics are identical. The two textured regions are not preattentively discriminable. His later counter-examples to this conjecture were the result of a careful construction of texture pairs that have identical second-order statistics (see Fig. 4(b)) [14,15,16].

Julesz proposed the "theory of textons" to explain the preattentive discrimination of texture pairs. Textons are visual events (such as collinearity, terminations, closure, etc.) whose presence is detected and used in texture discrimination. Terminations are endpoints of line segments or corners. Using his theory of textons, Julesz explained the examples in Fig. 4 as follows. Recall that both texture images in Fig. 4 have two regions that have identical second-order statistics. In Fig. 4(a), the number of terminations in both the upper and lower regions is the same (i.e. the texton information in the two regions is not different), therefore the visual system is unable to preattentively discriminate the two textures. In Fig. 4(b), on the other hand, the number of terminations in the upper half is three, whereas the number of terminations in the lower half is four. The difference in this texton makes the two textured regions discriminable. Caelli has also proposed the existence of perceptual analyzers by the visual system for detecting textons [17]. Beck *et al.* [18] have conducted experiments and argue that the perception of texture segmentation in certain types of patterns is primarily a function of spatial frequency analysis and not the result of higher level symbolic grouping processes.

Studies in psychophysiology have suggested that a multi-channel, frequency and orientation analysis of the visual image formed on the retina is performed by the brain. Campbell and Robson [19] performed psychophysical experiments using various grating patterns. They suggested that the visual system decomposes the image into filtered images of various frequencies and orientations. De Valois *et al.* [20] have studied the brain of the macaque monkey which is assumed to be close to the human brain in its visual processing. They recorded the response of the simple cells in the visual cortex of the monkey to sinusoidal gratings of various frequencies and orientations and concluded that these cells are tuned to narrow ranges of frequency and orientation. These studies have motivated vision researchers to apply multi-channel filtering approaches to texture analysis.

2.2. *Applications*

Texture analysis methods have been utilized in a variety of application domains. In some of the mature domains (such as remote sensing) texture already has played a major role, while in other disciplines (such as surface inspection) new applications of texture are being found. We will briefly review the role of texture in automated inspection, medical image processing, document processing, and remote sensing. Images from two application domains are shown in Fig. 5. The role that texture plays in these examples varies depending upon the application. For example, in the SAR images of Figs. 5(b) and (c) texture is defined to be the local scene heterogeneity and this property is used for classification of land use categories such as water, agricultural areas, etc. In the ultrasound image of the heart in Fig. 5(a), texture is defined as the amount of randomness which has a lower value in the vicinity of the border between the heart cavity and the inner wall than in the blood filled cavity. This fact can be used to perform segmentation and boundary detection using texture analysis methods.

2.2.1. *Inspection*

There has been a limited number of applications of texture processing to automated inspection problems. These applications include defect detection in images of textiles and automated inspection of carpet wear and automobile paints.

In the detection of defects in texture images, most applications have been in the domain of textile inspection. Dewaele *et al.* [21] used signal processing methods to detect point defects and line defects in texture images. They have sparse convolution masks in which the bank of filters are adaptively selected depending upon the image to be analyzed. Texture features are computed from the filtered images. A Mahalanobis distance classifier is used to classify the defective areas. Chetverikov [22] defined a simple window differencing operator to the texture features obtained from simple filtering operations. This allows one to detect the boundaries of defects in the texture. Chen and Jain [23] used a structural approach to defect detection in textured images. They extract a skeletal structure from images, and by detecting

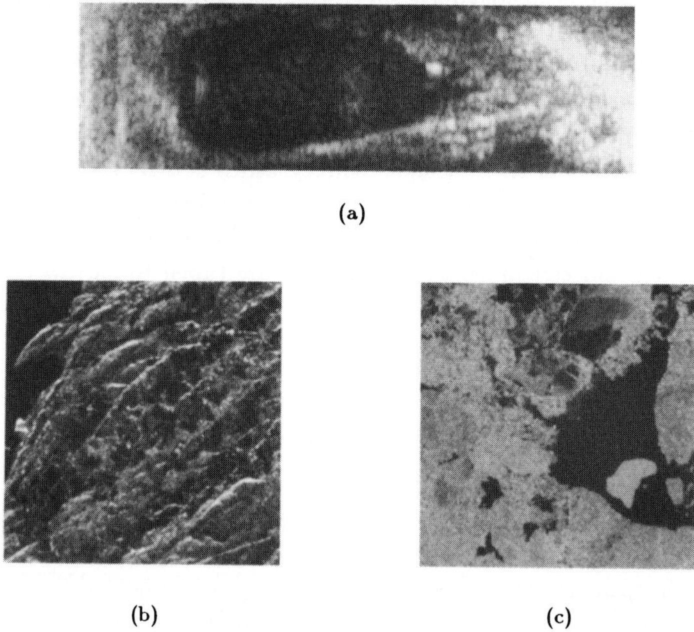

(a)

(b)   (c)

Fig. 5. Examples of images from various application domains in which texture analysis is important. (a) The ultrasound image of a heart. (b), (c) are example aerial images using SAR sensors.

anomalies in certain statistical features in these skeletons, defects in the texture are identified. Conners *et al.* [24] utilized texture analysis methods to detect defects in lumber wood automatically. The defect detection is performed by dividing the image into subwindows and classifying each subwindow into one of the defect categories such as knot, decay, mineral streak, etc. The features they use to perform this classification are based on tonal features such as mean, variance, skewness, and kurtosis of gray levels along with texture features computed from gray level co-occurrence matrices in analyzing pictures of wood. The combination of using tonal features along with textural features improves the correct classification rates over using either type of feature alone.

In the area of quality control of textured images, Siew *et al.* [25] proposed a method for the assessment of carpet wear. They used simple texture features that are computed from second-order gray level dependency statistics and from first-order gray level difference statistics. They showed that the numerical texture features obtained from these techniques can characterize the carpet wear successfully. Jain *et al.* [26] used the texture features computed from a bank of Gabor filters to automatically classify the quality of painted metallic surfaces. A pair of automotive paint finish images is shown in Fig. 6 where the image in (a) has a uniform coating of paint, but the image in (b) has a "mottled" or "blotchy" appearance.

(a)

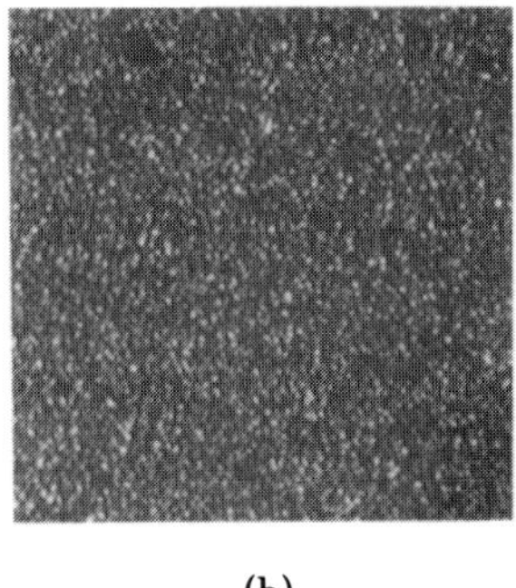

(b)

Fig. 6. Example images used in paint inspection. (a) A non-defective paint which has a smooth texture. (b) A defective paint which has a mottled look.

2.2.2. *Medical Image Analysis*

Image analysis techniques have played an important role in several medical applications. In general, the applications involve the automatic extraction of features from the image which are then used for a variety of classification tasks, such as distinguishing normal tissue from abnormal tissue. Depending upon the particular classification task, the extracted features capture morphological properties, color properties, or certain textural properties of the image.

The textural properties computed are closely related to the application domain to be used. For example, Sutton and Hall [27] discuss the classification of pulmonary disease using texture features. Some diseases, such as interstitial fibrosis, affect the lungs in such a manner that the resulting changes in the X-ray images are texture changes as opposed to clearly delineated lesions. In such applications, texture analysis methods are ideally suited for these images. Sutton and Hall propose the use of three types of texture features to distinguish normal lungs from diseased lungs. These features are computed based on an isotropic contrast measure, a directional contrast measure, and a Fourier domain energy sampling. In their classification experiments, the best classification results were obtained using the directional contrast measure.

Harms *et al.* [28] used image texture in combination with color features to diagnose leukemic malignancy in samples of stained blood cells. They extracted texture micro-edges and "textons" between these micro-edges. The textons were regions with almost uniform color. They extracted a number of texture features from the textons including the total number of pixels in the textons which have a specific color, the mean texton radius and texton size for each color and various texton shape features. In combination with color, the texture features significantly improved the correct classification rate of blood cell types compared to using only color features.

Landeweerd and Gelsema [29] extracted various first-order statistics (such as mean gray level in a region) as well as second-order statistics (such as gray level co-occurrence matrices) to differentiate different types of white blood cells. Insana *et al.* [30] used textural features in ultrasound images to estimate tissue scattering parameters. They made significant use of the knowledge about the physics of the ultrasound imaging process and tissue characteristics to design the texture model. Chen *et al.* [31] used fractal texture features to classify the ultrasound images of livers, and used the fractal texture features to do edge enhancement in chest X-rays.

Lundervold [32] used fractal texture features in combination with other features (such as response to edge detector operators) to analyze ultrasound images of the heart (see Fig. 7). The ultrasound images in this study are time sequence images of the left ventricle of the heart. Figure 7 shows one frame in such a sequence. Texture is represented as an index at each pixel, being the local fractal dimension within an 11 × 11 window estimated according to the fractal Brownian motion model proposed by Chen *et al.* [31]. The texture feature is used in addition to a number of other traditional features, including the response to a Kirsch edge operator, the gray level, and the result of temporal operations. The fractal dimension is expected to be higher on an average in blood than in tissue due to the noise and backscatter characteristics of the blood which is more disordered than that of solid tissue. In addition, the fractal dimension is low at non-random blood/tissue interfaces representing edge information.

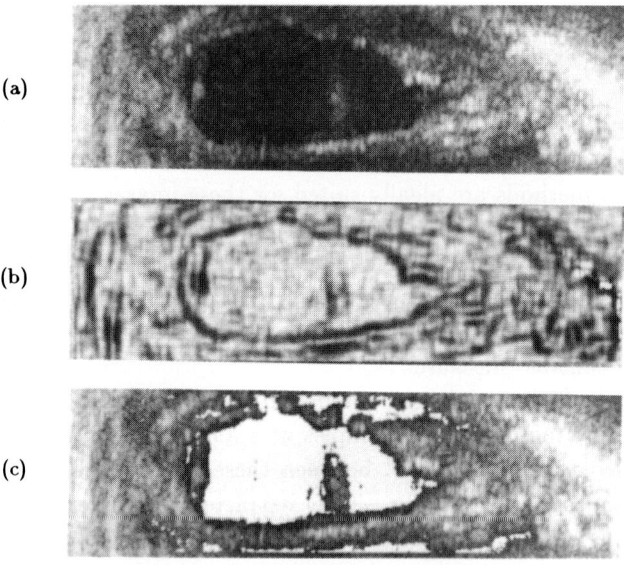

Fig. 7. The processing of the ultrasound images of the heart using textural features. (a) A 128×432 ultrasound image from the left ventricle of the heart. (b) The fractal dimension used as the texture feature. The fractal dimension is lower at the walls of the ventricle. (c) Image segmentation from a k-means clustering algorithm. The white region is cluster 2 which corresponds to the blood. The clustering uses four features, one of which is the fractal texture feature.

2.2.3. *Document Processing*

One of the useful applications of machine vision and image analysis has been in the area of document image analysis and character recognition. Document processing has applications ranging from postal address recognition to analysis and interpretation of maps. In many postal document processing applications (such as the recognition of destination address and zip code information on envelopes), the first step is the ability to separate the regions in the image which contain useful information from the background.

Most image analysis methods proposed to date for document processing are based upon the characteristics of printed documents and try to take advantage of these properties. For example, generally newspaper print is organized in rectangular blocks and this fact is used in a segmentation algorithm proposed in [33]. Many methods work on images based on precise algorithms which one might consider as having morphological characteristics. For example, Wang and Srihari [33] used projection profiles of the pixel values to identify large "text" blocks by detecting valleys in these profiles. Wahl *et al.* [34] used constrained run lengths and connected component analysis to detect blocks of text. Fletcher and Kasturi [35] used the fact that most text blocks lie in a straight line, and utilized Hough transform techniques to detect collinear elements. Taxt *et al.* [36] view the identification of print in document images as a two-category classification problem, where the categories are print and background. They use various classification methods to compute the segmentation including contextual classification and relaxation algorithms.

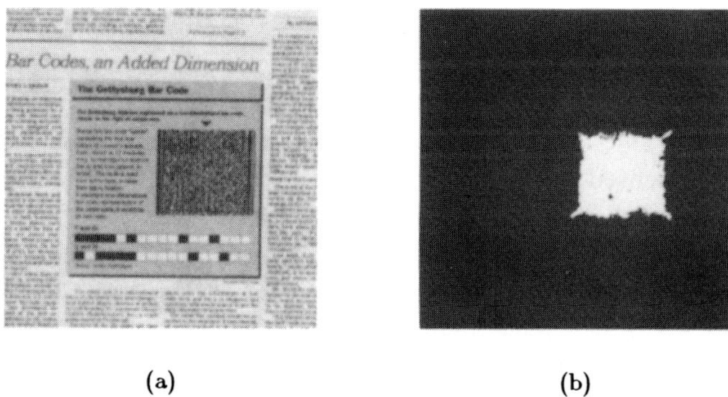

(a)   (b)

Fig. 8. Locating bar code in a newspaper image. (a) A scanned image of a newspaper that contains a bar code. (b) The two-class segmentation using Gabor filter features in [40]. The bar code region in the image has a distinct texture.

One can also use texture segmentation methods for preprocessing document images to identify regions of interest [37,38,39]. An example of this can be seen in Fig. 8. The texture segmentation algorithm described in [40] was used to segment a newspaper image. In the resulting segmentation, one of the regions identified as having a uniform texture, which is different from its surrounding texture, is the bar code block. A similar method is used for locating text blocks in newspapers. A segmentation of the document image is obtained using three classes of textures: one class for the text regions, a second class for the uniform regions that form the background or images where intensities vary slowly, and a third class for the transition areas between the two types of regions (see Fig. 9). The text regions are characterized by their high frequency content.

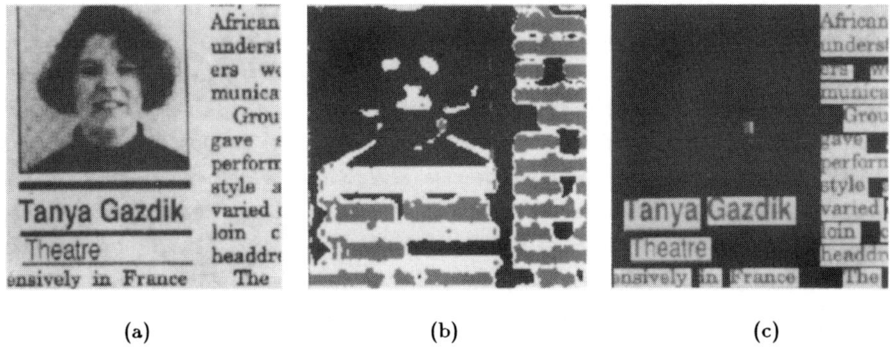

(a)   (b)   (c)

Fig. 9. Text/graphics separation using texture information. (a) An image of a newspaper captured by a flatbed scanner. (b) The three-class segmentation obtained by the Gabor filter based texture segmentation algorithm. (c) The regions identified as text.

2.2.4. *Remote Sensing*

Texture analysis has been extensively used to classify remotely sensed images. Land use classification where homogeneous regions with different types of terrains (such as wheat, bodies of water, urban regions, etc.) need to be identified is an important application. Haralick *et al.* [41] used gray level co-occurrence features to analyze remotely sensed images. They computed gray level co-occurrence matrices for a distance of one with four directions ($0°, 45°, 90°$, and $135°$). For a seven-class classification problem, they obtained approximately 80% classification accuracy using texture features.

Rignot and Kwok [42] have analyzed SAR images using texture features computed from gray level co-occurrence matrices. However, they supplement these features with knowledge about the properties of SAR images. For example, image restoration algorithms were used to eliminate the specular noise present in SAR images in order to improve classification results. The use of various texture features was studied for analyzing SAR images by Schistad and Jain [43]. SAR images shown in Figs. 5(b) and (c) were used to identify land use categories of water, agricultural areas, urban areas, and other areas. Fractal dimension, autoregressive Markov random field model, and gray level co-occurrence texture features were used in the classification. The classification errors ranged from 25% for the fractal based models to as low as 6% for the MRF features. Du [44] used texture features derived from Gabor filters to segment SAR images. He successfully segmented the SAR images into categories of water, new forming ice, older ice, and multi-year ice. Lee and Philpot [45] also used spectral texture features to segment SAR images.

3. A Taxonomy of Texture Models

Identifying the perceived qualities of texture in an image is an important first step towards building mathematical models for texture. The intensity variations in an image which characterize texture are generally due to some underlying physical variation in the scene (such as pebbles on a beach or waves in water). Modelling this physical variation is very difficult, so texture is usually characterized by the two-dimensional variations in the intensities present in the image. This explains the fact that no precise, general definition of texture exists in the computer vision literature. In spite of this, there are a number of intuitive properties of texture which are generally assumed to be true.

- Texture is a property of areas; the texture of a point is undefined. So, texture is a contextual property and its definition must involve gray values in a spatial neighborhood. The size of this neighborhood depends upon the texture type, or the size of the primitives defining the texture.
- Texture involves the spatial distribution of gray levels. Thus, two-dimensional histograms or co-occurrence matrices are reasonable texture analysis tools.
- Texture in an image can be perceived at different scales or levels of resolution [10]. For example, consider the texture represented in a brick wall. At a coarse resolution, the texture is perceived as formed by the individual bricks in the wall; the interior details in the brick are lost. At a higher resolution, when only a few bricks are in the field of view, the perceived texture shows the details in the brick.
- A region is perceived to have texture when the number of primitive objects in the region is large. If only a few primitive objects are present, then a group of countable objects is perceived instead of a textured image. In other words, a texture is perceived when significant individual "forms" are not present.

Image texture has a number of perceived qualities which play an important role in describing texture. Laws [47] identified the following properties as playing an important role in describing texture: uniformity, density, coarseness, roughness, regularity, linearity, directionality, direction, frequency, and phase. Some of these perceived qualities are not independent. For example, frequency is not independent of density and the property of direction only applies to directional textures. The fact that the perception of texture has so many different dimensions is an important reason why there is no single method of texture representation which is adequate for a variety of textures.

3.1. *Statistical Methods*

One of the defining qualities of texture is the spatial distribution of gray values. The use of statistical features is therefore one of the early methods proposed in the machine vision literature. In the following, we will use $\{I(x,y), 0 \le x \le N-1, 0 \le y \le N-1\}$ to denote an $N \times N$ image with G gray levels. A large number of texture features have been proposed. But, these features are not independent as pointed out by Tomita and Tsuji [46]. The relationship between the various statistical texture measures and the input image is summarized in Fig. 10 [46]. Picard [48] has also related the gray level co-occurrence matrices to the Markov random field models.

3.1.1. *Co-occurrence Matrices*

Spatial gray level co-occurrence estimates image properties related to second-order statistics. Haralick [10] suggested the use of gray level co-occurrence matrices (GLCM) which have become one of the most well-known and widely used texture features. The $G \times G$ gray level co-occurrence matrix $P_\mathbf{d}$ for a displacement vector $\mathbf{d} = (dx, dy)$ is defined as follows. The entry (i, j) of $P_\mathbf{d}$ is the number of occurrences of the pair of gray levels i and j which are a distance $\mathbf{d}$ apart. Formally, it is given as

$$P_\mathbf{d}(i,j) = |\{((r,s),(t,\nu)) : I(r,s) = i, I(t,\nu) = j\}| \qquad (3.1)$$

where $(r,s),(t,\nu) \in N \times N, (t,\nu) = (r + dx, s + dy)$, and $|\cdot|$ is the cardinality of a set.

As an example, consider the following 4×4 image containing three different gray values:

$$
\begin{array}{cccc}
1 & 1 & 0 & 0 \\
1 & 1 & 0 & 0 \\
0 & 0 & 2 & 2 \\
0 & 0 & 2 & 2
\end{array}
$$

The 3×3 gray level co-occurrence matrix for this image for a displacement vector of $\mathbf{d} = (1,0)$ is given as follows:

$$
P_\mathbf{d} = \begin{bmatrix} 4 & 0 & 2 \\ 2 & 2 & 0 \\ 0 & 0 & 2 \end{bmatrix} .
$$

Here the entry $(0,0)$ of $P_\mathbf{d}$ is 4 because there are four pixel pairs of that are offset by $(1, 0)$ amount. Examples of $P_\mathbf{d}$ for other displacement vectors is given below.

$$
\mathbf{d} = (0,1) \qquad P_\mathbf{d} = \begin{bmatrix} 4 & 2 & 0 \\ 0 & 2 & 0 \\ 2 & 0 & 2 \end{bmatrix}
$$

$$
\mathbf{d} = (1,1) \qquad P_\mathbf{d} = \begin{bmatrix} 3 & 1 & 1 \\ 1 & 1 & 0 \\ 1 & 0 & 1 \end{bmatrix}
$$

Notice that the co-occurrence matrix so defined is not symmetric. But a symmetric co-occurrence matrix can be computed by the formula $P = P_\mathbf{d} + P_{-\mathbf{d}}$. The co-occurrence matrix reveals certain properties about the spatial distribution of the gray levels in the texture image. For example, if most of the entries in the co-occurrence matrix are concentrated along the diagonals, then the texture is coarse with respect to the displacement vector $\mathbf{d}$. Haralick has proposed a number of useful texture features that can be computed from the co-occurrence matrix. Table 1 lists some of these features. Here μ_x and μ_y are the means and σ_x and σ_y are the standard deviations of $P_\mathbf{d}(x)$ and $P_\mathbf{d}(y)$, respectively, where $P_{\mathbf{d}(x)} = \sum_j P_\mathbf{d}(x, j)$ and $P_\mathbf{d}(y) = \sum_i P_\mathbf{d}(i, y)$.

Table 1. Some texture features extracted from gray level co-occurrence matrices.

Texture Feature	Formula
Energy	$\displaystyle\sum_i \sum_j P_\mathbf{d}^2(i, j)$
Entropy	$\displaystyle -\sum_i \sum_j P_\mathbf{d}(i, j) \log P_\mathbf{d}(i, j)$
Contrast	$\displaystyle\sum_i \sum_j (i - j)^2 P_\mathbf{d}(i, j)$
Homogeneity	$\displaystyle\sum_i \sum_j \frac{P_\mathbf{d}(i, j)}{1 + |i - j|}$
Correlation	$\displaystyle\frac{\sum_i \sum_j (i - \mu_x)(j - \mu_y) P_\mathbf{d}(i, j)}{\sigma_x \sigma_y}$

The co-occurrence matrix features suffer from a number of difficulties. There is no well established method of selecting the displacement vector $\mathbf{d}$ and computing co-occurrence matrices for different values of $\mathbf{d}$ is not feasible. For a given $\mathbf{d}$, a large number of features can be computed from the co-occurrence matrix. This means that some sort of feature selection method must be used to select the most relevant features. The co-occurrence matrix-based texture features have also been primarily used in texture classification tasks and not in segmentation tasks.

3.1.2. *Autocorrelation Features*

An important property of many textures is the repetitive nature of the placement of texture elements in the image. The autocorrelation function of an image can be used to assess the amount of regularity as well as the fineness/coarseness of the texture present in the image. Formally, the autocorrelation function of an image $I(x, y)$ is defined as follows:

$$\rho(x, y) = \frac{\displaystyle\sum_{u=0}^{N} \sum_{v=0}^{N} I(u, v) I(u + x, v + y)}{\displaystyle\sum_{u=0}^{N} \sum_{v=0}^{N} I^2(u, v)} . \tag{3.2}$$

The image boundaries must be handled with special care but we omit the details here. This function is related to the size of the texture primitive (i.e. the fineness of the texture). If the texture is coarse, then the autocorrelation function will drop off slowly; otherwise, it will drop off very rapidly. For regular textures, the autocorrelation function will exhibit peaks and valleys.

The autocorrelation function is also related to the power spectrum of the Fourier transform (see Fig. 10). Consider the image function in the spatial domain $I(x, y)$ and its Fourier transform $F(u, \nu)$. The quantity $|F(u, \nu)|^2$ is defined as the power spectrum where $|\cdot|$ is the modulus of a complex number. The example in Fig. 11 illustrates the effect of the directionality of a texture on the distribution of energy in the power spectrum. Early approaches using such spectral features would divide the frequency domain into rings (for frequency content) and wedges (for orientation content) as shown in Fig. 12. The frequency domain is thus divided into regions and the total energy in each of these regions is computed as texture features.

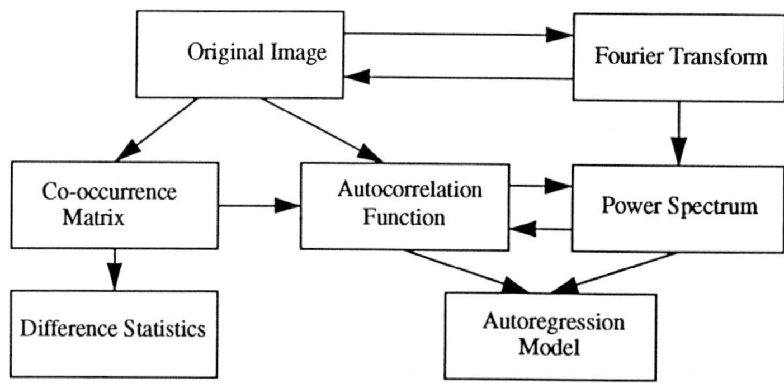

Fig. 10. The interrelation between the various second-order statistics and the input image [46]. © Reprinted by permission of Kluwer Academic Publishers.

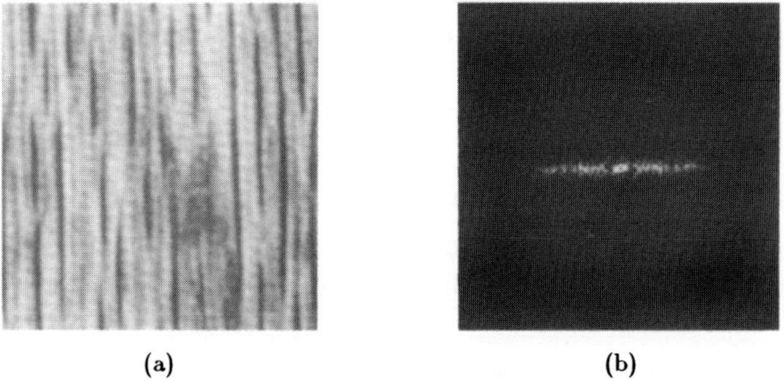

(a)   (b)

Fig. 11. Texture features from the power spectrum. (a) A texture image, and (b) its power spectrum. The directional nature of this texture is reflected in the directional distribution of energy in the power spectrum.

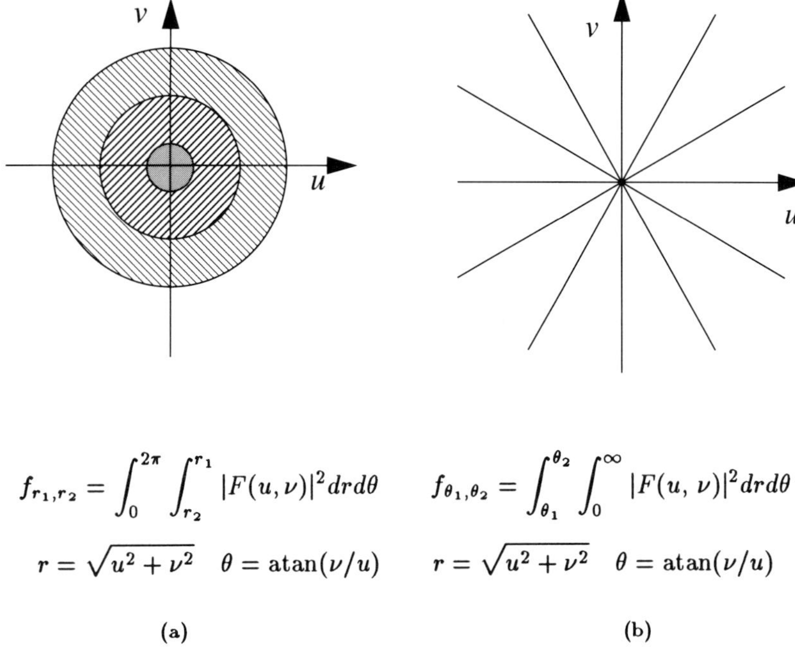

$$f_{r_1,r_2} = \int_0^{2\pi} \int_{r_2}^{r_1} |F(u,\nu)|^2 dr d\theta \qquad f_{\theta_1,\theta_2} = \int_{\theta_1}^{\theta_2} \int_0^{\infty} |F(u,\nu)|^2 dr d\theta$$

$$r = \sqrt{u^2 + \nu^2} \quad \theta = \mathrm{atan}(\nu/u) \qquad r = \sqrt{u^2 + \nu^2} \quad \theta = \mathrm{atan}(\nu/u)$$

(a)   (b)

Fig. 12. Texture features computed from the power spectrum of the image. (a) The energy computed in each shaded band is a texture feature indicating coarseness/fineness, and (b) the energy computed in each wedge is a texture feature indicating directionality.

3.2. Geometrical Methods

The class of texture analysis methods that falls under the heading of geometrical methods is characterized by their definition of texture as being composed of "texture elements" or primitives. The method of analysis usually depends upon the geometric properties of these texture elements. Once the texture elements are identified in the image, there are two major approaches to analyzing the texture. One computes statistical properties from the extracted texture elements and utilizes these as texture features. The other tries to extract the placement rule that describes the texture. The latter approach may involve geometric or syntactic methods of analyzing texture.

3.2.1. Voronoi Tessellation Features

Tuceryan and Jain [49] proposed the extraction of texture tokens by using the properties of the Voronoi tessellation of the given image. Voronoi tessellation has been proposed because of its desirable properties in defining local spatial neighborhoods and because the local spatial distributions of tokens are reflected in the shapes of the Voronoi polygons. First, texture tokens are extracted and then the tessellation is constructed. Tokens can be as simple as points of high gradient in the image or complex structures such as line segments or closed boundaries.

In computer vision, the Voronoi tessellation was first proposed by Ahuja as a model for defining "neighborhoods" [50]. Suppose that we are given a set S of three or more tokens (for simplicity, we will assume that a token is a point) in the Euclidean plane. Assume that these points are not all collinear, and that no four points are cocircular. Consider an arbitrary pair of points P and Q. The bisector of the line joining P and Q is the locus of points equidistant from both P and Q and divides the plane into two halves. The half plane $H_P^Q(H_Q^P)$ is the locus of points closer to $P(Q)$ than to $Q(P)$. For any given point P, a set of such half planes is obtained for various choices of Q. The intersection $\bigcap_{Q \in S, Q \neq P} H_P^Q$ defines a polygonal region consisting of points closer to P than any other point. Such a region is called the Voronoi polygon [51] associated with the point. The set of complete polygons is called the *Voronoi diagram* of S [52]. The Voronoi diagram together with the incomplete polygons in the convex hull define a *Voronoi tessellation* of the entire plane. Two points are said to be *Voronoi neighbors* if the Voronoi polygons enclosing them share a common edge. The dual representation of the Voronoi tessellation is the *Delaunay graph* which is obtained by connecting all the pairs of points which are Voronoi neighbors as defined above. An optimal algorithm to compute the Voronoi tessellation for a point pattern is described by Preparata and Shamos [53]. A simple 2-D dot pattern and its Voronoi tessellation are shown in Fig. 13.

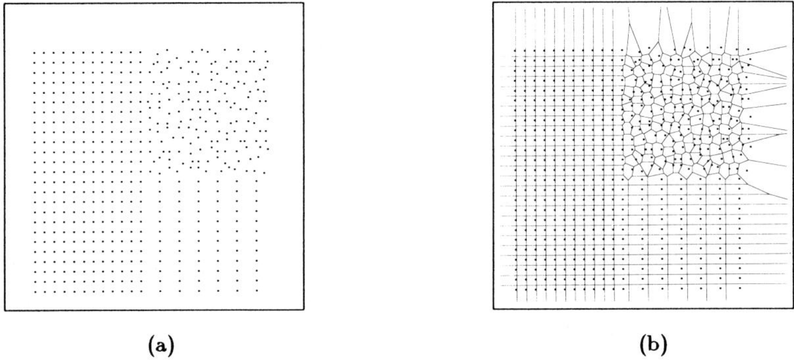

(a)   (b)

Fig. 13. Voronoi tessellation: (a) An example dot pattern, and (b) its Voronoi tessellation.

The neighborhood of a token P is defined by the Voronoi polygon containing P. Many of the perceptually significant characteristics of a token's environment are manifest in the geometric properties of the Voronoi neighborhoods (see Fig. 13). The geometric properties of the Voronoi polygons are used as texture features.

In order to apply geometrical methods to gray level images, we need to first extract tokens from images. We use the following simple algorithm to extract tokens from input gray level textural images.

1. Apply a Laplacian-of-Gaussian (LoG or $\nabla^2 G$) filter to the image. For computational efficiency, the $\nabla^2 G$ filter can be approximated with a difference of

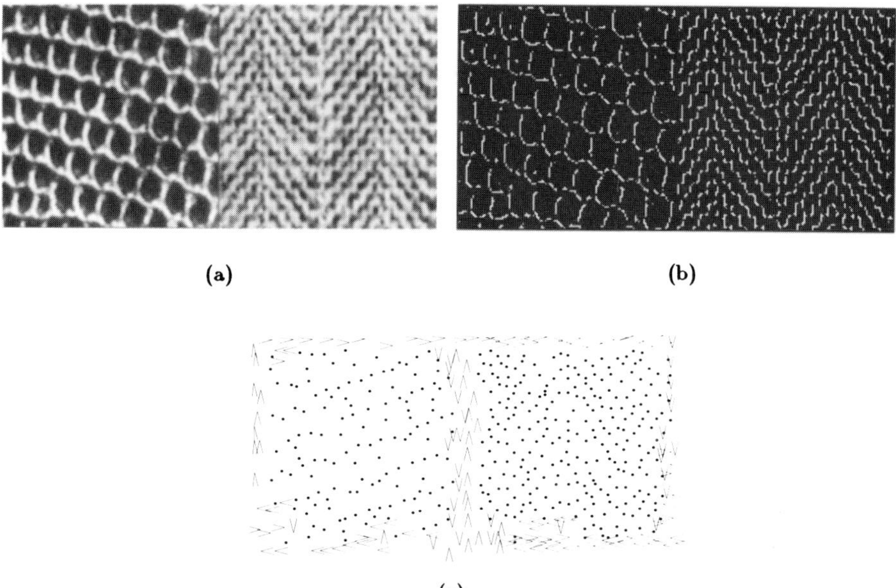

(a)   (b)

(c)

Fig. 14. Texture segmentation using the Voronoi tessellation. (a) An example texture pair from Brodatz's album [92], (b) the peaks detected in the filtered image, and (c) the segmentation using the texture features obtained from Voronoi polygons [49]. The arrows indicate the border direction. The interior is on the right when looking in the direction of the arrow.

Gaussians (DoG) filter. The size of the DoG filter is determined by the sizes of the two Gaussian filters. Tuceryan and Jain used $\sigma_1 = 1$ for the first Gaussian and $\sigma_2 = 1.6\sigma_1$ for the second. According to Marr, this is the ratio at which a DoG filter best approximates the corresponding $\nabla^2 G$ filter [54].

2. Select those pixels that lie on a local intensity maximum in the filtered image. A pixel in the filtered image is said to be on a local maximum if its magnitude is larger than six or more of its eight nearest neighbors. This results in a binary image. For example, applying steps 1 and 2 to the image in Fig. 14(a) yields the binary image in Fig. 14(b).

3. Perform a connected component analysis on the binary image using eight nearest neighbors. Each connected component defines a texture primitive (token).

The Voronoi tessellation of the resulting tokens is constructed. Features of each Voronoi cell are extracted and tokens with similar features are grouped to construct uniform texture regions. Moments of area of the Voronoi polygons serve as a useful set of features that reflect both the spatial distribution and shapes of the tokens in the textured image. The $(p + q)$th order moments of area of a closed region R with respect to a token with coordinates (x_0, y_0) are defined as [55]:

$$m_{pq} = \iint\limits_{R} (x - x_0)^P (y - y_0)^q \, dx \, dy \tag{3.3}$$

Table 2. Voronoi polygon features used by the texture segmentation algorithm [49]. Here, f_2 gives the magnitude of the vector from the token to the polygon centroid, f_3 gives its direction, f_4 gives the overall elongation of the polygon ($f_4 = 0$ for a circle), and f_5 gives the orientation of its major axis. $(\bar{x}, \bar{y})$ are the coordinates of the Voronoi polygon's centroid.

Texture Feature	Computation
f_1	m_{00}
f_2	$\sqrt{\bar{x}^2 + \bar{y}^2}$
f_3	$\mathrm{atan}(\bar{y}/\bar{x})$
f_4	$\dfrac{\sqrt{(m_{20} - m_{02})^2 + 4m_{11}^2}}{m_{20} + m_{02} + \sqrt{(m_{20} - m_{02})^2 + 4m_{11}^2}}$
f_5	$\mathrm{atan}\left(\dfrac{2m_{11}}{m_{20} - m_{02}}\right)$

where $p + q = 0, 1, 2, \ldots$. A description of the five features used is given in Table 2 where $(\bar{x}, \bar{y})$ are the coordinates of the Voronoi polygon's centroid.

The texture features based on Voronoi polygons have been used for segmentation of textured images. The segmentation algorithm is edge based, using a statistical comparison of the neighboring collections of tokens. A large dissimilarity among the texture features is evidence for a texture edge. This algorithm has successfully segmented gray level texture images as well as a number of synthetic textures with identical second-order statistics. Figure 14(a) shows an example texture pair and Fig. 14(c) shows the resulting segmentation.

3.2.2. *Structural Methods*

The structural models of texture assume that textures are composed of texture primitives. The texture is produced by the placement of these primitives according to certain placement rules. This class of algorithms, in general, is limited in power unless one is dealing with very regular textures. Structural texture analysis consists of two major steps: (a) extraction of the texture elements, and (b) inference of the placement rule.

There are a number of ways to extract texture elements in images. It is useful to define what is meant by texture elements in this context. Usually texture elements consist of regions in the image with uniform gray levels. Voorhees and Poggio [56] argued that blobs are important in texture perception. They have proposed a method based on filtering the image with Laplacian of Gaussian (LoG) masks at different scales and combining this information to extract the blobs in the image. Blostein and Ahuja [57] perform similar processing in order to extract texture tokens in images by examining the response of the LoG filter at multiple scales. They integrate their multi-scale blob detection with surface shape computation in order to improve the results of both processes. Tomita and Tsuji [46] also suggest a method of computing texture tokens by doing a medial axis transform on the connected components of a segmented image. They then compute a number of properties such as intensity and shapes of these detected tokens.

Zucker [58] has proposed a method in which he regards the observable textures (real textures) as distorted versions of ideal textures. The placement rule is defined for the ideal texture by a graph that is isomorphic to a regular or semiregular tessellation. These graphs are then transformed to generate the observable texture. Which of the regular tessellations is used as the placement rule is inferred from the observable texture. This is done by computing a two-dimensional histogram of the relative positions of the detected texture tokens.

Another approach to modeling texture by structural means is described by Fu [59]. In this approach the texture image is regarded as texture primitives arranged according to a placement rule. The primitive can be as simple as a single pixel that can take a gray value, but it is usually a collection of pixels. The placement rule is defined by a tree grammar. A texture is then viewed as a string in the language defined by the grammar whose terminal symbols are the texture primitives. An advantage of this method is that it can be used for texture generation as well as texture analysis. The patterns generated by the tree grammars could also be regarded as ideal textures in Zucker's model.

3.3. *Model Based Methods*

Model based texture analysis methods are based on the construction of an image model that can be used not only to describe texture, but also to synthesize it. The model parameters capture the essential perceived qualities of texture.

3.3.1. *Random Field Models*

Markov random fields (MRFs) have been popular for modeling images. They are able to capture the local (spatial) contextual information in an image. These models assume that the intensity at each pixel in the image depends on the intensities of only the neighboring pixels. MRF models have been applied to various image processing applications such as texture synthesis [60], texture classification [61,62], image segmentation [63,64], image restoration [65], and image compression.

The image is usually represented by an $N \times N$ lattice denoted by $L = \{(i,j)|1 \le i \le M, 1 \le j \le N\}$. $I(i,j)$ is a random variable which represents the gray level at pixel (i,j) on lattice L. The indexing of the lattice is simplified for mathematical convenience to I_t with $t = (i-1)N + j$. Let A be the range set common to all random variables I_t and let $\Omega = \{(x_1, x_2, \ldots, x_{MN})|x_t \in A, \forall t\}$ denote the set of all labellings of L. Note that A is specified according to the application. For instance, for an image with 256 different gray levels A may be the set $\{0, 1, \ldots, 255\}$. The random vector $I = (I_1, I_2, \ldots, I_{MN})$ denotes a coloring of the lattice. A discrete Markov random field is a random field whose probability mass function has the properties of positivity, Markovianity, and homogeneity.

The neighbor set of a site t can be defined in different ways. The first-order neighbors of t are its four-connected neighbors and the second-order neighbors are its eight-connected neighbors. Within these neighborhoods, sets of neighbors which form cliques (single site, pairs, triples, and quadruples) are usually used in the definition of the conditional probabilities.

A discrete Gibbs random field (GRF) assigns a probability mass function to the entire lattice:

$$P(\mathbf{X} = \mathbf{x}) = \frac{1}{z}e^{-U(x)} \quad \forall \mathbf{x} \in \Omega \tag{3.4}$$

where $U(\mathbf{x})$ is an energy function and Z is a normalizing constant called the partition function. The energy function is usually specified in terms of cliques formed over neighboring pixels. For the second-order neighbors the possible cliques are given in Fig. 15. The energy function is then expressed in terms of potential functions $V_C(.)$ over the cliques Q:

$$U(\mathbf{x}) = \sum_{c \in Q} V_C(\mathbf{x}) \ . \tag{3.5}$$

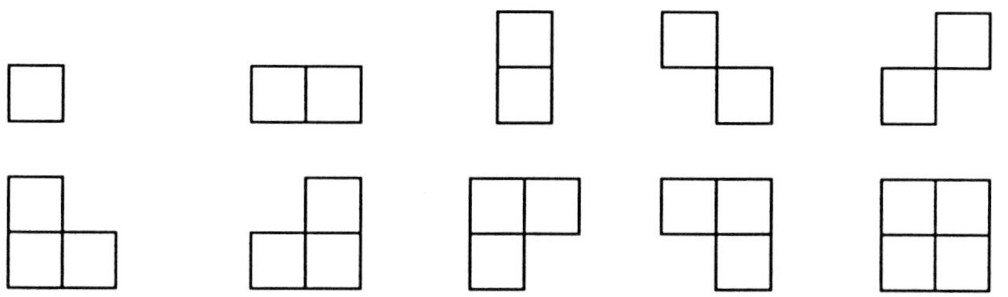

Fig. 15. The clique types for the second-order neighborhood.

We have the property that with respect to a neighborhood system, there exists a unique Gibbs random field for every Markov random field and there exists a unique Markov random field for every Gibbs random field [66]. The consequence of this theorem is that one can model the texture either globally by specifying the total energy of the lattice or model it locally by specifying the local interactions of the neighboring pixels in terms of the conditional probabilities.

There are a number of ways in which textures are modeled using Gibbs random fields. Among these are the Derin–Elliot model [67] and the auto-binomial model [66, 60] which are defined by considering only the single pixel and pairwise pixel cliques in the second-order neighbors of a site. In both models the conditional probabilities are given by expressions of the following form:

$$P(x_t | R_t) = \frac{1}{Z_t}e^{-\mathbf{w}(x_t | R_t)^T \theta} \tag{3.6}$$

where $Z_t = \sum_{g \in A} e^{-\mathbf{w}(g, R_t)^T \theta}$ is the normalization constant. The energy of the Gibbs random field is given by:

$$U(\mathbf{x}) = \frac{1}{2} \sum_{t=1}^{MN} \mathbf{w}(x_p R_t)^T \theta \tag{3.7}$$

where $\mathbf{w}(x_t, R_t) = [w_1(x_t)\ w_2(x_t)\ w_3(x_t)\ w_4(x_t)]^T$ and $\theta = [\theta_1\ \theta_2\ \theta_3\ \theta_4]^T$. The two models define the components of the $\mathbf{w}$ vector, $w_r(x_t)$, differently as follows:

Derin–Elliott model: $w_r(x_t) = I(x_t, x_{t-r}) + I(x_t, x_{t+r})\quad 1 \leq r \leq 4$.

Auto-binomial model: $w_r(x_t) = x_t(x_{t-r} + x_{t+r})\quad 1 \leq r \leq 4$.

Here r is the index that defines the set of neighboring pixels of a site t, and $I(a, b)$ is an indicator function as follows:

$$I(a, b) = \begin{cases} -1 & \text{if } a = b \\ 1 & \text{otherwise} . \end{cases} \tag{3.8}$$

The vector θ is the set of parameters that defines and models the textural properties of the image. In texture synthesis problems, the values are set to control the type of texture to be generated. In the classification and segmentation problems, the parameters need to be estimated in order to process the texture images. Textures were synthesized using this method by Cross and Jain [60]. Model parameters were also estimated for a set of natural textures. The estimated parameters were used to generate synthetic textures and the results were compared to the original images. The models captured microtextures well, but they failed with regular and inhomogeneous textures.

3.3.2. *Fractals*

Many natural surfaces have a statistical quality of roughness and self-similarity at different scales. Fractals are very useful and have become popular in modelling these properties in image processing. Mandelbrot [68] proposed fractal geometry and is the first one to notice its existence in the natural world.

We first define a deterministic fractal in order to introduce some of the fundamental concepts. Self-similarity across scales in fractal geometry is a crucial concept. A deterministic fractal is defined using this concept of self-similarity as follows. Given a bounded set A in a Euclidean n-space, the set A is said to be self-similar when A is the union of N distinct (non-overlapping) copies of itself, each of which has been scaled down by a ratio of r. The fractal dimension D is related to the number N and the ratio r as follows:

$$D = \frac{\log N}{\log(1/r)} . \tag{3.9}$$

The fractal dimension gives a measure of the roughness of a surface. Intuitively, the larger the fractal dimension, the rougher the texture is. Pentland [69] has argued and given evidence that images of most natural surfaces can be modelled as spatially isotropic fractals. Most natural surfaces and in particular textured surfaces are not deterministic as described above but have a statistical variation. This makes the computation of fractal dimension more difficult.

There are a number of methods proposed for estimating the fractal dimension D. One method is the estimation of the box dimension as follows [70]. Given a bounded set A in Euclidean n-space, consider boxes of size $L_{\max}$ on a side which cover the set A. A scaled down version of the set A by ratio r, will result in $N = 1/r^D$ similar sets. This new set can be covered by boxes of size $L = rL_{\max}$. The number of such boxes is then related to the fractal dimension by

$$N(L) = \frac{1}{r^D} = \left[\frac{L_{\max}}{L} \right]^D .$$ (3.10)

The fractal dimension is then estimated from Eq. (3.10) by the following procedure. For a given L, divide the n-space into a grid of boxes of size L and count the number of boxes covering A. Repeat this procedure for different values of L. Then estimate the value of the fractal dimension D from the slope of the line

$$\ln(N(L)) = -D\ln(L) + D\ln(L_{\max}) .$$ (3.11)

This can be accomplished by computing the least squares linear fit to the data, namely, a plot of $\ln(L)$ vs. $-\ln(N(L))$.

An improved method of estimating the fractal dimension was proposed by Voss [71]. Assume we are estimating the fractal dimension of an image surface A. Let $P(m, L)$ be the probability that there are m points within a box of side length L centered at an arbitrary point on the surface A. Let M be the total number of points in the image. When one overlays the image with boxes of side length L, then the $(M/m)P(m, L)$ is the expected number of boxes with m points inside. The expected total number of boxes needed to cover the whole image is

$$E[N(L)] = M \sum_{m=1}^{N} (1/m)P(m, L) .$$ (3.12)

The expected value of $N(L)$ is proportional to L^{-D} and thus can be used to estimate the fractal dimension D. Other methods have also been proposed for estimating the fractal dimension. For example, Super and Bovik [72] have proposed using Gabor filters and signal processing methods to estimate the fractal dimension in textured images.

The fractal dimension is not sufficient to capture all textural properties. It has been shown [70] that there may be perceptually very different textures that have very similar fractal dimensions. Therefore, another measure, called *lacunarity*

[68,71,70], has been suggested in order to capture the textural property that will let one distinguish between such textures. Lacunarity is defined as

$$\Lambda = E\left[\left(\frac{M}{E(M)} - 1\right)^2\right] \tag{3.13}$$

where M is the mass of the fractal set $E(M)$ and is the expected value of the mass. This measures the discrepancy between the actual mass and the expected value of the mass. Lacunarity is small when texture is fine and it is large when the texture is coarse. The mass of the fractal set is related to the length L by the power law:

$$M(L) = KL^D \ . \tag{3.14}$$

Voss [71] suggested computing lacunarity from the probability distribution $P(m, L)$ as follows. Let $M(L) = \sum_{m=1}^{N} mP(m, L)$ and $M^2(L) = \sum_{m=1}^{N} m^2 P(m, L)$. Then lacunarity Λ is defined as:

$$\Lambda(L) = \frac{M^2(L) - (M(L))^2}{(M(L))^2} \ . \tag{3.15}$$

This measure of the image is then used as a texture feature in order to perform texture segmentation or classification.

Ohanian and Dubes [73] have studied the performance of various texture features. They studied the texture features with the performance criteria: "which features optimized the classification rate?" They compared four fractal features, 16 co-occurrence features, four Markov random field features, and Gabor features. They used Whitney's forward selection method for feature selection. The evaluation was done on four classes of images: Gauss Markov random field images, fractal images, leather images, and painted surfaces. The co-occurrence features generally outperformed other features (88% correct classification) followed by fractal features (84% classification). Using both fractal and co-occurrence features improved the classification rate to 91%. Their study did not compare the texture features in segmentation tasks. It also used the energy from the raw Gabor filtered images instead of using the empirical nonlinear transformation needed to obtain the texture features as suggested in [40] (see also Section 3.4.3).

3.4. *Signal Processing Methods*

Psychophysical research has given evidence that the human brain does a frequency analysis of the image [19,74]. Texture is especially suited for this type of analysis because of its properties. This section will review the various techniques of texture analysis that rely on signal processing techniques. Most techniques try to compute certain features from filtered images which are then used in either classification or segmentation tasks.

3.4.1. *Spatial Domain Filters*

Spatial domain filters are the most direct way to capture image texture properties. Earlier attempts at defining such methods concentrated on measuring the edge density per unit area. Fine textures tend to have a higher density of edges per unit area than coarser textures. The measurement of edgeness is usually computed by simple edge masks such as the Robert's operator or the Laplacian operator [10,47]. The two orthogonal masks for the Robert's operator and one digital realization of the Laplacian are given below.

Robert's Operators   Laplacian Operator

$$M_1 = \begin{bmatrix} 1 & 0 \\ 0 & -1 \end{bmatrix} \quad M_2 = \begin{bmatrix} 0 & 1 \\ -1 & 0 \end{bmatrix} \qquad L = \begin{bmatrix} -1 & -1 & -1 \\ -1 & 8 & -1 \\ -1 & -1 & -1 \end{bmatrix}$$

The edgeness measure can be computed over an image area by computing a magnitude from the responses of Robert's masks or from the response of the Laplacian mask.

Malik and Perona [75] proposed spatial filtering to model the preattentive texture perception in the human visual system. Their proposed model consists of three stages: (i) convolution of the image with a bank of even-symmetric filters followed by half-wave rectification, (ii) inhibition of spurious responses in a localized area, and (iii) detection of the boundaries between the different textures. The even-symmetric filters they used consist of differences of offset Gaussian (DOOG) functions. The half-wave rectification and inhibition (implemented as leaders-take-all strategy) are methods of introducing a nonlinearity into the computation of texture features. A nonlinearity is needed in order to discriminate texture pairs with identical mean brightness and identical second-order statistics. The texture boundary detection is done by a straightforward edge detection method applied to the feature images obtained from stage (ii). This method works on a variety of texture examples and is able to discriminate natural as well as synthetic textures with carefully controlled properties. Unser and Eden [76] have also looked at texture features that are obtained from spatial filters and a nonlinear operator. Reed and Wechsler [77] review a number of spatial/spatial frequency domain filter techniques for segmenting textured images.

Another set of spatial filters are based on spatial moments [47]. The $(p+q)$th moments over an image region R are given by the formula

$$m_{pq} = \sum_{(x,y) \in R} x^p y^q I(x,y) \; . \tag{3.16}$$

If the region R is a local rectangular area and the moments are computed around each pixel in the image, then this is equivalent to filtering the image by a set of spatial masks. The resulting filtered images that correspond to the moments are then used as texture features. The masks are obtained by defining a window of size $W \times W$ and a local coordinate system centered within the window. Let (i,j) be the image coordinates at which the moments are computed. For pixel coordinates (m,n)

which fall within the $W \times W$ window centered at (i, j), the normalized coordinates (x_m, y_n) are given by:

$$x_m = \frac{(m - i)}{(W/2)} \quad y_n = \frac{(n - j)}{(W/2)} \ . \tag{3.17}$$

Then the moments within a window centered at pixel (i, j) are computed by the sum in Eq. (3.16) that uses the normalized coordinates.

$$m_{pq} = \sum_{n=-W/2}^{W/2} \sum_{m=-W/2}^{W/2} I(m,n) x_m^p y_n^q \ . \tag{3.18}$$

The coefficients for each pixel within the window to evaluate the sum is what defines the mask coefficients. If R is a 3×3 region, then the resulting masks are given below:

$$M_{00} = \begin{bmatrix} 1 & 1 & 1 \\ 1 & 1 & 1 \\ 1 & 1 & 1 \end{bmatrix} \quad M_{10} = \begin{bmatrix} -1 & -1 & -1 \\ 0 & 0 & 0 \\ 1 & 1 & 1 \end{bmatrix} \quad M_{01} = \begin{bmatrix} -1 & 0 & 1 \\ -1 & 0 & 1 \\ -1 & 0 & 1 \end{bmatrix}$$

$$M_{20} = \begin{bmatrix} 1 & 1 & 1 \\ 0 & 0 & 0 \\ 1 & 1 & 1 \end{bmatrix} \quad M_{11} = \begin{bmatrix} 1 & 0 & -1 \\ 0 & 0 & 0 \\ -1 & 0 & 1 \end{bmatrix} \quad M_{02} = \begin{bmatrix} 1 & 0 & 1 \\ 1 & 0 & 1 \\ 1 & 0 & 1 \end{bmatrix}$$

The moment-based features have been used successfully in texture segmentation [78]. An example texture pair and the segmentation are shown in Fig. 16.

(a)   (b)

Fig. 16.   The segmentation results using moment based texture features. (a) A texture pair consisting of reptile skin and herringbone pattern from the Brodatz album [92]. (b) The resulting segmentation.

3.4.2. *Fourier domain filtering*

The frequency analysis of the textured image is best done in the Fourier domain. As the psychophysical results indicated, the human visual system analyzes the textured images by decomposing the image into its frequency and orientation components [19]. The multiple channels tuned to different frequencies are also referred to as multi-resolution processing in the literature. The concept of multi-resolution processing is further refined and developed in the wavelet model described below. Along the lines of these psychophysical results, texture analysis systems have been developed that perform filtering in the Fourier domain to obtain feature images. The idea is similar to the features computed from the rings and wedges as described in Section 3.1.2, except that the phase information is kept. Coggins and Jain [79] used a set of frequency and orientation selective filters in multichannel filtering approach. Each filter is either frequency selective *or* orientation selective. There are four orientation filters centered at $0°, 45°, 90°$, and $135°$. The number of frequency selective filters depends on the image size. For an image of size 128×128 six filters with center frequencies at 1, 2, 4, 8, 16, 32, and 64 cycles/image were used. They were able to successfully segment and classify a variety of natural images as well as synthetic texture pairs described by Julesz with identical second-order statistics (see Fig. 4).

3.4.3. *Gabor and wavelet models*

The Fourier transform is an analysis of the global frequency content in the signal. Many applications require the analysis to be localized in the spatial domain. This is usually handled by introducing spatial dependency into the Fourier analysis. The classical way of doing this is through what is called the window Fourier transform. The window Fourier transform (or short-time Fourier transform) of a one-dimensional signal $f(x)$ is defined as:

$$F_w(u, \xi) = \int_{-\infty}^{\infty} f(x)w(x - \xi)e^{-j2\pi ux}dx \ . \tag{3.19}$$

When the window function $w(x)$ is Gaussian, the transform becomes a Gabor transform. The limits on the resolution in the time and frequency domain of the window Fourier transform are determined by the *time-bandwidth product* or the *Heisenberg uncertainty inequality* given by:

$$\Delta t \Delta u \geq \frac{1}{4\pi} \ . \tag{3.20}$$

Once a window is chosen for the window Fourier transform, the time-frequency resolution is fixed over the entire time-frequency plane. To overcome the resolution limitation of the window Fourier transform, one lets the Δt and Δu vary in the time-frequency domain. Intuitively, the time resolution must increase as the central frequency of the analyzing filter is increased. That is, the relative bandwidth is kept constant in a logarithmic scale. This is accomplished by using a window whose width changes as the frequency changes. Recall that when a function $f(t)$ is scaled in time by a, which is expressed as $f(at)$, the function is contracted if $a > 1$ and it is expanded when $a < 1$. Using this fact, the wavelet transform can be written as:

$$W_{f,a}(u, \xi) = \frac{1}{\sqrt{a}} \int_{-\infty}^{\infty} f(t)h^*\left(\frac{t - \xi}{a}\right)dt \ . \tag{3.21}$$

Here, the impulse response of the filter bank is defined to be scaled versions of the same prototype function $h(t)$. Now, setting in Eq. (3.21)

$$h(t) = w(t)e^{-j2\pi u t} \tag{3.22}$$

we obtain the wavelet model for texture analysis. Usually the scaling factor will be based on the frequency of the filter.

Daugman [80] proposed the use of Gabor filters in the modeling of the receptive fields of simple cells in the visual cortex of some mammals. The proposal to use the Gabor filters in texture analysis was made by Turner [81] and Clark and Bovik [82]. Later Farrokhnia and Jain used it successfully in segmentation and classification of textured images [40,83]. Gabor filters have some desirable optimality properties. Daugman [84] showed that for two-dimensional Gabor functions, the uncertainty relations $\Delta x \Delta u \geq \pi/4$ and $\Delta y \Delta v \geq \pi/4$ attain the minimum value. Here Δx and Δy are effective widths in the spatial domain and Δu and Δv are effective bandwidths in the frequency domain.

A two-dimensional Gabor function consists of a sinusoidal plane wave of a certain *frequency* and *orientation* modulated by a Gaussian envelope. It is given by:

$$f(x,y) = \exp\left(\frac{1}{2}\left[\frac{x^2}{\sigma_x^2} + \frac{y^2}{\sigma_y^2}\right]\right)\cos(2\pi u_0 x + \phi) \tag{3.23}$$

where u_0 and ϕ are the frequency and phase of the sinusoidal wave. The values σ_x and σ_y are the sizes of the Gaussian envelope in the x and y directions, respectively. The Gabor function at an arbitrary orientation θ_0 can be obtained from Eq. (3.23) by a rigid rotation of the x–y plane by θ_0.

The Gabor filter is a frequency and orientation selective filter. This can be seen from the Fourier domain analysis of the function. When the phase θ is 0, the Fourier transform of the resulting even-symmetric Gabor function $f(x,y)$ is given by

$$F(u,\nu) = A\left(\exp\left(-\frac{1}{2}\left[\frac{(u-u_0)^2}{\sigma_u^2} + \frac{\nu^2}{\sigma_\nu^2}\right]\right) + \exp\left(-\frac{1}{2}\left[\frac{(u+u_0)^2)}{\sigma_u^2} + \frac{\nu^2}{\sigma_\nu^2}\right]\right)\right)$$

$$\tag{3.24}$$

where $\sigma_u = 1/(2\pi\sigma_x), \sigma_\nu = 1/(2\pi\sigma_y)$, and $A = 2\pi\sigma_x\sigma_y$. This function is real-valued and has two lobes in the spatial frequency domain, one centered around u_0 and another centered around $-u_0$. For a Gabor filter of a particular orientation, the lobes in the frequency domain are also appropriately rotated.

Jain and Farrokhnia [40] used a version of the Gabor transform in which window sizes for computing the Gabor filters are selected according to the central frequencies of the filters. The texture features were obtained as follows:

(a) Use a bank of Gabor filters at multiple scales and orientations to obtain filtered images. Let the filtered image for the ith filter be $r_i(x,y)$.

(b) Pass each filtered image through a sigmoidal nonlinearity. This nonlinearity $\psi(t)$ has the form of $\tanh(\alpha t)$. The choice of the value of α is determined empirically.

(c) The texture feature for each pixel is computed as the absolute average deviation of the transformed values of the filtered images from the mean within a window W of size $M \times M$. The filtered images have zero mean, therefore, the ith texture feature image $e_i(x, y)$ is given by the equation:

$$e_i(x, y) = \frac{1}{M^2} \sum_{(a,b) \in W} |\psi(r_i(a, b))| \,. \tag{3.25}$$

The window size M is also determined automatically based on the central frequency of the filter. An example texture image and some intermediate results are shown in Fig. 17. Texture features using Gabor filters were used in texture segmentation and texture classification tasks successfully. An example of the resulting segmentation is shown in Fig. 18. Further details of the segmentation algorithm are explained in Section 4.1.

4. Texture Analysis Problems

The various methods for modelling textures and extracting texture features can be applied in four broad categories of problems: texture segmentation, texture classification, texture synthesis, and shape from texture. We now review these four areas.

4.1. *Texture Segmentation*

Texture segmentation is a difficult problem because one usually does not know *a priori* what types of textures exist in an image, how many different textures there are, and what regions in the image have which textures. In fact, one does not need to know which specific textures exist in the image in order to do texture segmentation. All that is needed is a way to tell that two textures (usually in adjacent regions of the images) are different.

The two general approaches to performing texture segmentation are analogous to methods for image segmentation: region-based approaches or boundary-based approaches. In a region-based approach, one tries to identify regions of the image which have a uniform texture. Pixels or small local regions are merged based on the similarity of some texture property. The regions having different textures are then considered to be segmented regions. This method has the advantage that the boundaries of regions are always closed and therefore, the regions with differ-ent textures are always well separated. It has the disadvantage, however, that in many region-based segmentation methods, one has to specify the number of dis-tinct textures present in the image in advance. In addition, thresholds on similarity values are needed.

The boundary-based approaches are based upon the detection of differences in texture in adjacent regions. Thus boundaries are detected where there are differences in texture. In this method, one does not need to know the number of textured regions in the image in advance. However, the boundaries may have

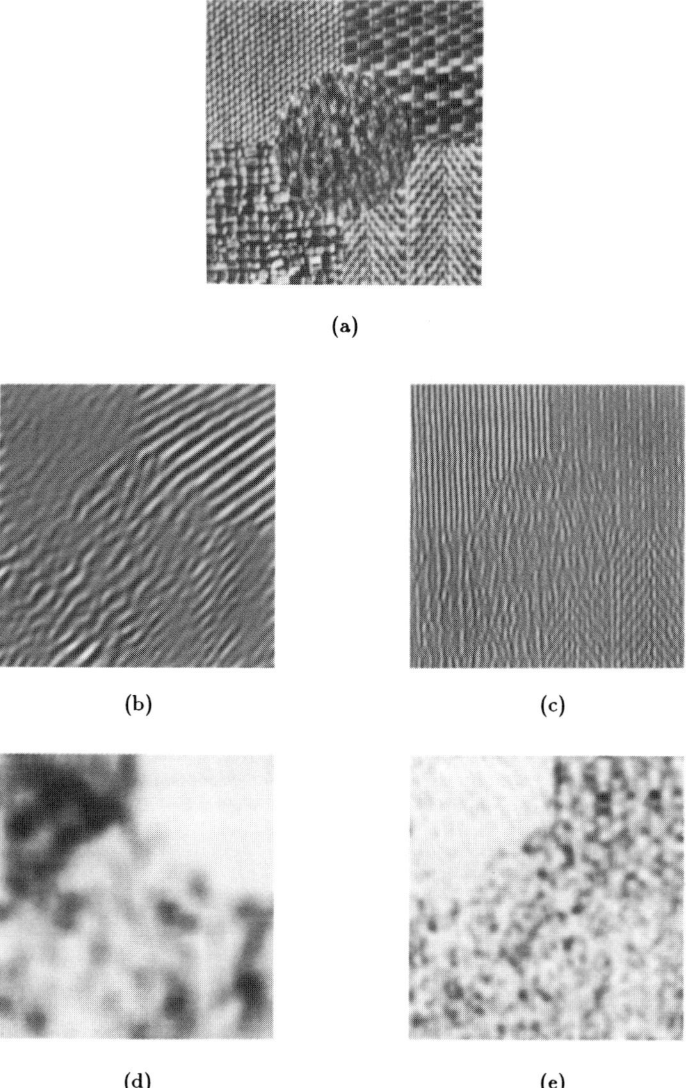

(a)

(b)   (c)

(d)   (e)

Fig. 17. Filtering results on an example texture image. (a) Input image of five textures. (b), (c) A subset of the filtered images each filtered with a Gabor filter with the following parameters. The filter in (b) has a central frequency at 16 cycles/image-width and $135°$ orientation. The filter in (c) has a central frequency of 32 cycles/image-width and $0°$ orientation. (d), (e) The feature images obtained corresponding to the filtered images in (b) and (c). The filtered image in (b) shows a lot of activity in the textured region of the top right quadrant and the image in (c) shows activity in the textured region of the top left quadrant. These are reflected in the feature images in (d) and (e).

gaps and two regions with different textures are not identified as separate closed regions. Strictly speaking, the boundary based methods result in segmentation only if all the boundaries detected form closed curves.

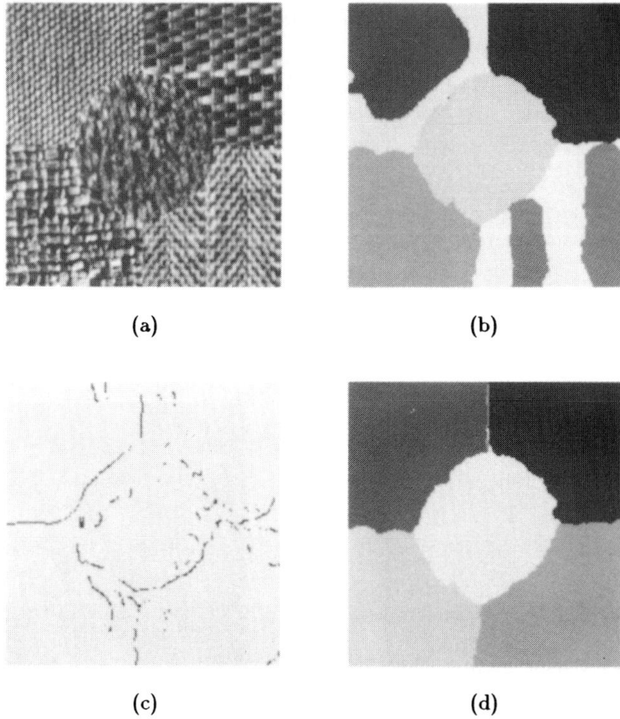

(a)　　　　　　　　　　(b)

(c)　　　　　　　　　　(d)

Fig. 18. The results of integrating region-based and boundary-based processing using the multi-scale Gabor filtering method. (a) Original image consisting of five natural textures. (b) Seven category region-based segmentation results. (c) Edge-based processing and texture edges detected. (d) New segmentation after combining region-based and edge-based results.

Boundary-based segmentation of textured images have been used by Tuceryan and Jain [49], Voorhees and Poggio [56], and Eom and Kashyap [85]. In all cases, the edges (or texture boundaries) are detected by taking two adjacent windows and deciding whether the textures in the two windows belong to the same texture or to different textures. If it is decided that the two textures are different, the point is marked as a boundary pixel. Du Buf and Kardan [86] studied and compared the performance of various texture segmentation techniques and their ability to localize the boundaries.

Tuceryan and Jain [49] use the texture features computed from the Voronoi polygons in order to compare the textures in the two windows. The comparison is done using a Kolmogorov-Smirnoff test. A probabilistic relaxation labeling, which enforces border smoothness, is used to remove isolated edge pixels and fill boundary gaps. Voorhees and Poggio extract blobs and elongated structures from images (they suggest that these correspond to Julesz's textons). The texture properties are based on blob characteristics such as their sizes, orientations, etc. They then decide whether the two sides of a pixel have the same texture using a statistical test called maximum frequency difference (MFD). The pixels where this statistic is sufficiently large are considered to be boundaries between different textures.

Jain and Farrokhnia [40] give an example of integrating a region-based and a boundary-based method to obtain a cleaner and more robust texture segmentation method. They use the texture features computed from the bank of Gabor filters to perform a region-based segmentation. This is accomplished by the following steps:

(a) Gabor features are calculated from the input image, yielding several feature images.

(b) A cluster analysis is performed in the Gabor feature space on a subset of randomly selected pixels in the input image (this is done in order to increase computational efficiency. About 6% of the total number of pixels in the image are selected). The number k of clusters is specified for doing the cluster analysis. This is set to a value larger than the true number of clusters and thus the image is oversegmented.

(c) Step (b) assigns a cluster label to the pixels (pattern) involved in cluster analysis. These labelled patterns are used as the training set and all the pixels in the image are classified into one of the k clusters. A minimum distance classifier is used. This results in a complete segmentation of the image into uniform textured regions.

(d) A connected component analysis is performed to identify each segmented region.

(e) A boundary-based segmentation is performed by applying the Canny edge detector on each feature image. The magnitude of the Canny edge detector for each feature image is summed up for each pixel to obtain a total edge response. The edges are then detected based on this total magnitude.

(f) The edges so detected are then combined with the region-based segmentation results to obtain the final texture segmentation.

The integration of the boundary-based and region-based segmentation results improve the resulting segmentation in most cases. For an example of this improvement see Fig. 18.

4.2. *Texture Classification*

Texture classification involves deciding what texture category an observed image belongs to. In order to accomplish this, one needs to have *a priori* knowledge of the classes to be recognized. Once this knowledge is available and the texture features are extracted, one then uses classical pattern classification techniques in order to do the classification.

Examples where texture classification was applied as the appropriate texture processing method include the classification of regions in satellite images into categories of land use [41]. Texture classification was also used in automated paint inspection by Farrokhnia [83]. In the latter application, the categories were ratings of the quality of paints obtained from human experts. These quality rating categories were then used as the training samples for supervised classification of paint images using texture features obtained from multi-channel Gabor filters.

4.3. *Texture Synthesis*

Texture synthesis is a problem which is more popular in computer graphics. It is closely tied to some of the methods discussed above, so we give only a brief summary here. Many of the modelling methods are directly applicable to texture synthesis. Markov random field models discussed in Section 3.3.1 can be directly used to generate textures by specifying the parameter vector θ and sampling from the probability distribution function [62,60]. The synthetic textures in Fig. 2(b) are generated using a Gaussian Markov random field model and the algorithm in [87].

Fractals have become popular recently in computer graphics for generating realistic looking textured images [88]. A number of different methods have been proposed for synthesizing textures using fractal models. These methods include midpoint displacement method and Fourier filtering method. The midpoint displacement method has become very popular because it is a simple and fast algorithm yet it can be used to generate very realistic looking textures. Here we only give the general outline of the algorithm. A much more detailed discussion of the algorithm can be found in [88]. The algorithm starts with a square grid representing the image with the four corners set to 0. It then displaces heights at the midpoints of the four sides and the center point of the square region by random amounts and repeats the process recursively. The iteration $n + 1$ uses the grid consisting of the midpoints of the squares in the grid for iteration n. The height at the midpoint is first interpolated between the endpoints and a random value is added to this value. The amount added is chosen from a normal distribution with zero mean and variance σ_n^2 at iteration n. In order to keep the self-similar nature of the surface, the variance is changed as a function of the iteration number. The variance at iteration n is given by

$$\sigma_n^2 = r^{2nH} \quad \text{where } r = 1/\sqrt{2} \ . \tag{4.1}$$

This results in a fractal surface with fractal dimension $(3 - H)$. The heights of the fractal surface can be mapped onto intensity values to generate the textured images. The example image in Fig. 2(c) was generated using this method.

Other methods include mosaic models [89,90]. This class of models can in turn be divided into subclasses of cell structure models and coverage models. In cell structure models the textures are generated by tessellating the plane into cells (bounded polygons) and assigning each cell gray levels according to a set of probabilities. The type of tessellation determines what type of textures are generated. The possible tessellations include triangular pattern, checkerboard patterns, Poisson line model, Delaunay model, and occupancy model. In coverage models, the texture is obtained by a random arrangement of a set of geometric figures in the plane. The coverage models are also referred to as bombing models.

4.4. *Shape from Texture*

There are many cues in images that allow the viewer to make inferences about the three-dimensional shapes of objects and surfaces present in the image. Examples of such cues include the variations of shading on the object surfaces or the relative configurations of boundaries and the types of junctions that allow one to infer three-dimensional shape from the line drawings of objects. The relation between the variations in texture properties and surface shape was first pointed out by Gibson [10].

Stevens observed that certain properties of texture are perceptually significant in the extraction of surface geometry [91]. There are three effects that surface geometry has on the appearance of texture in images: foreshortening and scaling of texture elements, and a change in their density. The foreshortening effect is due to the orientation of the surface on which the texture element lies. The scaling and density changes are due to the distance of the texture elements from the viewer. Stevens argued that texture density is not a useful measure for computing distance or orientation information because the density varies both with scaling and foreshortening. He concluded that the more perceptually stable property that allows one to extract surface geometry information is the direction in the image which is not foreshortened, called the *characteristic dimension*. Stevens suggested that one can compute relative depth information using the reciprocal of the scaling in the characteristic dimension. Using the relative depths, surface orientation can be estimated.

Bajcsy and Lieberman [92] used the gradient in texture element sizes to derive surface shape. They assumed a uniform texture element size on the three-dimensional surface in the scene. The relative distances are computed based on a gradient function in the image which was estimated from the texture element sizes. The estimation of the relative depth was done without using knowledge about the camera parameters and the original texture element sizes.

Witkin [93] used the distribution of edge orientations in the image to estimate the surface orientation. The surface orientation is represented by the slant (σ) and tilt (τ) angles. The Slant is the angle between a normal to the surface and a normal to the image plane. The Tilt is the angle between the surface normal's projection onto the image plane and a fixed coordinate axis in the image plane. He assumed an isotropic texture (uniform distribution of edge orientations) on the original surface. As a result of the projection process, the textures are foreshortened in the direction of steepest inclination (slant angle). Note that this idea is related to Stevens' argument because the direction of steepest inclination is perpendicular to the characteristic dimension. Witkin formulated the surface shape recovery by relating the slant and tilt angles to the distribution of observed edge directions in the image. Let β be the original edge orientation (the angle between the tangent and a fixed coordinate axis on the plane S containing the tangent). Let α^* be the angle between the x-axis in the image plane and the projected tangent. The α^* is related to the slant and tilt angles by the following expression:

$$\alpha^* = \operatorname{atan}\left(\frac{\tan\beta}{\cos\sigma}\right) + \tau \ . \tag{4.2}$$

Here α^* is an observable quantity in the image and (σ, τ) are the quantities to be computed. Witkin derived the expression for the conditional probabilities for the slant and tilt angles given the measured edge directions in the image and then used a maximum likelihood estimation method to compute the (σ, τ). Let $A^* = \{\alpha_1^*, \ldots, \alpha_n^*\}$ be a set of observed edge directions in the image. Then the conditional probabilities are given as:

$$P(\sigma, \tau | A^*) = \frac{P(\sigma, \tau)P(A^* | \sigma, \tau)}{\iint P(\sigma, \tau)P(A^* | \sigma, \tau)d\sigma d\tau} \tag{4.3}$$

where $P(\sigma, \tau) = \dfrac{\sin \sigma}{\pi^2}$. The maximum likelihood estimate of $P(\sigma, \tau | A^*)$ gives the desired surface orientation.

Blostein and Ahuja [57] used the scaling effect to extract surface information. They integrated the process of texture element extraction with the surface geometry computation. Texture element extraction is performed at multiple scales and the subset that yields a good surface fit is selected. The surfaces are assumed planar for simplicity. Texture elements are defined to be circular regions of uniform intensity which are extracted by filtering the image with $\nabla^2 G$ and $\frac{\partial}{\partial \sigma}(\nabla^2 G)$ operators and comparing the filter responses to those of an ideal disk (here σ is the size of the Gaussian G). At the extremum points of the image filtered by $\nabla^2 G$, the diameter (D) and contrast (C) of the best fitting disks are computed. The convolution is done at multiple scales. Only those disks whose computed diameters are close to the size of the Gaussian are retained. As a result, blob-like texture elements of different sizes are detected.

The geometry of the projection is shown in Fig. 19. Let σ and τ be the slant and tilt of the surface. The image of a texture element has the foreshortened dimension F_i and the characteristic dimension U_i. The area A_i of the image texel is proportional to the product $F_i U_i$ for compact shapes. The expression for the area A_i of the image of a texture element is given by:

$$A_i = A_C (1 - \tan \theta \tan \sigma)^3 \tag{4.4}$$

where A_C is the area that would be measured for the texel at the center of the image. The angle θ is given by the expression

$$\theta = \text{atan}((x \cos \tau + y \sin \tau)(r/f)) \, . \tag{4.5}$$

Here, r is the physical width of the image, r/f is a measure of the field of view of the camera, and (x, y) denotes pixel coordinates in the image. A_i can be measured in the image. To find the surface orientation, an accumulator array consisting of the parameters (A_C, σ, τ) is constructed. For each combination of parameter values, a possible planar fit is computed. The plane with the highest fit rating is selected as the surface orientation, and texture elements that support this fit are selected as

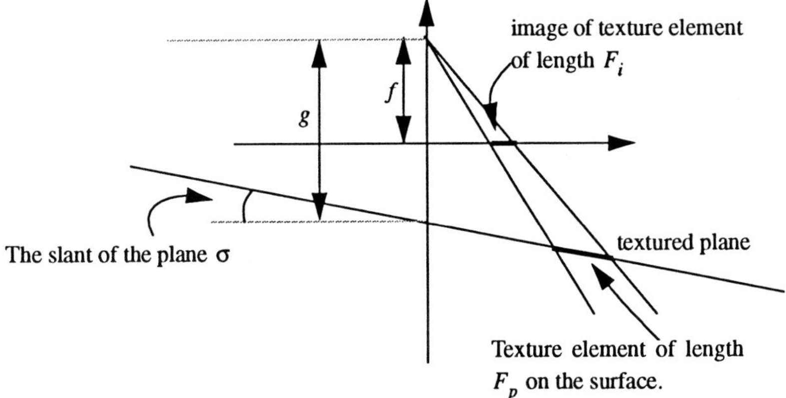

Fig. 19. The projective distortion of a texture element in the image.

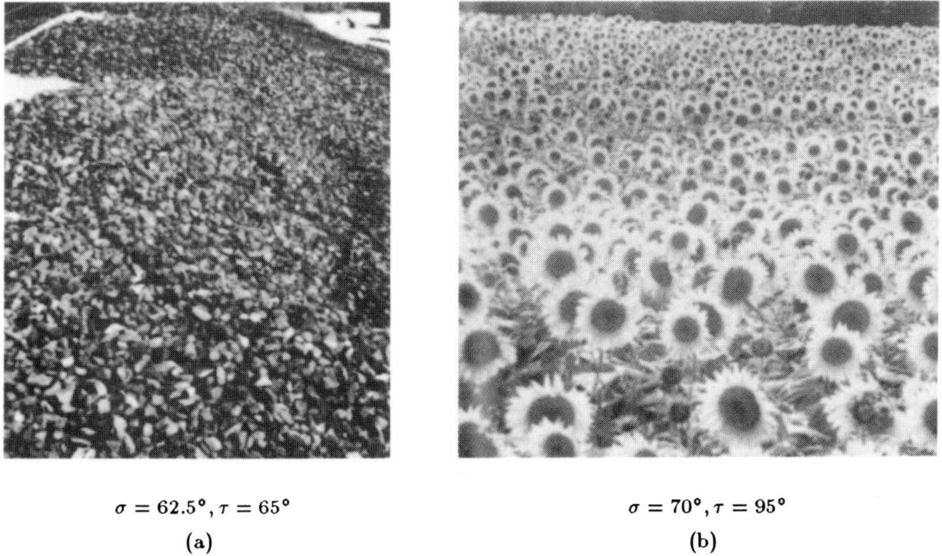

$\sigma = 62.5°, \tau = 65°$

(a)

$\sigma = 70°, \tau = 95°$

(b)

Fig. 20. Examples of shape from texture computation using Blostein and Ahuja's algorithm [57]. (a) An image of a field of rocks and the computed slant and tilt of the plane. (b) An image of a sunflower field and the extracted slant and tilt values.

the true texture elements. Some example images and the computed slant and tilt values are shown in Fig. 20.

5. Summary

This chapter has reviewed the basic concepts and various methods and techniques for processing textured images. Texture is a prevalent property of most physical surfaces in the natural world. It also arises in many applications such as satellite imagery and printed documents. Many common low level vision algorithms such as edge detection break down when applied to images that contain textured surfaces. It is therefore crucial that we have robust and efficient methods for processing textured images. Texture processing has been successfully applied to practical application domains such as automated inspection and satellite imagery. It is also going to play an important role in the future as we can see from the promising application of texture to a variety of different application domains.

Acknowledgment

The support of the National Science Foundation through grants IRI-8705256 and CDA-8806599 is gratefully acknowledged. We thank the Norwegian Computing center for providing the SAR images shown in Fig. 5. We also thank our colleagues Dr. Richard C. Dubes and Dr. Patrick J. Flynn for the invaluable comments and feedback they provided during the preparation of this document.

References

[1] J. M. Coggins, A Framework for Texture Analysis Based on Spatial Filtering, Ph.D. Thesis, Computer Science Department, Michigan State University, East Lansing, MI, 1982.

[2] H. Tamura, S. Mori and Y. Yamawaki, Textural features corresponding to visual perception, *IEEE Trans. Syst. Man Cybern.*, (1978) 460–473.

[3] J. Sklansky, Image segmentation and feature extraction, *IEEE Trans. Syst. Man Cybern.* (1978) 237–247.

[4] R. M. Haralick, Statistical and structural approaches to texture, *Proc. IEEE* **67** (1979) 786–804.

[5] W. Richards and A. Polit, Texture matching, *Kybernetic* **16** (1974) 155–162.

[6] S. W. Zucker and K. Kant, Multiple-level representations for texture discrimination, in *Proc. IEEE Conf. on Pattern Recognition and Image Processing*, Dallas, TX, 1981, 609–614.

[7] J. K. Hawkins, Textural properties for pattern recognition, in B. Lipkin and A. Rosenfeld (eds.), *Picture Processing and Psychopictorics* (Academic Press, New York, 1969).

[8] P. Brodatz, *Textures: A Photographic Album for Artists and Designers* (Dover Publications, New York 1966).

[9] C. C. Chen, Markov Random Fields in Image Analysis, Ph.D. Thesis, Computer Science Department, Michigan State University, East Lansing, MI, 1988.

[10] J. J. Gibson, *The Perception of the Visual World* (Houghton Mifflin, Boston, MA, 1950) .

[11] B. Julesz, E. N. Gilbert, L. A. Shepp and H. L. Frisch, Inability of humans to discriminate between visual textures that agree in second-order statistics — revisited, *Perception* **2** (1973) 391–405.

[12] B. Julesz, Visual pattern discrimination, *IRE Trans. Inf. Theory* **8** (1962) 84–92.

[13] B. Julesz, Experiments in the visual perception of texture, *Sci. Am.* **232** (1975) 34–43.

[14] B. Julesz, Nonlinear and cooperative processes in texture perception, in T. P. Werner and E. Reichardt (eds.), *Theoretical Approaches in Neurobiology* (MIT Press, Cambridge, MA, 1981) 93–108.

[15] B. Julesz, Textons, the elements of texture perception, and their interactions, *Nature* **290** (1981) 91–97.

[16] B. Julesz, A theory of preattentive texture discrimination based on first-order statistics of textons, *Biol. Cybern.* **41** (1981) 131–138.

[17] T. Caelli, *Visual Perception* (Pergamon Press, 1981).

[18] J. Beck, A. Sutter and R. Ivry, Spatial frequency channels and perceptual grouping in texture segregation, *Comput. Vision Graph. Image Process.* **37** (1987) 299–325.

[19] F. W. Campbell and J. G. Robson, Application of Fourier analysis to the visibility of gratings, *J. Physiol.* **197** (1968) 551–566.

[20] R. L. Devalois, D. G. Albrecht and L. G. Thorell, Spatial-frequency selectivity of cells in macaque visual cortex, *Vision Res.* **22** (1982) 545–559.

[21] P. Dewaele, P. Van Gool and A. Oosterlinck, Texture inspection with self-adaptive convolution filters, in *Proc. 9th Int. Conf. on Pattern Recognition*, Rome, Italy, Nov. 1988, 56–60.

[22] D. Chetverikov, Detecting defects in texture, in *Proc. 9th Int. Conf. on Pattern Recognition*, Rome, Italy, Nov. 1988, 61–63.

[23] J. Chen and A. K. Jain, A structural approach to identify defects in textured images, in *Proc. IEEE Int. Conf. on Systems, Man, and Cybernetics*, Beijing, 1988, 29–32.

[24] R. W. Conners, C. W. McMillin, K. Lin and R. E. Vasquez-Espinosa, Identifying and locating surface defects in wood: Part of an automated lumber processing system, *IEEE Trans. Pattern Anal. Mach. Intell.* **5** (1983) 573–583.

[25] L. H. Siew, R. M. Hodgson and E. J. Wood, Texture measures for carpet wear assessment, *IEEE Trans. Pattern Anal. Mach. Intell.* **10** (1988) 92–105.

[26] A. K. Jain, F. Farrokhnia and D. H. Alman, Texture analysis of automotive finishes, in *Proc. of SME Machine Vision Applications Conf.*, Detroit, MI, Nov. 1990, 1–16.

[27] R. Sutton and E. L. Hall, Texture measures for automatic classification of pulmonary disease, *IEEE Trans. Comput.* **21** (1972) 667–676.

[28] H. Harms, U. Gunzer and H. M. Aus, Combined local color and texture analysis of stained cells, *Comput. Vision Graph. Image Process.* **33** (1986) 364–376.

[29] G. H. Landeweerd and E. S. Gelsema, The use of nuclear texture parameters in the automatic analysis of leukocytes, *Pattern Recogn.* **10** (1978) 57–61.

[30] M. F. Insana, R. F. Wagner, B. S. Garra, D. G. Brown and T. H. Shawker, Analysis of ultrasound image texture via generalized Rician statistics, *Opt. Engin.* **25** (1986) 743–748.

[31] C. C. Chen, J. S. Daponte and M. D. Fox, Fractal feature analysis and classification in medical imaging, *IEEE Trans. Medical Imaging* **8** (1989) 133–142.

[32] A. Lundervold, Ultrasonic tissue characterization–A pattern recognition approach, Technical Report, Norwegian Computing Center, Oslo, Norway, 1992.

[33] D. Wang and S. N. Srihari, Classification of newspaper image blocks using texture analysis, *Comput. Vision Graph. Image Process.* **47** (1989) 327–352.

[34] F. M. Wahl, K. Y. Wong and R. G. Casey, Block segmentation and text extraction in mixed text/image documents, *Comput. Graph. Image Process.* **20** (1982) 375–390.

[35] J. A. Fletcher and R. Kasturi, A robust algorithm for text string separation from mixed text/graphics images, *IEEE Trans. Pattern Anal. Mach. Intell.* **10** (1988) 910–918.

[36] T. Taxt, P. J. Flynn and A. K. Jain, Segmentation of document images, *IEEE Trans. Pattern Anal. Mach. Intell.* **11** (1989) 1322–1329.

[37] A. K. Jain and S. K. Bhattacharjee, Text segmentation using Gabor filters for automatic document processing, *Mach. Vision and Appl.* **5** (1992) 169–184.

[38] A. K. Jain and S. K. Bhattacharjee, Address block location on envelopes using Gabor filters, in *Proc. 11th Int. Conf. on Pattern Recognition*, The Hague, Netherlands, Aug. 1992, Vol. B, 264–267.

[39] A. K. Jain, S. K. Bhattacharjee and Y. Chen, On texture in document images, in *Proc. IEEE Conf. on Computer Vision and Pattern Recognition*, Champaign, IL, Jun. 1992, 677–680.

[40] A. K. Jain and F. Farrokhnia, Unsupervised texture segmentation using Gabor filters, *Pattern Recogn.* **24** (1991) 1167–1186.

[41] R. M. Haralick, K. Shanmugam and I. Dinstein, Textural features for image classification, *IEEE Trans. Syst. Man Cybern.* **3** (1973) 610–621.

[42] E. Rignot and R. Kwok, Extraction of textural features in SAR images: Statistical model and sensitivity, in *Proc. Int. Geoscience and Remote Sensing Symp.*, Washington, DC, 1990, 1979–1982.

[43] A. H. Schistad and A. K. Jain, Texture analysis in the presence of speckle noise, in *Proc. IEEE Geoscience and Remote Sensing Symp.* Houston, TX, May 1992, 147–152.

[44] L. J. Du, Texture segmentation of SAR images using localized spatial filtering, in *Proc. Int. Geoscience and Remote Sensing Symp.*, Washington, DC, 1990, 1983–1986.

[45] J. H. Lee and W. D. Philpot, A spectral-textural classifier for digital imagery, in *Proc. Int. Geoscience and Remote Sensing Symp.*, Washington, DC, 1990, 2005–2008.

[46] F. Tomita and S. Tsuji, *Computer Analysis of Visual Textures* (Kluwer Academic Publishers, Boston, 1990).

[47] K. I. Laws, Textured Image Segmentation, Ph.D. thesis, University of Southern California, 1980.

[48] R. Picard, I. M. Elfadel and A. P. Pentland, Markov/Gibbs texture modeling: Aura matrices and temperature effects, in *Proc. IEEE Conf. on Computer Vision and Pattern Recognition*, Maui, Hawaii, 1991, 371–377.

[49] M. Tuceryan and A. K. Jain, Texture segmentation using Voronoi polygons, *IEEE Trans. Pattern Anal. Mach. Intell.* **12** (1990) 211–216.

[50] N. Ahuja, Dot pattern processing using Voronoi neighborhoods, *IEEE Trans. Pattern Anal. Mach. Intell.* **4** (1982) 336–343.

[51] G. Voronoi, Nouvelles applications des paramètres continus à la théorie des formes quadratiques. Deuxième mémoire: Recherches sur les parallélloèdres primitifs, *J. Reine Angew. Math.* **134** (1908) 198–287.

[52] M. I. Shamos and D. Hoey, Closest-point problems, in *16th Annual Symposium on Foundations of Computer Science*, 1975, 131–162.

[53] F. P. Preparata and M. I. Shamos, *Computational Geometry* (Springer-Verlag, New York, 1985).

[54] D. Marr, *Vision* (Freeman, San Francisco, 1982).

[55] M. K. Hu, Visual pattern recognition by moment invariants, *IRE Trans. Inf. Theory* **8** (1962) 179–187.

[56] H. Voorhees and T. Poggio, Detecting textons and texture boundaries in natural images, in *Proc. First Int. Conf. on Computer Vision*, London, 1987 250–258.

[57] D. Blostein and N. Ahuja, Shape from texture: Integrating texture-element extraction and surface estimation, *IEEE Trans. Pattern Anal. Mach. Intell.* **11** (1989) 1233–1251.

[58] S. W. Zucker, Toward a model of texture, *Comput. Graph. Image Process.* **5** (1976) 190–202.

[59] K. S. Fu, *Syntactic Pattern Recognition and Applications* (Prentice-Hall, New Jersey, 1982).

[60] G. C. Cross and A. K. Jain, Markov random field texture models, *IEEE Trans. Pattern Anal. Mach. Intell.* **5** (1983) 25–39.

[61] R. Chellappa and S. Chatterjee, Classification of Textures using Gaussian Markov random fields, *IEEE Trans. Acoust. Speech Signal Process.* **33** (1985) 959–963.

[62] A. Khotanzad and R. Kashyap, Feature Selection for texture recognition based on image synthesis, *IEEE Trans. Syst. Man Cybern.* **17** (1987) 1087–1095.

[63] F. S. Cohen and D. B. Cooper, Simple parallel hierarchical and relaxation algorithms for segmenting noncausal Markovian random fields, *IEEE Trans. Pattern Anal. Mach. Intell.* **9** (1987) 195–219.

[64] C. W. Therrien, An estimation-theoretic approach to terrain image segmentation, *Comput. Vision Graph. Image Process.* **22** (1983) 313–326.

[65] S. Geman and D. Geman, Stochastic relaxation, Gibbs distributions, and the Bayesian restoration of images, *IEEE Trans. Pattern Anal. Mach. Intell.* **6** (1984) 721–741.

[66] J. Besag, Spatial interaction and the statistical analysis of lattice systems, *J. Roy. Stat. Soc.* **B36** (1974) 344–348.

[67] H. Derin and H. Elliott, Modeling and segmentation of noisy and textured images using Gibbs random fields, *IEEE Trans. Pattern Anal. Mach. Intell.* **9** (1987) 39–55.

[68] B. B. Mandelbrot, *The Fractal Geometry of Nature* (Freeman, San Francisco, 1983).

[69] A. Pentland, Fractal-based description of natural scenes, *IEEE Trans. Pattern Anal. Mach. Intell.* **9** (1984) 661–674.

[70] J. M. Keller, S. Chen and R. M. Crownover, Texture description and segmentation through fractal geometry, *Comput. Vision Graph. Image Process.* **45** (1989) 150–166.

[71] R. Voss, Random fractals: Characterization and measurement, in R. Pynn and A. Skjeltorp (eds.), *Scaling Phenomena in Disordered Systems* (Plenum, New York, 1986).

[72] B. J. Super and A. C. Bovik, Localized measurement of image fractal dimension using Gabor filters, *J. Visual Commun. Image Represent.* **2** (1991) 114–128.

[73] P. P. Ohanian and R. C. Dubes, Performance evaluation for four classes of textural features, submitted to *Pattern Recogn.*

[74] M. A. Georgeson, Spatial Fourier analysis and human vision, Chapter 2, in N. S. Sutherland (ed.), *Tutorial Essays in Psychology, A Guide to Recent Advances*, vol. 2 (Lawrence Erlbaum Associates, Hillsdale, NJ, 1979).

[75] J. Malik and P. Perona, Preattentive texture discrimination with early vision mechanisms, *J. Opt. Soc. Am. Series A* **7** (1990) 923–932.

[76] M. Unser and M. Eden, Nonlinear operators for improving texture segmentation based on features extracted by spatial filtering, *IEEE Trans. Syst. Man Cybern.* **20** (1990) 804–815.

[77] T. R. Reed and H. Wechsler, Segmentation of textured images and Gestalt organization using spatial/spatial-frequency representations, *IEEE Trans. Pattern Anal. Mach. Intell.* **12** (1990) 1–12

[78] M. Tuceryan, Moment based texture segmentation, in *Proc. 11th Int. Conf. on Pattern Recognition*, The Hague, Netherlands, Aug. 1992, Vol. III, 45–48.

[79] J. M. Coggins and A. K. Jain, A spatial filtering approach to texture analysis, *Pattern Recogn. Lett.* **3** (1985) 195–203.

[80] J. G. Daugman, Two-dimensional spectral analysis of cortical receptive field profiles, *Vision Res.* **20** (1980) 847–856.

[81] M. R. Turner, Texture discrimination by Gabor functions, *Biol. Cybern.* **55** (1986) 71–82.

[82] M. Clark and A. C. Bovik, Texture segmentation using Gabor modulation/demodulation, *Pattern Recogn. Lett.* **6** (1987) 261–267.

[83] F. Farrokhnia, Multi-channel Filtering Techniques for Texture Segmentation and Surface Quality Inspection, Ph.D. thesis, Computer Science Department, Michigan State University, 1990.

[84] J. G. Daugman, Uncertainty relation for resolution in space, spatial-frequency, and orientation optimized by two-dimensional visual cortical filters, *J. Opt. Soc. Am.* **2** (1985) 1160–1169.

[85] Kie-Bum Eom and R. L. Kashyap, Texture and intensity edge detection with random field models, in *Proc. Workshop on Computer Vision*, Miami Beach, FL, 1987, 29–34.

[86] J. M. Du Buf, H. M. Kardan and M. Spann, Texture feature performance for image segmentation, *Pattern Recogn.* **23** (1990) 291–309.

[87] R. Chellappa, S. Chatterjee and R. Bagdazian, Texture synthesis and compression using Gaussian–Markov random field models, *IEEE Trans. Syst. Man Cybern.* **15** (1985) 298–303.

[88] H. O. Peitgen and D. Saupe, *The Science of Fractal Images* (Springer-Verlag, New York, 1988).

[89] N. Ahuja and A. Rosenfeld, Mosaic models for textures, *IEEE Trans. Pattern Anal. Mach. Intell.* **3** (1981) 1–11.

[90] N. Ahuja, Texture, in *Encyclopedia of Artificial Intelligence* (Wiley, 1987) 1101–1115.

[91] K. A. Stevens, Surface perception from local analysis of texture and contour, MIT Technical Report, Artificial Intelligence Laboratory, no. AI-TR 512, 1980.

[92] R. Bajcsy and L. Lieberman, Texture gradient as a depth cue, *Comput. Graph. Image Process.* **5** (1976) 52–67.

[93] A. P. Witkin, Recovering surface shape and orientation from texture, *Artif. Intell.* **17** (1981) 17–45.

Handbook of Pattern Recognition and Computer Vision, pp. 277–310
Eds. C. H. Chen, L. F. Pau and P. S. P. Wang

$\boxed{\text{CHAPTER 2.2}}$

MODEL-BASED TEXTURE SEGMENTATION
AND CLASSIFICATION

R. CHELLAPPA

*Department of Electrical Engineering, Center for Automation Research
Institute for Advanced Computer Studies, University of Maryland
College Park, MD 20742, USA*

R. L. KASHYAP

*School of Electrical Engineering, Purdue University
W. Lafayette, IN 47907, USA*

and

B. S. MANJUNATH

*Department of Electrical and Computer Engineering
University of California, Santa Barbara, CA 93106, USA*

Over the last ten years, several model based methods have been proposed for segmentation and classification of textured images. Models based on random field representations and psychophysical/neurophysiological studies have been dominant. In this chapter, we present examples drawn from both approaches. Related issues on implementation of the various optimal/suboptimal algorithms are also addressed.

Keywords: Texture segmentation, texture classification, artificial neural networks, Markov random fields, fractional differencing model, preattentive segmentation.

1. Introduction

Automatic segmentation and classification of textured images has several applications in landsat terrain classification [1], bio-medical applications [2] and aerial image understanding [3]. Previous approaches to segmentation have been based on correlation [4], Fourier transform features [5], Laws features and their extensions [6,7], fractal models [8], and features from co-occurrence matrix [9]. Recently, more emphasis has been given to methods using random field models such as the 2-D non-symmetric half plane models [10] and non-causal Gauss Markov random field models and their variations [11–18]. Both supervised and unsupervised methods have been developed. Although significant progress has been made using these methods, several problems remain as the methods are sensitive to illumination and resolution changes and transformations such as rotation. Also, these methods do not explain the role of preattentive segmentation as applied to textures. Preattentive segmen-

277

tation refers to the ability of humans to perceive textures without any sustained attention. Central to solving this problem are the issues of what features need to be computed and what kind of processing of these features is required for texture discrimination. Some of the early work in this field can be attributed to Julesz [19] for his theory of textons as basic textural elements. The spatial filtering approach has been used by many researchers for detecting texture boundaries not clearly explained by the texton theory [20]. Recently an elegant computational model for preattentive texture discrimination has been proposed by Malik and Perona [21]. Grossberg and Mingolla's Boundary Contour System (BCS) [22] is one of the first attempts to model the early processing stages in the visual cortex.

Texture classification refers to the problem of identifying the particular class label of the input texture and can operate on the output of the segmentation algorithm. Thus, standard pattern classification techniques may be applied by assuming that there is only one texture in the image, the image being constructed from a single segmented region. Features for texture classification have been derived from a variety of approaches such as co-occurrence matrices [1,23], textural features [5,24,25], runlength statistics [5], difference statistics [5], decorrelation methods [26], Fourier power spectrum [5], structural features [9,27], region based random fields [28–30], parametric Gaussian random field models [31–38], fractals and fractional models [36,39,40], etc. A major advantage of the features based on parametric Gaussian non-causal random field models is that they are information preserving in the sense that the features in conjunction with the discrete random field model can be used to synthesize an image which closely resembles the original. The chief disadvantage of the above model and all other related classification methods is that they are not rotation invariant, i.e. if we train the classifier with a set of texture data and test the classifier with a rotated version of the same image, the correct classification rate goes down. We give an approach for achieving rotational invariance in Section 4.

We illustrate the different approaches to texture segmentation and classification mentioned above using several deterministic and stochastic algorithms. The first method we describe in Section 2 stems from the idea of using Markov random field (MRF) models for texture in an image. We assign two random variables for the observed pixel, one characterizing the underlying intensity and the other for labeling the texture corresponding to the pixel location. We use the Gauss Markov Random Field (GMRF) model for the conditional density of the intensity field given the label field. Prior information about the texture label field is introduced using a discrete Markov distribution. The segmentation can then be formulated as an optimization problem involving minimization of a Gibbs energy function. Exhaustive search for the optimum solution is not possible because of the large dimensionality of the search space. For example, even for the very simple case of segmenting a 128×128 image into two classes, there are $2^{2^{14}}$ possible label configurations.

Derin and Elliott [13] have investigated the use of dynamic programming for obtaining the Maximum *a posteriori* (MAP) estimate while Cohen and Cooper [11] give a deterministic relaxation algorithm for the same problem. The optimal MAP solution can be obtained by using stochastic relaxation algorithms like simulated annealing [41]. However, the computational burden involved because of the theoretical requirements on the initial temperature and the impractical cooling schedules overweigh their advantages in many cases. Recently there has been considerable interest in using neural networks for solving computationally hard problems. Fast approximate solutions can be obtained by using a deterministic relaxation algorithm like the iterated conditional mode rule [42]. The energy function corresponding to this optimality criterion can be mapped into a Hopfield type network in a straightforward manner and it can be shown that the network converges to an equilibrium state, which in general will be a local optimum. The solutions obtained using this method are sensitive to the initial configuration and in many cases starting with a maximum likelihood estimate is preferred.

The second optimality criterion we discuss minimizes the expected percentage of classification error per pixel. This is equivalent to finding the pixel labels that maximizes the marginal posterior probability given the intensity data [43]. Since calculating the marginal posterior probability is very difficult, Marroquin [44] suggested the Maximum Posterior Marginal (MPM) algorithm (see Section 4) that asymptotically computes the posterior marginal. Here we use this method to find the texture label that maximizes the marginal posterior probability for each pixel.

In Section 3 we discuss a simple biologically motivated approach to detect texture boundaries within a more general context of boundary detection [45]. The input image is first processed through a bank of orientation selective bandpass filters at various spatial frequencies. The convolution of the image with these filters yields a representation which is localized in space as well as in frequency. A special class of this decomposition is the wavelet transformation where the filter profiles are all self-similar. Wavelets are families of basis functions obtained through dilations and translations of a *basic wavelet* and such a decomposition provides a compact data structure for representing information. Following the wavelet decomposition we introduce local feature interactions. Three distinct types of interactions are considered: competition between spatial neighbors in each orientation channel, competition between orientations at each spatial location, and interscale interactions. Interscale interactions are used in localizing line ends and play an important role in boundary detection. The second stage of interactions groups similar features in the neighborhood. This cooperative processing helps in the boundary completion process. The receptive fields of the cells in this stage have the same orientation selectivity as their inputs and have a larger receptive field, and the filter profiles are modeled by oriented Gaussians.

In Section 4, we discuss direct pattern classification strategies for classifying textures, assuming that there is only one texture in the image or in the segment of the image. The strategy is to fit varieties of parametric random field models, extract features from them, and use these features for classification using both standard algorithms and new procedures. In Section 5, a multi-level classification

method based on fractional differencing models with a fractal scaling parameter
is presented. This algorithm can handle arbitrary 3-D rotated textures. Since
the fractal scale is known to be a rotational and scaling invariant parameter, the
accuracy of classification from the procedure will not be affected by 3-D rotation of
the test texture. In the first level of classification, the textures are classified by the
first-order Fractional Differencing model with a fractal scale parameter, and in the
second level, classification is completed with the additional frequency parameters
of the second-order Fractional Differencing periodic model.

2. Texture Segmentation via Optimization and Artificial Neural Networks

The inherent parallelism of neural networks provides an interesting architecture
for implementing many computer vision algorithms [46]. Some examples are image
restoration [47], stereopsis [48] and computing optical flow [49–51]. Networks for
solving combinatorially hard problems like the Traveling Salesman problem have
received much attention in the neural network literature [52]. In all these cases
the networks are designed to minimize an energy function defined by the network
architecture. The parameters of the network are obtained in terms of the cost function which is to be minimized and it can be shown that [52] for networks having
symmetric interconnections, the equilibrium states correspond to the local minima
of the energy function. For practical purposes, networks with few interconnections
are preferred because of the large number of processing units required in any image
processing application. In this context MRF models for images play a useful role.
They are typically characterized by local dependencies and symmetric interconnections which can be expressed in terms of energy functions using Gibbs–Markov
equivalence. The artificial neural net (ANN) approach suggested here stems from
the idea of using MRF models for textures in an image.

2.1. *Markov Random Fields and the Image Model*

In modeling images consisting of more than one texture we have to consider two
random processes, one for the texture intensity distribution and the second for the
label distribution. Various models have been proposed in the literature for textured
images. In this section we discuss one such model based on Markov random fields.

In most image processing applications the input image is a rectangular array of
pixels taking values in the range 0–255. Let Ω denote such a set of grid points on
an $M \times M$ lattice, i.e. $\Omega = \{(i,j),\ 1 \leq i,j \leq M\}$. Let $\{Y_s, s \in \Omega\}$ be a random
process defined on this grid.

Definition. The process $\{Y_s\}$ is said to be strictly Markov if

$$P(Y_s | \text{all } Y_r, r \neq s) = P(Y_s | Y_r, r \text{ is a neighbor of } s) \tag{2.1}$$

The neighborhood set of site s can be arbitrarily defined. However in many image
processing applications it is natural to consider neighbors which are also spatial

neighbors of the site. The Markov process can further be classified as causal or non-causal depending on the relationship of these neighbors with respect to the site. The use of MRF in image processing applications has a long history (see for e.g. [53]) and MRF have been used in applications such as image restoration, segmentation, etc. Cross and Jain [54] provide a detailed discussion on the application of MRF in modeling textured images. In the following we use $\{L_s, s \in \Omega\}$ to denote the label process and $\{Y_s, \ s \in \Omega\ \}$ for the zero mean intensity process.

Intensity Process. We model the intensity process $\{Y_s\}$ by a Gaussian Markov random field (GMRF). Depending on the neighborhood set one can construct a hierarchy of GMRF models as shown in Fig. 1. The numbers indicate the order of the GMRF model relative to the center location x. Note that this defines a symmetric neighborhood set. We have used the fourth order model for the intensity process.

		7	6	7		
	5	4	3	4	5	
7	4	2	1	2	4	7
6	3	1	x	1	3	6
7	4	2	1	2	4	7
	5	4	3	4	5	
		7	6	7		

Fig. 1. Structure of the GMRF model. The numbers indicate the order of the model relative to x [54].

Let N_s denote the symmetric fourth order neighborhood of a site s. Let N^* be the set of one-sided shift vectors corresponding to the fourth order neighborhood, i.e. N^* is the set of shift vectors corresponding to a fourth order neighborhood system,

$$N^* = \{\tau_1, \tau_2, \tau_3, \ldots, \tau_{10}\}$$
$$= \{(-1,0), (0,1), (-1,1), (1,1), (-2,0), (0,2), (-1,2), (1,2), (-2,1), (2,1)\}$$

and

$$N_s = \{r : r = s \pm \tau, \ \tau \in N^*\} \tag{2.2}$$

where $s + \tau$ is defined as

$$s = (i,j), \ \tau = (x,y), \ s + \tau = (i+x, j+y).$$

Assuming that all the neighbors of s also have the same label as that of s, the conditional density of the intensity at the pixel s is:

$$P(Y_s = y_s \mid Y_r = y_r, r \in N_s, L_s = l) = \frac{e^{-U(Y_s = y_s \mid Y_r = y_r, r \in N_s, L_s = l)}}{Z(l \mid y_r, r \in N_s)} \qquad (2.3)$$

$$U(Y_s = y_s \mid Y_r = y_r, r \in N_s, L_s = l) = \frac{1}{2\sigma_l^2}\left(y_s^2 - 2\sum_{r \in N_s} \Theta_{s,r}^l y_s y_r\right). \qquad (2.4)$$

Equation (2.3) is a Gibbs distribution function, $U(.)$ is often referred to as a Gibbs measure and $Z(l \mid y_r, r \in N_s)$ is called the partition function. In (2.4), σ_l and Θ^l are the GMRF model parameters of the l-th texture class. A stationary GMRF model implies that the parameters satisfy $\Theta_{r,s}^l = \Theta_{r-s}^l = \Theta_{s-r}^l = \Theta_\tau^l$. There are several ways of estimating the GMRF parameters and a comparison of different schemes can be found in [53]. We have used the least squares method in our experiments. We view the image intensity array as composed of a set of overlapping $k \times k$ windows W_s, centered at each pixel $s \in \Omega$. In each of these windows we assume that the texture label L_s is homogeneous (all the pixels in the window belong to the same texture) and model the intensity distribution in the window by a fourth order stationary GMRF. Let $\mathbf{Y}_s^*$ denote the 2-D vector representing the zero mean intensity array in the window W_s. Using the Gibbs formulation and assuming a free boundary model, the joint probability density in the window W_s can be written as:

$$P(\mathbf{Y}_s^* = \mathbf{y}_s^* \mid L_s = l) = \frac{e^{-U_1(\mathbf{y}_s^* \mid L_s = l)}}{Z_1(l)}$$

where $Z_1(l)$ is the partition function and

$$U_1(\mathbf{y}_s^* \mid L_s = l) = \frac{1}{2\,\sigma_l^2}\sum_{r \in W_s}\left\{ y_r^2 - \sum_{\tau \in N^* \mid r+\tau \in W_s} \Theta_\tau^l y_r(y_{r+\tau} + y_{r-\tau}) \right\}. \qquad (2.5)$$

Label Process. The texture labels are assumed to obey a first or second order discrete Markov model with a single parameter β, which measures the amount of clustering between adjacent pixels. If $\hat{N}_s$ denotes the appropriate neighborhood for the label field, then we can write the distribution function for the texture label at site s conditioned on the labels of the neighboring sites as:

$$P(L_s \mid L_r, \ r \in \hat{N}_s) = \frac{e^{-U_2(L_s \mid L_r)}}{Z_2}$$

where Z_2 is a normalizing constant and

$$U_2(L_s \mid L_r, \ r \in \hat{N}_s) = -\beta \sum_{r \in \hat{N}_s} \delta(L_s - L_r), \ \beta > 0. \qquad (2.6)$$

In (2.6), β determines the degree of clustering, and $\delta(i-j)$ is the Kronecker delta. Using the Bayes rule, we can write

$$P(L_s \mid \mathbf{Y}_s^*, \, L_r, \, r \in \hat{N}_s) = \frac{P(\mathbf{Y}_s^* \mid L_s) \, P(L_s \mid L_r, \, r \in \hat{N}_s)}{P(\mathbf{Y}_s^*)}. \qquad (2.7)$$

Since $\mathbf{Y}_s^*$ is known, the denominator in (2.7) is just a constant. The numerator is a product of two exponential functions and can be expressed as

$$P(L_s \mid \mathbf{Y}_s^*, \, L_r, \, r \in \hat{N}_s) = \frac{1}{Z_p} \, e^{-U_p(L_s \mid \mathbf{Y}_s^*, \, L_r, \, r \in \hat{N}_s)} \qquad (2.8)$$

where Z_p is the partition function and $U_p(.)$ is the posterior energy corresponding to (2.7). From (2.5) and (2.6) we write

$$U_p(L_s \mid \mathbf{Y}_s^*, \, L_r, \, r \in \hat{N}_s) = w(L_s) + U_1(\mathbf{Y}_s^* \mid L_s) + U_2(L_s \mid L_r, \, r \in \hat{N}_s). \qquad (2.9)$$

Note that the second term in (2.9) relates the observed pixel intensities to the texture labels and the last term specifies the label distribution. The bias term $w(L_s) = \log Z_1(L_s)$ is dependent on the texture class and it can be explicitly evaluated for the GMRF model considered here using the toroidal assumption (the computations become very cumbersome if toroidal assumptions are not made). An alternate approach is to estimate the bias from the histogram of the data as suggested by Geman and Graffigne [15]. Finally, the posterior distribution of the texture labels for the entire image given the intensity array is

$$P(\mathbf{L} \mid \mathbf{Y}^*) = \frac{P(\mathbf{Y}^* \mid \mathbf{L}) \, P(\mathbf{L})}{P(\mathbf{Y}^*)}. \qquad (2.10)$$

Maximizing (2.10) gives the optimal Bayesian estimate. Though it is possible in principle to compute the right-hand side of (2.10) and find the global optimum, the computational burden involved is so enormous that it is practically impossible to do so. However we note that the stochastic relaxation algorithms discussed in Section 2.3 require only the computation of (2.8) to obtain the optimal solution. The deterministic relaxation algorithm given in the next section also uses these values, but in this case the solution is only an approximation to the MAP estimate.

2.2. A Neural Network for Texture Classification

We describe the network architecture used for segmentation and the implementation of deterministic relaxation algorithms. The energy function which the network minimizes is obtained from the image model discussed in the previous section. For convenience of notation let $U_1(i,j,l) = U_1(\mathbf{Y}_s^*, L_s = l) + w(l)$ where $s = (i,j)$ denotes a pixel site and $U_1(\,.\,)$ and $w(l)$ are as defined in (2.9). The network consists of K layers, each layer arranged as an $M \times M$ array, where K is the number of texture classes in the image and M is the dimension of the image. The elements (neurons) in the network are assumed to be binary and are indexed by (i,j,l) where

$(i, j) = s$ refers to their position in the image and l refers to the layer. The (i, j, l)-th neuron is said to be ON if its output V_{ijl} is 1, indicating that the corresponding site $s = (i, j)$ in the image has the texture label l. Let $T_{ijl;i'j'l'}$ be the connection strength between the neurons (i, j, l) and (i', j', l') and I_{ijl} be the input bias current. Then a general form for the energy of the network is [52]

$$E = -\frac{1}{2} \sum_{i=1}^{M} \sum_{j=1}^{M} \sum_{l=1}^{K} \sum_{i'=1}^{M} \sum_{j'=1}^{M} \sum_{l'=1}^{K} T_{ijl;i'j'l'} V_{ijl} V_{i'j'l'} - \frac{1}{2} \sum_{i=1}^{M} \sum_{j=1}^{M} \sum_{l=1}^{K} I_{ijl} V_{ijl} . \quad (2.11)$$

We note that a solution for the MAP estimate can be obtained by minimizing (2.10). Here we approximate the posterior energy by

$$U(\mathbf{L}|\mathbf{Y}^*) = \sum_{s} \{ U(\mathbf{Y}_s^*|L_s) + w_{L_s} + U_2(L_s) \} \quad (2.12)$$

and the corresponding Gibbs energy to be minimized can be written as

$$E = \frac{1}{2} \sum_{i=1}^{M} \sum_{j=1}^{M} \sum_{l=1}^{K} U_1(i, j, l) V_{ijl} - \frac{\beta}{2} \sum_{l=1}^{K} \sum_{i=1}^{M} \sum_{j=1}^{M} \sum_{(i',j') \in \hat{N}_{ij}} V_{i'j'l} V_{ijl} \quad (2.13)$$

where $\hat{N}_{ij}$ is the neighborhood of site (i, j) (same as the $\hat{N}_s$ in Section 2). In (2.13), it is implicitly assumed that each pixel site has a unique label, i.e. only one neuron is active in each column of the network. This constraint can be implemented in different ways. For the deterministic relaxation algorithm described below, a simple method is to use a *winner-takes-all* circuit for each column so that the neuron receiving the maximum input is turned on and the others are turned off. Alternately a penalty term can be introduced in (2.13) to represent the constraint as in [52]. From (2.11) and (2.13) we can identify the parameters for the network,

$$T_{ijl;i'j'l'} = \begin{cases} \beta & \text{if } (i', j') \in \hat{N}_{ij}, \forall\, l = l' \\ 0 & \text{otherwise} \end{cases} \quad (2.14)$$

and the bias current

$$I_{ijl} = - U_1(i, j, l) . \quad (2.15)$$

2.2.1. *Deterministic relaxation*

The above equations (2.14) and (2.15) relate the parameters of the network to that of the image model. The connection matrix for the above network is symmetric and there is no self feedback, i.e. $T_{ijl;ijl} = 0, \forall i, j, l$. Let u_{ijl} be the potential of neuron (i, j, l). (Note that l is the layer number corresponding to texture class l), then

$$u_{ijl} = \sum_{i'=1}^{M} \sum_{j'=1}^{M} \sum_{l'=1}^{K} T_{ijl;i'j'l'} V_{i'j'l'} + I_{ijl} \quad (2.16)$$

In order to minimize (2.13), we use the following updating rule:

$$V_{ijl} = \begin{cases} 1 & \text{if } u_{ijl} = \min{}_{l'}\{u_{ijl'}\} \\ 0 & \text{otherwise} \end{cases} \tag{2.17}$$

This updating scheme ensures that at each stage the energy decreases. Since the energy is bounded, the convergence of the above system is assured but the stable state will in general be a local optimum.

This network model is a version of the Iterated Conditional Mode algorithm (ICM) of Besag [42]. This algorithm maximizes the conditional probability $P(L_s = l | \mathbf{Y}_s^*, L_{s'}, s' \in \hat{N}_s)$ during each iteration. It is a local deterministic relaxation algorithm that is very easy to implement. We observe that in general any algorithm based on MRF models can be easily mapped onto neural networks with local interconnections. The main advantage of this deterministic relaxation algorithm is its simplicity. Often the solutions are reasonably good and the algorithm usually converges within 20–30 iterations. In the next section we study two stochastic schemes which asymptotically converge to the global optimum of the respective criterion functions.

2.3. *Stochastic Algorithms for Texture Segmentation*

We look at two optimal solutions corresponding to different decision rules for determining the labels. The first one uses simulated annealing to obtain the optimum MAP estimate of the label configuration. The second algorithm minimizes the expected misclassification per pixel. The parallel network implementation of these algorithms is discussed in Section 2.3.3.

2.3.1. *Searching for MAP solution*

The MAP rule [15] searches for the configuration L that maximizes the posterior probability distribution. This is equivalent to maximizing $P(\mathbf{Y}^* \mid L) \, P(L)$ as $P(\mathbf{Y}^*)$ is independent of the labels and $\mathbf{Y}^*$ is known. The right-hand side of (2.10) is a Gibbs distribution. To maximize (2.10) we use simulated annealing [41], a combinatorial optimization method which is based on sampling from varying Gibbs distribution functions

$$\frac{e^{-\frac{1}{T_k}U_p(L_s \mid \mathbf{Y}_s^*, \, L_r, r \in \hat{N}_s)}}{Z_{T_k}}.$$

In order to maximize

$$\frac{e^{-U_p(\mathbf{L} \mid \mathbf{Y}^*)}}{Z},$$

T_k being the time varying parameter, is referred to as the temperature. We used the following cooling schedule

$$T_k = \frac{T_0}{1 + \log_2 k}. \tag{2.18}$$

where k is the iteration number. When the temperature is high, the bond between adjacent pixels is loose, and the distribution tends to behave like a uniform distribution over the possible texture labels. As T_k decreases, the distribution concentrates on the lower values of the energy function which correspond to points with higher probability. The process is bound to converge to a uniform distribution over the label configuration that corresponds to the MAP solution. Since the number of texture labels is finite, convergence of this algorithm follows from [41]. In our experiment, we realized that starting the iterations with $T_0 = 2$ did not guarantee convergence to the MAP solution. Since starting at a much higher temperature will slow the convergence of the algorithm significantly, we use an alternative approach, viz., cycling the temperature [43]. We follow the annealing schedule till T_k reaches a lower bound then we reheat the system and start a new cooling process. By using only a few cycles, we obtained results better than those with a single cooling cycle. Parallel implementation of simulated annealing on the network is discussed in Section 2.3.3. The results we present in Section 2.4 were obtained with two cycles.

2.3.2. *Maximizing the posterior marginal distribution*

The choice of the objective function for optimal segmentation can significantly affect its result. The choice should be made depending on the purpose of the classification. In many implementations the most reasonable objective function is the one that minimizes the expected percentage misclassification per pixel. The solution to the above objective function is also the one that maximizes the marginal posterior distribution of L_s, given the observation $\mathbf{Y}^*$, for each pixel s.

$$P\{L_s = l_s \mid \mathbf{Y}^* = \mathbf{y}^*\} \propto \sum_{\mathbf{l}|L_s=l_s} P(\mathbf{Y}^* = \mathbf{y}^* \mid \mathbf{L} = \mathbf{l}) \, P(\mathbf{L} = \mathbf{l})$$

The summation above extends over all possible label configurations keeping the label at site s constant. This concept was thoroughly investigated in [44]. Marroquin [55] discusses this formulation in the context of image restoration, and illustrates the performance on images with few gray levels. The possibility of using this objective function for texture segmentation is also mentioned. In [42] the same objective function is mentioned in the context of image estimation.

To find the optimal solution we use the stochastic algorithm suggested in [44]. The algorithm samples out of the posterior distribution of the texture labels given the intensity. Unlike the stochastic relaxation algorithm, samples are taken with a fixed temperature $T = 1$. The Markov chain associated with the sampling algorithm converges with probability one to the posterior distribution. We define new random variables $g_s^{l,t}$ for each pixel ($s \in \Omega$):

$$g_s^{l,t}\{L_s^t\} = \begin{cases} 1 & L_s^t = l \\ 0 & \text{otherwise} \end{cases}$$

where L_s^t is the class of the s pixel, at time t, in the state vector of the Markov chain associated with the Gibbs sampler. The ergodic property of the Markov chain [56] is used to calculate the expectations for these random variables using time averaging:

$$E\{g_s^{l,t}\} = \lim_{N\to\infty} \frac{1}{N} \sum_{t=1}^{N} g_s^{l,t} = P_s\{L_s = l|\mathbf{Y}^*\}$$

where N is the number of iterations performed. To obtain the optimal class for each pixel, we simply chose the class that occurred more often than the others.

The MPM algorithm was implemented using the Gibbs sampler [41]. A much wider set of sampling algorithms such as Metropolis can be used for this purpose. The algorithms can be implemented sequentially or in parallel, with a deterministic or stochastic decision rule for the order of visiting the pixels. In order to avoid dependence on the initial state of the Markov chain, we can ignore the first few iterations. In the experiments conducted we obtained good results after five hundred iterations. The algorithm does not suffer from the drawbacks of simulated annealing. For instance we do not have to start the iterations with a high temperature to avoid local minima and the performance is not severely affected by enlarging the state space.

2.3.3. *Network implementation of the sampling algorithms*

All the stochastic algorithms described in the Gibbs formulation are based on sampling from a probability distribution. The probability distribution is constant in the MPM algorithm [44] and is time varying in the case of annealing. The need for parallel implementation is due to the heavy computational load associated with their use.

We now describe how these stochastic algorithms can be implemented on the network discussed in Section 2.2. The only modification required for the simulated annealing rule is that the neurons in the network fire according to a time dependent probabilistic rule. Using the same notation as in section 3, the probability that neuron (i, j, l) will fire during iteration k is

$$P(V_{ijl} = 1) = \frac{e^{-\frac{1}{T_k}u_{ijl}}}{Z_{T_k}} \tag{2.19}$$

where u_{ijl} is as defined in (2.16) and T_k follows the cooling schedule (2.18).

The MPM algorithm uses the above selection rule with $T_k = 1$. In addition, each neuron in the network has a counter which is incremented every time the neuron fires. When the iterations are terminated the neuron in each column of the network having the maximum count is selected to represent the label for the corresponding pixel site in the image.

2.4. *Experimental Results*

The segmentation results using the above algorithms are given on two examples. The parameters σ_l and Θ_l corresponding to the fourth order GMRF for each texture class were pre-computed from 64×64 images of the textures. The local mean (in an 11×11 window) was first subtracted to obtain the zero mean texture and the least square estimates [53] of the parameters were then computed from the interior of the image. The parameter values for the different textures used in our experiments is given in Table 1.

Table 1. GMRF texture parameters.

	calf	grass	pigskin	sand	wool	wood
θ_1	0.5689	0.5667	0.3795	0.5341	0.4341	0.5508
θ_2	0.2135	0.3780	0.4528	0.4135	0.2182	0.2498
θ_3	-0.1287	-0.2047	-0.1117	-0.1831	-0.0980	-0.1164
θ_4	-0.0574	-0.1920	-0.1548	-0.2050	-0.0006	-0.1405
θ_5	-0.1403	-0.1368	-0.0566	-0.1229	-0.0836	-0.0517
θ_6	-0.0063	-0.0387	-0.0494	-0.0432	0.0592	0.0139
θ_7	-0.0052	0.0158	-0.0037	0.0120	-0.0302	-0.0085
θ_8	-0.0153	0.0075	0.0098	0.0111	-0.0407	-0.0058
θ_9	0.0467	0.0505	0.0086	0.0362	0.0406	-0.0008
θ_{10}	0.0190	0.0496	0.0233	0.0442	-0.0001	0.0091
σ^2	217.08	474.72	79.33	91.44	126.22	14.44

The first step in the segmentation process involves computing the Gibbs energies $U_1(\mathbf{Y}^*{}_s|L_s)$ in (2.5). This is done for each texture class and the results are stored. For computational convenience these $U_1(.)$ values are normalized by dividing by k^2, where k is the size of the window. To ignore the boundary effects, we set $U_1 = 0$ at the boundaries. We have experimented with different window sizes and larger windows result in more homogeneous texture patches but the boundaries between the textures are distorted. The results reported here are based on windows of size 11×11 pixels. We obtained $w(l_s)$ by trial and error.

The choice of β plays an important role in the segmentation process and its value depends on the magnitude of the energy function $U_1(.)$. Various values of β ranging from 0.2–3.0 were used in the experiments. In the deterministic algorithm it is preferable to start with a small β and increase it gradually. Large values of beta usually degrade the performance. We also observed that slowly increasing β during the iterations improves the results for the stochastic algorithms. It should be noted that using a larger value of β for the deterministic algorithm (compared to those used in the stochastic algorithms) does not improve the performance.

The nature of the segmentation results depends on the order of the label model. It is preferable to choose the first order model for the stochastic algorithms if we know *a priori* that the boundaries are either horizontal or vertical. However for the deterministic rule and the learning scheme the second order model results in more homogeneous classification.

The MPM algorithm requires the statistics obtained from the invariant measure of the Markov chain corresponding to the sampling algorithm. Hence it is preferable to ignore the first few hundred trials before starting to gather the statistics. The performance of the deterministic relaxation rule of Section 2.2 also depends on the initial state and we have looked into two different initial conditions. The first one starts with a label configuration $\mathbf{L}$ such that $L_s = l_s$ if $U_1(\mathbf{Y}_s^*|l_s) = \min_{l_k}\{U_1(\mathbf{Y}_s^* \mid l_k)\}$. This corresponds to maximizing the probability $P(\mathbf{Y}^* \mid \mathbf{L})$ [12]. The second choice for the initial configuration is a randomly generated label set. Results for both the cases are provided and we observe that the random choice often leads to better results.

Example 1. This is a 256×256 image (Fig. 2(a)) having six textures: calf, grass, wool, wood, pigskin and sand. This is a difficult problem in the sense that three of the textures (wool, pigskin and sand) have almost identical characteristics and are not easily distinguishable even by the human eye. The ICM result obtained with the maximum likelihood estimate (MLE) as the initial condition is in Fig. 2(b). The MAP solution using simulated annealing is shown in Fig. 2(c). As mentioned before, cycling of temperature improves the performance of simulated annealing. The segmentation result was obtained by starting with an initial temperature $T_0 = 2.0$ and cooling according to the schedule (2.18) for 300 iterations. Then the system was reset to $T_0 = 1.5$ and the process was repeated for 300 more iterations. In the case of the MPM rule the first 500 iterations were ignored and Fig. 2(d) shows the result obtained using the last two hundred iterations. As in the previous example the best results were obtained by the simulated annealing and MPM algorithms. For the MPM case there were no misclassifications within homogeneous regions but the boundaries were not accurate and in fact, as indicated in Table 2, simulated annealing has the lowest percentage error in classification.

Table 2. Percentage misclassification for Example 1 (six class problem).

Algorithm	Percentage Error
Maximum Likelihood Estimate	22.17
Neural network (MLE as initial state)	16.25
Neural network (Random initial state)	14.74
Simulated annealing (MAP)	6.72
MPM algorithm	7.05

3. Preattentive Segmentation

In this section we discuss a simple biologically motivated approach to detect texture boundaries within a more general contex of boundary detection [45]. Previous approaches to this problem are discussed in [21,22]. In [21], Malik and Perona propose a three stage model involving convolution with even symmetric filters followed by half wave rectification, local inhibition, and texture boundary detection using odd symmetric filters. The BCS processes the intensity data and performs

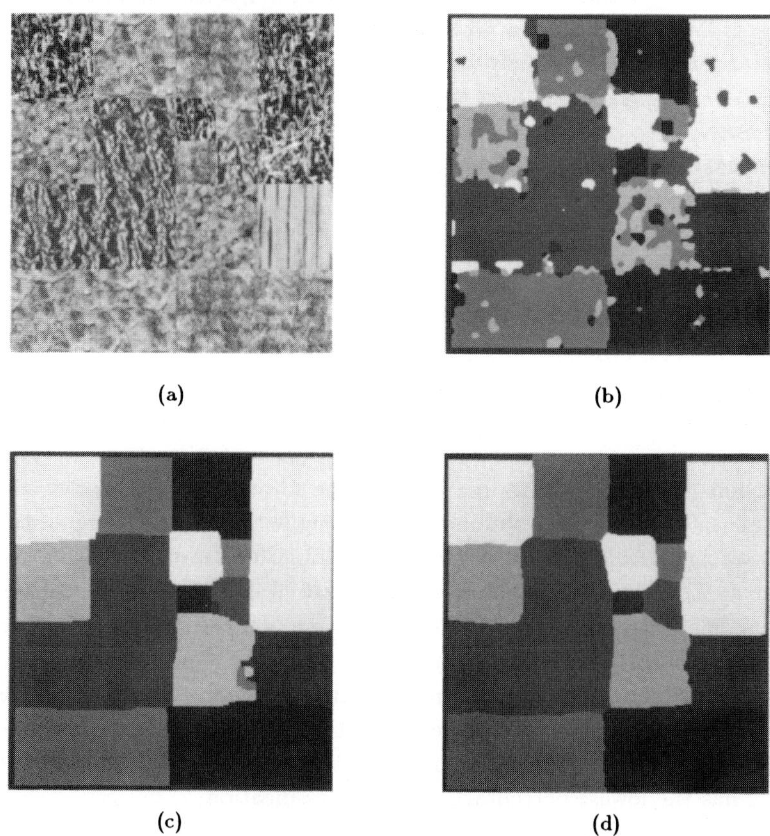

(a)　　　　　　　　　　　　　(b)

(c)　　　　　　　　　　　　　(d)

Fig. 2. Texture segmentation results for a six class problem. (a) original image. Segmentation results using ICM, MAP and MPM are given in (b)–(d), respectively.

preattentive segmentation of the scene. The first stage of the BCS consists of oriented contrast filters at various scales and orientations and extracts the contrast information from the scene. The outputs of the filters are then fed to a two-stage competitive network whose main goal is to generate end-cuts. Subsequent long range cooperative interactions and a positive feedback to the competitive stage help in boundary completion. The boundary detection takes place independently in different spatial channels.

The input image is first processed through a bank of orientation selective bandpass filters at various spatial frequencies. The convolution of the image with these filters yields a representation which is localized in space as well as in frequency. We then introduce three distinct types of local feature interactions for consideration: competition between spatial neighbors in each orientation channel, competition between orientations at each spatial location, and interscale interactions. Interscale interactions are used in localizing line ends and play an important role in boundary detection. The second stage of interactions groups similar features in the neighborhood. This cooperative processing helps in the boundary completion process. The final step involves identifying image boundaries.

3.1. *Gabor Functions and Wavelets*

Gabor functions are Gaussians modulated by complex sinusoids. Consider a wavelet transform where the *basic wavelet* is a Gabor function of the form

$$
\begin{aligned}
g_\lambda(x, y, \theta) &= e^{-(\lambda^2 x'^2 + y'^2) + i\pi x'} \\
x' &= x\cos\theta + y\sin\theta \\
y' &= -x\sin\theta + y\cos\theta
\end{aligned}
\tag{3.1}
$$

where λ is the spatial aspect ratio and θ is the preferred orientation. To simplify the notation, we drop the subscript λ and unless otherwise stated assume that $\lambda = 1$. For practical applications, discretization of the parameters is necessary. The discretized parameters must cover the entire frequency spectrum of interest. Let the orientation range $[0, \pi]$ be discretized into N intervals and the scale parameter α be sampled exponentially as α^j. This results in the wavelet family

$$
(g(\alpha^j(x - x_0, y - y_0), \theta_k)), \alpha \in \mathbf{R}, \ j = \{0, -1, -2, \ldots\}
\tag{3.2}
$$

where $\theta_k = k\pi/N$. The Gabor wavelet transform is then defined by

$$
W_j(x, y, \theta) = \int f(x_1, y_1)\, g^*(\alpha^j(x_1 - x, y_1 - y), \theta)\, dx_1 dy_1 \,.
\tag{3.3}
$$

3.2. *Local Spatial Interactions*

Following feature extraction using Gabor wavelets, we now consider local competitive and cooperative processing of these features. Competitive interactions help in noise suppression, and in reducing the effects of illumination.

These interactions are modeled by non-linear lateral inhibition between features. Two types of such interactions are considered. The first type includes competition between spatial neighbors within each orientation and scale. The second type involves competition between different orientations at each spatial position. For simplicity the transfer function $g(x)$ of all feature detectors is assumed to be the same. The following notation is used in explaining the interactions: The output of a cell at position $s = (x, y)$ in the ith spatial frequency channel with a preferred orientation θ is denoted by $Y_i(s, \theta)$, with $I_i(s, \theta)$ being the excitatory input to that cell from the previous processing stage. For example, $I_i(s, \theta)$ could be the energy in the filter output corresponding to feature (s, θ) in the ith frequency channel. For convenience we will drop the subscript i indicating the frequency channel whenever there is no ambiguity. Let N_s be the local spatial neighborhood of s. The competitive dynamics is represented by:

$$\dot{X}(s,\theta) = -a_{s,\theta}X(s,\theta) + I(s,\theta) - \sum_{s' \in N_s} b_{s,s'}Y(s',\theta) - \sum_{\theta' \neq \theta} c_{\theta,\theta'}Y(s,\theta') \quad (3.4)$$

$$Y(s,\theta) = h(X(s,\theta)) \quad (3.5)$$

where (a, b, c) are positive constants. In our experiments we have used a sigmoid non-linearity of the form $h(x) = 1/(1 + \exp(-\beta x))$. The dynamics of (3.4) can be visualized as follows : At each location within a single frequency channel, the corresponding cell receives an excitatory input from a similarly oriented feature detector (of the same spatial frequency). Further it also receives inhibitory signals from the neighboring cells within the same channel. We assume that all these interactions are symmetric ($b_{s,s'} = b_{s',s}$ and $c_{\theta,\theta'} = c_{\theta',\theta}$). The competitive dynamics of the above system can be shown to be stable. The Lyapunov function for the system [52] can be written as

$$E(Y) = \frac{1}{2}\sum_{s,s'} b_{s,s'}Y(s,\theta)Y(s',\theta) + \frac{1}{2}\sum_{\theta,\theta'} c_{\theta,\theta'}Y(s,\theta)Y(s,\theta')$$

$$+ \sum_{s,\theta} \int_0^{Y(s,\theta)} \left(a_{s,\theta}h^{-1}(y) - I(s,\theta)\right) dy. \quad (3.6)$$

Under the assumptions that the interactive synapses are symmetric and that $g(\cdot)$ is monotone non-decreasing, the time derivative of E is negative and the system represented by (3.4) always converges.

3.3. *Local Scale Interactions*

We now suggest a simple mechanism to model the end-inhibition property of hypercomplex cells. Hypercomplex cells in the visual cortex differ from simple and complex cells in that they respond to small lines and line endings [57]. For this the hypercomplex cell receptive field must have inhibitory end zones along the preferred orientation. Such a profile can be generated either by modifying the profile of the simple cell itself or through interscale interactions, discussed below. The fact that both simple and complex cells often exhibit this end-stopping behavior further suggests that both these mechanisms are utilized in the visual cortex. If $Q_{ij}(x,y,\theta)$ denotes the output of an end-inhibited cell at position (x,y) receiving inputs from two frequency channels i and j ($\alpha^i < \alpha^j$) with preferred orientation θ, then

$$Q_{ij}(x,y,\theta) = h(\|W_i(x,y,\theta) - \gamma W_j(x,y,\theta)\|) \quad (3.7)$$

where $\gamma = \alpha^{-2(i-j)}$ is the normalizing factor. The logic behind this is simple. At line ends, cells with shorter receptive fields will have a stronger response than those with larger fields, and consequently will be able to excite the hypercomplex cells. At other points along the line, both small and large receptive field cells are equally excited and in the process the response of the hypercomplex cells is inhibited. It appears that such scale interactions to generate end inhibition do exist in the visual cortex. Bolz and Gilbert [58] observe that connections between layers 6 and 4 in the cat striate cortex play a role in generating end inhibition. The cells in layer 4 are of hypercomplex type exhibiting end inhibition. Layer 6 cells have large receptive fields and require long bars (or lines) to activate them. In addition, cells in both layers show orientation selectivity. Inactivating layer 6 cells resulted in the loss of end-inhibition property of layer 4 cells, while preserving other properties such as orientation selectivity. Thus, in the absence of layer 6 activity, cells in layer 4 could be excited by short bars and their response did not decrease as the bar lengths increased, suggesting that layer 6 cells have an inhibitory effect on the cells of layer 4.

3.4. *Grouping and Boundary Detection*

The final stage involves grouping similar orientations. The grouping process receives inputs both from the competitive stage (3.4) and from the end detectors (hypercomplex cells) described in Section 3.3. Note that the orientation of the activating end-detector is orthogonal to the actual orientation of the grouping process. This incorporates the observation made in [59,60] that hypercomplex cells are responsible for detecting illusory contours. Abrupt line endings signal an occluding boundary almost orthogonal to the edge orientation, and this is represented by these end-inhibited cells providing input to the grouping process nearly orthogonal in their orientation preference. If $Z_i(s, \theta)$ represents the output of this process, then

$$Z_i(s, \theta) = h\left(\int d_i(s - s', \theta)(Y_i(s', \theta) + Q_{ij}(s', \theta')ds'\right). \qquad (3.8)$$

$d_i(s, \theta)$ represents the receptive field of $Z_i(s, \theta)$ and in our experiments we have used

$$d(s = (x, y), \theta) = \exp(-(2\sigma^2)^{-1}[\lambda^2(x\cos\theta + y\sin\theta)^2 + (-x\sin\theta + y\cos\theta)^2]) \quad (3.9)$$

where θ is the preferred orientation, θ' is the corresponding orthogonal direction, and λ is the aspect ratio of the Gaussian. The Z cells thus integrate the information from similar oriented cells within each frequency channel and from hypercomplex cells of appropriate orientation, and thus help in grouping the features and in boundary completion. Since the various frequency channels are sampled, the effective standard deviation of the Gaussian is σ/α^i, where α^i is the scale parameter for channel i.

To summarize, this approach consists of three distinct steps: (a) feature detection using Gabor wavelets, (b) local interactions between features and (c) scale interactions to generate end inhibition. The output $Z(.)$ from different frequency channels is now used to detect edges and texture boundaries.

3.5. *Experiments*

The performance of our approach is illustrated on several images. The following parameter values were used in our experiments described here: $\beta = 4.0$ in the transfer function $g(.)$. The strengths of the inhibitory synapses in (3.4) are $b_{s,s'} = 1/\parallel n_s \parallel$ and $c = 1/N$, where $\parallel N_s \parallel$ is the cardinality of the neighborhood set and n is the number of discrete orientations used. Unless otherwise stated, $N = 4$ and N_S consists of the four nearest neighbors of s. The aspect ratio of the Gaussian in both the Gabor wavelets (3.1),and in the receptive field of Z cells (3.8) is set to 0.5. If more than one channel is mentioned then the result shown is a superposition of the boundaries detected in the individual channels.

Regarding implementing the dynamics of competition, we used a simple gradient descent on the corresponding energy function (3.6) instead of solving the set of differential equations. The equilibrium points in general for these two methods will be different, but gradient descent on E in (3.6) will be much faster (typically it takes less than 50 iterations to converge on a 256×256 image).

Example 2 (Intensity edges). Figure 3 shows two examples of edge detection using the energy measures. Figures 3(a) and (c) show the original 256×256 images. The edges shown in Figure 3(b) are detected in channels $\alpha^i = [1/\sqrt{2}, 1/2]$ and in (d) they correspond to the channel $\alpha^i = 1/\sqrt{2}$. In both cases σ is set to 1.

Example 3. Figure 4 shows the boundaries detected in an aerial image consisting of four textures, grass, water, wood and raffia. The wood texture is present at two regions at different orientations. The parameter values used are $\alpha^i = \{1/2, 1/2\sqrt{2}, 1/4\}$ and $\sigma = 5.0$.

Example 4. Figure 5 shows the results on a synthetic texture which is often used in psychophysical experiments. The boundary between L and Ts is not easily perceived whereas that between straight and oriented Ts clearly stands out. This boundary can be easily detected in almost all frequency channels and the parameters values used are the same as in the previous example.

Example 5. This example illustrates the importance of end inhibition in texture boundary detection. Figure 6 shows another commonly used texture consisting of randomly oriented Ls and +s. Unlike the previous example, orientation information can be used for segmentation. The line segments forming Ls and +s have the same length (seven pixels). The two regions differ in the distribution of corners, line-ends and interactions. As we discussed in Sec. 3.2.1, scale interactions play an important role in detecting these features. None of the scales by themselves contain enough information to segment the two regions, but using these interscale interactions the boundary between the Ls and +s can be detected (Fig. 6(b)). The boundary shown is for the case of using the interactions between scales corresponding to $\{1/2, 1/4\}$ with $\sigma = 16$.

Example 6 (Illusory contours). The usefulness of scale interactions in detecting line endings and their subsequent grouping to detect illusory contours is illustrated in Figure 7. For the line (Fig. 7(d)) and sine wave (Fig. 7(e)) contours the results shown are for $\alpha^i = \{1/2, 1/4\}, \sigma = 8$. For the circle (Fig. 7(f)) $\alpha^i = \{1/\sqrt{2}, 1/2\}$ and $\sigma = 2$.

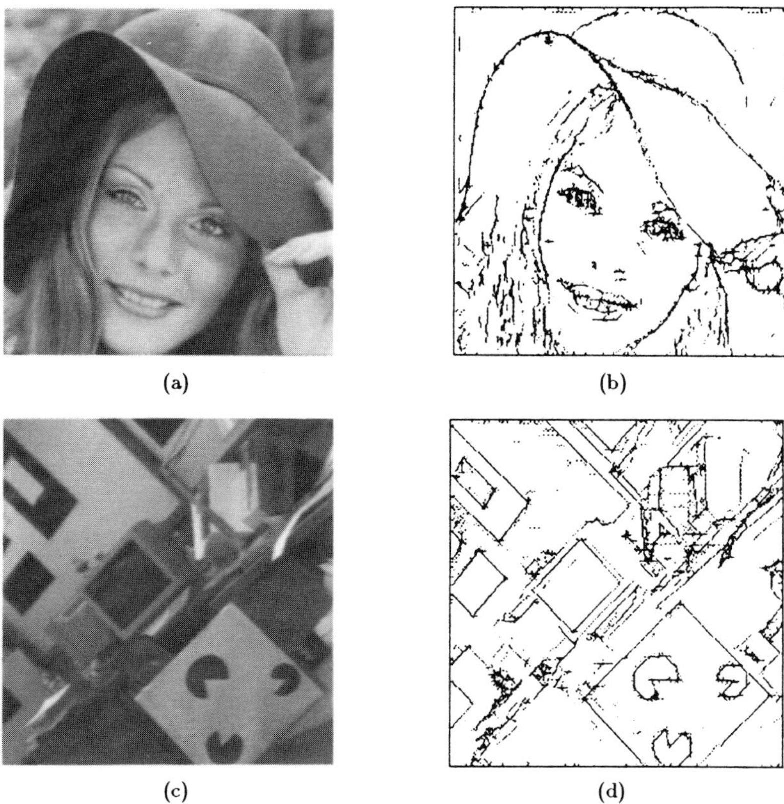

(a)   (b)

(c)   (d)

Fig. 3. (a) and (c) show two 256×256 images and the corresponding edges detected are shown in (b) and (d). In (b) the edges are from two channels $\alpha^i = \{1/\sqrt{2}, 1/2\}$ and in (d) $\alpha^i = 1/\sqrt{2}$. For both examples $\sigma = 1$.

4. Rotational Invariant Texture Classification

We discuss direct pattern classification strategies for classifying textures, assuming that there is only one texture in the image. The strategy is to fit varieties of parametric random field models, extract features from them, and use these features for classification using both standard algorithms and new procedures.

4.1. *Rotation Invariant Non-Causal AR Model*

The model used here is a modified version of a second-order non-causal autoregressive (NCAR) model, where the nearest eight neighbors are interpolated on a circle according to the following formula [61]:

$$y(s) = \alpha \sum_{r \in N_{2c}} g_r y(s \oplus r) + \sqrt{\beta} w(s),$$

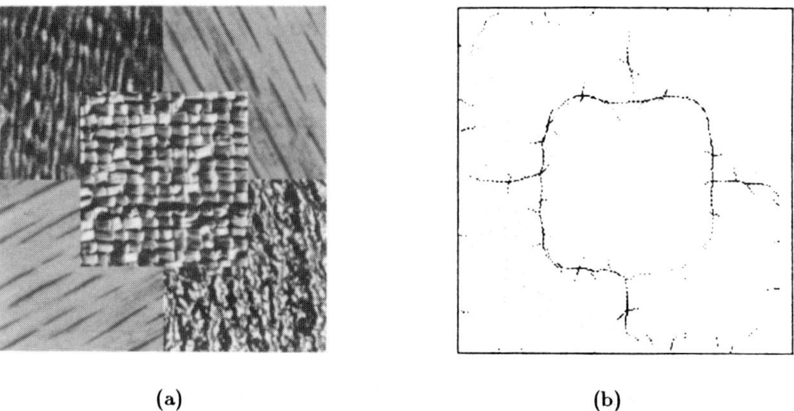

(a)   (b)

Fig. 4. (a) Image consisting of four natural textures, water, wood (in two regions at different orientations), raffia and grass. (b) texture boundary detected using the scales $\alpha^i = \{1/2, 1/2\sqrt{2}, 1/4\}$ and $\sigma = 5$ pixels.

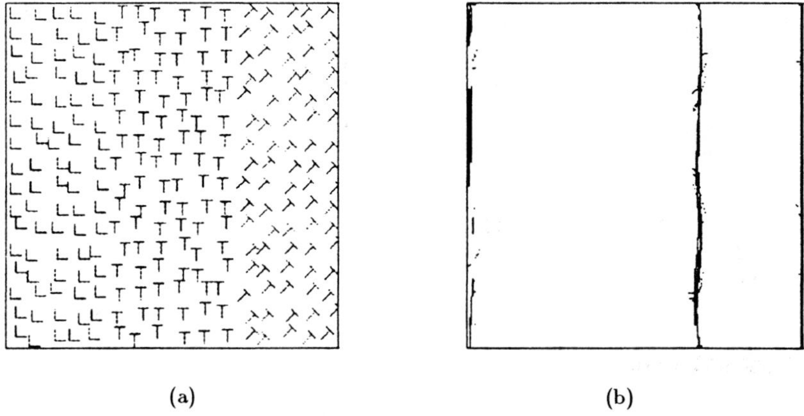

(a)   (b)

Fig. 5. Texture consisting of three regions, L, T and tilted T. The boundary between the Ls and Ts cannot be easily detected. However, the orientation difference between the two T regions is enough to discriminate between the two regions in almost all frequency channels. The boundary shown in (b) corresponds to the combined output from channels $\alpha^i = \{1/2, 1/2\sqrt{2}, 1/4\}$ and $\sigma = 5$ pixels.

where the neighborhood N_{2c} contains the lattice points

$$N_{2c} = (-1,-1), (-1,0), (-1,1), (0,-1), (0,0), (0,1), (1,-1), (1,0), (1,1)$$

and the interpolation kernel g_t is given by

$$g_r = \left\{ \begin{array}{ccc} 0.005 & 1.4336 & 0.4005 \\ 1.4336 & 0.6636 & 1.4336 \\ 0.4005 & 1.4336 & 0.4005 \end{array} \right\} .$$

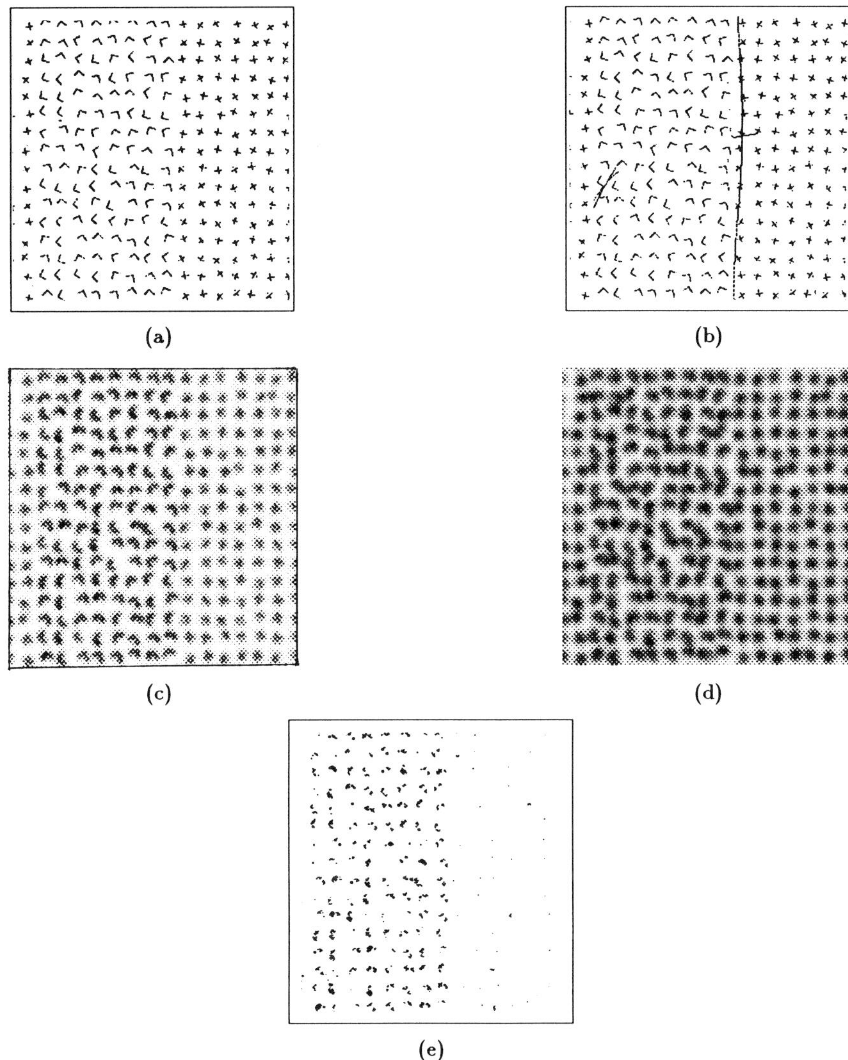

Fig. 6. Texture consisting of randomly oriented L and +. The boundary shown in (b) is detected using the output of the scale interactions with $\sigma = 16$. The scales used in this example are $\alpha^i = \{1/2, 1/4\}$, and figures (c) and (d) show the result of convolution and (e) shows the output after the interactions.

The parameters α and β can be estimated by least-squares technique and the estimates $\hat{\alpha}$, $\hat{\beta}$ can be used as discriminating features. $\hat{\beta}$ can be interpreted as a measure of the roughness of the texture.

Classification experiments performed using only these two features showed that there is room for improvement. Textures like wood have a strong degree of directionality, not captured by $\hat{\alpha}$ or $\hat{\beta}$. A feature which measures the degree of directionality can be obtained by fitting to the image two different simultaneous autoregressive

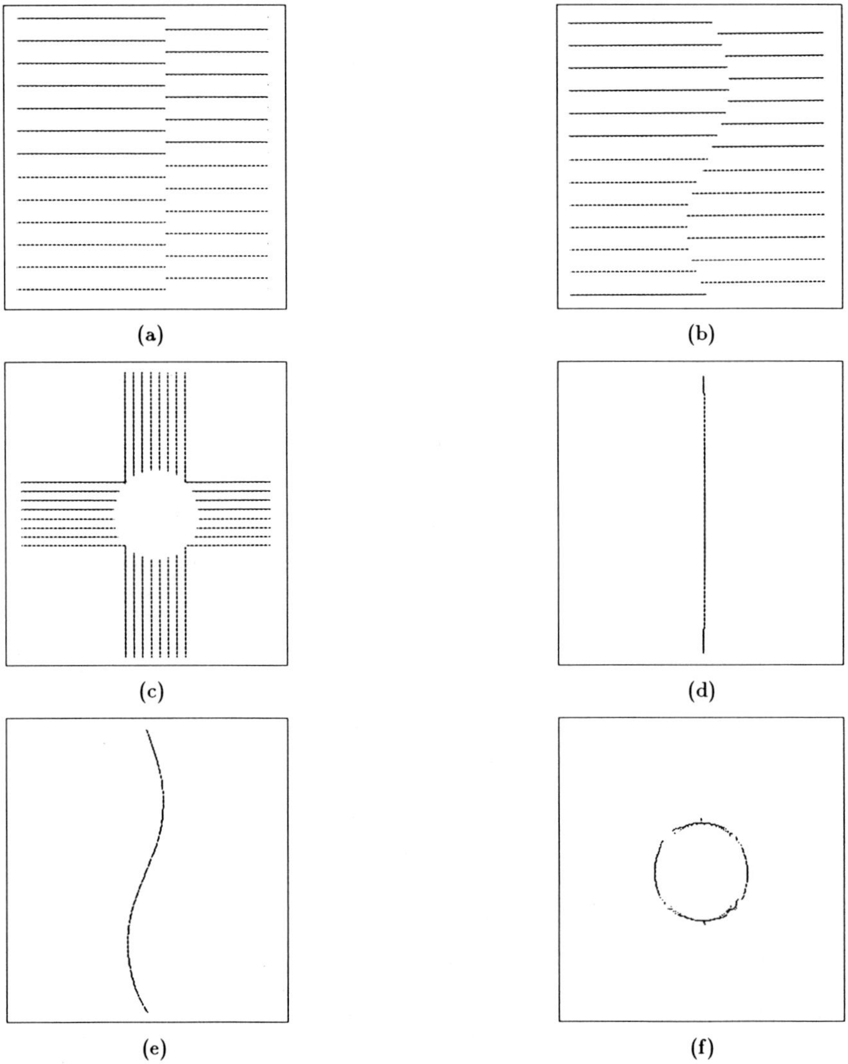

(a)　　　　　　　　　　　　　　(b)

(c)　　　　　　　　　　　　　　(d)

(e)　　　　　　　　　　　　　　(f)

Fig. 7. Some examples of illusory contours formed by line terminations (a), (b), and (c), and the corresponding detected contours (d), (e) and (f).

(SAR) models [31,62,61], having the following form:

$$y(s) = \sum_{r \in N} \theta_r y(s \oplus r) + \sqrt{\rho}\, w(s)$$

where $\theta_r = \theta_{-r}$ and $w(\dot{m})$ is (0,1) an identical, and independently distributed (IID) sequence. N is a neighbor set excluding (0,0). Let us first choose the neighbor set N to consist of four nearest neighbors, namely $N_a = [(0,1),(0,-1),(1,0),(-1,0)]$. Let $\theta^*_{(0,1)}$ and $\theta^*_{(1,0)}$ be the ML estimates of $\theta_{(0,1)}$ and $\theta_{(1,0)}$. Next, let us fit another SAR model with neighbor set N_b having the four nearest diagonal members, namely

$N_b = [(1,1),(1,-1),(-1,1),(-1,-1)]$. Let $\theta^*_{(1,1)}$ and $\theta^*_{(1,-1)}$ be the ML estimates of the corresponding parameters. Consider the feature ξ defined as

$$\hat{\xi} = \max[|\ \theta^*_{(1,0)} - \theta^*_{(0,1)}\ |, |\ \theta^*_{(1,1)} - \theta^*_{(1,-1)}\ |].$$

$\hat{\xi}$ measures the extent of variation in the orthogonal directions. For a texture having strong directionality like wood or straw, $\hat{\xi}$ will be very large. From a directionless texture like sand, it will be very small.

Thus, our feature set is $(\hat{\alpha}, \hat{\beta}, \hat{\xi})$.

A supervised recognition approach is used for the classification of textures. The inputs to the system are the digitized images from one of the m texture classes. The images are separated into test and training sets. The class of textures in the training set is known *a priori*. In the feature selection state, $\hat{\alpha}$, $\hat{\beta}$ and ξ are extracted from the processed images. The class parameterization phase computes the sample mean and standard deviation of each category training feature. The classifier is a distance classifier which measures a weighted distance between the features of the *test* image denoted by $\hat{\mathbf{X}}^{(t)} = [\hat{\alpha}^{(t)}, \hat{\beta}^{(t)}, \xi^{(t)}]$ and the mean feature of each of the m classes. The texture is then classified to class C_i^* for which such a distance is minimum, i.e.

$$i^* = \min_i d(\hat{\mathbf{X}}^{(t)}, i), \ i = 1, \ldots, m,$$

where

$$d(\hat{\mathbf{X}}^{(t)}, i) = \sum_{f = \hat{\alpha}, \hat{\beta}, \xi} \left\{ [f^t - \bar{f}^{(i)}]^2 / \sum_{j=1}^{m} [\sigma_f^2]^{(i)} \right\}$$

and $\bar{f}^{(i)}$ and $[\sigma_f^2]^{(i)}$ correspond to the sample mean and variance of class (i) feature, obtained from the training set, respectively.

4.2. *Experiments*

Twelve different textures, namely, calf leather (D24), wool (D19), beach sand (D29), pigskin (D92), plastic bubbles (D112), herringbone weave (D17), raffia (D84), wood grain (D68), grass (D9), straw (D15), brick wall (D95) and bark of tree (D12) were chosen from the photo album by Brodatz [63]. This selection includes both macrotextures (e.g. brick wall) and microtextures (e.g. sand). Seven rotated 512×512 - 8 bit (0–225) digitized images with relative angles of rotation of $0deg$, $30deg$, $60deg$, $90deg$, $120deg$, $150deg$, and $200deg$ are taken from each class of texture. Each 512×512 image was first reduced to a 128×128 one by averaging every 4×4 window into a single pixel. Each 128×128 image is then segmented into four 64×64 images. Thus the database has 28 64×64 images from each texture. One 64×64 digitized window of $0deg$ orientation of each texture is shown in Fig. 8. Figure 9 shows a 64×64 sample of raffia texture for all of the seven orientations.

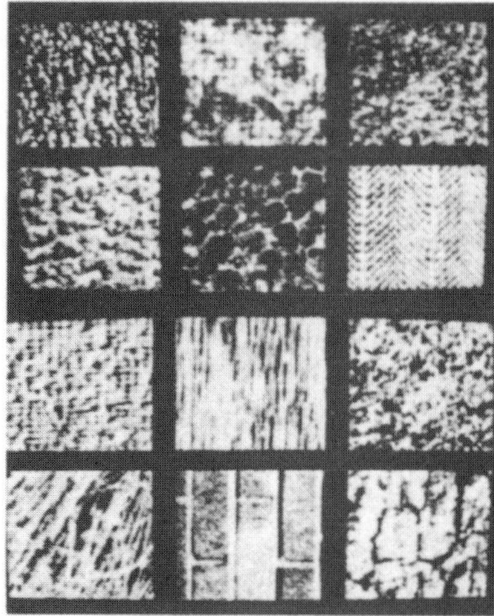

Fig. 8. A 64 × 64, 0*deg* digitized sample of each texture of the database. From left to right, first row: calf leather, wool, sand; second row: pigskin, plastic bubbles, herringbone weave; third row: raffia, wood, grass; fourth row: straw, brick wall, bark of tree.

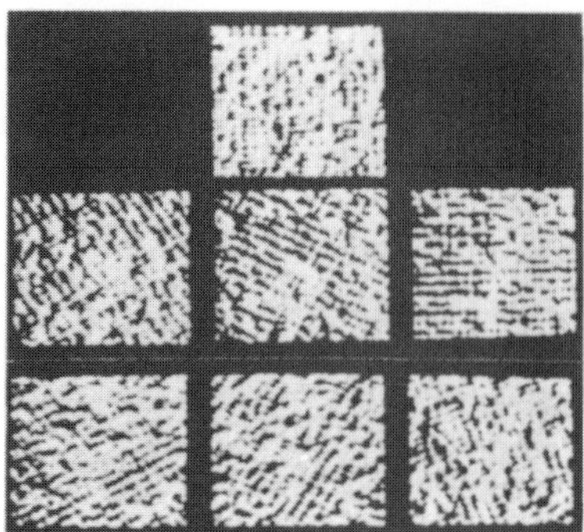

Fig. 9. A 64 × 64 digitized sample of each of the seven orientations of raffia texture. From top and from left to right: 0*deg*, 30*deg*, 60*deg*, 90*deg*, 120*deg*, 150*deg*, and 200*deg*.

To remove the variability in the image caused by illumination or quantization schemes, all the 64 × 64 images were first subjected to a gray scale normalization procedure and then normalized so that each image has zero empirical mean and unit empirical variance.

To illustrate the discriminating power of each individual feature, a range plot is presented for each of them in Fig. 10. The classes are first ordered for each feature according to the mean value of the respective features. Then the actual range of values that each feature takes for each category is plotted. Underneath

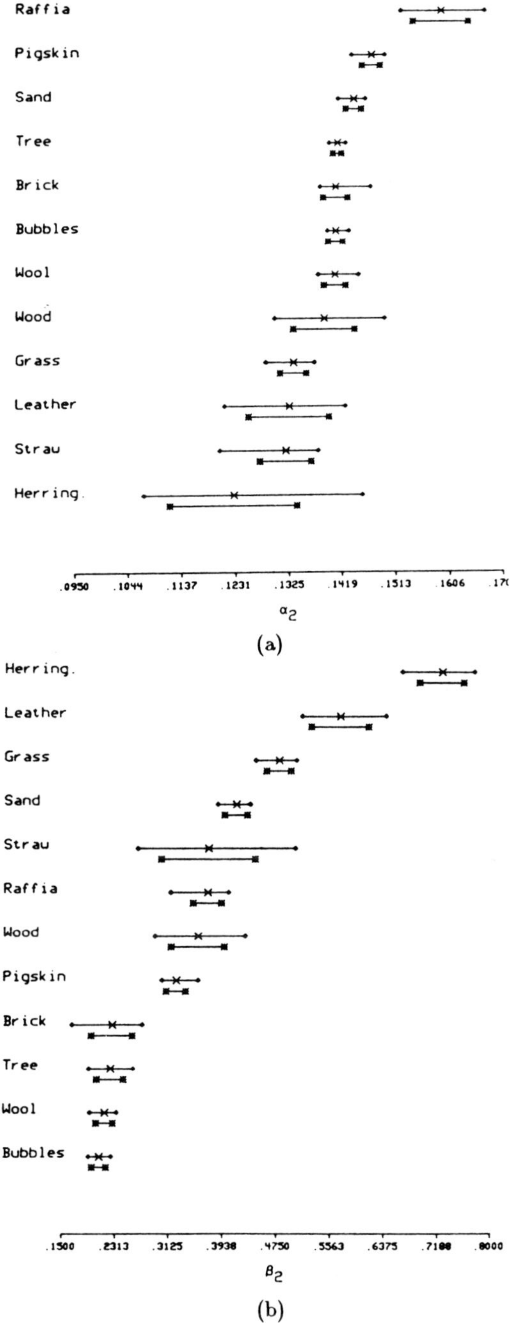

Fig. 10. (a) Range plots of $\hat{\alpha}$. (b) Range plots of $\hat{\beta}$. ✕: mean value. ●: range extrema. ∗: mean $\pm\sigma$.

each range plot the distance corresponding to two empirical standard deviations of the feature for that texture is also given. These range plots indicate how packed each respective feature is. The amount of vertical overlap between category range plots is an indication of the classification power of the causing feature. The less such an overlap, the better the feature. On the average, the $\hat{\alpha}$ values of each texture class overlap with $\hat{\alpha}$ values of four other classes. Raffia texture is an exception with very distinct $\hat{\alpha}$. Herringbone and leather textures have very distinct $\hat{\beta}$ features while the $\hat{\beta}$ of the rest of the categories overlap with an average of three other classes. Note that the mean value of $\hat{\beta}$ for highly circularly nonsymmetric features like herringbone is much higher than the mean value for plastic bubbles which has more of a circular symmetry property.

Several experiments were carried out [64] and only one is described here. Recall that we have 28 images with 7 orientations for each texture. The classifier for each texture is trained on samples from the images of three orientations (i.e. 12 images) and the classifier is tested using all other images (i.e. 16 images of that texture and 28 of all other textures). Thus the classifier has not "seen" the orientations it encounters in the test phase. The results are presented in Table 3. A total of ten experiments were carried out and the average classification accuracy obtained is 89 percent.

Table 3. Classification results for 12 classes in the database using $(\hat{\alpha}, \hat{\beta}, \xi)$ feature vector. In each experiment the available 28 samples from each class are divided into 12 training and 16 test samples.

Angle of rotation (degree)		
Training samples	Testing samples	Classification accuracy rate
0, 30, 60	90, 120, 150, 200	87%
30, 60, 90	0, 120, 150, 200	88%
60, 90, 120	0, 30, 150, 200	88%
90, 120, 150	0, 30, 60, 200	89%
120, 150, 200	0, 30, 60, 90	86%
0, 60, 120	30, 90, 150, 200	91%
30, 90, 150	0, 60, 120, 200	90%
0, 90, 200	30, 60, 120, 150	90%
0, 150, 200	30, 60, 90, 120	91%
30, 150, 200	0, 60, 90, 120	90%
	AVERAGE	89%

5. Classification Using Fractional Models

A multi-level classification method which can handle arbitrary 3-D rotated samples of textures is developed based on fractional differencing models with a fractal scaling parameter. In the first level of classification, the textures are classified by the first-order Fractional Differencing model with a fractal scale parameter, and in the second level, classification is completed with the additional frequency parameters of the second-order Fractional Differencing periodic model. This multi-level classification scheme has several advantages over the conventional approaches [31–39].

5.1. *Fractional Difference Models (FDM)*

The Fractional Difference model in one dimension is the discrete version of the continuous fractional Brownian motion process (FBM) introduced by Mandelbrot and Van Ness [65]. The FBM differs from the GMRF models introduced earlier in two respects, namely (i) its correlation function decays with lag much slower than that in the parametric GMRF models, and (ii) it has considerable power at low frequencies and can account for large periodicities unlike the GMRF models which have little power at low frequencies. The FDM possesses both these properties possessed by FBM. In many images, widely separated image pixels seem to display relatively high degrees of correlation.

We will first generalize the first-order FDM given in [65] for two dimensions as follows [66]:

$$y(m_1, m_2) = [(1 - z_1^{-1})(1 - z_2^{-1})]^{-c/2} \xi(m_1, m_2), \ m_1, \ m_2 = 0, \ 1, \ \dots, \ N - 1 \quad (5.1)$$

where z_1, z_2 are the unit lead variables in the two-dimensions, c is the fractional parameter, $0 < c < 1$, and $\xi(\dot{m}, \dot{m})$ is a two-dimensional independent, identically distributed sequence of random variables with zero mean and finite variance ρ.

The above model is stationary even though it has a zero unit circle. By taking the factor $(1 - z_1^{-1})^{-c/2}(1 - z_2^{-1})^{-c/2}$ on the left-hand side and expanding it in an infinite power series, one can interpret the above model as an infinite order (non-Markov) autoregressive model in two dimensions.

The above model has only two "tunable" parameters, c and ρ. Sometimes they are not enough to provide the level of classification. Then we go to the second-order FDM given below [66]:

$$y(m_1, m_2) = [(1 - 2z_1^{-1}\cos\omega_1 + z_1^{-2})(1 - 2z_2^{-1}\cos\omega_2 + z_2^{-2})^{-c/2}]\xi(m_1, m_2). \quad (5.2)$$

$(\cos\omega_1)$ and $(\cos\omega_2)$ are the two additional parameters. In addition, we can choose different scaling parameters c_1, c_2 in the two directions instead of one parameter c. The corresponding DFTs of these functions are

$$Y(k_1, k_2) = [(1 - e^{-j\pi\frac{k_1}{N}})(1 - e^{-j2\pi\frac{k_2}{N}})]^{-c/2}W(k_1, k_2),$$

and

$$Y(k_1, k_2) = [(1 - 2\cos\omega_1 e^{-j2\pi\frac{k_1}{N}} + e^{-j4\pi\frac{k_1}{N}})]$$

where z_i is the delay operator associated with m_i, $\xi(m_1, m_2)$ is an IID Gaussian sequence, and $W(k_1, k_2)$ is the corresponding DFT.

A key property of both these models is that the structure of their DFT given above and the associated parameters are unaltered even if the images are rotated, tilted and slanted. The details are in [67]. For any given image, the parameters c and ρ in the first-order model and the parameters c, ω_1, ω_2, ρ in the second-order model can be estimated [67,68].

5.2. *Multi-level 3-D Rotational Invariant Classification Scheme*

For this classification scheme, the images are separated into test and training sets. The class of textures and the number of classes in the training set is assumed to be known *a priori*.

In the first level, the different 3-D rotated texture images are classified into M different classes depending on their estimated values of the fractal scale. Actual classification is achieved by applying a distance classifier $d(c, i)$, which measures a weighted distance between the extracted feature of the test image denoted by $\hat{c}$ and the mean feature of each of M classes. Then the texture is classified to class A_i for which such a distance is minimum. That is,

$$i^* = \min_i [\hat{c} - \bar{c}_i]^2 \, i = 1, \ldots, M$$

where $\bar{c}_i$ corresponds to the sample mean of feature c in class A_i.

The class A_i can consist of several different texture classes since several different textures share the same fractal scale (the roughness of the surface). This means that the fractal scale only is not enough to distinguish the different textures. Thus, we need an additional classification scheme to distinguish textures contained in the same class A_i.

In the second level, the textures which were already classified to the same class in the first-level are split to the different subclasses, based on the values of pattern features ω_1, ω_2 in the second-order fractional differencing periodic function (5.2).

$$k^* = \min_k d(\hat{\Omega}^{(k)}, k), \, k = 1, \ldots, N$$

$$d(\hat{\Omega}^{(k)}, k) = \sum_{f = \hat{\omega}_1, \hat{\omega}_2} \left\{ \frac{[f - \bar{f}^k]^2}{\sum_{j=1}^{N} [\sigma_f^2]^j} \right\}$$

and $\bar{f}^{(i)}$ and $[\sigma_f^2]^{(k)}$ correspond to the sample mean and variance of subclass (k) features, respectively. Here, it should be noticed that since we have at most several subclasses from a first-level class, we need to compare only a small number of subclasses to complete the classification, instead of checking the feature distance of whole other texture classes.

5.3. *Experiments*

For these experiments, nine different classes of texture were taken from Brodatz's standard texture album for the training set. These are, namely, grass [D9], tree bark [D12], straw [D15], herringbone weave [D17], woolen cloth [D19], calf leather [D24], beach sand [D29], water [D37], and raffia [D84].

Table 4. The sample mean and variance of parameters c, ω_1, ω_2: 16 64 × 64 sample image data are taken for each different texture classes, and the parameter values are extracted from the first and second-order fractional differencing models.

Textures	c		ω_1		ω_2	
	$\bar{x}$	σ^2	$\bar{x}$	σ^2	$\bar{x}$	σ^2
grass	1.209	0.057	0.744	0.078	0.636	0.082
tree bark	1.530	0.073	0.691	0.199	0.601	0.324
straw	0.923	0.053	0.387	0.068	1.209	0.070
herringbone weave	1.003	0.072	1.263	0.114	1.175	0.167
woolen cloth	0.809	0.024	0.852	0.095	0.793	0.098
calf leather	1.064	0.044	1.175	0.114	0.935	0.122
beach sand	1.195	0.038	0.665	0.107	0.571	0.129
water	1.074	0.055	0.083	0.064	0.972	0.132
raffia	1.547	0.062	1.042	0.153	0.988	0.165

For the actual training, 16 64 × 64-sized sample image data were taken for each different texture pattern, and the sample mean and variance of parameters, c, ω_1, and ω_2 were obtained for each texture class, based on the first- and second-order fractional differencing models (Table 4). As we can see from Table 5, fractal scale c itself is not enough to classify the different textures, because some of the textures have similar values of c, even though they are different texture patterns. Based on these sample mean and variance values of the parameters c, nine textures are grouped into five classes as indicated in Table 6, which also indicates the corresponding sample mean and variance of each class. Notice that the herringbone weave texture belongs to classes 2 and 3, because of its high value of variance. The second level gives the recognized texture from each class.

2-D rotated texture case. In this experiment, the test input images were taken from the 2-D raffia textures rotated by various angle θs. Then, each 64 × 64 texture was classified by the proposed multi-level classification scheme. For the first level, the fractal scale parameter c was extracted based on the first-order Fractional Differencing model (5.1), and the parameters ω_1 and ω_2 were extracted from the second-order Fractional Differencing periodic model (5.2). Actual classification of the test images was done in each level by comparing weighted distances between the extracted features and the data base. The classification results are presented in Table 7, which shows the parameter values extracted from each rotated texture pattern and demonstrates the perfect result of classification based on these values.

Rotated and projected texture case. In this experiment, six 64 × 64 test input images were taken from the straw textures rotated and projected orthographically from the various tilted and slanted texture surfaces. Like in previous experiments, for the first level, the fractal scale parameter c was extracted based on the first-order Fractional Differencing model (5.1), and the parameters, ω_1 and ω_2, were

Table 5. Database of the first level of classification. $\bar{c}_i$ and σ_i^2 are the sample mean and the variance of class i, respectively.

Class	Textures	$\bar{c}_i$	σ_i^2
1	woolen cloth	0.809	0.024
2	straw, herringbone weave	0.963	0.063
3	herringbone weave, calf leather, water	1.047	0.055
4	grass, beach sand	1.202	0.045
5	tree bark, raffia	1.539	0.067

Table 6. Classification results from the 2-D rotated texture images. (Result indicates the result class after applying two-level classification method.)

Angles	$\hat{c}$	$\hat{\omega}_1$	$\hat{\omega}_2$	Result
20	1.523	1.132	1.098	raffia
40	1.517	1.144	1.102	raffia
60	1.535	1.138	1.119	raffia
80	1.537	1.142	1.120	raffia
100	1.532	1.139	1.118	raffia
120	1.529	1.138	1.120	raffia
140	1.527	1.135	1.097	raffia
160	1.533	1.140	1.113	raffia
180	1.525	1.133	1.099	raffia

Table 7. Classification results from the rotated and orthographically projected straw texture images. (Result indicates the result class after applying two-level classification method.)

Angles	$\hat{c}$	$\hat{\omega}_1$	$\hat{\omega}_2$	Result
$\theta = 0deg, \tau = 0deg, \sigma = 15deg$	0.914	0.365	1.189	straw
$\theta = 45deg, \tau = 0deg, \sigma = 30deg$	0.932	0.371	1.224	straw
$\theta = 90deg, \tau = 0deg, \sigma = 45deg$	0.928	0.373	1.218	straw
$\theta = 0deg, \tau = 45deg, \sigma = 15deg$	0.918	0.368	1.156	straw
$\theta = 45deg, \tau = 45deg, \sigma = 30deg$	0.922	0.375	1.191	straw
$\theta = 90deg, \tau = 45deg, \sigma = 45deg$	0.927	0.377	1.202	straw

extracted from the second-order Fractional Differencing periodic model (5.2). The classification results from this experiment are presented in Table 7. Table 7 shows the parameter values extracted from each rotated and projected texture pattern and demonstrates the perfect result of classification based on these values.

6. Summary

In this chapter we presented a number of techniques for texture segmentation and classification. Although significant progress has been made over the last thirty years, completely automated, unsupervised texture segmentation and classification algorithms that are invariant to transformations such as rotation scaling, illumination, etc. remain elusive.

References

[1] R. M. Haralick, Statistical and structural approaches to textures, *Proc. IEEE* **67** (1979) 786–804.

[2] G. H. Landerweerd and E. S. Gelsema, The use of nuclear texture parameters in the automatic analysis of leukocytes, *Pattern Recogn.* **10** (1978) 57–61.

[3] M. Nagao and T. Matsuyama, *A Structural Analysis of Complex Aerial Photographs* (Plenum Press, New York, 1980).

[4] P. C. Chen and T. Pavlidis, Segmentation by texture using correlation, *IEEE Trans. Pattern Anal. Mach. Intell.* **5** (1983) 64–69.

[5] J. Weszka, C. R. Dyer and A. Rosenfeld, A comparative study of texture measures for terrain classification, *IEEE Trans. Syst. Man Cybern.* **6** (1976) 269–285.

[6] K. Laws, Textured image segmentation, Ph.D. Thesis, University of Southern California, 1978.

[7] A. Ikonomopoulos and M. Unser, A directional filtering approach to texture discrimination, in *Proc. 7th Int. Conf. on Pattern Recognition*, Montreal, Canada, Jul. 1984, 87–89.

[8] A. P. Pentland, Fractal-based descriptions of natural scenes, *IEEE Trans. Pattern Anal. Mach. Intell.* **6** (1984) 661–674.

[9] S. W. Zucker and D. Terzopoulos, Finding structure in co-occurrence matrices for texture analysis, in Azriel Rosenfeld (ed.), *Image Modeling* (Academic Press, New York, 1981) 423–445.

[10] C. W. Therrien, An estimation-theoretic approach to terrain image segmentation, *Comput. Vision Graph. Image Process.* **22** (1983) 313–326.

[11] F. S. Cohen and D. B. Cooper, Simple parallel hierarchical and relaxation algorithms for segmenting noncausal Markovian fields, *IEEE Trans. Pattern Anal. Mach. Intell.* **9** (1987) 195–219.

[12] S. Chatterjee and R. Chellappa, Maximum likelihood texture segmentation using Gaussian Markov random field models, in *Proc. Computer Vision and Pattern Recognition Conf.*, San Francisco, CA, Jun. 1985.

[13] H. Derin and H. Elliott, Modeling and segmentation of noisy and textured images using Gibbs random fields, *IEEE. Trans. Pattern Anal. Mach. Intell.* **9** (1987) 39–55.

[14] P. B. Chou and C. M. Brown, Multi-model segmentation using Markov random fields, in *Proc. Int. Joint Conf. on Artificial Intelligence*, Seattle, WA, 1987, 663–670.

[15] S. Geman and C. Graffigne, Markov random fields image models and their application to computer vision, in A. M. Gleason (ed.), *Proc. Int. Congress of Mathematicians 1986*, Providence, RI, 1987.

[16] Z. Fan and F. S. Cohen, Textured image segmentation as a multiple hypothesis test, *IEEE Trans. Circuits and Syst.* **35** (1988) 691–702.

[17] B. S. Manjunath, T. Simchony and R. Chellappa, Stochastic and deterministic networks for texture segmentation, *IEEE Trans. Acoust. Speech Signal Process.* **38** (1990) 1039–1049.

[18] B. S. Manjunath and R. Chellappa, A note on unsupervised texture segmentation, *IEEE Trans. Pattern Anal. Mach. Intell.* **13** (1991) 472–483.

[19] B. Julesz, Visual pattern discrimination, *IRE Trans. Inf. Theory* **8** (1962) 84–92.

[20] J. R. Bergen and E. H. Adelson, Early vision and texture perception, *Nature* **333** (1988) 363–364.

[21] J. Malik and P. Perona, Preattentive texture discrimination with early vision mechanisms, *J. Opt. Soc. Am. A* **7** (1990) 923–932.

[22] S. Grossberg and E. Mingolla, Neural dynamics of surface perception: Boundary webs, illuminants, and shape-from-shading, *Comput. Vision Graph. Image Process.* **37** (1987) 116–165.

[23] L. S. Davis, M. Clearman and J. K. Aggarwal, An empirical evaluation of generalized co-occurrence matrices, *IEEE Trans. Pattern Anal. Mach. Intell.* **3** (1981) 214–221.

[24] D. Chetverikov, Experiments in the rotation-invariant texture discrimination using anisotropy features, in *Proc. 6th Int. Conf. on Pattern Recognition*, Munich, Germany, Oct. 1982, 1071–1073.

[25] L. S. Davis, Polograms: A new tool for image texture analysis, *Pattern Recogn.* **13** (1981) 219–223.

[26] O. D. Faugeras and W. K. Pratt, Decorrelation methods of texture feature extraction, *IEEE Trans. Pattern Anal. Mach. Intell.* **2** (1980) 323–332.

[27] F. Vilnrotter, Structural analysis of natural textures, Ph.D. Thesis, University of Southern California, 1981.

[28] B. J. Schacther, A. Rosenfeld and L. S. Davis, Random mosaic models for textures, *IEEE Trans. Syst. Man Cybern.* **9** (1978) 694–702.

[29] N. Ahuja and A. Rosenfeld, Mosaic models for textures, *IEEE Trans. Pattern Anal. Mach. Intell.* **3** (1981) 1–11.

[30] J. W. Modestino, R. W. Fries and A. L. Vickers, Texture discrimination based upon an assumed stochastic texture model, *IEEE Trans. Pattern Anal. Mach. Intell.* **3** (1981) 557–580.

[31] R. L. Kashyap, R. Chellappa and A. Khotanzad, Texture classification using features derived from random field models, *Pattern Recogn. Lett.* **1** (1982) 43–50.

[32] P. M. Lapsa, New models and techniques for synthesis, estimation and segmentation of random fields, Ph.D. Thesis, Purdue University, 1982.

[33] R. Chellappa and S. Chatterjee, Classification of textures using Gaussian–Markov random fields, *IEEE Trans. Acoust. Speech Signal Process.* **33** (1985) 959–963.

[34] A. Khotanzad and R. L. Kashyap, Feature selection for texture recognition based on image synthesis, *IEEE Trans. Syst. Man Cybern.* **17** (1987) 1087–1095.

[35] P. DeSouza, Texture recognition via autoregression, *Pattern Recogn.* **15** (1982) 471–475.

[36] R. L. Kashyap and K.-B. Eom, Texture boundary detection based on the long correlation model, *IEEE Trans. Pattern Anal. Mach. Intell.* **11** (1989) 58–67.

[37] J. Zhang and J. W. Modestino, Markov random fields with applications to texture classification and discrimination, *Conf. on Information Sciences and Systems*, Princeton, NJ, 1986.

[38] S. Chatterjee, Classification of natural texture using Gaussian Markov random field models, in R. Chellappa and A. K. Jain (eds.), *Markov Random Fields: Theory and Application* (Academic Press, 1992).

[39] C. Chen, J. S. Daponte and M. D. Fox, Fractal feature analysis and classification in medical imaging, *IEEE Trans. Medical Imaging* 8 (1989) 133–142.

[40] R. L. Kashyap and Y. Choe, Multilevel 3-D rotation invariant classification, in *Proc. 11th Int. Conf. on Pattern Recognition*, The Hague, Sept. 1992.

[41] S. Geman and D. Geman, Stochastic relaxation, Gibbs distributions, and Bayesian restoration of images, *IEEE Trans. Pattern Anal. Mach. Intell.* 6 (1984) 721–741.

[42] J. Besag, On the statistical analysis of dirty pictures, *J. Roy. Statist. Soc. B* 48 (1986) 259–302.

[43] U. Grenander, *Lectures in Pattern Theory* (Springer-Verlag, New York, 1981).

[44] J. L. Marroquin, Probabilistic solution of inverse problems, Ph.D. Thesis, Artificial Intelligence Laboratory, Massachusetts Institute of Technology, 1985.

[45] B. S. Manjunath and R. Chellappa, A unified approach to boundary perception: Edges, textures and illusory contours, *IEEE Trans. Neural Networks* 4 (1992).

[46] T. Poggio, V. Torre and C. Koch, Computational vision and regularization theory, *Nature* 317 (1985) 314–319.

[47] Y. T. Zhou, R. Chellappa, A. Vaid and B. K. Jenkins, Image restoration using a neural network, *IEEE Trans. Acoust. Speech Signal Process.* 36 (1988) 1141–1151.

[48] Y. T. Zhou and R. Chellappa, Stereo matching using a neural network in *Proc. IEEE Int. Conf. on Acoustics, Speech and Signal Processing*, New York, NY, Apr. 1988, 940–943.

[49] C. Koch, J. Luo, C. Mead and J. Hutchinson, Computation motion using resistive networks, in D. Z. Anderson (ed.), *Proc. Neural Information Processing Systems*, Denver, CO, 1987.

[50] Y. T. Zhou and R. Chellappa, Computation of optical flow using a neural network, in *Proc. IEEE Int. Conf. on Neural Networks*, San Diego, CA, Jul. 1988, 71–78.

[51] H. Bulthoff, J. Little and T. Poggio, A parallel algorithm for real-time computation of optical flow, *Nature* 337 (1989) 549–553.

[52] J. J. Hopfield and D. W. Tank, Neural computation of decisions in optimization problems, *Biol. Cybern.* 52 (1985) 114–152.

[53] R. Chellappa, Two-dimensional discrete Gaussian Markov random field models for image processing, in L. N. Kanal and A. Rosenfeld (eds.), *Progress in Pattern Recognition 2* (Elsevier Science Publishers, North Holland, 1985) 79–112.

[54] G. R. Cross and A. K. Jain, Markov random field texture models, *IEEE Trans. Pattern Anal. Mach. Intell.* 5 (1983) 25–39.

[55] J. Marroquin, S. Mitter and T. Poggio, Probabilistic solution of ill-posed problems in computer vision, in *Proc. Image Understanding Workshop*, Miami Beach, FL, Dec. 1985, 293–309.

[56] B. Gidas, Non-stationary Markov chains and convergence of the annealing algorithm, *J. Stat. Phys.* **39** (1985) 73–131.

[57] D. H. Hubel and T. N. Wiezel, Functional architecture of macaque monkey visual cortex, in *Proc. Royal Soc. of London, Ser. B* **198** (1977) 1–59.

[58] J. Bolz and C. D. Gilbert, Generation of end-inhibition in the visual cortex via interlaminar connections, *Nature* **320** (1986) 362–365.

[59] E. Peterhans and R. von der Heydt, Mechanisms of contour perception in monkey visual cortex. II. Contour bridging gaps, *J. Neuroscience* **9** (1989) 1749–1763.

[60] R. von der Heydt and E. Peterhans, Mechanisms of contour perception in monkey visual cortex. I. Lines of pattern discontinuity, *J. Neuroscience* **9** (1989) 1731–1748.

[61] R. L. Kashyap and R. Chellappa, Estimation and choice of neighbors in spatial interaction models, *IEEE Trans. Inf. Theory* **29** (1983) 60–72.

[62] R. L. Kashyap and K.-B. Eom, Robust image models and their applications, in P. Hawkes (ed.), *Advances in Electronics and Electron Physics*, Vol. 70 (Academic Press, 1988) 79–158.

[63] P. Brodatz, *Texture: A Photographic Album for Artists and Designers* (Dover, New York, 1956).

[64] R. L. Kashyap and A. Khotanzad, A model-based method for rotation invariant texture classification, *IEEE Trans. Pattern Anal. Mach. Intell.* **18** (1986) 472–481.

[65] B. B. Mandelbrot and J. W. Van Ness, Fractional Brownian motions, fractional noises and applications, *SIAM Rev.* **10** (1968) 422–437.

[66] R. L. Kashyap and P. M. Lapsa, Synthesis and estimation of random fields using long correlation models, *IEEE Trans. Pattern Anal. Mach. Intell.* **6** (1991) 800–808.

[67] Y. Choe and R. L. Kashyap, 3-D shape from a shaded and textural surface image, *IEEE Trans. Pattern Anal. Mach. Intell.* **13** (1991) 907–918.

[68] R. L. Kashyap and K.-B. Eom, Estimation in long-memory time series model, *J. Time Series Analysis* **9** (1988) 35–41.

Handbook of Pattern Recognition and Computer Vision, pp. 311–368
Eds. C. H. Chen, L. F. Pau and P. S. P. Wang
© 1993 World Scientific Publishing Company

CHAPTER 2.3

COLOR IN COMPUTER VISION

QUANG-TUAN LUONG

INRIA Sophia-Antipolis, 2004 route des Lucioles, 06561 Valbonne Cedex, France
Email: luong@sophia.inria.fr

The use of color in computer vision has received growing attention. This chapter gives the state-of-the-art in this subfield, and tries to answer the questions: *What is color? Which are the adequate representations? How is it computed? What can be done using it?*

The first section introduces some basic tools and models that can be used to describe the color imaging process. We first summarize the classical photometric and colorimetric notions: light measurement, intensity equation, color signal, color perception, trichromatic theory. The growing interest in color during the last few years comes from two new classes of models of reflection, physical models and linear models, which lead to highlight algorithms as well as color constancy algorithms. We present these models in detail and discuss some of their limitations.

The second section deals with the problem of color constancy. The term "color constancy" refers to the fact that the colors perceived by humans in real scenes are relatively stable under large variations of illumination and of material composition of scenes. From a computational standpoint, achieving color constancy is an underdetermined problem: computing the spectral reflectance from the sensor measurements. We compare three classes of color constancy algorithms, based on lightness computation, linear models, and physical models, respectively. For each class, the principle is explained, and one or two significant algorithms are given. A comparative study serves to introduce the others.

The third section is concerned with the use of color in *universal*, i.e. mainly low-level, vision tasks. We emphasize the distinction between tasks that have been extensively studied in monochromatic images and for which the contribution of color is just a *quantitative* generalization, and tasks where color has a *qualitative* role. In the first case, additional image features are obtained, and have to be represented and used efficiently. In the latter case, it is hoped that color can help recover intrinsic physical properties of scenes. We study successively three important themes in computer vision: edges, segmentation, matching. For each of them, we present the two frameworks for the use of color.

Keywords: Color, computer vision, modelization, reflectance, colorimetry, color constancy, edge detection, segmentation, matching, intrinsic properties, features.

1. Modelisation

This chapter introduces some basic tools and models that can be used to describe the color imaging process. The first section deals with the classical photometric and colorimetric notions. The growing interest in color during the last years comes

311

from two new classes of models which lead to highlight algorithms as well as color constancy algorithms. These models will be presented in the second section.

1.1. Basic Notions

This section gives some elementary facts and definitions. They are considerably elaborated in the reference books of Wyszecki and Stilles [126] and Judd and Wyszecki [72]. The first book elaborates more on certain topics and contains a lot of data. The second is more recent, and covers more topics, with a practical approach. The book by Horn [59] contains very good chapters on photometry.

1.1.1. Light measurement

In this short section we give some definitions to clarify the meaning of the word "intensity". This word is used both for the light sources and for the imaging devices outputs.

The light measurements can be done with two units:

- The Radiometric units, related to physical measurements of energy.
- The Photometric units, related to psychophysical measurements of luminance.

The relation between them is $u_p = K_m V(\lambda).u_r$ where $K_m = 679.6$ lumens/watt and $V(\lambda)$ is the relative photopic sensibility function, which gives the sensibility to different wavelengths of the human photoreceptors used for daily vision. See Fig. 9 the y function of the CIE system, which is exactly identical to $V(\lambda)$.

The three most important quantities are:

- The rate of energy W being emitted, transferred, or received in the form of radiation.

    radiant flux: $\Phi = dW/dt$, unit is watt (luminous flux unit is lumens).
- The energy received by a surface at a given point.

    irradiance: $I = d\Phi/dA$, unit is watt per square meter (illuminance unit is lumens per square meter)
- The radiant flux Φ emitted by a source in a given direction (at a point on the surface of a source or receptor, or at a point on the path of a beam)

    radiance: $L = d^2\Phi/(d\omega dA \cos\theta)$, unit is watt per steradian per square meter. (luminance, lux).

If the above quantities are given as a function of wavelength, the terms are preceded by the adjective *spectral* and the units become per unit wavelength interval per nanometer.

The relation between the intensity I measured by an imaging system (image irradiance) based on a lens, and the scene radiance is:

$$I = \frac{\pi}{4}\left(\frac{d}{f}\right)^2 \cos^4\alpha L$$

where d is the lens diameter, f its focal length, and α the angle between the optical axis and the direction of observation. It is important to notice that, given an orthographic projection hypothesis, $\alpha = 0$, so that the measured intensity is proportional to the physically significant value, the radiance.

1.1.2. *The intensity equation*

The photometric model. The radiations detected by an imaging system can be emitted directly by the object (light source), be transmitted (transparent or transluscent objects), or be reflected (opaque object). We will only consider the last case. The most accurate reflection model is the one with the bidirectional spectral reflectance distribution function (BSRDF), which indicates how a surface looks like, observed in a certain direction, when it is illuminated from another specified direction. The precise definition is:

$$f_r(\theta_i, \phi_i, \theta_e, \phi_e, \lambda) = dL(\theta_e, \phi_e, \lambda)/dE(\theta_i, \phi_i, \lambda) \qquad (1.1)$$

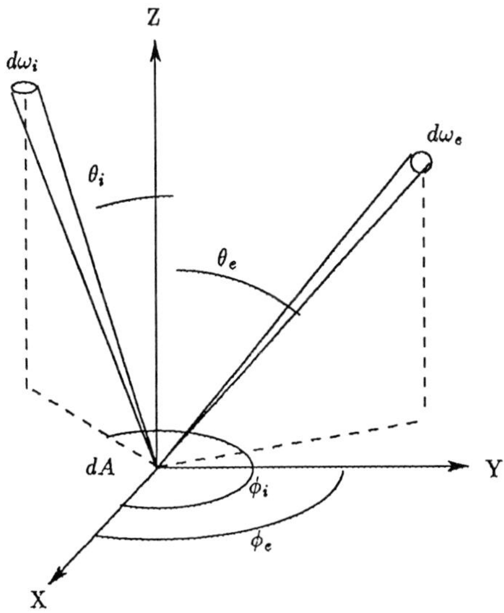

Fig. 1. Photometric local angles in the general case.

where dE is the spectral irradiance received in the incident direction (θ_i, ϕ_i) and dL is the spectral radiance in the observation direction (θ_e, ϕ_e). (θ, ϕ) is a local spherical coordinate system at the reflection point (Fig. 1). If the surface is not anisotropic, f_r depends of $\phi_e - \phi_i$ instead of (ϕ_e, ϕ_i). In this case, the spectral radiance reflected under an illumination of spectral radiance L_i of solid angle $d\omega_i$

is:

$$L_r = \int_{\omega_i} f_r(\theta_i, \phi_i, \theta_e, \phi_e, \lambda) L_i(\theta_i, \phi_i, \lambda) \cos \theta_i \, d\omega_i \ . \tag{1.2}$$

This model can deal with complex situations such as extended light sources and inter-reflections, but it has too many parameters for ordinary applications.

The simplified equation. The intensity equation used in almost all computer vision problems assumes a point light source and an isotropic surface. It looks like:

$$I(i, e, g, \lambda, \mathbf{r}) = R(i, e, g, \lambda, \mathbf{r}) E(\lambda, \mathbf{r}) \tag{1.3}$$

where (i, e, g) are the angles of incidence, observation, and phase (Fig. 2), and $\mathbf{r}$ is the position of the observed point (the material composition of the surface depends on this point). $E(\lambda)$ is the spectral energy distribution of the illuminant and $R(i, e, g, \lambda, \mathbf{r})$ is the reflectance function of the object. It is that function which is correlated with the observed color of the object.

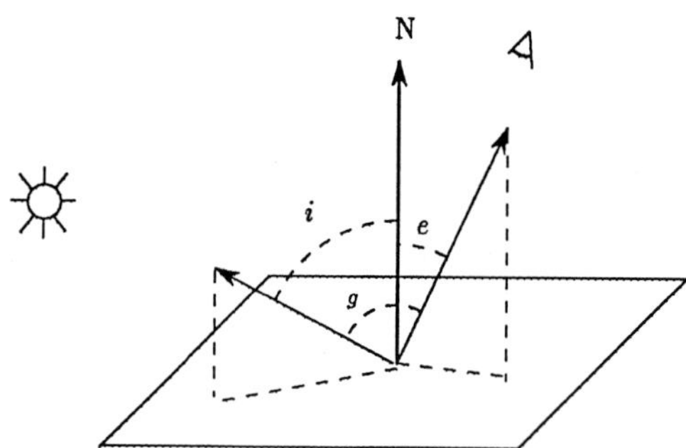

Fig. 2. Photometric angles in the isotropic case.

Most of the work has been done assuming an intensity equation where spatial factors and spectral factors are factorized:

$$I(\lambda, \mathbf{r}) = \rho(\lambda, \mathbf{r}) F(i, e, g) E(\lambda, \mathbf{r}) \tag{1.4}$$

- $\rho(\lambda, \mathbf{r})$, the albedo, depends only on the material properties of the surface at the reflection point. If the surface is white, $\rho(\lambda, \mathbf{r}) = 1$.
- $F(i, e, g)$ is a geometric factor which takes into account the illumination and observation directions. If the surface is perpendicular to the illuminant and to the observation direction, $F(i, e, g) = 1$.
- $I(\lambda, \mathbf{r})$ is the spectral energy distribution of the illuminant over space. If the light emitted by the illuminant is white, $I(\lambda, \mathbf{r}) = 1$ at the points where there are no shadows.

This equation is very important. Most of the present work, although based on more realistic models (NIR and unichromatic), use it after some simplifying assumptions. But we will see later that these assumptions are sometimes questionable.

1.1.3. *The color signal*

This section describes the color signal from a physical point of view, using the notions of wavelength and energy. A very brief word will be said about acquisition problems.

Photometry: the sensors' measurements. The signal perceived by the visual system is an electromagnetic wave. It is entirely characterized by its spectral energy distribution, which is a function $s(\lambda)$. The visible spectrum includes the wavelengths λ between 400 nm and 700 nm. Ordinary light is, in general, made of a continuum of monochromatic wavelengths, that is revealed by the prism experiment. The color of the monochromatic waves is a continuous function of the wavelength.

The color signal $s(\lambda)$ is not represented by the visual information processing systems. The sensors cannot directly gain access to the color signal (one needs spectrophotometers, which are expensive, slow, and fragile devices), but only to scalars of the form:

$$s_i = \int_{\lambda_1}^{\lambda_2} s(\lambda) r_i(\lambda) d\lambda \tag{1.5}$$

where $r_i(\lambda)$ is the spectral sensibility of the sensor number i, a function with values between 0 and 1. For the human sensors, as well as for the currently used artificial sensors, the passing bandwidth of the sensibility curve is so large that it is not possible to consider the s_i as values of $s(\lambda)$ at the wavelengths λ_i characterizing the maximum response of the sensors. But the response of a sensor of sensibility $s(\lambda)$ to a monochromatic signal of wavelength λ_0 is just $s(\lambda_0)$.

The fact that there are three sensors enables us to make distinctions between monochromatic signals of different wavelengths. We see now a first justification of the number three.[a] Let us consider first a system that has only one sensor type, facing two monochromatic signals, of wavelengths λ_1 and λ_2. As the effect of photon absorption is independent of wavelength, the sensor will respond identically to the signal of intensity 1 and wavelength λ_1, and to the signal of intensity $\frac{s(\lambda_1)}{s(\lambda_2)}$ and wavelength λ_1. Within a system with two sensor types, this kind of confusion would only occur between wavelengths λ_1 and λ_2 such that $\frac{s_1(\lambda_1)}{s_1(\lambda_2)} = \frac{s_2(\lambda_1)}{s_2(\lambda_2)}$. If there exists a wavelength λ_0 such that $s_1(\lambda_0) = s_2(\lambda_0)$, the monochromatic signal of wavelength λ_0 cannot be discriminated from the achromatic signal, which excites evenly the two sensors. These problems do not occur with three independent sensors. As the color signal space is infinite-dimensional, and as there is only a finite number of

---

[a]The most convincing justification will be given later, using psychophysical arguments from the color perception studies.

sensors, there will be an infinite number of general (not monochromatic) signals leading to an identical measurement triplet. The relation (1.5) between the sensors measurement and the color signal can constrain it. If we suppose further than it can be described by a few parameters, these relations can determine it, as we will see later.

Acquisition. The human visual system uses three types of cones for the high-intensity color vision. Their spectral sensibility curves can be found in the book by Wyszecki and Stiles [126] and other numerous references. These cones respond to, respectively, the short (blue), medium (green) and long (red) wavelengths. They give a natural decomposition of the spectrum which yields in a simple manner to the unicity of the decomposition in pure colors. In the field of computer vision, a set of filters is used to give a decomposition of the visible[b] spectrum. This decomposition is satisfying when the support-sets form a partition of the visible colors interval. Various technical solutions are found:

- Black-and-white cameras with colored optical filters, like the Kodak Wratten. Classically, one will use the 25, 58, and 47B.[c]
- Mono-CCD color cameras. Each CCD cell is used to obtain three values thanks to a filter mask. They are cheap, but there are important losses in dynamic range, essentially on the red and blue channel.
- Tri-CCD color cameras. A high precision prism makes three copies of the image, which are independently filtered before each arrives at a CCD cell.

A color image acquisition process consists in obtaining three (monochromatic) images representing the red, green, and blue components of the observed scene. As mentioned, the (r, g, b) triplet leads to an unambiguous reconstitution of each monochromatic color, so we can speak in this sense of the (R, G, B) sensor basis, where each primary R,G,B is defined by its spectral sensibility. The superposing of the three components gives back the original colored image.

Unfortunately most of the cameras are not photometrically exact. Before running an algorithm that relies on the scene photometric property, it is necessary to do a preprocessing. This will usually involve a linearization scheme and a white-balancing scheme. Some details about these techniques can be found in [32] and [75]. The latter reference contains a precise description of a camera model and preprocessing operations.

1.1.4. *Physiology and psychology of color perception*

The (R, G, B) sensor basis is distinct from the human experience of colors. However, the notion of color does not have an absolute existence; it is closely related to our perception. We shall describe in this section two other bases which can give a

---

[b]A filter is required to block the infrared radiations.
[c]The transmission curves are in the first edition of the book by Wyszecki and Stiles [126], or can be obtained from Kodak.

better account for it. The starting point for both of them will be the values

$$r = \int_{\lambda_1}^{\lambda_2} s(\lambda)R(\lambda)d\lambda \, , \quad g = \int_{\lambda_1}^{\lambda_2} s(\lambda)G(\lambda)d\lambda \, , \quad b = \int_{\lambda_1}^{\lambda_2} s(\lambda)B(\lambda)d\lambda \, .$$

Opponent colors. Several perceptual phenomena are hard to explain within the framework of a trichromatic theory. After staring at a yellow square, one sees a blue square when he looks at a white surface (these illusions are called afterimages). Four names is the minimum set for naming the entire visual spectrum, and while naming colors, combinations like blue-yellow or red-green are never used.

The opponent-color theory explains these matches. It combines the outputs of the R, G, B channels as in the Fig. 3 to give an achromatic channel (Black-W) and two chromatic channels, (Y-B) and (R-G). An analysis made by Gottschalk and Buchsbaum [49] points out that within the framework of the theory of information, this system is optimal, that is its components are orthogonal and therefore do not contain redundant information.

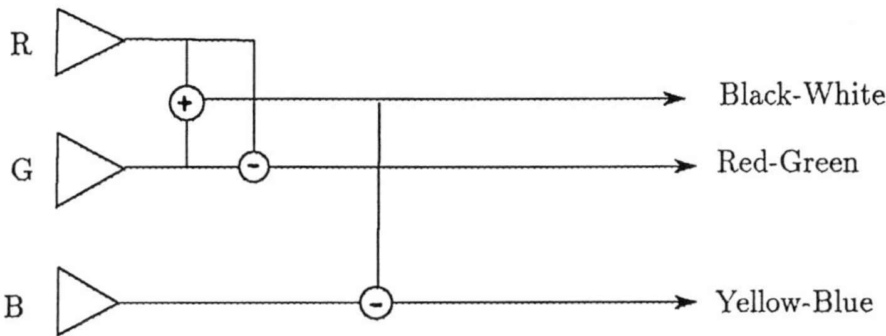

Fig. 3. The opponent-colors model.

A variant[d] of this model has been introduced by Faugeras [33,32] in the field of image processing. He considers that the cones non-linear response is proportional to the logarithm of the stimulus intensity. This yields the basis:

$$A = a(\alpha \log r + \beta \log v + \gamma \log b), C_1 = u_1 \log(r/v), C_2 = u_2 \log(r/b) \, . \qquad (1.6)$$

The constants are adjusted to match classical psychophysical data, in particular, to obtain a function A that matches V one uses $\alpha = 0.612, \beta = 0.369, \gamma = 0.019$. The functions (A, C_1, C_2) describe the responses of cells which have been effectively found in the visual cortex.[e]

---

[d]The existence of the achromatic channel and of the two opponents is certain, but the relative contributions of the different photoreceptors is not clear [88].

[e]The trichromatic coordinates and the opponent-color system can be seen as the first and the second stage of color perception. The opponent-color model describes how the three kinds of photoreceptors are grouped and connected in the retina and in the brain. Important correlations between psychophysical results and neurophysiological data have been shown first by De Valois [28]. Other classical references on the neurophysiology of color perception are [27] (it includes a discussion of the neurophysiological implications of the Retinex theory), [88], and [128].

The (A, C_1, C_2) space has also, with good precision, an interesting interpretation in perceptual terms, as shown in Fig. 4. This figure shows some quantities we shall now discuss.

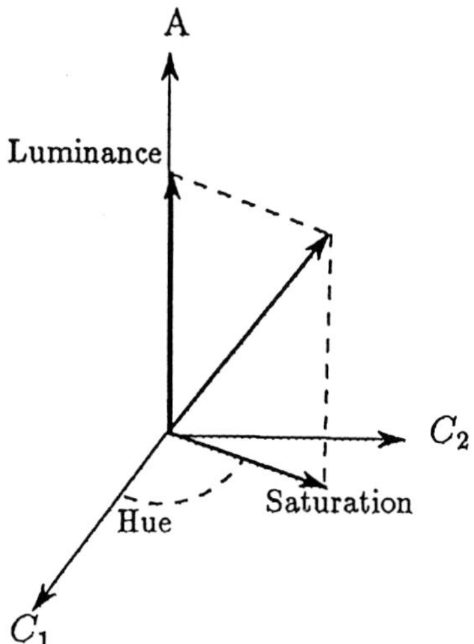

Fig. 4. Perceptual interpretation of the (A, C_1, C_2) space.

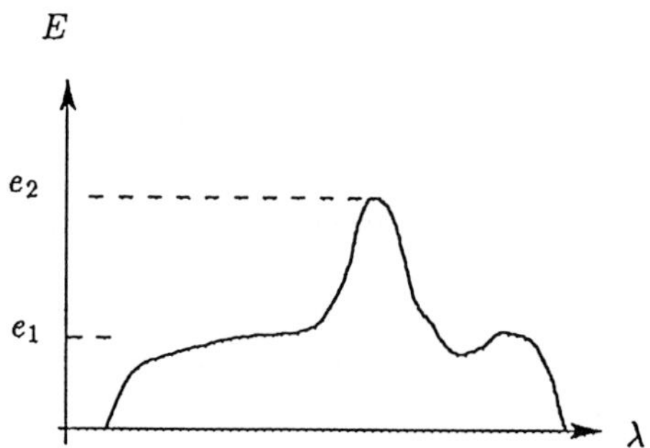

Fig. 5. Spectral power distribution showing the dominant wavelength (the energy peak at e_2), the purity (the ratio of e_1, the energy of white light in the signal e_2) and the luminance (the integral of the curve).

Luminance, hue, saturation. This triplet is the closest to human conscious perception. It has an (imprecise) interpretation in photometric terms, as shown in Fig. 5, which illustrates a general (not monochromatic) color signal.

The triplet can also be approximated by the values (L, λ, p), that we define in colorimetric terms in the next section. Another approximation is a coordinates system which can be obtained in the (R, G, B) space as a cylindrical system, so that a direct computation is possible from (r, g, b). Its axis is the main bisecting line, as shown in Fig. 6.

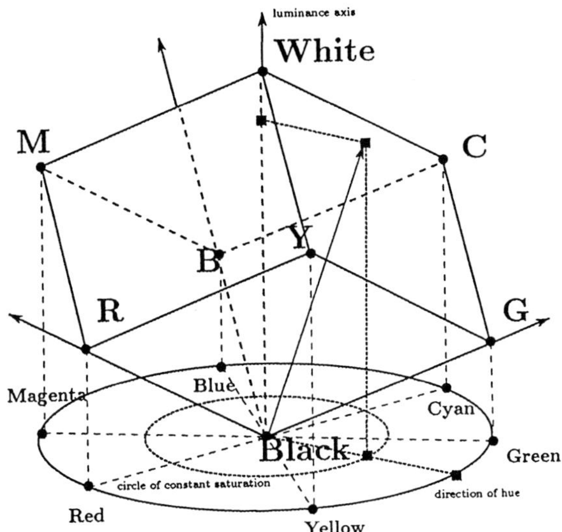

Fig. 6. The coordinate system (I, H, S) in the natural coordinate system of the color cube (R, G, B).

We notice that in all these approximations (as well as in the computation formulas derived from them), the three parameters are independents. This is not completely correct.

- Luminance: the colors are classified from "light" to "dark". This attribute distinguishes the gray levels. The eye discriminates more than a hundred levels. (L: the signal energy rate)

- Hue: red, yellow, green... There are more than a hundred hues that the human eye can discriminate. (Dominant wavelength λ: wavelength of the pure color that is observed in the signal).

- Saturation: a pure color has a 100% saturation, white and grays have a 0% saturation. This distinguishes red and pink. There are about twenty different saturation levels, depending on the hue. (Excitation purity p: proportion of light of dominant wavelength and of white light needed for the reproduction of the signal).

1.1.5. *The trichromatic theory*

We have seen that the color signals generate an infinite-dimensional space. The goal of this chapter is to show why satisfying three-dimensional representations can be used.

Psychophysics of color perception. Colorimetry is a well-worked psychophysical descriptive theory. A basic result is that under a significant number of observation conditions, most of the colors can be perfectly reproduced by a mixture[f] of three fixed colors, and that the proportions of the mixtures are uniquely determined. These colors can be broadly chosen, provided they are independent, in the sense that one of them should not be obtained by a mixture of the two others. A stronger result is that mixtures obey additive and proportionality laws (Grassman's laws). It is important to notice that everything depends on the color matching experimental paradigm, that *defines* the colorimetric concepts: each half of the optical field contains a color zone of little extension, the subject tunes controls to make them appear identical to him. The theory predicts matchings, not perceived colors. Another thing is that different spectral energy distributions can yield an identical color (metamerism). It is a consequence of the reduction of the color space dimensionality.

Colorimetric techniques. Two of the most important colorimetric tools are:

- The color space: thanks to experimental matching laws that have been stated previously, colors can be represented as vectors of a three-dimensional vector space. It enables one to do changes of coordinates very simply. Given three primary colors $\mathbf{C_i}$ and a test color $\mathbf{C}$, known by their spectral energy distribution $c_i(\lambda)$ and $c(\lambda)$, the coordinates C_i are given by the relation:

$$C_i = \int_{\lambda_1}^{\lambda_2} c(\lambda)c_i(\lambda)d\lambda \; . \tag{1.7}$$

This relation is the link between colorimetric color and color signal. The coordinates can be negative. In that case one has to subtract a primary.

- The chromatic diagrams: they represent chrominance by eliminating luminance. Starting from the three chromatic coordinates $c_i = C_i/(C_1 + C_2 + C_3)$, only the first two are plotted on a bidimensional diagram (the third is uniquely determined). Figure 7 shows, on the CIE XY diagram, the coordinates of the standard illuminants, the pure colors curve, and the purple line. All the colors that can be physically realized are in the convex. As Fig. 8 shows, the dominant wavelength and the excitation purity, psychophysical quantities corresponding respectively to hue and saturation, as well as the complementary pure color, can be easily obtained.

Another property illustrated by Fig. 7, is that the set of the colors resulting from the mixture of three (resp. two) given colors is the interior of the triangle (resp. segment) they define. It can be useful, for instance, to represent the gamut that can be obtained from an R–G–B filtering system. One just needs the chromatic coordinates of the primaries that are used.

---

[f]By mixture, one means addition or subtraction: if the primaries used in a field are green, yellow, and blue, and if the wanted color in the other field is red, the relation Yellow = Red + Green has to be used, by adding a *negative* quantity of Green (this is done by adding it to the other field). Mixtures are algebraic operations.

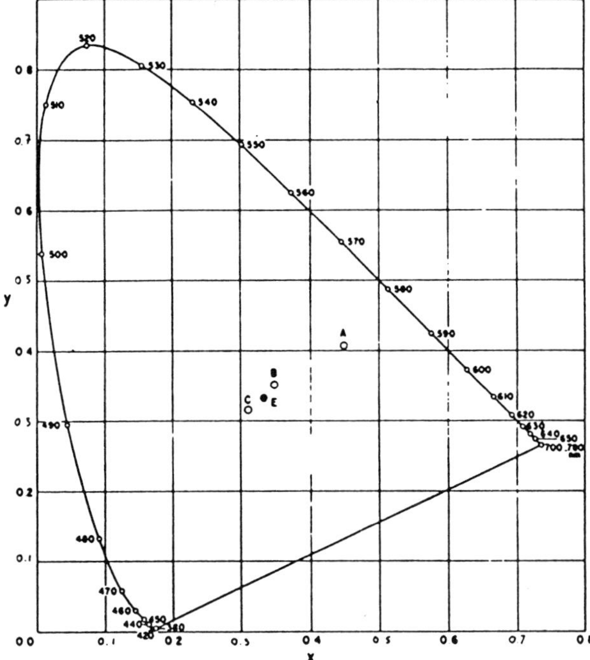

Fig. 7. The CIE (x,y) diagram.

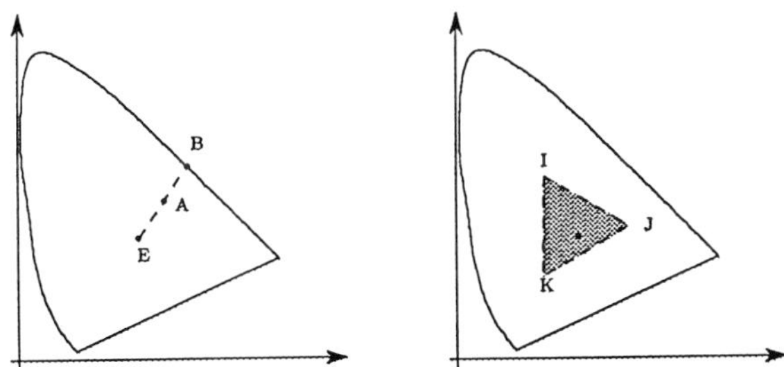

Fig. 8. Left: The dominant wavelength of the color A is the color B, the purity is $\frac{\overline{EA}}{\overline{EB}}$. Right: Colors that can be obtained by a mixture of I, J, and K.

The CIE defined in 1931 a system of three reference primaries (they are imaginary as they lie outside of the convex of the physically realizable colors) named XYZ (Fig. 9). The advantages of this system are:

- The color coordinates of real colors are always positive (this was not the case in the RGB-based systems).
- The X and Z primaries luminance is zero, so the Y component represents the luminance of the signal (in order to obtain this property, the choice $Y(\lambda) = V(\lambda)$ has been made, where $V(\lambda)$ is the relative spectral sensibility function).

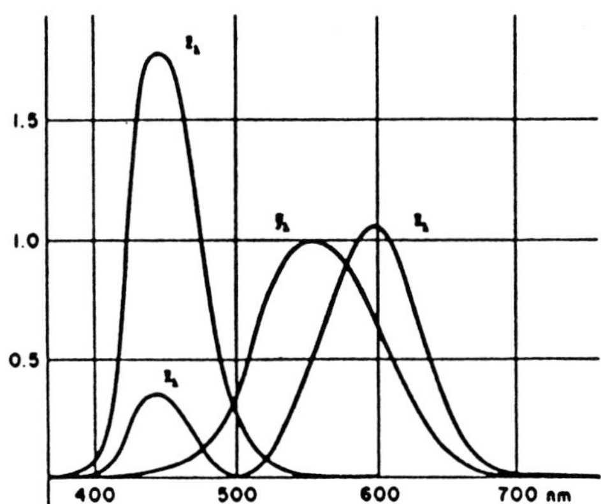

Fig. 9. Tristimulus values of monochromatic lights in the CIE X–Y–Z system.

- The white (defined by a radiant flux uniform over wavelengths) is represented by the point defined by an equal proportion mixture of the three primaries XYZ.

Another technique that is frequently used to classify colors is to use color atlases. The theory has been developed by Koenderink [80]. The best known is the Munsell book of color. The advantage of using colorimetric atlases over colorimetric techniques is that under a sufficient number of illuminants it is possible to compare directly reflectance functions, which yield to photometric classifications. The Munsell system is based on cylindrical coordinates, using the three perceptual attributes value, hue, and chroma. Note that value and intensity are different as are chroma and saturation, to account for the fact that when the lightness of an object changes, a simultaneous change in saturation is perceived (this fact is taken into account in the uniform systems presented above). As it is based on nearly uniformly spaced scale of color, the Munsell system is still very useful. A scale of ten values is defined. The hues are placed on a circle in a plane orthogonal to the value axis. The circle is divided into ten colors, obtained from red, yellow, green, blue, purple, and the mixture of two of these adjacent colors. The colors are placed so that two symmetrical colors are complementary. Each hue angular section is then divided in ten subsections. The chroma is uniform along concentric circles that start from chroma /0 (for the gray). (see Fig. 10). Thus the color defined by the Munsell notation $7.5YR6/2$ has hue $7.5YR$, value $6/$, and departs from the gray /6 of chroma /2. The set of all colors lies in a non-cylindrical volume, as the maximum chroma depends on the hue (for example: blue /8, red /14), and on the value (it is obtained for value /5). The color solid obtained from the Munsell system is shown in Fig. 10. The principal drawback of this system is that it is not very compatible with an automated colorimetric measurement, as it is difficult to obtain the correlation between a color signal and its Munsell notation. The relation between the value scale and the Y scale is given by the polynomial:

$$Y = 1.2219V - 0.2311V^2 + 0.23951V^3 - 0.021009V^4 + 0.0008404V^5 \ .$$

The conversion between Munsell notations and CIE (Y,x,y) coordinates can be done only using tables, which are for instance in [126].

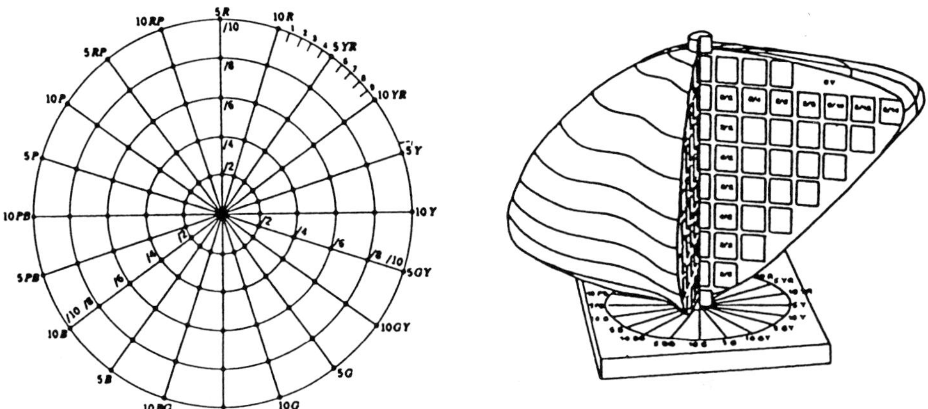

Fig. 10. Left: organization of a plane of constant value in the Munsell system. Right: the Munsell color solid.

We will conclude this presentation emphasizing the fact that colorimetric results rely on an experimental paradigm that is very special. They are not a theory of color vision, because color vision takes place in (spatially) complex scenes.

More color spaces. The X–Y–Z system has been very satisfying in allowing exchange and communication of chromatic informations. Many other color coordinates systems were devised for specific applications. The following formulas (except the first ones) are in Pratt [100].[8]

- R–G–B, C–M–Y:
- These are hardware-oriented systems. The R–G–B basis already discussed, is used by color cameras, display monitors, and the human eye. However, the primaries naturally attached to each of these devices are different. A procedure for calibrating monitors with respect to the CIE R–G–B system is described in [25]. The CIE R–G–B primary system is based on stimuli $R = 700.0$nm, $G = 546.1$nm, $B = 435.8$nm, for which:

$$\begin{pmatrix} R \\ G \\ B \end{pmatrix} = \begin{pmatrix} .735 & .265 & .000 \\ .274 & .717 & .009 \\ .167 & .009 & .082 \end{pmatrix} \begin{pmatrix} X \\ Y \\ Z \end{pmatrix} \ .$$

The C–M–Y primary system is used for color printing. Cyan, magenta, and yellow are the complements of red, green, and blue, respectively. They are called

---

[8] Insignificant differences exist in the literature.

subtractive primaries, because their effect is to subtract some color from white light. The relation between the R–G–B primary system and the C–M–Y primary system is just:

$$\begin{pmatrix} R \\ G \\ B \end{pmatrix} = \begin{pmatrix} 1 \\ 1 \\ 1 \end{pmatrix} - \begin{pmatrix} C \\ M \\ Y \end{pmatrix} .$$

A lot of information on color printing can be found in [61]. A recent work on calibrated color reproduction and an application to the printing of digital images is [108].

- I–H–S

  Intensity, hue, saturation:

$$I = R + G + B$$

$$H = \arccos\left(\frac{\frac{1}{2}((R-G) + (R-B))}{\sqrt{(R-G)^2 + (R-B)(G-B)}} \right)$$

and if $B > V$, $H = 2\pi - \arccos\left(\frac{\frac{1}{2}((R-G)+(R-B))}{\sqrt{(R-G)^2+(R-B)(G-B)}} \right)$

$$S = 1 - \min(R, G, B)/I .$$

This system has interesting properties: the independence of hue and saturation, and a straightforward interpretation in terms of human perception, as we have previously seen (Figs. 4 and 6). This last point has a big "ergonomic" importance, for instance in the segmentation schemes, where the automatic methods as well as the semi-automatic ones need long testing stages. Unfortunately the transformation from R–G–B to I–H–S is non-linear and therefore has two major drawbacks that are detailed by Kender [74]:

- there are irreducible singularities of the hue for the achromatic points ($R = G = B$) and of the saturation for the black ($R = G = B = 0$). In the neighborhood of these points a little perturbation on R, G, B can lead to important variations of H or S.
- the transformed values distribution is not uniform, and the digitalization can lead to spurious peaks or gaps in the repartition.

- L–a–b, U^*–V^*–W^*

  These are perceptually uniform systems, in which the Euclidean metrics are significant in terms of perceived color differences. They are obtained by weighting chrominance by luminance. The differences obtained are comparable to the Munsell notations.

$$L = 25(100Y/Y_0)^{1/3} - 16, a = 500((X/X_0)^{1/3} - (Y/Y_0)^{1/3}),$$

$$b = 200((Y/Y_0)^{1/3} - (Z/Z_0)^{1/3})$$

$$U^* = 13W^*(u - u_0), V^* = 13W^*(v - v_0), W^* = 25(100Y)^{1/3} - 17$$

where $u_0 = 0.199, v_0 = 0.308, u = 4X/(X + 15Y + 3Z), v = 6Y/(X + 15Y + 3Z)$, and X_0, Y_0, Z_0 are the reference white coordinates. These systems have the same drawbacks as the preceding one. They are not often useful in computer vision. One is more interested in measurable differences than in psychologically significant ones. But they allow simple computations of mean values. This fact is used for example by Westelius [120]. Tominaga [113] also used them and argues that they lead to proper spatial arrangement of clusters.

- Y–I–Q, $I1$–$I2$–$I3$

  These systems are obtained by a linear transformation from the initial values, derived by a principal-components analysis.

$$\begin{pmatrix} Y \\ I \\ Q \end{pmatrix} = \begin{pmatrix} .299 & .587 & .114 \\ .596 & -.273 & -.322 \\ .212 & -.522 & .315 \end{pmatrix} \begin{pmatrix} R \\ V \\ B \end{pmatrix}$$

$$I1 = (R + V + B)/3, I2 = (R - B)/2, I3 = (2V - R - B)/4$$

As the transformations are linear, singularities, instability, and non-uniformity problems are avoided. The first system is used by the television and was conceived to minimize the bandwidth of the signal, while keeping the color fidelity. It is based on psychophysical observations (achromaticity of the eye, and bichromaticity along an orange-cyan axis, at low angles). A color image is decomposed into a luminance signal (Y) and two chrominance signals (I,Q), so that compatibility with black-and-white television is achieved. The second one is derived by Ohta [97] from eight images. He uses a dynamic (applied at each iteration of the split-region recursive thresholding segmentation algorithm of Ohlander[96]) Karhunen-Loeve transformation, then he makes a statistic of the emerging color coordinates. Using only $I1, I2, I3$ that appear the most often, in this order, gives as efficient segmentations as the adaptive method. This means that in general (i.e. statistically), this system is the best to account for color differences, even if for a particular image, other coordinates systems would be more efficient. It is interesting to note that it coincides quite precisely with the Cohen characteristic vectors for describing reflectances: the best description of materials is given by the vectors which yield the best description of their images under relatively standard illuminants.

It is worth noting that the Karhunen-Loeve transform is an important statistical tool that can be used on each image to provide the most discriminating coordinate system for it. The vectors X_1, X_2, X_3 obtained are:

$$X_i = w_{Ri}R + w_{Vi}V + w_{Bi}B$$

where $W_i = (w_{Ri}, w_{Vi}, w_{Bi})^t$ is the normalized eigenvector of the R, G, B distributions covariance matrix, corresponding to the eigenvalue λ_i, where $\lambda_1 \geq \lambda_2 \geq \lambda_3$.

They are uncorrelated; X_1 is the optimal vector (the one with the biggest variance), X_2 is the best that is orthogonal to X_1, etc.

The properties of these classical color coordinates are summarized in Table 1.

For the segmentation-like tasks, color seems to be bidimensional information [97], therefore all the coordinates systems are barely equivalent. It is interesting, and quite straightforward, while using a three-dimensional representation for the color, to keep an intensity image and a bidimensional vector for chromaticity. In spite of the problems we mentioned, it is appealing to use normalized coordinates (for instance (x,y), (r,g), (H,S)) for it as it separates the intensity information from the chromaticity kind. Besides, an important advantage of normalized coordinates is, in the framework of the simplified (without highlights) model of Eq. (1.4), to discard the little spatial color variations caused by a change of the observation angle. This is an important point for the algorithm which uses different points of view on the same scene (for instance stereovision), and for the segmentation algorithm, when facing curved surfaces, and shadows. However, due to the singularity at $I = 0$, the normalized colors obtained with little intensities are very noisy and not significant.

Table 1. Properties of classical color spaces.

Color System	Transformation	Normalization	Uniformity
R–G–B		no	no
C–M–Y	linear	no	no
r–g–b	non-linear, non-one-to-one	yes	no
X–Y–Z	linear	no	no
x–y–z	non-linear, non-one-to-one	yes	no
Y–H–S	non-linear	yes (2 coordinates)	no
Y–r–g	non-linear	yes (2 coordinates)	no
Y–x–y	non-linear	yes (2 coordinates)	no
L–a–b	non-linear	no	yes
U^*–V^*–W^*	non-linear	no	yes
Y–I–Q	linear	no	no
$I1$–$I2$–$I3$	linear	no	no

It is the place to note a method for the computation of normalized color, due to Healey [54,51], that is photometrically sound and that can give precise results when several color filters are used. The idea is to look for an approximation of $I(\lambda)$ as a linear sum of n basis functions, $\sum_{j=1}^{n} x_j B_j(\lambda)$ from n measurements $s_i = \int_{\lambda_1}^{\lambda_2} F_i(\lambda)I(\lambda)d\lambda$ obtained with sensors of spectral sensibility $F_i(\lambda)$. One has just to solve the simultaneous linear equations:

$$s_i = \sum_{j=1}^{n} K_{ij} x_j \tag{1.8}$$

where $K_{ij} = \int_{\lambda_1}^{\lambda_2} F_i(\lambda)B_j(\lambda)d\lambda$. Each color corresponds in this way to a vector (x_i) of R^n, so the classical vector norms have in this framework, a physical interpretation.

1.2. *Recent Models*

The study of models of reflectance comes together with color vision research as the color of a surface is correlated with its reflectance properties. We first introduce some notions about reflection, and then discuss two general models. We next present the modeling of spectral properties by these models. The last subsection will be devoted to a different class of models which use a different approach to integrate physical information.

1.2.1. *Models of surface reflection*

Lambertian and specular surfaces. The two extreme cases of reflectance geometric properties are:

- Lambertian surfaces (perfectly diffuse, or isotropic, reflection). The reflected intensity does not depend on the observation angle. It depends only on the illumination angle i and on the albedo ρ.

$$f_r(\theta_i, \phi_i, \theta_e, \phi_e, \lambda) = \frac{\rho}{\pi} \qquad (1.9)$$

For a point source of radiance E, $L = \frac{\rho}{\pi} E \cos \theta_i$.
- The mirror (perfectly specular reflection). The reflected intensity is entirely concentrated in one direction, according to Descarte's law:

$$f_r(\theta_i, \phi_i, \theta_e, \phi_e, \lambda) = \frac{\delta(\theta_i - \theta_r)\delta(\phi_i - \phi_r - \pi)}{\sin \theta_i \cos \theta_i} \, . \qquad (1.10)$$

Surfaces were assumed to be Lambertian in a lot of previous computer vision work, but models appeared that can take into account highlights and, to a certain extent, imaging geometry. The first of these models was due to Phong [99], introduced in the field of computer graphics, which is only empirical. It used a parameterized continuous function to represent specular reflectance. The most precise models that are now available to describe color surfaces are, unlike the above, based on the physics of reflection.

Most of the surfaces have intermediary properties, and their reflectances are, geometrically speaking, the sum of a Lambertian-like term and of a specular-like term. Such a representation is justified by Nayar, Ikeuchi, and Kanade [92] as a "hybrid surface". From this modeling, they can recover the orientation and the Lambertian/specular ratio of surfaces using a photometric sampling method. The principle is to fix an observation direction and to obtain (working in a plane, so $g = i + e$) the function $I(g) = A \cos(i) + B\delta(i - e)$. From this function, it is possible to estimate, as shown in Fig. 11, A and B, the relative strength of the Lambertian and specular components, and e, which gives the direction of the normal. Practically these authors use extended light sources. The advantages are that you are sure to obtain the specular spike (which could be undetected otherwise due to the sampling process), and that the two components are measured on one image (with comparable intensities). This brings only some algorithmic changes.

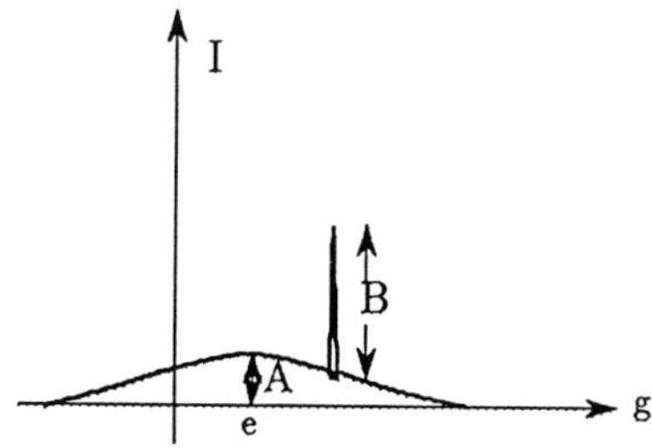

Fig. 11. Intensity as a function of the illumination angle, for a hybrid surface.

Another hybrid representation is used by Ikeuchi and Sato [66]. The difference is the modeling of the specular term by $B\frac{\exp(-k\alpha^2)}{\cos e}$, which is the value predicted by the Torrance-Sparrow model (see later). These authors give an algorithm which computes A, B, k (roughness parameter) from an intensity image and a range image. It is based on a function similar to the previous one.

Physical and geometrical models. The most exact models of surface reflection are obtained from physical optics theories. Physical models use directly Maxwell equations and consider light as a wave. The formulation of the reflection problem in terms of electromagnetic waves is very precise. Geometrical models consider it as a ray. They have simpler mathematical forms, and so they are easier to use. The manner in which light is reflected from a surface depends on the microscopic shape of the surface. A smooth surface may reflect the incident light in a single direction, while a rough surface tends to scatter light in various directions. As it is not possible to determine exactly the structure of each surface, they are described by a statistical distribution of either its height or its slope.

The Beckmann–Spizzichino model [4] assumes that surfaces are perfect conductors. This assumption is necessary to obtain a closed-form solution to the problem. There is no assumption about the roughness of the surface, thus the model is applicable to surfaces that vary from perfectly smooth to very rough. The surface height is modeled as continuous stationary random process with standard deviation σ_h (representing the roughness of the surface), and spatial frequency T. The incident light is assumed to be a plane electromagnetic wave with wavelength λ. This model predicts two primary reflection components:

- A specular spike, which is zero in all directions except for a very narrow range around the specular direction predicted from Descarte's law (delta function).
- A specular lobe, which spreads around the specular direction (Gauss function).

These two components together form the specular reflection. For a very smooth surface ($\sigma_h \ll \lambda$), the specular spike is dominant, for a rough surface, it can be neglected,and the specular lobe is dominant. The specular reflection is very concentrated for a smooth surface ($\sigma_h/\lambda < 1.5$) or a gently undulating one ($\sigma_h/T < 0.02$). The lobe and the spike are simultaneously significant for only a small range of roughness values.

The Torrance–Sparrow model [115] assumes that the law of geometrical optics are applicable, that is that the wavelength of incident light is much smaller than the dimensions of the surface irregularities ($\sigma_h \gg \lambda$). It is not valid when the surface roughness is comparable to the wavelength of incident light, so it cannot describe accurately smooth surfaces and the specular spike. There are no assumptions about polarization or conductivity, thus the model can be applied to dielectrics as well as metals. The surface is modeled as small, randomly oriented, specular facets. The slope of the micro-facets is a random variable, for instance, Gaussian with standard deviation σ_α. The resulting specular model is:

$$R_s = FDA \tag{1.11}$$

where

- F, amount of light reflected individually by the facets, is given by the Fresnel equations, which describe the reflected and transmitted components at the interface between two dielectrics (the details can be found for instance in the book by Born and Wolf [8]).
- D, facet orientation (relative to the average normal) distribution function is $C \exp(-\frac{\alpha^2}{2\sigma_\alpha^2})$.
- A, adjusted geometrical attenuation factor, quantifies the shadowing and masking of facets by adjacent facets, and is given by the Torrance and Sparrow equations.

To account for body reflection (see below) the Torrance–Sparrow model adds a Lambertian term (it gives a diffuse lobe modeled by a cosine function). The model has been successfully used (achromatically) by Healey and Binford [55] to recover the radius of cylinders in carefully controlled experiments.

A very detailed comparison between a physical model (Beckmann–Spizzichino) and a geometrical model (Torrance–Sparrow) using reflectance curves predicted by the two models, as well as a precise description of each model and of its conditions of validity can be found in the paper by Nayar, Ikeuchi, and Kanade [94]. The Lambertian model is used for the body component. The specular lobe is approximated by the Torrance–Sparrow model (which agrees well with the lobe predicted by the Beckmann–Spizzichino model, whose roughness parameters, though different, are well related). The specular spike is a very sharp function which can be approximated by a double-delta function. To follow the propositions of these authors, the resulting image irradiance equation can be written as a linear combination of the three reflection components already identified (the specular spike and lobe, and the body diffuse component):

$$I = C_{ss}\delta(\theta_i - \theta_r)\delta(\phi_i - \phi_r - \pi) + C_{sl}\exp(-\frac{\alpha^2}{2\sigma_\alpha^2}) + C_d\cos\theta_i$$

where the constants C_d, C_{ss}, C_{sl} are respectively the strengths of the diffuse component, specular spike and specular lobe components. The ratio C_{sl}/C_{ss} is dependent on surface roughness.

1.2.2. Physical models of color

Spectral properties of surface reflection. Within the framework of the Torrance–Sparrow model, Cook and Torrance [23] have explicitly studied issues related to color. Doing simulations, they find that F and A have a smooth variation, except for $i \to 90^o$. The color of the specular component depends both on the illuminant color and from the material color . The dependence from the incidence angle is:

for $0 \le i \le 70^o$, $R_s(\lambda)$ has little variation for $i \to 90^o$, $R_s(\lambda) \to 1$.

Qualitatively, the highlight color goes towards the illuminant color. However it is not easy to compute precisely the variation.

Body and surface reflection. When one is interested in spectral properties, the most important distinction is (shown in Fig. 12) between the reflection that takes place on the surface and the one which happens after penetration of the light to the material. It is not the same distinction as the *specular/diffuse* one, which is purely geometrical. However, as the main mechanism that produces Lambertian reflection is internal scattering,[h] Lambertian reflection and body reflection are often confounded. Indeed, a Lambertian model is very adequate to represent body reflection.

Healey and Binford [53] present a general reflectance model for color vision. They combine the Cook and Torrance model to describe the specular reflection, and the Kubelka–Munk model, with extensions due to Reichman [101] (a good description is given in [72] too) for the body reflection. Two material classes are differentiated:

- Homogeneous materials (metals) : $R = R_s$.
- Inhomogeneous materials (dielectrics): $R = R_s + R_p$. R_s depends only weakly on λ, R_p depends only weakly on i, highlights are well-localized (and have high irradiance). In consequence, in the matt areas, $R = R_p$ and in the highlight areas $R_p = cte$. The presence of R_p gives a basis to distinguish dielectrics from metals.

---

[h]Incident light rays penetrate the surface and encounter microscopic inhomogeneities in the material medium. The rays are repeatedly reflected and refracted, and some of them reach the surface with quasi-random direction.

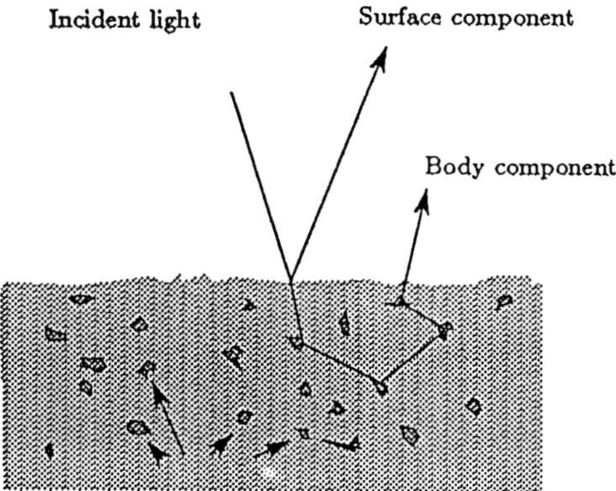

Fig. 12. Surface and body components of reflection.

The dichromatic model is for inhomogeneous materials.

$$R(i,e,g,\lambda) = R_s(i,e,g,\lambda) + R_p(i,e,g,\lambda) = m_s(i,e,g)C_s(\lambda) + m_p(i,e,g)C_p(\lambda)$$
$$(1.12)$$

The extra assumption is empirical. It is contained in the second equation, which means that there is a factorization where the geometry and the spectral factors are independent. The other hypotheses (and their consequences) are still valid. Practically, $m_s(i,e,g)$ is a function with zero values except on a peak, and $m_p(i,e,g)$ has a gentle variation. The NIR (neutral interface reflection) model assumes further $C_s(\lambda) = cte$, that means the specular color is the illuminant color, whereas the body color is the object color. This model is the most widely used. The unichromatic model, valid for homogeneous materials is the same as the dichromatic model, without the body term. We notice that within the framework of a dichromatic model, if the surface component can be neglected, or if it can be isolated by an algorithm, an intensity equation similar to the Eq. (1.4) is found.

The adequacy of the models, including the ones elaborated by physicists, is not easy to demonstrate, because there are a lot of physical causes to color. The exact equations are always very complicated. The three last presented models have been experimentally tested: Healey [56], working on 11 metals, found good agreement with the unichromatic model, and using 25 Munsell chips, found good agreement with the dichromatic model. Lee, Breeneman and Schulte [87] made a test of the NIR model on eight different materials. Results are good with plastics, plant leaves, painted surfaces, orange peel, and some glossy cloth, but they are weak for colored papers and ceramics. Tominaga [114] has also investigated experimentally the adequacy of the dichromatic reflection model. He finds results consistent with the previous ones, except for ceramic and cloth.

1.3. *Linear Models*

Finite-dimensional linear models use decompositions on the basis of which the vectors are fixed functions from the interval 400 nm–700 nm. The functions that are decomposed are:

- The illuminant energy spectral distribution function $\mathbf{E}(\lambda)$.
- The studied surfaces reflectance function $\mathbf{R}(\lambda)$.
- The sensibilities function of the sensors $\mathbf{S}(\lambda)$.

The advantage of these models is that they can represent the spectral information with a small number of parameters. The spatial factors (contained in the coefficients) are also separated from the spectral factors (contained in the basis functions). This separation is a feature also shared by the dichromatic model, but an important difference is that on the one hand more functions are used, and on the other they are *a priori* specified and are common to the set of studied surfaces. Note that the color signal (i.e. the spectral information) representation is necessary to modelize reflectance. Trichromatic representations are just inadequate.

A choice of three basis functions compatible with the NIR model is used by D'Zmura and Lennie [31] and is also examined by Wandel [119]. These functions are the three first basis function of a Fourier analysis (Fig. 13): $\mathbf{R}_1(\lambda)$ is constant, $\mathbf{R}_2(\lambda)$ is a Red-Green function, $\mathbf{R}_3(\lambda)$ is a Yellow-Blue function. However such a choice does not seem to enable a precise representation of the spectral information.

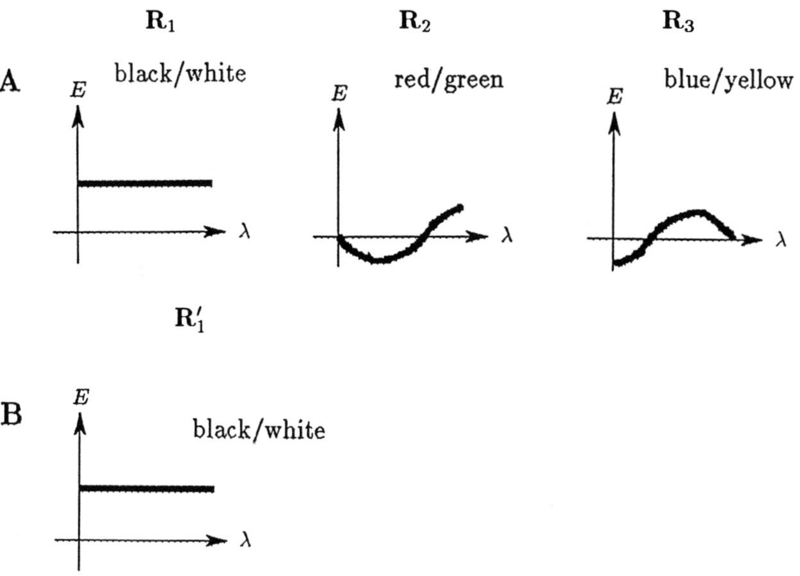

Fig. 13. Basis functions compatible with the dichromatic model, for the body (A) and surface (B) component.

It is more easy to build such models than to prove their validity as every model resulting from measures is automatically finite-dimensional. The interesting thing is to obtain a low dimensionality. One of the problems with these models is that the number of parameters needed for a correct representation of a big number of objects is greater than the "reasonable" number, that is three. Another drawback is that the determination of the basis functions is merely empirical; in consequence it depends largely on the sample used for the statistics.

Curves of the color spectra of some materials are given in the book by Wyszecki and Stiles [126] (pages 60–63): they include different building materials (brick, shingles, sheet metals, rocks, and enamel paints), and some typical natural objects. The last data are taken from the work of Krinov [81] who measured the spectral reflectance of samples of 370 natural materials, such as forests and shrubs, grass, mosses, field and garden crops, soils, roads, water surfaces, and snow. Very well known data are also the Munsell color atlas chips.

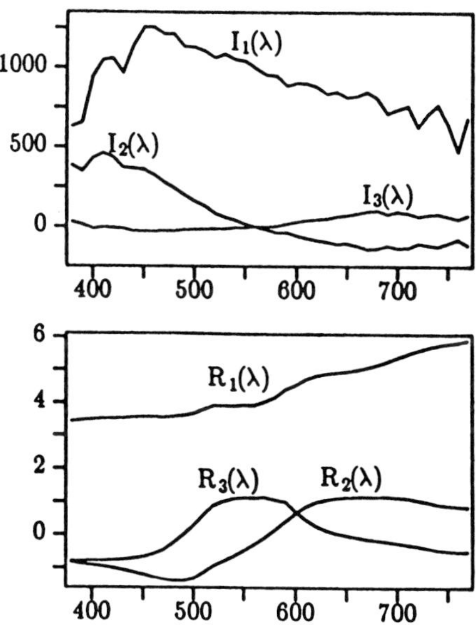

Fig. 14. Basis functions for the representation of illuminants [71] and reflectances [19].

The first studies are due to Judd et al. for the illuminant [71] (the tables are also in [126]) and to Cohen for the reflectance [19]. They use a characteristic vectors statistical analysis. These classical results are presented in Fig. 14. A more recent work is due to Maloney [89]. He extends the previous analysis to 462 Munsel chips and to 337 Krinov reflectance curves. His conclusion is that, generally speaking, five to seven parameters are necessary; but if one takes into account the human photoreceptors, sensibility curves and filtering properties, a model of three or four parameters is sufficient.

Jaaskelainen, Parkkinen, Kuittinen and Oja [67,98] have also done statistical work to determine basis functions to represent color, and their conclusions are very similar.

1.4. *Illumination Modeling*

All these models assume a point source illumination. For multiple illuminants one has to add the terms corresponding to each illuminant (there is no application within this framework; it seems very complicated). It is even more difficult to take into account the mutual illumination: each point of each object in the scene is to be considered as a light source. Practically, according to Nishita and Nakamae [95] mutual illumination represents 30% of the total illumination in indoors scenes. If the illuminants are chromatically neutral, mutual illumination can produce important color shifts as shown on a particular image by Gershon [45]. As long as it is not possible to take into account such illumination effects, it seems to be difficult to use very detailed models of reflectance.

These problems are the major obstacle to their use in a natural environment. The applications which make use of them take place in very well-controlled experimental set-ups. Except in the case of almost black surfaces or of a convex isolated surface, the interreflection problems have important qualitative effects as pointed out by Forsyth and Zissermann [35,36,40]. These authors use monochromatic images and compare the intensity profiles of pairs of scenes with identical geometry and different albedos: only the radiance discontinuities are significant,[i] the values themselves result from an interaction between surfaces, which are global and non-linear. The radiosity equation is

$$I(M) = I_0(M) + \rho(M) \int K(M, M')I(M')dM' \qquad (1.13)$$

where $I_0(M)$ is the component of the radiance at M due only to the light source, and $K(M, M')$ (the *kernel*, which in the Lambertian case is 0 if the points M and M' are not mutually visible, and $\frac{1}{\pi}(\mathbf{n}_{M'}.\mathbf{u}_{MM'})(\mathbf{n}_M.\mathbf{u}_{M'M})$ otherwise) represents the gain factor for the gain component at M caused by M'. It enables the explicit computation of radiance by a finite-element technique, from a model of the surfaces. For m facets, Eq. (1.13) becomes

$$I = I_0 + RKI \qquad (1.14)$$

where the m components of I and I_0 are respectively the radiances and radiance components caused only by the light source, and R, K are very simple matrices formed with albedos and kernels. This technique has been introduced in the field

---

[i]In a Lambertian framework they can come only from surface discontinuities, shadows, and changes in reflectance.

of computer graphics by Cohen and Greenberg [20] and experimentally verified by Forsyth and Zissermann [35]. In the case of achromatic images of Lambertian surfaces, Nayar, Ikeuchi, and Kanade [93] show that the Eq. (1.14) can be the basis for an algorithm which starts from estimates of shape and albedo given (inexactly) by a shape from shading algorithm, and converges iteratively towards the correct shape and albedo. This is an important work as it shows that the analysis (or vision) problem can be solved with a model introduced for the synthesis, that is not explicitly invertible. There is not related work on colored or non-Lambertian surfaces yet.

The problem of detecting interreflections has received recent attention. Jang [68] has proposed a method of identification in color images based on the dichromatic model. As he considers only a single-bounce interreflection produced by the body to body component only, he obtains equations that can be tested using pairs of areas in the image. This problem has also been addressed by Bajcsy, Lee and Leonardis [3] using the same model. The fact that they use a reference plate to achieve a form of color constancy allows then to detect local illumination induced by interreflections using some simple heuristics.

1.5. *Conclusion*

The colorimetric transformations have properties that are interesting, but of limited scope. A lot of color spaces are more or less equivalent. One cannot expect much from them.

Recent models are based on the formalization of the reflection process and of the color signal; they enable the representation of scene intrinsic physical properties. One of the big advantages of recent models (the linear ones and the dichromatic ones) is to factor spatial factors and spectral factors. This enables us to take into account both of them, which should theoretically result in simultaneous computation of color and geometrical features. In a *vision* framework this is very important. A local analysis of the interactions between the two factors at the level of biological operators has been done by Gershon [45]. Hurlbert [63] also gives a discussion of the algorithmic functions of chromatic cells which have been found in the brain.

It seems that the use of very sophisticated reflectance models is very delicate in environments which are not very well (or artificially) controlled. The limitations will come less from the models themselves than from the difficulty of using them in complex cases. More specifically, we lack an *illumination* model simple enough to be algorithmically exploitable, rich enough to go beyond the point source hypothesis, taking into account diffusion and mutual illumination problems.

2. Color Constancy

The term "color constancy" refers to the fact that the color perceived by humans in real scenes are relatively stable under large variations of illumination and of material composition of scenes. Such a phenomenon shows that color *vision* is a complex process, that requires processing beyond the measurement of the physical quantities described in the previous section. Without elaborating, it is possible to say that psychophysical experiments reveal strong spatial effects. From a computational standpoint, overcoming the color constancy problem is an underdetermined problem: computing the spectral reflectance, from the sensor measurements.

It is an important issue, as the mere color signal that is measured does not indicate anything very reliable about the world. On the other hand, if we can compute reflectance, we will obtain an intrinsic property of objects, which will be useful for the derivation of semantic descriptions, or the identification of physical characteristics. However, if we want to compute only image features (not scene features) such as edges, or color labels for matching, color constancy will not always be necessary.

The color constancy problem has been extensively studied. Most of the work done in color vision is devoted to this subject. The algorithms are too numerous to describe (or even mention). However if one considers the work that has been done in an algorithmic framework, one has to remark that:

- most of the work is based on restrictive hypotheses that are not very realistic,
- the few convincing realizations work only in simplified scenes.

For a very clear and comprehensive review (especially of Retinex algorithms), the reader is referred to [38]. Worthy of interest is also a chapter by Hurlbert [63].

2.1. *Lightness Algorithms*

The idea behind lightness algorithms is that it is possible to do the job of discarding the illuminant independently in each waveband, and then to combine the results.

2.1.1. *The Retinex idea for computing color*

Land has published numerous papers that have been both very influential, and much criticized. His work suffers from a lack of precise algorithmic definitions, and is not easy to evaluate, thus we will not discuss it in detail. However it is interesting to look at the experiments which illustrate well the issues of color constancy, and the sophistication of the color vision in complex scenes [82,85,83].

The algorithms presented in this section share some basic assumptions on which Land's Retinex algorithm was based. The three principles are:

- The color seen at a point does not depend only on the color signal at this point.
- The color seen at a point depends only on the combination of three "designators".
- The "designators" are computed *independently* in three wavebands.

Moreover, the "designators" should not depend on the composition of the observed scene, but only of the reflectance properties at the observed point. The computational problem is to recover lightness (an approximation to surface reflectance), by discarding the effects of the illuminant. The underlying intensity equation is

$$I(\lambda, \mathbf{r}) = \rho(\lambda, \mathbf{r}) E'(\lambda, \mathbf{r}) \ . \tag{2.1}$$

It is the intensity equation (1.4) where factors have been grouped together to isolate the surface properties by defining the *effective irradiance E'*, and where various dependencies have been suppressed. It is used only for three fixed values of λ.[j] Another basic assumption is that there exists an asymmetry between ρ and E', which enables one to solve Eq. (2.1): ρ consists of uniform patches with abrupt changes, whereas E' varies smoothly on the whole scene. It is the *Mondrian (micro) World.*

The two conditions required[k] for the algorithm to work are:

- Hypothesis 1 (Mondrian world): the scene is a flat Mondrian world, the effective irradiance varies slowly and smoothly, and is independent of the observer position.
- Hypothesis 2 (Gray world): The mean value of the scene reflectances in each waveband is the same.

The first hypothesis enables one to perform, at each spatial location, the decomposition of the intensity in these two components. The second hypothesis guarantees that the spectral normalization (that is needed because the previous process gives results only up to a multiplicative constant) will give a triplet corresponding to the surface color.

2.1.2. *Formalized algorithms*

Principles. Several propositions have been carried out for algorithms performing the same lightness computation as the Retinex, but in a well-defined computational framework. They are formulated directly in a two-dimensional framework, using parallel and local operations. They use the following method (see Fig. 15).

- Differentiate spatially the intensity.
- Use a threshold to eliminate the small values (caused by the little variations of the illuminant) while keeping the large values (caused by the abrupt changes in reflectance).
- Integrate to recover the reflectance (lightness).

The operations implied are of two different types:

- Differentiation, which is a *local* process doing the spatial decomposition.

---

[j]A problem common to all in this family of methods is the fact that the values which are used as the starting point for the algorithm are in fact integrals, as shown by Eq. (1.5). Thus the quotient of the intensities from one side to another of an edge is different from the quotient of reflectances.
[k]Clearly, they are not verified in real scenes. It seems difficult to do segmentation in Mondrian parts, as one has to solve the problems eliminated by the Mondrian world in order to achieve this kind of segmentation.

- Integration, which is a *global* process doing the spectral normalization using a large portion of the visual field to obtain a mean value.

These operations, which eliminate the low spatial frequencies, are physiologically done by the lateral inhibition phenomena (in which a cell inhibits the activity of neighboring cells of a quantity proportional to its excitation, and decreasing with distance).

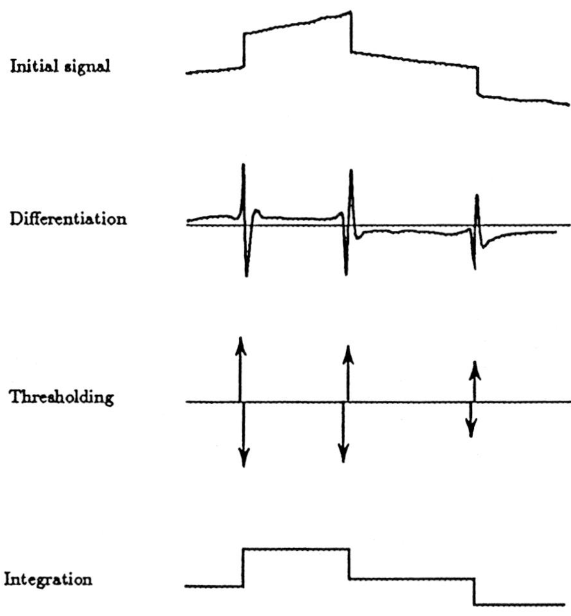

Fig. 15. Lightness computation.

The logarithm problem. This class of algorithms has been designed to work on gray-level data (wavelength is not a parameter). In the framework of color constancy, an important assumption is that the signal obtained from the sensors is decomposed to a *sum* of two components representing the reflectance and the effective irradiance. For a lightness computation, the sum is obtained by a mere application of the logarithm: if the original values are I and E, by taking $I' = \log I$, $\rho' = \log \rho$, $E' = \log E$, one obtains $I' = \rho' + E'$. The techniques presented enable the computation of ρ', and hence, of ρ. The interest of this application of the logarithm has been pointed out by the homomorphic model of Stockham [107]. The meaning of homomorphic is that the multiplicative structure of the image formation process (product of E by R) is mapped to the additive structure of the human visual system, by the sensibility functions of the retinal receptors, that are logarithmic. The A, C_1, C_2 model of Faugeras, already mentioned, is a color extension of the Stockham model. It provides a possible scheme to eliminate changes in illumination: if the illuminant changes uniformly on the image, the responses of the R, G, and B receptors will be multiplied respectively by k_R, k_G, and k_B. The channels A, C_1, and C_2 will send a value increased evenly by the constants $a(\alpha \log(k_R) + \beta \log(k_V) + \gamma \log(k_B))$, $u_1 \log(k_R/k_G)$, and $u_2 \log(k_R/k_B)$, respectively. The last one can be eliminated by spatial filtering through lateral inhibition. However, while changes in illumination can thus be taken into account by the perceptual system, the separation of reflectance and illumination cannot be completely performed by this method. There is a difficulty in the case of a color signal, as taking its logarithm will not cause any separation (it would be the case if the sensors could get access to values of the color signal, but unfortunately they have access only to integrals, so one is confronted with an integral of a product). The algorithm cannot compute the spectral reflectance ρ, even in the favorable case when the illuminant is separable in space and wavelength: one obtains with a logarithm, only a separation of spatial factors.

Algorithms for lightness computation. A comparison of the main features of existing algorithms is illustrated in Table 2, where we mention the original retinex scheme just to illustrate the analogy with formal schemes.[1] The difficult operation in all these schemes is the inversion of ∇^2, the two-dimensional Laplacian, which implies the resolution of a Poisson equation. In the discrete case, this is done by solving with a relaxation method a system of finite-differences simultaneous equations obtained by a discretization on a grid. The formulation of Blake is more precise, as the use of gradient allows retention of more information during the differentiation stage, and improves on the formulation of Horn in two points:

- The conditions on limits are more general. Horn's scheme assumes that lightness is constant on the border of the Mondrian.[m]
- The formulation is shown to have a unique solution, and to be well-behaved in the presence of noise.

Let us mention a different approach by Hurlbert and Poggio [65]. The idea is to estimate the linear operator L that maps an array of sensor values S to an array of known reflectances R using a learning procedure. The learned operator is similar to Land's last proposal.

2.2. Linear Models

The principle of these algorithms is to write all the reflectances and illuminants as linear combinations of a limited number of vectors. These techniques present

---

[1]The Poisson equation resulting from Blake's formulation can also be solved by computing $r(x, y) = \int \sigma \nabla I dl$ along a path joining (x_0, y_0), a reference point for r, and (x, y).

[m]Because the associated Poisson equation $\nabla^2 r(x, y) = \sigma(\nabla^2 I(x, y))$ imposes only the condition $\nabla^2 r(x, y) = 0$ inside patches, the solution could otherwise contain an arbitrary harmonic term. If the condition is not satisfied, the algorithm can yield to incorrect results.

Table 2. Lightness algorithms.

Algorithm	Operators	Tessellation of the plane	Experimentation
Retinex [84] (the most recent)	$R^\Lambda(i,j) = \sum_k \sigma_1 \left(\log \frac{I_{k+1}}{I_k} \right)$ "designator": $\overline{R}^\Lambda(i) = \dfrac{\sum_{j=1}^N R^\Lambda(i,j)}{N}$	stochastic selection of paths between zones i and j	McCann, McKee and Taylor [91] (one image); analysis by Brainard and Wandell [10]
Horn [57]	$(\nabla^2)^{-1}\sigma_1\nabla^2$ σ_1 is a one-dimensional thresholding operator	hexagonal grid	implemented using a multiresolution scheme by Terzopoulos [111]
Blake [5]	$(\nabla^2)^{-1}\nabla\sigma_2\nabla$ σ_2 is a two-dimensional thresholding operator	hexagonal grid	synthetic images
Brelstaff and Blake [11]	$(\nabla^2)^{-1}$ Canny edge detector	square grid	real images

over the Retinex the advantage to perform the computations simultaneously in each waveband, thus overcoming the problems caused by the logarithm and the normalization. These algorithms start from the same intensity equation, thus they also need the Mondrian world hypothesis. The basic idea is to solve an underdetermined system of equations, using various constraints. The minimum acceptable number of unknowns is three parameters for the illuminant, and three parameters for the reflectance in each different patch, while the number of sensors is generally three. In this section, we first present in detail two simple algorithms for color constancy. We then survey the other existing algorithms.

2.2.1. *Linear algorithms*

Invariant based algorithms. The idea of the algorithms of Buchsbaum and Gershon is to estimate the illuminant color using the straightforward hypothesis (closed to the gray-world hypothesis) that some average quantity $\mathbf{U}$ is constant across different scenes. The Buchsbaum algorithm relies on the fact that the mean value of the reflectances over the scene is a gray value. Gershon has slightly improved this algorithm by a different calculation of the invariants:

- The invariant is a mean value taken on Krinov's data of reflectances of natural surfaces. Gershon finds $\mathbf{U} = (0.1956, 0.000523, 0.0324)$ over the basis obtained with Cohen's characteristic vectors.
- The mean value in the image is computed over segmented regions, rather than by a spatial averaging.

The algorithm is presented below. The interest lies in its very simple mathematical form, requiring only linear calculations.

Buchsbaum–Gershon Algorithm: Color Constancy

Let $\mathbf{U}$ be a reflectance vector which is an invariant, and T the tensor defined by: $(T)_{i,j,k} = \sum_\lambda E_i R_j S_k$, where E_i, R_j, S_k are the fixed basis functions for the illuminant, the reflectance, and the sensors.

1. Compute $\mathbf{V}$ by a spatial averaging, or an averaging on segmented regions.
2. Compute the illuminant: $\epsilon = \Lambda_{\mathbf{U}}^{-1}.\mathbf{V}$ where $\Lambda_{\mathbf{U}} = T.\mathbf{U}$ is a representation of the reflectances.
3. For each sensor value (color measured) $\mathbf{s}$, compute the reflectance value: $\mathbf{r} = \Lambda_{\epsilon}^{-1}.\mathbf{s}$ where $\Lambda_{\epsilon} = T.\epsilon$ is a representation of the illuminant.

Dimensionality based algorithms. This family of algorithms does not need any assumption on the composition of the scenes. Here, the assumption is about the general structure of the sets of illuminants and reflectances. The fundamental equation, in each point $\mathbf{r}$ corresponding to a different surface reflectance, is a linear equation relating the responses of the p sensors $\mathbf{S}$ and the n coordinates of the reflectance $\mathbf{R}$:

$$S(\mathbf{r}) = \Lambda_{\mathbf{E}}.\mathbf{R}(\mathbf{r}) \tag{2.2}$$

where $\Lambda_E = T.\mathbf{E}$, the operator which depends only on the illuminant. The idea is illustrated in Fig. 16: under some conditions, discussed later, the responses observed in the sensor's space will be lying only in a proper subspace. This subspace depend only on the illuminant, whereas the positions of the responses in this subspace depend only on the reflectances. The model chosen for illuminants and reflectances features the following assumptions:

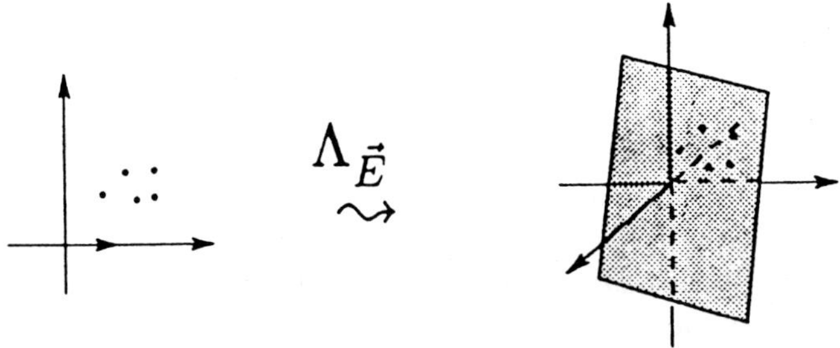

Fig. 16. The idea behind the Maloney and Wandell method.

- The number of sensors is strictly superior to the the dimension of the reflectance space. Using three sensors enables us only to recover two reflectance parameters, which is not sufficient.
- The mapping must also be such that two surfaces of different reflectances will always give different responses, whatever the illuminant is.

The algorithm presented below is also simple, and deals naturally with the case of Gaussian noise. The residuals obtained in the linear least-squares calculations are a good indication of the failure of the model.

Maloney and Wandell Algorithm: Color Constancy

1. Identify the sub-space $Vect(\Lambda_{\mathbf{E}}.\mathbf{R}(\mathbf{r}))_{\mathbf{r}}$. This is done by solving the linear least-squares problem min $M\mathbf{n}$, where M is the matrix whose rows are the sensor values, which gives the normal $\mathbf{n}$ to that subspace.

2. Compute the illuminant vector $\mathbf{E}$ *up to a scale factor*, by solving, in the least-squares sense, the system of N linear equations obtained with the N different surfaces $\mathbf{R}_i$:

$$\mathbf{n}^t.\Lambda_{\mathbf{R}_i(\mathbf{r})}.\mathbf{E} = 0 \quad 1 \le i \le N$$

where $(\Lambda_{\mathbf{R}_i(\mathbf{r})}) = T.\mathbf{R}_i$.

3. Compute the reflectances in each point $\mathbf{r}$ using a pseudo-inversion: $\mathbf{R}(\mathbf{r}) = \Lambda_{\mathbf{E}}^{-1}\mathbf{S}(\mathbf{r})$.

2.2.2. *More algorithms: a comparison*

The advantage of the previous algorithms is that they do only linear computations and thus they are easy to analyze. It is possible to evaluate simply the input and to see whether the algorithms will fail or not. The problem is that they need assumptions that are quite restrictive. To overcome the difficulties raised by these assumptions, a lot of improvements have been proposed. The common idea is to use more sophisticated constraints to solve the underdetermined system of equations. These constraints are more realistic and are based on weaker assumptions, thus the algorithms are theoretically superior: they can recover more degrees of freedom for the reflectance, or can accommodate the case of non-uniform illumination. However, they involve non-linear computations, that are iterative. The computational complexity is high, and it is not possible to predict *a priori* the performance. The number of sensors considered is generally three, but some algorithms allow for more. Table 3 below gives a comparison between some algorithms for color constancy based on linear models. From an experimental point of view, there has been published demonstrations only on synthetic images, except for the last algorithm. To end let us mention to finish a new approach by Forsyth [39, 34], whose sophisticated mathematical formulation gives good insight into the color constancy problem, and yields an efficient algorithm which has been tested on real images, when the sensors are narrowband.

2.3. *Physical Approaches*

These approaches are generally based on a physical model of reflection, almost exclusively the NIR model. The advantage over the previous algorithms is that here the Mondrian world hypothesis is not needed. The drawbacks are that:

- Highlights and inhomogeneous materials must be present in the scene. It will not be the case in the Mondrian world.
- The illumination conditions must be well-controlled to avoid multiple illuminants, interreflections, and shadows.
- These algorithms just compute the illuminant color, which is not exactly the relevant information, this being the illuminant spectral power distribution.

Using highlights. A first method is to observe directly the illuminant color in the specularities, assuming a NIR model. The idea has been proposed by Healey and Binford [53] and is very simple: if we can find a specular/diffuse boundary on an object, and if we assume that:

- $R_s(\lambda)$, the surface reflectance, has a little spectral variation so that it can be taken constant,
- $R_b(\lambda)$, the body reflectance has a little spatial variation, so that it does not change across the boundary,

then the illuminant is obtained up to a scale factor by: $E(\lambda) = I(\lambda) - I'(\lambda)$, where $I(\lambda) = (R_s + R_p(\lambda))E(\lambda)$ and $I'(\lambda) = R_p(\lambda)E(\lambda)$ are measured respectively on the

Table 3. Color constancy algorithms based on linear models.

Author(s)	Paradigm	Complexity	Reflectance	Illumination
Buchsbaum [15] Gershon [45]	computation based on an invariant	linear algorithm	$dim\mathcal{R} = 3$ the average of the reflectances in the image is an invariant	$dim\mathcal{E} = 3$ E is uniform on the entire image
Maloney–Wandell [90,119] Yuille [127]	limitation of the dimensionality of the reflectance space	linear least squares	$dim\mathcal{R} < dim\mathcal{S}$ two surfaces of $\neq$ reflectances always yield $\neq$ sensor responses	$dim\mathcal{E} < $ number of $\neq$ surfaces and $dim\mathcal{E} \leq dim\mathcal{S}$ $E(x,y)$ has a locally constant spectrum distribution (on areas with a sufficient number of $\neq$ surfaces)
Rubner–Schulten [103]	regularisation: $E(x,y) \to$ white average of reflectances $\to$ grey $E_x, E_y \to 0$	non-linear minimization	$dim\mathcal{R} = 3$	$dim\mathcal{E} = 3$ $E(x,y) = E + xE_x + yE_y$
Funt–Drew [41]	Retinex–Horn scheme	iterative solution to partial derivatives equations	$dim\mathcal{R} = dim\mathcal{S}$	$dim\mathcal{E} = dim\mathcal{S}$ $E(x,y)$ varies smoothly
Tsukada–Ohta [116]	multiple images of the same scene	system of non-linear equation	$dim\mathcal{R} = 3$ two surfaces are identified from one image to another	$dim\mathcal{E} = 3$ two constant illuminants, E_1, E_2

specular side and the diffuse side. Unfortunately, the choice of boundary and areas is not simple.

A second family of methods overcomes the difficulties raised by the spatial reasoning inplied in the above method. The idea is to use multiple objects of different colors. The observation of the histogram of the colors of each object yields a constraint on the illuminant color. As we want to determine it only up to a scale factor, a minimum of two objects are needed.

- Klinker, Shafer, and Kanade [76,77] first compute the dichromatic planes of the objects. If the surface reflection vector is the same, which is the case in a NIR model, these planes will intersect along a line which represents the illuminant color. As the determination of the dichromatic planes is quite tricky (see a discussion of their method in the section on physical segmentation), we describe a simpler method.
- Lee [86] has exploited directly the same idea: on a chromatic diagram, the colors of a monochromatic object lie on a line through which goes the illuminant color and the body color of the object. Using at least two objects of different colors, it is thus possible to obtain the illuminant color by taking the intersection of these lines.

Lee Algorithm: Illuminant Color from Highlights

1. Perform an edge detection in the three images G/R, G, B/R.
2. At each contour point, keep the values G/B and B/R corresponding to the directions of maximal variations for G.
3. Keep only the lines defined by parts of the same object: this is done by performing a linear regression on the sets of values G/B and B/R, and by checking the regression factor.
4. Compute (using an approximative method), the intersection of those lines.

Other methods. Let us just give pointers about using other sources of information to achieve color constancy:

- Chromatic aberration. The work of Funt and Ho [42] shows how to estimate the color signal from analysis of patterns resulting from chromatic aberration in some simple cases, using gray-level images. From the color signal a linear model gives easily the reflectance and illumination parameters. This approach needs a very precise model of the optics used.
- Inter-reflection. The idea of the work by Drew and Funt [30] is to observe in two neighboring areas, not only the radiance values coming from direct reflection, but also the values generated by mutual reflection of the two areas, which give some supplementary equations. A linear model with three degrees of freedom for the illuminant and for the reflectances can then be solved and a geometrical factor recovered, even if there is only one surface color.

- Polarization. Wolf has shown that using images taken with a polarizing filter can lead to very efficient solutions to classical problems in color vision like material classification [123], separation of reflection components [122], and physically-based edge labeling [9] even with a weak hypothesis on the illuminant. However, these powerful methods are a little beyond mere color vision.

2.4. *Conclusion*

After some successive improvements, there is now an algorithm for the computation of lightness that works well in gray-level images [11]. This algorithm does not give the exact albedo in complex scenes, because it will be misled by all the intensity discontinuities which are different from changes in albedo. Similarly, in the Mondrian world, the problem of the recovery of reflectance seems to have received a few satisfying solutions [34], although the case of variable illumination has been rarely implemented.

However, it seems that, by concentrating on the toy world, these two research directions miss the important problems of vision. In a real application these algorithms does not seem very useful. The main difficulties come from:

- Geometric factors: it can be expected that algorithms working under a variable illuminant will still work when there are smooth variations caused by shading, however they will not cope with changes in orientations and highlights.
- The illumination: shadows (abrupt changes), and mutual illumination (which causes changes in spectral composition of the illumination) are challenging problems.

To adapt all these algorithms to the real world, it will certainly be necessary to identify the physical origin of discontinuities to segment the image in areas where the assumptions are verified. This is a difficult task, as we will see later.

Physical approaches use more realistic assumptions, but the models are valid only under very well controlled illumination conditions.

A general remark is that the robustness of algorithms has not been really investigated, even for those which work on real images. There are two factors to be considered:

- accuracy when there is noise and various sensor distortions,
- accuracy when the simplifying assumptions of the underlying models are not verified in the scenes.

Only the first item has been (sometimes) studied. That limits a lot the practical utility of the algorithms. A second remark is that a change in illumination can affect seriously the quality of the sensors measurements. Forsyth [38] points out that as one proceeds with constant acquisition parameters that are adjusted for white light, for instance when the light becomes red, the signal dynamic range in the green channel becomes very narrow, thus the system becomes almost ignorant about the information measured in this channel. A color constancy system should control the parameters of its transducers using its estimates of the light color, as the human system does, with the phenomena of adaptation.

3. Using Color Information: From Image Features to Scene Intrinsic Properties

This section will present the use of color in *universal* (so mainly low-level) vision tasks. They include everything that can be computed without any *a priori* knowledge, except those of the physics of imaging systems, that is common to all scenes. We emphasize the distinction between tasks that have been extensively studied in monochromatic images and for which the contribution of color is just a *quantitative* generalization, and tasks where color has a *qualitative* role. In the first case, additional image features are obtained, and have to be represented and used efficiently. In the latter case, it is hoped that color can help recover the scene's intrinsic physical properties. This implies the use of generic *a priori* models. We study successively three important themes in computer vision. For each of them, we present the two frameworks for the use of color:

- three values instead of one.
- a key to intrinsic scenes' properties?

3.1. *Edges*

Edges are very important image features. We first study the benefits obtained by using color in performing their detection. We then try to examine if it is possible to go further, and to label them in a way that is related to intrinsic scene properties.

3.1.1. *Color edge detection*

Several methods have been experimented to improve intensity-based techniques. They can be classified into three categories, following the kind of representation used:

- A special metric on the color space (corresponding to psychophysical results, to quantify the notion of perceptible color difference) is defined. Then the edge detection uses this metric. This technique is illustrated by [18] and brings back the edge detection problem to a one-dimensional space[n] problem. It is unlikely to give better results than an intensity based detection, as the intensity image is the most significant one-dimensional representation of color changes, as seen previously. Another problem is that using a global metrics (a deformation of a color space as intensity-hue-saturation) would make it difficult to define derivatives. An improvement of this idea is presented by Huntsberger and Descalzi [62] who represent individual pixels in the image by fuzzy membership values to

---

[n]The term "one-dimensional" here refers to the dimensionality of the information contained in each pixel of the image, not the dimensionality of the image itself.

clusters in a color vector space. These fuzzy membership values are generated by an iterative segmentation scheme based on a fuzzy K-means algorithm. Thus they are related to the underlying color structure of the image.

- A coding on multiple (likely three) one-dimensional image. The detection is made independently by a classical edge detector in each of the images. For example Forsyth [37] proposes to use two opponent-color images (Blue–Yellow and Red–Green) and gives some interesting ideas to support this choice. The problem to be addressed is the one of fusion. It seems that it can be dealt with in a multisensorial fusion framework, and could lead to more stability and robustness.
- The combined use of multiple components. The alternatives are to do all the computations using vectors instead of scalars, or to make combinations (such as mean values, least squares) from differences computed on each component. Novak and Shafer (see [73] for an overview) use both the techniques and introduce a methodology to build different color operators n/m doing combinations at different stages:

— Perform independently the n first stages on each component.
— Combine using the m norm.
— Go on from the $n + 1$ stage with the combined (one-dimensional) values.

Nevatia has generalized the Huckel edge detector, using a constraint of edge orientation between the three components (the fitting parameters of the "step" are allowed to vary independently, the best fit is determined by a least-square minimization). A purely multidimensional method is used by Coutance, Baron, and Briot [24] and Shafer and Novak [73]. The key point is the computation of a multidimensional gradient (presented also by DiZenzo [29]) using the Jacobian matrix. Let the color image function be $f : (x,y) \mapsto \mathbf{C} = (C_1, C_2, C_3)$, and m the greatest eigenvalue of $J^t(f)J(f)$, where $J(f) = [\mathbf{C}_x, \mathbf{C}_y]$. The eigenvector associated to m gives the direction yielding to the greatest variation and $\sqrt{m}$ is the value of that variation. The formulas are:

$$\theta = \frac{1}{2} \arctan \frac{2\mathbf{C}_x \cdot \mathbf{C}_y}{\|\mathbf{C}_x\|^2 - \|\mathbf{C}_y\|^2}$$
$$m = (\mathbf{C}_x \cos(\theta) + \mathbf{C}_y \sin(\theta))^2 \ .$$

However Novak and Shafer find that the $2/\infty$ operator, which: (1) computes the partial derivatives in each image, (2) computes the direction and amplitude of edges in each image, and combines with L_∞, (3) suppresses the non-maxima by thresholding, gives almost the same contours as the vectorial operator.

A typical conclusion of these authors is that the use of color vs. black-and-white images does not give many new edges, but that the edges obtained are a little better: they correspond more often to significant changes in the image. Most of the detected color edges are also intensity edges, so that color would be of secondary use, to refine the detection. However it is difficult to quantitatively assess these results (as the authors just present side-by-side the images with the extracted edges), and this is an explanation for the differences. Perhaps the main interest of color is not to improve edge detection, but to enhance their description. Actually the surfaces photometric properties are linked with surfaces, not edges. Color is more naturally attached to regions. It is why the dual problem of color image segmentation has received more interest.

3.1.2. *Physical edge labeling*

The problem here is to classify edges that were detected as intensity, or color discontinuities, according to the type of physical event that caused then to appear. This task is very important to gain access to intrinsic scenes properties, because it is natural to start from contours to recover them, as the contours correspond effectively to physical discontinuities (they are unaffected by problems caused by sensors or mutual illumination, which are continuous distortions). It also seems to us that it is necessary to solve the color constancy problem in natural scenes, as the present algorithms have had their limitations examined previously. However it is a very difficult task.

Let us consider the intensity equation resulting from the NIR model[o]:

$$I(\lambda, \mathbf{r}) = (m_s(i, e, g) + m_p(i, e, g)C_p(\lambda, \mathbf{r}))E(\lambda, \mathbf{r}) \ . \tag{1.7}$$

Each of the terms of this equation can have a sharp variation,[p] giving the following discontinuities:

- Specular (highlight): discontinuity of $m_s(i, e, g)$ between an area where it can be neglected and an area where it is important.
- Orientation (vertex): discontinuity of $m_p(i, e, g)$.
- Reflectance (color marks): discontinuity of $C_p(\lambda, \mathbf{r})$.
- Illuminant (shadow): discontinuity of $E(\lambda, \mathbf{r})$.

Horn [58] has given a general discussion of the problem, but he did not give any classification method. There has been only a little work on this subject. It is well known that:

- from one side of a reflectance contour to the other, the direction of the intensity gradient is continuous, and the ratio of the intensities is equal to the ratio of the gradients.
- from one side of a shadow contour to the other, the intrinsic color[q] (that would result from a color constancy algorithm[r]) is constant, the texture is continuous, and the intensity contrast is high.

---

[o]Because it is more simple, Eq. (1.4), is often used. It means that the term $m_s(i, e, g)$ is just ignored.

[p]Depth is not explicit. The depth discontinuities are always combined with at least one of the three mentioned discontinuities. In the most general case, it combines with the three at the same time.

[q]It is sometimes incorrectly considered to be the hue.

[r]That shows why color constancy and edge labeling are mutually dependent.

The idea that color can serve to identify the physical nature of contours is due to Rubin and Richards [102]. The method is based on the use of the intensity equation (1.4) and of the color signals $I(\lambda)$ and $I'(\lambda)$ on each side of the contour. Each type of contour will be correlated with a variation of one of the terms of Eq. (1.4). For a contour due to:

- a shadow, the illuminant is just a diffuse component on the shadowed side, whereas on the lit side a direct component is added. This yields an additive relation $I(\lambda) = I'(\lambda) + k(\lambda)$, $k \geq 0$.
- a change in orientation, only the term F, which does not depend on λ varies, yielding a multiplicative relation between $I(\lambda)$ and $I'(\lambda)$.
- a change in pigmentation (on the same material), the two albedos $\rho(\lambda)$ and $\rho'(\lambda)$ are both a power of the same function (Beer's law).

The interesting remark (Fig. 17) is that these variations are characterized by the fact that for each wavelength λ, $I(\lambda) \geq I'(\lambda)$ (or always the opposite). It is then possible to discriminate between the contours caused by one of the mentioned causes and the contours caused by material changes using a very simple operator (it has the same form as double-opponent cells) which performs the test if $I(\lambda_1) > I'(\lambda_1)$ and $I(\lambda_2) < I'(\lambda_2)$.

This idea is interesting as it uses directly the intensity equation. Its sign comparison technique can be a robust solution to the problem posed by exact comparisons between regions (that are in general not uniform). Unfortunately it has not been implemented yet, so we do not know whether the following points are critical:

- The sensors cannot access directly to the value of the color signal at a precise wavelength.
- The physical model is not very accurate. The assumption on illumination is not verified if there is a lot of mutual illumination, as shown by Gershon[45].

Gershon[45] has proposed a method to avoid these difficulties, but his algorithm depends on an important threshold that depends on the scene characteristics. The difficulty that he shows[s] illustrates why it would be desirable to have color constancy. It shows also that it will be very difficult to find an algorithm capable of dealing with such scenes.

In recent work done by Gamble, Geiger, Poggio, and Weinshall [44] a new methodology has been suggested. Using a Markov random field, the output of each of four modules (stereo, motion, color, and texture) is processed to restore the lacking or noisy data, and to find the discontinuities, guided by the contour detection process. This gives a representation of the discontinuities, labeled by their observed effects. In order to obtain a labeling based on physical origin, instead of using *a priori* knowledge, as mentioned previously, derived from the intensity equation (and the underlying model), these authors consider a heuristic approach.

---

[s]He exhibits an image where an important part of the diffuse illumination is due to a colored object, so that its color is very different from the directly illuminated one.

ORIENTATION: multiplicative relation   ILLUMINATION: additive relation

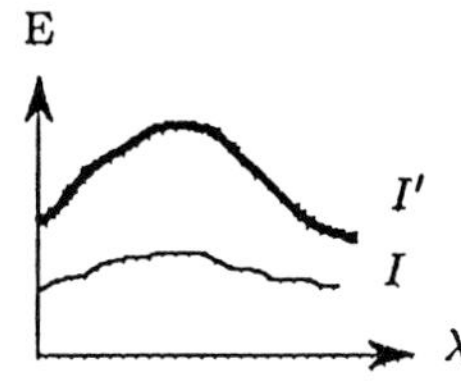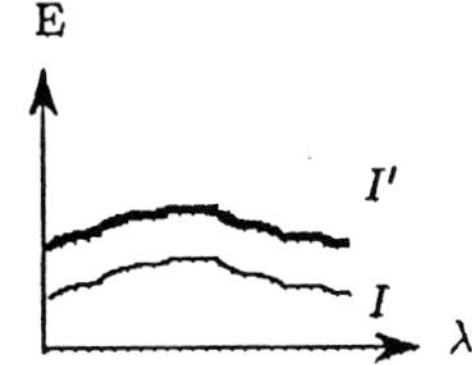

PIGMENTATION: power relation   OTHER: no constraint

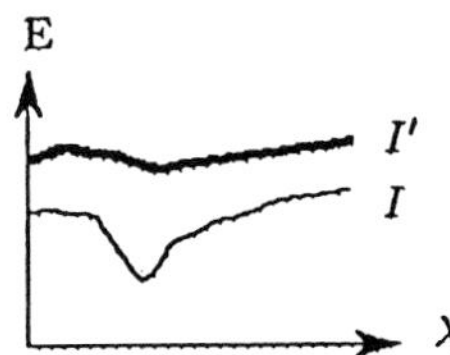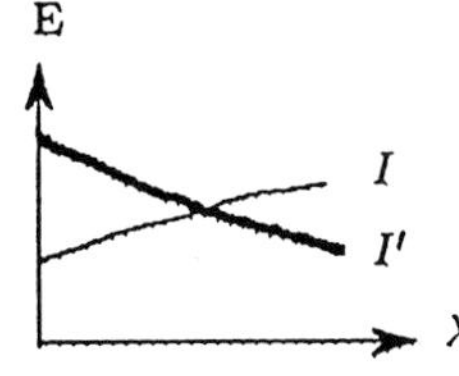

Fig. 17. Relations between the color signals in the different cases of contours [102].

They use a linear classificator. Its entries are the four units signaling presence, absence, or undetermination concerning the discontinuities detected by each module, plus units representing the average intensity on each side of the contour and the contour length. The outputs are five units representing each type of physical discontinuity. A learning phase has been done on a "still nature" image, which corresponds to thresholds tuning. The network will then give good labeling on images of the same type. It seems that the limits of this approach are the same as other learning networks. The good results seem to come more from the presence of dense and redundant information obtained by the four low-level modules than from the labeling technique itself.

3.2. *Segmentation*

This is perhaps the most important application of color techniques. Color is information which is naturally attached to regions. It has been used in early work to segment regions, with the hope that the obtained regions are more significant: color is a more stable[t] attribute than mere luminance, and it is a richer source of information. We first present methods for segmenting color images that are based only on the use of various color image features. It is worth noting that these methods will not always give significant segmentations: little differences caused uniquely by geometry can split uniform regions, as illustrated by the cylinder exhibited by Ohta et al. [97]. Generally speaking the images will not be segmented only along material boundaries, but also along other lines exhibiting color or intensity variations, such as

---

[t]A meaning that we will make more precise when examining "physical" segmentation methods.

highlights, and shadow boundaries, or internal object edges with significant shading changes. This problem is addressed by the physical segmentation methods that are presented subsequently, and that use a scene intrinsic model to attempt to obtain segmentations that are physically significant.

However, the segmentations obtained by merely using color features, suffer less from the problems caused by shadows and surface curvature, than the monochromatic segmentations, as shown by comparisons done by Gevers and Groen [47] using three test images segmented by a human expert. These authors compared different color coordinates, and two segmentation methods: split and merge, and a K-means clustering techique. They find that the first method is better. Color systems which are linear combinations of the same R–G–B basis provide similar segmentation results. As expected, normalized coordinates provide the best segmentation results if there are irrelevant changes of intensity in the image, but if the intensity is small, the segmentation yielded will be poor.

3.2.1. *Algorithms for image segmentation based on color features*

Color as a multidimensional feature. The first family of methods uses color as a feature which is multidimensional. It is a generalization of monochromatic methods. The main problem in transferring these methods to a multidimensional framework is to find an adequate metric, which supposes a choice of a color coordinates system. Another problem is the computational cost. The main segmentation methods are region growing, histogramming, and clustering (for a general discussion, which is very relevant as color segmentation is algorithms is often mere generalizations of monochromatic algorithms, see [50]). The first method emphasizes local geometric relations. It is illustrated by an adaptation (Gershon [45,47] of the split-and-merge algorithm introduced by Horowitz and Pavlidis [60]. It is the two last families of methods which have been extensively used to segment color images. They are global methods that typically suffer from a lack of important spatial knowledge in histograms or clusters and a dependence on thresholds.

Histogramming. These algorithms use color histogram analysis. The best known is Ohlander's [96] recursive region splitting method. In the case of a monochromatic image, a histogram of the gray-level values of the image elements is analyzed, and cut-off limits are obtained from prominent peaks which often correspond to gray-level values of significant regions in the picture. In the case of a color image, the method takes a region of the image, and using histograms of up to nine redundant attribute values, determines a threshold in one color component to split the region into smaller parts. In fact, many different image features can be used with a color image, and the algorithm can be optimized by a judicious choice of these chromatic features. Several features are already used by Ohlander, but the search for the most efficient color coordinate system was done systematically by Ohta et al. [97], whose work has already been described previously. This method is in fact a simple combination of several one-dimensional analyses.

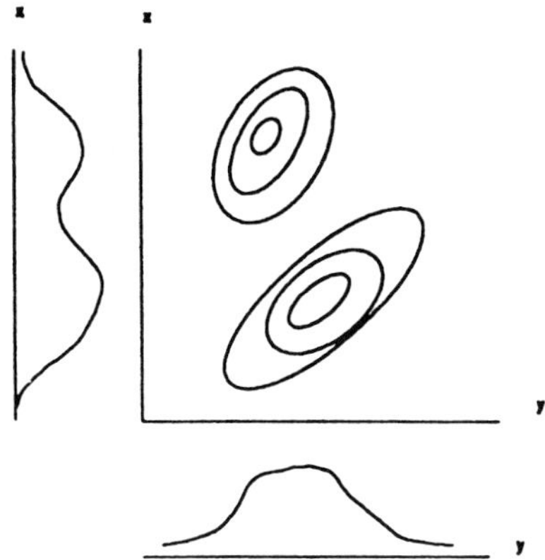

Fig. 18. Two-color clusters that yield components which are difficult to separate.

Clustering. Many attempts have been made to find segmentations using higher-dimensional analysis. The advantages of higher-dimensional analysis is that from the natural viewpoint of three-dimensional color space, image regions of near-constant color will form clusters, whereas under projections it is possible that some clusters which were separable in the three-dimensional space are no longer separable on many of these projections (see Fig. 18). The principle of clustering methods is to search for optimal cluster locations and the optimal number of clusters, by repeated iterations over the data. A statistical approach of the multidimensional clustering problem that is very accurate is presented by Coleman and Andrews [21]. Unfortunately, it is quite complicated. Generally speaking, since the feature space is three-dimensional, these methods are computationally expensive, and two kinds of approaches have been used to reduce the cost.

One solution is to project the feature space onto a lower-dimensional space. Some work using the bidimensional projection of color space onto the chromaticity triangle is reported by Tenenbaum *et al.* [110]. A bidimensional clustering technique described by Underwood and Aggarwal [117] and Ali and Aggarwal [1] (refined in [2] by the use of quadratic decision surfaces in an interactive operation), is based on the projections of the (x, y, I) normalized color space onto the x–y, x–I, and y–I planes. A more drastic dimensionality reduction, projecting the color space onto a given line, would of course result in a kind of Ohlander's method. However Celenk [16,17] has developed another approach based on repetition of projections on selected coordinate axes until the clusters are enclosed in some specified volume elements, which operates in the L^*–a^*–b^* uniform coordinate system.

The alternative solution is to develop efficient methods of storing and processing the information in the original three-dimensional color space. In a three-dimensional clustering technique presented by Schacter, Davis, and Rosenfeld [106], the three-dimensional image histogram is stored in a binary tree, with the key being

R–G–B values, and the information being the number of points with this key value. Clusters are detected if the number of points exceeds some threshold and if they lie within some distance from each other. A similar approach was used in the (x, y, I) normalized color space by Sarabi and Aggarwal [105].

Using Markov random fields. Statistical methods, such as the classical Bayes decision theory, which are based on previous observation have been used for a while. They depend on global *a priori* knowledge of the image content and organization. An important and recent family of algorithms has appeared, which considers a color image as a set of three monochrome images coupled by Markov random fields. It possesses several useful characteristics. Geometrical properties such as piecewise smoothness and continuity of color over an entire image can be enforced using only dependencies among local neighbors. Discontinuities which separate regions may be explicitly computed while smooth regions are being found. The inclusion of both the prior and posterior distributions, through Bayes' rule, establishes a relationship between noisy observed images and color segmentation results. As a triplet can be correlated at the pixel level without the need of a direct correlation between the different values, it is easy to use different representations for color (they are tested by Daily [26], who investigates also the influence of the use of different lattice structures). Even data from different sensors can be coupled, like the output of four different modules used at M.I.T. [44]), and it is possible to impose more or less coincidence between discontinuities from an image to another, as shown by Wright [125], which demonstrates the effect of different coupling values.

The drawbacks are that there is still a dependence on the choice of parameters (this is discussed in [26], whereas they are empirically determined in [44]). The most serious problem is the need of global optimization procedures (simulated annealing, Monte-Carlo techniques), which are computationally very expensive.[u]

3.2.2. *Physical segmentation*

Highlight detection. These algorithms operate even in areas of constant material composition, to separate significant types of reflections. It is useful to detect highlights, first in order to localize them, and second, in order to obtain the object (matt) intrinsic color:

- Highlights can be useful for shape computations: Blake has shown [6,7] that knowing their disparities yields strong constraints on the surfaces [6,7], while Healey and Binford [55] have shown that using the Cook and Torrance model enables recovery of the local curvature of a cylinder. However in natural scenes highlights are very sparse so that the most interesting techniques are those using active vision to fully exploit the information [104,129].

---

[u]Daily [26] speaks of 60 hours, using eight Lisp machines in parallel; Wright [125] uses only 32 × 32 images.

- On the other hand, highlights are view-point dependent and are troublesome for classical matching algorithms (the intensity values of the same three-dimensional surface will differ from one image to another) as well as for shape from shading techniques (they make the assumptions of Lambertian surfaces, see the book by Horn [59] for more details).
- In the framework of the dichromatic model, a normalized representation of color like the one of Healey and Binford [52,54] gets rid of the dependencies dues to geometric factors and keeps only those due to the illuminant and to the material surface. This is the key for a kind of physical segmentation.

Highlights differ from matt parts in two points:

- Their chromaticity is near the illuminant's one.
- Their intensity is greater

Recently some detection techniques based on color have been quite successful. It is worth noting their links with color constancy techniques.

Making very clever use of the dichromatic model as well as of a precise camera model, Klinker, Shafer, and Kanade [78] make the remark that on a (three-dimensional) histogram of the colors of an object made of a unique material, the points corresponding to the surface reflection, and the points corresponding to the body reflection will lie on two coplanar line segments forming a T as shown in Fig. 19. This kind of cluster was thoroughly analyzed by these authors, and is the basis for an algorithm which uses only chromatic information to identify these points.

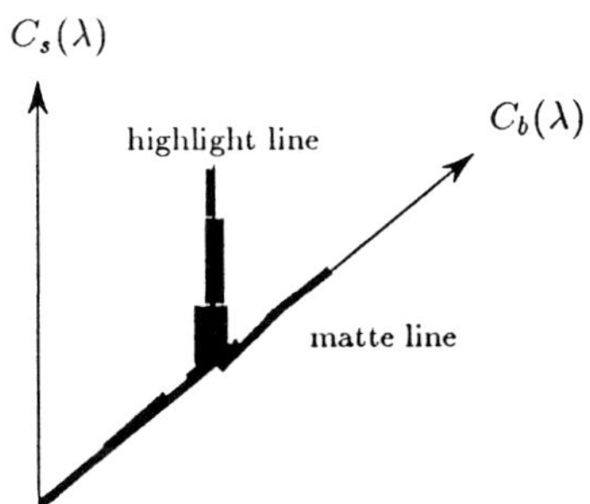

Fig. 19. The T-cluster in the dichromatic plane (Klinker–Shafer–Kanade) [78].

This first algorithm assumed the prior segmentation of the image in areas of constant material composition. It was successfully improved in [79] to avoid this problem as we will see in the next section. We just give an outline of the simpler version:

Klinker–Shafer–Kanade Algorithm: Highlight Detection

1. Compute the color histogram in the R–G–B cube.
2. Identify the dichromatic plane on which all the points lie.
3. Identify the two segments of the T-model to obtain the vectors $\mathbf{C}_p$ and $\mathbf{C}_s$.
4. Compute the pixel coordinates in this new basis: they are the body and surface components.

The approach of Gershon, Jepson, and Tsostsos [46] rests on the very basic observation that in a transition from a diffuse region to a specular region, there is color shift towards the illuminant color, resulting in a kind of inflexion in the color space, as illustrated by Fig. 20.

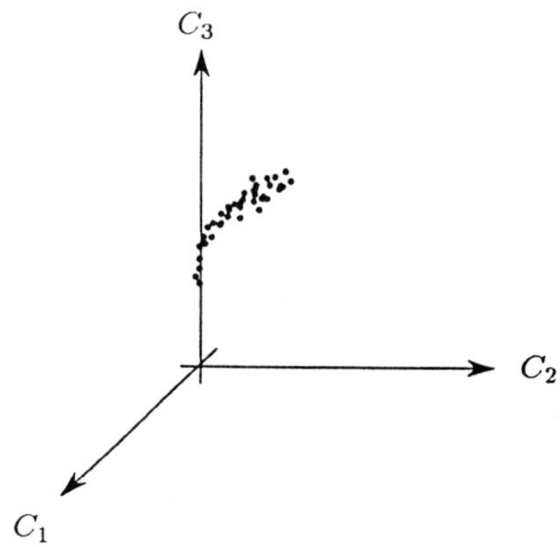

Fig. 20. Inflexion in the color cube [46].

The assumptions concerning the reflectance model are weaker, but the algorithm needs color constancy, which, as we have seen, is difficult to achieve in natural scenes. However these authors exhibit good results with some natural images.

These methods are in fact segmentation methods based on some special form of clustering. In consequence, they are computationally expensive due to the use of three-dimensional histograms, and make calculations in a very global manner.

It seems that a sufficient alternative is to work with images that are just monochromatic, without using any explicit highlight model. Brelstaff and Blake [12] argue that surfaces maintain quasi Lambertian properties except in the highlight areas. To make it more precise, they claim that the deviations from a BSRDF function f_r are within a factor 3, for every illumination and observation direction. Two kinds of tests are then proposed: the first detects the regions that are too bright to be Lambertian (a lightness computation is needed), the second detects the irradiance peaks that are too sharp to be Lambertian.

To conclude this section, we note that these problems could be efficiently solved using polarized light, as shown by Wolff[124], whose methods work without any assumption on the illuminant and object colors.

Material segmentation. Contrary to the segmentation algorithms previously presented, which made segmentations resulting in areas of constant image features (whatever they are), the methods described in this section aim to make segmentations that are physically significant, resulting in areas of constant reflectance (which is related to material composition). Note that highlight removal is necessary, as highlight areas introduce important discontinuities in areas of otherwise constant material composition. A unifying theoretical framework for material segmentation from color images, adapted from Nikolaev's work, is presented by Brill [13].

The last version of the algorithm of Klinker, Shafer, and Kanade [79] is a segmentation algorithm which can distinguish color changes at material boundaries from changes due to shading and highlights. It is much more difficult to analyze T-clusters from multiple objects than from a single object, because there is a mutual dependency between segmentation and physical interpretation. The algorithm solves this problem using a complicated generate-and-test analysis that at each stage looks in a bottom-up process for possible T-clusters, generates a hypothesis, then applies it to the image using a region-growing approach. It gives neat results with well-controlled images. However the conceptual limitations of this approach are those of the dichromatic model. The segmentation method will not distinguish between objects for which the matt lines are collinear, and it cannot operate in areas without highlights. More general problems are that the histograms will not be T in uncontrolled environments, due to local changes in illuminant chromaticity.

The approach of Bajcsy, Lee, and Leonardis [3] to the segmentation problem is to use the dichromatic model together with an intensity–hue–saturation representation of color. These authors use a reference plate, so that they can achieve a form of color constancy and have a white illuminant. Thus they provide the algorithm with important information. In these conditions, simple heuristics work well. The objects are segmented according to hue and saturation values. Shading and shadows do not change an object's color. Within an object, highlights are detected as change in saturation, and interreflections as changes in hue and saturation, with lower thresholds than those used to segment objects. This approach has been demonstrated by simple scenes containing objects with saturated colors. It can be expected that with objects with less saturated colors, distinguishing interreflection from material change will be more difficult.

These two methods operate only in color space, that is on a three-dimensional histogram of the color values present in the image, and therefore do not use any spatial information. Let us mention two other works which are both based on the conjoint use of normalized color and of the intensity equation (1.4), and, unlike the previous ones, represent spatial information.

The work of Healey aims to classify surfaces according to their material composition. The basic idea is that if one assumes that the intensity equation is like (1.4), the normalization

$$\frac{\rho(\lambda, \mathbf{r})F(i, e, g)E(\lambda)}{\|\rho(\lambda, \mathbf{r})F(i, e, g)E(\lambda)\|} = \frac{\rho(\lambda, \mathbf{r})E(\lambda)}{\|\rho(\lambda, \mathbf{r})E(\lambda)\|}$$

will eliminate the geometric dependencies, so that under the assumption of a unique illuminant $\rho(\lambda, \mathbf{r})$, characterization of the surface can be computed. As this property is conserved under integrals, it is possible to use a sensor model such as (1.5). A first version of the algorithm consisted in a clustering technique in the sensor space using presegmented regions [56]. A more sophisticated one is described in [52]: an edge detection is performed, then a division process examines regions that are smaller and smaller, until it finds regions containing no edges, which are then assumed to be of constant material composition. For each of these surfaces, a statistical classification technique either attaches it to a material class already found, or adds its material class to the list. The algorithm is not designed to work in the presence of highlights or of shadows.

The work of Hurlbert and Poggio [63] also makes use of the intensity contours to guide the segmentation which is based on the model of the Eq. (1.4) as well. Color is represented by the normalized coordinates

$$u = \frac{R}{R + G + B} \quad \text{and} \quad v = \frac{G}{R + G + B} \, .$$

Under the assumption of Lambertian surfaces illuminated *in each point* by a light source of constant spectrum,[v] these coordinates are intrinsic characteristics of surfaces. The goal of the algorithm is to find the discontinuities of u and of v using as a help the discontinuities of the intensity. It is necessary to combat noise (which is always important, as previously seen, with normalized color coordinates), using the piecewise regularity. Techniques based on Markov random field have been examined, but because of the computational complexity, an iterative algorithm based on a network method has been preferred. The network operates in the image of the values u (or v) by replacing each pixel value by the mean of the value of its neighbors provided that the values are similar and that they are not separated by an edge. The result is an averaging which suppresses noise to yield regions of constant colors by a process of filling-in blocked by edges, that has similarities with human perception. The authors show some good results on simple real images, however it seems that the possibilities of this algorithm is also limited by the underlying model.

---

[v] This hypothesis does not seem in fact to be sufficient: in general the spectral composition of direct illumination is not the same as that of the indirect illumination received by a shadowed surface. The consequence is that the normalized color will change from one side of the shadow to another, even if the surface remains of constant reflectance. The algorithm will not work in the presence of shadows.

3.3. *Matching*

In the first application that we will present, image tokens are to be matched from different images. The description of these tokens can be made richer thanks to color, to improve the matching process. The second application is very different: it involves matching from an image to a model of objects in the world.

3.3.1. *Stereovision*

The main problem in stereovision is the matching of corresponding tokens between the different views. The use of color yields additional features which can help disambiguate the matches. Jordan and Bovik [69] report a match counting experiment (performed on 3 pairs of images) with line segments. They compare the matches obtained with only the constraints of proximity, contrast sign, orientation and those obtained by adding the constraint of chromatic gradient in the R–G, G–B, B–R, normalized images. Their conclusion is that there is on the one hand a significant reduction of the number of segments matched (-40%) and the total number of candidates matched (-60%), and on the other hand an increase of the number of unique matches ($+70\%$) and the number of correct matches ($+1\%$). The same authors [70] have done the same experiment using a more sophisticated chromatic gradient matching constraint, based on an error analysis (they now just use the original R,G,B images to reduce problems caused by noise), and above all, a less simplistic framework for matching, the PMF stereo algorithm.[w] Four images were used. For the first stage (extraction) of the algorithm there was a reduction of the number of potential matches (-17% to -36%), and an increase of the number of unique matches ($+50\%$ to $+300\%$), as well of the number of correct unique matches ($+50\%$ to $+500\%$). These figures indicate that the use of chromatic information can significantly reduce match ambiguity. The analysis of the last stage of the algorithm (selection) gives the ultimate effect upon algorithm accuracy and speed. The final results depend on a parameter of the algorithm (the matching-strength support neighborhood radius), thus the authors give plots of the numbers and percentages of correct matches as well as execution time, as a function of this parameter. They notice a significant improvement: in the best case (small radius), for instance, the increase of number of matches was 20% and the percentage of correct matches was 60%.

Another thorough investigation on this subject is that of Brockelbank and Yang [14], whose approach consists in combining operators at different stages. These operators are: edge detection, feature map building, matching (a rather complicated method by relaxation and labeling). The models studied are:

- *Achromatic.*

---

[w] Also tested was a modified version of the PMF, which incorporates a gray-level gradient constraint. Its performance was between that of the classical PMF and that of the color PMF.

- *Three channels*: the processing of the achromatic model is done in each of the three R,G,B channels.
- *Trichromatic*: the edge detection is performed in the R,G,B images, the edges are combined in one feature map with chromatic attributes (which are used for the matching process).
- *Opponent*: the R,G,B images are combined to produce opponent images. The processing goes on as in the precedent model.

The tests have been run on three images: a random-dot stereogram with decorrelated colors, a random-dot stereogram with edges correlated between colors, and a natural scene. Because of the different nature of the images, the results are not very consistent (the ratio of the well-matched edges and of the detected edges is, in image 1, 48% for the achromatic model, and 73% for the chromatic ones, in image 2 90%, 55%, 75%, 91%, and in image 3, always 47.5%). However the authors do many other counts and conclude that:

- the achromatic model detects far less edges (it is the main difference for the authors, but it seems to me to be an artifact; tests are to be conducted extensively on real images) but the matching seems very near.
- the three channel model gives results that are sometimes not very consistent from one channel to another.
- the representation of features is better with opponent colors than with trichromatic ones: the R,G,B components have a bandwidth that is less that the opponent components, and can miss some edges. This point confirms the usefulness of the representation scheme "Intensity/Color-feature1/Color-Feature2".

This kind of approach used for stereovision can also be useful for all the algorithms based on the matching of features between multiples images, like motion analysis or fusion of multiple views. One can certainly expect a reduction of the combinatorial complexity, but it is unclear if it is worth the additional preprocessing and storage.

3.3.2. *Indexing models*

Color is a very natural recognition cue. It has been studied very early and is well used in some specialized applications. For example when there a *priori* knowledge of the scene, the segmentation process is a decisional one: the knowledge is materialized by several clusters, and each pixel has to be assigned to one cluster, based on a probability computed from a particular metric. This approach is often used for applications such as road following [112], where only a very simple form of scene modeling (road/non-road) is required.

Given that reasonable color constancy can be achieved, color has enormous value in recognition because it is a local surface property that is view invariant and largely independent of resolution. However, for general use, it has been largely neglected as a useful cue. One reason is that it may not be as intrinsically related to the object's identity as geometric properties are. But the more important reason is the lack of good algorithms for color constancy. Another reason why color may not have been so successful is that it has been associated with a Mondrian-like view: one color per object. But many objects are multi colored.

A first work in this framework is the one by Wixson and Ballard [121] which used color to find multicolored objects with a mobile camera. The idea is to represent an object by its color histogram. The matching technique consisted in comparing ratios of peaks in the model and image histograms (it is scale invariant). It failed for uni-colored objects, and was very affected by occlusion which cuts across most of the colored regions. Another matching technique has been proposed by Swain and Ballard [109], that is histogram intersection: given a pair of histograms I and M, the intersection is defined to be: $\sum_j \min(I_j, M_j)$, where j ranges over each color in the histograms. The intersection is the number of pixels from the model that have corresponding pixels of the same color in the image. To obtain a match value between 0 and 1, it is normalized by the number of pixels in the model histogram $\sum_j M_j$. This match value has useful properties for identifying an object: it is not sensible to distractions in the background of the object, change of viewpoint, and occlusion. Another simple algorithm, histogram backprojection, enables efficient location of a known object.

3.4. *Conclusion*

Let us now examine from a global viewpoint the contribution of color to computer vision. One can consider that the goal of this field of research is to compute an intrinsic description of the environment from visual sensors outputs. Most of the effort has concentrated on low-level representations and the following themes:

- features extraction
- segmentation
- 3D reconstruction
- motion analysis
- shape representation
- object recognition.

To begin from the end, object recognition using color now seems promising, but it needs color constancy. Color is an important attribute, provided its intrinsic value can be computed. This is still the color constancy problem. We have seen that this is very difficult to achieve in real environments. Other less important features are the reflection components and the highlights. As to features and segmentations that could be obtained by monochromatic process, it seems that adding color leads to limited, however significant, improvements. They can be explained by a simple increase in available information, without a noticeable conceptual progress. These works rely mainly on colorimetry. Judicious choices of chromatic representations are useful because they determine the quality of features and segmentations. As the preprocessing can be obviously done in parallel, it can be interesting to develop real-time applications. Except for some histogramming or clustering techniques, the increase in algorithmic complexity is not very important. However, the cost of the hardware is important, and there will be some additional problems with the cameras, which are often less precise and more difficult to use. On the other hand, the use of formalizations of reflectance can enable segmentations that are physically significant, and more useful. Some convincing algorithms begin to appear.

As to purely geometric problems, like 3-D reconstruction or motion analysis, color can be considered as a mere feature, used to help the (geometric) matching process. In this case, its role can be useful thanks to its stability and its relative independence from the geometry, but it is of secondary importance as color is then used only as numerical values without direct physical significance. On the other hand, one can consider that there is an interaction between the form process and the color process. In this framework, *qualitative* progress will only result from model-based algorithms devised to recover physical and geometrical intrinsic properties. The idea to simultaneously recover shape (orientation) and reflectance (albedo) of Lambertian achromatic objects has already been thoroughly explored (shape from shading). These algorithms have always needed well-controlled experimental conditions. Mutual illumination has just begun to be studied. How do we generalize to colored objects? The first challenge is to model real environments. The second challenge for this kind of task, is the need for a form of color constancy. The problem is that the discontinuities that we want to identify (using color among other cues) are precisely what makes it difficult to work on color constancy with actual algorithms. It is only by overcoming these difficulties that the question *"What can the universal use of color be?"* will find an answer.

References

[1] M. Ali and J. Aggarwal, Automatic inspection of infrared aerial color photographs of citrus orchards having infestations of insect pests and diseases, *IEEE Trans. Geosci. Electron.* **15**, 3 (1977) 170–179.

[2] M. Ali, W. Martin and J. Aggarwal, Color-based computer analysis of aerial photographs, *Comput. Graph. Image Process.* **9** (1979) 282–293.

[3] R. Bajcsy, S. W. Lee and A. Leonardis, Color image segmentation with detection of highlights and local illumination induced by inter-reflections, in *Proc. Int. Conf. on Pattern Recognition*, Atlantic City, NJ, 1990, 785–790.

[4] P. Beckmann and A. Spizzichino, *The Scattering of Electromagnetic Waves from Rough Surfaces* (The Macmillan Company, 1963).

[5] A. Blake, Boundary conditions for lightness computation in Mondrian world, *Comput. Vision Graph. Image Process.* **32** (1985) 314–327.

[6] A. Blake, Inferring surface shape by specular stereo, in *Proc. Int. Joint Conf. on Artificial Intelligence*, Los Angeles, CA, 1985, 973–976.

[7] A. Blake and G. Brelstaff, Geometry from specularities, in *Proc. Int. Conf. on Computer Vision*, Tampa, FL, 1988, 394–403.

[8] M. Born and E. Wolf, *Principles of Optics* (Pergamon Press, 1959).

[9] T. E. Boult and L. B. Wolf, Physically-based edge labeling, in *Proc. Computer Vision and Pattern Recognition*, Maui, Hawaii, 1991, 656–662.

[10] D. H. Brainard and B. A. Wandell, Analysis of the Retinex theory of color vision, *J. Opt. Soc. Am. A* **3**, 10 (1986) 1651–1661.

[11] G. Brelstaff and A. Blake, Computing lightness, *Pattern Recogn. Lett.* **5** (1987) 129–138.

[12] G. Brelstaff and A. Blake, Detecting specular reflection using Lambertian constraints, in *Proc. Int. Conf. on Comput. Vision*, Tampa, FL, 1988, 297–302.

[13] M. H. Brill, Image segmentation by object color: A unifying framework and connection to color constancy, *J. Opt. Soc. Am. A* **7** (1990) 2041–2047.

[14] D. Brockelbank and Y. H. Yang, An experimental investigation in the use of color in computational stereopsis, *IEEE Trans. Trans. Pattern Anal. Mach. Intell.* **19**, 6 (1989) 1365–1383.

[15] G. Buchsbaum, A spatial processor model for object colour perception, *J. Franklin Inst.* **310** (1980) 1–26.

[16] M. Celenk, Color image segmentation by clustering and parametric-histogramming technique, in *Proc. IEEE Int. Conf. on Pattern Recognition*, 1986, 883–886.

[17] M. Celenk, A color clustering technique for image segmentation, *Comput. Vision Graph. Image Process.* **52** (1990) 145–170.

[18] R. R. Claxon and E. K. Kwok, The use of colour to segment and label images, in *Proc. Alvey Vision Conf.*, Cambridge, UK, 1987, 295–302.

[19] J. Cohen, Dependency of the spectral reflectance curves of the Munsell color chips, *Psychol. Sci.* **1** (1964) 369–370.

[20] M. F. Cohen and D. P. Greenberg, The hemi-cube: A radiosity solution for complex environments, in *Proc. SIGGRAPH, Comput. Graph.* **19**, 3 (1985) 31–40.

[21] G. Coleman and H. Andrews, Image segmentation by clustering, *Proc. IEEE* **67**, 5 (1979) 773–785.

[22] R. Cook, T. Porter and L. Carpenter, Distributed ray tracing, in *Proc. SIGGRAPH, Comput. Graph.* **18**, 3 (1984) 137–145.

[23] R. L. Cook and K. E. Torrance, A reflectance model for computer graphics, in *Proc. SIGGRAPH, Comput. Graph.* **15**, 3 (1981) 307–316.

[24] V. Coutance, T. Baron and M. Briot, Segmentation of color images in robotics, in *Proc. Reconnaissance des formes et intelligence artificielle*, 1989, 1115–1122.

[25] W. B Cowan, An inexpensive method for the CIE calibration of color monitors, *Comput. Graph.* **11**, 3 (1983) 314–321.

[26] M. Daily, Color image segmentation using Markov random fields, in *Proc. IEEE Conf. on Computer Vision and Pattern Recognition*, San Diego, CA, 1989, 304–312.

[27] N. W. Daw, The psychology and physiology of colour vision, *Trends in Neurosci.* **7** (1984) 330–335.

[28] R. L. De Valois, Central mechanisms of color vision, in *Handbook of Sensory Physiology*, Vol. VII/3, 1973, 209–253.

[29] S. DiZenzo, A note on the gradient of a multi-image, *Comput. Vision Graph. Image Process.* **33** (1986) 116–125.

[30] M. Drew and B. Funt, Calculating surface reflectance using a single-bounce model of mutual reflection, in *Proc. Int. Conf. on Computer Vision*, 1990, 394–399.

[31] M. D'Zmura and P. Lennie, Mechanisms of color constancy, *J. Opt. Soc. Am. A* **3**, 10 (1986) 1662–1672.

[32] O. D. Faugeras, Digital Color Image Processing and Psychophysics within the Framework of a Human Visual Model, Ph.D. thesis, Univ. of Utah, Salt Lake City, Jun. 1976.

[33] O. D. Faugeras, Digital color image processing within the framework of a human visual model, *IEEE Trans. Acoust. Speech Signal Process.* **27**, 4 (1979) 380–393.

[34] D. Forsyth, A novel algorithm for color constancy, *Int. J. Comput. Vision* **5**, 1 (1990) 5–36.

[35] D. Forsyth and A. Zissermann, Mutual illumination, in *Proc. IEEE Conf. on Computer Vision and Pattern Recognition*, San Diego, CA, 1989, 466–473.

[36] D. Forsyth and A. Zissermann, Shape from shading in the light of mutual illumination, *Image Vision Comput.* **8**, 1 (1990) 42–49.

[37] D. A. Forsyth, A system for finding changes in colour, in *Proc. Alvey Vision Conf.*, Cambridge, UK, 1987, 285–294.

[38] D. A. Forsyth, Colour Constancy and its Applications in Machine Vision, Ph.D. thesis, Univ. of Oxford, 1988.

[39] D. A. Forsyth, A novel approach to colour constancy, in *Proc. Int. Conf. on Computer Vision*, Tampa, FL, 1988, 9–18.

[40] D. A. Forsyth and A. Zissermann, Reflections on shading, *IEEE Trans. Pattern Anal. Mach. Intell.* **13**, 7 (1991) 671–679.

[41] B. Funt and M. S. Drew, Color constancy computation in near-Mondrian scenes using a finite-dimensional linear model, in *Proc. IEEE Conf. on Computer Vision and Pattern Recognition*, Ann Arbor, MI, 1988, 544–549.

[42] B. Funt and J. Ho, Color from black and white, in *Proc. Int. Conf. on Computer Vision*, Tampa, FL, 1988, 2–8.

[43] A. Gagalowicz, Collaboration between computer graphics and computer vision, in *Proc. Int. Conf. on Computer Vision*, Osaka, Japan, 1990, 733–739.

[44] E. Gamble, D. Geiger, T. Poggio and D. Weinshall, Integration of vision modules and labeling of surface discontinuities, *IEEE Trans. Syst. Man Cybern.* **19** (1989) 1576–1581.

[45] R. Gershon, The Use of Color in Computational Vision, Ph.D. thesis, Dept. of Computer Science, Univ. of Toronto, 1987.

[46] R. Gershon, A. D. Jepson and J. K. Tsostsos, Highlight identification using chromatic information, in *Proc. Int. Conf. on Computer Vision*, 1987, 161–170.

[47] T. Gevers and F. Groen, Segmentation of color images, in *Proc. SCIA*, 1991, 1170–1177.

[48] C. Goral, K. Torrance, D. Greenberg and B. Battaille, Modeling the interaction of light between diffuse surfaces, in *Proc. SIGGRAPH, Comput. Graph.* **18**, 3 (1984) 213–222.

[49] A. Gottshalk and G. Buchbaum, Information theoretic aspects of color signal processing in the visual system, *IEEE Trans. Syst. Man Cybern.* **13**, 5 (1983) 864–873.

[50] R. Haralick and L. Shapiro, Image segmentation techniques, *Comput. Vision Graph. Image Process.* **29** (1985) 100–132.

[51] G. Healey, Color discrimination by computer, *IEEE Trans Pattern Anal. Mach. Intell.* **19**, 6 (1989) 1613–1617.

[52] G. Healey, A parallel color algorithm for segmenting images of 3-D scenes, in *Proc. ARPA Image Understanding Workshop*, Palo Alto, CA, 1989, 1038–1041,

[53] G. Healey and T. O. Binford, The role and use of color in a general vision system, in *Proc. ARPA Image Understanding Workshop*, 1987, 599–613.

[54] G. Healey and T. O. Binford, A color metric for computer vision, in *Proc. IEEE Conf. on Computer Vision and Pattern Recognition*, Ann Arbor, MI, 1988, 10–17.

[55] G. Healey and T. O. Binford, Local shape from specularity, *Comput. Vision Graph. Image Process.* **42** (1988) 62–86.

[56] G. Healey and T. O. Binford, Predicting material classes, in *Proc. ARPA Image Understanding Workshop*, Cambridge, MA, 1988, 1140–1146.

[57] B. K. P. Horn, Determining lightness from an image, *Comput. Graph. Image Process.* **3** (1974) 277–299.

[58] B. K. P. Horn, Understanding image intensities, *Artif. Intell* 2, 8 (1977) 201–231.

[59] B. K. P. Horn, *Robot Vision* (MIT Press, 1986).

[60] S. L. Horowitz and T. Pavlidis, Picture segmentation by a directed split-and-merge procedure, in *Proc. 2nd Int. Joint Conf. on Pattern Recognition*, 1974, 424–433.

[61] R. W. G. Hunt, *The Reproduction of Color*, 3rd edn. (Wiley, 1975).

[62] T. L. Huntsberger and M. F. Descalzi, Color edge detection, *Pattern Recogn. Lett.* **3** (1985) 205–209.

[63] A. Hurlbert, The Computation of Color, Ph.D. thesis, MIT, AI Lab, 1989.

[64] A. Hurlbert and T. Poggio, A network for image segmentation using color, in *Proc. Denver Conf. on Neural Networks*, 1988.

[65] A. Hurlbert and T. Poggio, Synthesizing a color algorithm from examples, *Science* **239** (1988) 482–485.

[66] K. Ikeuchi and K. Sato, Determining reflectance parameters using range and brightness images, in *Proc. Int. Conf. on Computer Vision*, Osaka, Japan, 1990, 12–20.

[67] T. Jaaskelainen, J. Parkkinen and E. Oja, Color discriminaton by optical pattern recognition, in *Proc. Int. Conf. on Pattern Recognition*, Paris, France, 1986, 766–768.

[68] Y. Jang, Identification of interreflection in color images using a physics-based reflection model, in *Proc. Computer Vision and Pattern Recognition*, Maui, Hawaii, 1991, 632–637.

[69] J. Jordan and A. Bovik, Computational stereo vision using color, *IEEE Control Syst. Mag.* **8** (1988) 31–36.

[70] J. R. Jordan and A. C. Bovik, Using chromatic information in edge-based stereo correspondence, *Comput. Vision Graph. Image Process.: Image Understanding* **54**, 1 (1991) 98–118.

[71] D. Judd, D. MacAdam and G. Wyszecki, Spectral distribution of typical daylight as a function of correlated color temperature, *J. Opt. Soc. Am. A* **54** (1964) 1031–1040.

[72] D. Judd and G. Wyszecki, *Color in Business, Science and Industry* (John Wiley and Sons, 1975).

[73] T. Kanade, Image understanding research at CMU, in *Proc. ARPA Image Understanding Workshop*, Los Angeles, CA, 1987, 35–37.

[74] J. Kender, Saturation, Hue, and Normalized Color: Calculation, Digitization Effects, and Use, Master's thesis, Department of Computer Science, Carnegie-Mellon Univ., 1976.

[75] G. J. Klinker, A Physical Approach to Color Image Understanding, Ph.D. thesis, Department of Computer Science, Carnegie-Mellon Univ., 1988.

[76] G. J. Klinker, S. A. Shafer and T. Kanade, Using a color reflection model to separate highlights from object color, in *Proc. Int. Conf. on Computer Vision*, 1987, 145–150.

[77] G. J. Klinker, S. A. Shafer and T. Kanade, Color image analysis with an intrinsic reflection model, in *Proc. Int. Conf. on Computer Vision*, Tampa, FL, 1988, 292–296.

[78] G. J. Klinker, S. A. Shafer and T. Kanade, The measurement of highlights in color images, *Int. J. Comput. Vision* **2**, 1 (1988) 7–32.

[79] G. J. Klinker, S. A. Shafer and T. Kanade, A physical approach to color image understanding, *Int. J. Comput. Vision* **4**, 1 (1990) 7–38.

[80] J. Koenderink, Color atlas theory, *J. Opt. Soc. Am. A* **4**, 7 (1987) 1314–1321.

[81] E. L. Krinov, Spectral reflectance properties of natural formations, Technical Report Technical translation TT-439, National Research Council of Canada, 1947.

[82] E. Land, Color vision and the natural image, in *Proc. Nat. Acad. Sci.*, Vol. 45, 1959, 115–129, 636–645.

[83] E. H. Land, The retinex theory of color vision, *Sci. Am.* **237** (1977) 108–128.

[84] E. H. Land, Recent advances in Retinex theory, *Vision Res.* **26**, 1 (1986) 7–21.

[85] E. H. Land and J. J. McCann, Lightness and Retinex theory, *J. Opt. Soc. Am. A* **61** (1971) 1–11.

[86] H.-C. Lee, Method for computing the scene-illuminant chromaticity from specular highlights, *J. Opt. Soc. Am. A* **3**, 10 (1986) 1694–1699.

[87] H.-C. Lee, E. J. Breneman and C. P. Schulte, Modeling light reflection for computer color vision, *IEEE Trans. Pattern Anal. Mach. Intell.* **12**, 4 (1988) 402–409.

[88] M. S. Livingstone and D. H. Hubel, Anatomy and physiology of a color system in the primate visual cortex, *J. Neurosci.* **4** (1984) 309–356.

[89] L. T. Maloney, Evaluation of linear models of surface spectral reflectance with small numbers of parameters, *J. Opt. Soc. Am. A* **3**, 10 (1986) 1673–1683.

[90] L. T. Maloney and B. A. Wandell, Color constancy: a method for recovering surface spectral reflectance, *J. Opt. Soc. Am. A* **3**, 1 (1986) 29–33.

[91] J. J. McCann, S. P. McKee and T. H. Taylor, Quantitative studies in Retinex theory, *Vision Res.* **16** (1976) 445–458.

[92] S. Nayar, K. Ikeuchi and T. Kanade, Extracting shape and reflectance of hybrid surfaces by photometric sampling, in *Proc. ARPA Image Understanding Workshop*, Palo Alto, CA, 1989, 563–583.

[93] S. Nayar, K. Ikeuchi and T. Kanade, Shape from interreflections, in *Proc. Int. Conf. on Computer Vision*, Osaka, Japan, 1990, 1–11.

[94] S. K. Nayar, T. Ikeuchi and K. Kanade, Surface reflection: Physical and geometrical perspectives, *IEEE Trans. Pattern Anal. Mach. Intell.* **13**, 7 (1991) 611–634.

[95] T. Nishita and E. Nakamae, Continuous tone representation of three-dimensional objects taking account of shadows and interreflection, in *Proc. SIGGRAPH, Comput. Graph.* **19**, 3 (1985) 23–30.

[96] R. Ohlander, K. Price and D. Raj Reddy, Picture segmentation using a recursive region splitting method, *Comput. Graph. Image Process.* **8** (1978) 313–333.

[97] Y.-I. Ohta, T. Kanade and T. Sakai, Color information for region segmentation, *Comput. Graph. Image Process.* **13** (1980) 222–241.

[98] J. Parkkinen, T. Jaaskelainen and M. Kuittinen, Spectral representation of color images, in *Proc Int. Conf. on Pattern Recognition*, Rome, Italy, 1988, 933–935.

[99] B. T. Phong, Illumination for computer generated pictures, *Commun. ACM* **18** (1975) 311–317.

[100] W. Pratt, *Digital Image Processing* (John Wiley and Sons, 1978).

[101] J. Reichman, Determination of absorption and scattering coefficients for nonhomogeneous media, 1: Theory, *Appl. Opt.* **12**, 8 (1973) 1811–1815.

[102] J. M. Rubin and W. A. Richards, Color vision and image intensities: When are changes material? Technical Report AI Memo 631, AI Lab, MIT, 1981. Also *Biol. Cybern.* **45** (1982) 215–226.

[103] J. Rubner and K. Schulten, A regularized approach to color constancy, *Biol. Cybern.* **61** (1989) 29–36.

[104] A. C. Sanderson, L. E. Weiss and K. N. Nayar, Structured highlight inspection of specular surfaces, *IEEE Trans. Pattern Anal. Mach. Intell.* **10**, 1 (1988) 44–55.

[105] A. Sarabi and J. K. Aggarwal, Segmentation of chromatic images, *Pattern Recogn.* **13** (1981) 417–427.

[106] B. Schacter, L. Davis and A. Rosenfeld, Scene segmentation by cluster detection in color space, Technical Report 424, Computer Science Center, University of Maryland, 1975. Also *SIGART Newsletter* **58** (1975) 16–17.

[107] T. Stockham, Image processing in the context of a visual model, *IEEE (special issue on picture processing)* **60** (1972) 828–842.

[108] M. C. Stone, W. B. Cowan and J. C. Beatty, Color gamut mapping and the printing of digital color images, *ACM Trans. Graphics* **7**, 4 (1988) 249–292.

[109] M. Swain and D. Ballard, Indexing via color histograms, in *Proc. Int. Conf. on Computer Vision*, Osaka, Japan, 1990, 390–393. Also color indexing, *Int. J. Comput. Vision* **7**, 1 (1991) 11–32.

[110] J. Tenenbaum, T. Garvey, S. Weyl and H. Wolf, An interactive facility for scene analysis research, Technical Report 87, AIC-SRI, 1974.

[111] D. Terzopoulos, Efficient multiresolution algorithms for computing lightness, shape-from-shading, and optical flow, in *Proc. AAAI*, Austin, Texas, 1984, 314–317.

[112] C. Thorpe, T. Hebert, T. Kanade and S. A. Shafer, Vision and navigation for the Carnegie-Mellon Navlab, *IEEE Trans. Pattern Anal. Mach. Intell.* **10**, 3 (1988).

[113] S. Tominaga, A color classification method for color images using a uniform color space, in *Proc. Int. Conf. on Pattern Recognition*, Atlantic City, NJ, 1990, 803–806.

[114] S. Tominaga, Surface identification using the dichromatic reflection model, *IEEE Trans. Pattern Anal. Mach. Intell.* **13**, 7 (1991) 658–670.

[115] K. Torrance and E. Sparrow, Theory for off-specular reflection from roughened surfaces, *J. Opt. Soc. Am. A* **57** (1967) 1105–1114.

[116] M. Tsukada and Y. Ohta, An approach to color constancy using multiple images, in *Proc. Int. Conf. on Computer Vision*, Osaka, Japan, 1990, 385–389.

[117] S. Underwood and J. Aggarwal, Interactive computer analysis of aerial color infrared photographs, *Comput. Graph. Image Process.* **6** (1977) 1–24.

[118] J. R. Wallace, M. F. Cohen and D. P. Greenberg, A two-pass solution to the rendering equation: A synthesis of ray tracing and radiosity method, in *Proc. SIGGRAPH, Comput. Graph.* **21**, 4 (1987) 311–320.

[119] B. A. Wandel, The synthesis and analysis of color images, *IEEE Trans. Pattern Anal. Mach. Intell.*, **9**, 1 (1987) 2–13.

[120] C. Westelius and C. Westin, A colour representation for scale-spaces, in *Proc. Scandinavian Conf. on Image Analysis*, 1989, 890–893.

[121] L. Wixson and D. Ballard, Color histograms for real-time object search, in *Proc. SPIE Sensor Fusion II: Human and Machine Strategies Workshop*, Philadelphia, PA, 1989, 435–446.

[122] L. B. Wolf, Using polarization to separate reflections components, in *Proc. IEEE Conf. on Computer Vision and Pattern Recognition*, San Diego, CA, 1989, 363–369.

[123] L. B. Wolf, Polarization-based material classification from specular reflection, *IEEE Trans. Pattern Anal. Mach. Intell.* **12**, 11 (1990) 1059–1071.

[124] L. Wolff, Using polarisation to separate reflection components, in *Proc. IEEE Conf. on Computer Vision and Pattern Recognition*, San Diego, CA, 1989, 363–369.

[125] W. A. Wright, A Markov random field approach to data fusion and colour segmentation, *Image Vision Comput.* **7**, 2 (1989) 144–150.

[126] G. Wyszecki and W. S. Stiles, *Color Science, Concepts and Methods, Quantitative Data and Formulas* (John Wiley and Sons, 1967).

[127] A. Yuille, A method for computing spectral reflectance, *Biol. Cybern.* **56** (1987) 195–201.

[128] S. Zeki, The representation of colours in the cerebral cortex, *Nature* **284** (1980) 412–418.

[129] A. Zisserman, P. Giblin and A. Blake, The information available to a moving observer from specularities, *Image Vision Comput.* **7**, 1 (1989) 38–42.

Handbook of Pattern Recognition and Computer Vision, pp. 369–393
Eds. C. H. Chen, L. F. Pau and P. S. P. Wang
© 1993 World Scientific Publishing Company

CHAPTER 2.4

PROJECTIVE GEOMETRY AND COMPUTER VISION

ROGER MOHR

*Lifia–Irimag, 46 Av. Félix Viallet
38031 Grenoble Cedex, France*

This chapter surveys the contributions of projective geometry to computer vision. Projective geometry deals elegantly with the general case of perspective projection and therefore provides interesting understanding of the geometric aspect of image formation. It also provides useful tools like perspective invariants. First the major definitions and results of this geometry are presented. Applications are then provided for several domains of 3-D computer vision, including location of the viewer for uncalibrated cameras, properties of epipolar lines in stereovision and object recognition.

Keywords: 3-D vision, geometry, stereovision, invariant.

1. Introduction

The objectives of this chapter are to provide the reader with the geometric background which will enable him to understand the imaging system and to derive tools for working in 3-D vision. Here we consider the image formation system to be a pure perspective projection, i.e. the camera model we adopt is the pin-hole model. This is a good approximation of existing image acquisition systems. Sometimes this model has to be corrected by using radial corrections [1], and the photogrammetrists use even more sophisticated corrections [2]. It has to be mentioned that these last models mainly correct the image in order to simulate the pure pin-hole model.

Therefore the properties of central projection have to be studied. This will be done in Section 2 for general geometrical consideration, and in Section 3 for the camera calibration problem. Applications to 3-D vision problems will then follow in Sections 4, 5 and 6.

Larger developments of what is presented here can be found in the book [3] and for the particular case of invariants in [4].

1.1. *Some Historical Considerations*

The ancient Greek school of mathematicians already knew some mathematical properties of the projections. Using Thales' theorem (600 BC) they were able to prove that the cross ratio of four points on a line remains invariant after a perspective projection (see Fig. 2). In fact the cross ratio is the key invariant in projective geometry as we will see in Section 6. It is not clear when this result was established, but Appolonius of Perga (200 BC) was already using it.

The Italian painters of the Renaissance in the 16th century mainly studied the properties of geometry in order to reproduce correctly on their pictures the projection of the three-dimensional world they were observing. They made large use of the vanishing points, and derived some geometric construction techniques for their practical use, as for instance how to split a projected square into four equal subsquares, or how to find the projection of the corner of a parallelogram when the projection of two side surfaces are known.

Photography was discovered in France in 1839 (Nièpce, Daguerre, Arago). At the same period of time, people studied independently how to make measurements using perspective drawings of scenes. The meeting of the two techniques led naturally towards photogrammetry. The mathematician Lambert headed a committee stemming from Académie des Sciences de Paris for studying how three-dimensional measures could be made using two photographs (1859). From there Europe became a place of active development, particularly in Austria and Germany. Meydenbauer is considered as the one who got the first successful results and opened up the wide area of photogrammetry applications.

During the same century, the mathematicians developed a new kind of geometry which was able to deal with points at infinity and perspective projections, i.e. projective geometry. This study was almost completed at the beginning of the 20th century and it is now no longer considered as an investigation domain for mathematicians. However the 20th century mathematical contribution was to present it in a very clear algebraic way which can now be read in the excellent book by Semple and Kneebone [5].

1.2. *What the Chapter is About*

All of us have experienced, when looking at the image of a straight road, the feeling that the parallel borders meet at "the end of the road" (see Fig. 1). Walking outside in the night, we can also observe that the moon follows us, i.e. being far enough, its position in our coordinate frame is not modified by our limited translation. These are some of the properties of the strange world of projective geometry that we are going to address. Other differences are that the lengths and even the ratios of length are not preserved.

Our goal will be to explore what remains invariant with perspective projections, and what are the properties that can be computed in order to provide quantitative information for computer vision. As we shall see, the underlying mathematics are easy enough to do symbolic computation, from which can be derived also qualitative results.

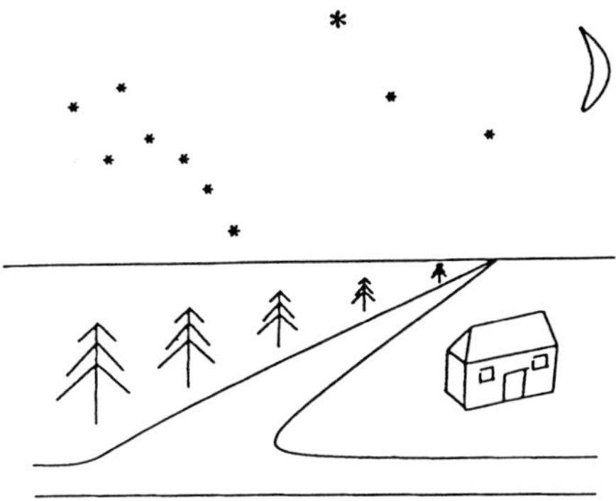

Fig. 1. Infinity points may be very present in perspective projection.

So after a first section on basic results and notations, we will show how they can be used to solve some 3-D vision problems. First we will discuss the geometry of a stereovision system. In Section 5, 3-D positioning from images is investigated and finally a short presentation of how projective invariants can be used for object recognition is given in Section 6.

2. A Few Results from Projective Geometry

2.1. *Preliminary Definitions*

We provide here a short introduction to projective geometry definitions and vocabulary. The reader is referred to [5] for a gentle introduction or to [6] for advanced vision-oriented considerations on projective geometry. A new book [3] covers parts of what is presented here and presents many other geometric considerations on vision.

We consider the $n+1$ dimensional space $\mathcal{R}^{n+1} - \{(0, \ldots, 0)\}$ with the equivalence relation:

$$(x_1, \ldots, x_{n+1}) \sim (x_1', \ldots, x_{n+1}') \text{ iff}$$
$$\exists \lambda \neq 0 \text{ such that } (x_1', \ldots, x_{n+1}') = \lambda(x_1, \ldots, x_{n+1}). \tag{2.1}$$

The quotient space obtained from this equivalence relation is the projective space $\mathcal{P}^n$. Thus the $(n+1)$-tuples of coordinates $(x_1, \ldots, x_{n+1})$ and $(x_1', \ldots, x_{n+1}')$ represent the same point in the projective space.

The usual n-dimensional affine space $\mathcal{R}^n$ is mapped into $\mathcal{P}^n$ by the correspondence Ψ:

$$\Psi \; : \; (x_1, \ldots, x_n) \rightarrow (x_1, \ldots, x_n, 1). \tag{2.2}$$

Notice that Ψ is a one-to-one mapping and that only the points represented by $(x_1, \ldots, x_n, 0)$ are not reached. Ψ provides us with an understanding for the points

$(x_1, \ldots, x_n, 1)$, which caan be viewed as the usual points in the Euclidean space; it also provides us an intuitive understanding for the remaining points, if we consider $(y_1, \ldots, y_n, 0)$ as the limit of $(y_1, \ldots, y_n, \lambda)$ while $\lambda \to 0$, i.e. the limit of $\sim (y_1/\lambda, \ldots, y_n/\lambda, 1)$. This is the limit of a point in $\mathcal{R}^n$ going to infinity in the direction $(y_1, \ldots, y_n)$. Therefore we will consider in the remainder $(y_1, \ldots, y_n, 0)$ as the point at infinity in this direction.

A hyperplane H in $\mathcal{P}^n$ is defined by the $n+1$-tuple of its homogeneous coefficients $H = (a_1, \ldots, a_{n+1})$. It defines the set of points whose coordinates satisfy

$$\sum_{1}^{n+1} a_i x_i = HX^t = 0 \,.$$

A particular case is the hyperplane $x_{n+1} = 0$: this is the hyperplane with all points at infinity.

A *collineation* or projective transformation is any mapping from $\mathcal{P}^n$ into $\mathcal{P}^n$ defined by a regular $(n+1) \times (n+1)$ matrix $\mathbf{A}$ such that the image of $(x_1, \ldots, x_{n+1})$ is defined in the usual way by:

$$\begin{pmatrix} y_1 \\ \ldots \\ y_{n+1} \end{pmatrix} = \mathbf{A} \begin{pmatrix} x_1 \\ \ldots \\ x_{n+1} \end{pmatrix} \,.$$

Notice that as the column vector is defined up to a scaling factor, so is the matrix $\mathbf{A}$. Collineations map hyperplanes on hyperplanes and therefore lines on lines. If B is the scalar vector defining a projective hyperplane, i.e. the set of points X such that $B^t \cdot X = 0$, the image of this hyperplane is defined by $\mathbf{A}^{-1^t} \cdot B$ where $\mathbf{M}^t$ denotes the transpose of $\mathbf{M}$.

A *basis* of the projective space $\mathcal{P}^n$ is given by $n + 2$ points, with no $n + 1$ of them lying in the same hyperplane. The canonical basis usually chosen is $(1, 0, \ldots, 0), \ldots, (0, 0, \ldots, 0, 1)$ augmented with the "unity point" $(1, 1, \ldots, 1)$. For the regular 3-D projective spaces, these four first points are respectively the point at infinity on the x-axis, on the y-axis, on the z-axis and the origin. It has to be mentioned that a collineation has $(n + 1) \times (n + 1) - 1$ degrees of freedom. Knowing the image of each point of the basis provides us with $n + 1$ equations up to a scaling factor, i.e. only n independent equations. So for $n + 2$ points in the basis, this provides us with $n^2 + 2n$ equations, exactly the number of unknowns for the collineation matrix. For a proof of the uniqueness of the solution, see [5].

Standard *affine transformation* maps easily into projective transformation. For instance in the 3-D space the translation by the vector (a, b, c), is extended in $\mathcal{P}^3$ by the collineation defined by the matrix

$$\begin{pmatrix} 1 & 0 & 0 & a \\ 0 & 1 & 0 & b \\ 0 & 0 & 1 & c \\ 0 & 0 & 0 & 1 \end{pmatrix} \,.$$

In the general case an affine transformation in $\mathcal{R}^3$ is defined by a translation $t = (a, b, c)$, and a linear 3×3 matrix $\mathbf{M}$ in the vectorial 3-D space. The associated collineation is then defined by its matrix:

$$\begin{pmatrix} \mathbf{M} & t^t \\ 0\,0\,0 & 1 \end{pmatrix}.$$

Notice in such a case that each point at infinity is mapped onto a point at infinity. Reversely all the collineations mapping the infinity points on infinity points are affine transformations.

2.2. *The Basic Projective Invariant*

The cross ratio is the basic invariant in projective geometry: all other projective invariants can be derived from it [7].

Theorem 1. Let A, B, C, D be four collinear points; their cross ratio defined as:

$$[A, B; C, D] = \frac{\overline{AC}}{\overline{AD}} \times \frac{\overline{BD}}{\overline{BC}}, \tag{2.3}$$

is invariant under any collineation.

The notation $\overline{AC}$ stands for the algebraic measure of the segment AC. This result was already established by the ancient Greek mathematicians. It can be extended in the projective space by using the following computation rules which deal with infinity:

$$\frac{\infty}{\infty} = 1, \quad \frac{a}{\infty} = 0, \quad \frac{\infty}{a} = \infty.$$

The cross ratio $[A, B; C, D]$ does not rely on the choice of the unity vector taken on the line; in fact, changing the origin and the unity vector is just an affine transformation on this line. It is often easier to take barycentric coordinates, that is considering each point as row vector of dimension $n + 1$ we can write:

$$\begin{aligned} C &= A + \lambda_C B \\ D &= A + \lambda_D B \\ A &= A + 0 \times B & &: \lambda_A = 0 \\ B &= \lim_{\lambda_B \to \infty} A + \lambda_B B & &: \lambda_A = \infty \end{aligned} \tag{2.4}$$

and the cross ratio (2.3) is then rewritten:

$$\frac{\lambda_C - 0}{\lambda_D - 0} \times \frac{\lambda_D - \infty}{\lambda_C - \infty} = \frac{\lambda_C}{\lambda_D}. \tag{2.5}$$

This theorem has an immediate application for locating a point on a line. Knowing three points, the position of the fourth one is uniquely defined by the cross ratio of these four points. So three points are a projective basis for the projective line.

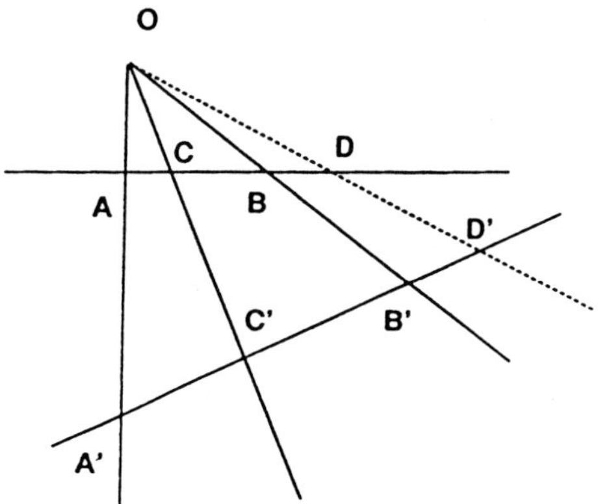

Fig. 2. Cross ratio of a pencil of lines.

Let us now consider a pencil of four lines $L_i, i = 1, \ldots, 4$ (see Fig. 2). Let A, B, C, D be the intersection of this pencil with a first line L and A', B', C', D' be the intersection with a second line L'. The central projection mapping from A onto A' is a projective mapping and therefore the cross ratios are the same:

$$[A, B; C, D] = [A', B'; C', D'].$$

Therefore the cross ratio of a pencil of lines can be defined as:

$$[L_1, L_2; L_3, L_4] = [A, B; C, D].$$

A more geometric proof can be established considering only the magnitude of segment lengths and using standard Euclidean relations on triangles; it is proved that (see [5]):

$$\frac{\overline{AC}}{\overline{AD}} \times \frac{\overline{BD}}{\overline{BC}} = \frac{\sin(OA, OC)}{\sin(OA, OD)} \times \frac{\sin(OB, OD)}{\sin(OAB, OD)}. \tag{2.6}$$

Such a ratio is obviously not related to the secant line.

Computing the cross ratio of a pencil of lines in the way suggested by this theorem is tedious. It is generally preferred to compute it using the following theorem.

Theorem 2. Let O be the origin of a pencil of lines L_1, L_2, L_3, L_4. Let A_i be points on L_i, $A_i \neq O$. Then

$$[L_1, L_2; L_3, L_4] = \frac{|OA_1A_3|}{|OA_1A_4|} \times \frac{|OA_2A_4|}{|OA_2A_3|}.$$

where $|OA_iA_j|$ stands for the determinant of the 3×3 matrix where each column is the column of homogeneous coordinates of the points O, A_i, A_j.

Proof. ($\square$. Old known result) If $(a,b), (x,y)$ and (u,v) are the coordinates of O, A_i and A_j we have:

$$\begin{vmatrix} a & x & u \\ b & y & v \\ 1 & 1 & 1 \end{vmatrix} = \begin{vmatrix} a & x-a & u-a \\ b & y-b & v-b \\ 1 & 0 & 0 \end{vmatrix} = \vec{OA_i} \times \vec{OA_j} \,.$$

It is straightforward to see that $\mid OA_iA_j \mid$ is equal to the cross product $\vec{OA_i} \times \vec{OA_j}$, up to a scaling factor which disappears in the cross ratio.

The cross product is twice the algebraic measure of the triangle associated with the two vectors and therefore the previous cross ratio is equal to a cross ratio of areas, and therefore of sines as the lengths of the sides simplify in the ratio:

$$\frac{\mid OA_1A_3 \mid}{\mid OA_1A_4 \mid} \times \frac{\mid OA_2A_4 \mid}{\mid OA_2A_3 \mid} = \frac{\sin(OA_1, OA_3)}{\sin(OA_1, OA_4)} \times \frac{\sin(OA_2, OA_4)}{\sin(OA_2, OA_3)}$$

which, using (2.6) leads to the final result.

2.3. *Projective Coordinates*

We already mentioned that if three points A, B, C lie on a line, each point D of L is uniquely defined by the cross-ratio $[A, B; C, D]$. So this cross ratio is the projective coordinate for D with respect to the basis (A, B, C).

In a projective plane $\mathcal{P}^2$, any four points A, B, C, D (no three are collinear), define a projective coordinates system (see Fig. 3). Given a point P of $\mathcal{P}^2$, let (x_1, x_2, x_3) be a triplet of real numbers defined up to a scaling factor, and such that

$$\frac{x_1}{x_2} = [CA, CB; CD, CP] \tag{2.7}$$

$$\frac{x_2}{x_3} = [AB, AC; AD, AP] \,. \tag{2.8}$$

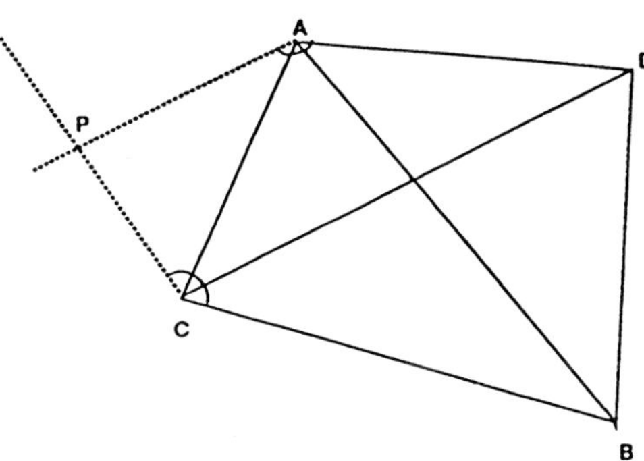

Fig. 3. Projective coordinates in the plane.

$(x_1,\ x_2,\ x_3)$ are called the projective coordinates of P in the coordinate system $(A,\ B,\ C,\ D)$. Naturally we also have $x_3/x_1 = [BC,\ BA;\ BD,\ BP]$.

In a projective plane with four known points we can uniquely reference any point of the plane by their projective coordinates so defined. In fact only the two cross ratios $k_1 = x_1/x_2$ and $k_2 = x_2/x_3$ are necessary to uniquely define a point as long as this point does not lie on the line AC.

2.4. *Cross Ratio and Conics*

We consider here the projective plane $\mathcal{P}^2$. The general equation for a conic is the second degree homogeneous polynomial

$$a_{11}x_1^2 + a_{22}x_2^2 + a_{33}x_3^2 + a_{12}x_1x_2 + a_{13}x_1x_3 + a_{23}x_2x_3 = 0 \tag{2.9}$$

which can be rewritten

$$\begin{aligned}
&a_{11}x_1^2 + a'_{12}x_1x_2 + a'_{13}x_1x_3 + a'_{21}x_2x_1 + a_{22}x_2^2 + a'_{23}x_2x_3 \\
&+ a'_{31}x_3x_1 + a'_{32}x_3x_2 + a_{33}x_3^2 = 0\,.
\end{aligned} \tag{2.10}$$

Equation (2.10) can be written as a matrix product

$$X\mathbf{A}X^t = 0$$

with $\mathbf{A}$ being a 3×3 symmetrical homogeneous matrix; its degree of freedom is therefore 5.

Theorem 3. [Chasles] In the projective plane, let A, B, C, D be four points, no three of them being collinear. The locus of the center of a pencil of a line passing through these four points and having a given cross ratio is a conic. Reciprocally, if M lies on a conic passing through A, B, C and D, the cross ratio of the four lines MA, MB, MC, MD is independent of the point M on the conic.

Figure 4 illustrates this result: if P and Q are two points on a conic, we have

$$[PA,\ PB;\ PC,\ PD] = [QA,\ QB;\ QC,\ QD]\,.$$

This conic can easily be derived from the data. Let L_{AB} be the first degree polynomial equation of the line going through A and B:

$$L_{AB} = (x_A - x)(y_A - y_B) - (y_A - y)(x_A - x_B)\,.$$

Notice then that

$$C_\lambda = \lambda L_{AB}L_{CD} + (1-\lambda)L_{AC}L_{BD} \tag{2.11}$$

defines a second degree polynomial in x and y which has A, B, C and D as roots. C_λ defines exactly the family of conics passing through these four points. A direct computation proves that C_k is Chasles' conic for the cross ratio k.

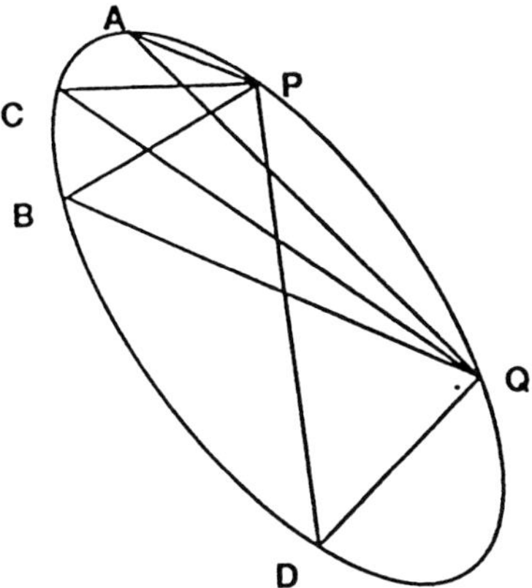

Fig. 4. Invariance of cross ratio on a conic.

3. Camera Calibration

"Camera calibration" is the process of computing the projective mapping (i.e. a 3×4 homogeneous matrix) from the 3-D space onto the image. Once the camera parameters are known, the problem of the 3-D reconstruction becomes much easier (see for instance [8,9,10] for recent contributions).

Notice that each 3-D point with coordinates $X = (X_1, X_2, X_3, 1)$ projects in the image on a point $x = (\lambda x_1, \lambda x_2, \lambda)$. The projection matrix $\mathbf{M} = (m_{ij})$ is defined up to a scaling factor and this leads to the following two equations:

$$
\begin{aligned}
x_1 &= \frac{m_{11}X_1 + m_{12}X_2 + m_{13}X_3 + m_{14}}{m_{31}X_3 + m_{32}X_2 + m_{33}X_3 + m_{34}} \\[2mm]
x_2 &= \frac{m_{12}X_1 + m_{22}X_2 + m_{23}X_3 + m_{24}}{m_{31}X_3 + m_{32}X_2 + m_{33}X_3 + m_{34}} .
\end{aligned}
\tag{3.1}
$$

So if $\mathbf{M}$ is known, the image point provides us with the view line defined by the two linear equations (3.1) in the space coordinates. On the other side, when a calibration point is known with its image, it provides us with two linear equations relating the camera parameters. There are 12 unknowns up to a scaling factor, and therefore the degree of freedom is 11. So at least 11 independent equations are needed, i.e. at least six calibration points.

Notice that finding $\mathbf{M}$ is a linear problem and therefore it can be easily approached with standard least squares methods using redundant data in order to correct by measure noise.

It is often proposed to use methods that separate what are called the intrinsic or interior parameters which depend only on the camera from the parameters

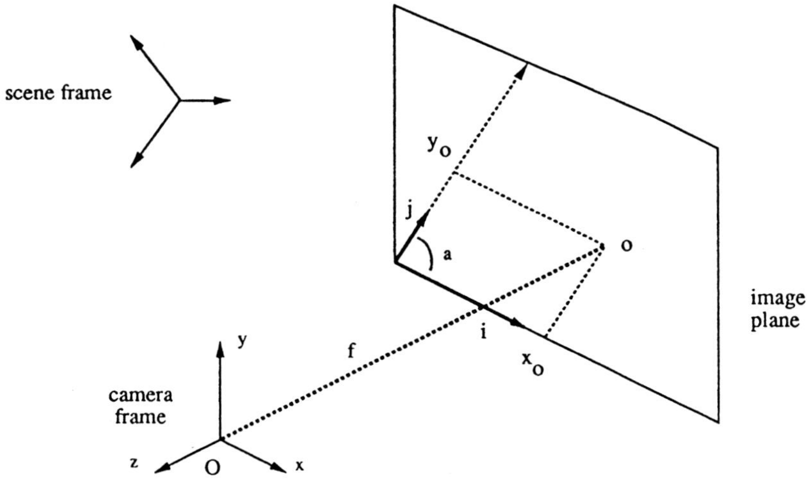

Fig. 5. The intrinsic or interior parameters.

which depend only on position; the latter are therefore called extrinsic or exterior parameters. The first terminology comes from the computer vision community (see for instance [11] or [12], but the second is more than 50 years old and comes from photogrammetrists.

Figure 5 depicts the standard reference frame for a pure perspective imaging system. The image plane has its own reference frame $(\vec{\imath}, \vec{\jmath})$. The image plane is at a distance f from the principal point O. f is called the principal axis distance, but also sometimes improperly called focal length. O is the origin of the camera reference frame $(\vec{x}, \vec{y}, \vec{z})$, which is oriented as in the figure.

If the 3-D word reference frame coincides with the camera frame and if the camera coordinate axis $(\vec{x}, \vec{y})$ is parallel to the axis of the image frame, the perspective projection matrix $\mathbf{P}$ can be written as:

$$\mathbf{P} = \begin{pmatrix} k_x & 0 & u_0 & 0 \\ 0 & k_y & v_0 & 0 \\ 0 & 0 & 1 & 0 \end{pmatrix} .$$

k_x and k_y are the scaling factor; they rely on the value of f and on the image scaling factor on each image axis. u_0 and v_0 are the coordinates of the projection of the optical center onto the image plane. It has to be noted that if the image frame is not orthogonal as it is in Fig. 5, the total number of these camera parameters are then five: u_0, v_0, k_x, k_y and the angle a. So if we add the six degrees of freedom for the three-dimensional positioning of this camera frame in a world frame, we reach the total number of 11 degrees of freedom for the camera, which is to be related to the 11 degrees of freedom of a projective transformation from $\mathcal{P}^3$ on $\mathcal{P}^2$.

The general projection matrix $\mathbf{P}'$ can be written as the product of a Euclidean transformation with the projection matrix $\mathbf{P}$, the Euclidean transformation mapping the world coordinate frame in the camera coordinate frame:

$$\mathbf{P}' = \begin{pmatrix} k_x & 0 & u_0 & 0 \\ 0 & k_y & v_0 & 0 \\ 0 & 0 & 1 & 0 \end{pmatrix} \times \begin{pmatrix} R & T^t \\ 0\,0\,0 & 1 \end{pmatrix}. \tag{3.2}$$

Given an estimation for $\mathbf{P}'$, the computation of the estimation for $\mathbf{P}$ and for the rotation $\mathbf{R}$ and translation T satisfying (3.2) is a less easy and stable problem. References [11] or [12] provide solutions and other new methods have been developed using for instance the properties of vanishing points [13]. It has to be pointed out that, even in the case of a moving camera, such a decomposition is unnecessary. For instance if the camera is calibrated in two positions with the resulting projection matrices $\mathbf{P}'$ and $\mathbf{P}''$, the matrix associated to the motion to be estimated is just a rotation and translation matrix $\mathbf{M}$ containing a rotational orthogonal matrix $\mathbf{R}$ and a translation T such that

$$\mathbf{P}'' = \mathbf{P}' \times \begin{pmatrix} \mathbf{R} & T^t \\ 0\,0\,0 & 1 \end{pmatrix}.$$

4. Application to Stereovision

As it was presented in the previous section, a point in a image corresponds to a line in the space, and this line in completely determined if the system is calibrated. Let us now consider the case of two cameras observing the same scene. If we are able to find the projection in the two images of a 3-D point M, then its position in space is simply defined by the intersection of the two lines associated with each image. Usually such an intersection is computed using least square methods, as errors are always introduced in all the steps of the process: calibration, image acquisition, image point determination.

Stereovision thus implies several steps:
- camera calibration,
- determination of points correspondence from one image to the other,
- 3-D reconstruction.

The reader is referred to books concerned with the subject like the one describing the pioneer work of Marr and Grimson [14] or the book written by Ayache where he describes the use of three cameras [15].

4.1. *The Epipolar Geometry*

We only address here the problem of the geometry of such a stereoscopic system. Figure 6 displays the configuration. The 3-D point M observed by the two cameras defines a plane which intersects the image planes respectively by line l and l'. Notice that when M moves, all these lines l pass through the intersection of the

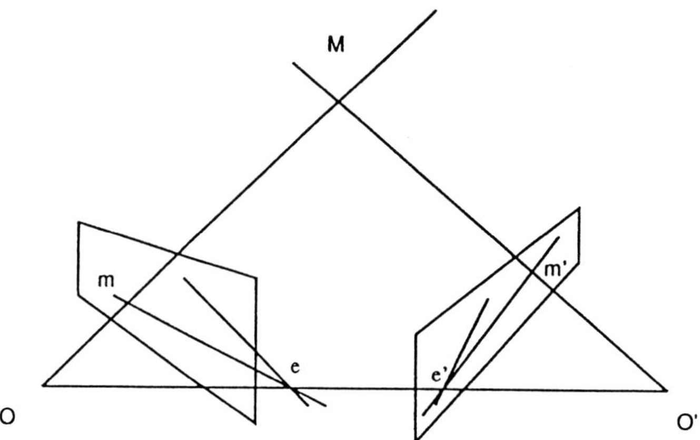

Fig. 6. Epipolar lines for two images.

image plane P and the intersection of the line OO'. This point e is called the epipole of image 1 with respect to image 2. Similarly, e' is the epipole of image 2 with respect to image 1. l and l' are the corresponding epipolar lines for these two images.

Let m and m' be the projection of M on each image. It has to be noticed that the line Om is projected on image 2 as the line l', so each possible point m' corresponding to the projection m of M has to be on the epipolar line l' associated to l. Such a geometrical constraint reduces nicely the search for corresponding matches in the two images.

Consider now the two pencils of epipolar lines when M moves through the space. Let us consider four points M_i providing four distinct corresponding epipolar lines l_i and l'_i. As these pencils are obtained by the intersection of the pencil of planes passing through OO', their cross ratios are the same; in fact this cross ratio is by definition the cross ratio of the pencil of planes. Therefore the pencil of the corresponding epipolar lines are in a projective correspondence. In conclusion, if three of the corresponding epipolar lines are known, the epipolar line correspondence for a fourth line is deduced in a straightforward manner from the cross ratio of the four lines in the pencil.

The problem of epipolar geometry has seven degrees of freedom: 2 x 2 for the coordinates of the epipoles e and e', and three for the three epipolar lines in the second image corresponding to three arbitrarily epipolar lines going through e in the first image. So, the correspondence of between seven points in the two images is enough for defining the epipolar geometry. How it can be done effectively was recently established by Maybank and Faugeras [16].

4.2. *A Linear Computation of the Epipolar Geometry [3]*

In the case of eight point matches between the two images, the computation of the epipolar geometry becomes much simpler. This elegant construction is inspired by [17]. Let $m = (x, y, t)$ be a point in the first image and let $e = (u, v, w)$ be the epipole point with respect to image 2. The three homogeneous coordinates (a, b, c) of the epipolar line l going through e and m are $m \times e$ where $\times$ denotes the cross product: obviously $l.m^t = l.e^t = 0$. The mapping $m = (x, y, z)^t \longrightarrow m \times e = (a, b, c)^t$ is linear and can be represented by a matrix $\mathbf{C}$ of rank 2:

$$\begin{pmatrix} a \\ b \\ c \end{pmatrix} = \begin{pmatrix} yw - zv \\ zu - xw \\ xv - yu \end{pmatrix} = \begin{pmatrix} 0 & w & -z \\ -w & 0 & u \\ z & -u & 0 \end{pmatrix} \begin{pmatrix} x \\ y \\ z \end{pmatrix} . \tag{4.1}$$

The mapping of each epipolar line l from image 1 to its corresponding epipolar line l' in image 2 is a collineation defined in the dual space of lines in $\mathcal{P}^2$. Let $\mathbf{A}$ be one such collineation: $l'^t = \mathbf{A} l^t$.

$\mathbf{A}$ is defined by the correspondence of three distinct epipolar lines. The first two correspondences provide four constraints as the degree of freedom of a line is 2. As the third line in correspondence belongs to the pencils defined by the two first ones, the third correspondence only adds one more constraint. So $\mathbf{A}$ only has five constraints for eight degrees of freedom.

Let $\mathbf{E} = \mathbf{AC}$. Using (4.1) we get

$$l'^t = \mathbf{A} \cdot \mathbf{C}.m^t \tag{4.2}$$

As $\mathbf{A}$ has rank 3 and $\mathbf{C}$ has rank 2, $\mathbf{E}$ has rank 2. As the kernel of $\mathbf{C}$ is obviously $\lambda e \sim e$, the epipole is the kernel of $\mathbf{E}$.

Let m' be the corresponding point of m. Using (4.1) the epipolar constraint $m'l'^t = 0$ can be rewritten $m'\mathbf{E}m = 0$. So each matching between the two images provides a constraint on $\mathbf{E}$, and as $\mathbf{E}$ is defined up to a scaling factor, eight independent constraints will allow us to linearly compute $\mathbf{E}$ and therefore get the epipolar geometry. Notice that $\mathbf{E}$ is defined by seven degrees of freedom: $\mathbf{C}$ has two (the epipole position) and $\mathbf{A}$ has five. But allowing a redundant set of constraints provides a unique solution which can be linearly computed.

4.3. *Bringing Epipolar Lines in Parallel: Image Rectification*

A visually interesting case occurs when two image planes are parallel: the epipoles are at infinity and the epipolar lines are therefore parallel. Many people working in computer vision use image planes which are the same for the two images, which is an even stronger constraint than parallelism. This makes computation a bit simpler, but adds an unnecessary technical constraint to the vision system. As these constraints are hardly satisfied with the needed precision, this has to be avoided for real applications where the goal is precision in reconstruction.

If parallel epipolar lines are wanted for easy human visual matching, one would prefer the following method:
- calibration of the stereovision system,
- computation of the epipoles,
- computation of the image transformation which provides parallel epipolar lines,
- reconstruction of all the image features after such a transformation.

The transformation computation is easy (see [15] for another explanation and illustration). Let $e = (a, b, 1)^t$ be the epipole of the first image. We have to find a projective mapping which sends e to infinity along the image $\vec{x}$ axis, i.e. a 3×3 homogeneous matrix $\mathbf{A}$ such that

$$\begin{pmatrix} 1 \\ 0 \\ 0 \end{pmatrix} = \mathbf{A} \begin{pmatrix} a \\ b \\ 1 \end{pmatrix} .$$

The images of four points completely define $\mathbf{A}$. As only one is presently set, we can add some more constraints, for instance leave three of the four corners of the image invariants. Such a choice allows the features to move not too far out of the image border lines.

The same process can then be applied on the second image. However people prefer to have the epipolar not only parallel to the $\vec{x}$ axis, but also that the corresponding epipolar line have the same coordinates. Therefore we chose three epipolar lines in the first rectified image, each having the equation $y = y_i$. On the corresponding epipolar lines on image 2 three points can be chosen and their image specified with coordinates (x_i, y_i), where the x_i are arbitrarily chosen. This allows enough freedom to have the rectified second image with reasonable coordinates.

Figure 7 displays such rectified images. It is interesting to notice that such rectifications were already done optically with old photogrammetrist material a hundred years ago: as a perspective projection is just the general case of a projective transformation, this was done by choosing interactively a new projection of the previous image.

4.4. *The Transfer Problem*

Having located a 3-D point in two images, the transfer problem is to determine how it can be located in a third one. In order to solve it, we need some knowledge of the three images, and here we assumed that we have the matches of several features within the three images. Computing the epipolar geometry of the imaging systems provides a direct solution. Let p_i be the location of the considered point in image i. p_1 and p_2 are already located. So p_3 has to be on the epipolar line corresponding to p_1 in image 3, and on the epipolar line corresponding to p_2. Thus it lies at their intersection. This fact is widely used in trinocular stereovision [15].

The fact that epipolar geometry can be computed with at least seven point matches was already mentioned in the previous subsection. However a simple case

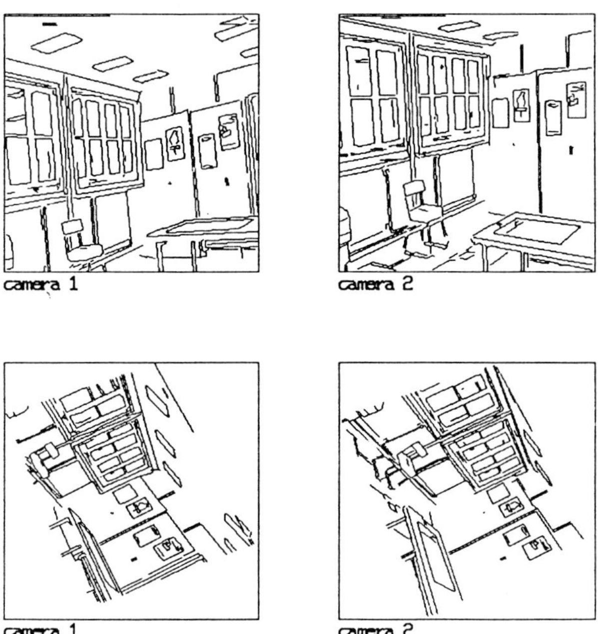

Fig. 7. Rectification of two stereo images. The corresponding epipolar lines are now horizontal lines with equal coordinates (courtesy of N. Ayache).

can be considered here when only six such matches are known, in the three images, and four of these points correspond to coplanar 3-D points.

In what remains in this section we suppose that we shall never encounter degenerate cases (for instance two lines coinciding instead of the general case of two different lines). Let A, B, C, D be the four coplanar 3-D points and F, G the two remaining reference points. O_i, $i = 1, 2, 3$ are the principal points of each of the three imaging systems we consider. a', a'', a''' are the projections of A in the images 1, 2, 3. The intersection F' of the view line $O_1 F$ with the plane $ABCD$ is defined by its projective coordinates measured in image 1, taking the projections a', b', c', d' as reference frame (see Fig. 8).

Now consider image 2. Using a'', b'', c'', d'' and the projective coordinate of F', we can locate its projection ϕ in the second image. As we also have the image f'' of F, we have therefore in image 2 the projection of two points from the line $O_1 F$, i.e. we have the epipolar line associated with F (see Fig. 8).

If we proceed similarly with G, the intersection of these two epipolar lines provides the epipole e_{12} of image 2 with respect to image 1. Of course the process is symmetrical and allows us to find the epipole e_{21} of image 1 with respect to image 2. Three epipolar lines are needed to complete the epipolar correspondence: using the

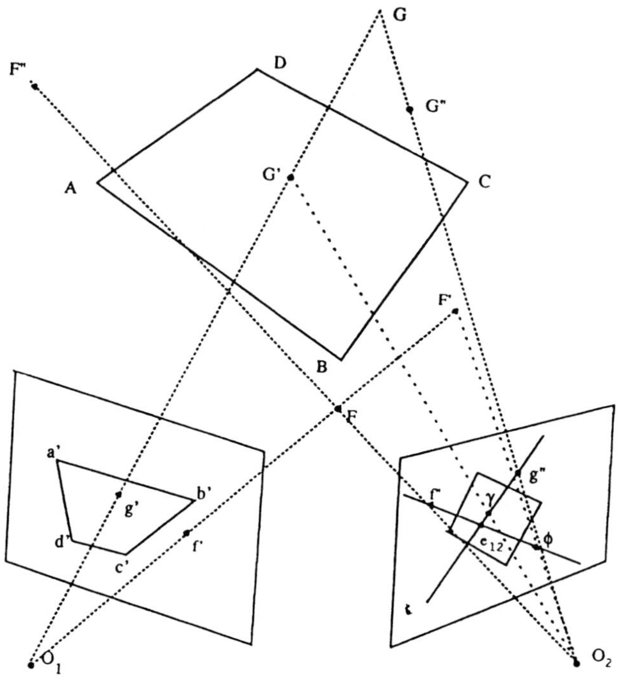

Fig. 8. Reconstruction of the epipolar geometry.

reference point matches we have plenty of them: $e_{21}a_1$ with $e_{12}a_2$, $e_{21}b_1$ with $e_{12}b_2$, and so on.

Now consider the third image. From the epipolar geometry the position of each point matched in the two first images is straightforward. Using the previous construction, the epipolar geometry between images 1 and 3 and between images 2 and 3 is constructed, and the epipolar lines corresponding to the location of the point in images 1 and 2 intersects in only one possible position.

5. Application to 3-D Positioning

5.1. *Relative Positioning*

Let us consider first the simple case of four points P_i lying on a line and viewed on an image where we can compute the cross ratio. We know that the fourth point is uniquely defined from the position of the first three and from the computed cross ratio. So, taking the first point as the origin, the position of the fourth point can be expressed, using as parameters the position of the second one and the third one, and using the cross ratio. The resulting expression is

$$k = \frac{\overline{P_1 P_3}}{\overline{P_1 P_4}} \times \frac{\overline{P_2 P_4}}{\overline{P_2 P_3}} \implies \overline{P_1 P_4} = \frac{\overline{P_1 P_2} \cdot \overline{P_1 P_3}}{\overline{P_1 P_3} - k\overline{P_2 P_3}}. \tag{5.1}$$

This simple example shows how relative positioning is possible. Similar construction can be done in the plane using the projective coordinates defined by the cross ratios (2.7) and (2.8). In the more simple case when the four points are the vertices of a parallelogram, the relation simplifies as we can easily choose two sides as reference axis (see Fig. 9).

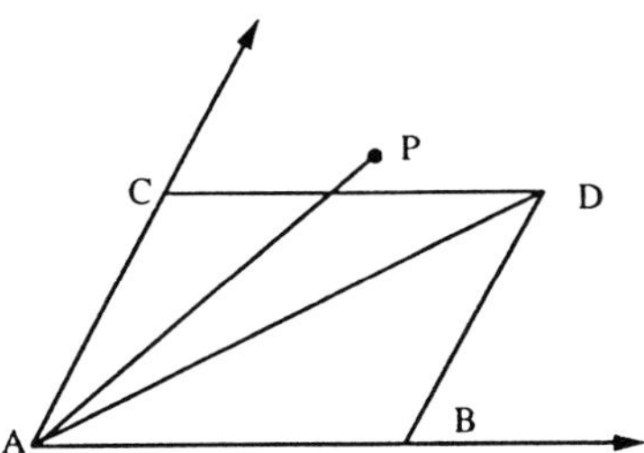

Fig. 9. Relative positioning using a parallelogram.

In such a case the position of P in the frame $(\vec{AB}, \vec{AC})$ is easily deduced:

$$x = \frac{-k_1}{k_1 + k_2}$$

$$y = \frac{1}{k_1 + k_2} \tag{5.2}$$

$$k_1 = [AB, AC;\ AD, AP],\ k_2 = [BA, BD;\ BC, BP].$$

As no 3-D position can be deduced from a single image [18], extra assumptions have to be added: the alignment in the space of four points for (5.1) or coplanarity for (2.7) and (2.8).

5.2. *Where is the Camera?*

We consider here the problem of finding the location of the principal point (sometimes called optical center) of the viewing system. We first consider the case of seeing six points in the scene, with four of them coplanar.

First we are derive the view line associated with an image point relative to a reference point in the scene. Let m be the projection of a point M on an image where the projection of the planar configuration $ABCD$ is projected as $abcd$ (see Fig. 10).

As we mentioned (Section 2.3), we can compute the projective coordinates of f with respect to the basis a, b, c, d. From the definition, these coordinates are the same for F', where the view line OF intersects with the plane $ABCD$. So the view line goes through F and F' and is defined.

Proceeding in a similar way, we can compute the view line coming through E, and therefore the principal point O is the intersection of these two lines.

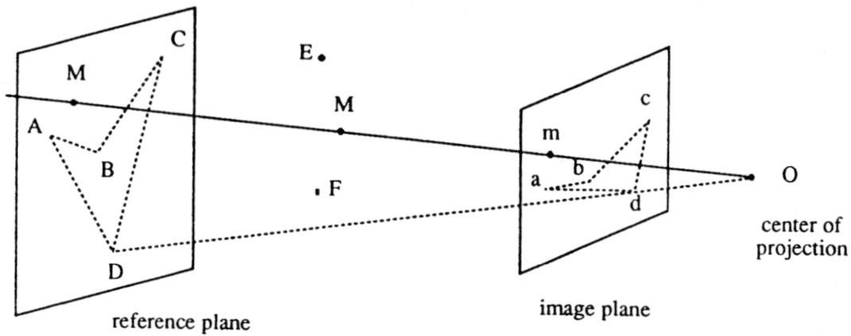

Fig. 10. The back projection of the image point m.

Having the 3-D position for O, we deduce easily the viewline associated with each point m in the image.

Such a computation can also be done using non-coplanar points, but the demonstration is a bit tedious and the reader is referred to [19] for the details. The hint of the technique can however be provided using a planar configuration: we suppose here that the image is restricted to a line and that we are taking such a picture in a planar world. We observe five reference points A, B, C, D, E with their images a, b, c, d, e. Measuring the cross ratio $[a, b; c, d]$, we deduce from Chasles' theorem that the principal point lies on a conic passing through A, B, C and D and completely defined by $[a, b; c, d]$ (see Fig. 11). We can do it again with A, B, C, E and the two conics intersect in four points, three of them already known: A, B, C. So the remaining intersection is the desired position and is computed algebraically from formula (2.11).

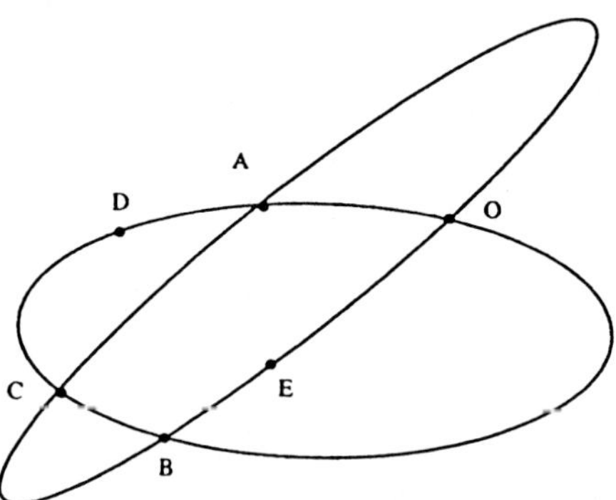

Fig. 11. The camera location lies at the two conic intersections.

5.3. *Choosing Points as References in the Scene*

The techniques presented may lead to 3-D position estimation of points in the scene. However such an estimation needs at least two images when no constraints on the scene are given. We describe here a simple experiment of computation of the location with two views.

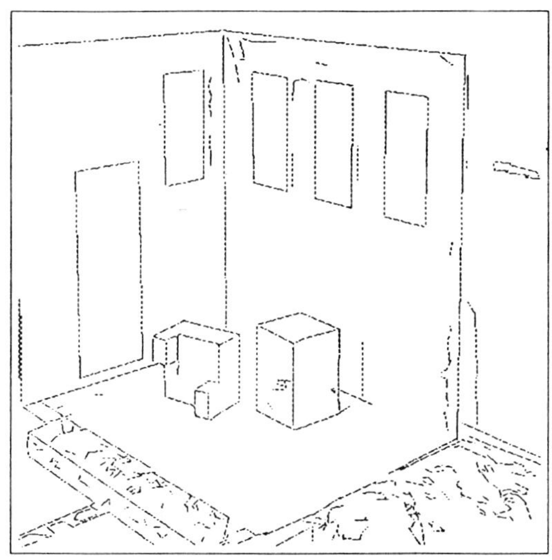

Fig. 12. Contour image of a scene.

Let us consider the scene described in Fig. 12. It displays contours of an image taken approximately at a distance of 1 m with a regular Pulnix camera. Contours were fitted with straight lines and corner point coordinates were computed as intersections of these lines. The same process was applied on a second image. Taking as reference points six points from the background rectangles, the view line associated with each contour was computed using the technique presented in the previous section.

Matches between the images was performed by hand as matching was not the primary concern of the present study. Intersection of the view lines associated with two corresponding image points was then computed using least squares and this provided us with the 3-D coordinates of the corresponding point in the scene.

Table 1 describes the results for the cube vertices. The exact location has no real meaning, it corresponds to the reference frame of the chosen point whose locations were measured with a standard ruler. Much more interesting are the edge lengths computed from these coordinates. As the exact size of the cube is 50 mm, the computed results are accurate within 4% of the value, and this without camera modeling and subpixel edge extractor.

Table 1. Experimental results for 3-D reconstruction of the cube.

Points	x	y	z	Edges	Length
0	78.9	140	48.5	0–1	50.5
1	79.1	141	-2	0–2	49.1
2	81.3	189	47.5	0–6	48.9
3	82.0	188	-1.5	1–3	47.1
4	33.2	195	48.5	2–3	49.5
5	34.4	194	-1.5	2–4	48.9
6	30.3	145	49.0	3–5	48.0
				4–5	49.8
				4–6	50.1

6. Recognition Using Projective Invariant

In order to classify patterns, standard pattern recognition techniques use numerical measures which are invariant under the experimental conditions like for instance the movement of the observing camera (see [20] or Chapter 1.2 "Statistical Pattern Recognition" in this book). Therefore such invariants can be applied directly in classification methods. More recently researchers developed indexing for selecting a subset of possible candidate models using hashing techniques based on geometric invariants [21,22].

The interesting point with the geometrical approach is that partial information on the image is sufficient to recover points, straight lines, conics, etc. and therefore to compute the invariants. This is not the case for standard global invariant measures like moments.

We will first explore some results of the invariant theory and derive from there some invariants in the second subsection.

6.1. *Results on Invariant Theory*

Only a simple introduction of this theory can be provided in this chapter. The reader is referred to the standard textbook on the subject like the second part of [5] or to the more vision application-oriented ones [4].

Let $\mathcal{G}$ be a group which acts on a set E, and $\circ$ the composition operator of $\mathcal{G}$. For instance $\mathcal{G}$ can be the Euclidean transformations in the plane and E the set of circles in this plane. $\circ$ is in this case the composition of such transformations. $\mathcal{G}$ acts on E means that

$$\forall x \in E, \ \forall g, h \in \mathcal{G}, \ g(h(x)) = g \circ h(x).$$

Finding an invariant for E means computing a measure m that is constant for all $x \in E$: $\forall x, x' \in E \, m(x) = m(x')$. Of course if $m(\cdot)$ is such a function, so is $f(m(\cdot))$. We are only interested in such independent invariant functions.

Let us consider the example of E being the set of circles with radius r. E is generated from a single circle by applying all the Euclidean transformations. There is an obvious invariant here: the radius r. The area a is also an invariant, but it is not independent with r: $a = 2\pi r^2$. On the other hand if we consider the set of all points in the plane under the Euclidean transformation, there are no invariants.

Before stating the basic result, we need few more notations. Let $D_{\mathcal{G}}$ be the degree of freedom of $\mathcal{G}$ (i.e. more formally its dimension). Let D_x be the degree of freedom of the subgroup which leaves an element $x \in E$ invariant (such a subgroup is called the isotropic subgroup of x), and let D_E be the degree of freedom of E, then the number I of independent invariants is:

$$I = D_E - \left(D_{\mathcal{G}} - \min_{x \in E} D_x\right). \tag{6.1}$$

In the previous example, the degree of freedom for the planar Euclidean transformation is 3, a circle is defined by three parameters, and the subgroup which leaves a circle invariant is the one-dimensional subgroup of rotations centered at the circle center. So we get one independent invariant.

Notice that we are only dealing with groups here. So we are not addressing the problem of the projection of the 3-D space into a 2-D image. But this result is applicable to planar shapes projected onto an image: the group is then the group of 2-D collineations. In fact there is no invariant in the case of 2-D projection of 3-D data [18] without additional conditions such as coplanarity.

6.2. *Computing the Invariant Using the Cross Ratio*

Formula (6.1) provides us only with the number of possible independent invariants. Here we explore how they can be computed easily in the projective case using the cross ratio. Recall that the degree of freedom for the collineation in $\mathcal{P}^2$ is 8, as a collineation in the projective plane is defined by a 3×3 homogeneous matrix.

6.2.1. *Invariant for two conics*

Each conic has five degrees of freedom; this provides us with ten parameters for two conics. As there is no collineation which leaves two conics invariant in the general case, two invariants have to be discovered. The two conics intersect in four points, and as stated in Section 2, four points on a conic define a cross ratio. Each of these two cross ratios (one for each conic) are obviously independent. From (6.1) it is then possible to conclude that all other invariants can be obtained as a combination of these two measures.

Such invariants are very useful as conics can be found by conic approximation to different shapes [23].

6.2.2. *Two points and two lines*

Let A and B be two points and α and β be two lines intersecting in O. This provides us with an eight degrees of freedom configuration (see Fig. 13). There is

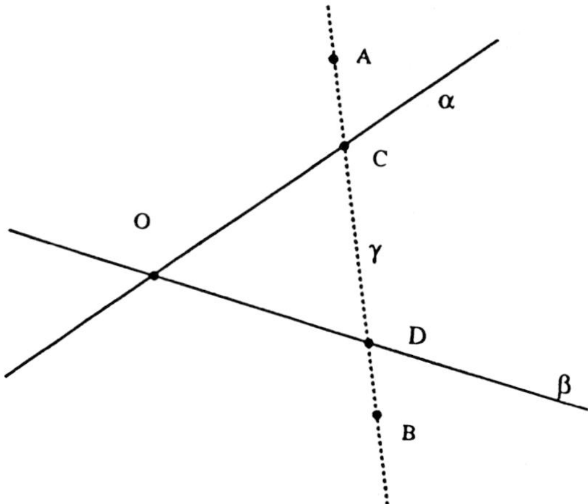

Fig. 13. The two points and two lines configuration.

an obvious invariant cross ratio: the line γ defined by A and B intersects α and β in C and D, and this defines four points on a line; four points on a line provide us with a cross ratio $[A, B, C, D]$.

Formula (6.1) indicates therefore that they should be a collineation subgroup leaving this configuration invariant and with degree of freedom at least equal to 1. In fact if A and B are at infinity, it is easy to see that the only collineations which leave this configuration invariant are the uniform scaling transformations (similitudes) with origin at O. This obviously is a one-dimensional subgroup and so there is only one independent invariant: $[A, B; C, D]$ is a solution.

6.2.3. *Implementation*

Experiments were conducted on this kind of invariants at the University of Oxford [24]. Figure 14 shows the relevant features used. In fact these authors computed these invariants using the general algebraic tools from the invariant theory. These algebraic invariants are nicely related to the one presented here [25].

Using such invariants may however lead to small combinatorial problems. For instance five points in a plane have two invariants, the two cross ratios provided by (2.7) and (2.8). However, having five points we have to choose which four points are going to be used as basis, and in which order they have to be considered. This leads us to $5! = 120$ possibilities.

The solution to this combinatorial problem is the use of the symmetrical polynomials. For instance we know that if k is the cross ratio of four points, then all possible cross ratios obtained by taking these four points in different orders are:

$$k, \ \frac{1}{k}, \ 1 - k, \ \frac{1}{1 - k}, \ \frac{k - 1}{k} \ \text{or} \ \frac{k}{k - 1} \, . \tag{6.2}$$

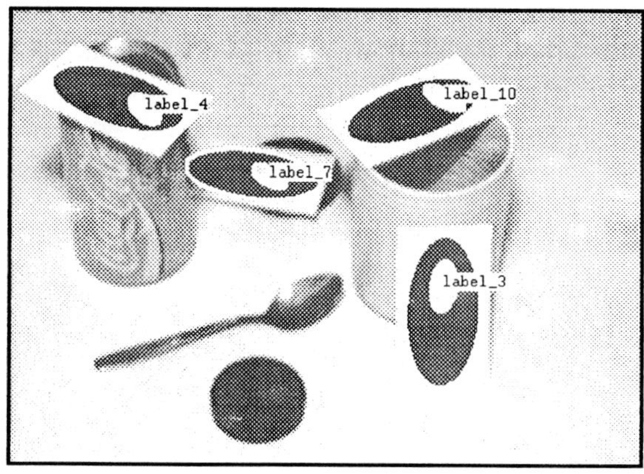

Fig. 14. Recognition using conic fitting and conic invariants (courtesy of D. Forsyth et al.).

So for getting an invariant which does not depend on the order of these points, we have to look for a symmetrical polynomial with six variables, each for a value of (6.2). One of the simplest symmetrical polynomials which is not constant is

$$\sum_{i=1}^{6} x_i^2 = \frac{2k^6 - 6k^5 + 9k^4 - 8k^3 + 9k^2 - 6k + 2}{k^2(k-1)^2}.$$

Finding such symmetrical polynomials avoids the combinatorics of sorting the feature in a feature set. There still remains the combinatorial problem of collecting the right set of features, for instance the right set of five points. No general answer exists for this problem.

7. Discussion

This chapter provided a short introduction to the geometry of the image formation system in the case of a pure perspective projection. For real images, optics and electronics provide differences with this ideal model and this can reach some pixels when using standard CCD cameras. For this reason methods are proposed in calibration for correcting the image, bringing the geometry back to the original perspective projection [26,1].

Projective geometry offers the right tool for dealing with such perspective projections. Its basic invariant is the cross ratio. Computing cross ratios can be done easily with image points, lines or conics. Such sets of features provide invariants which can be used in two ways: by indexing models for finding the possible models which can be associated with the invariant measured in a scene, or by finding the relative 3-D location of an object with reference to another object. The latter case is called relative positioning and has proved to be more flexible and robust than standard 3-D positioning in a camera reference frame.

New kinds of geometric invariants are presently under investigation. In [27] the reader may find studies of differential invariants, i.e. invariants obtained on a curve using derivatives of different orders. Cross ratios on areas can also be computed [28]. However few experiences were reported on the stability of the values computed in the different cases. Such practical evaluations still remain to be done.

Acknowledgements

The Esprit program "Basic Research" and the French national project "Orasis" provided financial and intellectual support to many parts of the work reported here. E. Arbogast, P. Gros, L. Morin, and L. Quan are kindly acknowledged for their insightful discussions and contributions. Figure 7 is displayed with courtesy of N. Ayache, and Fig. 14 with courtesy of A. Zisserman, J. Mundy, D. Forsyth, and Ch. Rothwell. I would like to thank them all for their cooperation.

References

[1] R. Y. Tsai, A versatile camera calibration technique for high-accuracy 3D machine vision metrology using off-the-shell TV cameras and lenses, *IEEE Trans. Robotics and Automation* **3**, 4 (1987) 323–344.

[2] K. W. Wong, Mathematical formulation and digital analysis in closerange photogrammetry, *Photogrammetric Eng. Remote Sensing* **41** (1975) 1355–1373.

[3] O. D. Faugeras, *3-D Computer Vision* (MIT Press, Cambridge, MA, 1992).

[4] J. Mundy and A. Zisserman (eds.), *Applications of Invariance in Computer Vision* (MIT Press, Cambridge, MA, 1992).

[5] J. G. Semple and G. T. Kneebone, *Algebraic Projective Geometry* (Oxford Science Publication, 1952).

[6] S. J. Maybank, The projective geometry of ambiguous surfaces, Technical Report 1623, Long Range Laboratory, GEC, Wembley, Middlesex, UK, Jul. 1990.

[7] N. Efimov, *Advanced Geometry* (MIR, Moscow, 1978).

[8] R. Horaud, B. Conio, O. Leboulleux and B. Lacolle, An analytic solution for the perspective 4-point problem, *Comput. Vision Graph. Image Process.* **47** (1989) 33–44.

[9] J. S. C. Yuan, A general photogrammetric solution for determining object position and orientation, *IEEE Trans. Robotics and Automation* **5**, 2 (1989) 129–142.

[10] Y. Liu, T. S. Huang and O. D. Faugeras, Determination of camera location from 2-D to 3-D line and point, *IEEE Trans. Pattern Anal. Mach. Intell.* **12**, 1 (1990) 28–37.

[11] R. K. Lenz and R. Y. Tsai, Techniques for calibration of the scale factor and image center for high accuracy 3-D machine vision metrology, in *Proc. IEEE Int. Conf. on Robotics and Automation*, Raleigh, USA, 1987, 68–75.

[12] O. D. Faugeras and G. Toscani, Camera calibration for 3-D computer vision, in *Proc. Int. Workshop on Machine Vision and Machine Intelligence*, Tokyo, Japan, 1987.

[13] B. Caprile and V. Torre, Using vanishing points for camera calibration, *Int. J. Comput. Vision* **4** (1990) 127–140.

[14] W. E. L. Grimson, *From Images to Surfaces. A Computational Study of the Human Early Visual System* (MIT Press, Cambridge, MA, 1981).

[15] N. Ayache, *Stereovision and Sensor Fusion* (MIT Press, Cambridge, MA, 1990).

[16] S. Maybank, O. Faugeras and Q. T. Luong, Camera self-calibration: Theory and experiments, in *Proc. Second European Conf. on Computer Vision*, Santa Margherita, May 1992.

[17] O. Faugeras, What can be seen in three dimensions with an uncalibrated stereo rig? in *Proc. Second European Conf. on Computer Vision*, Santa Margherita, May 1992.

[18] J. B. Burns, R. Weiss and E. M. Riseman, View variation of point-set and line-segment features, in *Proc. DARPA-ESPRIT Workshop on Applications of Invariants in Computer Vision*, Reykjavik, Iceland, Mar. 1991, 55–108.

[19] R. Mohr, L. Morin and E. Grosso, Relative positioning with poorly calibrated cameras, in *Proc. DARPA-ESPRIT Workshop on Applications of Invariants in Computer Vision*, Reykjavik, Iceland, Mar. 1991, 7–45.

[20] J. T. Tou and R. C. Gonzalez, *Pattern Recognition Principles* (Addison-Wesley, 1974).

[21] P. C. Wayner, Efficiently using invariant theory for model-based matching, in *Proc. Conf. on Computer Vision and Pattern Recognition*, Maui, Hawaii, Jun. 1991, 473–478.

[22] H. L. Wolfson, Model-based object recognition by geometric hashing, in O. Faugeras, (ed.), *Proc. 1st European Conf. on Computer Vision*, Antibes, France (Springer-Verlag, 1990) 526–536.

[23] D. Forsyth, J. L. Mundy, A. Zisserman and C. M. Brown, Projectively invariant representation using implicit algebraic curves, in O. Faugeras (ed.), *Proc. 1st European Conf. on Computer Vision*, Antibes, France (Springer-Verlag, Apr. 1990) 427–436.

[24] D. Forsyth, J. L. Mundy, A. Zisserman and C. Rothwell, Invariant descriptors for 3-D object recognition and pose, in *Proc. DARPA-ESPRIT Workshop on Applications of Invariants in Computer Vision*, Reykjavik, Iceland, Mar. 1991, 171–208.

[25] L. Quan, P. Gros and R. Mohr, Invariants of a pair of conics revisited, in P. Mowforth (ed.), *Proc. British Machine Vision Conf.*, Glasgow, Scotland (Springer Verlag, 1991) 71–77.

[26] C. C. Slama (ed.), *Manual of Photogrammetry*, fourth ed. (American Society of Photogrammetry and Remote Sensing, Falls Church, VA, 1980).

[27] A. Zisserman and J. Mundy (eds.), *Proc. DARPA-ESPRIT Workshop on Applications of Invariants in Computer Vision*, Reykjavik, Iceland, Mar. 1991.

[28] E. B. Barrett, P. M. Payton, N. N. Haag and M. H. Brill, General methods for determining projective invariants in imagery, *Comput. Vision Graph. Image Process.: Image Understanding* **53**, 1 (1991) 46–65.

Handbook of Pattern Recognition and Computer Vision, pp. 395–441
Eds. C. H. Chen, L. F. Pau and P. S. P. Wang
© 1993 World Scientific Publishing Company

CHAPTER 2.5

3-D MOTION ANALYSIS FROM IMAGE SEQUENCES USING POINT CORRESPONDENCES

JOHN. J. WENG

Department of Computer Science, Michigan State University
East Lansing, Michigan 48824, USA

and

THOMAS S. HUANG

Beckman Institute, University of Illinois at Urbana-Champaign
Urbana, Illinois 61801, USA

The objective is to analyze the motion between a rigid scene and the camera. The temporal correspondences between consecutive images are established by a procedure of image matching. Such temporal correspondences are then used for the estimation of the three-dimensional (3-D) interframe motions, as well as the 3-D structure of the scene. Long term motion that covers many image frames is modeled using object dynamics, and the model parameters are determined from the interframe motions. Thus, smooth 3-D motion can be predicted using the model parameters.

Keywords: Image matching, optical flow, 3-D motion estimation, structure from motion, motion modeling, motion prediction.

1. Introduction

The projection of a dynamic 3-D scene onto an image plane contains rich dynamic and geometric information about the scene. The projections at different time instants can be recorded by a sequence of images. To extract the information from the image sequence, several basic subtasks are identified: image matching, interframe motion estimation, motion modeling and prediction.

1.1. *Image Matching*

The first subtask is to establish the correspondences between images. Its objective is to identify image elements in different images that correspond to the same element of the sensed scene. The matching elements, or tokens, can vary significantly from one approach to another. Existing techniques for image matching roughly fall into two categories: continuous and discrete.

395

(1) Continuous approaches. Although the objective of the approaches in this category is to determine image velocity field instead of performing explicit matching between images, the computed velocity field amounts to image matching. Each velocity vector approximates the correspondence between two points in different images. Ideally, one needs the projection of 3-D velocity on the image plane. However, since such a projection is not directly available from visual sensors, an optical flow field (the field representing the apparent motion of the brightness pattern) is used to approximate the actual image plane velocity field. The techniques in this category typically need the assumption that the interframe motion is small and the intensity function is smooth and well-behaved [1–5].

(2) Discrete approaches. The techniques in this category treat the images as samples of the scene taken at discrete times, and select discrete features as tokens that are to be matched. Points with high intensity variation are often used as the matching tokens [6,7]. Other features used for matching include closed contours of zero crossings of Laplacian-of-Gaussian images to compute velocity field [8], edges for stereo matching [9–12], lines for stereo matching [13], correlation of intensity patterns [14,15], local phase information [16–18], or some aspects of higher level scene structure [19–21]. Discrete approaches allow either small motion or relatively large motion.

The image matching algorithm presented here belongs to the discrete approach, but it takes the advantages of implicit matching which is common in continuous approaches. It associates multiple attributes with the images to obtain an overdetermined system of matching constraints. This accommodates, to varying degrees, image noise and slight variations in image intensity that result from changes in viewing position, lighting, shading, reflection, etc. More importantly, the displacement vectors are determined in this overdetermined system without resorting to smoothness constraint. A multi-resolution multi-grid computational structure is employed to deal with relatively large image disparities caused by large interframe motions. The approach is capable of dealing with uniform non-textured object surfaces that are often present in real world images. We also address the problem of discontinuities in the field of displacement, and occlusion. The algorithm computes the displacement field and occlusion maps along a dense pixel grid, based on two perspective images of a scene. This algorithm has been tested on images of real world scenes which contain significant occlusions and depth discontinuities [22].

1.2. *3-D Motion Estimation*

3-D motion estimation has been investigated also under two types of approach: discrete and continuous. In the discrete approaches, the motion is treated as a displacement from one time instant to the next. Therefore, the time separation between the two time instants can be either long or short. The parameters of interframe motion are called two-view motion parameters. The result of image matching, used as input for 3-D motion estimation, is given as the displacement vectors between the corresponding image points. In the continuous approaches, the interframe motion is approximated by motion velocity and, therefore, in order for such an approximation to be reasonable, the interframe motion must be very small. The 3-D motion is formulated as velocity. The result of image matching, which is needed as input for motion estimation, is given as optical flow. Since the discrete approach more accurately models what actually happens than the continuous approach, we present a discrete approach in this chapter.

The possibility of recovering the 3-D motion and structure of a scene from its monocular views has been known to photogrammetrists for quite long. This subject attracted investigations in the computer vision area around the early 80's. A few iterative algorithms were proposed [23–27]. One drawback of these iterative algorithms is that the solution is not guaranteed because the iterative search may be trapped at local extrema.

Two linear algorithms were developed independently by Longuet-Higgins [28], and Tsai and Huang [29]. The linear algorithms guarantee a unique solution if certain nondegeneracy conditions are met. Yen and Huang [30] reported a vector-geometric approach to this problem. Because these algorithms were designed primarily for noise-free cases, a high sensitivity to noise has been reported [29,31]. In the framework of continuous approach, closed-form solutions for motion velocity from optical flow have been presented by Zhuang et al. [32,33] and Waxman et al. [34].

Since then, improvements have been made in reducing the sensitivity to noise while still keeping the algorithm linear. The post-consideration of the constraint in E through a constrained matrix fitting was independently reported by Faugeras, Lustman and Toscani [35], and Weng, Huang and Ahuja [36]. The latter algorithm is almost the same as the one presented in this chapter (Section 3). It eliminates the need to compute three false solutions and also uses other measures to improve the stability of the solution.

While the above linear algorithms require the solution of only linear systems and therefore no iteration is needed, further improvement of the solution requires a globally optimal nonlinear solution and thus a nonlinear algorithm. The optimal solution is presented in Section 3.4.

1.3. *Motion Modeling and Prediction*

The trajectory of a moving object can be used to understand the motion pattern and predict future motion. Section 4 presents a framework for motion modeling, understanding and prediction. Based on dynamics, a locally constant angular momentum (LCAM) model is introduced [42]. The model is local in the sense that it is applied to a limited number of image frames at a time. Specifically, the model constrains the motion, over a local frame subsequence, to be a superposition of precession and translation. Thus, the instantaneous rotation axis of the object is allowed to change with time. The trajectory of the rotation center is approximated by a vector polynomial. The parameters of the model evolve in time so that they can adapt to long term changes in motion characteristics. Based on the assumption that the motion is smooth, object position and motion in the near future can be predicted, and short missing subsequences can be recovered.

2. Image Matching

Two images, I and I', are two functions: $i: U \to B$ and $i': U \to B$, where U is a subset of 2-D space, and B is a subset of 1-D space for monochrome images (3-D space for color images). U defines the image plane. Functions i and i' map each point in the image plane to an intensity value.

The occlusion map, O for image I consists of those image points in image I whose corresponding points are not visible in image I'. Similarly, we define the occlusion map, O' for image I'.

An image matching from I to I' is a mapping $\kappa : U \to U$ such that for any $\mathbf{u} \in U - O$ (the symbol "−" denotes set subtraction), $\mathbf{u}$ and $\kappa(\mathbf{u})$ are the projections of the same point of the scene onto images I and I', respectively. Notice that the mapping from an occluded point $\mathbf{u} \in O$ is arbitrary. Similarly we define κ' as the matching from I' to I. The displacement field is defined by $\mathbf{d} = \kappa - \mathbf{e}$, where $\mathbf{e}$ is an identity mapping $\mathbf{e}(\mathbf{u}) = \mathbf{u}$ for all $\mathbf{u}$ in 2-D space. Therefore, the matched image point for $\mathbf{u}$ is $\mathbf{u}' = \kappa(\mathbf{u}) = \mathbf{u} + \mathbf{d}(\mathbf{u})$. We will use the term "displacement field" to refer to the result of image matching.

2.1. *Image Attributes*

Image attributes are defined for image matching: the matching points should have similar attributes. Some simple image attributes are defined in the following.

Image intensity is a simple image attribute. Under certain conditions, e.g. from matte surfaces illuminated by extended light sources, the image intensity value of a scene is in fact quite stable under motion.

However, if matching is based on intensity only, a point can be matched to any point with the same or similar intensity. Although intensity may vary, certain relationships among intensity values of nearby points may be relatively stable. These relationships provide some structural information of the scene. A candidate of such image structural information is a sharp transition of intensity, or edge. To get a continuous measure of edgeness, we define *edgeness* as the magnitude of the gradient of intensity, namely, $e - \|\nabla i\|$.

Similarly, the edgeness and intensity are generally not sufficient to reliably determine the correct match. The features that relate to the shape of the local intensity surface are useful in distinguishing otherwise similar looking points. For example, different points on the border of a region may have the same intensity and edgeness values, but the local border shape may vary from point to point on the border. A point at a geometrical corner may be clearly distinguished from others. The cornerness or the curvature of a region border thus can be used as a matching criterion. We define the *cornerness* in the following way that does not use computationally expensive polynomial fitting but achieves very good performance on real world images. As we mentioned earlier, we define positive and negative cornerness separately. Roughly speaking, the edgeness at a point $\mathbf{u}$ measures the change in the direction of the gradient at two nearby points, weighted by the gradient at the point. These two points, $\mathbf{u} + \mathbf{r}_a$ and $\mathbf{u} + \mathbf{r}_b$ are located on a circle centered at $\mathbf{u}$. The radius of the circle is determined by the level of image resolution. We choose $\mathbf{r}_a$ and $\mathbf{r}_b$ such that the directional derivative along the circle reaches the minimum and the maximum values, respectively. Let $\mathbf{a} = \nabla i(\mathbf{u} + \mathbf{r}_a)$, $\mathbf{b} = \nabla i(\mathbf{u} + \mathbf{r}_b)$, and angle $(\mathbf{a}, \mathbf{b})$ be the angle from $\mathbf{a}$ to $\mathbf{b}$ measured in radians counter-clockwise, ranging from $-\pi$ to π. The closer the angle is to $\pi/2$, the higher the positive cornerness measure should be. In addition, the measure should be weighted by the magnitude of gradient at the point $\mathbf{u}$ since the direction of the gradient in a uniform region is very unreliable. Mathematically, the *positive cornerness* and *negative cornerness* are defined, respectively, by

$$
p(\mathbf{u}) = \begin{cases} e(\mathbf{u})(1 - |1 - 2/\pi \text{ angle}(\mathbf{a}, \mathbf{b})|) & 0 \le \text{angle}(\mathbf{a}, \mathbf{b}) \le \pi \\ 0 & \text{otherwise} \end{cases} \tag{2.1}
$$

and

$$
n(\mathbf{u}) = \begin{cases} e(\mathbf{u})(1 - |1 + 2/\pi \text{ angle}(\mathbf{a}, \mathbf{b})|) & -\pi \le \text{angle}(\mathbf{a}, \mathbf{b}) \le 0 \\ 0 & \text{otherwise} \end{cases} \tag{2.2}
$$

where column vectors $\mathbf{a}$ and $\mathbf{b}$ are intensity gradients at $\mathbf{u} + \mathbf{r}_a$, and $\mathbf{u} + \mathbf{r}_b$, respectively:

$$
\mathbf{a}^t = \left. \frac{\partial i(\mathbf{s})}{\partial \mathbf{s}} \right|_{\mathbf{s}=\mathbf{u}+\mathbf{r}_a},
$$
$$
\mathbf{b}^t = \left. \frac{\partial i(\mathbf{s})}{\partial \mathbf{s}} \right|_{\mathbf{s}=\mathbf{u}+\mathbf{r}_b},
$$

where $\mathbf{r}_a$ and $\mathbf{r}_b$ are such that $\|\mathbf{r}_a\| = \|\mathbf{r}_b\| = r$ and

$$
\left. \frac{\partial i(\mathbf{v})}{\partial \mathbf{v}} \right|_{\mathbf{v}=\mathbf{u}+\mathbf{r}_a} \cdot \mathbf{r}_a^\perp = \min_{\|\mathbf{r}\|=r} \left. \frac{\partial i(\mathbf{v})}{\partial \mathbf{v}} \right|_{\mathbf{v}=\mathbf{u}+\mathbf{r}} \cdot \mathbf{r}^\perp \tag{2.3}
$$

and

$$
\left. \frac{\partial i(\mathbf{v})}{\partial \mathbf{v}} \right|_{\mathbf{v}=\mathbf{u}+\mathbf{r}_b} \cdot \mathbf{r}_b^\perp = \max_{\|\mathbf{r}\|=r} \left. \frac{\partial i(\mathbf{v})}{\partial \mathbf{v}} \right|_{\mathbf{v}=\mathbf{u}+\mathbf{r}} \cdot \mathbf{r}^\perp \tag{2.4}
$$

where the superscript "$\perp$" denotes the corresponding perpendicular vector: if $\mathbf{r} = (r_u, r_v)^t$, then $\mathbf{r}^\perp = (-r_v, r_u)^t$. If $\mathbf{r}_a$ and $\mathbf{r}_b$ that correspond to the minimum in (2.3) and the maximum in (2.4), respectively, are not unique, we choose those that minimize $p(\mathbf{u})$ in (2.1) and (2.2), in addition to satisfying (2.3) and (2.4). The cornerness is defined only if the involved derivatives exist. The value of r is a parameter of cornerness, and is directly related to image resolution. In the discrete version, r is equal to the pixel size.

The framework described below does not depend very much on the type of image attributes used. Different image attributes can be used according to the actual applications. The attributes defined in this section are planar rigid motion invariant (PRMI) in the sense that if the image is rigidly moved in the image plane, the attributes defined at the two corresponding points (before and after the 2-D motion) have the same value.

2.2. *Smoothness*

Smoothness constraints impose some similarity of the displacement vectors over a neighborhood. In addition to considering the smoothness of the overall displacement vectors, we separately consider the smoothness of the orientation of these vectors. The reason for emphasizing orientation smoothness is that (1) the orientation of the displacement vectors projected from a coarse level is generally more reliable than their magnitude, and (2) at a fine level, the local attribute gradient perpendicular to the displacement vector can easily lead the displacement vector in a wrong direction if the orientational smoothness is not emphasized.

Clearly, the smoothness constraint should be enforced only over points whose displacements are related, e.g. over adjacent points from the same surface. To selectively apply the smoothness constraint to two points, we use the similarity of intensities and the similarity of available displacement vector estimates at the two points. We represent the displacement vector field in the vicinity of a point $\mathbf{u}_0$ by a vector $\overline{\mathbf{d}}(\mathbf{u}_0)$, which is intended to approximate the displacement field within the region that $\mathbf{u}_0$ belongs to. In the implementation, $\overline{\mathbf{d}}(\mathbf{u}_0)$ is computed as

$$\overline{\mathbf{d}}(\mathbf{u}_0) = \iint_{0<||\mathbf{u}-\mathbf{u}_0||<r} w(i(\mathbf{u}) - i(\mathbf{u}_0), \mathbf{d}(\mathbf{u}) - \mathbf{d}(\mathbf{u}_0))\mathbf{d}(\mathbf{u})d\mathbf{u} \qquad (2.5)$$

where $0 < ||\mathbf{u} - \mathbf{u}_0|| < r$ denotes a region around $\mathbf{u}_0$, and $w(\cdot, \cdot)$ is a weight. In the digital implementation, the integration is replaced by a summation over $\mathbf{u}_0$'s eight-neighboring pixels. The weight is a function of the intensity difference $i(\mathbf{u}) - i(\mathbf{u}_0)$ and the displacement vector difference $\mathbf{d}(\mathbf{u}) - \mathbf{d}(\mathbf{u}_0)$. The objective that $\overline{\mathbf{d}}(\mathbf{u}_0)$ represents the neighboring displacement vectors of the region of $\mathbf{u}_0$ suggests the following requirements on the weight.

(1) The weight is large if the intensity difference is small. We assume that small intensity difference is observed when two neighboring points $\mathbf{u}$ and $\mathbf{u}_0$ belong to the same region, and therefore, their displacement vectors should be similar.

(2) If $\mathbf{u}$ and $\mathbf{u}_0$ have similar intensity but the corresponding displacement vectors are different, the weight should remain large. This case occurs when the displacement field is projected from a coarse level to the finer level. Two adjacent points with the same intensity may take quite different initial displacement vectors if they belong to different grid points at the coarse level.

(3) If $\mathbf{u}$ and $\mathbf{u}_0$ have different intensities and their displacement vectors are very different, the weight should be extremely small to suppress the influence of $\mathbf{u}$ on $\overline{\mathbf{d}}(\mathbf{u}_0)$.

Let $\eta_i = |i(\mathbf{u}) - i(\mathbf{u}_0)|$ and $\eta_{\mathbf{d}} = \mathbf{d}(\mathbf{u}) - \mathbf{d}(\mathbf{u}_0)$. A definition of weight that satisfies the above criteria is as follows:

$$w(\eta_i, \eta_{\mathbf{d}}) = \frac{c}{\epsilon + |\eta_i|(1 + ||\eta_{\mathbf{d}}||^2)} \tag{2.6}$$

where ϵ is a small positive number to reduce the effects of noise in intensity and prevent the denominator from becoming 0, and c is a normalization constant which makes the integration of weights equal to 1:

$$\iint\limits_{0<||\mathbf{u}-\mathbf{u}_0||<r} w(i(\mathbf{u}) - i(\mathbf{u}_0), \mathbf{d}(\mathbf{u}) - \mathbf{d}(\mathbf{u}_0))\, d\mathbf{u} = 1\,.$$

To ensure that requirement (2) is met, a small scale factor can be applied to the term $||\eta_{\mathbf{d}}||^2$, or alternatively, it can be set to zero which gives a simpler form:

$$w(\eta_i, \eta_{\mathbf{d}}) = \frac{c}{\epsilon + |\eta_i|}\,. \tag{2.7}$$

When the displacement field is computed with a computed occlusion map, the weights in (2.6) and (2.7) should be modified if, in (2.5), $\mathbf{u}_0$ is not an occluded point but $\mathbf{u}$ is. In this case, the weight corresponding to the occluded point $\mathbf{u}$ should be zero, $w = 0$, since $\overline{\mathbf{d}}(\mathbf{u}_0)$ should not take the meaningless $\mathbf{d}(\mathbf{u})$ into account. If $\mathbf{u}_0$ is an occluded point, the weight need not be set to zero no matter whether $\mathbf{u}$ is an occluded point or not, since the displacement vector at an occluded point may conveniently take the value of such a $\overline{\mathbf{d}}(\mathbf{u}_0)$.

Thus, the weight is automatically determined based on the intensity difference and the displacement difference. The smoothness constraint imposes similarity between $\mathbf{d}(\mathbf{u}_0)$ and $\overline{\mathbf{d}}(\mathbf{u}_0)$. The larger the difference in intensity, the more easily the fields for two adjacent regions can differ. If two regions get different displacements after some iterations, the quadratic term $||\eta_{\mathbf{d}}||^2$ results in a very small weight to reduce their interactions. On the other hand, the displacement vectors in the same region will be similar since the corresponding weight is large. Because intensity difference is usually much larger than the magnitude of displacement difference, $|\eta_i|$ is not squared in (2.6) (unlike $\eta_{\mathbf{d}}$), otherwise the weight will be too sensitive to small changes in intensity. The weights, thus, implicitly take into account discontinuities and occlusions. The registered value $\overline{\mathbf{d}}(\mathbf{u}_0)$ allows us to perform matching using uniform numerical optimization despite the presence of discontinuities and occlusions. This is discussed below.

2.3. *Matching Based on Image Attributes*

Given a displacement vector field, some measure of similarity, or residual error, between the attributes of estimated corresponding points can be defined. The residual of intensity is defined by:

$$r_i(\mathbf{u},\, \mathbf{d}) = i'(\mathbf{u} + \mathbf{d}) - i(\mathbf{u})\,.$$

Similarly, we define the residual of edgeness $r_e(\mathbf{u},\, \mathbf{d})$, that of positive cornerness $r_p(\mathbf{u},\, \mathbf{d})$, and that of negative cornerness $r_n(\mathbf{u},\, \mathbf{d})$. The residual of orientation smoothness is defined by

$$r_o(\mathbf{u},\, \mathbf{d}) = \|\mathrm{cross}\{\mathbf{d}(\mathbf{u}),\, \overline{\mathbf{d}}(\mathbf{u})\}\| / \|\overline{\mathbf{d}}(\mathbf{u})\|\,,$$

where $\mathrm{cross}\{(a,\, b),\, (c,\, d)\} = ac - bd$. The residual of displacement smoothness is defined by

$$r_d(\mathbf{u},\, \mathbf{d}) = \|\mathbf{d}(\mathbf{u}) - \overline{\mathbf{d}}(\mathbf{u})\|\,.$$

These residuals account for changes of a wide variety of factors. Under the conditions we discussed above, the similarity of attributes approximately holds. So, we determine displacement vector $\mathbf{d}$ such that the weighted sum of squares of residuals is minimized:

$$\min_{\mathbf{d}} \sum_{\mathbf{u}} \{r_i^2(\mathbf{u},\, \mathbf{d}) + \lambda_e r_e^2(\mathbf{u},\, \mathbf{d}) + \lambda_p r_p^2(\mathbf{u},\, \mathbf{d}) + \lambda_n r_n^2(\mathbf{u},\, \mathbf{d}) + \lambda_o r_o^2(\mathbf{u},\, \mathbf{d}) + \lambda_d r_d^2(\mathbf{u},\, \mathbf{d})\}$$

where r_e, r_p, r_n, r_o and r_d are weighting parameters that are dynamically adjusted at different levels. Let

$$\mathbf{r} \triangleq (r_i,\, r_e,\, r_p,\, r_n,\, r_o,\, r_d)^t\,.$$

With the previous estimate of the displacement vector $\mathbf{d}$ (initially $\mathbf{d}$ is a zero vector at the highest level), we need to find increment $\delta_{\mathbf{d}}$. Expanding $\mathbf{r}(\mathbf{u},\, \mathbf{d} + \delta_{\mathbf{d}})$ at $\delta_{\mathbf{d}} = 0$, we have (suppressing the variable $\mathbf{u}$ for conciseness)

$$\mathbf{r}(\mathbf{d} + \delta_{\mathbf{d}}) = \mathbf{r}(\mathbf{d}) + \frac{\partial \mathbf{r}(\mathbf{d})}{\partial \mathbf{d}} \delta_{\mathbf{d}} + o(\|\delta_{\mathbf{d}}\|) \triangleq \mathbf{r} + J\delta_{\mathbf{d}} + o(\|\delta_{\mathbf{d}}\|) \qquad (2.8)$$

where

$$J = \frac{\partial \mathbf{r}(\mathbf{d})}{\partial \mathbf{d}} = \begin{bmatrix} \dfrac{\partial i'}{\partial u} & \dfrac{\partial i'}{\partial v} \\[2mm] \dfrac{\partial e'}{\partial u} & \dfrac{\partial e'}{\partial v} \\[2mm] \dfrac{\partial p'}{\partial u} & \dfrac{\partial p'}{\partial v} \\[2mm] \dfrac{\partial n'}{\partial u} & \dfrac{\partial n'}{\partial v} \\[2mm] -\overline{d}_v/\|\overline{\mathbf{d}}\| & \overline{d}_u/\|\overline{\mathbf{d}}\| \\[2mm] 1 & 0 \\[2mm] 0 & 1 \end{bmatrix}\,,$$

$(\overline{d}_u, \overline{d}_v)^t = \overline{\mathbf{d}}$, and the partial derivative $\frac{\partial i'}{\partial u}$ denotes the partial derivative of $i'(u, v)$ with respect to u at point $\mathbf{u} + \mathbf{d}$, and so on. Define a diagonal matrix which specifies the weights on different residuals

$$\Lambda = diag(1, \lambda_e, \lambda_p, \lambda_n, \lambda_o, \lambda_d)\,. \tag{2.9}$$

We need to solve for $\delta_{\mathbf{d}}$ such that the sum of squared residuals is minimized. Neglecting high order terms and minimizing $||\Lambda(\mathbf{r} + J\delta_{\mathbf{d}})||^2$, from (2.8) we get the formula for updating $\mathbf{d}$:

$$\delta_{\mathbf{d}} = -(J^t \Lambda^2 J)^{-1} J^t \Lambda^2 \mathbf{r}(\mathbf{u})\,.$$

For each grid point along which the displacement vectors are to be computed at a resolution level (see Fig. 1), the displacement vector $\mathbf{d}$ is replaced by $\mathbf{d} + \delta_{\mathbf{d}}$. An iteration consists of such an updating for every grid point. At each resolution level, a fixed number of iterations (e.g. 20) are performed before the displacement field along the grid is projected to the next finer level. The final displacement field is obtained at the original image resolution.

2.4. *Multi-Resolution and Multi-Grid*

To find matches over a large disparity requires that we know the approximate locations of the matches, since otherwise multiple matches may be found. One solution to this problem is blurring the image to filter out high spatial frequency components. However, blurred intensity images have very few features left, and their locations are unreliable. Therefore, instead of blurring the image first and then measuring edgeness and cornerness, we blur the original edgeness and cornerness images (called attribute images here). Since the cornerness measure has a sign, nearby positive and negative corners may be blurred to give almost zero values, which is the same as the result of blurring an area without corners. We therefore separate positive and negative corners into two attribute images. Blurring is done for positive and negative images separately. Such blurred edgeness and cornerness images are not directly related to the blurred intensity images. They are related to the strength and frequency of the occurrence of the corresponding features, or to the texture content of the original images. While texture is lost in intensity images at coarse levels, the blurred edgeness and cornerness images retain a representation of texture, which is used for coarse matching. The intra-regional smoothness constraint at coarse levels applies to blurred uniform texture regions (with averaged intensity). When the computation proceeds to finer levels, the sharper edgeness and cornerness measures lead to more accurate matching. Therefore, in general the algorithm applies to both textured or non-textured surfaces.

At a coarse resolution, the displacement field only needs to be computed along a coarse grid, since the displacement computed at a coarse resolution is not accurate, and a low sample rate suffices. A coarse grid also helps to speed up the propagation of results within uniform regions. In the approach described in this paper, the coarse displacement field is projected to the next finer level (copied to the four corresponding grid points), where it is refined, according to the above discussion. Such a projection-and-refinement procedure continues down to finer levels successively until we get the final results at the original resolution. The computational structure and data flow used in this process are shown in Fig. 1.

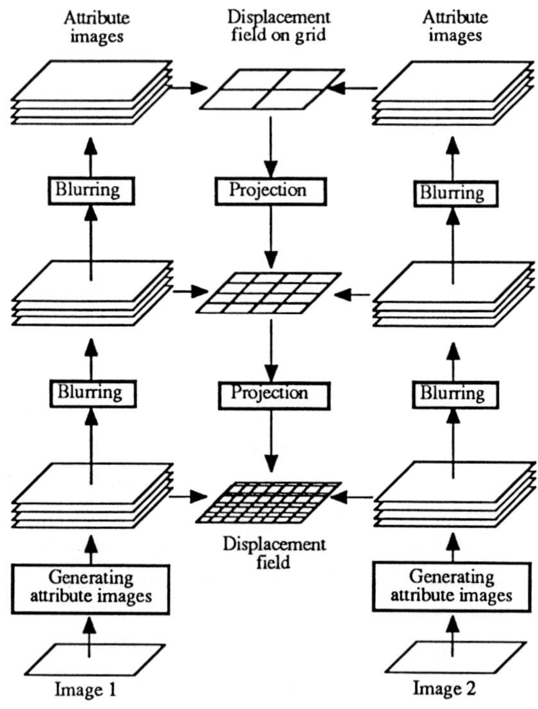

Fig. 1. The computational structure and the data flow.

The partial derivatives of the entries of J in (2.9) are computed by a finite difference method in the implementation. Let s denote the distance between two adjacent points on a grid, along which the finite deference of the attributes is computed, assuming a unit spacing between adjacent pixels. Then s should vary with the resolution. In addition, s should also vary with successive iterations within a resolution level. A large spacing is necessary for a rough displacement estimate when iterations start at each level. As iterations progress, the accuracy of the displacement field increases and s should be reduced to measure local structure more accurately. The mask to compute the finite differences is shown in Fig. 2, where spacing s at level l is equal to 2^l for the first one-half number of iterations at level l, and is reduced by a factor of 2 for the second half, except for $l = 0$. At the original resolution ($l = 0$), the spacing is always equal to 1, since no smaller spacing is available on pixel grid.

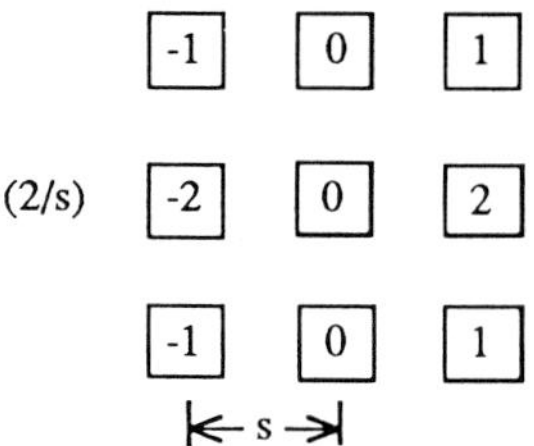

Fig. 2. Mask for computing derivatives.

2.5. *Preprocessing, Normalization, and Recursive Blurring*

The matching algorithm has to cope with images of a wide variety of scenes. The purposes of preprocessing are (1) to normalize the images so that the algorithm can use a set of standard parameters for different scenes and (2) to filter out noise in the images.

The pair of intensity images to be matched is first normalized by a linear function so that the minimum and the maximum intensities are equal to 0 and 255, respectively. (This range from 0 to 255 is to adapt to the representation with 8 bits/pixel, but it can be changed as needed.) Then it is filtered with a small (3×3) low pass filter to suppress gray level noise.

Similarly the edgeness and the cornerness also need to be normalized. The following considerations motivate the normalization. First, small gradients are more susceptible to intensity noise and are not reliable. Second, strong gradients may overwhelm moderate gradients in the edgeness measurement. Third, different scenes have different ranges of gradient magnitude and the algorithm should treat them in a systematic way. Therefore, we slightly modify the definition of edgeness defined in Section 2.1. Edgeness is the magnitude of the gradient normalized and transformed by a function f shown in Fig. 3

$$e(\mathbf{u}) = f(\|\nabla i(\mathbf{u})\|) \,. \tag{2.10}$$

The function f maps the magnitude of the gradient onto the range $[0, 255]$. It has two transition points x_0 and x_1. From $x = 0$ to $x = x_0$, $f(x) \approx 0$ to suppress noise. From $x = x_0$ to $x = x_1$, $f(x)$ increases from near 0 to almost 255 gradually and smoothly. The smooth transition interval $[x_0, x_1]$ allows continuous variation of edgeness for the gradient with a moderate magnitude. For $x > x_1$, $f(x) \approx 255$, to limit strong edges and relatively enhance the moderate edges. The values of two transition points x_0 and x_1 are determined automatically through an analysis of the histogram of gradient magnitudes such that the fractions of the pixels in the edgeness images that have values below $f(x_0)$ and above $f(x_1)$ are maintained at predetermined levels.

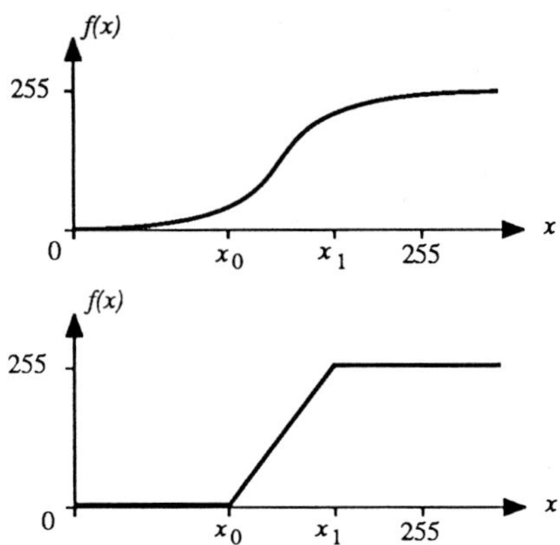

Fig. 3. Two normalization functions for the edgeness.

The edgeness $e(\mathbf{u})$ used in the definition of cornerness, (2.1) and (2.2), should also use the modified definition (2.10) as well. Note that such modified edgeness and cornerness are still PRMI attributes.

The preprocessing and normalization steps enable the algorithm to perform consistently for a wide variety of images using a set of standard parameters, which are selected based on a moderate number of image examples. In the implementation, the parameters can be determined through trials. A set of parameters, e.g. those in (2.6) or (2.7) and (2.9), are determined for each level of resolution. At coarse levels, the edgeness, cornerness and smoothness have relatively large weights. Their weights are reduced gradually down to finer levels, since smoothness constraint should be reduced at finer levels where details of the displacement are obtained, and cornerness and edgeness measurements at finer levels are more susceptible to noise than significantly blurred measurements.

The original images are first preprocessed by the methods discussed above. Then as shown in Fig. 1, four pairs of attribute images are generated (intensity, edgeness, positive cornerness and negative cornerness). The attribute images are extended in four directions to provide context for the points that are near the image border. The extension is made by replicating the border row or column. We use recursive blurring to speed up computation. Only integer summations and a few integer divisions are needed to perform such a simple blurring. The blurring for level $l + 1$ is done using the corresponding attribute image at level l: For each pixel at level $l + 1$, the value is equal to the sum of the values of four pixels at level l divided by k ($k = 4$ for the intensity, $k = 3$ for the edgeness and $k = 2$ for the cornerness). The locations of these four pixels are such that each is centered at a quadrant of a square of $a \times a$. a is equal to 2^l at level l. Therefore, the blurred intensity image at level l is equal to the average over all pixels in a square of size $a \times a$. To enhance sparse edges and corners, k is smaller than 4 for the edgeness and the cornerness. So, the results can be larger than 255. If this occurs, the resulting value is limited to 255. This multilevel recursive normalization is useful for the algorithm to adapt to different scenes.

2.6. *Occlusion*

To correctly match two images, those scene regions which are occluded in one or the other image must be identified. Occlusion occurs when a part of the scene visible in one image is occluded in the other by the scene itself, or a part of the scene near the image boundary moves out of the field of view in the other image. If the occluded regions are not detected, they may be incorrectly matched to nearby regions, interfering with the correct matching of these regions. To identify the occluded regions, we define two occlusion maps, occlusion map 1 showing parts of image 1 not visible in image 2, and similarly occlusion map 2 for image 2 (see Fig. 4, where black areas denote the occluded regions). We first determine the displacement field from image 2 to image 1, without occlusion information. The objective of this matching process is to compute occlusion map 1. This matching may "jam" the occluded parts of image 2 (e.g. the right-most section in Fig. 4) into parts of image 1 (e.g. the right-most section in Fig. 4). This generally will not affect the computation of the occlusion map 1, since the occluded regions of image 1 may only occur on the opposite side across the "jammed" region (in Fig. 4, e.g. the occluded region of image 1 is to the right of a "jammed" region). Those regions in image 1 that have not been matched (in Fig. 4, no arrows are pointing to them) are occluded in image 2 and are therefore marked in occlusion map 1 (black in Fig. 4). These unmatched patches may also be located at the center of the images, if they are occluded by other parts of the scene. Once the occlusion map 1 is obtained, we then compute the displacement field from image 1 to image 2 except for the occluded regions of image 1. The results of this step determine occlusion map 2 (see Fig. 4).

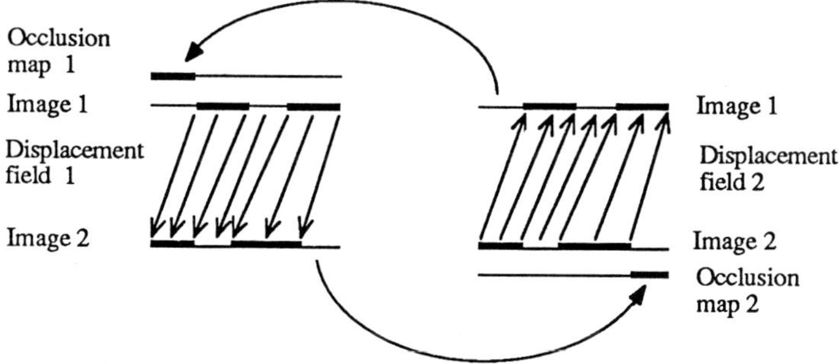

Fig. 4. A 1-D illustration of determining occlusion maps (see text). Images are represented by lines as one-dimensional images. The displacement fields shown just illustrate the correspondences between two 1-D images, and are not the actual displacement fields.

From the definition of κ and κ', it is clear that κ and κ' are one-to-one correspondences from $U - O$ to $U - O'$, and from $U - O'$ to $U - O$, respectively. Therefore, the occlusion map O can be determined by $O = U - \kappa'(U - O')$, and similarly $O' = U - \kappa(U - O)$. However, this procedure is recursive. Once one occlusion map is determined, the other can also be determined. The procedure outlined in Fig. 4 used preliminary κ' that is computed to determine O without information about O'. Since regions in O and O' are generally far apart, this preliminary κ' may be good enough to determine O.

2.7. *Outline of the Algorithm*

The following summarizes the steps of the procedure that computes the displacement field from one image to the other (see Fig. 1):

(1) Filter the two images using a 3×3 low pass filter to remove noise and normalize the pair of images as described in Section 2.5. .

(2) Compute the image attributes: intensity, edgeness, positive cornerness and negative cornerness as described in Sections 2.1 and 2.5.

(3) Set the level to the highest e.g. $l = 6$, and set the displacement field on the grid of level 6 to zero.

(4) Blur the attribute images to level l as described in Section 2.5. The scale of the blurring filter at level l is 2^l.

(5) Compute the displacement field along the grid. Perform a number of iterations as discussed in Section 2.3.

(6) If $l = 0$, the procedure returns with the resulting displacement field. Otherwise go to 7.

(7) Project the displacement field on the grid of level l to the grid of level $l - 1$ (replicating the vector at each grid point to the four corresponding grid points of level $l - 1$); decrement l by one and go to (4).

Suppose we need to determine the displacement field from image 1 to image 2. In order to obtain occlusion map 1, first compute the displacement field from image 2 to image 1 using the above procedure, without occlusion information (assuming image 2 has no occluded region in image 1). The displacement field computed is used to determine the occlusion map 1 for image 1. In the implementation, the occlusion maps are filtered by 3×3 median filters to remove single-pixel-wide occlusion and noise. Then, the displacement field from image 1 to image 2 is computed using the occlusion map 1 by calling the above procedure starting from step (4). In step (6), if a point in image 1 is marked in the occlusion map 1, it is not visible in image 2, and so, the displacement vector from this point cannot be determined. We just copy the vector $\bar{d}$ to this occluded point. The final computed displacement field assigns a displacement field to every pixel in image 1.

In summary, the matching algorithm computes a displacement vector for every pixel in the source image. This vector points to the matching point in the target image. Since subpixel precision is used, the two components of the displacement vector use real value prepresentation. Mathematically, this is equivalent to computing point correspondences: For each point in the source image, the algorithm determines the corresponding point in the target image so that these two points are projections of the same point in the scene.

3. Motion Estimation

This section first presents a linear algorithm that exploits redundancy in the available data to improve accuracy of the solution. Then, the optimization is discussed. We first define a mapping $[\cdot]_\times$ from a 3-D vector to a 3×3 matrix:

$$[(x_1,\, x_2,\, x_3)^t]_\times = \begin{bmatrix} 0 & -x_3 & x_2 \\ x_3 & 0 & -x_1 \\ -x_2 & x_1 & 0 \end{bmatrix}. \tag{3.1}$$

Using this mapping, we can express cross operation of two vectors by the matrix multiplication of a 3×3 matrix and a column matrix:

$$\mathbf{X} \times \mathbf{Y} = [\mathbf{X}]_\times \mathbf{Y}. \tag{3.2}$$

3.1. *Problem Statement*

Let the coordinate system be fixed on the camera with the origin coinciding with the projection center of the camera, and the z-axis coinciding with the optical axis and pointing toward the scene (Fig. 5). Since we are only interested in the ratio of image coordinates to the focal length and one can always measure the image coordinates in the unit of focal length, we assume, without loss of generality, that the focal length is unity. We call such a camera model *normalized* camera model. Thus, in the normalized camera model, the image plane is located at $z = 1$. Visible objects are always located in front of the camera, i.e. $z > 0$. Notice that $0 < z < 1$ may occur since the camera model is normalized.

Consider a point P on the object which is visible at two time instants. The following notation is used for the spatial vectors and the image vectors.

$$\mathbf{x} = (x,\, y,\, z)^t \qquad \text{spatial vector of P at time } t_1;$$

$$\mathbf{x}' = (x',\, y',\, z')^t \qquad \text{spatial vector of P at time } t_2;$$

$$\mathbf{X} = (u,\, v,\, 1)^t = \left(\frac{x}{z},\, \frac{y}{z},\, 1\right)^t \qquad \text{image vector of P at time } t_1;$$

$$\mathbf{X}' = (u',\, v',\, 1)^t = \left(\frac{x'}{z'},\, \frac{y'}{z'},\, 1\right)^t \qquad \text{image vector of P at time } t_2;$$

where $(u,\, v)$ and $(u',\, v')$ are the image coordinates of the point. Therefore, the spatial vector and image vector are related by

$$\mathbf{x} = z\mathbf{X}, \quad \mathbf{x}' = z'\mathbf{X}'.$$

Figure 5 shows the geometry and the camera model of the setup. From the figure we can see that the image of a point determines nothing but the projection line, the line that passes through the point and the projection center. The direction of this projection line is all that we need, and the position of the image plane is immaterial. That is why we can normalize the focal length to unity. It is obvious that the model in Fig. 5 is not meant to describe the optical path in a conventional camera. But rather, it is a simple geometrical model that is mathematically equivalent to an ideal pin-hole camera. A conventional camera can be calibrated so that every point in the actual image plane can be transformed to a point in the image plane of this normalized model.

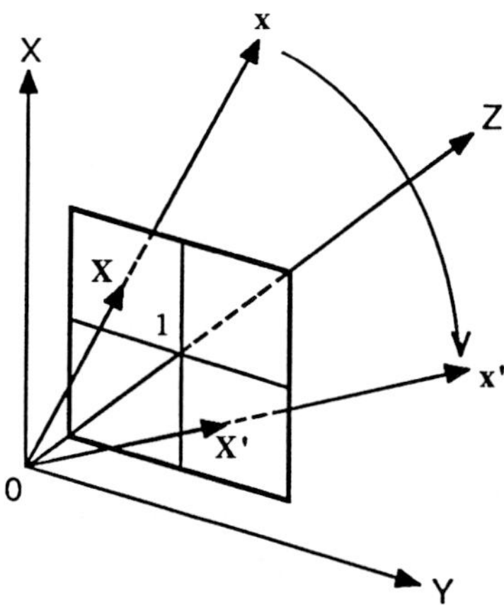

Fig. 5. The geometry and the camera model of the setup.

Let R and $\mathbf{T}$ be the rotation matrix and the translational vector, respectively. The spatial points at the two time instants are related by

$$\mathbf{x}' = R\mathbf{x} + \mathbf{T}$$

or for image vectors:

$$z'\mathbf{X}' = zR\mathbf{X} + \mathbf{T}. \qquad (3.3)$$

If $\|\mathbf{T}\| \neq 0$, from (3.3) we get

$$\frac{z'}{\|\mathbf{T}\|}\mathbf{X}' = R\frac{z}{\|\mathbf{T}\|}\mathbf{X} + \mathring{\mathbf{T}} \qquad (3.4)$$

where

$$\mathring{\mathbf{T}} = \frac{\mathbf{T}}{\|\mathbf{T}\|}.$$

Given n corresponding image vector pairs at two time instants, $\mathbf{X}_i$ and $\mathbf{X}'_i$, $i = 1, 2, \ldots, n$, the algorithm solves for the rotation matrix R. If the translation vector $\mathbf{T}$ does not vanish, the algorithm solves for the translational direction represented by a unit vector $\mathring{\mathbf{T}}$ and the relative depths $\frac{z_i}{\|\mathbf{T}\|}$ and $\frac{z'_i}{\|\mathbf{T}\|}$ for object points $\mathbf{x}_i$ and

$\mathbf{x}'_i$, respectively. The magnitude of the translational vector $\|\mathbf{T}\|$, and the absolute depths of the object points, z_i and z'_i, cannot be determined by monocular vision. This can be seen from (3.4), which still holds when $\|\mathbf{T}\|$, z_i and z'_i are multiplied by any positive constant. In other words, multiplying the depths and $\|\mathbf{T}\|$ by the same scale factor does not change the images.

3.2. *Algorithm*

We shall first state the algorithm, and then justify each of the steps.

Step (i). Solving for E. Let $\mathbf{X}_i = (u_i, v_i, 1)^t$, $\mathbf{X}'_i = (u'_i, v'_i, 1)^t$, $i = 1, 2, \ldots, n$, be the corresponding image vectors of n $(n \geq 8)$ points, and

$$A = \begin{bmatrix} u_1 u'_1 & u_1 v'_1 & u_1 & v_1 u'_1 & v_1 v'_1 & v_1 & u'_1 & v'_1 & 1 \\ u_2 u'_2 & u_2 v'_2 & u_2 & v_2 u'_2 & v_2 v'_2 & v_2 & u'_2 & v'_2 & 1 \\ \vdots & \vdots & \vdots & \vdots & \vdots & \vdots & \vdots & \vdots & \vdots \\ u_n u'_n & u_n v'_n & u_n & v_n u'_n & v_n v'_n & v_n & u'_n & v'_n & 1 \end{bmatrix}, \qquad (3.5)$$

and

$$\mathbf{h} = (h_1, h_2, h_3, h_4, h_5, h_6, h_7, h_8, h_9)^t . \qquad (3.6)$$

We solve for unit vector $\mathbf{h}$ in

$$\min_{\mathbf{h}} \| A\mathbf{h} \|, \text{ subject to: } \| \mathbf{h} \| = 1 . \qquad (3.7)$$

The solution of $\mathbf{h}$ is a unit eigenvector of $A^t A$ associated with the smallest eigenvalue. (Alternatively, the above problem can be transformed to a linear least squares problem by setting a nonzero nonvanishing component of $\mathbf{h}$ to one and moving the corresponding column to the right hand side.) The matrix E is determined by

$$E = [\mathbf{E}_1\ \mathbf{E}_2\ \mathbf{E}_3] = \sqrt{2} \begin{bmatrix} h_1 & h_4 & h_7 \\ h_2 & h_5 & h_8 \\ h_3 & h_6 & h_9 \end{bmatrix} . \qquad (3.8)$$

Step (ii). Determining a unit vector $\mathbf{T}_s$ with $\overset{\circ}{\mathbf{T}} = \pm\mathbf{T}_s$. Solve for unit vector $\mathbf{T}_s$ in

$$\min_{\mathbf{T}_s} \| E^t \mathbf{T}_s \|, \quad \text{subject to: } \| \mathbf{T}_s \| = 1 . \qquad (3.9)$$

The solution of $\mathbf{T}_s$ is a unit eigenvector of $E E^t$ associated with the smallest eigenvalue. If

$$\sum_i (\mathbf{T}_s \times \mathbf{X}'_i) \cdot (E \mathbf{X}_i) < 0 , \qquad (3.10)$$

---

then $\mathbf{T}_s \leftarrow -\mathbf{T}_s$. The summation in (3.10) is over several values of i's to suppress noise (usually three or four values of i will suffice).

Step (iii). Determining rotation matrix R. Without noise, it follows that

$$E = [\mathbf{T}_s]_\times R \tag{3.11}$$

or

$$R^t[-\mathbf{T}_s]_\times = E^t. \tag{3.12}$$

In the presence of noise, we find rotation matrix R in

$$\min_R \| R^t[-\mathbf{T}_s]_\times - E^t \|, \quad \text{subject to: } R \text{ is a rotation matrix.} \tag{3.13}$$

Alternatively, we can find R directly: Let

$$\begin{aligned} W &= [\mathbf{W}_1\ \mathbf{W}_2\ \mathbf{W}_3] \\ &= [\mathbf{E}_1 \times \mathbf{T}_s + \mathbf{E}_2 \times \mathbf{E}_3 \quad \mathbf{E}_2 \times \mathbf{T}_s + \mathbf{E}_3 \times \mathbf{E}_1 \quad \mathbf{E}_3 \times \mathbf{T}_s + \mathbf{E}_1 \times \mathbf{E}_2]. \end{aligned} \tag{3.14}$$

Without noise, $R = W$. In the presence of noise, we find rotation matrix R such that

$$\min_R \| R - W \|, \quad \text{subject to: } R \text{ is a rotation matrix.} \tag{3.15}$$

We can use either (3.13) or (3.15) to compute R. They both have the form

$$\min_R \| RC - D \|, \quad \text{subject to: } R \text{ is a rotation matrix} \tag{3.16}$$

where $C = [\mathbf{C}_1\ \mathbf{C}_2\ \mathbf{C}_3]$, $D = [\mathbf{D}_1\ \mathbf{D}_2\ \mathbf{D}_3]$. The solution of (3.16) is as follows:
Define a 4×4 matrix B by

$$B = \sum_{i=1}^{3} B_i^t B_i \tag{3.17}$$

where

$$B_i = \begin{bmatrix} 0 & (\mathbf{C}_i - \mathbf{D}_i)^t \\ \mathbf{D}_i - \mathbf{C}_i & [\mathbf{D}_i + \mathbf{C}_i]_\times \end{bmatrix}. \tag{3.18}$$

Let $\mathbf{q} = (q_0, q_1, q_2, q_3)^t$ be a unit eigenvector of B associated with the smallest eigenvalue. The solution of rotation matrix R in (3.16) is

$$R = \begin{bmatrix} q_0^2 + q_1^2 - q_2^2 - q_3^2 & 2(q_1 q_2 - q_0 q_3) & 2(q_1 q_3 + q_0 q_2) \\ 2(q_2 q_1 + q_0 q_3) & q_0^2 - q_1^2 + q_2^2 - q_3^2 & 2(q_2 q_3 - q_0 q_1) \\ 2(q_3 q_1 - q_0 q_2) & 2(q_3 q_2 + q_0 q_1) & q_0^2 - q_1^2 - q_2^2 + q_3^2 \end{bmatrix}. \tag{3.19}$$

Step (iv). Checking $\mathbf{T} \neq \mathbf{0}$. *If* $\mathbf{T} \neq \mathbf{0}$, *determine the sign of* $\overset{\circ}{\mathbf{T}}$. Let α be a small threshold ($\alpha = 0$ without noise). If

$$\frac{\| \mathbf{X}'_i \times R\mathbf{X}_i \|}{\| \mathbf{X}'_i \| \, \| \mathbf{X}_i \|} \leq \alpha$$

for all $1 \leq i \leq n$, then report $\mathbf{T} \approx \mathbf{0}$. Otherwise determine the sign for $\overset{\circ}{\mathbf{T}}$ as follows. If

$$\sum_i (\mathbf{T}_s \times \mathbf{X}'_i) \cdot (\mathbf{X}'_i \times R\mathbf{X}_i) > 0 \,, \tag{3.20}$$

then $\overset{\circ}{\mathbf{T}} = \mathbf{T}_s$. Otherwise $\overset{\circ}{\mathbf{T}} = -\mathbf{T}_s$. Similar to (3.10), summation (3.20) is over several values of i.

Step (v). If $\mathbf{T} \neq \mathbf{0}$, *estimate relative depths.* For $i, 1 \leq i \leq n$, find relative depth

$$\mathbf{Z}_i = \left(\frac{z'_i}{\| \mathbf{T} \|}, \frac{z_i}{\| \mathbf{T} \|} \right)^t = (\tilde{z}'_i, \tilde{z}_i)^t \tag{3.21}$$

to minimize

$$\| [\mathbf{X}'_i \quad - R\mathbf{X}_i] \mathbf{Z}_i - \overset{\circ}{\mathbf{T}} \| \tag{3.22}$$

using a standard least squares method for linear equations.

A simple method to correct structure based on rigidity constraint is as follows. The corrected relative 3-D position (scaled by $\| \mathbf{T} \|^{-1}$) of point i at time t_2 equals to $\tilde{\mathbf{x}}'_i = (R(\tilde{z}_i \mathbf{X}_i) + \overset{\circ}{\mathbf{T}} + \tilde{z}'_i \mathbf{X}'_i)/2$. Its relative 3-D position (scaled by $\| \mathbf{T} \|^{-1}$) at time t_1 equals to $\tilde{\mathbf{x}}_i = R^{-1}(\tilde{\mathbf{x}}'_i - \overset{\circ}{\mathbf{T}})$.

3.3. Justification of the Algorithm

We now justify each step of the algorithm.

For Step (i). Let $\mathbf{T}_s$ be a unit vector that is aligned with $\mathbf{T}$, i.e.

$$\mathbf{T}_s \times \mathbf{T} = \mathbf{0} \,. \tag{3.23}$$

Pre-crossing both sides of (3.4) by $\mathbf{T}_s$ we get, using (3.1) and (3.2),

$$\frac{z'}{\|\mathbf{T}\|} \mathbf{T}_s \times \mathbf{X}' = \frac{z}{\|\mathbf{T}\|} [\mathbf{T}_s]_\times R\mathbf{X} \,. \tag{3.24}$$

Pre-multiplying both sides of (3.24) by $\mathbf{X}'^t$ (inner product between vectors), we get:

$$\mathbf{X}'^t [\mathbf{T}_s]_\times R\mathbf{X} = 0 \tag{3.25}$$

since $\mathbf{X}'^t (\mathbf{T}_s \times \mathbf{X}') = 0$ and $z > 0$. Geometrically, (3.25) means that three vectors $\mathbf{X}'$, $\mathbf{T}_s$ and $R\mathbf{X}$ are coplanar, which can be seen from (3.3). Define E to be

$$E = [\mathbf{T}_s]_\times R = [\mathbf{T}_s \times \mathbf{R}_1 \quad \mathbf{T}_s \times \mathbf{R}_2 \quad \mathbf{T}_s \times \mathbf{R}_3] = [\mathbf{E}_1 \ \mathbf{E}_2 \ \mathbf{E}_3] \tag{3.26}$$

where $R = [\mathbf{R}_1\ \mathbf{R}_2\ \mathbf{R}_3]$. From the definition of $\mathbf{T}_s$, the sign of E is arbitrary since the sign of $\mathbf{T}_s$ is arbitrary (as long as the sign of $\mathbf{T}_s$ and that of E match such that (3.26) holds). Using (3.26), the definition of E, we rewrite (3.25) as

$$\mathbf{X}'^t E \mathbf{X} = 0. \tag{3.27}$$

Our objective is to find E from the image vectors $\mathbf{X}$ and $\mathbf{X}'$. Each point correspondence gives one equation (3.27) which is linear and homogeneous in the elements of E. n point correspondences give n such equations. Let

$$E = [e_{ij}], \quad \mathbf{E} = (e_{11}, e_{21}, \ldots, e_{33})^t.$$

Given n point correspondences, we rewrite (3.27) as linear equations in the elements of E and get

$$A\mathbf{E} = \mathbf{0}, \tag{3.28}$$

where the coefficient matrix A is given in (3.5). In the presence of noise, we use (3.7). The solution of $\mathbf{h}$ in (3.7) is then equal to $\mathbf{E}$ up to a scale factor provided rank $(A) = 8$. The rank of the $n \times 9$ matrix A cannot be larger than 8 since $\mathbf{E}$ is a non-zero solution of (3.28). Longuet-Higgins [37] gives a necessary and sufficient condition for the rank of A to fall below. Assuming the relative motion is due to motion of the camera, the condition is that the feature points do not lie on any quadratic surface that passes through the projection center of the camera at the two time instants. To satisfy this condition, at least eight points are required. More points are needed to combat noise.

Since the sign of E is arbitrary, we need only to find the Euclidean norm of E to fully determine E (equivalently $\mathbf{E}$) from $\mathbf{h}$. Let $\mathbf{T}_s = (s_1, s_2, s_3)^t$. Noticing $\mathbf{T}_s$ is a unit vector and using (3.26), we get

$$\begin{aligned}
||E||^2 &= \operatorname{trace}\{EE^t\} \\
&= \operatorname{trace}\{[\mathbf{T}_s]_\times R([\mathbf{T}_s]_\times R)^t\} \\
&= \operatorname{trace}\{[\mathbf{T}_s]_\times ([\mathbf{T}_s]_\times)^t\} \\
&= ||[\mathbf{T}_s]_\times||^2 \\
&= 2(s_1^2 + s_2^2 + s_3^2) = 2.
\end{aligned}$$

So, $\mathbf{E} = \sqrt{2}\mathbf{h}$. This gives (3.8).

For Step (ii). We determine $\mathbf{T}_s$. From (3.26), $\mathbf{T}_s$ is orthogonal to all three columns of E. We get $E^t\mathbf{T}_s = \mathbf{0}$. With noise, we use (3.9).

It is easy to prove that the rank of E is always equal to 2. In fact, let $\mathbf{Q}_2$ and $\mathbf{Q}_3$ be such that $Q = [\mathbf{T}_s\ \mathbf{Q}_2\ \mathbf{Q}_3]$ is an orthonormal 3×3 matrix. $S = R^t Q$ is then also orthonormal. Post-multiplying the two sides of the first equation of (3.26) by S, we get

$$ES = [\mathbf{T}_s]_\times RS = [\mathbf{T}_s]_\times Q = [\mathbf{0}\quad \mathbf{T}_s \times \mathbf{Q}_2\quad \mathbf{T}_s \times \mathbf{Q}_3].$$

We see the second and the third columns of ES are orthonormal, according to the definition of Q. Thus, rank $\{E\}$ = rank $\{ES\}$ = 2.

Since rank $\{E\}$ = 2, the unit vector $\mathbf{T}_s$ is uniquely determined up to a sign by (3.9). To determine the sign of $\mathbf{T}_s$ such that (3.26) holds, we rewrite (3.24) using $E = [\mathbf{T}_s]_\times R$:

$$\frac{z'}{\|\mathbf{T}\|}\mathbf{T}_s \times \mathbf{X}' = \frac{z}{\|\mathbf{T}\|}E\mathbf{X}. \tag{3.29}$$

Since $z > 0$ and $z' > 0$ for all the visible points, from (3.29) we know the two vectors $\mathbf{T}_s \times \mathbf{X}_i'$ and $E\mathbf{X}_i$ have the same directions. If the sign of $\mathbf{T}_s$ is wrong, they have the opposite directions. Thus, if (3.10) holds, the sign of $\mathbf{T}_s$ should be changed.

For Step (iii). In steps (i) and (ii) we found E and $\mathbf{T}_s$ that satisfy (3.11). R can be determined directly by (3.14). We now prove W in (3.14) is equal to R without noise:

$$R = [\mathbf{R}_1 \ \mathbf{R}_2 \ \mathbf{R}_3]$$
$$= [\mathbf{E}_1 \times \mathbf{T}_s + \mathbf{E}_2 \times \mathbf{E}_3 \quad \mathbf{E}_2 \times \mathbf{T}_s + \mathbf{E}_3 \times \mathbf{E}_1 \quad \mathbf{E}_3 \times \mathbf{T}_s + \mathbf{E}_1 \times \mathbf{E}_2].$$

Using the identity equation $(\mathbf{a} \times \mathbf{b}) \times \mathbf{c} = (\mathbf{a} \cdot \mathbf{c})\mathbf{b} - (\mathbf{b} \cdot \mathbf{c})\mathbf{a}$ and (3.26), we get

$$\mathbf{E}_1 \times \mathbf{T}_s + \mathbf{E}_2 \times \mathbf{E}_3$$
$$= (\mathbf{T}_s \times \mathbf{R}_1) \times \mathbf{T}_s + (\mathbf{T}_s \times \mathbf{R}_2) \times (\mathbf{T}_s \times \mathbf{R}_3)$$
$$= (\mathbf{T}_s \cdot \mathbf{T}_s)\mathbf{R}_1 - (\mathbf{R}_1 \cdot \mathbf{T}_s)\mathbf{T}_s + (\mathbf{T}_s \cdot (\mathbf{T}_s \times \mathbf{R}_3))\mathbf{R}_2 - (\mathbf{R}_2 \cdot (\mathbf{T}_s \times \mathbf{R}_3))\mathbf{T}_s$$
$$= \mathbf{R}_1 - (\mathbf{R}_1 \cdot \mathbf{T}_s)\mathbf{T}_s + (\mathbf{R}_2 \cdot (\mathbf{R}_3 \times \mathbf{T}_s))\mathbf{T}_s$$
$$= \mathbf{R}_1 - (\mathbf{R}_1 \cdot \mathbf{T}_s)\mathbf{T}_s + ((\mathbf{R}_2 \times \mathbf{R}_3) \cdot \mathbf{T}_s)\mathbf{T}_s$$
$$= \mathbf{R}_1 - (\mathbf{R}_1 \cdot \mathbf{T}_s)\mathbf{T}_s + (\mathbf{R}_1 \cdot \mathbf{T}_s)\mathbf{T}_s$$
$$= \mathbf{R}_1 .$$

This proves that the first column of R is correct. Similarly we can prove that the remaining columns of R are correct.

In the presence of noise, however, the estimated E has errors, and so does the matrix determined by (3.14). In particular, W in (3.14) does not give a rotation matrix in general. For the same reason, generally, one cannot find a unit vector $\mathbf{T}_s$ and a rotation matrix R so that $[\mathbf{T}_s]_\times R = E$ if E has errors. This can be understood by considering degrees of freedom in a correct E (3 for rotation and 2 for a unit T_s), which is smaller than the degrees of freedom, 8, in a unit $\mathbf{h}$ in (3.7). In other words, in solving for $\mathbf{h}$ in (3.7), we neglect the constraint in $\mathbf{h}$. This is necessary to be able to derive a linear algorithm. The alternative steps, (3.13) and (3.15), re-consider such a constraint through matrix fitting.

To solve the problem of (3.16), we represent the rotation matrix R in terms of a unit quaternion $\mathbf{q}$. R and $\mathbf{q}$ are related by Eq. (3.19). We have [38]

$$\|RC - D\|^2 = \mathbf{q}^t B\mathbf{q} \tag{3.30}$$

where B is defined in (3.17) and (3.18). The problem of (3.16) is then reduced to the problem of minimization of a quadratic. The solution of the unit vector $\mathbf{q}$ in (3.30) is then a unit eigenvector of B associated with the smallest eigenvalue.

Note that R is uniquely determined in (3.12), since the rank of $[-\mathbf{T}_s]_\times$ is two and the positions of any two non-collinear vectors completely determine a rotation: If $R\mathbf{X}_1 = \mathbf{Y}_1$, $R\mathbf{X}_2 = \mathbf{Y}_2$, and $\mathbf{X}_1 \times \mathbf{X}_2 = \mathbf{0}$, then we have the third equation:

$$R(\mathbf{X}_1 \times \mathbf{X}_2) = \mathbf{Y}_1 \times \mathbf{Y}_2 ,$$

and $[\mathbf{X}_1 \quad \mathbf{X}_2 \quad \mathbf{X}_1 \times \mathbf{X}_2]$ has a full rank.

For Step (iv). Pre-crossing both sides of (3.3) by $\mathbf{X}'$, we get

$$\mathbf{0} = z\mathbf{X}' \times R\mathbf{X} + \mathbf{X}' \times \mathbf{T} . \tag{3.31}$$

If $\mathbf{T} = \mathbf{0}$, for any point $\mathbf{X}'$ we have (note $z > 0$)

$$\mathbf{X}' \times R\mathbf{X} = \mathbf{0} . \tag{3.32}$$

If $\mathbf{T} \neq \mathbf{0}$, $\mathbf{X}' \times \mathbf{T} \neq \mathbf{0}$ holds for all the points $\mathbf{X}'$ (except at most one). Therefore, (3.32) cannot hold for all points by virtue of (3.31). In the algorithm, we normalize the image vectors in (3.32) and give a tolerance threshold α in the presence of noise.

From (3.31), if $\overset{\circ}{\mathbf{T}} = \mathbf{T}_s$ then $\mathbf{T}_s \times \mathbf{X}'$ and $\mathbf{X}' \times R\mathbf{X}$ have the same directions. Otherwise they have opposite directions since $\overset{\circ}{\mathbf{T}} = -\mathbf{T}_s$. We use the sign of the inner product of the two vectors in (3.20) to determine the sign of $\overset{\circ}{\mathbf{T}}$.

For Step (v). The equations for the least-squares solution (3.21) follow directly from (3.4). The idea for correcting structure based on rigidity is as follows. Moving the recovered 3-D points at time t_1 using the estimated rotation and translation, their new positions should coincide with the recovered position at time t_2, if the data is noise free. However, in the presence of noise, the positions do not coincide. Here we adopt a simplistic way of removing this discrepancy: the midpoint between these two positions of a point at time t_2 is chosen as the corrected solution for the position of the point at time t_2. Moving the midpoint back gives the corrected 3-D position of the point at time t_1.

In summary, we have proved that if rank $(A) = 8$, the solution of R and $\overset{\circ}{\mathbf{T}}$ is unique, and we have derived the close-form solution. Given eight or more point correspondences, the algorithm first solves for the essential parameter matrix E. Then the motion parameters are obtained from E. Finally the spatial structure is derived from the motion parameters. All the steps of the algorithm make use of the redundancy in the data to combat noise. As the results of determining the signs in (3.10) and (3.20), the computations of three false solutions [28,29] are avoided. These steps for determining signs are stable in the presence of noise, since the decisions are made based on the signs of the inner product of the two vectors which are in the same or opposite direction without noise. Summations over several points in (3.10) and (3.20) suppress the effects of the cases where two noise-corrupted small vectors are used, whose inner products are close to zero and the signs are unreliable.

If $\mathbf{T} \neq \mathbf{0}$ and the spatial configuration is nondegenerate, the rank of A is 8. In this case, we can determine the unit vector $\mathbf{h}$ in (3.7) up to a sign, and determine R and $\overset{\circ}{\mathbf{T}}$ uniquely. If $\mathbf{T} = \mathbf{0}$, any unit vector $\mathbf{T}_s$ satisfies (3.24) and so matrix E, and correspondingly the unit vector $\mathbf{h}$, have two degrees of freedom (notice $\mathbf{T}_s$ and $\mathbf{h}$ are restricted to be unit vectors). Therefore, A in (3.5) has a rank less than or equal to 6. If $\mathbf{T} = \mathbf{0}$, relative depths of the points cannot be determined. However, the rotation parameters can be determined even if $\mathbf{T} = \mathbf{0}$.

3.4. *Optimal Motion Estimation*

The optimization is motivated by the following observations on the linear algorithms (including the one presented in Section 3.2):

(a) With certain types of motion, even pixel level perturbations (such as digitization noise of conventional CCD video cameras) may override the information characterized by the epipolar constraint, which is a key constraint used for determining motion and structure by linear algorithms. The epipolar constraint restricts only one of the two components in image point displacement. The other component is related to the depth of the point and the motion. If this component is also used for motion estimation, the accuracy of the estimated motion parameters can be considerably improved.

(b) Existing linear algorithms give closed-form solution to motion parameters. However, the constraints in the intermediate parameter matrix (essential matrix E) are not fully used. The use of these constraints can improve the accuracy of the solution in the presence of noise.

The above considerations are unified under a general framework of optimal estimation: Given the noise-contaminated point correspondences, we need the best estimator for motion and structure parameters.

In reality, the image coordinates of an object point as well as the corresponding displacement vector in the image plane are the results from a feature detector and the corresponding matcher, whose accuracy is influenced by a variety of factors including lighting, structure of the scene, image resolution and the performance of the feature matching algorithms. Thus, the observed 2-D image plane vectors $\mathbf{u}_i$ of image 1 and $\mathbf{u}_i'$ of image 2 are noise-contaminated versions of the true ones. Let $(\mathbf{u}_i, \mathbf{u}_i')$ be the observed value of a pair of random vectors $(\mathbf{U}_i, \mathbf{U}_i')$. (With n point correspondences over two time instants, we add subscripts i to denote the ith point. A subscript-free letter denotes a general example of the vectors.) What we obtain is a sequence of the observed image vector pairs

$$\mathbf{u} \triangleq (\mathbf{u}_1^t, (\mathbf{u}_1')^t, \mathbf{u}_2^t, (\mathbf{u}_2')^t, \ldots, \mathbf{u}_n^t, (\mathbf{u}_n')^t)^t$$

of a sequence of random vector pairs

$$\mathbf{U} \triangleq (\mathbf{U}_1^t, (\mathbf{U}_1')^t, \mathbf{U}_2^t, (\mathbf{U}_2')^t, \ldots, \mathbf{U}_n^t, (\mathbf{U}_n')^t)^t .$$

We need to estimate the motion parameter vector $\mathbf{m}$ and the 3-D positions of the feature points (scene structure)

$$\mathbf{x} \triangleq (\mathbf{x}_1^t, (\mathbf{x}_1')^t, \mathbf{x}_2^t, (\mathbf{x}_2')^t, \ldots, \mathbf{x}_n^t, (\mathbf{x}_n')^t)^t .$$

We assume that the errors are uncorrelated between the different components of a point and between different points. Let $\mathbf{h}_i(\mathbf{m}, \mathbf{x})$ be the noise-free projection of the ith point in the first image, given motion $\mathbf{m}$ and structure $\mathbf{x}$, and $\mathbf{h}_i'(\mathbf{m}, \mathbf{x})$ be the corresponding projection in the second image. Then, according to the principle of minimum variance estimator, the optimal estimate of $\mathbf{m}$ and $\mathbf{x}$ is the one that minimizes

$$\sum_{i=1}^{n} (\|\mathbf{u}_i - \mathbf{h}_i(\mathbf{m}, \mathbf{x})\|^2 + \|\mathbf{u}_i' - \mathbf{h}_i'(\mathbf{m}, \mathbf{x})\|^2) \tag{3.33}$$

which is just the sum of discrepancies between the observed projection and the inferred projections. The value of (3.33) measures the differences in the observed images and the inferred images.

Equation (3.33) involves both motion parameters and the 3-D position of every feature point. The maximum is over all the possible motion parameters and scene structures. The parameter space for iteration is huge and the computation is very expensive. However we do not have to iterate on the structure of the scene.

In fact, given motion parameters $\mathbf{m}$, the structure $\mathbf{x}$ that minimizes the value of (3.33) can be estimated analytically. That is, we can compute

$$\min_{\mathbf{x}} \{\|\mathbf{u}_i - \mathbf{h}_i(\mathbf{m}, \mathbf{x})\|^2 + \|\mathbf{u}_i' - \mathbf{h}_i'(\mathbf{m}, \mathbf{x})\|^2\} \triangleq g_i(\mathbf{m}) \tag{3.34}$$

from a given $\mathbf{m}$. In fact,

$$\min_{\mathbf{m}, \mathbf{x}} \{\sum_{i=1}^{n} (\|\mathbf{u}_i - \mathbf{h}_i(\mathbf{m}, \mathbf{x})\|^2 + \|\mathbf{u}_i' - \mathbf{h}_i'(\mathbf{m}, \mathbf{x})\|^2)\}$$

$$= \min_{\mathbf{m}} \left\{ \sum_{i=1}^{n} \min_{\mathbf{x}} \{\|\mathbf{u}_i - \mathbf{h}_i(\mathbf{m}, \mathbf{x})\|^2 + \|\mathbf{u}_i' - \mathbf{h}_i'(\mathbf{m}, \mathbf{x})\|^2\} \right\} = \min_{\mathbf{m}} \sum_{i=1}^{n} g_i(\mathbf{m}) .$$

So computationally, structure $\mathbf{x}$ will not be included in the parameter space of iteration. Given an $\mathbf{m}$, $\mathbf{x}$ is computed directly as we will discuss in the following paragraph. This drastically reduces the amount of computation. Otherwise it is computationally extremely expensive to iterate on this huge $(\mathbf{m}, \mathbf{x})$ space (iterations on n points needs $(3n + 5)$-dimensional parameter space!). Since the optimal structure $\mathbf{x}$ can be determined from motion parameters, we can exclude $\mathbf{x}$ from the notation for parameters to be estimated. That is, symbolically, the parameters to be determined are just $\mathbf{m}$.

To derive the closed-form expression for $\mathbf{x}$ that gives $g_i(\mathbf{m})$ in (3.34), we use the following methods. From motion parameter vector $\mathbf{m}$ and the observed projections of point i, the two observed projection lines are determined. These two observed projection lines do not intersect in general. If the true 3-D point is on the observed projection line of the first image, the discrepancy $\|\mathbf{u}_i - \mathbf{h}_i(\mathbf{m}, \mathbf{x})\|^2$ is equal to zero, but $\|\mathbf{u}'_i - \mathbf{h}'_i(\mathbf{m}, \mathbf{x})\|^2$ generally is not. If the true 3-D point is on the other observed projection line, $\|\mathbf{u}'_i - \mathbf{h}'_i(\mathbf{m}, \mathbf{x})\|^2$ is equal to zero while $\|\mathbf{u}_i - \mathbf{h}_i(\mathbf{m}, \mathbf{x})\|^2$ is not. Given the motion parameters, we need to find a 3-D point for each feature point such that the corresponding term $\|\mathbf{u}_i - \mathbf{h}_i(\mathbf{m}, \mathbf{x})\|^2 + \|\mathbf{u}'_i - \mathbf{h}'_i(\mathbf{m}, \mathbf{x})\|^2$ is minimized. Obviously, under a normal configuration the point lies in the shortest line segment L that connects the two observed projection lines, because otherwise the perpendicular projection of a 3-D point onto L is better than the 3-D point. An exact solution of the optimal point requires solving a fourth order polynomial equation. It can be shown that using a reasonable approximation, we can get a closed-form solution. The optimal point is generally not far from the midpoint of the line segment L, unless the distance to the object and the viewing angle differ a lot between two images. For computational efficiency, we may just use the midpoint of the line L as an approximated optimal point, which is the solution in (3.22).

Computationally, a two-step approach is proposed here. First, a linear algorithm is applied which gives a closed-form solution. Then in the second step, this solution is used as an initial guess for an iterative algorithm which improves the initial guess to minimize the objective function (3.33). This two-step approach has the following advantages:

(1) A solution is generally guaranteed. The linear algorithm always gives a solution provided that degeneracy does not occur. Unless the noise level is very high, this solution is close to the true one. As long as the initial guess is within the convergent region to a globally optimal point, iteration leads to the optimal solution.

(2) The approach yields reliable solutions. The linear algorithms use only the epipolar constraint and so, the solution is sensitive to noise and the reliability of solutions varies with motion types. The optimization in the second step employs more global constraints and achieves significant improvements over the first step.

(3) The computation is faster than straight iterative methods that start with a "zero" initial guess. Generally, a linear algorithm is fast, and a nonlinear algorithm is slow. When a linear algorithm is followed by a nonlinear algorithm, the amount of computation is not simply equal to the sum of those needed by each algorithm individually. Since the linear algorithm provides a good initial guess, the time taken by the nonlinear algorithm to reach a solution is greatly reduced.

4. Motion Modeling and Prediction

In general, the moving objects exhibit a smooth motion, i.e. the motion parameters between consecutive image pairs are correlated. From this assumption and given a sequence of images of a moving rigid object, we determine what kind of local motion the object is undergoing. A Locally Constant Angular Momentum model, or LCAM model for short, is introduced. The model assumes short term conservation of angular momentum and a polynomial curve as the trajectory of the rotation center. This constraint is the precise statement of what we mean by smoothness of motion. However, we allow the angular momentum, and hence, the motion characteristics of the object to change or evolve over the long term. Thus, we do not constrain the object motion by some global model of allowed dynamics.

We will give a closed-form solution to motion parameters and structure from a sequence of images. As a result of the analysis presented in this section, some of the questions that we can answer are: whether there is precession or tumbling; what the precession is if it exists; how the rotation center of the object (which may be an invisible point!) moves in space; what the future motion would probably be; where a particular object point would be located in image frames or in 3-D at the next several time instants; where the object would be if it is missing from an image subsequence, and what the motion before the given sequence could be.

This approach of motion modeling and prediction is based on the two-view motion analysis of image sequences consisting of either monocular images, or stereo image pairs. Generally, two-view motion does not represent actual continuous motion undergone by the object between the two time instants. The physical location of the rotation axis is not determined by such a two-view position transformation. Using a a single camera, the 3-D translation and the range of the object can be determined up to a scale factor. If stereo cameras are used, we can determine the absolute translation velocities and the ranges of object points.

The approach presented in this section is independent of the type of algorithms used to determine two-view motion parameters. To be specific, feature points are used for the discussion here. We assume that there is a single rigid object in motion, the correspondences of feature points between images are given, and the motion does not exhibit any discontinuities such as those caused by collisions.

4.1. *Motion of a Rigid Body in 3-D*

We first present the laws of physics that govern the motion of a rigid body. All external forces acting on a body can be reduced to a total force **F** acting on a suitable point Q, and a total applied torque **N** about **Q**. For a body moving freely in space, the center of mass is to be taken as the point Q. If the body is constrained to rotate about a fixed point, then that point is to be taken as the point Q. That point may move with the supports. Letting m be the mass of the body, the motion of the center of mass is given by

$$\mathbf{F} = \frac{d}{dt}\left(m\mathbf{V}\right).\tag{4.1}$$

Let $\mathbf{L}$ be the angular momentum of the body. The torque $\mathbf{N}$ and the angular momentum $\mathbf{L}$ satisfy [39,40]:

$$\mathbf{N} = \frac{d\mathbf{L}}{dt}.\tag{4.2}$$

The rotation is about the point Q, which will be referred to as the rotation center. In the remainder of this subsection, we concentrate on the rotation part of the motion. The motion of the rotation center Q will be discussed in the next subsection.

In matrix notation, the angular momentum $\mathbf{L}$ can be represented by

$$\mathbf{L} = G\boldsymbol{\omega}$$

or writing in components:

$$\begin{bmatrix} L_x \\ L_y \\ L_z \end{bmatrix} = \begin{bmatrix} g_{xx} & g_{yx} & g_{zx} \\ g_{xy} & g_{yy} & g_{zy} \\ g_{xz} & g_{yz} & g_{zz} \end{bmatrix} \begin{bmatrix} \omega_x \\ \omega_y \\ \omega_z \end{bmatrix}$$

where

$$g_{xx} = \int (y^2 + z^2)dm\,, \quad g_{yy} = \int (z^2 + x^2)dm\,, \quad g_{zz} = \int (x^2 + y^2)dm\,,$$

$$g_{zx} = g_{xz} = -\int xz\,dm\,, \quad g_{yx} = g_{xy} = -\int xy\,dm\,,$$

$$g_{zy} = g_{yz} = -\int zy\,dm\,.$$

The above integrals are over the mass of the body.

If the coordinate axes are the principal axes of the body [39,40], the inertia tensor G takes the diagonal form:

$$G = \begin{bmatrix} g_{xx} & 0 & 0 \\ 0 & g_{yy} & 0 \\ 0 & 0 & g_{zz} \end{bmatrix}.\tag{4.3}$$

Referring to a coordinate system fixed on such a rotating body, (4.2) becomes

$$n_x = g_{xx}\dot{\omega}_x + \omega_y\omega_z(g_{zz} - g_{yy})\,,$$
$$n_y = g_{yy}\dot{\omega}_y + \omega_z\omega_x(g_{xx} - g_{zz})\,,$$
$$n_z = g_{zz}\dot{\omega}_z + \omega_x\omega_y(g_{yy} - g_{xx})\,,$$

where $(n_x, n_y, n_z) = \mathbf{N}$. These are known as Euler's equations for the motion of a rigid body. These equations are nonlinear and have generally no closed-form solutions. Numerical methods are generally needed to solve them.

Clearly the motion of a rigid body under external forces is complicated. In fact even under no external forces, the motion remains complex. Perspective projection adds further complexity to the motion as observed in the image. However, in a short time interval, realistic simplifications can be introduced. One simplification occurs if we ignore the impact of the external torque over short time intervals. If there is no external torque over a short time, there is no change in the angular momentum of the object. Thus, if we have a dense temporal sequence of images, we can perform motion analysis over a small number of successive frames under the assumption of locally constant angular momentum. Another simplification occurs if the body possesses an axis of symmetry. The symmetry here means that at least two of i_{xx}, i_{yy}, i_{zz} in (4.3) are equal. Cylinders and disks are such examples. Most satellites are also symmetrical or almost symmetrical in this sense.

Under the above two simplifications, Euler's equations are integrable [39,40]. The motion is such that the body rotates about its axis of symmetry **m**, and at the same time the axis rotates about a spatially fixed axis **l**. The motion can be represented by a rotating cone that rolls along the surface of a fixed cone without slipping as shown in Fig. 6, where the body is fixed on the rolling cone, the axis of symmetry coincides with that of rolling cone, and the center of mass or the fixed point Q of the body coincides with the apices of the cones. Then, the motion of the rolling cone is the same as the motion of the body. Figure 6 gives three possible configurations of the rolling cone and the fixed cone.

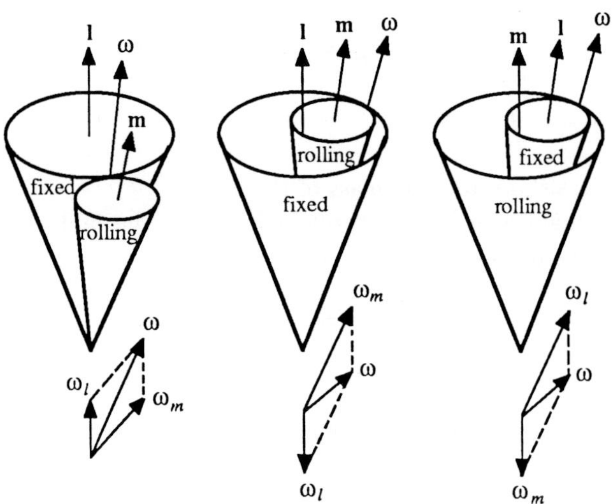

Fig. 6. The precessional motion of a symmetrical rigid body.

Let ω_l be the angular velocity at which the rolling cone rotates about **l**, and ω_m be the angular velocity at which the rolling cone rotates about its own axis of symmetry **m**. Then the instantaneous angular velocity ω is the vector sum of ω_l and ω_m as shown in Fig. 6. The magnitudes of ω_m and ω_l are constant. Thus, the magnitude of the instantaneous angular velocity is also constant. This kind of motion about a point is called precession in the following sections and it represents the restriction imposed by our model on the allowed object rotation.

A special case occurs when $\mathbf{m}$ is parallel to $\mathbf{l}$. Then $\boldsymbol{\omega}$ is also parallel to $\mathbf{l}$. Therefore, the instantaneous rotation axis does not change its orientation in motion. This type of motion is called motion without precession.

4.2. *Motion of Rotation Center*

The location of rotation center $\mathbf{Q}(t)$ changes with time. Assume the trajectory of the rotation center is smooth, or specifically, it can be expanded into a Taylor series:

$$\mathbf{Q}(t) = \mathbf{Q}(t_0) + \frac{1}{1!}\frac{d\mathbf{Q}(0)}{dt}(t - t_0) + \frac{1}{2!}\frac{d\mathbf{Q}(0)}{dt}(t - t_0)^2 + \cdots . \qquad (4.4)$$

If the time intervals between image frames are short, we can estimate the trajectory by the first k terms. We get a polynomial of time t. The coefficients of the polynomial are three-dimensional vectors. Letting

$$\frac{1}{j!}\frac{d^j\mathbf{Q}(0)}{dt^j} = \mathbf{b}_j + 1 \, ,$$

$j = 0, 1, 2, \ldots, k - 1$, we have

$$\mathbf{Q}_i = \mathbf{b}_1 + \mathbf{b}_2(t_i - t_0) + \mathbf{b}_3(t_i - t_0)^2 + \cdots + \mathbf{b}_k(t_i - t_0)^{k-1} \, . \qquad (4.5)$$

For simplicity, we assume the time intervals between image frames are constant c, i.e. $t_i = ci + t_0$. From (4.5) we get

$$\mathbf{Q}_i = \mathbf{b}_1 + c\mathbf{b}_2 i + c^2\mathbf{b}_3 i^2 + \cdots + c^{k-1}\mathbf{b}_k i^{k-1} \, . \qquad (4.6)$$

Letting $\mathbf{a}_j = c^{j-1}\mathbf{b}_j$, $j = 1, 2, \cdots, k$, we get

$$\mathbf{Q}_i = \mathbf{a}_1 + \mathbf{a}_2 i + \mathbf{a}_3 i^2 + \cdots + \mathbf{a}_k i^{k-1} \, . \qquad (4.7)$$

Equation (4.7) is the model for the motion of the rotation center. The basic assumption we made is that the trajectory can be approximated by a polynomial. If the motion is smooth and the time interval covered by the model is relatively short, Eq. (4.7) is a good approximation of the trajectory. In the sense of dynamics, (4.7) implies that the total force acting on the center of rotation has zero high order temporal derivatives.

A polynomial trajectory of center of rotation in (4.7) together with the precession model presented in the previous subsection, gives the complete LCAM model [42]. The model is characterized by locally constant angular momentum, i.e. the angular momentum of the moving object can be treated as constant over short time intervals.

A point should be mentioned here. Though we derive the model from the assumption of constant angular momentum and object symmetry, the condition leading to such motion is not unique. In other words, the motion model we derived applies to any moving object whose rotation can be locally modeled by such motion: the rotation about a fixed-on-body axis that rotates about a spatially fixed axis, and whose translation can be locally modeled by a vector polynomial. It is important to motivate the kinematics from dynamic conditions. But in reality, many different dynamic conditions may result in the same type of motion.

Our goal here is to understand 3-D motion of an object over an extended time period using the two-view motion analysis of images taken at consecutive time instants. Thus we would first estimate the motion parameters of the moving object from the images taken at two time instants, using the method presented in the previous section. Such motion parameters give the displacement between two time instants and do not describe the actual motion, since the object can move arbitrarily between the two time instants. The displacement can be represented by a rotation about an axis located at the origin of a world coordinate system, and a translation [41]. We have called this displacement two-view motion.

Let the column vector $\mathbf{p}_0$ be the 3-D coordinates of any object point at time t_0; let $\mathbf{p}_1$ be that of the same point at time t_1, R_1 be the rotation matrix from time t_0 to t_1, and $\mathbf{T}_1$ be the corresponding translation vector. Then, $\mathbf{p}_0$ and $\mathbf{p}_1$ are related by

$$\mathbf{p}_1 = R_1\mathbf{p}_0 + \mathbf{T}_1 \tag{4.8}$$

where R_1 represents a rotation about an axis through the origin.

Given a set of point correspondences, R_1 and $\mathbf{T}_1$ can be determined by two-view motion analysis. In the case of monocular vision, the translation vector can only be determined up to a positive scale factor, i.e. only the direction of $\mathbf{T}$, $\mathring{\mathbf{T}} = \mathbf{T}/\|\mathbf{T}\|$, can be determined from the perspective projection.

In Eq. (4.8), letting $\mathbf{p}_0$ be at the origin, it is clear that $\mathbf{T}_1$ is just the translation of the point at origin. For any point $\mathbf{Q}_0$, we can translate the rotation axis so that it goes through $\mathbf{Q}_0$ and rotate $\mathbf{p}_0$ about the axis at the new location. Mathematically, from (4.8) it follows that

$$\mathbf{p}_1 = R_1(\mathbf{p}_0 - \mathbf{Q}_0) + (R_1\mathbf{Q}_0 + \mathbf{T}_1). \tag{4.9}$$

Compared with (4.8), (4.9) tells us that the same motion can be represented by rotating $\mathbf{p}_0$ about $\mathbf{Q}_0$ by R_1, and then translating by $R_1\mathbf{Q}_0 + \mathbf{T}_1$. Because $\mathbf{Q}_0$ is arbitrarily chosen, there are infinitely many ways to select the location of the rotation axis. This is an ambiguity problem in motion understanding from image sequences. If we let the rotation axis always be located at the origin, the trajectory described by R_i and $\mathbf{T}_i$, $i = 1, 2, 3 \ldots$ would be like what is showed in Fig. 7, which is very unnatural.

In Fig. 7 the real trajectory of the center of the body is the dashed line. However, neither the rotation nor the translation components show this trajectory. As

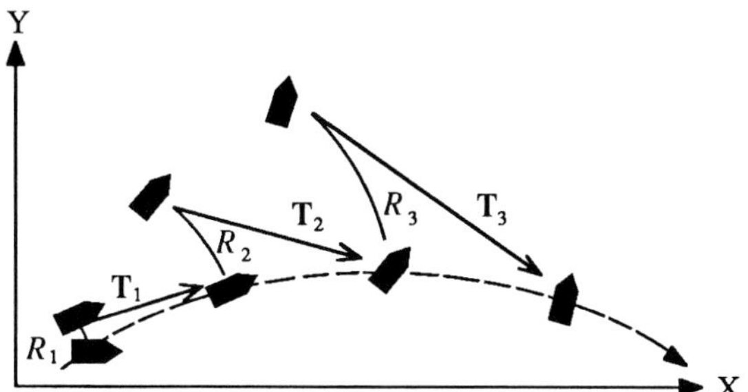

Fig. 7. Trajectory described by R_i and $\mathbf{T}_i$ if the rotation axis is always located at the origin.

we discussed in Section 4.1, the center of mass of a body in free motion satisfies Newton's equation of motion of a particle (4.1). Rotation is about the center of mass (or fixed point if it exists). Thus, motion should be expressed in two parts, the motion of the rotation center (the center of mass or the fixed point), and the rotation about the rotation center.

Let $\mathbf{Q}_i$ be the position vector of the rotation center at time t_i, R_i be the rotation matrix from t_{i-1} to t_i, and $\mathbf{T}_i$ be the translation vector from t_{i-1} to t_i. From (4.8) it follows that

$$\mathbf{Q}_1 = R_1\mathbf{Q}_0 + \mathbf{T}_1\,,$$

or,

$$-R_1\mathbf{Q}_0 + \mathbf{Q}_1 = \mathbf{T}_1\,.$$

Similarly we get equations for the motion from t_{i-1} to t_i, $i = 1, 2, \ldots, f$:

$$-R_1\mathbf{Q}_0 + \mathbf{Q}_1 = \mathbf{T}_1\,,$$
$$-R_2\mathbf{Q}_1 + \mathbf{Q}_2 = \mathbf{T}_2\,,$$
$$\cdots\cdots$$
$$-R_f\mathbf{Q}_{f-1} + \mathbf{Q}_f = \mathbf{T}_f\,. \tag{4.10}$$

Equations (4.10) give the relationship among the locations of the rotation center, the two-view rotation matrices and the two-view translation vectors.

Substituting (4.7) into (4.10), we get

$$(I - R_1)\mathbf{a}_1 + \mathbf{a}_2 + \mathbf{a}_3 + \cdots + \mathbf{a}_k = \mathbf{T}_1\,,$$
$$(I - R_2)\mathbf{a}_1 + (2I - R_2)\mathbf{a}_2 + (4I - R_2)\mathbf{a}_3 + \cdots + (2^{k-1}I - R_2)\mathbf{a}_k = \mathbf{T}_2\,,$$
$$\cdots\cdots$$
$$(I - R_f)\mathbf{a}_1 + (fI - (f-1)R_f)\mathbf{a}_2 + (f^2I - (f-1)^2R_f)\mathbf{a}_3 + \cdots$$
$$+ (f^{k-1}I - (f-1)^{k-1}R_f)\mathbf{a}_k = \mathbf{T}_f\,. \tag{4.11}$$

Vector equations (4.11) are referred to as the coefficient equations. Both sides of the equations are three-dimensional vectors. There are f equations in k unknown three-dimensional vectors. Let $\mathbf{A} = (a_1^t, a_2^t, \ldots, a_k^t)^t$, $\mathbf{T} = (\mathbf{T}_1^t, \mathbf{T}_2^t, \ldots, \mathbf{T}_f^t)^t$, and D be the coefficient matrix of the unknowns in (4.11). Let the element of D at the ith row and jth column be the 3×3 matrix D_{ij}, i.e. $D = [D_{ij}]_{f \times k}$. We have

$$D_{ij} = i^{j-1}I - (i-1)^{j-1}R_i \,.$$

We can rewrite the coefficient equations (4.11) as

$$DA = T \,. \tag{4.12}$$

D and $\mathbf{T}$ are determined by two-view motion analysis. The problem here is to determine $\mathbf{A}$, the coefficients of the polynomial in (4.7).

4.3. *Solutions of the Coefficient Equation*

Let $f = k$ in (4.11). Then the matrix D is a square matrix. We wish to know whether the linear equations (4.12) have a solution. If a solution exists, is it unique? If it is not unique, what is the general solution?

The solution of the coefficient equations depends on the types of motion, or the rotation matrices R_i and the translation vectors $\mathbf{T}_i$. Let us first consider a simpler case, where $k = 2$. This means that the trajectory of the rotation center is locally approximated by a motion of constant velocity. Three frames are used in this case. The coefficient equations become

$$(I - R_1)\mathbf{a}_1 + \mathbf{a}_2 = \mathbf{T}_1 \,, \tag{4.13}$$
$$(I - R_2)\mathbf{a}_1 + (2I - R_2)\mathbf{a}_2 = \mathbf{T}_2 \,. \tag{4.14}$$

Solving for $\mathbf{a}_2$ in (4.13) and substituting it into (4.14), we get

$$(I - 2R_1 + R_2R_1)\mathbf{a}_1 = (2I - R_2)\mathbf{T}_1 - \mathbf{T}_2 \,. \tag{4.15}$$

If $I - 2R_1 + R_2R_1$ is nonsingular, $\mathbf{a}_1$ can be uniquely determined from (4.15):

$$\mathbf{a}_1 = (I - 2R_1 + R_2R_1)^{-1}((2I - R_2)\mathbf{T}_1 - \mathbf{T}_2) \,.$$

Then $\mathbf{a}_2$ is determined from (4.13):

$$\mathbf{a}_2 = \mathbf{T}_1 - (I - R_1)\mathbf{a}_1 \,.$$

It can be shown [42] that $(I - 2R_1 + R_2R_1)$ is nonsingular if and only if the following two conditions are both satisfied: (1) the axes of rotations, represented by R_1 and R_2, respectively, are not parallel; (2) neither rotation angle is zero. Condition (2) is usually satisfied if the motion is not pure translation. If condition (1) is not satisfied, the solution of Eqs. (4.13) and (4.14) is not unique and has some structure. To show this, assume the rotation axes of R_1 and R_2 are parallel. Let

w be any vector parallel to these axes. Because any point on the rotation axis remains unchanged after rotation, we have $R_1\mathbf{w} = \mathbf{w}$, $R_2\mathbf{w} = \mathbf{w}$. For any solution $\mathbf{a}_1$ and $\mathbf{a}_2$, $\mathbf{a}_1 + c\mathbf{w}$ and $\mathbf{a}_2$ is another solution, where c is an arbitrary real constant. Therefore, there exist infinitely many solutions.

The following theorem presents the results for the general case.

Theorem 1 [42]. In coefficient equations, let $f = k$. Define S_k^j to be a 3 × 3 matrix :

$$S_k^j = \sum_{l=0}^{k-j} (-1)^l \binom{k}{l} R_{k-l} R_{k-l-1} \dots R_{j+1} I, \quad j = 0, 1, 2, \dots, k.$$

Define number $u_{i,j}$:

$$u_{i,j} = \sum_{m=1}^{i} (-1)^{i-m} m^{j-1} \binom{i}{m}, \quad j = i+1, i+2, \dots, k.$$

Then

$$S_k^0 \mathbf{a}_1 = -\sum_{l=1}^{k} S_k^l \mathbf{T}_l,$$

$$\mathbf{a}_k = \frac{1}{(k-1)!}\left(\sum_{m=1}^{k-1} S_{k-1}^m \mathbf{T}_m + S_{k-1}^0 \mathbf{a}_1 \right),$$

$$\mathbf{a}_{k-1} = \frac{1}{(k-2)!}\left(\sum_{m=1}^{k-2} S_{k-2}^m \mathbf{T}_m + S_{k-2}^0 \mathbf{a}_1 - u_{k-2,k}\mathbf{a}_k \right),$$

$$\mathbf{a}_{k-2} = \frac{1}{(k-3)!}\left(\sum_{m=1}^{k-3} S_{k-3}^m \mathbf{T}_m + S_{k-3}^0 \mathbf{a}_1 - u_{k-3,k}\mathbf{a}_k - u_{k-3,k-1}\mathbf{a}_{k-1} \right),$$

$$\dots \dots$$

$$\mathbf{a}_3 = \frac{1}{2!}\left(\sum_{m=1}^{2} S_2^m \mathbf{T}_m + S_2^0 \mathbf{a}_1 - u_{2,k}\mathbf{a}_k - u_{2,k-1}\mathbf{a}_{k-1} - \dots - u_{2,4}\mathbf{a}_4 \right),$$

$$\mathbf{a}_2 = \frac{1}{1!}\left(\sum_{m=1}^{1} S_1^1 \mathbf{T}_1 + S_1^0 \mathbf{a}_1 - u_{1,k}\mathbf{a}_k - u_{1,k-1}\mathbf{a}_{k-1} - \dots - u_{1,3}\mathbf{a}_3 \right). \qquad \square$$

If S_k^0 is not singular, the first equation given by Theorem 1 uniquely determines $\mathbf{a}_1$. Then $\mathbf{a}_k$, $\mathbf{a}_{k-1}$, $\dots$, $\mathbf{a}_2$ can be determined, sequentially, by the second, third, $\dots$, and last equations in Theorem 1. Thus, if S_k^0 is not singular, the solution is unique.

Theorem 2 [42]. In the case of rotation without precession, let w be any column vector parallel to the rotation axes, then

$$S_k^0 \mathbf{w} = 0, \tag{4.16}$$

and for any vector $\mathbf{a}$

$$(S_k^0 \mathbf{a}) \cdot \mathbf{w} = 0. \qquad (4.17)$$

$\square$

Using Theorem 1 gives

$$S_k^0 \mathbf{a}_1 = -\sum_{l=1}^{k} S_k^l \mathbf{T}_l. \qquad (4.18)$$

In the case of rotation without precession, Eq. (4.16) implies S_k^0 is singular. From (4.17), the left-hand side of (4.18) is orthogonal to $\mathbf{w}$. However if the real trajectory of the rotation center is not exactly a jth degree polynomial with $j \le k-1$ in (4.7), the right-hand side of (4.18) can be any vector, which may not be orthogonal to $\mathbf{w}$. This means that no solution exists for Eq. (4.18). If the real trajectory is a jth degree polynomial with $j \le k-1$, then Eq. (4.18) has a solution by our derivation of (4.18). Since Eq. (4.7) is usually only an approximation of the real trajectory, a least-squares solution of (4.18) can serve our purpose. Let $\hat{\mathbf{a}}_1$ be a least-squares solution of (4.18) which is solved by using independent columns of S_k^0. If the rank of S_k^0 is 2, which is generally true for motion without precession, the general solution is then $\mathbf{a}_1 = \hat{\mathbf{a}}_1 + c\mathbf{w}$, where c is any real number. All general solutions $\{\hat{\mathbf{a}}_1 + c\mathbf{w}\}$ form a straight line in 3-D space. From Eq. (4.7), this line gives the location and direction of the two-view rotation axis of the motion between time instants t_0 and t_1. From Theorem 2 it follows that

$$S_{k-1}^0 \mathbf{w} = 0, \ S_{k-2}^0 \mathbf{w} = 0, \ \ldots, \ S_1^0 \mathbf{w} = 0.$$

Then

$$S_{k-1}^0 \mathbf{a}_1 = S_{k-1}^0 \hat{\mathbf{a}}_1, \ S_{k-2}^0 \mathbf{a}_1 = S_{k-2}^0 \hat{\mathbf{a}}_1, \ \ldots, \ S_1^0 \mathbf{a}_1 = S_1^0 \hat{\mathbf{a}}_1.$$

Based on the equations given by Theorem 1, the unknowns $\mathbf{a}_k$, $\mathbf{a}_{k-1}$, $\ldots$, $\mathbf{a}_2$ are determined without knowing the undetermined number c.

If the motion is pure translation without rotation, all the rotation matrices R_i, $i = 1, 2, \ldots, k$, are unit matrix I. S_k^0 is the zero matrix. The first three columns of D are zero. $\mathbf{a}_1$ cannot be determined by coefficient equations. From Theorem 1, $\mathbf{a}_2, \mathbf{a}_3, \ldots, \mathbf{a}_k$, can still be determined by coefficient equations. Because no rotation exists, any point can be considered as a rotation center. Equation (4.7) can be used to approximate the trajectory of any object points.

Thus the solutions of the coefficient equations can be summarized as follows.

(1) In the case of rotation with precession, the solution of the coefficient equations is generally unique. The trajectory of the rotation center is described by (4.7).

(2) In the case of rotation without precession, the general solution of $\mathbf{a}_1$ gives the two-view rotation axis of the first two-view motion. All other coefficients $\mathbf{a}_2, \mathbf{a}_3, \ldots, \mathbf{a}_k$ are generally determined uniquely by Theorem 1. Thus, the two-view rotation axes of all two-view motions are determined by (4.7). Because no precession exists, any point on the rotation axis can be considered as

the rotation center. This is the meaning of the general solution $\mathbf{a}_1$. Once a particular point on the rotation axis is chosen as the rotation center, its trajectory is described by Eq. (4.7). There are infinitely many possible "parallel" trajectories of the rotation center depending on which point on the axis is chosen as the rotation center.

(3) In the case of pure translation without rotation, $\mathbf{a}_2, \mathbf{a}_3, \ldots, \mathbf{a}_k$ can still be determined by coefficient equations. However $\mathbf{a}_1$ cannot be determined by coefficient equations. $\mathbf{a}_1$ can be chosen to be the position of any object point at time t_0. Then Eq. (4.7) describes the trajectory of this point.

In the presence of noise, both a large number of point correspondences and a large number of image frames provide overdetermination. The algorithm presented in Section 3 can be used for the closed-form least-squares solution of two-view motion parameters. To use overdetermination based on a large number of frames, we let $f > k$ in the coefficient equations (4.11). In fact, the coefficient matrix S_k^0 is essentially a high order deference [42]. S_k^0 tends to be ill-conditioned when k gets large. This means $f > k$ is more important when k is large. If $f > k$, Eq. (4.12) can be solved by a least-squares method. We find a solution $\mathbf{A}$ to minimize

$$\| D\mathbf{A} - \mathbf{T} \| .$$

In the case of motion with precession, all the columns of D are generally independent. The least-squares solution is

$$\mathbf{A} = (D^t D)^{-1} D^t \mathbf{T} .$$

In the case of motion without precession, the column vectors of D are linearly dependent. This can be shown by letting $\mathbf{a}_1$ in Eq. (4.11) be a non-zero vector parallel to the two-view rotation axes. Then the first three columns of D linearly combined by $\mathbf{a}_1$ is a zero vector. To get the least-squares solution of the coefficient equations (4.11), the largest set of independent columns of D should be found or tolerance-based column pivoting should be made. Theorem 1 solves $\mathbf{a}_2, \mathbf{a}_3, \ldots, \mathbf{a}_k$. This means the last $3k - 3$ columns of D are always independent. In the presence of noise the columns of D are very unlikely to be exactly linearly dependent even in the case of motion without precession.

4.4. *Continuous and Discrete Motions*

The LCAM model we discussed is based on continuous precessional motion. We must find the relationship between continuous precession and two-view motion, before we can estimate the precessional parameters of our model based on discrete two-view motions.

As we discussed in Section 4.1, a precession can be considered as the motion of a rolling cone which rolls without slipping upon a fixed cone. The angular frequency

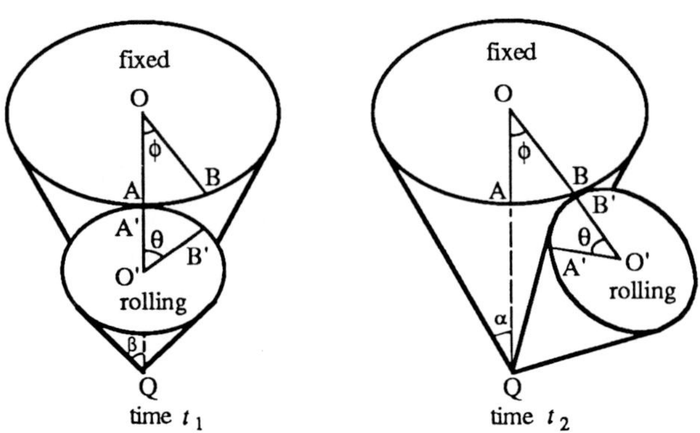

Fig. 8. The relation between rotation angles θ and ϕ.

at which the symmetrical axis of the rolling cone rotates about the fixed cone is constant.

Assumed at time t_1, that an edge point A$'$ on the rolling cone touches an edge point A on the fixed cone as shown in Fig. 8. After a certain amount of rolling, the touching points become B$'$ on the rolling cone and B on the fixed cone at time t_2. Let θ be the central angle of points A$'$ and B$'$, and ϕ be that of A and B. Let r and r' be the radii of circles O and O$'$, respectively. The arc length between A and B is equal to that between A$'$ and B$'$. Thus, $\phi r = \theta r'$ or $\phi \sin \alpha = \theta \sin \beta$, where α and β are generating angles of the fixed cone and the rolling cone, respectively. We get

$$\frac{\theta}{\phi} = \frac{\sin \alpha}{\sin \beta} \,. \tag{4.19}$$

The precession consists of two rotational components. One is the rotation of the rolling cone about its own symmetrical axis. The other is the rotation of the rolling cone about the fixed cone. From Fig. 8 it can be readily seen that the relative position of the rolling cone and the fixed cone is uniquely determined if the touching points of the two cones are determined. Or alternatively, starting from the previous position, the new position of the rolling cone is determined if the two angles ϕ and θ are determined. Thus, no matter how we order these two rotational components, the final positions are identical as long as the angle ϕ and θ are kept unchanged. We can first rotate the rolling cone about its axis **m** and then rotate the rolling cone about the axis of the fixed cone, **l**, or vice versa.

We hope to find the equivalent two-view rotation axis of this continuous motion between two frames at time t_1 and time t_2, respectively in Fig. 8. If we can find two fixed points which stay in the same positions before and after the motion, then the two-view rotation axis must go through these points. One trivial fixed point is the apex Q of the cones. Another fixed point can be found as follows: In Fig. 9 let the midpoint of arc AB touch the rolling cone (at time $(t_1 + t_2)/2$). Extend line OB

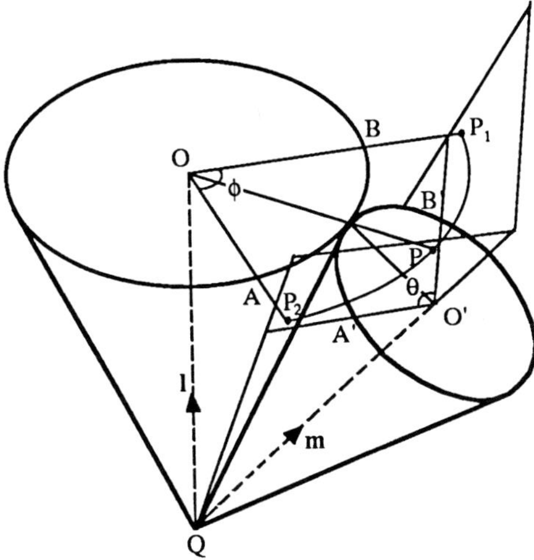

Fig. 9. Finding fixed points for two-view rotation.

so that it intersects the plane containing Q, O′ and B′ at a point P_1. Extend line OA so that it intersects the plane containing Q, O′ and A′ at a point P_2. Draw a circle centered at O and passing through P_1 and P_2. Then the midpoint P of arc $P_1 P_2$ is a fixed point. This can be seen by noting that the rolling cone can also reach its position at the next time instant t_2 in an alternative manner as follows. First, rotate the rolling cone (slipping along the fixed cone) about l by angle $\phi/2$, thus rotating P to its new position at P_1, and axis m reaches the position shown in Fig. 9. Then rotate the rolling cone (slipping on the fixed cone) about its own axis m by angle θ. Point P now reaches position P_2. Finally, rotate the rolling cone (slipping along the fixed cone) about l again by angle $\phi/2$, taking the rolling cone to the position at time instant t_2. This takes the point P back to its starting position. Therefore, the two-view rotation axis ϕ found by two-view motion analysis from two image frames, goes through Q and P. Notice that the angular frequency at which the symmetrical axis of the rolling cone rotates about the fixed cone is constant. From the way of finding P, it is clear that the two-view rotation axis also rotates about l by a constant angle between consecutive frames. Thus, we have the following theorem:

Theorem 3. If a rigid body undergoes a precessional motion of the LCAM model, the two-view rotation axis between constant time intervals changes by rotating about the precessional vector by a constant angle.   □

Without loss of generality, we assume the time intervals between consecutive image frames are of unit length. We define the *precessional vector* to be a unit vector l parallel to the symmetrical axis of the fixed cone, the *precessional angular frequency* ϕ to be the angular frequency at which the symmetrical axis of the rolling cone rotates about the precessional axis, the *ith body vector.* $\mathbf{m}_i$ to be a unit vector parallel to the symmetrical axis of the rolling cone at time t_i, and the *body rotation angular frequency* θ to be the angular frequency at which the rolling cone rotates about its symmetrical axis (see Fig. 10).

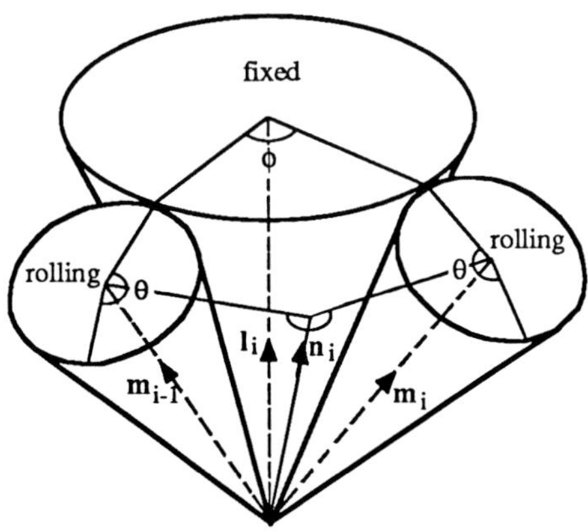

Fig. 10. Parameters of continuous precession and discrete two-view motion.

From image sequences we find estimates of two-view motion parameters. They are the *ith two-view rotation axis vector* $\mathbf{n}_i$, a unit vector parallel to the two-view rotation axis between time instants t_{i-1} and t_i; the corresponding *ith two-view rotation angle* ψ_i and the *ith two-view translation vector* $\mathbf{T}_i$. Figure 10 shows the precession parameters of continuous motion and discrete two-view motion.

Let $R(\mathbf{n},\ \theta) = [r_{ij}]$ denote the rotation matrix representing a rotation with axis unit vector $\mathbf{n} = (n_x, n_y, n_z)$ and rotation angle θ, then $R(\mathbf{n},\ \theta)$ is given by

$$
\begin{bmatrix}
(n_x^2 - 1)(1 - \cos\theta) + 1 & n_x n_y(1 - \cos\theta) - n_z \sin\theta & n_x n_z(1 - \cos\theta) + n_y \sin\theta \\
n_y n_x(1 - \cos\theta) + n_z \sin\theta & (n_y^2 - 1)(1 - \cos\theta) + 1 & n_y n_z(1 - \cos\theta) - n_x \sin\theta \\
n_z n_x(1 - \cos\theta) - n_y \sin\theta & n_z n_y(1 - \cos\theta) + n_x \sin\theta & (n_z^2 - 1)(1 - \cos\theta) + 1
\end{bmatrix} .
$$

$$(4.20)$$

Theorem 4. The continuous precession parameters and discrete two-view motion parameters are related by

$$R(\mathbf{l},\ \phi)R(\mathbf{m}_{i-1},\ \theta) = R(\mathbf{n}_i,\ \psi_i)\,, \tag{4.21}$$

$$R(\mathbf{m}_i,\ \theta)R(\mathbf{l},\ \phi) = R(\mathbf{n}_i,\ \psi_i)\,. \tag{4.22}$$

Proof. From time t_{i-1}, to time t_i, the body moves from its previous position to a new position. From Fig. 10 the new position of the rolling cone (or the body) can be reached in the following way: First, the rolling cone rotates about its body vector $\mathbf{m}_{i-1}$ by angle θ. Then, the rolling cone rotates about the precessional vector $\mathbf{l}$ by angle ϕ. The two-view motion combines these two motions into one, which is the rotation about the two-view rotation axis vector $\mathbf{n}_i$ by angle ψ_i. We get Eq. (4.21). Similarly if we change the order of these two rotational components we get Eq. (4.22). $\qquad\square$

From Theorem 3, the two-view rotation axis rotates about the precessional vector. Therefore, the precessional vector $\mathbf{l}$ is perpendicular to $\mathbf{n}_i - \mathbf{n}_{i-1}$ and $\mathbf{n}_{i-1} - \mathbf{n}_{i-2}$. The sign of $\mathbf{l}$ is arbitrary. Thus, $\mathbf{l}$ can be determined by

$$\mathbf{l} = \frac{(\mathbf{n}_i - \mathbf{n}_{i-1}) \times (\mathbf{n}_{i-1} - \mathbf{n}_{i-2})}{\|(\mathbf{n}_i - \mathbf{n}_{i-1}) \times (\mathbf{n}_{i-1} - \mathbf{n}_{i-2})\|} . \tag{4.23}$$

We will assume that precessional angular frequency, body rotation angular frequency and two-view rotation angle are not larger than half a turn between every two consecutive frames. This assumption is necessary in practice, since the rotation must be small enough for matching to be possible. The precessional angular frequency ϕ is equal to the the angle between $\mathbf{n}_i \times \mathbf{l}$ and $\mathbf{n}_{i-1} \times \mathbf{l}$:

$$|\phi| = \cos^{-1} \frac{(\mathbf{n}_i \times \mathbf{l}) \cdot (\mathbf{n}_{i-1} \times \mathbf{l})}{\|\mathbf{n}_i \times \mathbf{l}\| \, \|\mathbf{n}_{i-1} \times \mathbf{l}\|} . \tag{4.24}$$

The sign of ϕ is the same as the sign of

$$(\mathbf{n}_{i-1} \times \mathbf{n}_i) \cdot \mathbf{l}. \tag{4.25}$$

After $\mathbf{l}$ and ϕ are found by Eqs. (4.23), (4.24) and (4.25), $R(\mathbf{l}, \phi)$ can be calculated by (4.20). $R(\mathbf{m}_{i-1}, \theta)$ and $R(\mathbf{m}_i, \theta)$ can be determined by (4.21) and (4.22):

$$R(\mathbf{m}_{i-1}, \theta) = R^{-1}(\mathbf{l}, \phi) R(\mathbf{n}_i, \psi_i) , \tag{4.26}$$

$$R(\mathbf{m}_i, \theta) = R(\mathbf{n}_i, \psi_i) R^{-1}(\mathbf{l}, \phi) . \tag{4.27}$$

We can determine $\mathbf{m}_{i-1}$, $\mathbf{m}_i$ and θ by (4.26) and (4.27), because $\mathbf{n}$ and θ can be determined from $R(\mathbf{n}, \theta)$ [41]:

$$\theta = \pm \cos^{-1}\left(\frac{r_{11} + r_{22} + r_{33} - 1}{2}\right) ,$$

$$\mathbf{l} = \frac{[r_{32} - r_{23}, \, r_{13} - r_{31}, \, r_{21} - r_{12}]^t}{\|[r_{32} - r_{23}, \, r_{13} - r_{31}, \, r_{21} - r_{12}]\|} .$$

Thus, we get the following theorem.

Theorem 5. The precessional vector, precessional angular frequency, body axes and body rotation angular frequency which define the precession part of the LCAM model can all be determined from three consecutive two-view motions, or four consecutive image frames. $\qquad\square$

In addition to these basic parameters which uniquely determine the motion of the model, some other parameters can also be determined from these basic parameters.

For example, the generating angles α and β of the fixed cone and the rolling cone, respectively, in Fig. 8 can also be determined from $\mathbf{l}$, ϕ, $\mathbf{m}_i$, θ and Eq. (4.19).

4.5. *Estimation and Prediction*

The LCAM model is applied to subsequences of the images successively. The parameters of the model are estimated for every (overlapping) subsequence. The estimated model parameters can then be used to describe the current local motion. The following questions can be answered. Is there precession? If so, what are the precession parameters? What are the current or previous body vectors? What is the body rotation angular frequency? What is the probable motion for the next several time intervals? What are the probable locations of the feature points at the next several time instants? If the moving object is occluded in some of the previous image frames, what are the motion and the locations of these feature points during that time period?

The number of frames covered by an LCAM model can be made adaptive to the current motion. The number can be changed continuously to cover as many frames as possible so long as the constant angular momentum assumption is approximately true during the time period to be covered. The value of the number of frames chosen can be based on the accuracy with which the model describes the current set of consecutive frames. The residuals of least-squares solutions and the variances of the model parameter samples indicate the accuracy. The noise level also affects the residuals and the variances of parameter samples. However, the noise level is relatively constant or can be measured. The resolution of the cameras and the viewing angle covering the object generally determine the noise level. The noise can be smoothed by determining the best time intervals and the number of frames covered by the model, according to the current motion. Because the LCAM model is relatively general, the time interval an LCAM model can cover is expected to be relatively long in most cases.

The following part deals with the estimation of model parameters using overdetermination. Although one can derive formulation for minimum variance estimator here, the computation of the estimates requires iterations. We will discuss this optimal solution in Section 4.7. Here we give a closed-form solution that uses overdetermination. The solution can be directly computed without resorting to iterations.

After finding two-view rotation axis vectors $\mathbf{n}_1, \mathbf{n}_2, \ldots, \mathbf{n}_f$, precessional vector $\mathbf{l}$ should be orthogonal to $\mathbf{n}_2 - \mathbf{n}_1, \mathbf{n}_3 - \mathbf{n}_2, \ldots, \mathbf{n}_f - \mathbf{n}_{f-1}$. However, because of noise, this may not be true. Thus, we find $\mathbf{l}$ such that the sum of squares of the projections of $\mathbf{l}$ onto $\mathbf{n}_2 - \mathbf{n}_1, \mathbf{n}_3 - \mathbf{n}_2, \ldots, \mathbf{n}_f - \mathbf{n}_{f-1}$ is the smallest. Let

$$A = \begin{bmatrix} (\mathbf{n}_2 - \mathbf{n}_1)^t \\ (\mathbf{n}_3 - \mathbf{n}_2)^t \\ \cdots\cdots \\ (\mathbf{n}_f - \mathbf{n}_{f-1})^t \end{bmatrix} .$$

We are to find unit vector $\mathbf{l}$ in

$$\min_{\mathbf{l}} \|A\mathbf{l}\|, \text{ subject to: } \|\mathbf{l}\| = 1 . \tag{4.28}$$

The solution $\mathbf{l}$ of (4.28) is the unit eigenvector corresponding to the smallest eigenvalue of $A^t A$.

Let the precessional angular frequency determined from (4.24) and (4.25) be ϕ_i. The precessional angular frequency of the model ϕ can be estimated by the mean

$$\phi = \frac{1}{f-1} \sum_{i=2}^{f} \phi_i .$$

Let the body rotation angular frequency determined by (4.27) be θ_i. Body rotation angular frequency of the model can be estimated by the mean

$$\theta = \frac{1}{f} \sum_{i=1}^{f} \theta_i .$$

Body vectors are estimated by averaging two consecutive two-view motion using (4.26) and (4.27), respectively.

Two-view angular frequency can also be estimated by mean

$$\psi = \frac{1}{f} \sum_{i=1}^{f} \psi_i .$$

According to the motion model, the $(f+1)$st two-view rotation axis vector $\mathbf{n}_{f+1}$ is $R(\mathbf{l}, (f-i+1)\phi)\mathbf{n}_i$ for any $1 \leq i \leq f$. In the presence of noise, we use the mean over all previous two-view motions to predict the next two-view rotation axis vector:

$$\mathbf{n}_{f+1} = f^{-1} \sum_{i=1}^{f} R(\mathbf{l}, (f-i+1)\phi)\mathbf{n}_i .$$

From (4.9) the next position of point $\mathbf{x}_f$ in the fth frame is predicted by

$$\mathbf{x}_{f+1} = R(\mathbf{n}_{f+1}, \psi)(\mathbf{x}_f - \mathbf{Q}_f) + \mathbf{Q}_{f+1}$$

where $\mathbf{Q}_f$ and $\mathbf{Q}_{f+1}$ are determined by (4.7). The prediction can be made for more than $p \geq 2$ frames by using the following equations successively.

$$\mathbf{n}_{f+p} = R(\mathbf{l}, \phi)\mathbf{n}_{f+p-1} ,$$
$$\mathbf{x}_{f+p} = R(\mathbf{n}_{f+p}, \psi)(\mathbf{x}_{f+p-1} - \mathbf{Q}_{f+p-1}) + \mathbf{Q}_{f+p} .$$

If the object was occluded in parts of image sequences,the positions and orientations of the object as well as the locations of the feature points on the object can be recovered by an interpolation similar to the prediction procedure discussed above. For the motion of the rotation center, occlusion just means that some rows in the coefficient equations are missing. The solution can still be found if we have enough rows. For the precession part of the emotion, the interpolation can be made in a way similar to prediction or extrapolation. When making interpolation we use both the "history" and the "future" of the missing part. For prediction, only the "history" is available. Furthermore, we can also extrapolate backwards to find "history", i.e. to recall what has not been seen before. The essential assumption is that the motion is smooth.

4.6. *Monocular Vision*

For the monocular case, 3-D positions can be predicted only up to a global scale factor from two images. When more interframe motions are involved, how many scale factors are unable to be determined? The answer is one, provided that at least one point is visible among every three consecutive image frames. In other words, from point correspondences over a sequence of monocular image sequences, the depth of any visible points and translation between any two image frames can be determined up to a scale factor c. Therefore, although the 3-D position of the points can only be determined up to a scale factor, the image coordinates of the points can be predicted without knowing the scale factor, since the scale factor c is canceled out in image coordinates. In the following, we derive these results.

Suppose a point P is located at $\mathbf{x}_i = (x_i, y_i, z_i)^t$ at time t_i, $i = 0, 1, 2, \ldots$. The image vectors are defined by $\mathbf{x}_i = z\mathbf{X}_i$. From image frame f_i to image frame f_{i+1} the motion, called ith motion, is a rotation represented by R_i followed by a translation represented by $\mathbf{T}_i$.

$$\mathbf{x}_i = R_i \mathbf{x}_{i-1} + \mathbf{T}_i\,,$$

or

$$\frac{z_i}{\|\mathbf{T}_i\|}\mathbf{X}_i = R_i \frac{z_{i-1}}{\|\mathbf{T}_i\|}\mathbf{X}_{i-1} + \overset{\circ}{\mathbf{T}}_i\,,$$

$i = 1, 2, \ldots, n$. As discussed in Section 3, we can determine relative depths

$$\tilde{z}_i \triangleq \frac{z_i}{\|\mathbf{T}_i\|}\,, \tag{4.29}$$

and

$$\tilde{z}'_{i-1} \triangleq \frac{z_{i-1}}{\|\mathbf{T}_i\|}\,,$$

for $i = 1, 2, \ldots, n$, assuming the point P is visible for t_0 to t_n. We have

$$\frac{\tilde{z}_i}{\tilde{z}'_i} = \frac{\|\mathbf{T}_{i+1}\|}{\|\mathbf{T}_i\|}\,. \tag{4.30}$$

Multiplying both sides for $i = 1$ to $i = k$ yields

$$\prod_{i=1}^{k} \frac{\tilde{z}_i}{\tilde{z}'_i} = \frac{\|\mathbf{T}_k\|}{\|\mathbf{T}_1\|}. \tag{4.31}$$

Letting $\|\mathbf{T}_1\| \triangleq s$ be the unknown scale factor, (4.31) gives

$$\|\mathbf{T}_k\| = s \prod_{i=1}^{k} \frac{\tilde{z}_i}{\tilde{z}'_i}. \tag{4.32}$$

That is, the norm of the kth translation, $k = 1, 2, \ldots, n$, is a product of the scale factor s and a number

$$\prod_{i=1}^{k} \frac{\tilde{z}_i}{\tilde{z}'_i} \tag{4.33}$$

which can be determined from the relative depths. Therefore, although many interframe motions are involved in a long monocular sequence, only one unknown scale factor exists, instead of many. If the norm of translation in any interframe motion is known, s is determined from (4.31) and then motion and structure in the entire sequence is determined completely. Similarly, if the absolute depth of a point at a time instance is known, the norm of the translation vector is determined from (4.29), and then so does motion and structure in the entire sequence.

Now what happens if there exists no point that is visible through the entire sequence? We can see from (4.30) that (4.31) and (4.32) still hold true if each factor $\tilde{z}_i / \tilde{z}'_i$ corresponds to a different point. For $\tilde{z}_i$ and $\tilde{z}'_i$ to be determined for a point P, the point P must be visible from t_{i-1} to t_{i+1} in three consecutive image frames. Therefore, as long as through any three consecutive frames there is at least one point visible, the norm of any translation vector can be completely determined from s as in (4.32). Now we have proved the following theorem:

Theorem 6. Suppose the rotation matrix and direction of the translation between every consecutive monocular image pair can be determined. The magnitude of any interframe translation and the depths of visible points can be determined up to the same scale factor s, provided that through every three consecutive images at least one point is visible. $\qquad\square$

Since the depth of every point can be determined up to the same scale factor s, the 3-D position of the points can be predicted up to s as we discussed in the previous section. Since the image coordinates of a point cancel out this scale factor, the image coordinates of the point can be predicted without knowing the scale factor. For example, we can let $s = 1$ and compute the predicted 3-D position in the next frame based on the previous motion trajectory. Then by projecting the predicted 3-D point onto the image plane, we get the predicted image position of the point. This predicted position is the same for any positive s.

In the presence of noise, the error in a single point may significantly influence the accuracy of the product in (4.33). Therefore, the product should be determined based on many points instead of one. For example, the value of $\tilde{z}_i/\tilde{z}_i'$ can be averaged over many points before it is used to evaluate (4.33).

4.7. *Optimization*

The algorithm discussed above gives closed-form solutions for the model parameters. A simple least-squares solution is obtained when redundant data are available. Those solutions are generally good preliminary estimates. However, since the statistics of noise distribution is not employed, the solution is not optimal. If iterations are allowed, one can obtain higher accuracy through optimization.

The optimization for more than two image frames is very similar to the case of two frames (either monocular or stereo). We just need a natural extension. The two-step approach can be used. First, the algorithm discussed above provides initial guesses. Then the initial guesses are improved through an iterative optimization. Similar to the notation in Section 3.4. Let $\mathbf{m}$ denote the motion model parameter vector, $\mathbf{x} = (\mathbf{x}_1, \mathbf{x}_2, \ldots, \mathbf{x}_n)$ denote the structure of the scene at time t_0, $\mathbf{u}_{ijk}$ denote the observed ith image point in the jth camera (e.g. left: 1st, right: 2nd) at time t_k $(k = 0, 1, \ldots, f)$, and $\mathbf{h}_{ijk}(\mathbf{m}, \mathbf{x})$ denote the computed projection of the ith point in the jth camera at time t_k. Suppose that the additive noise in the coordinates of the image point is uncorrelated,

$$\hat{\mathbf{u}}_{ijk} = \mathbf{h}_{ijk}(\mathbf{m}, \mathbf{x}) + \delta_{ijk}\,.$$

According to the minimum variance estimation, the optimal estimate of $\mathbf{m}$ and $\mathbf{x}$ is the one that minimizes image plane errors:

$$\sum_{i=1}^{n}\sum_{j=1}^{2}\sum_{k=0}^{f} \|\hat{\mathbf{u}}_{ijk} - \mathbf{h}_{ijk}(\mathbf{m}, \mathbf{x})\|^2\,.$$

To keep the dimension of the iterative search space low, only the independent model parameters should be included into $\mathbf{m}$. They include *precessional velocity* vector defined as $\phi\mathbf{l}$, 0th *body velocity* vector defined as $\theta\mathbf{m}_0$, and coefficient vectors in the coefficient equation $\{\mathbf{a}_i\}$. Those parameters uniquely determine the two-view motion parameters through (4.21) and (4.22). Since the optimal 3-D position of a point $\mathbf{x}_i$ at time t_0 depends only on model parameters and the observations of the point in image sequences, the optimal $\mathbf{x}_i$ can be determined by minimizing

$$g_i(\mathbf{m}) \triangleq \min_{\mathbf{x}_i} \sum_{j=1}^{2}\sum_{k=0}^{f} \|\hat{\mathbf{u}}_{ijk} - \mathbf{h}_{ijk}(\mathbf{m}, \mathbf{x}_i)\|^2\,. \tag{4.34}$$

The solution for $\mathbf{x}_i$ that minimizes (4.34) can be estimated in a closed-form as in Section 3.4. Then, using the space decomposition technique gives

$$\min_{\mathbf{m}, \mathbf{x}}\left\{\sum_{i=1}^{n}\sum_{j=1}^{2}\sum_{k=0}^{1} \|\hat{\mathbf{u}}_{ijk} - \mathbf{h}_{ijk}(\mathbf{m}, \mathbf{x})\|^2\right\} = \min_{\mathbf{m}} \sum_{i=1}^{n} g_i(\mathbf{m})\,.$$

This decomposition significantly reduces the dimension of search space. If the two-view motion parameters used to compute the model parameters are optimized, the initial guess of **m** is usually very good. This will significantly reduce the number of iterations in computing the optimal **m**.

It is clear that either using monocular vision or any multi-ocular vision, we just need to change the upper limit of j accordingly.

Computationally, the minimization of the above function can be performed using a recursive-batch approach [43] which is a revised version of the Kalman filtering approach [44]. The recursive-batch approach is useful for improving the performance and efficiency when the image sequence is very long, or virtually infinite.

References

[1] B. K. P. Horn and B. G. Schunck, Determining optical flow, *Artif. Intell.* **17** (1981) 185–203.

[2] A. M. Waxman, An image flow paradigm, in *Proc. Workshop on Computer Vision: Representation and Control*, Annapolis, MD (IEEE Computer Society Press, Washington D.C., 1984) 49–57.

[3] H.-H. Nagel and W. Enkelmann, An investigation of smoothness constraints for the estimation of displacement vector fields from image sequences, *IEEE Trans. Pattern Anal. Mach. Intell.* **8** (1986) 565–593.

[4] J. K. Kearney, W. B. Thompson and D. L. Boley, Optical flow estimation: An error analysis of gradient-based methods with local optimization, *IEEE Trans. Pattern Anal. Mach. Intell.* **9** (1987) 229–244.

[5] D. J. Heeger, Optical flow using spatiotemporal filters, *Int. J. Comput. Vision* **2** (1987) 279–302.

[6] S. T. Barnard and W. B. Thompson, Disparity analysis of images, *IEEE Trans. Pattern Anal. Mach. Intell.* **2** (1980) 333–340.

[7] L. Dreschler and H.-H. Nagel, Volumetric model and 3-D trajectory of a moving car derived from monocular TV frame sequences of a street scene, *Comput. Graph. Image Process.* **20** (1982) 199–228.

[8] E. C. Hildreth, *The Measurement of Visual Motion* (MIT Press, Cambridge, MA, 1983).

[9] D. Marr and T. Poggio, A theory of human stereo vision, *Proc. Royal Society of London* **B204** (1979) 301–328.

[10] J. E. W. Mayhew and J. P. Frisby, Psychophysical and computational studies towards a theory of human stereopsis, *Artif. Intell.* **17** (1981) 349–385.

[11] W. E. L. Grimson, *From Images to Surfaces: A Computational Study of the Human Early Visual Systems* (MIT Press, Cambridge, MA, 1981).

[12] Y. Ohta and T. Kanade, Stereo by intra- and inter-scanline search using dynamic programming, *IEEE Trans. Pattern Anal. Mach. Intell.* **7** (1985) 139–154.

[13] N. Ayache and B. Faverjon, Efficient registration of stereo images by matching graph descriptions of edge segments, *Int. J. Comput. Vision* **1** (1987) 107–131.

[14] H. P. Moravec, Towards automatic visual obstacle avoidance, in *Proc. 5th Int. Joint Conf. on Artificial Intelligence* (William Kaufmann, Los Angeles, LA, 1977).

[15] F. Glazer, G. Reynolds and P. Anandan, Scene matching by hierarchical correlation, in *Proc. IEEE Conf. on Computer Vision Pattern Recognition* (IEEE Computer Society Press, Washington D.C., 1983) 432–441.

[16] T. D. Sanger, Stereo disparity computation using Gabor filters, *Biol. Cybern.* **59** (1988) 405–418.

[17] A. D. Jepson and M. R. M. Jenkin, The fast computation of disparity from phase differences, in *Proc. IEEE Conf. on Computer Vision Pattern Recognition*, San Diego, CA (IEEE Computer Society Press, Washington D.C., 1989) 398–403.

[18] J. Weng, A theory of image matching, in *Proc. Third Int. Conf. on Computer Vision*, Osaka, Japan (IEEE Computer Society Press, Washington D.C., 1990) 200–209.

[19] J. J. Hwang and E. L. Hall, Matching of featured objects using relational tables from stereo images, *Comput. Graph. Image Process.* **20** (1982) 22–42.

[20] W. K. Gu, J. Y. Yang and T. S. Huang, Matching perspective views of a polyhedron using circuits, *IEEE Trans. Pattern Anal. Mach. Intell.* **9** (1987) 390–400.

[21] H. S. Lim and T. O. Binford, Stereo correspondence: A hierarchical approach, in *Proc. Image Understanding Workshop* (Science Applications Corp., Mclean, VA, 1987) 234–241.

[22] J. Weng, N. Ahuja and T. S. Huang, Two-view matching, in *Proc. 2nd Int. Conf. on Computer Vision* (IEEE Computer Society Press, Washington D.C., 1988) 64–73. Also, Matching two perspective views, *IEEE Trans. Pattern Anal. Mach. Intell.* **14** (1992) 806–825.

[23] R. Jain and H.-H. Nagel, On the analysis of accumulative difference pictures from image sequences of real world scenes, *IEEE Trans. Pattern Anal. Mach. Intell.* **1** (1979) 206–214.

[24] J. W. Roach and J. K. Aggarwal, Determining the movement of objects from a sequence of images, *IEEE Trans. Pattern Anal. Mach. Intell.* **2** (1980) 554–562.

[25] A. R. Bruss and B. K. Horn, Passive navigation, *Comput. Vision Graph. Image Process.* **21** (1983) 3–20.

[26] G. Adiv, Determining three-dimensional motion and structure from optical flow generated by several moving objects, *IEEE Trans. Pattern Anal. Mach. Intell.* **7** (1985) 348–401.

[27] A. Mitiche and J. K. Aggarwal, A computational analysis of time-varying images, in T. Y. Young and K. S. Fu (eds.), *Handbook of Pattern Recognition and Image Processing* (Academic Press, New York, 1986).

[28] H. C. Longuet-Higgins, A computer program for reconstructing a scene from two projections, *Nature* **293** (1981) 133–135.

[29] R. Y. Tsai and T. S. Huang, Uniqueness and estimation of 3-D motion parameters of rigid bodies with curved surfaces, *IEEE Trans. Pattern Anal. Mach. Intell.* **6** (1984) 13–27.

[30] D. L. Yen and T. S. Huang, Determining 3 D motion and structure of a rigid body using the spherical projection, *Comput. Vision Graph. Image Process.* **21** (1983) 21–32.

[31] J. Q. Fang and T. S. Huang, Some experiments on estimating the 3-D motion parameters of a rigid body from two consecutive image frames, *IEEE Trans. Pattern Anal. Mach. Intell.* **6** (1984) 547–554.

[32] X. Zhuang and R. M. Haralick, Rigid body motion and the optic flow image, in *Proc. IEEE 1st Conf. on Artificial Intelligence Applications*, Denver, CO (IEEE Computer Society Press, Washington D.C., 1984) 366–375.

[33] X. Zhuang, T. S. Huang, N. Ahuja and R. M. Haralick, A simplified linear optic flow-motion algorithm, *Comput. Vision Graph. Image Process.* **42** (1988) 334–344.

[34] A. M. Waxman, B. Kamgar-Parsi and M. Subbarao, Closed-form solutions to image flow equations for 3-D structure and motion, *Int. J. Comput. Vision* **1** (1987) 239–258.

[35] O. D. Faugeras, F. Lustman and G. Toscani, Motion and structure from point and line matches, in *Proc. Int. Conf. on Comput. Vision*, London, UK (IEEE Computer Society Press, Washington D.C., 1987) 25–34.

[36] J. Weng, T. S. Huang and N. Ahuja, Error analysis of motion parameter determination from image sequences, in *Proc. 1st Int. Conf. on Computer Vision*, London, UK (IEEE Computer Society Press, Washington D.C., 1987) 703–707.

[37] H. C. Longuet-Higgins, The reconstruction of a scene from two projections — configurations that defeat the 8-point algorithm, in *Proc. IEEE 1st Conf. on Artificial Intelligence Applications*, Denver, CO (IEEE Computer Society Press, Washington D.C., 1984) 395–397.

[38] J. Weng, T. S. Huang and N. Ahuja, Motion and structure from two perspective views: Algorithms, error analysis and error estimation, *IEEE Trans. Pattern Anal. Mach. Intell.* **11** (1989) 451–476.

[39] G. R. Fowles, *Analytical Mechanics*, 3rd ed. (Holt, Rinehart and Winston, New York, 1977).

[40] W. D. Macmillan, *Dynamics of Rigid Bodies* (McGraw-Hill, New Jersey, 1936).

[41] O. Bottema and B. Roth, *Theoretical Kinematics* (North-Holland, New York, 1979).

[42] J. Weng, T. S. Huang and N. Ahuja, 3-D motion estimation, understanding and prediction from noisy image sequences, *IEEE Trans. Pattern Anal. Mach. Intell.* **9** (1987) 370–389.

[43] J. Weng, P. Cohen and N. Rebibo, Motion and structure estimation from stereo image sequences, *IEEE Trans. Robotics and Automation* **8**, 3 (1992) 362–382.

[44] G. S. Young and R. Chellappa, 3-D motion estimation using a sequence of noisy stereo images: Models, estimation, and uniqueness results, *IEEE Trans. Pattern Anal. Mach. Intell.* **12** (1990) 735–759.

Handbook of Pattern Recognition and Computer Vision, pp. 443–456
Eds. C. H. Chen, L. F. Pau and P. S. P. Wang
© 1993 World Scientific Publishing Company

CHAPTER 2.6

SEGMENTATION TOOLS IN MATHEMATICAL MORPHOLOGY

SERGE BEUCHER

Centre de Morphologie Mathématique — Ecole des Mines
35 Rue Saint-Honoré, 77305 Fontainebleau, France

This paper presents a general methodology for picture segmentation using tools provided by mathematical morphology. This methodology is based on the marking of the objects to be segmented. The marking (using techniques which may differ according to the kind of picture to be analyzed) provides a "marker set" which is used to modify the gradient of the image. This modification using geodesic image reconstruction produces a new gradient image. The main characteristic of this modified gradient is that its minima exactly fit the various connected components of the "marker set".

In a second step, a morphological transform called "watersheds" is performed on this gradient image. The watershed transform produces a partition of the image into homogeneous regions called "catchment basins". Every catchment basin contains only one marker and its boundary corresponds to the pixels of the image where the contrast is locally maximum. Thus, the transformed image exhibits the contours of the marked objects.

Some examples illustrate the use of this process when objects marking is not too complex. Then, we extend this method to situations where the marking step is not obvious, and we show how the watershed transform together with the simplification of the image can provide efficient tools for detecting homogeneous regions in an image.

Introduction

Image segmentation by mathematical morphology is performed in two steps. The first one consists in marking the objects in the image to be segmented. The second one uses a morphological tool named watershed transformation. This transformation produces a partition of the image into regions called catchment basins. The watershed transformation was applied to segmentation problems for the first time by Beucher and Lantuéjoul [1]. Unfortunately, this transformation very often leads to an over-segmentation of the image. This over-segmentation can be avoided by marking as shown by Meyer [2]. The marking of the objects provides a marker set which is used to change the homotopy of the function in the watershed transformation. This function, very often, corresponds to the gradient image, but this is not compulsory. We may use other functions depending on the problem to be

---

443

solved. The first part of this paper will be devoted to the introduction of these basic tools. Some algorithms of watershed transformation will be described. This transformation will be applied to a simple case, then to a more complicated one, where over-segmentation occurs. The concept of markers and the modification of the homotopy of the gradient function solve this problem. Other examples will be described to illustrate the methodology.

The second part of this presentation will introduce the notion of image simplification which leads to a representation of a picture in terms of graph. We will show that the basic morphological transformations can be defined on any graph, and in particular the watershed transformation. The watershed becomes then a powerful tool for a hierarchical segmentation of complex pictures.

1. Basic Tools for Segmentation in Mathematical Morphology

For the sake of simplicity, we will consider digital pictures only. A grey-tone image can be represented by a function $f\colon \mathbb{Z}^2 \to \mathbb{Z}$. $f(x)$ is the grey value of the image at point x. The points of the space $\mathbb{Z}^2$ may be the vertices of a square or an hexagonal grid.

A section of f at level i is a set $X_i(f)$ defined as:

$$X_i(f) = \{x \in \mathbb{Z}^2 : f(x) \geq i\}. \tag{1}$$

In the same way, we may define the set $Z_i(f)$:

$$Z_i(f) = \{x \in \mathbb{Z}^2 : f(x) \leq i\}. \tag{2}$$

We obviously have:

$$X_i(f) = Z^c_{i+1}(f). \tag{3}$$

1.1. *The Watershed Transformation*

The set of all the points $\{x, f(x)\}$ belonging to $\mathbb{Z}^2 \times \mathbb{Z}$ can be seen as a topographic surface S. The lighter the grey value of f at point x, the higher the altitude of the corresponding point $\{x, f(x)\}$ on the surface.

Various characteristic features can be defined on this topographic surface. Among them are the *minima*, also called *regional minima*, of f. Consider two points s_1 and s_2 of this surface S. A path between $s_1(x_1, f(x_1))$ and $s_2(x_2, f(x_2))$ is any sequence $\{s_i\}$ of points of S, with s_i adjacent to s_{i+1}. A non-ascending path is a path where:

$$\forall\ s_i(x_i, f(x_i)),\ s_j(x_j, f(x_j))\ i \geq j \leftrightarrow f(x_i) \leq f(x_j). \tag{4}$$

A point $s \in S$ belongs to a minimum iff there exists no ascending path starting from s. A minimum can be considered as a sink of the topographic surface (Fig. 1a). The set M of all the minima of f is made of various connected components $M_i(f)$. Let us define the *catchment basins* of f and the *watershed lines* by means of a

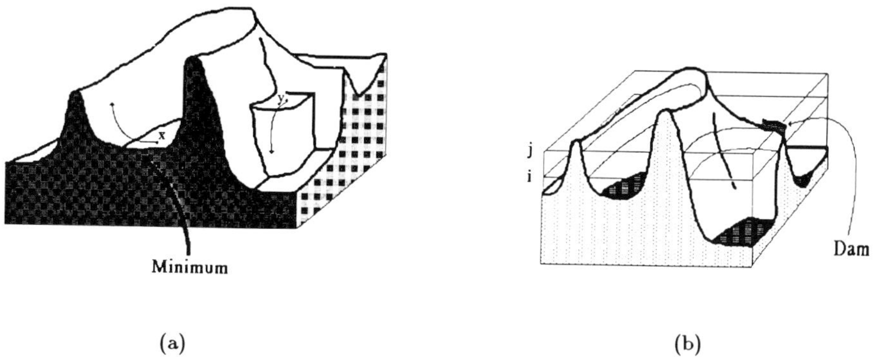

Fig. 1. Minima of a function (a), flooding of the relief and construction of dams (b).

flooding process. Imagine that we pierce each minimum $M_i(f)$ of the topographic surface S, and that we plunge this surface into a lake with a constant vertical speed. The water entering through the holes floods the surface S. During the flooding, two or more floods coming from different minima may merge. We want to avoid this phenomenon and we build a dam on the points of the surface S where the floods would merge (Fig. 1b). At the end of the process, only the dams emerge. These dams define the watershed of the function f. They separate the various catchment basins $CB_i(f)$, each one containing one and only one minimum $M_i(f)$ (Fig. 2).

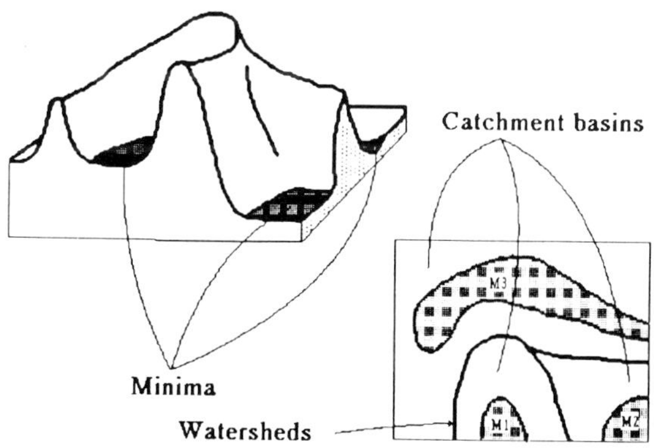

Fig. 2. Regional minima, catchment basins and divide lines.

1.2. *Building the Watershed*

This definition of the watershed transformation has a great advantage: it can be performed on the sections of the function. The watershed algorithms can be divided into two groups. The first group contains algorithms which simulate the flooding process. The second group consists of procedures aiming at detecting directly the points of the watershed lines.

Let us describe the algorithm based on the sections (it belongs to the first group). But, before, we must introduce some geodesic transformations.

1.2.1. *Geodesy, geodesic zones of influence*

Let $X \subset \mathbb{Z}^2$ be a set, and x and y be two points of X. We define the *geodesic distance* $d_X(x, y)$ between x and y as the length of the shortest path (if it exists) included in X and linking x and y (Fig. 3a).

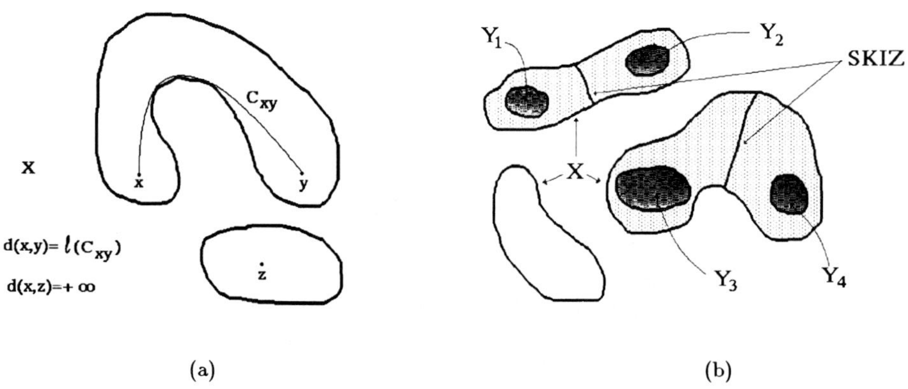

(a)   (b)

Fig. 3. Shortest path and geodesic distance (a); geodesic skeleton by zones of influence (b).

Many basic morphological transforms can be redefined with this distance. Let Y be any set included in X. We can compute the set of all points of X which are at finite geodesic distance from Y:

$$R_X(Y) = \{x \in X : \exists\, y \in Y,\ d_X(x, y)\ \text{finite}\}. \qquad (5)$$

$R_X(Y)$ is called the *X-reconstructed set* by the marker set Y. It is made of all the connected components of X which are marked by Y.

Suppose now that Y is composed of n connected components Y_i. The *geodesic zone of influence* $z_X(Y_i)$ of Y_i is the set of the points of X that are at a finite geodesic distance from Y_i and closer to Y_i than to any other Y_j (Fig. 3b):

$$z_X(Y_i) = \{x \in X : d_X(x, Y_i)\ \text{finite and}\ \forall j \neq i,\ d_X(x, Y_i) < d_X(x, Y_j)\}. \qquad (6)$$

The boundaries between the various zones of influence give the *geodesic skeleton by zones of influence* of Y in X.

We shall write:

$$SKIZ_X(Y) = \bigcup_i z_X(Y_i). \qquad (7)$$

1.2.2. *Watersheds and sections of f*

Consider (Fig. 4) a section $z_i(f)$ of f at level i, and suppose that the flood has reached this height. Consider now the section $Z_{i+1}(f)$. We immediately see that the flooding of $Z_{i+1}(f)$ is performed in the zones of influence of the connected components of $Z_i(f)$ in $Z_{i+1}(f)$. Some connected components of $Z_{i+1}(f)$ which are not reached by the flood are, by definition, minima at level $i+1$. These minima must therefore be added to the flooded area. Denoting by $W_i(f)$ the section at level i of the catchment basins of f, and by $M_{i+1}(f)$ the minima of the function at height $i+1$, we have:

$$W_{i+1}(f) = [SKIZ_{Z_{i+1(f)}}(X_i(f))] \cup M_{i+1}(f) . \qquad (8)$$

The minima at level $i+1$ are given by:

$$M_{i+1}(f) = Z_{i+1}(f)/R_{Z_{i+1(f)}}(Z_i(f)) \qquad (9)$$

where / stands for the set difference.

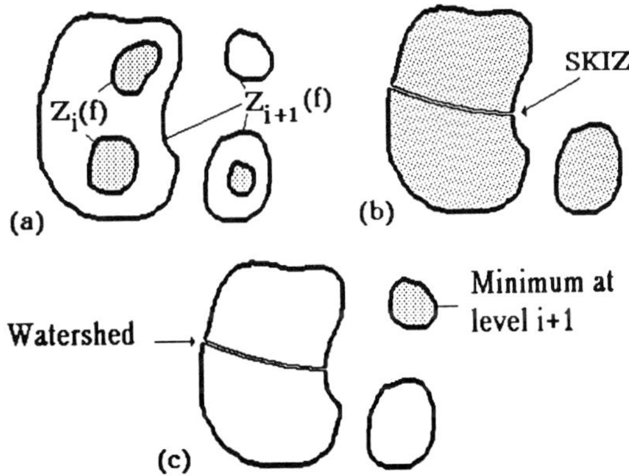

Fig. 4. Successive steps of the watershed construction using geodesic *SKIZ*.

This iterative algorithm is initialized with $W_{-1}(f) = \emptyset$. At the end of the process, the watershed line $DL(f)$ is equal to:

$$DL(f) = W_N^c(f) \text{ (with } \max(f) = N) . \qquad (10)$$

1.2.3. *Arrowing and watersheds*

The previous algorithm belongs to the first group: it simulates the flooding of the surface S starting from the minima of f. We will now present briefly another algorithm that belongs to the second group and which is based on the *arrowing representation* of a function f.

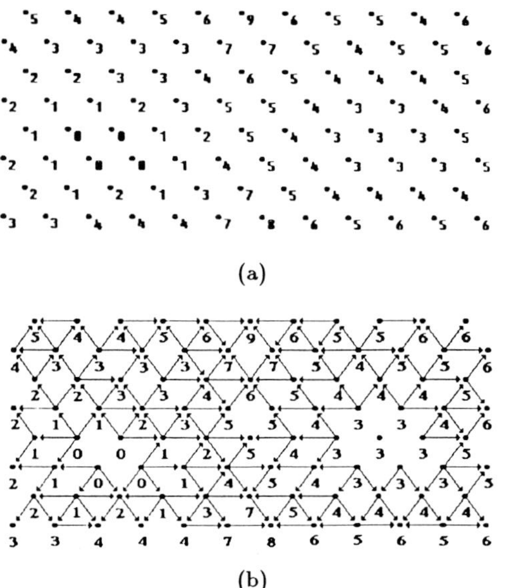

(a)

(b)

Fig. 5. Function f (a) and its complete graph of arrows (b).

From f_2: $\mathbb{Z}^2 \to \mathbb{Z}$, we may define an oriented graph whose vertices are the points of $\mathbb{Z}^2$ and equipped with edges (or arrows) from x to any adjacent point y iff $f(x) < f(y)$ (Fig. 5) [3].

The definition does not allow the arrowing of the plateaus of the topographic surface. This arrowing can be performed by means of geodesic dilations. The operation is called the *completion* of the graph of arrows. We may, then, select on the complete graph some configurations which, locally, correspond to divide lines. These configurations are represented on Fig. 6 for the 6-connectivity neighborhood of a point (up to a rotation).

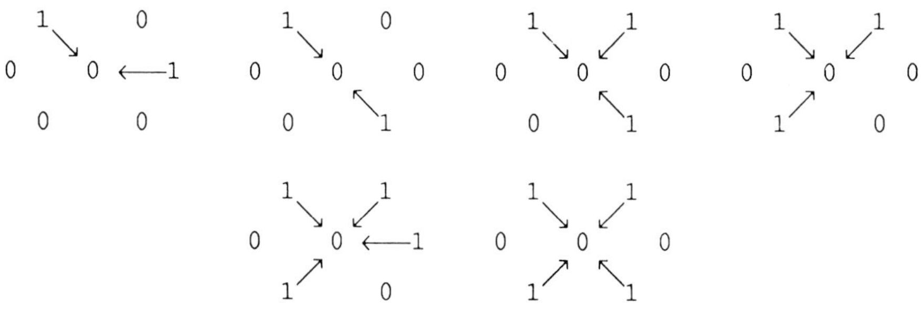

Fig. 6. Configurations of arrows corresponding to possible divide points.

Any point receiving arrows from more than one connected component of its neighborhood may be flooded by different lakes. Consequently, this point may belong to a divide line. In a second step, the arrows starting from the selected points must be suppressed. These points, in fact, cannot be flooded, so they cannot propagate the flood. Doing so, we change the arrowing of the neighbor points. Some new divide points may then appear. The procedure is re-run until no new divide point is selected (Fig. 7).

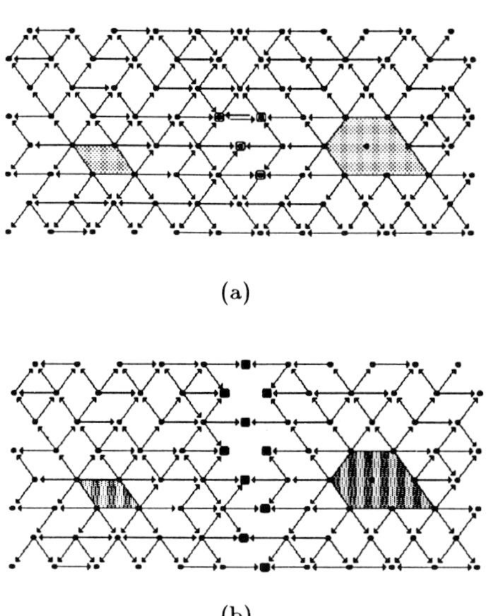

(a)

(b)

Fig. 7. Watersheds by arrowing. (a) Selection of primary divide points, (b) final result and corresponding graph of arrows.

This algorithm produces local watershed lines. The true watersheds can be extracted easily. They are the only ones that form closed curves.

3. Use of Watersheds in Picture Segmentation

3.1. *A Real Example*

The use of watershed transformations for picture segmentation will be explained by means of a real example: the contouring of proteins in an electrophoresis gel (Fig. 8a). Each blob can be characterized by a sink in the topographic surface drawn by the grey-tone image f. The corresponding gradient image should present a volcano-type topography as depicted in Fig. 8b. The contours of the proteins blobs correspond therefore to the watershed lines of the gradient image $g(f)$. This gradient is defined as:

$$g(f) = (f \oplus B) - (f \ominus B) \tag{11}$$

where $f \oplus B$ and $f \ominus B$ are respectively elementary dilation and erosion of f [4].

Unfortunately, the real watershed transform of the gradient, given in Fig. 9a, presents many catchment basins; there are as many of them as there are minima

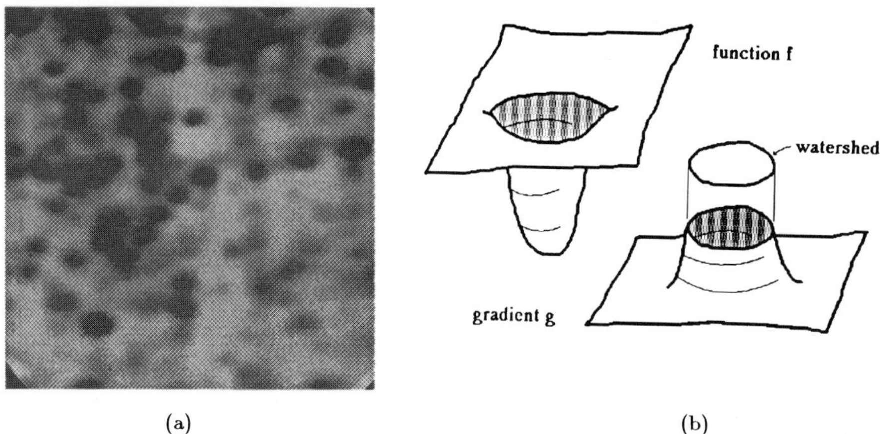

(a)   (b)

Fig. 8. Electrophoresis gel (a), topographic surface of the initial function and of the gradient image (b).

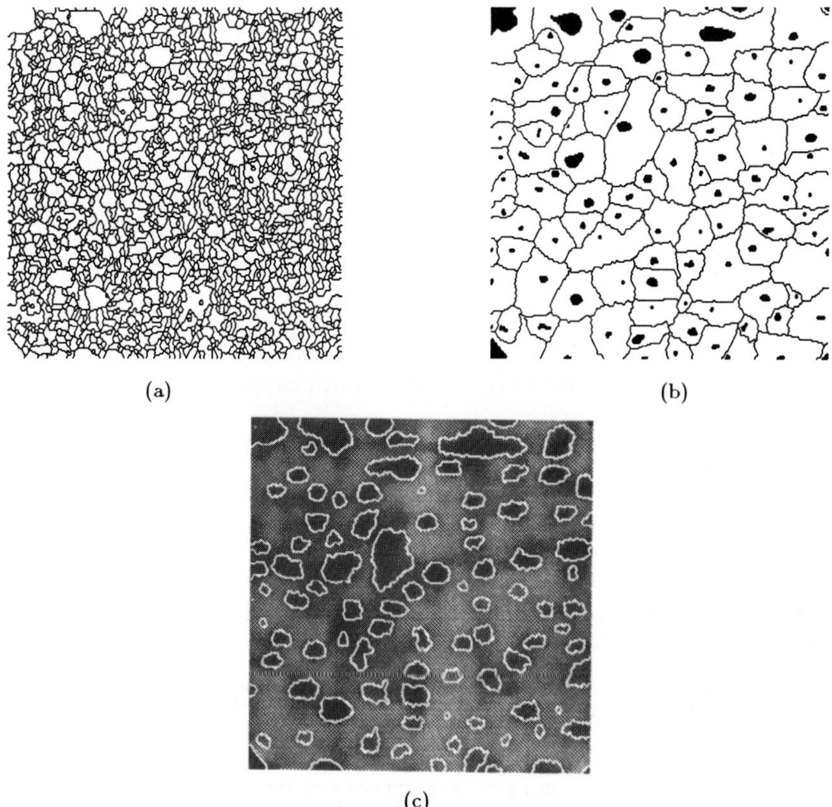

(a)   (b)

(c)

Fig. 9. Watersheds of the gradient image (a), set of selected markers M (inner markers of blobs, and one outer marker for the background) (b), final segmentation (c).

in the gradient. These minima are produced by small variations in the grey values. This over-segmentation could be reduced by appropriate filtering. But a better result will be obtained if we mark the patterns to be segmented before performing the watershed transformation of the gradient. Suppose that we mark each blob of protein of Fig. 8a. This marking can be performed by extracting the minima of f. We must also define a marker for the background. In order to get a connected marker surrounding the blobs, the watershed transform of the initial image is performed. Then, we obtain a set of markers M (Fig. 9b). We consider again the topographic surface of the gradient image and the flooding process, but, instead of piercing the minima of this surface, we will only make holes through the components of the marker set M. The flooding will invade the surface and produce as many catchment basins as there are markers comprised in the markers set. Moreover, the watershed lines will correspond to the crest lines of this topographic surface which themselves correspond to the contours of the objects (Fig. 9c).

We can show that this algorithm may be written as follows.

If $W_i(g)$ is the section at level i of the new catchment basins of g, we have:

$$W_{i+1}(g) = SKIZ_{Z_{i+1}} \cup M(W_i(g)) \tag{12}$$

with:

$$W_{-1}(g) = M, \text{ markers set}$$

Surprisingly, this algorithm is simpler than the pure watershed algorithm, because we do not take the real minima of g into account.

This procedure may be split into two steps. The first one consists in modifying the gradient function g in order to produce a new gradient g'. This new image is very similar to the original one, except that its initial minima have disappeared and have been replaced by the set M. This image modification, also called *homotopy modification*, can be performed by reconstructing the sections of g with the markers M.

We have:

$$\forall i, \ Z_i(g') = R_{Z_j(g) \cup M}(M). \tag{13}$$

The second step simply consists in performing the watershed transform of the modified gradient g' [2].

2.2. *Towards a Methodology of the Segmentation*

This first example of segmentation leads to a general scheme. Image segmentation consists in selecting first a marker set M pointing out the objects to be extracted, then a function f quantifying a segmentation criterion (this criterion can be, for instance, the changes in grey values). This function is modified to produce a new function f' having as minima the set of markers M. The segmentation of the initial image is performed by the watershed transform of f' (Fig. 10).

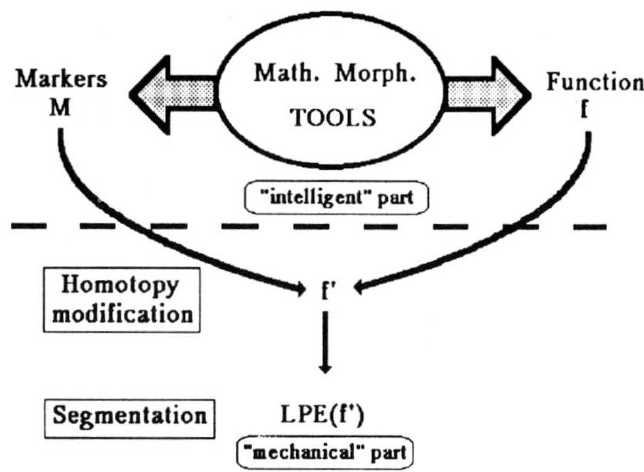

Fig. 10. Synopsis of the morphological segmentation methodology.

The segmentation process is therefore divided into two steps: an "intelligent" part whose purpose is the determination of M and f, and a "straightforward" part consisting in the use of the basic morphological tools which are watersheds and image modification.

A lot of segmentation problems may be solved according to this general scheme [5]. Let us illustrate this procedure with two examples.

The first example is a part of a road traffic sensor able to compute various parameters from a road traffic scene for each traffic lane [6]. To achieve the segmentation of the traffic lanes, two images are generated. The first one is an average picture of a sequence of images (Fig. 11a) and the second one is the average of the first derivative of the sequence along the time axis (Fig. 11b). These two images are used to produce a marker set (Fig. 11c) and the function to be segmented (Fig. 11d). The latter function is the geodesic distance function of the ground layout. The final segmentation is given in Fig. 11e.

The second example is a problem of segmentation of cleavage facets in a SEM micrograph of a steel fracture (Fig. 12a). The function used for watersheds (Fig. 12b) along with the marker set (Fig. 12c) are built by combining a photometric criterion (contrast between facets due to blazing ridges) and a shape criterion (facets are supposed to be more or less convex). The final result (Fig. 12d) is obtained after a watershed transformation and an elimination of some irrelevant arcs separating markers belonging to the same facet [5].

3. Watersheds and Hierarchical Segmentation

Very often, especially for complex and noisy pictures, the markers selection is difficult. To overcome this problem, we may simplify the initial image and try to extract homogeneous regions from this simplified picture. Both image simplification and region extraction make intensive use of the watershed transformations.

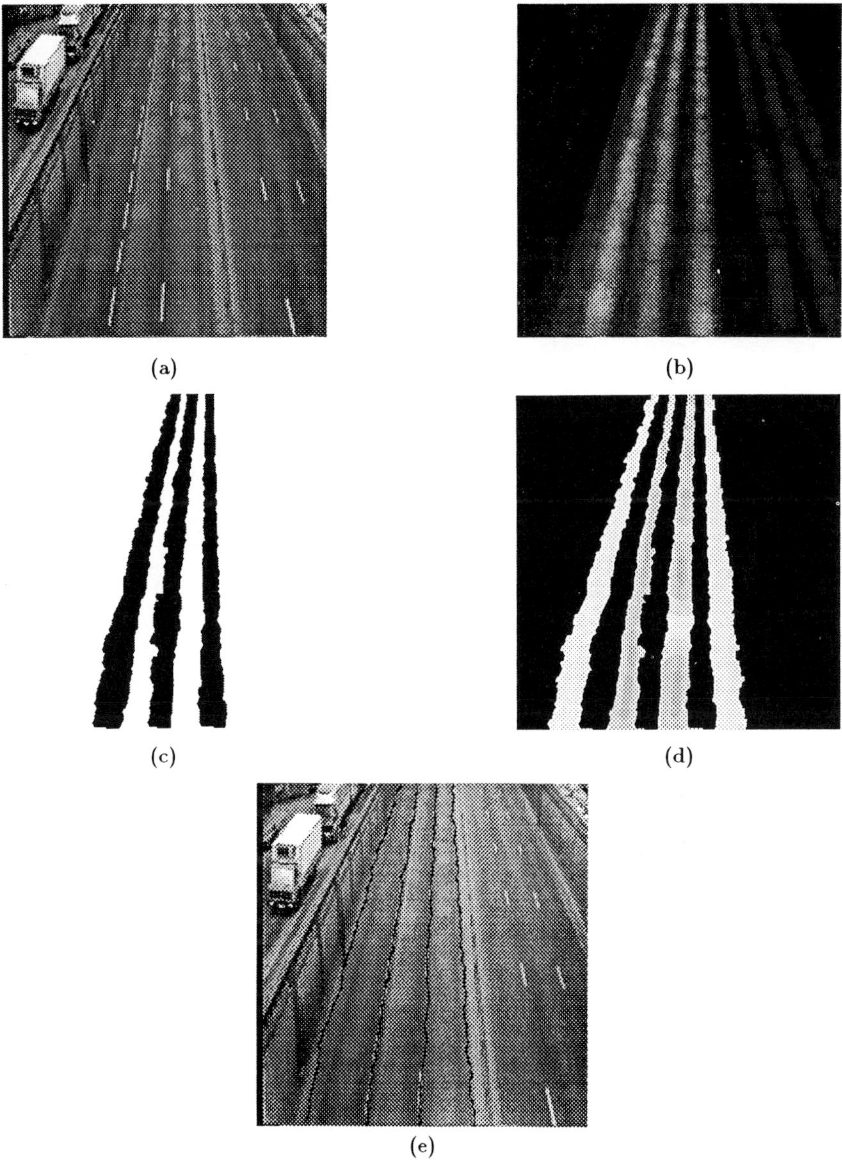

Fig. 11. First image (a), second image (b), markers of traffic lanes (c), geodesic distance of ground layout (d), segmentation of the traffic lanes (e).

3.1. *Image Simplification*

Consider a grey-tone image f, and its corresponding morphological gradient image $g(f)$. A simplified image can be computed in the following way:

- First, we calculate the watersheds of the gradient image.

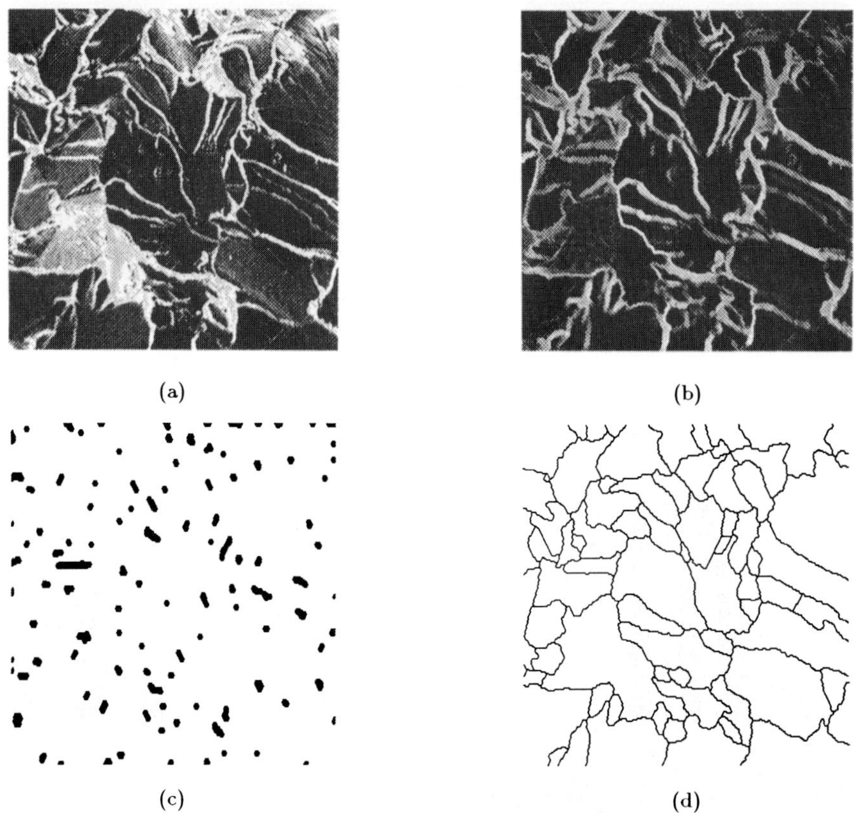

Fig. 12. SEM image of a metallic fracture (a), function used for segmentation (b), markers of facets (c), final result with facets detection (d).

- Second, we label every catchment basin of the watershed transform with the grey value in the initial image f corresponding to the minima of $g(f)$.

The result is a simplified image (Fig. 13), made of a mosaic of pieces (the catchment basins) of constant grey levels, where no information regarding the contours has been lost. Then, this simplified image, also called *mosaic image*, may be used to define a valued graph, on which the morphological transformations, and in particular the watersheds, can be extended [7].

3.2. Hierarchical Segmentation

Consider the previous mosaic image. First, the boundaries between adjacent tiles of the mosaic image are valued with the difference of their grey values. This produces a gradient image whose support is the watersheds of the image $g(f)$. Each wall of this gradient image is considered as a vertex of a valued graph (Fig. 14b). Two vertices of this graph are neighbors if the corresponding boundaries surround the same tile of the mosaic picture. A watershed transformation can be applied

Fig. 13. Original image (a), simplified mosaic image (b).

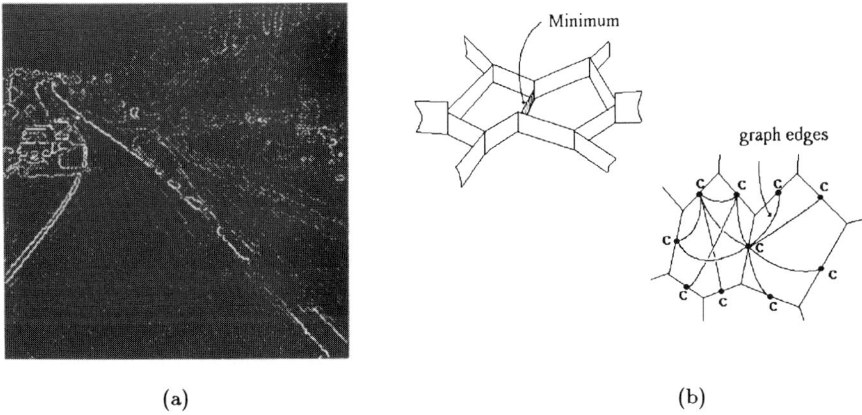

Fig. 14. Gradient of the mosaic image (a), corresponding graph used for the hierarchical segmentation (b).

to this graph. The weakest boundaries of the mosaic image correspond to regional minima of our valued graph (Fig. 14a).

The result of the watershed transformation leads to a hierarchical segmentation of the image, as illustrated with the example given in Fig. 15. A selection of markers can be made at this level to segment features in the image (for example, the road in our case). Further levels of hierarchy may also be defined by iterating this procedure [8].

Conclusion

The watershed transformation can be considered as an all-purpose tool in the approach of segmentation problems by mathematical morphology. This tool, combined with the marker selection of the features to be extracted, leads to a general methodology for the segmentation process. First, by means of the markers selec-

(a)   (b)

Fig. 15. Detection of the road: (a) First level of hierarchy, (b) marker of the road.

tion, we point out what we want to extract from the picture. Then, we have to define the criteria used to segment the image. This means that image segmentation cannot be performed accurately and adequately if we do not build the objects we want to detect. In this approach, the picture segmentation is not the primary step of image understanding. On the contrary, a fair segmentation can be obtained only if we know exactly what we are looking for in the image.

References

[1] S. Beucher and C. Lantuéjoul, Use of watersheds in contour detection, in *Proc. Int. Workshop on Image Processing, Real-Time Edge and Motion Detection/Estimation*, CCETT/INSA/IRISA, IRISA Report n°132, pp. 2.1–2.12, Rennes, France, 17–21 Sept. 1979.

[2] F. Meyer and S. Beucher, Morphological Segmentation, to be published in *Journal of Visual Communication and Image Representation*.

[3] F. Maisonneuve, Sur le partage des eaux, CMM Internal report, Paris School of Mines, Dec. 1982.

[4] S. Beucher and F. Meyer, Méthodes d'analyse des contrastes à l'analyseur de texture, in *Proc. of Congrès AFCET/IRIA, Reconnaissance des Formes et Traitement des Images*, Tome 1, pp. 378–384, Chatenay-Malabry, France, 21–23 Feb. 1978.

[5] S. Beucher, Segmentation d'images et morphologie mathématique, Doctorate Thesis, Paris School of Mines, France, June 1990.

[6] S. Beucher, J. M. Blosseville and F. Lenoir, Traffic spatial measurements using video image processing, in *Proc. of SPIE, Advances in Intelligent Robotics Systems, Cambridge Symposium on Optimal and Optoelectronic Engineering*, Vol. 848, pp. 648-655, Cambridge, Mass., USA, 1–6 Nov. 1987.

[7] L. Vincent, Graphs and Mathematical Morphology, *Signal Processing*, Vol. 16, no. 4, pp. 365–388, April 1989.

[8] S. Beucher, M. Bilodeau and X. Yu, Road Segmentation by watershed algorithms, in *Proc. PROMETHEUS Workshop*, Sophia-Antipolis, France, April 1990 (in press).

Handbook of Pattern Recognition and Computer Vision, pp. 457–490
Eds. C. H. Chen, L. F. Pau and P. S. P. Wang
© 1993 World Scientific Publishing Company

| CHAPTER 2.7 |

PARALLEL THINNING ALGORITHM
FOR BINARY DIGITAL PATTERNS*

YUNG-SHENG CHEN

*Department of Electrical Engineering, Yuan-Ze Institute of Technology
135 Yuan-Tung Road, Nei-Li, Taoyuan, Taiwan 320, Republic of China*

and

WEN-HSING HSU

*Institute of Electrical Engineering, National Tsing-Hua University
101 Sec. 2, Kuang-Fu Road, Hsinshu, Taiwan 300, Republic of China*

To develop a parallel thinning process which has the fewest number of iterations and
the least time complexity of an iteration, capably produce the perfect 8-connected thin
line including T-junction and prevent excessive erosion, we present a systematic approach
which can induce not only 2-subcycle/iteration but also pseudo 1-subcycle/iteration
parallel thinning algorithms. When using this novel approach in designing parallel thinning algorithms, the property of dividing an iteration into two subcycles is obtained.
The 2-subcycle/iteration parallel algorithm can be easily reduced to the pseudo 1-
subcycle/iteration version by a so-called extended local connecting function. Perfect
8-connected skeletons can be always produced by means of a so-called local connecting
function and the shape invariant property of a local straight line. In this chapter, we also
present the improvements of the proposed algorithm to produce the perfect 8-connected
thin line excluding T-junction and to obtain the isotropic skeleton of an L-shaped pattern. Experiments show that the presented algorithms are feasible.

Keywords: Parallel thinning algorithm, local connecting function, extended local connecting function, erosive direction number, shape invariant property, thinning window,
perfect 8-connected thin line, side effect, isotropic property.

1. Introduction

1.1. *Computer Processing of Line Images*

It is known that one of the general problems in the field of pattern recognition
is the extraction of characterizing elements from a given pattern. In general, it
is difficult to state the nature of characterizing elements, and general methods
available to solve these problems are not many. It is also well known that the
effectiveness of a pattern recognition method depends largely on how significant the
set of extracted features is.

---

*The contents of this chapter are principally condensed from our original works [43,44].

457

If a two-dimensional (2-D) binary image consisting of line-like objects is to be recognized, e.g. alphanumeric printed or handwritten characters, chromosomes, etc., the thickness of the strokes which constitute the objects generally do not contribute to the recognition. In general, fundamental to computer processing of line images is the concept of *thinning*, which is the most common name for the process of transforming a line-like object which is many pixels wide to just a single pixel. Other terms commonly used to describe this process are "skeletonization", "medial axis transformation" or (MAT), and "symmetric transformation".

Since the idea was first developed about thirty years ago [1], thinning has become an important process in pattern recognition. It has been used as an aid in the inspection of printed circuit boards [2], electrical schematic and logic diagram interpretation [3], counting of asbestos fibers on air filters [4], analysis of chromosome shapes [5], examination of soil cracking patterns [6], classification of fingerprints [7–9], recognition of characters [10–15], three-dimensional (3-D) object description [16], application in intelligent copying and facsimile transmission systems [17], data reduction of map storage [18–20], etc. The major advantages of thinning in image processing and pattern recognition are (i) reduction of the data amount of an input binary image which will help decrease the data storage and the data transmission time, and (ii) preservation of the fundamental skeleton, which is topologically equivalent to the original object, which will facilitate the extraction of fundamental features of the object.

Given the definition of thinning alone, the skeleton only has a meaning when applied to lines which have considerably greater length than width. For instance, it is not immediately clear what the skeleton of a square should look like or even whether the skeleton of a square can be of any practical use [21].

1.2. *Review of Thinnings*

1.2.1. *Local operations in line thinning*

Many algorithms developed were based on a successive deletion of contour points rather than on the concept of distance. Hence, the transformed line is commonly called a "medial line" or "thinned line" rather than "skeleton". The thinning algorithm is usually a technique of iterative edge-point erosion, where a 3×3 window is moved over the entire image and a set of rules is applied to the contents of the window. The most important requirement of the thinning operation is "connectivity". In general, three types of thinned line are focused on, i.e. 4-connected, imperfectly 8-connected, and perfectly 8-connected [22]. The 4-connected version of the thinning algorithm often yields an extremely noisy medial line which needs a special method to prune [23]; and the imperfectly 8-connected version results in trouble in postprocessings such as tracking the thin line [22]. The preferred thin line is the perfectly 8-connected one [22,24]. Two often-used connectivity measures are *crossing number* and *connectivity number*, which were proposed by Rutovitz [25] and Yokoi *et al.* [26,27], respectively. The discussion of these measures had been made by Tamura [22]. The natural concepts and simple-connectedness defined for subsets of a digital picture were proposed and discussed in a major way by Rosenfeld [28]. A characterization of parallel thinning algorithms was also discussed by Rosenfeld [29].

The thinning algorithms designed by local operations are reviewed as follows: Rutovitz [25] first proposed a thinning algorithm, which is defined by the crossing number, and allows parallel operations. The iteration of this algorithm is not divided into subcycles. Thus the algorithm can erode the whole layer of the contour. Rutovitz's algorithm was modified by Deutsch [30] in order to improve the thinness of diagonal lines and prevent their successive shrinking. However, Deutsch's algorithm will yield highly biased thin lines as Fraser indicated [31].

A well-known skeletonization approach is Hilditch's algorithm [5]. Hilditch described in detail the criteria that must be satisfied before a black pixel of a pattern is deleted. However, she did not present her approach in a compact algorithmic form. The algorithm produces perfect 8-curves. It performs in sequential operations. Stefanelli and Rosenfeld [32] presented a "simplified version" of Hilditch's approach as a formal algorithm. However, according to the investigations by Naccache and Shinghal [33], the Stefanelli–Rosenfeld version does not reflect exactly the approach described by Hilditch. In 1984, Zhang and Suen [34] also presented a fast parallel algorithm which was derived from the "simplified version" by Stefanelli and Rosenfeld [32] and divided an iteration into two subiterations. However, the algorithm has the demerits of serious shrinking and the problem of line connectivity problem. Lü and Wang proposed an improved algorithm to overcome these demerits by preserving the necessary and essential structures for certain patterns [35]. Chen and Hsu [36] also presented a modified algorithm by the table mapping strategy to solve such problems. Both algorithms can maintain efficient operations.

Stefanelli and Rosenfeld [32] have presented some parallel thinning algorithms for digital pictures. They noted that the removal of all the contour points in parallel has the disadvantage that it can yield nonconnected or even empty medial lines for connected figures, and therefore two parallel algorithms were concerned in their article, one is the 4-subcycle version, the other is the 2-subcycle version. They used the concept of final-points which are prohibited from deletion at any subsequence once they are detected. Because there were several mistakes in the algorithm, Tamura [37] has corrected all these mistakes, and the redundancy in the final-points of Stefanelli and Rosenfeld's algorithm are reduced. Other related parallel algorithms are presented by Arcelli *et al.* [38,39].

Deutsch [40] developed three algorithms with rectangular, hexagonal, and triangular array, respectively. He found that the algorithm operating with the triangular array is the most sensitive to image irregularities and noise, yet it will yield a thinned image with an overall reduced number of points. He concluded that the algorithm operating in conjunction with the hexagonal array has features which strike a balance between those of the other two arrays.

Tamura [22] presented a detailed comparison of several thinning algorithms from the digital geometric viewpoint. Naccache and Shinghal [41] proposed a skeletonization algorithm called safe-point thinning algorithm (SPTA) and compared the SPTA with fourteen other existing algorithms. Chu and Suen [42] presented a two phases thinning algorithm; and compared it with two other research groups and then with nine other existing algorithms. Smith [21] gave a detailed survey for computer processing of line images. And recently we [43] proposed a systematic approach to designing 2-subcycle and pseudo 1-subcycle parallel thinning algorithms, in which five 2-subcycle and four 1-subcycle existing thinning algorithms are compared. The new approach has been further improved [44]. We [45] also derived a generalized expression for comparison among some one-pass parallel thinnings proposed by Holt *et al.* [46], Chin *et al.* [47], and us [43].

1.2.2. *Other thinning algorithms*

Several special algorithms were also proposed. For example, Triendl [48] proposed a scheme for skeletonization of noisy handdrawn symbols by using parallel operations which basically consist of *clean, connected, clean,* and *thin* steps. Davies and Plummer [49] described a procedure for thinning which includes *propagate, mark, slim, thin, clean,* and *purge.* Stentifold and Mortimer [50] presented a similar algorithm based on some heuristics, i.e. performing some preprocessings (*hole removal, smoothing, actual angle emphasis*) before thinning binary handprinted characters for OCR (optical character recognition). In 1986, Chu and Suen [42] also proposed a two-phase algorithm: one for thinning the pattern (*fill, delete, label, strip*), the other for adjusting the skeleton (*propagate, move*). And, in 1989, Wang and Zhang [51] presented a fast serial and parallel algorithm by several provided functions.

There were several algorithms based on the data-structure-type representation for skeletons whose composing elements (points) are linked to each other and may not necessarily coincide with the pixels, i.e. any pair of the elements linked to each other may not be 4- or 8-connected. In such a type of representation, one can easily obtain versatile kinds of thin line representation for *syntactical* or *semantical* structures of thin line (e.g. an analysis of the LAG (line adjacency graph) in order to find the skeleton by Naito *et al.* [52]; a core-line tracing algorithm based on maximal square moving by Wakayama [53]; a parallel syntactic thinning based on recoding of binary pictures by Favre and Keller [54]), and a vectorizer and feature extractor for document recognition [55]. However, it is interesting to note that although structural descriptions were proposed quite early (as far back as 1959), they have been found to be of limited use in practice as Pavlidis [56] indicated. The most likely reason is that they tend to have more extensive computational requirements than purely heuristic techniques. As the price of computing decreases, though, one expects their implementation to become inexpensive. Therefore, Pavlidis [57] suggested that they should be kept in mind as potential candidates in any system design.

As argued by Pavlidis [57], purely parallel processing is not very efficient for images because most processing algorithms operate, in effect, near edges, so that processors assigned to the pixel inside large uniform areas would be idle most of the time. Hence, an asynchronous thinning algorithm was proposed [57]. Recently, such a concept has also been implemented in the iterative parallel 2-subcycle thinning algorithm by Suzuki and Abe [58]. However, from the viewpoint of special hardware design, it takes the same minimum time for both processings of pattern and background pixels as discussed by Chin *et al.* [47] and us [36,43,59]. Hence, parallel operations are preferable in the thinning algorithm in practical applications, e.g. the special architectures proposed by us [59–62].

Several algorithms were designed with the boundary information of objects. Shapiro *et al.* [63] described a technique for generating a skeleton of a ribbon-like or tree-like object using sequential data for all or part of the boundary. Shinha [64] presented an algorithm for estimation of skeletons of thick characters. The author directly identified the core pixels of the skeleton forming the core skeletal segments based on labeling of the character boundary with some local properties. Martínez-Pérez *et al.* [65] presented a thinning algorithm based on the manipulation of the polygons that represent the borders of thin structures in digital images. And Baruch [66] proposed a line following technique as a means to perform line thinning. All these algorithms were implemented and analyzed on the conventional computer.

The 3-D object thinning algorithms have also been investigated by several authors. The sources of 3-D pictures may be either stacks of 2-D images obtained by computerized tomography, echocardiography or other technologies, or sequences of 2-D time-varying pictures. 3-D object thinning can also be applied to feature extraction, boundary surface thinning, and many potential applications as 3-D digital pictures become more common. Lobregt *et al.* [67] gave a principle and an algorithm for 3-D skeletonization. And Tsao and Fu [68] also proposed a parallel algorithm for 3-D object thinning. In this paper, the concept of connectivity in 3-D digital pictures was studied in which path connectivity and surface connectivity were discussed, and the criteria to avoid excessive deletion and preserve connectivity were described.

1.3. *Some Problems in Thinning*

In general, there exist several main problems in the thinning process (presented by Shinji *et al.*, [11]) such as: (i) the phenomenon of shrinking on medial lines, (ii) the subtle changes on the border of a pattern which may yield noisy branches or affect the positions of medial lines, and (iii) two distinct branching points which may be yielded after thinning crossing lines, and Y-shape distortion which may be produced in the neighborhood of a branching point.

If the above problems influence the thinning results greatly, in the case of OCR, the strokes cannot be extracted reasonably in the postprocessing. Hence, a better method which can overcome these problems is desirable [36]. The desirable thin lines should satisfy three basic requirements, i.e. the preservation of line connectivity, the satisfaction of isotropy, and the avoidance of excessive erosion or serious shrinking [43].

Through Tamura's investigations [22], 4-connected versions of thinning algorithms usually yield noise branches and excessive erosion. Other detailed illustrations can also be found in Naccache and Shinghal's paper [33]. Excessive erosion may also appear in the imperfectly 8-connected version, such as the efficiency-oriented algorithm proposed by Zhang and Suen [34] and its improved version by Holt *et al.* [46], and the Chin *et al.*'s algorithm [47]. For providing a convenient abstraction of line-like patterns, the thin line is always expected to be perfectly 8-connected [24].

Among several efficiency-oriented thinning algorithms [32–36,41,46], we recommend the parallel version for practicability as Smith [21] pointed out. In general, the efficiency of an algorithm is tested by a general-purpose computer in CPU-time [32–35,41], or an array processor in a number of time-units, i.e. the complexity of an iteration or subcycle [43,46]; and commonly in the number of iterations. We have proposed a *table mapping strategy* [36] so that its efficiency can be evaluated only by the number of iterations. Obviously, the most efficient algorithm must be the one which spends the fewest time-units and the fewest iterations under the premises of maintaining the perfect 8-curve and preventing excessive erosion. However, as Stefanelli and Rosenfeld [32] indicated, a 1-*subcycle/iteration* parallel version has the disadvantage that it may yield non-connected or even empty medial lines for connected figures. For instance, a two-pixels-wide straight stroke will be entirely eliminated after a single iteration. Therefore, the 4-*subcycle/iteration* and 2-*subcycle/iteration* versions performed in parallel are of interest too, and have been developed by many researchers [32,34–40,58,69].

Several 1-*subcycle/iteration* parallel algorithms have been developed [25,30,43, 44,46,47]. Deutsch modified the original Rutovitz scheme and overcame the deficiency of excessive erosion, but the modified version would yield a highly biased thin line. Holt *et al.*'s algorithm would yield the serious shrinking and imperfect 8-curve. And Chin *et al.*'s algorithm also had the two problems of higher bias and an imperfect 8-curve. All the demerits have been discussed and overcome by our works [43,44].

As a result, in this chapter, the design of an efficient and effective thinning algorithm will be presented and discussed in the following sections, in which the following fundamental requirements should be met: (i) The algorithm should be a parallel version. (ii) The number of subcycles (subiterations) and the time-units (complexity) per subcycle should be as small as possible. Note here that the term "subcycle" is more suitable than the term "iteration" for the evaluation of a multi-*subcycle/iteration* or a 1-*subcycle/iteration* parallel algorithm. (iii) The thin lines must be perfectly 8-connected, possess the property of isotropy, and should avoid excessive erosion (or serious shrinking).

2. Basic Framework, Definitions and Functions

2.1. *Basic Framework*

A binary pattern matrix, whose size is $M \times N$ pixels, consists of only two-level pixels: one is the pattern pixel (denoted by "1") and the other is the background pixel (denoted by "0"). For any pixel $P_{x,y}$ in row x and column y of the image matrix, let $N(0)$, $N(1)$, ... , $N(7)$ be the values of its neighbors from $P_{x,y-1}$ in clockwise order as shown in Fig. 1. The patterns are 8-neighbor connected. With these eight nearest neighbors of pixel $P_{x,y}$, we define an eight-digit number, called $\mathcal{N}$-*number*, to indicate the value of the combination of these neighbors. The expression of $\mathcal{N}$-*number* for any pixel $P_{x,y}$ is given below:

$$\mathcal{N}(P_{x,y}) = \sum_{n=0}^{7} N(n) \cdot 2^n \, . \tag{2.1}$$

Here for each $N(n)$, the value is either 1 or 0.

$N(7) = P_{x-1,y-1}$	$N(0) = P_{x,y-1}$	$N(1) = P_{x+1,y-1}$
$N(6) = P_{x-1,y}$	$P_{x,y}$	$N(2) = P_{x+1,y}$
$N(5) = P_{x-1,y+1}$	$N(4) = P_{x,y+1}$	$N(3) = P_{x+1,y+1}$

Fig. 1. Designation of a 3 × 3 square array.

As we know, thinning may be defined as the successive erosion of the outermost layers of a pattern until only a connected "skeleton" or "medial line" of unit width remains. Such an iterative process can be defined as the first-order recursive filter, named a **thinning filter**, i.e.

$$P_{x,y}^{j+1} = \sim \left\{ \sum_{i=-\infty}^{\infty} T(i) \delta[\mathcal{N}(P_{x,y}^j) - i] \right\} , \tag{2.2a}$$

for $x = 0, 1, \ldots, M - 1$, $y = 0, 1, \ldots, N - 1$; where "$\sim$" represents NOT logical operation. $T(i)$ is called the **thinning window**, to be discussed later in Section 3. The δ-function is defined as follows:

$$\delta[\mathcal{N}(P_{x,y}^j) - i] = \begin{cases} 0, & \text{for } \mathcal{N}(P_{x,y}^j) \neq i \text{ or } P_{x,y}^j = 0, \\ 1, & \text{for } \mathcal{N}(P_{x,y}^j) = i \text{ and } P_{x,y}^j = 1. \end{cases} \tag{2.3}$$

Since the total number of combinations of $\mathcal{N}$-*number* is 256 $(= 2^8)$ in Eq. (2.1), the Eq. (2.2a) can be written as

$$P_{x,y}^{j+1} = \sim \left\{ \sum_{i=0}^{255} T(i) \delta[\mathcal{N}(P_{x,y}^j) - i] \right\} , \tag{2.2b}$$

for $x = 0, 1, \ldots, M - 1$, $y = 0, 1, \ldots, N - 1$.

In addition, a halting condition for the thinning filter in Eq. (2.2b) which checks whether the **Sum of Absolute Differences (SAD)** between the filtered patterns at the jth iteration (or subcycle) and those at the $(j+1)$th iteration (or subcycle) becomes zero or not, is defined as follows:

$$\textbf{SAD} = \sum_{x=0}^{M-1} \sum_{y=0}^{N-1} \left| P_{x,y}^j - P_{x,y}^{j+1} \right|. \qquad (2.4)$$

Based on the above framework, three new functions named **local connecting (LC)**, **extended local connecting (ELC)** and **erosive direction number (EDN)**, as well as two properties of **shape invariance** of *local edges* and *local straight lines* will be defined in Section 2.3 and will be used to derive the thinning windows $T(i)'s$ in Section 3.

2.2. *Classical Definitions*

In this section, we review several classical definitions for image processing. Basically, all the definitions are centered on the discrete image. The reviewed terms include genus and Euler formular, 4- and 8-path, 4- and 8-connected, 4- and 8-deletable points, crossing number and connectivity number, shrinking and thinning, 4- and 8-curve, isotropic skeleton, sequential and parallel process, and subcycle.

Definition 2.1 (Discrete image). The most common grid used in picture (image) processing is the *square grid* (or called rectangular array) consisting of square cells arranged as a chessboard. This is suggested by the conventional scanning technique which operates in a line-by-line fashion. The image discussed in this article is a discrete (bilevel or binary) one. One level is called the pattern component, the other is the background component. In general, a major concern in the study of such images is the concept of *shape*, which is not easy to define quantitatively [56]. One faces this problem when sampling an analog image. Hence, to preserve the image shape, the discretization of an analog image should be concerned with the sampling effect (e.g. the size of the cells of the sampling grid) and the topological property (e.g. the connectivity).

Definition 2.2 (Genus and Euler formula). For any binary image, special methods can be used to compute the number of pattern components minus the number of background components $+1$; this number is called the *genus* of the image [28,40]. Application of the *Euler formula* $V - E + F$ to the pattern should give its genus. Here V, E, and F denote the number of vertices, edges, and faces on a polygonal image, respectively. A very important term, called connectivity, in image processing is just discussed by whether the Euler number agrees with the genus number or not for both pattern and background in an image.

Definition 2.3 (4- and 8-path). Let I^2 denote the set of all pairs (i, j) of integers, which may be regarded as points (pixels) in the plane (binary image), and let

$A = (i_1, j_1), \ldots, (i_t, j_t)$ be any t-tuple of $(i, j)'s$ where $t \geq 1$. We call A a *4(or 8)-path* if for each r, where $1 \leq r < t$, we have $|i_r - i_{r+1}| + |j_r - j_{r+1}| \leq 1$ (or $\max(|i_r - i_{r+1}|, |j_r - j_{r+1}|) \leq 1$, respectively) [28]. The first means that (i_{r+1}, j_{r+1}) is either the same as (i_r, j_r) or is one of its four horizontal and vertical neighbors. Similarly, the second means that (i_{r+1}, j_{r+1}) is either the same as (i_r, j_r) or is one of its eight horizontal, vertical, and diagonal neighbors. And let $E_{i,j}$ denote the set of eight neighbors of (i, j) and $F_{i,j}$ denote the set of four horizontal and vertical neighbors of (i, j), respectively.

Definition 2.4 (4- and 8-connected). We say that the elements (h, k) and (m, n) of pattern S are *4(or 8)-connected* in S if there exists a 4(or 8)-path having (h, k) as its first term, (m, n) as its last term, and all its terms in S [28]. Now, there exists a problem: "how do we choose the corresponding connectivity for pattern S and the background $\bar{S}$ respectively ?" The answer is that if 4-neighbor connectivity is assumed for the pattern and 8-neighbor connectivity for the background (or *vice versa*), then the Euler number will agree with the genus number. Otherwise, these two terms disagree mutually. Incidentally, the *order* of 4(8)-connectivity of the 4(8)-connected set S is defined to be the number of 8(4)-components of $\bar{S}$ (if finite). If the order of 4(8)-connectivity of S is 1, we call it *simply* 4(8)-connected.

Definition 2.5 (4- and 8-deletable point). If the removal of a point x will not destroy the pattern connectivity, then we call the point x deletable. The definition of deletable point is given by Rosenfeld [28]. An element x of S which satisfies (i) $F_x \cap S \neq \phi$, (ii) $E_x \cap \bar{S} \neq \phi$, and (iii) $F_x \cap S$ is contained in a 4-component of $E_x \cap S$, will be called *4-deletable point*. To obtain analogous results in the 8-case, we simply interchange "4" and "8", "F", and "E" in the foregoing; except that for the part of the definition of "deletable," we replace "$F_x \cap S$ is contained in a 4-component of $E_x \cap S$" by "$E_x \cap S$ 8-connected."

Definition 2.6 (Crossing number and connectivity number). For any pixel $P_{x,y}$, in row x and column y of a given image matrix, let $N(0), N(1), \ldots, N(7)$ be the value of its neighbors starting from $P_{x,y-1}$ in clockwise order as Fig. 1 shows. So the patterns are 8-neighbor connected. The *crossing number* [25], **CN** is defined as

$$\mathbf{CN} = \sum_{k=0}^{8} |N(k+1) - N(k)|, \tag{2.5}$$

where k has a period of eight and **CN** indicates the number of distinct 4-neighbor connected groups of black and white (pattern and background) elements around $P_{x,y}$. The neighbors' sum **NS** is also defined as below:

$$\mathbf{NS} = \sum_{k=0}^{7} N(k). \tag{2.6}$$

Yokoi's *connectivity numbers* [26–27] are defined for 4-connectedness and 8-connectedness respectively as follows:

$$\mathbf{N}_{c4} = \sum_{k \in S_e} \left[N(k) - N(k)N(k+1)N(k+2) \right], \text{(4-connectivity case)} \qquad (2.7a)$$

$$\mathbf{N}_{c8} = \sum_{k \in S_e} \left[\bar{N}(k) - \bar{N}(k)\bar{N}(k+1)\bar{N}(k+2) \right], \text{(8-connectivity case)} \qquad (2.7b)$$

where S_e is a set of 4-neighbors and $\bar{N}(k)$ means $1 - N(k)$.

Let $\mathbf{CN}'$ be $\mathbf{CN}/2$, since the value of $\mathbf{CN}$ must be even. The values of $\mathbf{CN}'$, $\mathbf{N}_{c4}$, $\mathbf{N}_{c8}$ characterize the property of a point in the same way as follows. $\mathbf{CN}' = 0$ denotes interior or isolated point. $\mathbf{CN}' = 1$ denotes edge point. $\mathbf{CN}' = 2$ denotes connecting point. $\mathbf{CN}' = 3$ denotes branching point. $\mathbf{CN}' = 4$ denotes crossing point. It had been proved that a point of $\mathbf{N}_c = 1$, i.e. $\mathbf{CN}' = 1$, is deletable [22,26,27].

Definition 2.7 (Other connectivities). There are other two connectivities which are often discussed. They are arranged in *hexagonal* or *triangular* arrays [40]. The first has the perfect property that there is no choice of connectivity for either the pattern or the background; both must be 6-neighbor connected. However, the structure of the second is much more complicated. There are three neighborhood connectivities; 3, 9, or 12, to be chosen. Since these structures are rarely implemented, we do not apply them to the design of thinning algorithms.

Definition 2.8 (Shrinking and thinning). The process of *shrinking* is described as follows [27]: A picture is scanned in a certain way and at every "1" pixel (black or pattern pixel) the value of $\mathbf{CN}'$ or $\mathbf{N}_c$ is computed. If $\mathbf{N}_c = 1$ for the "1" pixel, then the pixel is removed (changed into the "0" pixel). This procedure is repeated until no 4(8)-deletable point is found in the picture.

Since the connectivity is a topological property [22], it cannot distinguish the endpoint from the simple point. (Note here that a 4(8)-*endpoint* is defined to be a point if exactly one of its 4(8)-neighbors is 1. Also, an edge point is called 4(8)-*simple*, i.e. $\mathbf{N}_c = 1$, if changing it from "1" to "0" does not change the 4(8)-connectedness of "1"'s in its neighbors [23,29]). Furthermore, the endpoints are a subset of simple points and make no sense topologically, hence they cannot be detected uniquely by $\mathbf{N}_c$. In accordance with the investigations of Tamura [22], the 4-endpoint is inadequate for the purpose of thinning since it may result in the extremely noisy medial line and serious shrinking. Accordingly, the *thinning* process is different from the shrinking process in that even though the concept of endpoint cannot be presented topologically, it must be embedded explicitly or implicitly into a scheme of line thinning. Otherwise the contour erosion process works not as a thinning but a shrinking operation.

Definition 2.9 (4-curve and 8-curve). 4-connectedness is a stricter condition than 8-connectedness. Hence, a 4-curve must not contain 8-connected points, while an 8-curve may have 4-connected parts. Such 4-connected points on an 8-curve are all 8-deletable. Accordingly, an 8-curve is necessarily defined in a strict sense [22]. We call it the *perfectly 8-connected curve* if it has no 8-deletable points; otherwise, we call it *imperfect*. However, from the geometric viewpoint, the T-junction reasonably exists on a thin line [24]. Furthermore, whether or not the deletable point is removed in a T-junction will not affect the branching feature point among these contributed thin lines. So, a type of the perfect 8-curve allowing the existence of the T-junction on a thin line is named *perfect 8-curve including T-junction* (P8IT)-type. The original perfect 8-curve *excluding T-junction* is thus called P8ET-type.

Definition 2.10 (Isotropic skeleton). Since the thin line should preserve the fundamental structure of the original picture, the thin line must be isotropic or symmetric. It is often called the medial line [40]. That is, if the thin line produced is biased, many geometric features may be distorted which will result in the reduction of the performance of the following postprocessings.

Definition 2.11 (Sequential and parallel processing). The processing can be either sequential or parallel [32]. In sequential processing, one point at a time is processed; the result of processing a point at the zth iteration depends on a set of points for some of which the result of the zth iteration is known. Sequential processing can be more efficient than parallel processing when it is implemented on a general purpose computer. As to parallel processing, the value to a point at the zth iteration depends on the values given to the point and its eight neighbors at the $(z-1)$th iteration for the thinning process discussed here. Fundamentally, parallel processing is very suitable for implementation on a highly parallel architecture which can provide high speed operation, such as cellular networks. Incidentally, for the convenience of parallel computations, the neighbors' calculation can be performed by table mapping fashion [36].

Definition 2.12 (Subcycle). A general method for extracting the medial line of a picture consists in removing, at each iteration, all the deletable points (or contour points) of the picture, except the ones that might belong to the line. Such a scheme is called *1-subcycle* [32]. Because such a method may have the disadvantage that it can yield nonconnected or even empty medial lines for a connected picture, each iteration is usually subdivided into four or two subcycles to prevent this disadvantage. They are called 4-subcycle and 2-subcycle, respectively. Essentially, the number of iterations needed for a thinning process depends proportionally on the subcycles used. Of course, the time complexity in each subcycle should also be considered.

2.3. *Some Other Definitions and Functions*

Following the designation of a 3×3 square array as shown in Fig. 1, where $N(n)$ for $n = 0, 1, \ldots, 7$ denotes the values of eight neighbors of the central pixel $P_{x,y}$, let S_e and S_o denote two sets of integers $\{0, 2, 4, 6\}$ and $\{1, 3, 5, 7\}$, respectively. Let S_x denote a set of eight integers, i.e. $S_x = S_e \cup S_o$, and S_b denote a set of integers

$\{b|b = 0, 1, \dots, T_b - 1, T_b = \text{NS}\}$. Here T_b denotes the total number of black neighbors of the central pixel P, computed by Eq. (2.6). In order to facilitate the following calculations, let a mapping function $B : S_b \to S_x$ be defined by $B(b) = n$, where $b = 0, 1, \dots, T_b - 1$, and $n = 0, 1, \dots, 7$, denotes the location of the bth black neighbor from $P_{x,y-1}$ in clockwise order as shown in Fig. 1. For convenience, the inverse relation B^{-1} is also used. Note that the variables b and n are treated modulo T_b and 8, respectively.

Before introducing the *local connecting function* (**LC**-*function* for short) of a 3×3 local pattern, we first define *local pattern connectivity*, the set of *connecting elements*, and a binary operator named the *connecting operator* (represented by symbol "©").

Definition 2.13. Let a 3×3 local pattern be 8-neighbor connected. Then the pattern connectivity of the local pattern is still preserved if removal of the black central pixel P will not break the pattern into two or more parts. Conversely, we say that the pattern connectivity is destroyed.

Definition 2.14. For any nonzero neighbor $N(n)$, let the connecting set be $CE(n) = \{n + 1\}$, if $n \in S_o$ or $CE(n) = \{n + 1, n + 2\}$, if $n \in S_e$.

Definition 2.15. For any two consecutive elements in S_b, take the connecting set $CE(B(b))$ of the former element and take the location $B(b + 1)$ of the latter. Then the connecting operation © is given by:

$$CE(B(b)) © B(b + 1) = \begin{cases} 1, & \text{if } B(b + 1) \in CE(B(b)), \\ 0, & \text{if } B(b + 1) \notin CE(B(b)). \end{cases} \tag{2.8}$$

If the operation of © on all $B(b)'s$ results in one value of zero, we give the *starting pointer* SP and *ending pointer* EP to denote the value of $B(b + 1)$ and $B(b)$, respectively. These expressions will facilitate the following calculations.

Definition 2.16. The **LC**-function of a 3×3 local pattern, whose central pixel P is black, is given as:

$$\mathbf{LC}(P) = \sum_{b=0}^{T_b-1} CE(B(b)) © B(b + 1). \tag{2.9}$$

The **LC**-function is a function to evaluate those useful local patterns referred to in Definitions 2.18 and 2.19, and therefore is used to generate the **first thinning window** referred to in Eq. (2.15). According to the above definition, there are three main different values of $\mathbf{LC}(P)$ to be discussed:

(1) $\mathbf{LC}(P) = T_b$. This case indicates that the pixel P is an *interior point* ($T_b \neq 0$) or an *isolated point* ($T_b = 0$). The skeleton only has meaning when it is applied to line-like patterns which have considerably greater length than width, and the binary pattern is always smoothed beforehand [21]. Removing the interior

point will make a hole, and removing the isolated point will make us lose the objective for preserving such a point. Hence, these points are not removable.

(2) $\mathbf{LC}(P) = T_b - 1(\neq 0)$. In this case, the local pattern connectivity will not be destroyed if the pixel P is removed. However, for the purpose of parallel processing, we will further discuss this case in detail. Note that if $\mathbf{LC}(P) = 0$ then the pixel P is an *end-point* which must be preserved.

(3) $\mathbf{LC}(P) \leq T_b - 2$. It is inevitable that all such cases will destroy the local pattern connectivity if the pixel P is removed.

In case (2), there intuitively exists a property of **shape invariance** for three possible local patterns, i.e. the *local edge*, the *local straight line*, and the *local branch*. A property of a 3 × 3 local pattern is called shape invariance if the pattern whose central pixel P is nonzero has shape S and it still has S after P has been removed.

Shape invariance of the local edge is always true. The local branch should always be preserved in the thinning results. However, for the local straight line, those *line*-like patterns which will result in *curve*-like patterns after P is removed must be pruned, because they cannot preserve the property of shape invariance in the thinning results. In order to further illustrate the case of local straight line, we have the following definition.

Let S_{1b} and S_{1a} be two connecting sets which are the *shortest paths* from SP to EP in a 3 × 3 local pattern before and after pixel P is removed, respectively. Therefore, S_{1b} must be the union of set $\{SP, EP\}$ and the singleton set containing the location of the central black pixel; and S_{1a} must be a subset of the set S_b containing the locations of all the black neighbors in the local pattern.

Definition 2.17. Let $p(= SP)$, $q(= EP)$ be points of the set S_{1b} (or S_{1a}), and let pq denote the (real) line segment between p and q. We say that pq *lies near* S_{1b} (or S_{1a}), if for any (real) point (x, y) of pq, there exists a (lattice) point (i, j) of S_{1b} (or S_{1a}) such that the Euclidean distance $\sqrt{(i - x)^2 + (j - y)^2} < 1$. If pq *lies near* both S_{1b} and S_{1a} then we claim that the local pattern (local straight line) satisfies the property of shape invariance. (This definition is modified from [70].)

Definition 2.18. A local pattern is called a local edge if $\mathbf{E}(P)=\mathbf{LC}(P)$. The formula of $\mathbf{E}(P)$ is given as:

$$\mathbf{E}(P) = \sum_{b=B^{-1}(SP)}^{B^{-1}(SP)+T_b-2} \left| B(b+1) + C - B(b) \right|, \tag{2.10}$$

where

$$C = \begin{cases} 0, & \text{if } B(b+1) > B(b), \\ 8, & \text{if } B(b+1) < B(b). \end{cases}$$

Here $\mathbf{E}(P)$ is used to calculate the sum of all *location differences between two consecutive black pixels* starting from SP to EP in clockwise order. Because the pattern containing *a local edge* has only two distinct parts (i.e. *a connected pattern* and *a connected background*), we can easily use the function $\mathbf{E}(P)$ to evaluate whether the local pattern is a local edge or not. If the difference of each pair is 1, then $\mathbf{E}(P)$

must be equal to $\mathbf{LC}(P)$ and the local pattern is a local edge. Otherwise, it is not a local edge.

Definition 2.19. A local pattern is called a local straight line if $\mathbf{S}_4(P) = 2$ and $\mathbf{L}(P) = 1$. The formulas of $\mathbf{S}_4(P)$ and $\mathbf{L}(P)$ are given below:

$$\mathbf{S}_4(P) = \sum_{\substack{b=0 \\ B(b) \in S_e}}^{T_b - 1} N(B(b)), \tag{2.11}$$

and

$$\mathbf{L}(P) = \sum_{\substack{b=0 \\ B(b) \in S_e}}^{T_b - 1} N(B(b)) \cdot \bar{N}(B(b+1)) \cdot N(B(b+2)). \tag{2.12}$$

The pattern containing *a local straight line* consists of two disjoint parts of *connected background* which are divided by *a connected pattern*. Thus, we only have the following four types of local straight lines generated by $\mathbf{S}_4(P) = 2$ and $\mathbf{L}(P) = 1$ to satisfy the condition $\mathbf{LC}(P) = T_b - 1$ and Definition 2.17 for a 3×3 local pattern (see Fig. 2). Note that the symbol "X" denotes *"don't care"*.

X	1	0		0	0	X		X	0	0		0	1	X
0	P	1		0	P	1		1	P	0		1	P	0
0	0	X		X	1	0		0	1	X		X	0	0
	Type 1				Type 2				Type 3				Type 4	

Fig. 2. Four types of local straight lines.

There also exists the useful information called the *"direction of erosive breach"* on the local patterns satisfying the condition $\mathbf{LC}(P) = T_b - 1$. A function of $\mathbf{EDN}$ (*erosive direction number*) will be defined as the following definition and plays an important role for designing parallel thinning algorithms in Section 3.

Definition 2.20. Let $\mathbf{DF}(P)$ be a direction function,

$$\mathbf{DF}(P) = \left(\sum_{k=EP+1}^{SP+M-1} k \right) / (SP + M - EP - 1), \tag{2.13}$$

where

$$M = \begin{cases} 0, & \text{if } SP > EP, \\ 8, & \text{if } SP < EP. \end{cases}$$

Let $\mathbf{DF}(P)$ be equal to $Int[\mathbf{DF}(P)] + Frac[\mathbf{DF}(P)]$, the first term denotes the integral part of $\mathbf{DF}(P)$ and the second term denotes the fractional part of $\mathbf{DF}(P)$, respectively. Then, the $\mathbf{EDN}$ of pixel P is defined by the following equation:

$$\mathbf{EDN}(P) = \begin{cases} \mathbf{DF}(P), & \text{if } Frac[\mathbf{DF}(P)] = 0, \\ Int[\mathbf{DF}(P)], & \text{if } Frac[\mathbf{DF}(P)] \neq 0 \text{ and } EP \in S_o, \\ Int[\mathbf{DF}(P) + 1], & \text{if } Frac[\mathbf{DF}(P)] \neq 0 \text{ and } SP \in S_o. \end{cases} \tag{2.14}$$

Note that all **EDN**s are computed modulo 8.

For clarity, three examples are used to illustrate the calculations of $\mathbf{DF}(P)$ and $\mathbf{EDN}(P)$ [43]; the reader can refer to them.

Accordingly, with the **LC**-*function* and the two properties of shape invariance of local edges and local straight lines, the *first thinning window* T_1 is obtained and expressed as:

$$T_1(\mathcal{N}(P)) = \begin{cases} 1, \text{if } [\mathbf{LC}(P) = T_b - 1(\neq 0)] \text{ and} \\ [\mathbf{E}(P){=}\mathbf{LC}(P)] \text{ or } [\mathbf{S}_4(P) = 2 \text{ and } \mathbf{L}(P) = 1], \\ 0, \text{elsewhere} . \end{cases} \qquad (2.15)$$

Recall that $\mathcal{N}(P)$ denotes the $\mathcal{N}$-*number* of pixel P in Section 2.1. Here $T_1(\mathcal{N}(P)) = 1$ denotes that pixel P is a candidate for removal; conversely, $T_1(\mathcal{N}(P)) = 0$ denotes that pixel P cannot be removed.

For the purpose of parallel processing, we must further consider the property of *extended local connectivity* because so far we have only dealt with the local connectivity. There are *strong* and *weak* properties on the extended local connectivity.

Definition 2.21. That two adjacent removable pixels cannot be rashly deleted simultaneously is called **weak connectivity** if they are a horizontal or vertical adjacent pair.

Definition 2.22. That two adjacent removable pixels can be deleted simultaneously is called **strong connectivity** if they are a diagonal adjacent pair.

Based on the above two definitions, the *extended local connecting function* (**ELC**-*function* for short) for a 3 × 3 local pattern is given by:

$$\mathbf{ELC}(P) = \sum_{\substack{b=0 \\ B(b)\in S_e}}^{T_b-1} T_1[\mathcal{N}(N(B(b)))]\Bigg|_{T_1(\mathcal{N}(P))=1} . \qquad (2.16)$$

If $\mathbf{ELC}(P) = 0$, then the pixel P can be exactly removed in parallel processing. Conversely, if $\mathbf{ELC}(P) \neq 0$, by definition the pattern connectivity will be destroyed as the pixel P and its removable neighbor(s) are deleted at the same time. Accordingly, two questions may be raised in designing parallel thinning algorithms: First, how many subcycles in an iteration are sufficient for designing parallel thinning algorithms? Secondly, which removable candidate should be assigned to which subcycle? The corresponding answers will be detailed in the next section. In addition, the pseudo 1-*subcycle/iteration* parallel thinning algorithm will also be introduced.

3. Parallel Thinning Algorithms

3.1. *Thinning Windows*

In this section, two *types* of parallel thinning algorithms will be introduced. First, the 2-*subcycle/iteration* version is constructed by a checking procedure of *off-line* **ELC**-*function*. Secondly, with the developed results of the first version as well as the use of *on-line* **ELC-*function***, the pseudo 1-*subcycle/iteration* version can be easily constructed. Note that the meaning of on-line and off-line is concerned with whether the **ELC-*function*** is being applied to the thinning process or not.

As mentioned in Section 2.3, if all removable candidates shown by $T_1[\mathcal{N}(P)] = 1$ are deleted simultaneously, then whether the pattern connectivity is destroyed or not is checked by whether there exists the nonzero $\mathbf{ELC}(P)$. Therefore, for a black pixel P, we must provide a procedure to check all possible cases of the $\mathcal{N}$-*number* for their $\mathbf{ELC}(P)$ value. If the value of $\mathbf{ELC}(P)$ is zero, then the pixel P can always be deleted. Otherwise, we have to know which pair of $\mathcal{N}$-*numbers* cannot co-exist, and mark the pair by the values of $\mathbf{EDN}(P)$ and $\mathbf{EDN}(N(\cdot))$ which is opposite to $\mathbf{EDN}(P)$. The procedure can be described in Algorithm 3.1.

Algorithm 3.1. Off-line checking procedure of **ELC-*function***. Input is all possible $\mathcal{N}$-*numbers* of a black pixel P in the range $[0, 255]$. Output is a list of the pairs of **EDN** and their opposite values.

> **For** all possible $\mathcal{N}$-*numbers* of a black pixel P **do:**
> **Begin.**
> Calculate $T_1[\mathcal{N}(P)]$.
> **If** $T_1[\mathcal{N}(P)] = 1$ **then** calculate $\mathbf{EDN}(P)$ **else** do nothing.
> > **Begin.**
> > Set $\mathbf{ELC}(P)$ to zero.
> > **For** b from 0 to $T_b - 1$ **do:**
> > **If** $B(b) \notin S_e$ **then** do nothing.
> > > **Begin.**
> > > **For** all possible $\mathcal{N}$-*number* of the black neighbor $N(B(b))$ **do:**
> > > > **Begin.**
> > > > Calculate $T_1[\mathcal{N}(N(B(b)))]$.
> > > > **If** $T_1[\mathcal{N}(N(B(b)))] = 1$ **then** increase $\mathbf{ELC}(P)$ by one and calculate $\mathbf{EDN}(N(B(b)))$.
> > > > **End.**
> > > **End.**
> > **End.**
> **End.**
> **End of ALGORITHM.**

After performing Algorithm 3.1, we can obtain four pairs of **EDN**s. They are $0 \leftrightarrow 4$ (or $4 \leftrightarrow 0$), $1 \leftrightarrow 5$ (or $5 \leftrightarrow 1$), $2 \leftrightarrow 6$ (or $6 \leftrightarrow 2$), and $3 \leftrightarrow 7$ (or $7 \leftrightarrow 3$). They can be regarded as a product set $\{1, 5\} \times \{2, 6\} \times \{3, 7\}$ starting from the node $0 \leftrightarrow 4$. Obviously, there are eight possible cases of the 2-*subcycle/iteration* parallel thinning algorithm to be constructed [43]. Consequently, according to Algorithm 3.1, we have empirically shown the following conclusion:

Conclusion 3.1. Division of an iteration into two subcycles is sufficient for designing the parallel thinning algorithm. The pattern connectivity will not be destroyed if all the removable candidates satisfying $T_1[\mathcal{N}(P)] = 1$ are deleted simultaneously except that half the candidates whose $\mathbf{ELC}(P)$ values are nonzero are excluded in the current subcycle.

Let L_1 and R_1 be the two sets of the mutually opposite $\mathbf{EDN}$s $\{0,1,2,3\}$ and $\{4,5,6,7\}$ respectively, L_2 and R_2 be the sets of the mutually opposite $\mathbf{EDN}$s $\{0,1,2,7\}$ and $\{4,5,6,3\}$ respectively, etc. Accordingly, by Conclusion 3.1, we first have one common subwindow T_c and sixteen different subwindows T_{1t} and T_{2t} for $t = 1, 2, \ldots, 8$. They are:

$$T_c(i) = \begin{cases} 1, & \text{if } \mathbf{ELC}(P) = 0, \\ 0, & \text{elsewhere}, \end{cases} \tag{3.1}$$

$$T_{1t}(i) = \begin{cases} 1, & \text{if } \mathbf{ELC}(P) \neq 0 \text{ and } \mathbf{EDN}(P) \in L_t, \\ 0, & \text{elsewhere}, \end{cases} \tag{3.2}$$

and

$$T_{2t}(i) = \begin{cases} 1, & \text{if } \mathbf{ELC}(P) \neq 0 \text{ and } \mathbf{EDN}(P) \in R_t, \\ 0, & \text{elsewhere}, \end{cases} \tag{3.3}$$

for $t = 1, 2, \ldots, 8$, and i is the $\mathcal{N}$-number of P.

Accordingly, eight thinning windows $T2W_t$, for $t = 1, 2, \ldots, 8$ are found for the thinning filter in Eq. (2.2b). The so-called *2-subcycle/iteration* parallel thinning algorithm is constructed from them. The eight thinning windows are expressed as follows:

$$T2W_t(i) = \begin{cases} 0, & T_c(i) \vee T_{1t}(i), \text{ if } j \text{ is even}, \\ 1, & T_c(i) \vee T_{2t}(i), \text{ if } j \text{ is odd}, \end{cases} \tag{3.4}$$

for $t = 1, 2, \ldots, 8$; where "$\vee$" represents OR logical operation and j is the jth subcycle referred to in Eq. (2.2b).

Theorem 3.1. Consider any candidate P^* being removed in the on-line thinning process. Whichever subwindow T_{1t} or T_{2t} the process takes, the pixel can be exactly deleted iff

$$\mathbf{ELC}(P^*) = \left. \sum_{\substack{b=0 \\ B(b) \in S_e}}^{T_b-1} \bar{T}_2[\mathcal{N}(N^*(B(b)))] \right|_{T_2(\mathcal{N}(P^*))=1} \tag{3.5}$$

is zero. Here T_2 and $\bar{T}_2$ represent two mutually opposite subwindows either T_{1t} or T_{2t}, and N^* is the neighbor of P^* being computed.

Proof. Assume that two candidates P_1^* and P_2^* are voted by the subwindows T_{1t} and T_{2t}, respectively, in the on-line thinning process, and they can be deleted simultaneously. Then it implies that the candidate P_2^* is not excluded by the co-used subwindow T_{1t}, and the candidate P_1^* is not excluded by the co-used subwindow T_{2t}. But, this fact is contrary to Conclusion 3.1. Accordingly, it implies that Eq. (2.16) is reduced to the on-line $\mathbf{ELC}$-*function* in Eq. (3.5) which is zero.

On the other hand, suppose both $\mathbf{ELC}(P_1^*)$ and $\mathbf{ELC}(P_2^*)$ are zero. It evidently implies that deleting simultaneously both candidates P_1^* and P_2^* will neither affect nor destroy the pattern connectivity. $\square$

Therefore, according to Theorem 3.1, the other eight thinning windows $T1W_t$, for $t = 1, 2, \ldots, 8$ are found for the thinning filter (2.2b). They are:

$$T1W_t(i) = \begin{cases} T_c(i) \vee T_{1t}(i) \vee T_{2t}(i), & \text{if } \mathbf{ELC}(P^*) = 0, \\ T_c(i) \vee T_{1t}(i), & \text{if } \mathbf{ELC}(P^*) \neq 0 \text{ and } j \text{ is even}, \\ T_c(i) \vee T_{2t}(i), & \text{if } \mathbf{ELC}(P^*) \neq 0 \text{ and } j \text{ is odd}, \end{cases} \qquad (3.6)$$

for $t = 1, 2, \ldots, 8$.

Because, in general, most of the earlier iterations for on-line thinning (uniform pattern in particular) are in the case of $\mathbf{ELC}(P^*) = 0$, and only the window $T_c(i) \vee T_{1t}(i) \vee T_{2t}(i)$ is used until the case of $\mathbf{ELC}(P^*) \neq 0$ appears. Accordingly, we claim that the thinning windows $T1W_t$, for $t = 1, 2, \ldots, 8$ construct the **pseudo 1-*subcycle/iteration* parallel thinning algorithm**.

It is worth emphasizing that the perfect 8-connected (P8IT-type) skeletons can be exactly produced by using these algorithms. This good effect is due to the use of the local connecting function in Eq. (2.9) and the property of shape invariance of the local straight line in Definition 2.17 of Section 2.3.

3.2. *Results*

As mentioned in Section 1, an efficient and effective thinning algorithm should satisfy the following requirements: (i) The algorithm should be a parallel version. (ii) The number of subcycles and the time-units (complexity) per subcycle should be as small as possible. (iii) The thin lines must be perfectly 8-connected, possess a good isotropy, and should avoid excessive erosion.

Because, empirically, all the subwindows (T_{1t} *versus* T_{2t}) are *changeable*, the other 16 different cases (whose thinning windows are denoted by $T2W_t^c$ and $T1W_t^c$, for $t = 1, 2, \ldots, 8$, respectively) are constructed. Hence, in order to confirm the presented approach, we tested all the 32 different algorithms in detail, and all the proposed algorithms were applied to several patterns [43]. The experiments show that the pseudo 1-subcycle version can approximately meet the above requirements. The 2-subcycle version is slightly inferior to the pseudo 1-subcycle version but superior to many other analogous algorithms.

4. Further Improvements

In this section, we further focus on the considerations of the perfect 8-curve in the 1-subcycle parallel thinning algorithm. We present two improved versions of our algorithm introduced in the previous section so that the P8ET-type thin line can be obtained in Section 4.2 and the isotropic skeleton in the L-shape pattern can also be produced in Section 4.3. In order to facilitate the comparison among these algorithms, a *two-stage* structure (including a thinning table and a control unit) of the proposed 1-subcycle parallel algorithm is first introduced in Section 4.1, and, in Section 4.3, we give a discussion.

4.1. *A Two-Stage Structure*

The structure is shown in Fig. 3. It consists of a *thinning table* and a *control unit*. The thinning table is used to provide the attributions an input 3 × 3 local pattern has. The control unit is used to further check the removal of the center "1" pixel of this local pattern. Note that the inputs of the control unit also comprise the outputs of other neighboring thinning tables. In the next two subsections, we will discuss the thinning table and the control unit, respectively.

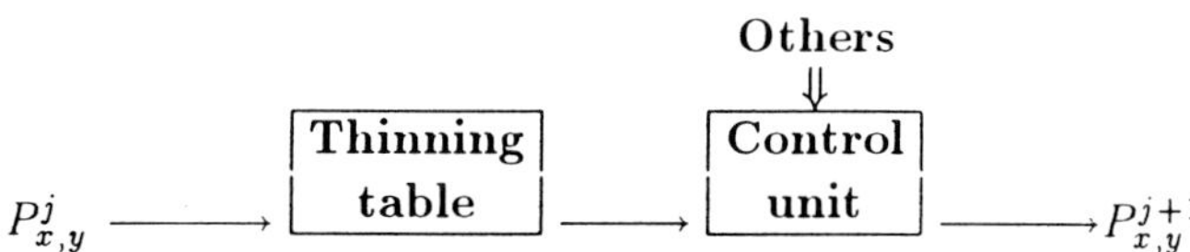

Fig. 3. Two-stage structure of the 1-subcycle parallel thinning process.

4.1.1. *Thinning table*

The thinning table of the case $t = 3$ of our proposed algorithm is shown in Fig. 4. Because the operational window is 3 × 3, and whether the "1" pixel is deleted or not is decided by its eight neighbors, the number of all the various combinations is $2^8(= 256)$. For clarity, the table is illustrated by a 16 × 16 matrix, where both the address and the data of the table are denoted in hexadecimal. For each combination of the eight neighbors of a pixel P, we convert it into an address of the thinning table by using the expression $\mathcal{N}(P)$ in Eq. (2.1). The corresponding content of the address will reveal the attributions of the related 3 × 3 local pattern. The "attributions" are defined by a data format.

The data format of this table is also shown in Fig. 4. Here three bits $D_2 - D_0$ represent the **EDN** in Eq. (2.14) since it only has eight cases. $D_3 = 1$ denotes that the currently presented 3 × 3 combination belongs to T_c. And $D_4 = 1$ denotes that the currently presented 3 × 3 combination belongs to T_{13} or T_{23}. If $D_3 = 0$ and $D_4 = 0$, then the "1" pixel P cannot be removed. The remaining three bits $D_7 - D_5$ will be introduced in Section 4.2.

For example, given a 3 × 3 local pattern (Fig. 5), where $\mathcal{N}(P) = 87$ and the corresponding content of this address of the table is 0D. It reveals **EDN** = 5 (i.e. $D_2 D_1 D_0 = 101$) and $D_3 = 1$. Therefore we know that this local pattern belongs to T_c, and P can be removed. However, if $D_4 = 1$ then whether the "1" pixel P should be removed or not must be further checked by Eq. (3.5) mentioned in Section 3.1. Hence, besides the first stage (thinning table), we require the second stage (control unit) to realize the 1-subcycle parallel algorithm.

$$\underbrace{\{N(7)N(6)N(5)N(4)}\quad\underbrace{N(3)N(2)N(1)N(0)\}}\ \Longleftarrow\ \{i\ =\ \mathcal{N}(P)\}$$

	0	1	2	3	4	5	6	7	8	9	A	B	C	D	E	F
0	00	00	00	0C	00	0D	0E	0D	00	00	00	00	0E	15	0E	0D
1	00	00	00	00	0F	26	17	00	08	00	00	00	0F	00	0F	16
2	00	00	00	00	00	00	00	00	00	00	00	00	00	00	00	00
3	08	00	00	00	17	26	17	00	08	00	00	00	0F	00	0F	16
4	00	0B	00	13	00	24	00	00	00	00	00	00	00	24	00	00
5	09	22	00	22	20	00	20	00	11	22	00	22	00	00	00	00
6	0A	13	00	13	00	24	00	00	00	00	00	00	00	24	00	00
7	09	00	00	00	00	00	00	00	09	00	00	00	10	00	10	40
8	00	0C	00	0C	00	15	00	0D	00	00	00	00	00	15	00	0D
9	00	00	00	00	00	26	00	00	00	00	00	00	00	00	00	16
A	00	00	00	00	00	00	00	00	00	00	00	00	00	00	00	00
B	00	00	00	00	00	26	00	00	00	00	00	00	00	00	00	16
C	0A	0B	00	0B	00	00	00	14	00	00	00	00	00	00	00	14
D	11	00	00	00	20	00	20	00	11	00	00	00	00	00	00	40
E	0A	0B	00	0B	00	00	00	14	00	00	00	00	00	00	00	14
F	09	12	00	12	00	00	00	40	09	12	00	12	10	40	10	80

$T_i\,T_r\,T_j$	$T_{13}\,(or\,T_{23})$	T_c	**EDN**
$D_7\,D_6\,D_5$	D_4	D_3	$D_2\,D_1\,D_0$

Data format:

Fig. 4. The thinning table of the case $t = 3$.

1	1	1
0	P	1
0	0	0

Fig. 5. Example.

4.1.2. *Control unit*

The control unit is composed of three *control gates*, which are used to check whether or not the removal of a nonzero pixel $P_{x,y}$ will destroy the line connectivity under parallel processing. Let $G_1(x,y)$ be a control gate and let $C_1(0)$ and $C_1(1)$ denote the two sets of mutually opposite **EDNs** $\{4,5,2,7\}$ and $\{0,1,6,3\}$ corresponding to T_{13} and T_{23} mentioned in Section 3.1. If any one of the following conditions is satisfied ($G_1(x,y) = 1$,) then the "1" pixel $P_{x,y}$ associated with $D_4(x,y) = 1$ can be removed. (For convenience, we use (x,y) to stand for $P_{x,y}$.)

(a) **EDN**$(x,y) \in C_1(j \bmod 2)$,

(b) **EDN**$(x,y) \in C_1(j+1 \bmod 2)$ and there is no "1" neighbor $P_{m,n}$ associated with $D_4(m,n) = 1$ such that **EDN**$(m,n) \in C_1(j \bmod 2)$,

where (m,n) may be $(x,y-1)$, $(x+1,y)$, $(x,y+1)$, or $(x-1,y)$, and j is the number of current iterations. In practice, $(j \bmod 2)$ and $(j+1 \bmod 2)$ can be replaced by

0	0	0	0	0	0
0	0	0	0	0	0
1	1	R	0	0	0
0	0	P	Q	0	0
0	0	0	1	0	0
0	0	0	1	0	0

$$\mathcal{N}(P) = 8D; \ D_4(P) = 1; \ \mathbf{EDN}(P) = 5$$
$$\mathcal{N}(Q) = D0; \ D_4(Q) = 1; \ \mathbf{EDN}(Q) = 1$$
$$\mathcal{N}(R) = 58; \ D_4(R) = 1; \ \mathbf{EDN}(R) = 1$$

Fig. 6. Example.

a flip-flop. For example, a parallel processing is performed on the given pattern shown in Fig. 6.

Assume that the number j of current iterations is even. For the "1" pixel P, $\mathbf{EDN}(P) = 5 \in C_1(0)$ belongs to the condition (a), therefore it can be removed. But for the "1" pixels Q and R, $\mathbf{EDN}(Q) = 1 \in C_1(1)$ and $\mathbf{EDN}(R) = 1 \in C_1(1)$ belong to the condition (b), and both of them have a "1" neighbor P associated with $D_4 = 1$ (see the address $\mathcal{N}(P) = 8D$ in the thinning table for reference) such that $\mathbf{EDN}(P) = 5 \in C_1(0)$, so they cannot be removed in this iteration.

Consequently, the control gate $G_1(x, y)$ performs the function of Eq. (3.5) which deals with those local patterns labeled by $D_4 = 1$. The above conditions are easily implemented by the combinational logics and therefore the realized form of the proposed 1-subcycle parallel thinning algorithm can be expressed by:

$$P_{x,y}^{j+1} = P_{x,y}^j \cdot \bar{D}_3(x, y) \cdot \bar{G}_1(x, y) \tag{4.1}$$

where "$\cdot$" and "$-$" represent AND and NOT, respectively.

4.1.3. Results and comments

In this subsection we apply the realization of Eq. (4.1) to some experiments. Figure 7 presents the results of our 1-subcycle algorithm, where pattern "A" in [32] is frequently used in comparative study [22,35,43–45,47] and the other patterns are those in our original work [43].

From the illustrative results, we can observe that the thin line belongs to P8IT-type, i.e. there are no 8-deletable points on the thin line except for the T-junction. Comparing these results with the skeletons obtained by Holt *et al.*'s algorithm in Fig. 8, we find that serious shrinking does not appear in our algorithm. The higher biased skeleton obtained by Chin *et al.*'s algorithm in Fig. 9 is also reduced in our algorithm.

Even though the thinning results of the proposed algorithm are quite good, the algorithm is worthy of further improvement in the following two directions:

(a) 6 iterations   (b) 5 iterations

(c) 12 iterations   (d) 8 iterations

Fig. 7. The skeletons obtained by our algorithm (see Section 3).

the production of P8ET-type thin line and the production of an isotropic skeleton for an *L*-shape pattern. In Section 4.2.1 we shall present the first improvement based on our previous algorithm to produce the P8ET-type thin line which is well-defined [22]. Also we observe that most of the parallel algorithms cannot produce an isotropic thinning result for an *L*-shape pattern. This can be illustrated by the skeletons in Figs. 7–9. The reason will be detailed in Section 4.2.2 and a further improvement will also be presented.

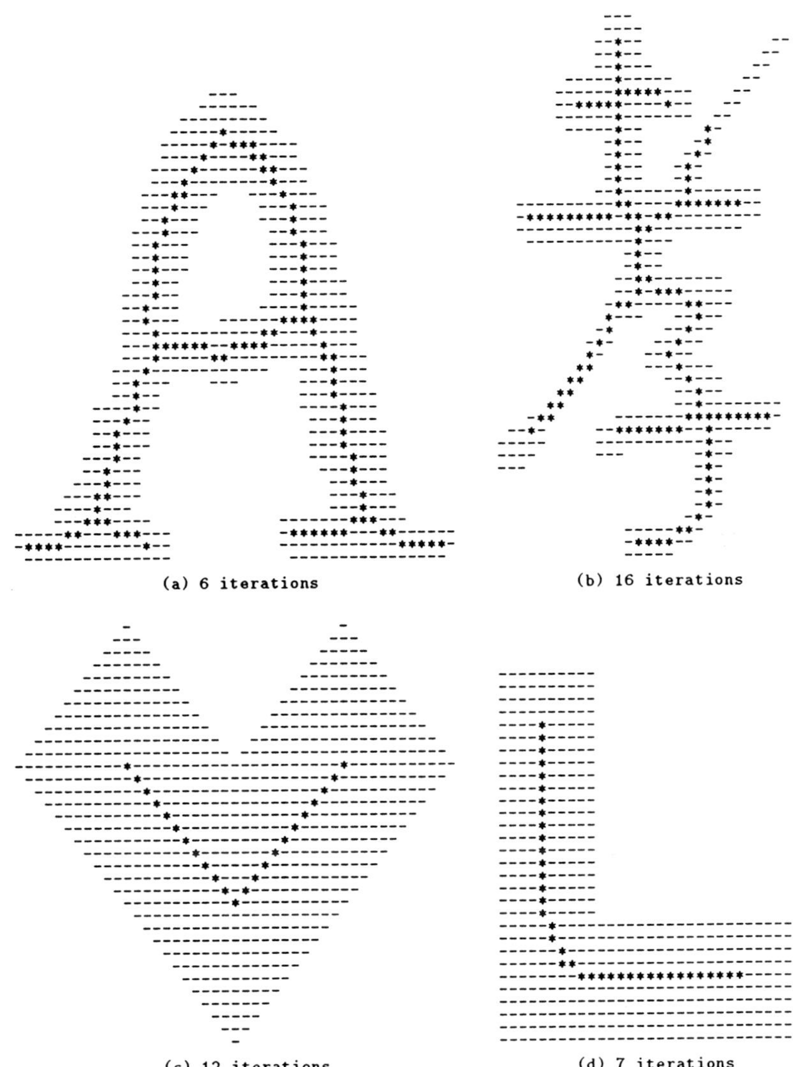

(a) 6 iterations

(b) 16 iterations

(c) 12 iterations

(d) 7 iterations

Fig. 8. The skeletons obtained by Holt *et al.*'s algorithm [46].

4.2. *Improvements*

4.2.1. *Production of P8ET-type thin line*

Since the local branches occurring in the case $\mathbf{LC}(P) = T_b - 1(\neq 0)$ mentioned in Section 2.3 are not designed as a thinning condition in our previous work [43], the P8IT-type thin line is produced. In fact, for a 3×3 local pattern, only the

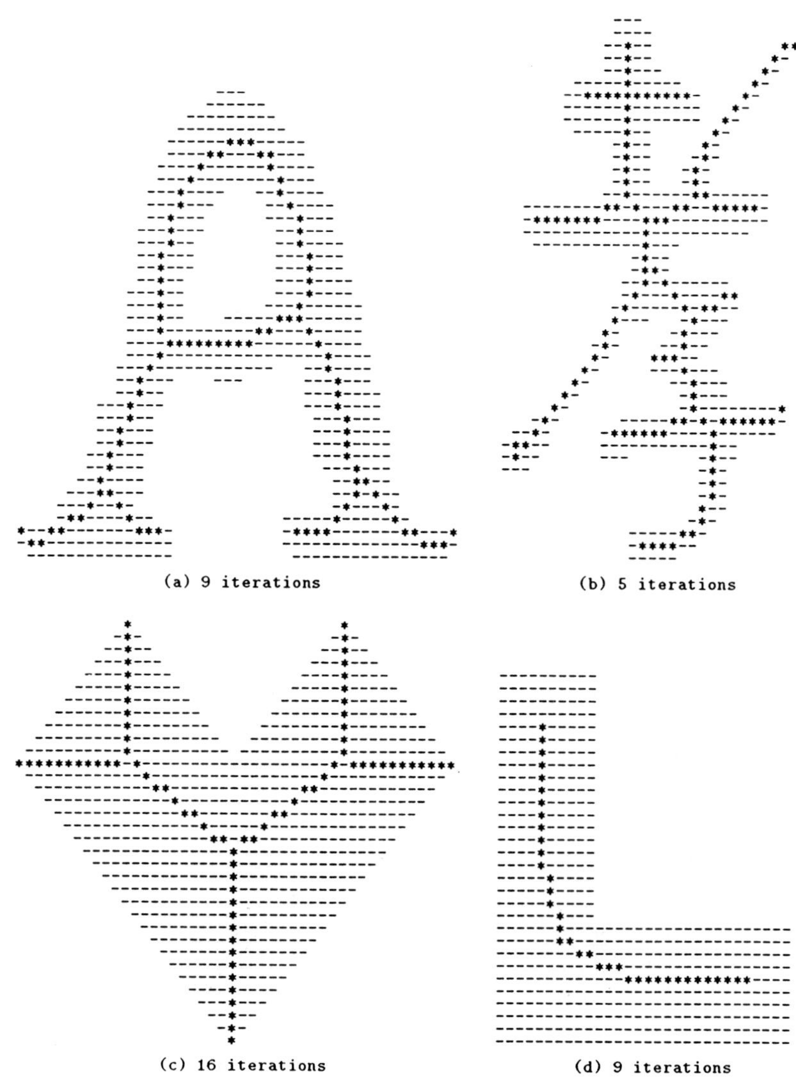

(a) 9 iterations   (b) 5 iterations

(c) 16 iterations   (d) 9 iterations

Fig. 9. The skeletons obtained by Chin *et al.*'s algorithm [47].

T-junction or *quasi* T-junction belongs to the case of local branches. We can list all of such cases as follows (Fig. 10), where P, Q, and R denote "1" pixels, and Xs are "don't cares". For parallel processing, since we have *a priori* information of the mutually opposite **EDN**s $C_1(0) = \{4, 5, 2, 7\}$ and $C_1(1) = \{0, 1, 6, 3\}$ and the **EDN**s listed above are only 0, 2, 4, and 6, we therefore have the information that those local patterns associated with **EDN**s 2, 4 are opposite to those associated with **EDN**s 0, 6 for the above cases. All these cases are assigned another thinning

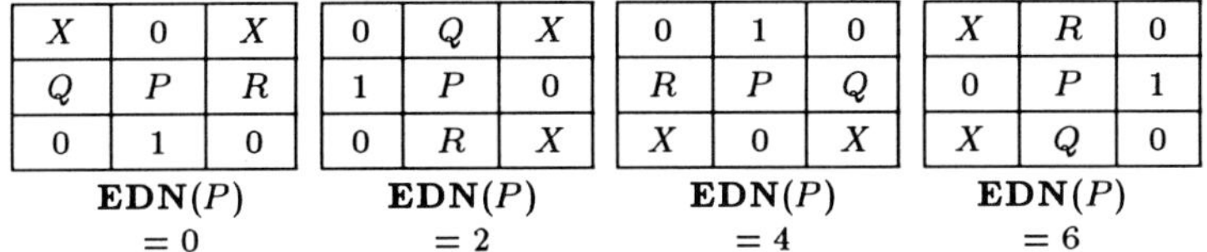

Fig. 10. All cases of T-junction or *quasi* T-junction.

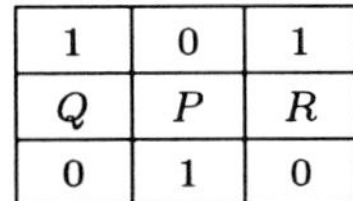

Fig. 11. Example.

Fig. 12. The mutually opposite **EDN**s given the example shown in Fig. 11.

subwindow T_j and addressed in the thinning table as shown in Fig. 4, where bit D_5 is assigned "1" for each case.

If we further examine briefly the cases of "1" neighbors for each case mentioned above, we will discover other mutually opposite **EDN**s. For example, given a 3 × 3 local pattern (a quasi T-junction) shown in Fig. 11, the mutually opposite **EDN**s may occur in following cases as Fig. 12 shows. (According to the weak connectivity mentioned in Section 2.3, we only need to examine the neighbors $N(0)$, $N(2)$, $N(4)$, and $N(6)$ for the "1" pixel P.) Note that these cases only belong to T_{13}, T_{23}, or T_j. After these examinations, which are similar to our proposed checking procedure (see Algorithm 3.1), we obtain the relationships of the new mutually opposite pairs of **EDN**s shown in Table 1.

Table 1. Relationships of the newly mutually opposite **EDN**s.

EDN(P)	$\leftrightarrow$	**EDN**(Q)	or	**EDN**(R)
$D_5 = 1$		$D_4 = 1$		$D_5 = 1$
0		3 or 5		4
2		5 or 7		6
4		1 or 7		0
6		1 or 3		2

Since $\mathbf{EDN}(P) = 2, 4$ belong to a set said to be $C_1(0)$, and $\mathbf{EDN}(P) = 0, 6$ belong to the other set said to be $C_1(1)$, we let $C_2(0)$ and $C_2(1)$ be the sets of $\{0, 1, 5, 6, 7\}$ and $\{1, 2, 3, 4, 5\}$, respectively. Let $G_2(x, y)$ be the second control gate. A P8ET-type thin line can be produced by performing the following expression:

$$P_{x,y}^{j+1} = P_{x,y}^{j} \cdot \bar{D}_3(x, y) \cdot \bar{G}_1(x, y) \cdot \bar{G}_2(x, y), \qquad (4.2)$$

where $G_2(x, y)$ is designed as follows: If any one of the following conditions is satisfied $(G_2(x, y) = 1,)$ then the "1" pixel $P_{x,y}$ associated with $D_5(x, y) = 1$ can be removed.

(a') $\mathbf{EDN}(x, y) \in C_1(j \bmod 2)$ and there is no "1" neighbor $P_{m,n}$ associated with $D_4(m, n) = 1$ such that $\mathbf{EDN}(m, n) \in C_2(j \bmod 2)$,

(b') $\mathbf{EDN}(x, y) \in C_1(j + 1 \bmod 2)$ and there is no "1" neighbor $P_{m,n}$ associated with $D_4(m, n) = 1$ or $D_5(m, n) = 1$ such that $\mathbf{EDN}(m, n) \in C_2(j + 1 \bmod 2)$,

where (m, n) may be $(x, y - 1)$, $(x + 1, y)$, $(x, y + 1)$, or $(x - 1, y)$.

We had applied the realized structure in Eq. (4.2) to several patterns. Figure 13 illustrates the thinning results of the same patterns in Fig. 7 obtained by this improved version, and confirms that the first improved version can produce the P8ET-type thin line.

4.2.2. *Production of isotropic skeleton for L-shape patterns*

A reason for resulting in the bias for an L-shape skeleton was mentioned in Chin *et al.*'s paper [47]. That is, a *side effect* of the thinning templates: they remove pixels from convex corners faster than from concave corners. In that paper, it did not show what thinning templates for concave corners should be added to deal with this situation. In this subsection, we will present how these thinning conditions are designed.

Let us observe the following 3 × 3 local pattern shown in Fig. 14. This local pattern will appear in most of the concave patterns especially in the case of the L-shape pattern because it belongs to the case $\mathbf{LC}(P) = T_b$ (see Section 2.3, it cannot be designed as a thinning condition in general.) If such a local pattern can be designed as a thinning condition under the preservation of pattern connectivity, then the side effect mentioned by Chin *et al.* [47] will be reduced and therefore a more isotropic skeleton of an L-shape pattern can be obtained.

Consider a 5 × 5 local pattern shown in Fig. 15. Here P, Q, R, S, and Ts are "1" pixels, and Xs are "don't cares". Since the removal of "1" pixels labeled by "T" is apparent (refer to the realization in Eq. (4.1) or (4.2) and the thinning table shown in Fig. 4) the eventual removal of the center "1" pixel P is also certain. Hence, all such cases and their rotated versions by multiples of 90° can be exactly designed as a thinning condition.

In order to facilitate the operation of our proposed two-stage structure in Fig. 3, we let T_r be a set containing the 3 × 3 local patterns shown in Fig. 16, and address them in the thinning table as shown in Fig. 4, where bit D_6 is assigned "1" for these

(a) 7 iterations

(b) 6 iterations

(c) 12 iterations

(d) 8 iterations

Fig. 13. The skeletons obtained by the first improved algorithm (see Section 4.2.1).

1	1	0
1	P	1
1	1	1

Fig. 14. Example.

cases. The case shown in Fig. 17 is denoted by the set T_i and the bit D_7 is assigned for this case in the thinning table.

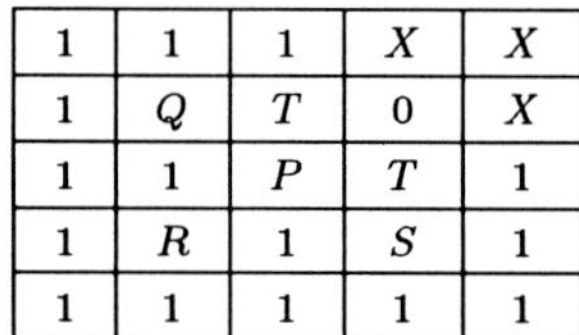

Fig. 15. Illustration.

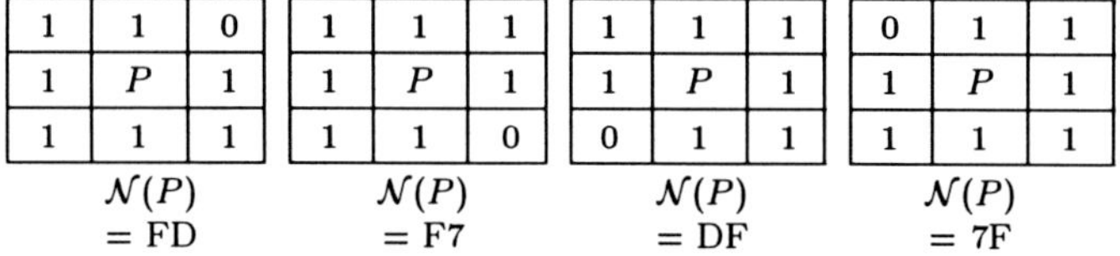

Fig. 16. Four cases contained in T_r.

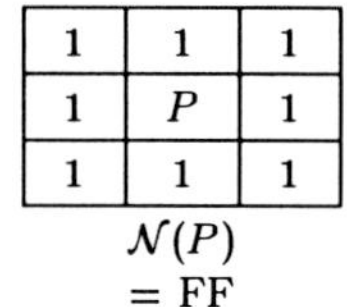

Fig. 17. The case contained in T_i.

From the 5×5 local pattern mentioned above, we can simply detect this pattern by applying the 3×3 cases belonging to T_r and T_i. It is obviously shown that the 3×3 local pattern with the center pixel P belongs to T_r, and those with the center pixels Q, R, and S belong to T_i. The pixels Q, R, and S are the neighbors of P. It is not necessary to consider other "1" neighbors of P. Let $G_3(x, y)$ be the third control gate. If the $G_3(x, y) = 1$ condition is satisfied, then the "1" pixel $P_{x,y}$ associated with $D_6(x, y) = 1$ can be removed.

(c) There exist three "1" neighbors $(P_{m,n})s$ associated with $D_7 = 1$, where (m, n) may be $(x - 1, y - 1)$, $(x + 1, y - 1)$, $(x - 1, y + 1)$, or $(x + 1, y + 1)$.

Hence the improved version which can produce an isotropic skeleton of an L-shape pattern is expressed by

$$P_{x,y}^{j+1} = p_{x,y}^{j} \cdot \bar{D}_3(x, y) \cdot \bar{G}_1(x, y) \cdot \bar{G}_2(x, y) \cdot \bar{G}_3(x, y). \tag{4.3}$$

Applying this improved version to the same set of patterns in Fig. 7, we see the corresponding results in Fig. 18. In comparision with those in Fig. 13, the results are close to the original patterns from the nontopological viewpoint especially with respect to the position of lines. The comparison also shows that Eq. (4.3) requires fewer iterations than Eq. (4.1) or (4.2). To further check the algorithm, two challenging patterns "X" and "Q" used in [51] and [33] respectively are processed by this algorithm. The results shown in Fig. 19 confirm that the algorithm is effective. Accordingly, the special set of thinning conditions presented in this subsection can lead to the production of isotropic skeletons even for an L-shape pattern so that

(a) 5 iterations

(b) 4 iterations

(c) 12 iterations

(d) 6 iterations

Fig. 18. The skeletons obtained by the second improved algorithm (see Section 4.2.2).

the visual quality of the skeleton is more satisfactory. It also makes the improved algorithm more efficient.

4.3. *Discussions*

In this section, two further improved versions based on the pseudo 1-subcycle parallel thinning algorithm have been presented and a two-stage structure is also described to realize the proposed 1-subcycle parallel algorithm. The first improved

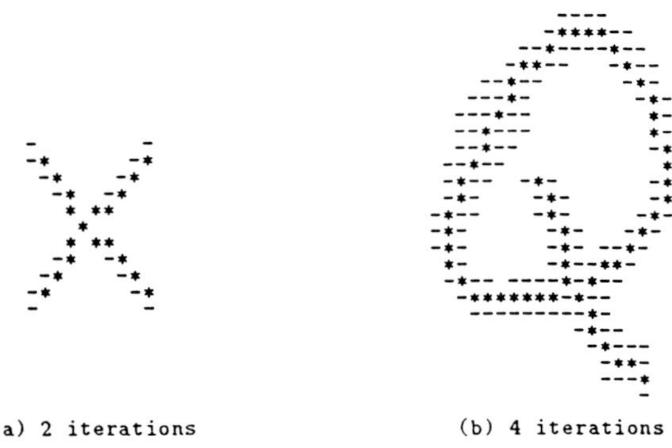

(a) 2 iterations   (b) 4 iterations

Fig. 19. Results of applying the second improved algorithm to the challenging patterns "X" [51] and "Q" [33].

version can exactly produce the well-defined perfect 8-curve thin line, and the second improved version can further obtain an isotropic skeleton for an L-shape pattern, so that the skeletons obtained are a better approximation of the original pattern from the nontopological viewpoint especially with respect to the position of thin lines.

5. Conclusions

The computer algorithms described in this chapter are thinning algorithms. Thinning is an important technique for transforming the thickness of a line-like object from many pixels wide to just a single pixel. The abstracted information of a line image will facilitate the extraction of features for further pattern description and recognition. Several related algorithms have been reviewed. The fundamental requirements for the design of an efficient and effective thinning algorithm are also given. Before introducing the systematic approach to designing a parallel thinning algorithm, we presented the basic framework of the thinning method, reviewed several classical related defintions, and defined some new definitions and functions. Three new functions called the local connecting (**LC**) function, the extended local connecting (**ELC**) function, and the erosive direction number (**EDN**) are principally used to design the thinning windows. With these defined functions and the property of shape invariance, all the possible cases of the 2-subcycle parallel thinning algorithm are constructed. By further using the **ELC** function, the 2-subcycle version can be reduced to the pseudo 1-subcycle version. The experiments showed that the skeletons produced by the systematic approach are always perfectly 8-connected. To facilitate the postprocessing of a line pattern, we further improved the developed algorithm, which can produce the well-defined perfect 8-curve thin line and obtain an isotropic skeleton for an L-shape pattern, so that the skeletons obtained are a better approximation of the original pattern from the nontopological viewpoint especially with respect to the position of thin lines.

Acknowledgements

The authors are grateful to the Prof. P. S. P. Wang for his helpful comments and suggestions. The first author also owes a special thanks to his wife Mrs. Tsuey-Ping Chung for her helpful suggestions, never-failing support and love.

References

[1] H. Sherman, A quasi-topological method for the recognition of line patterns, in *Information Processing, Proc. UNESCO Conf.* (Butterworths, London, 1959) 232–238.

[2] A. P. Pullen, Automatic visual inspection of complex industrial components, paper read at BPRA Meeting, University College, London, 1977.

[3] J. F. Jarris, The line drawing editor: schematic diagram editing using pattern recognition techniques, *Comput. Graph. Image Process.* **6** (1977) 452–484.

[4] R. N. Dixon and C. J. Taylor, Automated asbestos fibre counting, in *Proc. IOP Conf. on Machine-aided Image Analysis* (Institute of Physics, London, 1979) 178–185.

[5] C. J. Hilditch, Linear skeletons from square cupboards, in B. Metzer and D. Michie (eds.), *Machine Intelligence* **IV** (University Press, Edinburgh, 1969) 403–420.

[6] J. F. O'Callaghan and J. Loveday, Quantitative measurements of soil cracking patterns, *Pattern Recogn.* **5** (1973) 83–98.

[7] C. V. K. Rao, On the fingerprint pattern recognition, *Pattern Recogn.* **10** (1978) 15–18.

[8] W. C. Liou, J. Y. Jong and W. H. Hsu, Automatical finger-prints identification system with no-ink input method, in *Proc. of National Computer Symposium*, Kaohsiung, Taiwan, ROC, 1985, 760–768.

[9] C. C. Chien, and W. H. Hsu, Automatic fingerprint identification — a planar point pattern matching approach, in *Proc. of National Computer Symposium*, Taipei, Taiwan, ROC, 1987, 806–815.

[10] H. Ogawa and K. Taniguchi, Thinning and stroke segmentation for handwritten Chinese recognition, *Pattern Recogn.* **15** (1982) 229–308.

[11] T. Shinji et al., Thinning algorithms for digital pictures and their application to handprinted characters recognition, *Trans. IECE* **J66-D** (1983) 526–532, in Japanese.

[12] W. H. Hsu and F. H. Cheng, Recognition of handwritten Chinese by structure analysis of strokes, *Comput. Process. of Chinese and Oriental Lang.* **2** (1985) 101–112.

[13] F. H. Cheng and W. H. Hsu, Radical extraction from handwritten Chinese characters by background thinning method, *IEICEJ Trans.* **71-E** (1988) 88–98.

[14] F. H. Cheng, W. H. Hsu and C. A. Chen, Fuzzy approach to solve the recognition problem of handwritten Chinese characters, *Pattern Recogn.* **22** (1989) 133–141.

[15] F. H. Cheng, W. H. Hsu and M. Y. Chen, Recognition of handwritten Chinese character by modified Hough transform technique, *IEEE Trans. Pattern Anal. Mach. Intell.* **11** (1989) 429–439.

[16] W. K. Gu and T. S. Huang, Connected line drawing extracted from a perspective view of a polyhedron, *IEEE Trans. Pattern Anal. Mach. Intell.* **7** (1985) 422–430.

[17] I. D. Judd, Compression of binary images by stroke encoding, *Comput. Digital Techniques* **2** (1979) 41–48.

[18] G. F. P. Deeker and J. P. Penny, On iterative map storage and retrieval, *Information* **10** (1972) 62–74.

[19] T. Kreifelts, Skelettierung und linienverfolgung in raster digitalisierten linienstruk-turen, *GL/NTG Congress on Digital Image Processing*, Münich, Informatik-Fachberichte, Nr. 8 (Springer, Berlin, 1977).

[20] P. Seuffert, An application of line and character recognition in cartography, in *Proc. IEEE Congress on Pattern Recogn.*, Troy, New York, 1988, 338–343.

[21] R. W. Smith, Computer processing of line images: a survey, *Pattern Recogn.* **20** (1987) 7–15.

[22] H. Tamura, A comparison of line thinning algorithms from digital geometry viewpoint, in *Proc. Int. Joint Conf. on Pattern Recognition*, Kyoto, Japan, 1978, 715–719.

[23] A. Rosenfeld and L. S. Davis, A note on thinning, *IEEE Trans. Syst. Man Cybern.* **6** (1976) 226–228.

[24] S. H. Y. Hung and T. Kasvand, Critical points on a perfectly 8- or 6-connected thin binary line, *Pattern Recogn.* **16** (1983) 297–306.

[25] D. Rutovitz, Pattern recognition, *J. Roy. Statist. Soc. Ser.* **A 129** (1966) 504–530.

[26] S. Yokoi et al., Topological properties in digitized binary pictures, *Trans. IECE* **J56-D** (1973) 662–669, in Japanese.

[27] S. Yokoi, J. T. Toriwaki and T. Fukumura, An analysis of topological properties of digitized binary pictures using local features, *Comput. Graph. Image Process.* **4** (1975) 63–73.

[28] A. Rosenfeld, Connectivity in digital pictures, *J. ACM* **17** (1970) 146–160.

[29] A. Rosenfeld, A characterization of parallel thinning algorithms, *Inf. Control* **29** (1975) 286–291.

[30] E. S. Deutsch, Comments on a line thinning scheme, *British Comput. J.* **12** (1969) 142.

[31] J. G. Fraser, Further comments on a line thinning scheme, *British Comput. J.* **13** (1970) 221–222.

[32] R. Stefanelli and A. Rosenfeld, Some parallel thinning algorithms for digital pictures, *J. ACM* **18** (1971) 255–264.

[33] N. J. Naccache and R. Shinghal, An investigation into the skeletonization approach of Hilditch, *Pattern Recogn.* **17** (1984) 279–284.

[34] T. Y. Zhang and C. Y. Suen, A fast parallel algorithm for thinning digital patterns, *Commun. ACM* **27** (1984) 236–239.

[35] H. E. Lü and P. S. P. Wang, A comment on "a fast parallel algorithm for thinning digital patterns", *Commun. ACM* **29** (1986) 239–242.

[36] Y. S. Chen and W. H. Hsu, A modified fast parallel algorithm for thinning digital patterns, *Pattern Recogn. Lett.* **7** (1988) 99–106.

[37] H. Tamura, Further considerations on line thinning schemes, *Paper of IECEJ Technical Group on Pattern Recognition and Recognition* **PRL75-66** (1975) 49–56, in Japanese.

[38] C. Arcelli, L. P. Cordella and S. Levialdi, Parallel thinning of binary pictures, *Electron. Lett.* **11** (1975) 148–149.

[39] C. Arcelli, L. P. Cordella and S. Levialdi, More about a thinning algorithm, *Electron. Lett.* **16** (1979) 51–53.

[40] E. S. Deutsch, Thinning algorithms on rectangular, hexagonal, and triangular arrays, *Commun. ACM* **15** (1972) 827–837.

[41] N. J. Naccache and R. Shinghal, SPTA: a proposed algorithm for thinning binary patterns, *IEEE Trans. Syst. Man Cybern.* **14** (1984) 409–418.

[42] Y. K. Chu and C. Y. Suen, An alternate smoothing and stripping algorithm for thinning digital binary patterns, *Signal Process.* **11** (1986) 207–222.

[43] Y. S. Chen and W. H. Hsu, A systematic approach for designing 2-subcycle and pseudo 1-subcycle parallel thinning algorithms, *Pattern Recogn.* **22** (1989) 267–282.

[44] Y. S. Chen and W. H. Hsu, A 1-subcycle parallel thinning algorithm for producing perfect 8-curves and obtaining isotropic skeleton of the *L*-shape pattern, in *IEEE Proc. of Computer Vision and Pattern Recognition*, San Diego, 1989, 208–215.

[45] Y. S. Chen and W. H. Hsu, A comparison on some one-pass parallel thinnings, *Pattern Recogn. Lett.* **11** (1990) 35–41.

[46] C. M. Holt, A. Stewart, M. Clint and R. H. Perrott, An improved parallel thinning algorithm, *Commun. ACM* **30** (1987) 156–160.

[47] R. T. Chin, H. K. Wan, D. L. Stover and R. D. Iverson, A one-pass thinning algorithm and its parallel implementation, *Comput. Vision Graph. Image Process.* **40** (1987) 30–40.

[48] E. E. Triendl, Skeletonization of noisy handdrawn symbols using parallel operations, *Pattern Recogn.* **2** (1970) 215–226.

[49] E. R. Davies and A. P. N. Plummer, Thinning algorithms: a critique and a new methodology, *Pattern Recogn.* **14** (1981) 53–63.

[50] F. W. M. Stentiford and R. G. Mortimer, Some new heuristics for thinning binary handprinted characters for OCR, *IEEE Trans. Syst. Man Cybern.* **13** (1983) 81–84.

[51] P. S. P. Wang and Y. Y. Zhang, A fast and flexible thinning algorithm, *IEEE Trans. Comput.* **38** (1989), 741–745.

[52] S. Naito, H. Arakawa and I. Masuda, Recognition of hand-printed alphanumerics and symbols based on centroid lines, in *Proc. 4th Int. Joint Conf. on Pattern Recognition*, Kyoto, Japan, 1978, 797–801.

[53] T. Wakayama, A core-line tracing algorithm based on maximal square moving, *IEEE Trans. Pattern Anal. Mach. Intell.* **4** (1982) 68–74.

[54] A. Favre and H. Keller, Parallel syntactic thinning by recoding of binary pictures, *Comput. Vision Graph. Image Process.* **23** (1983) 99–112.

[55] T. Pavlidis, A vectorizer and feature extractor for document recognition, *Comput. Vision Graph. Image Process.* **35** (1986) 111–127.

[56] T. Pavlidis, *Algorithms for Graphics and Image Processing* (Computer Science Press, 1982).

[57] T. Pavlidis, An asynchronous thinning algorithm, *Comput. Graph. Image Process.* **20** (1982) 133–157.

[58] S. Suzuki and K. Abe, Binary picture thinning by an iterative parallel two-subcycle operation, *Pattern Recogn.* **20** (1987) 297–307.

[59] Y. S. Chen and W. H. Hsu, A multi-function parallel processor for binary image processing, *Journal of Chinese Institute of Engineers* **11** (1988) 73–86.

[60] P. N. Chen, Y. S. Chen and W. H. Hsu, A computing architecture of adjustable convolution system for image processing, *Journal of Information Science and Engineering* **3** (1987) 63–79.

[61] P. N. Chen, Y. S. Chen and W. H. Hsu, Reduced processing element architecture (RPEA) for parallel local image processing, *Journal of the Chinese Institute of Engineers* **10** (1987) 701–707.

[62] Y. S. Chen and W. H. Hsu, A simplified high-speed parallel processor for binary image processing, in *Proc. of National Computer Symposium*, Taipei, Taiwan, ROC, 1987, 766–770.

[63] B. Shapiro, J. Pisa and J. Sklansky, Skeleton generation from x, y boundary sequences, *Comput. Graph. Image Process.* **15** (1981) 136–153.

[64] R. M. Shinha, A width-independent algorithm for character skeleton estimation, *Comput. Vision Graph. Image Process.* **40** (1987) 388–397.

[65] M. P. Martínez-Pérez, J. Jiménez and J. L. Navalón, A thinning algorithm based on contours, *Comput. Vision Graph. Image Process.* **39** (1987) 186–201.

[66] O. Baruch, Line thinning by line following, *Pattern Recogn. Lett.* **8** (1988) 271–276.

[67] S. Lobregt, W. Verbeet and F. C. A. Groen, Three-dimensional skeletonization: principle and algorithm, *IEEE Trans. Pattern Anal. Mach. Intell.* **2** (1980) 75–77.

[68] Y. F. Tsao and K. S. Fu, A parallel thinning algorithm for 3-D pictures, *Comput. Graph. Image Process.* **17** (1981) 315–331.

[69] H. Tamura and K. Mori, A parallel thinning algorithm for binary pictures and its connectivity, *Nat. Conr. Rec. IECEJ. No. 1539* (1974) 1390, in Japanese.

[70] A. Rosenfeld, Digital straight line segments, *IEEE Trans. Comput.* **23** (1974) 1264–1269.

PART 3

RECOGNITION APPLICATIONS

Handbook of Pattern Recognition and Computer Vision, pp. 493–509
Eds. C. H. Chen, L. F. Pau and P. S. P. Wang
© 1993 World Scientific Publishing Company

CHAPTER 3.1

PATTERN RECOGNITION IN NONDESTRUCTIVE EVALUATION OF MATERIALS

C. H. CHEN

Department of Electrical and Computer Engineering
University of Massachusetts Dartmouth, N. Dartmouth, MA 02747, USA

Nondestructive evaluation (NDE) of materials is now widely used in defect detection and classification, material characterization and discrimination, and machine inspection. To improve the capability of NDE instrumentation, pattern recognition is the key to automating the inspection process as well as providing information for making objective decisions. This chapter presents the major activities and results of pattern recognition in NDE, including both traditional statistical pattern recognition and modern neural network classifiers for ultrasonic, acoustic emission and eddy current signals and radiographic images.

Keywords: Nondestructive evaluation, ultrasonic signals, acoustic emission, eddy current, radiographic images, defect detection, statistical and neural network classifiers.

1. Introduction

Nondestructive evaluation (NDE), also called nondestructive testing (NDT) or nondestructive inspection (NDI), of materials refers to the characterization, discrimination and prediction of material defects nondestructively. Early effort in NDE was limited to visualization or simply knocking the material being tested. It was only about fifty years ago when ultrasonic sensors and radiographic methods were developed that more reliable NDE instrumentation became available. This progress was marked by the birth of the American Society of Nondestructive Testing (ASNT) in Boston in 1941. Since the late 70's when digital processing of signals became popular, pattern recognition techniques have been increasingly used in NDE problems. Some early examples of pattern recognition in NDE using eddy current and acoustic emission signals are [1–4].

Generally speaking the goals of pattern recognition and signal processing in NDE are to improve inspection reliability, to improve defect detection and characterization, to automate inspection tasks, and to generate information about the material properties to assess the remaining life of a structure. The materials tested vary from bonding adhesives, ceramics, composites, to metals, weldings, and many others for a wide range of applications in the aerospace industry, chemicals, electronics, nuclear reactors, ships, etc.

NDE sensors and methods include: ultrasonics, acousto-ultrasonics, radiography (X-ray, neutron, etc.), acoustic emission, eddy current, magnetics, visual, liquid penetrants, lasers and holograms, electromagnetics, thermal imaging, computed tomography, etc. Some useful references in NDE methods are in [5–8]. Also ASNT has published a series of NDT handbooks that describe in detail the NDE methods. For each method, features can be extracted from the digitized waveform or image data and pattern recognition techniques are employed to help achieve one or more of the goals stated above. In the last few years, there has been significant progress to demonstrate the feasibility of pattern recognition in NDE. Many challenges remain however before reliable recognition procedures can be fully implemented in operational NDE systems.

In this chapter emphasis will be placed on pattern recognition with the ultrasonic NDE, though other methods like eddy current, acoustic emission and radiography will also be examined. Examples are based on the specific system making use of the software package IUNDE (for interactive ultrasonic NDE), which we have developed [9,10].

2. Pattern Recognition in Ultrasonic NDE Systems

Ultrasonic methods of nondestructive testing are comparatively less expensive, easy to use and reliable. The center frequency of transducers employed in NDE typically ranges from 2MHz to 15MHz or higher depending on the size of defects considered. A single trace of ultrasonic pulse echo is called an A-scan. A sequence of pulse echoes taken as the transducer moves along a line is called a B-scan. The peak value of the pulse echo can give an indication of a hidden flaw or defect. The thickness can also be measured from the spacing between successive echoes. Mathematically the characterization of the defect from the pulse echo is an inverse problem which is not easy to solve except for some very simple defect geometry. To formulate this as a pattern recognition problem, we assume that the defect can be classified as one of several specified categories. Then features are extracted from the digitized data for classification. A simpler recognition problem can be a detection of the existence of a significant defect. The recognition method may also be used to estimate the most probable defect size.

Figure 1 is an example of a complete ultrasonic NDE system. The system consists of an ultrasonic pulser/receiver, an IBM PC/AT compatible, a high resolution digital scope which communicates with both pulser/receiver and computer, and an immersion tank for immersion mode operation, in addition to the usual contact mode operation. A typical set of test specimens with different hidden defect geometries in aluminum blocks is shown in Fig. 2. Here T15 refers to a transducer of center frequency 15MHz. For each defect geometry, an A-scan signal is obtained. By using the system as shown in Fig. 1, a C-scan ultrasonic image can be generated by using a mechanical movement of the immersion probe and a peak detector. A high resolution acoustic image may be obtained by further using digital image processing.

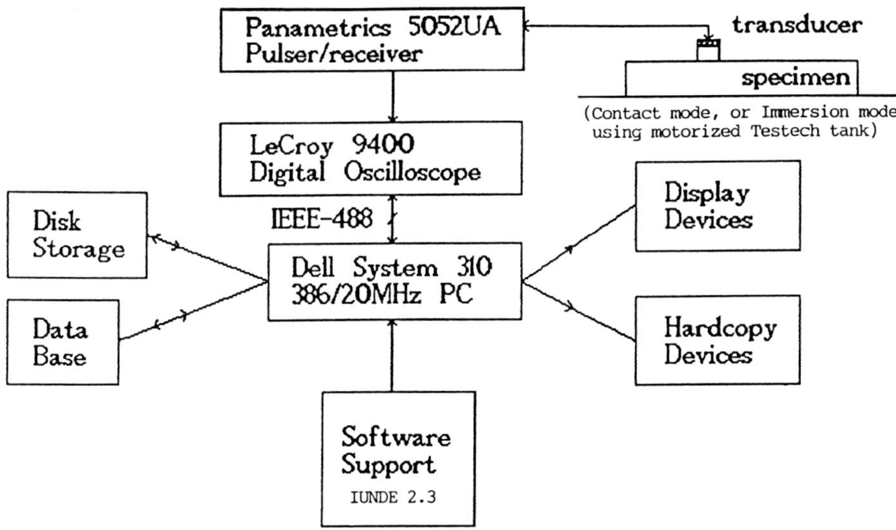

Fig. 1. The block diagram of a complete high resolution ultrasonic NDE system.

Image segmentation techniques can also be used to isolate the defect regions of hidden flaws not visible from the material surfaces. Software support is much needed throughout the entire system.

The digital system as shown in Fig. 1 has the advantages of providing high resolution data using a high sampling rate (typically 50MHz), automatic processing of such data, and flexibilty to be configured for different requirements. The digital operations can also compensate to some extent for the limitation of the pulser/receiver bandwidth and the transducer frequency response. Of course the best data are provided by the best instruments which can be very expensive. The detailed operation of this system is described in [9,10]. Other NDE systems that incorporate pattern recognition and artificial intelligence capability employ the software packages ICEPAK [11] and TestPro [12].

Before features are computed, signal processing functions are needed to present different knowledge domains of the signal [13], such as the time domain, frequency domain, the correlation structure, and the impulse response. Features can then be extracted from these domains. A detailed discussion of feature extraction and pattern classification is presented in the next section. On the subject of signal processing in NDE, there are now extensive research publications (see e.g. [14–16]). Here spectral analysis, deconvolution and time-frequency analysis are the three main topics. There is a close relationship between the spectrum and the hidden geometrical defects, as presented in the work on ultrasonic spectroscopy [17,18]. Modern spectrum analysis makes it possible to determine a high resolution and a reliable spectrum [19]. Good spectral features can be determined from the high resolution spectrum. However the problem is the lack of quantitative relationship

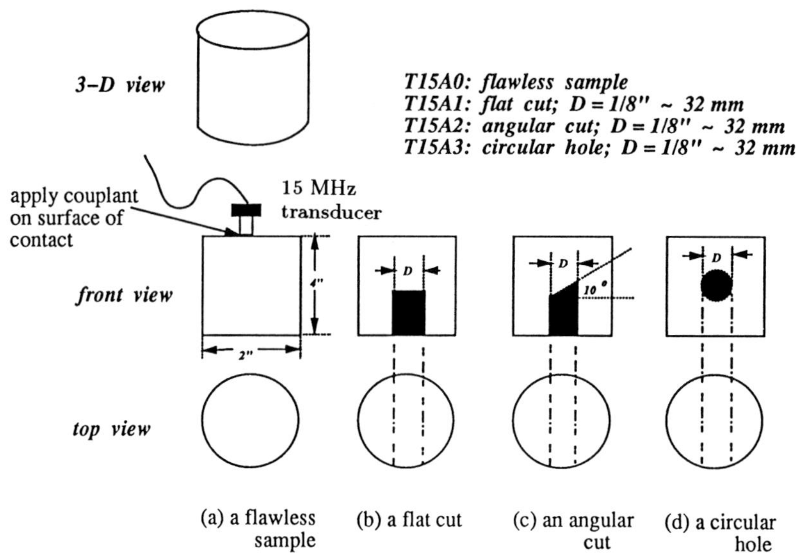

Fig. 2. Test specimens with different hidden-defect geometries.

available, except in very special cases [20], to calculate defect parameters from the spectrum.

The main objective of deconvolution is to determine the impulse response of the defect [21–23], which can be the internal discontinuities of a test specimen. With the effect of source signal removed, the impulse response presumably has a better characterization of the defect. For thickness and depth measurement, the impulse response can be very reliable. It is difficult to determine other parameters such as size and shape of a defect from the impulse response. For different defect categories, the impulse responses should be different and thus a good set of features may be derived from the impulse responses. In general it is difficult to obtain an accurate impulse response, especially in the presence of noise. However deconvolution always brings out some useful information not available from the original signal. To illustrate signal processing functions as provided by IUNDE, Fig. 3 shows, for the test specimens described in Fig. 2, signal processing results in spectrum analysis and deconvolution.

The ultrasonic signals normally experience a nonhomogeneous media and thus are time varying in nature which requires time-frequency representation. The short term Fourier analysis, Wigner distribution, and the Wavelet transform are most often used in time-frequency analysis. The pseudo-Wigner distribution can be used to decompose an ultrasonic signal into components [24] and to estimate accurately the bondline reflector thickness [25]. Both the wavelet transform and the Wigner distribution are also useful to extract features for ultrasonic signal classification [26]. The work reported on time-frequency analysis with the ultrasonic signals so far has been very limited, and this is a research topic that remains to be explored.

3. Feature Extraction and Pattern Classification in Ultrasonic NDE

Some of the best features that have good physical significance can be listed as follows:

(1) amplitude ratio, defined as the ratio of the cumulative sum of the absolute amplitude of the test specimen to that of a reference specimen.

(2) frequency ratio, defined as the ratio of the cumulative sum of the amplitude spectrum of a higher frequency band to that of a lower frequency band.

(3) maximum peak correlation value and the root mean square value of the correlation function between the test specimen and the reference specimen.

(4) the kurtosis and skewness, normally used as parameters of a probability density, of an amplitude spectrum. Kurtosis is the ratio of the fourth moment to the square of the second moment. Skewness is the ratio of the third moment to 1.5 power of the second moment of the amplitude spectrum.

(5) the pulse duration, defined as the time difference between the intercepts of the pulse envelope with a line at 10% of the peak amplitude in each waveform.

(6) the fractional powers over a certain number (say 8) of frequency bands.

(7) the peak spectral value, and the bandwidth of the power spectrum. It is noted that the IUNDE can automatically provide a tabulation of some features listed above, for a given ultrasonic trace, to form a feature vector, in addition to the statistical parameters.

Other mathematical features are (see e.g. [13,26,27]):

(1) width between major peaks of the impulse response, and the power deconvolution coefficients, defined as the mean value of the deconvolved amplitude spectrum,

(2) number of peaks above 25% of the maximum signal amplitude,

(3) the position and half pulse width of the largest peak,

(4) percentage of area under the largest peak,

(5) rise time and fall time of the largest peak,

(6) distance between the two largest peaks and the largest to the third peak,

(7) percentage of partial power in the first and fourth octant in the cepstral domain,

(8) number of peaks above the base line in the phase domain,

(9) fractal dimension of the signal,

(10) multichannel time/frequency decomposition features [28],

(11) partial sum of the derivative of the Wigner distribution, and the Laplacian of the Wigner distribution,

etc. Many other choices are possible which fully exploit the time and frequency and time-frequency domain structures of the signal. These features of course are useful in general in waveform classification.

As an example of the "feature-based" method in ultrasonic NDE, an experiment was conducted [10] on plastic balls of diameters 8/32", 12/32", 16/32" and 1"

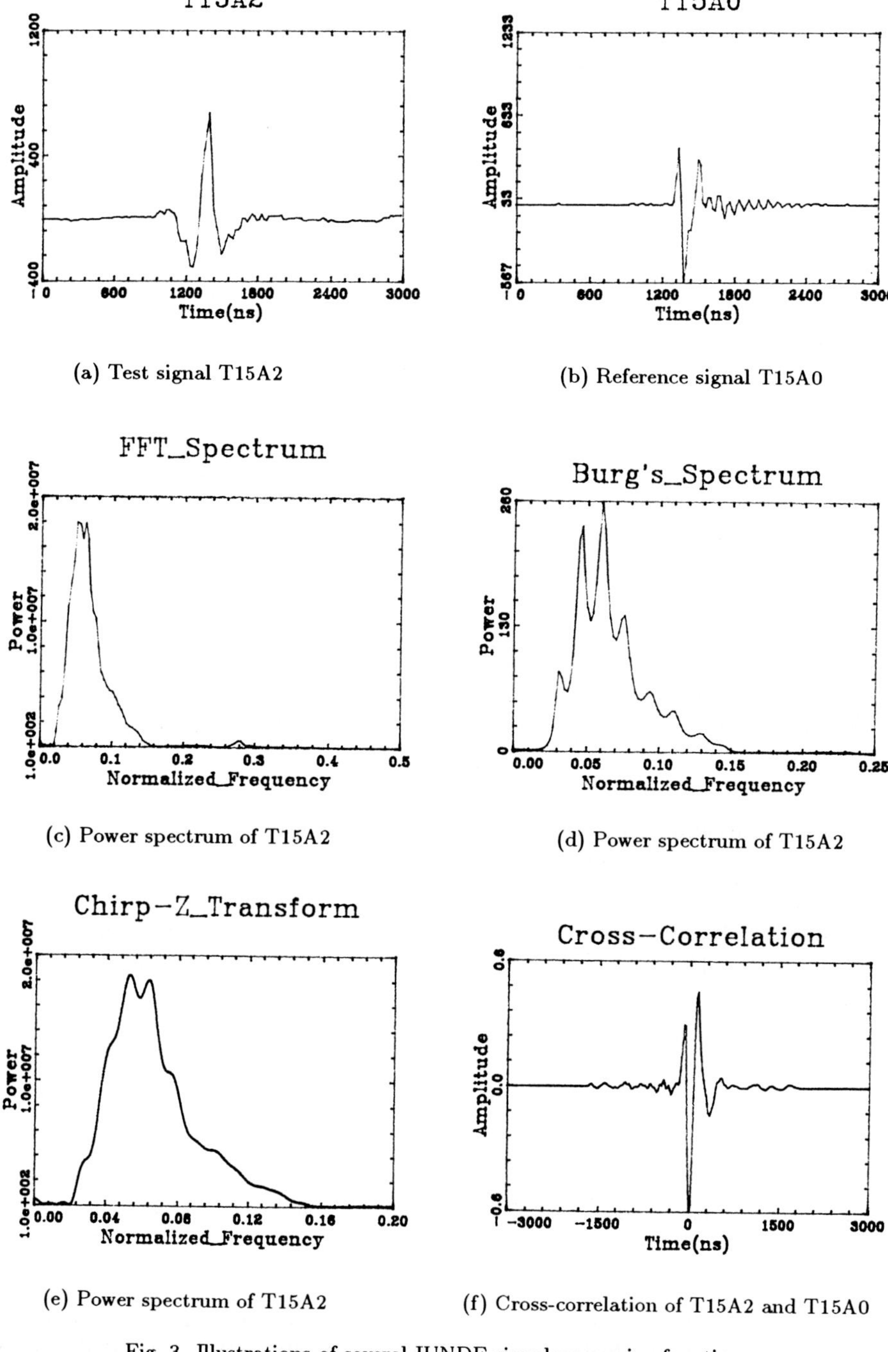

(a) Test signal T15A2

(b) Reference signal T15A0

(c) Power spectrum of T15A2

(d) Power spectrum of T15A2

(e) Power spectrum of T15A2

(f) Cross-correlation of T15A2 and T15A0

Fig. 3. Illustrations of several IUNDE signal processing functions.

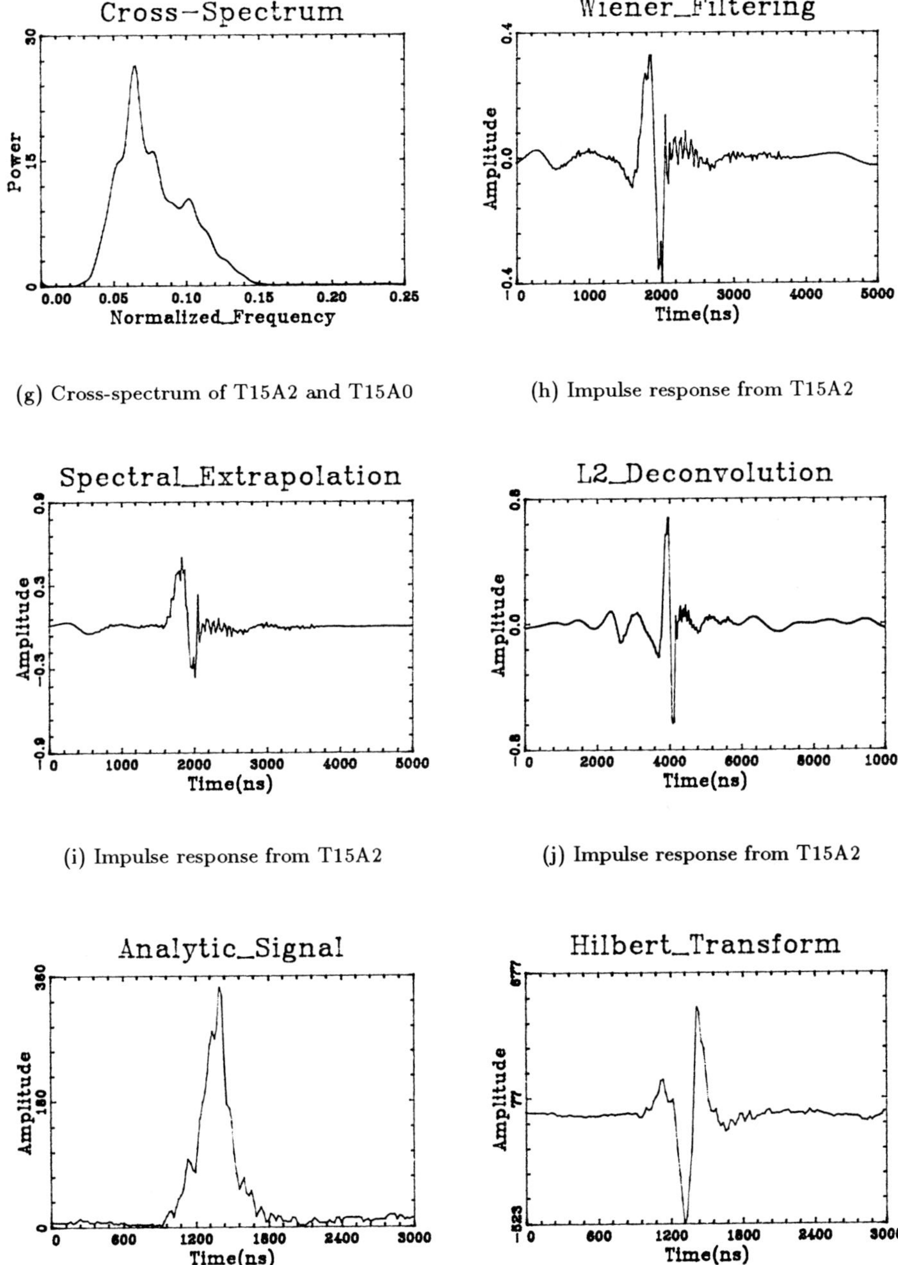

(g) Cross-spectrum of T15A2 and T15A0

(h) Impulse response from T15A2

(i) Impulse response from T15A2

(j) Impulse response from T15A2

(k) Analytic signal of T15A2

(l) Hilbert transform of T15A2

Fig. 3. Illustrations of several IUNDE signal processing functions (continued).

suspended inside a water-filled immersion tank. The controlled geometries created provide artificial discontinuities between the water and the balls. A tabulation of major feature values such as the amplitude ratio, frequency ratio, kurtosis of spectrum , and frequency of peak power shows an almost linear relationship between the feature values and the ball diameter. This along with similar experiments demonstrate that vector measurements of the same defect geometry tend to be clustered together.

In pattern classification, only a small number of carefully selected features are used. Evaluation of individual features can be done by using the Fisher criterion [14], or by examining empirically their effectiveness from percentage error. The traditional pattern recognition techniques typically employed in NDE classification [29] are the minimum distance classifier, the Fisher linear discriminant, the maximum likelihood classifier, and the K-mean clustering algorithm. For the hidden defect geometries shown in Fig. 2, both the nearest neighbor decision rule and the neural networks have been employed for classification experiments [10,30]. The neural network classifiers used include the RCE (Reduced Columb Energy) network of Nestor, Inc. [31], and the popular multilayer backpropagation network. Both the nearest neighbor decision rule and the two neural networks provide the same 83.3% correct recognition for the limited data available. Some other results of using neural networks in ultrasonic NDE classification are reported in [32–34]. Generally speaking, different neural networks require different training time. The best available classification results from different networks are fairly similar, and may not always be significantly better than the best available result from the traditional statistical classifiers. However neural networks do not require any assumption of the probability distributions of the data, and are computationally very efficient. For a limited amount of data available, which is typically the case in ultrasonic NDE, neural networks with proper training offer the possibility to greatly outperform the statistical classifiers. Classification of defects in composite materials, for example, offers a particular challenge and neural network classifiers when fully developed will provide a means to determine whether the material is suitable for the intended structural application [32].

4. Pattern Recognition in Eddy Current NDE

The use of eddy current is another cost effective method to detect and locate the defects especially if they are near the metal surface. For this reason, eddy current probes have been used in nuclear reactor and power plant inspection for detection of cracks and corrosions, well before the ultrasonic method became popular in NDE in the early 80's. Eddy current signals can be displayed in impedance contour plots, or a sequence of waveforms. Features extracted can take the form of Fourier descriptors (see eg. [35]) for impedance contour, or waveform features. Consider the eddy current scan along the circumference of a tube (Y-direction), as the probe moves along the axis (X-direction). The spectral features of a single scan (see e.g.

[36]) can form a feature vector including as components the frequency of the spectral peak in the amplitude spectrum of the Y-component signal, the ratio of the X and Y spectral amplitudes at this frequency, the phase difference between the X and Y spectral phases at the frequency, the amplitude spectral areas in three frequency ranges, normalized with respect to the total spectral areas. Other procedures for extraction of mathematical features are available. When the multi-frequency probes are used, features must be extracted to include essential information from all probe frequencies. Feature dimension reduction is always needed to simplify the classifier structure. Based on the signal extrema as features, the eddy current methods can also be used to classify objects with different shapes such as holes and cracks [37].

Early eddy current signal classification made use of the adaptive learning network [38] and the Fisher linear discriminant approach [1]. More recently, neural networks have proven to be very effective [39] for eddy current signal classification using Fourier descriptors as features. In one experiment reported, a set of 61 signals was generated by scanning each defect several times, and each signal is represented by eight Fourier descriptors which serve as input to the neural network classifier. A two-layered artificial neural network was trained by backpropagation algorithm, using a training set of 40 signals to identify four different classes. The remaining 21 signals were used for testing. The neural network classifier classified all signals correctly while the classification using k-means algorithm had one error. It is noted that one advantage of the neural network is that it is easy for working with a large-dimensional feature set. The network itself can also give us an indication which features are most important as larger weights are established on such features after significant training.

5. Pattern Recognition in Acoustic Emission NDE

Pattern recognition methods have been used for classifying acoustic emission (AE) signals according to their source types [40,41]. Simple time and frequency domain features of the AE waveforms are used in the classification to distinguish one type from another. Sources of the AE in the monitoring application considered are crack growth, crack face rubbing, fastener fretting, mechanical impacts, electrical transients, and hydraulic noise. For each AE event, two simultaneous waveforms were recorded, one from each transducer. For the waveform of an individual transducer, the major features are arrival time and amplitude of the peak, amplitude in six time intervals around and after the trigger, energy in several frequency bands, and total energy in the spectrum. The two-transducer features include ratio of peak amplitudes, ratio of energy in signals, ratio of energies in frequency bands, etc. The mean and variance of each feature are computed, from which the distance of each event from a given class is computed as the sum of squares of the difference between the value of the feature and the mean, normalized by the feature variance. The decision is based on the minimum distance.

In another reported work, neural networks using backpropagation training are used for leak location [42], i.e. to monitor the source of leaks in the shell of a space station. Again neural networks are shown to be feasible for pattern recognition with AE signals.

6. Pattern Recognition in Radiographic NDE

The improvement in radiography has now made it cost effective to use the radiographic NDE even at real time operation [43]. The pictorial information about the defects provided by the imagery certainly far exceeds what is available from the waveform data. For pattern recognition, the imagery must be digitized first. But then the large amount of image enhancement and processing techniques can be used to improve greatly our ability to interpret the defects and the material properties. To detect the local inhomogeneities in a fiber reinforced composite structure, the segmentation of both X-ray radiography and the ultrasonic C-scan of the same specimen was considered by Jain et al. [44,45]. Four segmentation techniques, viz. simple thresholding, the adaptive thresholding scheme of Chow and Kaneko (see e.g. [46]), the iterative conditional modes method of Besag [47], and the adaptive thresholding scheme of Yanowitz and Bruckstein [48] were examined, but found to be unsatisfactory. A new algorithm based on the adaptive thresholding method proposed by Yanowitz and Bruckstein and the Canny edge detector [49] was proposed for segmentation of real X-ray and C-scan images. Further improvement was obtained by a simple fusion technique which takes the X-ray and C-scan images and the location distribution histogram of events from the acoustic emission to separate the real defects from the spurious components resulting from segmentation, so that a more complete defect map of the specimen can be obtained.

To illustrate the use of computer vision in radiographic NDE, we use the excellent results from [44] (courtesy of A. K. Jain) which are shown in Figs. 4–7. Figure 4

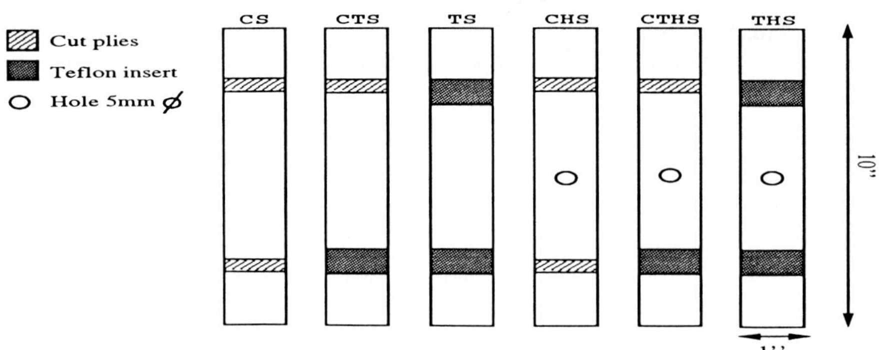

Fig. 4. Set of test specimens showing defects (after [44], reprinted with permission).

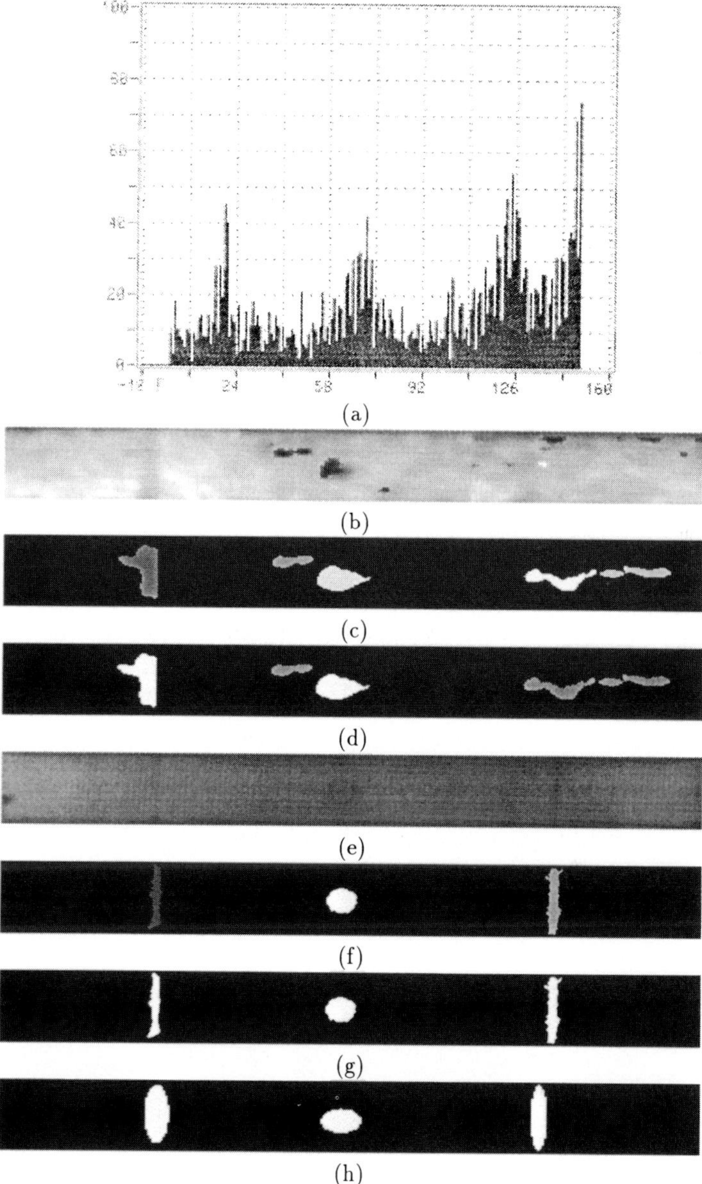

Fig. 5. Results for the specimen CHS (after [44], reprinted with permission).

shows the six test specimens with three kinds of defects inserted: cut plies, teflon insert, and a 5 mm diameter hole. Figures 5–7 show the results of three of the specimens (CHS, CTHS, and TS). In each figure, (a) is the acoustic emission graph, (b) is the C-scan image, (c) is the segmentation of the C-scan image, (d) is the extraction of the defects (in white) in the C-scan image, (e) is the X-ray image,

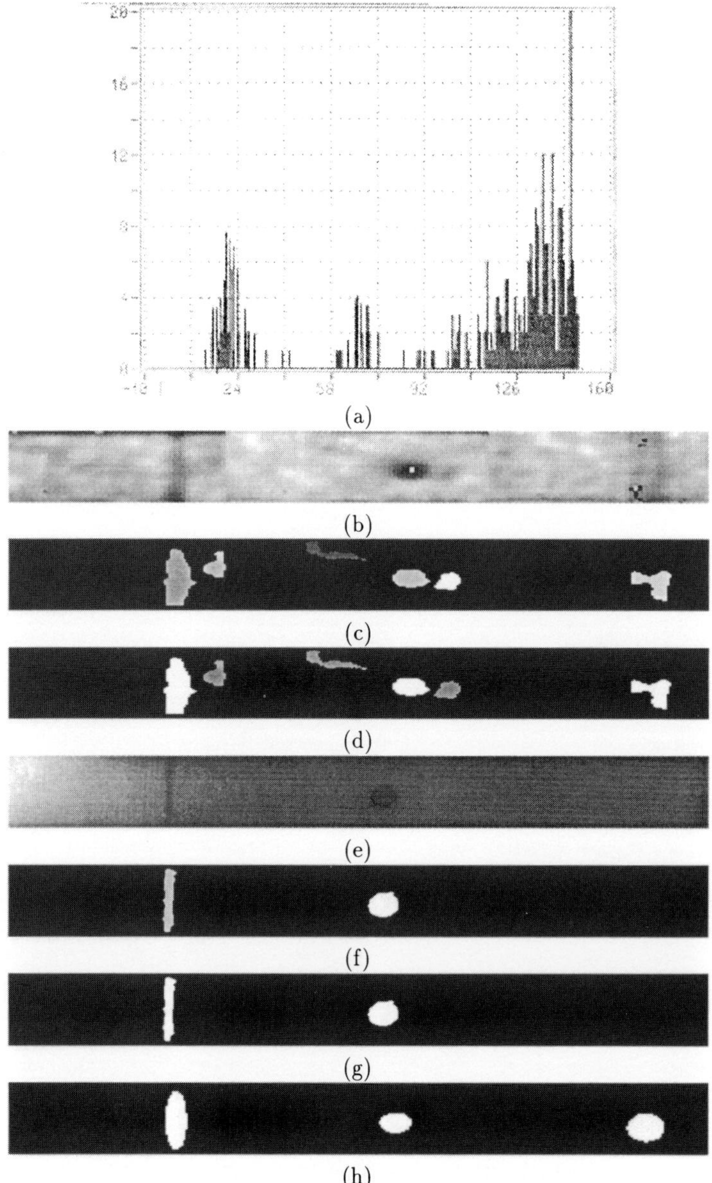

Fig. 6. Results for the specimen CTHS (after [44], reprinted with permission).

(f) is the segmentation of the X-ray image, (g) is the extraction of the defects (in white) in the X-ray image, and (h) is the defect map of the specimen. It is noted that the defect map is obtained by drawing an ellipse around each identified defect [44]. The ellipse is centered at the centroid of the connected component and its major and minor axes are determined from the eigenvectors and eigenvalues of the connected component, averaged over the two images.

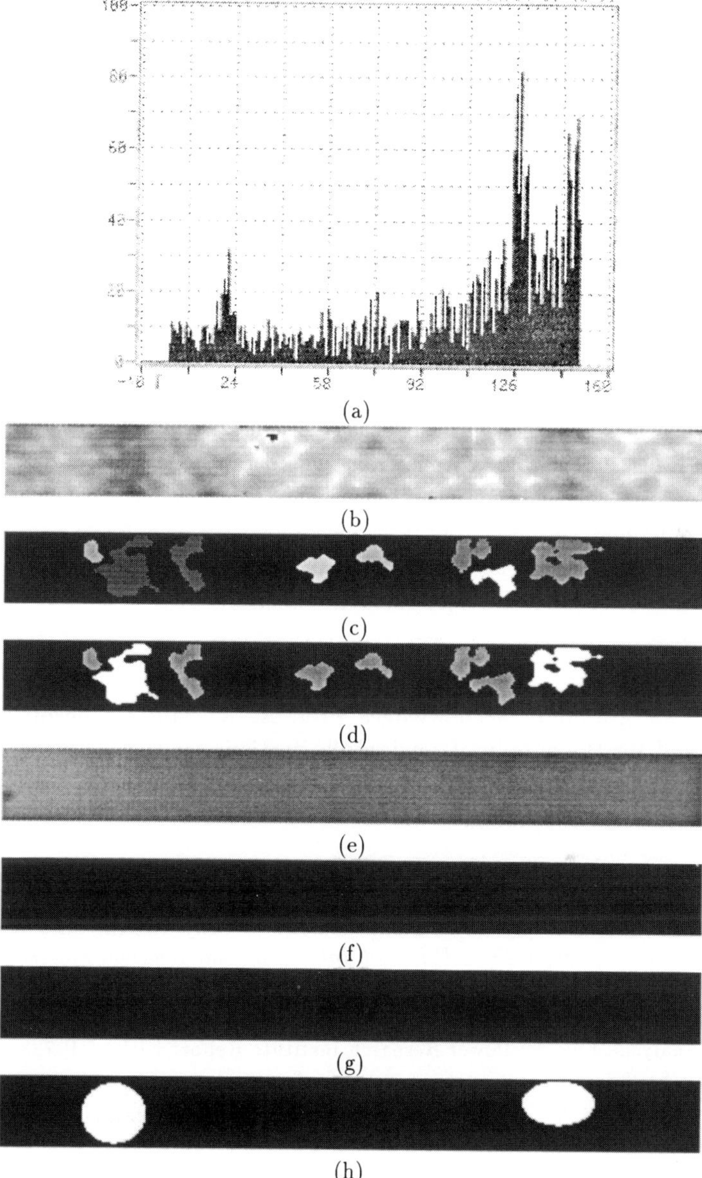

Fig. 7. Results for the specimen TS (after [44], reprinted with permission).

An interesting comparison between the neural network and Markov random field image segmentation is made in [50] for radiographic images. The paper also mentioned several hybrid approaches. Recently a hybrid approach using the probabilistic neural network for segmentation of wafer inspection images [51] has been proposed. Neutron radiography testing is, for certain applications, a useful alternative to the standard X-ray testing methods. Digital image processing can increase such an advantage [52], for example in detection of defects in microchips. The enormous progress on computer vision as reported in Part 2 of this book will certainly be significant in making digital radiography a dominant approach in NDE.

7. Comments and Further Work

Undoubtedly most progress on pattern recognition in NDE has been made only very recently. The interest and demand for reliable pattern recognition in NDE will certainly increase. This presents both a challenge and an opportunity to pattern recognition and related areas. A fully automated NDE system is not an unreasonable expectation and several successes have been reported. A major effort is needed to improve the recognition reliability under the cost constraint.

Only a few NDE methods have been considered in this chapter. There are numerous NDE instrumentations which can use digital processing and recognition to improve effectiveness. Also for one type of specimen being tested, several NDE methods can be feasible. Fusion of information from various NDE sensors or methods can be the solution for the best NDE results in many problems. This is certainly another area that requires a major research effort.

Acknowledgements

The author gratefully acknowledges Prof. A. K. Jain for permission to use Figs. 4–7, and for the supply of original illustrations for these figures. This work was supported by the Information Research Laboratory, Inc. through SBIR Phase III with internal R&D funding.

References

[1] P. G. Doctor and T. P. Harrington, Analysis of eddy current data using pattern recognition methods, in *Proc. IEEE 5th Int. Joint Conference on Pattern Recognition*, Miami, FL, Dec. 1980, 137–139.

[2] R. Shanker et al., Feasibility of using adaptive learning methods for eddy current signal analysis, Electric Power Research Institute Report EPRI NP-723, TPS77-723, Mar. 1978.

[3] R. K. Elsley and L. J. Graham, Pattern recognition techniques applied to sorting acoustic emission signals, in *IEEE Ultrasonic Symp. Proc.*, Sept.–Oct. 1976, 147–150.

[4] W. Y. Chan, D. R. Hay, C. Y. Suen and O. Schwelb, Application of pattern recognition techniques in the identification of acoustic emission signals, in *Proc. IEEE 5th Int. Joint Conference on Pattern Recognition*, Miami Beach, FL, Dec. 1980, 108–111.

[5] R. Halmshaw, *Non-destructive Testing* (Edward Arnold, London, 1987).

[6] R. C. McMaster, *Nondestructive Testing Handbooks*, Vols. 1 and 2 (American Society for Nondestructive Testing, Columbus, OH, 1959).

[7] J. Krauthramer and H. Krautramer, *Ultrasonic Testing of Materials, Fourth Ed.* (Springer-Verlag, New York, 1990).

[8] D. E. Bray and R. K. Stanley, *Nondestructive Evaluation: A Tool in Design, Manufacturing and Service* (McGraw-Hill, New York, 1989).

[9] C. H. Chen, On a high resolution ultrasonic inspection system, in D. O. Thompson and D. E. Chimenti (eds.), *Review of Progress in Quantitative Nondestructive Evaluation (QNDE)*, Vol. 9A (Plenum Press, New York,1990) 959–965.

[10] C. H. Chen, High resolution ultrasonic spectroscopy system for nondestructive evaluation, Final Report on Contract DAAL04-88-C-0003, submitted to US Army Materials Technology Lab., Jan. 1991.

[11] D. R. Hay et al., ICEPAK (Intelligent Classifier Engineering Package) pattern recognition software package, Tektrend International Inc. 1989.

[12] A. N. Mucciardi et al., TestPro software package, Informetrics, 1987.

[13] C. H. Chen, Pattern recognition for the ultrasonic nondestructive evaluation of materials, *Int. J. Pattern Recogn. Artif. Intell.* 1 (1987) 251–260.

[14] C. H. Chen, Signal processing in nondestructive evaluation of materials, in C. H. Chen (ed.), *Signal Processing Handbook* (Marcel Dekker, New York, 1988) 661–682.

[15] C. H. Chen, High resolution spectral analysis NDE techniques for flaw characterization, prediction and discrimination, in C. H. Chen (ed.), *Signal Processing and Pattern Recognition in Nondestructive Evaluation of Materials* (Springer-Verlag, Berlin-Heidelberg, 1988) 155–173.

[16] C. H. Chen, Time series analysis for ultrasonic nondestructive testing, in C. H. Chen (ed.), *Applied Time Series Analysis* (World Scientific, Singapore, 1989) 121–136.

[17] O. R. Gericke, Determination of the geometry of hidden defects by ultrasonic pulse analysis testing, *J. Acoustical Society of America* 35 (1963) 364–368.

[18] O. R. Gericke, Ultrasonic spectroscopy, U.S. Patent 3538753, Nov. 1970.

[19] C. H. Chen and W. L. Hsu, Modern spectral analysis for ultrasonic NDT, in *Proc. Conf. on Nondestructive Testing of High-Performance Ceramics*, Boston, MA, Aug. 1987, 401–407.

[20] K. Honjoh, Y. Sudoh and J. Masuda, Evaluation technique for metal by analysing ultrasonic spectrum, in J. Boogaard and G.M. van Dijk (eds.), *Proc. 12th World Conference on Non-Destructive Testing* (Elsevier Science Publishers, Amsterdam, 1989).

[21] C. H. Chen and S. K. Sin, On effective spectrum-based ultrasonic deconvolution techniques for hidden flaw characterization, *J. Acoustical Society of America* 87 (1990) 976–987.

[22] C. H. Chen and S. K. Sin, High-resolution deconvolution techniques and their applications in ultrasonic NDE, *Int. J. Imaging Systems and Technology* 1 (1989) 223–242.

[23] S. K. Sin and C. H. Chen, A comparison of deconvolution techniques for the ultrasonic nondestructive evaluation of materials, *IEEE Trans. Image Process.* 1 (1992) 3–10.

[24] P. Flandrin, Non-destructive evaluation in the time-frequency domain by means of the Wigner-Ville distribution, in C. H. Chen (ed.), *Signal Processing and Pattern Recognition in Nondestructive Evaluation of Materials* (Springer-Verlag, Berlin-Heidelberg, 1988) 109–116.

[25] C. H. Chen and J. C. Guey, On the use of Wigner distribution in ultrasonic NDE, in D. O. Thompson and D. E. Chimenti (eds.), *Review of Progress in Quantitative Nondestructive Evaluation*, Vol. 11A (Plenum Press, New York, 1992) 967–974.

[26] C. H. Chen and G. G. Lee, On the wavelet transform and its applications to ultrasonic NDE, unpublished report submitted to the US Army Materials Technology Lab., Jun. 1992.

[27] R. W. Y. Chan, D. R. Hay, J. R. Matthews, and H. A. MacDonald, Automated ultrasonic system for submarine pressure hull inspection, in C. H. Chen (ed.), *Signal Processing and Pattern Recognition in Nondestructive Evaluation of Materials* (Springer-Verlag, Berlin-Heidelberg, 1988) 176–186.

[28] M. Desai and D. J. Shazeer, Acoustic transient analysis using wavelet decomposition, *Proc. IEEE Conf. on Neural Networks for Ocean Engineering*, Washington, D.C., Aug. 1991, 29–40.

[29] *Nondestructive Testing Handbook*, Vol. 7: *Ultrasonic Testing*, second edn., chapter on pattern recognition methods (American Society of Nondestructive Testing, 1991).

[30] C. H. Chen, Applying and validating neural network technology for nondestructive evaluation of materials, in *Proc. IEEE Systems, Man and Cybernetics Society Conf.*, Cambridge, MA, Nov. 1989.

[31] Nestor Development System (NDS 1000), Nestor, Inc. 1988.

[32] L. M. Brown, R. W. Newman, R. DeNale, C. A. Lebowitz and F. G. Arcella, Graphite epoxy defect classification of ultrasonic signatures using statistical and neural network techniques, in D. O. Thompson and D. E. Chimenti (eds.), *Review of Progress in Quantitative Nondestructive Evaluation*, Vol. 11A (Plenum Press, New York, 1992) 677–684.

[33] K. Shahani, L. Udpa and S. S. Udpa, Time delay neural networks for classification of ultrasonic NDT signals, in D. O. Thompson and D. E. Chimenti (eds.), *Review of Progress in Quantitative Nondestructive Evaluation*, Vol. 11A (Plenum Press, New York, 1992) 693–670.

[34] M. Kitahara et al., Neural network for crack-depth determination from ultrasonic backscatter data, in D. O. Thompson and D. E. Chimenti (eds.), *Review of Progress in Quantitative Nondestructive Evaluation*, Vol. 11A (Plenum Press, New York, 1992) 701–708.

[35] S. S. Udpa, Signal processing for eddy current nondestructive evaluation, in C. H. Chen (ed.), *Signal Processing and Pattern Recognition in Nondestructive Evaluation of Materials* (Springer-Verlag, Berlin-Heidelberg, 1988) 129–144.

[36] J. E. S. Macleod, Pattern classification in the automatic inspection of tubes scanned by a rotating eddy-current probe, in *Proc. IEEE 5th Int. Joint Conf. on Pattern Recognition*, Munich, Germany, 1982, 214–216.

[37] K. Grotz and T. W. Guettinger, Fast pattern recognition method for eddy current testing, in D. O. Thompson and D. E. Chimenti (eds.), *Review of Progress in Quantitative Nondestructive Evaluation*, Vol. 11A (Plenum Press, New York, 1992) 919–926.

[38] A. N. Mucciardi, Elements of learning control systems with applications to industrial processes, in *Proc. IEEE Conf. on Decision and Control*, New Orleans, LA, 1972.

[39] L. Upda and S. S. Udpa, Eddy current defect characterization using neural networks, *Materials Evaluation* **48** (1990) 342–353.

[40] L. J. Graham and R. K. Elsey, AE source identification by frequency spectral analysis for an aircraft monitoring application, *J. Acoustic Emission* **2** (1983) 47–55.

[41] R. K. Elsley and L. J. Graham, Pattern recognition in acoustic emission experiments, in *Proc. SPIE Symp. on Pattern Recognition and Acoustic Imaging*, Newport Beach, CA, Feb. 1987.

[42] K. Grotz and T. W. Guettinger, Fast pattern recognition method for eddy current testing, in D. O. Thompson and D.E. Chimenti (eds.), *Review of Progress in*

Quantitative Nondestructive Evaluation, Vol. 11A (Plenum Press, New York, 1992) 919–926.

[43] R. Grimm, Progress in real-time radiography, in J. Boogaard and G.M. van Dijk (eds.), *Proc. 12th World Conf. on Non-Destructive Testing* (Elsevier Science Publishers, Amsterdam, 1989),

[44] A. K. Jain, M.-P. Dubuisson and M. S. Madhukar, Multi-sensor fusion for nondestructive inspection of fiber reinforced composite materials, in *Proc. of the American Society for Composites*, Albany, NY, Oct. 1991, 941–950.

[45] A. K. Jain and M.-P. Dubuisson, Segmentation of X-ray and C-scan images of fiber reinforced composite materials, *Pattern Recogn.* **25** (1992) 257–270.

[46] A. Rosenfeld and A. C. Kak, *Digital Picture Processing*, Vols. 1 and 2 (Academic Press, Orlando, FL, 1982).

[47] J. Besag, On the statistical analysis of dirty pictures, *J. Roy. Stat. Soc.* **48** (1986) 259–302.

[48] S. D. Yanowitx and A. M. Brackstein, A new method for image segmentation, *Comput. Graph. Image Process.* **46** (1989) 82–95.

[49] J. Canny, A computational approach to edge detection, *IEEE Trans. Pattern Anal. Mach. Intell.* **8** (1986) 679-698.

[50] F. G. Smith, K. R. Jepsen and P. F. Lichtenwalner, Comparison of neural network and Markov random field image segmentation techniques, in D. O. Thompson and D. E. Chimenti (eds.) *Review of Progress in Quantitative Nondestructive Evaluation*, Vol. 11A (Plenum Press, New York, 1992) 717–724.

[51] C. H. Chen and G. H. You, Pattern wafer image processing research, unpublished final project report submitted to Inspex, Inc., Jul. 1992.

Handbook of Pattern Recognition and Computer Vision, pp. 511–539
Eds. C. H. Chen, L. F. Pau and P. S. P. Wang
© 1993 World Scientific Publishing Company

CHAPTER 3.2

PATTERN RECOGNITION IN GEOPHYSICAL SIGNAL PROCESSING AND INTERPRETATION

YANDA LI, ZHAOQI BIAN, PINFAN YAN and TONG CHANG

Department of Automation, Tsinghua University, Beijing 100084, China

The task of geophysical signal processing and interpretation is very complicated in its nature. Usually, the explorationists explain geophysical data not only based on information contained in the geophysical data, but also on other related geological knowledge. Knowledge and expertise play very important roles. Although it is extremely difficult to establish an automatic geophysical data interpretation system, much effort has been made to introduce the technology of pattern recognition and expert system to geophysical signal processing and interpretation. In order to expose the possibility and effectiveness of exploiting pattern recognition techniques in the field of exploration of hydrocarbon reservoirs, a tentative geophysical signal interpretation system has been developed in our group. This system consists of four parts, for the following purposes:

(1) Detection of horizons from real seismic data and seismic configurations classification.
(2) Feature extraction and classification of seismic data for the sedimentary facies inference based on synthetic seismograms obtained from the corresponding modeling.
(3) Lithology recognition and sedimentary environment interpretation from geophysical wireline logs.
(4) Geophysical signal correlation.

Some real seismic data and well log data have been used to evaluate the effectiveness of the proposed approaches. From the experimental results we may conclude that the pattern recognition technique will provide explorationists with some effective means in reducing their labor intensities and improving the quality of interpretation.

Keywords: Pattern recognition, artificial intelligence, oil exploration, geophysical signal processing, seismic data interpretation

1. Introduction

Geophysical signals provide us with much information on the geologic structure and rock properties of the earth subsurface. The progress of geophysical prospecting for petroleum is closely associated with geophysical signal processing and interpretation. Usually, geophysical signal interpretation is very complicated. It requires not only in-depth understanding of physical principles about wave propagation inside the earth, but also general knowledge of geology at given regions, and personal experience in analyzing seismograms and well log data, particularly in the presence of noises of various kinds. In order to make seismic data interpretation coherent and consistent with other physical measurements, geophysical interpreters often need to

511

design the corresponding seismic model and do very tedious work in finding the real geologic structures contained in the seismic sections. Recent developments in the fields of pattern recognition and artificial intelligence have stimulated many researchers to introduce the technology of PR and AI to geophysical signal processing and interpretation [1–3]. Although it is extremely difficult to establish an automatic geophysical signal interpretation system, much effort has been made and many significant results have been reported. In our group, an experimental system used for detection of horizons and configuration classification, seismic facies classification, inference of three kinds of sedimental environment and lithology recognition from wireline logs, has been developed. From the results obtained in our system, we can conclude that the PR and AI techniques have great potential in aiding an explorationist to extract useful information from seismograms and well log data, as well as to complete some arduous work during the interpretation process. In the following section, we give a brief review on some approaches of pattern recognition to geophysical signal classification. After that, we present a detailed description of our system for further exposing the effectiveness of pattern recognition in the field of petroleum exploration.

2. A Brief Discussion on the Pattern Recognition Approaches to Geophysical Signal Classification

Several approaches have been proposed and tested for the application of pattern recognition to seismic events recognition. The simplest task is to identify a given kind of seismic event from seismograms, using a set of features extracted and selected by means of evaluation under some appropriate criteria. For example, Kubichek and Quincy [4,5] implemented a Bayes classifier to decide for each point of a given seismogram, whether it belongs to a specific stratigraphic trap (in their case, the sandstone lens) or not. They defined a data window for each point, and, in order to design the classifier based on 1-NN metric with minimum error rate, adopted the following three features computed within this window: (1) the ratio of autocorrelation at the first minimum to the zero lag value, (2) a measure of dominant polarity, and (3) the first principal component of instantaneous phase. Huang and Fu [6,7] first realized a tree classifier and then proposed a syntactic method to detect bright spots in the seismic regions. Based on their observations, a sequence of seismic signals which have high amplitude, low frequency, negative polarity, and which are from a continuous reflection layer, constitutes a bright spot with large probability. Some real data of the Mississippi Canyon and High Island in the United States have been tested to show the effectiveness of their approaches.

Bois [8] described an approach of determining the nature of reservoirs in petroleum prospection by using pattern recognition technique with prior learning. As a training set, he used 20 traces of a known reservoir whose nature had been determined by drilling and was located not far from another reservoir with unknown properties. Each of these two reservoirs is represented in a Cartesian graph by a set of 20 dots, which are the coefficients of the Burg prediction filters of 20 trace sectors belonging to one of the two reservoirs. By using clustering analysis, Bois [8] suggested a decision rule to determine whether or not these two reservoirs have the same nature. Dumay [9] applied multivariate statistical analysis to seismic facies recognition. His method is based upon two steps. The first step, learning step, begins with the definition of learning seismic traces for each facies we wish to recognize. The choice of learning traces is based upon either well data or a seismic stratigraphic interpretation. A large number of features such as the positive peaks and corresponding times, etc., are then estimated from the autocorrelation function of the trace, the power spectrum, and the analytical signal modulus; multidimensional analysis, such as clustering and discriminant factor analysis, are carried out in order to validate the choice of learning traces and to select, among all the available features, those that discriminate best. At this stage, a modeling step may be carried out to relate the seismic features to the geologic features. The second step is a predictive step. Dumay computed the seismic features of unknown traces and classified the traces with regard to the learning traces.

Fournier [10] presented a statistical methodology for deriving quantitative geological information from seismic data by means of multidimensional statistical analysis applied both to geological and geophysical data. Firstly, he computed the geological parameters from well data in the interval that we wish to analyze through averaging (porosities) and simplifying (lithofacies). These parameters globally represent the pattern of the reservoir and generate the "geological space". In this space, multidimensional analysis is carried out in order to find reliable well groups and detect the geological meaning of each group by a set of explicative features. The seismic traces are then analyzed on the time window corresponding to the geological interval. The seismic data under analysis include field seismic traces, synthetic traces computed from well data (velocity and density logs) and model traces expressing the seismic response of the principal geological pattern. The traces are represented by points in a K-dimensional space which is generated by the first K factors from a principal components analysis carried out on the amplitude series of the traces. The field seismic traces are then projected onto the K factors space. The traces belonging to the centers of the groups will be selected as learning traces. The traces are then inverted towards the geological space by an affine mapping. This method requires a large amount of data but is still useful even in complex environments. The classifiers described above are based on the collection of training samples, and their performances greatly depend on the size of the training set and its representative characteristics. Generally, it is difficult or costly to obtain sufficient real seismic data with known seismic significance. This problem can be alleviated by creating synthetic traces based on the corresponding geologic model and wavelets [4,5,11].

Sinvhal and Khattri [11] discussed a model for simulating sedimentary formations in which the cyclic pattern was presumed during deposition of a sedimentary sequence. They considered a stratigraphic sequence as a series of partially interdependent finite number of lithologies. From the well log data, in terms of thickness of various sedimentary rocks, they calculated the transition probability matrices characterizing some parts of a sedimentary basin in India. Many synthetic stratigraphic sequences thus could be produced and the corresponding seismograms with known properties of lithology were obtained. Because a sufficient number of seismograms with given classification were available, the statistical discriminant analysis could be well realized and the seismic attributes related to lithology were determined effectively. Although certain assumptions required for discriminant analysis were not probably satisfied for field seismograms, their experiments on real data showed the effectiveness of the proposed method in hydrocarbon exploration. The same idea can be extended into the lithology model using a Monte Carlo approach [12]. However, many factors such as lateral variations in wave velocity, downdip thinning of reflection intervals, geometric focusing produced by reflector curvature, and various kinds of noises with unknown properties, cannot be considered fully in the above synthetic models, so it is usually difficult to estimate the performances of these approaches.

The second class of approaches for predicting geological information from seismic data consists in an inversion of the seismic data at the reservoir level [13–15]. A process of calibration of the acoustic impedances is then carried out with porosity and impedances data available from a few wells. The results provided by this method are fairly good as long as the geological setting is simple, i.e. a geological parameter which represents variations and the size of the reservoir is consistent with the resolution power of the seismic survey.

Some researchers applied pattern recognition techniques to seismic data interpretation under the consideration of the seismic section as a two-dimensional picture image. Various techniques of image processing, such as texture analysis, run-length statistics, and template matching, have been proposed for segmenting a seismic section into regions of common signal character [2]. For example, Love and Simaan [16] successfully developed a run-length algorithm augmented with heuristic rules for segmentation of the Gulf of Mexico stacked section into four large zones of common signal character. In this approach, no training set is required, and the knowledge concerning the structural and geologic properties of a given region can be easily incorporated into the system. In the last few years, an expert system for identifying the horizon, anticline traps, faults, salt domes, and reefs has been developed by Pitas and Venetsanopoulos [17]. This system is based on the frame knowledge representation and on the hypothesize-and-test control structure. They have given much attention to various signal processing routines to filter the seismic data for obtaining the useful information required for interpretation. To increase the level of utilization of expert systems in the oil industry, Aminzadeh, Wong and Ruspini [18] suggested integration of data sets and knowledge systems from different sources using the "Evidential Reasoning" framework.

Recently, artificial neural networks (ANN) has been applied to geophysical signal processing and interpretation. Liu, Xue and Li [19] proposed a neural network method for tracing seismic events. The experimental result on synthetic records and real data showed that the proposed method can recognize the event correctly even in the case of low SNR. Moreover, it has computation parallelism, net fault tolerance and weight adaptability. McCormark [20] illustrated with two examples the application of ANN to seismic data processing and interpretation. One is to estimate lithology using two synthetic logs. The other is seismic trace editing. Zhang and Li [21] also reported their work on seismic trace editing. The difficulties of trace editing are the vast data size and the many different characters of bad traces. The idea of the method is to recognize the good traces instead of the bad ones. The artificial neural network used is a simple single-layer model with feedback, called novelty filter model which uses minus-Hebb-rule as its learning rule. The experiments showed that this approach is effective and the editing results are quite acceptable.

Pattern recognition techniques have also been applied to well-log interpretation and correlation. Weiss and Kulikowski [22] have developed an Expert Log Analysis System (ELAS) for different log-interpretation tasks. Smoilar [23] used a three-stage method (formalization, confrontation against intuition, and correction) for quantitative well-log interpretation. Hohn and Fontana [24] developed a system to match lithologic units on drilling logs with formation tops derived from geophysical logs. Wu and Nyland [25] also described an approach for well-log interpretation using an artificial intelligence technique. Lineman, Mendelson and Toksoz [26] developed an expert system for well-to-well log correction. They used dynamic programming to find an optimal depth matching between two sets of well log data. The program also uses a knowledge-based system to integrate the breadth of information usually available for log correction. These data include digitized wireline logs, simple lithologic information, seismic lines, interpreted dipmeter logs, and local geologic models. The system uses rules stored in the knowledge base to analyze these data and impose geologic constraints on the correction. Also, see Olea and Davis [27] for the correlation of geophysical well logs.

From our experience in exploiting the pattern recognition techniques for geophysical signal interpretation, the signal processing of seismic data is the first step for its application to seismic events interpretation. We have to pay more attention to various signal processing routines to filter the seismic data for obtaining the useful information required for interpretation. Secondly, the integration of various types of information (or data fusion) plays the key role of reducing the ambiguity and nonuniqueness issues inherent in many exploration problems. Thirdly, the problem of feature extraction and selection becomes more important, owing to the complexity of geophysical signals. Finally, more and more attention has been paid to lithology prediction owing to the strong need from reservoir engineering. In this chapter we will discuss the detection of horizons and configuration classification, the application of statistical pattern recognition to inference of sedimentary facies, wireline logs interpretation, and geophysical signal waveform correlation in detail.

We will give a detailed discussion on our approaches for realizing the above goals, in the following sections.

3. Detection of Horizons and Configuration Classification

From the above discussion, we can conclude that most of the tasks in seismic data interpretation can be formalized as problems of pattern classification. We also pay much attention to signal processing, and feature selection and extraction. In the following sections we will describe details of an experimental system for seismic configurations classification and some sedimentary facies recognition in conjunction with the approaches and algorithms of signal processing developed for the above purposes.

A seismic horizon is generally viewed as a line representation of a sequence of reflective waves coming from the same reflecting interface and is characterized by its length, orientation, strength (reflection amplitude), and shape of the waveforms. Pitas and Venetsanopoulos [17] developed a line follower tracking the reflection horizons in their system for automated geophysical interpretation of seismic data. Some filtering techniques are required to make the lines neat. Roberto, Peron and Fumis [28] presented some low-level processing modules of a knowledge-based system for the task of semantic primitive extraction in seismic sections. In their system, some typical image processing approaches such as image enhancement and texture analysis were implemented on a seismic section consisting of 500 vertical time samples at 4 ms sampling period and 660 horizontal distance samples. After that, some algorithms for line-pattern following, region formation and clustering were realized for obtaining high-level representations used in geophysical interpretation. For our purpose of classifying the seismogram into one of the basic configurations suggested by Sangree and Widmier [29] (see Fig. 1), we have developed an automatic horizon system which consists of the following parts.

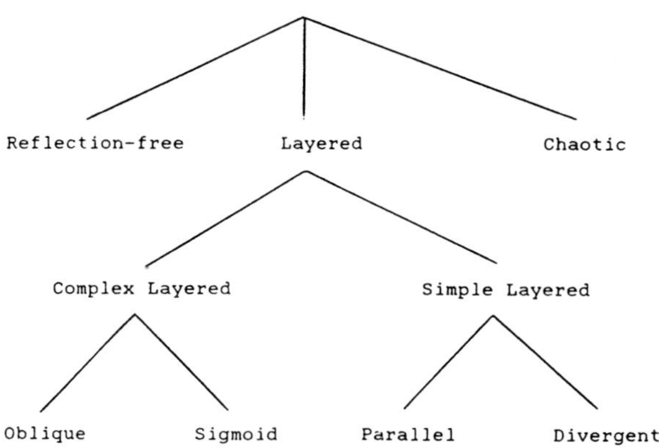

Fig. 1. Seismic configurations classification.

3.1. *Direction Filtering for Noise Reduction*

The detection of horizons is generally based on the coherence measure of the traces and the constraint imposed from geological considerations. However, if one calculates coherence or the similarity measure of the traces in the stacked seismogram, some difficulties would arise due to various noises and interferences which remained after stacking. To decrease the error rate of horizon detection, a heuristic noise-reduction procedure is necessary.

Some researchers [30,31] in the field of seismic exploration concluded that the signal could be distinguished from the noises by its greater spatial coherence. Starting from this point, we can define a data set containing $2M+1$ adjacent traces and approximate the events formed by corresponding reflection signals with the same phases by a line segment with its slope in a limited range. Suppose a line segment fitting an event with the same phase passes point i of the trace $Y(0)$ and point j of the trace $Y(M)$. We define the right slope $K(r)$ of the line segment involving the trace $Y(0)$ and its right adjacent M traces by Eq. (3.1)

$$K(r) = (j - i)/M \; . \tag{3.1}$$

Similarly, if the left line segment passes the point k of the trace $Y(-M)$, then

$$K(l) = (i - k)/M \; . \tag{3.2}$$

Therefore, the point X at which the line segment intersects the trace $Y(m)$ can be calculated by Eq. (3.3).

$$\begin{aligned}
X(m) &= i + K(l) \cdot m \qquad \text{if } -M \le m \le 0 \\
X(m) &= i + K(r) \cdot m \qquad \text{if } 0 \le m \le M
\end{aligned} \tag{3.3}$$

Along the line segment, we can define a window of width W and compute the similarity of seismic signals within this window. Let $S_r(i, K(r))$ denote the right similarity of signals with the line segment passing point i, then

$$S_r(i, K(r)) = \frac{\sum_{\tau=W/2}^{W/2} \left(\sum_{m=0}^{M} \text{data}(X(m) + \tau, Y(m)) \right)^2}{(M+1) \sum_{\tau=-W/2}^{W/2} \sum_{m=0}^{M} \left(\text{data}(X(m) + \tau, Y(m)) \right)^2} \tag{3.4}$$

Similarly,

$$S_l(i, K(l)) = \frac{\sum_{\tau=-W/2}^{W/2} \left(\sum_{m=-M}^{0} \text{data}(X(m) + \tau, Y(m)) \right)^2}{(M+1) \sum_{\tau=-W/2}^{W/2} \sum_{m=-M}^{0} \left(\text{data}(X(m) + \tau, Y(m)) \right)^2} \; , \tag{3.5}$$

where data $(X(m) + \tau, Y(m))$ is the magnitude of a signal in position $X(m) + \tau$ of trace $Y(m)$.

Suppose $K(r)$ and $K(l)$ can only take discrete values in the interval $[-R, R]$, then we have

$$S_r(i, \alpha_r(i)) = \max_{-R \leq K(r) \leq R} S_r(i, K(r))$$

$$S_l(i, \alpha_l(i)) = \max_{-R \leq K(l) \leq R} S_l(i, K(l))$$

and

$$S(i, \alpha_j(i)) = \max\{S_r(i, \alpha_r(i)), \quad S_l(i, \alpha_l(i))\}$$

where j denotes either r or l. Now we can use a pair of slope parameters $\{\alpha(i), j(i)\}$ to characterize the direction of coherence for each point i of trace $Y(0)$.

Generally, the events extracted from the same stratigraphic layer should have approximately the same direction of coherence. This observation can be used to designate a directional median filter for eliminating the sudden change of the slope parameters caused by random noises and other disturbances within the same stratigraphic layer, while keeping the natural change in the slope parameters from layer to layer. The size of the window used for median filtering is less than or equal to W, the width of the window for computing the coherence measure. From our experiences, 50 ms is a suitable value. Now we can estimate the signals from seismic data. Suppose the signals change linearly along the direction of coherence. Within the data set consisting of $M + 1$ adjacent traces, the magnitude at $X(m)$ of trace $Y(m), G[X(m), Y(m)]$, is calculated according to the following expression:

$$G[X(m), Y(m)] = am + b, \qquad 0 \leq m \leq M \text{ or } -M \leq m \leq 0.$$

Using least square error criteria, b can be determined from Eqs. (3.6) or (3.7):

$$b = \frac{\sum_{m=0}^{M} m^2 \sum_{m=0}^{M} \text{data}(X(m), Y(m)) - \sum_{m=0}^{M} m \sum_{m=0}^{M} m \cdot \text{data}(X(m), Y(m))}{(M+1) \sum_{m=0}^{M} m^2 - \left(\sum_{m=0}^{M} m\right)^2}$$

$$\text{if } \alpha_j(i) = \alpha_r(i) \qquad (3.6)$$

$$b =$$

$$\frac{\sum_{m=-M}^{0} m^2 \sum_{m=-M}^{0} \text{data}(X(m), Y(m)) - \sum_{m=-M}^{0} m \sum_{m=-M}^{0} m \cdot \text{data}(X(m), Y(m))}{(M+1) \sum_{m=-M}^{0} m^2 \left(\sum_{m=-M}^{0} m\right)^2}$$

$$\text{if } \alpha_j(i) = \alpha_r(i) \qquad (3.7)$$

and where a is equal to $\alpha_r(i)$ or $\alpha_l(i)$ respectively.

Using this algorithm, the reflection signals are greatly enhanced, and by giving a suitable interval of slope values of coherence direction, the constraint from geologic consideration is imposed on the procedure so that the interferences produced by different sources are effectively suppressed. After this processing, the real seismogram becomes suitable for seismic horizon extraction.

3.2. *Extraction of the Seismic Horizon*

The early work on automatic seismic horizon extraction proposed by Bois [1] is based on the following three criteria:

(a) Criterion of energy: The energy of reflection signals is greater than that of background noises.
(b) Criterion of waveform similarity: The degree of similarity between waveforms reflecting from the same layer is greatest.
(c) Criterion of continuity: The signals reflecting from the same layers are laterally continuous and change smoothly.

The algorithm of horizon extraction proposed by Bois [1] has the following steps:

(a) Detect the peaks with amplitudes exceeding some threshold for every trace of the seismogram.
(b) Determine 14 parameters for describing the detected peaks which are of the trace i according to Fig. 2.
(c) For a given detected peak i, search for an adjacent peak $i+1$ located in a given area of the next trace with maximum similarity of waveforms with the detected peak. The similarity calculation is based on the Mahalanobis distance between two vectors composed of 14 parameters of corresponding peaks.
(d) Connect these two peaks with a line segment and from the peak $i+1$, search the peak $i+2$ according to step (c).

This step is repeated until no suitable peak can be found in the given area of the next trace. Then we come back to the first trace and begin searching for another given detected peak. Finally, a horizon picture of the seismogram can be obtained.

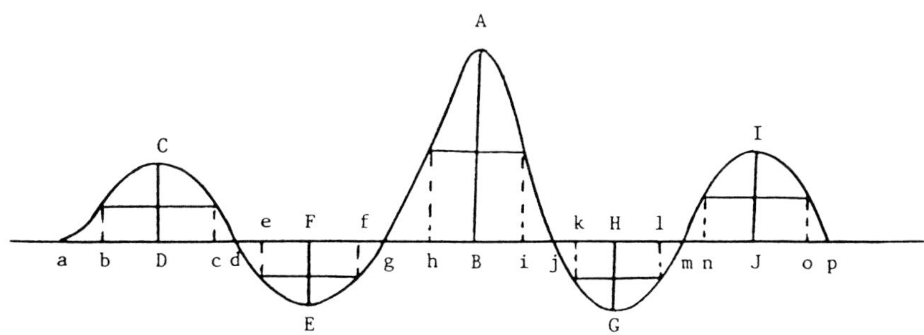

Fig. 2. The detected peak A described by 14 parameters which are: d-a, g-d, j-g, m-j, p-m, c-b, f-e, i-h, l-k, o-n, CD/AB, EF/AB, CH/AB, IJ/AB.

There are several problems which must be considered in this algorithm:

(a) The threshold for detecting the peaks is critical. A higher threshold value may cause the horizons with low energy to be undetected. On the other hand, a lower threshold value may produce incorrect horizons in the presence of noises.

(b) The range of a given area of the next trace for searching the peak with maximum similarity is also critical for correct extraction of horizons. A large window may cause erroneous picking, but a small window is not suitable for horizons with great lateral variation.

A new approach to extracting the horizons automatically from the seismogram after direction filtering has been developed in our system (see Figs. 3(a) and (b)). It

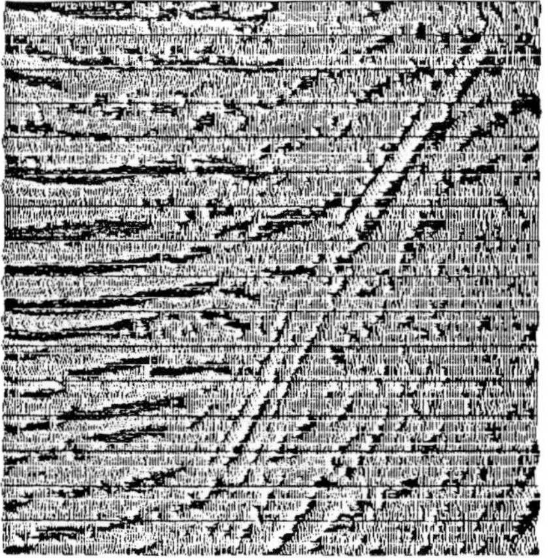

Fig. 3. (a) A seismic section before filtering.

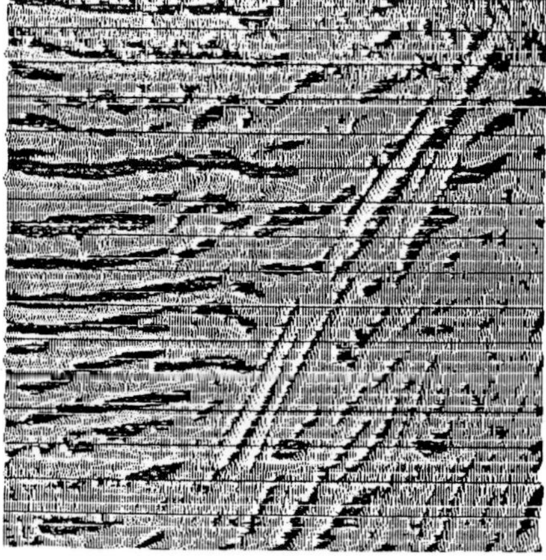

Fig. 3. (b) A seismic section after filtering.

is based on segmenting the seismogram into a set of groups. Each group consists of ten adjacent traces, and there is some overlap in traces between the two successive groups. We call the reflection event within a group a group event. If there is no fault presented in a group, the group event can be represented by a line segment. It can be picked up by the following steps:

(1) For each trace of the group, detect the positive and negative peaks and calculate the waveform parameters within a certain window centered at these peaks.

(2) Let $P_i(1)$ be the position of a given peak of the first trace. Find the peaks of the second trace nearest to $P_i(1)$ and denote its position by $P_i(2)$. Then find the peak of the third trace nearest to $P_i(2)$ and so on. Finally, a data set of peak positions $P_i = \{P_i(1), P_i(2), \ldots, P_i(10)\}$ can be obtained.

(3) Fit the best-squares line to the data set and calculate the square errors by this approximation.

(4) Compare the square errors with a given threshold. If it is greater than T, then P_i is considered a false event and discarded.

After extraction of group events for all groups of the seismogram, an operation of merging the group events is needed for obtaining the basic elements required for horizon searching.

Suppose the line segment representing the group event P_i of group j is expressed by Eq. (3.8):

$$Y_{ik}^{(j)} = a_i^{(j)} \cdot k + b_i^{(j)} \tag{3.8}$$

where

$$a_i^{(j)} = \frac{10 \cdot \sum_{k=1}^{10} k P_i^{(j)}(k) - \sum_{k=1}^{10} P_i^{(j)}(k) \sum_{k=1}^{10} k}{10 \cdot \sum_{k=1}^{10} k^2 - \left(\sum_{k=1}^{10} k\right)^2}$$

$$b_i^{(j)} = \frac{\sum_{k=1}^{10} k^2 \sum_{k=1}^{10} P_i^{(j)}(k) - \sum_{k=1}^{10} k \sum_{k=1}^{10} k P_i^{(j)}(k)}{10 \sum_{k=1}^{10} k^2 - \left(\sum_{k=1}^{10} k\right)^2} .$$

To determine whether the end point of the group event i of group j denoted by $e(i,j)$ can be merged with the starting point of group event s of the next group t denoted by $b(s,t)$ which is nearest to the group event i, one should calculate the similarity between two waveforms of given length which are centered at $e(i,j)$ and $b(s,t)$ respectively. If the similarity exceeds some given threshold and the distance between $e(i,j)$ and $b(s,t)$ is below some value, then $e(i,j)$ and $b(s,t)$ can be connected by a line segment to form a so-called merging event. Otherwise, $e(i,j)$ and $b(s,t)$ are left disconnected.

After completing the merging operation for all events of all groups, the resultant events (including those group events which are not connected to any other events) are represented by the nodes in the graph, and two nodes are connected by an edge only if intersection of the neighborhoods of the end point of one resultant event and the starting point of another resultant event is not empty. The end point of one resultant event must be located at the left side of the starting point of another resultant event. The size of neighborhoods should be determined from the geological considerations and can be adjusted experimentally. A loss is assigned to the edge connecting the nodes i and j by the following equation:

$$\lambda_{ij} = (a \cdot D_A(1 - S_{ij}) + b \cdot D_{ij}) \cdot W_{ij}$$

where $D_A = |X_e^{(i)} - X_s^{(j)}|$ is the absolute difference between the signal magnitude of the end point of resultant event i and that of the starting point of resultant event j. Also, in the above expression

$$S_{ij} = \frac{\sum_{t=-N}^{N} X_t^{(j)} X_t^{(j)}}{\left(\sum_{t=-N}^{N}(X_t^{(i)})^2 \sum_{t=-N}^{N}(X_t^{(j)})^2\right)^{1/2}}$$

is a similarity measure between the waveforms of length $2N + 1$ centered at the end point of resultant event i and the starting point of resultant event j, D_{ij} is a distance measure between the resultant events i and j, W_{ij} is a factor considering the influence of the lengths of resultant events on the loss in connecting the events, and a and b are two weights.

Now by using a dynamic programming approach, a path from a node to another node with minimum loss can be searched. Under the constraints that (i) the loss must be below a given threshold value T; (ii) any node is not allowed to be present in more than one path; (iii) if we denote the path by a sequence of nodes $d_1, d_2, \ldots, d_i, d_{i+1}, \ldots, d_n$, then the end point of the event corresponding to d_i must be at the left side of the starting point of the event corresponding to d_{i+1}; and (iv) the length of a path is defined as the location of the end point of its last node which must exceed a given value T_e, a set of paths corresponding to the horizons in the seismogram can be extracted from the graph. Obviously, the number of horizons depends on the thresholds T and T_e, and it can be adjusted interactively. Figures 4–6 show a result from a real seismic section. As an example, T and T_e are adjusted in such a manner that only one horizon can be obtained from the seismogram (see Fig. 6). Finally, the pattern recognition approach for configuration classification is applied to the picture of resultant events shown in Fig. 5. Because the picture is composed of only line segments with different lengths and orientations, by using texture analysis, one of the three basic configurations (that is, reflection-free, layered, or chaotic) defined by Sangree and Widmier [29] will be easily identified. However, a more complicated system must be developed for seismic signal classification. This is the subject of our next section.

4. The Application of Statistical Pattern Recognition to Inference of Sedimentary Facies

As we know, the seismic sections corresponding to different sedimentary facies zones may present different characteristics of seismic facies, i.e. different patterns

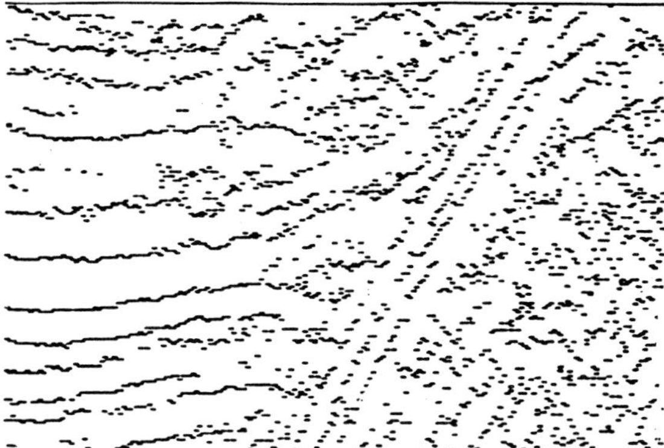

Fig. 4. Image of detected peaks obtained from the seismic section shown in Fig. 3(b).

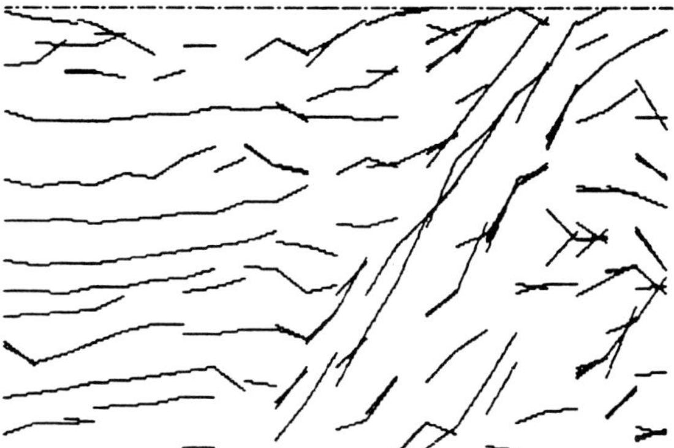

Fig. 5. The result after the merging operation.

Fig. 6. One horizon obtained by adjusting the threshold.

of seismic data. Therefore, it is possible to extract the reflection characteristics of the seismic sections for the purpose of classifying the seismic data into one of the given seismic facies. Although the interpretation of sedimentary facies requires other geological information, part of which can only be obtained from analyzing the well log data, designing a seismic facies classifier is still significant for deepening our knowledge on the effectiveness of various features. In cooperation with the Computing Center of the Geological Ministry of the People's Republic of China, the models of three kinds of sedimentary facies (Alluvial Fan, Lake Basin, and Delta) have been created (see Fig. 7), and synthetic seismograms were produced from the convolution of the presumed wavelet with the sequences of reflection coefficients calculated from the geological models. Several original synthetic seismograms are shown in Fig. 8. Various noises and disturbances with different characteristics are considered in producing the synthetic seismogram. The primary features or descriptions of the patterns are extracted based on geological and mathematical considerations. They can be grouped into five categories:

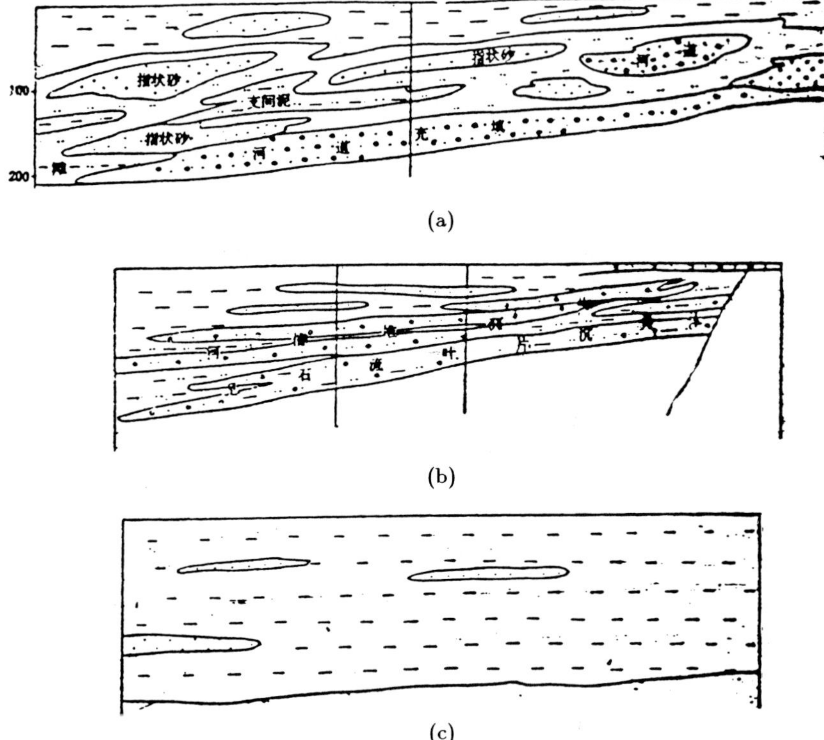

(a)

(b)

(c)

Fig. 7. Sedimentary facies models: (a) Delta, (b) Alluvial Fan, (c) Lake Basin.

4.1. *Spectrum of Seismic Traces*

The sample power spectrum $P(w_i), i = 1, 2, \ldots, N$ of seismic trace Xt can be obtained by some spectral estimation method, (e.g. for simplicity of computation,

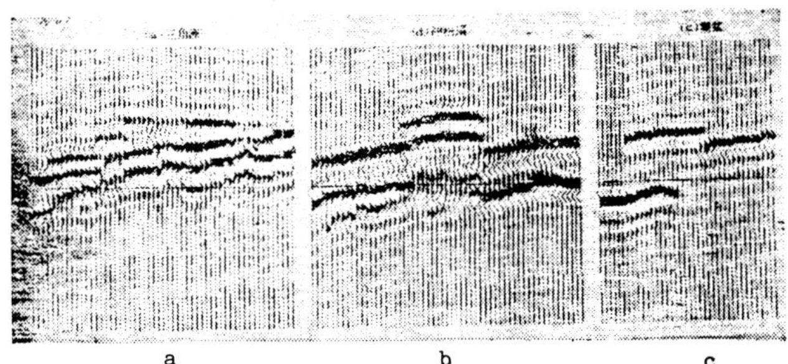

Fig. 8. The synthetic seismograms obtained from the modeling shown in Fig. 7.

the usual periodogram method may be used). From $P(w_i)$, 20 features are extracted which can be divided into two subgroups. One is the frequency feature subgroup in which there are 14 features, the other is the energy feature subgroup in which there are six features.

The frequency feature subgroup has 14 features:

(1) The frequency at which the maximum value is reached:

$$f_1 = w_m \ , \quad P(w_m) = \max_i P(w_i) \ .$$

(2) The first moment of frequency:

$$f_2 = \frac{\sum_{i=1}^{N} w_i P(w_i)}{\sum_{i=1}^{N} P(w_i)} \ .$$

(3) The width-of-frequency band:

$$f_3 = \left\{ \frac{\left[\sum_{i=1}^{N}(w_i - f_2)^2 P(w_i)\right]}{\sum_{i=1}^{N} P(w_i)} \right\}^{1/2} \ .$$

(4) The normalized third central moment of frequency:

$$f_4 = \frac{\sum_{i=1}^{N}(w_i - f_2)^3 P(w_i)}{f_3^{3/2}} \ .$$

(5) The normalized fourth central moment of frequency:

$$f_5 = \frac{\sum_{i=1}^{N}(w_i - f_2)^4 P(w_i)}{f_3^2} \ .$$

(6) The frequency f_6: It is the first frequency at which $P(w_i)$ becomes higher than half of the value $P(w_m)$ as w_i is increased from w_m to w_n.

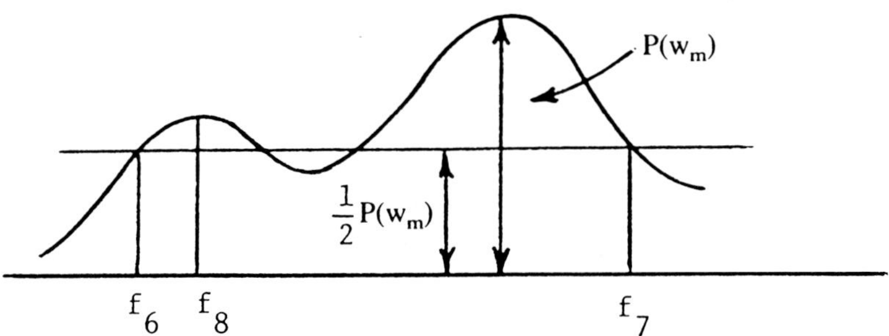

Fig. 9. Features f_6, f_7, f_8.

(7) The frequency f_7: It is the first frequency at which $P(w_i)$ becomes lower than half of the value $P(w_m)$ as w_i is increased from w_m to w_n.

(8) The frequency f_8: Within the frequency interval between f_6 and f_7, f_8 is the first frequency at which $P(w_i)$ reaches the first extreme value as w_i increases from f_6. (f_6, f_7 and f_8 above are shown in Fig. 9.)

(9) The first moment frequency f_9 of the low-frequency interval $[w_1, w_{N/4}]$:

$$f_9 = \frac{\sum_{i=1}^{N/4} w_i P(w_i)}{\sum_{i=1}^{N/4} P(w_i)} \, .$$

(10) The first moment frequency f_{10} of the middle-frequency interval $[w_{N/4+1}, w_{3N/4}]$:

$$f_{10} = \frac{\sum_{i=N/4+1}^{3N/4} w_i P(w_i)}{\sum_{i=N/4+1}^{3N/4} P(w_i)} \, .$$

(11) The first moment frequency f_{11} of the high-frequency interval $[w_{3N/4+1}, w_N]$:

$$f_{11} = \frac{\sum_{3N/4+1}^{N} w_i P(w_i)}{\sum_{3N/4+1}^{N} P(w_i)} \, .$$

(12) The frequency f_{12} which is the 25th percentile of summed energy of the spectrum:

$$f_{12} = w_{R_1} \, , \quad \text{where} \quad \sum_{i=1}^{R_1} P(w_i) = 0.25 \sum_{i=1}^{N} P(w_i) \, .$$

(13) The frequency f_{13} which is the 50th percentile of summed energy of the spectrum:

$$f_{13} = w_{R_2} \, , \quad \text{where} \quad \sum_{i=1}^{R_2} P(w_i) = 0.5 \sum_{i=1}^{N} P(w_i) \, .$$

(14) The frequency f_{14} which is the 75th percentile of summed energy of spectrum:

$$f_{14} = w_{R_3}, \quad \text{where} \quad \sum_{i=1}^{R_3} P(w_i) = 0.75 \sum_{i=1}^{N} P(w_i).$$

The energy feature subgroup has six features:

(15) The ratio of the maximum $P(w_m)$ to the total energy:

$$f_{15} = \frac{\max P(w_i)}{\sum_{i=1}^{N} P(w_i)}.$$

(16) The ratio of $P(f_8)$ to the total energy:

$$f_{16} = \frac{P(f_8)}{\sum_{i=1}^{N} P(w_i)}.$$

(17) The ratio of $P(f_2)$ to the total energy:

$$f_{17} = \frac{P(f_2)}{\sum_{i=1}^{N} P(w_i)}.$$

(18) The ratio of summed energy in the low-frequency interval $[w_1, w_{N/4}]$ to the total energy:

$$f_{18} = \frac{\sum_{i=1}^{N/4} P(w_i)}{\sum_{i=1}^{N} P(w_i)}.$$

(19) The ratio of summed energy in the middle-frequency interval $[w_{N/4+1}, w_{3N/4}]$ to the total energy:

$$f_{19} = \frac{\sum_{i=N/4+1}^{3N/4} P(w_i)}{\sum_{i=1}^{N} P(w_i)}.$$

(20) The ratio of summed energy in the high-frequency interval $[w_{3N/4+1}, w_N]$ to the total energy:

$$f_{20} = \frac{\sum_{i=3N/4+1}^{N} P(w_i)}{\sum_{i=1}^{N} P(w_i)}.$$

4.2. Autoregressive Coefficients

For each trace, the coefficients of the AR model with order p are computed. They constitute a $p + 1$ vector together with the predictive square error.

4.3. Reflection Coefficients

By deconvolution of seismic traces with a given wavelet, a sequence of reflection coefficients can be obtained. To characterize its distribution of coefficient magnitudes, several statistics such as mean, second moment, etc., are computed and adopted as initial features.

4.4. *Correlation Analysis*

Correlation analysis may be one of the most effective methods for obtaining the features used in sedimentary facies inference. Sinvhal and Khattri [11] have established a correlation between lithology and quantitative parameters extracted from seismic data. They used the autocorrelation function of the impulse response of models depicting subsurface lithologies for calculating A_1/A_0, A_2/A_0 in lithology recognition, where A_i denotes the autocorrelation functions at the subscripted lag. We also calculated these features in our models and developed a new class of L_p autocorrelation functions to further exploit the effectiveness of correlation analysis to seismic data interpretation. The L_p autocorrelation function is defined as

$$R^p(t_1, t_2) = \frac{1}{2^p}(E[|x(t_1) + x(t_2)|^p] - E[|x(t_1) - x(t_2)|^p])$$

for every t_1 and t_2, where p is a positive real or integer value, and $E[.]$ is the expectation operator.

If p is equal to 2, the above expression can be rewritten as

$$R(t_1, t_2) = E[x(t_1)x(t_2)]$$

which is the original autocorrelation function.

Similarly, the L_p cross-correlation can be expressed as

$$R^p_{xy}(t_1, t_2) = \frac{1}{2^p}(E[|x(t_1) + y(t_2)|^p] - E[|x(t_1) - y(t_2)|^p]) \ .$$

It is interesting to note that by using L_p autocorrelation with different positive p values, more features can be obtained to characterize the seismic traces. Particularly, we have found that the discriminant power of the features extracted from the L_1 (that is, $p = 1$) correlation function seems better than those from the ordinary correlation function. This is perhaps because the L_1 correlation function may contain more phase information than the L_2 correlation function. We will be doing further work on the application of the L_p correlation function to seismic signal interpretation.

4.5. *Other Physical Properties*

The most important features from lithological considerations can be obtained from the velocity spectrum and the absorption coefficients computed by the various techniques of seismic signal processing. In our case, these values are given or estimated directly from synthetic models. A stepwise discriminant analysis method is chosen to do feature selection. In this procedure, the Wilks statistic $\lambda = |S_w|/|S_t|$

is selected as the feature performance metric, where S_w is the innerclass covariance matrix and S_t is the total covariance matrix. Because λ is easy to calculate and its distribution function can be obtained when each class is assumed to be from a Normal distribution, it can be used not only for comparing the different feature subsets but also for testing the classification ability of each subset. The stepwise discriminant analysis method has just made full use of the advantages of λ.

From the experimental results based on 30 synthetic seismograms from three kinds of sedimentary facies, only five to nine features are good enough to discriminate between these three classes with an acceptable error rate. Either a minimum distance measure or a linear discriminant function can be used in this classifier.

To check the performance of this classifier in practical situations, the real seismic data recorded from the regions in the northern part of Jiangsu Province in China have been tested, and the classification results are obtained and analyzed. Under the condition that the sections belonging to one of the sedimentary facies in the seismogram are initially approximately segmented by geologists, the classification results basically coincide with the interpretations of the experts. Some errors may arise from the improper processing of real seismic data and the difference in some regional characteristics between the training samples and real data.

In our opinion, the following problems must be treated carefully in order to further develop a system for computer-aided sedimentary facies classification:

(1) Seismic facies classification is only partially correlated to sedimentary environment interpretation. Therefore, an expert system approach is probably needed to improve the ability of an automated interpretation system based on geological knowledge and the features of seismic signals extracted by pattern recognition techniques.

(2) A carefully selected collection of seismic facies properly chosen for a given region and its corresponding descriptions are required to make the results consistent with the geological structure of the region. In this respect, one should fully employ the information obtained from the well log data located in the same region.

(3) Image processing algorithms are probably very useful in identifying stratigraphic traps from the seismograms needed for sedimentary facies classification. The descriptions of the texture of the traps from both statistical and syntactical methods are important for different traps detection.

(4) The seismic signals recorded in the field must be properly preprocessed for the preservation of amplitude information. Otherwise, the features calculated from the seismic signals will be obscured by a series of factors such as spherical divergence, ray path curvature, scattering, etc. A better feature extraction system must consider the reliability of the records and have the ability to delete bad traces if necessary.

5. Lithology Recognition and Sedimentary Environment Interpretation from Geophysical Wireline Logs

Geophysical wireline logs play an important role in seismic data interpretation. Well logs represent measures of a wide range of physical properties, such as acoustic, electrical, and nuclear, as a function of depth. One use of logs is to derive lithology from measured physical properties at a given well [32]. Moreover, we can interpret depositional sequence and environment using well logs in combination with core data and other information. We developed a lithology recognition and sedimentary environment interpretation system as shown in Fig. 10.

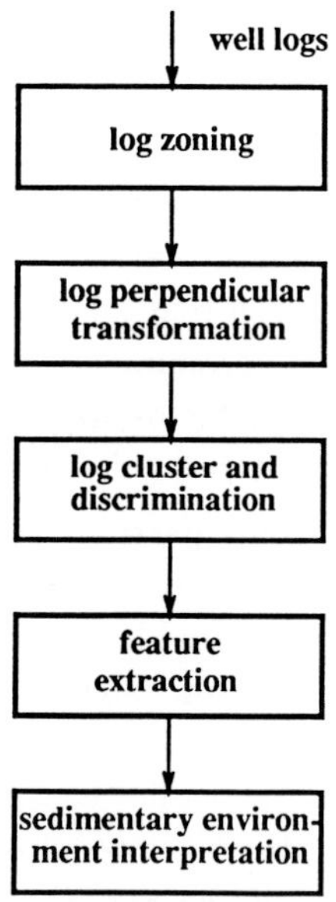

Fig. 10. A lithology recognition and sedimentary environment interpretation.

The procedure consists of the following steps:

(1) Log zoning
(2) Log perpendicular transformation
(3) Log cluster and discrimination
(4) Features extraction
(5) Sedimentary environment interpretation.

The principle of deriving lithology from well logs at a given well is to use a set of specific mathematical criteria to group a series of well log data into a geological meaning zone according to core data, then deduce the lithology from the well logs. The lithology recognition procedure includes step 1 to step 3, and the sedimentary environment interpretation procedure includes step 1 to step 5.

5.1. *Log Zoning*

Logs are first environmentally corrected to suppress the errors caused by temperature, pressure, etc. To account for amplitude difference between different types of logs, a normalization of logs is needed. After the logs are properly normalized, they will be automatically cut into several intervals which represent different geophysical meaning zones. Automatic zoning is an optimization cut-apart method based on cutting N samples into several intervals such that the differences among intervals are as large as possible and the differences within an interval are as small as possible. The method can be described as follows:

Define the log data matrix (X) of P log responses as

$$X = \begin{bmatrix} X_{11} & X_{21} & \cdots & X_{P1} \\ X_{12} & X_{22} & \cdots & X_{P2} \\ X_{13} & X_{23} & \cdots & X_{P3} \\ \cdots & \cdots & \cdots & \cdots \\ X_{1N} & X_{2N} & \cdots & X_{pN} \end{bmatrix}.$$

Then the difference of one sample interval $(X_{Mi}, X_{M,i+1}, \ldots, X_{Mj})$ is

$$D(i,j) = \sum_{K=i}^{j} \sum_{M=1}^{P} (X_{M_K} - \overline{X}_M)$$

where

$$\overline{X}_M = \sum_{K=i}^{j} X_{MK}/(j - i + 1)$$

$$1 \leq M \leq P,\ 1 \leq i \leq j \leq N\ .$$

The total difference of two-cut is:

$$TD(N, 2) = \min_{i=k}^{N}\{D(1, i-1) + D(i, N)\}\ .$$

The recurrence formula of K-cut is:

$$TD(N, k) = \min_{i=k}^{N}\{TD(i-1, k-1) + D(i, N)\}\ .$$

5.2. *Log Perpendicular Transformation*

The log perpendicular transformation algorithm converts P log responses to $m(m \leq P)$ independent log components in order to reduce the redundance of log responses. For example, for the gamma tool after perpendicular transformation, we can express its response as follows:

$$GR = a_{11}F_1 + a_{12}F_2 + \cdots + a_{1m}F_m$$

where $F_1, F_2, \ldots, F_m$ are independent of each other.

The simplified model of P log responses is as follows:

$$\begin{cases} X_1 &= a_{11}F_1 + a_{12}F_2 + \ldots + a_{1m}F_m \\ X_2 &= a_{21}F_1 + a_{22}F_2 + \ldots + a_{2m}F_m \\ \ldots & \quad \ldots \quad\quad \ldots \quad\quad \ldots \quad\quad \ldots \\ X_P &= a_{P1}F_1 + a_{P2}F_2 + \ldots + a_{Pm}F_m \end{cases}$$

Because m is less than P, we cannot calculate F_i precisely. We construct the F-regression modified functions by:

$$F_i = [a_{1i}, a_{2i}, \ldots, a_{Pi}]R^{-1}[C_1X_1, C_2X_2, \ldots, C_PX_P]'$$

where

R^{-1} : the converse matrix of interrelation coefficient

a_{ji} : regression coefficients

C_j : log evaluation coefficients

X_j : log responses

$$(i = 1, 2, \ldots, m), \quad (j = 1, 2, \ldots, P)$$

The regression functions represent the most information of the log data.

5.3 *Log Cluster and Discrimination*

Log cluster and discrimination is the last step for lithology recognition. After comparing the log responses clustering against the core data, we obtain the meaningful clusters which represent several different formations. We then form the discriminant functions of each group and classify the lithology types from log responses by reference to the groups above using Bayes decision rules. For example, for the gth group, the Bayes modified equation can be expressed as follows:

$$B_g(X) = \ln(q_g) + \sum_{k=1}^{P} C_{kg} * E_k * X_k + C_{0g}$$

where

X_k : log response values

q_g : *a priori* probability

C_{0g}, C_{kg} : Bayes coefficients

E_k : log quality coefficients

The principle of discriminant analysis is to attach a probability distribution of each group to lithology, and then identify the lithology from the group that the given set of log readings is most likely to be form.

5.4. *Features Extraction*

Log response also contains vast qualitative information, such as depositional sequence and sedimentary environment. These can not only be used for well-to-well correlation, but also for depositional environment interpretation. In order to interpret the environment, we have to extract the features first. The procedure of feature extraction is to divide the logging section into several intervals by use of restraint conditions, such as log activity, log derivative, log shale baseline etc., then determine the interpretation window length of different intervals, and finally, extract the features from these intervals.

Six types of logging intervals can be classified by the number of red, blue and green models and by the combination of these models.

The red, blue and green models are defined in reference to the first derivative:

$$\begin{array}{ll} \text{red model} & f'(x) > 0 \\ \text{blue model} & f'(x) < 0 \\ \text{green model} & f'(x) = 0 \end{array}$$

We also describe each interval with ten features as follows:

 (1) Curvename: GR, THOR, etc.
 (2) Depth: start-depth, end-depth
 (3) Shape: bell, funnel, cylinder, finger, gear, etc
 (4) Amplitude: very large, large, medium, small, very small
 (5) Boundary: (top and bottom) abrupt, gradation
 (6) Smooth: serrated, smooth
 (7) Sequence: up-fine, up-coarse, etc.
 (8) Lithology: sandstone, silt, shale, etc.
 (9) Total thickness: thickness (numbers)
(10) Single thickness: thickness (numbers)

Therefore, a logging interval can be expressed with a vector: vector ={Curvename, Depth, Shape, Amplitude, Boundary, Smooth, Sequence, Lithology, Total-thickness, Single-thickness}

5.5. *Sedimentary Environment Interpretation*

The term "sedimentary environment" covers a wide range of phenomena. Here, we only deal with continental deposits which include five depositional sandbodies: River Delta, Fan Delta, Turbidities, Subaqueous Fan and Beach-Bar in China. Terrestrial sediments consist mainly of fluvial and lacustrine facies. The best reservoir accumulation zone is the channel deposits of these facies. So our main research interest focuses on the recognition of channel deposits by use of the features extracted above and other geological information, such as field experience, core data, etc.

By means of rule-based knowledge, our method simulates human thought for interpreting sedimentary environment and sequence.

In this system, "Production rule" is used for knowledge expression and a two-stage model, knowledge model, is constructed in order to avoid "crossfacies". The first stage is to recognize the major environment, and the second is to interpret

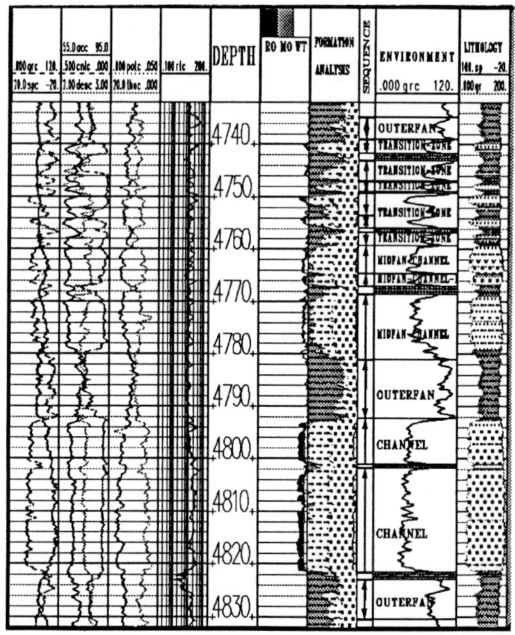

Fig. 11. Results applied to wireline logs.

the sub-environment. In the knowledge model, the logging features extracted above are the main knowledge. The core data, field experience, etc. are also considered. Backward inference strategy is implemented for searching the best path from the objective state to the primitive state.

As an example, Fig. 11 shows the results applied to wireline logs with this system. The lithology determined from the geophysical wireline in one well is mainly shaly sand which has been verified by core analysis. The sedimentary environment consists mainly of turbidities in lacustrine deposit. The hydrocarbon accumulation zone exists in channel deposits from 4792.3 to 4801.0 meters and from 4801.7 to 4821.6 meters. These results have been proven by the field data.

6. Geophysical Signal Correlation

Lithostratigraphic correlation is vital for subsurface interpretation but extremely difficult to establish with certainty. Recently, much effort has been made to develop a computer system for the determination of lithostratigraphic correlation, such as a pattern recognition algorithm proposed by Cheng and Lu [33], a dynamic programming method combined with AI technique proposed by Lineman et al. [26] and an expert system for well-to-well log correlation by Olea and Davis [27]. But heavy geologic distortions resulting from missing and breaking strata still challenge most existing algorithms. There are several problems handling geophysical signal correlation. Firstly, one kind of algorithm usually suits only a specific kind of data, but a computer system must be applied using a variety of data. Secondly, mismatches are usually inevitable and mismatches at higher levels will be duplicated in later processing. Thirdly, automated correlation techniques, no matter how powerful, will have very limited applications unless they can be guided in some way by geologic knowledge. These stimulate us to develop a computer system with a hierarchical processing structure, optimized algorithm, information integration, and interactive interface. The hierarchical scheme is an imitation of the human thought process which is coarsely described as event detection, feature extraction and sequence matching. The procedure begins with the most significant event, the first level matching which results in a segmentation of the signal. Then the same procedure is repeated in segmented intervals. The matching becomes more dense with each step. Moreover, if the segmented signal and extracted sequences are much more regular, this improves the effectiveness of the algorithms.

Also, the hierarchical scheme permits an optimized data-driven selection of correlation algorithms. For each step, each iteration, each section of signal, the choice of algorithm and its parameters are generated automatically by a rule machine which makes decisions on the basis of some easily measured signal features and information *a priori*. Each rule is fired accordingly to give a recommendation about algorithms. These recommendations are then synthesized to give a decision. The rules have the following model, for example:

If (no information and full-length well log) then (1st level alg. = DP) with (recommendation = 0.9).

The working model generated on-line is called a "boss" algorithm. It consists of the choice of algorithm and the algorithm parameters. Another advantage of hierarchical processing is error control. The user's access to step results increases the system credibility. To handle correlation across missing and discontinuous rock units, information other than signal shape and context is necessary, i.e. knowledge and constraint learned from seismic data, chronological and historical data survey and the user's personal observation. The information is summed up in three descriptive constraints which guide the correlation procedure: missing portion, obvious markers and sectional match tendency. In this system, an interactive interface permits easy information input, either manual or automatic, when connected to a general processing system. A processing frame chart is shown in Fig. 12. Because mismatches are usually inevitable, and mismatch at a higher level will be duplicated in lower levels, an interactive interface is established with the help of graphics tools to avoid mismatch in every level. The interactive system displays the mapping results in each level and the user can choose his comments from among several options: very bad, good enough, generally coarse and locally coarse. The user can also give markers on the correct and wrong matching points or adjust the tolerance of the correlation algorithm. Then the system will react accordingly by adjusting the "boss" algorithm continuing or returning back to the last coarse level. The system is established on a SUN workstation. A synthetic data correlation is

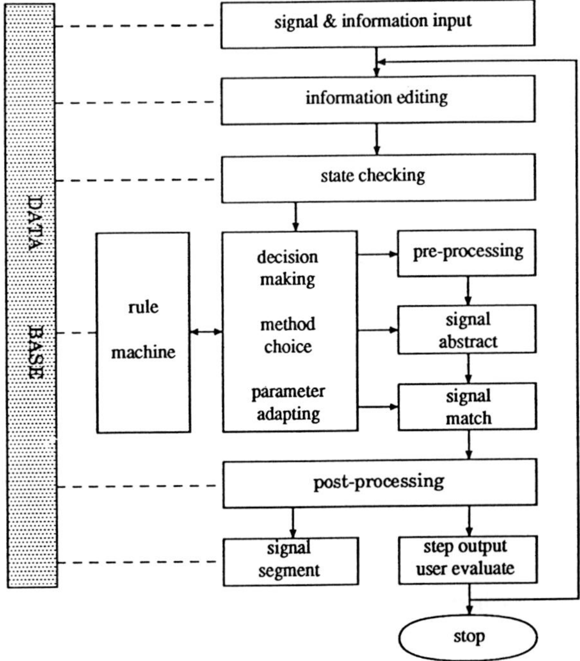

Fig. 12. Processing flow chart.

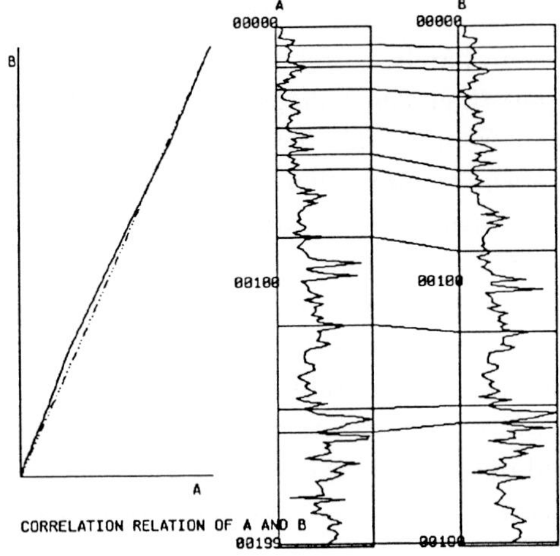

Fig. 13. A synthetic data correlation.

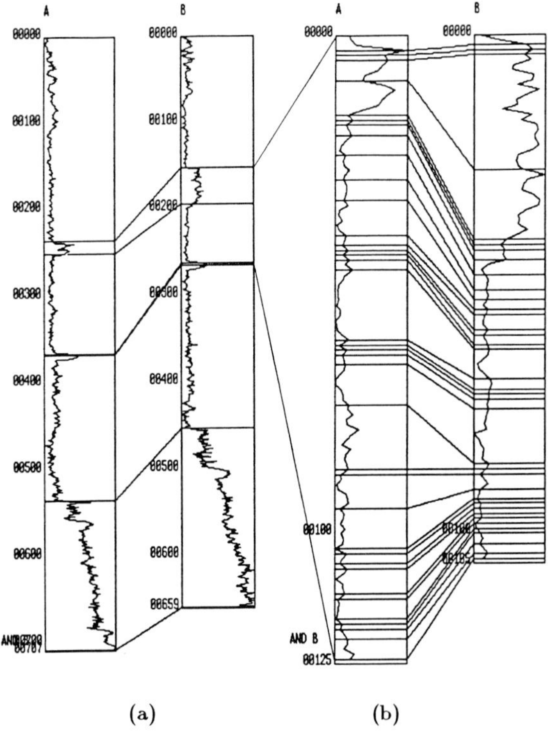

(a)   (b)

Fig. 14 A real data correlation.

shown in Fig. 13. A real data correlation of well logs is shown in Figs. 14(a), (b), and is acceptable to interpreters.

Our system has studied the effect of hierarchical structure, optimized algorithm, information integration and interaction interface. It has been shown from our experience that the adaptability and effectiveness of correlation are both improved by this system.

7. Conclusion

Four different approaches of pattern recognition applied to seismic signal classification have been proposed and realized in our group. Although the seismic patterns are very complicated in their nature and the interpretation of seismic data must be based on both the information extracted from the real data and the geological knowledge of experts, we can conclude that the pattern recognition technique will provide the interpreters with an effective means of reducing their labor intensive work and improving the quality of interpretation. It is hoped that we can incorporate pattern recognition techniques with expert systems, so that the construction of an automated seismic data interpretation system may be possible. We will make efforts in this direction.

538   *Y. Li et al.*

Acknowledgement

The authors would like to acknowledge Mr. Wang Weizhong, Mr. Xu Lei, Mr. Liu Yexin and Ms. Li Nan for their fruitful work on this project. This work was sponsored by the National Scientific Foundation under the contract No. 6865013 and No. 68995001.

References

[1] P. Bois, Applications of pattern recognition to oil and exploration, *IEEE Trans. Geoscience and Remote Sensing* **21**, 4 (1983) 416-426.

[2] F. Aminzadeh (ed.), *Pattern Recognition and Image Processing in Oil Exploration* (Geophysical Press, Amsterdam, 1987).

[3] M. Simaan and F. Aminzadeh (eds.), *Advances in Geophysical Data Processing*, Vol. 3 (JAI Press Inc., 1989).

[4] R. Kubichek and E. Quincy, Statistical modeling and feature selection for seismic pattern recognition, *Pattern Recogn.* **18**, 6 (1985) 441–448.

[5] R. Kubichek and E. Quincy, Identification of seismic stratigraphic traps using statistical pattern recognition, *Pattern Recogn.* **18**, 6 (1985) 449–458.

[6] K. Huang and K. Fu, Detection of bright spots in seismic signal using tree classifiers, *Geoexploration* **23** (1985) 121–145.

[7] K. Huang and K. Fu, Syntactic pattern recognition for the recognition of bright spots, *Pattern Recogn.* **18**, 6 (1985) 421–428.

[8] P. Bois, Determination of nature of reservoirs by use of pattern recognition algorithm with prior learning, *Geophys. Prosp.* **29** (1981) 687–701.

[9] J. Dumay and F. Fournier, Multivariate statistical analyses applied to seismic facies recognition, *Geophysics* **53**, 9 (1988) 1151-1159.

[10] F. Fournier, Extraction of quantitative geologic information from seismic data with multidimensional statistical analyses, *59th Ann. Int. Meeting SEG, Expanded Abstracts*, 1989, 726-733.

[11] A. Sinvhal and K. Khattri, Application of seismic reflection data to discriminate surface lithostratigraphy, *Geophysics* **48**, 11 (1983) 1498–1513.

[12] P. M. Doyen, T. Guidish and M. H. de Buyl, Lithology prediction from seismic data, a Monte Carlo approach, *58th Ann. Int. Meeting SEG, Expanded Abstracts*, 1988.

[13] T. Guidish and M. de Buyl, Well calibration of seismically derived petrophysical parameters: a sensitivity analysis, *58th Ann. Int. Meeting SEG, Expanded Abstracts*, 1988.

[14] M. Solano and W. Schneider, Rock properties estimation in the Vivian sand in northern Peru, *57th Ann. Int. Meeting SEG, Expanded Abstracts*, 1987.

[15] M. H. de Buyl, T. Guidish and F. Bell, Reservoir description from seismic lithologic parameter estimation, *J. Petroleum Technology* **40**, 4 (1988) 475-482.

[16] P. L. Love and M. Simaan, Segmentation of a seismic section using image processing and artificial intelligence techniques, *Pattern Recogn.* **18**, 6 (1985) 409–420.

[17] I. Pitas and A. Venetsanopoulos, Toward a knowledge-based system for automated geophysical interpretation of seismic data, *Signal Process.* **13** (1987) 229–253.

[18] F. Aminzadeh, F. S. Wong and E. H. Rusipini, A practical view of expert systems for oil exploration: integration of multiple knowledge sources, in M. Simaan and

F. Aminzadeh (eds.), *Advances in Geophysical Data Processing*, Vol. 3 (JAI Press Inc., 1989) 1–18.

[19] X. Liu, P. Xue and Y. Li, Neural network method for tracing seismic events, in *59th Ann. Int. Meeting SEG, Expanded Abstracts*, Dallas, TX, 1989.

[20] M. D. McCormark, Neural computing in geophysics, *The Leading EDGE of Exploration* **10**, 1 (1991) 11–15.

[21] X. Zhang and Y. Li, Automatic editing of noisy seismic data using an artificial neural network approach, in *Proc. Int. Symposium of Computer Application in Geoscience*, Beijing, China, 1991.

[22] S. M. Weiss and C. A. Kulikowski, *A Practical Guide to Designing Expert Systems* (Rowman and Allanheld Publishers, Totowa, NJ, 1984).

[23] S. W. Smoilar, Problem solving in the domain of quantitative well log interpretation, in *Proc. 2nd IEEE Computer Science Society Conf. on Artificial Intelligence Applications*, Miami Beach, FL, 1985, 55–59.

[24] M. E. Hohn and M. V. Fontana, Geostatics and artificial intelligence applied to stratigraphic correlation, *Ann. AAPG-SEPM-EMD-DPA Convention*, Atlanta, GA, 1986.

[25] X. Wu and E. Nyland, Well log interpretation using artificial technique, in *Trans. Society of Professional Well Log Analysis (SPWLA) 27th Ann. Logging Symposium*, paper M, 1987.

[26] D. Lineman, J. Mendelson and M. Toksoz, An expert system for well-to-well log correlation, in M. Simaan and F. Aminzadeh, (eds.), *Advances in Geophysical Data Processing*, Vol. 3 (JAI Press Inc., 1989) 235–278.

[27] R. A. Olea and J. C. Davis, An expert system for the correlation of geophysical well logs, in M. Simaan and F. Aminzadeh (eds.), *Advances in Geophysical Data Processing*, Vol. 3 (JAI Press Inc., 1989) 279–307.

[28] V. Roberto, A. Peron and P. L. Fumis, Low-level processing techniques in geophysical image interpretation, *Pattern Recogn. Lett.* **10** (1989) 111–122.

[29] J. Sangree and J. Widmier, Interpretation of depositional facies from seismic data, *Geophysics* **44** (1979) 131–160.

[30] W. S. Harlan, J. F. Claerbout and F. Rocca, Signal/noise separation and velocity estimation, *Geophysics* **49** (1984) 1869–1880.

[31] S. W. Kong, R. A. Phinney and K. R. Chowdhury, A nonlinear signal detector for enchancement of noisy seismic record sections, *Geophysics* **50** (1985) 539–550.

[32] M. Wolff, Faciolog — Automatic electrofacies determination, *Trans. Society of Professional Well Log Analysis 23rd Ann. Logging Symposium*, 1982.

[33] Y. Cheng and S. Lu, Waveform correlation by tree matching, *IEEE Trans. Pattern Anal. Mach. Intell.* **7**, 3 (1985) 229–305.

Handbook of Pattern Recognition and Computer Vision, pp. 541–568
Eds. C. H. Chen, L. F. Pau and P. S. P. Wang
© 1993 World Scientific Publishing Company

CHAPTER 3.3

SIGNAL TRANSIENT ANALYSES AND CLASSIFICATION TECHNIQUES

R. CRAIG OLSON

*Engineering & Science Associates, Inc., 6110 Executive Boulevard, Suite 315
Rockville, Maryland 20852, USA*

Short-duration signals (transients) are observed in many fields such as acoustics, biomedical signal processing, and seismic signal processing. In many of these areas, transient signals have increased in significance and importance in recent years. Oft times it is considered essential to detect and to classify transient signals concurrently with minimal time delays.

In this chapter, transient signal detection and classification techniques are presented. The required steps needed to be undertaken for the development of a suitable pattern recognition system for transient signals are identified and described.

Keywords: Transients, pattern analysis, pattern recognition, feature extraction, feature selection, classification.

1. Introduction

A transient signal may be defined as a waveform of arbitrary shape with a time duration that is short compared with the observation interval. Transient signals may be observed in many areas [1]. Some of these areas include the following: (1) speech processing [2–4]; (2) electrocardiography [5]; (3) electroencephalography [6]; (4) seismic signal processing; (5) control and communications theory; (6) biomedical engineering [7]; (7) sonar; and (8) radar. The detection and recognition of such short-duration signals oft times in the presence of noise may provide the only significant information on the operational conditions of the source of these signals.

Up to the present time considerable reliance has been placed upon the oral and/or visual recognition skills of human observers to detect and to classify such transient signals. In many areas it is becoming more important for transient signals to be detected and concurrently recognized in a near-real time mode, i.e. the detection/recognition tasks should be performed within a small time fraction of the occurrence of the transient signal.

This paper will address generically the problems associated with the concurrent detection/recognition of individual transient signals (events) and sequences of transient signals (evolutions).

The major sections of this paper cover: detection, pattern recognition system, system implementation. A summary is given at the end.

2. Detection

The detection of a short duration signal may be addressed generically in the context of time-series analysis. In such a case, it is of paramount importance to detect any change in specific time-series parameters. Such a change should provide the necessary information that a transient signal has been observed. Later localization of the region where there has been observed changes in the time-series parameters will aid in the definition of the possible transient signal. Such an area of the time series then may be examined in detail to determine its characteristics and establish its classification. This localization process which will establish the boundaries of the transient signal (when it started and when it stopped) is termed "segmentation".

An algorithm which performs the detection/segmentation function can work off-line by batch processing, or on-line as new samples come in. Depending upon the particular application, there may be different criteria regarding the performance which the algorithm should fulfill.

One such criterion which applies only to on-line processing of a signal is that a "segment boundary" should be detected as soon and as rapidly as possible. That is, the time delay between the occurrence and the detection of a segment boundary should be minimal. Implementation of such a requirement relative to the allowable time lapse for detection, in all likelihood, will result in an increase in the observed false alarm rate.

Another criterion may be to minimize the false alarm rate when a detection fast reaction time is not a primary factor. Segment boundaries should not be falsely detected. This situation cannot be avoided completely due to the finite observation intervals that are used. The false alarm rate, however, should not exceed a suitable upper bound. Short segments with distinct parameter jumps should nevertheless be detected reliably and not be "smeared out."

A third criterion close to the previous one is to localize segment boundaries after the detection as exactly as possible; that is, the mean and the variance of the difference between the "real" and estimated segment boundaries should be as small as possible. Again, in on-line processing of the incoming signals, this can be achieved only by allowing a substantial delay between the real occurrence and the final decision about the localization of a boundary. This property is important for effective and exact signal modeling purposes where a pattern recognition algorithm follows the segmentation process.

The demand for detection of short segments and for the best possible localization of the associated boundaries makes the choice of an appropriate decision measure as important as that of reasonable time-series observation windows. Both factors should be considered so the maximum amount of information can be extracted from a possible signal.

As the interest in nonstationary signal processing has increased in recent years, a considerable number of detection/segmentation algorithms have been developed for use in many areas [8–29].

In recent years, a considerable amount of effort has gone into the development of techniques which may be used in those cases where the signal and/or the background noise fields do *not* have a Gaussian distribution. A fundamental tool in digital signal processing has been the estimation of the power spectral density (PSD) or simply the power spectrum of discrete-time deterministic and stochastic processes. The information contained in the power spectrum is that which is present in the autocorrelation sequence; this would suffice for the complete statistical description of a Gaussian process of a known mean value. The power spectrum is, in fact, a member of the class of higher order spectra, i.e. it is a second-order spectrum. There are practical situations where one would have to look beyond the power spectrum to obtain information regarding deviations from Gaussianness and presence of nonlinearities. Higher order spectra (also known as polyspectra), defined in terms of higher order cumulants of the process, do contain such information. Particular cases of higher order spectra are the third-order spectrum also called the bispectrum (by definition, this is the Fourier transform of the third-order cumulant sequence), and the trispectrum (fourth-order spectrum), which is the Fourier transform of the fourth-order cumulant sequence of a stationary random process. The general motivation behind the use of higher order spectra in signal processing is threefold: to extract information due to deviations from Gaussianness; to estimate the phase of non-Gaussian parametric signals; and to detect and characterize the nonlinear properties of mechanisms that generate time series via phase relations of their harmonic components [30–34].

Maranda and Fawcett [35] investigated the performance of a fourth-moment detector for a burst-noise signal in background noise. This detector's performance was compared with that of a conventional quadratic detector when a fixed-length observation window was employed. The results quantified the signal-to-noise ratio advantage of the fourth-law detector over its square-law counterpart when the signal duration was much shorter than the integration time.

The ability to provide rapid segmentation of transient signals is essential for their processing. This segmentation capability should be achieved as near as possible to the time of actual detection. Thus, the transient signal can be detected and at least initially segmented in near to real time as possible. Various segmentation techniques may be employed which will provide rapid but coarse segmentation capabilities on one hand and on the other fine segmentation capability may be provided but may require some off-line processing to achieve any improved accuracy.

A number of researchers have recently started to investigate the application of neural networks to this concurrent detection/classification problem. Malkoff and Cohen [36] utilize time-frequency representations modified so their entry location into the network of nodes is independent of the starting time of the transient. They have stipulated four basic requirements for establishing a pattern that will act as input to the neural network: the pattern must have features which reveal the characteristics of the signal in a robust and significant manner; the pattern must remain the same (except for the change in the possible realizations of the noise) as it moves across the observation window; the pattern should be independent of arrival time since the precise time of arrival or its exact location within the observation window will not be known beforehand; and the representation should discriminate well between different signals. The representation has the form of a two-dimensional array. Each cell of the array corresponds to a single input node of the network. The determination of the presence of a signal is triggered when a new sample deviates from the mean and standard deviation of the 30 previous samples. A deviation is based upon some threshold of those statistical parameters. Deviation in only one node is sufficient to trigger the presence of a signal. They employed a three-layered and feed-forward algorithm, capable of training or testing in a single-pass. Hero and Kim [37] have developed an optimal technique for performing simultaneous signal detection and signal classification when the probability of false alarm is constrained to be below a prespecified threshold. A constrained max–min strategy has been adopted. The constrained max–min procedure which has been derived has the property of ensuring the best minimum level of performance among detection/classification procedures which satisfy the constraint. The procedure compares a set of weighted likelihood-ratios to a threshold and if the threshold is exceeded it chooses the signal class with the highest weighted likelihood.

3. Pattern Recognition System

3.1. *Background*

In view of the complex patterns which exist in many of the transient signals fields, detailed collated analyses of all the available components of the signal signature are required. Such detailed analyses should develop a symbolic description of the various transient sequences generated in the applicable field. This description should include, when it applies, those features and transient event structures which would provide an individual source class recognition capability. A pattern analysis system should be developed to satisfy the unique analyses associated with the requirement to classify the various complex patterns of transient sequences or clusters. Once the pattern analysis system has been developed, it will also provide the required classification capabilities.

3.2. *Pattern Analysis System*

A pattern analysis system is needed when the patterns are complex in nature. Transient signals may be very complex in nature. Individual transient signals may be generated due to a particular source mechanism. For a particular evolution there may be several individual transient events which will produce a time sequence of transient signals. The individual transient events may be detected and classified by statistical pattern recognition methods based upon the selection of suitable feature sets. The identification of the evolution at the source by recognition of individual transient events may require additional insight unless a single transient event describes fully the evolution. The additional insight may be obtained from the implementation of an expert system. The ability to achieve the individual transient signal event recognition and the identification of the source-generated evolution may be developed by the implementation of a suitable pattern analysis system.

A system for pattern analysis should have four basic components: a data base which contains the *results* obtained so far during the analysis of the pattern; a data base which contains the *methods* for processing the patterns; a data base which contains *information* (or *knowledge*) about the structural properties of the patterns; and a module which executes *control*. Figure 1 shows the interrelationships of the various components of a pattern analysis system. Such a system provides the maximum flexibility in the application of different processing methods so the various transient sequences, clusters, events and evolutions generated by the source can be recognized.

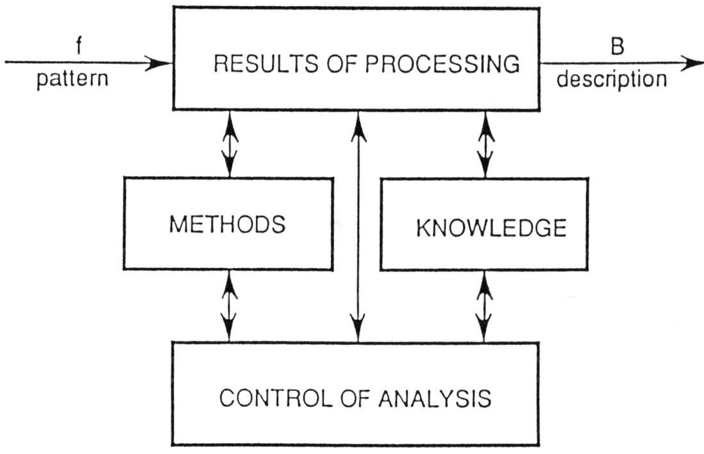

Fig. 1. Component interrelationships.

This system will permit a modular approach for analysis of the specific patterns without adopting one particular structure. This system also overcomes the problems associated with fixed control structures such as in a hierarchical system. In a hierarchical system, an error occurring in a low level module is passed on to all higher level modules with no possibility of being corrected.

The analysis of the various transients from specific source classes should be guided by the *Control Module* which selects the most promising processing methods on the basis of the problem-dependent knowledge and the hitherto existing results of processing.

One sequence of methods or processing steps, suited for a particular pattern, need not be optimal for another pattern. The *Control Module* should find this optimal sequence, or at least a good sequence of processing steps depending on the pattern offered to the system.

Pattern analysis may be viewed as a problem-solving activity. The initial state of the problem is defined by the input pattern of the system. By a sequence of actions (processing modules) which are ordered according to sequence (or step) number, the initial state undergoes a sequence of state transitions which leads to a sequence of new states being defined by the contents of the *Results Data Base*. The system stops if either a goal state (where a distinctive description of the pattern has been obtained) is reached or no further action is possible.

In a well-defined pattern analysis system, one would expect that for many patterns belonging to a particular field of problems there is at least one path which leads from the input through the various processing method alternatives to a distinctive description of the patterns. It is the task of the *Control Module* to find this path. If the same sequence of actions is suited for all patterns in a particular field of problems, this sequence may be specified once and for all, and no *Control Module* is necessary. In this case the system has a fixed control structure. A *Control Module* normally should be employed to provide the maximum flexibility now and in the future.

A state-space search may be used in the *Control Module*. A "Branch-and-Bound" method [38–40] is ideally suited for such a state-space search. The branch-and-bound algorithm is the only optimal search method in which all the possible subsets are implicitly inspected without the exhaustive search. It is basically a top-down search procedure but with a backtracking facility which allows all the possible combinations of features to be examined.

Consideration should be given to the development also of an expert system to help the user in the choice and the use of different feature extraction algorithms [41]. The choice between different types of feature extraction techniques: nonparametric, parametric, frequency, time, time-frequency, etc. may be highly dependent upon the characteristics of the signal and its associated background. Feature extraction techniques should be chosen based upon an understanding of the signal and background characteristics which are pertinent. An expert system should be implemented to provide the needed capability for transient signal characterization. This capability would be of immeasurable assistance to the primary *Control Module*.

For a complex transient evolution, which may consist of multiple simple events, additional tools will be required. One approach that may be used in this context is the creation of an expert system specifically geared to rapid recognition of complex transient signal patterns [42].

At the end of the analyses, the *Results Data Base* should contain a description of the pattern. This description should contain the unique information necessary for recognition of transient events and evolutions generated by various classes of sources.

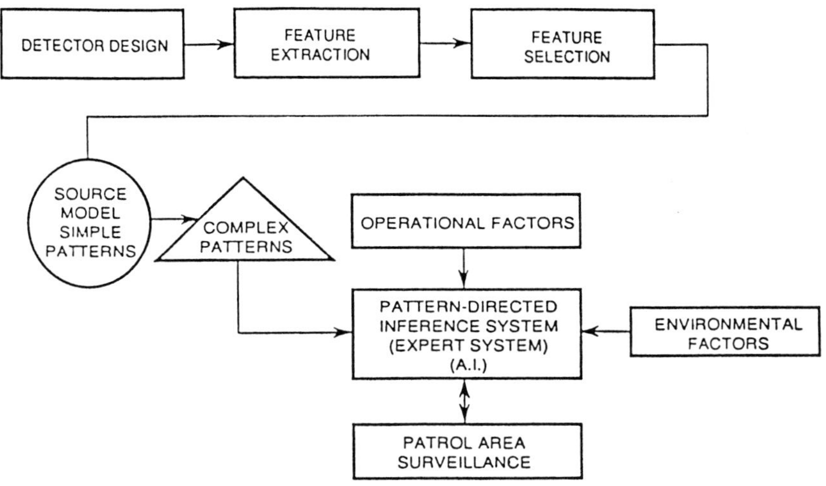

Fig. 2. Example of general pattern recognition.

Another example of the general pattern recognition methodology to be used is shown in Fig. 2.

A pattern recognition system may be composed of two primary parts: a feature extractor and a classifier [43]. The primary function of the feature extractor is to develop a set of features that will provide the maximum discriminator capability. The function of the classifier is to assign a pattern class designator to each input sample.

The transient signal classification process is basically a threefold process. The first process involves *feature extraction*; that is, the identification of quantitative and qualitative exploitable characteristics of the detected transient signal. The second process is associated with *feature selection*; that is, the determination of a minimum number of features which provides the maximum separation of a particular transient signal from all others (maximum discrimination capability). The third process involves the actual *recognition* of a particular transient signal. This capability is achieved by a classifier. Various types of classifiers are available. The type to be selected is dependent to some degree on the type of signals to be classified, the *a priori* knowledge of signal class characteristics and the execution speed desired. The major contributors to a highly successful recognition system are found in the feature extraction/selection areas. The determination of highly discriminatory features is the key to a successful transient signal recognition system.

3.3. *Characterization of Nonstationary Signals*

The following section provides background information about how nonstationary signals may be characterized. It should provide the basis of the feature extraction effort associated with any transient signal characterization effort.

Analysis of a signal in the time domain is based on the study of its periodic components. Such information also can be obtained through the Fourier transformation of the signal and expressed in the frequency domain as the signal's frequency spectrum. Although these domains are related by the Fourier transform pair, providing the true representation of a signal's characteristics is constrained by the limitation of the finite length of available data, as the original definition of the Fourier transform is determined by the complete time history from minus to plus infinity. The time-varying nature of a signal has been generalized in terms of being deterministic or random according to its origination. The implementation, however, of such classification of a finite length of signal is very much related to the time frame of observation and the selection of ensemble size for the analysis. Meaningful interpretation of the analysis results depends on the validity of the assumption of periodicity or stationarity during the Fourier transform processing.

Nonparametric methods of nonstationary spectrum estimation have been developed in an attempt to overcome identified limitations. These methods include narrowband filtering, complex demodulation and short-time Fourier transforms (STFT) [44]. The STFT is evaluated by applying a suitable windowing function to the original signal and then evaluating the conventional Fourier transform of the resulting finite length sequence. It is assumed that the signal is stationary during the short time interval specified. The time-frequency resolution of the STFT technique is inversely related to the window length. Increasing the window length increases the frequency resolution, while at the same time it reduces the frequency tracking capability of the representation.

Parametric spectral estimation methods [45] have been developed during the last two decades to overcome the problems associated with nonparametric techniques. These methods have the following capabilities as compared to nonparametric techniques: frequency resolution is independent of the inverse of the signal's time duration; estimation accuracy is improved at high signal-to-noise ratios; and analysis and synthesis are considerably more flexible. Thus, it is then possible to estimate the spectrum of signals which have short duration with good resolution in frequency.

Although the data samples used in parametric spectral estimation techniques may be considerably smaller in duration than those required for nonparametric techniques, there still is a strong limitation of these methods due to the necessary assumption of a stationary signal. Extensions of several well-known parametric techniques of stationary spectral estimation to the nonstationary case have been made [46–49]. Time-varying autoregressive (AR) models have been identified by means of a fast [50] algorithm which is suitable also for the AR part of a mixed autoregressive moving average (ARMA) model. An extension of Cadzow's ARMA method [51] has also been developed. Lattices with time-dependent reflection coefficients have been identified through an algorithm which is similar to Burg's maximum entropy method [52]. Prony's method [53] has also been adapted to the nonstationary context.

A common way of representing transient signals is to model them as impulse responses of time-invariant linear systems as in the AR, and ARMA models. Equivalently, the signals can be represented as a sum of real or complex damped exponentials. Prony's method seeks to fit a deterministic exponential to the data, in contrast to autoregressive (AR) and autoregressive moving average (ARMA) models that seek to fit a random model to the second-order data statistics. Prony presented a method of fitting exactly as many purely damped exponentials as needed to fit the available data points. The modern version of Prony's method has been generalized to contain only damped sinusoidal models. A modification of the modern Prony method can also fit a purely sinusoidal model with no damped components to the data. There are three basic steps to be taken in the Prony method: (1) determine the linear prediction parameters that fit the available data; (2) estimate the damping and frequencies of each of the exponential sinusoidal terms based upon the roots of a polynomial formed from the linear prediction coefficients; and (3) solve a second set of linear equations to obtain the estimates of the exponential amplitude and initial sinusoidal phase. Prony's method, however, is highly sensitive to additive measurement noise. Prony's method thus is statistically inefficient, i.e. the variance of the estimated parameters often exceeds the Cramer–Rao lower bound (CRB) [54].

Kumaresan and Tufts (K–T) [55,56] have proposed a method which offers considerable improvement over Prony's method, at the expense of greater computational complexity. The K–T method has the following features: (1) uses an overdetermined set of linear equations; (2) overestimates the order of the assumed linear model; (3) applies a singular value decomposition (SVD) to the data matrix, and then truncates the set of singular values; and (4) estimates the backward predictor polynomial and then uses its roots to separate the signal poles from the poles introduced by the noise. Porat and Friedlander's [57,58] modification to the K–T method uses the forward and backward predictors to select the signal poles, and then combines the two sets of poles to form the final estimates. The modified algorithm exhibits an improved robustness and smaller bias in test cases.

For a time-varying signal, whether a deterministic transient or a nonstationary random signal, a single-domain representation does not reveal all the information content and may lead to erroneous results such as the loss of desired characteristic features or misinterpretation for the wrong conclusion.

To alleviate the shortcomings of the single-domain representation, some other efforts have been directed toward developing a joint time-frequency representation. Kodera et al. [59] have developed four different methods for analyzing time-varying signals. These methods employ a joint time-frequency representation. The signal is characterized by a three-dimensional surface defined by the energy of the signal. The methods which Kodera used included the following: (1) Amplitude Maximum of the Spectrum (MS); (2) Amplitude Maximum of the Envelope (ME); (3) the Moving Window Method (MWM); and (4) the Modified Moving Window Method (MMWM). These methods are based upon Short-Time Fourier Transforms (STFT) and the nonstationary situation is treated as a concatenation of quasi-stationary ones. Short-time analyses are known [60] to suffer drawbacks, especially according to the quasi-stationarity assumptions.

A generalized representation is needed to give a more complete description of a type of time-varying signal, whether it is a deterministic transient or a nonstationary random signal [61].

In recent years, alternative time-frequency representations have been investigated. The conclusion of these investigations is that the Wigner–Ville Distribution (WVD) function is the most powerful and fundamental time-frequency representation [62–69].

The implementation of the Wigner–Ville Distribution function [70] may be achieved as follows: (1) compute successively the analytical signal corresponding to the input signal; (2) form a weighted kernel function; and (3) analyze the kernel function using a discrete Fourier transform (DFT).

The Wigner distribution (WD) can provide for high frequency- or time-resolution, but its nonlinear property poses problems when applied to signals with multiple frequency components. Kobayashi and Suzuki [71] first convert the observed data to analytic signals, which are then subjected to Fourier transforms after squaring. Results obtained using this approach reveal its superiority over WD for multicomponent signals. Allard et al. [72] and also Garudadri et al. [73] have employed smoothing to reduce the interferences resulting from the different frequency components present in a pseudo-Wigner distribution presentation. A new nonstationary analysis technique has been developed by Atlas et al. [74] which makes use of a kernel that allows finite-time support while suppressing interference terms. O'Shea and Boashash [75] have developed an instantaneous frequency estimation technique using the Cross Wigner–Ville Distribution for use in the detection of nonstationary transient signals in a high noise environment.

Nikias and Raghuveer in 1987 [76], and Nikias in 1989 [77] reported on the application of bispectrum signal processing to parameter estimation. They identified three general reasons behind the use of bispectrum in signal processing. These were outlined in the section on Detection above.

3.4. *Feature Extraction*

Various signal processing methods and techniques should be applied to the transient signals of interest so that spatial (if applicable), temporal, and frequency relationships may be developed. These relationships should provide significant recognition capabilities for the various transients. Features or attributes will be developed or identified which are the most important for classification of simple patterns, have the highest expected reliability, require the minimum computational time, and represent source generation mechanisms. It should be recognized that the feature extraction processes are domain-dependent and may not be directly transferred from one investigative area to another. Where there are similarities between areas there should be at least an examination of relative feature extraction techniques. The methods which should be considered for use in general transient signal investigations include the following: signal time-waveform analysis; signal-frequency spectra analysis; and time-frequency analysis.

A fairly comprehensive list of applicable feature extraction algorithms which may be applied to transient signals in general is presented in Appendix A. It includes nonparametric methods, parametric methods and waveform measurement techniques for both time-waveform representation and frequency-waveform representation. Time-frequency representation techniques are also included. The methods to be employed are dependent upon the characteristics of the transient signals, the nature of the background noise fields and the acceptable computational times. Ideally, the methods selected should match the signal pattern and have minimal computational requirements.

Almost all of the feature extraction techniques listed in Appendix A have been used by one or more investigators. A systematic analysis of the effectiveness of these features has not been conducted for any of the transient signals which may be encountered on a regular basis. This pattern analysis effort associated with feature extraction/selection needs to be undertaken.

3.5. *Classification*

3.5.1. *General*

Four principal approaches are possible for the implementation of automatic pattern recognition systems: heuristic, mathematical, syntactic, and dynamic models [78,79].

3.5.2. *Mathematical approach*

The major emphasis has been placed to date on mathematical implementations for classification of transient signals. The following are typical mathematical implementation techniques:

- Bayes classifier,
- Fisher classifier,
- Minimum distance classifier,
- K-nearest-neighbor method,
- Minimum squared error procedure,
- Error correction method with fixed and varying increment.

Often the required separation between pattern classes for adequate recognition cannot be achieved by means of a linear function relative to the pattern space. The linear and/or non-linear transformation of the pattern space features may be accomplished by implementing or developing a set of Potential Functions [80]. This approach for a classifier will result in linear decision boundaries.

In recent years considerable effort has been given to the application of neural networks to pattern recognition [81–85]. Most researchers have used the backpropagation algorithm [86–88] operating on a perceptron with hidden layers. The various neural network algorithms may be equated to appropriate mathematical techniques. In the case of a multi-layer perceptron, it may be equated to a k-Nearest Neighbor Mixture algorithm [89–90].

In 1988, Gorman et al. reported on the use of neural networks in the classification of sonar targets [91].

3.5.3. *Dynamic model approach*

Shields and Therrien [92] describe a system for modeling and classifying acoustic transient signals based on Hidden Markov Models (HMMs), which were developed initially for speech processing. They have used various features related to the short-time power spectrum including bandpass spectral energy, linear prediction parameters, and cepstral features.

4. Interactive Pattern Analysis and Classification System Implementation

4.1. *General*

The development of a practical and workable pattern recognition system is often a formidable task. Considerable interaction between the researcher and the available tools and techniques is required for feature extraction/selection and also for the definition of the appropriate decision logic. Figure 3 illustrates how such an interactive process would take place. The advantages of human interaction and intervention in all phases of the iterative design process and the important role of interactive computing and display technology in making this feasible have been elaborated upon by Kanal [93]. He has given the following reasons for the desirability of an Automated Interactive Pattern Analysis and Classification System (IPACS):

- No single technique is suited for all pattern recognition problems.
- Feature evaluation and classification should be linked in a feedback mechanism.
- Structure analysis is best achieved if suitable graphics are easily available.
- In an IPACS the human is in charge of the design and evaluation process, whereas the computational burden is left to the computer.

Chien [94] enumerated the following general capabilities and design considerations for an IPAC system:

- *Easy Communication with the System.* Communication and control of the system through simple procedures, such as: selection of options displayed at each stage of the design process in the form of a menu on the side of the graphic display; selection of options through a simple language using an alphanumeric keyboard.
- *Quick Response.* Quick response in an on-line mode, allowing rapid formulation, insertion, and testing of alternate hypotheses.

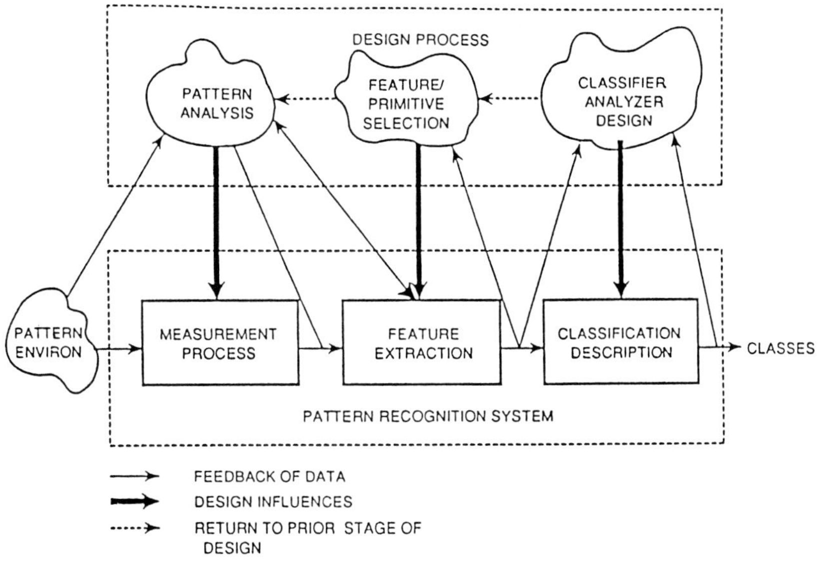

Fig. 3. Pattern recognition system.

- *Easy Generation and Modification of Algorithms.* Easy on-line generation and modification of algorithms and programs; selecting, labeling, merging, and splitting of data sets; performing all types of set operations on data sets and subsets; retrieving selected data for visual inspection and trial design of algorithms.
- *Dynamic Allocation of Core to Data and Programs.* Allocation of programs and data dynamically to main and auxiliary storage. This capability is essential to the success of an IPACS due to the large amounts of data which have to be stored in a structured manner and the many programs for implementing user options.
- *Options Availability.* Storage and comparison of the results of applying various optional procedures on a data set.
- *Implementation of Data Structure to Provide a Vehicle Between the Various Options.* Provision of capability to define and examine "structure" in large data sets of high-dimensional multivariate data.

4.2. *IPACS Implementation*

Several IPACS have been implemented in support of various investigations. These include among others: PAL – A system developed for analysis and recognition of seismic data [95]; DX-1–"The Experimental Dynamic Processor". A system to study on-line interactive sensor data processing [96]; FACEL – A feature analysis comparison and evaluation library [97]; IDSS – An interactive decision structuring system [98]; ILS – A system developed primarily for speech analysis [99]; ISPAHAN

[100] – An interactive pattern analysis system patterned after OLPARS [101] and MIPACS [102]; IPACS – A general software system for statistical pattern recognition. The last has been used for recognition of objects in digital images and classification of waveforms [103].

Currently there are systems available which may be used to solve in part the pattern recognition problems associated with the rapid detection and classification of transient signals. The known systems include the following: HYPERSIGNAL – A time-domain and frequency-domain digital signal processing interactive system [104]; MONARCH – A signal processing and digital filter design and analysis development system [105]; SACALC – A signal analysis system [106]; TUSA – A sonar signal analysis system for transient analysis based upon a combination of conventional signal processing techniques and neural network paradigms [107].

5. Summary

The detection and recognition of short-duration signals (transients) is a problem of increasing importance in a number of fields including acoustics, biomedicine and, seismic analysis. Furthermore, there is additional emphasis for the concurrent detection/recognition of these signals. Detection and classification techniques have been presented for the general field of transient signals. The particular detection algorithms, feature extraction techniques and classification methods are dependent at least in part upon the particular domain of interest. A general method pattern analysis system, which should provide an efficient recognition of transient signals has been presented.

References

[1] H. T. Le and E. J. Wegman, Transient signal detection and estimation: A survey, Tech. Rep. No. 31, Center for Computational Statistics and Probability, George Mason University, Fairfax, VA, 1988.

[2] H. F. Silverman and D. P. Morgan, The application of dynamic programming to connected speech recognition, *IEEE ASSP Mag.* **7** (1990) 7–25.

[3] J. Picone, Continuous speech recognition using Hidden Markov Models, *IEEE ASSP Mag.* **7** (1990) 26–41.

[4] R. J. Niederjohn, A mathematical formulation and comparison of zero- crossing analysis techniques which have been applied to automatic speech recognition, *IEEE Trans. Acoust. Speech Signal Process.* **23** (1975) 373–380.

[5] S. M. Blanchard and R. C. Barr, Comparison of methods for adaptive sampling of cardiac electrograms and electrocardiogram, *Med. Biol. Eng. Comput.* **23** (1985) 377–386.

[6] G. Bodenstein and H. M. Praetorins, Feature extraction from the encephalogram by adaptive segmentation, *Proc. IEEE* **65** (1977) 642–652.

[7] H. Yamada and K. Yamamoto, Recognition of echocardiograms by dynamic programming matching method, in *Proc. 9th Int. Conf. on Pattern Recognition*, Rome, Italy, 1988, 685–688.

[8] A. S. Willsky, A survey of design methods for failure detection in dynamic systems, *Automatica* **12** (1976) 601–611.

[9] J. B. Anderson and C. W. Law, Real-number convolutional codes for speech-like quasi-stationary sources, *IEEE Trans. Inf. Theory* **23**, 6 (1977) 778–782.

[10] G. Bodenstein and H. M. Praetorius, Feature extraction from the electroencephalogram by adaptive segmentation, *Proc. IEEE* **65**, 5 (1977) 642–652.

[11] A. C. Sanderson, J. Segen and E. Richey, Hierarchical modeling of EGG signals, *IEEE Trans. Pattern Anal. Mach. Intell.* **2**, 5 (1980) 405–415.

[12] B. H. Jansen, A. Hasman and R. Lenten, Piecewise analysis of EEGs using AR modeling and clustering, *Comput. Biomed. Res.* **14**, 168–178.

[13] T. van Eck and L. G. Ahlbom, Automatic event detection applied to single channel seismic records, in *Proc. IEEE Int. Conf. on Acoustics, Speech, and Signal Processing*, Paris, France, 1982, 1894–1897.

[14] M. Bassevillle and A. Benveniste, Sequential detection of abrupt changes in spectral characteristics of digital signals, Res. Rep. No. 129, IRISA, Campus du Beaulieu, Rennes, France, 1982.

[15] A. Von Brandt, Detecting and estimating parameter jumps using ladder algorithms and likelihood ratio tests, in *Proc. IEEE 1983 Int. Conf. on Acoustics, Speech, and Signal Processing*, Boston, MA, 1983, 14–16.

[16] U. Appel and A. Von Brandt, Adaptive sequential segmentation of piecewise stationary time series, *Inf. Sci.* **29** (1983) 27–56.

[17] D. Michael and J. Houchin, Automatic EEG analysis: A segmentation procedure based on the autocorrelation function, *Electroenceph. Clin. Neurophysiol.* **46** (1981) 512–525.

[18] G. Bodenstein and W. Schneider, Pattern recognition of clinical electroencephalograms, in *Proc. Int. Conf. on Digital Signal Processing*, Florence, Italy, 1981, 206–211.

[19] K. Kumamaru, S. Sagara, K. Inoue and S. Takagi, Recognition-identification of non-linear systems with unknown variations in the dynamics' pattern and its application to the EEG analysis, in *Proc. 5th IFAC Symp.*, Vol. 2, 1979, 891–898.

[20] A. S. Willsky and H. L. Jones, A generalized likelihood ratio approach to the detection and estimation of jumps in linear systems, *IEEE Trans. Automatic Control* **21** (1976) 108–112.

[21] B. Porat and B. Friedlander, Adaptive detection of transients, *IEEE Trans. Acoust. Speech Signal Process* **34** (1986) 1410–1418.

[22] S. M. Kay and L. L. Scharf, Invariant detection of ARMA signals with unknown initial conditions, in *Proc. 1984 Int. Conf. on Acoustics, Speech, and Signal Processing*, San Diego, CA, 1984, 38.4.1–38.4.4.

[23] B. Porat and B. Friedlander, Parametric techniques for adaptive detection of gaussian signals, *IEEE Trans. Acoust. Speech Signal Process.* **32** (1984) 780–790.

[24] B. Friedlander and B. Porat, Detection of transient signals by the Gabor Representation, *IEEE Trans. Acoust. Speech Signal Process.* **37** (1989) 169–180.

[25] U. Appel and A. v. Brandt, A comparative study of three sequential time series segmentation algorithms, *Signal Processing* **6** (1984) 45–60.

[26] M. Basseville and A. Benveniste, Design and comparative study of some sequential jump detection algorithms for digital signals, *IEEE Trans. Inf. Theory* **20** (1983) 709–723.

[27] M. Basseville and A. Benveniste (eds.), *Detection of Abrupt Changes in Signals and Dynamical Systems* (Springer-Verlag, Berlin, 1986).

[28] M. Basseville and A. Benveniste, Sequential segmentation of nonstationary digital signals using spectral analysis, *Inf. Sci.* **29** (1983) 57–73.

[29] S. L. Sclove, Time-series segmentation: A model and a method, *Inf. Sci.* **29** (1983) 7–25.

[30] C. L. Nikias and M. R. Raghuveer, Bispectrum estimation: A digital signal processing framework, *Proc. IEEE* **75** (1987) 869–891.

[31] M. L. Hinich and G. R. Wilson, Detection of non-gaussian signals in non-gaussian noise using the bispectrum, *IEEE Trans. Acoust. Speech Signal Process* **38** (1990) 1126–1131.

[32] M. J. Hinich, Detecting a transient signal by bispectral analysis, *IEEE Trans. Acoust. Speech Signal Process.* **38** (1990) 1277-1283 (1990).

[33] E. J. Sullivan and M. J. Hinich, Active-sonar and transient detection using polyspectra, presented at 119th Meeting: Acoustical Society of America, May 1990.

[34] G. B. Giannakis and M. K. Tsatsanis, Signal detection and classification using matched filtering and higher order statistics, *IEEE Trans. Acoust, Speech Signal Process.* **38** (1990) 1284–1296.

[35] B. H. Maranda and J. A. Fawcett, The performance analysis of a fourth-moment detector, in *Proc. 1990 Int. Conf. on Acoustics, Speech, and Signal Processing,* Albuquerque, NM, 1990, 1357–1360.

[36] D. B. Malkoff and L. Cohen, A neural network approach to the detection problem using joint time-frequency distributions, in *Proc. 1990 Int. Conf. on Acoustics, Speech, and Signal Processing,* 1990, 2739–2742.

[37] A. O. Hero and J. K. Kim, Simultaneous signal detection and classification under a false alarm constraint, in *Proc. 1990 Int. Conf. on Acoustics, Speech, and Signal Processing,* 1990, 2759–2762.

[38] H. M. Wagner, *Principles of Operations Research with Application to Managerial Decisions* (Prentice-Hall, Englewood Cliffs, NJ, 1969) 466–480.

[39] R. C. Olson, Feature extraction in an adaptive multiclass pattern recognition system, Ph.D. Dissertation, The Catholic University of America, Washington, D.C. (1978).

[40] B. S. Gottfried and J. Weisman, *Introduction to Optimization Theory* (Prentice-Hall, Englewood Cliffs, NJ, 1973) 320–326.

[41] G. P. Marizet-Mahoudeaux, Expert system use in signal processing: User aid in spectral density estimation methods, *Onde Electr. (France)* **68** (1988) 90–97.

[42] A. Raper and J. K. Hammond, An expert system for transient data analysis using a model based architecture developed with POPLOG, in *Proc. 1987 Int. Conf. on Acoustics, Speech, and Signal Processing,* 1987, 1871–1874.

[43] T. Y. Young and T. W. Calvert, *Classification, Estimation and Pattern Recognition* (American Elsevier Publishing Co., New York, 1974).

[44] S. H. Nawab, T. F. Quatieri and J. S. Lim, Signal reconstruction from short-time fourier transform magnitude, *IEEE Trans. Acoust. Speech Signal Process.* **31** (1983) 986–998.

[45] H. Fargetton, R. Gendrin and J. L. Lacoume, Adaptive methods for spectral analysis of time varying signals, in M. Kunt and F. de Coulon (eds.), *Signal Processing: Theory and Applications* (North-Holland, Amsterdam, 1980) 777–792.

[46] Y. Grenier, Time-dependent ARMA modeling of nonstationary signals, *IEEE Trans. Acoust. Speech Signal Process.* **31** (1983) 899–911.

[47] N. Martin, An AR spectral analysis of non-stationary signals, *Signal Processing* **10** (1986) 61–74.

[48] Y. Grenier and M.-C. Omnes-Chevalier, Autoregressive models with time-dependent log area ratios, *IEEE Trans. Acoust. Speech Signal Process.* **36** (1988) 1602–1612.

[49] M. J. E. Salami, St. Nichols and M. R. Smith, A SVD-based transient error method for analyzing noisy multicomponent exponential signals, *Proc. 1987 Int. Conf. on Acoustics, Speech, and Signal Processing*, Dallas, TX, Vol. 2, 1987, 677–680.

[50] N. Levinson, The Wiener (root mean square) error criterion in filter design and prediction, *J. Math. Phys.* **25** (1947) 261–278.

[51] J. A. Cadzow, ARMA spectrum estimation: A model equation error procedure, in *Proc. IEEE 1980 Int. Conf. on Acoustics, Speech, Signal Processing*, Denver, CO, 1980, 598–601.

[52] J. P. Burg, A new analysis technique for time-series data, NATO Advanced Study Institute on Signal Processing with Emphasis on Underwater Acoustics, 1968.

[53] F. B. Hildebrand, *Introduction to Numerical Analysis* (McGraw-Hill, New York 1956).

[54] R. F. Barrett and D. R. A. McMahon, Comparison of frequency estimators for underwater acoustic data, *J. Acoust. Soc. Am.* **79** (1986) 1461–1471.

[55] R. Kumaresan, Estimating the parameters of exponentially damped or undamped sinusoidal signals in noise, Ph.D. dissertation, Univ. Rhode Island, Kingston, Oct. 1982.

[56] R. Kumaresan and D. W. Tufts, Estimating the parameters of exponentially damped sinusoids and pole-zero modeling in noise, *IEEE Trans. Acoust. Speech Signal Process.* **30** (1982) 833–840.

[57] B. Friedlander and B. Porat, An accuracy analysis of the Kumaresan-Tufts method for estimating complex damped exponentials, in *Proc. 1987 Int. Conf. on Acoustics, Speech, and Signal Processing*, Dallas, TX, 1987, 665–668.

[58] B. Porat and B. Friedlander, A modification of the Kumaresan-Tufts method for estimating rational impulse responses, *IEEE Trans. Acoust. Speech Signal Process.* **34** (1986) 1336–1338.

[59] K. Kodera, R. Gendrin and C. De Villedary, Analysis of time-varying signals with small BT values, *IEEE Trans. Acoust. Speech Signal Process.* **26** (1978) 64–76.

[60] P. Flandrin and B. Escudie, An interpretation of the pseudo-Wigner-Ville distribution, *Signal Processing* **6** (1984) 27–36.

[61] Hung T. Le and Edward J. Wegman, Generalized function estimation of underwater transient signals, *J. Acoust. Soc. Am.* **89**, 1 (1991) 274–279.

[62] B. Boashash, Theory, implementation and application of time-frequency signal analysis using the Wigner-Ville distribution, *J. Electr. Electron. Eng. Aust.* **7** (1987) 166–177.

[63] J. Ville, Theories et application de la notion de signal analytique, *Cables et Transmission* **A1** (1984) 61–74.

[64] B. Bouachache and F. Rodriquex, Recognition of time-varying signals in the time-frequency domain by means of the Wigner distribution, in *Proc. 1984 Int. Conf. on Acoustics, Speech, and Signal Processing*, San Diego, CA, 1984, 22.5.1–22.5.4.

[65] B. Bouachache, Sur la possibilite d'utilizer la representation conjointe en temps et frequence de ville aux signaux vibrosimiques, presented at the Colloque Nat Trait Sign, Gretsi 121/1, 121/6, Nice, France, 1979.

[66] B. Bouachache and P. Flandrin, Wigner-Ville analysis of time-varying signals, in *Proc. Int. Conf. on Acoustics, Speech, and Signal Processing 82*, Paris, France, 1982, 1329–1332.

[67] W. Martin and P. Flandrin, Wigner-Ville spectral analysis of nonstationary processes, *IEEE Trans. Acoust. Speech Signal Process.* **33** (1985) 1461–1470.

[68] S.-C. Pei and T.-Y. Wang, The Wigner distribution of linear time-variant systems, *IEEE Trans. Acoust. Speech Signal Process.* **36** (1988) 1681–1684.

[69] P. Rao and F. J. Taylor, Detection and localization of narrow-band transient signals using the Wigner distribution, *J. Acoust. Soc. Am.* **90**, 3 (1991) 1423–1434.

[70] B. Bouachache and P. J. Black, An efficient real-time implementation of the Wigner-Ville distribution, *IEEE Trans. Acoust. Speech Signal Process.* **35** (1987) 1611–1618.

[71] F. Kobayashi and H. Suzuki, Time-varying signal analysis using squared analytic signals, in *Proc. 1987 Int. Conf. on Acoustics, Speech, and Signal Processing*, Vol. 3, Dallas, TX, 1987, 1525–1512.

[72] J. F. Allard, J. C. Valiere and R. Bourdier, Broadband signal analysis with the smoothed pseudo-Wigner Distribution, *J. Acoust. Soc. Am.* **83** (1988) 1041–1044.

[73] H. Garudadri, M. P. Beddoes, A.-P. Benguerel and J. H. V. Gilbert, On computing the smoothed Wigner distribution, in *Proc. 1987 Int. Conf. on Acoustics, Speech, and Signal Processing*, Vol. 3, Dallas, TX, 1987, 1521–1524.

[74] L. Atlas, W. Koolman, P. Loughlin and R. A. Cole, New nonstationary techniques for the analysis and display of speech transients, in *Proc. 1990 Int. Conf. on Acoustics, Speech, and Signal Processing*, Albuquerque, NM, 1990, 385–388.

[75] P. O'Shea and B. Boashash, Instantaneous frequency estimation using the cross Wigner-Ville distribution with application to non-stationary transient detection, in *Proc. 1990 IEEE Int. Conf. on Acoustics, Speech, and Signal Processing*, 1990, 2887–2890.

[76] C. L. Nikias and M. R. Raghuveer, Bispectrum estimation: a digital signal processing framework, *Proc. IEEE* **75** (1987) 869–891.

[77] C. L. Nikias, Transient signal analysis via higher-order spectra, in *Proc. First Acoustic Transient Workshop*, Naval Research Laboratory, 152–5100, 1989.

[78] J. T. Tou and R. C. Gonzalez, *Pattern Recognition Principles* (Addison-Wesley, Reading, MA, 1974).

[79] L. F. Pau, Intelligent man-machine interfaces in instrumentation, in *Proc. Finland Artificial Intelligence Conf.*, Univ. Helsinki, Vol. 1, 1988, 12–19; and *J. Japanese Society for AI* **5**, 1 (1990) 106–109.

[80] W. S. Meisel, *Computer-Oriented Approaches to Pattern Recognition* (Academic Press, New York, 1972).

[81] T. King, Using neural networks for pattern recognition, *Dr. Dobbs Journal* #147 (1989) 14–28.

[82] R. P. Lippmann, Pattern classification using neural networks, *IEEE Commun. Mag.* (1989) 27–62.

[83] T. Kohonen, G. Barna and R. Chrisley, Statistical pattern recognition with neural networks: Bench mark studies, in *Proc. 1988 Int. Conf. on Acoustics, Speech, and Signal Processing*, New York, NY, 1988, 61–68.

[84] C.-J. Wang, M. A. Wickert and C.-H. Wu, Three-layer neural network for spectral estimation, in *Proc. 1990 Int. Conf. on Acoustics, Speech, and Signal Processing*, Albuquerque, NM, 1990, 881–884.

[85] L. F. Pau and F. S. Johansen, Neural network signal understanding for instrumentation, *IEEE Trans. Instrumentation* (1990).

[86] R. P. Lippmann, An introduction to computing with neural nets, *IEEE ASSP Mag.* April (1987) 4–22.

[87] D. E. Rumelhart, J. L. McClelland (eds.), *Parallel Distributed Processing: Exploration in the Microstructure of Cognition* (MIT Press, Cambridge, MA, 1986).

[88] W. P. Jones and J. Hoskins, Backpropagation: A generalized delta learning rule, *BYTE* **12**, 1 (1987) 155–162.

[89] R. P. Lippman, An introduction to computing with neural nets, *IEEE ASSP Mag.* April (1987) 4–22.

[90] R. J. Brown, An artificial neural network experiment, *Dr. Dobbs Journal* April (1987) 16–71.

[91] R. P. Gorman and T. J. Sejnowski, Analysis of hidden units in a layered network trained to classify sonar targets, *Neural Networks* **1** (1988) 75–89.

[92] M. K. Shields and C. W. Therrien, A Hidden Markov Model approach to the classification of acoustic transients, in *Proc. 1990 Int. Conf. on Acoustics, Speech, and Signal Processing*, 1990, 2731–2734.

[93] L. N. Kanal, Interactive pattern analysis and classification systems: A survey and commentary, *Proc. IEEE* **60** (1972) 1200–1215.

[94] Y.-T. Chien, *Interactive Pattern Recognition* (Marcel Dekker, New York, 1978).

[95] R. B. Ives, PAL a highly tutorial interactive pattern recognition program, in *Proc. Int. Symp. on Computer Aided Seismic Analysis and Discrimination*, Hyannis, MA, 1977, 119–121.

[96] C. M. Walter, The experimental dynamic processor DX-1, *IRE Int. Conv. Rec.* **10** (1962) 151–156.

[97] ____, FACEL, Recognition Systems, Inc., 1981.

[98] W. C. Liles and H. J. Payne, *IDSS (Interactive Decision Structuring System) User's Manual*, Technology Service Corporation TSC-PD-142-7, 1975.

[99] ____, *Interactive Laboratory System Users Guide*, Signal Technology, Inc., 1991.

[100] G. Eden and E. S. Gelsema, Investigation of multidimensional data using the Interactive Pattern Analysis ISPAHAN, *Pattern Recogn.* **11** (1979) 391–399.

[101] J. W. Sammon, Jr., On-line Pattern Analysis and Recognition System (OLPARS) Rome Air Dev. Ctr. Tech. Rpt. TR-68-263, 1968.

[102] G. C. Stockman, Maryland Interactive Pattern Analysis and Classification System: Part I: Concepts, Comp. Sci. Tech. Rpt.TR–408, University of Maryland, 1975.

[103] I. Dyrdal, IPACS – Interactive Pattern Analysis and Classification System, in C. H. Chen (ed.), *Applied Time Series Analysis* (World Scientific, Singapore, 1989).

[104] ____, *HYPERCEPTION DSP Sourcebook*, Hyperception, Inc., 1991.

[105] ____, *MONARCH DSP Software*, The Athena Group, Inc., 1990.

[106] W. T. Hardy, SACALC – *Signal Analysis Calculator User's Guide* (Artech House, 1990).

[107] D. Greenwood, F. Stevenson, R. Taber and S. Deiss, Learning environment for neural networks and transient acoustics, Netrologic, Inc. Report TR-89-1-ONR, 1990.

Appendix A. Transient Signal Feature Extraction Techniques

Technique	Reference for description of algorithm	Source code available
• Time-Waveform Representation		
Nonparametric Methods		
Short-time processing techniques – Autocorrelation analysis – Average magnitude Difference function – Average zero crossing rate – Energy	L. R. Rabiner and R. W. Schafer, *Digital Processing of Speech Signals* (Prentice-Hall, Englewood, NJ, 1978)	Not included.
Parametric Methods		
Autoregressive Moving Average (ARMA) Model	E. A. Robinson, *Time Series Analysis* *and Applications* (Goose Pond Press, Houston, TX, 1981)	FORTRAN
Kumaresan's Method	R. Kumaresan, Estimating the Parameters of Exponentially Damped or Undamped Sinusoidal Signals in Noise, Ph.D. dissertation, Department of Electrical Engineering, University of Rhode Island, Kingston, RI, 1982	Not included.
Linear Predictive Coding (LPC) Method	Digital Signal Processing Committee, IEEE Acoustics, Speech, and Signal Processing Society, *Programs for* *Digital Signal Processing* (IEEE Press, New York, NY, 1979)	FORTRAN
Waveform Measurements		

Duration
  – Burst
  – High signal-to-noise
  – Trailing edge
Power envelope
  – Detection peak
  – Number of detection crossings
  – Number of peak crossings		

Rise time
  – Rise time
  – Rise rate
  – Peak rise time
  – Peak rise rate
Fall time
  – Fall time
  – Fall rate
  – Peak fall time
  – Peak fall rate
Burst interval
	Appendix B	Not included.

Kurtosis of time series	W. H. Press, B. P. Flannery, S. A. Teukolsky and W. T. Vetterling, *Numerical Recipes – The Art of* *Scientific Computing* (Cambridge University Press, Cambridge, 1986)	FORTRAN

Technique	Reference for description of algorithm	Source code available
• Frequency-Waveform Representation		
Nonparametric Methods		
Complex Demodulation	Digital Signal Processing Committee, IEEE Acoustics, Speech, and Signal Processing Society, *Programs for Digital Signal Processing* (IEEE Press, New York, NY, 1979)	FORTRAN
Discrete Fourier Transform	W. H. Press, B. P. Flannery, S. A. Teukolsky and W. T. Vetterling, *Numerical Recipes – The Art of Scientific Computing* (Cambridge University Press, Cambridge, 1986)	FORTRAN
Discrete Hartley Transform	H. V. Sorensen, D. L. Jones, C. S. Burrus and M.T. Heideman, On Computing the Discrete Hartley Transform, *IEEE Trans. Acoust. Speech Signal Process.* **33** (1985) 1231–1238	FORTRAN
Narrow-band Filtering	Digital Signal Processing Committee, IEEE Acoustics, Speech, and Signal Processing Society, *Programs for Digital Signal Processing* (IEEE Press, New York, NY, 1979)	FORTRAN
Short-time Fourier Transform (STFT)	L. R. Rabiner and R. W. Schafer, *Digital Processing of Speech Signals* (Prentice-Hall, Englewood Cliffs, NJ, 1978)	Not included.
Short-time Periodogram	L. R. Rabiner and R. W. Schafer, *Digital Processing of Speech Signals* (Prentice-Hall, Englewood Cliffs, NJ, 1978)	Not included.
Parametric Methods		
ARMA Model Spectral Estimation	S. L. Marple, Jr., *Digital Spectral Analysis* (Prentice-Hall, Englewood Cliffs, NJ, 1987)	FORTRAN
Burg's Method for Spectral Estimation	S. L. Marple, Jr., *Digital Spectral Analysis* (Prentice-Hall, Englewood Cliffs, NJ, 1987)	FORTRAN
Kumaresan–Prony Method for Spectral Estimation	R. F. Barrett and D. R. A. McMahon, Comparison of frequency estimators for underwater acoustic data, *J. Acoust. Soc. Am.* **79** (1986) 1461–1471	Not included.

Technique	Reference for description of algorithm	Source code available
Pisarenko Harmonic Decomposition (PHD)	S. L. Marple, Jr., *Digital Spectral Analysis* (Prentice-Hall, Englewood Cliffs, NJ, 1987)	FORTRAN
Prony's Method for Spectral Estimation	S. L. Marple, Jr., *Digital Spectral Analysis* (Prentice-Hall, Englewood Cliffs, NJ, 1987)	FORTRAN

Waveform Measurements
Specified Tonals
  – Number of tonals
  – Center frequency
  – Peak S/N
  – Bandwidth
  – Tonal power		

Broadband (BB)
  – Number of broadbands
  – BB power weighted
  – Center frequency
  – BB peak S/N
  – BB bandwidth
  – BB power sum
  – Percent BB power
	Appendix B	Not included.

• Time-Frequency Representation		
Amplitude Maximum of the Envelope (ME)	K. Kodera et al., An analysis of time-varying signals with small BT values, *IEEE Trans. Acoust. Speech Signal Process.* **26** (1978) 64–76	Not included.
Amplitude Maximum of the Spectrum (MS)	K. Kodera et al., An analysis of time-varying signals with small BT values, *IEEE Trans. Acoust. Speech Signal Process.* **26** (1978) 64–76	Not included.
Modified Moving Window Method (MMWM)	K. Kodera, et al. An analysis of time-varying signals with small BT values, *IEEE Trans. Acoust. Speech Signal Process.* **26** (1978) 64–76	Not included.
Moving Window Method (MWM)	K. Kodera et al., An analysis of time-varying signals with small BT values, *IEEE Trans. Acoust. Speech Signal Process.* **26** (1978) 64–76	Not included.
Wigner–Ville Distribution (WVD)	N. Yen, Time and frequency representation of acoustic signals by means of the Wigner distribution function: Implementation and interpretation, *J. Acoust. Soc. Am.* **81** (1986) 1841-1850	Not included.

Appendix B. Waveform Measurements

B.1. Introduction

The purpose of this appendix is to present time and frequency domain features which may be used to characterize transient signals. This grouping of features is defined as a waveform measurement.

All features are measured on each individual burst. A burst is defined as a continuous time sequence which contains sufficient energy in at least one of the frequency bands of interest. The feature extraction algorithms operate on an edited time segment which contains lead-in and trailing noise. This edited time segment must be provided by a separate detection program.

B.2. Time Domain Waveform Measurements

An edited time segment is obtained from the output of the transient detection program. The data samples are blocked with a blocking size equal to the FFT size used in the detection program. A prescribed number of lead-in blocks and also a minimum number of trailing blocks are transmitted from the detection program.

The lead-in blocks are assumed to contain noise only. They are used to estimate the background noise statistics. The mean and variance of the noise power are computed from samples in each of the lead-in blocks. Samples in the first half of the block adjacent to the signal will be used in these computations in order to protect against bursts which actually start near the end of this block.

Most of the time domain features are measured on the power envelope of the received signal. The only exceptions are the mean and variance of the modulation frequency which are measured from the autocorrelation function. The first step in the feature extraction process is an exponential average of the power time series. The envelope sequence is obtained from the power sequence by

$$e(t) = (1 - \alpha)e(t - \Delta t) + \alpha p(t) \tag{B.1}$$

where α is an input parameter that controls the averaging time. The time averaging is initiated by setting $e(0)$ equal to the noise mean just computed.

B.2.1. *Start/Stop Times*

Although neither the start time nor the stop time are reported features, both are used in the definition of measured features. Both are defined in terms of a detection threshold against noise given by

$$T_{\mathrm{N}} = \mu + N_{\mathrm{SD}} \sqrt{\frac{\alpha}{2 - \alpha}} \, \sigma_{\mathrm{N}} \tag{B.2}$$

where N_{SD} is the number of standard deviations above the mean noise level to set the threshold. The variance in the noise has been reduced by the factor $\alpha/(2 - \alpha)$

due to the exponential time averaging. The default value for N_{SD} should be set to achieve the desired false alarm probability.

The start time is defined basically as the time where the power envelope crosses the detection threshold.

The stop time is the time beyond which the power envelope remains predominantly below the detection threshold.

B.2.2. *Duration*

There are four features which measure the burst duration.

- *Block Duration.* This feature is simply the number of blocks which passed the detection threshold as determined by the detection program. No computation is performed in the feature extractor. The value of this feature should be passed from the detection program.

- *Burst Duration.* If both the start time and the stop time were found, then the Burst Duration is defined as the difference of these two times.

- *High Signal-to-Noise Duration.* This feature is determined by measuring the time difference between the first and last points which have power sufficiently close to the peak power of the burst. The Peak Threshold is defined by

$$T_{\mathrm{P}} = T_{\mathrm{N}} + K_{\mathrm{R}}(P - T_{\mathrm{N}}) , \tag{B.3}$$

where T_{N} is the noise threshold obtained from Eq. (B.1), P is the peak power, and k_{R} is an input parameter which specifies how close to the peak to set the threshold. If $k_{\mathrm{R}} = 0.25$, then at high signal-to-noise ratios, the Peak Threshold is approximately 6 dB down from the peak, and the High Signal-to-Noise Duration corresponds to the outermost points which are within 6 dB of the peak. For bursts where the peak power is small (less than 6 dB), the definition in Eq. (3) still allows the High Signal-to-Noise Duration to be measured, as long as the peak is above the detection threshold.

- *Trailing Edge Duration.* This feature is a measure of how much longer the end of the burst is detectable in the time domain than in the frequency domain. It is defined only when the stop time has been found. Specifically, it is the difference between the stop time as defined above and the time corresponding to the end of the stop block. If the stop time occurs during the stop block, then the Trailing Edge Duration feature is set equal to zero.

B.2.3. *Power Envelope*

This set of features relates to variations in the power envelope.

- *Detection Peak.* This feature is defined as the peak power level within the burst divided by the mean noise level.

- *Number of Detection Crossings.* This feature is determined by the number of times the power envelope sequence falls below the detection threshold T_{N} in Eq. (B.2) (not including the final drop which indicates the end of the burst).

- *Number of Peak Crossings.* This feature is defined as the number of times the power envelope sequence falls below the Peak Threshold T_{P} in Eq. (B.3) (not including the final drop which indicates the end of the burst).

B.2.4. *Rise Time*

- *Rise Time.* This feature is defined as the time difference between the first crossing of the Peak Threshold and the start time.

- *Rise Rate.* This feature is determined by the rate at which the power level increases. It is given by

$$\text{Rise Time} = \frac{10 \, \log(\text{Peak Threshold/Detection Threshold})}{\text{Rise Time}} \tag{B.4}$$

- *Peak Rise Time.* This feature is defined as the time difference between the peak in the power sequence and the start time.

- *Peak Rise Rate.* This feature is given by

$$\text{Peak Rise Rate} = \frac{10 \, \log(\text{Detection Peak/Detection Threshold})}{\text{Peak Rise Time}} \tag{B.5}$$

B.2.5. *Fall Time*

- *Fall Time.* This feature is the time difference between the stop time and the last downward crossing of the Fall Threshold. The Fall Threshold T_{f} is defined by

$$T_{\mathrm{f}} = T_{\mathrm{N}} + K_{\mathrm{f}}(P - T_{\mathrm{N}}) , \tag{B.6}$$

where T_{N} is the noise threshold (Eq. (B.2)), P is the peak power, and k_{f} is an input parameter which specifies how close to the peak to set the threshold.

- *Fall Rate.* This feature measures the rate at which the power level falls off. It is given by

$$\text{Fall Rate} = \frac{10 \, \log(\text{Fall Threshold/Detection Threshold})}{\text{Fall Time}} \tag{B.7}$$

- *Peak Fall Time.* This feature is determined by the time difference between the stop time and the peak in the power sequence.

- *Peak Fall Rate.* The Peak Fall Rate is given by

$$\text{Peak Fall Rate} = \frac{10 \, \log(\text{Dection Peak/Detection Threshold})}{\text{Peak Fall Time}} \tag{B.8}$$

B.2.6. *Burst Interval*

All of the previously defined parameters are measured for a single burst as determined by the detection code.

- *Burst Interval.* This feature is determined by the time difference between the start times of the consecutive bursts. It is an array of time intervals between each of the detected bursts.

B.3. Frequency Domain Waveform Measurements

B.3.1. *Introduction*

The power spectrum is obtained by first performing an FFT on the time series data. The power spectrum is normalized by the background noise before any measurements are made. Each burst is divided into three regions: a start region, an end region, and a region encompassing the entire burst. Measurements are made for each region. When the start time cannot be determined from the time series data, then the blocking for the FFT is the same as the original blocking from the detection code.

Depending on the burst duration and the choices for input parameters, Start Blocks (N_S) and End Blocks (N_L), the start and end regions may overlap. Whenever either the start region or the end region is identical to the entire event, then parameters are reported only for the event region.

When the start time can be determined from the data, the time series data are reblocked prior to performing the FFT. The data sample corresponding to the start time becomes the first time sample of the reblocked data for the first FFT. Thus, the first FFT is not contaminated by lead-in noise. In general, the stop time will not occur at the end of the last FFT block and thus a percentage of time samples for the last FFT block could be noise. If the percentage of time samples which contain signals is less than some input parameter value, then the last block is not used for spectral measurements.

Spectral parameters are measured for each non-redundant region. Three types of parameters are measured in each region: parameters associated with specified tonals, parameters associated with the broadband spectrum, and parameters associated with tonals other than in specified bands. All parameters are measured on the spectrum after averaging the FFT's over the region of interest. For comparison, the parameters associated with the specified tonals are also measured on each individual FFT and the average of the individual measurements is reported.

B.3.2. *Specified Tonals*

This set of parameters measure features associated with tonals in specific frequency bands of interest. The number of bands to be searched, the minimum and maximum frequency for each band must be specified upon program initiation.

The strongest tonal in each band is reported if it satisfies certain criteria as outlined below.

For each specified band, the bin with the highest signal-to-noise ratio is found. If this peak signal-to-noise ratio is below the specified detection threshold, then missing values are reported for the tonal in the band. The detection threshold is given by

$$T = \frac{T_{\mathrm{T}}}{\sqrt{\mathrm{Nr\ FFTs\ Integrated}}} \tag{B.9}$$

where the tonal threshold T_{T} is an input which corresponds to the detection threshold with no integration.

- *Peak S/N.* This feature is determined if the peak signal-to-noise ratio exceeds the threshold.

- *Center Frequency.* This feature is the frequency of the peak bin.

- *Bandwidth.* This feature's measurement algorithm depends on the peak S/N. If the S/N is less than 3 dB, a missing value is reported for the bandwidth. If the S/N is greater that 9 dB, then the 6 dB bandwidth is measured. This is done by finding the first bin on either side of the peak bin which is at least 6 dB below the peak S/N and converting the bin separation to a frequency bandwidth. If the peak S/N is between 3 dB and 9 dB, then the 3 dB bandwidth is measured and converted to a 6 dB bandwidth by multiplying by $\sqrt{2}$. To ensure that a tonal has been found and not just some broadband energy, the requirement is made that the measured bandwidth be less than some maximum allowed tonal bandwidth specified in an input parameter.

- *Tonal Power.* This feature is defined as the total power contained within the 6 dB points of the tonal. Its measurement requires that the bandwidth not be a missing value.

- *Number of Tonals.* This feature is defined as the number of specified bands that contain a tonal with the feature, Peak S/N, not set to missing value.

B.3.3. *Broadband (BB)*

Events which may be of interest may be characterized by broad bands of energy. A spectrum may have bands of energy which lie above a threshold given by

$$T = \frac{T_{\mathrm{BB}}}{\sqrt{\mathrm{Nr\ FFTs\ Integrated}}} \tag{B.10}$$

where the broadband threshold T_{BB} is an input parameter which corresponds to the detection threshold with no integration.

Each band is specified by the lower, f_{l} , and upper, f_{u}, frequencies where the threshold is crossed.

- *Number of Broadbands.* This feature identifies the edited number of broad bands of energy present in the spectrum.

- *BB Power Sum.* The total power in each band is computed by summing the power for all bins between f_l and f_u. This feature represents the power in each of the two strongest bands.

- *Percent BB Power.* This feature represents the BB Power Sum for each of the two bands divided by the power in all accepted bands.

- *BB Peak S/N.* This feature represents the peak signal-to-noise level in the band.

- *BB Power Weighted Center Frequency.* This feature provides a measure of the center frequency of the band. It is defined as

$$
f_\mathrm{BB} = \frac{\displaystyle\sum_{i=1}^{\mu} f_i, P_i}{\displaystyle\sum_{i=1}^{\mu} P_i} \, ,
\tag{B.11}
$$

where f_i, P_i are the frequency of the ith bin.

- *BB Bandwidth.* This feature is determined by the frequency difference between the outermost crossings of a peak threshold defined by

$$
T_\mathrm{P} = T + k_\mathrm{BB}(\text{BB Peak S/N} - T) \, ,
\tag{B.12}
$$

where k_BB is an input. If $k_\mathrm{BB} = 0.25$, then at high S/N, the BB Bandwidth feature measures the outermost 6 dB down points.

Handbook of Pattern Recognition and Computer Vision, pp. 569–594
Eds. C. H. Chen, L. F. Pau and P. S. P. Wang

CHAPTER 3.4

ANALYSIS OF ECONOMIC AND BUSINESS INFORMATION

CLAUDIO GIANOTTI

Via R. Birolli 7, 20125 Milano, Italy

Real-world economic and business applications are in general demanding information processing tasks, whereby high volumes of incomplete, noisy data and high information costs are often the most remarkable features. Hence the need for advanced information analysis methods, such as those developed in the pattern recognition literature. This chapter shows real-world applications of a number of methods, most of them still quite new to the economic and financial analysts. The focus is not on the full coverage of all relevant information analysis approaches (a challenging task indeed), rather on the understanding of how the underlying data structures and data representations influence the interpretation activity. To this purpose, the presentation is organized by application domains, where we address broadly different areas including as examples real-time trading, financial analysis and long-term economic analysis, as well as the related data and interpretation goals. Correspondingly, several different methods used in these application domains are described and shown at work, including: statistics, grammars, neural networks, and qualitative modeling.

Keywords: Finance, trading, economic reasoning, syntactic pattern recognition, correspondence analysis, neural networks, qualitative reasoning.

1. Introduction

Several considerations suggest that pattern recognition is relevant as a theoretical approach, and that pattern recognition algorithms can be turned into viable tools for the analysis of economic and financial data.

First, pattern recognition is useful to overcome the lack of theoretical models, in that model structures are replaced by classes of models, thus avoiding the need to provide substantial details on these structures beyond a class label [1]. As one example, the exercise of classifying institutions into broad risk classes for insurance or lending purposes do often rely on the statistical analysis of past cases, the causal impact of each financial ratio being mostly obscure (see Section 3.2.1 below). As another example, graphical patterns in financial time series are identified and empirically related to the underlying economic or psychological trading motivations, and then used for buy/sell decisions (see Section 2 below).

Second, a distinguishing feature of most economic and financial applications, including the ones mentioned in the above examples, is the high cost of knowledge and information. As a consequence, the investment in advanced data interpretation

569

tools is generally more than compensated by the savings in data acquisition and the increased success rate of the decision making process. More specifically, pattern recognition allows the selection of the most relevant features, thus leading to the savings induced by collecting only the raw information needed to estimate these features. Under this viewpoint, pattern recognition has a twofold advantage: from the one side, it paves the way to sound and viable data interpretation tools; from the other side, the said tools tend to be robust with respect to incomplete and/or noisy data, thus further relaxing the need for precise, and potentially costly, information or modeling work. This is not the case with other popular analysis tools, such as numeric models or econometric or business modeling.

Third, pattern recognition methods can in general be used incrementally on a sequence of patterns, and are easily coupled with learning facilities, thus leading to adaptive tools (see Section 3.2 below). Learning is again quite a desirable capability, since it eases the data acquisition bottleneck, provides a way to tackle real-time applications, and reduces the need for sound data. It is furthermore attractive from a theoretical standpoint as well, since financial and economic experts do indeed adapt their decision criteria to the status of the environment, and only agree on class definitions (qualitative) rather than on more detailed model structures. Typical examples are investment decisions vs. inflation, or trading decisions vs. market liquidity and volatility.

Finally, the flexibility to deal with both numeric and qualitative patterns greatly enhances the application domains of pattern recognition.

In spite of the above-mentioned advantages, there has been only limited use of pattern recognition theory in the economic and financial community, except for statistical pattern recognition, and the related concepts of taxonomy and clustering, with discriminant analysis as the most popular method: see the classical example in [2], as well as [3]. More recent application-oriented developments tend to focus on adaptive algorithms and especially neural networks [4–6], as well as on the need to integrate pattern recognition methods into more complex computer programs, also addressing:

(i)   feature extraction using expert guidance or knowledge [7–9], or advanced natural language processing methods [10, 11], or finally causal models [12–14];

(ii) inference of new qualitative knowledge, typically through a logic formalism [15,16];

(iii) handling methods for different types of information, e.g. qualitative and quantitative, certain and uncertain, etc., coming from different, sometimes inconsistent, data sources [17–20];

(iv) interfaces to knowledge-based systems, typically rule-based [21] or frame-based [22,23].

The know-how to design, implement and interface the above-listed components, while available within the pattern recognition or artificial intelligence communities, is in some cases not mature for field applications, and in others not sufficiently widespread to warrant consideration among economic and financial practitioners.

This chapter takes an application-oriented approach by presenting a number of representative worked-out case studies, whereby pattern recognition methods are embedded into full decision-support systems, whenever feasible. Consequently, it is organized by application domain, rather than by the nature of the tools used:

- Section 2 addresses the rapidly growing field of pattern recognition in financial trading,
- Section 3 highlights some applications to financial analysis,
- Section 4 deals with economic modeling.

This organization is just indicative: first, other application domains exist, including insurance, tax planning and banking, see [4] for a survey; second, useful approaches in one domain may be quite valuable in other domains as well. However, the key point here is to stress the dependency of methods on data and problem specifications, rather than the opposite.

2. Applications to Financial Trading

One increasingly popular method in analyzing time series of traded stocks or financial indexes is technical, or chart, analysis, whereby the curves representing price, index, ratio, and volume fluctuations over time are studied, in order to infer some investment decisions from the local and/or global shape of the curves [24]. It is therefore a two stage process, with:

(i) visual segmentation of the curve(s) into primitive shapes significant to the chart theory, such as valleys, peaks, steep rise or fall, tops and bottoms, etc.

(ii) a knowledge-based correspondence established between the time sequence of such primitive shapes found in the curve, and specific investment decisions, including forecasts or trend assessment.

This approach marks a significant shift from the classical statistical analysis of time series, mostly aiming at summarizing the huge amount of numerical data into some significant indicators (such as averages, variances, etc.), or at estimating selected parameters. It also marks a change in perspective from fundamental analysis, i.e. forecasting based on macro- and micro-economic indicators (inflation, balance sheets, industry growth rate). The purpose here is not to compare the relative merits of the different approaches, but rather to show that automatic curve interpretation according to technical analysis is feasible and can lead to useful tools. As of today, chart analysis is mostly performed by hand and off-line; by increasing trading activity across different time zones, however, back-office processing is getting less important compared to real-time capabilities. Technical analysis has the further advantage of lending itself well to automation: chartist trading tools are quite manageable, since very little information is needed besides time series.

Sections 2.1 to 2.6 below are largely based on [4]. Although specifically developed for the trading of interest rate instruments, the described system is applicable to most time series, or more generally, to pattern recognition tasks in which patterns can be partially ordered according to their structure (such as time, volume, levels, risks, etc.). Section 4 below shows a similar example of this.

2.1. *Technical Analysis through Syntactic Pattern Recognition*

The relevant curve shapes are described through a grammar G [25]. Its role is to provide a method for relating the available price curve(s) to technical patterns. The set of technical patterns significant to the analyst is first defined: this is the set V_T of terminal symbols. Different sets V_T may be specified according to the purpose of the analysis and the specific experience of the analyst. However, there is a very limited number of basic graphic components relevant to all technical patterns, and these are the most obvious choices for the elements of V_T (terminal symbols are conventionally written in uppercase):

$$V_T = \{\text{UPTREND, DOWNTREND, FLAT, GAP-UP, GAP-DOWN, ...}\}.$$

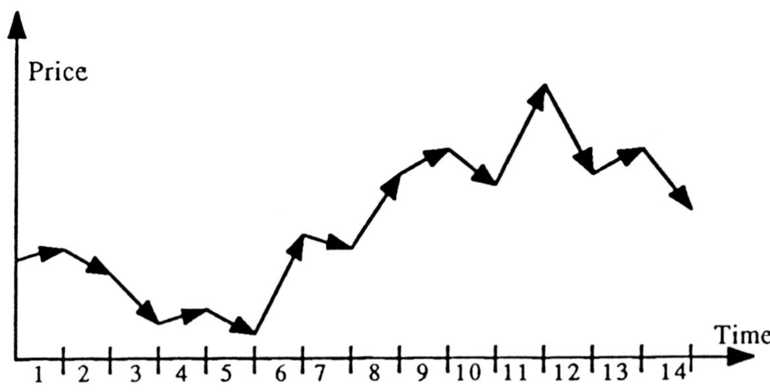

Fig. 1. A price curve as a sequence of terminal symbols.

A curve described as a sequence of terminal symbols is pictured in Fig. 1. However, chart analysts generally look for more complex and informative patterns. These are sequences of terminal symbols complying with given specifications, and are represented in G as nonterminal symbols. Referring again to Fig. 1, the sequence of terminal symbols in time intervals three to six is a significant pattern called "double bottom". Nonterminal symbols are partially ordered in a hierarchy, so that simpler nonterminal symbols are the building blocks of other, more complex ones. Quite expectedly, the set V_N of nonterminal symbols may vary widely among different applications. A simple example of this is:

$$V_N = \{\text{peak, valley, head-and-shoulders top/bottom, double top/bottom, ...}\}.$$

Nonterminal symbols are conventionally written in lowercase. The initial curve segment itself is a nonterminal symbol conventionally referred to as the initial symbol, and denoted s.

Finally, a set P of rewriting rules specifies how a nonterminal symbol (including the initial symbol) is to be substituted for terminal or nonterminal symbols. Each rewriting rule p_N is thus a formal and explicit definition of a pattern as a sequence of one or more simpler patterns. The analysis is completed once the curve is rewritten as a sequence of terminal symbols from V_T, i.e. as a sentence. Examples of rewriting rules are:

p_1:	valley	$\rightarrow$	DOWNTREND UPTREND
p_2:	peak	$\rightarrow$	UPTREND DOWNTREND
p_3:	down	$\rightarrow$	down DOWNTREND | DOWNTREND
p_4:	up	$\rightarrow$	up UPTREND | UPTREND

where the symbol "$\rightarrow$" means "can be substituted with" or "can be rewritten as" and the symbol " $\vert$ " stands for the exclusive OR (i.e. "a $\vert$ b" means: a or b, but not both).

The rewriting rules P describe not only the patterns, but also the relations among them, as anticipated by the technical analysis theory. For example, a head-and-shoulders bottom may be followed by uptrends, flags, or other bullish configurations, but may not be followed by downtrends, double bottoms or other bearish configurations. Should this be the case, then either an alternative interpretation for the head-and-shoulders pattern is found, or the input curve is rejected, i.e. not every input curve is a valid curve according to the above defined grammar G.

The process of interpreting a price curve through a grammar G is called parsing. Examples of simple parsers are readily available in the computer science literature, especially in books about formal languages [26,27]. The process is basically one of tree construction, in which the root of the tree is the initial symbol s and the leaves of the tree are the terminal symbols in the segmented sequence, see Fig. 2. The most interesting part of the algorithm however is the identification of the intermediate nodes of the tree, i.e. the relevant nonterminal symbols, whereby the parser carries out the pattern recognition process.

The parsing output is then either the parsing tree itself, or the ordered sequence $\pi = (p_0, p_1, \ldots, p_q)$ of substitutions. In the case of context-free grammars, i.e. grammars whose rewriting rules have the form:

$$a \in V_N \rightarrow b \in (V_T \cup V_N)^*,$$

simple parsing algorithms can be given [28], where the initial symbol s is expanded by successively substituting nonterminals to try to fit the sequence to be parsed [29]. More complex algorithms are needed in the case of context sensitive grammars, in which substitutions are subject to restrictions.

The above procedure does not fully specify all the parameters available to the analyst. For instance, the time frame of the analysis is still to be settled, by associating a time duration to the terminal symbols. But even after all parameters

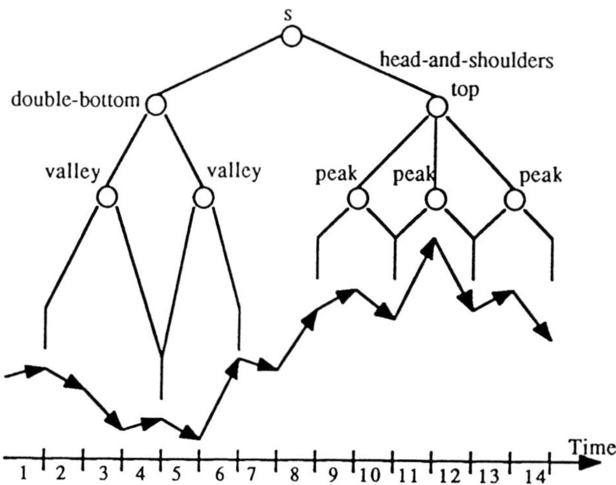

Fig. 2. Parse tree of a price curve.

have been specified, the parser output need not be unique, and in general it is not. Alternative parsings correspond to different curve interpretations consistent with technical analysis.

2.2. *Curve Segmentation*

The input to the parser described in Section 2.1 above is a sequence of terminal symbols, derived from the available market data through segmentation. As the whole burden of the pattern recognition task is on the grammar G and the associated parsing algorithm, the segmentation algorithm need not be a complicated one. In one simple implementation, it would just partition the input curve into time intervals of the desired length and assign one terminal symbol to each interval, depending on the price difference at the interval ends (increasing, decreasing, stable price). This process may be preceded by averaging, filtering or other curve smoothing methods.

Noise in the price curve patterns may nevertheless lead to incorrect segmentations. A measure of likelihood or similarity is then required to make the comparisons, whereby the parser must look for allowable segmentations according to the grammar G, which are the most similar to the given noisy one. The parser can then perform substitutions, deletions and replacements of terminal symbols within the input sequence, according to the following rules:

(i)   substitution rule p in V_T:

   p substitution: $A, B \in V_T, A \neq B$: $\alpha A \beta \rightarrow \alpha B \beta$

(ii) deletion rule p in V_T:
$$p \text{ deletion:} \qquad A \in V_T: \qquad \alpha A \beta \to \alpha \cdot \beta$$
(iii) insertion rule p in V_T:
$$p \text{ insertion:} \qquad A \in V_T: \qquad \alpha \beta \to \alpha A \beta \,,$$

where α and β denote any sequence of terminal symbols. The most likely interpolation for the noisy input sequence is then the closest (most similar) allowable sequence within G. One such similarity measure is the Levenshtein distance $d(x, y)$ between two sequences of terminal and nonterminal symbols [30]:

$$d(x, y) = \text{Min}\,(n_s, n_d, n_i)\,,$$

which is the smallest number of transformations required to derive one sentence from the other, where:

- n_s is the number of substitutions
- n_d is the number of deletions
- n_i is the number of insertions.

For the application at hand, it is convenient to improve the definition of $d(x, y)$ by allowing the possibility of weighting the terminal symbols to be replaced, inserted or deleted according to their position within a candidate pattern. This is because the technical analyst is more likely to accept noise in non-critical pattern features than in critical ones. Interpolations assuming noise in key pattern features should therefore be given a lower priority, even though they result in the lowest $d(x, y)$ value. Allowable noisy sections within each pattern may then be used to focus the minimum distance computations.

$d(x, y)$ in its plain or weighted form is then used as the basis for error-correcting parsing such that, given a noisy segmentation Y, this is replaced by the allowable segmentation W with minimum distance from Y [31,32]:

$$d(W, Y) = \min_{z} \{d(Z, Y)|Z \in L(G)]\}\,,$$

where $L(G)$ denotes the set of all correct segmentations. References [31,32] give calculation algorithms for $d(W, Y)$. The overall result is an error-correcting parser, which will again work top-down, but with provisions for operating on sequences derivable from the ob served curve by substitution, deletion, and insertion error grammar rules, and for accumulating the similarity values.

2.3. *Trading Decisions*

Decisions based on technical analysis are derived from a study of the curve shape and the price levels at critical positions. Given a sequence of primitive curve patterns (i.e. terminal symbols), two filtering procedures can be defined, one for shape and one for price levels:

(i) shape-filters count the number of terminal symbols in the parsed sequence, their relative positions and their durations in time, and produce a list of decisions relevant to the situation at hand;

(ii) level-filters define a set of intervals on the price scale, assign the terminal symbols to the intervals, and make it possible to detect the crossing of significant price levels.

The final decision is a result of the filter outputs, as well as of expert rules, which are extracted from experts and collected into a knowledge base. More precisely, filters help to select relevant rules and to weight them. Rules can be widely classified into:

(i) *Analysis rules.* These are rules which complement the analysis by generating overall Buy (resp. Sell) signals or other derived indicators. For example,
   - a Buy signal is generated if the price $\text{Close}(N+1)$ exceeds the highest close of the last N days; a Sell signal is generated if the price $\text{Close}(N+1)$ is lower than the lowest close of the last N days

(ii) *Decision rules.* These are rules which suggest a trading as well as portfolio management decisions. For example:
   - When a new Buy or Sell signal is generated, the old position is liquidated simultaneously.
   - If a peak peak-1 is followed by a valley, and the bottom of the valley-1 is above 62% of the top of the peak; AND, if a subsequent peak-2 following valley-1 exceeds peak-1, peak-1 is impulsive, then buy (Elliot Wave Theory rule, [33]).

Conflicting trade indications are quite normal in the daily practice of analysis, and may also arise within the knowledge base, as the result of conflicting rules: examples include concurrent Buy/Sell signals, and buy, sell, hold advices. They are usually resolved by attributing weights (i.e. credibility measures) to the supporting evidence for each competing decision and by cumulating the weights over non-conflicting decisions. The best-supported course of action is then selected. An alternative approach would relate conflicting evidence to trading risk, and use competing, but insufficiently supported, decisions as a suggestion that the transaction's amount, time horizon or stop-loss policies need to be reviewed and made more conservative.

2.4. *Multiple Curve Analysis*

Chart analysis is rarely limited to just one curve: instead, a number of indicators based on several price, earnings, volume, and interest rate curves are first generated. Decisions then summarize the overall results of the analysis. Typical examples are the validation of price patterns through volume indicators, and the well-know interrelations between a stock index (e.g. the Standard and Poor index), short and long term interest rates (e.g. the 3-month T-Bill resp. the 30-year T-Bond future contracts) and the price of commodities (e.g. the Commodity Research Bureau index). Other common examples involve the joint study of a price curve and of one or more derived curves, usually moving averages.

Multiple curves can be analyzed within the framework in Sections 2.1 and 2.2 above, provided each element in V_T is replaced by a set, consisting of possible combinations of terminal symbols, one for each curve to be part of the analysis:

$$V_T^N = \otimes \, V_T = \{(A_1, \ldots, A_N) | A_i \in V_T\} \, .$$

2.5. *Learning*

Learning is carried out off-line and aims at optimizing the parameters of the analysis, adjusting them for:

(i)   patterns, volumes, volatility typical of a specific market (e.g. market behaviour close to settlement dates)

(ii) major market shifts due to critical events, changes in the regulations, changes in the definitions (e.g. introduction of a future contract on a traded stock or commodity)

(iii) changes in the analysis goals (e.g. shifts in the time horizon).

Parameters to be optimized include the smoothing and threshold detection algorithms, the parsing rules (e.g. the definition of the nonterminal symbols), the decision rules, the time basis of moving averages, etc. Optimization criteria over a given time span include the number of successful trades, the return generated by each trade, etc.

Due to the large amount of parameters involved, only limited learning is feasible by today's technology and understanding. What is especially missing is a theoretical guidance for which parameters should be varied (and over which range), in order to optimize a set of trading objectives.

2.6. *Conclusion*

A system similar to the one described in this section was developed over 1987–1988 as a part of a government sponsored project [34]; more recently, a similar product, however with emphasis on portfolio management, was launched by Wyatt Software in 1989; very recently also, the idea of using a syntactic grammar has been presented again [35]. The implementation in [34] uses a mixed object-oriented programming (Smalltalk/V) and a logic programming environment (Prolog/V) both by Digitalk [36], running on a standard personal computer with accelerator board to enhance the real time performances.

3. Applications to Financial Analysis

Financial analysis is an important domain of the application of pattern recognition, and the one which has attracted the most interest since the very beginning of pattern recognition applications to economics [2] or finance. This is due to the fact that financial institutions are naturally described by a set of quantitative or qualitative features (balance sheet entries, financial ratios, organizational structure), mostly changing over time, which can be easily understood as patterns, and consequently processed globally, rather than sequentially feature by feature.

Furthermore, it is an analyst's goal to compare and evaluate the performance of a number of companies or stocks, in order to group companies and stocks with similar economic or financial behaviour and evolution. Such an exercise is for instance important in portfolio selection based on fundamental analysis. One good example is the classification of a company according to its development stage (conquesting, improving, implosive, development, bankruptcy, declining), based on the industry's growth rate as well as e.g. a 12-feature vector consisting of the following company data: size, return on equity, return on total capital, debt ratio, profit margin on sales, capital investment, reinvested earnings, P/E ratio, Beta ratio, stock price to book value, export rate, resource utilization [37,38].

With respect to the trading applications described in Section 2 above, financial analysis features longer time horizons as well as high-dimensional pattern vectors. Data compression then plays a key role, both as a visualization technique, and as an analysis tool. Section 3.1 shows how correspondence analysis can be used to achieve both goals. Section 3.2 on the contrary stresses learning as a method of inferring causalities when theoretical models are lacking, and neural networks as a suitable computational tool.

3.1. *Correspondence Analysis*

Correspondence analysis [39,40] is a statistical compression, learning as well as pattern recognition method applicable to random correspondences among two or more sets, e.g. a set of individuals and a set of observations/measurements on the individuals. Correspondence analysis is strongly related to other statistical methods, such as discriminant analysis, canonical analysis, etc., while being in a certain sense more general and flexible.

Its primary purpose is to highlight the correlations among observations, by computing a set of independent random variables (called factors) able to describe the structures of the data at hand and to maximize the sample variance; both the individuals and the observations/measurements are then represented in the factors' space. The end result is a set of quantitative correspondences among individuals, observations, as well as individuals and observations, which are captured as distances in the factors' space. Class assignment based on proximity then becomes possible. The method can also be used incrementally, in the sense that the factors are computed from a training set, and the number of factors is likewise incrementally increased to higher detail or subtlety levels, while new data are easily fitted into the factors' space through a linear transformation. The whole analysis can be easily implemented in a computer program, although the interpretation of the factors may be critical and require some skills.

The role of correspondence analysis in financial analysis is shown through a time dependent example [41], whereby eight Danish banks are studied over the years 1969–1973 based on 33 indicators and ratios. For a few of them information was obtained by referring to the Danish monetary market, and for the remainder it was taken from each bank's annual report. Let J be the set of features (indicators and ratios) and I the set of individuals (banks). Then:

- $\text{card}(J) = p = 33$
- $\text{card}(I) = n = 8 \times 5 = 40$.

Note how each of the five discrete time measurements of a bank's features (one per year in the period 1969–1973) is considered as a new individual, thus leading to the shown cardinality of I. In this way, an analysis in the discrete time domain can be transformed into a time-independent one, and time can be ignored for the remainder of the discussion, except for the final interpretation and display of the results. In the following, whenever reference is made to an "individual", this extended definition is always meant.

Sections 3.1.1 to 3.1.4 below explain in a step-by-step fashion how correspondence analysis is carried out.

3.1.1. *Definition of the contingency table*

The available data for each individual can be represented in a $p * n$ table, with elements $t(i, j)$, $i \in I$, $j \in J$. It is customary to standardize the measure units for the features j, since the analysis is sensitive to the absolute value levels. In the present case, all absolute values are transformed into ratios by using total assets as a normalization factor. However, domain independent normalizations are also available, e.g. based on the standard deviation of a given feature. A discrete probability measure $p(i, j)$ can now be defined from the standardized $t(i, j)$ as follows:

$$p(i, j) = \frac{t(i, j)}{\sum_{i,j} t(i, j)} \, .$$

The values $p(i, j)$ build a $I * J$ table, the contingency table, which is the starting point of correspondence analysis. Weights and other corrections can be introduced at this stage, by applying a function g to the $p(i, j)$ before entering them into the contingency table:

$$r(i, j) = g[i, j, p(i, j)] \, ,$$

with:

$$r(i, j) \geq 0$$
$$\sum_{i,j} r(i, j) = 1 \, ,$$

i.e. r must be a probability measure.

3.1.2. *Representation in the feature space*

Banks are represented as weighted points in the feature space, with coordinates $x(i, j)$ and weight M_i defined as follows:

$$\forall j \in J \qquad x(i, j) = \frac{p(i, j)}{p(i, .)p(., j)} - 1 = \frac{p(j/i)}{p(., j)} - 1$$

$$X(I, J) \triangleq \{x(i, j)\}$$

$$M_i = p(i, .), \tag{3.1}$$

with

$$p(i, .) : \qquad \text{the marginal probability of } i$$
$$p(., j) : \qquad \text{the marginal probability of } j$$
$$p(j/i) : \qquad \text{the conditional probability of } j \text{ on } i.$$

Definition (3.1) has the following properties:

(i)   Individuals whose features have the same conditional probabilities are mapped into the same point of the feature space, in spite of different feature values. This is seen for instance in the case of two banks having equal balance sheet data up to a scaling factor.

(ii)   In the case of independence, i.e.

$$p(i, j) = p(i)\, p(j),$$

the point coordinates $i \in I$ are all zero, and the analysis is not meaningful.

(iii) The definition for $x(i, j)$ is symmetric in i and j: hence it also represents the coordinates of feature points in the space of individuals (banks), with weights:

$$M_j = p(., j),$$

The "distance" h in between the two pattern vectors associated to banks i, is defined as a weighted sum of the Euclidean distance between components:

$$d^2(i, h) = \sum_j p(., j)[x(h, j) - x(i, j)^2. \tag{3.2}$$

It is easily shown that the above definition satisfies the usual axioms for a distance measure. Based on (3.2), similarities among individuals can be expressed as proximity relations.

3.1.3. *Data compression*

Like most linear signal compression methods, correspondence analysis considers a pattern vector $\mathbf{x}(i, .)$ as the weighted summation of a number of basis vectors, and provides a way to select the said basis vectors, so that all or most of the variance of $X(I, J)$ is retained. The general idea is, given the point distribution in the original feature space, to find a different reference system whose axes are positioned along the directions of maximum variance in the said point distribution: hopefully, just a few of the newly computed basis vectors will capture most of the sample variance, while the remaining ones can be dropped. Mathematically, the problem above is formalized as follows:

$$\mathrm{Max}(\mathrm{Var}\ (\mathbf{z}(i, .))$$
$$\mathbf{z}(i, .) = \mathbf{x}(i, .)\ A$$
$$^t AA = I \qquad A^{-1} = {}^t A, \tag{3.3}$$

where $z(i, .)$ is an orthonormal transformation of the row vector $\mathbf{x}(i, .)$, corresponding to a geometrical rotation of the feature space axes, and A is an orthonormal transformation matrix.

It is well-known that variance maximization is achieved if and only if the columns of the transformation matrix A are proportional to the eigenvectors of the covariance matrix C of X:

$$C = \sum_{i=1}^{n} p(i, .)t[\mathbf{x}(i, .) - \mathbf{x}_{\mathrm{av}}][\mathbf{x}(i, .) - \mathbf{x}_{\mathrm{av}}], \tag{3.4}$$

where

$$\mathbf{x}_{\mathrm{av}} = \sum_{i} p(i, .)\mathbf{x}(i, .).$$

In the computation of the variance, care must be taken to use the distance definition in (3.2). Since the average vector $\mathbf{x}_{\mathrm{av}}$ is the null vector at the origin, the variance of $X(I, J)$ is computed as follows:

$$\mathrm{Var}(X(I, J)) = \sum_{i} p(i, .) \sum_{j} p(., j)\left[\frac{p(j/i)}{p(., j)} - 1\right]^2$$
$$\mathrm{Var}(X(I, J)) = \sum_{i} \sum_{j} \left[\frac{p(i, j)}{\sqrt{p(i, .)p(., j)}} - \sqrt{p(i, .)p(., j)}\right]^2, \tag{3.5}$$

which suggests the following definition for the covariance matrix C of X:

$$C = {}^t VV, \tag{3.6}$$

where the elements of V are

$$v(i, j) = \frac{p(i, j)}{\sqrt{p(i, .)p(., j)}} - \sqrt{p(i, .)p(., j)}. \tag{3.7}$$

The variance of the transformed sample Z, $Z(I, J) = \{z(i, j)\}$, defined in (3.3), is then maximized if the columns of the transformation matrix A are equal, up to a normalization factor, to the eigenvectors $\mathbf{u}_i$ of C, defined in (3.6). These are often called the factorial axes, and represent "synthetic features" spanning a new space. The factorial axes, and also the columns of A, can be easily ordered by the amount of variance captured by each of them. To see how this can be done, let's first recall that the total variance of X is given by:

$$\mathrm{Var}(X(I, J)) = \mathrm{Trace}\ (C) = \mathrm{Sum}\ \lambda_i, \tag{3.8}$$

where λ_i are the eigenvalues of C, λ_i is then a measure of the sample variance in the direction pointed to by the corresponding eigenvector $\mathbf{u}_i$. The feature space dimensions can now be reduced, in that only the first m, $m < p$ factorial axes, associated to the m largest eigenvectors, are retained, thus leading to a reduced transformation matrix A_m and reduced transformed sample z_m, equal to the sum in (3.3) restricted to the first m columns of A. The amount of sample variance retained in the reduced space can be precisely computed as follows:

$$\mathrm{Var}(Z_m(I, J) = \frac{\sum_{i=1}^{m} \lambda_i}{\mathrm{Trace}\ (C)}. \tag{3.9}$$

Equation (3.9) is the basis for an acceptance test of the reduced space, since it provides a measure of how much discriminant information is retained (resp. lost) in it.

As a final remark, note that $v(i, j)$, defined in (3.7), and V, defined in (3.6), are symmetric in I and J, which means that:

$$C' = V^{\,t}V$$

can be used to define a reduced, synthetic space of individuals in which features are represented as points. The eigenvalues of C and C' are the same, although the eigenvectors are not. By appropriate scaling, however, the eigenvectors corresponding to the same eigenvalue in both spaces can be superimposed, so that features and individuals can be represented in the same reference system, and proximity relations between individuals and features can be defined. These are significant mainly in the analysis of the causality between observations and individual behaviour.

3.1.4. *Interpretation of correspondence analysis*

Conceptually, each factorial axis corresponds to a "synthetic feature" of the individuals, which is generally not directly observable or measurable, but is derived from a linear combination of the initial pattern features $j \in J$. These "synthetic features" must nevertheless be interpreted. This is an often delicate process, and is illustrated here referring to the Danish bank example introduced in Section 3.1, and described in [41]. As it turns out, the first two factorial axes capture more than 60%

of the total sample variance, which makes it possible to represent the total sample of dimension 40 × 33 in a plane. Figure 3 is a simplified version of the resulting distribution, showing just two typical banks. Note that points corresponding to the features of the same individual bank, at different times, are connected in the order of increasing accounting years to form trajectories over time.

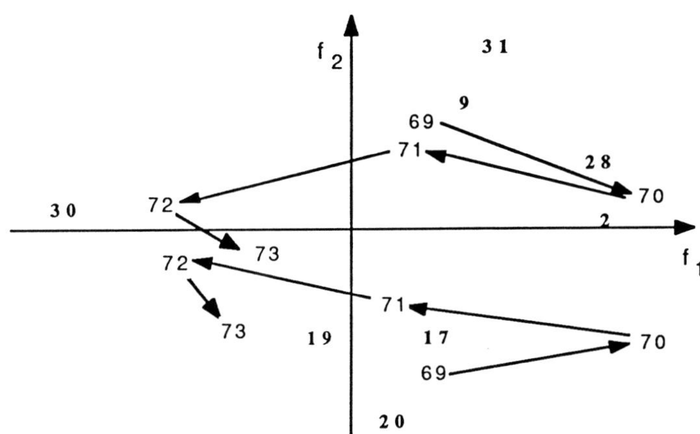

Fig. 3. Time evolution of two banks in the synthetic feature space.

The two factorial axes are then interpreted by studying the coordinates of the pattern features $j \in J$ with respect to them. Most relevant are those features positioned close to each axis and with large positive or negative coordinates:

(i) Positive correlation with f_1 : liquidity/total investment in bonds and shares (feature no. 28); financial revenues/total investment in bonds and shares (feature no. 2). Both show reduced investment in bonds and stocks, and increased portfolios of loans.
Negative correlation with f_1: the monetary mass M_2 (feature no. 30)

(ii) Positive correlation with f_2: bank guarantees/mortgage deeds registered to all commercial banks (feature no. 31); bank guarantees (feature no. 9); liquidity/total investment in bonds and shares (feature no. 28). All of them show increased bank guarantees and decreased dividends.
Negative correlation with f_2 : price of shares/book value (feature no. 19); dividend paid/pre-tax profit (feature no. 17); P/E ratio (feature no. 20). All of them show increased investment in high-yield securities and increased dividends.

The axis f_1 is then a measure of the banks' sensitivity to money market indicators and the corresponding portfolio decisions. Axis f_2 is related to the banks' growth and dividend distribution policy. This interpretation is very interesting by itself for financial analysts as it derives the critical synthetic features useful for comparative stock analysis of banks.

The sharp shift of all trajectories toward the negative end of the f_1 axis shows the impact of the Danish policy, especially the regulatory ceilings on bank lending, approved in 1972. Note how major banks (upper curve) started with a growth oriented policy, followed by a period of consolidation. Smaller banks (lower curve) have on the contrary favoured distribution to the shareholders.

3.2. *Neural Network Applications*

As most economic and financial analysis and decision making problems are characterized by frequently changing conditions, such as economic climate, regulatory framework, competitive situation, it is crucial for most knowledge-based applications to be supplemented by some knowledge acquisition capabilities. Unfortunately, this knowledge acquisition is almost invariably still carried out today by a combination of interviewing, data analysis, and database retrieval techniques. The parameters in numerical models can be re-estimated based on recent past observations by statistical parameter estimation techniques, econometrics, or by model identification algorithms, including adaptive control. In some instances, search may be added to estimation or parameter fitting.

However, three promising approaches for automatic learning have recently emerged and led to a number of significant economic and financial applications. They are neural networks, inductive learning and case-based reasoning which relies on both neural networks and inductive learning plus an information retrieval technique [42]. These are adequate for inferring or extracting patterns, regularities and classifications from large amounts of noisy data, in applications in which there is no theory, i.e. where correlation dominates as opposed to causality. It turns out that useful, sometimes surprising, regularities can be detected, often leading to a restricted number of rules and/or classes, grouping large amounts of data. In particular, neural network applications have gained wide popularity largely because of the following attractive features:

(i)   usefulness in both supervised and unsupervised learning tasks;
(ii) easy adaptation to changing conditions: upgrades of knowledge represented symbolically are on the contrary rather cumbersome;
(iii) robust with respect to the quality of input data, provided enough hidden layers are defined, and a possibly long training time is affordable;
(iv) relatively high speed, once the training phase is over, and therefore suitable for real time applications;
(v)   more flexibility than most competitive data estimation and classification techniques;
(vi) easy to use.

There is a cost to be paid, however, with a number of negative features compensating for part of the above-listed advantages; some of them due to the still immature technology, some others to the non-causal approach typical of this technology, namely:

(i)   huge computation time in the training phase, unless the network architecture and the input data are carefully controlled;

(ii) scarce theoretical guidance toward the selection of the optimum network topology for a well-defined task;

(iii) difficult interpretation and validation of the results;

(iv) poor interaction with the user, e.g. lack of a straightforward explanation facility (see however [43] for an early attempt);

(v)   limited capability to interface with the other software components of a typical decision support system.

The presentation below concentrates on two examples of how neural networks can be put to work in economic and financial tasks; there is no claim to give a complete coverage of the technology, which is anyway fast-growing and not easily summarized.

Applications based on inductive learning and case-based reasoning are on the contrary not addressed in this presentation: the interested reader will find a theoretical coverage of the topic in [44–49]. Inductive learning and neural network application areas tend to overlap. Examples of inductive learning applications are:

(i)   bankruptcy prediction [50–52],

(ii) stock market trading [53,49],

(iii) business loan risk classification [51],

(iv) credit card loan [54].

3.2.1. *Investment rating*

Investment rating is the process of grading bonds [55], convertible bonds [56] or stocks [4] into classes, and describing their suitability for investment. To this purpose, each security to be rated is described as a set (pattern) of features, referring to the issuer's ability to pay the interests and the principal (bonds), or to the issuer's financial strength and growth potential (stocks), or to a combination of both (convertible bonds). Risk classes are defined in advance, either by the experts, or by international rating agencies, such as Moody's and Standard & Poor. The rating goal then amounts to the identification of a function mapping patterns into ratings, in a way which is consistent with expert advice or rating agencies assignments. To this purpose, both statistical methods and the supervised training of neural networks have been used, and the resulting performances compared [55].

A typical statistical solution to the investment rating problem involves multiple regression, whereby a set of financial ratios and other indicators showing high correlation with the ratings is first selected, followed by the regression between the set of indicators and the ratings. In spite of several variations and improvements, it turns out that regression methods do rarely exceed 60% correctness when applied to a test set. This is due to the fact that regression analysis can only optimize the parameters of an *a priori* specified functional dependency between ratios and ratings, which is unfortunately unknown in this application: it is no surprise then that a wrong assumption on the functional form is bound to provide poor classifications [55].

This is not the case for neural networks: while it is true that the network's topology (i.e. the number of layers and the number of nodes in each layer) does influence the discriminating power of the network, i.e. the network's mapping capabilities, it turns out that a network with just one hidden layer can discriminate arbitrary open or closed convex regions in the feature space, and one with two hidden layers can discriminate arbitrary, non-contiguous regions [57].

In a neural network solution, the securities are first grouped into three sets, the training and test sets containing previously rated securities, and the working set, containing the securities to be rated. The training set is used to perform the supervised learning of the network's weights, while the test set is used to measure the network's performance. Each security is again described as a pattern of financial measures which varies according to the security to be rated:

(i)   bonds [55]:   6 or 10 variables
(ii) stocks [4]:   3 variables
(iii) convertible bonds [56]:   13/16 variables (manufacturing/electric utilities).

It is interesting to note that the results of statistical analysis, especially the correlations of the financial ratios with the ratings, can be used as a criterion for selecting the input variables, an often difficult task [55].

Finally, the network architecture is defined. This is a step largely carried out in a trial-and-error fashion, whereby large final errors, slow or no convergence or bad results on test data are early warnings of a wrong architecture. All the three examples above show however a remarkably similar architecture, based on networks with one hidden layer, a back-propagation learning algorithm or a modification [56], and a sigmoid node transfer function. In detail:

(i)   bonds [55]:   input layer: 6 or 10 nodes
                                hidden layer: unknown
                                output layer: 1 node
(ii) stocks [4]:   input layer: 3 nodes
                                hidden layer: 9 nodes
                                output layer: 3 nodes
(iii) convertible bonds [56]:   input layer: 13 nodes
                                hidden layer: 5 nodes
                                output layer: 1 node.

Note that in [4] one output node is defined for each security investment class, while in [56] classes are associated to different numeric values of just one output node.

Both [55] and [56] report a success rate of about 80% on the test set, far above the best performance of any statistical method. The same success rate is achieved in [55] with a network model without a hidden layer, i.e. the bonds are separable by half planes in the selected feature space [5].

Investment rating is typical for a number of financial examples, in which a set of individuals must be classified according to some financial criteria, but no or limited explicit models exist for such a classification. Credit scoring and other lending decisions, financial statements analysis, etc. fall into this category (one application in credit card lending is described in [58]).

3.2.2. *Forecasting with neural networks*

The classification capabilities of neural networks can be readily exploited to provide forecasts, whereby the input to the network includes the past values of the variable to be forecasted, and the output is the desired forecast. Needless to say, this possibility has attracted a lot of attention in the financial trading environments, due to the potentially high return from an even limited improvement in the trading success rate. In practice, training a neural network on a forecasting task can be a major challenge, because of one or more of the following problems:

(i)   large amounts of data,
(ii) high data volatility and noise,
(iii) difficulty in selecting a set of relevant inputs, with a clear causal impact on the variable to be forecasted,
(iv) scanty theoretical guidance on how to design and train the network.

Consequently, the hardware resources engaged in the training tasks are quite extensive, and the use of supercomputers is common practice. At the same time, technical details about such applications are rather scanty, although some banks and security houses claim good performance improvements [56,59]. Other known systems, listed in [4], include the Neural Trader's Assistant by Concepts Logiciels Experts, Paris, as well as the one by Fusion Group (N.Y.) and the Hecht-Nielsen Corporation.

It is furthermore still open how neural networks forecasting performance compares to other knowledge-based forecasting approaches, as well as to genetic algorithms and inductive learning.

4. Applications to Economic Modeling

Moving toward larger economic aggregates, the causal relations between data, classes and decisions are in general better understood, so that the inference of dependency relations becomes less important. What is not known is on the one hand the exact functional specification of a causal relation, and on the other the relative importance of a causal relation within a given model.

A typical example is policy decision making, in which one of the instrument variables is changed, causing a change in the endogenous variables, according to expressed and implied policy goals. The problem can again be represented as one of mapping. But as opposed to the examples presented in Section 3.2 above, the theoretical models on which the decision process is based are either known, or can be inferred, although in general they cannot be completely specified. The resulting mapping is a fairly structured one, conceptually similar to the example in Section 2 above, in which the underlying structure can be exploited with advantage, although care must be taken to avoid potentially explosive computational tasks.

Sections 4.1 to 4.4 present a worked out example.

4.1. *Definition of a Causal Model*

It is customary in macroeconomics, and also quite often in microeconomics, to formalize a numerical model in terms of the following quantities [4]:

(i)   a set of state variables X, where each state has properties attached to it; a state variable is normally an identified quantity in terms of economic concepts and official statistics or accounts;

(ii)   a set of instrumental variables U, which are a subset of X, restricted to those variables under the control of a decision-maker which may set their values;

(iii) a set of endogenous variables, which are a subset of X, restricted to those variables in $(X - U)$ which are not under the control of the decision-maker;

(iv) a set of exogenous quantities E, which describe the economic context and its parameters, and thus impact the state variables.

With the relations between state, instrumental, exogenous variables, their time distributed values, and time itself, the model is built, including a set of constants t, functions, constraints, attached to it.

Causality in a model is an asymmetric relation between two entities, such that a change in one entity causes a change in the other, but not vice versa. Although models are built around a set of causal relations, these relations are lost once they are formalized in mathematical terms. Equations are non-directional constraints, and as such symmetric with respect to the variables involved: variables can be moved freely between the left and right sides of the equation without altering its mathematical content.

In the following, therefore, our attention will be restricted to causal models, i.e. those models for which the causal relations within the set (X, U, E) are known. A causal relation is fully specified if the state being the cause, the state being the effect, and the functional form of the causal impact (i.e. the partial derivative of the effect with respect to the cause) are known. A causal model is partly specified if only part of the information about the causal relations in the model is known; in the following, it is assumed that at least the causes and the effects are always specified.

4.2. *Building a Causal Model*

Given a mathematical model, the causal structure underlying it can be determined by, e.g. "causal ordering" [60], a method based on a purely syntactical analysis of which variables appear in which equations, and is fully independent of the model parameters. A causal model derived from a mathematical model is always fully specified.

Alternatively, the model can be derived from judgemental knowledge about economic relations, like the one contained in descriptive texts, such as speeches, articles and official statements. Furthermore, implicit to each application domain and its model, is a decision structure, a management organization, and possibly legal conditions, which dictate a significant part of the causality relations between elements of U and X. This fact is very often overlooked in many qualitative models, although it must be emphasized to be of overriding importance: the same set (X, U, E) can be governed in entirely different ways, not because causalities are free, but because the decision and legal structures are most diverse. Much of these constraints are not available in mathematical form, but are easily captured from the analysis of natural language text, such as corporate policies and political statements. A semi-automatic method for inferring causal relations from natural language is described in [61].

4.3. *Causal Analysis*

A causal representation of the IS-LM model, see [62], is shown in Fig. 4. Causalities are visualized by a graph having as many nodes as the states and endogenous variables, with a directed arc going between two variables if and only if a change in the first variable causes a direct change in the second variable. The arc will be directed from the variable closest to the decision making (i.e. closest to the instrument variables), to the one closest to the endogenous outputs. The arcs may be labeled, either with the sign of the partial derivative of the downstream node w.r.t. changes in the upstream node (as in Fig. 4), and/or by the qualitative assessment of the impact. Any allowable judgemental reasoning, or causal path, corresponds to a path in the graph.

The graph shows the equilibrium conditions of the model. Causal analysis then starts when this equilibrium is disturbed, e.g. by a change in one or more instruments (model inputs). The purpose of the analysis is to get a qualitative appreciation for the expected changes in the endogenous variables (the model outputs). Note however that the model can also be used the other way around, by considering changes in the endogenous variables, and inferring changes in the instrument variables (forecasting).

The input/output relation is further constrained by consistency criteria. Assume that the decision making process imposes an increase in one endogenous variable, due to a measure on some instrument, although the model tells that a decrease is to be expected: then, a trend inconsistency has been detected, and the change on that instrument can be discarded from the set of likely policy measures. Next, assume that model dynamics are introduced on the state variables, and that overshoots are detected, as a consequence of a policy decision: if these exceed the allowable values, then there is an amplitude inconsistency. Also, instrumental inconsistency occurs if, when selected instrument variables are added or retracted from U, the amplitude change constraints on some goals are not met. Finally, model parametric

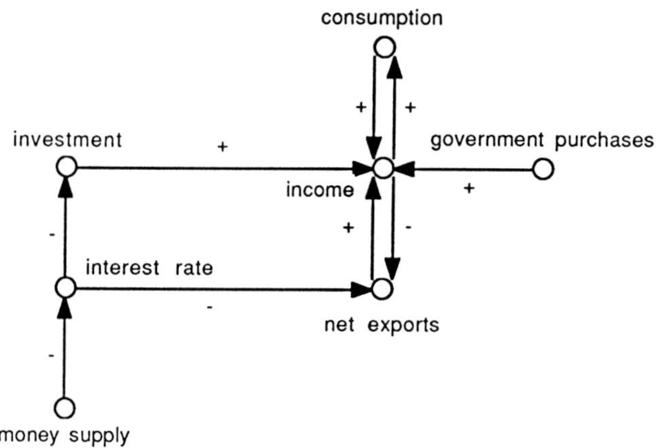

Fig. 4. Causal representation of the IS-LM model.

inconsistency corresponds to the case where the values of some states or instrumental variables exceed the limits on them for the model itself to be correctly defined, or to be estimated correctly from the econometric viewpoint.

An obvious causal analysis algorithm would follow each active causal path, i.e. each sequence of variables affected by a change in the exogenous variables. This is in general not feasible, because of cascaded multiple effects, which make the number of the causal paths grow exponentially, and become unmanageable for both humans and computers. Two related questions then arise:

(i)   which judgemental reasoning should be followed, given a well-specified use of the model,

(ii) how can judgemental reasonings be compared, and ranked, in order to select the most promising ones.

The first question can be answered by considering the time horizon of the analysis. If this is short, i.e. only the short-term consequences of an exogenous change are of interest, then multiple causalities can be disregarded, and depth-first analysis [4,63] is the corresponding reasoning method: this is often the case in financial analysis. By longer time horizons, or by detailed analysis of causal impacts, then all multiple causalities must be taken into account, their effects on the output variables duly cumulated, and breadth-first analysis [4,63] is the appropriate reasoning method: this is the case of economic analysis. Psychological as well as sociological considerations may lead to the identification of further allowable causal reasonings on the same model: there is no *a priori* optimum causal reasoning, but a trade-off among completeness, time and storage must be found depending on the goals of the decision making.

The second question is addressed by one more basic principle in causal analysis, i.e. that the causality is the strongest if the length of the decision path is the shortest. This means that if a given state variable is causally influenced by two others belonging to two different allowable causal paths, then in case of a tie in their effects, the shortest path will dominate. If furthermore a qualitative assessment of the magnitude of the causal impact is associated to the causal arcs, then the relative strength of their effects can be calculated, and only those causal paths with the highest value in the calculation are selected for further propagation.

4.4. An Algorithm for Causal Analysis: Beam-Search

The considerations in Section 4.3 above lead to the definition of an algorithm for causal analysis with the capability to limit the number of reasoning paths being explored, in a way which is consistent with the above-mentioned principles.

In beam-search, only the k most important causal chains are followed. This approach may seem psychologically unsound: in human reasoning the number of causal chains to be followed is not defined in advance, but rather dynamically adjusted depending on the interest in the current situations. It is however relatively simple to modify beam-search to retain at each level either k nodes (cognitive limitation), or all nodes below a given threshold of a ranking function measuring the interest in the current situation, whichever is smaller.

Table 1. The beam-search algorithm in pseudo-code.

1	Put the start node s on OPEN; CLOSED is empty.
2	If OPEN is empty, return a failure message and STOP.
	For each node n_i on OPEN, starting from the topmost:
3	Remove it from OPEN and put it on CLOSED.
4	If n_i is a target node, follow the pointers back to s.
	Return the solution path, issue a message of successful search completion and STOP.
5	If n_i has no effects, remove it from CLOSED and go to step 2.
6	Expand n_i, generating all its effects.
7	For each successor m_i of n_i:
7a	Calculate $f(m_i)$.
7b	If m_i is neither on OPEN nor on CLOSED, direct its pointer to n_i and put it on OPEN.
7c	If m_i is already on OPEN or CLOSED, compare it to the newly calculated one; if the former value is smaller, redirect the pointer to n_i and assign the new value of $f(m_i)$.
7d	If m_i was on CLOSED, put it on OPEN.
8	Sort the nodes on OPEN in descending order of their evaluation functions (the node with the smallest evaluation function on top). Retain only a number "breadth" of nodes choosing them from among those with smallest evaluation function; discard the other.
9	Go to step 2.
END	

The algorithm is described in pseudo-code in Table 1. $f(n)$ represents a ranking or heuristic function computed at the current state which is monotonic decreasing with preference: it is intended to capture all knowledge likely to influence the search process.

The beam-search is the basis for a simple qualitative simulation, whose computer code is listed in [4].

Acknowledgements

I would like to thank Prof. L. F. Pau for basic contributions to the ideas in this chapter, as well as for continuous support and help throughout its development.

References

[1] P. Mertens, Die Theorie der Mustererkennung in den Wirtschaftwissenschaften, *Schmalenbachs Zeitschrift für betriebwirtschaftliche Forschung* **29** (1977) 777–794.

[2] E. I. Altman, Financial ratios, discriminant analysis and the prediction of corporate bankruptcy, *J. Finance* **23** (1968) 589–609.

[3] K. V. Smith, Classification of investment securities using multiple discriminant analysis, Working Paper, Krannert Research Institute, Purdue Univ. 101, 1969.

[4] L. F. Pau and C. Gianotti, *Economic and Financial Knowledge-based Processing* (Springer, Berlin, 1990).

[5] Y. H. Pao, *Adaptive Pattern Recognition and Neural Networks* (Addison-Wesley, Reading, 1989).

[6] L. F. Pau, J. Motiwalla, Y. H. Pao and H. H. Teh (eds.), *Expert Systems in Economic, Banking and Management* (North-Holland, Amsterdam, 1989).

[7] M. Greenwell, *Knowledge Engineering for Expert Systems* (Ellis Horwood, Chichester, 1988).

[8] D. Diaper (ed.), *Knowledge Elicitation: Principles, Techniques and Applications* (Ellis Horwood, Chichester, 1989).

[9] A. L. Kidd, *Knowledge Acquisition for Expert Systems: A Practical Handbook* (Plenum, 1987).

[10] R. C. Schank and R. Abelson, *Scripts, Plans, Goals and Understanding* (Lawrence Erlbaum, Hillsdale, 1977).

[11] E. Rich, Natural-Language Interfaces, *Computer* **17** (1984) 39–47.

[12] F. Harary, R. Z. Norman and D. Cartwright, *Structural Models: An Introduction to the Theory of Directed Graphs* (J. Wiley & Sons, New York, 1965).

[13] J. de Kleer, An assumption-based truth maintenance system, *Artif. Intell.* **29** (1986) 241–288.

[14] Y. Shoham, *Reasoning About Change in Time and Causation from the Standpoint of Artificial Intelligence* (MIT Press, Cambridge, 1988).

[15] D. J. Israel, The role of logic in knowledge representation, *IEEE Comput.* **16**, 10 (1983) 37–41.

[16] M. R. Genesereth and N. J. Nilsson, *Logical Foundations of Artificial Intelligence* (Morgan Kaufmann, Los Altos, 1987).

[17] D. Dubois and H. Prade, Handling uncertainty in expert systems: pitfalls, difficulties, remedies, in *ATV Seminar on Safety and Risk in the Use of Expert Systems*, Danish Academy of Sciences, Copenhagen, May 1988.

[18] G. Shafer, The combination of evidence, *Int. J. Intell. Syst.* **1** (1986) 155–179.

[19] J. Pearl, *Probabilistic Reasoning in Intelligent Systems: Networks of Plausible Inference* (Morgan Kaufmann, Los Altos, 1988).

[20] G. J. Klir and T. A. Folger, *Fuzzy Sets, Uncertainty and Information* (Prentice Hall, Englewood Cliffs, 1988).

[21] F. Hayes-Roth, Rule-based systems, *Commun. ACM* **28** (1985) 921–932.

[22] R. E. Fikes and T. Kehler, The role of frame-based reasoning, *Commun. ACM* **28** (1985) 904–920.

[23] R. E. Fikes, Odyssey: A knowledge-based assistant, *Artif. Intell.* **16** (1981) 331–361.

[24] P. J. Kaufman, *Technical Analysis in Commodities* (J. Wiley & Sons, New York, 1978).

[25] K. S. Fu (ed.), *Syntactic Pattern Recognition Applications* (Springer, New York, 1979).

[26] A. V. Aho and J. D. Ullman, *Principles of Compiler Design* (Addison-Wesley, Reading, 1977).

[27] N. Wirth, *Compilerbau* (B. G. Teubner, Stuttgart, 1984).

[28] J. Earley, An efficient context-free parsing algorithm, *Commun. ACM* **13**, 2 (1970) 94–102.

[29] F. Giannesini, H. Kanoui, R. Pasero and M. van Caneghem, *Prolog* (Addison-Wesley, Reading, 1986).

[30] V. I. Levenshtein, Binary codes capable of correcting deletions, insertions and reversals, *Soviet Phys. Dokl.* **10**, 8 (1966).

[31] A. V. Aho and T. G. Peterson, A minimum distance error-correcting parser for context-free languages, *SIAM J. Comput.* **1**, 4 (1972) 305–312.

[32] E. Tanaka and K. S. Fu, Error-correcting parsers for formal languages, *IEEE Trans. Comput.* **27**, 7 (1978) 605–616.

[33] G. A. Neely, *Elliot Waves Motion* (Elliot Wave Institute, 1988).

[34] L. F. Pau et al., KEMEX Expert system, TUP Program report, Industry and Technology agency, Copenhagen, 1988.

[35] R. M. Miller, *Computer Aided Financial Analysis* (Addison-Wesley, Reading, 1990).

[36] *Smalltalk/V and Prolog/V*, Digitalk, 9841 Airport Boulevard, Los Angeles, CA 90045, USA, 1983.

[37] F. Goronzy, A factor analysis of selected variables of manufacturing business enterprises, *Management Int. Rev. (Germany)* **6** (1969) 71–96.

[38] R. S. Stich, How well do multinational companies perform, *Management Int. Rev. (Germany)* **11** (1971) 33–44.

[39] L. F. Pau, *Diagnostic des Pannes dans les Systèmes: Approche par la Reconnaissance des Formes* (Cepad, Toulouse, 1975).

[40] J. P. Benzecri et al., *L'analyse des Données* (Dunod, Paris, 1973).

[41] L. F. Pau and P. Valstorp, Feature extraction in the time-domain: application to the analysis of financial data and strategies over time, in K. S. Fu and A. B. Whinston (eds.), *Pattern Recognition Theory and Application*, NATO ASI Series E-22 (Noordhoff, Leyden, 1977) 75–90.

[42] C. K. Riesbeck and R. C. Schank, *Inside Case-Based Reasoning* (Lawrence Erlbaum, Hillsdale, 1989).

[43] L. F. Pau and T. Götzsche, An explanation facility to neural networks, *Int. J. Intell. Robotic Syst.* **5**, 2 (1992) 193–206.

[44] R. S. Michalski, A theory and methodology of inductive learning (AQ-Star algorithm), in R. Michalski, J. Carbonell and T. Mitchell (eds.), *Machine Learning* (Tioga Publ., Palo Alto, 1983).

[45] T. Mitchell and R. Keller, Explanation based generalization: a unifying view, *Mach. Learning J.* **1** (1986) 47–80.

[46] L. Rendell, A general framework for induction and a study of selective induction (PLS algorithm), *Mach. Learning J.* **1** (1986) 177–226.

[47] J. R. Quinlan, Discovering rules from large collections of examples (ID3 algorithm), in D. Michie (ed.), *Expert Systems in the Micro Electronic Age*, (Edinburgh University Press, Edinburgh, 1979).

[48] J. R. Quinlan, Induction of decision trees (ID3 algorithm), *Mach. Learning J.* **1** (1986) 81–106.

[49] L. Breiman, *Classification and Regression Trees* (Wadsworth & Brooks, Monterey, 1984).

[50] J. A. Gentry and P. Newbold, Classifying bankrupt firms with funds flow components, *J. Accounting Research* **23** (1985) 146–160.

[51] M. J. Shaw, J. A. Gentry and S. Piramuthu, Inductive learning for risk classification, *IEEE Expert*, Feb. (1990) 47–53.

[52] W. Messier and J. V. Hansen, Inducing rules for expert system development, *Management Science* **34**, 12 (1988) 1403–1415.

[53] K. C. Lee, Applying machine learning to building stock market strategy, *Journal of Computer Science in Economics and Management* (1990).

[54] C. Carter and J. Catlett, Assessing credit card applications using machine learning, *IEEE Expert* **2**, 3 (1987) 71–79.

[55] S. Dutta and S. Shekhar, An artificial intelligence approach to predicting bond ratings, in L. F. Pau, J. Motiwalla, Y. H. Pao and H. H. Teh (eds.), *Expert Systems in Economics, Banking and Management* (North-Holland, Amsterdam, 1989) 59–68.

[56] T. Kimoto, Neural networks in investment, in *Proc. 4th European Seminar on Neural Computing — Putting Neural Nets to Work*, London, UK, Feb. 1991 (ICB Technical Services, London, 1991).

[57] R. P. Lippman, An introduction to computing with neural nets, *IEEE ASSP Mag.* **4** (1987) 4–22.

[58] *Proc. SGAICO Symp. on Commercial Expert Systems in Banking and Insurance*, Lugano, May, 1989.

[59] A. Colin, Neural networks for exchange rate forecasting, in *Proc. 4th European Seminar on Neural Computing — Putting Neural Nets to Work*, London, UK, Feb. 1991 (ICB Technical Services, London, 1991).

[60] H. A. Simon, *Models of Discovery* (Reidel, Dordrecht, 1977).

[61] L. F. Pau, Inference of functional economic model relations from natural language analysis, in L. F. Pau (ed.), *Artificial Intelligence in Economics and Management*, (North-Holland, Amsterdam, 1986).

[62] R. E. Hall and J. B. Taylor, *Macro-economics* (Norton, New York, 1988).

[63] P. H. Winston, *Principles of Artificial Intelligence* (Addison-Wesley, Reading, 1984).

Handbook of Pattern Recognition and Computer Vision, pp. 595–624
Eds. C. H. Chen, L. F. Pau and P. S. P. Wang
© 1993 World Scientific Publishing Company

CHAPTER 3.5

OPTICAL HANDWRITTEN CHINESE CHARACTER RECOGNITION

JUN S. HUANG

Institute of Information Science, Academia Sinica, Taipei, Taiwan, Republic of China

Optical handwritten Chinese character recognition is a difficult and challenging problem. The major difficulties encountered in solving this problem are the large number of characters, the high complexity, many mutually similar characters, and the large variations in writing from person to person. In general, handwritten Chinese characters can be classified into two categories: the first is constrained handwriting where all strokes in each character are clearly visible and are written in a regular way as learned in elementary school; the second is unconstrained handwriting where some strokes are not clearly visible, are mixed up and are not separable. In this chapter the constrained handwriting category is considered and a stroke extraction method based on thinning and curve fitting is described. After stroke extraction structural matching is developed. The information utilized here is the geometric relationships between strokes. Two methods of structural matching are described. One is deterministic and is called invariant transformation matching based on least square method. The other is probabilistic and is called modified relaxation matching based on iterative updating of probabilities of matches. The knowledge-base approach is also briefly discussed. Finally, a description of Chinese radicals and the standard database for experimentation is given in detail.

Keywords: Optical character recognition, handwritten Chinese characters, stroke extraction, thinning, invariant transformation matching, relaxation matching, knowledge-base approach, Chinese radicals, standard database.

1. Introduction

Chinese characters are ideographic in nature and represent a kind of high quality pictorial art. Each of them has a structural meaning and in general is written in square form. Basically they are composed of a certain number of writing strokes, which can be roughly classified into 33 categories. There are about 5401 daily used characters in Taiwan. The advancement of computer technologies, both in hardware and software, within the last two decades enabled the Chinese in Taiwan to build their own Chinese computers and to distribute them to all levels of society. This achievement has promoted office automation as well as factory automation. The Chinese computer seems almost perfect now, but by careful observation one will notice a drawback, that the keyboard input of a Chinese computer is not as simple as that of an English one and to get fast data input one needs specially trained

595

operators. Thus the optical recognition of Chinese characters (Chinese OCR) is crucial to the development of the Chinese computer since it provides a way of input which is fast and simple. The success of Chinese OCR will also help many related business areas such as mail-reading in post offices, production automation, and check-reading in banking, etc.

Handwritten Chinese OCR is a difficult problem. We classify handwritten characters into two categories: the first is constrained handwriting where all strokes in each character are clearly visible and are written in a regular way as learned in elementary schools; the second is unconstrained handwriting where some strokes are not clearly visible, are mixed up, or are linked together and not separable. The recognition of the first category can be treated in several ways which will be explained in the next few sections. There is however, no report so far for recognition of the second category. The major difficulties in the optical character recognition of constrained Chinese handwriting are due to the large number of characters, the high complexity, many mutually similar characters, and the large variations in writing from person to person.

Research on OCR of constrained Chinese handwriting has been going on since 1980 in Japan and a good survey was given by Mori, Yamamoto and Yasuda [1] in 1984, where they suggested four approaches to this problem: (1) using a combination of a few simpler feature extraction methods, (2) using feature matching, (3) using high level techniques such as relaxation matching and knowledge-base matching, (4) using high level feature extraction. In Taiwan the research in this area started only a few years ago and experiences show that the first two approaches suggested by Mori et al. seem to work only for certain cases with limited number of characters. Most researchers here emphasize the last two approaches, especially stroke extraction and stroke matching, since Chinese characters are written stroke by stroke. In this article a reliable stroke extraction method based on thinning and two stroke matching methods based on invariant transformation and modified relaxation will be described in detail. Some experimental results are also given to show the effectiveness of these methods. The knowledge-base approach is also briefly discussed. Finally, a description of Chinese radicals and the standard database for experimentation is given in detail.

2. Filtering and Thinning

When a binary character image is input to the computer, the first step is to filter out the noise and smooth the boundary. The isolated single black pixel is deleted and the isolated single white pixel is filled by heuristic methods. Here the character pixel is black and the background pixel is white. The boundary pixels are traced and smoothed by averaging the coordinates of five consecutive pixels and replacing the coordinates of the middle pixel by the average ones (note that five pixels are proper for the resolution of 100×100 and if the resolution is higher then a higher number of pixels should be used). In certain cases where the quality of the character image is bad and some strokes are broken, the dilation operator in morphological filtering operations [2] may be used to make the broken strokes connected again.

There are basically two types of approaches for stroke extraction: one is with thinning [3–5] and the other is without thinning [6–7]. From the computational point of view the one with thinning is much simpler than the one without thinning. Here thinning is adopted. There are many thinning algorithms (e.g. [8–10]) and Lee [11] gives a performance evaluation of 19 thinning algorithms for oriental character recognitions. Since almost all thinning algorithms use local neighborhood properties to delete pixels, a serious problem arises, that is the thinned skeleton will contain spurious branches, have a cross point split into two fork points, and show some distortion around the junction points. This problem will cause the failure of stroke extraction.

The idea of thinning adopted here follows a modified version of Chu and Suen's [8]. Its basic idea is to strip the boundary pixels alternately until the character cannot be further stripped (i.e. a single pixel wide skeleton appears). This method seems to produce less spurious branches than other methods. An example is shown in Fig. 1.

(a)   (b)

Fig. 1. (a) Original character. (b) Thinned character of (a).

After thinning, some actions for correcting the above mentioned problems should be taken. Let us define a 1-fork point as an end point, a 2-fork point as a break point (or corner point), a 3-fork point as a T-junction point, a 4-fork point as a cross point, and so on. Also let us define a cluster as the class of fork points that should be merged together. Then we can obtain the center of a cluster by averaging the coordinates of these fork points in the cluster and use this center point to represent the cluster. The algorithm for finding a cluster is described in the following six steps:

Step 1. Let S be the original character and T the thinned character.

Step 2. For every fork point f (*no matter what kind of fork point it is*), figure out the radius of the largest circle within S that is centered at f. If the radius is less than one (*when the stroke is very thin*), we set the radius of this circle to 1. Let R_f represent the radius of the fork point f. An example is shown in Fig. 2(a).

Step 3. For every pair of fork points f_1 and f_2 calculate the distance $d_{f_1 f_2}$ between them. If $d_{f_1 f_2}$ is less than or equal to $R_{f_1} + R_{f_2}$, we say f_1 and f_2 are connected; that is to say the two largest circles of f_1 and f_2 intersect each other as shown in Fig. 2(b).

Step 4. If f_1 and f_2 are connected and f_2 and f_3 are also connected, we say f_1, f_2 and f_3 are all connected. Using this equivalent relation we can finally partition all the fork points into several clusters, and a fork point only connects with those fork points in the same cluster. An example is shown in Fig. 2(b).

Step 5. Erase all pixels within each circle of each fork point, except the fork point itself, as shown in Fig. 2(c). For every cluster K, average the coordinates of all fork points in K to get the center C_K. C_K is used to represent this cluster. Now we reconnect each stroke with the center C_K, and a new thinned character is formed as shown in Fig. 2(d).

Step 6. We can determine what kind of fork C_k is by the following procedure:

If the cluster K contains only one 1-fork point,

```
        then      counter = 1;
        else
            {       counter = 2;
                    for every fork point f in K do
                    { if f is 1-fork
                          counter = counter −1;
                      else
                          counter = counter + KIND(f) −2;
                    }
            }
    end.
```

The result is that C_K is a counter-fork point, where KIND is a function returning the kind of fork point: e.g. KIND (5-fork point) = 5, KIND (3-fork point) = 3. An example is depicted in Fig. 2(d).

Every spurious 3-fork point f usually has one short branch S_1 or two short branches S_1 and S_2 connecting to itself (see F_4 in Fig. 2(b)). We will consider the case of two short branches as an example. Let E_1 and E_2 be the end point of S_1 and S_2 respectively. E_1, E_2 and f are close to each other. Then the maximum circles of E_1, E_2 and f will overlap each other since thinning is done by stripping the boundary points. Thus E_1, E_2 and f belong to the same cluster. By Step 6 we can

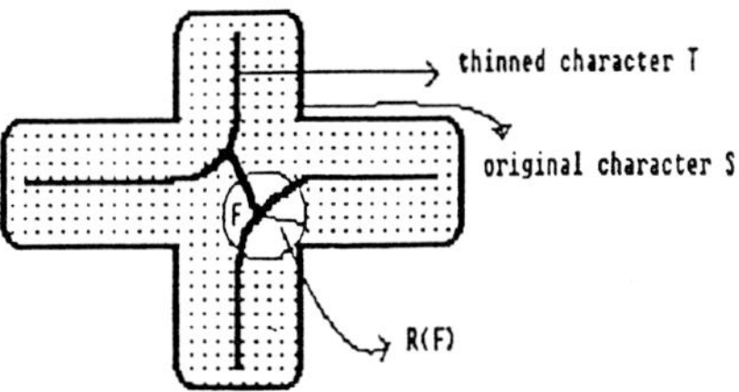

Fig. 2(a).

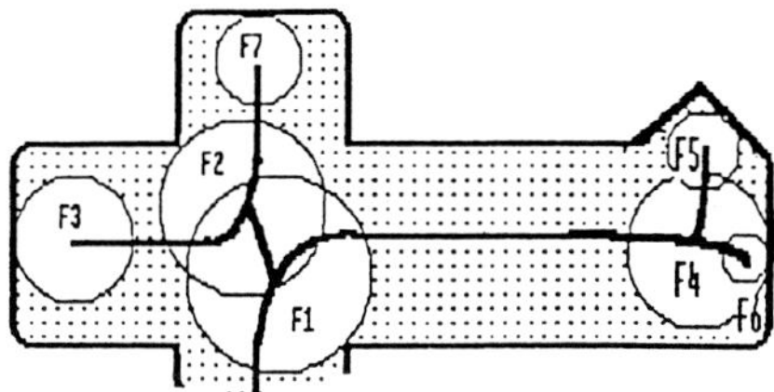

Fig. 2(b). F_3 forms a cluster and F_7 forms another cluster. F_2 is connected to F_1, so they form a cluster. F_4 is connected to F_5 and F_6, so F_4, F_5 and F_6 form a cluster.

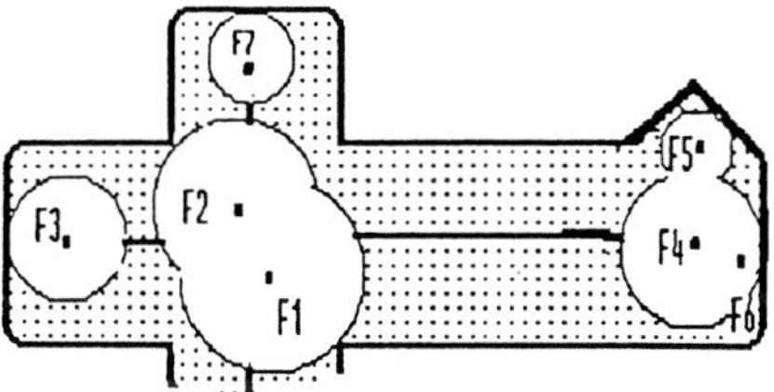

Fig. 2(c). All fork points and strokes are disconnected.

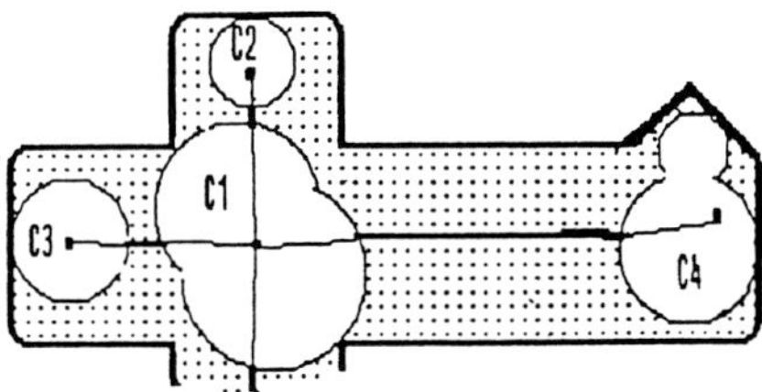

Fig. 2(d). C_3 is equal to F_3. C_3 is an end point (1-fork point). C_2 is equal to F_7. C_2 is an end point (1-fork point). C_1 is equal to the average of F_2 and F_1. Since $2 + (3 - 3) + (3 - 2) = 4$, so C_1 is a 4-fork point. C_4 is equal to the average of F_4, F_5 and F_6. Since $2 + (3 - 2) - 1 - 1 = 1$, so C_4 is an end point (1-fork point).

have counter = 1 for this cluster. Therefore f is in fact an end point. An example is shown in the point C_4 of Fig. 2(d). The reason why we set the radius of every circle to be greater than 1 is that when the stroke is very thin and a 4-fork point is split into two 3-fork points, these two 3-fork points will not be merged together if either one of two radii of these two 3-fork points is zero.

3. Stroke Extraction and Size Normalization

After thinning and corrections the whole character can be considered as a graph with vertices corresponding to m-fork points, $m \geq 1$. Since Chinese characters are written by smooth strokes except at 2-fork points where sharp turns occur, we shall use the smooth property and the sharp turn property to merge proper edges connected at the same m-fork point, $m > 2$ and to find 2-fork points, i.e. to extract strokes. The extraction procedure consists of two stages; each contains several steps and are described as follows:

STAGE 1: Merging edge pairs connected at the same n-fork point, $n > 2$, by curve fitting.

Step 1. For every n-fork point f, $n > 2$, find out all possible combinations of edge pairs connected at f. There are $l_1, l_2, \ldots, l_h$ edge pairs, $h = \binom{n}{2}$.

Step 2. For every l_i, find a Bernstein–Bezier curve best fitted to l_i and this curve has the same start and end points as those of l_i. This step consists of the following two substeps:

Step 2.1. Let $P(0), P(1), \ldots, P(k)$ be the points of l_i traced in order where k is the total number of points of l_i; $P(0)$ is the start point and $P(k)$ is the end point. The Bernstein–Bezier curve is a polynomial with parameter t and is represented by

$$B(t) = \sum_{i=0}^{m} \binom{m}{i} P_i\, t^i (1-t)^{m-i}, \quad 0 \leq t \leq 1,$$

where P_o and P_m are end points and $P_1, \ldots, P_{m-1}$ are control points. Here m is set to be $\lfloor k/c \rfloor$ for a proper constant $c > 1$, and $P_o = P(o) = B(o)$, $P_m = P(k) = B(1)$. What we want here is that $B(j/k)$ should be as close to $P(j)$ as possible for $0 < j < k$. Since the coordinates of every point are X and Y, we first try to find out the X component of every control point of the best fit Bernstein–Bezier curve, then we deal with the Y-component in the same manner. Let $B_x(t) = \sum_{i=0}^{m} \binom{m}{i} t^i (1 - t)^{m-i} P_{xi}$, $0 < t < 1$. $B_x(o) = P_x(o) = P_{xo}$ and $B_x(1) = P_x(k) = P_{xm}$. Here the subscript x means the X component (i.e. $P(i) = (P_x(i), P_y(i))$). By least square error method, let $E(P_{x1}, P_{x2}, \ldots, P_{x[m-1]}) = \sum_{i=0}^{k}(B_x(i/k) - P_x(i))^2$, and set $\partial E/\partial P_{x1} = 0, \ldots, \partial E/\partial P_{x[m-1]} = 0$. Since there are $m - 1$ variables and $m - 1$ linear equations, we can find $P_{x1}, P_{x2}, \ldots, P_{x[m-1]}$ easily. The computation of the Y components $(P_{y1}, \ldots, P_{y[m-1]})$ of the control points can be done in the same manner. Thus we obtain all the control points of the Bernstein–Bezier curve best fitted to l_i.

Step 2.2. Use these control points obtained in Step 2.1 to reconstruct the Bernstein–Bezier curve BB_i approximating l_i.

Step 3. Since every point on BB_i is influenced by all points on l_i, not just a local interval, the local zigzag curve in l_i always corresponds to a smooth curve in BB_i. Thus for every curve BB_i find out the point Q_i on BB_i that is closest to the fork point f and compute the radius of curvature r_i at Q_i where

$$r_i = |\,(\dot{X}_i^2 + \dot{Y}_i^2)^{1.5}/(\dot{X}\ddot{Y} - \ddot{X}\dot{Y})\,|,$$

$Q_i = (X_i, Y_i)$, and the dot means differential with respect to t.

Step 4. Considering all $l_i's$ and $r_i's$, we retain those l_i, say $l_{j1}, \ldots, l_{js}$, having $r_i > T_1$, a properly chosen threshold. If for some $jh, jk, 1 \leq jh, jk \leq s, l_{jh}$ and l_{jk} have an edge in common then retain the one with the larger radius of curvature and drop the other one. Merge the edge pairs of the retained $l_{jh}'s$. We call a substroke for each merged edge pair and each unmerged edge. Please note that the selected value of T_1 is important because at a 4-fork point if two edges are merged the other two edges may not be merged. An example is shown in Fig. 3 where the 4-fork point is a K-type junction.

Step 5. Use Step 1 to Step 4 to find out all the substrokes of all fork points except the 1-fork points and the 2-fork points. We say that two substrokes are connected if they share one edge in common before edge merging. Thus by connectedness property we can partition all substrokes into several mutually exclusive classes. Thus each class represents a stroke. We call a stroke with one single edge an isolated stroke and a stroke with more than two edges a compound stroke. An example is shown in Fig. 4 where E_7 and E_8 are isolated strokes, and (E_1, E_4, E_9), (E_2, E_3), (E_5, E_6) are compound strokes.

Step 6. Store both kinds of isolated and compound strokes. These strokes are called 1*st*-stage strokes. The strokes extracted here may contain corner points (also called 2-fork points, inflection points) (see Fig. 4). This is the end of STAGE 1.

Since some Chinese strokes may contain several corner points this phenomenon causes some difficulties in stroke matching. Thus it is essential to find these corner-points. This leads to the procedure of STAGE 2.

STAGE 2: Finding corner-points and splitting a stroke by corner points.

Step 1. Let the current 1st-stage stroke S contain $n + 1$ points: $S(0)$, $S(1)$, $\ldots, S(n)$. Use STAGE 1 to generate a Bernstein–Bezier curve $BS(t)$ best fit to S, $0 \leq t \leq 1$. $BS(i/n)$ is close to $S(i)$. For a long stroke the degree of $BS(t)$ is chosen to be large, and for a short stroke to be small. A corner point on S will correspond to a point on $BS(t)$ with a very small radius of curvature. Hence we find out all points having radii of curvature smaller than a given threshold T_2 and register them as corner points.

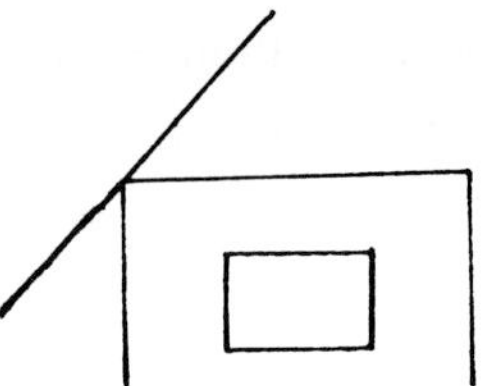

Fig. 3. A K-type junction.

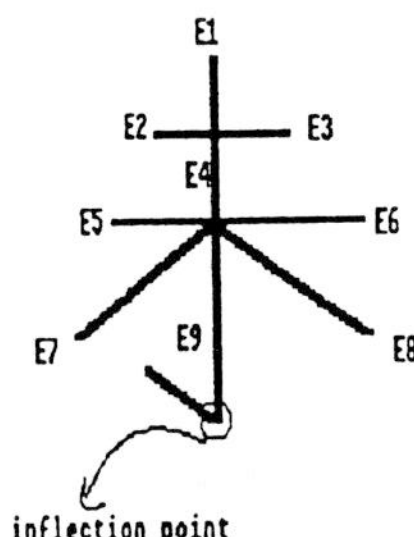

Fig. 4. A character with nine edges.

Step 2. There are some corner points that cannot be found in Step 1. Thus we try to find more corner points from a global view. A curve is said to be flat at some point if the radius of curvature at that point is greater than some threshold T_3. We define a bending curve portion to be a part of the curve that is flat in the vicinities of its two end points and the angle between the two slope directions at these two end points must be greater than some threshold T_4. Now we trace $BS(i/n)$, $i = 0, 1, \ldots, n$, to find all the bending curve portions, and for every bending curve portion we find the point Q_j on it with the minimum radius of curvature. We say Q_j is a corner point (actually it is a bending point) and register the parameter t_j of Q_j. Since $BS(i/n)$ is almost equal to $S(i)$ for all i, $S(nt_j)$ is a corner point of S. Thus we can find all the corner points of each stroke.

Step 3. Split each stroke into several smaller strokes by corner points if they exist. The smaller strokes will be very flat and smooth. We call these strokes the 2nd-stage strokes. This is the end of STAGE 2.

It is thinning that sometimes makes stroke extraction unreliable. We find out that the thicker the strokes are the higher the possibility of causing distortions in thinning. Thus if the strokes of a character are very thin we can extract strokes more stably and correctly. Most strokes of a machine printed character are much thicker than those of the same character written with a ball pen. In general, thinning the handwritten character will generate less distortion, and stroke extraction for machine printed characters is not obviously easier than that for handwritten characters. Here two machine printed characters are given as examples and the results of thinning, corrections, Bernstein–Bezier curve fitting, 1st-stage strokes, and 2nd-stage strokes are shown in Figs. 5–10.

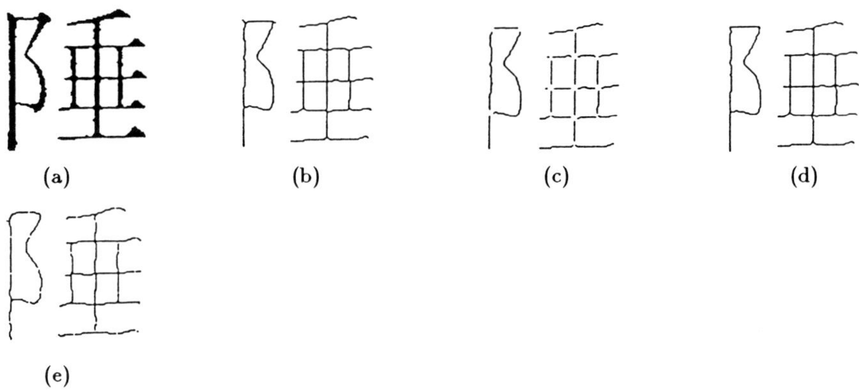

Fig. 5. (a) A Chinese character. (b) Result after thinning. (c) Erase the pixels near every fork point. (d) Reconnect each stroke to the fork point. (e) Use the Bernstein–Bezier curve to represent (a).

In Step 1 of STAGE 1, all combinations of edge pairs connected at an n-fork point are considered for curve fitting. This is time consuming. We can eliminate some edge pairs before curve fitting by heuristics. An example is that if the angle formed by two edges (in a heuristic way) is less than $100°$ then eliminate this edge pair. This can save much computing time.

After stroke extraction each stroke is fairly flat and smooth, so we can use a straight line segment to approximate each stroke (by connecting the start and the end points). Since each straight line segment is uniquely represented by its center point, slope angle and length, the normalization of the size of a character is straightforward and is done by the scaling up or down of the length and the shifting of the center point. The normalization of the size to a standard size, say 150 × 150, is essential for character matching which will be discussed in the following sections.

4. Structural Matching

Structural matching utilizing substrokes, full-strokes, and geometric relationships among the strokes, may be the only way for successful recognition of handwritten Chinese characters. Some matching methods adopt feature points (such as end points, cross points, etc.) and boundary approximation, and also base components (+, [], ⊓, etc.). However, feature points and boundary approximation are rather unstable because of handwriting whereas base components need complicated subgraph matching and the method is no better than radical matching to be discussed later. In general, structural matching includes: relaxation [12–15,18,23] which is the most frequently used, linear programming [16], dynamic programming

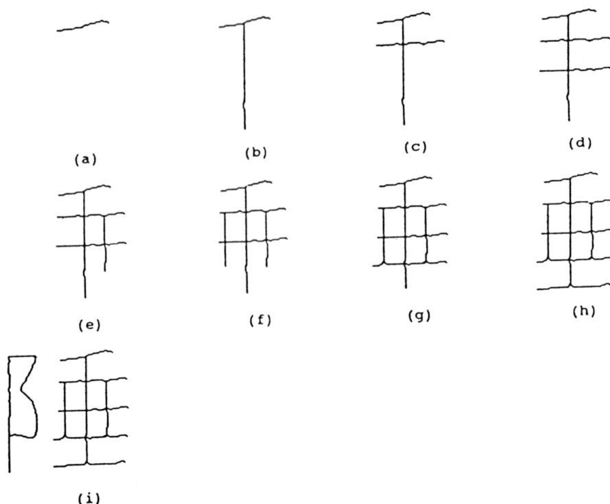

Fig. 6. The stroke extraction of the Chinese character (shown in Fig. 5) in the first stage.

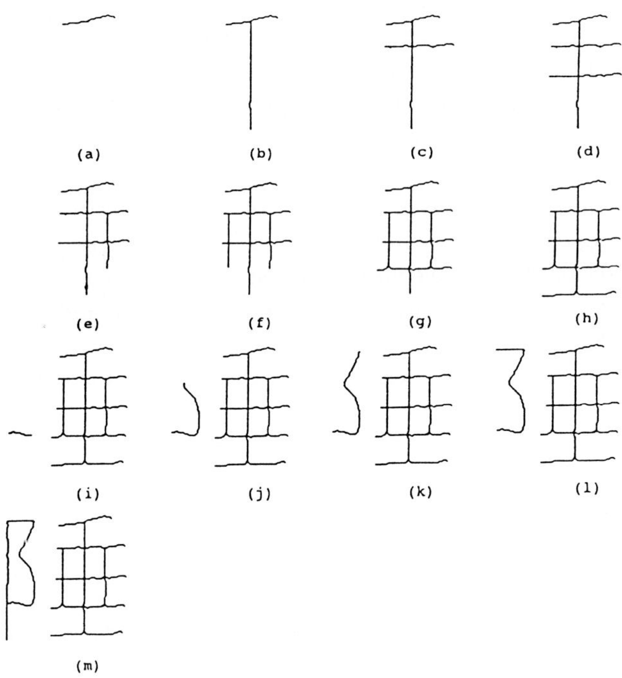

Fig. 7. The stroke extraction of the Chinese character (shown in Fig. 5) in the second stage.

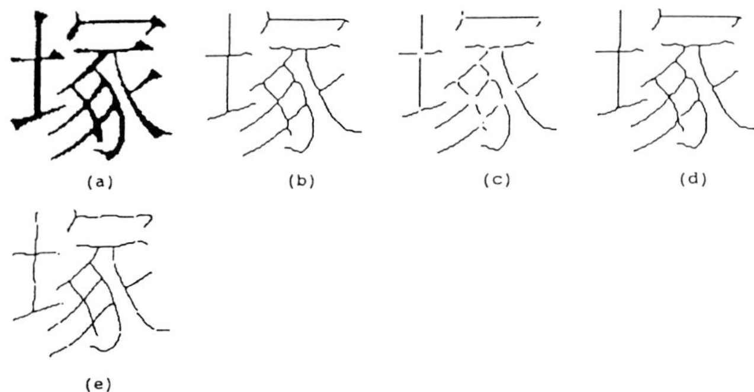

Fig. 8. (a) A Chinese character. (b) Result after thinning. (c) Erase the pixels near every fork point. (d) Reconnect each stroke to the fork point. (e) Use the Bernstein–Bezier curve to represent (a).

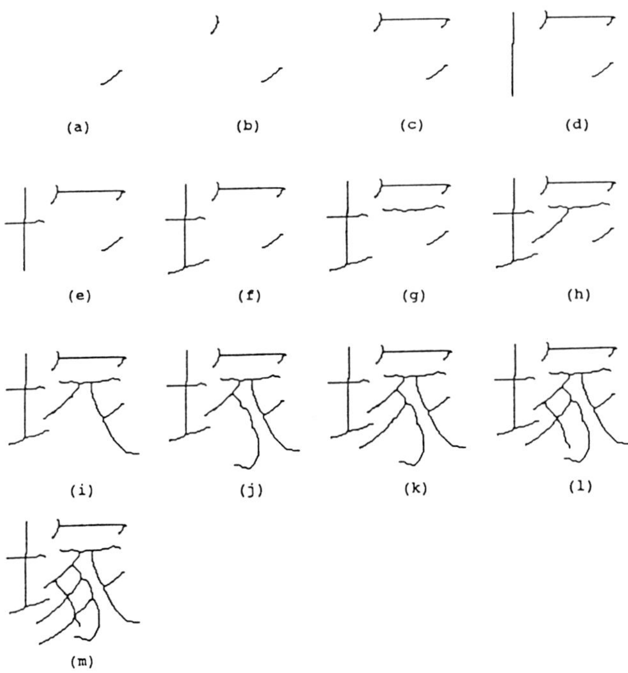

Fig. 9. The stroke extraction of the Chinese character (shown in Fig. 8) in the first stage.

[17], knowledge-base approach [18], fuzzy method [19], attributed graph matching (by A^* algorithm in AI [20], by tree search [21], by invariant transformation matching [22], and by relaxation on random graphs [23]), mutually-best match strategy

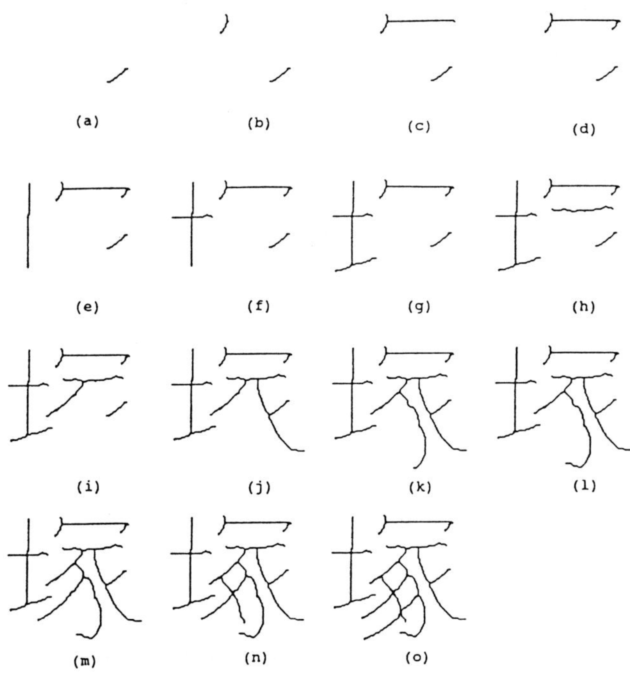

Fig. 10. The stroke extraction of the Chinese character (shown in Fig. 8) in the second stage.

[24], 2-D extended attribute grammar method [25], on-line model guided matching [26], and neural networks [27–31]. Here, we shall describe two promising methods: one is deterministic, and is called invariant transformation matching. The other is probabilistic and is called modified relaxation matching. Finally, we shall discuss the knowledge-base approach in Section 5.

4.1. *Invariant Transformation Matching*

All Chinese characters are composed of some fundamental characters, called radicals (see Section 6). Here we present an invariant transformation matching method to match the radicals, stored in the database, with the input character. The name "invariant transformation matching" means that a matching is invariant under rotation, scaling and translation of the input character.

From Section 3 each stroke extracted is a straight line segment and is uniquely determined by its two end points. Let the input character C_1 contain l strokes and the radical C_2 contain m strokes, $m \leq l$. There are n $(n = l \cdot (l - 1) \cdot (l - 2) \cdots (l - m + 1))$ permutations (not combinations) for matching C_1 with C_2; that is, there are n ways to select m strokes from C_1. An example is shown in Fig. 11. If m strokes have been selected from C_1 to match C_2 and these m strokes

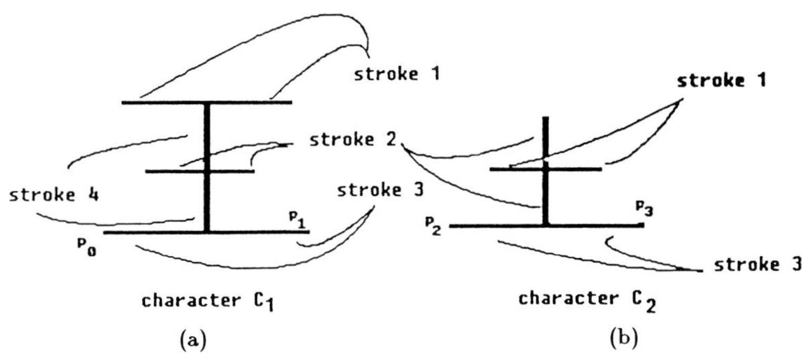

Strokes in C_2	1	2	3
Strokes in C_1	1	2	3
	1	2	4
	1	3	2
	1	3	4
	1	4	2
	1	4	3
	2	1	3
	2	1	4
	2	3	1
	2	3	4
	2	4	1
	2	4	3
	3	1	2
	3	1	4
	3	2	1
	3	2	4
	3	4	1
	3	4	2
	4	1	2
	4	1	3
	4	2	1
	4	2	3
	4	3	1
	4	3	2

(c)

Fig. 11. There are four strokes in C_1 shown in (a), and three strokes in C_2 shown in (b), so there are $4 * (4 - 1) * (4 - 2) = 24$ kinds of permutations for corresponding the strokes of C_1 with those of C_2. These 24 permutations are shown in (c).

constitute a subcharacter $C_{m-strokes}$ of C_1, then we use $X'_{2i-1}, Y'_{2i-1}, X'_{2i}$ and Y'_{2i} to represent the ith stroke of the m selected strokes ($C_{m-strokes}$) and $P_{x_{2i-1}}, P_{y_{2i-1}}, P_{x_{2i}}, P_{y_{2i}}$ to represent the ith stroke of C_2, respectively.

If $C_{m-strokes}$ is rotated by θ degrees, scaled by k_x and k_y and translated by t_x and t_y in the X and Y components, respectively, then the new coordinates, after transformation of the ith end point with coordinates (X_i', Y_i'), will be changed into $(k_x X_i + t_x, k_y Y_i + t_y)$ where $X_i = X_i' \cos\theta - Y_i' \sin\theta$ and $Y_i = X_i' \sin\theta + Y_i' \cos\theta$. The reason why we use two scaling factors k_x and k_y for X and Y components respectively is that handwritten Chinese characters are sometimes scaled differently in height and width. The evaluation for the difference between C_2 and transformed $C_{m-strokes}$ is defined as the sum of squares of errors of the coordinate differences associated with any two corresponding end points, and is denoted by $\xi(\theta, k_x, k_y, t_x, t_y)$:

$$\xi(\theta, k_x, k_y, t_x, t_y) = \sum_{i=1}^{2m} [(k_x X_i + t_x - P_{x_i})^2 + (k_y Y_i + t_y - P_{y_i})^2] \, .$$

Our object is to find θ, k_x, k_y, t_x and t_y that can minimize ξ. If the minimum ξ has a very small value, then we say that $C_{m-strokes}$ matches C_2. Differentiating ξ with respect to θ, k_x, k_y, t_x, and t_y, we then set the results to zero.

$\dfrac{\partial \xi}{\partial t_x} = 0$ implies

$$t_x = \frac{\sum_{i=1}^{2m} P_{x_i}}{2m} + \frac{k_x}{2m} \cdot (-\cos\theta \cdot \Sigma X_i' + \sin\theta \cdot \Sigma Y_i') \, . \tag{4.1}$$

$\dfrac{\partial \xi}{\partial t_y} = 0$ implies

$$t_y = \frac{\sum_{i=1}^{2m} P_{y_i}}{2m} + \frac{k_y}{2m} \cdot (-\sin\theta \cdot \Sigma X_i' - \cos\theta \cdot \Sigma Y_i') \, . \tag{4.2}$$

From (4.1) and (4.2) we can easily know that t_x and t_y are the functions of θ, k_x and k_y. From (4.1) and $\frac{\partial \xi}{\partial k_x} = 0$ we get

$$k_x = \frac{\sum_{i=1}^{2m} X_i \cdot (P_{x_i} - a_x)}{\sum_{i=1}^{2m} (X_i^2 + X_i \cdot (b \cdot \cos\theta + c \cdot \sin\theta))} \, . \tag{4.3}$$

From (4.2) and $\frac{\partial \xi}{\partial k_y} = 0$ we get

$$k_y = \frac{\sum_{i=1}^{2m} Y_i \cdot (P_{y_i} - a_y)}{\sum_{i=1}^{2m} (Y_i^2 + Y_i \cdot (b \cdot \sin\theta - c \cdot \cos\theta))} \, , \tag{4.4}$$

where

$$a_x = \frac{\sum_{i=1}^{2m} P_{x_i}}{2m} \, , a_y = \frac{\sum_{i=1}^{2m} P_{y_i}}{2m} \, , b = \frac{-\sum_{i=1}^{2m} X_i'}{2m} \, ,$$

and

$$c = \frac{\sum_{i=1}^{2m} Y_i'}{2m} \, .$$

From Eqs. (4.1), (4.2), (4.3) and (4.4) we know that t_x, t_y, k_x and k_y are the functions of θ . If we differentiate ξ with respect to θ and set the result to zero, we shall get a nonlinear equation with only one variable θ because t_x, t_y, k_x and k_y are all functions of θ. If we use a numerical method to solve this nonlinear equation, we cannot make sure that the solution of θ will converge after many iterations. Thus we make two assumptions: that θ is between $max\,\theta$ and $-max\,\theta$, and that $max\,\theta$ is much less than $90°$. Dividing the interval $(-max\,\theta, max\,\theta)$ equally into h subintervals, we get $\theta_0(= -max\,\theta), \theta_1, \theta_2, \ldots, \theta_h(= max\,\theta)$. For every θ_i, $0 \le i \le h$, work out the corresponding error ξ_i and find θ_{min} with minimum error $\xi_{local-min}$; h is a pre-defined integer.

If these two characters are the same and are written by the same person, every angle between the corresponding strokes in $C_{m-strokes}$ and C_2 should be less than some threshold $max\,\theta$. So it is reasonable for us to confine θ in this interval $(-max\,\theta, max\,\theta)$.

There are n possible matches between characters C_1 and C_2 (n depends on the configurations of C_1 and C_2), so we will match n times and get n $\xi_{local-min}$'s. From these n $\xi_{local-min}$'s we can get a global minimum $\xi_{global-min}$. The transformation resulting in $\xi_{global-min}$ is called the *optimal transformation*. The subcharacter in C_1 with $\xi_{global-min}$ is called the *optimal-matching* subcharacter, and we say that this subcharacter is the most similar subcharacter in C_1 to C_2. If $\xi_{global-min}$ is greater than some threshold ($m \cdot average\text{-}error$, where average-error is predetermined by experience), then C_2 is not a subcharacter of C_1. The more strokes the radical contains, the larger the error ξ may be, so this threshold is proportional to the number of strokes in C_2.

Because performing n possible matches is too time consuming, we use three reducing properties, as stated below, to reduce the number of possible matches significantly:

(1) The angle between any corresponding strokes in C_1 and C_2 should be less than $max\,\theta$.

(2) Let S_1 and S_2 be two strokes in C_2. If S_1 should be written above (below, at right of, at left of) some other stroke S_2 no matter how C_2 is written, the same kinds of relations must also exist between their corresponding strokes S_1' and S_2' in C_1.

(3) Let S_1 and S_2 be two strokes in C_2. If S_1 should or should not intersect some other stroke S_2 no matter how C_2 is written, the same kinds of relations must also exist between their corresponding strokes S_1' and S_2' in C_1.

After using the properties stated above, the number of possible matches is largely reduced. We take C_1 and C_2 in Fig. 11 as examples of *three reducing properties*. Stroke 1 in C_1 is almost normal to stroke 2 in C_2, all the permutations containing this kind of correspondence should be deleted, and this is an example of property 1. According to the structure of C_2 and the habit of handwriting, stroke 1 is always written above stroke 3. All the permutations that have their corresponding strokes in C_1 not satisfying this relationship should be deleted. This is an example of property 2. In C_2, stroke 1 should intersect stroke 2 and should not intersect stroke 3. All the permutations that have their corresponding strokes in C_1 not satisfying these relationships should also be deleted. This is an example of property 3.

Suppose that $\overline{P_0 P_1}$ and $\overline{P_2 P_3}$ are the corresponding strokes in C_1 and C_2 respectively. There are two ways to compare these two strokes; the first is to compare P_0 with P_2 and P_1 with P_3, and the second is to compare P_0 with P_3 and P_1 with P_2. How can we know which way of comparison is right? A wrong comparison between strokes may prevent this matching algorithm from finding the most similar subcharacter in the input Chinese character. We have made an assumption that if two input characters are the same and are written by the same person, the angle between the corresponding strokes in these two characters should be less than $max\,\theta$. So move $\overline{P_0 P_1}$ so that the center point of $\overline{P_0 P_1}$ coincides with the center point of $\overline{P_2 P_3}$, and if the angle between $\overline{P_0 P_1}$ and $\overline{P_2 P_3}$ is less than $90°$, P_0 is compared with P_2 and P_1 is compared with P_3, else P_0 is compared with P_3 and P_1 is compared with P_2. Two characters in Fig. 12 are taken as an example. When $\overline{P_0 P_1}$ is compared with $\overline{P_2 P_3}$, it is obvious that the angle between $\overline{P_0 P_1}$ and $\overline{P_2 P_3}$ is much less than $90°$, so we choose P_0 to correspond with P_2, and P_1 with P_3.

Suppose $C_{optimal-matching}$ is the optimal-matching subcharacter in C_1, and $C_{optimal-matching}$ after transformation results in another character C_3. We now re-check every corresponding stroke in C_2 and C_3 to know for sure whether C_2 is equal to C_3. The *re-checking procedure* has three steps and is shown below:

(1) If not all the angles between all the corresponding strokes in C_2 and C_3 are less than a threshold $\theta_{threshold}$ ($\theta_{threshold}$ should be less than $max\,\theta$), C_2 is not equal to C_3.

(2) If there exists a stroke such that both of its end points are very far away from those of its corresponding stroke, C_2 and C_3 are not the same.

(3) Suppose C_1 contains a subcharacter C_4 that is the same as C_2. It often happens that some stroke S_1 in C_1 but not in C_4 intersects with some stroke S_2 in C_4. If S_1 and S_2 are not collinear or if they do not have a common end point, these two strokes will be segmented into two different strokes, and this matching method will not be affected. This kind of intersection is called *evident-accidental-connection*. If S_1 and S_2 are almost collinear and connected at an end point, they will be segmented into one stroke, then this matching method will fail due to this mistake. We call this kind of intersection *vague-accidental-connection*. An example is depicted in Fig. 12. In this example, Fig. 12(a) is the normal form of the Chinese word "beat", and strokes 1 and 2, 3 and 4 are not connected with each other. Figure 12(b) is an example of the vague-accidental-connection, with stroke 1 and 2 connecting at an end point and collinear to each other. These two strokes are usually merged into a single stroke after the process of stroke segmentation. When it is matched with the radical shown in Fig. 12(d), we get an optimal matching subcharacter. We can see that P_1 is close to P_3, and P_0 is far away from P_2. Since $\overline{P_0 P_1}$ has length

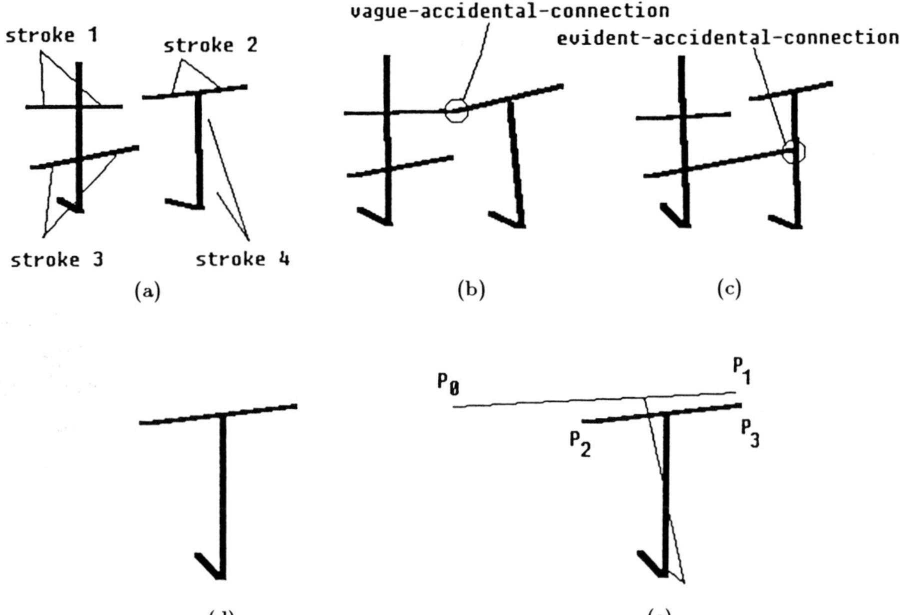

Fig. 12. (a) is the normal form of the Chinese word "beat", and strokes 1, 2, 3 and 4 are not connected with one another. (b) is an example of vague-accidental-connection, with strokes 1 and 2 connecting at an end point and collinear to each other. These two strokes are usually merged into a single stroke after the process of stroke segmentation. When it is matched with the radical shown in (d), we get an optimal matching subcharacter. (e) shows the comparison between (d) and the optimal matching sub-character. We can see that P_0 is close to P_2, and P_1 is far away from P_3. (c) is an example of evident-accidental-connection, with strokes 3 and 4 intersecting each other and not collinear to each other.

twice that of $\overline{P_2 P_3}$ and $\overline{P_0 P_1}$ has connection with a stroke not in C_4, then we can split $\overline{P_0 P_1}$ into two parts of equal size and complete the matching. Figure 12(c) is an example of the evident-accidental-connection, with strokes 3 and 4 intersecting each other and not collinear to each other. We sometimes allow at most k vague-accidental-connections, and k is usually very small (1 or 2). After transformation, the stroke resulting from evident-accidental-connection often has one end point close to and the other far away from those of its corresponding stroke in C_2 as shown in Fig. 12. So if C_3 contains more than k strokes that have one end point close to and the other far away from those of its corresponding stroke in C_2, C_3 and C_2 are not the same. The larger k is, the higher the possibility for this matching method to make a wrong judgment.

If C_3 satisfies the above three conditions, then C_3 is the same as C_2 and the matching is successful. Of course, since handwriting has a lot of variations there are some other conditions to be added for the validity of matching when needed. This will make the recognition system very complicated.

Some experimental results are given here. A tablet is used to input 114 characters and 62 radicals to test this *invariant transformation* matching method, called M_1. The orientations and the handwriting styles of these characters and radicals are not all the same; that is, translation, scaling and rotation of every character or every radical are not necessarily the same. Because every character is tested against every radical, M_1 is tested 62 114 = 7068 times.

We now show the values of the parameters in our experiments: Input Chinese characters are about the size 360 × 360 and the radicals are 100 × 100. The vague-accidental-connection and the evident-accidental-connection are set to 1; $max\,\theta$ is 30°; average-error is 5; and $\theta_{threshold}$ is 20°. These parameters should be updated if the degree of difference of handwriting styles between the input Chinese characters and the radicals is changed. M_1 treats a radical as a subcharacter of an input character if three re-checking procedures and the total error (number-of-strokes-in-radical × average-error) are satisfied. If M_1 can tell correctly whether a radical exists in a character, M_1 is successful; otherwise, M_1 has failed. In our experiments the success rate is above 99%. The tested radicals and Chinese characters are shown in Fig. 13. The computation time for M_1 depends highly on the three reducing properties of the radicals. If the three reducing properties are strong and can delete many redundant permutations when the radicals are matched with the input Chinese character, the computation time for M_1 is largely reduced. Otherwise, M_1 will be very time consuming.

From our experiments we know this algorithm is very reliable, and if we write characters carefully, it is possible for this algorithm to make no mistakes.

4.2. *Modified Relaxation Matching*

Relaxation matching is an elastic matching and it can tolerate considerable distortion of characters. The drawback is the heavy computation involved. However, due to recent advances in hardware speed and memory size, and the lower cost of workstations, this computational factor seems to be less influential than before. Our main concern here is to find a more reliable method (say with very high recognition rate and tolerable rejection rate), and the relaxation method is one of the best.

The best introduction to the relaxation technique is given in a book by Rosenfeld and Kak [32]. A good survey of relaxation is given by Kittler and Illingworth [33]. There are several versions of relaxation. We will adopt the average scheme since if an initial probability is 0 we require that its update probability always be 0, and if the initial probability is 1 that its update probability always be 1.

4.2.1. *Initial probability*

Let a_i be the ith stroke of an input character to be matched with b_j, the jth stroke of a model character stored in the database, $i, j = 1, 2, \ldots, n$. In defining the initial probability $P_{ij}^{(0)}$ of a_i matching b_j, note that the short line segment has great variation in slope angle due to quick handwriting. Let a_i be represented by

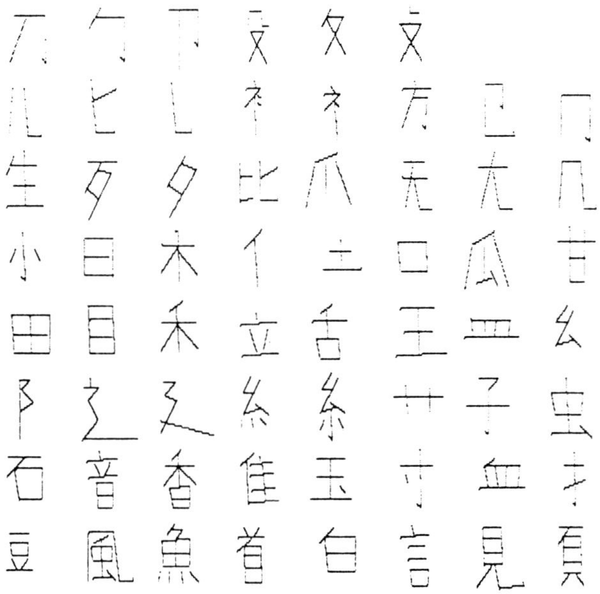

(a)

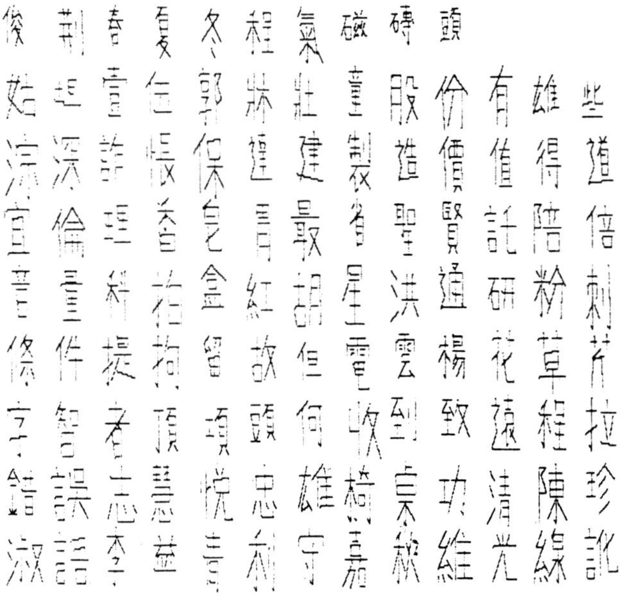

(b)

Fig. 13. (a) 62 tested radicals of approximate size 100 × 100. (b) 114 tested Chinese characters of approximate size 360 × 360.

the center point (X_{ci}, Y_{ci}), the slope angle θ_i, and the length l_i. Similarly b_j is represented by (X_{cj}, Y_{cj}), θ_j and l_j. Then:

Case 1. If l_i and l_j are both less than a threshold t_1 (say 10, with resolution 150 $\times$ 150).

$$P_{ij}^{(0)} = \frac{1}{1 + C_2 \mid l_i - l_j \mid + C_3 d_{ij}},$$

where

$$d_{ij} = \sqrt{(X_{ci} - X_{cj})^2 + (Y_{ci} - Y_{cj})^2},$$

$$C_2 = 0.01$$

and

$$C_3 = \begin{cases} 0 & \text{if} \quad d_{ij} \leq 15, \\ 0.02 & \text{if} \quad 15 < d_{ij} \leq 50, \\ \infty & \text{otherwise}. \end{cases}$$

Case 2. If either l_i or l_j is larger than the threshold t_1.

$$P_{ij}^{(0)} = \frac{1}{1 + C_1 \mid \theta_i - \theta_j \mid + C_2 \mid l_i - l_j \mid + C_3 d_{ij}},$$

where

$$C_1 = \begin{cases} 0 & \text{if} \quad \mid \theta_i - \theta_j \mid \leq 30° \\ 0.02 & \text{if} \quad 30° < \mid \theta_i - \theta_j \mid \leq 60° \\ \infty & \text{otherwise}, \end{cases}$$

and

$$C_2 = \begin{cases} 0 & \text{if} \quad \mid l_i - l_j \mid \leq 10, \\ \infty & \text{if} \quad \mid l_i - l_j \mid > l_i \ \text{or} \ l_j, \\ 0.02 & \text{otherwise}, \end{cases}$$

and C_3 is defined as before in Case 1. Here the values of C_1, C_2 and C_3 are determined heuristically to allow some variations of the input character. If the difference of angle sizes of two matching strokes is small (say less than 30°), the difference of lengths of two matching strokes is small (say less than 10), and the distance between two center points is small (say less than 15), then $C_1 = C_2 = C_3 = 0$ (i.e. $P_{ij}^{(0)} = 1$). If the angle size difference is too large (say larger than 60°), or the length difference is too large (say larger than l_i or l_j), or the distance between two center points is too long (say larger than 50), then the corresponding C_i ($i = 1$, or 2, or 3) is set to ∞ (i.e. $P_{ij}^{(0)} = 0$). In the other cases the match or no-match of two strokes is not clear and some probability value between 0 and 1 is assigned to $P_{ij}^{(0)}$ to allow some chance of match.

Next, the normalization of the initial probability is considered and a problem arises. If the stroke a_i is to match three strokes b_j, $j = 1, 2, 3$ with initial probabilities 0.1, 0.001, 0.001 respectively, then after normalization the initial probabilities will become 0.98, 0.0098, 0.0098, which means a_i will match b_1. This is a contradiction to the evidence provided by the very low initial probability 0.1. Thus we need to introduce an initial probability of no-match, which is defined by

$$Q_i^{(0)} = 1 - \max_{1 \le j \le n} P_{ij}^{(0)}.$$

Then we normalize the initial probabilities to be

$$P_{ij}^{(0)} = \frac{P_{ij}^{(0)}}{\sum_j P_{ij}^{(0)} + Q_i^{(0)}}$$

$$Q_i^{(0)} = \frac{Q_i^{(0)}}{\sum_j P_{ij}^{(0)} + Q_i^{(0)}}$$

where $i, j = 1, 2, \ldots, n$; $\sum_j P_{ij}^{(0)} + Q_i^{(0)} = 1$ for all i.

4.2.2. *Compatibility measure*

Before defining the compatibility measure the neighboring strokes of a given stroke should be defined. In general, a neighboring stroke of a given stroke is defined as the stroke that crosses it or touches it. But since the 3-fork point and the 2-fork point (corner point) are unstable feature points the neighboring relation is therefore unstable. Since each character has been normalized to 150 $\times$ 150 (as described at the end of Section 3), we can roughly describe the situations of being touched by another stroke. For each end point of a given stroke draw a circle of radius t_2 (say 7). Any stroke touching this circle is a neighboring stroke. Also, any stroke connected to a given stroke is naturally a neighboring stroke of the given stroke. For an isolated stroke its neighboring stroke is defined as the stroke with the shortest center to center distance.

Let a_i and b_j have neighboring strokes a_h and b_k respectively. Then the compatibility measure of a_i matched to b_j given a_h matched to b_k is

$$C(i,j \mid h,k) = \frac{2}{1 + C_4 \mid \theta_{ih} - \theta_{jk} \mid + C_5 \mid l_i + l_h - l_j - l_k \mid + C_6 \mid d_{ih} - d_{jk} \mid} - 1,$$

where

    θ_{ih} is the value of the angle between a_i and a_h;

    θ_{jk} is the value of the angle between b_j and b_k;

    d_{ih} is the distance between two center points of a_i and a_h;

    d_{jk} is the distance between two center points of b_j and b_k;

$$C_4 = \begin{cases} 0 & \text{if} \quad \mid \theta_{ih} - \theta_{jk} \mid \le 30° \\ 0.02 & \text{if} \quad 30° < \mid \theta_{ih} - \theta_{jk} \mid \le 60° \\ \infty & \text{otherwise}, \end{cases}$$

$$C_5 = \begin{cases} 0 & \text{if} \quad |\, l_i + l_h - l_j - l_k \,| \leq 30\,, \\ \infty & \text{if} \quad |\, l_i + l_h - l_j - l_k \,| > (l_i + l_h) \text{ or } (l_j + l_k)\,, \\ 0.02 & \text{otherwise}\,, \end{cases}$$

$$C_6 = \begin{cases} 0 & \text{if} \quad |\, d_{ih} - d_{jk} \,| \leq 20\,, \\ 0.02 & \text{if} \quad 20 \leq |\, d_{ih} - d_{jk} \,| \leq 40\,, \\ \infty & \text{otherwise}\,. \end{cases}$$

In defining neighboring relations please note that two strokes crossing each other is a rather stable relation, and hence if a_i has a_h crossing it and b_j has no b_k crossing it then a_i does not match b_j.

4.2.3. *Updating probabilities*

As stated before, we adopt the average scheme for updating probabilities because once an initial probability is 0 (or 1) then its updated probabilities should be 0 (or 1 correspondingly). Let the support function of a_i matched to b_j at time t be

$$S_{ij}^{(t)} = \frac{1}{n_{ij}} \sum_h \sum_k C(i,j \mid h,k) P_{hk}^{(t)}\,,$$

where $t = 0, 1, 2, \ldots$, and n_{ij} is sum of the number of h's and the number of k's in the two neighborhoods of a_h and b_j respectively. The updated probabilities are given by

$$P_{ij}^{(t+1)} = \frac{P_{ij}^{(t)}(1 + S_{ij}^{(t)})}{\sum_{k=1}^{n} P_{ik}^{(t)}(1 + S_{ik}^{(t)}) + Q_i^{(t)}}\,,$$

$$Q_i^{(t+1)} = \frac{Q_i^{(t)}}{\sum_k P_{ik}^{(t)}(1 + S_{ik}^{(t)}) + Q_i^{(t)}}\,,$$

where $i = 1, 2, \ldots, n$, and $\sum_j P_{ij}^{(t+1)} + Q_i^{(t+1)} = 1$. If $S_{ij}^{(t)}$ is negative but

$$\sum_k P_{ik}^{(t)} S_{ik}^{(t)} \approx 0$$

then

$$P_{ij}^{(t+1)} < \frac{P_{ij}^{(t)}}{\sum_k P_{ik}^{(t)} S_{ik}^{(t)} + 1} \approx P_{ij}^{(t)}\,.$$

Conversely, if $S_{ij}^{(t)}$ is positive and

$$\sum_k P_{ik}^{(t)} S_{ik}^{(t)} \approx 0$$

then

$$P_{ij}^{(t+1)} > P_{ij}^{(t)}\,.$$

The iteration for updating probabilities will be carried out ten times and then stopped. The limit of ten times is a heuristic measure based on the fact that too many iterations will result in the updated probabilities being too far away from the initial probabilities and this makes the probabilities meaningless, and also similar characters tend to be indistinguishable.

4.2.4. *Recognition rule*

If there are m model characters to be matched with the input character, then m distances can be computed as follows:

$$D_l = \sum_{i=1}^{n} Q_i^{(t+1)}, l = 1, 2, \ldots, m .$$

The model character with the minimum distance D_{min} among $\{D_l, \ l = 1, 2, \ldots, m\}$ is the recognized character for the input character. If D_{min} is greater than some given threshold we may reject the match and say that the input character is not recognized.

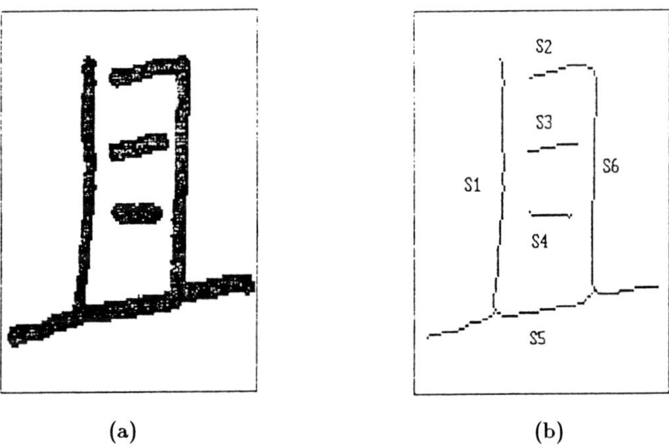

(a)   (b)

Fig. 14. (a) Input Chinese character image "and". (b) Thinned image of (a).

4.2.5. *Some experimental results*

Figure 14(a) shows an input Chinese character "and" which has zero cross points and six strokes. Hence this character will match those with the same number of cross points and the same number of strokes in the database. There are 27 model radicals stored in the database as shown in the left column of Table 1. After ten iterations of relaxation the distance values between the input character and the model characters are obtained as shown in the right column of Table 1, where the minimum distance has value 0.36 and corresponds to the correct match. Two similar characters "eye" and "moon" have distance values 3.52 and 1.95 respectively. They are shown in Figs. 15 and 16. The updated probabilities are shown in Tables 2(a), (b), (c).

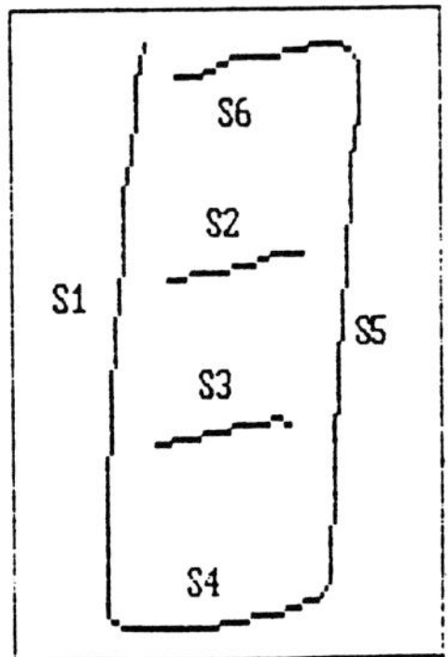

Fig. 15. Model character "eye".

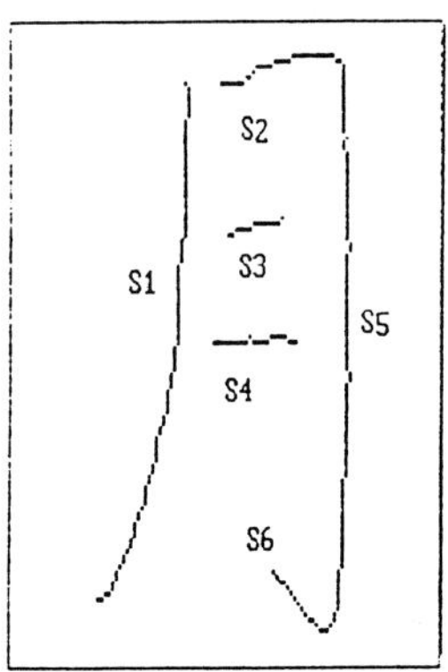

Fig. 16. Model character "moon".

5. Knowledge-Base Approach

The knowledge-base approach has been briefly studied by Leung, Cheung and Wong [18]. They developed some specific writing rules for the purpose of removing inconsistency with a higher efficiency in stroke matching, and they also adopted a two-level relaxation strategy to speed up the matching process. However, the organization of rules and the inference engine are not clearly described. Their idea is far from complete. A general description of the knowledge-base approach to solving computer vision problems is given in part 4 of a book by Ballard and Brown [34].

Rules incorporating the specific knowledge of writing Chinese characters can be used in any recognition method. For example, in the method of invariant transformation matching described in Section 4 some rules are used to make corrections and simplification. Of course rules can be used in relaxation matching to check the validity of match and to resolve ambiguities. For example, Fig. 17 shows a character with two different forms where the character in (b) has two very short strokes on the bottom side. This phenomenon happens to many characters. In this case rules can be used after relaxation matching to delete these short strokes. Another example is the accidental connection of two strokes where they should be separated in normal writing (see Fig. 18). Rules for splitting a long stroke into two parts when accidental connection happens are complicated since recognition (or structural matching) is needed to make proper judgements. A conclusion can be made in this section, that many rules can be introduced to deal with many specific events. The problem is "When and where should these rules be incorporated? In stroke segmentation? or in relaxation matching? Or after relaxation matching?" The whole logic (or system) will be very complicated and needs rigorous study.

Table 1. Model characters with zero cross points and six strokes.

Model Characters 樣版中文字編號	Distance Values 距離函數值
109 竹	3.278871
113 衤	5.232983
115 示	5.347677
116 石	5.441993
→ 117 目	→ 3.520669
119 四	4.193898
120 白	5.476106
123 氺	5.240956
< 128 且 >	<0.360000>
129 肖	4.661739
130 氺	5.092935
131 疋	3.674326
136 气	4.656476
137 辶	3.554282
138 勿	4.807496
141 乃	3.711839
145 方	4.023672
→ 146 月	→ 1.950906
147 己	4.994345
148 巛	4.459152
149 元	5.434395
150 分	4.908054
151 令	4.193570
185 巳	5.418605
232 穴	5.555163
236 丞	4.276927
237 巴	4.930367

6. Chinese Radicals and the Standard Database

Chinese characters have developed and evolved from oracle bone scriptures. Each character has structural meaning. As pointed out by Wang [35], Chinese characters are not only artistically elegant and culturally rich but also semantically meaningful and intelligently sound. There are several authors [25,36–40] trying to use the grammatical approach to give a formal description of Chinese characters by simple components. The problem with this approach is that once two strokes are accidentally connected there seems little hope of handling the character since little information is provided by a simple component. A better way is to use a subcharacter containing more strokes and having definite structure. Thus the idea of using radicals, instead of simple components, arises.

Each Chinese character is composed of some structural parts, called radicals. A Chinese input method, named Tsang-Chi input method, was developed several years ago [41]. It is based on radicals but the number of radicals used is limited by the size of the keyboard because each key on the keyboard corresponds to only one

Table 2. The updated probabilities after ten iterations.

Table 2. (a) Matching input "and" with model "and".

Model stroke j / Input stroke i	1	2	3	4	5	6	No-match Prob.
1	1.00	0.00	0.00	0.00	0.00	0.00	0.00
2	0.00	0.76	0.00	0.00	0.00	0.00	0.24
3	0.00	0.00	1.00	0.00	0.00	0.00	0.00
4	0.00	0.00	0.42	0.47	0.00	0.00	0.10
5	0.00	0.00	0.00	0.00	1.00	0.00	0.00
6	0.00	0.00	0.00	0.00	0.00	0.98	0.02

Table 2. (b) Matching input "and" with model "eye".

Model stroke j / Input stroke i	1	2	3	4	5	6	No-match Prob.
1	0.30	0.00	0.00	0.00	0.00	0.00	0.70
2	0.00	0.00	0.00	0.00	0.00	0.28	0.72
3	0.00	0.65	0.00	0.00	0.00	0.00	0.35
4	0.00	0.17	0.17	0.00	0.00	0.00	0.65
5	0.00	0.00	0.00	0.51	0.00	0.00	0.49
6	0.00	0.00	0.00	0.00	0.40	0.00	0.60

Table 2. (c) Matching input "and" with model "moon".

Model stroke j / Input stroke i	1	2	3	4	5	6	No-match Prob.
1	0.95	0.00	0.00	0.00	0.00	0.00	0.05
2	0.00	0.38	0.37	0.00	0.00	0.28	0.25
3	0.00	0.00	0.98	0.02	0.00	0.00	0.01
4	0.00	0.00	0.00	1.00	0.00	0.00	0.00
5	0.00	0.00	0.00	0.00	0.00	0.00	1.00
6	0.00	0.00	0.00	0.00	0.36	0.00	0.64

or two radicals. This means that Tsang-Chi can only use very simple and primitive radicals and a Chinese character must be divided into 1, 2, 3, 4, or 5 parts for input, with each part corresponding to a radical, while a key may correspond to two radicals which do not appear in the same character together. However, the radicals used by Tsang-Chi are not sufficient for optical character recognition, and some of them should be deleted. The main problem here is that we scan an image in a sequential way, and not a parallel way. Thus we have to create some new radicals suitable for optical character recognition. An example is given in Fig. 19 where the character "spring" 春 is composed of two radicals "big" 大 and "sun" 日 in Tsang-Chi input but it is more convenient to replace 大 by 夫 for image recognition.

(a)   (b)

Fig. 17. A character with two different forms.

(a)   (b)

Fig. 18. Characters with an accidental connection of two strokes.

Fig. 19. Character "spring".

Let a main radical be defined as a subpattern that appears in the left side or top side of a character, and is independent as well as representative (e.g. 忄 in 憶 , 隹 in 集). Let a secondary radical be defined as a subpattern that appears in the right side or bottom side of a character, and is independent as well as representative (e.g. 心 in 憶 , 木 in 集). Let an extra pattern be a subpattern that is neither a main radical nor a secondary radical (e.g. 韭 in 懺). According to 5401 daily used characters there are 290 main radicals, 32 secondary radicals, and 36 extra patterns. Thus we can classify 5401 characters into 290 classes from their main radicals and each class is further divided into some subclasses from the 32 secondary radicals. This classification will largely reduce the recognition time if we try to match radicals instead of the whole character. The list of all radicals as well as extra patterns is given in a technical report by Huang and Chang [42].

In evaluating the performance of an OCR system a standard database is required. The Japanese have an ETL-8 database containing about 1000 handwritten Chinese characters where each character has 160 writing variations. This is not sufficient for our use here since we have 5401 daily used characters. The Computer and Communication Research Laboratory of the Industrial Technology Research Institute in Taiwan, has recently compiled a Chinese database containing 5401 characters written by about 2000 writers. Each character in the database has a sample of size 214 to 284 handwritten character images, and each image has a resolution of 144 × 150 pixels. Each character sample is sorted according to the quality of a character image, and each character image has a Big-5 code associated with it. The total database is stored in six SONY 8 mm metal particle tapes. The announcement of this database is an important step for research in optical handwritten Chinese character recognition.

7. Discussion

A stroke extraction method based on thinning and two structural matching methods, deterministic and probabilistic, have been described above for the recognition of constrained handwritten Chinese characters. A suggestion is proposed for matching radicals instead of the whole character. Since handwriting has great variations many unexpected situations can happen. The most critical situation is when two strokes which are supposed to be separate are accidentally connected. This will cause the failure of stroke extraction as well as structural matching. Some rules need to be introduced to handle this situation. In general, many rules are needed to deal with different kinds of writing conditions, and a complicated knowledge-base system containing both rules and structural matching methods will be good for Chinese OCR. However, the development of such a complicated system is still in its infancy. We look forward to seeing such a system in the near future.

As for unconstrained handwritten Chinese characters, where stroke extraction is not feasible, the neural network approach may be a way to do the recognition job. However, neural networks are not well understood and depend largely on experiments. Since the writing quality is bad we seem to be helpless at this present stage. When there is a breakthrough on the recognition theory in cognitive science one day in the future we may then be able to handle unconstrained handwritten Chinese characters.

Acknowledgement

The author thanks Ms. C. M. Lin and Ms. Y. C. Lee for their skillful typing of this manuscript .

References

[1] S. Mori, K. Yamamoto and M. Yasuda, Research on machine recognition of hand-printed characters, *IEEE Trans. Pattern Anal. Mach. Intell.* **6**, 4 (1984) 386–405.

[2] C. R. Giardina and E. R. Dougherty, *Morphological Methods in Image and Signal Processing* (Prentice Hall, New Jersey, 1988).

[3] H. Ogawa and K. Taniguchi, Thinning and stroke segmentation for handwritten Chinese character recognition, *Pattern Recogn.* **15**, 4 (1982) 299–308.

[4] F. H. Cheng and W. H. Hsu, Three stroke extraction methods for recognition of handwritten Chinese Characters, in *Proc. Int. on Conf. Chinese Computing*, Singapore, 1986, 191–195.

[5] C. W. Liao and J. S. Huang, Stroke segmentation by Bernstein–Bezier curve fitting, *Pattern Recogn.* **23**, 5 (1990) 475–484.

[6] Y. S. Chen and W. H. Hsu, An interpretive model of line continuation in human visual perception, *Pattern Recogn.* **22**, 5 (1989) 619–639.

[7] F. Chang and S. H. Lai, Stroke segmentation for Chinese character recognition, in *Proc. First Nat. Workshop on Character Recognition*, Taiwan, Rep. of China, 1991, 1–3.

[8] Y. K. Chu and C. Y. Suen, An alternate smoothing and stripping algorithm for thinning digital binary patterns, *Signal Process.* **11** (1986) 207–222.

[9] P. S. P. Wang and Y. Y. Zhang, A fast and flexible thinning algorithm, *IEEE Trans. Comput.* **38**, 5 (1989) 741–745.

[10] Y. S. Chen and W. H. Hsu, A modified fast parallel algorithm for thinning digital patterns, *Pattern Recogn. Lett.* **7** (1988) 99–106.

[11] S. W. Lee, Performance evaluation of thinning algorithms for oriental character recognition, to appear in *IEEE Trans. Pattern Anal. Mach. Intell.* (1993).

[12] K. Yamamoto and A. Rosenfeld, Recognition of handprinted KANJI characters by a relaxation method, in *Proc. Int. Conf. on Pattern Recognition*, 1982, 395–398.

[13] I. Sekita, K. Toraichi, R. Mori, K. Yamamoto and H. Yamada, Feature extraction of handwritten Japanese characters by spline functions for relaxation matching, *Pattern Recogn.* **21**, 1 (1988) 9–17.

[14] S. L. Xie and M. Suk, On machine recognition of handprinted Chinese characters by feature relaxation, *Pattern Recogn.* **21**, 1 (1988) 1–7.

[15] M. Kimura, T. Ejima, H. Aso, H. Yashiro, N. Son and M. Suzuki, An intelligent character recognition system with high accuracy and high speed by integrating image-type and logical-type information processing, in *Proc. Int. Conf. on Pattern Recognition*, Rome, Italy, 1988, 38–40.

[16] M. C. Kuo, Recognition of handprinted Chinese characters by stroke relaxation algorithm, Master Thesis, Department of Electrical Engineering, National Tsing Hua University, Taiwan, R.O.C., 1989.

[17] F. H. Cheng, W. H. Hsu and M. Y. Chen, Recognition of handwritten Chinese characters by modified Hough transform techniques, *IEEE Trans. Pattern Anal. Mach. Intell.* **11**, 4 (1989) 429–439.

[18] C. H. Leung, Y. S. Cheung and Y. L. Wong, A knowledge-based stroke-matching method for Chinese character recognition, *IEEE Trans. Syst. Man Cybern.* **17**, 6 (1987) 993–1003.

[19] F. H. Cheng, W. H. Hsu and C. A. Chen, Fuzzy approach to solve the recognition problem of handwritten Chinese characters, *Pattern Recogn.* **22**, 2 (1989) 133–141.

[20] Y. S. Tsai, Handwritten character recognition by graph matching, Master Thesis, Institute of Information Science, National Chiao Tung University, Taiwan, R.O.C., 1988.

[21] S. W. Lu, Y. Ren and C. Y. Suen, Hierarchical attributed graph representation and recognition of handwritten Chinese characters, *Pattern Recogn.* **24**, 7 (1991) 617–632.

[22] C. W. Liao and J. S. Huang, A transformation invariant matching algorithm for handwritten Chinese character recognition, *Pattern Recogn.* **23**, 11 (1990) 1167–1188.

[23] L. H. Chen and J. R. Lieh, Handwritten character recognition using a 2-layer random graph model by relaxation matching, *Pattern Recogn.* **23**, 11 (1990) 1189–1205.

[24] S. L. Chou and W. H. Tsai, Recognizing handwritten Chinese characters by stroke-segment matching using an iteration scheme, *Int. J. Pattern Recogn. Artif. Intell.* **5**, 1&2 (1991) 175–189.

[25] M. Zhao, Two-dimensional extended attribute grammar method for the recognition of hand-printed Chinese characters, *Pattern Recogn.* **23**, 7 (1990) 685–695.

[26] C. C. Hsieh and H. J. Lee, Off line recognition of handwritten Chinese characters by on-line model-guided matching, in *Proc. First Nat. Workshop on Character Recognition*, Rep. of China, 1991, 55–75.

[27] C. J. Wu and W. H. Tsai, A decision-tree approach to recognition of printed Chinese characters by neural networks using neocognitrons, in *Proc. First Nat. Workshop on Character Recognition*, Rep. of China, 1991, 76–106.

[28] Y. Kimura, Distorted handwritten Kanji character pattern recognition by a learning algorithm minimizing output variation, in *Proc. Int. Joint Conf. on Neural Networks*, Vol. I, 1991, 103–106.

[29] J. F. Wang, H. D. Chang and J. H. Tseng, Handwritten Chinese radical recognition via neural networks, in *Proc. Int. Conf. on Computer Processing of Chinese and Oriental Languages*, Taiwan, ROC, 1991, 92–97.

[30] Y. Yong, Handprinted Chinese character recognition via neural networks, *Pattern Recogn. Lett.* **7** (1988) 19–25.

[31] H. Y. Liao, J. S. Huang and S. T. Huang, Stroke-based handwritten Chinese character recognition using neural networks, Technical Report, Institute of Information Science, Academia Sinica, Taiwan, Rep. of China, 1991.

[32] A. Rosenfeld and A. C. Kak, *Digital Picture Processing*, Vol. 2 (Academic Press, New York, 1982).

[33] J. Kittler and J. Illingworth, Relaxation labeling algorithms – a review, *Image Vision Comput.* **3**, 4 (1985) 206–216.

[34] D. H. Ballard and C. M. Brown, *Computer Vision* (Prentice-Hall, Englewood Cliffs, New Jersey, 1982).

[35] P. S. P. Wang, Knowledge pattern representation of Chinese characters, *Int. J. Pattern Recogn. Artif. Intell.* **2**, 1 (1988) 161–179.

[36] W. Stallings, The morphology of Chinese characters: A survey of models and applications, *Computer Humanities* **9** (1975) 13–24.

[37] B. Rankin and S. Siegal, A grammar for component combination in Chinese characters, NBS Tech. Note 296 (1966).

[38] K. S. Fu, *Syntactic Pattern Recognition and Applications* (Prentice-Hall, Englewood Cliffs, New Jersey, 1982).

[39] P. S. P. Wang, A new character recognition scheme with lower ambiguity and higher recognizability, *Pattern Recogn. Lett.* **3** (1985) 431–436.

[40] T. Agui and H. Nagahashi, A coding method of Chinese characters, *IEEE Trans. Pattern Anal. Mach. Intell.* **1**, 4 (1979) 333–341.

[41] *Tsang-Chi Chinese Input Method* (The Third Wave Co., Taipei, Taiwan, R.O.C., 1980).

[42] J. S. Huang and H. L. Chang, Classification of Chinese characters by radicals for image recognition, Technical Report TR-91-019, Institute of Information Science, Academia Sinica, Taipei, Taiwan, Rep. of China, 1991.

Handbook of Pattern Recognition and Computer Vision, pp. 625–654
Eds. C. H. Chen, L. F. Pau and P. S. P. Wang
© 1993 World Scientific Publishing Company

CHAPTER 3.6

AUTOMATIC ANALYSIS AND UNDERSTANDING
OF DOCUMENTS

YUAN Y. TANG

Centre for Pattern Recognition and Machine Intelligence
Concordia University, 1455 de Maisonneuve Blvd. West
Montreal, Quebec H3G 1M8, Canada
Email: tang@concour.cs.concordia.ca.

and

CHANG D. YAN, M. CHERIET, CHING Y. SUEN
Centre for Pattern Recognition and Machine Intelligence
Concordia University, 1455 de Maisonneuve Blvd. West
Montreal, Quebec H3G 1M8, Canada

A basic model for document processing is presented in this chapter. In this model, document processing can be divided into two phases: document analysis and document understanding. A document has two structures: geometric (layout) structure and logical structure. Extraction of the geometric structure from a document refers to document analysis; mapping the geometric structure into logical structure deals with document understanding. Both types of document structures and the two areas of document processing are discussed in this chapter.

Top-down and bottom-up approaches have been used in document analysis. Tree transform, formatting knowledge and description language approaches have been used in document understanding. All the above approaches are presented.

A particular case — form document processing — is discussed. Form description and form registration approaches are presented. A form processing system is also introduced.

Finally, many techniques, such as Hough transform, projection, crossing counts, form definition language, etc. which have been used in these approaches are also discussed here.

Keywords: Geometric and logical structures, top-down and bottom-up approaches, tree transform, formatting knowledge, description languages, document processing.

1. Introduction

Since the 1960's, much research on document processing has been done based on Optical Character Recognition (OCR) [5,45]. The study of automatic text segmentation and discrimination started about two decades ago [34,45]. With rapid development of modern computers and the increasing need to acquire large volumes of data, automatic text segmentation and discrimination have been widely studied since the early 1980's [1,64,71]. To date, many methods have been proposed, and many document processing systems have been described [14,20,28,46,49,66]. The

First International Conference on Document Analysis and Recognition was held in autumn 1991, in which many papers dealing with new achievements of the research on document processing were published [10,12,30,36,38,42,54,72].

What is document processing? Different definitions have caused a bit of confusion. In this handbook, the definition is chosen from a *basic document processing model* proposed by [57,60,61]. The principal ideas of this model will be seen throughout the entire chapter. The chapter is organized into six sections according to the model:

 (i) A Basic Model for Document Processing
 (ii) Document Structure
     (a) Strength of Structure
     (b) Geometric Structure
     (c) Logical Structure
(iii) Document Analysis
     (a) Top-down Approach
     (b) Bottom-up Approach
(iv) Document Understanding
     (a) Tree Transform Approach
     (b) Formatting Knowledge Approach
     (c) Description Language Approach
 (v) Form Document Processing
     (a) Characteristics of Form Documents
     (b) Form Description Language Approach
     (c) Form Registration Approach
     (d) A Form Document Processing System
(iv) Major Techniques

2. A Basic Model for Document Processing

A basic model for document processing was first proposed by [61] in the *First International Conference on Document Analysis and Recognition*. A graphical illustration can be shown in Fig. 1.

The following principal concepts are proposed in this model:

- Document processing is divided into two phases: *document analysis* and *document understanding*.
- A document is considered to have two structures: *geometric (layout) structure* and *logical structure*.
- Extraction of the geometric structure from a document refers to document analysis; mapping the geometric structure into logical structure is defined as document understanding. Once the logical structure has been captured, knowledge can be acquired from the document.

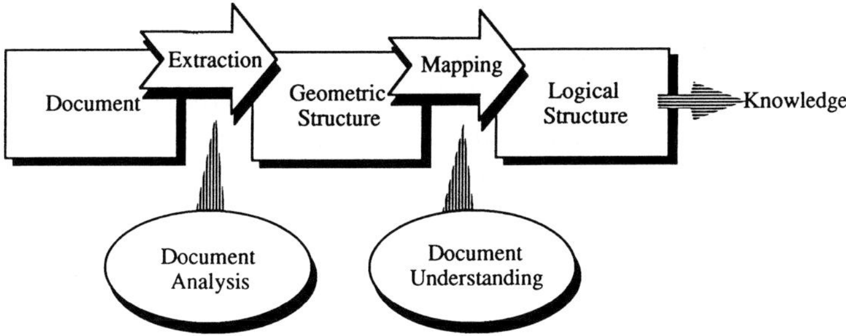

Fig. 1. Basic document processing model.

- But in some cases, there is no clear boundary between the two phases just described. For example, the document logical structure may also be found during an analysis of bank cheques by knowledge rules.

The relationship among geometric structure, logical structure, document analysis and document understanding can also be shown in the figure.

The basic model of document processing can be formally described below [58]:

Definition 1. A document Ω is specified by a quintuple

$$\Omega = (\Im, \Phi, \delta, \alpha, \beta) \tag{2.1}$$

such that

$$\Im = \{\Theta^1, \Theta^2, \ldots, \Theta^i, \ldots, \Theta^m\} \tag{2.2}$$

where

$$\Theta^i = \{\Theta^i_j\}^*$$

and

$$\Phi = \{\varphi_l, \varphi_r\}$$
$$\alpha = \{\alpha^1, \alpha^2, \ldots, \alpha^p\} \subseteq \Im$$
$$\beta = \{\beta^1, \beta^2, \ldots, \beta^q\} \subseteq \Im$$
$$\delta = \Im \times \Phi \rightarrow 2^{\Im} \tag{2.3}$$

where

- $\Im$ is a finite set of document objects which are sets of blocks Θ^i ($i = 1, 2, \ldots, m$).
- $\{\Theta^i_j\}^*$ denotes repeated sub-division.
- Φ is a finite set of linking factors. φ_l and φ_r stand for leading linking and repetition linking respectively.
- δ is a finite set of logical linking functions which indicate logical linking of the document objects.
- α is a finite set of heading objects.
- β is a finite set of ending objects.

Definition 2. *Document processing* is a process to construct the quintuple represented by Eqs. (2.1–2.3). *Document analysis* refers to extracting elements $\Im$, Θ^i and Θ^i_j in Eq. (2.2), i.e. extraction of the geometric structure of Ω. *Document understanding* deals with finding Φ, δ, α, and β in Eq. (2.3), considering the logical structure of Ω.

A simple example is illustrated in Fig. 2. We have

$$\Im = \{\Theta^1, \Theta^2, \Theta^3, \Theta^4, \Theta^5\}$$
$$\Theta^4 = \{\Theta^4_j\}^* = \{\Theta^4_1, \Theta^4_2\}, \ \Theta^5 = \{\Theta^5_j\}^* = \{\Theta^5_1, \Theta^5_2, \Theta^5_3\}$$
$$\alpha = \{\Theta^1, \Theta^2\}, \ \beta = \{\Theta^4, \Theta^5\}$$
$$\delta(\Theta^1, l) = \Theta^3, \ \delta(\Theta^2, l) = \Theta^4, \ \delta(\Theta^3, l) = \Theta^5, \ \delta(\Theta^4, r) = \Theta^{4*}_i, \ \delta(\Theta^5, r) = \Theta^{5*}_i .$$

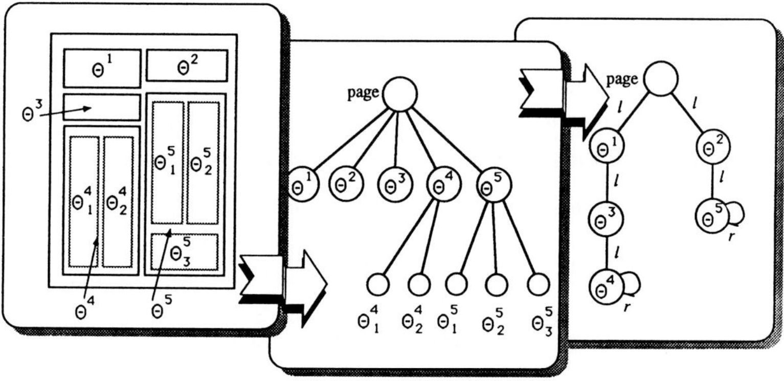

Fig. 2. A simple example of document processing described by the basic model.

From the above definition, it is obvious that there is a nondeterministic mapping from the geometric structure into the logical structure. However, as the geometric structure is extracted, its deterministic mapping can be achieved. It is formally described below:

Theorem 1. Let Ω be a document defined by a quintuple

$$(\Im_i, \Phi_i, \delta_i, \alpha_i, \beta_i)$$

having nondeterministic mapping from geometric structure into logical structure, then there exists a quintuple $(\Im_j, \Phi_j, \delta_j, \alpha_j, \beta_j)$ which contains a deterministic mapping from the geometric structure of Ω into a logical structure.

The proof of this theorem can be found in [58].

3. Document Structures

The key concept in document processing is that of structure. Document structure is the division and repeated subdivision of the content of a document into increasingly smaller parts which are called *objects*. An object which cannot be subdivided into smaller objects is called a *basic object*. All other objects are called *composite objects*. Structure can be realized as a geometric (layout) structure in terms of its geometric characteristics, or a logical structure due to its semantic properties.

3.1. *Strength of Structure*

To measure a document structure, a *Strength of Structure S_s* has been introduced [70].

Definition 3. Suppose a document is divided into n objects associated with n variables. H_i stands for the partial entropy of the ith variable, and H for the entropy of the whole document. The strength of structure is

$$S_s = \sum_{i=1}^{n} H_i - H \, . \tag{3.1}$$

For instance, if the entire document consists of four composite objects associated with the variables x_1–x_4, the strength will be

$$S_s = -\sum_{i=1}^{4} \sum_{j=1}^{n} p_j(x_i) \, log \, p_j(x_i) + \sum_{j=1}^{n} p_j(x_1, x_2, x_3, x_4) \, log \, p_j(x_1, x_2, x_3, x_4) \, .$$

$$\tag{3.2}$$

3.2. *Geometric Structure*

Geometric structure represents the objects of a document based on the presentation, and connection among these objects. According to the International Standard ISO 8613-1:1989(E) [31], the geometric or layout structure can be defined below:

Definition 4. Geometric or layout structure is the result of dividing and subdividing the content of a document into increasingly smaller parts, on the basis of the presentation.

Geometric (Layout) Object is an element of the specific geometric structure of a document. The following types of geometric objects are defined:

- *Block* is a basic geometric object corresponding to a rectangular area on the presentation medium containing a portion of the document content;
- *Frame* is a composite geometric object corresponding to a rectangular area on the presentation medium containing either one or more blocks or other frames;
- *Page* is a basic or composite geometric object corresponding to a rectangular area, if it is a composite object, containing either one or more frames or one or more blocks;
- *Page set* is a set of one or more pages;

- *Document Geometric (Layout) Root* is the object at the highest level in the hierarchy of the specific geometric structure. The root node in the above example represents a page.

3.2.1. *Document Geometric Model (DGM)*

The geometric structure can be formally described as a *document geometric model (DGM)* according to the basic model Eqs. (2.1) and (2.2). To facilitate document analysis (see the next section), an entropy function will be used in the following definition.

Definition 5. A DGM is described by a document space $\Omega = (\Im, \beta_U, H_\Im)$, where $\Im$ is the set of geometric objects which are either basic objects or composite objects; β_U is a set of operations which are performed in $\Im$, and $H_\Im$ stands for entropy function, such that

$$
\begin{aligned}
\Im &= \{\Im_T, \Im_G\} \\
\beta_U &= \{\cup, \cap\} \\
\forall_{i \neq j}(\Im_i \cup \Im_j) &\subseteq \Omega) \\
\forall_{i \neq j}(\Im_i \cap \Im_j) &= \phi) \\
H_\Im &= -\sum P(\Im_T, \Im_G) \, log \, P(\Im_T, \Im_G)
\end{aligned}
\tag{3.3}
$$

where $\Im_T$ represents *Text Area*, and $\Im_G$ stands for *Graphic Area*. Each area can be defined as follows:

$$
\begin{aligned}
\Im_T &= \{\Theta^1, \Theta^2, \ldots, \Theta^m\} \\
\Im_G &= \{\Theta^G, \Theta^C, \Theta^R\}
\end{aligned}
$$

where

- $\Theta^1, \Theta^2, \ldots, \Theta^m$ show different *Text Blocks*, e.g. Θ^1 shows a *Headline Block*, Θ^2 indicates a *Text Line Block*, etc.;
- Θ^G indicates *Geometric Graphics Block* such as points, arcs, and lines;
- Θ^C presents *Graphic Characters Block* such as accented letters and special symbols;
- Θ^R presents *Raster Graphics (Picture) Block*;

and

$$
\Theta^j = \{\Theta_i^j\}^*, \quad \Theta_i^j = \begin{cases} \{\sigma_1^C, \sigma_2^C, \ldots, \sigma_r^C\} & \Theta_i^j \subseteq \Im_T \\ \{\sigma_1^G, \sigma_2^G, \ldots, \sigma_s^G\} & \Theta_i^j \subseteq \Im_G \end{cases}
\tag{3.4}
$$

where

- σ_i^C indicates a *Character*;
- σ_i^G represents a *Graphic Element* including geometric graphics, graphic character elements and raster graphics elements.

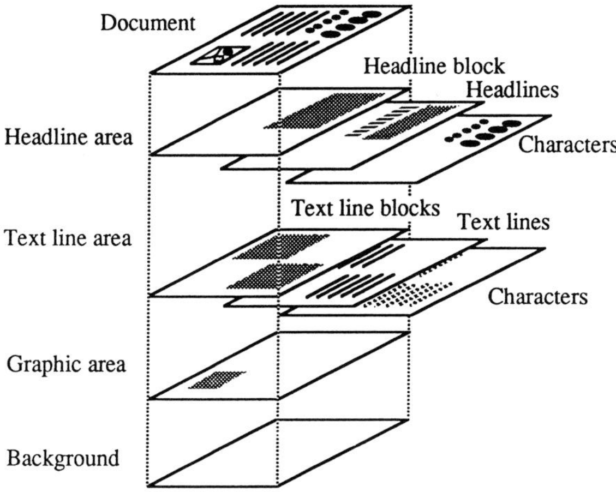

Fig. 3. Geometric model for a specific document.

This is a general description of the DGM. Different types of specific documents
have their specific form. For example, for a specific document shown at the top of
Fig. 3, from the above general model, its specific document geometric model can be
presented graphically as seen in the figure. In this model, a document is divided into
several areas: headline area, text line area, graphic area and background. Several
headlines occupying a single rectangle area are referred to as a *headline block*, a
series of continuous text lines is called a *text line block*, etc.

3.2.2. *Geometric Complexity*

The geometric complexity of a document can be measured by a *complexity function* μ which is defined below:

Definition 6. Let $|\Im_T|$ and $|\Im_G|$ be the number of elements in sets $\Im_T$ and $\Im_G$
respectively. Complexity function μ can be presented as

$$\mu = |\Im_T| + |\Im_G|. \tag{3.5}$$

In terms of complexity, documents can be classified into four categories:

- Documents without graphics (e.g. editorials): $\Im_G = \phi$;
- Document forms (e.g. bank cheques and other business forms): $\Im_G = \{\Theta_i^G\}$;
- Documents with graphics (e.g. general newspaper articles): $\Im_G \neq \phi$;
- Documents with graphics as the main elements (e.g. advertisements, front page
  of magazine): $|\Im_T| \leq |\Im_G|$.

3.3. *Logical Structure*

Document understanding emphasizes the finding of logical relations between the objects of a document. To facilitate this process, a logical structure and its model have been developed in our early work [61] which can be summarized below.

Logical structure represents the objects of a document based on the human-perceptible meaning, and connection among these objects. According to the International Standard ISO 8613-1:1989(E), the logical structure can be defined as follows [31]:

Definition 7. Logical structure is the result of dividing and subdividing the content of a document into increasingly smaller parts, on the basis of the *human-perceptible meaning* of the content, for example, into chapters, sections, subsections, and paragraphs.

Logical Object is an element of the specific logical structure of a document. For logical object, no classification other than *Basic logical object, Composite logical object* and *document logical root* is defined. Logical object categories such as *Chapter, Section* and *Paragraph* are application-dependent and can be defined using the *Object class* mechanism [31].

According to the basic model Eqs. (2.1) and (2.3), a formal description of the logical structure termed *document logical model (DLM)* is presented as follows:

Definition 8. A DLM is described by a tree, $\mho=(\Theta,\Re)$. Θ denotes a nonempty set of nodes which represent the logical objects. $\Re$ expresses a set of edges representing relations between the logical objects.

$$\Theta = \{\Theta^1, \Theta^2, \ldots, \Theta^n\}$$
$$\Re = \Im \times \Im$$
$$\Re = \{\Re_1, \Re_2, \ldots, \Re_m\}$$

$\mho$ can be represented as an *Incidence Matrix* with size $m \times n$:

$$\mho = \begin{cases} 1 & \text{when } \Re_j \text{ is incident with } \Theta^i \\ 0 & \text{otherwise}. \end{cases} \tag{3.6}$$

For a permissible specific logical structure as shown in Fig. 4, the incidence matrix can be expressed as

$$\mho = \begin{array}{c} \\ \Theta^1 \\ \Theta^2 \\ \Theta^3 \\ \Theta^4 \\ \Theta^5 \\ \Theta^6 \end{array} \begin{array}{ccccc} \Re_1 & \Re_2 & \Re_3 & \Re_4 & \Re_5 \\ \left[\begin{array}{ccccc} 1 & 1 & 0 & 0 & 0 \\ 0 & 0 & 1 & 1 & 0 \\ 0 & 0 & 0 & 0 & 1 \\ 0 & 0 & 0 & 0 & 0 \\ 0 & 0 & 0 & 0 & 0 \\ 0 & 0 & 0 & 0 & 0 \end{array}\right] \end{array}. \tag{3.7}$$

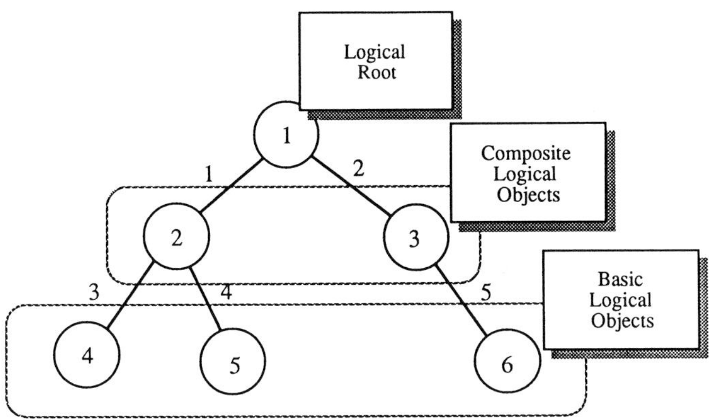

Fig. 4. A permissible specific logical structure.

In this figure, a page may contain two articles, the logical root Θ^1 may represent a page, composite logical objects Θ^2 and Θ^3 may indicate titles, and $\Theta^4 - \Theta^6$ may denote paragraphs.

4. Document Analysis

Document analysis is defined as the extraction of the geometric structure of a document. In this way, a document image is broken down into several blocks, which represent coherent components of a document, such as text lines, headlines, graphics, etc. with or without the knowledge regarding the specific format [61,66].

Top-down and bottom-up approaches have been used in document analysis. Each has its advantages and disadvantages. The top-down approach is fast and very effective for processing documents that have a specific format. On the other hand, the bottom-up approach is time consuming. But it is possible to develop algorithms which are applicable to a variety of documents. A better result may be achieved by combining the two approaches [47].

4.1. *Top-Down Approach*

The top-down (knowledge based) approach proceeds with an expectation of the nature of the document. It divides the document into major regions which are further divided into subregions, etc. [24,25,30,39,40,49,50]. The top-down approach is fast and very effective for processing documents that have a specific format.

The geometric structure of a document can be represented by a tree. Suppose this tree contains K levels. Figure 5 indicates the ith and $(i+1)$th levels. Suppose the upper layer has nodes $N_1^i, N_2^i, \ldots, N_m^i$; and the lower layer has nodes N_1^{i+1}, $N_2^{i+1}, \ldots, N_n^{i+1}$. The relations between these two layers are expressed by edges between the nodes. They can also be represented in the form of

$$
\begin{bmatrix} N_1^i \\ N_2^i \\ \cdot \\ \cdot \\ \cdot \\ N_m^i \end{bmatrix} \iff \begin{bmatrix} 1 & 1 & \ldots & 1 & 0 & 0 & \ldots & 0 & 0 & 0 & \ldots & 0 \\ 0 & 0 & \ldots & 0 & 1 & 1 & \ldots & 1 & 0 & 0 & \ldots & 0 \\ & & \ldots & & & & \ldots & & & & & \\ & & \ldots & & & & \ldots & & & & & \\ & & \ldots & & & & \ldots & & & & & \\ 0 & 0 & \ldots & 0 & 0 & 0 & \ldots & 0 & 1 & 1 & \ldots & 1 \end{bmatrix} . \tag{4.1}
$$

Values 1's in Eq. (4.1) correspond to the edges in Fig. 5 meaning that

$$
\begin{aligned}
N_1^i &\iff (N_1^{i+1}, N_2^{i+1}, \ldots, N_r^{i+1}) \\
N_2^i &\iff (N_{r+1}^{i+1}, N_{r+2}^{i+1}, \ldots, N_s^{i+1}) \\
\cdots \quad &\cdots \quad \cdots \\
N_m^i &\iff (N_{p+1}^{i+1}, N_{p+2}^{i+1}, \ldots, N_n^{i+1}) .
\end{aligned}
$$

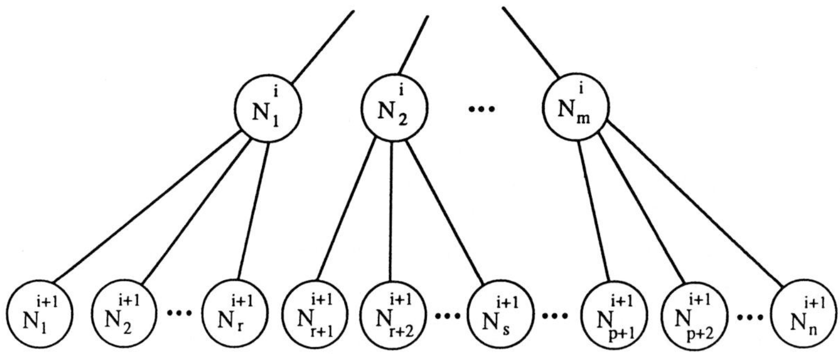

Fig. 5. The ith and $(i+1)$th level of a structure tree.

Equation (4.1) gives two ways: "$\Longrightarrow$" from left to right corresponding to "from top to bottom" in the tree structure (Fig. 5), and "$\Longleftarrow$" from right to left corresponding to "from bottom to top" in the same structure. In the top-down approach, the former way is used, and a document is divided into several regions each of which can be recursively divided into smaller subregions. Let $\Im$ be the set of objects which can be split into v disjoint subsets $\Theta^1, \Theta^2, \ldots, \Theta^p, \ldots, \Theta^v$,

$$
\Theta^p \subset \Im, \qquad p = 1, 2, \ldots, v
$$

such that

$$
\bigcup_{p=1}^{v} \Theta^p = \Im, \qquad \forall_{p \neq q}(\Theta^p \cap \Theta^q = \phi).
$$

A *C-function* [70] has been defined as

$$
C(\Theta^p) \geq 0, \qquad p = 1, 2, \ldots, v
$$

such that

$$C(\Theta^p \cup \Theta^q) \geq C(\Theta^p) + C(\Theta^q) \, .$$

From (3.1), the strength of structure S_s will be

$$S_s(\Theta^p, \Theta^q) \equiv C(\Theta^p \cup \Theta^q) - C(\Theta^p) - C(\Theta^q) \geq 0 \, . \tag{4.2}$$

The criterion of top-down splitting is that we should divide $\Theta^\tau = \Theta^p \cup \Theta^q$ into two subsets Θ^p and Θ^q such that the strength of structure S_s becomes minimum. This policy will maximize the intra-subset cohesion and minimize the inter-subset cohesion.

For multiple splitting, the strength of structure $S_s(\Theta^p, \Theta^q, \ldots, \Theta^y)$ can be derived by repeating Eq. (4.2):

$$\Theta^\tau = \Theta^p \cup \Theta^q \cup \ldots \cup \Theta^y$$
$$\forall_{p \neq q}(\Theta^p \cap \Theta^q = \phi)$$
$$C(\Theta^\tau) \geq C(\Theta^p) + C(\Theta^q) + \cdots + C(\Theta^y)$$
$$S_s(\Theta^p, \Theta^q, \ldots, \Theta^y) = C(\Theta^\tau) - C(\Theta^p) - C(\Theta^q) - \cdots - C(\Theta^y) \geq 0 \, . \tag{4.3}$$

To achieve a good splitting, $S_s(\Theta^p, \Theta^q, \ldots, \Theta^y)$ should be minimized.

Many methods have been employed in the top-down approach, e.g. smearing [34,35,71], projection profile cut [4,33,48], Fourier transform detection [27], template [17], and form definition language (FDL) [24,25].

4.2. *Bottom-Up Approach*

The bottom-up (data-driven) approach progressively refines the data by layered grouping operations. The bottom-up approach is time consuming. But it is possible to develop algorithms which can be applied to a variety of documents [4,14,18,23,28,29,33,71].

The bottom-up approach corresponds to the direction of "$\Longleftarrow$" in Eq. (4.1). In this way, basic geometric components are extracted and connected into different groups in terms of their characteristics, then the groups are combined into larger groups, etc.

An analysis of this approach based on the entropy theory is given in terms of the *dynamic coalescence model* [70]. In this model, we start with $N(0)$ objects of equal "mass". Suppose a region is formed by m original objects, such that this region has a mass m. $N(t)$ stands for the number of regions at time t. $X^{(\alpha)}$, $R^{(\alpha)}$ and $M^{(\alpha)}$ represent the position, size and mass of the αth region respectively, R_0 indicates a constant called *coalescence parameter*. We have

$$N(0) > N(t) > N(2t) > \ldots N(nt)$$

$$R^{(\alpha)} = \sqrt[n]{(M^{(\alpha)})R_0} \, .$$

The dynamic equation can be represented in the form

$$\frac{dX^\alpha}{dt} = F^{(a)}$$

where

$$F^{(a)} = A \sum_\beta \frac{X^{(\beta)} - X^{(\alpha)}}{|X^{(\beta)} - X^{(\alpha)}|} f_{\alpha\beta}^{(1)}$$

$$f_{\alpha\beta}^{(1)} = (M^{(\beta)} M^{(\alpha)})^\rho g(|X^{(\beta)} - X^{(\alpha)}|) \,. \tag{4.4}$$

If we want to include the second order effect in the equation in order to enhance the chain effect, then Eq. (4.4) can be replaced by the following formula

$$F^{(a)} = A \sum_\beta \frac{X^{(\beta)} - X^{(\alpha)}}{|X^{(\beta)} - X^{(\alpha)}|} [f_{\alpha\beta}^{(1)} + \varepsilon f_{\alpha\beta}^{(2)}] \tag{4.5}$$

where ε is a constant to be adjusted.

Two blocks α and β coalesce into a new block γ when they satisfy the following condition:

$$|X^{(\beta)} - X^{(\alpha)}| = R^{(\beta)} - R^{(\alpha)}$$

$$X^{(\gamma)} = \frac{(X^{(\alpha)} M^{(\alpha)} + X^{(\beta)} M^{(\beta)})}{(M^{(\beta)} + M^{(\alpha)})}$$

$$M^{(\gamma)} = (M^{(\beta)} + M^{(\alpha)}) \,. \tag{4.6}$$

There are two practical bottom-up methods: (1) neighborhood line density (NLD) indicating the complexity of characters and graphics [32,33,40]; and (2) connected components analysis indicating the component properties of the document blocks [8,23,43,56].

5. Document Understanding

As document analysis extracts geometric structures from a document image by using the knowledge about the general document and/or the specific document format, document understanding maps the geometric structures into logical structures considering the logical relationship between the objects in specific documents. There are several kinds of mapping methods in document understanding: [66] proposed a tree transformation method for understanding multi-article documents. [64] discussed the extraction of Japanese newspaper articles using a domain specific knowledge. [29] constructed a special purpose machine for understanding Japanese documents. [25] proposed a flexible format understanding method, using a form definition language. Our research [59,63,73] has led to the development of a form description language for understanding financial documents. These mapping methods are based on specific rules applied to different documents with different formats. A series of document formatting rules are explicitly or implicitly used in all these understanding techniques.

In this section, document understanding based on *tree transformation,* document *formatting knowledge* and document *description language* will be discussed.

5.1. *Document Understanding Based on Tree Transformation*

This method defines document understanding as the transformation of a geometric structure tree into a logical structure tree [66].

A document has an obvious hierarchical geometric structure, represented by a tree as shown in Fig. 6(b). And the logical structure of a document is also represented by a tree which is illustrated in Fig. 6(c). In this example, three kinds of blocks are defined: H (head), B (body) and S (either body or head). During the transformation, a label is attached to each node. Labels include title, abstract, sub-title, paragraph, header, footnote, page number, and caption.

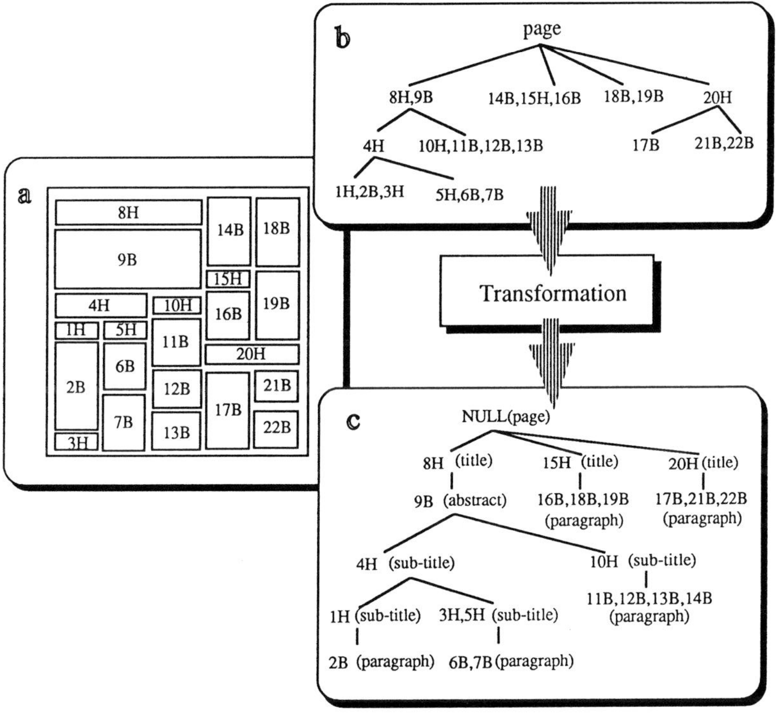

The transformation, which moves the nodes in the tree, is based on four transformation rules. These rules are created according to a layout desigend according to the manner in which humans read. Rules 1 and 2 are based on the observation that a title should have a single set of paragraphs as a child in the logical structure. The paragraph body in another node is moved to the node under the body title by these rules. Rule 3 is mainly for the extraction of characters or sections headed by a subtitle. By rule 4, a unique class is attached to each node.

This method was implemented on a SUN-3 workstation. Pilot experiments were carried out using 106 documents taken from magazines, journals, newspapers, books, manuals, letters, scientific papers, and so on. The results show that only 12 out of 106 tested documents were not interpreted correctly.

5.2. *Document Understanding Based on Formatting Knowledge*

Since a logical structure can correspond to a variety of geometric structures, the generation of logical structure from the geometric structure is difficult. One of the promising solutions to this problem is the use of *formatting knowledge*. The formatting rules may differ from each other because of the type of document and language to be used in it. However, for a specific kind of document, once the formatting knowledge is acquired, its logical structure can be deduced. An example can be found in [64] where a method of extracting articles from Japanese newspapers has been proposed. In this method, six formatting rules of Japanese newspaper layout are summarized. An algorithm for extracting articles from Japanese newspaper has been designed based on the formatting knowledge.

Another example can be found in [16] where a business letter processing approach has been developed. Because business letters are normally established in a single-column representation, letter understanding is mainly the identification of the logical objects, like sender, receiver, date, etc. In this approach, the logical objects of the letter are identified according to a *Statistical Database (SDB)*. As the author reported, the SDB consists of about 71 rule packages derived from the statistical evaluation of a few hundred business letters.

Other knowledge, like the shape, size and pixel density, etc. of the image block can also be used for document understanding. References [19,74] use statistical features of connected components to identify the address blocks on envelopes.

5.3. *Document Understanding Based on Description Language*

One of the most effective ways to describe the structures of a document is the use of a description language. [25] detects the logical structure of a document and makes use of the knowledge rules represented by a *form definition language (FDL)*. The basic concept of the form definition language is that both the geometric and logical structures of a document can be described in terms of a set of rectangular regions. For example, a part of a program in form definition language coded for the United Nations' (UN) documents is listed below:

```
(defform UN-DOC#
         (width 210) (height 297)
         (if (box (? ? ? ?)
                 (mode IN Y LESS)
                 (area (0 210 60 100))
```

```
                    (include (160 210 1 5)))
                 (form UN-DOC-A
                    (0 210 0 297))
                 (form UN-DOC-B
                    (0 210 0 297))))
           (defform UN-DOC-A ...)
           (defform UN-DOC-B ...)
```

It means that the UN documents have a width of 210 mm and a height of 297 mm. The *if* predicate is one of the control structures. If the box predicate succeeds, the document named UN-DOC# is compared with UN-DOC-A and UN-DOC-B, and analyzed as UN-DOC-A. Otherwise, it is analyzed as UN-DOC-B. The box states that a rule line should exist inside the region (0 210 60 100) and satisfy the conditions that the width of the ruled line is between 160 mm and 210 mm and the height is between 1 mm and 5 mm (defform UN-DOC-A ...) and (defform UN-DOC-B ...) will give the definition of the UN documents with and without a ruled line with the properties stated above.

According to the definition, a form dividing engine will analyze the document and produce the images of some logical objects, such as the organization which issued the document, document number, and section, etc. More details about this method can be found in [25].

6. Form Document Processing

Form document is a type of special-purpose documents commonly used in our daily life. For example, millions of financial transactions take place every day. Associated with them are form documents such as bank cheques, payment slips and bills. For this specific type of document, according to their specific characteristics, it is possible to use a specific method to acquire knowledge from it.

6.1. *Characteristics of Form Documents*

Specific characteristics of form documents have been identified and analyzed in our early work [59,62,63,73] which are listed below:

- In general, form document may consist of straight lines which are oriented mostly in horizontal and vertical directions.
- The information that should be acquired from a form is usually the filled data. The filling positions can be determined by the above lines as references.
- Texts in form documents often contain a small set of known machine-printed, hand-printed and handwritten characters, such as legal and numeric amounts. They can be recognized with current character recognition techniques.

6.2. *Form Document Processing Based on Form Description Language*

According to the above analysis, a form document processing method based on form description has been proposed in [59,62,63,73]. A block diagram of this method is illustrated in Fig. 7. The goal of this method is to extract information called *items* from the form documents.

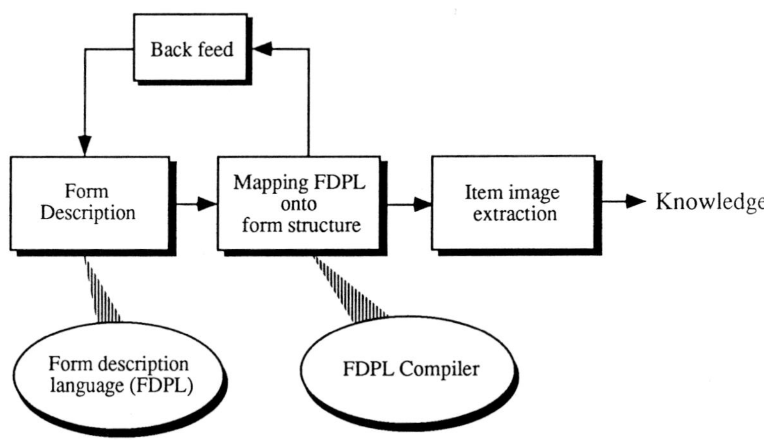

Fig. 7. Diagram of form processing based on the FDPL.

An example of a form document is given in Fig. 8(a) which is a Canadian bank cash withdrawal slip. It consists of six lines. The first line is described as (L, H, TM, 10, 60, 30, 1). It means that the beginning point of the first line L_1 is located at about 10 percent of the document length from the top edge of the document and 60 percent of the document width from the left edge of the document. The length of this line is about 30 percent of the width of this document. The complete form structure description can be found in Fig. 8(b).

To acquire the items from the form documents, the item description (IDP) has been developed [63,73]. Suppose there exists a finite set of relations $\Gamma = \{ \Gamma_1, \Gamma_2, \ldots, \Gamma_k \}$ between the finite set of items $\alpha = \{ \alpha_1, \alpha_2, \ldots, \alpha_m \}$ and the finite set of graphs $\Sigma = \{ \Sigma_1, \Sigma_2, \ldots, \Sigma_n \}$, and it can be represented by 0-Γ_i matrix. We call it an Item Description Matrix: M_{ID}, such that

$$M_{ID} = \begin{cases} \Gamma_l & \text{if } (\alpha_i, \Sigma_j) \in \Gamma \\ 0 & \text{if } (\alpha_i, \Sigma_j) \notin \Gamma \end{cases}$$

satisfying the following condition:

$$\forall_l (\Gamma_l = (\alpha \Re \Sigma)), \qquad \Re = \{R, L, A, B\},$$

where R, L, A and B represent Right, Left, Above and Below respectively.

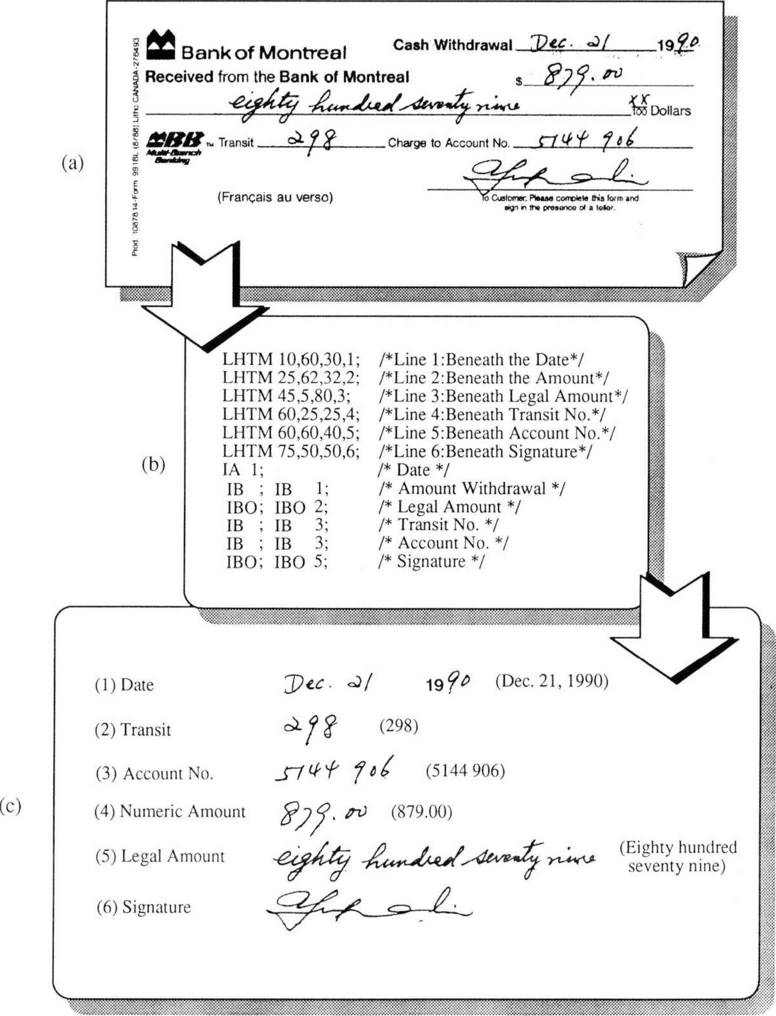

Fig. 8. An example of form processing based on the FDPL.

For example, the finite set of items and the finite set of graphs are given by $\alpha = \{\alpha_1, \alpha_2, \alpha_3, \alpha_4\}$ and $\Sigma = \{ L_1, L_2, L_3, L_4, L_5, L_6\}$ respectively. Let $\Gamma = \{ R, L, A, B\}$. M_{ID} is represented by the following matrix:

$$
M_{ID} = \begin{array}{c} \\ \alpha_1 \\ \alpha_2 \\ \alpha_3 \\ \alpha_4 \end{array}
\begin{array}{c} \begin{array}{cccccc} L_1 & L_2 & L_3 & L_4 & L_5 & L_6 \end{array} \\
\left[\begin{array}{cccccc}
A & 0 & 0 & L & 0 & 0 \\
B & A & 0 & R & L & 0 \\
0 & 0 & B & 0 & R & L \\
0 & 0 & B & 0 & 0 & R
\end{array} \right] \end{array}.
\tag{6.1}
$$

Equation (6.1) means that

(1) α_1 is located above line L_1 and also on the left of line L_4;
(2) α_2 is located below line L_1 and above line L_2 and also on the right of line L_4 and the left of line L_5;
(3) α_3 is located below line L_3 and also on the right of line L_5 and the left of line L_6;
(4) α_4 is located below line L_3 and also on the right of line L_6.

The result of acquiring knowledge from a Canadian bank cash withdrawal slip shown in Fig. 8(a) can be found in Fig. 8(c).

6.3. *Form Document Processing Based on Form Registration*

A form document processing system based on the pre-registered empty forms has been developed in [49]. The process includes two steps: (1) empty form registration, and (2) data-filled form recognition.

During the registration step, a form sample without any data is first scanned and registered with the computer. Through line enhancement, contour extraction and square detection, both the label and data fields are extracted. The relationships among these fields are then determined. Man-machine conversation is required during this registration process. The result of registration is stored as the format data of the form sample. During the recognition step, only the data fields are extracted according to the locations indicated by the format data.

6.4. *Form Document Processing System*

An intelligent form processing system (IFPS) has been described in [9]. It provides capabilities for automatically indexing form document for storage/retrieval to/from a document library, and for capturing information from scanned form images using OCR. The IFPS also provides capabilities for efficiently storing form images. The overall organization of IFPS is shown in Fig. 9, which contains two parallel paths, one for image applications such as retrieval, display and printing of a form document, the other for data processing applications that deal with information contained on a form.

IFPS consists of six major processing components:

- Defining form model;
- Storing the form model in a form library;
- Matching input form against the model stored in the form library;
- Registering the selected model to the input form;
- Converting the extracted image data to symbol code for input to data base;
- Removing the fixed part of a form, and retaining only the data filled in for storage.

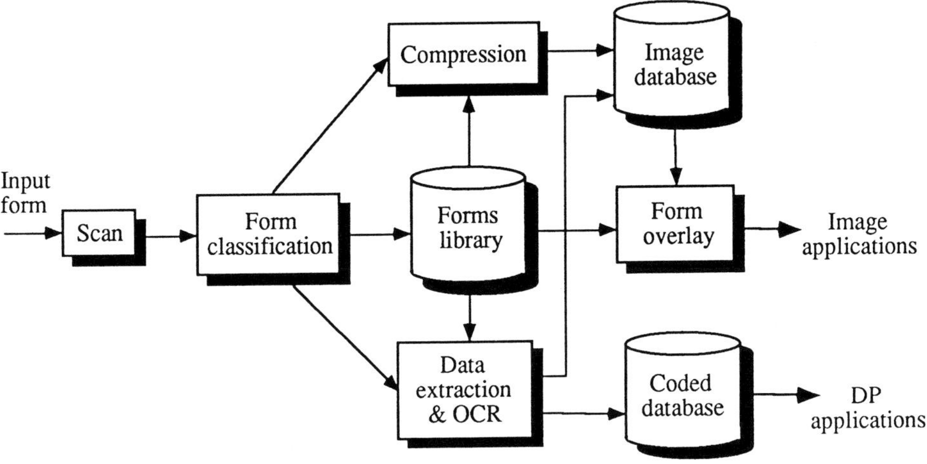

Fig. 9. An intelligent document form processing system.

7. Major Techniques

To implement the above approaches, many practical techniques have been developed. In this section, the major techniques will be presented.

- Hough Transform,
- Projection Profile Cuts,
- Run-Length Smoothing Algorithm (RLSA),
- Connected Components Algorithm,
- Crossing Counts,
- Form Description Language (FDL),
- Segmentation.

7.1. *Hough Transform*

The Hough transform maps points of the cartesian space (x, y) into sinusoidal curves in a $\rho\theta$ space via the transformation:

$$\rho = x \cos \theta + y \sin \theta .$$

Each time a sinusoidal curve intersects another at particular values of ρ and θ, the likelihood that a line corresponding to these $\rho\theta$ coordinate values is present in the original image also increases. An accumulator array (consisting of R rows and T columns) is used to count the number of intersections at various ρ and θ values. Those cells in the accumulator array with the highest number of counts will correspond to lines in the original image. Because text lines are actually thick lines of sparse density, the Hough transform can be used to detect them and their orientation.

Three major applications of the Hough transform in document analysis are listed below:

- *Skew Detection.* An important application of the Hough transform is skew detection. A typical method can be found in [26]. It detects the document skew by applying the Hough transform to a "burst image". At first, the resolution of the document image is reduced from 300 dpi (dots per inch) to 75 dpi. Next, a vertical and a horizontal burst image will be produced based on the reduced document image. The Hough transform is then applied to either the vertical or the horizontal burst image according to the orientation of the document. Compared to the original image, the number of black pixels in the burst image is significantly reduced compared to the original image. It speeds up the skew detection procedure. In order to eliminate the negative effects of the large run-length contributed by the figures and black margins, only small run-lengths of between 1 and 25 pixels are mapped to the $\rho\theta$ space. The skew angle can then be calculated according to the accumulator array. In [26], all skews have been detected correctly for the 13 test images of five different types of documents.
- *Text block identification.* The accumulator array produced by the transform has different properties corresponding to the different contents of the document images. The high peaks in the array correspond to graphics in the document, while the cells with regular value and uniform width in the array correspond to texts in the document [52,55]. Thus, the different document contents can be identified according to these properties.
- *Grouping the characters in a line for text/graph separation.* The Hough transform can also be used to detect the text lines by means of grouping the characters together and separating them from the graphics [23].

7.2. *Projection Profile Cuts*

Projection refers to the mapping of a two-dimensional region of an image into a waveform whose values are the sums of the values of the image points along some specified directions. A projection profile is obtained by determining the number of black pixels that fall onto a projection axis. Projection profiles represent a global feature of a document. They play a very important role in document element extraction, character segmentation and skew normalization.

Let $f(x, y)$ be a document image, and let R stand for an area of the document image. Assume that $f(x, y) = 0$ lies outside the image. $\delta[\ldots]$ denotes a delta function. $t = x \sin \phi - y \cos \phi$ gives the Euclidean distance of a line from the origin [51]. If the projection angle from the x-axis is ϕ, the projection can be defined as follows:

$$p(\phi, t) = \int_R f(x, y)\delta[x \sin \phi - y \cos \phi - t]dxdy . \tag{7.1}$$

Three directional projection profiles: (a) horizontal, (b) vertical and (c) diagonal, are commonly used:

$$p(0°, t) = \int_R f(x, t)dx$$

$$p(90°, t) = \int_R f(t, y)dy$$

$$p(45°, t) = \int_R f(t, x - \sqrt{2}t)dx$$

$$p(135°, t) = \int_R f(t, \sqrt{2}t - x)dx$$

For a digitized image, the symbol $\int_R$ should be replaced by $\sum_R$.

All objects in a document are contained in rectangular blocks. Blanks are placed between these rectangles. Thus, the document projection profile is a waveform whose deep valleys correspond to the blank areas of the documents. A deep valley with a width greater than an established threshold, can be cut as the position corresponding to the edge of an object or a block. Because a document generally consists of several blocks, the process of projection should be done recursively until all of the blocks have been located. An example can be shown in Fig. 10. More details about the various applications of this technique in document analysis can be found in references [4,33,48,65,67,69].

7.3. *Run-Length Smoothing Algorithm (RLSA)*

The basic RLSA is applied to a binary sequence in which white pixels are represented by 0's and black pixels by 1's. It transforms a binary sequence x into an output sequence y according to the following rules:

(1) 0's in x are changed to 1's in y, if the number of adjacent 0's is less than or equal to a predefined limit C.
(2) 1's in x are unchanged in y.

For example, with C = 4 the sequence x is mapped into y as follows:

$$x \ : \ 00010000010100001000000011000$$
$$y \ : \ 11110000011111111000000011111$$

When applied to pattern arrays, the RLSA has the effect of linking together neighboring black areas that are separated by less than C pixels. With an appropriate choice of C, the linked areas will be regions of a common data type. The degree of linkage depends on the following factors: (a) the threshold value C, (b) the distribution of white and black pixels in the document, and (c) the scanning resolution.

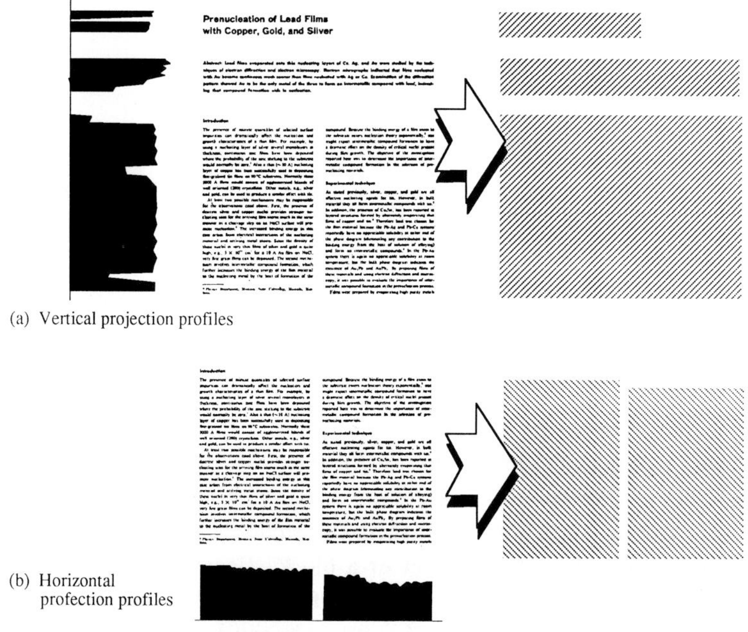

(a) Vertical projection profiles

(b) Horizontal profection profiles

Fig. 10. Projection profiles for extracting geometric structure.

On the other hand, the RLSA may also be applied to the background. It has the effect of eliminating black pixels that are less than C in length [34].

The choice of the smoothing threshold C is very important. Very small horizontal C values simply *close* individual characters. Slightly larger values of C merge individual characters into a word, but are not large enough to bridge the space between two words. Too large values of C often cause sentences to join to non-text regions, or to connect to adjacent columns. In general, threshold C is set according to the character height, gap between words and interline spacing [22,34].

The RLSA was first proposed by Johnston [34] to separate text blocks from graphics. It has also been used to detect long vertical and horizontal white lines [1,68]. This algorithm was extended to obtain a bit-map of white and black areas representing blocks which contain various types of data [71]. Run-length smoothed document images can also be used as basic features for document analysis [20,22,24].

7.4. *Neighbourhood Line Density (NLD)*

For every pixel on the document, its NLD is the sum complexity of its four directions.

$$NLD = \sum_{i \in \aleph} C_i$$

$$C_i = \sum_{i \in \aleph} (1/L_{ij})$$

$$\aleph = \{L, R, U, D\}$$

where, L, R, U and D stand for the four directions, i.e. left, right, up and down respectively. C_i indicates the complexity of a pixel for the direction i. L_{ij} represents the distance from the given pixel to its surrounding stroke j in the direction i.

Based on the following features, the NLD can be used to separate characters from graphics including the situation in which some characters are touching the graphics: (1) NLD is higher for character fields than graphic fields, and (2) there are high peaks of NLD in the character fields and their height is affected by the character's size and pitch [41].

The NLD consists of three processing steps. First, the NLD for all the black pixels of the input document is calculated using the method stated above. Second, an NLD emphasis processing is carried out in order to enlarge the NLD difference between the graphic fields and character fields. The third step is thresholding, the pixels which have an NLD value greater than a threshold θ are classified as character fields, otherwise they are classified as graphic fields.

7.5. *Connected Components Analysis (CCA)*

A connected component is a set of connected black or white pixels such that an 8-connected path exists between any two pixels. Different contents of the document tend to have connected components with different properties. Generally, graphics consist of large connected components. Texts consist of connected components with regular and relatively smaller size. By analyzing these connected components, graphics and texts in the document can be identified, grouped together to different blocks and separated from each other.

The size and location of the connected component can be represented by a four-tuple [64]. The analysis of a document can be regarded as the process of merging these four-tuples. Take the newspaper as an example. Its content is classified into several regions like index, abstract, article body, picture and figure, etc. During image analysis, the four-tuples are merged and classified into these regions using the features found in the regions. In [64], 13 features about the six regions of a Japanese newspaper are summarized. According to these features, a table is created summarizing the properties of the four-tuples in each region. All the four-tuples can be classified and merged following the rules described in this table. Since the four-tuples contain information about the location of the components, all the regions can be classified and located at the end of the four-tuple merging process.

Two typical applications of the CCA in document processing can be illustrated below.

- *Envelope processing.* An important application is automatic envelope processing [6,7,15,19,74]. By placing the connected components into several groups and further analyzing the components in them, CCA has been used to locate address blocks on envelopes [74].
- *Mixed text/graphics document processing.* [23] describes the development and implementation of a *Robust algorithm* where the CCA is successfully used to separate a text string from a mixed text/graphics document image. This algorithm consists of five steps: (a) connected component generation, (b) area/ratio filter, (c) collinear component grouping, (d) logical grouping of strings into words and phrases, and (e) text string separation.

7.6. *Crossing Counts*

A crossing count is the number of times the pixel value turns from 0 (white pixel) to 1 (black pixel) along horizontal or vertical raster scan lines. It can be expressed as a vector whose components are defined as follows.

(1) Horizontal crossing counts:

$$CC_h(i) = \sum_j \overline{f(i,j)} f(i,j+1)$$

(2) Vertical crossing counts:

$$CC_v(j) = \sum_i \overline{f(i,j)} f(i+1,j)$$

Crossing counts can be used to measure document complexity. In [4], crossing counts have been used as one of the basic features to separate and identify the document blocks.

7.7. *Form Definition Language (FDL)*

In [25] a top-down knowledge representation was proposed, called *Form Definition Language (FDL)*, to describe the generic layout structure of document. The structure can be represented in terms of rectangular regions, each of which can be recursively defined in terms of smaller regions. An example is given in Fig. 11. These generic descriptions are then matched to the preprocessed input document images. This method is powerful, but is complicated to implement. In [24] developed a simplified version of FDL was developed so that it may be implemented more easily.

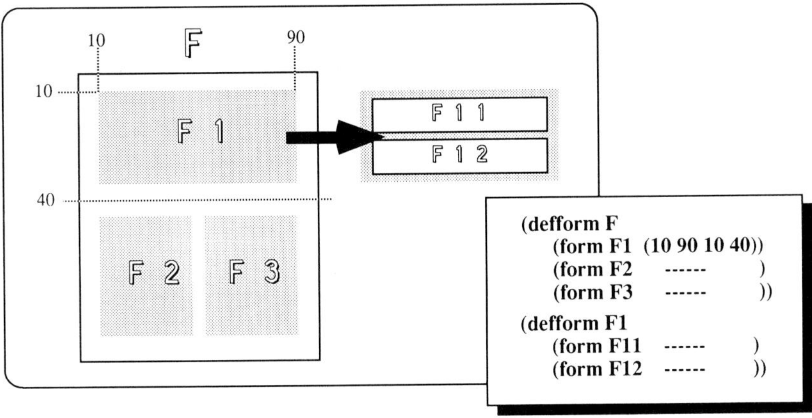

Fig. 11. Representation of structure using the FDL.

7.8. *Segmentation Techniques*

Segmentation techniques can be roughly categorized as [3,2,11,44,21,37,53]:

- projection-based,
- pitch-based,
- recognition-based,
- region-based.

The first two techniques are suitable for typewritten texts where characters are equally spaced and there is a significant gap between adjacent characters. In the "recognition-based" methods, segmentation is performed by recognizing a character in a sequential scan. For handwritten or handprinted texts where variations in handwriting are unpredictable, the performance of these methods is dubious. The "region-based" method is the only alternative for the segmentation of totally unconstrained handwritten characters. This category of techniques consists of finding and analyzing the input image components as well as how these components are related in order to detect suitable regions for segmentation. Also, segmentation techniques can be categorized as the following types by the sort of pixels to be worked on:

- Methods for working on foreground pixels (black pixels) [3,11,44,21,37,53],
- Methods for working on background pixels (white pixels) [13].

8. Conclusions

Everyday, millions of documents including technical reports, government files, newspapers, books, magazines, letters, bank cheques, etc. have to be processed. A great deal of time, effort and money will be saved if it can be executed automatically. However, in spite of major advances in computer technology, the degree of automation in acquiring data from such documents is very limited and a great deal of manual labour is still needed in this area. Thus, any method which can speed up this process will make a significant contribution.

This chapter deals with the essential concepts of document analysis and understanding. It begins with a key concept, document structure. The importance of this concept can be seen in the whole chapter: constructing a geometric structure model and a logical structure model; considering document analysis as a technique of extracting the geometric structure; regarding document understanding as a mapping from geometric structure into logical structure; etc. This chapter attempts to theoretically analyze document structure and top-down, bottom-up approaches which are commonly used in document analysis, in terms of entropy function.

Some open questions and problems still exist, especially in document understanding. Any practical document can be viewed differently depending on its geometric structure space and logical structure space. Because there is no one-to-one mapping between these two spaces, it is difficult to find a correct mapping to transform a geometric structure into a logical one. For example, rules based on knowledge may vary in different documents, and how to find the correct rules is a profound subject for future research.

References

[1] L. Abele, F. Wahl and W. Scheri, Procedures for an automatic segmentation of text graphic and halftone regions in document, in *Proc. 2nd Scandinavian Conf. on Image Analysis,* 1981, 177–182.

[2] P. Ahmed and C. Y. Suen, Computer recognition of totally unconstrained handwritten Zipcodes, *Int. J. Pattern Recogn. Artif. Intell.* 1, 1 (1987) 1–15.

[3] P. Ahmed and C. Y. Suen, Segmentation of unconstrained handwritten postal zipcodes, in *Proc. 6th Int. Conf. on Pattern Recognition,* Munich, Germany, 1982, 545-547.

[4] T. Akiyama and N. Hagita, Automated entry system for printed documents, *Pattern Recogn.* **23**, 11 (1990) 1141–1153.

[5] R. N. Ascher, G. M. Koppelman, M. J. Miller, G. Nagy and G. L. Shelton Jr., An interactive system for reading unformatted printed text, *IEEE Trans. Comput.* **20**, 12 (1971) 1527–1543.

[6] N. Bartneck, Knowledge based address block finding using hybrid knowledge representation schemes, in *Proc. 3rd USPS Advanced Technology Conf.,* Washington, DC, May 1988, 249–263.

[7] A. Bergman, E. Bracha, P. G. Mulgaonkar and T. Shaham, Advanced research in address block location, in *Proc. 3rd USPS Advanced Technology Conf.,* Washington, DC, May 1988, 218–232.

[8] J. P. Bixler, Tracking text in mixed-mode document, in *Proc. ACM Conf. on Document Processing Systems,* 1988, 177–185.

[9] R. G. Casey, D. R. Ferguson, K. M. Mohiuddin and E. Walach, An intelligent forms processing system, to appear in 1992.

[10] R. G. Casey and G. Nagy, Document analysis — A broader view, in *Proc. First Int. Conf. on Document Analysis and Recognition*, Saint-Malo, France, Sept. 1991, 839–850.

[11] M. Cesar and R. Shinghal, An algorithm for segmentation of handwritten postal codes, *Int. J. Man-Machine Stud.* **33** (1990) 63–80.

[12] Y. Chenevoy and A. Belaid, Hypothesis management for structured document recognition, in *Proc. First Int. Conf. on Document Analysis and Recognition*, Saint-Malo, France, Sept. 1991, 121–129.

[13] M. Cheriet, Y. S. Huang and C. Y. Suen, Background region-based algorithm for the segmentation of connected digits, Technical Report, Centre for Pattern Recognition and Machine Intelligence, Concordia University, 1991.

[14] G. Ciardiello, M. T. Degrandi, M. P. Poccotelli, G. Scafuro and M. R. Spada, An experimental system for office document handling and text recognition in *Proc. 9th Int. Conf. on Pattern Recognition*, Rome, Italy, 1988, 739–743.

[15] V. Demjanenko, Y. C. Shin, R. Sridhar, P. Palumbo and S. Srihari, Real-time connected component analysis for address block location, in *Proc. 4th USPS Advanced Technology Conf.*, Washington, DC, Nov. 1990, 1059–1071.

[16] A. Dengel, Document image analysis — expectation-driven text recognition, in *Proc. Workshop on Syntactic and Structural Pattern Recognition (SSPR90)*, 1990, 78–87.

[17] A. Dengel and G. Barth, Document description and analysis by cuts, *Proc. RIAO*, MIT, 1988.

[18] W. Doster, Different states of a document's content on its way from the Gutenbergian world to the electronic world, in *Proc. 7th Int. Conf. on Pattern Recognition*, Montreal, Canada, 1984, 872–874.

[19] A. C. Downton and C. G. Leedham, Preprocessing and presorting of envelope images for automatic sorting using OCR, *Pattern Recogn.* **23**, 3/4 (1990) 347–362.

[20] F. Esposito, D. Malerba, G. Semeraro, E. Annese and G. Scafuro, An experimental page layout recognition system for office document automatic classification: an integrated approach for inductive generalization, in *Proc. 10th Int. Conf. on Pattern Recognition*, Atlantic City, NJ, 1990, 557–562.

[21] R. Fenrich, Segmentation of automatically located handwritten words, in *Proc. 3rd International Workshop on Frontiers in Handwriting Recognition*, Chateau de Bonas, France, 1991, 33–44.

[22] J. L. Fisher, S. C. Hinds and D. P. D'Amato, A rule-based system for document image segmentation, in *Proc. 10th Int. Conf. on Pattern Recognition*, Atlantic City, NJ, 1990, 567–572.

[23] L. A. Fletcher and R. Kasturi, A robust algorithm for text string separation from mixed text/graphics images, *IEEE Trans. Pattern Anal. Mach. Intell.* **10**, 6 (1988) 910–918.

[24] H. Fujisawa and Y. Nakano, A top-down approach for the analysis of document images, in *Proc. Workshop on Syntactic and Structural Pattern Recognition (SSPR90)*, 1990, 113–122.

[25] J. Higashino, H. Fujisawa, Y. Nakano and M. Ejiri, A knowledge-based segmentation method for document understanding, in *Proc. 8th Int. Conf. on Pattern Recognition*, Paris, France, 1986, 745–748.

[26] S. C. Hinds, J. L. Fisher and D. P. D'Amato, A document skew detection method using run-length encoding and the Hough transform, in *Proc. 10th Int. Conf. on Pattern Recognition*, Atlantic City, NJ, 1990, 464–468.

[27] M. Hose and Y. Hoshino, Segmentation method of document images by two-dimensional Fourier transformation, *System and Computers in Japan* **16**, 3 (1985) 38–47.

[28] N. Hagita I. Masuda, T. Akiyama, T. Takahashi and S. Naito, Approach to smart document reader system, in *Proc. CVPR'85*, 1985, 550–557.

[29] K. Inagaki, T. Kato, T. Hiroshima and T. Sakai, MACSYM: A hierarchical parallel image processing system for event-driven pattern understanding of documents, *Pattern Recogn.* **17**, 1 (1984) 85–108.

[30] R. Ingold and D. Armangil, A top-down document analysis method for logical structure recognition, in *Proc. First Int. Conf. on Document Analysis and Recognition*, Saint-Malo, France, Sept. 1991, 41–49.

[31] ISO. 8613: *Information Processing-Text and Office Systems-Office, Document Architecture (ODA) and Interchange Format*, International Organization for Standardization, 1989.

[32] O. Iwaki, H. Kida and H. Arakawa, A character/graphic segmentation method using neighbourhood line density, *Trans. Institute of Electronics and Communication Engineers of Japan*, Part D **J68D**, 4 (1985) 821–828.

[33] O. Iwaki, H. Kida and H. Arakawa, A segmentation method based on office document hierarchical structure, in *Proc. IEEE Int. Conf. on Systems, Man and Cybernetics*, Alexandria, VA, Oct. 1987, pp. 759–763.

[34] E. G. Johnston, Short note: printed text discrimination, in *Comput. Graph. Image Process.* **3**, 1 (1974) 83–89.

[35] J. Kanai, M. S. Krishnamoorthy and T. Spencer, Algorithms for manipulating nested block represented images, in *Advance Printing of Paper Summaries, SPSE's 26th Fall Symposium*, Arlington, VA, Oct. 1986, 190–193.

[36] S. M. Kerpedjiev, Automatic extraction of information structures from documents, in *Proc. First Int. Conf. on Document Analysis and Recognition*, Saint-Malo, France, Sept. 1991, 32–40.

[37] F. Kimura and M. Shridhar, Recognition of connected numerals, in *Proc. 1st Int. Conf. on Document Analysis and Recognition*, Saint-Malo, France, 1991, 731–739.

[38] J. Kreich, A. Luhn and G. Maderlechner, An experimental environment for model based document analysis, in *Proc. First Int. Conf. on Document Analysis and Recognition*, Saint-Malo, France, Sept. 1991, 50–58.

[39] J. Kreich, A. Luhn and G. Maderlechner, Knowledge based interpretation of scanned business letters, in *Proc. IAPR Workshop on Computer Vision*, 1988, 417–420.

[40] K. Kubota, O. Iwaki and H. Arakawa, Document understanding system, in *Proc. 7th Int. Conf. on Pattern Recognition*, Montreal, Canada, 1984, 612–614.

[41] K. Kubota, O. Iwaki and H. Arakawa, Image segmentation techniques for document processing, in *Proc. 1983 Int. Conf. on Text Processing with a Large Character Set*, 1983, 73–78.

[42] S. W. Lam and S. N. Srihari, Multi-domain document layout understanding, in *Proc. First Int. Conf. on Document Analysis and Recognition*, Saint-Malo, France, Sept. 1991, 112–120.

[43] H. Makino, Representation and segmentation of document images, in *Proc. IEEE Comput. Soc. Conf. on Pattern Recognition and Image Processing*, 1983, 291–296.

[44] B. T. Mitchell and A. M. Gillies, A model-based computer vision system for recognizing handwritten ZIP codes, *Machine Vision and Applications* **2** (1989) 231–243.

[45] G. Nagy, A preliminary investigation of techniques for the automated reading of unformatted text, *Commun. ACM* **11**, 7 (1968) 480–487.

[46] G. Nagy, Towards a structured-document-image utility, in *Proc. Workshop on Syntactic and Structural Pattern Recognition (SSPR90)*, 1990, 293–309.

[47] G. Nagy, J. Kanai and M. Krishnamoorthy, Two complementary techniques for digitized document analysis, in *Proc. ACM Conf. on Document Processing Systems*, 1988, 169–176.

[48] G. Nagy, S. C. Seth and S. D. Stoddard, Document analysis with an expert system, in E. S. Gelsema and L. N. Kanal (eds.), *Pattern Recognition Practice II* (Elsevier Science Publishers B. V. (North-Holland), 1986) 149–159.

[49] Y. Nakano, H. Fujisawa, O. Kunisaki, K. Okada and T. Hananoi, A document understanding system incorporated with character recognition, in *Proc. 8th Int. Conf. on Pattern Recognition*, Paris, France, 1986, 801–803.

[50] D. Niyogi and S. N. Srihari, A rule-based system for document understanding, in *Proc. AAAI'86*, 1986, 789–793.

[51] T. Pavlidis, *Algorithm for Graphics and Image Processing*, (Computer Science Press, Maryland, 1982).

[52] A. Rastogi and S. N. Srihari, Recognizing textual blocks in document images using the Hough transform, Technical Report TR 86-01, Dept. of Computer Science, SUNY Buffalo, NY, 1986.

[53] M. Shridhar and A. Badreldin, Recognition of isolated and simply connected handwritten numerals, *Pattern Recogn.* **19**, 1 (1986) 1–12.

[54] J. C. Simon and K. Zerhouni, Robust description of a line image, in *Proc. First Int. Conf. on Document Analysis and Recognition*, Saint-Malo, France, Sept. 1991, 3–14.

[55] S. N. Srihari and V. Govindaraju, Analysis of textual images using the Hough transform, *Machine Vision and Application* **2** (1989) 141–153.

[56] S. N. Srihari, C. H. Wang, P. W. Palumbo and J. J. Hull, Recognizing address blocks on mail pieces: specialized tools and problem-solving architecture, *AI Mag.* **8**, 4 (1987) 25–40.

[57] C. Y. Suen, Y. Y. Tang and C. D. Yan, Document layout and logical model: A general analysis for document processing, Technical Report, Centre for Pattern Recognition and Machine Intelligence (CENPARMI), Concordia University, 1989.

[58] Y. Y. Tang, C. Y. Suen and C. D. Yan, Basic models for document analysis and understanding, Technical Report, Centre for Pattern Recognition and Machine Intelligence (CENPARMI), Concordia University, 1990.

[59] Y. Y. Tang, C. Y. Suen and C. D. Yan, Chinese form pre-processing for automatic data entry, in *Proc. Int. Conf. on Computer Processing of Chinese and Oriental Languages*, Taipei, Taiwan, Aug. 1991.

[60] Y. Y. Tang, C. Y. Suen and C. D. Yan, Document processing for automatic knowledge acquisition, to appear in *IEEE Trans. on Knowledge and Data Engineering*.

[61] Y. Y. Tang, C. D. Yan, M. Cheriet and C. Y. Suen, Document analysis and understanding: a brief survey, in *Proc. First Int. Conf. on Document Analysis and Recognition*, Sept. 1991, Saint-Malo, France, 17–31.

[62] Y. Y. Tang, C. D. Yan, M. Cheriet and C. Y. Suen, Financial document analysis and understanding, Technical Report, Centre for Pattern Recognition and Machine Intelligence (CENPARMI), Concordia University, 1990.

[63] Y. Y. Tang, C. D. Yan and C. Y. Suen, Form description language and its mapping onto form structure, Technical Report, Centre for Pattern Recognition and Machine Intelligence (CENPARMI), Concordia University, 1990.

[64] J. Toyoda, Y. Noguchi and Y. Nishimura, Study of extracting Japanese newspaper article, in *Proc. 6th Int. Conf. on Pattern Recognition*, Munich, Germany, 1982, 1113–1115.

[65] Y. Tsuji, Document image analysis for generating syntactic structure description, in *Proc. 9th Int. Conf. on Pattern Recognition*, Rome, Italy, 1988, 744–747.

[66] S. Tsujimoto and H. Asada, Understanding multi-articled documents, in *Proc. 10th Int. Conf. on Pattern Recognition*, Atlantic City, NJ, 1990, 551–556.

[67] M. Viswanathan, Analysis of scanned documents — a syntactic approach, in *Proc. Workshop on Syntactic and Structural Pattern Recognition (SSPR90)*, 1990, 450–459.

[68] F. Wahl, L. Abele and W. Scheri, Merkmale fuer die segmentation von dokumenten zur automatischen textverarbeitung, in *Proc. 4th DAGM-Symposium*, 1981.

[69] D. Wang and S. N. Srihari, Classification of newspaper image blocks using texture analysis, *Comput. Vision Graph. Image Process.* **47** (1989) 327–352.

[70] S. Watanabe, *Pattern Recognition: Human and Mechanical* (Wiley-Interscience Publications, 1985).

[71] K. Y. Wong, R. G. Casey and F. M. Wahl, Document analysis system, *IBM J. Res. Dev.* **26**, 6 (1982) 647–656.

[72] A. Yamashita, T. Amano, H. Takahashi and K. Toyokawa, A model based layout understanding method for document recognition system (DRS), in *Proc. First Int. Conf. on Document Analysis and Recognition*, Saint-Malo, France, Sept. 1991, 130–138.

[73] C. D. Yan, Y. Y. Tang and C. Y. Suen, Form understanding system based on form description language, in *Proc. First Int. Conf. on Document Analysis and Recognition*, Saint-Malo, France, Sept. 1991, 283–293.

[74] P. S. Yeh, S. Antoy, A. Litcher and A. Rosenfeld, Address location on envelopes, *Pattern Recogn.* **20**, 2 (1987) 213–227.

Handbook of Pattern Recognition and Computer Vision, pp. 655–665
Eds. C. H. Chen, L. F. Pau and P. S. P. Wang
© 1993 World Scientific Publishing Company

CHAPTER 3.7

PATTERN RECOGNITION AND VISUALIZATION OF SPARSELY SAMPLED BIOMEDICAL SIGNALS

CHING-CHUNG LI, T. P. WANG
Department of Electrical Engineering, University of Pittsburgh
Pittsburgh, PA 15261, USA

and

A. H. VAGNUCCI, M.D.
Department of Medicine, University of Pittsburgh
Pittsburgh, PA 15261, USA

A variety of biomedical signals such as hormonal concentrations in peripheral blood can only be sampled and measured infrequently over a limited period of time; hence, they are considered as sparsely sampled non-stationary short time series. Discrete pseudo Wigner distribution is a transform which can be applied to such signals to provide time-dependent spectral information at an improved frequency resolution in comparison to the short-time Fourier transform. When appropriately clipped and scaled, it can be visualized as an image showing the characteristic pattern of the signal. Spectral features can be extracted from the Wigner distribution for use in automatic pattern recognition. The basic technique is described in this article along with an example of its application to cortisol time series.

Keywords: Biomedical signal; cortisol; pattern recognition; pattern visualization; short time series; Wigner distribution.

1. Introduction

Various biological signals are often measured in a clinical setting for providing information to aid medical diagnosis. Some signals, such as EEG and ECG, etc., can be continuously measured with relative ease; it is well known that their spectra and other analyses have been successfully applied in characterizing the state of health [1,2]. Other types of biological signals, such as chemical signals in blood samples, can be measured only infrequently for a very limited period of time; such sparsely sampled data constitute short time series which are of non-stationary nature [3]. The short-time Fourier transform gives some crude spectral information at a coarse resolution. However, the pseudo Wigner distribution can be applied to provide a better estimate of the time-dependent spectral information. This time-frequency domain analysis and its use in biomedical pattern recognition will be discussed in the following sections.

The Wigner distribution was introduced by E. P. Wigner [4] in 1932 in the context of quantum mechanics, and then applied to signal theory by J. Ville [5] in 1948. During the past ten years, the methods and applications of the Wigner distribution to non-stationary signals have been developed rapidly [6-13]. An exposition of the important mathematical background of the Wigner distribution can be found in a series of three papers by Claasen and Mecklenbrauker [6], and a recent review is contained in a paper by Hlawatsch and Boudreaux–Bartels [14]. We will summarize some of the most useful properties of the Wigner distribution and the techniques of applying the discrete pseudo Wigner distribution to sparsely sampled biomedical signals. The plasma cortisol time series is taken as an example to illustrate its application to recognition and visualization of normal and abnormal patterns.

2. Wigner Distribution

2.1. *Continuous Wigner Distribution*

Let $f(t)$ be a continuous function of time variable t; $f(t)$ may be either real or complex, and $f^*(t)$ is the complex conjugate of $f(t)$. The Wigner distribution of $f(t)$ is defined by

$$W_f(t,\omega) = \int_{-\infty}^{\infty} f(t + \frac{\tau}{2})f^*(t - \frac{\tau}{2})e^{-j\omega\tau}\,d\tau \tag{2.1}$$

where τ is the correlation variable, $+\frac{\tau}{2}$ and $-\frac{\tau}{2}$ denote the time advance and time delay respectively. $f(t + \frac{\tau}{2})f^*(t - \frac{\tau}{2})$ forms a kernel function of the time variable t and the correlation variable τ. The Fourier transform of this kernel function with respect to τ gives the Wigner distribution $W_f(t,\omega)$ which is a real-valued continuous function of both time t and frequency ω.

If $F(\omega)$ is the Fourier transform of $f(t)$ and $F^*(\omega)$ is its complex conjugate, the Wigner distribution $W_F(\omega, t)$ can be defined as

$$W_F(\omega,t) = \frac{1}{2\pi} \int_{-\infty}^{\infty} F(\omega + \frac{\xi}{2})F^*(\omega - \frac{\xi}{2})e^{jt\xi}\,d\xi. \tag{2.2}$$

It can be shown that $W_f(t,\omega) = W_F(\omega, t)$. The reconstruction of $f(t)$ from $W_f(t,\omega)$ is given by

$$f(t) = \frac{1}{2\pi f^*(0)} \int_{-\infty}^{\infty} W_f(\frac{t}{2},\omega)e^{j\omega t}\,d\omega \tag{2.3}$$

and the reconstruction of $F(\omega)$ from $W_f(t,\omega)$ is given by

$$F(\omega) = \frac{1}{F^*(0)} \int_{-\infty}^{\infty} W_f(t, \frac{\omega}{2})e^{-j\omega t}\,dt. \tag{2.4}$$

The Wigner distribution is a bilinear transformation; if $f(t) = \sum_{k=1}^{K} f_k(t)$, then·

$$W_f(t,\omega) = \sum_{k=1}^{K} W_{f_k}(t,\omega) + 2Re\left(\sum_{i=k+1}^{K}\sum_{k=1}^{K-1} W_{f_k f_i}(t,\omega)\right) \tag{2.5}$$

where $W_{f_k f_i}(t,\omega)$ is the cross Wigner distribution of $f_k(t)$ and $f_i(t)$,

$$W_{f_k f_i}(t,\omega) = \int_{-\infty}^{\infty} f_k(t + \frac{\tau}{2}) f_i^*(t - \frac{\tau}{2}) e^{-j\omega\tau} d\tau \,. \tag{2.6}$$

Furthermore, integration of $W_f(t,\omega)$ with respect to t gives the energy density of $f(t)$ at frequency ω,

$$\int_{-\infty}^{\infty} W_f(t,\omega) dt = |F(\omega)|^2 \tag{2.7}$$

and integration of $W_f(t,\omega)$ with respect to ω gives the instantaneous power at time t,

$$\frac{1}{2\pi} \int_{-\infty}^{\infty} W_f(t,\omega) d\omega = |f(t)|^2 \,. \tag{2.8}$$

2.2. *Discrete-time Wigner Distribution*

Consider a discrete-time signal $f(nT)$ which is sampled from $f(t)$ with a sampling period T, where $t = nT$ and n is an integer. If T is equal to one time unit, the discrete-time signal can be simply denoted by a sequence $f(n)$. The discrete-time Wigner distribution is then given by

$$W_f(n,\omega) = 2 \sum_{k=-\infty}^{\infty} f(n+k)f^*(n-k) e^{-j2k\omega} \,. \tag{2.9}$$

$W_f(n,\omega)$ is a real-valued function of the discrete variable n and the continuous variable ω; it is periodic in ω with its period equal to π. The sum of $W_f(n,\omega)$ over the time index n gives

$$\sum_{n=-\infty}^{\infty} W_f(n,\omega) = |F(\omega)|^2 + |F(\omega + \pi)|^2 \,. \tag{2.10}$$

The instantaneous signal power is given by

$$|f(n)|^2 = \frac{1}{2\pi} \int_{-\frac{\pi}{2}}^{\frac{\pi}{2}} W_f(n,\omega) d\omega \,. \tag{2.11}$$

To compute the Wigner distribution, a symmetric window function $h(k)$ with a finite interval $[-N+1, N-1]$ is applied to the discrete-time signal $f(n)$, with its origin $(k = 0)$ being placed at the time instant n,

$$h(k) = \begin{cases} g(k) & -N+1 \leq k \leq N-1 \\ 0 & \text{elsewhere} \end{cases} \tag{2.12}$$

where $g(k)$ can be any symmetric function, for example, $g(k) = 1$. The kernel function used for computing the pseudo Wigner distribution is then equal to $h(k)h^*(-k)f(n+k)f^*(n-k)$ within the time window of length $2(N-1)$.

2.3. *Discrete Pseudo Wigner Distribution*

If the frequency variable ω is also discretized with $\omega = m\Delta\omega$, where the frequency quantization $\Delta\omega$ is equal to $\frac{\pi}{2(N-1)}$, then the discrete pseudo Wigner distribution $W(n,m)$ is given by

$$W(n,m) = W_f(n, m\Delta\omega)$$
$$= 2 \sum_{k=-N+1}^{N-1} |g(k)|^2 f(n+k)f^*(n-k)e^{-j2km\Delta\omega} \cdot \qquad (2.13)$$

$W(n,m)$ is a function of discrete-time n and discrete frequency $m\Delta\omega$. The frequency resolution is increased by a factor of two in comparison to that of the discrete Fourier transform. In practical applications, most signals are real-valued and, with $g(k) = 1$, Eq. (2.13) can be simply rewritten into

$$W(n,m) = 2 \sum_{k=-N+1}^{N-1} f(n+k)f(n-k)e^{-jkm\frac{\pi}{N-1}} . \qquad (2.14)$$

The discrete pseudo Wigner distribution has many useful properties, among which six are listed below [6]:

(i) $W(n,m)$ is real-valued.

(ii) $W_f(n, m\Delta\omega)$ is periodic in frequency with period π, i.e.

$$W_f(n, m\Delta\omega) = W_f(n, m\Delta\omega + \pi) . \qquad (2.15)$$

This is different from the discrete-time Fourier spectrum which has periodicity with period equal to 2π.

(iii) $W_f(n, m\Delta\omega)$ has higher frequency resolution by a factor of two as compared to the discrete Fourier transform.

(iv) $W(n,m)$ is a bilinear transformation with respect to $f(n)$. If

$$f(n) = \sum_{k=1}^{K} f_k(n) \qquad (2.16)$$

then

$$W(n,m) = \sum_{k=1}^{K} W_{f_k}(n,m)$$
$$+ 2Re\left[\sum_{j=k+1}^{K} \sum_{k=1}^{K-1} W_{f_k f_j}(n,m) \right] \qquad (2.17)$$

(v) The sum of $W(n, m)$ over its discrete frequency index m for one period is equal to the instantaneous signal power.

$$|f(n)|^2 = \frac{1}{4(N-1)} \sum_{m=-(N-1)}^{N-1} W(n, m). \qquad (2.18)$$

(vi) The sum of $W_f(n, m\Delta\omega)$ over the time index n gives the energy density at the discrete frequency $m\Delta\omega$,

$$E(m\Delta\omega) = \sum_{n=-N+1}^{N-1} W_f(n, m\Delta\omega)$$
$$= |F(m\Delta\omega)|^2 + |F(m\Delta\omega + \pi)|^2 \qquad (2.19)$$

where $F(m\Delta\omega)$ is the discrete Fourier transform of $f(n)$. This implies that if we want to evaluate the energy density from $W_f(n, m\Delta\omega)$, the signal should be sampled with a Nyquist frequency larger than twice the bandwidth so that there will be no aliasing problem.

3. Recognition and Visualization of Characteristic Patterns

A signal generally has multiple components with distinct individual time and frequency characteristics. Because the kernel function of the Wigner distribution contains multiplication of shifted signals, this multiplication produces two types of products: auto-products resulting from the individual signal components, and cross-products resulting from interaction between different signal components. These two types of products are then transformed into the frequency domain, giving the so-called auto-components and cross-components, respectively, of the Wigner distribution. The auto-components are mainly positive, while the cross-components are oscillatory, have both positive and negative values, and each is located at the midpoint between two corresponding auto-components. Cross-components of large magnitude will contribute peculiar patterns to obscure the auto-components. One would like to remove or suppress those cross-components in order to obtain a better measurement of auto-components in the Wigner spectrum. Several methods have been developed to achieve this purpose, among which is the auto-component selection (ACS) method which is discussed below [10].

In the ACS method, $W(n, m)$ is processed by two different filters. One is an averaging filter with a large support $(P \times Q)$ to filter out the oscillatory cross-components and give output $G(n, m)$. The other is a pre-processing filter of small support $(U \times V)$ to appropriately smooth out the original discrete pseudo Wigner distribution and give output $R(n, m)$. The ratio $\frac{G(n,m)}{R(n,m)}$ is compared with a threshold value t_s where $t_s < 1$. If the ratio is greater than t_s and, at the same time, the value of $W(n, m)$ is positive, then the original $W(n, m)$ is accepted as an auto-component value and is designated by $S(n, m)$; otherwise, $S(n, m)$ is set to zero. The resulting distribution $S(n, m)$ is considered to represent only the positive auto-component in the original discrete pseudo Wigner distribution. If both filters are simple averaging filters with different support sizes ($P > U, Q > V$), the combining action of these two filters in this selection process can be represented by a simple mask of size $P \times Q$ where all elements are equal to one, except the central $U \times V$ elements each of which is given by $D = 1 - \frac{PQ}{UV} t_s$. For example, we may use $P = Q = 7$ and $U = V = 3$, so the filter mask is

$$
\begin{array}{ccccccc}
1 & 1 & 1 & 1 & 1 & 1 & 1 \\
1 & 1 & 1 & 1 & 1 & 1 & 1 \\
1 & 1 & D & D & D & 1 & 1 \\
1 & 1 & D & D & D & 1 & 1 \\
1 & 1 & D & D & D & 1 & 1 \\
1 & 1 & 1 & 1 & 1 & 1 & 1 \\
1 & 1 & 1 & 1 & 1 & 1 & 1
\end{array}
$$

where the value of threshold parameter t_s is selected empirically. If the filter output is positive, then $S(n, m) = W(n, m)$; otherwise, $S(n, m) = 0$. With its negative values being clipped to zero and positive values being appropriately scaled, $S(n, m)$ may be presented as an image for visualization of the characteristic pattern of the signal in the time-frequency plane. For quantitative analysis, however, the energy density $E(m\Delta\omega) = \sum_{n=-N+1}^{N-1} W(n, m\Delta\omega)$ at various frequencies $m\Delta\omega$ can be examined and selected as discriminatory features to be used in automatic pattern recognition. Both aspects will be illustrated in the next section.

4. Pattern Recognition of Plasma Cortisol Signal

As an example, let us consider the application of the above described method to the problem of pattern recognition of plasma cortisol data. The circadian variation of cortisol concentration in peripheral blood is believed to manifest normality or abnormality in regard to a disease called Cushing's syndrome. There are three categories of the disease, each associated with a different tumor location: in the pituitary, in the adrenal, or elsewhere. They are denoted by "pituitary", "adrenal", and "ectopic", respectively. Although CT or MRI scans are routinely used to detect such tumors, they could be missed in the examination due to their small size, especially during the early stages. It would be desirable to detect the disease and recognize the disease class from the circadian cortisol pattern so as to infer the tumor location prior to confirmation by CT or MRI examination and surgical operation. Blood samples can be drawn and cortisol concentration be measured every half hour over a period of 25 to 28 hours, providing 50 to 56 data points in each measured cortisol signal. Such signals are sparsely sampled short-time series.

The short-time Fourier transform and Karhunen-Loeve expansion were applied to these cortisol time series, of both normal subjects and patients with Cushing's syndrome, in order to extract discriminatory features, and an automatic pattern recognition system was developed to recognize a cortisol pattern as normal or abnormal, and in the case of the latter, to define the category of the disease [3].

Recently, we also applied the discrete pseudo Wigner distribution to the cortisol time series for their pattern recognition [15,16]. Altogether a set of 90 cortisol time series, including 41 normal subjects, 28 "pituitary", 12 "adrenal" and 9 "ectopic", were processed. The results are summarized below as an illustration. $W(n,m)$ was computed from each cortisol time series. We chose $N = 25$ and, hence, the observation window length was 48 and the frequency quantization was $\Delta\omega = \frac{\pi}{48}$. The auto-component selection was performed with threshold t_s empirically set at 0.75. After clipping negative values to zero and scaling the magnitude to be within 8 bits, the resulting auto-component of the discrete pseudo Wigner distribution, $S(n,m)$, can be presented as images in the time-frequency plane. For eight example cortisol times series given in Fig. 1, their corresponding Wigner distributions $S(n,m)$, clipped and scaled, are shown in Fig. 2. In each image, the horizontal axis represents the time index n, $(n = 0, 1, 2, \ldots, 60)$, the vertical axis represents the frequency $m\Delta\omega$, $(m = -18, -17, \ldots, -1, 0, 1, \ldots, 17, 18)$, and the darker region indicates a larger magnitude of $S(n, m)$. In Fig. 2, from the top to the bottom, each pair of images are respectively normal, "pituitary", "adrenal" and "ectopic" spectral patterns. It is interesting to note that they show similar patterns for the cortisol time series of the same category, and distinct patterns for different categories. They provide a good visualization potential for physicians to consider.

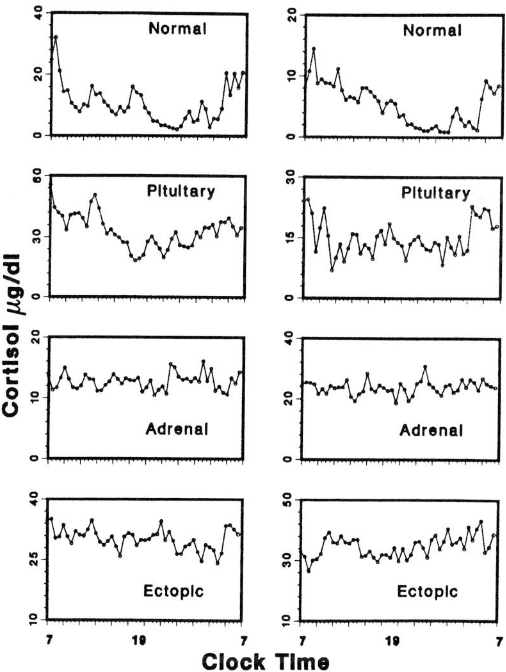

Fig. 1. Eight cortisol time series of normal subjects and patients with Cushing's syndrome; from top to bottom, two in each category: normal, "pituitary", "adrenal" and "ectopic". (From Li et al. [16], Copyright © 1990 New York University, reprinted by permission of New York University Press.)

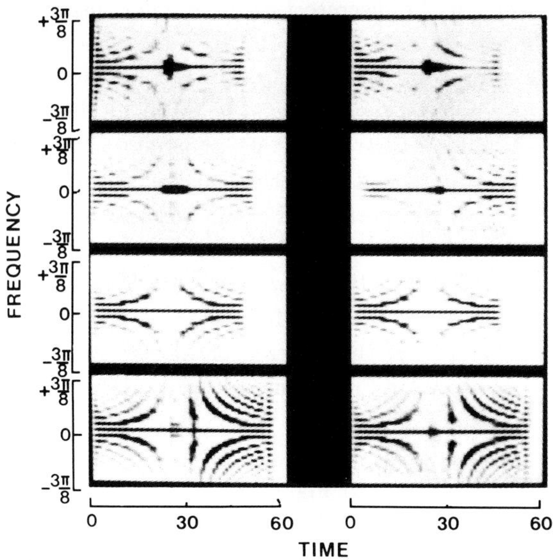

Fig. 2. Wigner distribution of eight cortisol time series shown in Fig. 1, presented here as images in the time-frequency plane with negative values clipped to zero and positive values scaled to within 255; from top to bottom, two in each category: normal, "pituitary", "adrenal" and "ectopic". (From Li et al. [16], Copyright © 1990 New York University, reprinted by permission of New York University Press.)

Examining these time-frequency characteristics, one can find that the major differences are shown in the central portion of the time-frequency domain ($n = 13$ to 37) where $W(n, m)$ is most reliably computed from the summation of all 49 non-zero products of data points. It supports the observation that $W(n, m)$ has the most significant intensity information in the time interval from $n = 13$ to $n = 37$. Let us examine the energy density profile along the frequency axis and compute the essential energy density at $m\Delta\omega$ by summing up $W(n, m)$ over the time index n from 13 to 37

$$E_n(m) = \sum_{n=13}^{37} W(n, m) \tag{4.1}$$

These $E_n(m)$'s are examined for selection of discriminating features. The normal patterns and Cushing's syndrome patterns can be distinguished by using two features: $E_n(0)$ and $E_n(4)$. Their distributions are shown in Fig. 3. Among the Cushing's syndrome patterns, "adrenal" and "ectopic" categories can also be differentiated by using these two features. $E_n(0)$, $E_n(2)$ and $E_n(3)$ were selected for discriminating "pituitary" from "adrenal". "Pituitary" and "ectopic" categories can be classified by using four features: $E_n(0)$, $E_n(3)$, $E_n(7)$ and $E_n(8)$. Altogether, six spectral features were selected for automatic pattern recognition of cortisol signals. By using a similar structure as the one used in [3], another pattern recognition system shown in Fig. 4 was trained with 100% accuracy. The weight vectors W_1,

W_2, W_3 and W_4 of component classifiers in the system are given in Table 1, where the last component in each weight vector is the threshold weight. Linear decision functions $d_i = (y_i', 1)W_i$, $(i = 1, 2, 3, 4)$, are used in the system. Joint decisions assign an abnormal category, for example, "pituitary" is classified when $d_1 < 0$, $d_2 > 0$ and $d_3 > 0$.

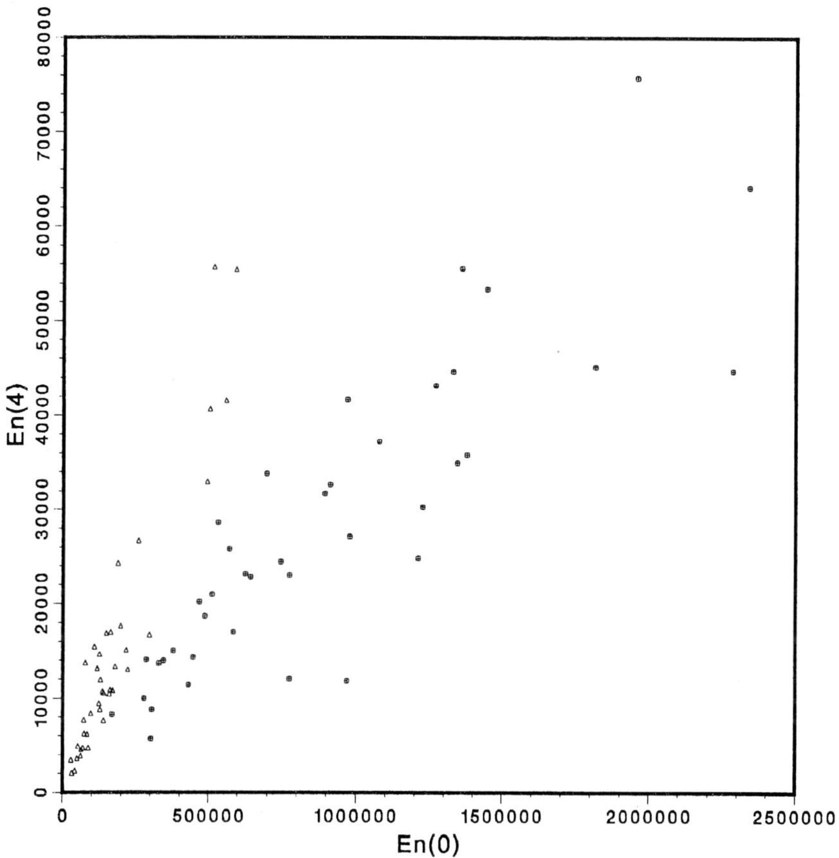

Fig. 3. Distributions of 41 normal patterns and 49 Cushing's syndrome patterns in $E_n(0)$–$E_n(4)$ feature space (triangle: Normal; circle: Cushing's syndrome).

In summary, we have shown that the discrete pseudo Wigner distribution provides an effective method for analyzing sparsely sampled biomedical signals. On one hand, its presentation in the time-frequency plane, after appropriate post-processing, may provide a means for pattern visualization for physicians. On the other hand, spectral information can be obtained with an increased frequency resolution, and thus contributes to the effective and efficient feature extraction for automatic pattern recognition.

Table 1. Augmented weight vectors for cortisol pattern recognition system shown in Fig. 4.

Classifier	Normal/ Patient	"pituitary"/ "adrenal"	"pituitary"/ "ectopic"	"adrenal"/ "ectopic"
Feature	$E_n(0)$	$E_n(0)$	$E_n(0)$	$E_n(0)$
Vector	$E_n(4)$	$E_n(2)$	$E_n(3)$	$E_n(4)$
y_i		$E_n(3)$	$E_n(7)$	
			$E_n(8)$	
Augmented	-0.3345	0.0745	-0.0680	-0.0095
Weight	-5.5846	3.1639	-0.6749	0.1780
Vectors	9994.5571	-2.5136	-1.5909	9206.8272
W_i		-9401.63	2.3334	
			41225.1457	

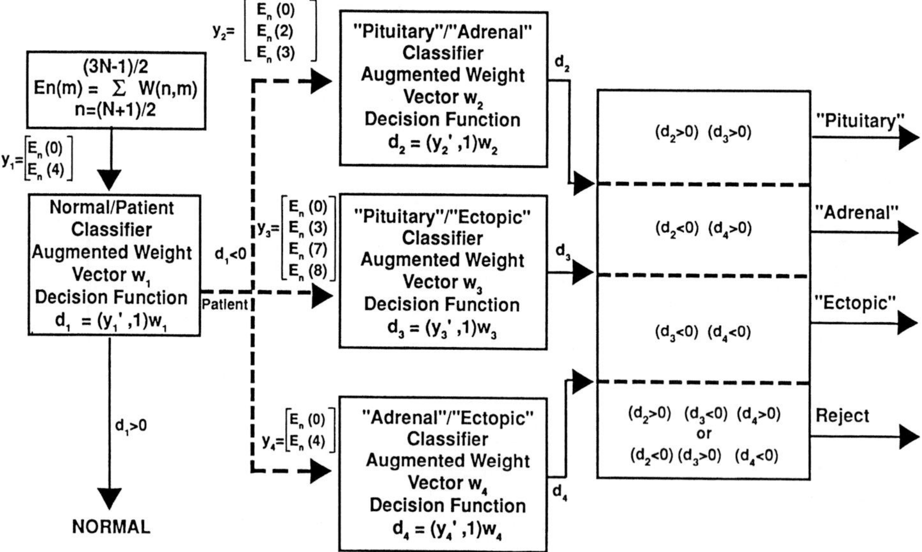

Fig. 4. Block diagram of a pattern recognition system for cortisol time series using spectral features extracted from discrete pseudo Wigner distribution.

References

[1] R. G. Shiavi and J. R. Bourne, Methods of biological signal processing, in T. Y. Young and K. S. Fu (eds.), *Handbook of Pattern Recognition and Image Processing* (Academic press, New York, 1986) 545–568.

[2] N. V. Thakor (guest ed.), Biomedical Signal Processing, *IEEE Engineering in Medicine and Biology Magazine* **9**, March (1990).

[3] A. H. Vagnucci, T. P. Wang, V. Pratt and C. C. Li, Classification of plasma cortisol patterns in normal subjects and in Cushing's syndrome, *IEEE Trans. Biomed. Eng.* **38** (1991) 113–125.

[4] E. P. Wigner, On the quantum correction for thermodynamic equilibrium, *Phys. Rev.* **40** (1932) 749–759.

[5] J. Ville, Theorie et applications de la notion de signal analytique, *Cables et Transmission* **2A** (1948) 61–74.

[6] T. A. C. M. Claasen and W. F. G. Mecklenbrauker, The Wigner distribution — A tool for time-frequency signal analysis, Part I, Part II, Part III, *Philips J. Res.* **35** (1980) 217–250, 276–300, 372–389.

[7] G. F. Boudreaux-Bartels, Time-frequency Signal Processing Algorithms: Analysis and Synthesis Using Wigner Distributions, Ph.D. Thesis, Rice University, 1984.

[8] W. Martin and P. Flandrin, Wigner–Ville spectral analysis of nonstationary processes, *IEEE Trans. Acoust. Speech Signal Process.* **33** (1985) 1461–1470.

[9] J. C. Andrieux, M. R. Feix, G. Mourgues, P. Bertrand, B. Izrar and V. T. Nguyen, Optimum smoothing of the Wigner–Ville distribution, *IEEE Trans. Acoust. Speech Signal Process.* **35** (1987) 764–769.

[10] M. Sun, The Discrete Pseudo Wigner Distribution: Efficient Computation and Cross-Component Elimination, Ph. D. Thesis, University of Pittsburgh, 1989.

[11] M. Sun, C. C. Li, L. N. Sekhar and R. J. Sclabassi, Efficient computation of discrete pseudo Wigner distribution, *IEEE Trans. Acoust. Speech Signal Process.* **37** (1989) 1735–1742.

[12] R. M. S. S. Abeysekera, Time-frequency domain features of ECG signals: An interpretation and their application in computer aided diagnoses, Ph. D. Thesis, University of Queensland, Australia, 1989.

[13] S. Usui and H. Araki, Wigner distribution analysis of BSPM for optimal sampling, *IEEE Engineering in Medicine and Biology Magazine* **9**, March (1990) 29–32.

[14] F. Hlawatsch and G. F. Boudreaux-Bartels, Linear and quadratic time-frequency signal representations, *IEEE Signal Processing Magazine* **9**, April (1992) 21–68.

[15] T. P. Wang, M. Sun, C. C. Li and A. H. Vagnucci, Classification of abnormal cortisol patterns by features from Wigner spectra, in *Proc. 10th Int. Conf. on Pattern Recognition*, Atlantic City, NJ, June, 1990, 228–230.

[16] C. C. Li, A. H. Vagnucci, T. P. Wang and M. Sun, Pseudo Wigner distribution for processing short-time biological signals, in D. C. Mikulecky and A. M. Clarke (eds.), *Biomedical Engineering: Opening New Doors, Proc. 1990 Annual Fall Meeting of Biomedical Engineering Soc.* (New York University Press, New York, 1990) 191–200.

Handbook of Pattern Recognition and Computer Vision, pp. 667–693
Eds. C. H. Chen, L. F. Pau and P. S. P. Wang
© 1993 World Scientific Publishing Company

CHAPTER 3.8

UNDERSTANDING MICROVESSELS IN TWO AND THREE DIMENSIONS

CARL E. WICK

Department of Weapons and Systems Engineering, U.S. Naval Academy
Annapolis, MD 21402-5000, USA

and

Department of Electrical Engineering and Computer Science, George Washington University
Washington, DC 20052, USA

MURRAY H. LOEW

Department of Electrical Engineering and Computer Science, George Washington University
Washington, DC 20052, USA

JOSEPH KURANTSIN-MILLS

Departments of Medicine and Physiology, George Washington University
Washington, DC 20052, USA

Automated morphometry of the microcirculation requires robust image processing programs which can identify and track microvessels in video or photographic images obtained by transillumination. We describe a model which replicates the illumination process contributing to a film or video image of the microvessels of the conjunctiva. The model provides a foundation for microvessel detection algorithms, for precise measurement of vessel dimensions and depth within a diffuse medium, and for separating neighboring vessels in complex images. In this model, a cylindrical vessel is embedded in a diffuse medium which is on a reflecting background. A light source illuminating the scene is reflected by scene components and passes through a pinhole to an image plane, which records these reflections as intensity values at discrete pixel locations. Fundamental physical principles which include Lambert's cosine law governing the illuminance of diffuse light sources and reflectors, isotropic spreading, Fresnel's reflection law, and Beer's law governing the effects of a translucent medium were systematically applied to the model. The direct and the reflected illumination at each point in the model was calculated using geometric relationships present in the scene. A video apparatus and a phantom was constructed to analyze different illumination conditions, to determine the contribution each scene component makes to the final image and to verify the completed model. Relative reflectivity data determined from video signals was used in a computer simulation of the image model. The results of the simulation compared favorably with experimental data. The validated image process model provides much needed information about the intensity values present in microvessel images. This information will be useful in finding solutions to problems which exist in vessel detection and tracking approaches based on idealized image models.

Keywords: Image processing, image modeling, microcirculation, conjunctiva.

1. Introduction

Computerized image processing is now applied to many clinical and research tasks. Its use already assists in the presentation, storage, transmission and analysis of all forms of images generated in biomedical science. Indeed, potential uses for systems that dramatically reduce the time, tedium, and subjectivity of detections and measurements from images seems almost boundless.

Image processing, however, particularly image analysis, is not easy. Tasks which seem almost trivial for experienced individuals to perform, may be time consuming, and routinely give poor or mixed results when they are automated. One area which currently limits our ability to automate the analysis of complex situations is our own knowledge about the information present in an image. In our development of image analysis applications, we frequently turn to heuristics and regional or global operations on the image to reduce the information content and cause it to take on more "ideal" characteristics. As image structures become more complicated and distinctions become more subtle, we find that the more we idealize an image, the less satisfactory results we get.

In our research effort to develop an automated procedure for the extraction of the morphology and topography of vessels of the microcirculation from photographic images, we encountered the problematic circumstances outlined above. Previous attempts by others to reduce the labor and to automate the extraction of blood vessel parameters had met with only partial success [1,2,3]. Figure 1(a) is a photograph of the human bulbar conjunctiva showing several types and sizes of blood vessels. Figure 1(b) is the graphical presentation of image intensity values taken from one horizontal line of the image. Discerning blood vessels in the image seems easy to us. When we examined the data, however, there was very little consistency which could be exploited to determine answers to complex questions such as the boundary limits of blood vessels, or the precise locale of a corresponding blood vessel when vessels intersect. We believe that in order to improve this particular image analysis process, and image analysis in general, we must have a better understanding of the type of information present in the intensity values of an image. In other words, what type of information is present in the three-dimensional reality of an image?

In an attempt to answer this question we elected to construct a comprehensive model of the illumination–reflection processes involved in forming an image. In this instance the image is one of the microvessels in a translucent membranous tissue such as the bulbar conjunctiva, the mesentery, or the cremaster muscle for which transillumination is the optical procedure for generating the image. In this study, we have utilized the microvessels of the bulbar conjunctiva as a typical example for the modeling. In the modeling processes, we apply first principles to a simplified physical model of the conjunctiva, accounting for each known effect. During modeling, an experimental apparatus which duplicated the physical model allowed various illumination and reflection effects to be explored in detail. When it was completed, the model was verified through data taken from images of a specifically

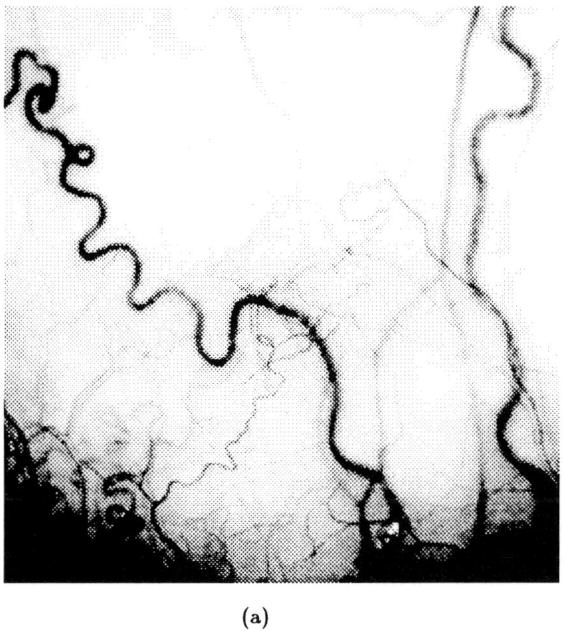

(a)

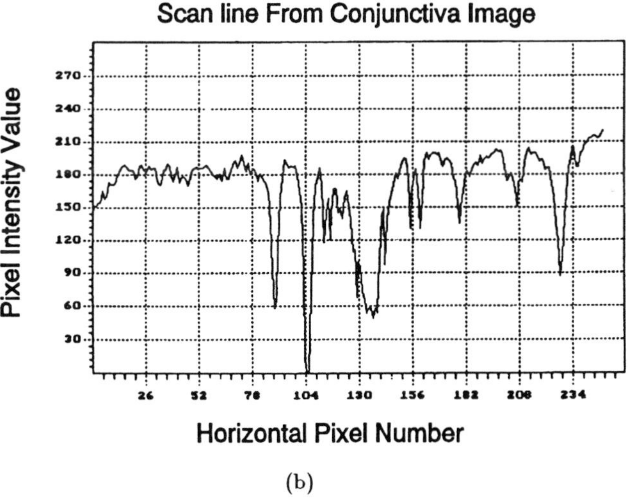

(b)

Fig. 1. Conjunctiva image data. (a) An example image of a portion of the human conjunctiva. Vessels seen embedded in the thin conjunctival membrane include arterioles, venules, and capillaries. Vessels deeper in the membrane and those which penetrate scleral tissue appear faded in comparison to vessels which are closer to the surface. (b) An example of the intensity values found in one horizontal scan line of the same image, taken at a point about half-way down the image. The intensity data shows a consistent white background level from the conjunctival membrane and sclera, contrasted with a marked variation among the intensity values corresponding to the vessels present in the image.

constructed phantom which also duplicated the basis physical model. The verified model provides a mapping from image intensity values to causal physical properties of the three-dimensional image. The mapping provides much useful information about the intensity values seen in the image. This information, in turn, provides an avenue for using intensity values as cues in subsequent image analysis to solve some problems which seem intractable in an idealized environment.

2. Modeling Methods

2.1. *Physical Model*

The physical model is the foundation of the mathematical analysis. It must represent the circumstance being modeled to the greatest degree possible, yet not be unduly complex. The physical model should also be realizable so that the modeling processes may be experimentally verified throughout the modeling process.

Figure 2 depicts the simplified physical model used in this study. The anatomical components of the model consist of a cylinder V representing a blood vessel contained within a translucent conjunctival membrane M. The membrane is thicker than the blood vessel, so the model must accommodate different vertical vessel positions within the membrane. The membrane and blood vessel rests on the diffusely reflecting background of the sclera S.

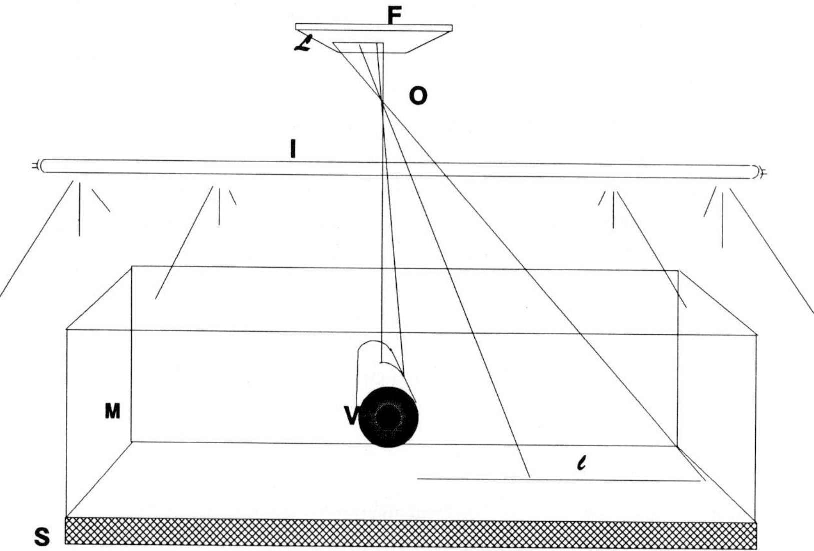

Fig. 2. The physical model. The physical model simulates the essential elements present in an image of the conjunctiva. The conjunctival membrane is represented by a diffuse medium M, the blood vessels by a cylinder V embedded in the medium, and the sclera S by a diffuse reflecting background. Light from a source l illuminates the scene from above, and reflects components from the scene through optics O onto a focal plane F.

The scene of the blood vessel, membrane and background is illuminated from above by an extended diffuse light source I. The horizontal dimension and the height of the light source are adjustable parameters. Light from the source is reflected off the scene and is imaged through the pinhole O and recorded at the focal plane F. The intensity value at a particular pixel position on F corresponds to illumination reflected from components which lie on a ray from the pixel through O to the scene.

Although the physical model is three-dimensional, any row of pixels on F record intensity values from rays which pass through an essentially two-dimensional plane at a right angle to the blood vessel. The image may then be viewed as an assemblage of these rows of pixels. This point of view simplifies the modeling process without loss of generality by reducing the modeling dimensions to two. It also allows relatively easy verification of effects through the use of line scanning hardware.

2.2. *First Principles*

The fundamental physical principles which were systematically applied to the physical model are Lambert's cosine law governing the illuminance of diffuse light sources and reflectors, isotropic spreading, Fresnel's reflection law [4–9], and Beer's law governing the effects of a translucent medium [8,9].

Lambert's law and the effects of isotropic spreading are illustrated in Figs. 3(a) and (b). By definition, the luminance of a diffusely emitting Lambertian point source in a particular direction is proportional to the cosine of an angle formed between the surface normal at the point and a ray in a chosen direction. Isotropic spreading from the point source to a receiving area decreases energy density at a receiving area by a factor of $1/R^2$, where R is the distance from light source to receiving area. At the receiving surface the collected illuminance is again a function of Lambert's law and is proportional to the projection of that surface toward the source of illumination. The receiving illuminance is therefore again proportional to the relative angle between ray and surface normal. An extended linear source of illumination, as in the physical model, allows some simplifications to be made in modeling. In Fig. 3(b), one can see that the projection of a receiving element towards the source at an angle $\beta(\gamma = 0)$ results in an increase in the area of a differential source element as seen by the receiving area. The increase in source area is a function of the distance R and the secant of the projected angle β (and γ). The result, as will be seen in a later section, is that the increased source area offsets the effects of Lambert's law and distance. The diffuse source then appears to have equal uniform luminance from all aspects.

Fresnel's equations express the behavior of light energy reflected at a surface. The equations characterize the fractional amount of energy which reflects in a specular manner (mirror reflection) as opposed to reflecting in a diffuse manner. These equations also specify the polarization of the reflected energy [4,5,8,9]. Each of these factors can be computed for different angles of incidence at a surface. Fresnel's equations predict a significant shift in reflective behavior from mainly diffuse to

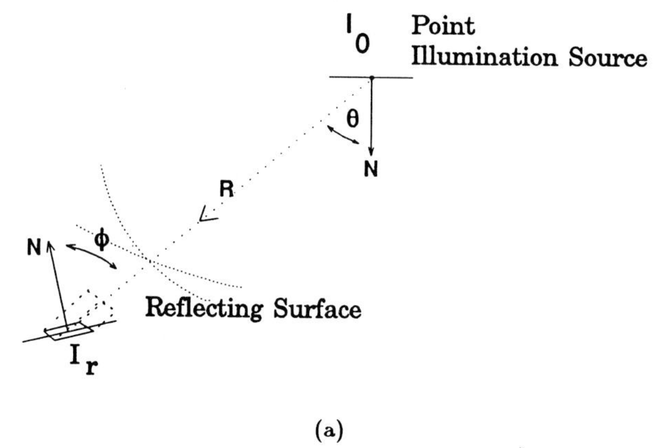

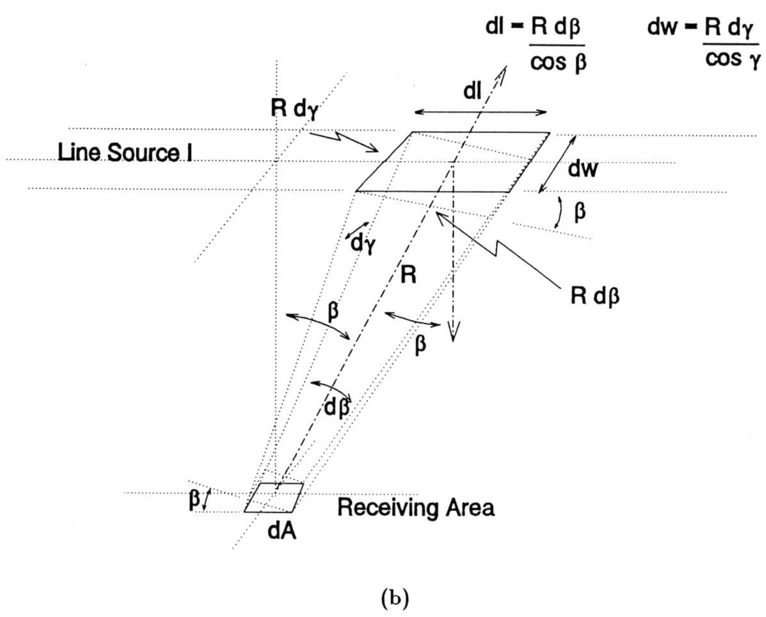

Fig. 3. Lambert's law effects. (a) Lambert's law defines the behavior of diffuse sources and reflecting surfaces. A diffuse point source radiates in an isotropic manner. Illumination from the source spreads spherically, and at some radius R intersects a reflecting surface. The amount of illuminance which is received by the surface (and which may be subsequently reflected) is dictated by the area in which it projects toward the source. Maximum illumination is received when the receiving area is perpendicular to the point source and varies for other geometries according to the cosine of the angle between the source and the receiving surface normal. (b) When an extended area source is used, the effects of the projected area cause a large differential area of the source to be seen by the receiving surface if the two surfaces are not aligned. This increase in effective illumination offsets the effects of angle and distance and the source appears uniform from all angles.

mainly specular as incident angles increase towards 90°. This shift was used to describe some observed reflective behavior at the limbus of the blood vessel in the physical model. The effects of polarization were not used. Fresnel effects were modeled by an approximating function in this effort (see Fig. 4). The approximating function provided an easier method to find the diffuse and specular components of reflections without the complexity of computing Fresnel laws for each instance.

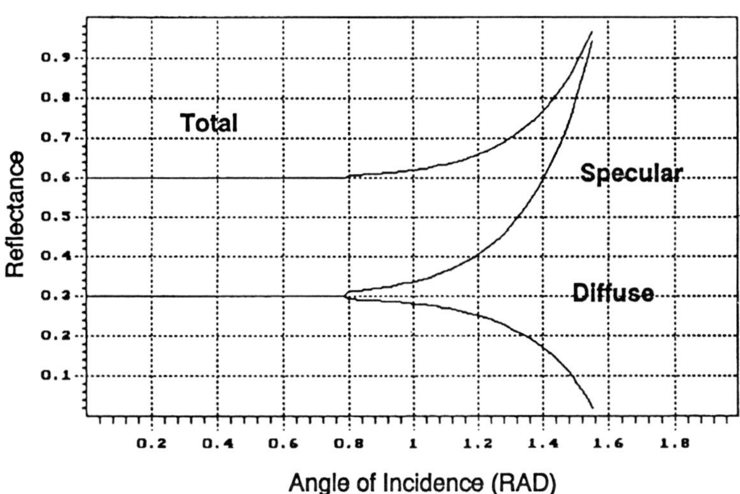

Fig. 4. Fresnel's approximation. Fresnel's law allows the polarization and the diffuse or specular nature of reflections to be determined from reflectivity coefficients and surface geometry. In general, reflections tend to become more specular and the reflective index approaches one as the angle of incidence approaches 90°. Because polarization information was not used in the model, an approximation of Fresnel behavior could be used to facilitate calculations. The approximation splits reflections into diffuse and specular components. These components are multiplied by a reflectivity constant which approaches one for the specular component and zero for the diffuse component as the angle of incidence approaches 90°.

Beer's law, sometimes referred to as the Bouguer–Lambert law, describes the extinction of illuminance with depth in a translucent material due to absorption and scattering (see Fig. 5). Provided single collisions prevail in the material, the differential change in illuminance with a change in path length through the material is proportional to the incident illumination, material optical properties, and the distance the light has already traveled. In general, the illuminance at a depth x in a translucent medium with optical distance $1/k$ is

$$I_x = I_0 e^{-kx} \; . \tag{2.1}$$

Refractive (Snell's law) effects at material interfaces were considered to be an additional first principle. However, in the course of model development, experimental evidence suggested that these effects were not significant enough to warrant including them in the final model.

2.3. *Illumination Model*

The modeling process proceeds from the physical model to the mathematical model by applying first principles to all geometric paths taken by light as it travels from its source to the focal plane. This is a multi-step calculation, similar to the radiosity approach used in computer image rendering [4,5], which involves the following (see Fig. 6). First, the illuminance at a point P in the scene is calculated by applying Lambert's and Beer's laws between P and each point on the extended light source I, and integrating the results over the entire extent of I visible from P. The visibility of I from P may be limited by the presence of an obscuring object V, or by the fact that the distance through M is so great that essentially no illumination from a particular location on I could penetrate to P. Once the illuminance at P is calculated, it is multiplied by the reflectance of the surface at P. Fresnel's law effects are applied if the angle of incidence approaches 90° at its surface, or if the angle of reflection required to place a ray onto focal plane F approaches 90°. Finally, Lambert's and Beer's law relationships are applied to the ray which reaches F from P through O. Added to the illumination reaching the focal plane by this path is illumination which is reflected by the translucent membrane. This back-scattered illumination from the medium may also be calculated by integrating Beer's law effects over the distance from the surface to point P.

In this basic manner, illumination from the source reflected back to the focal plane was found for the following areas of the scene: the scleral background, the blood vessel, from reflections of the background secondarily reflected off the limbus of the blood vessel, and from the translucent medium itself.

To further illustrate the process involved in this model, consider the reflection of the extended source I at a point P' on the scleral background. The illuminance at P' is the integral of Lambert's law applied to all points on I which can be seen from P'. If membrane M were transparent, then the illuminance arriving at P would be due to Lambertian effects between I and P' and due to spreading effects over distance R:

$$I_{P'} = \int^{W} \int_{-l_0}^{l_1} \frac{I_0 \cos\beta \cos\gamma}{R^2} \cos\beta \cos\gamma \, dl \, dw \; . \tag{2.2}$$

If the integration variables are changed from linear distances on I to angles β from P, and I is constrained to a line source ($\gamma = 0$) then

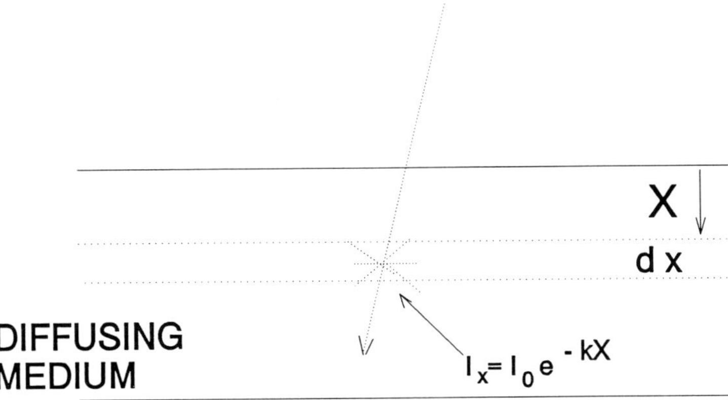

Fig. 5. Beer's law effects. Beer's law explains the loss of illuminance which occurs as depth is increased in a diffusing medium. The change in illuminance seen in a differential layer at a depth X is proportional to the illuminance arriving at that depth the concentration of reflecting particles in the differential layer, and the reflecting and absorbing properties of the particles. Solving this differential equation leads to Beer's law ($l_x = l_0 e^{-kX}$).

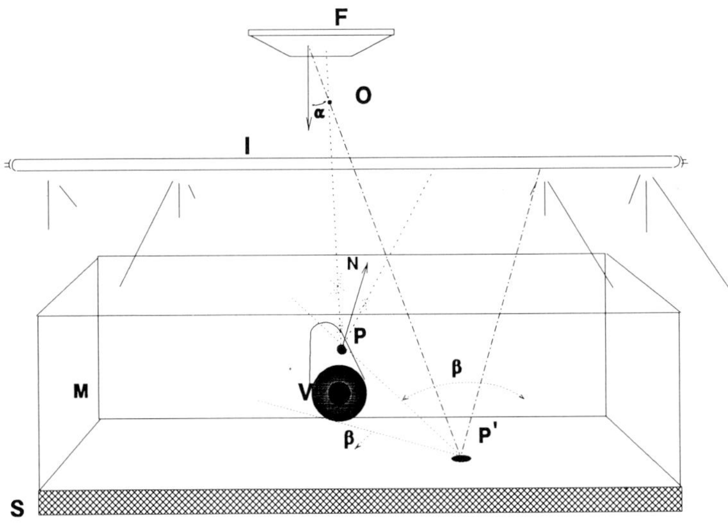

Fig. 6. Illumination model. The illumination model explores the types of reflections which may occur for light emitted at a point on the illumination source and its eventual destination at the focal plane. Illuminance arriving at different points in the scene (P and P') are influenced by the unobstructed angular extent of the light source β, and by the geometric relations between illumination source l and the objects through the application of Lambert's law and Beer's law. Light reflected by objects in the scene towards the focal plane is again influenced by the same relationships.

$$dl = \frac{R\,d\beta}{\cos\beta} \;,\; d\omega = R\,d\gamma$$

$$I_{P'} = I \int_{-\beta_0}^{\beta_1} \cos\beta\,d\beta$$

$$= I(\sin\beta_1 + \sin\beta_0) \tag{2.3}$$

where angles β are limited by the visible extent of I, or by vessel V obstructing a portion of the source. When I is obscured by V, a penumbra or shadow forms in the area receiving reduced illumination. The illuminance at point P is also moderated by the effects of absorption and scattering in membrane M which lies upon the background.

2.4. *Diffuse Medium Effects*

The illumination at point P is also moderated by the effects of absorption and scattering in membrane M which lies upon the background. Since membrane M is not totally transparent, it will tend to scatter and absorb incident light energy within its volume. The effect will be to reduce the available illuminance with increasing object depth. Thus, objects or points which are deeper will receive less illumination to reflect than objects or points which are closer to the surface. The effect holds in both directions, so light reflected from points within a diffusing medium will be further diminished by material scatterers and absorption as it is reflected back to the surface. This phenomena, which can be predicted in translucent materials by Beer's law, is believed to be the principal reason for differences seen in the apparent reflectivity of blood vessels in conjunctiva images. It should be noted here that the Beer's law model was chosen over the more rigorous transport theory model [10,11], because the relative transparency of the tissue indicates that single collisions will likely be the dominant mode of scattering and the exact spatial distribution of scattered light was not believed to be important for this particular problem.

Figure 7 illustrates the expected reflective behavior of a diffuse medium like the conjunctiva epithelia. The epithelial material which is not transparent contains non-homogeneous areas or "particles" which tend to reflect incident light with a factor ρ_p and absorb incident light with a factor α_p. If a differential layer dL in the material contains a concentration C of these particles, then the net change in illuminance due to the layer at a distance L from the surface can be expressed as

$$dI = I(\alpha_p + \rho_p)C\,dL \;.$$

Solving for I:

$$I_L = I_0 e^{-(\alpha_p + \rho_p)CL}$$

$$= I_0 e^{-kL} \;. \tag{2.4}$$

An object V at light ray distance L in a diffusing medium will reflect the light energy remaining at that distance according to its own reflectivity characteristic ρ_V.

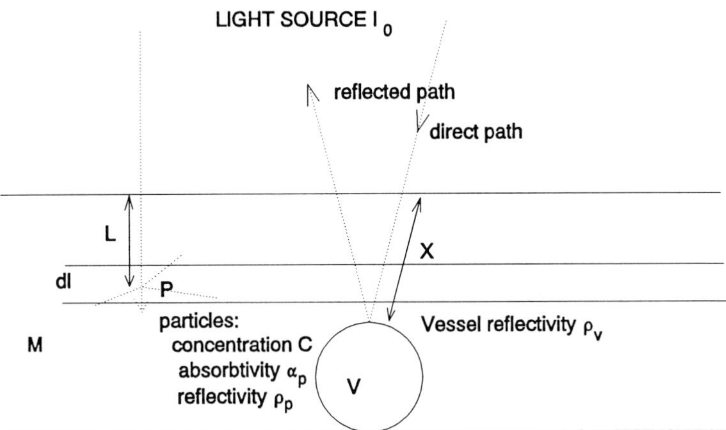

Fig. 7. Diffuse medium effects. When Beer's law is used to describe light reflected from a scene containing a diffuse medium, two separate cases must be considered. The first case is the loss of effective illuminance on the path from the source to the object to the focal plane. Losses on this path are due to absorption and scattering by particles within the medium. In the second case a certain amount of the incident light is reflected by the medium toward the focal plane. The illuminance which arrives at the focal plane is a combination of these two effects.

Light reflected from the object then travels back through the medium until it reaches the surface, where it is observed with illuminance I. If the return ray distance through the medium is the same distance L, then

$$I = I_0 \rho_V e^{-2kL} \ . \tag{2.5}$$

Incident light is also reflected by the individual particles of the medium. Some of this energy is reflected towards the surface and focal plane. If the available illuminance at some depth L is as shown in Eq. (2.4), and a particle reflects light in any direction with characteristic $\rho_{p'}$, then the total assemblage of particles constituting the medium reflects with

$$I_p = \int_0^L I_0 \rho_{p'} e^{-2kl} dl$$
$$= I_0 \hat{\rho}_p (1 - e^{-2kL}) \ . \tag{2.6}$$

The total illuminance seen by an observer at the surface of the diffuse medium is then the sum of the illumination reflected by objects and the medium itself

$$I = I_0 (\hat{\rho}_p + (\rho_V - \hat{\rho}_p) e^{-2kL}) \ . \tag{2.7}$$

To accommodate diffuse medium effects in the illumination model, the length of each light path in the medium from light source to reflecting point must be calculated. If an arbitrary ray at an angle β is chosen, then the path length for that ray in a medium of depth L is

$$\text{Path length} = L \sec \beta \,. \tag{2.8}$$

Returning to the previous example, the illuminance at a point P' on the background in a diffusing medium now becomes

$$I_{P'} = I_0 \int_{-B_0}^{B_1} \cos \beta e^{-kL \sec \beta} d\beta \tag{2.9}$$

and the resulting illuminance at the focal plane from point P' at look angle α becomes

$$I_F = I_0 \cos \alpha e^{-kL \sec \alpha} \int_{-B_0}^{B_1} \cos \beta e^{-kL \sec \beta} \, d\beta \,. \tag{2.10}$$

The integral in this instance has no known closed form solution. However, a Taylor series expansion gives a close approximation over a meaningful range of β:

$$\int_{-B_0}^{B_1} \cos \beta e^{-K \sec \beta} d\beta$$
$$\sim \frac{e^{-K}}{120} ((3K^2 + K + 1)\beta^5 - (20K + 20)\beta^3 + 120\beta) \tag{2.11}$$

where

$$K = kL \quad \text{and} \quad |\beta| \leq \cos^{-1} \left(\frac{K}{3.8} \right) \,.$$

The limits of β represent a path length through the medium which represents a range over which the Taylor series approximation very closely fits the integral. It also represents a range which results in nearly total extinction of illuminance due to diffusion effects.

2.5. *Direct Blood Vessel Reflections*

Direct reflection of the illumination source off the physical model blood vessel V and onto focal plane F is much like that of the background. The major dissimilarity between these reflections and the background is that the angles between the local normals at the light source and at the blood vessel are different (see Fig. 8). The surface normal of the cylindrical blood vessel may be found as a function of look angle α, the angle by which a ray from a pixel on the focal plane passes through pinhole O to terminate at point P on the vessel. The normal angle ϕ may be found through application of the law of sines:

$$\phi = \pi - \alpha - \sin^{-1} \left(\frac{H_{o\nu}}{r} \sin \alpha \right) \,. \tag{2.12}$$

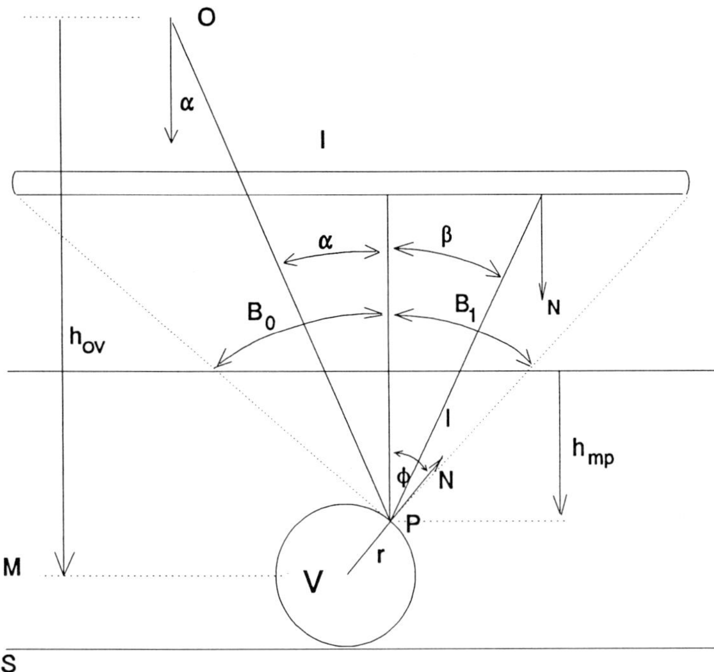

Fig. 8. Direct reflections. A fraction of all light energy which arrives at a point on the vessel is reflected to arrive at the focal plane. The total amount of light arriving at a point P is influenced by the angular extent of the light source (B_0 and B_1), by the angle between the surface normal at P and a point on the source (β and ϕ), and the distance the light travels through the diffuse medium. Light energy reflected at P arrives at a focal plane pixel position through a look angle α after a return trip through the medium.

To accommodate the effects of a diffuse medium in these reflections, the path length through the medium for each light ray must be calculated. The general concept behind these calculations is the same as outlined in the previous section on background reflections. If a point P on vessel V is located at a distance $L = h_{mp}$ from the top surface of a diffusing medium, then the illuminance at P will be

$$I_p = I \int_{-B_0}^{B_1} \cos(\phi - \beta) e^{-kL \sec \beta} d\beta \ .$$

If $K = kL$ then (2.13)

$$I_p \approx \frac{e^{-K}}{720} ((\cos\phi((18K^2 + 6K + 6)\beta^5 - (120K + 120)\beta^3 + 720\beta))$$
$$+ (\sin\phi((15K^2 + 15K + 1)\beta^6 - (90K + 30)\beta^4 + 360\beta^2))) \ .$$

In this approximation the angle β must be limited to the same range as the approximation used in background reflections. Furthermore, light reflected off V reaching the focal plane will be diminished along the return path by $\cos\alpha e^{-kL\sec\alpha}$.

2.6. *Indirect Blood Vessel Reflections*

Indirect reflections in a diffuse medium differ from background and direct blood vessel reflections only in the path that must be considered. Here, the path of light from the background to the focal plane must be broken into two segments (see Fig. 9); a segment from the background to the limbus of the vessel and a segment from the vessel to the focal plane. Light energy diminished along the segment from the vessel to the focal plane is a function of look angle α and the same formula presented in the previous paragraph suffices. Light energy on the path segment from background to vessel limbus is dependent upon the reflected illuminance at background point $l_{d,s}$, angle β, and the distance of point P from the background (h_{Ps}):

$$I_p = I_{l_{s,d}} \cos\beta e^{-Kh_{Ps}\sec\beta}$$

where   (2.14)

$$h_{Ps} = r(1 + a + \cos\phi) \ .$$

The illuminance arriving at point P is broken into specular and diffuse components. The specular component is determined from the background according to the incident angle required for a mirror reflection of the background off V onto F. The diffuse component is the remainder of the background visible from P. Each component is then multiplied by its corresponding Fresnel approximation reflectivity component before propagating the total illuminance to the focal plane. Fresnel reflectivity of the vessel surface was approximated by the use of two separate reflectivity values, one for specular reflections and one for diffuse reflections (see Fig. 4). Both reflectivity values were made equal to one-half vessel reflectivity for low angles of incidence (0–45°). At higher angles of incidence, the specular component approaches one while the diffuse component approaches zero in the limit:

$$\left(\psi \le \frac{\pi}{4}\right) \Rightarrow \rho_{Ps} = \frac{\rho_v}{2} \ , \quad \rho_{Pd} = \frac{\rho_v}{2}$$

$$\text{otherwise} \ \Rightarrow \rho_{Ps} = \frac{\rho_v}{2} + \left(1 - \frac{\rho_v}{2}\right)e^{-\frac{16\psi}{\pi}}$$ (2.15)

$$\rho_{Pd} = \frac{\rho_v}{2}\left(1 - e^{-\frac{16(\frac{\pi}{2}-\psi)}{\pi}}\right) \ .$$

The expressions for this approximation of Fresnel behavior were derived empirically by comparing the illumination levels seen at the limbus of a cylinder in reflecting and non-reflecting backgrounds. A diffuse medium will sharply reduce

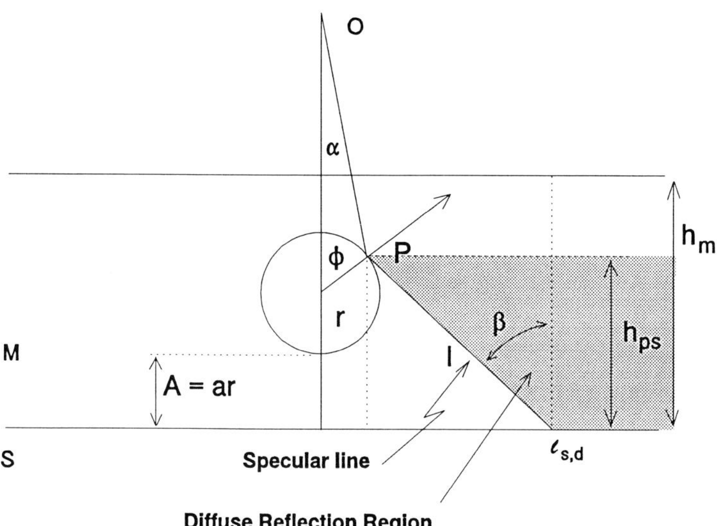

Fig. 9. Indirect reflections. Some of the light energy diffusely reflected by the background is re-flected a second time by the vessel and eventually reaches the focal plane. This indirect reflection activity occurs principally near the limbus of the vessel and makes the limbus appear brighter than it would against a dark background. In this region of the vessel, incident light angles from the background approach 90° and Fresnel reflection properties must be considered. The Fresnel approximation used in this study requires that the contributing reflection point from the back-ground be broken into two components: a specular reflection from a background point to a focal plane pixel and a diffuse component from all other contributing background points.

the indirect illumination effects seen at the limbus regions of the model vessel. While this source of illumination diminishes, the next effect, reflections of the medium itself, become dominant.

2.7. *Diffuse Medium Reflections*

If the medium is translucent, it must absorb and reflect some of the light energy which falls upon it. This is the basis for Beer's law. If the reflective properties of the medium are significant, then the medium itself will provide a substantial part of the total reflected energy which reaches the focal plane. To properly account for the contributions of particles within the medium, the illuminance for each particle along a look angle α must be calculated (see Fig. 10). In modeling, a numerical integration must be performed for all depths in the medium along a constant look angle (α) path

$$I_\alpha = \int_0^M \int_{-\beta_0}^{\beta_1} \cos\beta e^{-ky\,\sec\beta} dy d\beta \tag{2.16}$$

where $y = h_{ms}$ represents the vertical distance from the surface of M to point P along a constant α line, and β_0 and β_1 both represent the angular limits of visibility

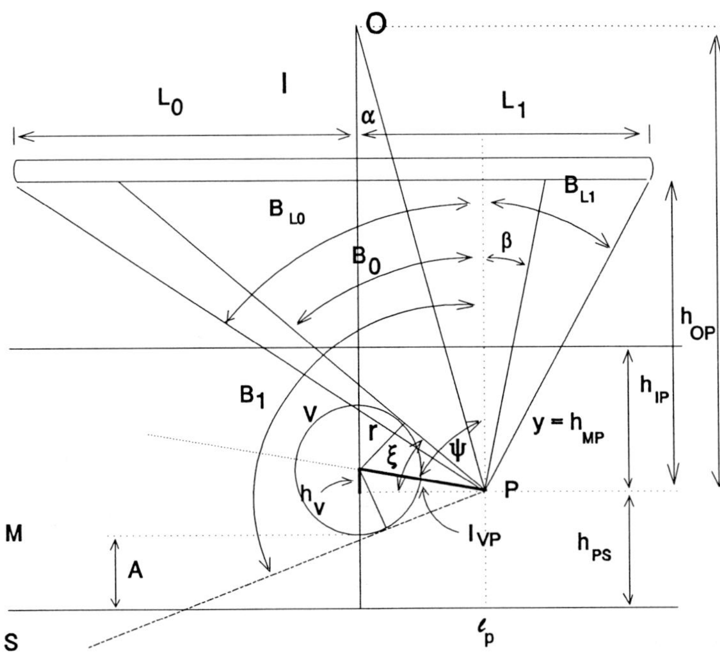

Fig. 10. Diffuse medium effects. Light reflected by particles within the medium itself contributes to the illuminance which arrrives at a pixel position on the focal plane. The amount of light energy reflected by a point in the medium is influenced by the depth of the medium at the point h_{IP}, the unobstructed angular extent of the light source from P (B_0 and B_{L1}), and the distance the light travels through the medium. Light reflected at P travels through the medium a second time and arrives at a focal plane pixel position through look angle α. A numerical integration of all points in the medium along α gives the total reflected light from the medium for a particular pixel position.

of light source I at position P. The visibility angles are limited by three factors; the physical extent of light source I, the limits of useful angles in the Taylor series approximation for the diffuse integral, and the obstruction that the cylindrical vessel V may place in a path from P to I:

$$\beta_0 = \min\{B_0, B_{l0}, B_{\text{diffuse}}\} \quad \beta_1 = \min\{B_1, B_{l1}, B_{\text{diffuse}}\}$$

where

$$B_{l0} = \tan^{-1}\left(\frac{L_0 + l_p}{h_{IP}}\right) \quad B_{l1} = \tan^{-1}\left(\frac{L_1 - l_p}{h_{IP}}\right) \quad B_{\text{diffuse}} = \cos^{-1}\left(\frac{h_{mp}}{3.8}\right)$$

$$B_0 = (\psi - \xi) \quad B_1 = (\psi + \xi) \,. \tag{2.17}$$

Obstruction angles ξ and ψ may be determined from some geometric relationships between point P and vessel V:

$$\xi = \sin^{-1}\left(\frac{r}{l_{vp}}\right)$$

$$\psi = \frac{\pi}{2} + \tan^{-1}\left(\frac{h_v}{l_p}\right) \tag{2.18}$$

where

$$l_p = h_{op}\tan\alpha \ , \quad h_v = h_{Ps} - A - r \ , \quad l_{vp} = \sqrt{l_p^2 + h_v^2} \ .$$

Integration is carried out in the "y" direction for the entire depth of medium M, except for those values of α which intersect cylinder V at some depth. In this instance, integration stops upon reaching the outside of the vessel. In the model the integration was restarted at the depth the ray left the vessel and was continued for the remaining M depth. This second value represents the amount of reflected illumination available underneath the vessel. This illumination may be partially transmitted by a vessel which is not opaque.

2.8. *Translucent Cylinder Effects*

If vessel V is not opaque, it will allow a certain amount of the light reflected by the medium and background below it to pass through and add to the vessel illuminance produced by direct and indirect reflections and the illuminance of the medium above it. The contribution of light energy passing through the vessel to the total illuminance is a function of the path length the light takes through the vessel, as predicted by Beer's law. In the case of this model, the path used through the model blood vessel is the constant look angle α line. This is a reasonable approximation for the path distance provided the index of refraction for both M and V are close to the same value, so that the vessel does not cause severe bending of the look angle line by refraction.

Illuminance transmitted through the vessel is added to the direct and indirect effects accumulated at point P on the model vessel. The net effect is an altering of the illuminance profile near the vessel apex, causing a general increase in illuminance for increasing look angles between the vessel apex and limbus. The net change in illuminance of a translucent over an opaque vessel closely matches behavior observed experimentally and the signal shape seen in scanned conjunctiva images.

3. Experimental Methods

3.1. *Experiment 1: Analysis of Illumination Effects*

There are many possible interactions between the illumination source and the elements in the scene which can potentially contribute to an image generated by the physical model used in the present study (Figs. 6, 8, 9 and 10). In order to explore, determine and measure the effects of the elements within the scene, a simple system was constructed which enabled direct viewing of the effects of different illumination situations on the physical model. This tool was instrumental in isolating and determining the effects of each of the many possible contributing elements in this problem and also served to verify the completed model.

In order to elucidate the interaction of the reflections of the scene components several reflection experiments were conducted. These experiments used

(a) a non-reflecting plastic cylinder (0.32 cm in diameter, 10.16 cm in length), which was positioned on three different types of surfaces: (i) a flat non-reflecting surface; (ii) a white diffuse reflecting surface; and (iii) a flat non-reflecting surface adjoined to a white diffuse reflecting surface. This allowed us to explore background reflections, shadow, and Fresnel's reflections.

(b) a reflecting plastic cylinder of the same dimensions which was placed on the same three diffuse surfaces. This allowed us to explore reflective properties of the cylinder itself and diffuse reflections off the background onto the cylinder.

(c) a plastic cylinder of the same dimensions with longitudinal axis divided equally to provide reflective and non-reflective surfaces, which was placed on the same three background surfaces. This allowed us to compare the illuminance seen from reflective and non-reflective cylinder surfaces at the same time, confirming background reflection and Fresnel reflection effects.

The apparatus used to obtain the intensity values from the cylinder and the background consisted of a CCD television camera (Panasonic WV-CD1BW), mounted above a surface where backgrounds and objects could be placed and moved. A fluorescent lamp on a movable arm provided an adjustable height illumination to the work surface. The output of the camera was sent to a monitor, to the vertical channel of an oscilloscope, and to a synchronization separator circuit. In this circuit the vertical synchronization signal was separated from the composite video signal, was delayed, and then used to trigger the oscilloscope. With this set-up, one single horizontal scan line in a video frame could be displayed—which was exactly the physical configuration of the model. The device also provided a means for verifying the mathematical model of the transparent medium of the model before the complication of a diffuse medium was included in the computation.

3.2. *Experiment 2: Verification of the Model*

The addition of a diffuse medium to the model required an additional physical method to simulate these effects for model verification. The method chosen was to build a phantom model of the diffuse medium scene (see Fig. 11). The phantom was constructed from a poured slab casting of polyester resin with a dark-colored translucent plastic tube linearly inclined and supported by an internal wire for stability. This configuration allowed the depth of the tube in the resin to be determined at any point by measuring the distance from one end of the casting. A small amount

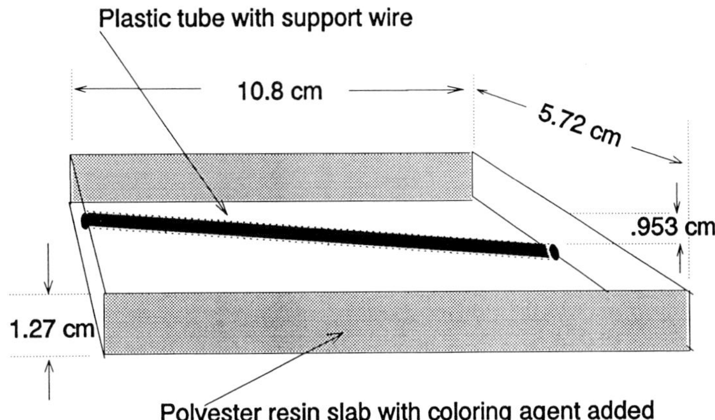

Fig. 11. Phantom model. To test diffuse medium theories, a duplicate of the physical model was manufactured from a dark-red colored polyethylene plastic tube and polyester casting resin. The plastic tube was inclined in the resin and supported with a steel wire to ensure that the depth of the tube progressed in a linear fashion along the length of the casting. A small amount (6–7 drops) of white polyester resin coloring agent was added to the resin before casting to increase the light diffusing properties of the medium. When hardened, the plastic tube was just visible at its deepest point in the resin. The hardened casting was placed on a flat bed scanner and images were made at resolutions of 75 dpi and 150 dpi.

of white resin coloring agent (Polyester/Epoxy White Coloring Agent, 50% coloring agent, 50% plasticizer) was added to the resin before casting to provide additional diffusing scatterers within the material. The size of the casting was approximately 5.72 cm by 10.80 cm by 1.27 cm deep, which was arbitrarily set by the casting container. The embedded 0.318 cm diameter tube was 10.16 cm in length and was embedded to a minimum depth of approximately zero centimeters (skim covering), and a maximum depth of approximately 0.953 cm in the resin, with a resulting 5° inclination. After the casting hardened, a 256 × 256 pixel image of it was produced by scanning the phantom on the bed of a flat bed scanner. The resolution of the image was 75 dots per inch (dpi) spatial resolution and 256 gray level intensity resolution. The phantom and its image provided a relatively constant record for determining and verifying the additional effects present when a translucent membrane was considered in the physical model.

3.3. *Computer Tools*

Although the majority of model and simulation software was locally developed in Borland C++ language, several other commercial software tools were also utilized in the numerical computation and data analysis during the development and verification of the illumination model. These include Pro-Matlab (by Math Works,

Inc., Natick, MA, USA), a matrix manipulation software package that was used in many estimations and non-linear curve fit applications. Derive (by Soft Warehouse (Honolulu, HI, USA), a symbolic mathematics package that solves symbolic and numerical problems, was used to determine and simplify approximate forms for diffuse effect integrals. The development and simulation of the numerical results of the mathematical modeling were accomplished on an Intel 486/33 mhz based microcomputer.

4. Results

4.1. *Experiment 1: Analysis of Illumination Effects*

Figure 12 is an example of the data provided by an oscilloscope trace of a single line from a CCD camera, as discussed in Experiment 1. The data is from a partially reflecting tube lying on a white diffuse reflecting background upon which a strip of black tape was placed as a black reference. In the trace, one can see the change in background illuminance due to the dimensions of the illumination source, the shadow effect caused by the tube obstructing the illumination source, the reflectance properties of the tube, and the low reflectance of the black tape.

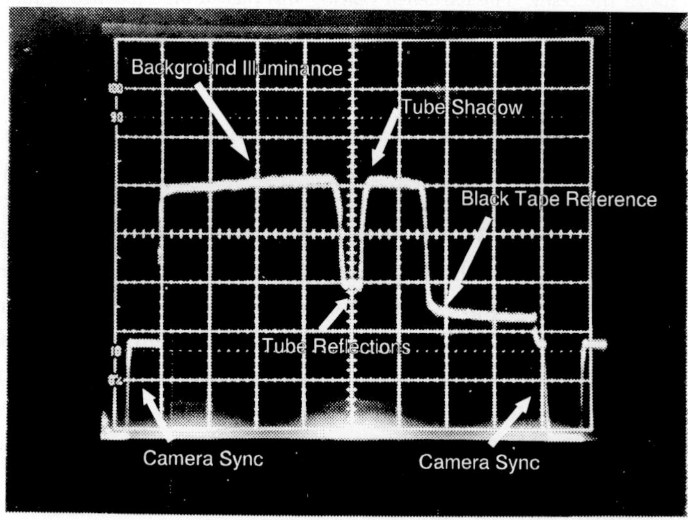

Fig. 12. Oscilloscope trace of CCD camera scan line. The reflective behavior of scene components in a transparent medium was observed through an apparatus which consisted of a fluorescent light source, a CCD television camera and plastic tubing on a white diffusely reflecting background. The signal from the camera was synchronized to an oscilloscope such that the scope displayed only one horizontal scan line from the camera. With this apparatus many different reflection experiments could be performed to determine the principal reflections present in the model scene.

By manipulating tubular objects in this environment, as discussed above, empirical evidence was gathered which supported the types and effects of reflections which were used in this study. Additionally, the data also provided a method to determine the relative reflectance properties of tube and background which were then used in simulations. The simulations were then compared to the scene to determine the extent to which the model reflected reality.

4.2. *Experiment 2: Beer's Law Effect*

The scanned image of the phantom model provided a known set of data which were used to test the applicability of Beer's law toward the particular set of circumstances indicated in the diffuse medium physical model. An image display and manipulation software that was locally developed during these studies was used to sample the phantom image along the apex of the embedded tube. The series of samples were then used as data in a locally developed MATLAB non-linear estimation program. This application is based on an iterative procedure where the partial derivatives of the basic Beer's law equation (Eq. (2.7)) and an error vector are used to compute new estimates of the equation parameters.

Figure 13(a) depicts the sampling methodology for the acquisition of the data displayed in Fig. 13(b). The data was sampled along the longitudinal axis of the cylinder. The expected data distribution was an exponential function (Eq. (2.7)). Figure 13b displays the results of this curve fit on phantom data. It clearly demonstrates that the expected effects on the image due to Beer's law holds for phantom data, and leads to the hypothesis that this phenomena is also a major contributor to the effects seen in conjunctiva data.

A computer simulation was constructed from the illumination–reflection relations found for the two-dimensional physical model. This simulation was provided dimension data from the phantom and other optical properties data estimated from scanned phantom image data. Figure 14(a) depicts the sampling methodology for the acquisition of the data displayed in Fig. 14(b). The data was sampled along the transverse axis of the cylinder. Figure 14(b) is a single scan line from the phantom image. It displays the signals present in the transverse slice at a point in the phantom where the tube is immersed approximately 3 mm into the diffusing resin. The horizontal extent of the phantom in the image is approximately 165 pixels or 82 pixels either side of center. The discontinuities seen at the left and right of center are due to the edges of the phantom slab casting a shadow on the white scanner background. The anomaly seen near the apex of the tube is due to an air bubble in the casting. Figure 13(c) displays the results of the computer simulation for a simulated vessel with depth and optical parameters equal to the phantom cylinder shown in Fig. 11. A total of 256 simulations were performed under the same set of optical conditions. The depth of the tube in the simulation was incrementally decreased to span the depth of the plastic substrate. The results of these simulations

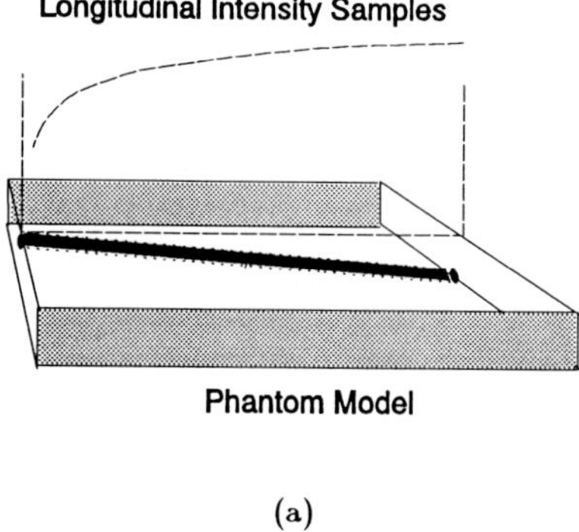

(a)

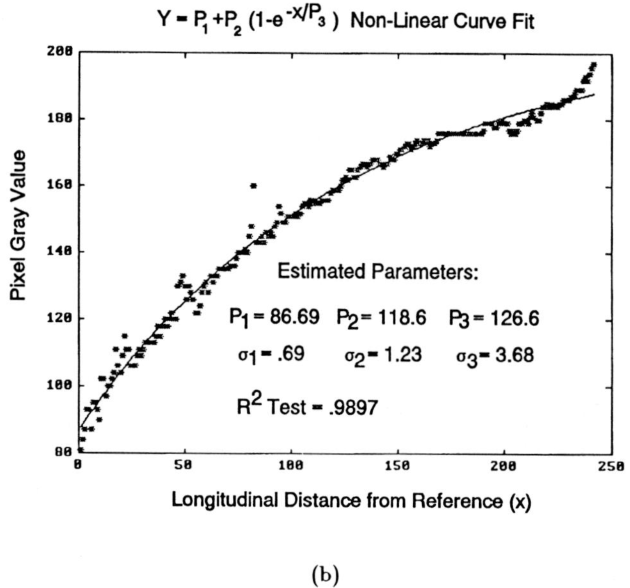

(b)

Fig. 13. Beer's law effects. The phantom provided a known environment to test the applicability of Beer's law to the physical model of this study. (a) A set of image intensity samples were taken along the longitudinal axis of the embedded plastic tube at its apex. The expected distribution of values by Beer's law for an object of linearly increasing depth was $Y = P_1 + P_2(1 + e^{-\lambda X})$. (b) The intensity values were processed by a non-linear curve fit routine and confirmed the predicted result. Thus, Beer's law provides a method for determining the depth of an object in a diffuse medium.

were assembled into a two-dimensional gray-scale array and compared to the data that were scanned from the phantom.

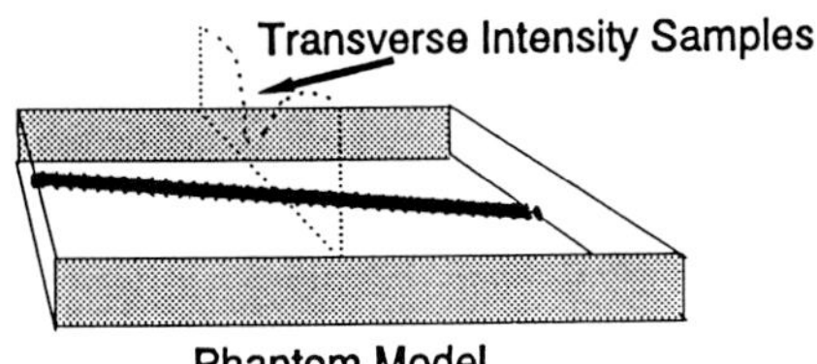

(a) Lambert's Law and spreading effects.

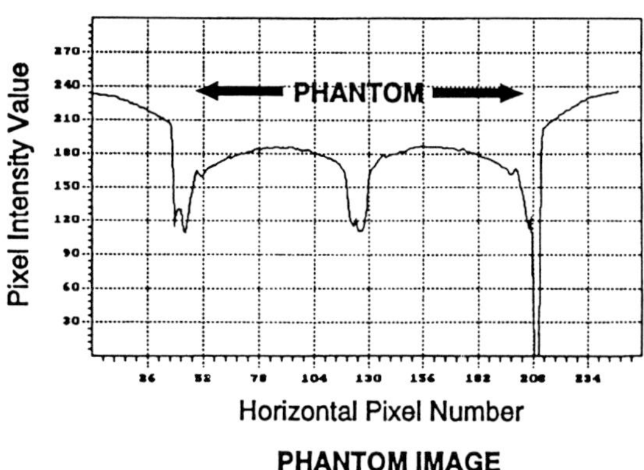

(b) Physical model illumination effects.

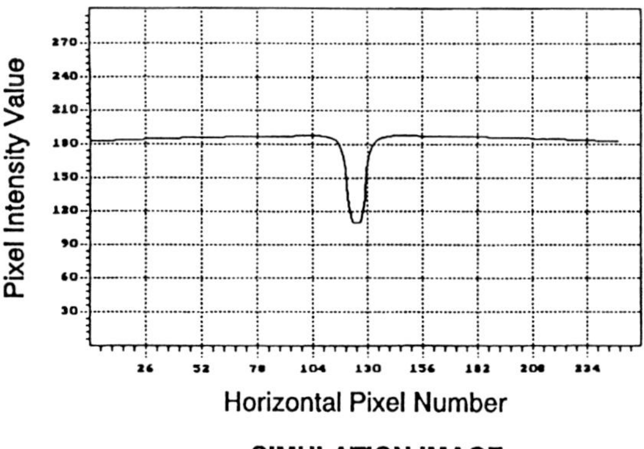

(c) Physical model illumination effects.

Fig. 14. Simulation results. To test the theories presented in this modeling effort, pixel intensity data was taken from the phantom, sampling was transverse to the embedded plastic tube (a). The data obtained from this sampling (b) was then used to arrive at relative reflectivity values for the image components. These data were then used in a simulation of the transverse scene section by the mathematical model (c).

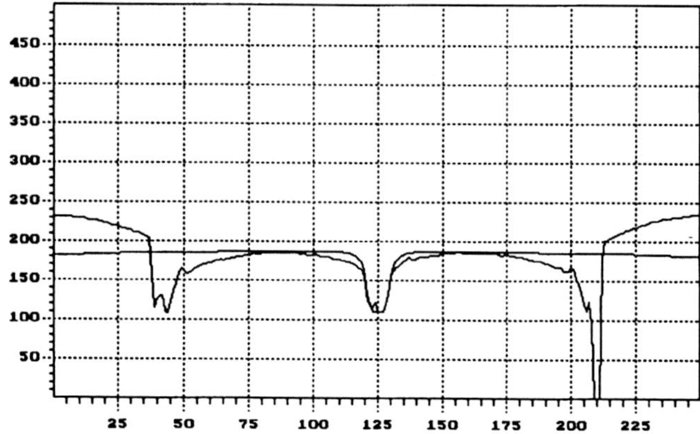

(a) Phantom and simulation overlay.

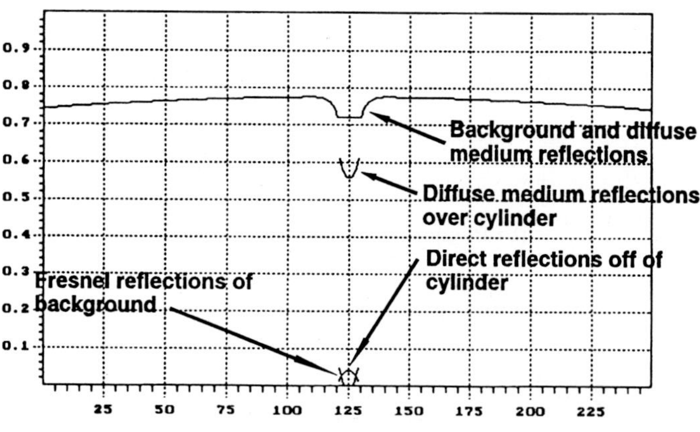

(b) Simulation component values.

Fig. 15. Simulation summary. An overlay of data taken from a transverse section of the phantom and a model based simulation of the same scene (a) graphically displays how well the model has captured the essential illumination and reflection characteristics of the scene. (b) The individual components of the simulation show the relative contribution each makes to the final value arriving at the focal plane. The dominance of the diffuse medium components presents the possibility of simplifying the model for practical use in determining object depth and other parameters, like vessel diameter.

Figure 15(a) displays simulation data overlaid by phantom image data for the same vessel depth. As can be seen in this presentation, the simulation closely corresponds to the phantom data at its center, where the effects of the edges of the phantom slab are minimal. Differences seen in the shadow area near the vessel are believed to be due to the finite nature of the phantom slab and other refractive and diffractive effects which were not modeled. When simulation parameters were adjusted to best fit the observed data, absolute errors of 2.7 per cent of the maximum intensity value were observed over the valid range of the phantom image (pixel numbers 75–175). The standard deviation of the error in this region was approximately 4.3 per cent of the range of intensity values. Figure 15(b) displays each modeled reflection's contribution to the simulation in a representative transverse section located at horizontal line 127 (out of 256 simulations). The figure shows that the major portion of illumination effects in this area of the image is due to reflections from the diffuse medium. As the cylinder approaches close to the surface of the medium, direct reflections become more prominent in the model, causing the illumination characteristics to change near the apex of the cylinder. This behavior was not observed in photographic images of the conjunctiva. It leads to the possibility that diffuse medium reflections alone are sufficient as a descriptor for the intensity values seen in conjunctiva images, substantially simplifying the model and its use in blood vessel detection and tracking.

5. Discussion

This model presented here stems from our efforts to develop automated tools to extract the morphology and topography of blood vessels present in photographic images of the conjunctiva. In the course of our research we discovered, as did several others before us, that treating images in an idealized manner often leads to inconsistent performance or to results of questionable value.

Examples of idealized approaches to extraction of morphology include several earlier works on quantitative morphometry of the conjunctival vessels through the application of stereological principles [3,13], and a semi-automated image processing approach [2]. In the instances of stereology, the problem of image analysis was idealized by treating it in essentially a two-dimensional manner [12]. Thus, observations and calculations could be expressed in terms of unit area rather than unit volume, and volume parameters were then extrapolated from the unit area data. The reasoning behind this approach was based on the fact that two or three layers of blood vessels occupy a region about 60 um thick; this dimension is very small in comparison to the lengths and widths of the volume studied. In this simplification, however, quantitative descriptions of the microvasculature were complicated by differences of focus of vessels in different layers, by variations in tissue transparency, and by obstruction of view of underlying vessels by the large vessels [12]. Other stereological studies on the conjunctival microvessels of normal subjects and diabetic patients by some investigators [3,12] have attempted to minimize some of these biases by having multiple observers examine the enlarged images. In Chen's attempts to automate the extraction of morphological data from images [2], ambiguities caused by crossing blood vessels prevented the linking of detected vessel segments into whole vessels and the diameters of vessels could not be accurately established.

We believe that real improvement in performance and accuracy in the extraction of morphological data will come from a better understanding of the information which is present in the intensity values recorded in an image. Algorithms to detect and track blood vessels may then use this information to measure and to resolve ambiguities which cannot be satisfactorily resolved in an idealized setting. Our approach was to develop a model which depicts to the maximum extent possible the physical reality of a scene representing the microvascular structure in translucent tissues. This physical model then became the basis for a mathematical model which describes the complete illumination–reflection process present in the image, from illumination source to the image plane.

Each component of this mathematical model was determined through the application of first physical principles to the physical model. This was accomplished through a two-step modeling process. First, a mathematical model was constructed for a simplified scene containing only a blood vessel and background; the medium the blood vessel rests in was regarded as transparent. An apparatus was constructed from a CCD television camera, plastic tubing, illumination source, and various backgrounds. The apparatus duplicated the salient features of the transparent medium physical model and allowed the empirical validation of each illumination and reflection component found for the mathematical model. It additionally provided a means to validate the completed simplified model. Next, the simplified model was extended to include the effects of a blood vessel immersed in a layer of light diffusing tissue. The extended model required the addition of Beer's law effects for all relations found in the transparent tissue model and required additional effects for the reflective and transmissive characteristics of the medium itself. The extended model was validated through the use of a phantom consisting of a plastic tube embedded in polyester resin made artificially diffuse by the addition of a few drops of standard white resin coloring agent. This phantom model was constructed to duplicate the diffuse medium physical model and to have known and directly measurable properties. By precisely angling the tube within the resin material, the phantom also allowed the exploration of the effects of different tube depths in a diffusing medium. The phantom was scanned on a flat bed scanner to yield a computer readable image which was used for empirical observations and for model validation.

The culmination of the mathematical modeling process was its exercise in the form of a simulation. In this simulation, data estimated or measured from the phantom image were used as parameters for the mathematical model. The model was run for each of 256 possible tube depths, spanning the same range as the phantom. These simulation runs were then juxtaposed to form a simulated image which could then be compared with the phantom image visually and by measurement. Comparison of the simulated image with the phantom demonstrated that an excellent fit between the two could be obtained (less than 3% error over the valid portions of both images), indicating that the mathematical model indeed captures the essential features of the imaging process.

The superiority of this approach is due to its ability to provide a link between observed intensity values in an image to corresponding morphological and topographical features in the subject of the image. This mathematical linkage provides us with the basis for more accurate measurements of some features which remain illusive in idealized models, for example, vessel diameter. The diffuse medium portion of the model provides us with meaningful information which could potentially allow recovery of relative three-dimensional structures present in the image. This recovery will be important to addressing ambiguities, like vessel crossings or bifurcations, which typically arise when we attempt to detect and track blood vessels.

References

[1] B. W. Fenton, Topographical Simulation of the Blood Vessels of the Bulbar Conjunctiva and Applications to Pressure-Flow, Dissertation, University of California, 1980.

[2] P. C. Y. Chen, S. W. Kovalcheck and B. W. Zweifach, Analysis of microvascular network in bulbar conjunctiva by image processing, *Int. J. Microcirc.: Clinical and Experimental* **6** (1987) 245–255.

[3] G. W. Schmid-Schoenbein, B. W. Zweifach and S. Kovalcheck, The application of stereological principles to morphometry of the microcirculation in different tissues, *Microvascular Research* **14** (1977) 303–317.

[4] R. Hall, Illumination and color in computer generated imagery, in D. F. Rogers (ed.), *Monographs in Visual Communications* (Springer-Verlag, New York, 1989).

[5] J. Foley et al., *Computer Graphics Principles and Practice*, 2nd ed. (Addison-Wesley, Reading, MA, 1990).

[6] T. Nishita, I. Okamura and E. Nakamae, Shading models for point and linear sources, *ACM Trans. Graphics* **4**, 2 (1985) 124–146.

[7] C. Verbeck and D. Greenburg, A comprehensive light-source description for computer graphics, *IEEE Trans. Comput. Graph. Appl.* **4** (1984) 66–75.

[8] J. R. Meyer-Arendt, *Introduction to Classical and Modern Optics*, 2nd ed. (Prentice-Hall, Englewood Cliffs, NJ, 1984).

[9] C. S. Williams and O. A. Becklund, *Optics: A Short Course for Engineers and Scientists* (Wiley-Interscience, New York, 1972).

[10] A. Ishimaru, Diffusion of light in turbid material, *Appl. Opt.* **28**, 12 (1989) 2210–2215.

[11] A. E. Profio, Light transport in tissue, *Appl. Opt.* **28**, 12 (1989) 2216–2222.

[12] B. M. Fenton, B. W. Zweifach and D. M. Worthen, Quantitative morphometry of conjunctival microcirculation in diabetes mellitus, *Microvasoular Research* **18** (1979) 153–166.

[13] W. A. Aherne and M. S. Dunhill, *Morphometry* (Edward Arnold, London 1982).

PART 4

INSPECTION AND ROBOTICS APPLICATIONS

Handbook of Pattern Recognition and Computer Vision, pp. 697–718
Eds. C. H. Chen, L. F. Pau and P. S. P. Wang
© 1993 World Scientific Publishing Company

CHAPTER 4.1

COMPUTER VISION IN FOOD HANDLING AND SORTING

HÖRÐUR ARNARSON and MAGNÚS ÁSMUNDSSON
Marel hf., Höfðabakka 9
IS-109 Reykjavík, Iceland

The need for automation in the food industry is growing. Some industries such as the poultry industry are now highly automated whereas others such as the fishing industry are still highly dependent on human operators. At the same time consumers are demanding increased quality of the products. In the food industry the objects are often of varying size and shape, and often flexible and randomly oriented when presented to the automation system. To automate handling of these objects, an intelligent system such as a vision system is needed to control the mechanical operations to ensure optimum performance and quality.

This chapter describes vision techniques that can be used to detect and measure shape and quality of food products. It stresses the specific implementation context, needed performance, sensors, optics, illumination as well as vision algorithms. Algorithms include those for the size measurement of flexible objects and for the colour measurement of objects with nonuniform colour. Some results are given.

Keywords: Industrial computer vision, image acquisition, image processing, size sorting, colour measurements.

1. Introduction

1.1. *Motivation*

The food industry is still highly dependent on the manual operation and manual feeding of machinery. The operations that are performed by humans are often very repetitive and the working conditions are difficult. The industry in many places is facing difficulties in getting skilled people to work, and therefore it is important to increase automation. Increased automation can also improve quality, increase the speed of production and simplify registration of production information. To increase automation in the food industry, intelligent sensing through computer vision will play a major role, as mechanical solutions are not able to automate handling of products of varying size and shape, without guidance from an intelligent system.

Computer vision is today used in several industries to sort and control handling of products. Most of these applications deal with objects of fixed size often also at a fixed place, with a known orientation. Examples of this are found in the electronic industry and the pharmaceutical industry, where computer vision techniques are used for quality control in production. Examples are also found in the food industry, but not many successful applications exist where the operation involves handling of objects of varying size and shape, and where there is little *a priori* knowledge of an accurate position of the object when it is feed to the automation system.

1.2. *Survey*

There have been several successful applications in agriculture. These include guiding a robot to pick fruits from trees [1], quality inspection of surface defects of fruits [2], and quality control and length measurement of french fries [2]. In the meat industry recent work includes guiding robots to cut meat [3], to evaluate the amount of fat in a piece of meat [4], the sorting of meat pieces based on shape using computer vision [5], and quality evaluation of chicken carcasses [6]. Other applications include measuring the thickness of chewing gum [2], evaluating shape and surface of pizza crusts [2], and inspection of packing quality [7].

In the fish industry several applications [8] have been reported, these include sorting whole fish by length independent of its orientation [9], species sorting of dead fish [9,10], biomass estimation of live fish [8] and guidance of a robot portioning fish fillets in the optimum way [11,12].

Some of the above applications have been very successful, but others rely too much on a manual operation, which limits the operation speed and the economical impact of the automation.

1.3. *Organisation of the Chapter*

This chapter deals with the use of computer vision for food handling and sorting. Section 2 describes the main implementation aspects for these applications. In Section 2.1 we discuss the very important issue of image acquisition; this includes definition of object characteristics, selection of sensors, lenses, filters and viewing and lighting techniques. In Section 2.2 the general characteristics of the harsh environment often encountered in the food industry are described. Section 2.3 highlights the main characteristics of algorithms used in real-time applications in the food industry. In Section 2.4 the criteria for selecting hardware for industrial applications are discussed.

In Section 3 we give two examples, which show real-time implementation of computer vision in the food industry. The first one deals with size sorting of whole fish, where the measurements are done independent of the fish orientation and its skewness. The other example is fish sorting by quality, based on the evaluation of flesh colour and surface defects of fish fillets, where the fillets are classified based on size, shape, and position of the defect.

2. Implementation Aspects

2.1. *Image Acquisition*

One of the most important tasks in any machine vision application is to obtain a good image of the object under investigation. This rather obvious point cannot be over emphasised. Sometimes a little effort spent on improving the quality of the raw image can be worth any amount of signal or image processing.

2.1.1. *Object characteristics*

Before the image acquisition part of a system is defined the optical and physical characteristics of the object have to be studied carefully. It is very important to regard the object as an integrated part of the optical system.

Optical characteristics of food products are different. The most important features that have to be identified before the acquisition part of the vision system can be defined are:

- Transparency of the object. Transparency can be a major obstacle especially when using backlighting techniques.
- Uniformity of the surface colour of the object. When using front lighting techniques it can be difficult to obtain good contrast between the object and the background if the surface colour is non-uniform.
- Reflectance from the object. High reflectance causes a mirror-like effect which reduces the contrast when inspecting the surface of the object.

The physical characteristics of the object that are of special importance are:

- The size of the object defines the size of the needed field of view. In the food industry the size is often varying, e.g. some pieces are a quarter of the size of others. When dealing with large objects (> 50 cm) special care has to be taken to get good image quality over the whole field of view.
- The shape of the object, to guide the selection of features to be identified. This can be a difficult task because food products are often non-rigid and easily damaged.

2.1.2. *Sensors*

There are several important characteristics one has to take into consideration when selecting cameras for vision systems. In this section the most important ones, when selecting between Charge Transfer Devices (CTD) [13] cameras and tube cameras, will be described.

(i) *Shape of the sensor.* When using CTD cameras it is possible to select between different shapes of sensors. The three most common types are: array, line and disk shaped sensors. Tube cameras are limited to array shaped sensors. The shape of the sensor is important, especially if the objects are moving. When the object is stationary or slow moving an array shaped sensor can be used.

For rapidly moving objects improved performance is obtained by using linear or disk shaped sensors [14] coupled to a motion synchroniser.

(ii) *Sensor resolution.* In array sensors the resolution is normally expressed as the number of lines per pictures height. In CTD cameras the limit is set by the pixels available in the image area. In tube cameras resolution is influenced by the type and size of the photoconductive layer, the image size on the layer, beam and signal levels, and the spot size of the scanning beam.

(iii) *Spectral sensitivity.* Spectral sensitivity is the sensor's relative response at different wavelengths of light. Usually CTD cameras cover wavelengths in the range 0.3–1.2 μm, while tube cameras cover 0.2–14 μm (not by one tube).

(iv) *Sensitivity.* Sensitivity is the efficiency of the light to the charge conversion of the sensor. There are several ways of measuring this sensitivity. The two most frequently used are luminous sensitivity and radiant sensitivity.

- Luminous sensitivity is measured at a specific colour of light, usually 2856 K. The output is expressed in mA/(lumen mm^2) or V/(mW mm^2).
- Radiant sensitivity is measured over a range of wavelengths, usually from 400 to 1000 nm. The output is expressed in mA/(Wmm^2).

In CTD cameras, sensitivity is influenced by variables such as quantum efficiency, the length of integration time and the dominant source of noise in the device. Tube camera sensitivity is dependent on the type and size of the photoconductive layer. It also varies with the target voltage level in certain types of tube cameras.

(v) *Dynamic range.* This represents the overall usable range of the sensor. It is usually measured as the ratio between the output signal at saturation and the RMS value of the noise of the sensor (sometimes peak to peak noise). In CTD cameras this RMS noise does not take into account dark signal nonuniformities [13]. In CTD cameras the saturation voltage is proportional to the pixel area. Factors influencing the dynamic range of tube cameras include photoconductive characteristics of the faceplate, as well as scanning rate and electronic gun characteristics.

Among other important characteristics of cameras are: signal to noise ratio, geometric distortion, lag, nonuniformities, readout speed, camera synchronisation, mean time between failure, operating temperature, damage by overlighting, operating power, operating voltage, size, weight, price.

Table 1 lists typical performances of CTD and tube (Vidicon) cameras currently available on the market.

2.1.3. *Lighting and viewing techniques*

Selection of illumination equipment and viewing geometry is an important step in the development of the acquisition part of a vision system [13,14]. Based on the application (inspection, handling, sorting) to be implemented and the characteristics

Table 1. Performance of CTD and tube cameras.

		CTD camera		Tube camera	
	Units	Typical value	Max. value	Typical value	Max. value
Resolution	lines	500	1000	750	2000
Dynamic range	peak sign /ms noise	4000 : 1	10000 : 1	100 : 1	1000 : 1
Max. sensitivity	lux	*	10^{-6}	*	20
Geometric distortion	%	0	0.1	1	2
Nonuniformity	%	2	12	10	20
Lag	%	0	0.1	10	15–20
Spectral sensitivity	nm	300–1200	*	200–14000	*
Mean time between failure	hours	unlimited	*	10000	*
Frame rate	frames/s	25	400	25	2000
Damage by overlighting	*	No	*	Yes	*
Price	USD	2500	*	1500	*
Supply voltage	V	15	*	500	*

of the object, both the physical and optical characteristics, the optimum lighting and viewing technique is defined.

In one- and two-dimensional size and shape measurements, diffused or direct backlighting are most likely to give good image quality. Although special care has to be taken with some food products, e.g. fish where the fins can be partly transparent. In three-dimensional size and shape measurements, structured light [15] is often used, but the use of two or more sensors can also give robust and accurate three-dimensional measurements.

When doing surface inspection the most appropriate set-up is diffused front lighting, where the contrast is often enhanced using coloured light and colour filters (Section 2.1) in front of the camera. Using front lighting techniques it can be difficult to cope with variations in the color of the object.

Inspection inside the food object, includes search for parasites and bones. In these applications it is generally very difficult to develop the lighting and viewing part of the vision system, because of the optical characteristics of the food [16]. In the fish industry different lighting techniques have been tested. This includes X-rays for bone detection [17], laser scanning for bones and parasites [18], ultrasound for bones and parasites [19], and fluorescence of fish bones [20]. Today it is possible to detect bones inside meat and fish flesh using soft X-rays, while the problem of parasites in fish still remains unsolved [18].

2.1.4. Optics

The optical front end of a vision system must be designed with equal care to that applied to electronics, otherwise there is a risk that an apparently precise measurement will hide a significant error caused by the limitation in optics. Special care has also to be taken, because applications in the food industry involve sensing of large images outside the optical axis of the lens system. In this section important characteristics of lenses for food handling and sorting will be discussed (see Fig. 1).

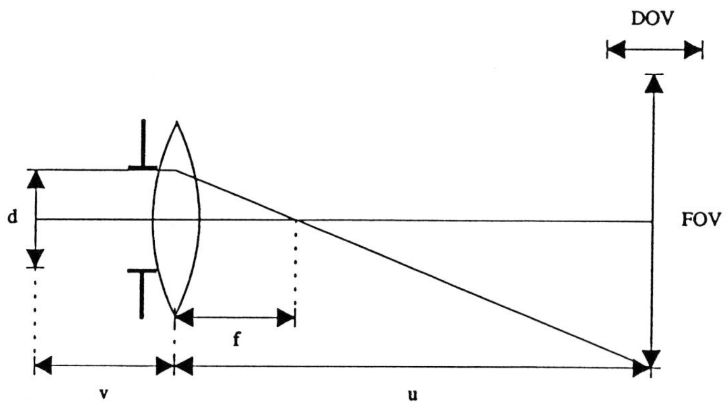

Fig. 1. Image forming basics.

(i) *Magnification m.* The optical magnification is defined as the image distance v over object distance u or Field-Of-View (FOV) over the sensor size d.

$$m = \text{FOV}/d = v/u. \qquad (2.1)$$

The FOV should be large enough to see the object, and because of object movement which is very often the case in the food industry an FOV 30% larger than the largest object is recommended.

(ii) *Focal length f.* The optimum focal length for each application is related to u and v through the well known lens equation:

$$1/f = 1/u + 1/v. \qquad (2.2)$$

Equation (2.2) assumes the light is perpendicular to the optical plane of the lens. In practice, for many applications in handling and sorting in the food industry, $u \gg v$ so a good approximation of Eq. (2.2) is :

$$1/f \approx 1/v. \qquad (2.3)$$

(iii) *Lens quality.* There are two main factors that influence lens quality. Special care has to be taken when working on applications involving large objects.

- Resolution r. Because of the diffraction effect of the light going through the lens, there is a theoretical limitation on the resolution of the lens. For lenses working at high demagnification, this theoretical value is given by [13]:

$$r = 1.22 * \lambda * f/A \qquad (2.4)$$

where

$$\lambda : \text{wavelength of light}$$
$$f : \text{focal length of lens}$$
$$A : \text{diameter of the aperture of the lens.}$$

- Aberration. There are two kind of aberrations: monochromatic and chromatic [21]. Monochromatic aberrations are divided into five subclasses and can be calculated theoretically using a lens formula assuming oblique line directions [22]. The chromatic aberrations are caused by the changing diffraction index of the lens material, with wavelength of light. All the aberrations get worse as the lens aperture is increased, and all of them except one subclass of monochromatic aberrations get worse with increased field angle. Monochromatic aberrations need special attention when doing accurate measurements outside the optical axis of the lens system.

  Typically, no information on resolution or aberrations are provided from the lens producer, instead a measure of the Modulation Transfer Function (MTF) is given. The MTF is the ability of a lens to image a particular sine wave pattern. The MTF is determined by measuring, through a lens, the contrast of such a sine wave pattern image, while changing the aperture and the off axis position of the object.

(iv) *Depth of View* (DOV) is defined as the distance along the optical axis on which the object can be located and still be properly imaged :

$$\text{DOV} = cu/(A - c) + cu/(A + c) \tag{2.5}$$

where

$$A : \text{lens aperture diameter}$$
$$u : \text{object distance}$$
$$c : \text{blur circle diameter at object.}$$

The blur circle is the amount of blur which can be tolerated, often set at one pixel. From Eq. (2.5), it can be seen that there is a maximum A for a given DOV.

2.1.5. *Filtering*

Filtering is used to improve image quality, reduce noise, and enhance features of interest. Three types of filtering are described in this section: neutral density filtering, polarisation filtering, and colour filtering.

(i) *Neutral density filtering.* Neutral density filters [23] are used to attenuate the intensity of a beam of light over a broad spectral region, without altering its spectral distribution. A neutral density filter can thereby for example be used to decrease the light intensity incident on a photodetector. Because of optical resolutions it is important to allow a large enough aperture of the lens (Section 2.1). Using a neutral density filter allows a larger aperture of the lens. A neutral density filter is characterised by its optical density D:

$$D = log_{10}\, I_0/I_T = -log_{10}T \qquad (2.6)$$

where

$$I_0 : \text{incident power}$$
$$I_T : \text{transmitted power}$$
$$T : \text{transmittance.}$$

(ii) *Polarisation filtering.* Light travels as a transverse electromagnetic wave, the electric and magnetic fields being perpendicular to each other as well as to the direction of propagation. A light beam is said to be linearly polarised if its electric field vectors are oriented in the same direction. A substance can affect the polarisation of light, reflected or transmitted, giving a significant feature for that same substance. The polarisation state of the resulting light beam can be detected with the aid of polarising filters, and by comparing it to the polarisation of the incident light information regarding the substance can be obtained.

    A polarisation filter can also be used to reduce glinting in an image. Dichroic film polarisers, fabricated from sheets made of long grain organic molecules are probably the most convenient type of polarisers for image processing purposes. They are inexpensive and have a convenient shape.

(iii) *Colour filtering.* Colour filtering [23] may be of the most obvious importance in image processing for the food industry. With colour filtering it is possible to extract information from well defined bands of the spectrum or to increase the amount of information in the image by examining more than one different band (wavelength regions). Colour images, as we know them (for example, TV images), are often based on the combination of three images in separate bands, which all together cover the visible spectrum. These bands are referred to as Red, Green and Blue (RGB) [23]. Such images are most often acquired using three well defined colour filters. A three-band colour image can sometimes have more information than necessary in the processing to come, or even unwanted information and, in that way, will slow down the processing. It is therefore essential to know what one is looking for and thereby be able to choose a band for measurement/acquisition and use the necessary colour filtering. Often a much narrower band than R, G or B is more effective, where the wave bands are selected using spectroradiographic study of the product to be investigated.

    Different types of colour filters are available. Coloured glass filters operate through ionic absorption or via absorptive and scattering crystallites formed within the glass. They are available as Long Wave Pass filters (LWP) with a relatively sharp cut and a variety of bandpass filters which are not so sharp.

Gelatin filters have similar characteristics to glass filters. They operate through absorption as well. They are commonly used in photography and are inexpensive. Gelatin is a "plastic-like" material and therefore gelatin filters are vulnerable to scratches.

Interference filters operate through interference to select a range of wavelengths. Wavelengths not falling within this range are reflected. They are fabricated as thin coatings of various dielectric materials on a glass plate. Interference filters are available as LWP, SWP (short wave pass) and BP (bandpass) filters with very sharp cut characteristics. By tilting an interference filter its characteristics are changed, the cut wavelength(s) being displaced. This effect can also occur when observing an object which is not lying on the system's optical axis, through such a filter. This should be noted or taken into account when used with cameras.

2.2. *Environment*

The environment in the food industry is generally harsh. The main characteristics are:

- The humidity is often high (95%–100%). This is caused by continuous washing of the machinery for sanitary reasons.
- It is frequently recommended to keep the temperature in the processing plants between 5–10°C.
- There are strict limitations on what types of waste are allowed from machines in the food industry.
- There are regulations on what types of materials are allowed in the food processing plants. For example, it is often forbidden to use conventional glass for direct contact with the food.

2.3. *Image Processing for Food Products*

All algorithms used in sorting and handling food products, use *a priori* knowledge, although at different levels. This *a priori* knowledge is used to build up a model of the process and provide strategies for the algorithms to be designed. Some of this knowledge is imposed on the process by selecting colour and texture of the background and by the viewing angle of the light source and the camera. Another part is controlled by the feeding system which determines the direction of motion of the object and whether or not the objects are overlapping. Also the object to be sorted gives information on what kind of algorithm should be used, for example, for fish, the fish has a head and a tail and some fins that can be used for classification. It is desirable to use as much *a priori* information on the object and the process as possible. In that way the algorithms can be simplified, the hardware requirements reduced, and the possibility of satisfying the needs of the industry at a cost and speed it accepts are increased.

Algorithms used in the food industry are made of the same basic elements as in most other industries, i.e.

- pre-processing
- feature extraction
- classification.

However the emphasis on these basic elements can be quite different compared to other types of applications.

2.3.1. *Pre-processing*

Although in real-time industrial applications special care is taken in designing the optimum image acquisition part, there is often a need to improve the image quality before extracting the feature of interest from the image.

In applications where the results are presented to the user in an image format, image enhancement techniques such as histogram equalisation, and look-up table operations are used to improve the contrast of the feature of interest in the image. On the other hand, in automatic control systems the computer controls some actions. Based on results from the image processing this type of enhancement technique is of no use and can in fact degrade the quality of the image because of quantization effects.

The nature of noise in applications in the food industry is different from what most textbooks discuss, where the focus is on random noise or spot noise. In applications in the food industry the noise usually has some physical explanation, e.g. dirt on the background or shadows because the camera has a different viewing angle than the light source. [9] describes methods based on mathematical morphology for filtering out noise, where the noise has some predefined form and some maximum size. In Section 3.2 on colour inspection, results are shown on how noise can be filtered out using this method when detecting surface defects on fish fillets.

The primary goal in pre-processing images is to reduce the amount of data in the image, for example by binarizing [24] the image. Global thresholding is used when possible. Otsu [25] describes a method for calculating the optimum threshold between classes. His method is theoretically well based but requires too much computation to be used on-line in a real-time application especially when using more than two classes. It can however be very useful in a training phase of an automatic system.

When the Field Of View (FOV) is large it is difficult to get even lighting in the whole FOV. In these cases it is necessary to use local thresholding, especially when the performance of the application is dependent on accurate thresholding.

2.3.2. *Feature extraction*

When selecting features to be measured it is important to select features that can be measured with good accuracy and good repeatability. Generally there are two kinds of errors that affect the feature extraction:

- Measurement error, because of limited accuracy of the sensing equipment, or the sensing process. This includes limited resolution of the sensor and optics, blur caused by the movement of the object, and quantization error in the A/D conversion process. The measurement error is controlled by selecting the appropriate sensing equipment.
- Presentation error, because of variations in the way the object is presented to the vision system. This error needs special attention when dealing with food products of non-uniform shape, varying size, flexibility and imperfect operation of feeding systems dealing with these kind of products.

It is important, based on knowledge of the products to be processed and also very importantly on the nature of the feeding system, to select features to be extracted. Generally features such as location, dimension, and orientation, are common to most handling and sorting problems in the food industry. These features are used to localise the parts to be classified. Further feature extraction includes identification of corners, lines, holes, and curves. It is very useful to use information on object location to reduce the amount of data to be processed, on dimensions of the object to get size invariance and on orientation of the object to reduce dependency on orientation. In this way it is possible to focus the attention of the vision system to Areas of Interest (AOI) and in that way speed up processing.

The algorithms used to extract the features selected have to be able to work on objects of random orientation and in real time.

A number of algorithms are used for feature extraction. A good overview of these are in [26]. One example of algorithms used is based on identifying the contour of the object. Edge detectors are used to enhance the edge pixels which are then connected in a chain code and further connected into shape primitives which are used to describe the object. These algorithms are very time consuming and of limited use in real-time applications in the food industry. Another type of feature extraction algorithm is a space domain technique like skeleton algorithms, where the object is characterised by its skeleton. These algorithms provide useful feature descriptions of the object using a limited amount of data. Of special interest is the distanced labelled skeleton [27], which can give a complete description of binary images. Another example of feature extraction algorithms is scalar transform techniques, such as moment invariants [28] and Fourier transform techniques.

Mathematical morphology [29] is a technique well suited for real-time applications in the food industry. This is due to the parallel nature of its basic operations. It is a set-theoretical approach to image analysis and its purpose is the quantitative description of geometrical structures. Mathematical morphology extracts information about the geometrical structures of image objects by transforming the object through its interaction with another object (structuring element) which is of simpler shape and size than the original image object. Information about size, spatial distribution, shape, connectivity, smoothness, and orientation can be obtained by transforming the image object using different structuring elements.

In [30] the Hit or Miss transform [29] from mathematical morphology is used to extract information on the presence and position of shape primitives (line, corner, convex, concave) in a fast and reliable way.

2.3.3. *Classification*

Based on the features extracted from the image, the object is classified into one of the possible classes. There exist numerous methods for classification based on features extracted from an image.

Statistical pattern classification [31] is a very sound theoretical method for classification of patterns. It is well suited in applications where a limited number of features is used. However when using many features it can be difficult and time consuming to design the classifier.

Graph matching [32] is a method where the presence and position of features in relation to other features is used to classify the object. The features used could for example be corners and lines used to recognise fish species.

Neural networks [30] is a suitable method, when a large number of features are available, but it is difficult to identify which are the most important features for classification. Of special interest is the possibility of training the classifier, in such a way that the classification rules are determined automatically.

2.4. *Hardware*

The performance of conventional sequential computer architectures is inadequate for the majority of machine vision applications in the food industry. The problem arises from the sheer amount of data presented in the image. Simple real time neighbourhood operations require 20 million operations per second (MOPS). The typical computational power of a sequential computer is less (e.g. 1–5 MOPS), and therefore they are too slow. Confronted with such computational problems numerous researchers and manufacturers have sought to develop new computer architectures to provide the necessary computational power required by real time machine vision applications [33,34]. One approach is to develop more powerful processors to handle the workload, typified by the newest Digital Signal Processor (DSP) chips. Another approach is to create architectures which allow many processors to work on the image data in parallel at the same time. It is important to note that algorithms have quite different possibilities of being implemented in parallel, and right from the beginning it is important to focus on the software side on algorithms that are parallel in nature.

2.4.1. *Image processing hardware*

There is no single architecture that is the optimum one for all vision algorithms or industrial applications [35]. Therefore it is important that there is a flexibility in the selection of arithmetic units that can be installed in an industrial vision system.

Figure 2 shows an example of a modular hardware structure, available from several companies (ITI, Vicom, Datacube, Eltec) today at a price of less than 25K USD.

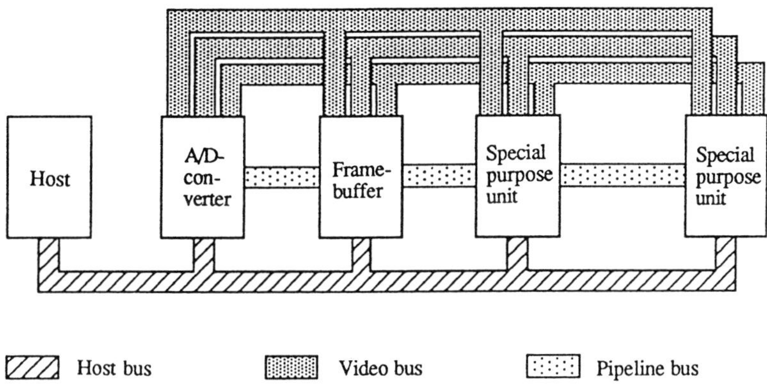

Fig. 2. Example of a modular hardware structure in an industrial vision system.

The basic blocks of this kind of industrial vision system are:

(1) Host computer which controls the system. This is typically an Intel 80x86 or a Motorola (MC 680x0) based computer.
(2) Analogue/Digital interface, to provide an interface to cameras. This is typically an 8-bit flash A/D converter with a 10 MHz sampling rate.
(3) Frame buffer, to store images. Often it is possible to install up to four frame buffers, where each frame buffer stores a $512 \times 512 \times 8$ image. It is important that there is more than a single port access to the frame buffer.
(4) Special purpose arithmetic units. It is very important that it is possible to select between different types of architectures dependent on the algorithms to be performed at each time. An example of the arithmetic units available are:
   (i) Pipeline processors, well suited for simple arithmetic, logical, conditional and bit-plane operations, that can be performed in real time.
   (ii) Rank value filters which perform real time median filtering and grey scale morphological operations.
   (iii) Binary correlators which perform real binary operations including convolution, correlation, erosion and dilation.

(iv) Signal processors, general purpose vision algorithms.
(v) RISC processors, for general purpose vision algorithms.

Which of the modules described above are used in each application is highly dependent on both the application and the way the object is presented to the vision system.

2.4.2. *Complexity of the vision system*

The levels of complexity for a vision system for food products is highly determined by the feeding part of the system. These levels are mainly determined by:

(i) Distance between the objects. Is there a minimum distance between the objects? Can they be side be side, or overlapping?
(ii) Orientation of the object. Is the object oriented, or not?

If objects are fed to the system on a conveyor and there is no minimum distance between the objects, then there is a need for at least two processes, one which constantly searches for the object while the other which measures the features of interest of the object. The orientation on the other hand directly influences the complexity of the algorithm. Table 2 lists the different levels of complexity in a vision based sorting system.

Table 2. Levels of complexity in the vision part of a sorting system.

Level	Feeding System
1	Objects oriented, and there is a minimum distance between objects.
2	Objects not oriented, and there is a minimum distance between objects.
3	Objects oriented, no minimum distance between, not overlapping.
4	Objects random, not overlapping.
5	Objects random, and overlapping.

In the food industry the practical levels are mainly levels 2–4. Level 1 is excluded because of the orientation demand which is difficult to obtain for an elastic object like food. Level 5 is excluded because it normally results in high sorting errors, and although the food products can be measured accurately, it is difficult to direct it mechanically to different places.

The compromise, which has to be made when selecting a working level for a vision based sorting system, lies between the requirements (cost) of the feeding system and the complexity and the speed of the algorithm.

The level of complexity selected when specifying a vision application, does not only determine the cost of the system, but also the possible accuracy of the features to be measured.

3. Applications

3.1. *Size Sorting of Fish*

3.1.1. *Motivation*

Sorting dead or dying fish is required on board fishing boats for packaging and storage purposes. Typically, the catch must be sorted by species, length or weight before going into boxes, the contents of which are compatible with the auctioning process. At the processing level, the machines (filleting and head cutters) still cannot handle in one batch diverse fish types or sizes without reduction in yield. Any set-up due to such variations is both time consuming and costly. By sorting the fish by size the fishing industry is able to get both increased yield and added production control [36].

3.1.2. *Image acquisition*

There are different size parameters that can be measured on a fish using computer vision, these include volume, area, length, thickness and width [37,38]. Much depends on the feeding system as to how difficult it is to measure these features. Here we will assume that the feeding system is working on level 4 (Section 2.4), that is the fish is lying randomly but not overlapping when fed to the vision system. Further we assume that the fish is round (e.g. cod, haddock).

When measuring the volume and the area, a high ($\pm$ 15%) presentation error (Section 2.3) is observed due to the irregular position of fins and belly flaps [9], whereas the length can be defined and measured with a low presentation error. Therefore the length is selected as a size feature when sorting round fish by size, where the length of the fish is defined as the length of a line starting at the middle of the tail to the top of the head, following the bone structure of the fish.

A fish is a highly reflecting object when under direct illumination. Fish colour varies for many species. Usually the fish is dark on the back, and white or greyish on the belly. Because of this it is very difficult to get a good contrast in an image using front lighting techniques. Diffused backlighting is used, but special care has to be taken because of transparency of fins, especially the tail fin.

This application has to be able to work on board rolling ships. This fact excludes the use of line-scan and circular-scan sensors, because of their dependency on object motion. A frame camera which is able to sense the whole fish is therefore selected. A CTD camera is selected here mainly because of its robustness.

3.1.3. *Image processing*

A block diagram of the algorithm is shown in Fig. 3. In start-up the system goes through a training phase where the threshold for the background and for the fish are automatically determined using the method in [25]. In the training phase the optical magnification of the system is determined, by measuring n objects of a known size. This training phase can also be entered into interactively by the user.

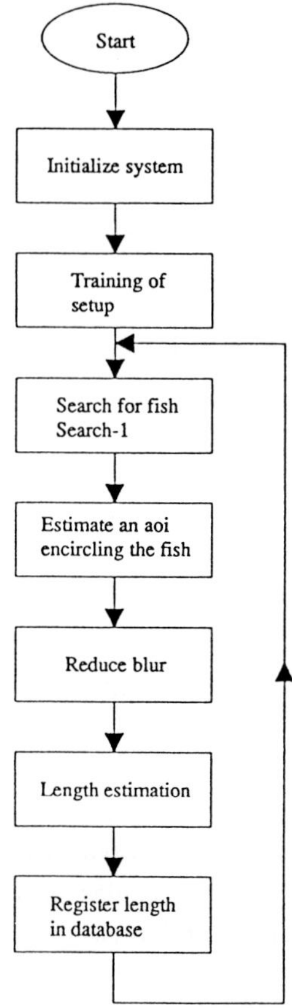

Fig. 3. Block diagram of an algorithm for length sorting of fish.

The algorithm starts by searching for a fish, in binary images that are snapped continuously. As soon as a whole fish is detected inside the field of view, its position is registered and a rectangular area of interest encircling the fish is determined.

Based on *a priori* knowledge on the shape of the fish, that the fish is an elongated object and that the fish is thicker close to the head than close to the tail, the position of the head, tail, fins and belly flaps are determined. Then the position of the length estimation line can be determined accurately.

The length is then measured using piecewise linear approximation and knowledge on the optical magnification of the system. Based on sorting criteria programmable by the user the fish is then classified as belonging to different groups based on the length measured. The measured length is also registered in a database.

3.1.4. *Results*

The length estimation system is now a commercial system [5]. See Fig. 4.

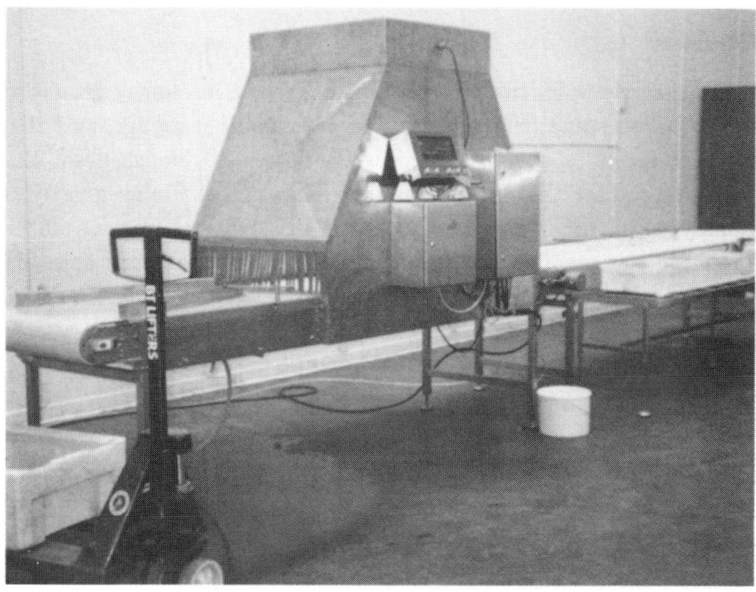

Fig. 4. Prototype for length estimation of whole fish.

Fish are fed to the vision system on a conveyor running at 1.2 m/s. The system is able to length estimate whole fish with an accuracy of ± 0.3 cm (one standard deviation), independent of fish orientation (Fig. 5). The processing time for each fish is 0.2–0.3 seconds, depending on fish size.

Fig. 5. Length estimation of cod fish.

3.2. *Colour Inspection*

3.2.1. *Motivation*

Fish flesh (for example, that of cod fish) is graded in quality groups according to: colour, coloured spots (blood spots and liver spots), gaping, and shape. The most important factor in quality control is the colour of the fish flesh. Briefly, one can say that the lighter the flesh the better the quality. Today quality control is done manually in all processing plants and under different circumstances in each place. Therefore the manual quality control is bound to be very dependent upon the individual performing it and the circumstances it is performed under.

The benefits of automation in quality control in the fish industry are evident. Coordination of control and standardisation will benefit both sellers and buyers.

3.2.2. *Image acquisition*

A first proposal for sensing equipment for a "colour grader" would presumably be a colour camera or a colorimeter. A wide variety of colorimeters are available on the market [39], some of them have been successfully applied in the food industry, for example, in inspection of fruit. Most colorimeters feature three sensors as the sensing equipment: these sensors are light sensitive in the visible (VIS) range but filtered with red, green, and blue filters respectively. Furthermore most colorimeters are point measurement devices. This is not a feasible alternative for the purpose of grading fish as none of the R, G, and B ranges fit the narrow range of wavelengths representing the difference between quality groups. Point measurement is not attractive either since the measurement must be more "intelligent". The colour must be measured locally in certain areas of the fish and other areas or picture elements must be avoided if they do not represent the colour of the healthy fish flesh, for example, blood spots, bones and skin. A colour camera could be an alternative, but it gives excessive and unwanted information in spectral ranges we do not want to measure.

Because no theoretical colour standard is available for the different quality groups of the fish, the most important issue is to define the colour of the fish and the colour difference between quality groups. The most accurate way to represent colour is by its reflectance or transmittance of different wavelengths of light.

In an effort to characterise the colour of fish, a considerable amount of fish was chosen, from each of the quality groups used, as a sample for the measurement. The fish was graded by five quality control personnel. Three samples were cut from each fish and the spectrum of each sample was measured with a spectrophotometer. The measurement covered all of the VIS spectrum and stretched into the NIR. All samples were measured in the range 350–1050 nm, with a 5 nm resolution, and some also in the range 1050–1600 nm. The results from the measurement showed that the spectral difference between groups was high in a certain narrow range of wavelengths in the VIS spectrum while there was little or no difference outside this range.

From results of the spectrum measurements the optimum lighting and sensing equipment was selected. For lighting we choose diffused front lighting, light sources with spectral characteristics strong in the range where the difference between groups was most evident and weaker outside this range, thereby exaggerating the difference. A sensing equipment that fits our purpose is a black and white CTD frame camera with the appropriate bandpass filter in the specific wavelength range.

Another colour feature that is to be taken into account when estimating the quality of fish is reddish bloodspots [40] that can occur in the fish flesh and which decrease the quality of the fish. These bloodspots must be detected locally in the fish flesh in some well defined areas, since the position of the spot plays a role concerning the weight of the defect (a blood spot on the more expensive loin piece of the fish is a more serious defect than a spot on the tail). A camera is therefore also suitable for detecting bloodspots. When using a black and white CTD camera to detect reddish bloodspots on the light fish flesh, the use of a bluish filter is appropriate to exaggerate the difference between healthy flesh and blood, making the discrimination easier.

3.2.3. *Image processing*

As the fish arrives on a conveyor under the camera an image of it is snapped. The fish position and orientation in the image is determined and then the image is segmented into predefined areas based on the form and the aspect ratio of the fish. The segmentation is necessary because of the different weights the fish pieces have in the quality evaluation. The colour of the fish flesh is computed individually for each area. A grey scale histogram is computed for the area and after smoothing the histogram with a moving average, two thresholds are computed deciding the interval of grey values belonging to the healthy fish flesh. The colour of the area is characterised by the average grey value of the healthy fish flesh pixels (in this case however the "grey values" of the image represent a very narrow range in the spectrum since the image is filtered).

Bloodspots are also tackled locally in predefined areas. The area is thresholded with a local thresholding operator, and a binary image of blood spots on healthy fish flesh is produced. Morphological operators are then used to evaluate the size and shape of the bloodspots (Fig. 6).

4. Concluding Remarks

By studying the work effort that people perform in the food industry, it is clear that one of the main obstacles in automation is the need of intelligent human-like operation of the machines. That is the machine has to be able to sense the food product to adjust and optimise the handling of the food. If increased automation in

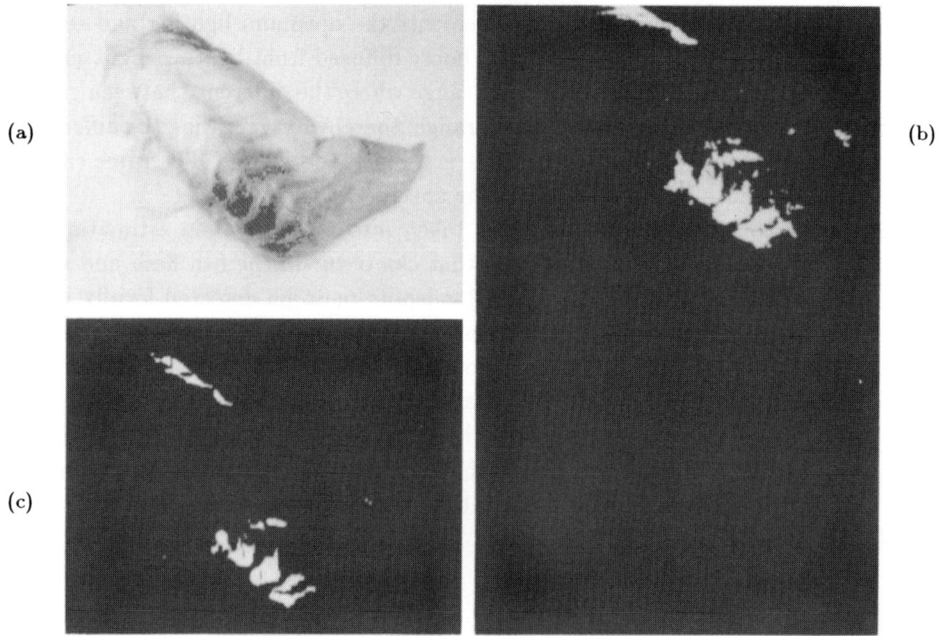

Fig. 6. Noise reduction, and detection and classification of surface defects of fish fillets. (a) Original image of fillet, (b) binary image of fillet, (c) results from classification of spots by size and shape.

the food industry is to come, it has to rely on intelligent sensing, where computer vision will play a major role.

In this chapter we have discussed the use of computer vision in the food industry. To be successful in this type of application special attention has to be put into the development of the image acquisition part of the vision system. This includes study of the object characteristics, lighting and viewing techniques, sensors and optics. The image processing algorithms have to be able to work in real time on randomly oriented objects of varying size, and shape. This processing demand limits what type of algorithms can be used, and imposes the need for special purpose arithmetic units to perform the processing.

There exist several commercial applications today where computer vision is used to guide food handling and sorting. Nevertheless it is a fact that this field has been growing slower than expected in the past five years. The main reason being that people underestimated the difficulties of applying this technique to objects of varying size and shape as food products are. These characteristics in fact demanded a processing power that was not available at a price acceptable by the food industry.

The evolution of the computer industry is also clear, as price is still going down and the performance of the systems are increasing. At the same time the sensors have been improving, and today random scan solid state cameras are available on the market [41]. These cameras, called Charge Injection Devices (CID), open new possibilities in intelligent scanning which can play a major role in simplifying the processing needed by the computer. Therefore we believe that it is only a question of time before computer vision will play a major role in controlling the handling and sorting of food products.

References

[1] R. C. Harrell, D. C. Slaugter and P. D. Adsit, A fruit-tracking system for robotic harvesting, *Machine Vision and Applications* 2 (1989) 69–80.

[2] C. Pellerin, CRE cross the pond with a DAB hand for food inspection, *Sensor Review* 11, 4 (1991) 17–19.

[3] K. Khodabandeloo, Getting down to the bare bones, *The Industrial Robot* 16, 3 (1989) 160–165.

[4] A. MacAndrew and C. Harris, Sensors detect no food contamination, *Sensor Review* 11, 4 (1991) 23–26.

[5] Marel H/F, 1989. Product Information, Reykjavik, Iceland.

[6] W. V. D. Sluis, A camera and PC can now replace the quality inspector, *Misset-World Poultry* 7, 10 (1991) 29–31.

[7] R. K. Dyche, INEX, 100 per cent on-line visual inspection of consumer products, *Sensor Review* 11, 4 (1991) 14–17.

[8] L. F. Pau and R. Olafsson (eds.), *Fish Quality Control by Computer Vision* (Marcel Dekker, New York 1991).

[9] H. Arnarson, Fish Sorting Using Computer Vision, Ph.D. report LD 78, EMI, Technical University of Denmark, 1990.

[10] N. J. C. Strachan and C. K. Murray, Image analysis in the fish and food industries, in [5].

[11] Lumitech, 1988. Product Information, Copenhagen, Denmark.

[12] Baader, 1990. Product Information, Lubeck, Germany.

[13] B. G. Batchelor, D. A. Hill and D. C. Hodgson, *Automated Visual Inspection* (IFS, Bedford, UK, 1985).

[14] A. Novini, Fundamentals of machine vision lighting, *Proc. SPIE*, Vol. 728, 1987, 84–92.

[15] D. Poussard and D. Laurendeau, 3-D sensing for industrial computer vision, in J. L. C. Sanz (ed.), *Advances in Machine Vision* (Springer, New York, 1988).

[16] J. Pétursson, Optical spectra of fish flesh and quality defects in fish, in L. F. Pau and R. Olafsson (eds.), *Fish Quality Control by Computer Vision* (Marcel Dekker, 1991) 45–70.

[17] Pulsar, 1990. Product Information, Eindhoven, Holland.

[18] D. L. Hawley, Final Report: Fish Parasite Research, Federal grant No. NA-85-ABH-00057, USA, 1988.

[19] H. Hafsteinsson and S. S. H. Rizvi, *Journal of Food Protection* 50, 1 (1987) 70–84.

[20] H. H. Huss, P. Sigsgaard and S. A. Jensen, Fluoresence of fish bones, *Journal of Food Protection* **48**, 5 (1984) 393–396.

[21] K. Harding, Lighting & Optics Tutorial, *VISION'87, SME*, Detroit, Jun. 1987.

[22] W. T. Welford, *Aberration of the Symmetrical Optical System* (Academic Press, New York, 1974).

[23] Oriel Corporation, 1990. *Optics and Filters*, Vol. III, Stratford, CT, 1990.

[24] J. S. Weszka, A survey of threshold selection techniques, *Comput. Graph. Image Process.* **7** (1978) 259–265.

[25] N. Otsu, A threshold selection for gray-level histograms, *IEEE Trans. Syst. Man Cybern.* **9**, 1 (1979) 62–66.

[26] M. D. Levine, *Vision in Man and Machine* (McGraw-Hill, New York, 1985).

[27] P. Maragos and R. W. Schafer, Morphological skeleton representation and coding of binary images, *IEEE Trans. Acoust. Speech Signal Process.* **34** (1986) 1228–1244.

[28] M. K. Hu, Visual pattern recognition by moment invariants, *IRE Trans. Inf. Theory* **8** (1962) 179–187.

[29] S. Serra, *Image Analysis and Mathematical Morphology* (Academic Press, New York, 1982).

[30] H. Arnarson and L. F. Pau, Shape classification in computer vision by the syntactic, morphological and neural processing technique PDL-HM, in *Proc. ESPRIT-BRA Workshop on Specialized Processors for Real Time Image Analysis*, Barcelona, Spain, Sept. 1991.

[31] K. Fukunaga, *Introduction to Statistical Pattern Recognition* (Academic Press, New York, 1972) 260–267.

[32] A. K. C. Wong, Knowledge representation for robot vision and path planning using attributed graphs and hypergraphs, in A. K. C. Wong and A. Pugh (eds.), *Machine Intelligence Knowledge Engineering Robotic Applications* (Springer-Verlag, New York, 1977).

[33] J. Kittler and M. J. B. Duff (eds.), *Image Processing System Architectures* (Research Studies Press Ltd, UK, 1985).

[34] L. Uhr, K. Preston, S. Levialdi and M. J. B. Duff (eds.), *Evaluation of Multicomputers for Image Processing* (Academic Press, Orlando, 1986).

[35] J. L. C. Sanz, Which parallel architectures are useful/useless for vision algorithms? *Machine Vision and Applications* **2**, 3 (1989).

[36] J. Heldbo, Information teknologi og Productionsstyring i Konsumfiske industrien (in Danish), Ph.D. Report, EF201, Technical University of Denmark, 1989.

[37] H. Arnarson, K. Bengoetxea and L. F. Pau, Vision applications in the fishing and fish product industries, *Int. J. Pattern Recogn. Artif. Intell.* **2**, 4 (1988) 657–673.

[38] H. Arnarson, Fish and fish product sorting, in [5].

[39] Honeywell, USA, Product Information.

[40] K. Bengoetxea, Lighting setup in the automatic detection of ventral skin and blood spots in cod fish fillets, Report No. 497, EMI, Technical University of Denmark, 1988.

[41] CID Technologies Inc., 1988. Product Information, Liverpool, USA.

Handbook of Pattern Recognition and Computer Vision, pp. 719–739
Eds. C. H. Chen, L. F. Pau and P. S. P. Wang
© 1993 World Scientific Publishing Company

$\boxed{\text{CHAPTER 4.2}}$

IMAGE INFORMATION RETRIEVAL SYSTEMS

ANG YEW-HOCK, ARCOT DESAI NARASIMHALU* and SULIMAN AL-HAWAMDEH

Institute of Systems Science, National University of Singapore
Heng Mui Keng Terrace, Kent Ridge, Singapore 0511

Progress in storage, communication, compression and high quality input and output technologies have accelerated the development and deployment of Image Information Retrieval (IIR) systems. Document Image Management (DIM) systems are being marketed successfully. However, there are a number of other IIR systems that have as big if not bigger markets. In this chapter we discuss the issues related to such image retrieval systems, present the key technologies in image matching and retrieval, summarize some of the research carried out in this area, and list some of the products and applications.

Keywords: Image management systems, image retrieval, image indexing, image database, feature-based retrieval, text-based retrieval.

1. Motivations and Applications

Due to advances in image technologies and retrieval methods many new application areas involving image information retrieval (IIR) have emerged over the last few years. Technological developments supporting this emergence are high resolution display, image compression and its emerging standards, high bandwidth communication, progressive image browsing, feature analysis and classification techniques, and evolving retrieval techniques which include free-text indexing and intelligent knowledge base.

The benefits of combining visual information with traditional text-based information systems are apparent from the application view point. Some of these are:

- Visual features (image details) description using high-level textual concept is inadequate. These detailed features are more appropriately characterised using (low-level) image feature processing.
- Image abstraction (visual concept) from low-level image features is technically unreliable. This, however, can be easily achieved with textual description.
- Direct visual access facilitates fast image browsing. This provides a natural (visual) interface between users and IIRs.

---

*To whom all correspondence should be addressed.

719

- Retrieval accuracy is improved by visual interaction. This is due to the consistency in query (input) specifications and retrieval (output) representation, both in the visual form.

In sourcing for IIR systems it is important to understand the limitations arising due to different levels of image abstraction. While high-level image concepts can be easily understood using textual descriptions, subtle visual differences in image details are more efficiently detected with low-level image features. For these reasons, it is common for IIR applications to adopt a two-tier approach to image indexing. That is, an initial coarse classification of the images using textual description followed by finer levels of classification based on their low-level image features.

1.1. *Example of IIR Systems*

Some examples of IIR applications are listed below:

- *Multimedia Documents.* Multimedia encyclopedias will require indexing based on free-text along with images classified according to the textual description. Images will include both stills and videos of varying resolution, and will require high compression for efficient storage.
- *Transaction Systems.* Catalogue-sales application as in tele-shopping require only a simple indexing scheme based on domain specific keywords, but must employ high compression algorithms along with fast image browsing capabilities. Similarly, inventory systems such as for museum artifacts and drama props will require only simple reference codes as indexes, but must support high image resolution.
- *Trademark Systems.* Trademark registration applications require use of contours as an indexing mechanism to locate groups of trademarks containing similar patterns. Visual indexing is important in this application as trademarks may be designed to closely resemble other popular ones, and may be highly abstract which may cause inconsistency in the classification if high-level concepts are attempted.
- *Medical Applications.* Medical records management requires large database search based on patient's records and keyword(s) indexing, and fast browsing of gray scale images. Diagnostic support uses visual features as the search pattern for similar medical cases.
- *Criminal Identification.* Keyword indexing of criminal particulars with free-text indexing on side-information such as the scene and pattern of the crime. Classification of criminal databases and criminal identification based on the characteristics of facial features and photofit images, respectively.

1.2. *Classification of IIR Systems*

Image retrieval systems can be classified in many dimensions. The primary data stored in the system can be either image only or image combined with any other data type (for example text). An IIR system may be built primarily for either query

Table 1. Typical image information retrieval applications.

	Document imaging systems
	Police mugshot systems
	Engineering library systems
	Museum artefact inventory systems
QUERY	Drama production inventory systems
	Trademark and patent retrieval systems
	Multimedia document retrieval systems
	Medical picture archival and communication systems
	General multimedia encyclopedia
	Medical encyclopedia
	Music encyclopedia
BROWSING	Electronic books
	Engineering handbooks
	Photographic banks
	Product libraries/catalogues

purposes or browsing purposes. Queries can be for obtaining either exact matches or partial matches. Browsing may be either navigational as in hypermedia or visual feedback based. Table 1 lists the different types of applications that such systems will support and Table 2 lists the underlying technologies that these systems will use.

2. Requirements for an Image Retrieval System

The following are the requirements for the design and development of good and usable IIR systems.

2.1. *Image Signature*

Every image that is to be stored in an IIR system has to be assigned some kind of index or signature. This code or signature should preferably be unique for each image. However, systems that use a unique signature for every image will require vast amounts of resources. For example, the index for each image will have to be very complex and large so that there is sufficient index space to represent every possible image that may be stored in such an IIR system. As a result, the ratio of the index space to the data space in such an IIR system might be relatively high as compared to those that allow overlaps in image signatures. Image indexes may be natural or artificial. Natural indexes correspond to either descriptions of the image through text or the features of the image. They are different from artificial indexes such as an employee number in an employee database that stores employees photographs.

Table 2. Technologies used in image information retrieval systems.

HARDWARE	Write once and erasable optical disks
	Juke boxes
	Interactive laser disks
	CD-audio
	Compression chips
	Image cards
SOFTWARE	Retrieval engines
	User interface builders
	Image analysis software
ALGORITHMS	Image classification
	Image indexing
	Similarity measures
	Image clustering
	Compression techniques
	Image matching

Image signatures may be of different kinds. For an image only IIR system, it may be an ordered list of key image features or it may be an authenticated description of an image. Sometimes an IIR system may store a number of images for a given entity. The concept of an ordered list of key images can still be used for such systems except that the list will be made of sublists generated from each of the images. In such a case, both the sublist and the features within each sublist will be ordered. It may also be required that the relationships between features in some sublists be identified. For an IIR system that requires images to be stored with accompanying text the signature will be a combination of image features and text.

2.2. *Image Similarity Measures*

Exact match search is sometimes used by IIR systems that use artificial image indexes. All other IIR systems rely on partial match given that there are likely to be small nuances between two different descriptions of the same image. The second type of IIR systems requires the definition of an image similarity measure which will define the "Image distance" between two given images. If the image distance is large then the two images are said to be dissimilar and if small they are said to be almost similar. When the image distance is zero, then the two images are the same. It is therefore important to define a good similarity measure for a given set of images. It is true that there cannot be an efficient universal similarity measure for all types of images. Similarity measures will have to be derived for each of the image application domains. Once the image distances of all the stored images are calculated against the image submitted as the query, the results can be ranked according to the increasing degree of dissimilarity. This offers systems designers the option of not displaying retrieved images that have their image distances beyond a defined threshold.

2.3. *Image Retrieval Engines*

Once image signatures are generated and images stored, a retrieval engine is required to search for the images and retrieve them. Image retrieval engines use image similarity measures to service either exact or partial match requests. For example, in the case of an employee database, images may be indexed by employee numbers. In such a case, the retrieval engine may be a relational or any other database retrieval engine. On the other hand if an image index is the description of images, then that retrieval engine will be a free-text retrieval engine. When image indexes are lists of image features, the retrieval engine may have to be more complex given that it may be required to identify the relationships within some sublists.

2.4. *Image Query Environment*

The query environment for an IIR system should offer the option to initiate a query using any or all of the data types that the application supports. For example, for a system like a Criminal Identification System that has image and text as components of a record, the query environment should allow a query to be invoked using text alone or image alone or a combination of the two. Such an environment should also support incremental query refinement, once again using any of the data types supported by the application. Such a query environment should allow for direct manipulation of the images and also provide for easy specification of relevant feedback.

2.5. *Image Knowledge Base*

Specific knowledge about the image database can significantly improve the search efficiency of general IIR systems. One of the most common knowledge representations used is the semantic network. A semantic network is a directed graph where the nodes represent objects and labeled arcs represent relations between objects. Structured graph is ideally suited for processing relational queries, especially in Graphical Information Systems, where relative locations of picture objects such as roads, trees, rivers, cities can be described as a query graph and, matches with existing graphs can be compared based on their vertices and junctions.

Image knowledge base may also be a representation which allows effective access to images at an intermediate (symbolic) level of vision. Symbolic representation provides an active interface to the higher-level inference processes that construct and image's interpretation. An example of symbolic knowledge representation is a hierarchical feature-based retrieval based on attribute relations maintained at picture, object, object-components and image regions. For example, a picture of a face would contain facial attributes about the eyes, nose and mouth, which in turn contain low-level features which can be characterised into shape and texture features without knowledge of the image content.

2.6. *Image Compression for Storage Management and Communication*

Images are large data items and are sometimes called BLOBS (Binary Large Objects). A 1000 × 1000 pixels color image would require 3 megabytes if it is in full color. The storage of such images will have to be optimized using JPEG [1] or MPEG [2]. JPEG (Joint Photographic Expert Group) is the standard for storing still images and MPEG (Motion Pictures Expert Group) is likely to become the standard for moving images or video. There may be applications where the images are required with their original resolution and details and hence some lossless compression techniques have to be used.

Even when gigabit networks become available as backbone networks, if a large number of users use IIR type of systems, the network traffic is bound to be high. One solution to the high volume of traffic caused by large images being transmitted across a network for selection purposes is to use compressed images in place of actual images. Where the loss in detail and resolution due to compression is not acceptable one can either organize an image in multiple resolutions so that a coarse image is sent first and the image is progressively refined until the desired effect is achieved or to have small icons of the images for selection purposes only.

3. Image Matching Algorithms

Except the exact match algorithm described in this section all other matching algorithms are used to retrieve similar images. The reason for this is obvious since in image retrieval systems, even the query may not be exact. If only exact match algorithms are used, then the actual image being sought may not be retrieved. Therefore, it is important to remember that in most image retrieval applications, it is better to retrieve a limited number of similar images rather than zero exact image.

3.1. *Text-Based Matching Techniques*

Where the number of details in an image is very large it may be futile to approach such a retrieval application based on any of the image features since the level of detailed features stored for such retrievals may be far too many to get a reasonable response. Hence, it is suggested that images be represented using text descriptions of the images and the retrieval be based on text descriptions.

3.1.1. *Exact keyword match*

As explained in an earlier section the exact match algorithm is best used in applications that have an artificial index for images. The search for an exact match will be carried out on an alphanumeric field of a record. The field that is to be used as the key will be indexed and a good hashing algorithm will help the speedy location of the required record from the disk.

3.1.2. *Boolean match*

In a typical text retrieval environment, a user query is formulated by linking the search terms together using the logical Boolean operators AND, OR and NOT. The disadvantage of this approach is that Boolean queries are very difficult to formulate. For example, the use of nested parenthesis to build up a query is considered to be a problem even for those with some experience in online searching [3]. The records in Boolean search are only retrieved if the attached index terms match the query specifications exactly and the search results in partitioning the image object collection into two sets: image objects that satisfy the query and image objects that do not. Therefore, all the records that are retrieved are presumed to be of equal usefulness to the searcher. There is no obvious means by which one can reflect the relative importance of the retrieved image objects to the query.

3.1.3. *Probabilistic match*

A number of probabilistic retrieval models have been developed based on Bayes decision rule and on the assumption that the binary terms are assigned independently to the image object representations [4,5]. One of these models is the probability ranking principle proposed by Robertson and Spark-Jones [6]. They defined a weight W_i for ranking the documents in the database given the ith term in the query as

$$W_i = \log \frac{p_i(1 - q_i)}{q_i(1 - p_i)}$$

where p_i, q_i are the estimated probabilities that the ith terms occurs in relevant and nonrelevant sets respectively.

According to this model, the primary function of the image object retrieval system is to compute for each user the probability that he will judge an image object to be relevant and then rank the image objects in order of their relevance. The probabilistic model represents a major contribution to the development of information retrieval systems since it has provided a firm theoretical basis for the use of many statistical techniques which have been developed previously on a purely empirical basis.

The simplest method of ranking retrieved image objects is to consider the presence or absence of a term in each image object and to assign weights to these terms. The image objects can then be ranked in descending order of the sum of term weights. The top ranked image objects are retrieved first from the ranked list; these image objects are judged by the system to be the most relevant to the query. Term weighting schemes allocate numerical values to each of the index terms in a query or an image object to demonstrate their relative importance. Similarity coefficients are then used to calculate the overall degree of similarity between the query and each of the image objects in the collection.

3.1.4. *Best match*

A best match search algorithm that minimizes the number of accesses to the image object file was first proposed by Noreault et al. [7]. The basic idea of this algorithm is to process the query lists against the inverted files, allocating a counter to each image object encountered and setting it to one. Every time an image object appears again, its counter is incremented by one; the result in each counter at the end is the number of matching terms in common between the query and the corresponding image object. If the query and image object terms have attached weights, then the result in each counter is incremented by the product of such weights rather than by one. Term weighting schemes are used to assess relevance information and improve precision [8]. The term weighting functions can be used to weight either query terms or document terms or both. If W_{di} or W_{qi} represents the weight of term t_i in document D or query Q vectors then the query-document similarity value can be obtained by comparing the two vectors using for example the conventional vector product formula

$$similarity(Q, D) = \sum_i = 1^t W_{qi} W_{di} \, .$$

The matching of the query against the file of image objects and the inverted file can be represented as:

```
FOR each Query term Qi DO
      isolate the ith Query list;
      calculate the corresponding weight Wi;
FOR each image object Di in the Query list DO
      IF new image object THEN
          allocate counter C(Di) and set to Wi;
      ELSE increment the appropriate counter by Wi
END
```

The algorithm computes the image object-query similarity for each image object that appears in the inverted file lists.

3.2. *Feature-Based Matching Techniques*

Computerized automated recognition of images involves low-level extraction of primitive features such as edges, regions, contours and gray-levels. These features are characteristics of the images and may be parameterized in terms of its shape, gray-level density profiles, principle-components and inter-feature distances, which form the basis for image classification and subsequent image retrieval based on similarity measures on their characteristics.

3.2.1. *Shape features*

In some image retrieval applications such as the trademark systems, it may not be necessary to have matching carried out on finer details. For such applications, it is preferable to use contour-based algorithms. A typical contour-based algorithm is described in [9]. For any polygon they generate a turn function. A turn function starts from a reference point on a polygon and keeps track of the quantum of turn to the left and right. To ensure that the function does not become overly large in value, often the left turns are represented by a positive value and the right turns by a negative value. The length of a value will correspond to the length of a side of the polygon before another turn takes effect. The turn function is used as an index or signature for matching a query image with that of the stored images.

The challenge often is one of how many details ought to be captured in the turn function. As can be seen in Fig. 1, where one might be simply interested in the fact that the two polygons are triangular in shape, the turn functions of the second polygon may in fact be a lot more complex than the first. Hence,

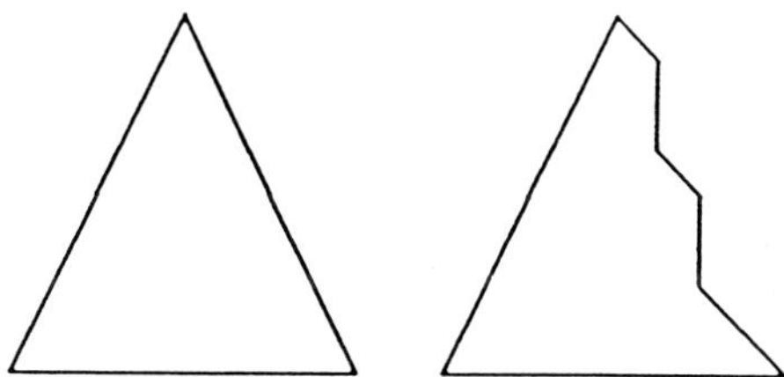

Fig. 1. Defining shape similarity.

there ought to be some clear definition of how and when some of the sides of a polygon may be approximated? The selection of this definition (called a similarity function) will in turn decide whether images can be compared at a cruder resolution or at a finer resolution.

Alternatively, approximate feature shapes may be described by the number of acute angles, or the number of approximated geometric shapes, etc. In most of these cases, it is important to develop a unique set of features for a given application, for there is no general set of features that can be considered optimal across applications. In [10], shapes are approximated by rectangular covers and the rectangular cover descriptions of the shapes are considered to be the signature of an image. Rectangular cover signatures are used for matching a query image with a set of stored images.

More generally, the gross shape of image regions can be described using classical shape analyses [11]. These single value measures can be rank-ordered according to its shape complexity for speedier image browsing, and as indexes for database image matching. For general shape analysis it is important that the descriptors should be robust and relatively invariant to size variation, translation and rotation of image regions. Examples of such invariant shape measures are:

(i) *Normalised second order moment.* The moment (or statistical variability) of order $p + q$ for the shape bounding the region R is defined as

$$\mu_{p,q} = \sum_{(x,y)\in R} (x - \bar{x})^p (y - \bar{y})^q$$

where $\bar{x} = \frac{1}{N} \sum_{x \in R} x$, $\bar{y} = \frac{1}{N} \sum_{y \cap R} y$ is the center of mass, and N is the total number of pixels in the region R. The normalised second moment is then expressed as

$$\eta_{p,q} = \frac{\mu_{p,q}}{\mu_{0,0}^2} \, .$$

The normalised second moment invariant used in this paper is

$$\phi = \eta_{0,2} + \eta_{2,0} \, .$$

(ii) *Compactness of region shape.* This measures the "roundness" or compactness of the region shape using the definition

$$C = \frac{T^2}{(4\pi A)}$$

where T is the perimeter and A is the area of the region.

(iii) *Fourier power-spectra distribution.* Power-spectra can be used to describe the regularities of region shapes by noting the distribution of their Fourier coefficients, given as

$$\Im(k) \triangleq \sum_{n=0}^{N-1} u(n) \exp\left(\frac{-j2\pi kn}{N}\right), 0 \leq k \leq N - 1$$

where $u(n) \triangleq x(n) + jy(n), n = 0, 1, \ldots, N - 1$ is the one-dimensional signal representation in complex pairs of the boundary co-ordinates.

3.2.2. *Gray-level density profiles*

One of the approaches based on gray-level density profiles is to draw gray level iso-density lines on an image such as a human face. Comparison is made using the shape of the iso-density lines. An example of such an approach can be found in [12].

The matching is based on differential marginal distribution at the coarser level and the local characteristics of the iso-density maps at the finer level. To check whether two pictures referred to the same person, they would first calculate the differential marginal distributions which are the projection profiles onto the x- and y-axes of constant gray-level areas after quantizing a human face.

Global matching is based on the inter-correlation coefficient C, computed on the density profiles of the retrieved and query pictures.

$$C = \sum_{k=1}^{N-1} C_x(k) + \sum_{k=1}^{N-1} C_y(k)$$

where N is the number of quantization levels, and $C_x(k), C_y(k)$ are the intercorrelation coefficients of the x- and y-axis profiles given as follows,

$$C_x(k) = \frac{P_x^{(r)}(k, k+1) \cap P_x^{(q)}(k, k+1)}{P_x^{(r)}(k, k+1) \cup P_x^{(q)}(k, k+1)}$$

$$C_y(k) = \frac{P_y^{(r)}(k, k+1) \cap P_y^{(q)}(k, k+1)}{P_y^{(r)}(k, k+1) \cup P_y^{(q)}(k, k+1)}$$

where $P_x^{(r)}(k, k+1), P_x^{(q)}(k, k+1)$ are the differential marginal distributions between the k and $k+1$ gray levels of the retrieved and query pictures computed along their respective x-axis profiles.

If $C \geq upper\_threshold$ the retrieved picture is deemed to be the same as the picture under examination. If $C \leq lower\_threshold$, the examined picture is deemed to belong to someone different from the one in the retrieved picture. If the value of C falls within the two thresholds, the picture under examination is taken up for a finer level of matching. Finer grain matching is carried out based on the local direction and the compactness of the iso-density lines within each non-overlapping 8×8 pixel block, averaged over the entire image.

3.2.3. *Feature distances*

Feature-based algorithms were one of the earliest matching algorithms explored for matching of faces. Harmon et al. [13] reported a series of studies using feature-based matching that were very successful for small domains. In general, feature based matching algorithms identify some invariant features of an image and tend to develop some relationships among these features. Time invariant features are especially important in the case of human faces where the bone structures could change over time. One of the commonly used features is a function of the distance between the pupils of eyes in a human face to the length from its midpoint to the tip of the nose. However, there are a number of other combinations of features that can also be considered for matching purposes. For human faces in particular, it is not wise to use shadows since they can be altered using make-up or plastic surgery.

More generally, inter-distances between distinctive points, such as sharp corners of man-made objects, which can be easy to extract [14] can also be used for image matching. However, the matching will be successful only if the amount of rotation (θ) is relatively small. For example, Fang and Huang [15] obtained good matching results if $\theta < 5\,\mathrm{deg}$.

In any case, pairwise similarities and differences of feature-distance vectors may be calculated using normalized Euclidean distances. The Euclidean distance between two sets of retrieved $\{r_i; i = 1, 2, \ldots, N\}$ and query $\{q_i; i = 1, 2, \ldots, N\}$ feature vectors is defined as

$$D(R,Q) = \sqrt{\left\{\sum_{i=1}^{N}\left[\frac{r_i - q_i}{s_i}\right]^2\right\}}$$

where N is the total number of feature vectors in the set, and s_i is the normalization factor for the ith feature-distance given by

$$s_i = \sqrt{\left\{\frac{1}{M}\sum_{j=1}^{M}(r_i^j - \bar{r}_i)^2\right\}}$$

where $\bar{r}_i$ is the mean feature-distance of the ith feature in the entire set of M images.

For a given query feature vector Q_j the pairwise Euclidean distances to all retrieved vectors R_j in the database, $D(R_j, Q); j = 1, 2, \ldots, M$ are ranked for image classification, or the smallest distance may be used to identify the best-matched image retrieved.

3.2.4. *Principle components*

Principle Component Analysis (PCA) is useful for decorrelating a given set of correlated variables, and optimizing their representation with a smaller set of statistically independent linear combinations having certain unique properties with regard to characterizing individual differences. The principle components computed on the covariance matrix of the input samples represent new composite variables which account for or describe a maximum amount of the total variability among individuals on all the original samples. Optimality in the approach is preserved by ensuring that the mean-square error introduced in truncating the least significant principle components is a minimum.

The PCA of a set of vectors can be computed based on the Karhunen-Loeve (K-L) expansion.

Let $U_i = \{u_j; j = 1, 2, \ldots, M\}$, be the vector which represents or describes the ith image in a set of N images.

- Form the mean vector, $\bar{U}$ by taking the averaged sum of U_i, i.e.

$$\bar{U} = \frac{1}{N} \sum_{i=1}^{N} U_i$$

- Compute the covariance matrix Φ using the zero-mean vectors, $\phi_i = U_i - \bar{U}$, i.e.

$$\Phi = \phi_i \phi_i'\,.$$

where $'$ indicates matrix transposition.
- Find the eigenvectors $\mathbf{a_j}$ using the equation

$$\Phi \mathbf{a_j} = \lambda_j \mathbf{a_j}$$

where the scalar λ_j are the corresponding eigenvalues of Φ.

A Fortran program for computing the eigenvectors and eigenvalues using an iterative solution can be found in [16].

The PCA technique has two useful properties. First, vector components are decorrelated and second, the M-uncorrelated (principle) components are compressed into a small number of K-L axes, i.e. into only a few coefficients of the K-L expansion. The first property is associated with the exponential distribution of eigenvalues λ_j. This means many of the eigenvectors $\mathbf{a_j}$ which have corresponding low eigenvalues may be disregarded, hence (the second property) without significantly affecting the K-L's ability to discriminate differences among a given set of variables.

The reduced set of $M'(\ll M)$ eigenvectors $\hat{\mathbf{a}} = \{\mathbf{a_j}; j = 1, 2, \ldots, M'\}$ are the desired weighting coefficients to be applied to original variables. For image database matching, the M-dimensional query image U can be efficiently represented into a few components $\omega_j; j = 1, 2, \ldots, M'$ by taking the Cartesian sums of the query image weighted by the eigenvectors,

$$\omega_j = \hat{\mathbf{a}}_{\mathbf{j}}'(U - \bar{U})\,.$$

From the eigen-images, $\Omega = \{\omega_1, \omega_2, \ldots, \omega_{M'}\}$, computed on the given query and retrieved images, image matching can be easily carried out following the Euclidean distance measure described in the previous section.

PCA has been shown to be efficient for feature extraction, image compression, and noise filtering [17]. Sirovich and Kirby [18] have applied PCA to human face analysis. They have demonstrated that face images can be efficiently represented and reconstructed to within 4% error using only the 40 largest terms in the K-L expansion. This is a significant reduction in data representation which would otherwise require 128 × 128 (pixels) data points. PCA has also been applied to face recognition [19], and in general, can be used for any information retrieval applications which require database classification.

3.3. Knowledge-Based Matching Techniques

3.3.1. *Low-level feature representation*

Sometimes it is useful to have a set of images classified according to some class of definitions so that when a query image is submitted for matching, its class(es) can be first determined and hence the search tree is considerably reduced. AGNESS [20] takes such an approach wherein a computation network for image correspondence problem is defined. Comparisons are carried out both on physical components and the spatial components and matching is carried out on both edges and regions. By defining a class hierarchy any time a query image is deemed to belong to a class, the properties of the class are derived from the knowledge bases to be the union of the property of the query image with those of the superclasses.

3.3.2. *High-level knowledge representation*

In contrast with AGNESS, high-level representation of the symbolic picture using a data structure called a 2-D string, which preserves the objects' spatial knowledge embedded in images, has also been proposed [21]. The 2-D string records each object in the original image and its relative spatial location with respect to other objects. It provides object-oriented search rather than search based on the low-level image primitives of objects. Image query represented by a 2-D string can be matched with those in the database based on different criteria: the existence of objects, pairwise spatial relationships between objects, and object-oriented picture or sub-picture.

3.3.3. *Intermediate symbolic representation*

An intermediate symbolic knowledge representation which links the high-level interpretation and low-level feature extraction of images is proposed by Brolio et al. [22]. Intermediate-level data may be regions, straight lines, line-region intersections, lines lying along region boundaries, and region-boundaries, and represented as a collection of hierarchical frames. The number of intermediate levels represents the accuracy or the amount of detail at which image matching can be performed, and may be altered by splitting, merging, adding, or deleting connected-nodes in the graph. A line-grouping algorithms which groups short lines to form longer ones has been proposed by Boldt et al. [23], and another which takes account of the perceptual organization of neighboring lines is proposed by Reynolds [24]. New nodes created may inherit or possess new properties possessed by any of its components. Fast graph query can then be performed through spatial proximity search over fixed 2-D grids imposed on the image, and by improving the search only in those areas which lie within the radius of interest.

4. Visual Feedback in Image Retrieval

Efficient management of pictorial information requires more than just the ability to retrieve keywords or indexes of image filenames. It is equally important that images can be efficiently accessed, transmitted, displayed, and browsed. Fast presentation of hit-images allows direct visual confirmation of the search results, and in turn enhances query specification using currently retrieved images as visual examples (Fig. 2). Because visual information can be recognized and understood faster than text description, direct visual access can result in retrieving more relevant images.

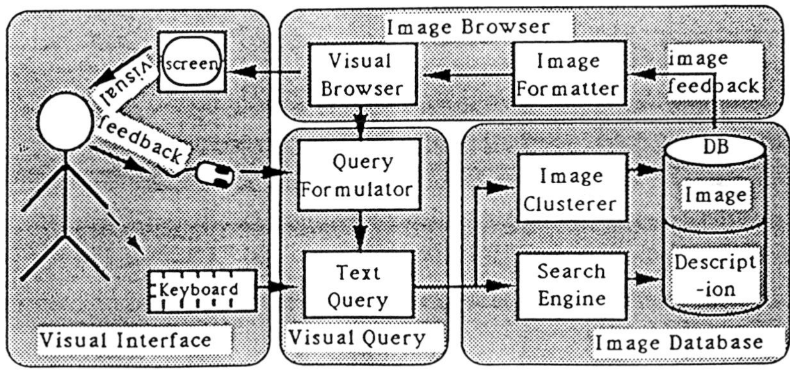

Fig. 2. Visual oriented image retrieval system.

In visual feedback we can exploit the unique characteristics of image data to improve the information retrieval process in ways not possible with standard text-based retrieval systems. Images can be examined and evaluated much more quickly than text. This characteristic of image data can be used to further facilitate the information retrieval process. We have already seen that icons can be used to improve browsing and evaluation of search results: they can also be employed to facilitate query re-formulation and refinement. In a Picture Archival System (PAS) [25], the user can formulate the initial query using natural language, Boolean or a knowledge-based system. The results of the search are then returned in a resizable icon window. At this point, the user can modify the query through text entry or expand the query using an attached thesaurus. However, the user may not be able to expand the query effectively either because (1) he is not able to anticipate the specific words (indexing language) used to describe the images of interest, or (2) the thesaurus-based expansion of a specific query may not be possible if the relevant knowledge is not available. These problems can be alleviated by using direct manipulation of relevant image icons to modify a query. Standard text-based relevance feedback techniques can then be employed to modify the original query.

Keywords are extracted from the descriptions associated with the selected icons and ranked using weights derived from word frequency measures [6]. The weight of each keyword is calculated using the following formula:

$$\text{weight} = \log \frac{(r + 0.5)(N - n - R + r + 0.5)}{(n - r + 0.5)(R - r + 0.5)}$$

where N = total number of documents (in the collection);
  n = total number of documents with the keyword;
  R = number of documents selected as being relevant;
  r = number of relevant documents with the keyword.

The top-ranked keywords are then used to reformulate or refine the query. Query refinement is used to increase recall of the initial query: the keywords are added to the original query terms to form the new query. Query re-formulation can be used to change the focus of the initial query, for example, by selecting one or more icons relating to a subset of the original query.

5. Research Prototypes

5.1. *Nearest Neighbor Search*

The picture archival system (PAS) [26] is based on the probabilistic retrieval model. The system employs the nearest neighbor or best match searching strategy with inverted file organization which can overcome many of the problems associated with the use of Boolean operators. The retrieved records are ranked in decreasing similarity with the query and the user only needs to look at those ranked at the top of the list. The nearest neighbor problem can be expressed as: given a set of N points D_i in n-space and a specific query point Q, find the set $R(R \subset N)$ of points $D_1...D_r$ closest to Q, where the closeness is measured by some sort of similarity measure. The obvious way to carry out the nearest neighbor search according to the above expression is to match the query terms against the sets of terms representing each of the image objects in the collection in turn, calculate the similarity measure for each image object and hence obtain the closest neighbors. This method requires $O(N)$ computations and is impractical for large collections. One approach for solving this problem is based on the inverted file organization which reduces the number of image objects that must be considered as potential candidates for the query in a nearest neighbor search.

5.2. *Fast Image and Video Browsing*

Images can be inspected faster and more easily than textual information. Therefore, an interface which allows the user to interact visually with the system is very important in an image retrieval system. Ang et al. [27] suggested a scheme for fast browsing of images. The browser permits multiple images to be quickly displayed onto equal and fixed sized windows at low resolution, but allows the viewer to progressively improve its iconic resolution as desired. Progressive resolution browsing is appropriate because (i) low detailed images can be adequately represented with less resolution, (ii) exploratory browsing requires only coarse representation of images, and (iii) experienced users have increased recognition ability to identify lower resolution images. The browser also allow the search context to be updated using image characteristics from one or more selected image examples.

Content oriented visual browsing of video sequences has also been suggested. Tonomura [28] described several ways to achieve fast video content browsing through variable speed playback, sampling flash, rush, and time-space. In fast sequence browsing, video segments are detected as histogram differences of intensity between adjacent frames.

5.3. *2-D String Image Matching*

Another example is the IIDS system which uses AI techniques to support image retrieval. IIDS is a prototype Intelligent Image Database based on 2-D string iconic indexing [29]. The system supports spatial reasoning, flexible image retrieval, visualization, and traditional image database operations. The system uses spatial reasoning to allow spatial queries and to construct a graphic representation from the 2-D string without referring to the original image. The user may construct queries based on the keywords or the spatial relations between objects in the image. The user can also retrieve images using icons. In such a case, the user arranges icons representing objects on the screen, and the images which have similar spatial relations are retrieved.

5.4. *Logical Pictures*

The concept of logical pictures have been introduced by researchers. Chang and Liu [30] described a model for indexing pictures using logical pictures. In this model logical pictures consist of picture objects and relational objects. A picture object consists of a set of attribute triples: attribute name, attribute value, and an evaluation procedure. The relational object also consists of a set of attribute triples: attribute name, attribute value, and an evaluation procedure. A relational object always has a type attribute or attribute set which characterizes the relation and is unique for this relation. A relational object class is defined as a set of relational objects having the same type. Starting with a collection of picture objects V and relational objects R, an abstraction operation can be applied to construct abstracted objects and index objects, where the corresponding picture predicates are obtained using the syntactic and semantic abstraction rules given in the paper. The picture query is expressed in terms of various index objects, picture objects, and relational objects.

5.5. *Image Query Languages*

Several query languages for pictorial information systems have been proposed. One of these is PSQL or Pictorial Structure Query Language [31]. PSQL is a query language which allows pictorial domains to be presented to the user in their analog form and allows him to do direct manipulation on the objects found in those domains. The ISQL prototype was developed to handle medical imaging [32]. A prototype system was implemented with a VAX 11/780 running VMS, a COMTAL VISION ONE/20 image processing system with ORACLE as the underlying textual DBMS. ISQL provides an extended data dictionary which allows for the description of images. A typical query in ISQL might look like this,

SELECT IMAGE pat_name, date
WHERE modality = 'NMR' AND
pat_name = 'ALLAN'
DISPLAY WITH SCALE =2;

PICQUERY is a high level query language built on top of PICDMS (Picture Database Management System) [33]. The PICQUERY commands operate on the whole pictorial database or a set of picture-object identifiers. A picture-object is a named region, line, point, or parts of a picture. Objects are identified for PICDMS/PICQUERY with the use of feature extraction techniques.

Query by Picture example (QBPE) is the most popular form of querying in pictorial databases [34]. QBPE is developed for querying relational databases by specifying examples. Although the query approach is graphical, QBE does not use the picture format, instead it uses the tabular information stored into the database and corresponding to the picture.

6. Prototypes and Products

Free-text retrieval systems are also used to enhance image retrieval through the use of image description. The first free text based image retrieval system is PICTURE-BASIS [35]. PICTURE-BASIS is a large picture and text archiving system. The system software consists of three parts: the full-text database system (BASIS), a document and image file management software which integrates text data and images, and an image and graphics processing package whereby the retrieved images can be processed. BASIS supports a wide range of bibliographic, full-text and numeric databases. The system provides structured query using relational fields and unstructured keyword-based query using Boolean searching. Other facilities such as word proximity, phrase searching, singular, plural searching, embedded search, synonyms using thesaurus are provided.

Another example of a free text based image retrieval system is the Picture Archival System (PAS) [25]. PAS is a general purpose system developed for archiving and retrieving pictures. Images may contain X-rays, photographs, thumbprints, handwritten signatures, CAD/CAM drawings, engineering blueprints, etc. The system is based on the probabilistic retrieval model which involves ranking the retrieved images in order of descending similarity with the query, where the similarity for each image is determined by the number of terms the description of the image has in common with the query. The system is visually oriented, in the sense that the user need only state the initial query in text format. After the first search is completed, the user can use any one of the retrieved and relevant images to browse for more relevant images. Alternatively, relevant images can be used to refine the original query and conduct a relevant feedback search.

In PAS, small pictures are generated from the original pictures and used for browsing. The small pictures are still distinctly clear at the reduced size and sufficient for the selection of the relevant pictures. After the initial search, the retrieved images are displayed on the screen in decreasing order of similarity with the query. The user can then select those images which are most relevant to the request. This information can then be used later to invoke browsing to find more relevant images. This is carried out by augmenting the original query by the terms extracted from the image description, repeating the search and ranking the retrieved images in decreasing order of similarity with the new query. This process is done internally by the system and is invisible to the user. Alternatively, the user can use the relevant images to conduct a relevance feedback search. In relevance feedback, the query is refined using the terms extracted from the relevant image descriptions and the search is repeated using the modified query.

Examples of other implementations of IIR systems are given in Table 3.

Table 3. Some examples of the image retrieval systems.

System	Data Model	Implementation	Application
CDPS	Free Text	Commercial	Document Image
EDICON	Relational	Commercial	Colour Photo
FASTFOTO	Relational	Commercial	Colour photo
FILENET	Relational	Commercial	Document Image
IIDS	Relational	Prototype	General
IMAGEEXPRESS	Relational	Commercial	Document Image
IMAGEFOLDER	Relational	Commercial	Document Image
IMAGEPLUS	Relational	Commercial	Document Image
ISQL	Relational	Prototype	Medical
PICTURE-BASIS	Free Text	Commercial	General
PAS	Free Text	Prototype	General
PROBE	Object Oriented	Prototype	Spatial
PICDBMS	Relational	Commercial	General
WIIS	Relational	Commercial	Document

References

[1] G. K. Wallace, The JPEG still picture compression standard, *Commun. ACM* **34**, 4 (1991) 30–44.

[2] D. Le Gall, MPEG: A video compression standard for multimedia applications, *Commun. ACM* **34**, 4 (1991) 45–58.

[3] P. Willett, *Document Retrieval Systems* (Taylor Graham, London, 1989).

[4] C. J. Van Rijsbergen, *Information Retrieval* (Butterworths, London, 1979).

[5] G. Salton and M. J. McGill, *Introduction to Modern Information Retrieval* (McGraw-Hill, New York, 1983).

[6] S. E. Robertson and K. Spark-Jones, Relevance weighting of search terms, *Journal of the American Society for Information Science* May-June (1976) 129–145.

[7] T. Noreault, M. Koll and M. J. McGill, Automatic ranked output from Boolean Searches in SIRE, *Journal of the American Society for Information Science* **28** (1977) 333–339.

[8] S. Al-Hawamdeh and P. Willett, Comparison of index term weighting schemes for the ranking of paragraphs in full-text documents, *International Journal of Information and Library Research* **1**, 2 (1989) 116–130.

[9] E. Arkin et al., An efficiently computable metric for comparing polygonal shapes, *IEEE Trans. Pattern Anal. Mach. Intell.* **13**, 3 (1991) 209–216.

[10] H. V. Jagadish, A retrieval technique for similar shapes, in *Proc. ACM SIGMOD*, Denver, Colorado, May 1991, 208-217.

[11] A. K. Jain, *Fundamentals of Digital Image Processing* (Prentice-Hall, 1989) chapter 9.

[12] K. Takahashi et al., Description and matching of density variation for personal identification through facial images, in *Proc. SPIE on Visual Communications and Image Processing '90*, Vol. 1360, 1990, 1694-1704.

[13] L. D. Harmon et al., Machine identification of human faces, *Pattern Recogn.* **13**, 2 (1981) 97–110.

[14] J. Q. Fang and T. S. Huang, A corner finding algorithm for image analysis and registration, in *Proc. AAAI-82*, Pittsburgh, Pennsylvania, Aug. 1982, 46–49.

[15] J. Q. Fang and T. S. Huang, Some experiments on estimating the 3-D motion parameters of a rigid body from two consecutive image frames, *IEEE Trans. Pattern Anal. Mach. Intell.* **6**, 5 (1984) 547–554.

[16] J. E. Overall and J. C. Kiett, *Applied Multivariate Analysis*, McGraw Hill Series in Psychology (McGraw Hill, 1971) Chapters 2–3.

[17] M. H. Savoji and R. E. Burge, On different methods based on the Karhunen-Loeve expansion and used in image analysis, *Comput. Vision Graph. Image Process.* **29** (1985) 259–269.

[18] L. Sirovich and M. Kirby, Low-dimensional procedure for the characterization of human faces, *J.Opt. Soc. Am. A* **4**, 3 (1987) 519–524.

[19] M. Turk and A. Pentland, Eigenfaces for recognition, *Journal of Cognitive Neuroscience* **3**, 1 (1991) 71–86.

[20] Lee Chung-Mong, et al., A knowledge-based system for the image correspondence problem, *Int. J. Pattern Recogn. Artif. Intell.* **4**, 1 (1990) 45-55.

[21] S. K. Chang, Q. Y. Shi and C. W. Yan, Iconic indexing by 2-D Strings, *IEEE Trans. Pattern Anal. Mach. Intell.* **9**, 3 (1987) 413–427.

[22] J. Brolio et al., ISR: A data for symbolic processing in computer vision, *IEEE Comput.* Dec. (1989) 22–29.

[23] R. Weiss and M. Boldt, Geometric grouping applied to straight lines, in *Proc. IEEE Conf. on Computer Vision and Pattern Recognition*, 1986 (IEEE Computer Society Press, Los Alamitos, CA) Order No.721, 489–495.

[24] G. Reynolds and J. R. Beveridge, Searching for geometric structure in images of natural scenes, *Proc. DARPA Image Understanding Workshop*, Feb. 1987, 257–271.

[25] S. Al-Hawamdeh and B. C. Ooi, Semantic-based query formulation in PAS, in *Proc. RIAO'91 Conf. on Intelligent Text and Image Handling*, Barcelona, Spain, Apr. 1991.

[26] S. Al-Hawamdeh et al., Nearest neighbour searching in a picture archival system, in *Proc. ACM Int. Conf. on Multimedia and Information Systems*, Singapore, Jan. 1991, 17–33.

[27] Y. H. Ang, P. S. Ng and H. C. Loke, Image retrieval through fast browsing and visual query using progressive resolution images, in *Proc. ACM Int. Conf. on Multimedia Information Systems*, Singapore, Jan. 1991, 161–174.

[28] Y. Tonomura and S. Abe, Content oriented visual interface using video icons for visual database systems, *J. Visual Lang. Comput.* **1** (1990) 183–198.

[29] S. K. Chang et al., An intelligent image database system, *IEEE Trans. Softw. Eng.* **14**, 5 (1988) 681–688.

[30] S. K. Chang and S. H. Liu, Picture indexing and abstraction techniques for pictorial databases, *IEEE Trans. Pattern Anal. Mach. Intell.* **6**, 4 (1984) 475–484.

[31] N. Roussopoulos, C. Faloutsos and T. Sellis, An efficient pictorial database system for PSQL, *IEEE Trans. Softw. Eng.* **14**, 5 (1988) 639–650.

[32] A. Assmann, R. Venema and K.H. Hohne, The ISQL language: A software tool for the development of pictorial information systems in medicine, in S. K. Chang (ed.), *Visual Languages* (Plenum Press, 1986) 261–284.

[33] T. Joseph and A. F. Cardenas, PICQUERY: A high level query language for pictorial database management, *IEEE Trans. Softw. Eng.* **14**, 5 (1988) 630–640.

[34] N. S. Chang and K. S. Fu, Query-by-pictorial example, *IEEE Trans. Softw. Eng.* **6**, 6 (1980) 519–524.

[35] L. F. Pau, A picture and text query and archiving system, *Pattern Recogn. Lett.* **4**, 6 (1986) 477–480.

Handbook of Pattern Recognition and Computer Vision, pp. 741–768
Eds. C. H. Chen, L. F. Pau and P. S. P. Wang
© 1993 World Scientific Publishing Company

CHAPTER 4.3

CONTEXT RELATED ISSUES IN IMAGE UNDERSTANDING

L. F. PAU

Digital Equipment Europe, P.O. Box 27, F06901 Sophia Antipolis, France

This chapter gives a formal model for scene understanding, as well as for context information; it helps in adapting image understanding procedures and software to varying contexts, when some formal assumptions are satisfied. We have defined and formalized context separation and context adaptation, which are essential for many applications, including to achieve the robustness of the understanding results in changing sensing environments. This model uses constraint logic programming and specialized models for the various interactions between the objects in the scene and the context. A comparison is made with, and examples are given of, the context models in more classical frameworks such as multilevel understanding structures, object based design in scenes, knowledge based approach, and perceptual context separation.

Keywords: Image understanding, computer vision, context models, scene models, constrained logic programming, object oriented design, prolog, object recognition, noise filtering

1. Introduction

1.1. *Context Definitions*

Biophysics as well as perceptual studies, and also image understanding/ computer vision research [7,46] continuously stumble over the issue of context adaptation and separation:

"Given a well defined image understanding task pertaining to objects or dynamic events in a scene, how do we render the formalization and implementation of this task independent from the scene and its varying parameters?"

Context adaptation means the ability to redesign an image understanding task and software by removing the context dependent information about one known context, and updating it with similar information for another known context.

Context separation means the ability to design an image understanding task not knowing the context and calibration information (e.g. when mapping 2-D information into 3-D information [27,36]).

If, exceptionally, only a finite number of contexts are assumed possible, and if context separation applies, then *context recognition* is the task of identifying in the specific scene the applicable context selected from that finite list.

741

If, furthermore, context adaptation applies, then image understanding redesign can be carried out for the recognized context.

In general, however, the number of possible contexts is infinite, even if scene, sensor, object and geometric calibration models are applied. The fundamental reasons for this are phenomena, geometric projections, or processes which violate the underlying required context separation:

- Object-object interactions with direct effects on the context, e.g. geometric occlusion.
- Object-context and context-object interactions, each obeying causality relations, e.g. shadows from objects onto the environment or, vice versa, from the environment onto the objects in the scene; this becomes even more complex when non visible phenomena are taken into account, such as induced irradiation.
- Context unstationarity, due to random or slowly changing events, e.g. weather or failure in the lighting systems.

Four basic approaches to context adaptation have been taken so far:

- multilevel image understanding structures
- object oriented design in scenes
- knowledge based approach
- perceptual context separation

as sometimes exemplified in defect recognition in machine vision, obstacle avoidance modeling in robot navigation [17], aerial imagery [15,18], and a diversity of other areas.

1.2. *Multilevel Image Understanding Structures*

The ability to represent information extracted from image data in a multilevel knowledge structure facilitates the hierarchical analysis needed for the image understanding (object detection, location, and completion of the understanding task at hand). In the now classical approaches, intermediate-level image processing operators (typically region and shape related) invoke lower-level operators (typically registration, feature extractors and measurement), which are then passed to higher-level operators to derive complex relations between objects and their task related meanings.

1.3. *Object Oriented Design in Scenes*

More recently, in relation to implementations of the previous multilevel understanding structures, object-oriented design has attempted to group similar low-level features or middle-level elements (such as regions or neighborhoods), while also separating those which are context related, into classes corresponding immediately to a hierarchical representation. In addition, the programming environments selected for the software solutions provide polymorphism, inheritance and encapsulation.

This has been easing the updating of the instances and operators (methods) when changing contexts and tasks or objects. Method and object inheritance [13,16] offer a code-sharing alternative to supplying special-purpose operators for handling specific classes of objects.

1.4. *Knowledge Based Approach*

Work has also taken place to break the hierarchical understanding structure by having a fully-fledged knowledge based system reason about all allowable combinations of low-level, intermediate level, and higher-level concepts or objects, but by introducing different depths into the selection and search according to the nature and ontology of these concepts or objects (e.g. [9]). Fundamentally, the image understanding task has become a goal, and backward inference is carried out to search for evidence along each possible explanation path. There was in this type of work an implicit hope, now largely lost, that the knowledge base itself could be segmented into context related and context independent pieces of knowledge; for example, it was hoped that generic rules would apply to, e.g. illumination, object centered geometrical transformations, clusters of physically related objects, etc.

1.5. *Perceptual Context Separation*

Perception and psychophysics research sometimes suggest that image understanding tasks can almost always be carried out by the human, with the exception of illusions, thanks to the filtering out of perceptual cues about the task irrespective of the context, thus carrying out at once both context separation and adaptation. For example, car driving in day and night time rely on a perceptual image flow and object distance cues which are analyzed equally well in both contexts. However, no one yet knows how to implement and generalize these perceptual cues or groupings (also called collated features), apart from some simple scenes or processes.

Some considerations have gone into using neural or Hopfield networks to coalesce and discriminate perceptual groupings such as edges and gaps between lines, line intersections, parallels, U's, rectangles, etc. The hope here was to be able to add or remove them according to the geometry of the problem and of the context in general. In the neural networks, after training of the understanding task, weights are trained for the links in a global competition between collated features.

1.6. *Review*

In the best case, image understanding work has focussed on the representation and control issues [24,30,35,42], such as those related to semantic network representations and their execution on distributed architectures; some work has focussed on the opposite of context modeling, that is, designing universal applications development environments able to cope with all kinds of specifics. As a result, context modeling has been largely ignored. When the context was not or was insufficiently known, the hypotheses were simply ranked by experimental tolerances or assigned likelihoods.

Experience proves that none of the first three approaches above, or combinations hereof, can deliver context adaptation and separation, except for very simple problems and scenes.

The multilevel image understanding structures fundamentally cannot allow for the lower-level feature parametrization and detection in changing contexts, even if mixed forward-backward reasoning is applied between levels. And the more cluttered the environment, the more numerous the interactions between levels.

The object oriented design in scenes is useful in highly structured environments, and especially for those understanding tasks which concern themselves with just a few objects with few interactions with the context (e.g. shadows, reflections, changes in reflection of). But that design is even more hierarchical, and thus more rigid, than the previous approach, and suffers from all the drawbacks hereof as well.

The knowledge based approach suffers from the well known knowledge elicitation and accumulation problems; it is probably a never-ending process to acquire heuristic information or models to cover all possible separate context relations and context related processes.

Perceptual context separation in humans and animals seems very powerful, especially as it achieves robustness versus perceptual deficiencies and anomalies. It is certainly a research goal of high importance to be able to formalize it, yet little is yet understood of the implementation sort for complex tasks.

1.7. *Plan*

In this chapter, we will formalize the context adaptation and separation problems, in both theoretical and practical ways, which have been shown to help out significantly, although not yet with resolution of the full range of context related issues. The formal models for the scene and context, and especially for their interactions, are given in Sec. 2. Sections 3, 4 and 5 illustrate those models, stressing especially the context modeling, via one example from car recognition in traffic images, by taking successively the multilevel understanding approach, the object oriented design of the same, and finally by addressing some perceptual context cues. Conclusions are given in Sec. 6, while two appendices give introductory definitions or explanations about object oriented design and constraint logic programming.

2. Formal Image Understanding and Context Description

2.1. *Approach*

The basic approach proposed here is to:

(i) provide a formal description of the scene images via logic
(ii) assume massive parallelism in both the spatial description as well as in the processing/understanding

(iii) describe each context as a set of logic predicates and constraints propagated through the formal description (i)

(iv) model the basic object $\leftrightarrow$ context interactions.

The need for the formal description is due to the context separation requirement; the need for the massive parallelism is due to the implementation requirement; while the need for the context model description and interaction modeling, is due to the context adaptation requirement.

It should be highlighted right away that image context simulation from physical processes has made significant progress, as evidenced by the flurry of image synthesis applications, and that they all contribute to the content of context modeling via call in-call out facilities to a battery of physical or other behavioral models.

In the following the notation in logic shall be the one from the Prolog language [11], although the image understanding task solution implementation may very well be done later on in other languages. The notation $a \Rightarrow b$ is a predicate saying that a is true iff b is true; the notation $A \leftarrow B$ is a rewriting rule saying that the list B is syntactically rewritten as A. The arity of a predicate is the number of arguments it has. One fundamental remark is also that, although difficult to achieve, the goal of these scene and context models is to help in image understanding tasks even in unstructured environments; this leads to the use of rather general context information data structures, i.e. the causal graphs and influencing domains (as defined below). This of course would be impossible unless the physical and causal image formation processes are not taken into account, and therefore we have to assume known the range of such processes existing in a given scene.

The other assumption is about the fact that the image understanding task relates to objects which are significant in terms of their overall presence in the scene, as e.g. measured by the total solid angle of these objects from the point of view of the sensor viewing the scene.

2.2. *Scene Model*

Assuming in general a four-dimensional space (x, y, z, t) each sensed pixel gray value/color code "pixel(x, y, z, t)" is true iff its value is true, which in logic corresponds to the fact/statement:

$$\text{pixel}\,(x, y, z, t)\,.$$

To each location (x, y, z, t) is attached a causal graph G of all other locations having an influence on its pixel code value/color. This dependency is explicitly shown by increasing the arity of the "pixel" predicate:

$$\text{pixel}\,(x, y, z, t) \;\Rightarrow\; \text{pixel}\,(x, y, z, t, G\,(x, y, z, t))\,.$$

The graph G is built from the causal influences mapped out pairwise on an influencing domain $D\,(x, y, z, t, p)$:

$$\text{influenced}\,(x, y, z, t, x', y', z', t')\,.$$

and this predicate is true iff (x', y', z', t') belongs to $D(x, y, z, t, p)$, where p is a causal process type. The influence "influenced" can in general not be related to a single process p, as the paths in the graph $G(x, y, z, t)$ leading to the location (x, y, z, t) may travel through a sequence of pixels each influenced by the previous pixel, but in different ways.

2.3. *Causal Processes p*

The range of causal processes $\{p\}$ is not bound, as they may be physical, relational, geometric, qualitative, behavioral [50], or model-based. It is here assumed that the same range of causal processes apply to the context related information.

A "default" set of causal processes to be considered are:

$$\{p\} = \{\text{lighting, sensor, optics, shadows, orthogonal-projection}\}.$$

In [48] is given an example of such process models in a simple case of context separation, irrespective of the image understanding task relating to objects in the scene.

2.4. *Image Understanding Task*

The image understanding task [33,35] is then a goal I to be satisfied in the scene in view of a finite number n of logical conditions applying to sets of pixels in the scene:

$$I \Rightarrow \text{cond-1}(\text{pixel}(.)), \text{cond-2}(\text{pixel}(.)), \dots, \text{cond-}n(\text{pixel}(.))$$

or equivalently via the composite condition (applying for example to a composite region [29,33]):

$$I \Rightarrow \text{cond}(\text{pixel}(.)).$$

The n logical conditions cond-1$, \dots,$ cond-n are here treated as constraints in a constraint logic programming framework (see Appendix B).

The understanding process itself is then the search process S (set-of (pixel), set-of (G), set-of (D), set-of (p)) needed to establish the previous goal I as true or false. The predicate "set-of" is self-explanatory. For reasons of clarity we assume here that S is the sequential ordered list of all nodes traversed in the total image, although of course a fundamental assumption made here is that a massively parallel architecture is used and reflected by a propagation scheme in this architecture.

In an earlier work [21], the satisfaction of the conditions cond(pixel(.)) was defined as a truth maintenance problem [31,32], in view of sensor fusion and of the disambiguation of scene contexts in a three-dimensional fusion task.

2.5. *Context Model*

The context is another massively parallel field "context-pixel (x, y, z, t)" with the corresponding causal graphs "Context-$G(x, y, z, t)$" and influencing domains "Context-$D(x, y, z, t, p)$".

We can then formalize the basic assumptions and definitions:

(i) there is context separation iff the following implication holds true:

$$\{I => \text{cond} \, (\text{pixel} \, (.\,,.\,,.\,, \text{Context-}G)), \text{ for all Context-}G\}$$

which means that all constraints "cond-i (pixel (.))" arc independent of all "Context-G" for the range of processes $\{p\}$.

(ii) context adaptation, assuming context separation, can be carried out by the following rewriting process:

$$S(\text{set-of (pixel)}, \text{ set-of (Context-}G), \text{ set-of }(D), \text{ set-of }(p)) \leftarrow$$
$$S(\text{set-of (pixel}'), \text{ set-of (Context-}G'), \text{ set-of }(D'), \text{ set-of }(p))$$

where the primed symbols pertain to the same problem/goal but in an old context.

2.6. Interaction Models: Object-Object

Defining an object is done easily by defining the "influenced" predicate for influencing domains $D(.\,,.\,,.\,, \text{object-name})$ covering the spatial and time extent of this object. Context objects are defined equivalently.

The influence of an object on a context object, or vice versa, is a predicate and rewriting rule, which in the most general form is in two parts:

$$\text{new-}D(.\,,.\,,.\,, \text{new-object-name}) \Rightarrow \text{intersect}(D(.\,,.\,,.\,, \text{object-name}),$$
$$\text{Context-}D(.\,,.\,,.\,, \text{context-object-name})).$$
$$\text{new-object-name} \leftarrow (\text{object-name} \quad \text{context-object-name})$$

where the "intersect" predicate says whether the two sets indeed intersect. The last rewriting rule is a possible, but not compulsory, object relabeling.

Example: Intersections of two objects

We find the intersections between objects A and B; these intersections divide the boundary of each object into contour segments. The contour segments of each object are then assigned to one of three disjoint sets, one containing segments that lie outside the other object, one containing segments that lie inside the other object, and one containing segments shared by the two objects. The relations between various collated features are represented in the context-graph G, which is labeled as a causal graph, in such a way that collated features which support each other perceptually are connected via positively weighted links, while mutually conflicting collations are linked via negatively weighted links.

The following cases exist, each modeled by specific predicates, rewriting rules, and attribute changes eventually described by an attributed grammar [22]; the definitions below apply to any pair of objects, but we are especially interested by the case where A is a real object and B a context-object:

(i) *Subsumption.* If the outside-segment set of a shape A is empty, and the shared-segment set non-empty, and the edge support for segments in the inside-segment set is non-existent, then we say that object A is subsumed by object B, and can be removed.

(ii) *Occlusion.* If the contour segments of A inside B have strong edge support, and those of B inside A have weak intensity edge support, then A occludes B. This applies even if the rest of the contour segments of A and B belong to the shared set or outside set.

(iii) *Merger compatibility.* If the segments in the inside-segment and shared-segment set for both objects A and B have poor edge support, then A and B represent segmentation of one object into two parts, and can thus be merged into one object.

(iv) *Disconnected.* If A and B have null inside-segment sets and null shared-segment sets, they are disconnected. If A and B have a non-empty shared-segment set, and null inside-segment sets, but the shared segments have good edge support, then A and B are still unrelated though adjoining.

(v) *Incompatible.* If A and B have non-empty inside-segment sets and the elements of the inside-segments of both A and B have strong edge support, then at least one of A and B is a wrong structural grouping and must be deleted.

2.7. *Interaction Models: Object $\leftrightarrow$ Context*

The influence between an object and the context is a predicate and rewriting rule, which in the most general form is in two parts:

$$\text{pixel}(.,.,., \text{new-}G) \leftarrow (\text{pixel}(.,.,.,G)\ \text{pixel}(.,.,., \text{Context-}G))$$
$$\text{new-}D(.,.,., \text{object-name}) \Rightarrow \text{intersect}(D(.,.,., \text{object-name}),$$
$$\text{Context-}D(.,.,., \text{object-name})).$$

which shows that the pixel value or code may be changed because of the change in the influenced domains.

2.8. *Interaction Models: Context Unstationarity*

This unstationarity is of course first achieved by the stochastic point processes linked to the location $(x,\ y,\ z,\ t)$ and thus to the domains G and D. The latter are of course the most interesting due to combining stochastic deviations made of spatial stationarity and temporal stationarity, to modify the influences. In practice, it is indeed very difficult to have or estimate the characteristics of these point processes, and thus to compensate for them in the search processes S. The simpler case is when $(x,\ y,\ z)$ is deterministic but where t is an independent variable driving the scene, task and context.

2.9. *Context Causal Graph G Operations*

The context causal graph Context-$G(.)$ can be manipulated by standard predicates operating on that causal graph and its attributes. It can for example be built (see [25,38] for complete predicate definitions) using:

 (i) causal graph merger, and adjacencies
 (ii) coalescence by graph join operations corresponding to overlaps between image scene contexts, with respect to an angle of view and perspective transformations
(iii) perception graph for the context, resulting from joining all context graphs for context-objects
(iv) extensions to sensor fusion tasks [21,49].

2.10. *Constraint Based Languages as Resolution Strategies*

Once the image understanding task has received a formal description as above, the big question is of course how to synthesize the search processes S. Here is where the impact of a new research field is felt the most, that is, of constraint based logic programming (see Appendix B for an introduction). These languages do exist and are in use in the industrial world under trade-names such as: Prolog III, CHIP, CHARME, PRINCE, etc. [1–6]. They include constraint domains (as formalized via the constraints cond(pixel$(.)$)) which can be both finite or infinite trees [5,14], linear algebras with infinite precision or rational numbers, boolean algebras, and lists. They also allow for domains such as finite domains (as related to the objects or the influencing domains D), and interval arithmetic (for pixel value rewriting rules such as most gray value "mixing" operations or thresholding). These languages also include the constraint solving algorithms right into their kernels (see Appendix B), while maintaining the declarative nature of the goal I and of all the predicates "influenced". Most of these languages have pre-compilers or compilers, which is most appreciated in applications development; the search strategies S may be synthesized interactively in the interpreted mode, or compiled [28], with all the underlying constraint propagation carried or by the constraint solving algorithms.

One area still unexplored is their implementation on massively parallel storage and processing architectures, although Digital Equipment is collaborating with some research partners on this subject.

2.11. *Implementation of the Context Adaptation and Separation*

This implementation follows from the logic formalism and problem specification described above:

- If there is no context separation over $\{p\}$, the assertion of the context separation definition will be false. This "fail" can in turn be used to authorize or deny further rewritings which assume this separation, via the standard "/" predicate, or via the delayed "dif" predicate [11]. If the "fail" happens, then the developer has the option to change the vocabularies in $\{p\}$ and change the range and types of processes.

- If there is context adaptation and this can be carried out, the simple rewriting rule of the context adaptation definition applies. This can be further eased by separating out all predicates and data structures for each Context-G and Context-D in separate "worlds" or "modules" of the asserted predicate knowledge base. This segmentation is precious for context adaptation and modularity. Incidentally, Prolog allows us to write very simply regular grammars and others to implement the rule rewriting.

It should also be noted, and this is very important in practice, that consistency of all "influenced" predicates is maintained, as dynamic updates in the "worlds" or "modules" will check out possible tautologies/contradictions and deny any if happening.

2.12. *Time Dependencies in the Context*

It is worth underlining once more that the context graph Context-$G\,(x,\,y,\,z,\,t)$ and the influencing domain Context-$D\,(x,\,y,\,z,\,t,\,p,\,\text{context-object-name})$ are both time dependent. This is mandatory as the context-objects move, and also as the causal graphs G change over time.

In the threat assessment [20], scene monitoring [34], or target tracking problems [20,37], there is an allowed domain attached to the transitions over time between spatial zones occupied by the objects in the scene, corresponding to constraint "scripts".

2.13. *Comparison*

This model is much more formal and powerful than the approaches surveyed in Sec. 1, except perceptual context separation. It opens one way to the latter by having "retinas" specified via the influencing domains D, and matching vision processes (see Sec. 5).

In Sec. 3, an example will show how easily the multilevel image understanding structures can be represented, with knowledge bases also, and Sec. 4 will show how object oriented design can be incorporated if needed.

3. Multilevel Image Context Representation in a Logic Programming Environment

This section describes in a simple case how a simple context information model can be combined with multilevel image understanding, as discussed in Sec. 1, to carry out a simple recognition task. The task I is to recognize car objects in a real-life scene (see Fig. 9). Extensions have been made to three-dimensional scenes in [21], with a full example therein.

All image processing predicates mentioned below are available as Prolog [11] predicates in an environment described in [8,38], and organized into a three-level hierarchy summarized in Table 1. The car objects are defined by clauses too, with orientation as a parameter (see Fig. 1). It should be noted that all predicates affected by the context are found in the upper Context level layer, and only there. About the implementation of the search process S, using the Prolog unification algorithms, see [2,8] for extensive details.

Table 1. Hierarchy of Principal Image Operators; all listed here are predicates which all allow for unification/backtracking. Parameters are explained in Sections 3 and 4.

```
CONTEXT    car (Img, Theta, ObjList)  /* ObjList forms a car in Img at < Theta */
LEVEL      carSide (W1, W2, Theta)    /* W1, W2 have similar orient< Theta */
           carCorner (W1, W2)              /* W1, W2 are roughly perpendicular */
           carWindow (Img, ObjNum, W)  /* car window W has pixval=ObjNum */


           trapezoid (Img, ObjNum, T)
           parallelogram (Img, ObjNum, P)
APPLIC.    rectangle (Img, ObjNum, R)
LEVEL      quadrilateral (Img, ObjNum, Q)
           orderSides (W, Edges)          /* Edges=Top,Bottom,L,R sides of W */
           aspectRatio (W, Ratio)            /* Ratio is Perim**2 / Area    */
           orientation (W, Or)              /* based on variance ratios */


           binarize (Src, Dest, Thresh)
           lopas (Src, Dest, Iter)
FEATURE    traceContour (Src, Dest, Obj, DIR) /* follows edge in DIR direction*/
(LOW)      closedPolygon (Corners)
LEVEL      locateCorners (Img, ObjNum, Corners, [SCAN, Thresh, COUNT])
```

```
car( Img, Orientation,
[W1, W2, W3]) :-
  carWindow( Img,
PixVal1, W1),
   nextTo( Img, W1, W2),
   carWindow( Img,
PixVal2, W2),
   carSide( W1, W2,
Orientation),
   nextTo( Img, W1, W3),
   carWindow( Img,
PixVal3, W3),
   carCorner( W1, W3).
```

Fig. 1. Example clause within 'car' predicate, showing one allowable transformation.

3.1. *Lower Level Predicates: Image Features*

A common characteristic of the predicates at this level is that each is task (I) and context (G) independent: edges, vertices, geometric features, etc. Predicates such as binary threshold and low-pass filter predicates preprocess the original image pixel gray level values. It is however object registration, scaling, labeling, contour tracking, and corner detection, which are the principal means for extracting information at this level. The attributes derived include, for each labeled object/region, its area, perimeter, centroid, x- and y- variances, chain-coded contour, number and locations of corners. Descriptions of the labeling and contour tracking algorithms are provided in [8]. For example, the general form of the corner location predicate could be [8]:

locateCorners (Src, Dest, ObjNum, Corners, [SCAN, Thres, COUNT])

in which Src, Dest are source and destination atoms, ObjNum is the object label number/name, Corners is the corner pixel location pointer pixel (x, y, z, t), and Thres is the gray level threshold for ObjNum. SCAN and COUNT are parameters which can be bound, unbound, or constrained. According to the way these bindings are specified at query time by constraints "cond (.)", then one can easily get declaratively, answers to questions such as (see Fig. 2):

- How many corners COUNT can be found using a scan window length of SCAN = 22 pixels?
- What scan length SCAN should be used to find exactly COUNT = 4 corners?

and any combinations of similar questions, including on other atoms.

```
           locateCorners(Src, Dest, ObjNum,
     Corners, [SCAN, Thresh, LINECOUNT]).

(a) locateCorners(Src, Dest, ObjNum,
Corners, [12, 0.75, LINECOUNT]).
               LINECOUNT = 5

(b) locateCorners(Src, Dest, ObjNum,
Corners, [SCAN, 0.75, 4]).
               SCAN = 12 ;
               SCAN = 16 ;
               SCAN = 20

(c) locateCorners(Src, Dest, ObjNum,
Corners, [SCAN, 0.75, LINECOUNT]).
               SCAN = 6, LINECOUNT = 5 ;
               SCAN = 8, LINECOUNT = 5 ;
               SCAN = 12, LINECOUNT = 4 ;
               SCAN = 24, LINECOUNT = 3
```

Fig. 2. Three predicate calls to illustrate effects of parameter bindings.

The search process yielding answers to these questions is based on unification and backtracking, and explained in [8,10,38]. Essentially, unification can, not only trigger a search for a suitable parameter value satisfying the goal constraints, but

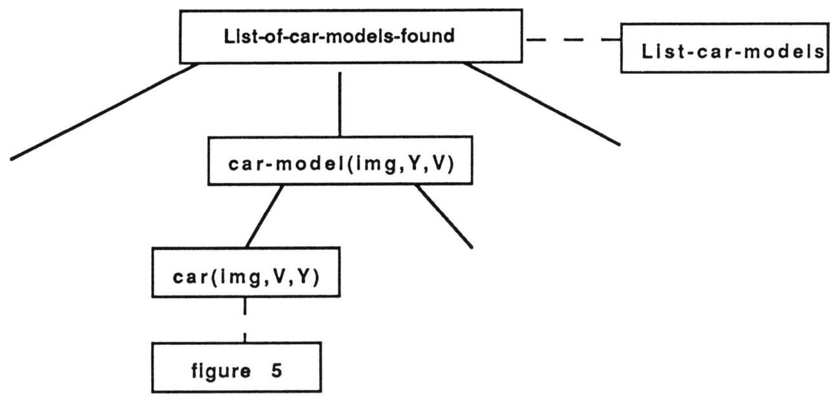

Fig. 3. Class allocation control structure.

can also match the unbound parameter against all possible values which satisfy the predicate's constraints.

3.2. *Intermediate Level Predicates: Application Dependent Predicate Knowledge Base*

The predicates defined at this level are all *I*-application specific and are employed to identify car windows as objects belonging to a particular class of shapes (trapezoid, rectangle, parallelogram), and with shape attributes (e.g. aspect ratio) conforming to specified ranges of values for cars. In addition, allowable transformations are defined, to permit the classification of shapes with incomplete contours. Spatial relationships between pairs of objects in the cars are also specified here; thus we see at this level, predicates for identifying adjacent objects in the cars, objects with the same orientation, etc. The same predicates can exclude objects which do not belong to a car although belonging to the same class of shapes.

These predicates altogether constitute what might be called a formal specification of the object model from regions [40], the objects being cars and car elements. They should be stored in a separate predicate base, or world; the use of such worlds is mandatory in sensor fusion tasks [49].

In [8,38] examples are given in detail as to how the search by unification/ backtracking allow detection of the shapes of the object model, if any exist, and to adapt the parameters as explained above for the lower level predicates:

- list of edges for a shape [8];
- region attributes for context dependent regions, producing attributes of the influencing domains Context-*D*.

<u>**definition**</u>

```
class polygon (Image, ObjNum)
  checks
    ( get_cornerData (Image, ObjNum, CornerList),
      closedPolygon (CornerList) )
  body
    img (Image) => (!).


quad (Image, ObjNum) class polygon
  checks
    ( get_cornerNum( Image, ObjNum, 4),
      orderEdges( Image, ObjNum, Edges),
      assert_once( quadrilateral(Image, ObjNum, Edges)))
  body
    edges( [T, B, L, R]) =>
      clause(quadrilateral(Image, ObjNum, [T, B, L, R]))
  -&-
    topBottomTheta( Theta) =>
      clause(quadrilateral(Image, ObjNum, [T,B|_]),
      transOrigin( T, B, Tnew, Bnew),
      rotateToXaxis( Tnew, Bnew, Theta).
```

<u>**creation**</u>

```
new(quad( image01, 14), Quad01)
```

<u>**messaging**</u>

```
Quad01#topBottomTheta( ThetaQ01 )
```

Fig. 4. Example class and subclass definitions, showing object creation and message passing. 'Body' predicates (methods) are inherited to subclasses. 'Checks' are also inherited, meaning that the call shown to create an instance of 'quad' will first evaluate the checks in 'polygon' and then in 'quad' before completing the instantiation.

3.3. *Higher Level Predicates: Goal Satisfaction Constraints*

At this level, coexisting in a multilevel representation are two very different types of predicates:

- the conditions "cond-i" which are constraints defining the image understanding task I
- all context related predicates, such as "influenced", "Context-G", "Context-D", etc.

As to the constraints, they essentially specify in the specific case at hand, that an object may be classified as a car of a given car model/type, if all component car windows are spatially dispersed in a certain way, specified for example by the constraints of the following car detection goal:

$I \Rightarrow$ cond (Img (.)).
$I =$ car (Img, Orientation, [W1, W2, W3])
cond-1 (Img (.)) = carWindow (Img, PixVal1, W1), nextTo (Img, W1, W2).
cond-2 (Img (.)) = carWindow (Img, PixVal2, W2), carSide (W1, W2, Orientation),
           nextTo (Img, W1, W3).
cond-3 (Img (.)) = carWindow (Img, PixVal3, W3), carCorner (W1, W2).

Unification again generates the search process S, satisfying the goal I, as well as all constraints on the objects or regions with specific characteristics, acting like special-purpose filters.

Other goals are then satisfied by other sets of constraints: for example, the initially mentioned sequential car recognition goal will be stated as (again allowing for identical predicates with variable arity):

$I \Rightarrow$ cond (Img (.)).
$I =$ list (Y1, match (Img, Y1 , Y2), List-car-types).
cond-1 (Img (.)) = different (Y1, Y2), car-model (Img, Y1, V1), car-model
           (Img, Y2, V2), element-of (Y1, list-car-models),
           element-of (Y2, list-car-models).
cond-2 (Img (.)) = car-model (Img, Y1, V1).
cond-3 (Img (.)) = car-model (Img, Y2, V2).
cond-4 (Img (.)) = equal (V1, [Theta1, Corners1, SCAN, Thresh1, COUNT1]).
cond-5 (Img (.)) = equal (V2, [Theta2, Corners2, SCAN, Thresh2, COUNT2]).

In the above, the search process S will return the list of car models seen in the image "Img", by ensuring that these car instances are spatially distinct, meaning that there is yet no object $\leftrightarrow$ object interaction. The car-model predicate will first unify the unbound V parameter lists before it can backtrack with one or several solutions. The predefined "different" predicate should guarantee the difference at the term level, and spatial distinction. Figure 5 illustrates the class allocation constraints nesting and hierarchy, and is made graphical to help in object oriented design. We have however to analyze this predicate "different" in more detail below.

3.4. *Context Model*

The above goal satisfaction constraints are still not fully specified, precisely because the "different" predicate referred to above is obviously context dependent, as it pertains to spatial distinction and non-occlusion, which falls into the class of object $\leftrightarrow$ object interaction models discussed in Sec. 2.

More precisely, the context separation in a multi-object recognition task can only be achieved by:

- first a scene model for isolated single objects alone
- next a context model for each additional object

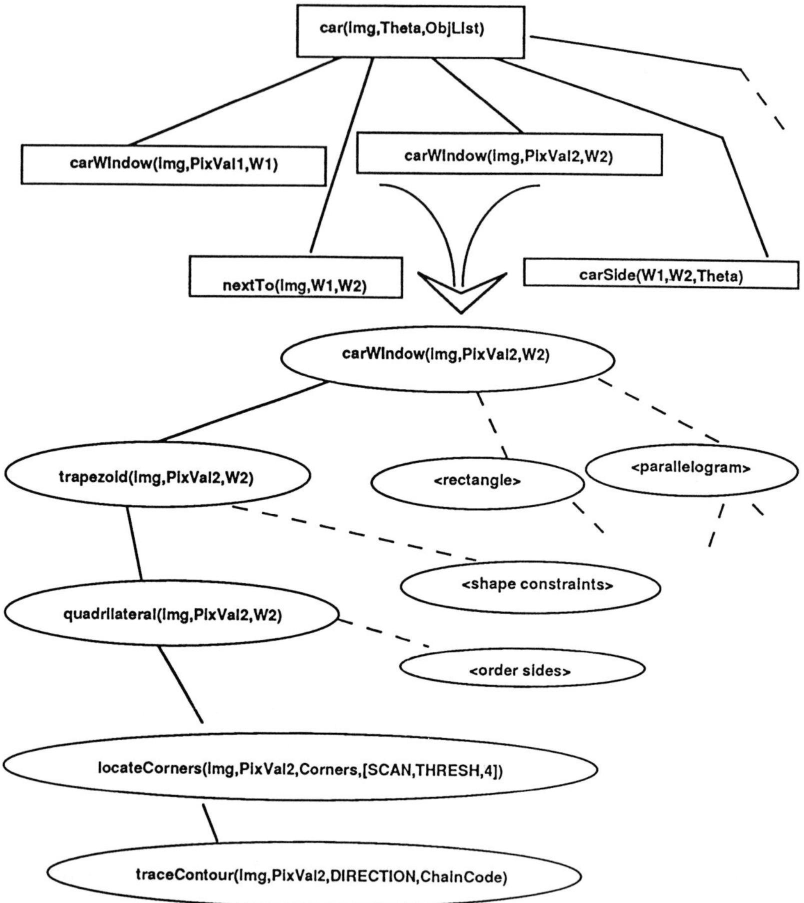

Fig. 5. Example. Invoking the 'car' predicate sequentially activates its subgoals. When the first call to 'carWindow' succeeds, W1 is bound to an object in 'img' with pixel assignment PixVal1. The subgoal 'nextTo' succeeds in finding a neighbor object, unifying it with W2. Now suppose that the second call to 'carWindow' succeeds (visiting the nodes shown in the expansion), but 'carSide' fails. Backtracking returns to the second 'carWindow' call, but since W2 is still bound, the search does not look for a new object. Instead, 'locateCorners' is invoked via backtracking to analyze the object with new scan parameters, to derive a new corner placement which may satisfy the 'carSide' constraints. A new object would be searched for if backtracking returned to 'nextTo', freeing W2 to be unified with a new neighbor object.

so that each isolated car is located and recognized individually, and overlapping cars are treated as an object ↔ object interaction as formalized in Sec. 2.

Reusing the goal specification for the car recognition task, and assuming the scene in which the isolated car must be located and recognized, is car-model (Img, Y1, V1). The context model for this object ↔ object interaction perfectly fits the generic definition:

$$\text{new-}D\,(.,.,.,\text{new-object-name}) \quad \Rightarrow \text{intersect}\,(D\,(.,.,.,\text{object-name}),$$
$$\text{Context-}D\,(.,.,.,\text{context-object-name})).$$
$$\text{new-object-name} \leftarrow (\text{object-name} \quad \text{context-object-name})$$

provided the application level specifies the predicates or definitions:

object-name $=$ car-model (Img, Y1, V1)
context-object-name $=$ car-model (Img, Y2, V2)
different (Y1, Y2) $\Rightarrow$ or (diff (new-object-name, Y1), diff (new-object-name, Y2)).

In case of spatial overlap, the rewriting rule must be defined otherwise, e.g. in relation to the attributes of the domains D-1 and D-2 and thus of the domain "new-D" (see the formal definitions above leading to the corresponding formal predicates).

In this car recognition example, the influencing domains D-1, D-2, new-D are explicitly described by the simple causal process of spatial, stationary, neighborhood, as explicated by the predicates "nextTo" in relation to the car windows.

In this example too, it is especially powerful to use the causal graphs $G(.)$ and Context-$G(.)$ to represent all possible relative attitudes of the "car-windows" and "car-corners" with respect to the sensor. For example, it is obvious that the car detection goal "car (Img, Orientation, [W1, W2, W3])" made explicit above, corresponds to one such causal graph.

In this specific example, as discussed in [8], there is no object $\leftrightarrow$ context interaction, nor context unstationarity:

- The object $\leftrightarrow$ context interaction would apply both to shades cast by the isolated cars, as well as to reflections between cars and the physical surroundings. However the causal graphs G and Context-G allow for the filtering out of the shade seen in Fig. 9 (once compared to Fig. 8), and no further object $\leftrightarrow$ context interaction model is needed.
- The context unstationarity would be capturing the randomness in the car speeds, but not speed (as pixel $(.,.,.,t)$ encapsulates time).

3.5. *Constraint Resolution Engine for Object Classification*

We can illustrate, in relation with the example treated in this section, how a constraint satisfaction engine would operate for the car classification goal I. We will further particularize this procedure, borrowed from [8], by jointly treating scene objects such as cars and context objects such as trees or road signs, assuming context separation.

Consider "obj" and "c-obj" as facts belonging to the lists "m" and "c-n" respectively, where the prefix c- applies to context information, and "a" is the context. The fact "r" as observed in the scene with its context will be resolved by the following predicate base which constitutes a constraint resolution engine, for the constraint that the object "obj" is found in that context "a":

(i) $r \Rightarrow$ obj c-obj.
(ii) class (r, a.l) $\Rightarrow$ obj c-obj class (obj, m) class (c-obj, c-n)
element-of (a, m) element-of (a, c-n).
(iii) class (r, nil) $\Rightarrow$ fail.
(iv) delete (r, obj c-obj) $\Rightarrow$ class (r, nil).
(v) add-predicate (no (r), obj c-obj) $\Rightarrow$.

where

- the first rule (i) belongs to the goal specification in the predicate base;
- the other rules (ii)–(v) belong to the constraint satisfaction engine by deleting inconsistent facts in the predicate base and adding conditions by (iv) and (v) to get smaller consistent fact lists;
- the notation "a.l" designates the list made of "a" followed by "l", "nil" the null fact; the other predicates are self-explanatory.

4. Image Understanding and Object Oriented Context Modeling

This section deals with the issue of showing how object oriented design can be used for context modeling, and the limitations hereof (see Sec. 1). To ease the reading, this is exemplified by extending the example of Sec. 3. Basic definitions of object oriented design terminology are given in Appendix A.

4.1. *Object Oriented Context Representation*

Even when using a logic based representation, as in Secs. 2 and 3, it is possible to extend the predicate representations by class definition capabilities, including mechanisms for inheritance and methods inheritance.

A class definition is composed of two groups of predicates:

- The group labeled "checks" is evaluated when an instance is requested via the predicate "new (⟨class name⟩)"; if these predicates are satisfied, the instantiation is successful;
- The group labeled "body" contains the predicates available as methods. Both groups are inherited to subclasses (see Fig. 4).

The context classes then correspond to classes of "context-object" names, the classes of influencing domains "Context-D", and the classes of causal processes $\{p\}$, as featured via the "Context-D (, , , context-object-name)" term in the formal model of Sec. 2. A more specific example of this, but by no means the only one, is the class of context regions shapes, found in a shape library as used in [9].

Method definitions allow a segment of Prolog code to be encapsulated within a class definition and invoked by sending a message to the class instance. Inheritance allows methods defined in a class to be available (inherited) to any of its subclasses.

Figure 3 illustrates definitions for a class (e.g. "car models") and subclass, as well as the syntax for object creation and message passing; "body" and "checks" of the corresponding class definitions are illustrated in Fig. 4; also [43] gives another example for ship classification. Methods applicable to context classes obviously include the rewriting rules specified above in the context model of Secs. 2 and 3, for context adaptation and object-context interactions.

```
?- car(0,Theta,ObjList).
1 CALL car(0,_361,[_452,_454])
2 CALL carWindow(0,_483,_452)
3 CALL locCorner(0,1,[_1488,_1490,_1492,img1],_1486)
4 EXIT locCorner(0,1,[16,0.5,4,img1],[[110,210],[180,170],[190,200],[120,250]])
5 EXIT carWindow(0,1,trapezoid(0,1,img1))
6 CALL nextTo(trapezoid(0,1,img1),_493,_494)
7 CALL locCorner(0,1,[_21696,_21698,_21700,img1],_21694)
8 FAIL locCorner(0,1,[16,0.5,4,img1],[[110,210],[180,170],[190,200],[120,250]])
9 REDO locCorner(0,2,[_21696,_21698,_21700,img2],_21694)
10 EXIT locCorner(0,2,[12,0.5,4,img2],[[200,160],[240,120],[270,130],[220,190]])
11 EXIT nextTo(trapezoid(0,1,img1),quad(0,2,img2),104.043)
12 CALL carWindow(quad(0,2,img2),_454)
13 CALL carWindow(0,2,_454)
14 CALL locCorner(0,2,[_29070,_29072,_29074,img2],_29068)
15 EXIT locCorner(0,2,[12,0.5,4,img2],[[200,160],[240,120],[270,130],[220,190]])
16 EXIT carWindow(0,2,trapezoid(0,2,img2))
17 EXIT carWindow(quad(0,2,img2),trapezoid(0,2,img2))
18 CALL carSide(trapezoid(0,1,img1),trapezoid(0,2,img2),_361)
19 FAIL carSide(trapezoid(0,1,img1),trapezoid(0,2,img2),_361)
20 REDO carWindow(0,2,trapezoid(0,2,img2))
21 REDO carWindow(quad(0,2,img2),trapezoid(0,2,img2))
22 CALL locCorner(0,2,[_29070,_29072,_29074,img3],_29068)
23 EXIT locCorner(0,2,[18,0.5,4,img3],[[200,150],[240,120],[280,130],[220,190]])
24 EXIT carWindow(0,2,trapezoid(0,2,img3))
25 EXIT carWindow(quad(0,2,img2),trapezoid(0,2,img3))
26 CALL carSide(trapezoid(0,1,img1),trapezoid(0,2,img3),_361)
27 EXIT carSide(trapezoid(0,1,img1),trapezoid(0,2,img3),-1.47424)
28 EXIT car(0,-1.47424,[trapezoid(0,1,img1),trapezoid(0,2,img3)])
Theta = -1.47424,
ObjList = [trapezoid(0,1,img1),trapezoid(0,2,img3)]
```

Fig. 6. Example Prolog trace showing top-level goal 'car' (1); subgoal 'carWindow' identifies an object as a car window (5); 'nextTo' finds a neighboring object (11); neighbor object identified as a car window (17); these two windows fail to satisfy 'carSide' (19); backtracking to 'carWindow' causes corner detection to retry same object with new parameters and derives a new corner placement (22); two windows satisfy the 'carSide' predicate (27).

The visualization of the search process S is displayed in Fig. 5, while Fig. 6 gives the trace of the "I" car recognition goal execution. Figure 7 displays the corner detection results achieved by this search process, for varying values of the bound SCAN parameter (see Sec. 3). Figure 8 displays the regions characterizing the car class instance, in the binary/thresholded image in Fig. 9. Please note that in Fig. 9 there are reflections from the roof and shadows, with the shadows eliminated by the context modeling, whereas the roof is treated as a supplementary "window" but not found to abide by the neighborhood graph Context-G, and thus is eliminated by the constraint satisfaction.

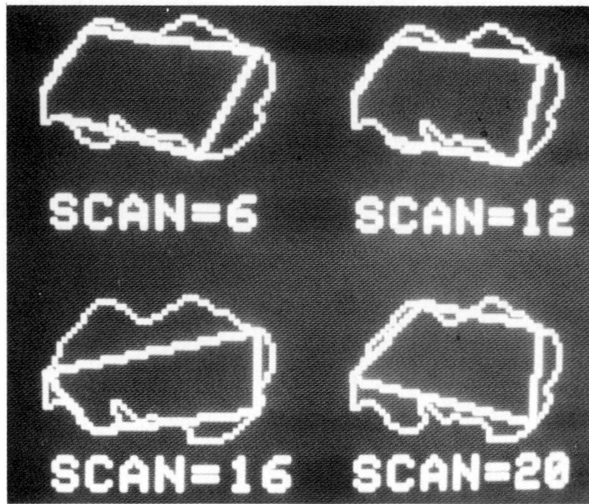

Fig. 7. Four corner detection results achieved by backtracking, varying the scan window length. Each result shows the same contour with a different corner placement.

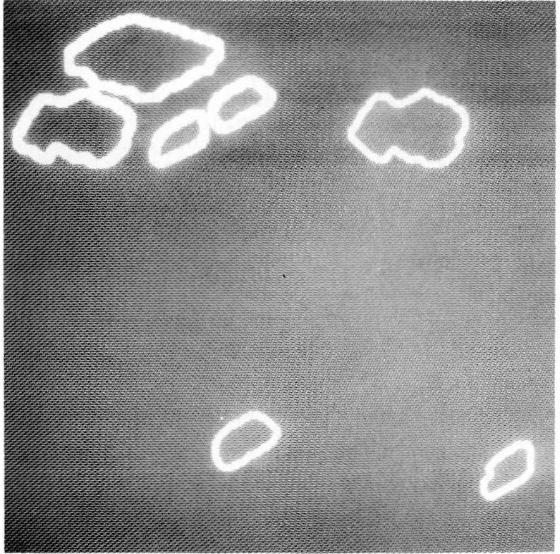

Fig. 8. Image of car after preprocessing (upper left) is identified as a car instance, matching the three extracted contours shown as car windows to satisfy one of the 'car' predicates.

4.2. *Extensions to Sensor Fusion*

The object oriented design comes in handy to represent context diversity and changes in the case of sensor fusion tasks [25,26,49], where different detection ranges of heterogeneous sensors overlap in the feature domains while having distinct attributes.

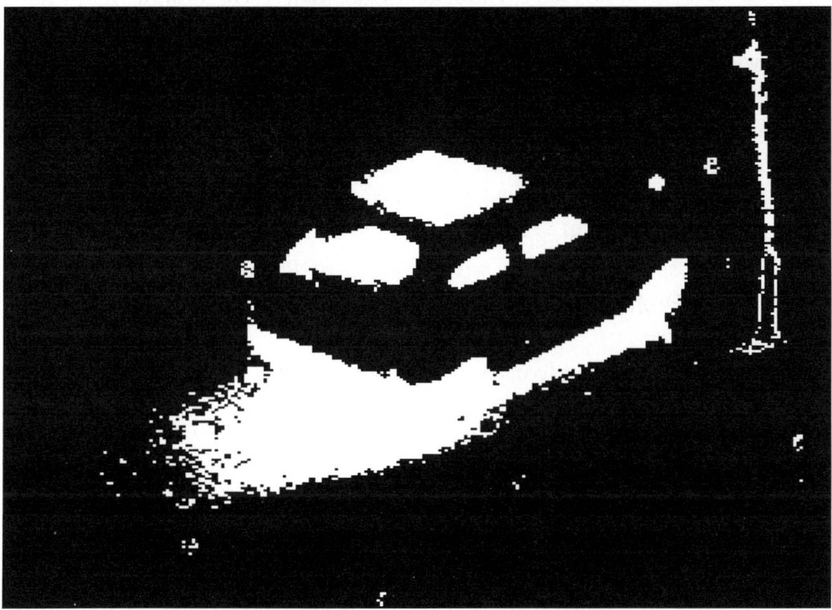

Fig. 9. Regions extracted by the understanding procedure in the car image. Some connected components have been filtered out thanks to context knowledge, kept separate from the generic one, and also the thresholds are adapted locally.

Above the context classes, a super-class must be defined for the instances of the same contexts according to different perceptual/sensor ranges. The sensor fusion tasks apply to this root class level. Inheritance applies for the context classes and the methods underneath, but the context causal graphs and influencing domains stay specific to each sensor.

4.3. *Comparisons*

A summary comparison of full object oriented design to the object oriented elements considered above, is presented in Table 2. But some comments are required.

Table 2. Summary comparison of full object oriented design and elements used here.

Attributes	Full OO Design	Current Image Understanding Environment
Objects/Classes	Yes	Yes
Inheritance	Full	Inheritance for methods
		No inheritance for instance variables
Encapsulation	Yes	No data in instances
		Methods exist only in class definitions
Last binding	Yes	Yes – inherent in Prolog's interpretive environment

An instantiation exists only within the predicate which created the object (with "new"). Thus we do not require here full object oriented design; this however is consistent with a formal object-oriented inheritance model such as [13].

Class inheritance is limited to methods; there are no instance variables *per se*. Furthermore, code is not actually encapsulated: objects, e.g. relating to the context, contain no code of their own, but forward messages to their class definitions. This type of behavior resembles "delegation" [16], but includes the message based inheritance presented in [13].

There is no loss of generality with respect to Prolog, as the class definitions are translated by Prolog into Prolog; inheritance is also implemented within Prolog [23,41,44,47].

Unification/backtracking/constraint satisfaction are fully applicable to class inheritances, especially for the context model, because of the object oriented modalities above.

The form of polymorphism presented here for context modeling is most flexible when the instances of influencing domains "Context-D", processes $\{p\}$, and possibly "context-object"-names, each strictly abide to a class tree structure. This holds if basically the image understanding context contains few context elements (i.e. few "Context-D" domains), but with a high variability within each class. This variability is well modeled by the subclasses, instances, and inheritance. Such an object oriented design is insufficient if the "Context-G" graphs are rich, with many arcs, labels, and loops all corresponding to contextual ambiguities.

5. Perceptual Context Modeling

5.1. *Perceptual Context Modeling*

This fourth approach is also covered by the model of Sec. 2, by a suitable joint selection of the topologies and of the causal structures in the context graphs "Context-G" and the influencing domains "Context-D".

Example: Perceptual noise filtering in images

Many image understanding tasks consist in removing the perceptual consequences of noise, as this interferes with the interpretation. Many noise removal algorithms rely on bandpass filtering of the gray levels, thus blurring or deleting or fragmenting, e.g. linear elements, such as the car element border lines in the example.

Context based modeling consists in representing the "influenced" process as a stochastic process, triggered by the local variations in gray values in the influencing domain "Context-D" around each pixel. This context model will be parametrized also by the orientation and curvature of edges or lines found in the influencing domain. Areas containing a lot of structure, with strong contrast between edges/lines and the background, have a higher gray value variance in local areas. This determines, by a context predicate, whether noise reduction by low-pass filtering is to be applied or not. The result is that noise can be reduced, while the edges in areas with prominent structures are kept sharp. By implementing separation of the context model and of the filter, noise removal filters can be designed with no regard to the structure of the image content.

5.2. *Ontologies*

One difficulty with perceptual context modeling is that, when this approach is used, it is often not clear what the categories, objects, attributes, entities and conceptual structures, are. This is what an ontology is about, i.e. about the study of the concepts and categories of the world. The understanding and semantic depth of an image in a domain depend on the richness of the ontology of that domain.

Most AI ontologies treat situations or states of the world as objects which can participate in relations; situations get changed by events and generate scripts. Underlying the ontologies are causal links which dictate the behavior: causal links are specialized relational links which indicate the propagation of change. The knowledge and mapping of the causal links driving perceptual changes is still not known (see however [50]).

6. Conclusions

Context modeling is of course difficult, but the time has come where the availability of context simulation models on one hand, and the urgent need for code sharing and reuse on the other hand, just simply impose the use of some still imperfect solutions. Until recently, there was little or no progress, just because of a lack of formal descriptions of the understanding task and of the context.

While the jury is still out on the specific forms of inheritance and polymorphism in object oriented design implementations, dynamic inheritance is clearly lacking in image understanding. By dynamic inheritance we mean allowing a method to change the inheritance specifications of the methods within an object. This is required to simplify the representation of context related physical phenomena and constraints, like changes in contrast, shape discontinuities, etc., and to be able to address perceptual cues better than now.

Furthermore, image understanding research should not ignore work on contexts in natural language [19,45]. In this field, a cohesive and coherent discourse relies on a three-tiered representation system based on linguistic and knowledge bases; semantic plausability relies finally on an overall discourse model, with the invocation of context specific handlers which:

- specify which types of interpretations are possible for each specific handler type;
- combine all information they get into a single text which reflects constraints on the plausability of a proposed interpretation.

This is very similar to the approach proposed here.

Finally, the extension of context modeling to sensor fusion should not necessarily we viewed as a "complication"; to the contrary, sensor diversity may often allow for disambiguation, provided the causal and physical processes are entirely known.

References

[1] A. Van Hentenryck, Constraint satisfaction in logic programming (CHIP) (MIT Press, Cambridge, MA, 1989).

[2] J. Cohen, Constraint logic programming languages, *J. ACM* **33**, 7 (1990) 52–67.

[3] J. Jaffar and J.-L. Lassez, Constraint logic programming, in *Proc. 14th ACM Symp. on Principles of Programming Languages (POPL-87)*, München, 1987, 111–119.

[4] W. Leler, *Constraint Programming Languages: Their Specification and Generation* (Addison Wesley, 1987).

[5] A. Colmerauer, An introduction to Prolog III, *J. ACM* **33**, 7 (1990) 67–90.

[6] P.-J. Gailly *et al.*, The Prince project and its applications, in G. Comyn and N. E. Fuchs (eds.), *Logic Programming in Action, Lecture Notes in Artificial Intelligence, Vol. 636* (Springer Verlag, Berlin, 1992) 55–63.

[7] D. H. Ballard and C. M. Brown, *Computer Vision* (Prentice-Hall, Englewood Cliffs, NJ, 1982).

[8] B. Bell and L. F. Pau, Contour tracking and corner detection in a logic programming environment, *IEEE Trans. Pattern Anal. Mach. Intell.* **12**, 9 (1990) 913–916.

[9] D. Cruse, C. J. Oddy and A. Wright, A segmented image data base for image analysis, *Proc. 7th Int. Conf. on Pattern Recognition*, Montreal, Canada (IEEE, 1984) 493–496.

[10] E. C. Freuder, Backtrack-free and backtrack-bounded search, in L. Kanal and V. Kumar (eds.), *Search in Artificial Intelligence* (Springer-Verlag, New York, NY, 1988) 343–369.

[11] F. Giannesini, H. Kanoui, R. Pasero and M. van Caneghem, *Prolog* (Addison Wesley, Reading, MA, 1986).

[12] A. Goldberg and D. Robson, *Smalltalk-80: The Language and Its Implementation* (Addison-Wesley, Reading, MA, 1983).

[13] B. Hailpern and Van Nguyen, A model for object-based inheritance, in B. Shriver and P. Wegner (eds.), *Research Directions in Object-Oriented Programming* (MIT Press, Cambridge, MA, 1987) 147–164.

[14] R. M. Haralick and G. L. Elliot, Increasing tree search efficiency for constraint satisfaction problems, *Artif. Intell. Journal* **14** (1980) 263-313.

[15] A. Huertas and R. Nevatia, Detecting buildings in aerial images, *Comput. Vision Graph. Image Process.* **41** (1988) 131–152.

[16] H. Lieberman, Using prototypical objects to implement shared behavior in object oriented systems, *Proc. ACM Conf. on Object Oriented Programming, Systems, Languages, and Applications*, Portland, OR, 1986, 214–223.

[17] S. Matwin and T. Pietrzykowski, Intelligent backtracking in plan-based deduction, *IEEE Trans. Pattern Anal. Mach. Intell.* **7**, 6 (1985) 682–692.

[18] D. M. McKeown, Jr., W. A. Harvey, Jr. and J. McDermott, Rule-based interpretation of aerial imagery, *IEEE Trans. Pattern Anal. Mach. Intell.* **7**, 5 (1985) 570–585.

[19] B. Neumann, Natural language description of time-varying scenes, in D. Waltz (ed.), *Advances in Natural Language Processes*, Vol. I (Morgan Kaufmann, 1984).

[20] L. F. Pau, Knowledge-based real-time change detection, target image tracking, and threat assessment, in A. K. C. Wong and A. Pugh (eds.), *Machine Intelligence and Knowledge Engineering for Robotic Applications, NATO ASI Series, Vol. F-33* (Springer Verlag, Berlin, 1987) 283–297.

[21] L. F. Pau, Knowledge representation for three-dimensional sensor fusion with context truth maintenance, in A. K. Jain (ed.), *Real Time Object Measurement and Classification* (Springer-Verlag, Berlin, 1988) 391–404.

[22] K. C. You and K. S. Fu, A syntactic approach to shape recognition using attribute grammars, *IEEE Trans. Syst. Man Cybern.* **9**, 6 (1979) 334–345.

[23] L. Leonardi, P. Mello and A. Natali, Prototypes in Prolog, *J. Object Oriented Programming* **2**, 3 (1989) 20–28.

[24] A. R. Rao and R. Jain, Knowledge representation and control in computer vision systems, *IEEE Expert*, Spring (1988) 64–79.

[25] L. F. Pau, Knowledge representation for sensor fusion, in *Proc. IFAC World Congress 1987* (Pergamon Press, Oxford, 1987).

[26] S. B. Pollard, J. E. W. Mayhew and J. P. Frisby, PMF: a stereo correspondence algorithm using a disparity gradient limit, *J. Perception* **14**, 449-470.

[27] R. A. Brooks, Model based 3-D interpretation of 2-D images, in *Proc. 7th Int. J. Conf. on Artificial Intelligence*, 1981, 619–623.

[28] L. Wes, R. Overbeck, E. Lusk and J. Boyle, *Automated Reasoning: Introduction and Applications* (Prentice Hall, Englewood Cliffs, NJ, 1984).

[29] L. Kitchen and A. Rosenfeld, Scene analysis using region-based constraint filtering, *Pattern Recogn.* **17**, 2 (1984) 189–203.

[30] Y. Ohta, *Knowledge Based Interpretation of Outdoor Natural Scenes* (Pitman Advanced Publishing Progr., 1985).

[31] J. Doyle, A truth maintenance system, *Artif. Intell. J.* **12** (1979) 231–272.

[32] J. De Kleer, Choices without backtracking, in *Proc. AAAI Nat. Conf. on Artificial Intelligence*, Aug. 1984.

[33] A. Rosenfeld et al., Comments on the Workshop on Goal-Directed Expert Vision Systems, *Comput. Vision Graph. Image Process.* **34**, 1 (1986) 98–110.

[34] Harbour change of activity analysis, AD 744332, NTIS, Springfield, VA, 1982.

[35] *Proc. DARPA Image Understanding Workshop*, Science Applications Report SAI-84-176-WA, or AD 130251, NTIS, Springfield, VA, June 1983.

[36] J. Ebbeni and A. Monfils (eds.), *Three-Dimensional Imaging, Proc. SPIE*, Vol. 402, Apr. 1983.

[37] N. Kazor, Target tracking based scene analysis, CAR-TR-88, CS-TR-1437, Univ. of Maryland, College Park, MD, Aug. 1984.

[38] B. Bell and L. F. Pau, Context knowledge and search control-issues in object oriented Prolog-based image understanding, *Pattern Recogn. Lett.* **13** (1992) 279–290.

[39] P. Coad and E. Yourdon, *Object Oriented Analysis* (Prentice Hall, Englewood Cliffs, NJ, 1991).

[40] A. Palaretti and P. Puliti, A Prolog approach to image segmentation, *J. Appl. Artif. Intell.* **3**, 4 (1990) 56–68.

[41] R. Knaus, Message passing in Prolog, *AI Expert*, May 21–27 (1990).

[42] D. T. Lawton, Image understanding environments, *Proc. IEEE* **76**, 8 (1988) 1036–1050.

[43] S.-S. Chen (ed.), *Image Understanding in Unstructured Environments* (World Scientific, Singapore, 1988).

[44] D. Pountain, Adding objects to Prolog, *BYTE*, Aug. (1990).

[45] S. Luperfoy and E. Rich, A computational model for the resolution of context-dependent references, MCC Technical report NL-068-92, MCC, Austin, TX, Mar. 1992.

[46] B.Jähne, *Digital Image Processing* (Springer Verlag, Berlin, 1991).

[47] B. Bell and L. F. Pau, Prolog object oriented embedded manager, Tech. Report, Technical University of Denmark, 21 Jul. 1989.

[48] G. Ciepel and T. Rogon, Background modelling in an object oriented, logic programming, image processing environment, Tech. Report, Technical University of Denmark, May 1990.

[49] L. F. Pau, *Sensor and Data Fusion* (Academic Press, NY, 1993).

[50] L. F. Pau, Behavioral knowledge in sensor and data fusion systems, *J. Robotic Syst.* **7**, 3 (1990) 295–308.

Appendix A. Object Oriented Definitions

A good introductory article and a more detailed glossary are found e.g. in [12,39].

Class: A set of elements sharing the same behavior and structure characteristics which are represented in a "class definition". A class which adopts the behavior and structure of another class, but specializes some characteristics to form a subcategory, is a "subclass".

Constraints: Predicates or parameters which control goal evaluation and backtracking so that the resulting object classification or scene understanding is consistent with the known physical characteristics of the object or class.

Context: A consistent subset of facts derived during the evaluation of a higher level goal. Context knowledge includes predicates to establish a context, i.e. to evaluate a top-level image understanding goal, and constraints to enforce consistency.

Instance: An element created from the descriptions in a class definition. An image object is classified when it is determined to be an instance of a class.

Method: A segment of code appearing within a class definition, which can be invoked by sending a message to any instance of that class to evaluate the named method.

Appendix B. Constraint Logic Programming

Logic is a powerful way of representing problems. Constraints appearing in logic programming are tests used for checking a solution. With CLP (Constraint Logic Programming), the constraints are part of the description of the problem, i.e. in this chapter. It is the image understanding task. The way they are used allows for a more efficient search for solutions. Further details on various CLP concepts and implementations are found in [1–6].

B.1. *Syntax*

A problem is represented in a CLP by a set of clauses (or rules), like in logic programming languages like Prolog [11]. However, the syntax of the clauses is different. The common part is that a clause consists of a term, the head of the clause, and a list of terms (which can be empty) in the body of the clause; in both cases it means "the head term is true if the body terms are true". The difference with respect to logic programming languages is that CLP clauses can also contain a list of constraints (see next section), and in this case the meaning becomes: "the head term is true if the body terms are true and the constraints are not violated".

B.2. *Constraints*

Constraints apply to terms, boolean values, identifiers, lists and trees, numbers (integers, rationals and/or reals, depending on the CLP language used). Constraints are equations or inequations or logicals or fixed lists. The variables in the constraints behave like unknown quantities in mathematical equations:

Examples: $X = X/2 + 1$, implies $X = 2$;

$\qquad\quad$ $X = X + 1$, has no solution;

$\qquad\quad$ $Y = X + 1$, means that, if the two variables X, Y are unbound, they belong to one line:

$\qquad\quad$ $A \Rightarrow B\ C$, says that A is true if B and C are;

$\qquad\quad$ $0 < T < 3X/4 + 5Y$, defines a region for the unbound variable T.

Execution efficiency depends very much on the time at which the constraint is treated, and on the algorithm used for testing the satisfiability of systems of constraints, in what is called the constraint solver.

B.3. *Resolution*

The resolution mechanism in CLP languages is based both on a constraint solving mechanism, which is in charge of testing if the constraints can have at least one solution, and upon a unification algorithm which attempts to prove each term of the goal by replacing it by an equivalent set of terms and constraints, as they appear in a clause. At each step of the attempt to prove a logical goal, the constraint solver must decide if there is at least a solution for the set of constraints on the variables which appear in the terms considered.

The mechanism is as follows: given a set of variables W (appearing in the query), a list of terms $t0, t1, \dots, tn$, and a list of currently satisfiable constraints S, two states are defined:

(1): $(W, t0, t1, \dots, tn, S)$

(2): $(W, s1, \ldots, sm, t1, \ldots, tn, (S \cup R \cup (s0 = t0)))$,   with $\cup =$ "union"

An inference step consists of making a transition from the state (1) to the state (2) by applying the program rewriting rule (r):

$r: s0 \leftarrow s1, \ldots, sm, R$

in which the (si)'s are terms and R is the set of constraints specified by the CLP rule. The new state after inference becomes (2) if the new set of constraints $(S \cup R \cup (s0 = t0))$ is satisfiable; it has at least one possible solution. Here, $(s0 = t0)$ represents the set of constraints applied to variables so that $s0$ and $t0$ become identical. If the new set of constraints is not satisfiable, another rule has to be tried in the CLP program to attempt to replace the term.

There are two types of non-determinisms that arise in the sequential interpretation of such CLP programs: the first is the selection of the term in the list of terms that will be processed first, and the second is the choice of an applicable rule in the CLP program.

The constraint solver must be incremental to minimize the computational effort required to check if the constraints remain satisfiable or not. If the set S of constraints has solutions, adding a new set of constraints R will not require to solve for $(S \cup R)$, but to transform the solutions of S into solutions of $(S \cup R)$.

Handbook of Pattern Recognition and Computer Vision, pp. 769–801
Eds. C. H. Chen, L. F. Pau and P. S. P. Wang
© 1993 World Scientific Publishing Company

CHAPTER 4.4

POSITION ESTIMATION TECHNIQUES FOR AN AUTONOMOUS MOBILE ROBOT – A REVIEW

RAJ TALLURI and J. K. AGGARWAL

Computer and Vision Research Center, Department of Electrical Engineering
University of Texas at Austin, Austin, Texas 78712, USA

In this paper, we review various methods and techniques for estimating the position and pose of an autonomous mobile robot. The techniques vary depending on the kind of environment in which the robot navigates, the known conditions of the environment, and the type of sensors with which the robot is equipped. The methods studied so far are broadly classified into four categories, landmark-based methods, methods using trajectory integration and dead reckoning, methods using a standard reference pattern, and methods using *a priori* knowledge of a world model which is matched the sensor data for position estimation. Each of these methods is considered and its relative merits and drawbacks are discussed.

Keywords: Autonomous navigation, mobile robots, position estimation, self-location, landmarks, world model.

1. Introduction

Autonomous mobile robots are one of the important areas of application of computer vision. The advantages of a vehicle that can navigate without human intervention are many and varied, ranging from providing access to hazardous industrial environments to battlefield surveillance vehicles. A number of issues and problems must be addressed in the design of an autonomous mobile robot, from the basic scientific issues to state-of-the-art engineering techniques. The tasks required for successful autonomous navigation by a mobile robot can be broadly classified as (1) sensing the environment; (2) building its own representation of the environment; (3) locating itself with respect to the environment; and (4) planning and executing efficient routes in this environment.

It is advantageous for a robot to use different types of sensors and sensing modalities to perceive its environment, since information available from one source can be used to better interpret information from other sources, and can be synergically fused to get a much more meaningful representation. Some of the different sensor modalities considered by previous researchers are visual sensors (both monocular and binocular stereo), infrared sensors, ultrasonic sensors, and laser range finders.

769

Building a world model also termed *map-making* is an important problem in mobile robot navigation. The type of spatial representation system used by a robot should provide a way to consistently incorporate the newly sensed information into the existing world model. It should also provide the necessary information and procedures for estimating the position and pose of the robot in the environment. Information to do path-planning, obstacle avoidance and other navigational tasks must also be easily extractable from the built world model. Section 3 presents a review of various map-making strategies and their associated position estimation methods.

Determining the position and the pose of a robot in its environment is one of the basic requirements for autonomous navigation. In this discussion, *position* refers to the location of the robot on the ground plane and the *pose* refers to the orientation of the robot. We use the term *position estimation* to refer to the estimation of both position and pose. The problem of self-location has received considerable attention, and many techniques have been proposed to address it. These techniques vary significantly, depending on the kind of environment in which the robot is to navigate, the known conditions of the environment, and the type of sensors with which the robot is equipped. Most mobile robots are equipped with wheel encoders that can be used to estimate the robot's position at every instant; however, due to wheel slippage and quantization effects, these estimates of the robot's position contain errors. These errors build up and can grow without bounds as the robot moves, and the position estimate becomes more and more uncertain. So, most mobile robots use an additional form of sensing, such as vision or range, to aid the position estimation process.

In this paper we review various techniques studied for estimating the position and pose of an autonomous mobile robot. Broadly, we classify the position estimation techniques into four categories, landmark-based methods, methods using trajectory integration and dead reckoning, methods using a standard reference pattern, and methods using *a priori* knowledge of a world model which is matched to the sensor data for position estimation. These four methods are briefly described below.

In landmark-based methods, typically the robot has a list of stored landmark positions in its memory. It then senses these landmarks using the onboard sensors and computes the position and pose using the stored and the sensor information. Section 2 reviews the different approaches using landmarks for self-location. In the second type of position estimation technique, the position and pose of a mobile robot are estimated by integrating over its trajectory and by dead reckoning, i.e. the robot maintains an estimate of its current location and pose at all times and, as it moves along, updates the estimate by dead reckoning. Section 3 reviews these methods. A third method of estimating the position and pose of the mobile robot accurately is to place standard patterns in known locations in the environment. Once the robot detects these patterns, the position of the robot can be estimated from the known location of the pattern and its geometry. Different researchers have used different kinds of patterns or marks, and the geometry of their methods and the associated techniques for position estimation vary accordingly. These methods are discussed in Section 4. Finally, some researchers consider the position estimation problem using *a priori* information about the environment in which the robot is to navigate, i.e. a *preloaded world model* is given. The approach is to sense the environment using onboard sensors and to match these sensory observations to the preloaded world model to arrive at an estimate of the position and pose of the robot with a reduced uncertainty. Section 5 presents a review of the different methods studied in solving these issues.

Once the robot has the capability to sense its environment, build a representation of it, and estimate its position accurately, then navigational tasks such as path-planning and obstacle avoidance can be performed.

2. Landmark-Based Methods

Using landmarks for position estimation is a popular approach. The robot uses the knowledge of its approximate location to locate the landmarks in the environment. Once these landmarks are identified and the range/attitude of these relative to the robot is measured, in general, the position and pose of the robot can be triangulated from these measurements with a reduced uncertainty.

Landmarks used for position estimation can include natural or man-made features in the outdoor environment, such as the tops of buildings, roof edges, hilltops, etc., or can be identifiable beacons placed at known positions to structure the environment. One basic requirement of the landmark-based methods is that the robot be able to identify and locate the landmarks, which is not an easy task. The position estimation methods based on landmarks vary significantly depending upon the sensors used (e.g. range or visual sensors); the type of landmarks (i.e. whether they are point sources or lines etc.); and the number of landmarks needed. Case [4] summarizes the landmark-based techniques quite well and presents a new method, called the *running fix* method, for position estimation. Case classifies the sensor data for navigation purposes as either angular or range type inputs. In general, any combination of two of these is sufficient to yield a fix.

In Fig. 1, for instance, the angle between the x-axis and each of the two landmarks is used to construct two lines of position (LOP) which intersect at the robot's location.

In Fig. 2, arcs are struck at the measured range corresponding to the two landmarks. The intersection points of these two arcs yield two possible positions for the robot, thus requiring either correlation with an estimated position or the use of a third landmark to resolve the ambiguity.

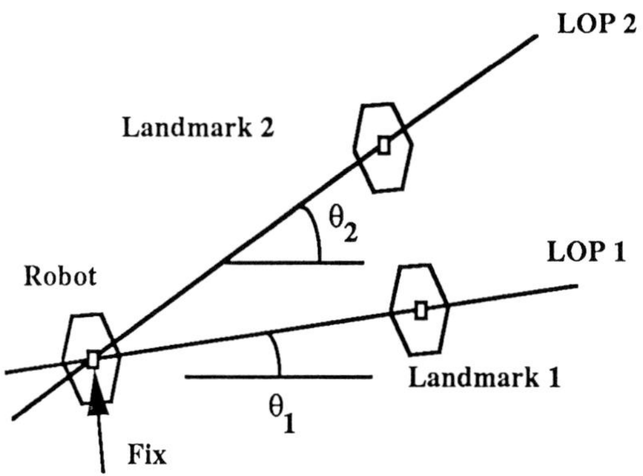

Fig. 1. Two landmarks and lines of position.

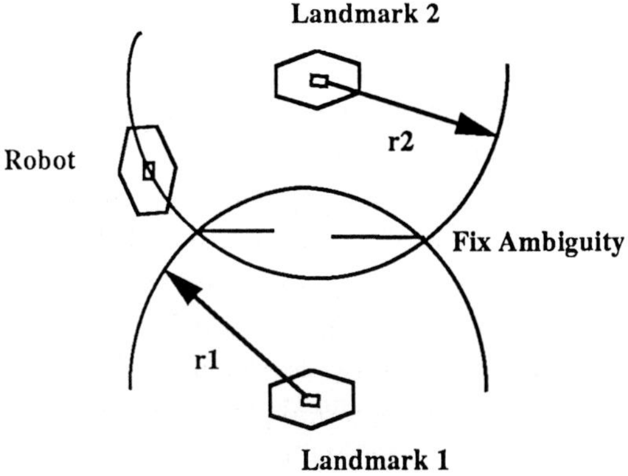

Fig. 2. Ranges from two landmarks.

A range and an angle may also be used, as in Fig. 3. This requires only one landmark, but requires either multiple sensors or a sensor capable of measuring both range and attitude. The angle measurements can be either absolute or relative. Absolute angle measurements require the robot to maintain an internal reference using a gyrocompass or an inertial sensor. Any error in this reference usually affects the position estimation accuracy. Case also presents a method called the *running fix* for use in areas with a low density of landmarks. The underlying principle of the technique in that an angle or range to a landmark obtained at a time $t - 1$ can be used at a time t. To do this the cumulative measurement vector recorded since the reading was obtained is added to the

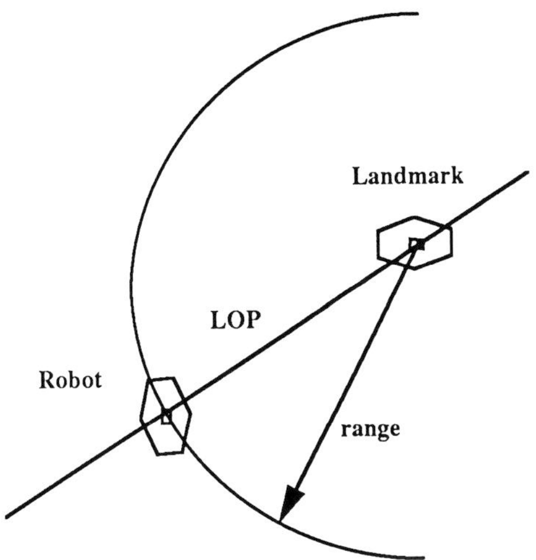

Fig. 3. LOP and range from one landmark.

position vector of the landmark, thus creating a virtual landmark. Case presents experimental results using an ARCTEC Gemini mobile robot with an infrared beacon/detector pair.

Clare D. McGillem et al. [35] also describe an infra-red location system for autonomous vehicle navigation. They present an efficient method of resection for position estimation using three infrared beacons to structure the environment and an optical scanner on the robot capable of measuring the angles between a pair of beacons. They also discuss the sensitivity of the method to errors. They point out that by judiciously placing the beacons in the environment, regions of high error sensitivity can be minimized or avoided. They demonstrate the feasibility of their approach by implementing it on an inexpensive experimental system. Nasr and Bhanu [42] present a new approach to landmark recognition based on the perception, reasoning, and expectation (PREACTE) paradigm for autonomous mobile robot navigation. They describe an expectation driven, knowledge-based landmark recognition system that uses *a priori* map and perceptual knowledge. Bloom [2] also describes a landmark-based system for mobile robot navigation that uses a grid-based terrain map (MAP), a landmark database, and a landmark visibility map (LVM). Bloom describes the landmarks by one or more of three distinctive attribute sets: a color attribute set, a textural attribute set, and a 2-D geometry attribute set. He then describes the contents of these attribute sets and shows how the vision system uses these attributes to recognize the landmarks.

Sugihara [47,48] presents algorithms for the position estimation of a mobile robot equipped with a single visual camera. He considers the problem of a robot given a map of a room in which it navigates. Vertical edges are extracted from the images taken by the robot's camera, with the optical axis parallel to the floor. The points from where the vertical edges can arise are assumed to be given. Sugihara then considers two classes of problems. In the first class, all vertical edges are identical, and he searches for the point where the image is taken by establishing a correspondence between the vertical edges in the images and those in the map. In the second class of problems, the vertical edges are not distinguishable from each other and the exact directions in which the edges are seen are not given; only the order in which they are found in the image is given. The problems are considered mainly from the point of view of computational complexity.

In the case where the vertical lines are distinguishable from one another, Sugihara shows that if we establish a correspondence between three image points and three poles (vertical lines) and measure the angles between the rays joining the image points to the lines, we can uniquely determine the camera's position.

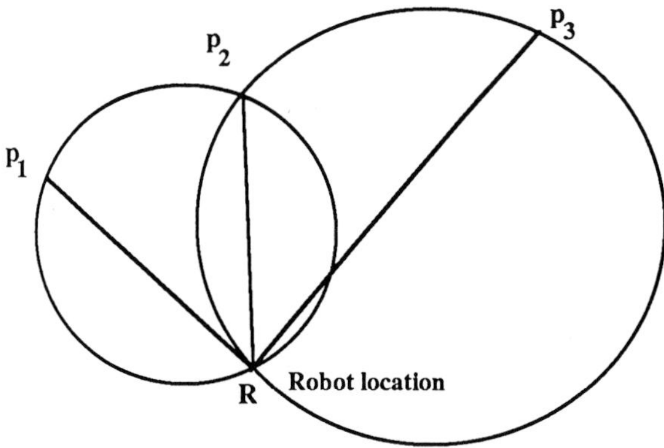

Fig. 4. The unique camera position determined by three rays and the corresponding mark points.

In Fig. 4, p_1, p_2, and p_3 are the three poles and R is the robot's position. In the case involving four poles, the solution is not necessarily unique. So, in general, when we have k poles and, hence, k rays, Sugihara suggests using the first three rays, r_1, r_2, r_3 to determine the position R and then using the other rays to check if the solution R is correct. Now, in the general case when the k lines are not distinguishable from one another, the suggested approach is: First, choose and fix any four rays, say r_1, r_2, r_3, r_4, and next, for any quadruplet (p_i, p_j, p_k, p_l) of marks (vertical lines), solve for the position on the assumption that r_1, r_2, r_3, r_4 correspond to (p_i, p_j, p_k, p_l), respectively. Then repeat for the $n(n-1)(n-2)(n-3)$ different quadruplets for a consistent solution. The above naive procedure can solve for the position in $O(n^4)$ time. He then gives a less naive algorithm for the position estimation, with n identical marks, which runs in $O(n^3 \log n)$ time with $O(n)$ space or in $O(n^3)$ time with $O(n^2)$ space. Sugihara also considers variations of this problem of n indistinguishable vertical lines, such as: (1) the existence of spurious edges; (2) the existence of opaque walls; (3) linearly arranged marks; and

(4) a case in which the robot has a compass. He discusses the possible solutions and simplifications of the original algorithm to these special cases. The case in which the marks are distinguishable from one another but the directions are inaccurate is considered in the second part of the paper. He shows that this case is essentially the same as the problem of forming a region which generates a *circular scan list* in a given order.

Krotkov [25] essentially followed Sugihara's work of localizing a mobile robot navigating on a flat surface with a single camera using the vertical lines in the image plane as landmarks. He formulates the problem as a search in a tree of interpretations (pairings of landmark directions and landmark points). The algorithm he uses is the naive algorithm, discussed by Sugihara, that runs in $O(n^4)$ time. In his work, Krotkov also considers the errors in the ray directions and, using the worst-case analysis, comes up with bounds on the position and pose estimated using this method of localization. He shows that in the case when the angles of the rays are erroneous, the robot position estimated lies not on one point but in a region of possible points, R (see Fig. 5).

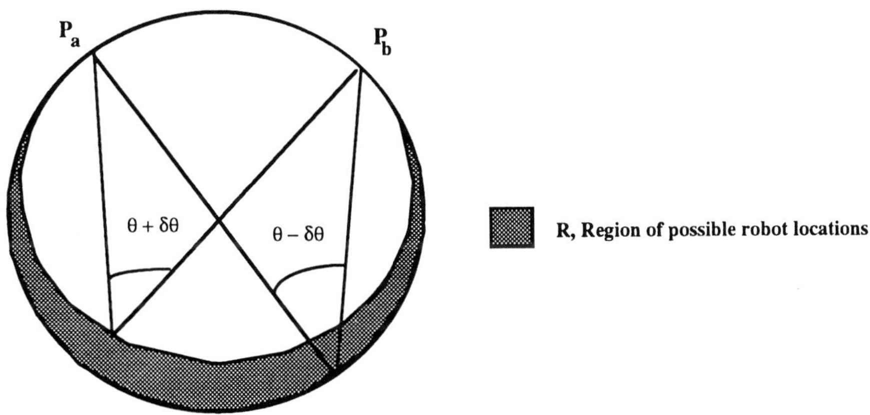

Fig. 5. Possible locations given by noisy rays.

He also presents simulation results with random ray errors and worst-case ray errors and makes the following observations from his analysis: (1) the number of solution poses computed by the algorithm depends significantly on the number k of angular observations and the observation uncertainty $\delta\phi$; and (2) the distribution of solution errors, given angular observation errors that are either uniformly or normally distributed, is approximately Gaussian, whose variance is a function of $\delta\phi$. Krotkov also presents real data results using a CCD imagery.

Most of the landmark-based approaches considered above suffer from the disadvantages of : (1) assuming the availability of landmarks in the scene around the robot; (2) depending on the visibility and the ability to recognize these landmarks from the image to estimate the range/attitude to them from the current location; (3) requiring an approximate starting location to check for the landmarks; and (4) needing a database of landmarks in the area to look for in the image.

2.1. *Photogrammetric Methods*

Photogrammetry generally deals with the mathematical representation of the geometrical relations between physical objects in three-dimensional space based on their images recorded on a two-dimensional medium. Over the years, photogrammetry has been routinely used in aerial photography, cartography, and remote sensing [61]. One of the problems of cartography is to determine the location of an airborne camera from which a photograph was taken by measuring the positions of a number of known ground objects or landmarks on the photograph. This problem is sometimes known as the *camera calibration problem*. The orientation and position of the camera in the object space are traditionally called the camera's *exterior orientation parameters* as opposed to its *interior orientation parameters*, which are independent of the co-ordinate system of the ground objects. The interior orientation parameters include such elements as the camera's effective focal length, lens distortion, decentering, image plane scaling, and optical axis orientation. These parameters generally do not vary as much, or as quickly, as the exterior orientation parameters and need not be updated at image sampling rates. For nonmetric cameras, standard off-line calibration procedures are available for determining the elements of the interior calibration.

The problem of estimating the position and pose of an autonomous mobile robot is, in essence, similar to the camera exterior orientation problem in photogrammetry. However, since the robot is ground-based and has position encoders and other sensors on it, these can be used to constrain the possible orientation and pose. In general, the exterior camera orientation problem involves solving for six degrees of freedom, three rotational and three translational. Traditionally, in single camera photogrammetry, by observing the object's feature points on the image, it is possible to solve the exterior orientation calibration problem using a traditional method known as *space resection* [12]. The method is based on the perspective geometry of a simplified camera model, derived from pinhole optics, in which the image of each feature point is projected onto the image plane by a ray connecting the feature point with the pinhole lens. This collinearity condition results mathematically in two nonlinear equations for each feature point. Hence at least three non-collinear points are required to solve for the six degrees of freedom. These collinearity equations are linearized and solved in an iterative fashion. When the images are noisy, more than three points can be used, with least squares criteria, to take advantage of data smoothing. These methods are now standard in the photogrammetry literature [61]. Iterative solutions are generally more computationally demanding, so that simplifying assumptions are usually necessary for real-time applications. Over the years, a number of alternate methods have been proposed in an effort to improve the efficiency of the camera calibration procedure. Some of these are reviewed below.

Szczepanski [49] surveys nearly 80 solutions, beginning with one by Schrieber of Karlsruhe in 1879. The first robust solution in computer vision literature is by Fischler and Bolles [15]. They studied the exterior calibration problem in connection with the concept of *random sample consensus* (RANSAC), a methodology proposed for processing large data sets with gross errors or outliers. They argue against the classical techniques of parameter estimation, such as least squares, that optimize (according to a specified objective function) the fit of a functional description (model) to *all* the presented data. Their argument is that the above techniques are usually averaging techniques that rely on the smoothing assumption, which is not usually valid when the data has outliers or gross errors. The RANSAC paradigm they present can be stated as follows :

Given a model that requires a minimum of n data points to instantiate its free parameters and a set of data points P such that the number of points in P is greater than n, randomly select a subset $S1$ of n data points from P and instantiate the model. Use the instantiated model $M1$ to determine the subset $S1^*$ of points in P that are within some error tolerance of $M1$. The set $S1^*$ is called the consensus set of $S1$.

If $\#(S1^*)$ is greater than some threshold t, which is a function of the estimate of the number of gross errors in P, use $S1^*$ to compute (possibly using least squares) a new model $M1^*$.

If $\#(S1^*)$ is less that t, randomly select a new subset $S2$ and repeat the above process. If, after some predetermined number of trials, no consensus set with t or more members has been found, either solve the model with the largest consensus set found or terminate in failure.

Fischler and Bolles then discuss methods to determine the three unspecified parameters in the RANSAC paradigm: (1) the error tolerance, (2) the number of subsets to try, and (3) the threshold t. They then present a new solution to the Location Determination Problem (LDP) based on the RANSAC paradigm. They reduce the LDP problem to the *perspective_n_point* problem, i.e. if we can compute the lengths of the rays from three landmarks to the center of perspective projection, then we can directly solve for the location and orientation of the camera. They obtain solutions in a closed form for three and four coplanar feature points; the latter, as well as the case of six points *in general position*, are demonstrated to be unique. Unfortunately, these analytic solutions cannot be extended to the general case involving more than four points. Nevertheless, the paper does demonstrate graphically the existence of multiple solutions with four or five noncoplanar points. Beyond these qualitative observations, however, no conclusion was offered regarding the existence and uniqueness in the general case. The four point solution has been implemented in a power line inspection system [29].

Ganapathy [19] presents a noniterative, analytic technique for recovering the six exterior orientation parameters as well as four of the interior orientation parameters (two for scaling and two for the location of the origin in the image plane). His method assumes that the *perspective transformation matrix* relating the world model and image plane points is determined by experimental means. Ganapathy essentially presents an algorithm to decompose the given transformation into the various camera parameters that constitute the components of the matrix. He linearizes the system of equations represented by the transformation matrix by increasing the number of unknowns. He then adds additional constraints, drawn from the properties of the rotation matrix, to solve these systems of equations. The algorithm is independent of the number or distribution of the feature points, since this information has already been distilled into the transformation matrix. Although the matrix may be obtained through experimental means, it is not known whether the effort will be feasible for operation in real time. Kumar and Hanson [28] report that their implementation of the method is extremely susceptible to noise, and suggest that the susceptibility may be due to the nonlinear least square minimization used, where it is assumed that all the parameters are linearly independent while they actually are not.

Tsai [58] presents a two stage technique for the calibration of both the exterior and interior parameters of the camera that is probably the most complete camera calibration method proposed so far. The interior parameters include the effective focal length, the radial lens distortion, and the image scanning parameters. The basic idea used is to reduce the dimensionality of the parameter space by finding a constraint or equation which is only a function of the subset of the calibration parameters. Tsai introduces a constraint called the *radial alignment constraint*, which is a function of only the relative rotation and translation (except for the z component) between the camera and the calibration points. Although the constraint is a nonlinear function of the above mentioned calibration parameters (called Group I parameters), a simple and efficient way exists for computing them. The rest of the calibration parameters (called Group II parameters) are computed with normal projective equations. A good initial estimate of the Group II parameters can be obtained by ignoring the lens distortion and using simple linear equations in two unknowns. The precise values for these Group II parameters can then be computed in one or two iterations, minimizing the perspective equation error. One of the limitations of this technique is that although the method calls for a minimum of five coplanar feature points (seven in the non-coplanar case), a much larger number is required for accuracy (60 points were used in the experiment). Furthermore, restrictions in the relative positions between the objects and the camera exist. For instance, the plane containing the feature points must not be exactly parallel to the image plane of the camera. Although these conditions can be easily arranged in a laboratory environment, they cannot be guaranteed to hold in a real life operating environment for a mobile robot. Finally, the range parameter (Group II) must still be generated by a nonlinear optimization procedure (specified only as a steepest descent), the choice of which could have a major influence on the efficiency of the algorithm.

Horaud et al. [21] consider the perspective-4-point problem. They derive an analytic solution for the case of four non-coplanar points, namely a biquadratic polynomial in one unknown. Roots of such an equation can be found in closed form or by an iterative method. Finding a solution for four non-coplanar points is equivalent to finding a solution to a pencil of three non-coplanar lines: The three lines share one of the four points. The authors show the various line and point configurations that are amenable to solving the P4P problem.

Liu, Huang, and Faugeras [31] present a new method for determining the camera location using straight line correspondences. Since the lines can be created from given points, the method can be used for point correspondences also. They show that the rotation matrix and the translation vector can be solved for separately. Both linear and nonlinear algorithms are presented for estimating the rotation. The linear method needs eight line correspondences or six point correspondences, while the nonlinear method needs three line or point correspondences. For the translation vector, the method needs three line correspondences or two point correspondences and the algorithm is linear. The authors argue that since the nonlinear methods need fewer correspondences and have a wide convergence range, they may be preferable in practical problems. The constraint used by Liu, Huang, and Faugeras is that the 3-D lines in the camera coordinate system must lie on the projection plane formed by the corresponding image line and the optical center. Using this fact the constraints of rotation can be separated from those of translation. They suggest two methods to solve for the rotation constraint. In the first, they represent the rotation as an orthonormal matrix and the device as an eigen-value solution. However, they do not enforce the six orthonormality constraints for an orthonormal matrix. The second method represents rotation by Euler angles and is a nonlinear iterative solution obtained by linearizing the problem about the current estimate by the output parameters. The translation constraint is solved by a linear least-squares method.

Kumar [27] argues that the decomposition of the solution into the two stages of solving first for rotation and then for translation does not use the set of constraints effectively. His argument is that since the rotation and translation constraints, when used separately, are very weak constraints, even small errors in the rotation stage become amplified into large errors in the translation stage. This, he says, is particularly true in the case of an autonomous mobile robot in an outdoor environment, where the landmark distances from the camera are large. He suggests solving for both the rotation and translation matrices simultaneously to achieve better noise immunity. He uses the same constraints as Liu, Huang, and Faugeras but a different nonlinear technique. The technique he uses is one adapted from Horn [22] to solve the problem of relative orientation. Kumar presents two algorithms, R_then_T and R_and_T. The former solves for the rotation first and then for the translation using the rotation matrix. The latter solves for both rotation and translation simultaneously. He presents experimental results which show that R_and_T performs better in all cases. In addition, he also develops a mathematical analysis of the uncertainty measure, which relates the variance in the output parameters to the noise present in the input parameters. For the analysis, he assumes that that there is no noise in the 3-D model data and that the only input noise occurs in the image data.

To handle the problem of outliers or errors in the data and landmark correspondences, Kumar and Hanson [28] present a technique that performs quite well even in the presence of up to 49.9% outliers or gross errors. The work is basically an extension of their previous work [27]. They present an algorithm called *Med_R_and_T* which minimizes the median of the square of the error over all lines, or the LMS (least median of squares) estimate. The outliers can be arbitrarily large. The algorithm is based on the robust algorithm by Rosseeuw [45]. LMS algorithms have been proven to have a 49.9% breakdown point.

Haralick et al. [20] summarize the various cases of the position estimation problem using point data. They consider the pose estimation problem to involve, essentially, the estimation of the object position and orientation relative to a model reference frame or relative to the object position and orientation at a previous time using a camera sensor or a range sensor. They divide the problem into four cases, depending on the type of model and sensor data: (1) 2-D model data and 2-D sensor data, (2) 3-D model data and 3-D sensor data, (3) 3-D model data and 2-D sensor data, and (4) two sets of 2-D sensor data.

All data considered is point data, and the correspondence between the model and sensor data is assumed. The 2-D sensor data is usually the camera perspective projection. The 3-D sensor data refers to range data. The authors refer to Case 3 as *absolute orientation* and Case 4 as *relative orientation*. Case 4 occurs in multi-camera imagery or time-varying imagery.

Haralick et al. present a solution to each of the above four problems and characterize their performance under varying noise conditions. They argue for robust estimation procedures in machine vision, since all machine vision feature extractors, recognizers, and matchers seem to make occasional errors which are indeed blunders. Their thesis is that the least square estimators can be made robust under blunders by converting the estimation procedure to an iterative, reweighted least squares procedure, where the weight for each observation depends on the residual error and its redundancy number. So, they first find the form of the least-square solution, establish their performance as a baseline reference, put the solution technique in an iterative reweighted form, and, finally, evaluate the performance using non-normal noise, such as slash noise. The least-squares solution for both the 2-D–2-D and the 3-D–3-D cases are constrained to produce rotation matrices guaranteed to be orthonormal.

Yuan [60] presents a general method for determining the 3-D position and orientation of an object relative to a camera based on a 2-D image of known feature points located on the object. The problem is identical to the camera exterior calibration problem. In contrast to the conventional approaches, however, the method described here does not make use of the collinearity condition, i.e. the condition of the pinhole camera and the perspective projection. Instead, the algebraic structure of the problem is fully exploited to arrive at a solution which is independent of the configuration of the feature points. Although the method is applicable to any number of feature points, Yuan says that no more than five points are needed from a numeric stand point and, typically, three or four points suffice. A necessary condition for the existence of the solution is presented and also a rigorous proof for the uniqueness of the solution in the case of four coplanar points. He shows with simulation results that in the case of four feature points, non-coplanar configurations generally outperform the coplanar feature point configurations, in terms of robustness, in the presence of image noise.

In a more recent work, Chen [6] describes a polynomial solution to the pose estimation problem that does not require an *a priori* estimate of the robot location, using line-to-plane correspondences. He describes the situations when such a problem arises. In the case of a mobile robot, the lines are the 2-D image features and the planes are the projection planes joining these lines to the 3-D world model features. As do Liu et al. [31], Chen also solves for the rotations first and then for the translations. The crux of the approach is that it converts a problem with three unknowns (the three rotation angles) into one that has two unknowns by transforming the co-ordinate system into a *canonical configuration*. The two unknowns are then computed by evaluating the roots of an eighth degree polynomial using an iterative method. Chen also presents closed form solutions for orthogonal, co-planar and parallel feature configurations. He also derives the necessary and sufficient conditions under which the line-to-plane pose determination problem can be solved.

3. Trajectory Integration and Dead Reckoning

In this section, we consider techniques for estimating the position and pose of a mobile robot by integrating over its trajectory and dead reckoning, i.e. the robot maintains an estimate of its current location and pose at all times and, as it moves along, updates the estimate by dead reckoning. In order to compute an accurate trajectory, the robot detects features from the sensory observations in one of the positions and these are used to form the world model. As the robot moves, these features are again detected, and correspondence is established between the new and the old features and the trajectory of the robot is computed. These techniques do not rely on the existence of landmarks and the robot's ability to identify them. However, to successfully implement such techniques a fundamental problem of environment perception and modeling must be addressed. Indeed, the model of the environment and the location model are the two basic data for position estimation, path planning, and all other navigation tasks involving interaction between the robot and its environment.

3.1. *Spatial Representation*

Using preloaded maps and absolute referencing systems can be impractical because they constrain the robot's navigation to a limited, static, and structured environment. In this section we survey the various approaches for map making and position estimation using trajectory integration and dead reckoning and evaluate their relative merits. The various approaches are influenced by the environment in which the robot navigates and the type of sensing used. Some approaches try to reason away errors and uncertainties to simplify the map-making process, while others take explicit account of errors and uncertainties using either static error factors or stochastic approaches that use probability distributions to model the errors. Most of the methods deal with an indoor factory or office-type environment made up of walls, corridors, and other man-made obstacles in which the robot navigates. Map-making in an outdoor scenario is a much more complex problem which relies on the existence of landmarks and digital elevation maps of the area.

The different methods of mobile robot map-making studied so far are quite varied and differ chiefly in terms of:

- The environment in which the mobile robot is to navigate. The map-making strategies for an indoor office type robot differ significantly from those of an outdoor terrain autonomous land vehicle.
- The type of world representation (either 2-D or 3-D). Most methods consider a 2-D representation or a *floor map* type approach. Since the mobile robot is essentially interested only in obstacle avoidance and path planning, a map of the vacant/occupied areas of the floor should suffice for these tasks.
- The types of sensors used. To a certain extent, the sensing modality affects the mapping strategies used. Typically, all mobile robots use some kind of range sensor. If a passive range sensor such as binocular stereo is used, the map so constructed will usually be sparse and feature-based. On the other hand, a laser range finder gives dense, high resolution depth estimates, which affect the mapping strategy differently. Sonar-based range finding techniques give less accurate and hence more uncertain depth estimates, so the map-making technique used should have the capability to deal with these uncertain readings.
- The navigational tasks to be accomplished by the robot. Most mobile robots consider tasks such as position estimation, obstacle avoidance, and path planning.

Keeping in view the above differences, map making approaches can be broadly classified into the following four types: (1) object feature-based methods; (2) graph-based approaches; (3) certainty grid-based approaches; and (4) qualitative methods These categories are not exacting, since some approaches do not fit into any of the categories and some have properties of more than one approach. However, such a classification may help put things in a better perspective.

3.2. *Object Feature-Based Methods*

In these methods, object features detected from the sensory observations in one of the robot's positions are used to form the world model. As the robot moves, these features are again detected, and correspondence is established between the new and the old features. Usually the motion of the robot is known to a certain degree of accuracy as given by its position sensors. These motion estimates are then used to predict the occurrence of the new positions for the features in the world model. The prediction is then used as an aid to limit the search space and to establish a correspondence between the detected features and those already in the current world model. A mechanism to consistently update the world model is also provided when new features are detected.

One significant advantage of the object feature-based methods is that after the position sensors are used to establish correspondence, the motion parameters of the robot between the old and the new positions can be solved for explicitly. The solution provides a much more accurate estimate of the robot's position. The loop then continues, and the world model is continuously updated. The type of sensing used is typically stereo triangulation or other types of visual sensing [38,39,33,43]. Crowley [8] uses a ring of 24 sonar sensors for a similar paradigm.

Moravec's *Cart* [38] was one of the first attempts at autonomous mobile robot navigation using a stereo pair of cameras. He defines an *interest operator* to locate the features in a given image. Essentially, the interest operator picks regions that are a local maxima of a directional variance and uses these to select a relatively uniform scattering of good features over the image. A coarse to fine correlation strategy is used to establish correspondence between the features selected by the interest operator between different frames.

The Cart uses a unique variable baseline stereo mechanism called *slider stereo*. At each pause, the computer slides its camera left to right on a 52 cm track, taking nine pictures at 6.5 cm intervals. A correspondence is established by using a coarse to fine correlation operator between the central image and the other eight images, so that the features' distance is triangulated in the nine images. These are then considered as 36 stereo pairings and the estimated (inverse) distance of the feature is recorded in a histogram. The distance to the feature is indicated by the highest peak in the histogram if it crosses a given threshold; otherwise, it is forgotten. Thus, the application of a mildly reliable (correlation) operator is used to make a very reliable distance measurement.

Position estimation in the Cart is carried out in exactly the same manner as described before, i.e. the features used to establish correspondence are then used to estimate the motion parameters and, hence, the location. The world model developed by the Cart is a set of these matched object features. The uncertainty and error modeling of the object features used in the Cart is a simple scalar uncertainty measure. This measure was proportional to the distance of the feature from the robot location; the further the feature, the larger the error associated with it, and, hence the less reliable the measure.

Matthies and Shafer [33] show that Moravec's approach is very similar to using a spherical probability distribution of error centered around the object feature. They argue that a 3-D Gaussian distribution is a much more effective way to explicitly deal with stereo triangulation errors and errors due to the image's limited resolution. They detail a method to estimate the 3-D Gaussian error distribution parameters (mean and covariance) from the stereo pair of images. They then present a method to consistently update the robot's position, explicitly taking into account the Gaussian error distribution of the feature points and motion parameters and their error covariances. A Kalman filter approach is used to recursively update the robot position from the detected features and the previously maintained world model. They assume the correspondence problem to be solved, and show by simulation data and experimental results that the Gaussian error model results in a more accurate stereo navigation paradigm.

The Cart suffers from the requirement of a huge memory to store the object features, the lack of speed (typically it moves in lurches of 1 meter in 10 to 15 minutes), and errors in position estimation due to insufficient error modeling. However, as one of the first autonomous mobile robots, it performed very well and made clear the various problems associated with autonomous navigation. The CMU Rover dealt with and corrected many of these problems [39].

Faugeras and Ayache [14,13,1] also address the problem of autonomous navigation. They use trinocular stereo to detect object features. The features they use are 3-D line segments. They propose a paradigm to combine coherently visual information obtained at different places to build a 3-D representation of the world. To prevent the system using line segments as primitives from running out of memory, they want their system to "forget intelligently" i.e. if a line segment "S" is detected at different positions 1, 2, 3, ..., n of the robot as S_1, S_2, ..., S_n, they want to establish a correspondence between all these, to form the line segment S from them, and to forget all others. Thus, the end result is a representation of the environment by a number of *uncertain* 3-D line segments attatched to co-ordinate frames and related by an uncertain rigid motion. The measurements are combined in the presence of these uncertainties by using the *Extended Kalman Filtering* technique. The authors present these ideas, and detail with experimental data the technique for building, registering, and fusing noisy visual maps.

A framework presented by Smith and Cheesman [46] for the representation and estimation of position uncertainty is relevant in this context. They describe a general method for estimating the nominal relationships and expected error (covariance) between coordinate frames representing the relative locations of objects. They introduce the concept of *Approximate Transformations* (ATs) consisting of an estimated mean of one co-ordinate frame relative to another and an error co-variance matrix that expresses the uncertainty of the estimate. They present two basic operations that allow the estimation of the relationship between any two coordinate frames given another relative transformation linking them. The first, *Compounding*, allows a chain of ATs to be collapsed (recursively) into a single AT. The final compounded AT has a greater uncertainty than its components. The second operation, *Merging*, combines information from parallel ATs to produce a single resulting AT with an uncertainty less than either of its components.

Crowley [8,9] has a similar approach to Ayache and Faugeras [14]; he also uses a line segment based representation of the free space using Extended Kalman filtering techniques for dealing with error covariances. However, he uses a circular ring of 24 polaroid ultrasonic sensors, while Faugeras and Ayache use trinocular stereo.

3.3. Graph-Based Approaches

Rodney Brooks [3] was one of the first to suggest the idea of using a relational map, which is rubbery and stretchy, rather than place observations in a 2-D coordinate system. The key idea is to represent free space as *freeways*, elongated rectangular regions, which naturally describe a large class of collision-free straight line motions of objects to be moved. Some places are described as convex regions and called *meadows*. So a map representation of free space is a graph; nodes of the graph are meadows; and arcs of the graph are freeways. Meadows and freeways are further described with metric and relational position and orientation properties.

Brooks also suggests a method for dealing with uncertainties in the position of the robot. He argues that the position uncertainty is a 2-D manifold in a 3-D space and that dealing with this explicitly makes it mathematically complex. He proposes to use instead an upper bound on the uncertainty which is cylindrical and mathematically easier to handle. Brooks also suggests how the uncertainty in the position estimation can be reduced if landmarks can be detected in a meadow.

Miller [37] presents a surface representation for real-world indoor robots equipped with a ranging device such as sonar and robot odometry as sensors. He assumes that the world consists of a flat, open plane on which walls and obstacles are placed. Since the robot is limited to motion on the plane of the floor, the projection of walls and obstacles on the plane of the floor captures all the relevant world information. The basic unit of the spatial representation system is the *map*, composed of linked *regions*. Regions have a local coordinate frame. Walls and obstacles are themselves represented by line segments, whose end point positions are designated by coordinates in the frame of the region. The borders of the regions are marked with labels that specify the adjoining regions.

Regions can be of four types, 0-F, 1-F, 2-F, and 3-F, since a floor dwelling mobile robot has three degrees of freedom, two translational (x and y), and one rotational (orientation θ). A type designation of j-F means that a sensor (here a sonar range sensor with a maximum range of $D_{\max}$) can be used to eliminate j degrees of freedom.

Regions are made up of a set of edges. Each edge is represented by a pair of end points, whose Cartesian coordinates are specified in the frame of reference of a particular region. The relative positions of features in two different regions cannot be known with great precision. The more 0-F, 1-F, and 2-F regions on the path between the two regions in question, the less the accuracy with which the two regions can be related. It is, however, possible to arrive at an approximate idea of the distance to be traveled between regions by using the lower bounds of the regions.

Having set the mapping scheme, Miller then presents methods for position estimation as a heuristic search paradigm. The type of region in which the robot operates determines the amount of position information that can be calculated. If the robot is in an 0-F region, then the only position information available would be extrapolations from the last known position, based on the robot's ability to do dead reckoning. If the robot is known to be in a region that is 1-F or greater, then position information can be found by taking several sensor readings and conducting a heuristic search over the tree of possible matches between the observations and the edges in the map.

Chatila and Laumond [5] present a world modeling and position referencing system on their mobile robot HILARE. They take a multisensor approach using a laser range finder for measuring depth and optical shaft encoders on the drive wheel axis for the trajectory integration. The random errors are modeled as Gaussian distributions and their parameters are determined experimentally. They present a three-layer model consisting of geometric, topological, and semantic levels. In the model construction paradigm, the robot at every instance has:

(1) a current environmental model with geometric, topological, and semantic levels related to an absolute reference frame,
(2) knowledge about the attitude and position of the robot, and
(3) a robot-centered geometric model of the environment perceived at that point.

The central problem is to update the models of (1) using (2) and (3), and to correct the information of (2), if possible.

3.4. *Certainty Grid-Based Methods*

Moravec and Elfes [11,40] use a grid-based representation for mapping the environment a mobile robot will inhabit. The basic idea is to represent the floor as a rectangular grid and to store the information about the occupancy of different portions of the floor on this grid as probability distributions. A sensor range reading provides information concerning empty and occupied volumes in a cone in front of the sensor. The readings are modeled as probability profiles and are projected onto a rasterized 2-D map where somewhere occupied and everywhere empty regions are represented. Range measurements from multiple points of view (taken from multiple sensors on the robot and from the same sensor after the robot moves) are symmetrically integrated into the map. Overlapping empty volumes reinforce each other and serve to condense the range of the occupied volumes. The map definition improves as more readings are added. The final map shows regions probably occupied, probably empty, and unknown areas. The method deals effectively with *clutter* and can be used for motion planning and extended landmark recognition. The system was tested and implemented on a CMU mobile robot called *Neptune.*

The authors also develop and present a fast algorithm for relating two maps of the same area to determine relative displacement, angle, and goodness of the match. These can then be used to estimate the position and pose of the robot. A measure of the goodness of the match between two maps at a trial displacement and a rotation is found by computing the sum of products of corresponding cells in the two maps. An occupied cell falling on an occupied cell contributes to a positive increment to the sum, as does an empty cell falling on an empty cell. An empty cell falling on an occupied one reduces the sum, and any comparison involving an unknown value causes neither an increase nor a decrease. Moravec and Elfes then offer more efficient versions of this naive algorithm, which take into account only the occupied cells and also use a hierarchy of reduced resolution versions of each map.

The authors argue that the advantages of the sonar maps are that they : (1) are much denser than stereo maps, (2) require less computation, (3) can be built more quickly, and (4) can be used for position estimation.

Of course, the disadvantages of sonar maps are that the large uncertainty areas associated with the features detected and the difficulties associated with active sensing.

Moravec [40,41] presents a new Bayesian statistical foundation for the map-making strategies in the certainty grid framework which seems to hold promise. The fundamental formula used is for the two occupancy cases of a cell o (cell is occupied) and $\bar{o}$ (cell is empty) with prior likelihoods $p(o)$ and $p(\bar{o})$ and new information M; Bayes' theorem can be expressed as

$$\frac{P(o/M)}{P(\bar{o}/M)} = \frac{P(M/o)}{P(M/\bar{o})} \times \frac{p(o)}{p(\bar{o})}. \tag{3.1}$$

The new information, M, occurs in terms of the probability of M in the situation that a cell is or is not occupied, i.e., $P(M/o)$ and $P(M/\bar{o})$, respectively. This inversion of o and M is the key feature of using the Bayesian framework, and it combines independent sources of information about o and M into a single quantity $P(o/M)$. Moravec then elaborates on this principle and derives formulas for the various cases of multiple sensor readings and presents a *Context-Free* and *Context-Sensitive* method. The former is much faster, but the latter is much more reliable. The former has a linear cost while the latter has a cost proportional to the cube of the volume. These methods are illustrated by simulations.

The certainty grid representation also provides an easy framework for fusing information from different sensing modalities, such as sonar, stereo, thermal, proximity, and contact sensors. Matthies and Elfes [34] present several approaches and results in integrating sonar and stereo in a certainty grid.

3.5. Qualitative Methods

Levitt et al. [30] and Kuipers et al. [26] argue that the existing robot navigation techniques use absolute range information and, hence, tend to be brittle, to accumulate error and to use little or no perceptual information. They propose qualitative methods which do not depend as much upon metrical information as on perceptual information to build a topological map.

Levitt et al. [30] describe a formal theory that depends on visual landmark recognition for the representation of environmental locations. They encode perceptual knowledge in structures called *viewframes*. Paths in the real world are represented as a sequence of sets of landmarks, viewframes, and other distinctive visual events. Approximate headings are computed between viewframes that have their lines of sight to common landmarks. Range-free, topological descriptions called *orientation regions* are rigorously abstracted from viewframes to yield a coordinate-free model of the visual landmark memory that can also be used for navigation and guidance. With this approach, a robot can opportunistically observe and execute visually cued *short-cuts*. Map and metric information are not required but, if available, are handled in a uniform representation with the qualitative navigation technique. Most of the examples they present are of simulated outdoor scenes using a visual sensor.

Kuipers et al. [26] present an approach similar in spirit for an indoor robot with a sonar sensor. They draw a parallel from cognitive science and argue that a powerful description of the environment is a topological description. Their topological description consists of a set of nodes and arcs. The nodes represent *distinctive places* and the arcs represent travel edges connecting them. A distinctive place is defined as the local maximum of some measure of distinctiveness appropriate to its immediate neighborhood and is found by a *hill climbing search*. Local travel edges are described in terms of local control strategies required for travel. How to find the distinctive places and how to follow edges is the procedural knowledge which the robot learns dynamically during the exploration stage and which guides the robot in the navigation stage. An accurate topological model is created by linking places and edges, and allows metrical information to be accumulated with reduced vulnerability to metrical errors. The authors describe a simulated robot called *NX* to illustrate the technique.

The position estimation strategies that use trajectory integration and dead reckoning thus rely on the robot's ability to sense the environment and to build a representation of it, and to use this representation effectively and efficiently. Each of the approaches detailed above has relative merits and works well in different environments. The sensing modalities used significantly affect the map-making strategy. Error and uncertainty analyses play an important role in accurate position estimation and map building. It is important to take explicit account of the uncertainties; modeling the errors by probability distributions and using Kalman Filtering techniques are good ways to deal with these errors explicitly. Qualitative methods propose to overcome the brittleness of the traditional approaches by relying on perceptual techniques. In general, a 2-D floor map of the environment is good enough for most navigation problems such as path planning and position estimation. This approach conserves memory and is easier to build. Certainty grid-based methods are novel and use the Bayesian probability techniques to advantage in combining information from various viewpoints consistently.

4. Techniques Using a Standard Pattern

Another method of estimating the position and pose of the mobile robot accurately is to place standard patterns in known locations in the environment. Once the robot detects these patterns, the robot's position can be estimated from the known location of the pattern and its geometry. The pattern itself is designed to yield a wealth of geometric information when transformed under the perspective projection. Ambiguous interpretations are avoided, and a minimum of *a priori* knowledge about the camera is desirable. These methods are particularly useful in those applications where a high degree of accuracy in the positioning of the robot is required only after it is near a particular workstation. Simple trajectory integration systems could be used to locate the robot near the work station. Then by identifying the mark (standard pattern) located near the workstation, the robot can be positioned more accurately. Researchers have used different kinds of patterns or marks, and the geometry of the method and the associated techniques for position estimation vary accordingly.

Fukui [18] uses a square mark rotated by 45 degrees. As the robot moves on the floor, Fukui determines the position of the robot by two co-ordinates, r and p, where r is the distance between the standard point and the robot and p is an angle between the r vector and the normal line to the mark. Figure 6 shows this situation.

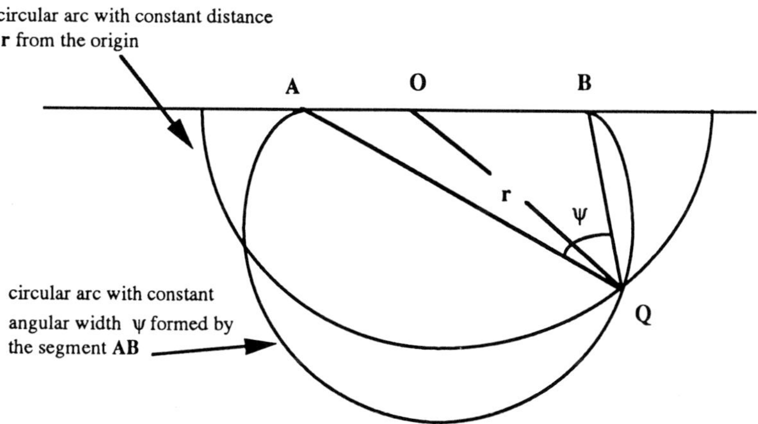

Fig. 6. Determination of point Q by r and ψ.

Two circles are drawn, one with the center at the standard point and with a radius of r, the other with an arc of a constant visual angle ψ made by watching a segment AB on the mark. Generally these two circles intersect at two points, and it is easy to judge in another way which is the real point. However, if ψ is a right angle, the two circles become the same and the position cannot be determined. The height of the camera is adjusted to the square mark $ACBD$, and it is imaged. If θ is the visual angle made by viewing CD in the square and ψ is that made by viewing AB, then the robot position in polar co-ordinates (p, r) can be determined from the following relations:

$$r = w\frac{(1 + \cos\theta)}{\sin\theta} \tag{4.1}$$

$$p = \pm\arctan\frac{\sqrt{(r^2 + w^2)(\cos\psi)^2 - (r^2 - w^2)^2}}{(r^2 - w^2)\sin\psi} \tag{4.2}$$

where AB is equal to CD, which equals $2w$ in length, and $r \neq w$ (see Fig. 7).

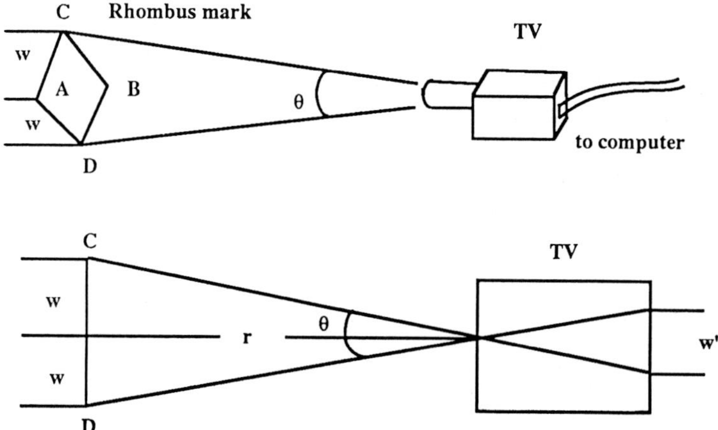

Fig. 7. Diagram to measure the distance from the origin.

To know the sign of p, Fukui measures the two angles in the image which correspond to $\angle CAD$ and $\angle CBD$, and decides if $\angle CBD \leq \angle CAD$, $p \leq 0$, or else $p > 0$. The angles ψ and θ are determined as follows:

Using all the data of the image and the method of least squares, the equations of the lines AC, AD, CB, and DB are determined on the image. Then the four points A, B, C, D are determined as the points of intersections of these lines. Next, assuming that ψ is proportional to the corresponding length AB on the image and that θ is proportional to CD, Fukui determines the proportional coefficients that can be used to convert the measured lengths into the desired angles.

Fukui also outlines image processing techniques to extract the lines of the pattern from the images. In addition, he presents experimental results to determine the camera position using this method and discusses the effects of errors in the measurement of the angles θ and ψ on the position (p, r).

Courtney, Magee, and Aggarwal [7] use the same mark as Fukui but relax the constraint of having the lens center at the same height as the mark center by partitioning the problem into two planes. Each plane passes through the lens center and either the vertical or the horizontal diagonal. Their results initially yield two equations in three unknowns, which must be further constrained by adding a second mark at a known height above the original mark or by assuming that the height of the camera relative to the mark is known. Since adding the second mark forces the solving of a system of six nonlinear equations, they opt for the later solution, which involves straightforward substitution.

Magee and Aggarwal [32] consider the use of a standard mark which would always directly produce at least one of the three position parameters (distance, elevation, or azimuth) and whose geometric properties would be such that its basic shape would be unchanged when its center is viewed along the optical axis. A sphere is such an object, and its projection is always a circle whose radius may be used to determine the distance. On the other hand, an unmarked sphere produces no information regarding the orientation, and so horizontal and vertical great circles are added to the sphere for computing the elevation and azimuth. The resulting self-locator system is mathematically quite simple. The preprocessing stage requires that four values be determined. These are the center and radius of the sphere's projected circle and the co-ordinates of the points on the projections of the great circle that are closest to the center of the sphere's outline. The three position estimation parameters used are: (1) the distance of the lens center D, (2) the elevation angle ϕ of the lens center above the horizontal great circle, and (3) the azimuth angle θ of the lens center with respect to the plane of the vertical great circle. The value of D can be computed from the relation

$$D = \frac{R}{r}\sqrt{(r^2 + f^2)} \tag{4.3}$$

where f is the focal length of the camera, R is the radius of the sphere, and r is the radius of the circular projection of the sphere on the image plane (see Figs. 8 and 9 for details).

Similarly, the authors give relations to determine the azimuth and the elevation angles from the projections of the great circles. The pre-processing used to extract these primitives from the images are also discussed and experimental results in estimating the position are shown. From the error analysis presented, the authors show that the errors in the computed distance increase as the camera is moved farther from the sphere and the errors in the computed angles increase as their respective great circles approach the edge of the sphere. This method is robust as long as the primary features are not lost in the sphere's shadow.

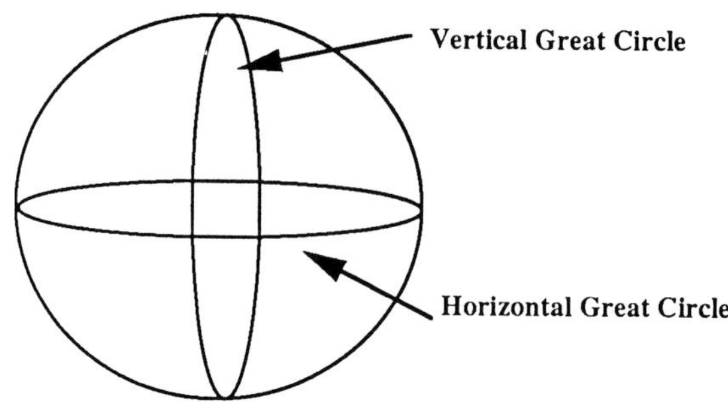

Fig. 8. The robot locator sphere.

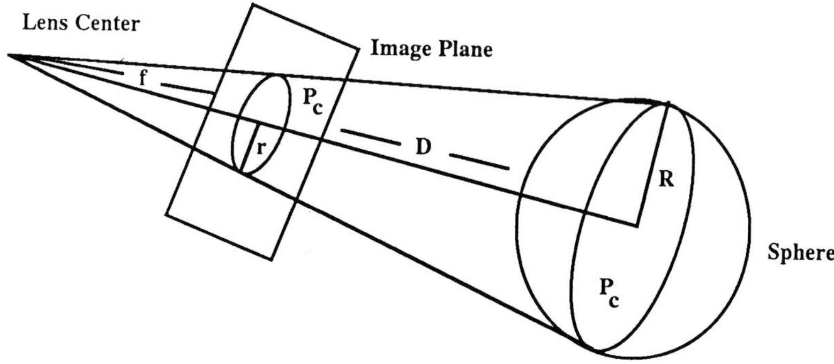

Fig. 9. Geometry for finding the distance to the center of the sphere.

Drake et al. [10] present a method of estimating the position and pose of a mobile robot using a *Navigation Line*, for use in factory environments. The navigation line is a long line with parallel edges on the floor, that does not intersect other lines. Once the line is imaged and detected by the robot, the position of the robot with respect to the line can be easily computed. The geometry used by the authors, illustrated in Figs. 10, 11, and 12 below, explains the method.

θ is the pan angle and ϕ is the tilt angle of the sensor. Two coordinate systems are shown; the unprimed coordinates (x, y, z) represent the global coordinate system and the primed coordinates (x', y') represent the coordinate system of the image plane. In Fig. 10, the gimbal center coincides with the focal point and is centered on the xy plane, and $z = 0$ is defined as the ground plane so that the sensor is at z_0. The authors also assume that the sensor is centered on the navigation line so that the pan angle $\theta = 0$. Since the navigation line is coincident with the y-axis, the line has the co-ordinates as shown in Fig. 11. The robot's position may be described by two parameters: the lateral position along the x-axis between the sensor and the navigation line (the x-shift) denoted by x_0, and the angle between the robot's

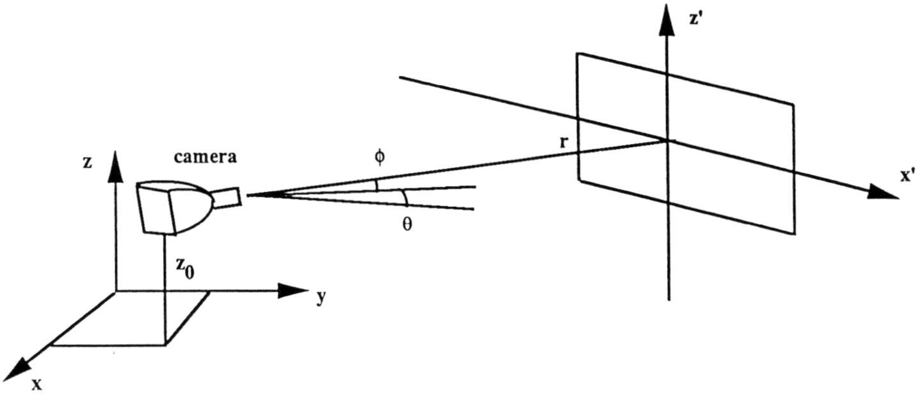

Fig. 10. The sensor geometry.

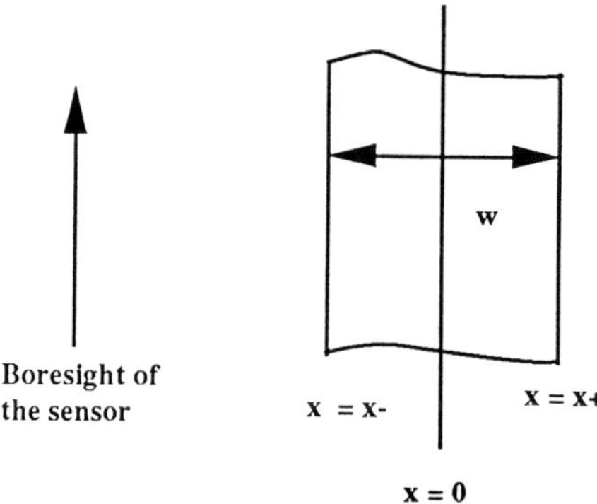

Fig. 11. Mobile robot with $-\theta$ orientation angle error and $-x_0$ x-shift position error.

orientation vector (the direction of travel) and the navigation line denoted by θ. The authors develop relations for these two parameters in terms of the focal length of the camera f, the image plane co-ordinates of the edges of the line x', and z', given below.

$$x = x_0 - \frac{z_0 x' \cos\theta + (z' \sin\phi - f \cos\phi)(z_0 \sin\theta)}{z' \cos\phi + f \sin\phi}. \tag{4.4}$$

While this equation is only one equation in two unknowns, by using a number of (x', z') points along the line and using numerical techniques, the values of x and θ can be solved for quite accurately. The authors also present a specialized operator to detect edges in an image that occur at a specific angle, and use the operator to detect the edges of the navigation line. In addition a Hough transform is used to completely segment the navigation line from the image. The authors also present experimental results to illustrate the robustness of the method.

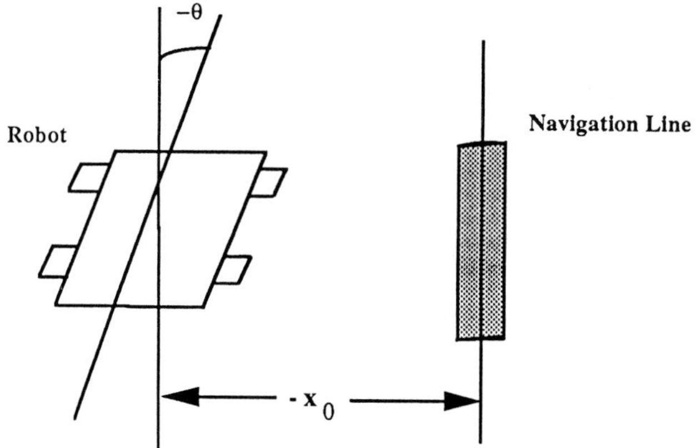

Fig. 12. Global coordinates of the navigation line.

Kabuka and Arenas [23] consider the problem that the robot might end up in a position that will not allow it to view the standard pattern. To alleviate the problem, they suggest using multiple patterns in the navigation environment. It is assumed that the location of each pattern in some standard world coordinate system is known. They associate a unique code with each pattern that will enable the robot to identify and distinguish that pattern from all the others. It consists of two parts: a relative displacement part and an identification code. The relative displacement pattern is used, as in the previous methods, to obtain the relative position of the viewing point with respect to the pattern by analysis of the particular geometric characteristics of its projection onto the image plane. The identification codes serve two purposes: they provide a unique code to discern the viewed pattern from other patterns in the environment, and they provide an aid to scan for the pattern in a minimal amount of time. The displacement pattern used by the authors is a circle, and the identification codes used are similar to bar codes. The authors present a detailed analysis of the application of this method and study the effects of errors in the input parameters on the position estimation.

5. Model-Based Approaches

Some researchers consider the problem of the position estimation of a mobile robot when *a priori* information is available about the environment in which the robot is to navigate. This could be provided in terms of a CAD model of the building (or a floor map, etc.) in the case of an indoor mobile robot, or a Digital Elevation Map (DEM) in the case of an outdoor robot. In these cases, the position estimation techniques used take on a different flavor. The basic idea is, of course, to sense the environment using onboard sensors on the robot and to match these sensory observations to the preloaded world model to arrive at an estimate of the position and pose of the robot with a reduced uncertainty.

One problem with such an approach is that the sensor readings and the world model may be in different forms. For instance, given a CAD model of the building and a visual camera, the problem is to match the 3-D descriptions in the CAD model to the 2-D visual images. This is the problem addressed by Kak et al. [24]. They present PSEIKI, a system that uses evidential reasoning in a hierarchical framework for image interpretation. They discuss how the PSEIKI system can be used for mobile robot self-location and how their approach is utilized by the navigational system of the autonomous mobile robot PETER. The robot's position encoders are used to maintain an approximate estimate of its position and heading at each point. However, to account for errors in the quantization effects of the encoders and the slippage of the wheels, a visual sensor in conjunction with a CAD model of the building is used to derive a more accurate estimate of the robot's position and pose. The basic idea is that the approximate position from the encoders is utilized to generate, from the CAD model, an estimated visual scene that would be seen. This scene is then matched against the actual scene viewed by the camera. Once the matches are established between the features of the two images (expected and actual), the position of the robot can be estimated with a reduced uncertainty.

Tsubouchi and Yuta [59] discuss the position estimation techniques used in their YAMABICO robot, which use a color camera and a map of the building in which the robot navigates. The authors propose a vision system using image and map information with consideration of real time requirements. This system consists of three operations. The first operation is the abstraction of a specified image from a TV camera. The image is processed, and highly abstracted information, called the *real perspective information,* is generated. The second operation is the generation of the *estimated perspective information* by coordinate transformation and map information, using information about the robot's position and direction. The third operation is the establishment of correspondence between the two perspectives. The authors use color images in their real perspective views. They argue for color images, saying that they are invariant under lightness and shadow. From the color images, the authors extract regions of *similar* color and fit trapezoids to these regions. From the map information, trapezoids are also extracted and, in the matching process, these trapezoids from the two sources are used as matching primitives. The authors provide a method of representing the map information efficiently and also discuss techniques for matching trapezoids. Real image data are provided as examples.

As pointed out earlier, one of the key issues involved in determining the position of a mobile robot given a world model is to establish a correspondence between the world model (map) and the sensor data (image). Once this correspondence is established, the position of the robot in the environment can be determined easily as a coordinate transformation. Indeed, this problem of image/map correspondence is of fundamental importance not only to the mobile robot position estimation problem, but also to many other computer vision problems, such as object recognition, pose estimation, airborne surveillance and reconnaissance, etc. Other work addressing this image/map correspondence problem is described in [30,24,36,16,17,44].

Freeman and Morse [17] consider the problem of searching a *Contour Map* for a given terrain elevation profile. Such a problem is encountered, for example, when locating the ground track of an aircraft (the projection of the flight path on the ground) given the elevation of the terrain below the aircraft during the flight. The authors describe a solution that takes advantage of the topological properties of the contour map. A graph of the map topology is used to identify all the possible contour lines that would have been intersected by the ground track. So, the topological constraints of the terrain elevation profile and the geometric constraints of the flight path are used in estimating the location of the elevation profile in the given map. Ernst and Flinchbach [16] consider the problem of determining the correspondence between maps and the terrain images in low altitude airborne scenarios. They assume that an initial estimate of the three-dimensional position is available. Their approach consists of partially matching the detected and expected curves in the image plane. Expected curves are generated from a map using the estimate of the sensor position and the simulated curves are matched with the curves in the image plane. Rodriguez and Aggarwal [44] consider the problem of matching aerial image to a Digital Elevation Map (DEM). They use a sequence of aerial images to perform stereo analysis on successive images and recover an elevation map. Then they present a method to match the recovered elevation map to the given DEM and thereby estimate the position and pose of the airborne sensor.

Talluri and Aggarwal [50–52] describe a position estimation technique for autonomous mobile robots navigating in outdoor, mountainous environment equipped with a visual camera that can be panned and tilted. A DEM of the area in which the robot navigates is provided to the robot. The robot is also assumed to be equipped with a compass and an altimeter to measure the altitude. Typical applications could be that of an autonomous land vehicle, such as a planetary rover. The approach presented formulates the position estimation problem as a constrained search problem. The authors also follow the idea of computing the expected image and comparing it to the actual image. In particular, the main idea of their work is to hypothesize a robot location, render the model (DEM) data, extract the Horizon Line Contour (HLC) and compare it to the HLC extracted from the camera images. In order to reduce the complexity of the search, the authors propose a two stage search strategy. First, all possible camera locations are checked by comparing the predicted (from the DEM) HLC height at the center of the image with the height computed from the camera image. This is done in the four geographic directions (N, S, E, and W). Only the candidate locations with the HLC height within some threshold of the actual height remain. Second, for each remaining candidate location the terrain image is rendered and the complete HLC is extracted and matched with the actual HLC (from the camera image). Examples of the position estimation strategy using real terrain data and simulated images are presented. The algorithm is made robust to errors in the imaging process by accounting for the worst case errors.

In a separate work, Talluri and Aggarwal [53–57] also consider the navigational aspects of an autonomous mobile robot navigating in an outdoor, urban environment consisting of polyhedral buildings. The 3-D descriptions of the rooftops of the buildings are assumed to be given as a world model and the robot is assumed to be equipped with a visual camera. The position and pose are estimated by establishing a correspondence between the lines that constitute the rooftops of the buildings (world model features) and their images. A tree search is used to establish a set of consistent correspondences. The tree is pruned using the geometric constraints between the world model features and their images. To effectively capture the geometric relations between the world model features with respect to their visibility from various positions of the robot, the free space of the robot is partitioned into a set of distinct, non-overlapping regions called the Edge Visibility Regions (EVRs). Associated with each EVR is a list of the world model features that are visible in this region called the Visibility List (VL). Also stored for each entry in the VL is a range of orientations of the robot for which this feature is visible. The uses of these EVRs in pruning the tree in searching for a consistent set of correspondences between the world model and the image features is discussed in this paper. An algorithm for forming such an EVR description of the environment from the given world model is presented. The authors also derive worst case bounds on the maximum number of EVRs that will be generated for a given world model and show that this is polynomial in the number of world model features. The uses of this EVR description in the path-planning tasks of the robot are also outlined. Results of the position estimation are provided using a model of a real airport scene.

6. Conclusions

In this paper we have illustrated the various aspects of the problem of estimating the position and pose of a mobile robot and provided a comprehensive review of the various methods and techniques used. These techniques vary significantly depending on the known conditions of the navigation environment and the type of sensors with which the robot is equipped. Landmark-based methods are suitable for robots with the ability to identify the landmarks and measure the range/attitude to them. This usually requires the robot to have a database of landmarks occurring in the environment and an approximate location to start to search the database. Computing the *exterior orientation parameters* in the camera calibration problem is dealt with in the photogrammetry literature. This problem is quite similar to the position estimation problem of a mobile robot using landmarks. Some of the techniques used in photogrammetry can thus be modified and applied in localizing the robot's position and orientation. Methods using trajectory integration and dead reckoning usually require the robot to address the problem of environment perception and modeling. Various methods of modeling the environment and forming a map of it for navigation tasks are also reviewed in this paper. The position estimation techniques used depend on the map-making strategy and representation used. Techniques which use a standard pattern to structure the environment by placing a standard reference pattern at known locations in the environment are particularly useful in those applications where a high degree of accuracy in positioning the robot is required only after it nears a particular workstation. Simple trajectory integration techniques could be used to locate the robot near the workstation, and then the standard pattern can be used. Model-based methods are best applied when *a priori* information of the robot's environment is available in the form of a world model. The problem to be solved in this instance is to match the model and the sensor observations, which may be in different forms.

Acknowledgments

This research was supported by the Army Research Office under contract DAAL03-91-G-0050.

References

[1] N. Ayache, O. D. Faugeras, Building a consistent 3-D representation of a mobile robot environment by combining multiple stereo views, in *Proc. 10th IJCAI*, 1987, 808–810.

[2] B. C. Bloom, Use of landmarks for mobile robot navigation, in *SPIE Proc., Intelligent Robots and Computer Vision*, Vol. 579, 1985, 351–355.

[3] R. A. Brooks, Visual map making for a mobile robot, in *Proc. IEEE Int. Conf. on Robotics and Automation*, St. Louis, MO, 1985, 824–829.

[4] M. Case, Single landmark navigation by mobile robots, in *SPIE Proc., Mobile Robots*, Vol. 727, Oct. 1986, 231–238.

[5] R. Chatila and J.-P. Laumond, Position referencing and consistent world modeling for mobile robots, in *Proc. IEEE Int. Conf. on Robotics and Automation*, St. Louis, MO, 1985, 138–145.

[6] H. H. Chen, Pose determination from line-to-plane correspondences: Existence condition and closed-form solutions, *IEEE Trans. Pattern Anal. Mach. Intell.* **13**, 6 (1991) 530–541.

[7] J. Courtney, M. Magee and J. K. Aggarwal, Robot guidance using computer vision, *Pattern Recogn.* **17**, 6 (1984) 585–592.

[8] J. L. Crowley, Dynamic world modeling for an intelligent mobile robot using a rotating ultra-sonic ranging sensor, in *Proc. IEEE Int. Conf. on Robotics and Automation*, St. Louis, MO, 1985, 128–135.

[9] J. L. Crowley, World modeling and position estimation for a mobile robot using ultra-sonic ranging, in *Proc. IEEE Int. Conf. on Robotics and Automation*, Scottsdale, May 1989.

[10] K. C. Drake, E. S. McVey and R. M. Iñigo, Experimental position and ranging results for a mobile robot, *IEEE Trans. Robotics and Automation* **3**, 1 (1987) 31–42.

[11] A. Elfes, Sonar based real-world mapping and navigation, *IEEE Trans. Robotics and Automation* **3**, 3 (1987) 249–265.

[12] I. M. El Hassan, Analytical techniques for use with reconnaissance from photographs, *Photogrammetric Eng. Remote Sensing* **47**, 12 (1981) 1733–1738.

[13] O. D. Faugeras, N. Ayache and B. Faverjon, Building visual maps by combining noisy stereo measurements, in *Proc. IEEE Conf. on Robotics and Automation*, San Francisco, CA, 1986, 1433–1438.

[14] N. Ayache and O. Faugeras, Maintaining representations of the environment of a mobile robot, *IEEE Trans. Robotics and Automation* **5**, 6 (1989) 804–819.

[15] M. A. Fischler and R. C. Bolles, Random sample consensus : A paradigm for model fitting with application to image analysis and automated cartography, *Commun. ACM* **24**, 6 (1981) 726–740.

[16] M. D. Ernst and B. E. Flinchbaugh, Image/map correspondence using curve matching, Texas Instruments Technical Report, CSC-SIUL-89-12, 1989.

[17] H. Freeman and S. P. Morse, On searching a contour map for a given terrain elevation profile, *Journal of the Franklin Institute* **284** (1967) 1–25.

[18] I. Fukui, TV image processing to determine the position of a robot vehicle, *Pattern Recogn.* **14**, 1–6 (1981) 101–109.

[19] S. Ganapathy, Decomposition of transformation matrices for robot vision, in *Proc. 1st IEEE Int. Conf. on Robotics*, Atlanta, GA, Mar. 1984, 130–138.

[20] R. M. Haralick et al., Pose estimation from corresponding point data, *IEEE Trans. Syst. Man Cybern.* **19**, 6 (1989) 1426–1445.

[21] R. Horaud, B. Conio and O. Leboulleux, An analytical solution to the perspective 4-point problem, in *Proc. IEEE Conf. on Computer Vision and Pattern Recognition, CVPR '89*, San Diego, CA, Jun. 1989, 500–507.

[22] B. K. P. Horn, Relative orientation, *Proc. Image Understanding Workshop*, Vol. 2, 1988, 826–837.

[23] M. R. Kabuka and A. E. Arenas, Position verification of a mobile robot using a standard pattern, *IEEE Trans. Robotics and Automation* **3**, 6 (1987) 505–516.

[24] A. Kak, K. Andress and C. Lopez-Abadia and M. S. Carroll, Hierarchical evidence accumulation in the PSEIKI system and experiments in model-driven mobile robot navigation, in *Uncertainty in Artificial Intelligence*, Vol. 5 (Elsevier Science Publishers B.V., North-Holland, 1990) 353–369.

[25] E. Krotkov, Mobile robot localization using a single image, in *Proc. IEEE Int. Conf. on Robotics and Automation*, Scottsdale, May 1989, 978–983.

[26] B. J. Kuipers and Y. T. Byun, A robust qualitative method for robot spatial learning, in *AAAI-88, The Seventh Nat. Conf. on Artificial Intelligence*, St. Paul/ Minneapolis, MI, 1988, 774–779.

[27] R. Kumar, Determination of the camera location and orientation, in *Proc. DARPA Image Understanding Workshop*, 1988, 870–881.

[28] R. Kumar and A. Hanson, Robust estimation of the camera location and orientation from noisy data having outliers, in *Proc. Workshop on Interpretation of 3-d scenes*, Austin, TX, Nov. 1989, 52–60.

[29] J. Lessard and D. Laurendeau, Estimation of the position of a robot using computer vision for a live-line maintenance task, in *Proc. IEEE Int. Conf. on Robotics and Automation*, Raleigh, NC, 1987, 1203–1208.

[30] T. S. Levitt, D. T. Lawton, D. M. Chelberg and P. C. Nelson, Qualitative navigation, in *Proc. DARPA Image Understanding Workshop*, 1987, 447–465.

[31] Y. Liu, T. Huang and O. Faugeras, Determination of the camera location from 2-d to 3-d line and point correspondences, *IEEE Trans. Pattern Anal. Mach. Intell.* **12**, 1 (1990) 28–37.

[32] M. J. Magee and J. K. Aggarwal, Determining the position of a robot using a single calibration object, in *Proc. 1st IEEE Int. Conf. on Robotics*, Atlanta, GA, Mar. 1984, 140–149.

[33] L. Matthies and S. A. Shafer, Error modeling in stereo navigation, *IEEE Trans. Robotics and Automation* **3** (1987) 239–248.

[34] L. Matthies and A. Elfes, Integration of sonar and stereo range data using a grid based representation, in *Proc. IEEE Int. Conf. on Robotics and Automation*, Philadelphia, PA, Apr. 1988, 727–733.

[35] C. D. McGillem and T. S. Rappaport, Infra-red location system for navigation of autonomous vehicles, in *Proc. IEEE Int. Conf. on Robotics and Automation*, Philadelphia, PA, Apr. 1988, 1236–1238.

[36] G. Medioni and R. Nevatia, Matching images using linear features, *IEEE Trans. Pattern Anal. Mach. Intell.* **6**, 6 (1984) 675–685.

[37] D. Miller, A spatial representation system for mobile robots, in *Proc. IEEE Int. Conf. on Robotics and Automation*, St. Louis, MO, 1985, 122–127.

[38] H. P. Moravec, *Robot Rover Visual Navigation* (UMI Research Press, Ann Arbor, MI, 1981).

[39] H. P. Moravec, The Stanford Cart and the CMU Rover, in *Proc. IEEE* **71**, 7 (1983) 872–884.

[40] H. P. Moravec, Sensor fusion in certainty grids for mobile robots, *AI Mag.* **9**, 2 (1988) 61–74.

[41] H. P. Moravec and D. W. Cho, A Bayesian method for certain grids, in *AAAI Spring Symposium Series on Mobile Robot Navigation*, Stanford, CA, Apr. 1989.

[42] H. Nasr and B. Bhanu, Landmark recognition system for autonomous mobile robots, in *Proc. IEEE Int. Conf. on Robotics and Automation*, Philadelphia, PA, Apr. 1988, 1218–1223.

[43] A. Robert de Saint Vincent, A 3-D perception system for the mobile robot HILARE, in *Proc. IEEE Conf. on Robotics and Automation*, San Francisco, CA, 1986, 1105–1111.

[44] J. J. Rodriguez and J. K. Aggarwal, Matching aerial images to 3-D terrain maps, *IEEE Trans. Pattern Anal. Mach. Intell.* **12**, 12 (1990) 1138–1149.

[45] P. J. Rosseeuw and A. M. Leroy, *Robust Regression and Outlier Detection* (John Wiley and Sons, NY, 1987).

[46] R. C. Smith and P. Cheeseman, On the representation and estimation of spatial uncertainty, *Int. J. Rob. Res.* **5**, 4 (1987) 56–58.

[47] K. Sugihara, Some location problems for robot navigation using a single camera, *Comput. Vision Graph. Image Process.* **42**, 1 (1988) 112–129.

[48] K. Sugihara, Location of a robot using sparse visual information, in Robert Bolles and Bernard Roth (eds.), *Robotics Research: The Fourth International Symposium* (MIT Press, 1987) 319–326.

[49] W. Szczepanski, Die Lösungsverchläge für den räumlichen Rückwärtseinschnitt, Deutche Geodätische Komission, Reiche C: Dissertationen-Heft Nr, 1958, 1–44.

[50] R. Talluri and J. K. Aggarwal, A position estimation for a mobile robot in an unstructured environment, in *Proc. IEEE Workshop on Intelligent Robots and Systems, IROS '90*, Tsuchiura, Japan, Jul. 1990, 159–166.

[51] R. Talluri and J. K. Aggarwal, A positional estimation technique for an autonomous land vehicle in an unstructured environment, in *Proc. AIAA/NASA Int. Symp. on Artificial Intelligence and Robotics Applications in Space, ISAIRAS '90*, Kobe, Japan, Nov. 1990, 135–138.

[52] R. Talluri and J. K. Aggarwal, Position estimation for an autonomous mobile robot in an outdoor environment, *IEEE Trans. Robotics and Automation* **8**, 5 (1992) 573–584.

[53] R. Talluri and J. K. Aggarwal, Edge visibility regions — a new representation of the environment of a mobile robot, in *Proc. IAPR Workshop on Machine Vision Applications, MVA '90*, Tokyo, Japan, Nov. 1990, 375–380.

[54] R. Talluri and J. K. Aggarwal, Positional estimation of a mobile robot using edge visibility regions, in *Proc. IEEE Conf. on Computer Vision and Pattern Recognition, CVPR '91*, Hawaii, Jun. 1991, 714–715.

[55] R. Talluri and J. K. Aggarwal, Positional estimation of a mobile robot using constrained search, in *Proc. IEEE Workshop on Intelligent Robots and Systems, IROS '91*, Osaka, Japan, Nov. 1991.

[56] R. Talluri and J. K. Aggarwal, Transform clustering for model-image feature correspondence, in *Proc. IAPR Workshop on Machine Vision Applications, MVA '92*, Tokyo, Japan, Dec. 1992, 579–582.

[57] R. Talluri and J. K. Aggarwal, Autonomous navigation in cluttered outdoor environments using geometric visibility constraints, in *Proc. Int. Conf. on Intelligent Autonomous Systems: IAS — 3*, Pittsburgh, PA, Feb. 1993.

[58] R. Y. Tsai, A versatile camera calibration technique for high accuracy 3-D machine vision metrology using off the shelf TV cameras and lenses, *IEEE Trans. Robotics and Automation* **3**, 4 (1987) 323–344.

[59] T. Tsuboushi and S. Yuta, Map assisted vision system of mobile robots for reckoning in a building environment, in *Proc. IEEE Int. Conf. on Robotics and Automation*, Raleigh, NC, 1987, 1978–1984.

[60] J. S.-C. Yuan, A general photogrammetric method for determining object position and orientation, *IEEE Trans. Robotics and Automation* **5**, 2 (1989) 129–142.

[61] P. R. Wolf, *Elements of Photogrammetry* (McGraw Hill, New York, 1974).

PART 5

ARCHITECTURES AND TECHNOLOGY

Handbook of Pattern Recognition and Computer Vision, pp. 805–815
Eds. C. H. Chen, L. F. Pau and P. S. P. Wang
© 1993 World Scientific Publishing Company

CHAPTER 5.1

VISION ENGINEERING:
DESIGNING COMPUTER VISION SYSTEMS

RAMA CHELLAPPA

*Department of Electrical Engineering, Center for Automation Research,
University of Maryland, College Park, Maryland 20742, USA*

and

AZRIEL ROSENFELD

*Center for Automation Research, University of Maryland
College Park, Maryland 20742, USA*

The goal of computer vision is to derive descriptive information about a scene by computer analysis of images of the scene. Vision algorithms can serve as computational models for biological visual processes, and they also have many practical uses; but this paper treats computer vision as a subject in its own right. Vision problems are often ill-defined, ill-posed, or computationally intractable; nevertheless, successes have been achieved in many specific areas. We argue that by limiting the domain of application, carefully choosing the task, using redundant data (multi-sensor, multi-frame), and applying adequate computing power, useful solutions to many vision problems can be obtained. Methods of designing such solutions are the subject of the emerging discipline of *Vision Engineering*. With projected advances in sensor and computing technologies, the domains of applicability and ranges of problems that can be solved will steadily expand.

Keywords: Computer vision, vision engineering.

1. Introduction

The general goal of computer vision is to derive information about a scene by computer analysis of images of that scene. Images can be obtained by various types of sensors; the most common kind are optical images obtained by a TV camera. An image is input to a digital computer by sampling its brightness at a regularly spaced grid of points, resulting in a digital image array. The elements of the array are called pixels (short for "picture elements"), and their values are called gray levels. Given one or more digital images obtained from a scene, a computer vision system attempts to (partially) describe the scene as consisting of surfaces or objects; this class of tasks will be discussed further in Section 2.

Animals and humans have impressive abilities to successfully interact with their environments — navigate over and around surfaces, recognize objects, etc. — using vision. This performance constitutes a challenge to computer vision; at the same time, it serves as an existence proof that the goals of computer vision are attainable. Conversely, the algorithms used by computer vision systems to derive information about a scene from images can be regarded as possible computational models for the processes employed by biological visual systems. However, constructing such models is not the primary goal of computer vision; it is concerned only with the correctness of its scene description algorithms, not with whether they resemble biological visual processes.

Computer vision techniques have many practical uses for analyzing images. Areas of application include document processing (e.g. character recognition), industrial inspection, medical image analysis, remote sensing, target recognition, and robot guidance. There have been successful applications in all of these areas, but many tasks are beyond current capabilities (e.g. reading unconstrained handwriting). These potential applications provide major incentives for continued research in computer vision. However, successful performance of specific tasks on the basis of image data is not the primary goal of computer vision; such performance is often possible even without obtaining a correct description of the scene.

Viewed as a subject in its own right, the goal of computer vision is to derive correct (partial) descriptions of a scene, given one or more images of that scene. Computer vision can thus be regarded as the inverse of computer graphics, in which the goal is to generate (realistic) images of a scene, given a description of the scene. The computer vision goal is more difficult, since it involves the solution of inverse problems that are highly underconstrained ("ill-posed"). A more serious difficulty is that the problems may not even be well defined, because many classes of real-world scenes are not mathematically definable. Finally, even well-posed, well-defined vision problems may be computationally intractable. These sources of difficulty will be discussed in Section 3.

In spite of these difficulties, vision systems have achieved successes in many domains. The chances of success are greatly increased by limiting the domain of application, simplifying the task to be performed, increasing the amount of image data used, and providing adequate computing power. These principles can be stated concisely as: *Define your domain*; *pick your problem*; *improve your input*; and *take your time*. They will be illustrated in Section 4.

Following these principles in attempting to solve vision problems provides a foundation for a discipline which we may call *Vision Engineering*, as discussed in Section 5.

2. Vision Tasks

If a scene could be completely arbitrary, not very much could be inferred about it by analyzing images. The gray levels of the pixels in an image measure the amounts of light received by the sensor from various directions. Any such set of brightness measurements could arise in infinitely many different ways as a result of light emitted by a set of light sources, transmitted through a sequence of transparent media, and reflected from a sequence of surfaces.

Computer vision becomes feasible only if restrictions are imposed on the class of possible scenes. The central problem of computer vision can thus be reformulated as follows: given a set of constraints on the allowable scenes, and given a set of images obtained from a scene that satisfies these constraints, derive a description of that scene. It should be pointed out that unless the given constraints are very strong, or the given set of images is large, the scene will not be uniquely determined; the images only provide further constraints on the subclass of scenes that could have given rise to them, so that only partial descriptions of the scene are possible.

Computer vision tasks vary widely in difficulty, depending on the nature of the constraints that are imposed on the class of allowable scenes and on the nature of the partial descriptions that are desired. The constraints can vary greatly in specificity. At one extreme, they may be of a general nature — for example, that the visible surfaces in the scene are all of some "simple" type (e.g. quadric surfaces with Lambertian reflectivities). [Constraints on the illumination should also be specified — for example, that it consists of a single distant light source. Note that the surfaces may be "simple" in a stochastic rather than a deterministic sense; for example, they may be fractal surfaces of given types, or they may be smooth sur-faces (e.g. quadric) with spatially stationary variations in reflectivity (i.e. uniformly textured surfaces).] At the other extreme, the constraints may be quite special-ized — for example, that the scene contains only objects having given geometric ("CAD") descriptions and given optical surface characteristics. Similarly, the de-sired scene descriptions can vary greatly in completeness. "Recovery" tasks call for descriptions that are complete as possible, but "recognition" and "navigation" tasks usually require only partial descriptions — for example, identification and location of objects or surfaces of specific types if they are present in the scene.

In its earliest years (beginning in the mid-1950s), computer vision research was concerned primarily with recognition tasks, and dealt almost entirely with single im-ages of (essentially) two-dimensional scenes: documents, photomicrographs (which show thin "slices" of the subject, because the depth of field of a microscope image is very limited), or high-altitude views of the earth's surface (which can be regarded as essentially flat when seen from sufficiently far away). The mid-1960's saw the beginnings of research on robot vision; since a robot must deal with solid objects at close-by distances, the three-dimensional nature of the scene cannot be ignored. Research on recovery tasks began in the early 1970's, initially considering only sin-gle images of a static scene, but by the mid-1970's it was beginning to deal with time sequences of images (of a possibly time-varying scene) obtained by a moving sensor.

By definition, recovery tasks require correct descriptions of the scene; but recog-nition and navigation tasks can often be performed successfully without completely describing even the relevant parts of the scene. For example, obstacles can often be detected, or object types identified, without fully determining their geometries.

Thirty-five years of research have produced theoretical solutions to many computer vision problems; but many of these solutions are based, explicitly or tacitly, on unrealistic assumptions about the class of allowable scenes, and as a result, they often perform unsatisfactorily when applied to real-world images. As we shall see in the next section, even for static, two-dimensional scenes, many vision problems are ill-posed, ill-defined, or computationally intractable.

3. Sources of Difficulty

3.1. *Ill-Posedness*

As already mentioned, the gray levels of the pixels in an image represent the amounts of light received by the sensor from various directions. If the scene does not contain transparent objects (other than air, which we will assume to be clear), the light contributing to a given pixel usually comes from a small surface patch in the scene (on the first surface intersected by a line drawn from the sensor in the given direction). This surface patch is illuminated by light sources, as well as by light reflected from other patches. Some fraction of this illumination is reflected toward the sensor and contributes to the pixel; in general, this fraction depends on the orientation of the surface patch relative to the direction(s) of illumination and the direction of the sensor, as well as on the reflectivity of the patch. In short, the gray level of a pixel is the resultant of the illumination, orientation, and reflectivity of a surface patch. If all these quantities are unknown, it is not possible to recover them from the image. Only under limited conditions of smoothly curved Lambertian surfaces with constant albedo can one recover estimates of illuminant direction, surface albedo and shape from a single image [1].

This example is a very simple illustration of the fact that most vision problems are "ill-posed", i.e. underconstrained; they do not have unique solutions. Even scenes that satisfy constraints usually have more degrees of freedom than the images to which they give rise; thus even when we are given a set of images of a scene, the scene is usually not uniquely determined. In some special cases, with the availability of singular points, unique solutions may be obtained [2].

In applied mathematics, a common approach to solving ill-posed problems is to convert them into well-posed problems by imposing additional constraints [3]. A standard method of doing this, known as regularization, makes use of smoothness constraints; it finds the solution that minimizes some measure of nonsmoothness (usually defined by a combination of derivatives). Regularization methods were introduced into computer vision in the mid-1980's, and have been applied to many vision problems [4]. Evidently, however, solutions found by regularization often do not represent the actual scene [5]; for example, the actual scene may be piecewise smooth, but may also have discontinuities, and a regularized solution tends to smooth over these discontinuities. To handle this problem, more general approaches have been proposed which allow discontinuities [6], but which minimize the complexity of these discontinuities — e.g. minimize the total length and total absolute curvature of the borders between smooth regions. In effect, these approaches [7] find solutions that have minimum-length descriptions (since the borders can be described by encoding them using chain codes). However, the actual scene is not necessarily the same as the scene (consistent with the images) that has the simplest description. Evidently, not all scenes of a given class are equally likely; but the likelihood of a scene depends on the physical processes that give rise to the class of scenes, not on the simplicity of its description, and certainly not on the simplicity of a description of its image.

As an alternative to the regularization approach, direct methods have been suggested for shape recovery from radar [8] and visible images [9]. For illumination sources near the camera, good results have been obtained on simple optical images. Direct methods are rigid, in that they cannot be easily generalized to arbitrary illumination directions or to incorporate additional information. In addition, the lack of smoothing may present problems in the presence of noise.

3.2. *Ill-Definedness*

It is often assumed in formulating vision problems that the class of allowable scenes is "piecewise simple", e.g. that the visible surfaces are all smooth (e.g. planar or quadric) and Lambertian. This type of assumption seems at first glance to strongly constrain the class of possible scenes (and images), but in fact, the class of images is not constrained at all unless a lower bound is specified on the sizes of the "pieces". If the pieces can be arbitrarily small, each pixel in an image can represent a different piece (or even parts of several pieces), so that the image can be completely arbitrary. For a two-dimensional scene, it suffices to specify a lower bound on the piece sizes; but for a three-dimensional scene, even this does not guarantee a lower bound on the sizes of the image regions that represent the pieces of surface; occlusions and nearly-grazing viewing angles can still give rise to arbitrarily small or arbitrarily thin regions in the image.

Lower bounds on piece sizes are important for another very important reason: they make it easier to distinguish between the ideal scene and various types of "noise". In the real world, piecewise simple scenes are an idealization; actual surfaces are not perfectly planar or quadric or perfectly Lambertian, but have fluctuating geometries or reflectivities. [Note that these fluctuations are in the scene itself; in addition, the brightness measurements made by the sensor are noisy, and the digitization process also introduces noise.] If the fluctuations are small relative to the piece sizes, it will usually be possible to avoid confusing them with "real" pieces. [Similarly, the noisy brightness measurements — assuming that they affect the pixels independently — yield pixel-size fluctuations, and digitization noise is also of at most pixel size; hence these types of noise too should usually not be confused with the pieces.] Of course, even if we can avoid confusing noise fluctuations with real scene pieces, their presence can still interfere with correct estimation of the geometries and photometries of the pieces.

Most analyses of vision problems (e.g. for piecewise simple ideal scenes) do not attempt to formulate realistic models for the "noise" in the scene; they usually assume that the noise in the image (which is the net result of the scene noise, the sensor noise, and the digitization noise) is Gaussian and affects each pixel independently. Examination of images of most types of real scenes shows that this is not a realistic assumption; thus the applicability of the resulting analyses to real-world images is questionable.

The problem of ill-definedness becomes even more serious if one attempts to deal with scenes containing classes of objects that do not have simple mathematical definitions — for example, dogs, bushes, chairs, alphanumeric characters, etc. Recognition of such objects is not a well-defined computer vision task, even though humans can recognize them very reliably.

3.3. *Intractability*

Even well-defined vision problems are not always easy to solve; in fact, they may be computationally intractable [10,11]. An image can be partitioned in combinatorially many ways into regions that could correspond to simple surfaces in the scene; finding the correct (i.e. the most likely) partition may thus involve combinatorial search. For example, even for scenes consisting of polyhedral objects, the problem of deciding whether a set of straight edges in an image could represent such a scene is NP-complete. Even identifying a subset of image features that represent a single object of a given type is exponential in the complexity of the object, if more than one object can be present in the scene, or if the features can be due to noise.

Parallel processing (e.g. [12]) is widely used to speed up computer vision computations; it is also used very extensively and successfully in biological visual systems. Very efficient speedup can be achieved through parallelism in the early stages of the vision process, which involve simple operations on the image(s); but little is known about how to efficiently speed up the later, potentially combinatorial stages. Practical vision systems must operate in "real time" using limited computational resources; as a result, they are usually forced to use suboptimal techniques, so that there is no guarantee of correct performance.

In principle, the computations performed by a vision system should be chosen to yield maximal expected gain of information about the scene at minimal expected computational cost. Unfortunately, even for well-defined vision tasks, it is not easy to estimate the expected gain and cost. Vision systems therefore usually perform standard types of computations that are not necessarily optimal for the given scene domain or vision task; this results in both inefficiency and poor performance.

4. Recipes for Success

4.1. *Define Your Domain*

Well-defined vision problems should involve classes of scenes in which both the ideal scene and the noise can be mathematically (and probabilistically) characterized. For example, in scenes that contain only known types of man-made objects, the allowable geometric and optical characteristics of the visible surfaces can be known to any needed degree of accuracy. If the objects are "clean", and the characteristics of the sensor are known, the noise in the images can also be described very accurately. In such situations, the scene descriptions that are consistent with the images are generally less ambiguous (so that the problem of determining these descriptions is relatively well-posed) because of the relatively specialized nature of the class of allowable scenes. If, in addition, the number of objects that can be present is limited, the complexity of the scene description task and the computational cost of recognizing the objects are greatly reduced. For example, it has been shown [11] that when all the features in the image can be assumed to arise from a single object, the expected search cost to recognize the object is quadratic in the number of features, and the number of possible interpretations drops rapidly to one as the number of features extracted from the image increases. The number of interpretations and the search cost are much higher when the scene is cluttered, so that the object of interest may be occluded and a significant part of the data may come from other objects in the scene.

4.2. *Pick Your Problem*

Even for specialized scene domains, deriving complete scene descriptions from images — the general recovery problem — can still be a very difficult task. However, there is no reason to insist on unique solutions to vision problems. The images (further) constrain the class of possible scenes; the task of the vision system is to determine these constraints. This yields a partial description of the scene, and for some purposes this description may be sufficient. In fact, in many situations only a partial description of the scene is needed, and such descriptions can often be derived inexpensively and reliably. A partial description may require only the detection of a specific type of object or surface, if it is present, or it may require only partial ("qualitative") characterizations of the objects that are present (e.g. are their surfaces planar or curved).

Two illustrations of the value of partial descriptions are:

(i) An autonomous vehicle can rapidly and accurately follow the markers on a road; it need not analyze the entire road scene, but need only detect and track the marker edges [13,14]. By using additional domain-specific knowledge about the types of vehicles, their possible motions, etc., significant improvements in 3-D object and motion estimation have been reported in [15].

(ii) An active observer, by shifting its line of sight so that the focus of expansion due to its motion occupies a sequence of positions, can robustly detect independent motion anywhere in the region surrounded by these foci [16]. In this region, independent motion is indicated by the sign of the normal flow being opposite to that of the expansion.

4.3. *Improve Your Inputs*

Vision tasks that are very difficult to perform when given only a single image of the scene generally become much easier when additional images are available. These images could come from different sensors (e.g. we can use optical sensors that detect energy in different spectral bands; we can use imaging sensors of other types such as microwave or thermal infrared; or we can use range sensors that directly measure the distances to the visible surface points in the scene). Alternatively, we can use more than one sensor of the same type — for example, stereo vision systems use two or more cameras. Even if we use only a single sensor, we can adjust its parameters — for example, its position, orientation, focal length, etc. — to obtain multiple images; control of sensor parameters in a vision system is known as *active vision* [17]. It has been shown that by using the active vision approach, ill-posed vision problems can become well-posed, and their solutions can be greatly simplified. These improvements are all at the sensor level; one can also consider improving the inputs to the higher levels of the vision process by extracting multiple types of features from the image data using different types of operators (e.g. several edge detectors).

This strategy leads to a situation where "less is required from more", i.e. where it is easier to derive the desired results if more input information is available, unlike the traditional situation where "more is required from less". Animals and humans integrate different types of sensory data, and control their sensory apparatus, to obtain improved or additional information (e.g. tracking, fixation). Obtaining additional constraints on the scene by increasing the amount of image data is evidently a sounder strategy than making assumptions about the scene (smoothness, simplicity, etc.) that have no physical justification.

Many successful computer vision systems have made effective use of redundant input data. In the following paragraphs we give three examples:

(i) In [18], thermal (8.5μ–12.5μ) and visual imagery are combined to identify objects or regions such as vehicles, buildings, areas of vegetation and roads. The visual image is used to estimate the surface orientation of the object. Using the surface orientation and other collateral information such as the ambient temperature, wind speed, and the date and time of image acquisition, an estimate of the thermal capacitance of the object is derived. This information, in conjunction with the surface reflectivity of the object (derived from the visual image) and the average object temperature (derived from the thermal image), is used in a rule-based system to identify the types of objects mentioned above.

(ii) Photometric stereo [19] is an excellent example of using more inputs to resolve the inherent ambiguities in recovering shape from shading using a single image irradiance equation. In this scheme, the viewing direction is held constant, but multiple images are obtained by changing the direction of illumination. One then generates as many coupled irradiance equations as there are illumination directions. By solving these equations, robust estimates of the surface orientation can be obtained. Photometric stereo can be very useful in industrial applications where the incident illumination can be controlled.

(iii) Stereo matching is the process of fusing two images taken from different viewpoints to recover depth information in the scene. The process involves identifying corresponding points or regions in two views and using their relative displacements together with camera geometry to estimate their depths. If the baseline (the distance between the two cameras) is large, accurate depth estimates can be obtained, but at considerable added computational cost in the feature matching process. With a short baseline the cost of matching is less, but the depth resolution is low. In [20] a method is described that uses multiple stereo pairs with different baselines generated by lateral displacements of a camera. A practical system with seven cameras has been developed. This is a very good example in which, by using more inputs, the complexity of the algorithms is considerably reduced, while at the same time the results are improved.

4.4. *Take Your Time*

Since the early days of computer vision, the power of general purpose computational resources has improved by many orders of magnitude. This, combined with special purpose parallel hardware, both analog [21] and digital (VLSI), has greatly expanded the range of tractable vision tasks. The availability of increasingly powerful computing resources allows the vision system designer much greater freedom to adopt an attitude of "take your time" in vision algorithms, as well as freedom to use redundant input data. With no end in sight as regards expected improvements in computing power, the required time to solve given vision problems will continue to decrease. Conversely, it will become possible to solve problems of increased complexity and problems that have wider domains of applicability.

5. Vision Engineering

Perception engineering has been defined by Jain [22] as the study of techniques common to different sensor-understanding applications, including techniques for sensing and for the interpretation of sensory data, and how to integrate these techniques into different applications. He pointed out the existence of a serious communication gap between researchers and practitioners in the area of machine perception, and proposed establishing the field of perception engineering to bridge this gap.

However, he did not formulate any principles that could serve as guidelines for the design of successful machine perception systems.

We believe that the principles discussed in Section 4 can serve as foundations for an approach to computer vision that we shall refer to as *Vision Engineering*. The central task of vision engineering is to make vision problems tractable by applying the four principles: carefully characterizing the domain, choosing the tasks to be performed (breaking a given problem up into subtasks, if necessary), and providing adequate input data and adequate computational resources. We feel that these principles and their extensions will find increasing application in the design and construction of vision systems over the coming years.

References

[1] Q. Zheng and R. Chellappa, Estimation of illuminant direction, albedo and shape from shading, *IEEE Trans. Pattern Anal. Mach. Intell.* **13** (1991) 680–702.

[2] J. Oliensis, Uniqueness in shape from shading, *Int. J. Comput. Vision* **6** (1991) 75–104.

[3] A. N. Tikhonov and V. Y. Arsenin, *Solution of Ill-Posed Problems* (Winston, New York, 1977).

[4] T. Poggio, V. Torre and C. Koch, Computational vision and regularization theory, *Nature* **317** (1985) 314–319.

[5] J. Aloimonos and D. Shulman, *Integration of Visual Modules: An Extension of the Marr Paradigm* (Academic Press, Boston, MA, 1989).

[6] D. Terzopoulos, Regularization of inverse visual problems involving discontinuities, *IEEE Trans. Pattern Anal. Mach. Intell.* **8** (1986) 413–426.

[7] Y. C. Leclerc, Constructing simple stable descriptions for image partitioning, *Int. J. Comput. Vision* **3** (1989) 73–102.

[8] R. L. Wildey, Topography from a single radar image, *Science* **224** (1984) 153–156.

[9] J. Oliensis, Direct method for reconstructing shape from shading, in *Proc. DARPA Image Understanding Workshop*, San Diego, CA, Jan. 1992, 563–571.

[10] L. M. Kirousis and C. H. Papadimitriou, The complexity of recognizing polyhedral scenes, *J. Comput. Syst. Sci.* **37** (1988) 14–38.

[11] W. E. L. Grimson, *Object Recognition by Computer* (MIT Press, Cambridge, MA, 1990) Chapter 10.

[12] V. K. Prasanna Kumar, *Parallel Architectures and Algorithms for Image Understanding* (Academic Press, New York, 1991).

[13] E. D. Dickmanns and V. Graefe, Dynamic monocular machine vision, *Mach. Vision Appl.* **1** (1988) 223–240.

[14] E. D. Dickmanns and V. Graefe, Applications of dynamic monocular machine vision, *Mach. Vision Appl.* **1** (1988) 241–261.

[15] J. Schick and E. D. Dickmanns, Simultaneous estimation of 3D shape and motion of objects by computer vision, *IEEE Workshop on Visual Motion*, Princeton, NJ, Oct. 1991, 256–261.

[16] R. Sharma and J. Aloimonos, Robust detection of independent motion: An active and purposive solution, Center for Automation Research Technical Report CAR-TR-534, University of Maryland, College Park, 1991.

[17] J. Aloimonos, I. Weiss and A. Bandophadhay, Active vision, *Int. J. Comput. Vision* **1** (1987) 333–356.

[18] N. Nandhakumar and J. K. Aggarwal, Integrated analysis of thermal and visual images for scene interpretation, *IEEE Trans. Pattern Anal. Mach. Intell.* **10** (1988) 469–481.

[19] R. J. Woodham, Photometric method for determining surface orientation from multiple images, in B. K. P. Horn and M. J. Brooks (eds.), *Shape from Shading* (MIT Press, Cambridge, MA, 1989).

[20] M. Okutomi and T. Kanade, A multiple-baseline stereo, in *Proc. IEEE Computer Society Conf. on Computer Vision and Pattern Recognition*, Miami, FL, June 1991, 63–69.

[21] C. Mead, *Analog VLSI and Neural Systems* (Addison-Wesley, Reading, MA, 1989).

[22] R. Jain, Perception engineering, *Mach. Vision Appl.* **1** (1988) 73–74.

Handbook of Pattern Recognition and Computer Vision, pp. 817–838
Eds. C. H. Chen, L. F. Pau and P. S. P. Wang
© 1993 World Scientific Publishing Company

CHAPTER 5.2

OPTICAL PATTERN RECOGNITION FOR COMPUTER VISION

DAVID CASASENT

Department of Electrical and Computer Engineering
Center for Excellence in Optical Data Processing
Carnegie Mellon University, Pittsburgh, Pennsylvania 15213, USA

Optical processors offer many useful operations for computer vision. The maturity
of these systems and the repertoire of operations they can perform is increasing rapidly.
Hence a brief updated overview of this area merits attention. Many of the new algorithms employed can also be realized in digital and analog VLSI technology and hence
computer vision researchers should benefit from this review. We consider optical morphological, feature extraction, correlation and neural network systems for different levels
of computer vision with image processing examples and hardware fabrication work in
each area included.

Keywords: Classifier neural net, correlator, distortion-invariant filters, feature extractor,
Hough transform, Hit-or-Miss transform, morphological processor.

1. Introduction

A book could be written on each aspect of optical pattern recognition. Thus,
only the highlights of selected optical processing operations can be noted here. The
reader is referred to the references provided, several texts [1-3], recent conference
volumes [4,5], journal special issues [6] and review articles [7,8] for more details
on each topic. To unify and best summarize this field, we consider (in separate
sections) optical systems for low, medium, high and very high-level computer vision
operations. Although the boundaries between these different levels are not rigid, we
distinguish low-level vision by noise and image enhancement operations, medium-
level vision by feature extractors, high-level vision by correlators and very high-level
vision by neural net operations. As we shall show, optical processing has a role in
each area. We will mainly emphasize recent work at Carnegie Mellon University in
these different areas.

Section 2 discusses the major optical processing architectures we consider (feature extractors, correlators and neural nets) and presents one possible unified hierarchical approach to the use of all techniques for scene analysis. Section 3 details
and provides examples of optical morphological processors for low-level vision and
for detection. Section 4 considers the role for optical processing in medium-level
vision with attention to feature extractors for product inspection and for subsequent analysis of regions of interest (ROIs). Section 5 details a variety of advanced

817

distortion-invariant optical correlation filters for several applications in high-level computer vision. We then consider in Section 6 very high-level vision operations with attention to optical neural nets for object identification and brief remarks on their use as production systems.

2. Operations Achievable

Many optical processing architectures exist that are of use in computer vision. The ability to compute the Fourier transform (FT) at P_2 of 2-D input data at P_1 with a simple lens (Fig. (1a)) is probably the most widely used concept in optical processing. To simplify analysis, the $|FT|^2$ is often sampled with a detector with wedge and ring shaped detector elements [9] as in Fig. 1(b). This is a very attractive feature space for analysis of an input object since the magnitude FT is shift invariant, the wedge samples are scale invariant and the ring samples are rotation invariant. The use of 32 wedge and 32 ring detector elements also greatly simplifies analysis by dimensionality reduction.

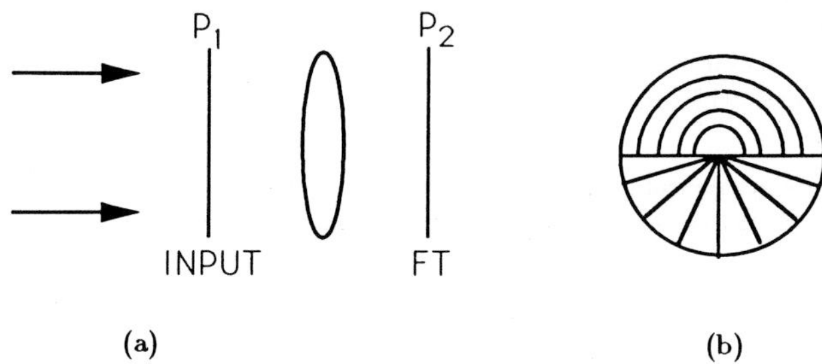

Fig. 1. Optical Fourier transform system (a) and wedge ring detector (b) [23].

Many other operations and feature space descriptions of an input object are possible and can be implemented optically [8]. These include: moments, chord distributions, polar-log FT spaces, and the Hough transform. From this we see that optical processors can implement a wide variety of image processing functions beyond the classic FT. Figure 2 shows an optical system that computes the Hough transform at TV frame rates. The input object at P_1 is imaged onto a computer generated hologram (CGH) at P_2 which forms the Hough transform at P_3 in parallel. The CGH consists of a set of N cylindrical lenses at different angles. The Hough transform input denotes the position, orientation and length of all lines in the input. Extensions to other curved shapes are possible and have been optically demonstrated. All of the aforementioned feature spaces can be optically produced using CGHs [8].

The optical correlator is also one of the most used optical processors. Figure 3 shows the schematic of a space and frequency multiplexed optical correlator. The input is placed at P_1, a set of spatially-multiplexed filters is shown at P_2.

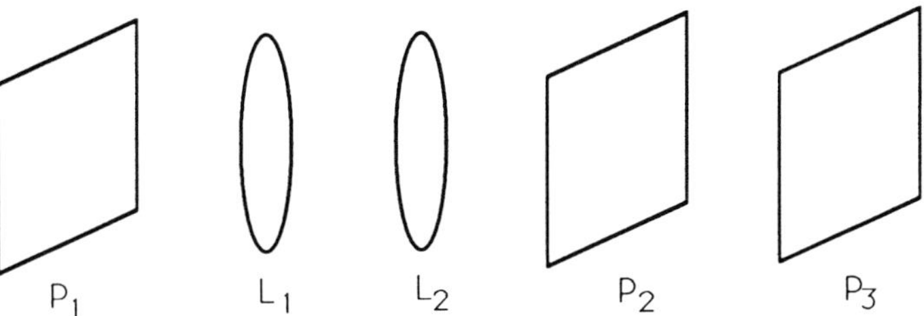

Fig. 2. Optical Hough transform system using a computer generated hologram.

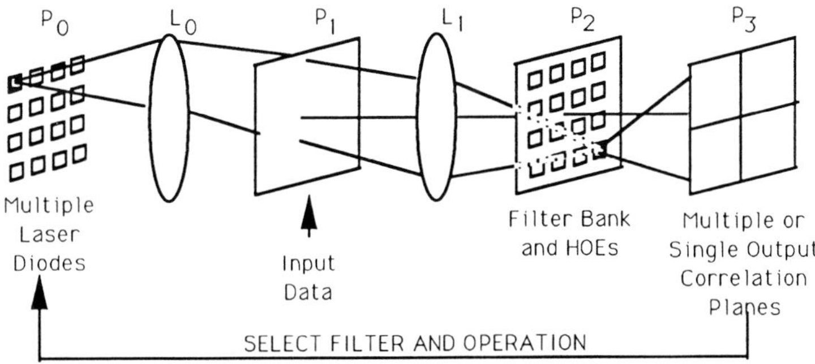

Fig. 3. Space and frequency-multiplexed optical correlator architecture [35].

Different laser diodes activated at P_0 allow different P_2 filters to be accessed. At each spatial P_2 location several (e.g. four) frequency-multiplexed filters are placed. When one P_0 laser diode is activated it selects a set of filters and the P_3 output is the correlation of the P_1 input and a set (e.g. four) of P_2 filters with the four correlations appearing in parallel in the four quadrants of P_3. With access to a large filter bank at P_2, many operations are possible (with a real-time device at P_2, adaptive filters are possible). Optical correlators have two major advantages in scene analysis: they can detect multiple objects in parallel (and are essential for parallel analysis of scenes containing multiple objects) with correlation peaks occurring at the locations of each object in the field of view and they are the optimum detector systems when noise is present.

The optical correlator is also quite versatile. With CGH filters at P_2, the P_3 output can be any of the feature spaces noted. With large banks of filters possible, one can use different filters and achieve detection, recognition and identification. When the P_2 filter used is a structuring element and when the P_3 output is properly thresholded, the P_3 output can be any morphological operation [10].

As we have just noted (to be detailed in subsequent sections), the optical correlator is a most versatile and multifunctional optical image processing architecture.
This is of major importance since optical correlators are rapidly reaching a significant level of maturity. As one example, we consider the solid optics correlator
fabricated by Teledyne Brown Engineering [11]. The system uses modular optical
elements for laser diode collimation, Fourier transform, imaging and beam splitter,
etc. components. These are assembled into a rugged optical correlator of small size
as shown in Figs. 4 and 5. In Fig. 4, the output from the laser diode light source on
the left is collimated and passes through the input spatial light modulator (SLM)
and its FT is formed at the right end where a reflective filter is placed. The light
reflected from the filter is Fourier transformed and reflected onto the output detector via the beam splitter (BS) to produce the output correlation. Figure 5 shows
the actual optical correlator system with a magneto-optic MO SLM input and a
dichromated gelatin (DCG) filter. This is typical of the high state of maturity that
this key optical architecture has reached [12]. With the advanced filters we describe,
this system will be most suitable for image processing.

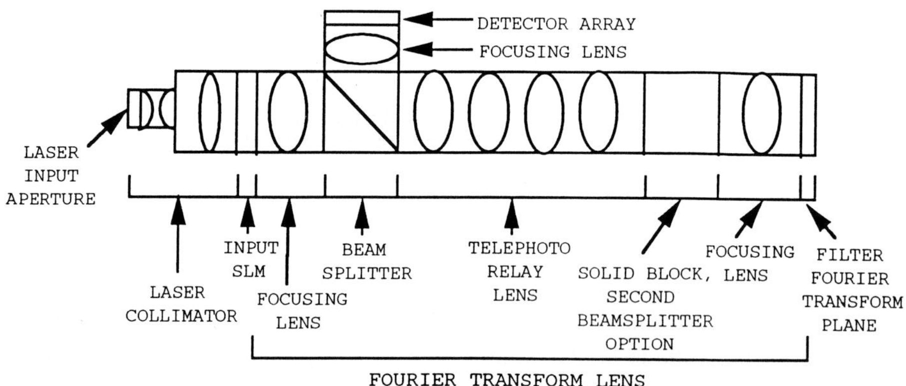

Fig. 4. Schematic diagram of the solid optics correlator [11].

The final basic optical processor architecture we consider is the optical matrix-
vector multiplier [13] of Fig. 6. The 1-D P_1 input vector $\underline{x}$ can be realized by a
linear LED or laser diode array or by a 1-D SLM. The light leaving P_1 is expanded
in 1-D to uniformly illuminate the columns of a 2-D matrix mask or SLM at P_2 with
transmittance $\underline{M}$ (a matrix). The light leaving P_2 is then integrated horizontally to
produce the output vector $\underline{y} = \underline{M}\underline{x}$ that is the matrix-vector product. We consider
the use of this system as the basic building block for an optical neural net for
object identification and as an artificial intelligence production system (Section 6).
As a multilayer neural net, the P_1 outputs are the input neurons, the matrix $\underline{M}$
is a set of weights and the P_3 outputs are the hidden layer neurons. A cascade

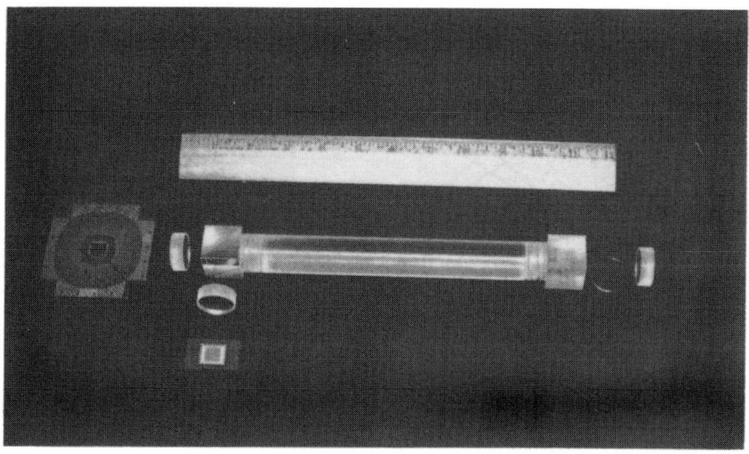

Fig. 5. Photograph of the solid optics correlator showing its major elements [11].

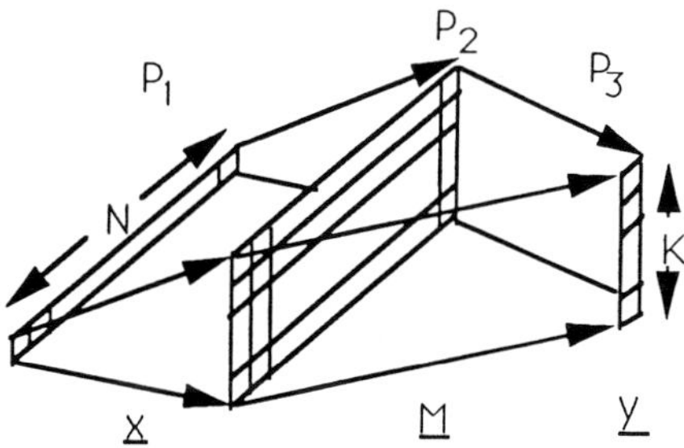

Fig. 6. Optical matrix-vector neural net processor.

of two such systems yields the standard multilayer neural net of Fig. 7 (one matrix-vector system is an associative processor) and with P$_3$ to P$_1$ feedback it is a production system (as we discuss in Section 6). The optical matrix-vector element has also achieved a high degree of maturity as seen in the schematic of Fig. 8 which shows this system component fabricated in integrated optics [14].

The basic optical image processing architectures can be viewed as low, medium, high and very high level computer vision modules. They can be used in many ways for computer vision. The approach we find to be the most useful is shown in Fig. 9. We consider the general scene analysis problem when multiple objects are present in high clutter. We separate the scene analysis problem into a hierarchy of detection, recognition and identification steps. For detection, we employ morphological correlator processors (Section 3). For recognition, we use distortion-invariant correlation filters (Section 5). For identification, we use feature extractors (Section 4) applied to the regions of interest (ROIs) obtained from detection and a neural net (Section 6) to analyze the feature space and provide the final object identification.

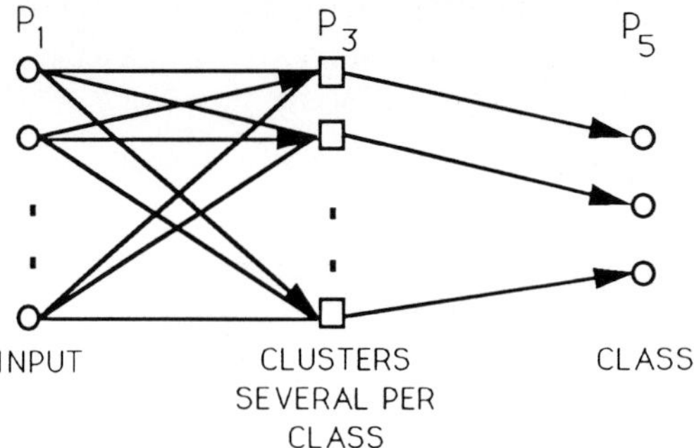

Fig. 7. Three-layer nonlinear neural net classifier used [23].

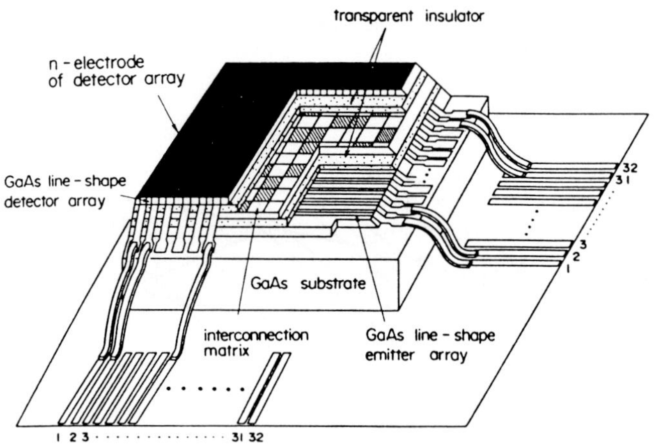

Fig. 8. Integrated optical matrix-vector processor schematic [14].

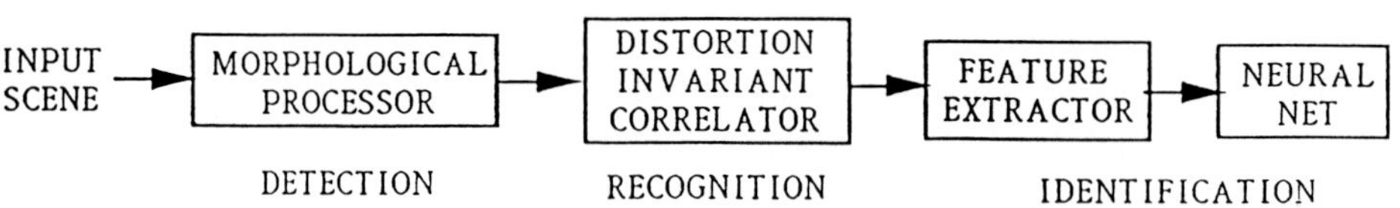

Fig. 9. One optical realization of three levels of scene analysis.

3. Low-Level Optical Morphological Processors

The two basic morphological operations are dilation (region growing) and erosion (region shrinking). We achieve both on a correlator using a filter that is a structuring

element (typically a disc), whose size determines the size of a hole or inlet to be
filled in or the size of a noise blob or protrusion to be removed. If the correlation
output is thresholded low (high) dilation (erosion) results [15]. Thus, including
structuring element filters at P_2 and an output threshold at P_3 allows the system
of Fig. 3 to also implement morphological operations. These are local operators.
Since filling in holes on a white object (dilation) and removing noise and regions
(erosion) distorts the boundary of the object, these operations are generally used
in pairs. A dilation followed by an erosion is a closure and an erosion followed by
dilation is an opening. Figure 10 shows examples of these operations. The noisy
input with holes (the treads of the tank) on the object is shown in Fig. 10(a).
The opening of it is shown in Fig. 10(b) (the erosion removes noisy background
smaller than the size of the structuring element used and the dilation restores the
boundary). The closure of Fig. 10(b) is shown in Fig. 10(c) (it fills in holes on the
object). Edge enhancement (Fig. 10(d)) is also easily achieved by the difference
between a dilation and an erosion and appears to be preferable to conventional
edge-enhancement methods [16]. Other operations such as removal of a nonuniform
background [16] etc. are also possible.

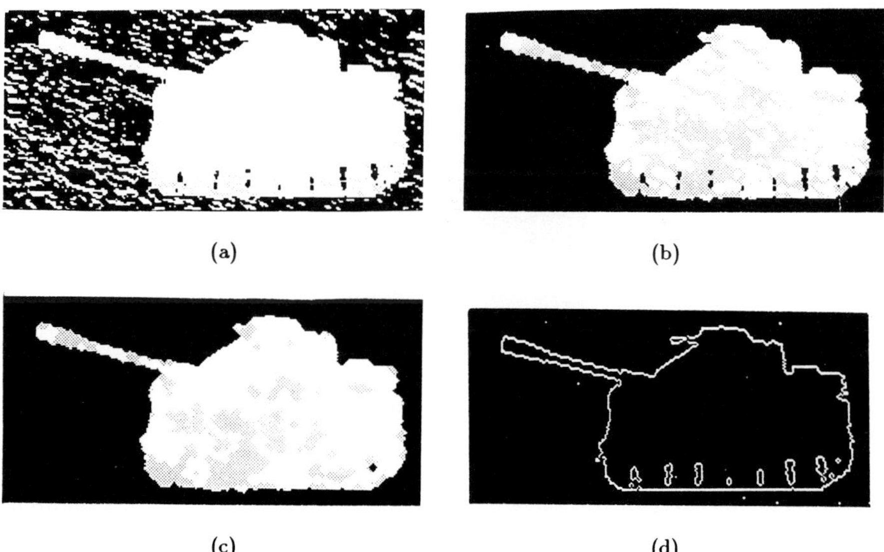

(a)   (b)

(c)   (d)

Fig. 10. Optical morphological image enhancement [35]. (a) input, (b) opening of (a), (c) closure
of (b), (d) edge-enhanced (b).

We find these standard morphological operations to be most useful to improve
the image of an object after detection. To achieve detection, we use a modified [17]
hit-or-miss (HOM) [18] morphological transform. In the basic HOM algorithm, the
input image is thresholded, correlated with a hit structuring element, and thresholded; the complement of the thresholded input is then correlated with a miss

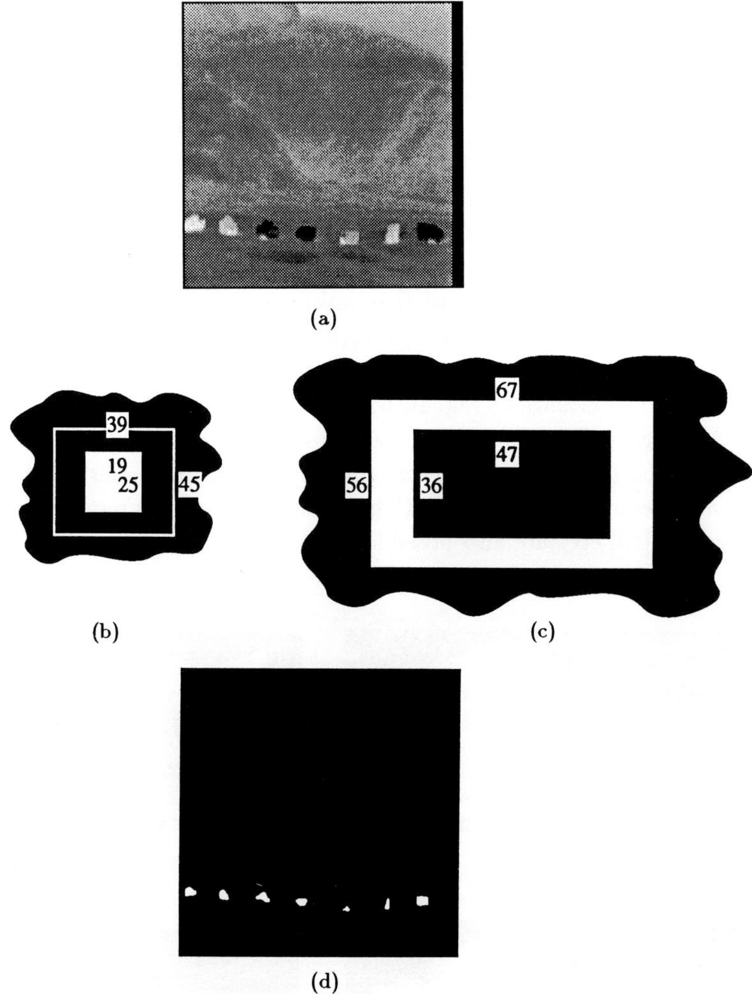

(a)

(b)   (c)

(d)

Fig. 11. Optical morphological HOM detection example. (a) Input scene, (b) H1 hit structuring element, (c) M1 miss structuring element, (d) output data.

structuring element (typically the complement of the hit element with a white border or background present) and thresholded; the intersection of the two correlations is the HOM result. Figure 11 shows an example of our new algorithm. Figure 11(a) shows a scene with hot (bright) and cold (dark) objects present. We threshold the image above the mean and perform an HOM correlation with the structuring element (not to scale with Fig. 11(a)) in Fig. 11(b). We then threshold the image below the mean and perform an MOH (miss or hit) correlation with the structuring element in Fig. 11(c). The union of the two correlations detects all objects (Fig. 11(d)). The hit filter (Fig. 11(b)) has a white region equal to the smallest object and the central dark part of the miss filter (Fig. 11(c)) is the size of the largest object (the size of the white border region in Fig. 11(c) depends upon the background expected). The HOM correlation detects hot objects and the MOH correlation detects cold objects. The hit correlation detects all objects larger than the smallest object, the miss correlation detects all objects less than the largest object and their union detects only objects within the desired range of sizes. We find this morphological function to be most attractive for the first (detection) phase of scene analysis in Fig. 9. When necessary, we use conventional image enhancement morphological operations prior to the last feature extraction step in Fig. 9.

4. Medium-Level Computer Vision (Feature Extraction)

Once regions of interest (ROIs) have been extracted (detection) from a scene, one must learn more about the contents of each such ROI. One technique that is very general (since it extends to a large number of multiple classes) is to calculate features associated with each ROI. These features include those noted in Section 2 and others. They are a reduced dimensionality description of each ROI and hence are easier to analyze (from a computation standpoint). They are generally also an in-plane distortion-invariant feature space. They almost always have shift invariance (this is essential since the location of the object in the ROI is not known) and this greatly simplifies training. In conventional pattern recognition, these features (as a feature vector) are input to a linear classifier (consisting of one or a number of linear discriminant functions, LDFs).

As an example of the power of a feature space processor, we consider the recognition of multiple classes of objects (two aircraft: an F4 and F104) with about 128×128 pixel resolution with four degree-of-freedom distortions (roll, pitch, and x and y translations). We considered $\pm 60°$ distortions in both pitch and roll at $2.5°$ increments (for each roll angle, all $\pm 60°$ pitch variations are considered). We trained a modified linear Ho-Kashyap classifier [19,20] on distortions every $5°$ in roll and pitch (625 distorted images per class). For each image, the 32-element wedge FT feature space was calculated and fed to the classifier algorithm. We then tested the classifier on 1152 distorted test images not present in the training set with $\sigma_n = 0.1$ of white Gaussian noise also present and obtained a very respectable 91.2% correct recognition. This demonstrates the ability of feature extractors to provide object discrimination in the face of very severe object distortions. For our present discussion, their major use is their potential to handle many classes of objects.

The wedge ring detector sampled FT is the most widely used optical feature space with many product inspection applications and with a well engineered system having been fabricated [21]. Here we describe a product inspection application of the Hough transform in which the specific locations and orientations of portions of a product to be inspected are of concern [22]. Figure 12 shows the product, a package of cigarettes. The specific issues of concern are that: (1) the package wrapper be aligned within $1.8°$, (2) the closure seal (A) at the top be present, aligned within $3.2°$, and that the bottom of it extends properly within 0.5 mm,

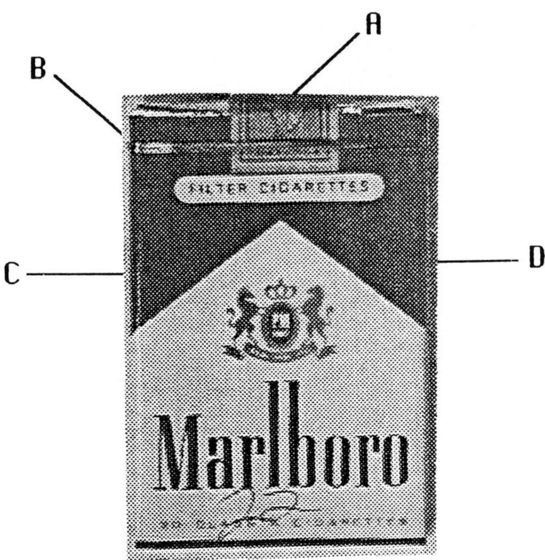

Fig. 12. Cigarette package to be inspected [22].

and (3) that the tear strip (B) be present, parallel to the top within tolerances, and be properly positioned within 0.5 mm. To achieve these inspection tasks, we form the Hough transform of each package as it is assembled. We form four slices of the Hough transform at $\theta = 38°$, $142°$, $0°$ and $90°$. The 38° and 142° angular slices denote the presence of and proper location of the two angular lines (C and D) and hence determine if the package is properly aligned. The 90° Hough transform slice has peaks corresponding to horizontal lines in the object (from top to bottom of the image, peaks occur due to the top of the package, the tear strip and the bottom of the closure seal). These indicate the presence of the tear strip and the seal and if they are at the proper location from the top of the package within tolerances. If either is at an angle, the corresponding Hough transform peak on the 90° slice becomes broader and its height decreases. The 0° slide of the Hough transform denotes vertical lines, specifically the two edges of the seal. If the seal is perfectly aligned, both Hough transform peaks will be of the same height and in the proper position horizontally on the package. If the seal is not aligned properly, the Hough transform peaks will be different in height. Figure 13 shows the Hough transform of a cigarette package with six regions along the four Hough transform slices noted with the portions of the product to which they correspond indicated. For each product, we thus investigate the six indicated Hough transform regions for a Hough transform peak and the value of each peak. The laboratory real-time Hough transform system assembled operated at 30 products per second and exhibited over 99% correct inspection. From errors in the Hough transform peak positions or heights, the nature of each product defect can be determined.

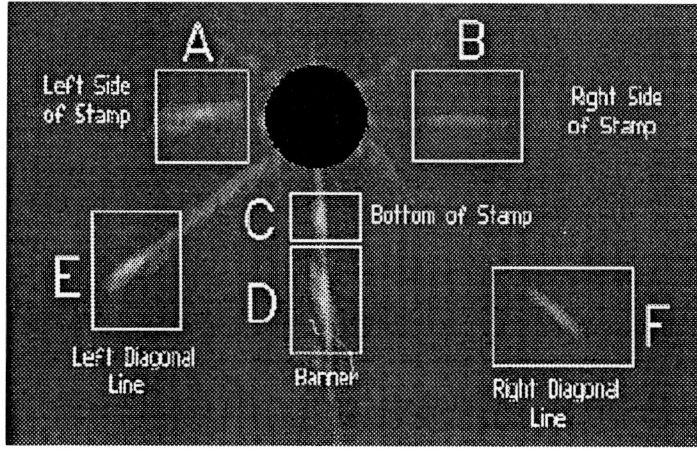

Fig. 13. Real time optical laboratory Hough transform of Fig. 12 [22].

It is important that only one object be present in the field of view and that noise be reduced when feature extractors are employed. The detection ROI location system achieves the one object requirement for scene analysis and LED or laser diode sensors achieve this for product inspection applications. Morphological processing techniques can be employed to reduce noise and improve the image if needed. Figure 9 allows for such operations prior to feature extraction and object identification.

5. High-Level Computer Vision (Correlators)

For this level of computer vision we consider advanced distortion-invariant filters used in correlators. Such correlation filters use internal object structure or the boundary shape of the object rather than simple rectangular filters as in the morphological HOM detection filters in Section 3. A wide variety of such filters exist and are generally extensions of the synthetic discriminant function (SDF) filters [24]. These SDF filters used a training set of different distorted images. The vector inner product matrix of the training set was used with a control vector that specified the correlation peak value to calculate the filter function. The filter is a linear combination of the training set of images.

5.1. *Filter Synthesis*

The synthetic discriminant function filters control only one or several points in the correlation plane and hence have limited storage capacity (number of training images N_T) before large sidelobes occur that cause false alarms. This filter clutter is due to [25] the reduced SNR that occurs for large N_T. The minimum average correlation energy (MACE) filter was the next significant development since its intent is to reduce correlation plane sidelobes. It achieves this by minimizing the correlation plane energy [26]

$$E = \underline{H}^+ \underline{\underline{D}}\, \underline{H},\tag{5.1}$$

where $\underline{H}$ is the vector version of the FT (Fourier transform) of the desired filter function and $\underline{\underline{D}}$ is a diagonal matrix with elements equal to the sum of $|FT|^2$ of the training images. We minimize (5.1) subject to a constraint on the correlation peak value for all training images

$$\underline{H}^+ \underline{\underline{X}} = \underline{u},\tag{5.2}$$

where $^+$ denotes the conjugate transpose, the columns of the matrix $\underline{\underline{X}}$ are the FTs $\underline{X}_i$ of the training set images and the elements of the control vector $\mathbf{u}$ are the correlation peak values specified for each training image (the elements of $\mathbf{u}$ are typically chosen to be one). The solution to (5.1) subject to the constraint in (5.2) is found by Lagrange multiplier techniques to be [26]

$$\underline{H} = \underline{\underline{D}}^{-1}\underline{\underline{X}}(\underline{\underline{X}}^+\underline{\underline{D}}^{-1}\underline{\underline{D}}\underline{\underline{X}})^{-1}\underline{u}.\tag{5.3}$$

The MACE filter solution yields a sharp correlation peak, which localizes the target's position well. However, such sharp correlation peaks result because the spectrum of the filter has been whitened emphasizing high frequencies. As a result, this filter has poor recognition of non-training set intra-class images and it is sensitive to noise.

To overcome these problems, we recently introduced the minimum noise and average correlation energy (MINACE) filter [27]. This uses a better bound on the spectral envelope of the images. And it also inherently uses a specified noise power spectrum $\underline{\underline{N}}$ in synthesis. For a filter with one training image i, the filter solution is

$$\underline{H} = \underline{\underline{T}}_i^{-1}\underline{\underline{X}}(\underline{\underline{X}}^+\underline{\underline{T}}_i^{-1}\underline{\underline{X}})^{-1}\underline{u},\tag{5.4}$$

and for N_T training images, the filter solution is

$$\underline{H} = \underline{\underline{T}}^{-1}\underline{\underline{X}}(\underline{\underline{X}}^+\underline{\underline{T}}^{-1}\underline{\underline{X}})^{-1}\underline{u}.\tag{5.5}$$

Its form is the same as in (5.3), however the preprocessing function $\underline{\underline{T}}_i$ is now a diagonal matrix with diagonal elements

$$T_i(u, v) = \max[D_i(u, v), N(u, v)]\tag{5.6}$$

and $\underline{\underline{T}}$ is a diagonal matrix with diagonal elements

$$T(u, v) = \max[T_1(u, v), T_2(u, v), \cdots, T_{N_T}(u, v)].\tag{5.7}$$

The key step is the choice of the preprocessing function $\underline{\underline{T}}$. Its elements are chosen *separately for each spatial frequency u and v* based on the magnitude of the spatial frequencies of the signal D and the noise N. Specifically, if the signal is above the noise at some spatial frequency, we select the signal; otherwise, we use the selected noise level N. This comparison is done separately for each spatial frequency and for all training images. This reduces the filter's response at high frequencies and other frequencies (where noise dominates) and hence improves intra-class recognition and performance in noise. This filter has another major advantage of use in our present problem: we can control the filter's recognition and discrimination performance. This is achieved by varying the amount of noise N (through its variance σ^2) used in filter synthesis. We define the control parameter

$$c = \sigma^2/DC \qquad (5.8)$$

to be the ratio of the noise energy (for white Gaussian noise) to the DC value of the signal energy. Large values of c emphasize lower spatial frequencies and provide filters that are good for detection (intra-class recognition and noise performance). Low c values emphasize higher spatial frequencies and such filters are good for identification. Medium c values prove to be useful for recognition. This provides the MINACE filter with a *flexibility* not found in other correlation filters which are quite *rigid*. Specifically, by varying the training set and the control parameter c, the same filter synthesis algorithm yields filters suitable for the three different levels in scene analysis (detection, recognition, and identification). We now provide initial examples of such results to demonstrate the concepts.

5.2. *Test Results*

Figure 14 provides an example of this multifunctional filter synthesis algorithm. Figure 14(a) shows the input scene. It contains 13 objects as noted in Fig. 14(b) (the values in parentheses indicate the orientation of each object). We formed a MINACE filter trained only on 36 orientations of the ZSU object at 10° intervals with a large $c = 0.1$ value. This object was chosen since it is the smallest one and we initially desire to only implement detection. Figure 14(c) shows the detection correlation results. We find peaks for all 13 objects and only one false alarm (lower left). Thus, this filter can achieve detection of all interesting ROIs independent of their orientation and in considerable noise. To achieve recognition of only the larger and more dangerous objects (the SCUD and FROG missile launchers), we trained a MINACE filter on only SCUDs and FROGs and used a lower $c = 0.05$ value. The results (Fig. 14(d)) show correlation peaks at the locations of these five mobile missile launchers. This filter thus achieves recognition of a subclass of objects (large missile launchers) independent of their orientation and in noise. To achieve identification of only the SCUD objects, we form another MINACE filter trained only on SCUDs and with a smaller $c = 0.001$ value (a lower c provides more discrimination). The results (Fig. 14(e)) locate the three SCUD objects and demonstrate identification.

Correlators are well-known to be ideal for detection in noise and when multiple objects are present. This example demonstrates how the same basic filter synthesis algorithm can achieve detection, recognition and identification and hence can solve quite complex scene analysis problems.

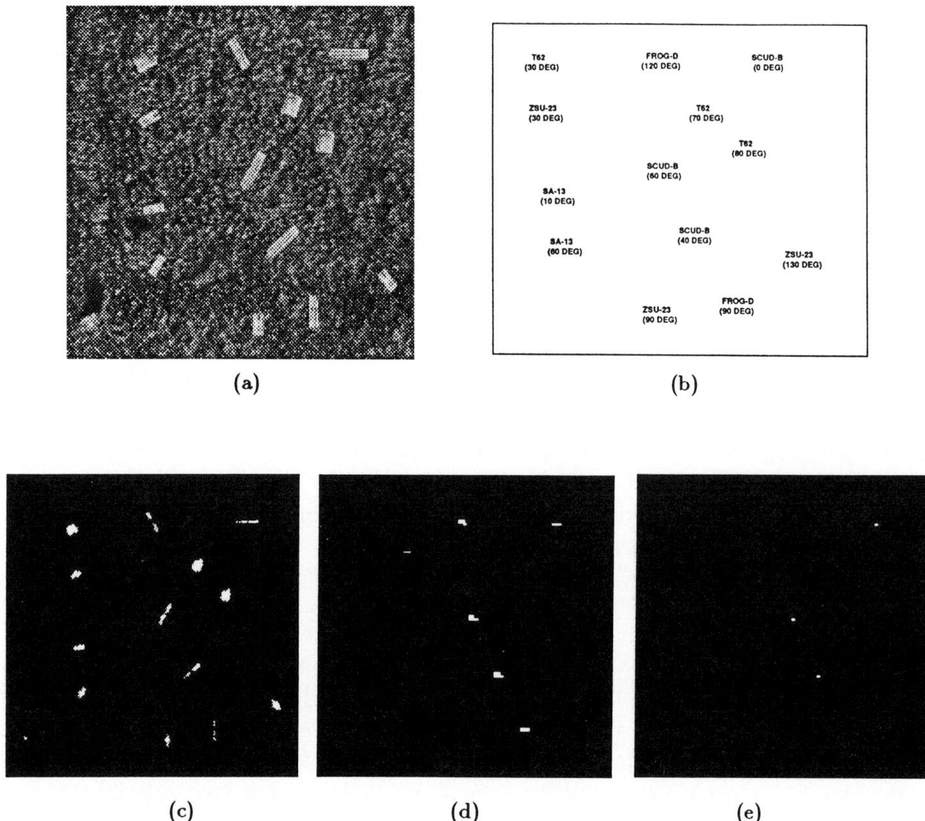

Fig. 14. Advanced MINACE distortion-invariant hierarchical correlation filter results. (a) Input, (b) input, (c) detection, (d) recognition (SCUDS/FROGS), (e) identification (SCUDS).

Another noteworthy example of filter performance is now briefly noted. For identification or discrimination between two very similar objects, correlation techniques using all object pixels rather than reduced dimensionality feature space methods are preferable. Figure 15 shows images of the SA-13 and ZSU-23 objects with about 32x12 pixel resolution. As seen, they are quite similar. To identify the SA-13 and discriminate it from the ZSU-23 object when 36 different rotated versions of each object are considered, we used a MINACE filter with c = 0.001 and $N_T = 19$ training images of the SA-13 at 19 of the 36 distorted angles. This filter successfully recognizes all true class SA-13 objects and yields no correlation peaks above 0.5 for any of the 36 false class ZSU-23 objects. Three other properties of the MINACE filter emerge from this example. As we increase c, we can reduce the size N_T of the required training set (e.g. $N_T = 19$ not 36 here). Use of a flat spectrum for our MINACE noise model thus also effectively models object distortions (e.g. controlling the spatial frequencies used to recognize an object in noise is similar to controlling

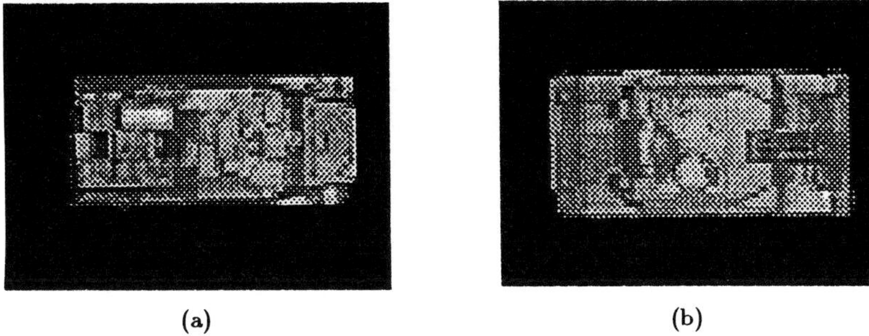

Fig. 15. Two similar objects for identification and discrimination (a) SA-13, (b) ZSU-23.

the spatial frequencies to achieve intraclass recognition, as this example has shown). Finally, no false class training images were used (i.e. we could have, but did not, train the filter to produce a zero or low output correlation value for troublesome false class images). This is attractive since one does not generally know every false class object that is possible. In multiple correlation stages of the identification portion of scene analysis, this may be allowable (and necessary) in some cases.

6. Very High-Level Computer Vision (Neural Nets)

Many potential applications for neural nets in computer vision have been advanced [28]. These include image enhancement and feature extraction. We find other techniques (Sections 3 and 4) to be preferable and sufficient for these operations. The major reason is the large number of neurons and interconnections required when the neural net input is an iconic (pixel-based) image representation. For example, one can achieve shift invariance in a neural net with N input neurons by the use of N^4 interconnections [29]. However, when $N = 512^2$, this is very excessive and since the same property can be achieved with the FT etc., we find such methods to be preferable.

When multiple objects are present in the field of view, no neural net can handle all objects in parallel. Conversely, a correlator (Section 5) easily achieves this. A correlator is in fact a most powerful neural net with the filter function being the set of weights applied to input iconic neurons (an image) with the unique property that the weights are applied in parallel to every region of the input scene. Thus, for such cases, we find a correlator using advanced distortion-invariant filters to be preferable.

In general, we find the use of such FT-based free-space optical interconnections to be preferable to other neural net approaches which achieve shift invariance with much more hardware with many hard-wired forced interconnections required (and are not easily achieved without optical processing techniques).

6.1. *Neural Net Classifier Algorithm*

In our opinion, one of the major uses of neural nets is their ability to provide an algorithm for determining nonlinear piecewise discriminant surfaces for classifiers. We now highlight our adaptive clustering neural net [30] and how it uses linear discriminant functions (linear classifiers) and neural net techniques to achieve a nonlinear classifier. As the input neuron representation space we use feature space neurons (Section 4) obtained for ROIs from a morphological detection processor. The classic three-layer neural net we use is shown in Fig. 7. The input P_1 neurons are a feature space (we use wedge $|FT$ samples in our example). The output P_5 neurons indicate the class of the input object. To determine the number of hidden layer neurons, we use standard clustering techniques [31] to select prototypes or exemplars for each class from the full training set. The number of prototypes decided upon is the number of hidden layer neurons N_3. We typically use three prototypes per class. We assign each of these to a hidden layer neuron (i.e. we use 3C hidden layer neurons, where C is the number of object classes). Each prototype and hence each P_3 hidden layer neuron corresponds to a feature vector or a point in the multidimensional feature space. As the initial weights from P_1 to each P_3 neuron (e.g. P_3 neuron i), we use the feature vector $\underline{p}_i$ for prototype i. This results in a set of P_1-to-P_3 weights that are classic linear discriminant functions as used in standard pattern recognition.

These are only the *initial* weights. They are then *adapted* into nonlinear discriminant functions by our neural net algorithm. To achieve this, we add an additional input neuron whose value is minus 0.5 times the sum of the squares of the other weights. Thus, with N_F features, we use $N_1 = N_F + 1$ input P_1 neurons with the weights w_{ij} (from P_1 input neuron j to P_3 neuron i) described by

$$w_{ij} = \begin{cases} p_{ij} & \text{for } j = 1 \cdots N_1 - 1 \\ -(1/2) \sum_{i=1}^{N_1-1} p_{ij}^2 & \text{for } j = N \end{cases} \tag{6.1}$$

where p_{ij} is element j of the prototype vector $\underline{p}_i$. This insures that the hidden layer neuron closest to the input vector at P_1 will be the most active one. We use a winner-take-all selection of the most active P_3 neuron during classification. We now use neural net training to adapt these initial P_1-to-P_3 weights (the neural net thus forms weights that are combinations of linear discriminant functions and hence it produces piecewise nonlinear discriminant surfaces as we shall show). To adapt the weights, we present each of the training set of image feature spaces to the neural net and we determine the P_3 neuron values for each input $\underline{x}$ (for P_3 neuron i this is simply the vector inner product $\underline{x}^T \underline{w}_i$ of the training set input vector $\underline{x}$ and the weight vector $\underline{w}_i$ from all P_1 neurons to P_3 neuron i). We then calculate the most active P_3 neuron $i(c)$ in class c of the input vector and the most active neuron $i(\bar{c})$ in any other class. We denote their weight vectors by $\underline{w}_{i(c)}$ and $\underline{w}_{i(\bar{c})}$. For each input, we then determine an error E for a perceptron error function as

$$E = \begin{cases} 0 & \text{if } \underline{w}_{i(c)}{}^T \underline{x} > \underline{w}_{i(\bar{c})}{}^T \underline{x} + S \\ S + (\underline{w}_{i(c)} - \underline{w}_{i(\bar{c})}{}^T)x & \text{otherwise} \end{cases} \qquad (6.2)$$

where $S = 0.05$ in our case. After each presentation of the training set, we calculate the derivative $\partial E / \partial \underline{w}_i$ and use it to adapt the weights using a conjugate gradient algorithm [32]. We then present the training set again, calculate E in (6.2) and continue to adapt the weights until convergence or negligible change occurs.

6.2. *Neural Net Classifier Results*

To best demonstrate the power of a neural net to produce piecewise nonlinear decision surfaces from linear discriminant functions, we consider the artificial problem in Fig. 16 with 383 samples in three classes (181 in class 1 on the left and bottom represented by a triangle; in class 2 in the center represented by a circle; and 105 in class 3 in the upper right represented by a diamond). We chose this 3-class example because it uses only two features and the results can thus be displayed. We used our ACNN algorithm to solve this problem using $N_1 = 3$ input P_1 neurons (the two features plus one bias neuron), $N_3 = 2C = 6$ hidden layer neurons and $N_5 = C = 3$ output neurons, the number of data classes. Figure 16 shows the piecewise nonlinear decision boundaries produced (they consist of six straight lines, modified combinations of the six initial linear discriminant functions associated with the six hidden layer neurons). The results obtained gave $P_C = 97\%$ correct recognition after only 80 iterations during training (in classification our ACNN algorithm is a one-pass non-iterative algorithm). We compared this neural net performance to that of the standard but very computationally expensive multivariate Gaussian

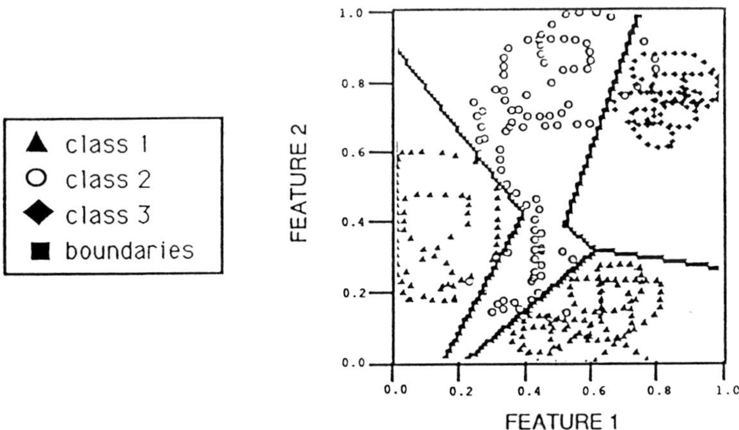

Fig. 16. Discrimination problem showing nonlinear decision surfaces automatically produced by our neural net algorithm [23].

classifier which achieved only $P_C = 89.5\%$ correct recognition. Thus, as expected a neural net is necessary to solve this problem. This 2-D (two feature) example is instructive to visually demonstrate the ability of a neural net algorithm to easily compute complex decision surfaces for difficult discrimination problems.

We now consider a more complex version of the pattern recognition problem in Section 4, one that requires the use of a neural net classifier. Specifically, we consider three not two aircraft (F4, F104 and DC-10) and a larger $\pm 85°$ range of roll and pitch distortions. Figure 17 shows several views of each aircraft. In each set of images, the top center image is top-down with no distortions in roll or pitch. Each row left-to-right corresponds to pitch angles of $-80°$, $-40°$, $0°$, $+40°$, and $+80°$. From top-to-bottom, they correspond to roll angles of $0°$, $40°$ and $80°$. We attempted to solve this multiclass pattern recognition problem using the linear classifier of Section 4 and obtained poor results ($P_C < 60\%$). We then used our ACNN algorithm with $N_1 = 33$ input neurons (32 wedge $|FT|$ features plus one bias neuron), $N_3 = 3C = 9$ hidden layer neurons and $N_5 = C = 3$ output neurons, one per class. The training set consisted of the feature spaces for 630 distorted objects per class ($3 \times 630 = 1890$ in total). The test set consisted of over 1800 distorted objects at intermediate roll and pitch distortions between those used in training. The results we obtained were excellent ($P_C = 98.6\%$ correct recognition). This example vividly demonstrates the advantage of a neural net over a linear classifier for complex discrimination problems. Thus, in our general block diagram (Fig. 9), we show a neural net classifier used on feature space data calculated for regions of interest (ROIs) obtained from the detection portion of our general scene analysis system.

6.3. *Production System Neural Net*

Another useful very high-level function in scene analysis is a production system. In this case the various facts learned about each ROI in the scene must be analyzed to obtain further data. To achieve this, one can write a set of IF-THEN rules, e.g.

$$\text{IF } a \rightarrow b$$
$$\text{IF } a \text{ and } c \text{ and } f \rightarrow g$$
$$\text{IF } b \rightarrow a$$
$$\text{IF } f \text{ and } g \rightarrow c$$

where the antecedents are the entries to the left, the consequents are those on the right and the arrow denotes THEN. More complex formulations with predicate calculus can be produced, but this example suffices to show the point. One can implement the above production system rules on a neural net as we now discuss [33]. We use a two-layer neural net (optical matrix-vector multipler) with each fact (antecedent or consequent) assigned to a specific neuron and with an equal number of input and output neurons. We encode the rules in the weights (matrix) as shown in Fig. 18 for the above example.

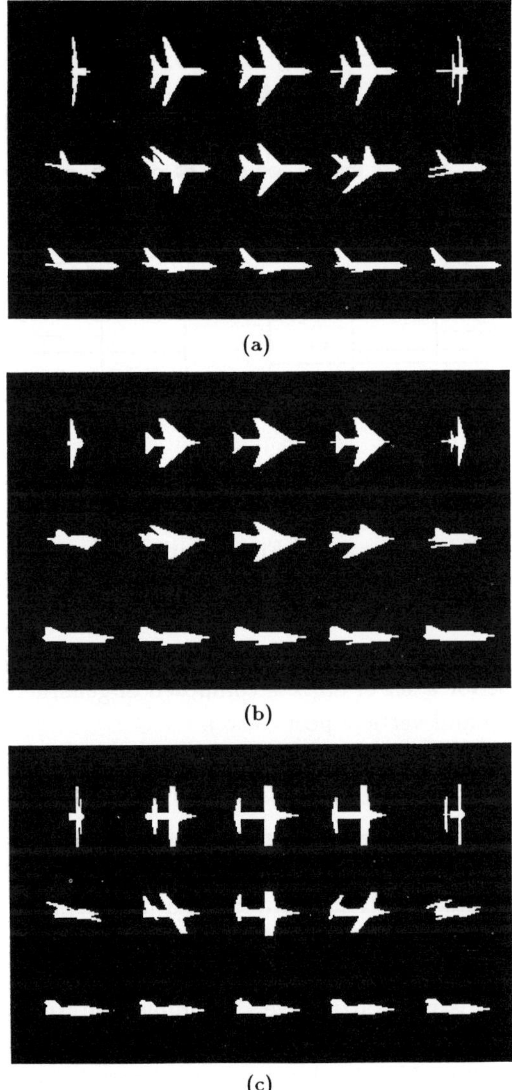

Fig. 17. Distorted images of the three aircraft used (a) F4, (b) F104, (c) DC10.

There are seven input and output neurons (a to g) for this simple example. The first matrix-vector multiplication and the neuron outputs after the first iteration indicate new facts learned from the initial input facts. We feed the output neurons back to the input neurons keeping previously activated input neurons (facts) still "on". These subsequent iterations allow the system to learn new rules not directly encoded in the original rules. The iterations continue until an output object "consequent" neuron has been activated in which case the object identification of the input scene region has been determined. The optical realization of this system is

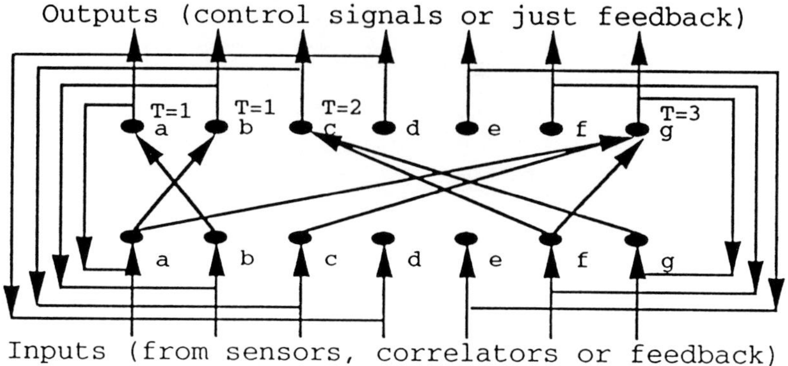

Fig. 18. Production system neural net [23].

the simple matrix-vector processor of Fig. 6 with feedback (Section 2). One can extend this basic system in many ways such as by using analog neurons proportional to the probabilities of each antecedent fact and by use of predicate calculus rather than propositional calculus formulations. We recently [34] demonstrated this system optically in real time for a set of objects composed of generic object parts (circles, rectangles, horizontal and vertical posts, etc.).

7. Summary

We have briefly reviewed the role for optics in four levels of general computer vision. As seen, optical processing has a significant role in each area, and optical hardware to achieve these functions is rapidly maturing. The algorithms described in each area of computer vision are novel and can also be implemented digitally. Our new morphological low-level vision algorithm for detection of regions of interest (ROIs) in a scene is most attractive. Its implementation and the realization of other low-level image enhancement operations on an optical correlator are also most attractive. We use a high-level vision optical correlator with new distortion-invariant filters to further analyze ROIs (and in some cases for detection and even object identification). For the general case, once ROIs have been detected, initially analyzed by a correlator and enhanced (if necessary) by morphological techniques, we perform feature extraction and finally use a neural net (for complex multiclass problems) for object identification of each ROI.

References

[1] H. Stark (ed.), *Applications of Optical Fourier Transforms* (Academic Press, 1982).
[2] S. H. Lee (ed.), *Optical Information Processing*, Vol. 28, Topics in Applied Physics (Springer-Verlag, 1981).

[3] G. I. Vasilenko and L. M. Tsibul'kin, *Image Recognition by Holography* (Consultants Bureau, 1989).

[4] D. Casasent (ed.), *Optical Pattern Recognition, Proc. SPIE*, Vol. 201, 1979. P. Schenker and H. K. Liu (eds.), *Optical and Digital Pattern Recognition, Proc. SPIE*, Vol. 754, 1987.

[5] D. Casasent and A. Tescher (eds.), *Hybrid Image Processing, Proc. SPIE*, Vol. 638, 1986. D. Casasent and A. Tescher (eds.), *Hybrid Image and Signal Processing, Proc. SPIE*, Vol. 939, 1989. D. Casasent and A. Tescher (eds.), *Hybrid Image and Signal Processing II, Proc. SPIE*, Vol. 1279, 1990.

[6] B. V. K. Vijaya Kumar (ed.), *Optical Engineering*, Special Issue on Optical Pattern Recognition **29**, 9 (1990).

[7] D. L. Flannery and J. L. Horner, Fourier optical signal processors, in *Proc. IEEE* **77** (1989) 1511–1527.

[8] D. Casasent, Coherent optical pattern recognition: A review, *Optical Engineering* **24** (1985) 26–32.

[9] G. G. Lendaris and G. L. Stanley, Diffraction-pattern sampling for automatic target recognition, *Proc. IEEE* **58** (1979) 198–205.

[10] P. Maragos, Tutorial: Advances in morphological image processing and analysis, *Optical Engineering* **26** (1987) 623–632.

[11] P. C. Lindberg and C. F. Hester, The challenge to demonstrate an optical pattern recognition system, *Proc. SPIE*, Vol. 1297, Apr. 1990, 72–76.

[12] D. A. Gregory, J. C. Kirsch and J. A. Loudin, Optical correlators: optical computing that really works, *Proc. SPIE*, Vol. 1296, Apr. 1990, 2–19.

[13] J. Goodman, A. R. Dias and L. Woody, Fully parallel high-speed incoherent optical method for performing discrete Fourier transforms, *Optics Letters* **2** (1983) 1–3.

[14] J. Ohta, M. Takahashi, Y. Nitta, S. Tai, K. Mitsunaga and K. Kyuma, A new approach to a GaAs/AlGaAs optical neurochip with three layered structure, in *Proc. IJCNN Int. Joint Conf. on Neural Networks*, Washington, D.C., Jun. 1989, Vol. II, II-477–II-480.

[15] D. Casasent and E. Botha, Optical symbolic substitution for morphological transformations, *Applied Optics* **27** (1988) 3806–3810.

[16] D. Casasent, R. Schaefer and J. Kokaj, Morphological processing to reduce shading and illumination effects, *Proc. SPIE*, Vol. 1385, 1990, 152-164.

[17] D. Casasent and R. Schaefer, Optical implementation of gray scale morphology, *Proc. SPIE*, Vol. 1658, Feb. 1992.

[18] D. Casasent, R. Schaefer and R. Sturgill, Optical hit-or-miss morphological transform, *Applied Optics* **31** (1992) 6255–6263.

[19] R. Duda and P. Hart, *Pattern Classification and Scene Analysis* (John Wiley and Sons, New York, 1973).

[20] B. Telfer and D. Casasent, Ho-Kashyap optical associative processors, *Applied Optics* **29** (1990) 1191–1202.

[21] D. Clark and D. Casasent, Practical optical Fourier analysis for high-speed inspection, *Optical Engineering* **27**, 5 (1988) 365-371.

[22] J. Richards and D. Casasent, Real-time optical Hough transform for industrial inspection, *Proc. SPIE*, Vol. 1192, 1989, 2–21.

[23] D. Casasent, Optical processing and hybrid neural nets, *Proc. SPIE*, Vol. 1469, Apr. 1991.

[24] D. Casasent, Unified synthetic discriminant function computational formulation, *Applied Optics* **23** (1984) 1620–1627.

[25] B. V. K. Vijaya Kumar and E. Pochapsky, Signal-to-noise ratio considerations in modified matched spatial filters, *J. Opt. Soc. Am. A* **3** (1986) 777–786.

[26] A. Mahalanobis, B. V. K. Vijaya Kumar and D. Casasent, Minimum average correlation energy (MACE) filters, *Applied Optics* **26** (1987) 3633–3640.

[27] G. Ravichandran and D. Casasent, Minimum noise and correlation energy (MINACE) optical correlation filter, *Applied Optics* **31** (1992) 1823–1833.

[28] H. Wechsler (ed.), *Neural Networks for Human and Machine Perception* (Academic Press, 1991).

[29] C. L. Giles, R. D. Griffen and T. Maxwell, Encoding geometric invariances in higher-order neural networks, in D. Anderson (ed.), *Neural Information Processing Systems*, Denver, CO (AIP, 1988) 301–309.

[30] D. Casasent and E. Barnard, Adaptive clustering optical neural net, *Applied Optics* **29** (1990) 2603–2615.

[31] T. M. Cover and P. E. Hart, Nearest neighbor pattern classification, *IEEE Trans. Inf. Theory* **13** (1967) 21–27.

[32] M. J. D. Powell, Restart procedures for the conjugate gradient method, *Mathematical Programming* **12** (1977) 241–254.

[33] E. Botha, D. Casasent and E. Barnard, Optical production systems using neural networks and symbolic substitution, *Applied Optics* **27** (1988) 5185–5193.

[34] D. Casasent and E. Botha, Optical correlator production system neural net, *Applied Optics* **31** (1992) 1030–1040.

[35] D. Casasent, Optical morphological processors, *Proc. SPIE*, Vol. 1350, 1990, 380–394.

Handbook of Pattern Recognition and Computer Vision, pp. 839–861
Eds. C. H. Chen, L. F. Pau and P. S. P. Wang
© 1993 World Scientific Publishing Company

$$\boxed{\text{CHAPTER 5.3}}$$

SPATIAL KNOWLEDGE REPRESENTATION
FOR ICONIC IMAGE DATABASE

SUH-YIN LEE

Department of Computer Science and Information Engineering
National Chiao Tung University, Hsinchu, Taiwan, Republic of China

and

FANG-JUNG HSU

Computer and Communication Research Laboratories, Industrial Technology Research Institute
Hsinchu, Taiwan, Republic of China

The perception of spatial relationships among objects in a picture is one important criterion to discriminate and retrieve images in an image database system. The data structure, called 2D string, to represent symbolic pictures was proposed by Chang et al. It allows a natural way of constructing iconic indexes for pictures. Jungert has extended 2D string to represent more types of spatial relationships, but the operators and the derived knowledge cannot be stored in a unified structure. Lee and Hsu proposed 2D C-string representation with a set of spatial operators and a more efficient cutting mechanism. 2D C-string is more characteristic of spatial knowledge and is more efficient in representation and manipulation of images. Since each symbolic picture can be represented by a 2D C-string, a picture query can also be specified by a 2D C-string. The problem of pictorial information retrieval then becomes the problem of 2D subsequence matching. Spatial relationship is a fuzzy concept. The capability of similarity retrieval for pictures is essential. Similarity measure and similarity retrieval of iconic images to different extents of precision is also presented.

Keywords: 2D C-string, spatial relationship, similarity retrieval, pictorial query, image database.

1. Introduction

In image information systems, one of the most important methods for discriminating the images is the perception of objects and the spatial relationships that exist among them in the desired images. Therefore, how images are stored and the capability of assembling queries on objects and their spatial relationships in a database are important issues of image database system design [1,2]. The data structure to represent the pictures should be object-oriented, and the spatial knowledge embedded in images should be preserved in the data structure [3,4,5]. So users can easily retrieve, visualize and manipulate objects in the image database systems [6].

Most systems of previous approaches provide search capability of simple table look up of image features and secondary information. The Intelligent Image Database System (IIDS) [6] provides high-level object-oriented search and supports spatial reasoning. The spatial reasoning is based on a data structure called 2D string [7,8] which preserves the objects' spatial knowledge embedded in images. The picture query can also be specified as a 2D string. The problem of pictorial information retrieval then becomes a problem of 2D string subsequence matching. This approach provides a natural way of constructing iconic indexes for pictures.

However, this representation is under challenge in solving the problems of spatial reasoning and planning in many applications. The spatial operators of 2D strings are not sufficient to give a complete description for a picture of arbitrary complexity. Jungert [9,10] introduced some local operators as compensation for handling more types of relations between pictorial objects in query reasoning. But these local operators and all the derived binary relations cannot be stored, in a unified structure with global operators, into a global 2D string. To overcome the problem, Chang et al. [11] introduced the generalized 2D string (2D G-string) with the cutting mechanism. The cuttings are performed at all extreme points of all the objects to segment the objects in the image. But it is not ideally economic for complex images in terms of storage space efficiency and navigation complexity in spatial reasoning.

Based on the above reasons, a set of spatial operators and a spatial knowledge representation 2D C-string were proposed [12]. All the spatial relations among objects with efficient segmentation are preserved with 2D C-string representation. It has been proved that this is more efficient than 2D G-string in storage space and in processing complexity. An algebraic point of view of 2D C-strings is presented in [13]. Transitive laws, distributive laws, and manipulation laws are discussed. From the 2D C-string representation of a symbolic picture, all the relationships among symbolic objects embedded in the picture can be derived. These laws form the theoretic basis for pictorial query inference and spatial reasoning.

To retrieve the images according to the spatial relationships, one problem may arise. Spatial relationship is a fuzzy concept and is thus often dependent on human interpretation. Also, the generation of 2D strings or 2D C-strings is sensitive to the shape, size and relative position of the objects in the images. Thus, similarity retrieval of images, which is one of the distinct functions different from a conventional database system, is essential.

In Section 2, a brief analysis of previous approaches is given. In Section 3, the spatial knowledge structure 2D C-string is introduced. The algebraic point of view of the 2D C-string is discussed in Section 4. The picture algebra provides the theoretic basis for spatial reasoning and pictorial query inference. In Section 5, we describe the spatial reasoning using 2D C-string and the powerful spatial 2D C-query. Similarity retrieval of images is discussed in Section 6. Conclusions and future works are summarized in the last section.

2. Spatial Query

Spatial relationship is a significant selection criterion when retrieving objects from an image. People often remember the relative spatial positions of the objects, rather than the absolute positions of the objects. The retrieval of an object by spatial relationship is called spatial query.

Spatial queries can be further classified into the following types:

(1) *Direction query.* Find the objects with directional relationship to the query objects. For example: "Find the hotels which are east of the city library and northeastern of the bus station."

(2) *Region query.* Find the objects with a regional relationship to the query objects. The regional relationships include covering, covered-by, intersection. For example: "Find the bridge which crosses the Mississippi River." or "Find the hotels which are located downtown."

(3) *Distance query.* Find the objects which are farthest from or nearest to the query objects. For example: "Find the hotels which are nearest to the bus station."

There exists two streams of approaches to process the spatial query. The first approach is based on the range query in conventional databases. The second approach is based on the iconic indexing technique of 2D string.

2.1. *Approaches of Range Queries*

The processing of the direction and the distance spatial query in the conventional database can be handled by the region query. For example, the spatial query to find the objects east of the house is to find the objects which are located in the eastern region of the house. Known methods for handling region queries of multi-dimensional objects are classified and briefly discussed below. Multi-dimensional objects include points, lines, rectangles, circles, or polygons, etc. Handling non-zero sized objects can be reduced to handling rectangles by finding the minimum bounding rectangle (MBR) of the given object. Two objects do not intersect if their corresponding MBRs do not intersect. This will reduce the cost of the potential intersection tests since the test on the intersection of two polygons or the intersection of a polygon and a sequence of line segments is more complicated than the test on the intersection of two rectangles.

The most common case of multi-dimensional data that has been studied in the past is points [3,14]. The main idea is to divide the whole space into disjoint subregions, usually in such a way that each subregion contains no more than C points. C is usually 1 if the data is stored in the core memory, or the capacity of a disk page, which is the number of data records one page can hold.

Insertions of new points may result in further partitioning of a region, known as a split. Split is performed by introducing one or more hyperplanes that partition a region further into disjoint subregions. The following attributes of a split help to classify the known methods:

(1) *Position.* In fixed methods, the position of the splitting hyperplane is predetermined, e.g. the region is cut in half as in the grid file method. In adaptable methods, the position of the hyperplane is determined by the data points as in the k–d trees or the K–D–B-trees methods.

(2) *Dimensionality.* In 1–d cut methods, the split is done with only one hyperplane. In k–d cut methods, the split is in all k dimensions with k hyperplanes, as the quad-trees and oct-trees do.

(3) *Locality.* The splitting hyperplane splits not only the affected region, but all the regions in this direction, as in the grid file. We shall call these methods grid methods. The opposite way is to restrict the splitting hyperplane to extend solely inside the region to be split. These methods will be referred to as brickwall methods. The brickwall methods usually do a hierarchical decomposition of the space, requiring a tree structure. The grid methods use a multi-dimensional array.

Table 1 illustrates some of the most well-known methods and their attributes according to the above classification. Notice that methods based on binary trees or quad-trees cannot be easily extended to work in secondary storage based systems. Since a disk page can hold pointers of the order of 50, trees with nodes of large fanout are more appropriate. Trees with two- or four-way nodes usually result in many (expensive) page faults.

Table 1. Illustration of the classification of methods for range query.

Method	Position	Dimensions	Locality
point quad-tree	adaptable	k–d	brickwall
k–d tree	adaptable	k–d	brickwall
grid file	fixed	1–d	grid
K–D–B tree	adaptable	1–d	grid

There are other methods of range queries based on the handling of rectangles. The main classes of the methods are the following:

(1) Methods that transform rectangles into points in a space of higher dimensionality: For example, a 2D rectangle (with sides-parallel to the axes) is characterized by four coordinates, and thus it can be considered as points in a 4D space. Therefore, one of the previously mentioned methods for storing points can be chosen.

(2) Methods that use space-filling curves to map a k–d space onto a 1–d space: Such a method, suitable for a paging environment, has been suggested, among others. The idea is to transform k-dimensional objects to line segments, using the so-called Z-transform. This transformation tries to preserve the distance, that is, points that are close in the k–d space are likely to be close in the 1–d transformed space. Improved distance-preserving transformations have been

proposed, which achieve better clustering of nearby points by using gray codes. The original Z-transform induces an ordering of the k–d points, which is the very same one as the ordering that a (k-dimensional) quad-tree takes to scan pixels in a k-dimensional space. The transformation of a rectangle is a set of line segments, each corresponding to a quadrant that the rectangle completely covers.

(3) Methods that divide the original space into appropriate sub-regions (overlapping or disjoint): If the regions are disjoint, any of the methods for points mentioned above can be used to decompose the space. The only complication to be handled is that a rectangle may intersect a splitting hyperplane. One solution is to cut the offending rectangle into two pieces and tag the pieces indicating that they belong to the same rectangle. Guttman [3] first proposed the use of overlapping subregions with R-trees. R-trees are an extension of B-trees for multi-dimensional objects that are either points or regions. Like B-trees, they are balanced (in the sense that all leaf nodes appear on the same level, which is a desirable feature) and guarantee that the space utilization is at least 50%.

2.2. *Approaches of Iconic Indexing*

The approach of iconic indexing by 2D string for spatial reasoning was proposed by Chang et al. [8] to represent symbolic pictures. First, after preprocessing by applying the techniques of image processing and pattern recognition, the objects in the original image are recognized and the symbolic names can be obtained. Then each object is enclosed by a minimum bounding rectangle (MBR) with boundaries parallel to the horizontal (x-) and vertical (y-) axes. The basic idea for obtaining the relation between the objects is to regard one of the objects as a "point of view object" (PVO) and then view the other objects in four directions (north, east, south and west). The subobjects "seen" by PVO are called orthogonal relation objects of the original object. After all the objects have been processed, the objects can be segmented according to their orthogonal relation objects respectively. The reference points of the segmented objects which are the centroids of each orthogonal relation object thus dominate the spatial relations of objects and constitute the symbolic picture. At last, the symbolic picture which preserves the spatial relationships among objects of the original image is converted to a 2D string representation which is stored in the pictorial database as an iconic index for the picture. The problem of pictorial information retrieval then becomes the problem of 2D string subsequence matching. This approach thus allows a natural way to construct an iconic index for pictures.

Three spatial relation operators "<", "=" and ":" are employed in 2D strings. The symbol "<" denotes the left-right or below-above spatial relationship. The symbol "=" denotes the "at the same spatial location as" relation and the symbol ":" stands for "in the same set as" relation. The symbolic picture f in Fig. 1 may be represented as 2D string $(A = D{:}E < B < C, A < B = C < D{:}E)$ or as $(A = DE < B < C, A < B = C < DE)$ where the symbol ":" can be omitted and is omitted.

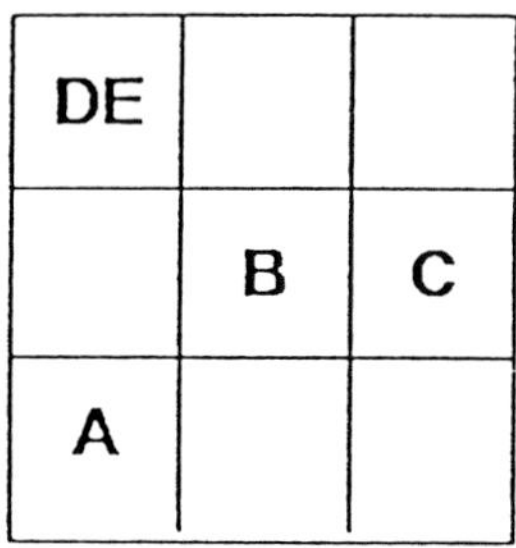

Fig. 1. A symbolic picture f.

However, the spatial operators "$<$" and "$=$" are not sufficient to give a complete description of spatial knowledge for pictures of arbitrary complexity. For complex images with many objects the 2D string representation is difficult and the reference points of the relational objects which are the centroids of each subparts cannot truly reflect their spatial locations. For example, in Fig. 2, the picture is segmented into f' by using the orthogonal relations method. The centroid of A_{Cs} is west of E_{Cn}, but the relational object A_{Cs} is not west of the relational object E_{Cn} along x-direction. A_{Cs} means object A is segmented from the point of view of object C and s stands for A being south of C.

The 2D string representation of f' is listed below.

2D-u-string(f'): $D_{Cw} = D_{Ew} < D_{Fw} < A_{Bw} < D_{An} = A_{Ds} < D_{Es} <$
$\qquad\qquad E_{An} = A_{Es} < D_{Cn} < A_{Cs} = C_{An} < E_{Cn} < C_{Es} < C_{De} <$
$\qquad\qquad B_{Es} = E_{Bn} < E_{De} < B_{Cs} = C_{Bn} < B_{Ae} < B_{Fs} < F_{De}$

2D-v-string(f'): $A_{Ds} = A_{Es} = A_{Cs} < A_{Bw} = B_{Ae} < B_{Es} = B_{Cs} = B_{Fs} <$
$\qquad\qquad D_{Cw} = C_{An} = C_{Es} = C_{De} = C_{Bn} < D_{Fw} = D_{An} = D_{Es} =$
$\qquad\qquad D_{Cn} = F_{De} < D_{Ew} = E_{An} = E_{Cn} = E_{Bn} = E_{De}$

To represent the spatial relationship between two non-zero sized objects, especially for the case of overlapping objects, Jungert [9,10] extended the operators of 2D strings as a global operator set and introduced a set of local operators to handle more types of spatial relationships among objects. These local operators can compensate 2D strings for more precise binary relations among objects, but they cannot be put unanimously as global operators into the global 2D string representation of symbolic pictures.

To overcome the problems in 2D strings and Jungert's work, Chang et al. [11] extended the concept of symbolic projection [7] and proposed generalized 2D string

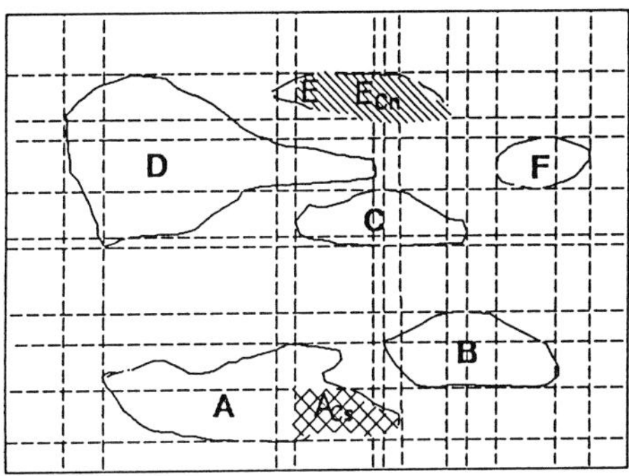

Fig. 2. The segmented picture f' using the orthogonal relations method.

(2D G-string) representation with a cutting mechanism to describe the objects of an image. $G_{op} = \{$ "$<$", "$=$", "$|$" $\}$ is the set of generalized relational operators. " $(,)$ " is a pair of separators used to describe a set of symbols as one local body and the content within which can be named and can always be regarded as first priority. It was pointed out that the edge to edge relation operator "$|$" is useful to solve the problem of overlapping objects. Using symbolic projections, the cutting lines are performed at all the extreme points of each picture object in the image viewing from x- and y- projection, respectively. Then every object may be partitioned into many smaller subparts at the bounding lines of other overlapping objects. For the same picture in Fig. 2 the 2D G-string representation is listed below and is shown in Figs. 3(a) and (b).

2DG-u-string(f'): $D \mid A = D \mid A = D = E \mid A = C = D = E \mid A = C = E \mid$
$\qquad\qquad A = B = C = E \mid B = C = E \mid B = C \mid B \mid B = F \mid F$

2DG-v-string(f'): $A \mid A = B \mid B < D \mid D = C \mid D = F \mid D \mid D = E$

Although 2D G-strings can represent the spatial relationships among objects in pictures and spatial reasoning can be carried out on generalized 2D strings using a set of reasoning rules, there still exist some unsolved problems. The number of segmented subparts of an object is dependent on the number of bounding lines of other objects which completely or partly overlap this target object. For the cases of objects with overlapping, the storage space overhead is high and it is time consuming in spatial reasoning if pictures are represented in 2D G-strings. In the following, a more efficient and economic cutting mechanism by employing a sound and characteristic set of spatial operators is described.

3. 2D C-String Spatial Knowledge Representation

The formal definition of the set of spatial operators used in 2D C-string representation is illustrated in Table 2 [9,10,12]. The notation 'begin(A)' denotes

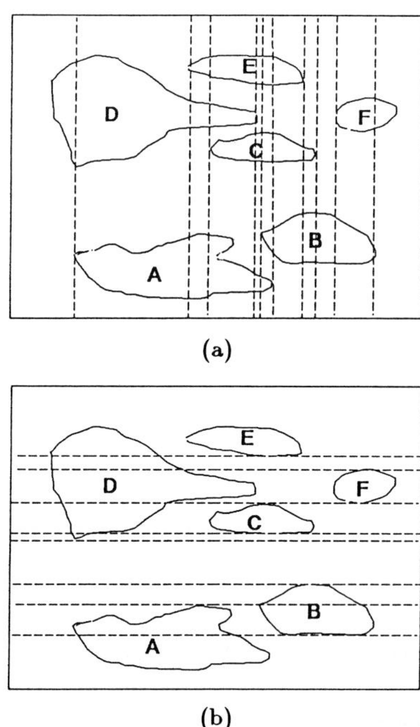

(a)

(b)

Fig. 3. The cutting lines of a 2D G-string. (a) The cutting lines of a 2D G-string along the x-axis direction. (b) The cutting lines of a 2D G-string along the y-axis direction.

the value of begin-bound of object A, and 'end(A)' denotes the value of the end-bound of object A. According to the begin-bound and end-bound of picture objects, spatial relationships between two enclosing rectangles can be categorized into 13 types, ignoring their length along the x-(or y-) coordinate axis as shown in Fig. 4. There are 169 types of spatial relationships between two rectangles in two-dimensional space as shown in Fig. 5. For example, $x : A\%B$, $y : B[A$ means

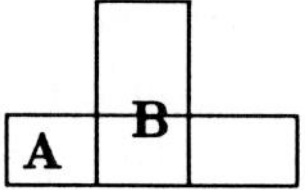

The seven operators in Table 2 are sufficient to describe precisely all the possible spatial relationships between any two MBRs in symbolic pictures.

For the characteristic spatial operators, considering x-axis or y-axis projection independently, five fundamental transformation laws can be observed as below. (TX-2), (TX-3), and (TX-4) are applied for the cases of completely overlapping objects and (TX-5) for the cases of partly overlapping objects. Thus, if the operators are fully utilized, no cutting or partitioning of objects into subparts is necessary.

(TX-1) $A = B \Leftrightarrow B = A$

(TX-2) $A[B \Leftrightarrow A = B \mid A$ or $B = A \mid A$

(TX-3) $A]B \Leftrightarrow A \mid A = B$ or $A \mid B = A$

(TX-4) $A\%B \Leftrightarrow A \mid A = B \mid A$ or $A \mid B = A \mid A$

$\qquad\qquad \Leftrightarrow A \,] \, B \mid A$

$\qquad\qquad \Leftrightarrow A \mid A \, [\, B$

(TX-5) $A/B \Leftrightarrow A \mid A = B \mid B$ or $A \mid B = A \mid B$

$\qquad\qquad \Leftrightarrow A \,] \, B \mid B$

$\qquad\qquad \Leftrightarrow A \mid B \, [A$

Table 2. The definition of characteristic spatial operators.

Notation	Condition	Meaning
$A < B$	$\text{end}(A) < \text{begin}(B)$	A disjoins B
$A = B$	$\text{begin}(A) = \text{begin}(B)$, $\text{end}(A) = \text{end}(B)$	A is the same as B
$A \mid B$	$\text{end}(A) = \text{begin}(B)$	A is edge to edge with B
$A \% B$	$\text{begin}(A) < \text{begin}(B)$, $\text{end}(A) > \text{end}(B)$	A contains B and they do not have the same bound
$A [B$	$\text{begin}(A) = \text{begin}(B)$, $\text{end}(A) > \text{end}(B)$	A contains B and they have the same begin-bound
$A] B$	$\text{begin}(A) < \text{begin}(B)$, $\text{end}(A) = \text{end}(B)$	A contains B and they have the same end-bound
A/B	$\text{begin}(A) < \text{begin}(B)$ $< \text{end}(A) < \text{end}(B)$	A is partly overlapping with B

Since transitivity does not hold in the inference of spatial reasoning when the derivation involves the partly overlapping operator "/", there might incur ambiguity. So the operator "/" is dropped from the set of spatial operators for unique representation. The "/" operator can be expressed in terms of the other six operators. The modified set of spatial operators is still characteristic of all possible spatial knowledge. As for the case of objects which are partly overlapping, for example A/B, $A] B \mid B$ can also be used according to the transformation law. In other words, an object will be segmented into two smaller subparts only when there are some other objects partly overlapping with it. It keeps the former object intact and partitions the latter object. The cuttings are performed along the x-axis and y-axis independently. In this way the 2D C-string representation of a picture is unique and minimal. The detailed algorithms to convert a symbolic picture to a 2D C-string and to reconstruct the symbolic picture uniquely

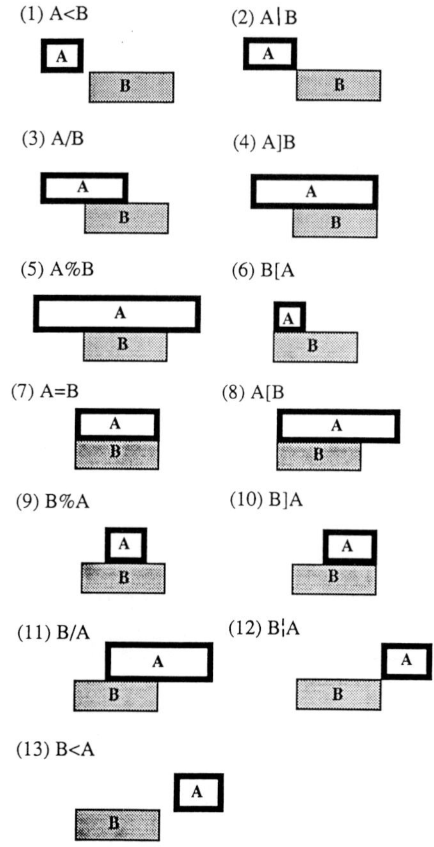

Fig. 4. The 13 types of spatial relations in one dimension.

from a 2D C-string can be found in [12]. The knowledge structure of 2D C-string for the representation and retrieval of symbolic pictures is defined as follows.

Definition 3.1. The knowledge structure of 2D C-string is a 5-tuple (S, C, R_g, R_l, "( )") where

1. S is the set of symbols in symbolic pictures of interest;
2. C is the cutting mechanism, which consists of cutting lines at the points with partial overlap from the x- and y-projection, respectively;
3. $R_g = \{$ "<", "|" $\}$ is the set of global relational operators;
4. $R_l = \{$ "=" , "[", "]" , "%" $\}$ is the set of local relational operators;
5. "()" is a pair of separators which is used to describe a set of symbols as one local body.

Basically, the cutting of 2D C-string is performed at the point of partial overlap. The former object is kept intact and the latter object is partitioned. The

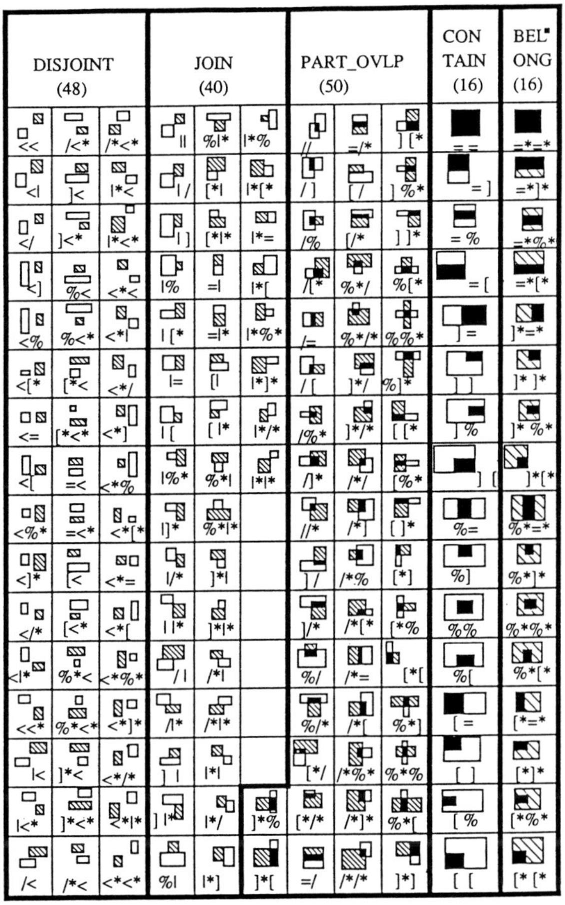

Fig. 5. The 169 types of spatial relations in two-dimensional space.

cutting mechanism is also suitable for pictures with many objects. Consider the example picture 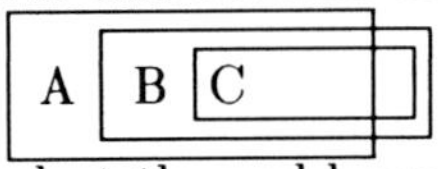 with three objects A, B and C. Only one cutting is performed at the end-bound of A and A is called a dominating object. The other objects partly overlapping with the dominating object will be segmented. Then the picture is represented as $A]B]C \mid B[C$ compared to $A \mid A = B \mid A = B = C \mid B = C \mid B$ in 2D G-string with four cuttings at begin(B), begin(C), end(A) and end(C).

Furthermore, the end-bound point of a dominating object does not partition other objects which contain the dominating object. Consider another example picture 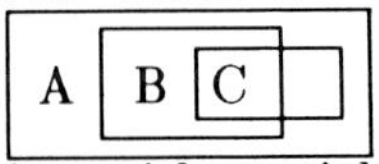 . Object B is the dominating object, because it is the former object with partial overlap. Object C will be segmented by B, but not for object A. Thus the 2D C-string representation is $A\%(B\ ]\ C\ |\ C)$. Actually, B and C constitute the local body of object A.

Less cuttings and no unnecessary cuttings in 2D C-strings will make the representation more efficient than 2D G-strings in the case of overlapping objects. Certainly, both mechanisms have the same result in the case of non-overlapping. It has been proved via simulation results that the number of segmented subparts of the 2D G-string is approximately $\log_2 N$ times that of the 2D C-string, where N is the number of objects in the image. The 2D C-string representation is more efficient in storage complexity at the expense of a little additional computation complexity only in the stage of converting a symbolic picture to a 2D G- or 2D C-string representation. For 2D G-string, it is more time consuming in the manipulation and integration of many partitioned subparts in order to derive the integral spatial relationship between objects in a picture. That is, the number of subparts directly influences the spatial reasoning in the query inference process. The simple spatial relationships such as north, south, east, west, over, under and the more complicated ones such as surrounded by, partly surrounded by, contain, belong, etc. can be derived naturally and directly from the 2D C-string representation. It is difficult to derive the complicated relationships directly from 2D G-strings. The 2D C-string representation of the picture in Figs. 6(a) and (b) is listed below.

$$\text{2D C-}u\text{-string}(f)\!: \quad D\ ]\ A\ ]\ E\ ]\ C\ |\ A = C = E\ ]\ B\ |$$
$$B = (C\ [\ E < F)\ |\ F$$

$$\text{2D C-}v\text{-string}(f)\!: \quad A\ ]\ B\ |\ B < D\ ]\ (C\ |\ F < E)$$

In some advanced application areas such as computer aided design systems and image understanding systems, pictorial objects of great complexity must be integrally stored and represented. 2D C-string can handle not only spatial relations among objects but can also support flexible description of compound objects. Consider a chip design database consisting of symbolic layout, masking layout and electrical specification database. Symbolic layout simplifies layout specification by allowing designers to work with symbols that represent primitive elements or components. A mask layout is made from a symbolic layout by expanding each symbol into the rectangles that form it, using coordinates of the symbols to guide the placement of rectangles. An 8 : 1 ratio inverter mask expressed in 2D C-string can be found in [12]. This description of a compound object is rather useful for image understanding as in automatic layout testing. We can retrieve the images under some constraints using the appropriate pictorial queries. For example, "Retrieve all chips that contain a-device and replace them with b-device".

4. Algebraic Point of View of 2D C-Strings

From the algebraic point of view of 2D C-strings, three kinds of fundamental laws, transitive laws, distributive laws, and manipulation laws are derived [13]. For

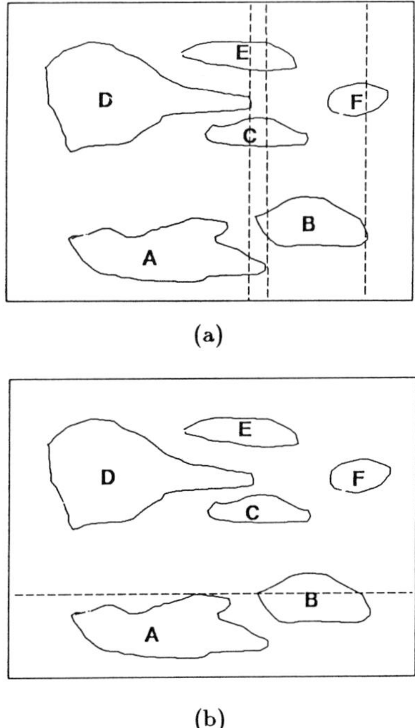

(a)

(b)

Fig. 6. The cutting lines of a 2D C-string. (a) The cutting lines of a 2D C-string along the x-direction. (b) The cutting lines of a 2D C-string along the y-direction.

pictorial query inference and spatial reasoning, all spatial relationships among objects can be derived based on these laws.

4.1. *Transitive Laws*

Suppose that a 2D C-string is expressed as

$$s_1 r_{12} s_2 r_{23} \cdots r_{(i-1)i} s_i \cdots r_{(n-1)n} s_n$$

where $s_1, \ldots, s_i, \ldots, s_n \in S$, $r_{(i-1)i} \in R_g \cup R_l$, and $i \in [2, n]$.

Can all the spatial relationships between any two objects, s_i and s_j, $i \neq j$, be derived from a 2D C-string? In other words, is the 2D C-string a characteristic representation of the spatial knowledge contained in a picture? The answer is yes and this is proved through the following derivations. First, we probe a 3-symbol string,

$$s_1 r_{12} s_2 r_{23} s_3 \, .$$

It is easy to derive three binary relations among s_1, s_2, and s_3:

(1) $s_1 r'_{12} s_2$,
(2) $s_2 r'_{23} s_3$, and
(3) $s_1 r'_{13} s_3$.

The three derived binary relational operators are shown in Table 3. For the example string $A \, [\, B \, | \, C$, we can get (1) $A \, [\, B$, (2) $B < C$, and (3) $A \, | \, C$.

Table 3. The derivation table of a 3-symbol string.

(a)

r'_{12}	r_{23}					
	<	|	=	[	]	%
r_{12} <	<	<	<	<	<	<
|	|	|	|	|	|	|
=	=	=	=	=	=	=
[	[	[	[	[	[	[
]	]	]	]	]	]	]
%	%	%	%	%	%	%

(b)

r'_{23}	r_{23}					
	<	|	=	[	]	%
r_{12} <	<	|	=	[	]	%
|	<	|	=	[	]	%
=	<	|	=	[	]	%
[	<	<	=	[	]	%
]	<	|	=	[	]	%
%	<	<	=	[	]	%

(c)

r'_{13}	r_{23}					
	<	|	=	[	]	%
r_{12} <	<	<	<	<	<	<
|	<	<	|	|	<	<
=	<	|	=	[	]	%
[	<	|	[	[	%	%
]	<	|	]	%	]	%
%	<	|	%	%	%	%

From Table 3, three facts can be observed:

(1) r'_{12}, is always the same as r_{12}.
(2) r'_{23} is the same as r_{23}, except for r_{23} being '|' and r_{12} being '[' or '%'.
(3) r'_{13} is the same as r_{23} when $r_{12} \in R_l$ and $r_{23} \in R_g$.

Any binary relationships among three symbols can be derived without difficulty. Based on the basic results, five transitive laws are presented in [13].

4.2. Distributive Law

In Definition 3.1, we have defined the knowledge structure of 2D C-strings. Included in the knowledge structure is a pair of separators '( )' which is used to describe some set of symbols as a local body. First we probe a three-symbol string with the separators, $s_1 r_{12}(s_2 r_{23} s_3)$, where $r_{12} \in R_l$ and $r_{23} \in R_g$, to illustrate the basis of the distributive law. It is easy to derive the following three binary relationships among s_1, s_2, and s_3.

(1) $s_1 r'_{12} s_2$,
(2) $s_2 r'_{23} s_3$, and
(3) $s_1 r'_{13} s_3$.

The three derived binary relational operators are shown in Table 4. For the example $A\,]\,(B\mid C)$, we can get (1) $A\,\%\,B$, (2) $B\mid C$, and (3) $A\,]\,C$. Based on the above results, two distributive laws are presented in [13].

Table 4. The distributive derivation table of 3-symbol string.

(a)

r'_{12}	r_{23}	
	<	|
=	[	[
[	[	[
r_{12}]	%	%
%	%	%

(b)

r'_{23}	r_{23}	
	<	|
=	<	|
[	<	|
r_{12}]	<	|
%	<	|

(c)

r'_{13}	r_{23}	
	<	|
=	]	]
[	%	%
r_{12}]	]	]
%	%	%

Based on transitive laws and distributive laws, all the binary spatial relationships among symbols in a 2D C-string can be derived. It means that the spatial relational operators of 2D C-strings preserve complete spatial knowledge of pictorial objects embedded in symbolic pictures. 2D C-strings are more efficient in the representation of spatial relationships than other knowledge structures in earlier approaches because of less cuttings.

4.3. *Manipulation Laws*

In the case of objects with partial overlap, a pictorial object must be cut to some segmented subparts at the bounding lines of other subjects partly overlap with it. It is necessary to integrate and manipulate these smaller subparts for the inference of spatial reasoning in pictorial query. The manipulation laws are for the inference of the segmented objects treating their relationships integrally [13].

The manipulation laws are simple and it is easy to manipulate the segmented subparts of objects. For example, objects A and B are partitioned relative to other objects in a symbolic picture and are represented as the 2D C-string shown below. It can be simplified by employing the manipulation laws. For example,

$$A \mid A \mid A] B \mid A = B \mid A = B \mid B [A \mid B$$

$$\Rightarrow \quad A \mid A] B \mid A = B \mid A = B \mid B [A \mid B$$
$$\Rightarrow \quad A] B \mid A = B \mid A = B \mid B [A \mid B$$
$$\Rightarrow \quad A] B \mid A = B \mid B [A \mid B$$
$$\Rightarrow \quad A] B \mid B [A \mid B$$
$$\Rightarrow \quad A] B \mid B [A$$
$$\Rightarrow \quad A / B$$

The final relationship between A and B is A/B. This gives demonstration and support for the theoretical basis for spatial reasoning.

5. Spatial Reasoning

Spatial reasoning means the inference of a consistent set of spatial relationships among the objects in an image. It is important in computer vision and robotics as well as in image database applications. When retrieving images from a database, one of the most powerful methods for discriminating images is the perception of spatial relationships that exist among objects in the desired image. The capability of making queries based on spatial relationships plays an important role in image database systems. A simple tabular account of these relationships soon overwhelms the system due to their combinatorial nature. Also, the addition of new facts may require a major reconfiguration of the database. For these reasons, a more practical approach is to store the information as facts from which these relations can be derived following a set of rules when they are needed.

However, the primary direction relationships are not sufficient for pictorial queries of various complex cases of objects with overlap in two-dimensional space.

According to the characteristics of spatial knowledge in two-dimensional space, all the spatial relationships between two non-zero sized objects, as shown in Fig. 5, can be categorized into five categories of relations. Suppose that two pictorial objects A and B are enclosed by minimum bounding rectangles. Then we have the five categories of relations below.

(1) A disjoins B. All parts of A are separated from all parts of B.
(2) A is edge to edge with B. The bound of A is edge to edge with the bound of B, and no part of A is overlapping with any part of B.
(3) A contains B. All parts of B are completely overlapping with some parts of A.
(4) A belongs to B. All parts of A are completely overlapping with some parts of B.
(5) A is partly overlapping with B.

The 2D C-string is characteristic of spatial knowledge and is complete in the sense that every spatial relation is derivable from the representation. Based on the transitive laws, distributive laws, and manipulation laws of picture algebra [13], it has been proved that all the binary relationships among objects in an image can be derived from a 2D C-string.

The problem of how to infer the spatial relations between two pictorial objects from a given 2D C-string representation in spatial reasoning is solved [15] by using the ranking mechanism, in which the ranks of pictorial objects in a 2D C-string can be defined. The rank values of objects stand for the relative sequencing in the u- or v-string representing the relative spatial positioning of the original symbolic picture along the x- and y-projection respectively. The rank plays an important role in 2D string subsequence matching [8]. The spatial knowledge is embedded in the ranks of the pictorial objects. In fact, the ranks become representative of the spatial knowledge of the pictorial objects in an image. The spatial relations between two symbols can be identified by their ranks according to the rules.

Because the spatial operators of 2D C-strings can directly support a richer spatial knowledge of images, the abundant pictorial query, called 2D C-query, is constructed by employing the set of operators [15]. The fundamentals of 2D C-query are based on the inference of spatial relationships among pictorial objects in a 2D C-string.

The objects may be divided into some subparts with the cutting mechanism. If the predicate (west, A, B) is true, it means there exist some subparts of A west of all subparts of B. But the converse predicate (east, B, A) cannot be established because there does not exist any subpart of B east of all subparts of A. It is useful to add an operator "*", name "reverse", for the purpose of spatial reasoning. $A <^* B$ means $B < A$. The fundamental direction relationships for each spatial operator have been reconsidered and are listed in Table 5. r^u_{AB} indicates the relationship between A and B along the x-direction. The relational operators r^v_{AB} of the v-string along the y-direction are analogously defined as r^u_{AB}.

As shown in Table 5, the primitive direction relationships can be inferred from the spatial operators of 2D C-strings. The following basic orthogonal directional aggregates are the main body of the 2D C-query.

(1) u: $Ar^u_{AB}B$, $r^u_{AB} \in \{<^*, |^*, [, \%, /^*\}$ iff (east, A, B)
(2) v: $Ar^v_{AB}B$, $r^v_{AB} \in \{<^*, |^*, [, \%, /^*\}$ iff (north, A, B)
(3) u: $Ar^u_{AB}B$, $r^u_{AB} \in \{<, |,], \%, /\}$ iff (west, A, B)
(4) v: $Ar^v_{AB}B$, $r^v_{AB} \in \{<, |,], \%, /\}$ iff (south, A, B)

Table 5. The direction predicates of spatial operators.

Predicate r^U_{AB}	<	|	=	[	]	%	/	<*	|*	=*	[*	]*	%*	/*
(west, A, B)	✓	✓			✓	✓	✓							
(east, B, A)	✓	✓					✓				✓		✓	
(east, A, B)						✓		✓	✓					✓
(west, B, A)								✓	✓			✓	✓	✓

The pictorial queries in 2D C-query can be summarized and classified into seven classes in the form of (RELATION, ?which_object, X) or (?which_relation, A, B).

(1) *Orthogonal direction object query.* The primary orthogonal direction aggregates can be combined to derive more direction aggregates. For example, from 2D C-string u: $A] B$ and v: A/B, three aggregates are inferred, (west, A, B), (south, A, B) and (north, B, A). Then the relationship between A and B are (south-west, A, B) and (north, B, A). For the orthogonal directions in two-dimensional space, there are 15 spatial queries about the orthogonal direction between two objects in the first class of 2D C-query.

(2) *Category relation object query.* The characteristic spatial operators are sufficient to describe the relationships among the non-zero sized objects. From the definition of the operators, there are twelve 1D relation aggregates along the x-direction or y-direction. Based on these relation aggregates, there are five queries of category relation, DISJOIN, EDGE, CONTAIN, BELONG, and PARTOVLP, in the second class of 2D C-query.

(3) *Auxiliary relation object query.* The relations of "same", "surround", "partly surround", "surrounded" and "partly surrounded" are important and useful in pictorial query.

The definitions are given below.

1. *A* is the same as B, if A is at the same location as B along the western, eastern, southern, and northern directions.

2. A surrounds B, if A contains B and A completely surrounds B along four orthogonal directions.

3. A partly surrounds B, if A contains B and A surrounds B along two or three orthogonal directions.

The relations "surround" and "partly surround" are with respect to "contain". The relations "surrounded" and "partly surrounded" are with respect to "belong".

(4) *Icon relation object query.* The fourth kind of 2D C-query is simple and natural. The query spatial relation can be specified by using an icon or a symbol. These queries are in the form of (rel_icon, ?object, X) .

The above four classes of 2D C-query, allow the users to retrieve all objects with a specified orthogonal direction or category relation or auxiliary relation or icon-relation in an image. There are three types of pictorial queries to examine the spatial relation between two specified objects in a given image. (?icon, A, B), (?category, A, B), and (?direction, A, B) stand for icon relation, category relation, and orthogonal direction query.

6. Similarity Retrieval

Similarity retrieval is one of the distinct functions of the image database systems. The target is to retrieve the images that are similar to the query image. The similarity between two patterns or pictures can be measured on the basis of the maximum-likelihood or minimum-distance criterion. The similarity between lD strings based upon the minimum-distance criterion has been developed in the techniques of pattern recognition [16]. The distance between two strings is defined in terms of the minimum number of error transformation used to derive one from the other. The alternative approach based on the the maximum likelihood criterion is defined in terms of the longest common subsequence between two strings. Adopting the maximum likelihood approach, the similarity retrieval of images represented in 2D C-strings is our concern.

Chang et al. [8] defined type-0, type-1, and type-2 2D subsequences to provide a simple approach to perform subpicture matching on 2D strings. Lee et al. [17] proposed a similarity retrieval algorithm, called 2D-string-LCS, to retrieve the most similar picture whose type-i similarity is the longest common subsequence among all the pictures stored in the image database. For representing the spatial relationships efficiently, 2D C-string is proposed and is applied to develop the pictorial query. Similarity retrieval based on 2D C-string is developed in [15].

Definition 6.1. Picture f' is a type-i unit picture of f, if (1) f' is a picture containing the two objects A and B, represented as u: $A\ r^{u'}_{AB}B$, v: $A r^{v'}_{AB}B$, (2) A and B are also contained in f, (3) the relations between A and B in f are represented as u: $A r^{u}_{AB}B$, v: $Ar^{v}_{AB}B$, then (type-0): $\text{Category}(r_{AB}^u, r_{AB}^v) = \text{Category}(r_{AB}^{u'}, r_{AB}^{v'})$;

(type-1): (type-0) and ($r_{AB}^u = r_{AB}^{u'}$ or $r_{AB}^v = r_{AB}^{v'}$) ;

(type-2): $r_{AB}^u = r_{AB}^{u'}$ and $r_{AB}^v = r_{AB}^{v'}$,

where $\text{Category}(r^u, r^v)$ denotes the relation category of the spatial relationships as shown in Fig. 5. The pair (A, B) is called a type-i similar pair.

Take the pictures f_1 and f_2 in Figs. 7(a) and (b) as an example. There are eight pictorial objects in these two pictures. The 2D C-string representations of the pictures are as below.

$$f_1: \quad \text{u-string:} \quad A\,]\,(B\,]\,E = H \mid E = H \mid C) < F\,]\,G \mid D\,[\,G,$$
$$ \text{v-string:} \quad A\,]\,(D\,[\,C\,[\,B \mid E) \mid E \mid F\,]\,G \mid H\,[\,G.$$

$$f_2: \quad \text{u-string:} \quad G\,]\,H\,]\,A \mid A\,]\,(B\,]\,E \mid E) \mid E < C \mid D\,]\,F \mid F,$$
$$ \text{v-string:} \quad H = C < F\,]\,A = B = D\,]\,G \mid A = (D\,[\,G \mid E) \mid E.$$

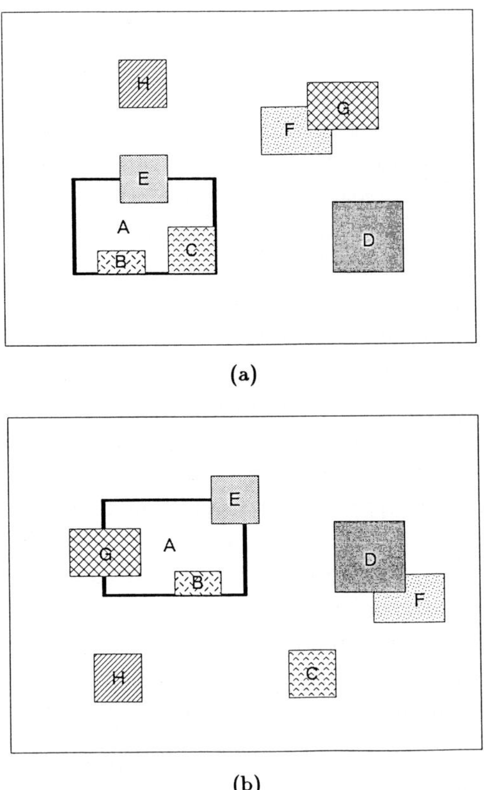

(a)

(b)

Fig. 7. An example of similarity retrieval. (a) An example of similarity retrieval (f_1). (b) An example of similarity retrieval (f_2).

By applying the reasoning rules, the spatial relationships among objects can be inferred by the ranks of symbols.

According to the definition of type-i similar picture in 2D C-string, we have the set of type-i similar pairs of pictures f_1 and f_2:

type-0: (A, B), (A, D), (A, E), (A, F), (A, H),
$\quad\quad$ (B, C), (B, D), (B, E), (B, F), (B, G),
$\quad\quad$ (B, H), (C, D), (C, E), (C, F), (C, G),
$\quad\quad$ (C, H), (D, E), (D, G), (D, H), (E, F),
$\quad\quad$ (E, G), (E, H), (F, H), (G, H).

type-1: (A, B), (A, D), (A, E), (B, C), (B, D),
$\quad\quad$ (B, E), (B, F), (C, F), (C, G), (D, E),
$\quad\quad$ (E, F), (F, H).

type-2: (A, B), (A, D), (B, D), (B, E), (C, F),
$\quad\quad$ (D, E).

As shown in Figs. 8(a), (b), and (c), the maximal complete subgraphs of type-0, type-1, and type-2 are found respectively. The corresponding type-i longest common subpictures of f_1 and f_2 are constructed from the following object sets:

type-0: $\{B, C, D, E, G, H\}$,
type-1: $\{A, B, D, E\}$,
type-2: $\{A, B, D\}$ *or* $\{B, D, E\}$.

In this example, f_1 is type-0, type-1, type-2 similar to f_2 with similar degree of 6, 4, and 3, respectively.

7. Conclusion

The approach of 2D strings opens a new area for iconic picture indexing and retrieval. Previous approaches of 2D strings were not powerful enough to give a complete description of spatial knowledge for pictures of arbitrary complexity. The spatial knowledge representation 2D C-string with a more efficient cutting mechanism is proposed to overcome the deficiencies. This representation supports flexible description and retrieval of compound objects or images with great complexity.

An algebraic point of view of 2D C-string is presented. Transitive laws, distributive laws, and manipulation laws are discussed. From the 2D C-string representation of symbolic pictures, all the spatial relationships among symbolic objects embedded in the pictures can be derived. These laws form the theoretic basis for pictorial query inference and spatial reasoning. The inference of spatial reasoning in 2D C-string by using the ranking mechanism is described. The powerful pictorial query 2D C-query is summarized. The similarity retrieval based on 2D C-string is also discussed.

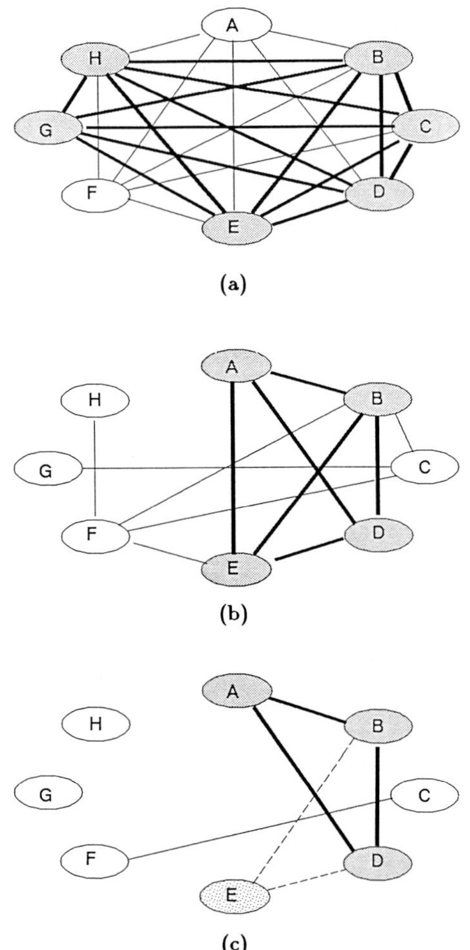

Fig. 8. Similar pairs between f_1 and f_2. (a) Type-0 similar pairs between f_1 and f_2. (b) Type-1 similar pairs between f_1 and f_2. (c) Type-2 similar pairs between f_1 and f_2.

The topic of how to detect picture objects which have similar shapes but different sizes needs further investigation. The extension of 2D C-string to 3D object representation, which is useful to object understanding and retrieval, is worth further study.

References

[1] H. Tamura and N. Yokoya, Image database systems: A survey, *Pattern Recogn.* **17**, 1 (1984) 29–43.

[2] S. K. Chang, *Principles of Pictorial Information Systems Design* (Prentice-Hall, Englewood Cliffs, NJ, 1989).

[3] A. Guttman, R-trees: A dynamic index structure for spatial searching, in *Proc. ACM-SIGMOD 1984 Int. Conf. on Management of Data*, Jun. 1984, 47–57.

[4] N. Roussopoulos and D. Leifker, Direct spatial search on pictorial database using packed R-tree, in *Proc. ACM-SIGMOD 1985 Int. Conf. on Management of Data*, May 1985, 17–31.

[5] S. K. Chang and S. H. Liu, Picture indexing and abstraction techniques for pictorial databases, *IEEE Trans. Pattern Anal. Mach. Intell.* **6**, 4 (1984) 475–484.

[6] S. K. Chang, C. W. Yan, D. C. Dimitrof and T. Arndt, Intelligent image database system, *IEEE Trans. Softw. Eng.* **14**, 5 (1988) 681–688.

[7] S. K. Chang and E. Jungert, A spatial knowledge structure for image information systems using symbolic projections, in *Proc. Fall Joint Computer Conf.*, Dallas, TX, Nov. 1986, 79–86.

[8] S. K. Chang, Q. Y. Shi and C. W. Yan, Iconic indexing by 2D strings, *IEEE Trans. Pattern Anal. Mach. Intell.* **9**, 3 (1987) 413–428.

[9] E. Jungert, Extended symbolic projection used in a knowledge structure for spatial reasoning, in *Proc. 4th BPRA Conf. on Pattern Recognition* (Springer Verlag, 1988).

[10] E. Jungert and S. K. Chang, An algebra for symbolic image manipulation and transformation, in T. S. Kunii (ed.), *Visual Database Systems* (North-Holland, 1989) 301–317.

[11] S. K. Chang, E. Jungert and Y. Li, Representation and retrieval of symbolic pictures using generalized 2D strings, in *SPIE Proc. on Visual Communications and Image Processing*, Philadelphia, Nov. 1989, 1360–1372.

[12] S. Y. Lee and F. J. Hsu, 2D C-string: A new spatial knowledge representation for image database systems, *Pattern Recogn.* **23**, 10 (1990) 1077–1087.

[13] S. Y. Lee and F. J. Hsu, Picture algebra for spatial reasoning of iconic images represented in 2D C-string, *Pattern Recogn. Lett.* **12**, 7 (1991) 425–435.

[14] T. Sellis, N. Rousspoulous and C. Faloutsos, The R+ tree: A dynamic index structure for multi-dimensional objects, in *Proc. 13th VLDB Conf.*, 1987, 507–518.

[15] S. Y. Lee and F. J. Hsu, Spatial reasoning and similarity retrieval of images using 2D C-string knowledge representation, *Pattern Recogn.* **24**, 3 (1992).

[16] K. S. Fu, *Syntactic Pattern Recognition and Applications* (Prentice Hall, Englewood Cliffs, NJ, 1982).

[17] S. Y. Lee, M. K. Shan and W. P. Yang, Similarity retrieval of iconic image database, *Pattern Recogn.* **22**, 6 (1989) 675–682.

Handbook of Pattern Recognition and Computer Vision, pp. 863–882
Eds. C. H. Chen, L. F. Pau and P. S. P. Wang
© 1993 World Scientific Publishing Company

$\boxed{\text{CHAPTER 5.4}}$

VIEWER-CENTERED REPRESENTATIONS IN OBJECT RECOGNITION: A COMPUTATIONAL APPROACH

RONEN BASRI

*Department of Applied Mathematics, The Weizmann Institute of Science
Rehovot 76100, Israel*

Visual object recognition is a process in which representations of objects are used to identify those objects in images. Recent psychophysical and physiological studies indicate that the visual system uses viewer-centered representations. In this chapter a recognition scheme that uses viewer-centered representations is presented. The scheme requires storing only a small number of views to represent an object. It is based on the observation that novel views of objects can be expressed as linear combinations of the stored views. This method is applied to rigid objects as well as to objects with more complicated structure, such as rigid objects with smooth surfaces and articulated objects.

Keywords: Alignment, linear combinations, 3-D object recognition, viewer-centered representations, visual object recognition.

1. Introduction

Visual object recognition is a process in which images are compared to stored representations of objects. These representations, their content and use, determine the outcome of the recognition process. The features stored in an object's model determine those properties that identify the object and overshadow other properties. It is not surprising, therefore, that the issue of object representation has attracted considerable attention (reviews of different aspects of object representations can be found in [1–5]).

For many objects, shape (as opposed to other cues, such as color, texture, etc.) is their most identifiable property. In shape-based recognition a model contains properties of the object that distinguish it from objects with different shapes. The wide range of possible shape representations is divided into two distinct categories, object-centered representations and viewer-centered ones. Object-centered representations describe the shape of objects using view independent properties, while viewer-centered representations describe the way this shape is perceived from certain views. Recent psychophysical studies indicate that viewer-centered representations are used in a number of recognition paradigms (see details in Section 2).

863

Recognition of 3-D objects from 2-D images is difficult partly because objects look significantly different from different views. A common approach to recognition, which received the name *alignment*, aligns the object's model to the image before they actually are compared [5] (see also [6–8]). We present a scheme that combines the use of viewer-centered representations with the alignment approach. The scheme, referred to as the "Linear Combinations" scheme (originally developed in [9]) represents an object by a small set of its views. Recognition is performed by comparing the image to linear combinations of the model views. The scheme handles rigid objects as well as more complicated objects, such as rigid objects with smooth bounding surfaces and articulated objects.

2. Viewer-Centered Representations

The issue of object representation is critical to recognition. It determines the information that makes an object stand out and the circumstances under which it can be identified. In addition, it divides the computational process into its on-line components, the "recognition" part, and off-line components, the "learning" or "model acquisition" part.

Object-centered representations describe the shape of objects using view independent properties. These representations usually include either view-invariant properties of the object (e.g. [10,11]) or structural descriptions defined within some intrinsic coordinate system, such as generalized cylinders [12,13], constructive solid modeling [14], and the vertices and edges in polyhedra [8,15]. Object-centered models in general are relatively concise. A single model is used to recognize the object from all possible views.

Viewer-centered representations describe the appearance of objects in certain views. Typically, a viewer-centered model consists of a set of one or more views of an object, possibly with certain 3-D shape attributes, such as depth or curvature (in a similar fashion to the $2\frac{1}{2}$-D sketch suggested by Marr and Nishihara [13]). Often, a viewer-centered representation covers only a restricted range of views of an object. A number of models is then required to represent the object from all possible views. Viewer-centered representations are in general easier to acquire, to store, and to handle than object-centered ones. For instance, with viewer-centered models there is no need to perform elaborate computations to account for self occlusion, since such occlusion is implicit in the model views.

Recent psychophysical and physiological studies indicate that in certain recognition paradigms the visual system uses viewer-centered representations. A number of experiments establish that the response time in recognition tasks varies as a function of the angular distance of the object to be recognized from either its upright position or a trained view. This effect, known as the *mental rotation* effect (originally shown in views comparison tasks by Shepard and Metzler [16]), was found in naming tasks of both natural and artificially made objects [17–23]. These effects considerably diminish with practice [18,20,23,24]. Namely, as subjects become more familiar with the objects, their response time becomes more and more uniform. Practicing the task on views of one object does not alter the performance for other objects [18,25], indicating that this is not a side effect resulting from the subjects' learning to perform the experiment better, but that indeed subjects attain richer representations of the objects with practice. Findings by Tarr and Pinker [23,26,27] suggest that massive exposure to different orientations of objects does not necessarily result in the formation of object-centered representations. They showed cases where the response time was linear with the angular separation between the observed object and its closest view in the training set.

Additional support to these findings was found in measuring the error rates in naming tasks. A few studies show that the number of incorrect namings increases with the angular separation between tested views and either trained views or the object's upright position [19,28,29]. Edelman and Bülthoff [28] found that error rates increase not only as a function of distance of the tested view to the training set, but they also depend on the specific relation between the tested view and the trained views. In their experiment subjects were trained on two views of an object. It was found that intermediate views, views that lie within the range between the trained views, were correctly recognized more often than extrapolated views, that is, views that lie outside this range. Interestingly, they also found that, unlike response time, error rates do not diminish with practice [30], indicating that even after practice subjects did not attain complete view-invariant representations.

Evidence consistent with the use of multiple viewer-centered descriptions was also found in single-cell activity recordings. Perret *et al.* [31] have investigated the response properties of face-sensitive cells in area STS of the macaque's visual cortex. They have found that cells typically respond to a wide range of 3-D orientations, but not to all viewing directions. A face-selective cell that responds to e.g. a face-on view will typically not respond to a profile view, but will respond to a wide range of intermediate orientations. The authors concluded that "High level viewer-centered descriptions are an important stage in the analysis of faces" ([31] p. 314).

It is important to remember that these experiments can be interpreted in more than a single way, and that the tested paradigms may not reflect the general recognition process. (See for example [32] where a case of dissociation of mental rotation from recognition is presented.) It seems, however, that a large number of experiments are consistent with the notion of viewer-centered representations.

3. Alignment

A major source of difficulty in object recognition arises from the fact that the images we see are two-dimensional, while the objects we try to recognize are three-dimensional. As a result, we always see only one face of an object at a time. The images of the same object may differ significantly from one another even when these

Fig. 1. Deformation of an image following a 15° rotation of a car. An overlaid picture of the car before and after rotation. Although the rotation is fairly small, the discrepancies between the two images are fairly large.

views are separated by a relatively small transformation (see for example Fig. 1). Cluttered scenes introduce additional complexity due to partial occlusion.

One approach to overcome these difficulties is to first recover the underlying 3-D shape of the observed object from the image (using cues like shading, stereopsis, and motion) and then to compare the result with the 3-D model (e.g. [13,33]) Although in recent years there has been tremendous progress in understanding early visual processes, current shape recovery algorithms still seem to be limited in their ability to provide accurate and reliable depth information. Moreover, people's ability to recognize objects seem to be fairly robust to elimination of depth cues (e.g. [30,34]). The ability to recognize objects from line drawings, which contain only sparse information about the shape of objects, demonstrates that shape recovery may not be essential for recognition.

The alignment approach avoids recovering the underlying 3-D shape of the observed object by comparing the object's model to the image in 2-D ("template matching"). To account for orientation differences between the stored model and the observed image these differences are compensated for before the model and the image are compared. The transformation that compensates for these differences is called "the *alignment transformation.*" Alignment is therefore a two-stage process. First, the position and orientation (pose) of the observed object is recovered, and then the model is transformed to this pose, projected to the image plane, and compared with the actual image.

A large number of studies use alignment-like algorithms to recognize 3-D objects from 2-D images [5–8,35–37]. These studies vary in the representations used and the method employed to recover the alignment transformation. Most of these studies use object-centered representations. When viewer-centered representations are used, the naive approach usually is taken; namely, the system can recognize only the stored views of an object (e.g. [37–39]). For example, in [37] an object is modeled by a large number of views (the representation includes a table of $72 \times 72 = 5184$ views). A view is recognized only if the image is related to one of these views by a rotation in the image plane, in which case this view and the image share the same appearance.

In the rest of this chapter we present an alternative to these approaches: an alignment scheme that recognizes objects using viewer-centered representations. The method requires only a small number of views to represent an object from all its possible views.

4. The Linear Combinations (LC) Scheme

The variability and richness of the visual input is overwhelming. An object can give rise to a tremendous number of views. It is not uncommon for humans to forget familiar views, perhaps because the visual system is incapable of storing and retrieving such huge amounts of information. Consequently, the visual system occasionally comes across novel views of familiar objects, whether these views have been forgotten, or they are entirely new. The role of the recognition process when a novel view is observed is to deduce the information that is necessary to recognize the object from its previously observed images. This relationship between the novel and the familiar views of objects is (implicitly) specified by the representation used by the recognition system.

The linear combinations (LC) scheme relates familiar views and novel views of objects in a simple way. Novel views in this scheme are expressed by linear combinations of the familar views. This property can be used to develop a recognition system that uses viewer-centered representations: an object is modeled in this scheme by a small set of its familiar views. Recognition involves comparing the novel views to linear combinations of the model views.

For such a representation to be feasible, the correspondence between the model views should first be resolved. Correspondence between views of objects is a source for understanding how the objects change between views. This information allows the system to track the location of feature points in the model images and predict their location in novel views of the object.

A view in the LC scheme is represented by the locations of feature points (such as corners or contour points) in the image. A model is a set of views with correspondence between the points. As already mentioned, novel views are expressed by linear combinations of the model views. When opaque objects are considered, due to self occlusion, different faces ("aspects") of the object appear in different views. A number of models (not necessarily independent) would then be required to predict the appearance of such objects from all possible viewpoints. The LC method applies to rigid objects as well as to more complicated objects, such as objects that undergo affine transformations, rigid objects with smooth bounding surfaces, and articulated objects. In this section we describe the main properties of the LC scheme. A more thorough presentation can be found in [9].

4.1. *Rigid Objects*

In this section we show that for rigid objects novel views can be expressed as linear combinations of a small number of views. We begin with the following definitions. Given an image I with feature points, $p_1 = (x_1, y_1), \ldots, p_n = (x_n, y_n)$, a *view* V_I is a pair of vectors $\mathbf{x}, \mathbf{y} \in \mathcal{R}^n$ where $\mathbf{x} = (x_1, \ldots, x_n)^T$ and $\mathbf{y} = (y_1, \ldots, y_n)^T$ contain the location of the feature points, $p_1, \ldots, p_n$, in the image. A *model* is a set of views $\{V_1, \ldots, V_k\}$. The location vectors in these views are ordered in correspondence, namely, the first point in V_1 is the projection of the same physical point on the object as the first point in V_2, and so forth. The objects we consider undergo rigid transformations, namely, rotations and translations in space. We assume that the images are obtained by weak perspective projection, that is, orthographic projection together with uniform scaling.

The proof of the linear combinations property proceeds in the following way. First, we show (Theorem 1) that the set of views of a rigid object is contained in a four-dimensional linear space. Any four linearly independent vectors from this space can therefore be used to span the space. Consequently, we show (Theorem 2) that two views suffice to represent the space. Any other view of the object can be expressed as (two) linear combinations of the two basis views. Next, we show (Theorem 3) that not every point in this 4-D space necessarily corresponds to a legal view of the object. The coefficients satisfy two quadratic constraints. These constraints depend on the transformation between the model views. A third view can be used to derive the constraints.

Theorem 1. *The views of a rigid object are contained in a four-dimensional linear space.*

Proof. Consider an object O with feature points $p_1 = (x_1, y_1, z_1), \ldots, p_n = (x_n, y_n, z_n)$. Let I be an image of O obtained by a rotation R, translation t, and scaling s, followed by an orthographic projection Π. Let $q_1 = (x'_1, y'_1), \ldots, q_n = (x'_n, y'_n)$ be the projected location in I of the points $p_1, \ldots, p_n$ respectively. For every $1 \leq i \leq n$

$$q_i = s\Pi(Rp_i) + t \,.$$

More explicitly, this equation can be written as

$$
\begin{aligned}
x'_i &= sr_{11}x_i + sr_{12}y_i + sr_{13}z_i + t_x \\
y'_i &= sr_{21}x_i + sr_{22}y_i + sr_{23}z_i + t_y
\end{aligned}
$$

where $\{r_{ij}\}$ are the components of the rotation matrix, and t_x, t_y are the horizontal and the vertical components of the translation vector. Since these equations hold for every $1 \leq i \leq n$, we can rewrite them in vector notation. Denote $\mathbf{x} = (x_1, \ldots, x_n)^T$, $\mathbf{y} = (y_1, \ldots, y_n)^T$, $\mathbf{z} = (z_1, \ldots, z_n)^T$, $\mathbf{1} = (1, \ldots, 1)^T$, $\mathbf{x'} = (x'_1, \ldots, x'_n)^T$, and $\mathbf{y'} = (y'_1, \ldots, y'_n)^T$, we obtain that

$$
\begin{aligned}
\mathbf{x'} &= a_1\mathbf{x} + a_2\mathbf{y} + a_3\mathbf{z} + a_4\mathbf{1} \\
\mathbf{y'} &= b_1\mathbf{x} + b_2\mathbf{y} + b_3\mathbf{z} + b_4\mathbf{1}
\end{aligned}
$$

where

$$
\begin{aligned}
a_1 &= sr_{11} & b_1 &= sr_{21} \\
a_2 &= sr_{12} & b_2 &= sr_{22} \\
a_3 &= sr_{13} & b_3 &= sr_{23} \\
a_4 &= t_x & b_4 &= t_y
\end{aligned}
$$

The vectors $\mathbf{x}'$ and $\mathbf{y}'$ can therefore be expressed as linear combinations of four vectors, $\mathbf{x}$, $\mathbf{y}$, $\mathbf{z}$, and $\mathbf{1}$. Notice that changing the view would result merely in a change in the coefficients. We can therefore conclude that

$$
\mathbf{x}', \mathbf{y}' \in span\{\mathbf{x}, \mathbf{y}, \mathbf{z}, \mathbf{1}\}
$$

for any view of O. Notice that if translation is omitted the views space is reduced to a three-dimensional one. $\qquad\square$

Theorem 2. The views space of a rigid object O can be constructed from two views of O.[a]

Proof. Theorem 1 above establishes that the views space of a rigid object is four-dimensional. Any four linearly independent vectors in this space can be used to span the space. The constant vector, $\mathbf{1}$, belongs to this space. Therefore, only three more vectors remain to be found. An image supplies two vectors. Two images supply four, which already is more than enough to span the space (assuming the two images are related by some rotation in depth, otherwise they are linearly dependent). Let $V_1 = (\mathbf{x}_1, \mathbf{y}_1)$ and $V_2 = (\mathbf{x}_2, \mathbf{y}_2)$ be two views of O, a novel view $V' = (\mathbf{x}', \mathbf{y}')$ of O can be expressed as two linear combinations of the four vectors $\mathbf{x}_1$, $\mathbf{y}_1$, $\mathbf{x}_2$, and $\mathbf{1}$. The remaining vector, $\mathbf{y}_2$, already depends on the other four vectors. $\qquad\square$

Up to this point we have shown that the views space of a rigid object is contained in a four-dimensional linear space. Theorem 3 below establishes that not every point in this space corresponds to a legal view of the object. The coefficients of the linear combination satisfy two quadratic constraints.

Theorem 3. The coefficients satisfy two quadratic constraints, which can be derived from three images.

Proof. Consider the coefficients $a_1, \ldots, a_4, b_1, \ldots, b_4$ from Theorem 1. Since R is a rotation matrix, its row vectors are orthonormal, and therefore the following equations hold for the coefficients.

$$
a_1^2 + a_2^2 + a_3^2 = b_1^2 + b_2^2 + b_3^2
$$

$$
a_1 b_1 + a_2 b_2 + a_3 b_3 = 0 .
$$

Choosing a different basis to represent the object (as we did in Theorem 2) will change the constraints. The constraints depend on the transformation that separates the model views. Denote by $\alpha_1, \ldots, \alpha_4, \beta_1, \ldots, \beta_4$ the coefficients that

---

[a]This lower bound was independently noticed by Poggio [40].

870   R. Basri

represent a novel view with respect to the basis described in Theorem 2, namely

$$\mathbf{x}' = \alpha_1\mathbf{x}_1 + \alpha_2\mathbf{y}_1 + \alpha_3\mathbf{x}_2 + \alpha_4\mathbf{1}$$
$$\mathbf{y}' = \beta_1\mathbf{x}_1 + \beta_2\mathbf{y}_1 + \beta_3\mathbf{x}_2 + \beta_4\mathbf{1}$$

and denote by U the rotation matrix that separates the two model views. By substituting the new coefficients we obtain new constraints

$$\alpha_1^2 + \alpha_2^2 + \alpha_3^2 - \beta_1^2 - \beta_2^2 - \beta_3^2 = 2(\beta_1\beta_3 - \alpha_1\alpha_3)u_{11} + 2(\beta_2\beta_3 - \alpha_2\alpha_3)u_{12}$$

$$\alpha_1\beta_1 + \alpha_2\beta_2 + \alpha_3\beta_3 + (\alpha_1\beta_3 + \alpha_3\beta_1)u_{11} + (\alpha_2\beta_3 + \alpha_3\beta_2)u_{12} = 0\,.$$

To derive the constraints the values of u_{11} and u_{12} should be recovered. A third view can be used for this purpose. When a third view of the object is given, the constraints supply two linear equations in u_{11} and u_{12}, and, therefore, in general, the values of u_{11} and u_{12} can be recovered from the two constraints. This proof suggests a simple, essentially linear structure from motion algorithm that resembles the method used in [41,42], but the details will not be discussed further here.   □

The scheme is therefore the following. An object is modeled by a set of views, with correspondence between the views, together with the two constraints. When a novel view of the object is observed the system computes the linear combination that aligns the model to the object. The object is recognized if such a combination is found and if in addition the constraints are verified. Figure 2 shows the application of the linear combination scheme to an artificially made object.

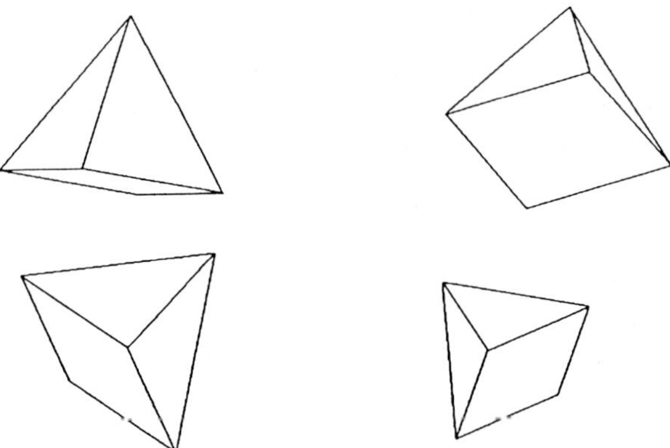

Fig. 2. Application of the linear combinations scheme to a model of a pyramid. Top: two model pictures of a pyramid. Bottom: two of their linear combinations.

For transparent objects a single model is sufficient to predict their appearance from all possible viewpoints. For opaque objects, due to self occlusion, a number of models is required to represent the objects from all aspects. These models are not necessarily independent. For example, in the case of a convex object as few as four images are sufficient to represent the object from all possible viewpoints. A pair of images, one from the "front" and another one from the "back" contains each object point once. Two such pairs contain two appearances of all object points, which is what is required to obtain a complete representation of all object points.

Note that positive values of the coefficients ("convex combinations") correspond to interpolation between the model views, while extrapolation is obtained by assigning one or more of the coefficients with negative values. This distinction between intermediate views and other views is important, since if two views of the object come from the same aspect then intermediate views are likely to also come from that aspect, while in other views other aspects of the objects may be observed.

4.2. *Additional Views*

In the previous section we have shown that two views of a rigid object are sufficient to represent an object from all possible viewpoints. All other views are linear combinations of the two views. In practice, however, because of noise and occlusion one may seek to use additional views to improve the accuracy of the model. In this section we present a method to build models from more than two views.

The idea is as follows. Each view provides two vectors, one for the x-coordinate and the other for the y-coordinate. These vectors can be viewed as points in $\mathcal{R}^n$. The space of views of the object is known to be four-dimensional. The objective, then, is to find the four-dimensional subspace of $\mathcal{R}^n$ that best approximates the input views. This subspace can be found using principal component analysis.

More formally, given l vectors, $\mathbf{v}_1, \ldots, \mathbf{v}_l$, we denote $F = [\mathbf{v}_1, \ldots, \mathbf{v}_l]$; F is an $n \times l$ matrix. The best k-dimensional space through these vectors (in a least-squared sense) is spanned by the k eigenvectors of FF^t that corresponds to its k largest eigenvalues. (A proof is given in [9], Appendix B.)

This method resembles the algorithm used by Tomasi and Kanade [43] to track features in motion sequences, with the exception that in our case the motion parameters do not need to be recovered since we are only interested in finding the linear space from which these views are depicted.

A method that approximates the space of views of an object from a number of its views using Radial Basis Functions [44] was recently suggested [45]. Similar to the LC method, the system represents an object by a set of its familiar views with the correspondence between the views. The number of views used for this approximation, between 10 to 100, is much larger than the number required under the linear combinations scheme. The system, however, can also approximate perspective views of the objects.

4.3. *Affine Objects*

In this section we extend the LC scheme to objects that undergo general affine transformations in space. In addition to the rigid transformations affine transformations include stretching and shearing. They are important since tilted pictures of objects appear to be stretched [46]. This effect is known as the La Gournerie Paradox (see [47]).

In order to extend the LC method to include affine transformations the same scheme can be used, but with the quadratic constraints ignored. Namely, the four-dimensional linear space contains all and only the affine views of the object. Two views are therefore sufficient to span the space with no further constraints.

4.4. *Rigid Objects with Smooth Surfaces*

In this section we extend the LC scheme to rigid objects with smooth bounding surfaces. These objects are considerably more difficult to recognize from their contour images than are objects with sharp edges (such as polyhedral objects). When objects with sharp edges are considered, the contours are always generated by those edges. With objects with smooth bounding surfaces, however, the silhouette (the boundary of the object) does not correspond to any particular edges on the object. That is, the *rim* (the set of object points that generates the contours) changes its position on the object with viewpoint, and its location therefore is difficult to predict (see Fig. 3).

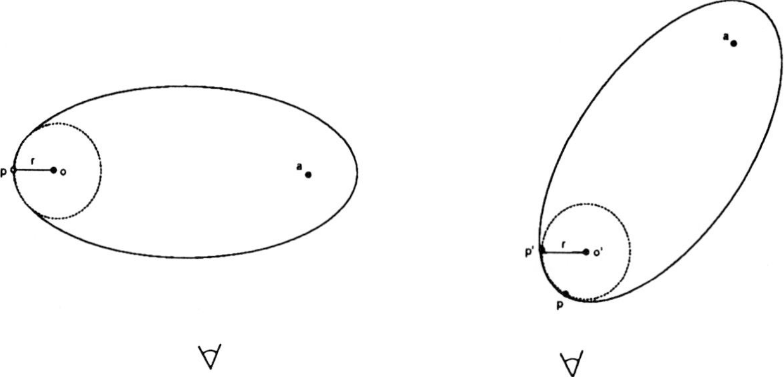

Fig. 3. The change of the rim of an object with smooth bounding surface due to rotation. Left: a horizontal section of an ellipsoid. p is a point on the rim. Right: the section rotated. p is no longer on the rim. Instead p' is the new rim point. The method described in Section 4.4 approximates the position of p' using the curvature circle at p. (See [48] for details.)

The position change of the rim depends largely on the 3-D curvature at the rim points. When this curvature is high the position change is relatively small. (In the case of a sharp edge, the curvature is infinite and the position change vanishes.) When the curvature is low the position change is relatively large.

Following this observation a method to approximate the position change of the rim using the surface curvature was developed [48]. In the original implementation a model contained a single contour image of the object. Each point along the contour was associated with its depth coordinate and its radial curvature (the curvature at the section defined by the surface normal and the line of sight). It was shown that a small number of images (at least three) is sufficient to recover this curvature. Using this information the system could approximate the appearance of objects with smooth bounding surfaces for relatively large transformations.

In a later paper Ullman and Basri [9] showed that this approximation method is linear in the model views. They concluded that objects with smooth bounding surfaces can be represented by linear combinations of their familiar views. The space of views in this case is six-dimensional (rather than four), and at least three views (rather than two) are required to span the space. Additional quadratic constraints apply to the coefficients of the linear combinations.

It should be noted that in order to handle objects with smooth bounding surfaces the definition of correspondence should be modified since contour points no longer represent the same physical points on the object from all views. Under the modified version, silhouette points in one image are matched to silhouette points in the second image that lie along the epipolar line. Ambiguities are resolved in a straightforward manner.

Note also that advance knowledge of the type of the object, whether it has sharp edges or smooth bounding surfaces, is not required. The views of a curved object span a larger space than the views of a polyhedral object. Thus, principal component analysis can be used to distinguish between the two (see Section 4.2).

Figure 4 shows the application of the method to real edge images of a car. It can be seen that the predictions obtained are fairly accurate even though the bounding contours are smooth.

4.5. *Articulated Objects*

An articulated object is a collection of links connected by joints. Each link is a rigid component. It can move independently of the other links when only its joints constrain its motion. The space of views of an articulated object with l links is at most $(4 \times l)$-dimensional. The joints contribute additional constraints, some of which may be linear, and they reduce the rank of the space, others are non-linear, in which case they are treated in the same way the quadratic constraints are treated in the rigid case.

Consider, for example, an object composed of two links connected by a rotational joint (e.g. a pair of scissors). The views space of a two-link object is at most eight-dimensional (four for each of the links). The rotational joint constrains the two links by forcing them to share a common axis. Denote by p and q two points along this axis, and denote by T_1 and T_2 the rigid transformations applied to the first and second links respectively, then the following two constraints hold:

$$T_1 p = T_2 p$$
$$T_1 q = T_2 q.$$

Fig. 4. Application of the linear combination scheme to a VW car. Top: three model pictures of the car. Middle: matching the model to a picture of the VW car. A linear combination of the three model images (left), an actual edge image (middle), and the two images overlaid (right). The prediction image and the actual one align almost perfectly. Bottom: matching the VW model to an image of another car. A linear combination of the three model images (left), an actual image of a Saab car (middle), and the two images overlaid (right). In this case, although the coefficients of the linear combination were chosen such that the prediction would match the actual image as much as possible, the obtained match is relatively poor.

These two constraints are linear, and therefore they reduce the dimension of the space from eight to six. In addition, there is one quadratic constraint that implies the two links are scaled by the same amount. To summarize, the space of views of an articulated object that is composed of two links connected by a rotational joint is contained in a six-dimensional linear space. Five additional quadratic constraints (two follow the rigidity of each of the two links and one follows the common scaling) apply to the coefficients.

As in the case of objects with smooth bounding surfaces, advance knowledge of the number of links and the type of the joints is not required. When sufficiently many views are presented, the correct rank of the views space can be recovered using principal components analysis.

Figure 5 shows the application of the linear combinations scheme to a pair of scissors. The images in this figure were obtained by different rigid transformations as well as articulations. It can be seen that the predictions match the real images also in the presence of articulations.

5. Recognition Using the LC Scheme

In the previous section we have presented a viewer-centered representation for object recognition. An object is modeled in this scheme by a small set of its views with the correspondence between the views. Novel views of the object are expressed

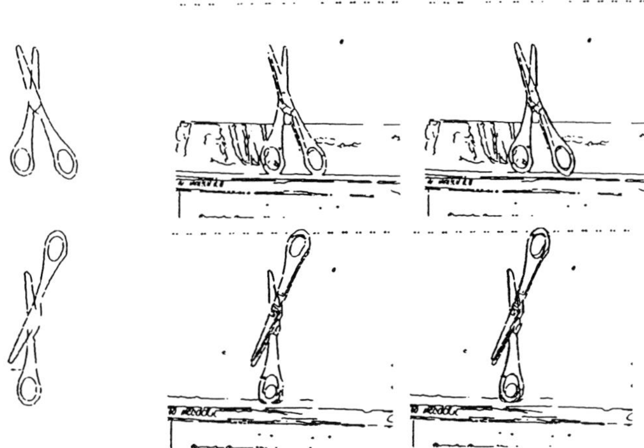

Fig. 5. Application of the linear combination method to a pair of scissors. Left: two linear combinations of the model views, Middle: actual edge images, Right: overlay of the predictions with the real images.

by linear combinations of the model views. In addition, the coefficients of these linear combinations may follow certain functional constraints.

In this section we discuss how this representation can be used in a recognition system. The task assigned to the recognition system is to determine, given an incoming image, whether the image belongs to the space of views of a particular model. In this section we discuss two principal methods to reach such a decision. The first involves alignment of the model to the image by explicitly recovering the coefficients of the linear combination, and the second involves the application of a "recognition operator".

5.1. *Recovering the Alignment Coefficients*

The alignment approach to object recognition identifies objects by first recovering the transformation that aligns the model with the incoming image, and then verifying that the transformed model matches the image. In the LC scheme, the observed image is expressed by linear combinations of the model views. The task is therefore to recover the coefficients of these linear combinations. In other words, given a view $\mathbf{v}'$ and a model $\{\mathbf{v}_1, \ldots, \mathbf{v}_k\}$ we seek a set of coefficients for which

$$\mathbf{v}' = a_1\mathbf{v}_1 + \cdots + a_k\mathbf{v}_k$$

holds. (In practice, to overcome noise, we may seek to minimize the difference between the two sides of this equation.)

To determine the coefficients that align a model to the image, either one of the two following methods can be employed. The first method involves recovering the correspondence between the model and the image, and the second method involves a search in the space of possible coefficients. In the first method correspondence is established between sufficiently many points so as to recover the coefficients. For a model that contains k views, at least k correspondences are required to solve a system of $2k$ linear equations (k equations for recovering the coefficients for the x-values, and another k equations for recovering the coefficients for the y-values). In this way, for example, four correspondences between model and image points are required to recover the coefficients for a rigid object by solving a linear system. If in addition we consider the quadratic constraints, this number is reduced to three. This is similar to the three-point alignment suggested by Huttenlocher and Ullman [5,7]. Applications of this method usually try to match triplets of model points to all combinations of triplets of image points to guarantee recognition.

An alternative approach to determine the coefficients involves a search in the space of possible coefficients. This method does not require correspondence between the model and the image. The idea is the following. Using global properties of the observed object, such as axes of elongation, an initial guess for the values of the coefficients can be made. This initial guess can be then improved by an iterative process. At every step in this process a new set of coefficients is generated. The model is transformed using these coefficients, and the result is compared to the actual image. If the two match, the observed object is recognized, otherwise the process is repeated until it converges. Minimization techniques such as gradient descent may be employed to reduce the complexity of the search. Such techniques, however, involve the risk of converging into a local minimum, which occasionally may be significantly worse than the desired solution.

It is interesting to note that the phenomenon of mental rotation seems to be consistent with the idea of search. The evidence for mental rotation suggests that recognition is not attained in an instance, but rather the response time increases with the angular separation between the observed object and its stored representation (see the discussion in Section 2).

5.2. *Recognition Operator*

A second approach to identify novel views of objects involves the application of "recognition operators" to these views. Such operators are essentially invariants for a given space of views, that is, they return a constant value for all views of the object, and different values for views of other objects. This method does not require the explicit recovery of the alignment coefficients. Still, it does require correspondence between the model and the image.

In the LC scheme a view is treated as a point in $\mathcal{R}^n$. A view contains the appearance of an object if it belongs to the space of views spanned by the object's model. A natural way to identify the object would be to determine how far apart the incoming view is from the views space of the object. The result of such a test would be zero if and only if the given view is a possible view of the object. By projecting the given view to the views space of the object we can generate a distance metric between the model and the view to be recognized.

Let $\mathbf{v}_1, \ldots, \mathbf{v}_k$ be the model views. Denote $M = [\mathbf{v}_1, \ldots, \mathbf{v}_k]$, M is a $k \times n$ matrix. Theorem 5 below defines a recognition operator L. L measures the distance of a view $\mathbf{v}'$ from the linear space spanned by the model views, $\mathbf{v}_1, \ldots, \mathbf{v}_k$, and ignores the nonlinear constraints.

Theorem 4. Let

$$L = I - MM^+$$

where $M^+ = (M^T M)^{-1} M^T$ denotes the pseudo inverse of M. Then $L\mathbf{v}' = 0$ if and only if $\mathbf{v}'$ is a linear combination of $\mathbf{v}_1, \ldots, \mathbf{v}_k$.

Proof. $L\mathbf{v}' = 0$ if and only if $\mathbf{v}' = MM^+\mathbf{v}'$. MM^+ is a projection operator; it projects the vector $\mathbf{v}'$ onto the column space of M. Therefore, the equality holds if and only if $\mathbf{v}'$ belongs to the column space of M, in which case it can be expressed by a linear combination of $\mathbf{v}_1, \ldots, \mathbf{v}_k$. The matrix L is therefore invariant for all views of the object; it maps all its views to zero. $\qquad\square$

Note that L only considers the linear envelope of the views space of the object. It does not verify any of the quadratic constraints. To verify in addition the quadratic constraints a quadratic invariant can be constructed. Weinshall [49] has recently presented a quadratic invariant for four points. This invariant can be modified to handle more points in a straightforward manner, but the details will not be discussed here.

The recognition operator can be made associative. The idea is the following. Suppose L is a linear operator that maps all model views to the same single vector, that is, $\mathbf{q} = L\mathbf{v}_1 = \ldots = L\mathbf{v}_k$. Since L is linear it maps combinations of the model to the same vector (up to a scale factor). Let $\mathbf{v}'$ be a novel view of the object, $\mathbf{v}' = \sum_{i=1}^{n} a_i \mathbf{v}_i$, then

$$L\mathbf{v}' = L\sum_{i=1}^{n} a_i \mathbf{v}_i = \sum_{i=1}^{n} a_i L\mathbf{v}_i = \left(\sum_{i=1}^{n} a_i\right) \mathbf{q}.$$

$\mathbf{q}$ serves as a name for the model, and it can be either zero (in which case we obtain an operator that is identical to the operator in Theorem 4 above) or it can be a familiar view of the object (e.g. $\mathbf{v}_1$).

A constructive definition of the associative operator is given below. Let $\{\mathbf{v}_1, \ldots, \mathbf{v}_n\}$ be a basis for $\mathcal{R}^n$ such that the first k vectors are composed of the model views. Denote

$$P = [\mathbf{v}_1, \ldots, \mathbf{v}_k, \mathbf{v}_{k+1}, \ldots, \mathbf{v}_n]$$
$$Q = [\mathbf{q}, \ldots, \mathbf{q}, \mathbf{v}_{k+1}, \ldots, \mathbf{v}_n].$$

(We filled the matrix Q with the vectors $\mathbf{v}_{k+1}, \ldots, \mathbf{v}_n$ so that the operator L would preserve the magnitude of noise if such is added to the novel view. These vectors can be replaced by any vectors that are linearly independent of $\mathbf{q}$.) We require that

$$LP = Q.$$

Therefore

$$L = QP^{-1}$$

(Notice that since P is a basis for $\mathcal{R}^n$ its inverse exists.) We have implemented the associative version of the recognition operator and applied it to the pyramid from Fig. 2. The results are given in Fig. 6. It can be seen that when this operator is applied to a novel view of the pyramid it returns a familiar view of the pyramid, and when it is applied to some other object it returns an unknown view.

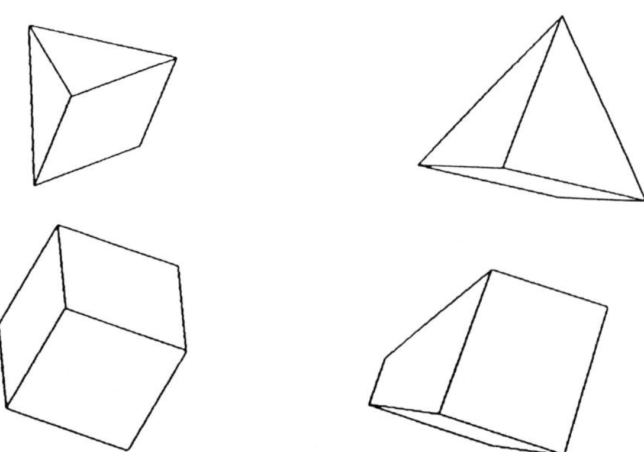

Fig. 6. Top: applying an associative "pyramidal" operator to a pyramid (left) returns a model view of the pyramid (right, compare with Fig. 2, top left). Bottom: applying the same operator to a cube (left) returns an unfamiliar image (right).

Both versions of the recognition operator can be implemented by a linear neural network with simple structure [50]. The network contains only input and output layers with no hidden units. The weights are set to be the components of L (see Fig. 7). The network operates on novel views of some object and returns either zero or a familiar view of the object, according to the operator it implements. It should be noted that for such an operator to be applicable the correspondence between the image and model must first be resolved.

6. Summary

Visual object recognition is a process in which images are compared to stored representations of objects. While recent psychophysical and physiological studies indicate that the visual system uses viewer-centered representations, most computational approaches to recognition use object-centered representations. The few existing methods that use viewer-centered representations require a large number of views to represent an object from all possible viewpoints.

A scheme was presented in which objects are recognized using viewer-centered models. The scheme is based on the observation that the novel views of an object

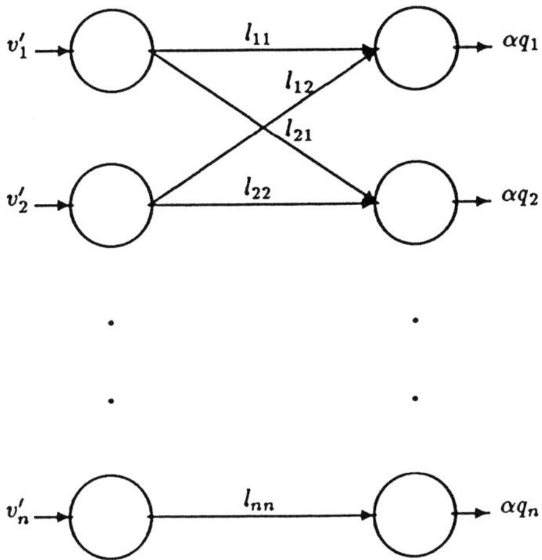

Fig. 7. A neural network architecture that implements the recognition operator L. The input to this network is composed of the elements of the novel view $\mathbf{v}'$, and the output is the "name" vector $\mathbf{q}$ (up to a scale factor α).

can be expressed as linear combinations of a small set of its familiar views. An object is modeled by a set of views with correspondence between the views and possibly with some functional constraints. A novel view is recognized if there exists a linear combination of the model views that aligns the model to the image, and if the coefficients of this combination satisfy the functional constraints.

The method was applied to rigid objects as well as to objects that undergo affine transformations, rigid objects with smooth bounding surfaces (in which case the method only approximates the appearance of these objects), and articulated objects. The number of views required to represent an object depends on the shape of the object, whether it has sharp edges or smooth surfaces, in the case of a rigid object, and on the type of joints that connect the links in the case of an articulated one. This number can be deduced from the set of views of the object.

To recover the alignment coefficients, a small number of points in the image and their corresponding points in the model can be used, or a search can be conducted in the space of possible coefficients. Alternatively, if the complete correspondence between the model and the image can be recovered, a "recognition operator" can be applied to the image. This operator obtains as its input a novel view of the object and returns a constant value, either the zero vector or a familiar view of the object. Furthermore, the operator can be implemented in a neural network with simple structure. Finding the correspondence between the model and the image is the difficult problem in recognition. The phenomenon of apparent motion, however, demonstrates that the visual system can successfully solve the correspondence problem.

Acknowledgements

I wish to thank Shimon Ullman without whom this work would not have been possible, and to T. D. Alter, S. Edelman, W. E. L. Grimson, T. Poggio, and A. Yuille for helpful comments at different stages of this work. This report describes research done at the Weizmann Institute of Science and at the Massachusetts Institute of Technology within the Artificial Intelligence Laboratory and the McDonnell-Pew Center for Cognitive Neuroscience. Support for the laboratory's artificial intelligence research is provided in part by the Advanced Research Projects Agency of the Department of Defense under Office of Naval Research contract N00014-91J-4038. Ronen Basri is supported by the McDonnell-Pew and the Rothchild postdoctoral fellowships.

References

[1] I. Biederman, Recognition by components: a theory of human image understanding, *Psychol. Rev.* **94** (1987) 115–147.

[2] R. T. Chin and C. R. Dyer, Model-based recognition in robot vision, *Comput. Surv.* **18**, 1 (1986) 67–108.

[3] P. Jolicoeur, Identification of disoriented objects: A dual-systems theory, *Mind and Language* **5** (1990) 387–410.

[4] S. E. Palmer, Fundamental aspects of cognitive representation, in E. Rosch and B. B. Lloyd (eds.), *Cognition and Categorization* (Lawrence Erlbaum, Hillsdale, NJ, 1978) 259–303.

[5] S. Ullman, Aligning pictorial descriptions: An approach to object recognition, *Cognition* **32**, 3 (1989) 193–254.

[6] M. A. Fischler and R. C. Bolles, Random sample consensus: A paradigm for model fitting with application to image analysis and automated cartography, *Commun. ACM* **24**, 6 (1981) 381–395.

[7] D. P. Huttenlocher and S. Ullman, Object recognition using alignment, in *Proc. Int. Conf. on Computer Vision (ICCV)*, London, UK, 1987, 102–111.

[8] D. G. Lowe, *Perceptual Organization and Visual Recognition* (Kluwer Academic Publishers, Boston, MA, 1986).

[9] S. Ullman and R. Basri, Recognition by linear combinations of models, *IEEE Trans. Pattern Anal. Mach. Intell.* **13**, 10 (1991) 992–1006.

[10] R. C. Bolles and R. A. Cain, Recognizing and locating partially visible objects: The local feature focus method. *Int. J. Robot. Res.* **1**, 3 (1982) 57–82.

[11] M. K. Hu, Visual pattern recognition by moment invariants, *IRE Trans. Inf. Theory* **8** (1962) 169–187.

[12] T. O. Binford, Visual perception by computer, in *Proc. IEEE Conf. on Systems and Control*, Miami, FL, 1971.

[13] D. Marr and H. K. Nishihara, Representation and recognition of the spatial organization of three dimensional shapes, *Proc. Royal Society* **B200** (1978) 269–291.

[14] A. Requicha and H. Voelcker, Constructive solid geometry, Production Automation Project Tm-26, University of Rochester, NY, 1977.

[15] L. G. Roberts, Machine perception of three-dimensional solids, in J. T. Tippett et al. (eds.), *Optical and Electro-Optical Information Processing* (MIT Press, Cambridge, MA, 1965).

[16] R. N. Shepard and J. Metzler, Mental rotation of three dimensional objects, *Science* **171** (1971) 701–703.

[17] L. A. Cooper, Demonstration of a mental analog to an external rotation, *Perception and Psychophysics* **1** (1976) 20–43.

[18] P. Jolicoeur, The time to name disoriented natural objects, *Memory and Cognition* **13**, 4 (1985) 289–303.

[19] P. Jolicoeur and M. J. Landau, Effects of orientation on the identification of simple visual patterns, *Canadian J. Psychol.* **38**, 1 (1984) 80–93.

[20] R. Maki, Naming and locating the tops of rotated pictures, *Canadian J. Psychol.* **40** (1986) 368–387.

[21] R. N. Shepard and J. Metzler, Mental rotation: effects of dimensionality of objects and type of task, *J. Exper. Psychol.: Human Perception and Performance* **14**, 1 (1988) 3–11.

[22] S. P. Shwartz, The perception of disoriented complex objects, in *Proc. 3rd Conf. on Cognitive Sciences*, Berkeley, CA, 1981, 181–183.

[23] M. J. Tarr and S. Pinker, Mental rotation and orientation-dependence in shape recognition, *Cognitive Psychology* **21** (1989) 233–282.

[24] M. C. Corballis, Recognition of disoriented shapes, *Psychol. Rev.* **95** (1988) 115–123.

[25] P. Jolicoeur and B. Milliken, Identification of disoriented objects: Effects of context of prior representation, *J. of Exper. Psychol.: Learning, Memory, and Cognition* **15** (1989) 200–210.

[26] M. J. Tarr and S. Pinker, When does human object recognition use a viewer-centered reference frame? *Psychol. Sci.* **1** (1990) 253–256.

[27] M. J. Tarr, Orientation Dependence in Three-Dimensional Object Recognition, Ph.D. thesis, Massachusetts Institute of Technology, 1989.

[28] S. Edelman and H. H. Bülthoff, Viewpoint-specific representations in three-dimensional object recognition, Technical Report A. I. Memo 1239, The Artificial Intelligence Lab., M.I.T., 1990.

[29] I. Rock and J. DiVita, A case of viewer-centered object perception, *Cognitive Psychology* **19** (1987) 280–293.

[30] S. Edelman and H. H. Bülthoff, Orientation dependence in the recognition of familiar and novel views of 3d objects, *Vision Research* **32** (1992) 2385–2400.

[31] D. I. Perret, P. A. J. Smith, D. D. Potter, A. J. Mistlin, A. S. Head, A. D. Milner, and M. A. Jeeves, Visual cells in the temporal cortex sensitive to face view and gaze direction, *Proc. Royal Society* **B223** (1985) 293–317.

[32] M. J. Farah and K. M. Hammond, Mental rotation and orientation-invariant object recognition: Dissociable processes, *Cognition* **29** (1988) 29–46.

[33] R. J. Douglass, Interpreting three dimensional scenes: A model building approach, *Comput. Graph. Image Process.* **17** (1981) 91–113.

[34] J. E. Hochberg and V. Brooks, Pictorial recognition as an unlearned ability: A study of one child's performance, *Am. J. Psychol.* **75** (1962) 624–628.

[35] C. H. Chien and J. K. Aggarwal, Shape recognition from single silhouette, in *Proc. Int. Conf. on Computer Vision (ICCV)*, London, UK, 1987, 481–490.

[36] O. D. Faugeras and M. Hebert, The representation, recognition and location of 3-D objects, *Int. J. Robot. Res.* **5**, 3 (1986) 27–52.

[37] D. W. Thompson and J. L. Mundy, Three dimensional model matching from an unconstrained viewpoint, in *Proc. IEEE Int. Conf. on Robotics and Automation*, Raleigh, NC, 1987, 208–220.

[38] Y. S. Abu-Mostafa and D. Pslatis, Optical neural computing, *Sci. Am.* **256** (1987) 66–73.

[39] P. Van Hove, Model based silhouette recognition, in *Proc. IEEE Computer Society Workshop on Computer Vision*, 1987.

[40] T. Poggio, 3D object recognition: On a result by Basri and Ullman, Technical Report TR 9005-03, IRST, Povo, Italy, 1990.

[41] S. Ullman, *The Interpretation of Visual Motion*, (MIT Press, Cambridge, MA, 1979).

[42] T. S. Huang and C. H. Lee, Motion and structure from orthographic projections, *IEEE Trans. Pattern Anal. Mach. Intell.* **2**, 5 (1989) 536–540.

[43] C. Tomasi and T. Kanade, Factoring image sequences into shape and motion, in *Proc. IEEE Workshop on Visual Motion*, Princeton, NJ, 1991, 21–29.

[44] T. Poggio and F. Girosi, Regularization algorithms for learning that are equivalent to multilayer networks, *Science* **247** (1990) 978–982.

[45] T. Poggio and S. Edelman, A network that learns to recognize three-dimensional objects, *Nature* **343** (1990) 263–266.

[46] D. W. Jacobs, Space efficient 3D model indexing, in *Proc. CVPR Conference*, Urbana, IL, 1992.

[47] J. E. Cutting, *Perception with An Eye for Motion* (MIT Press, Cambridge, MA, 1986).

[48] R. Basri and S. Ullman, The alignment of objects with smooth surfaces, in *Proc. 2nd Int. Conf. Computer Vision*, Florida, 1988, 482–488.

[49] D. Weinshall, Model based invariants for linear model acquisition and recognition, Technical Report RC-17705 (#77262), IBM, 1992.

[50] R. Basri and S. Ullman, Linear operator for object recognition, in J. E. Moody, S. J. Hanson and R. P. Lippmann (eds.), *Advances in Neural Information Processing Systems 4* (Morgan Kaufmann, San Mateo, CA, 1991).

Handbook of Pattern Recognition and Computer Vision, pp. 883–920
Eds. C. H. Chen, L. F. Pau and P. S. P. Wang
© 1993 World Scientific Publishing Company

$$\boxed{\text{CHAPTER 5.5}}$$

CONNECTIONIST ARCHITECTURES IN LOW LEVEL IMAGE SEGMENTATION

W. EKKEHARD BLANZ, CHARLES E. COX and SHERI L. GISH

IBM Research Division, Almaden Research Center
650 Harry Road, San Jose, CA 95120-6099, USA

First, we will briefly review the state of the art in image segmentation, as performed by connectionist architectures. We will then investigate issues of scalability and real-time performance of such systems. Based on these considerations we will describe a scalable real-time image segmentation architecture which uses a connectionist classifier as a central building block. The system that we describe has been built in our research lab and is fully operational. It consists of a feature extraction module and a connectionist classifier module. We will devote a section to hardware design considerations of connectionist architectures in general, and then elaborate on the design points that led to the fastest known implementation of a digital connectionist classifier. Finally, we will give examples of the performance of the implemented architecture on a variety of real-world applications.

Keywords: Image segmentation, neural network, pattern recognition, classifier, texture, feature extraction, real-time machine vision.

1. Introduction

An important fundamental component of machine vision is image segmentation, the process of identifying individual pixels in an image matrix as being members of different objects or regions in a scene. This process can be viewed as a decision analysis task, in which certain objects are classified into different classes on the basis of a set of measurements which are taken from each object. This approach is difficult to implement as a general solution strategy because both the choice of the best measurements and the selection of the ideal classifier are typically highly problem dependent [4,26]. However, it has been shown that with a certain set of programmable pixel measurements and a trainable classifier one can achieve good performance for a large set of well defined real world image segmentation tasks. Even the construction of special hardware to perform real-time image segmentation as a fairly general hardware building block for machine vision systems is feasible.

A central building block for a decision analytic approach to image segmentation is the classifier. In this chapter we will concentrate on the use of neural networks, or connectionist classifiers, for that task. Classifiers, in general, are parameterized devices which group objects into one out of a set of predefined categories or *classes*.

The objects are all described and represented by a set of measurements or *features*. The grouping process, or *class assignment*, is based on the experience that was gained during an adaptation procedure. In this procedure an adaptation set of objects, again represented by their features, is presented to an adaptation algorithm. The correct class membership of each object in the adaptation set is known. The adaptation algorithm then automatically determines class specific feature commonalities and characteristic feature differences of objects from different classes. This knowledge about feature differences and commonalities is then automatically converted into a parameter set for the classifier. By virtue of this parameter set the classifier is adaptable to a variety of different classification tasks. The applicability of a certain classifier architecture to a given classification problem is theoretically only limited by the ability of the given architecture to form surfaces in the space of features that separate the given classes. These surfaces are referred to as *decision surfaces*. In practice, however, it is sometimes often just as hard to find the optimal parameter set for a given architecture as it is to find the proper classifier architecture.

A tremendous amount of work has been done in the area of classification problems (referred to as *discriminant analysis* and *pattern recognition*) since the pioneering work of Fisher in 1939 [13], and a plethora of algorithmic classification architectures have been developed since. However, comparably little work has been done so far in mapping these algorithms onto hardware architectures. The need for appropriate hardware architectures arose with the requirements for high speed pattern recognition, most notably in optical character recognition and machine vision.

In general, most hardware implementations of powerful classification architectures are rather costly. This is mostly due to the fact that with most classical statistical approaches, reasonably complex decision surfaces can only be realized when products of different features are used. For instance, to build quadratic surfaces, the products of all pairs of features (as well as the squares of the individual features) have to be computed. Multiplications of two (or more) variables, however, are expensive, especially for higher dimensional feature spaces.

In contrast to conventional approaches, such as Gaussian maximum likelihood classifiers, where decision surfaces are determined by polynomials [11], connectionist architectures can form rather complex decision surfaces without the need for multiplications of several variables. It turns out that this is the key feature that makes digital hardware implementations of neural networks attractive. So far it has not been shown that a purely software implementation of a neural network image segmentation scheme is generally superior to a conventional scheme, irrespective of insulated cases where connectionist classifiers performed slightly better than their classical counterparts [16,20]. Moreover, the lack of a closed-form training for feed-forward neural networks makes training these networks unreliable and unpredictable, and hence makes connectionist classifiers generally less desirable whenever one cannot exploit the advantages inherent in hardware implementations of neural networks.

2. Image Segmentation Methods Using Neural Networks

2.1. *Short Review of Connectionist Architectures*

A connectionist architecture, also referred to as an artificial neural network, in general, is a graph with no self loops, where each vertex or *node* represents a processing unit, and each edge is assigned a number called the *weight* of that edge. All processing units in the net perform the same operation with different operands. Of practical interest for image segmentation purposes are two interconnection schemes: feed-forward, layered nets [23] and unlayered or Hopfield nets [18]. Figure 1 shows a three-layer[a] feed-forward net with three units in the input layer, four units in the central or *hidden* layer, and two units in the output layer. Figure 2 illustrates a five-unit fully connected Hopfield net.

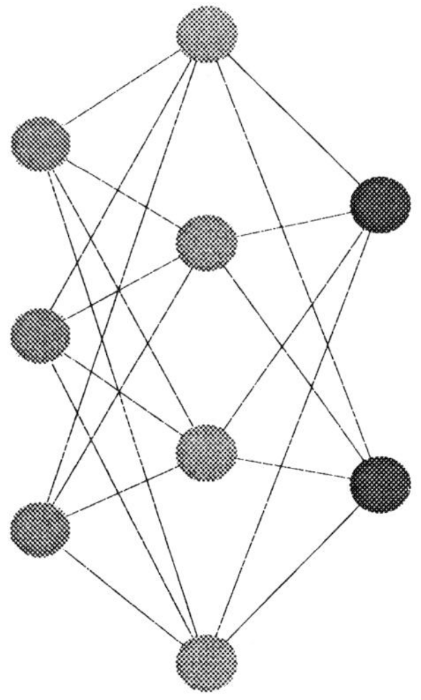

Fig. 1. Layered, feed-forward net.

In the layered net, edges in the graph of the network represent a unidirectional connection between processing units. The nodes of the graph are the processing units. Each processing unit in the hidden and the output layer computes a weighted sum of its inputs plus a bias value, applies an activation function, and takes the result as its current state. The current state is then passed to the connected nodes in the next layer as their input. The "output" of the net is the state of all units in the output layer. The nodes in the input layer do not perform any computation.

---

[a]We adhere to the numbering scheme used in graph theory, although some authors refer to the net sketched in Fig. 1 as a two-layer net.

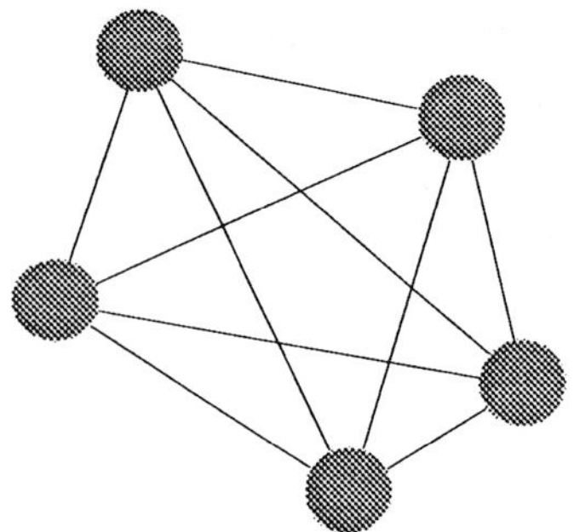

Fig. 2. Hopfield net.

Mathematically, the function of the processing units can be expressed as:

$$x_j^{(l)} = \sum_i a_{ij}^{(l)} s_i^{(l-1)} + b_j^{(l)} \tag{2.1}$$

$a_{ij}^{(l)}$ is the real-valued weight assigned to the edge between unit i in layer $l-1$ and unit j in layer l. $s_i^{(l-1)}$ is the current state of unit i in layer $l-1$ and $b_j^{(l)}$ is the bias value for unit j in layer l. The current state of the node is determined by applying a so-called activation function to $x_j^{(l)}$. For a variety of reasons [23] it is advantageous to use a sigmoid function as an activation function. Sigmoid functions are characterized by approaching 0 asymptotically if the argument approaches $-\infty$ and 1 if the argument approaches $+\infty$ with only one point of inflection where the argument is 0 (see Fig. 3). Most authors use the so-called "logistic" activation function

$$s_i^{(l)} = \frac{1}{1 + e^{-x_i^l}} \tag{2.2}$$

to produce the state $s_i^{(l)}$ (a value between 0 and 1) of each node.

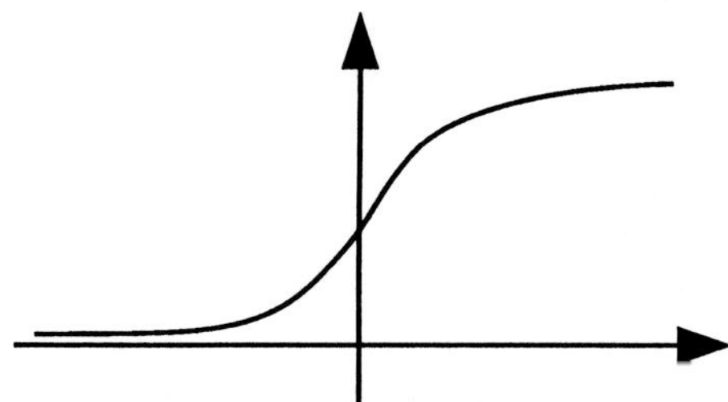

Fig. 3. Activation function.

Unlike layered nets, each node in a Hopfield net can be connected to every other node in the graph. Each connection between two nodes of the graph represent two communications paths, one from the first unit to the second, and one from the second unit to the first. In other words, each vertex of the Hopfield net is typically connected to all other vertices by two parallel edges. Although it would be possible to assign different weights to the two parallel edges, most authors assign the same weight to both parallel edges and draw only one edge, representing a bi-directional communications path (as done in Fig. 2). Unit processing in the Hopfield net is the same as the processing in the layered feed-forward net. The "output" of the Hopfield net is the state of all units in the net.

With only few exceptions [27] most authors prefer the layered net for image segmentation purposes. This is due to three main reasons: (1) The interconnection of the layered feed-forward net is much easier to implement than the full interconnection scheme of a Hopfield net. (2) The layered net requires examination of only a few nodes in the output layer to determine the result; in the case of a Hopfield net all nodes have to be considered. (3) The activation of a layered feed-forward net is a one-shot systolic process where the output can be determined immediately after the states of the nodes in the output layer have been computed. In the case of a Hopfield net, however, the final state of all nodes is only obtained after an asynchronous (hopefully) convergent process after which a stable state of all nodes is achieved. The number of processing steps for each node cannot be determined *a priori*.

For these reasons the layered feed-forward net is mainly used for classification purposes, whereas the application domain of the Hopfield net is mostly in the area of associative memories [21].

2.2. *Review of Image Segmentation Methods Using Neural Networks*

Much of the work on applying connectionist architectures to vision documented in the literature draws heavily on biological models of vision. Some authors present the biological models as their motivation while others simply compare their systems to biological vision systems. When concentrating on works describing neural network based image segmentation systems, one finds that many of these systems share a common input model, with the image fed directly into an artificial neural network with center-surround spot receptors. The center-surround spot receptors have excitatory centers surrounded by an inhibitory region and thus have a maximal output when the center spot is bright surrounded by darkness. Some authors propose analog network implementations and some digital network implementations. While this review of the state of the art does not claim to be complete and in particular does not include Hopfield networks, it is generally observed that there are a small number of architectures proposed and sometimes simulated, but that there is an obvious lack of neural network based image segmentation systems actually implemented in hardware in the public literature.

The oldest form of image segmentation is thresholding [10]. Here it is assumed that all objects lie in different gray level domains. In other words, the only measurement or feature describing each pixel is its gray value, and the classifier can be simply built out of two comparators for each class. A very simple form of using neural networks to do image segmentation is to apply them only during the adaptation to find appropriate thresholds for this method. This approach was taken by Scherf and Roberts [24], and they demonstrate their results on three different infrared scenes. Thresholding methods are comparably easy and inexpensive to implement in hardware, however, their applicability is limited by the fact that often the gray levels of different objects overlap in a scene.

Mesrobian and Skrzypek [19] use a network architecture to segment images based on regions of common texture. They use overlapping center-surround sensors to detect edges in certain orientations. Responses from the edge detector nodes feed line segment, line termination, and corner detectors. The outputs of these nodes are used to locate boundaries between differing textures (in this case regions of edges with a primary orientation). The architecture has no provision for labeling the segmented regions, but rather provides boundaries between them. The authors simulate their architecture on a workstation and present the results of processing a single synthetic 64 × 64 pixel binary image.

Cortes and Hertz [7] propose a network based architecture for reconstructing images distorted by blurring and noise. The image is fed directly to the network with one input node per pixel in the image. The inputs are not center-surround, but rather have edge detectors between each pair of pixels. There is a separate network for each orientation to be detected. The authors use one horizontal network and one vertical network but note that practical systems would have more. The next stage takes inputs from the orientation networks and the raw image. Within a region delineated by edges from the previous stage, this stage tends to pass the average pixel value of the raw image out. Results of the simulated architecture are shown on a synthetic 50 × 50 pixel image containing only horizontal and vertical edges.

An architecture proposed by Dupaguntla and Vemuri [12] also uses edge orientation as the primary means of discrimination between regions. They take their architecture a step further and attempt to label the segmented regions. An important step from a systems point of view is taken in this paper. The authors divide the problem into two tasks: feature extraction and classification. The feature extraction network draws its inputs directly from the input image through center-surround sensors and outputs some number of features, each of which corresponds to a particular edge orientation. The classification, or texture discrimination network, is trained to recognize each of the possible input textures. Since the only features used in the texture discrimination are based on edge orientations, the system is not rotation invariant, unless trained for all possible orientations of the textures.

A very interesting and promising approach to neural network based texture image segmentation which does not use the neuron-per-pixel paradigm has been proposed by Desmouceaux and Derycke [9]. They describe a much more elaborate feature extraction method in which 24 features are computed in 32 × 32 pixel sliding windows, i.e. they compute 24 features for each pixel in the scene. For classification they use a standard feed-forward net with 24 nodes in the input layer, 16 nodes in the hidden layer, and as many nodes in the output layer as they have texture classes (three in their application). This net, of course, is re-used for every pixel. The system is implemented in software, and one real-world 512×512 image is shown to demonstrate their segmentation result.

A very similar approach was taken by Özkan, Sprenkels and Dawant [20] to segment biomedical magnetic resonance images. The number of features used by these authors is three, determined by the physical nature of the image generation, i.e. no texture features are created in windows, but rather gray values are taken from three different channels, corresponding to different physical properties of the objects. They also use a feed-forward net with one hidden layer as the classification component of their system. The authors present impressive results on two different real-world MR images from cross-sections of human brains. They also discuss influences of the number of units in the hidden layer and compare the results obtained with the neural network classifier to those obtained with a classical Gaussian maximum likelihood classifier. Although the authors do not mention any hardware implementation of their system, the size of their net and the ease of obtaining their features would make this system very amenable for actual hardware implementation.

3. A Scalable Real-Time Neural Network Segmentation Machine

As we have seen in the previous section not many segmentation systems proposed in literature have actually been implemented in hardware and used for real-world applications. Most of the neuron-per-pixel based systems also would not scale up nicely to full TV-screen images, let alone much bigger images, such as those typically created by line scanners in many industrial machine vision applications. Also, while it is obvious that a single pixel cannot have a texture, and therefore information from its neighborhood has to be used to do texture segmentation, the center-surround spot technique is only one way of obtaining that neighborhood information. Which method is best for computing texture information is certainly application dependent, and flexible systems should somehow account for that. Furthermore, it is not clear yet, whether systems that use the neuron-per-pixel approach will ever get into a price range where they could economically compete against non-connectionist systems, or against human operators.

In this section we describe a system that is not based on the model of biological vision at all, much like the system proposed by Desmouceaux and Derycke or Özkan, Sprenkels and Dawant. Unlike their approach ours goes directly to the heart of the segmentation task, treating it as a task of classifying pixels into different *predefined* categories. This limits these systems to tasks where the objects which are anticipated in a scene are known *a priori*. The assumption of predefined object classes, however, is made implicitly or explicitly by most other authors in the field who use supervised training methods to adapt their networks. This is exactly the situation that we find in most industrial and medical inspection applications. We also go one step further than Desmouceaux and Derycke or Özkan, Sprenkels and Dawant and describe a complete hardware architecture that has been built, is functional, and in the process of being transferred to the manufacturing floor. Furthermore, there has been a fair amount of flexibility designed into our hardware to obtain texture information, thus making the system adaptable to different applications not only at the classifier level, but even at the feature extraction level. Needless to say methods to select the appropriate features for a given application have to go along with this built-in flexibility, and we will briefly describe our feature selection method as well.

3.1. *Overall Architecture*

The two major building blocks of our architecture are a pixel feature extraction unit and a classification unit. If a segmentation problem requires more than one input channel (e.g. different color bands, bright field and dark field channels on a microscope, or different physical properties in MR or satellite images), we use a feature extraction unit for each band. In our hardware implementation each channel is represented by an incoming datastream of pixels, each of which is described by eight bits. The feature extraction units extract up to ten pixel descriptors per band, each feature is also eight bits wide, per pixel. Up to 12 of the most powerful descriptors are then connected to our classification unit. In principal, the classification unit can be based on either a conventional scheme [5] or a connectionist scheme. In this chapter we will concentrate on the connectionist scheme, since it provides considerable advantages when implemented in hardware. The final classification result is again encoded in eight bits. The architecture is heavily pipelined to keep up with a datastream of 20 million pixels per second per channel. The latency of the entire system is the time equivalent of less than nine rows of the image matrix; this makes it possible to use our segmentation engine in robotics applications. An example of our segmentation engine configured for four input channels is shown in Fig. 4. However, almost all experimental results reported in this chapter are derived using a single input channel; only the thin film images were obtained using three different channels.

3.2. *Feature Extraction Block*

In this section we present RUBBER HOSE, a high performance feature extraction card. The key features of the design are its programmable flexibility and high throughput. The programmability of the card makes it applicable to a wide variety of machine vision problems. The card can take image data in at a rate of up to 20 million eight-bit pixels per second, and outputs ten eight-bit features in parallel. Frames can be up to 2048 pixels wide and essentially arbitrarily long.

3.2.1. *Background*

In most industrial machine vision applications (as well as in many other types of machine vision applications), objects and background differ either in gray levels, in their textures, or in a combination of both. Therefore, we have defined pixel descriptors which capture these two basic properties. While the gray level is certainly a feature of a single pixel, texture is not. Therefore, to get texture information on a pixel basis, we have to incorporate information from the neighboring pixels. This

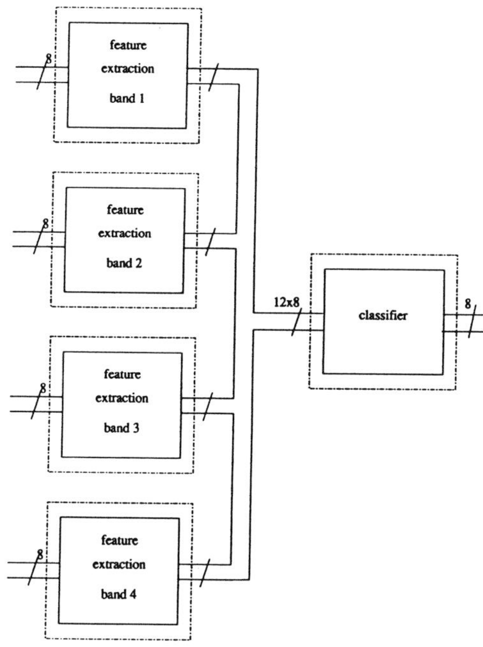

Fig. 4. Overall architecture of our segmentation engine.

is done in window operations where all the pixels in a certain window around the pixel of interest contribute to a description of that pixel.

The commitment to gray level and texture descriptors defines the application domain of our segmentation system; our real-time image segmentation engine can be applied whenever objects of interest differ from their background and other objects in the scene on the basis of gray level, texture, or both. Therefore, solely the architecture described in this section will not be sufficient to solve segmentation tasks which require the incorporation of further information about objects, such as shape. However, methods exist to complement our engine so that other information such as shape or some physical *a priori* knowledge can be included in a solution strategy which includes our segmentation engine [26].

3.2.2. *Technology*

In selecting our design point for RUBBER HOSE, we carefully considered what was feasible to be used with existing technology. Since we wanted to build a working system, architectures that may be academically interesting, but not practical to build were not considered. For example, available television cameras and line scanners provide image data as intensity information in row major order, so we cannot use center-surround spot sensors or assume that the entire image is available for presentation to the hardware at a single instant.

We also wanted to avoid full custom silicon, and so restricted ourselves to goals we could achieve using off the shelf logic. We rely heavily on two commercial products from LSI Logic, the L64220 Rank-Value Filter and the L64240 Multi-bit Filter for our actual processing capabilities. These two chips operate on neighborhoods of up to 8 × 8 pixels, and, hence, so does our card. Larger window sizes would obviously give us more flexibility, but would also add considerably to the system cost. The density of Field-Programmable Gate Arrays, specifically the XC3000 series of Logic Cell Arrays from Xilinx, allowed us to pack the required control logic and flexible data path onto the single card.

RUBBER HOSE is implemented on a single 9U VME card. A photograph of the card is given in Fig. 5. The card uses the VMEbus for set-up and control information, and MAXbus Data Port compatible connections for image data.

Fig. 5. Photograph of RUBBER HOSE.

3.2.3. *RUBBER HOSE Architecture*

A block diagram of the feature extraction card is given in Fig. 6. The major components on the block diagram are the boxes labeled "delay", "rank value", and "convolver". The boxes labeled "delay" are line delays that buffer eight lines of image data and output the lines in parallel allowing downstream devices to form 8 × 8 windows. The maximum line width is 2048 pixels.

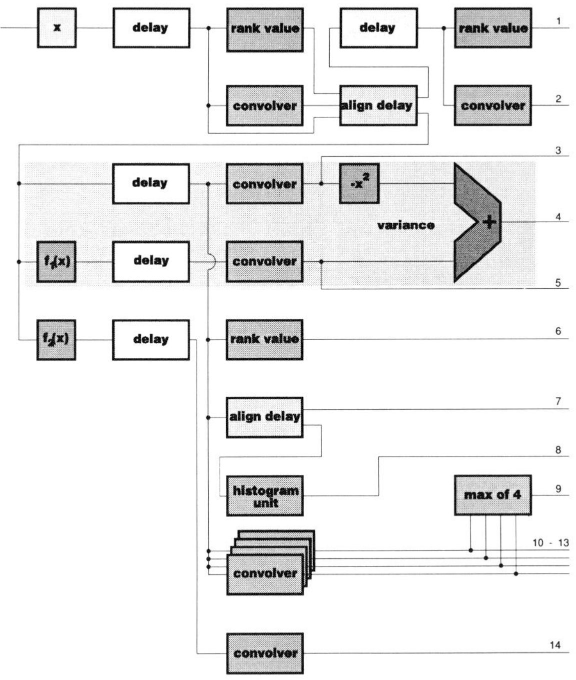

Fig. 6. Feature extraction architecture.

The majority of features generated on the feature extraction card are either convolution features or rank value features. The convolution features have programmable eight-bit kernel elements and window sizes of up to 8 × 8 pixels. The convolutions are programmed individually and may have differing window sizes as well as different kernels. The rank value features operate within a programmable window size of up to 8 × 8 pixels and can be any rank within that window (typically the minimum, median, or maximum). The window size of the three rank value processors on the card can be adjusted independently of each other as well as independently of the convolution processors.

The data path on RUBBER HOSE is designed to allow a great deal of flexibility in the selection of features to be extracted from an image. A total of five sliding windows are passed over the image data or transformations of the image data. The data path allows the cascading of convolution and rank value processors to generate second order features on the card. For example, the image data may be passed through a minimum filter followed by a maximum filter in one pass through the card. All features computed on the card are time aligned as they leave the card such that they can be presented in parallel to the classification unit.

The two boxes "$f_1(x)$" and "$f_2(x)$" in Fig. 6 are loadable look-up tables that can be used to transform the input data before neighborhood processing. The box labeled "max of 4" takes inputs from four convolution filters and outputs the maximum value of the four convolutions. This can be used as a multiple orientation edge detector by programming the four convolution kernels as edge detectors in four different orientations. The shaded block in Fig. 6 can be programmed to compute the variance within a window.

The histogram unit on RUBBER HOSE is different from all the other processors on the card because it cannot generate features in real time. By its very nature, a histogram is a global measure as opposed to a local measurement. The histogram unit may be programmed to take a histogram on one frame and then use the data generated to do a histogram normalization on the next frame. In industrial inspection tasks that may require multiple frames to inspect a single part, using histogram data from the previous frame is sufficient to track slowly varying parameters such as lighting. The histogram unit may be programmed to compute a histogram on any rectangular subset of an image. It can compute normal histograms, or histograms including only pixels that are greater than, less than, or equal to, a convolution of the neighborhood surrounding that pixel.

A summary of the pixel descriptors which can be computed by the card is given in Table 1.

Table 1. Features computed on RUBBER HOSE.

Feature	Description
f_1	rank value or
	rank value of rank value or
	rank value of convolution
f_2	convolution or
	convolution of rank value or
	convolution of convolution
f_3	convolution
	(mean if feature 4 is variance)
f_4	sum of $-(f_3)^2$ and f_5 or variance if
	f_3 and f_5 are programmed appropriately
f_5	convolution of look-up table function $f1(x)$
	or mean of gray levels squared if f_4 is variance
f_6	rank value
f_7	gray value
f_8	look-up table result
	(LUT loaded by histogram unit)
f_9	maximum of f_{10} through f_{13}
f_{10}	convolution
f_{11}	convolution
f_{12}	convolution
f_{13}	convolution
f_{14}	convolution of look-up table $f2(x)$

The fourteen features shown in Fig. 6 are all generated in parallel with a 20MHz throughput. Only ten of these features can actually be taken off of the card at a time. We have a programmable mapping of features to output buses.

To facilitate the later classification of each pixel, our feature extraction architecture determines and computes features with high discriminatory power in terms of a classification task [2]. Most of these pixel descriptors have parameters such as convolution kernels, rank order numbers, and window geometries. The selection of which features to use for a given problem (i.e. how our feature extraction unit is "programmed") will be described in Section 4.3 of this chapter.

3.3. *Neural Network Block*

In this section we present a hardware realization of a connectionist classifier architecture, called GANGLION. Key features of this architecture are its high speed of up to 4.48 billion interconnections[b] per second, its fully digital implementation without any loss of accuracy, and its reconfigurability and adaptability to different problems, making novel use of the reprogrammability of field programmable gate arrays. Another key aspect is the efficient realization of the multiply/accumulate function where the multiplication is one of a variable and a constant in field programmable gate arrays, with potential implications reaching far beyond connectionist classifiers into the area of digital filters.

3.3.1. *GANGLION Architecture*

At the highest level, GANGLION is a classifier that takes a set of up to 12 features and determines a proper class assignment for the object represented by these features. During an adaptation procedure all parameters of GANGLION are adjusted such that the misclassification over an adaptation set with known class assignments for each object is minimal. More specifically, GANGLION implements a feed-forward network with one hidden layer. The input layer consists of 12 channels, the hidden layer of 14 units, and the output layer of four units. Units of the various layers are fully interconnected between adjacent layers (see Fig. 7). The entire architecture is realized on a single 9U VME card (see Fig. 8) using Datacube MAXbus data ports for high speed data I/O and the VMEbus for control.

The units in the input layer do no processing, but simply buffer the data. The units in the other layers first form a weighted sum of their inputs. The eight-bit unsigned inputs are multiplied by eight-bit signed integer weights to form 16-bit signed products. The twelve (fourteen in the output units) products and a 16-bit signed, unit-specific, bias value are accumulated into a 20-bit result, to which the activation function is applied.

---

[b]Interconnections are defined as concurrent multiply accumulate operations in all nodes.

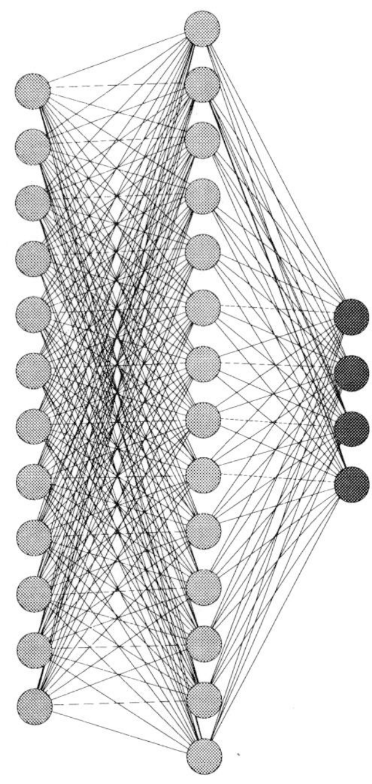

Fig. 7. GANGLION overall architecture.

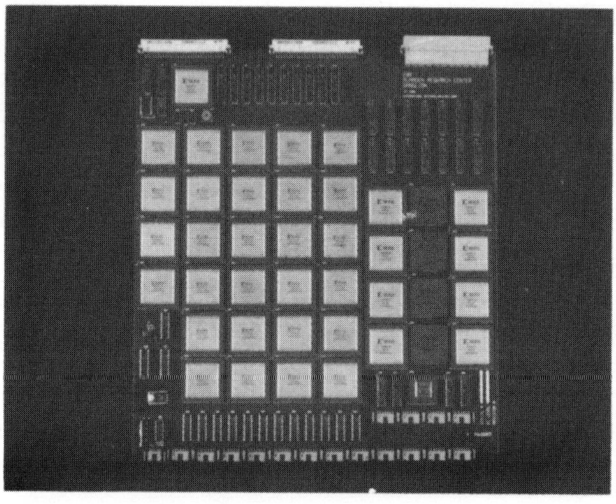

Fig. 8. Photograph of GANGLION.

According to Eq. (2.1) the node processing may be summarized by:

$$X_j^{(l)} = \sum_i A_{ij}^{(l)} S_i^{(l-1)} + B_j^{(l)}$$

with $A_{ij}^{(l)}$ being an eight-bit signed weight assigned to the edge of the net graph from node i in layer $l - 1$ to node j in layer l. $S_i^{(l-1)}$ is the eight-bit unsigned output (or *state*) of node i in layer $l - 1$. $B_j^{(l)}$ is a 16-bit signed bias added at node j in layer l. $X_j^{(l)}$ is the 20-bit result.

In the next step the 20-bit sum gets scaled to an 11-bit value, and passed through an arbitrary activation function. The activation function from Eq. (2.2) is realized as a look-up table (2K byte PROM), which produces the eight-bit output of each unit.

The integer weights assigned to each edge in the graph, the unit-specific bias values, and the scaling parameters for the sum are the adjustable parameters that allow the adaptation of GANGLION to a variety of different classification tasks.

3.3.2. *Technology*

Driving forces for our design included a desire for very rapid prototyping, and low cost for limited card production. We also had stringent throughput requirements imposed by our target machine vision application. We chose to build the architecture using almost entirely field programmable gate arrays. In particular, we used Xilinx Logic Cell Arrays (LCAs). These reconfigurable LCAs offer acceptable density without the cost and lengthy design cycles of full custom circuits.

The 3000 series of LCAs from Xilinx are composed of an array of Configurable Logic Blocks (CLBs) surrounded by a number of I/O pads. A user programmable interconnection scheme lies between the CLBs in the array and between the CLBs and the I/O pads. Each of the CLBs contains a function generator and two flip flops. The function generator can be programmed to produce two functions of four input variables each or a single function of five variables. Regardless of configuration, the function generator, actually a 32-bit look-up table, has at most five input variables. The outputs from the function generator can drive either the inputs to the D flip flops in the CLB or the outputs of the CLB. If not driven directly from the function generator, the CLB outputs may be driven from the flip flops. Outputs from CLBs are routed to inputs of other CLBs or I/O pads using the programmable interconnect resources. The programmable interconnection is achieved by using pass transistors to route signals from segment to segment. The configuration of the device is a matter of loading the look-up table function generators and selecting multiplexors in the CLBs, enabling the pass transistors in the interconnection, and selecting multiplexors in the I/O pads.

Since the Xilinx parts use static RAM to store configuration information instead of EPROM, fuse, or anti-fuse technology, they can easily be reconfigured *in system*.

We exploited this characteristic of the parts to good advantage. Instead of programming the parts to implement a generic connectionist architecture, we program the parts to implement a specific, trained connectionist architecture classifier. All weights, bias values and scaling parameters are "hard wired" for each particular application. In other words, we use different logical hardware on the same physical hardware for each application of GANGLION. In so doing, we realized the full potential power of the promise of programmable logic: custom silicon for every application. Narrowing the function of the silicon to a *specific application* of an architecture allows us to extract maximum performance from the silicon potential.

3.3.3. *Architectural Issues*

Multiplication. The architecture of GANGLION requires that 224 8×8 multiplications be performed every 50 ns cycle. Implementing 224 eight by eight-bit multipliers on a single card would be challenging. We take advantage of the fact that any specific application of GANGLION requires that 224 fixed multipliers of an eight-bit variable by an eight-bit constant be performed every 50 ns cycle. Implementing so many *fixed* multipliers on a single card is achievable using field programmable logic. We program the field programmable gate arrays for the specific application of the architecture rather than for the generic architecture.

Multiplying an eight-bit number by an eight-bit constant produces a 16-bit result. Each bit of that 16-bit result can be expressed as a function of the eight bits of the variable operand. An arbitrary function of eight bits is hard to implement using off the shelf logic short of a 256-bit look-up table. The standard look-up table approach would require 448 256×8 SRAMs just for the multipliers and could not be implemented on a single card to achieve our design goals.

An alternative approach is taken which involves breaking the eight-bit by eight-bit multiplication into two eight-bit by four-bit multiplications, and one addition. The eight by four multiplications require much less logic to implement than an eight by eight multiplication. Further, the required addition is collapsed into the summation of products already performed in the node processing.

Recall, that we are considering the multiplication of an eight-bit unsigned variable by an eight-bit signed constant. We call the eight-bit unsigned variable S and the eight-bit signed constant A. S can be broken into two nybbles, the upper four bits, U, and the lower four bits, L. Since the upper nybble is shifted by four bits (factor of 16) versus the lower nybble, S can be expressed as $16 \cdot U + L$. Note that U is a signed number since it has the sign bit in it while L is unsigned. The product of S and A is $S \cdot A = 16 \cdot U \cdot A + L \cdot A$. Of course, both partial products are signed now because A is signed. The full product can be computed by adding the two partial products.

A further savings in logic is achievable by ensuring that the lower partial product is always positive, thereby eliminating the need for sign extension of the lower partial product when adding it to the upper partial product. Recall that the lower partial product is $L \cdot A$, where L is an unsigned four-bit number, and A is a signed eight-bit number. The smallest possible product of the two is $15 \cdot (-128) = -1920$, while the largest is $15 \cdot (+127) = 1905$. We add 2048 to the lower partial product to ensure that it is always positive $((-1920) + 2048 = 128)$. The new largest partial product is now: $15 \cdot (+127) + 2048 = 3953$, a number that can be represented as an *unsigned* 12-bit number. Since we have added 2048 to the lower partial product, we must subtract 2048 from the upper partial product in order to get the correct full product. Since the upper partial product is shifted left four bits with respect to the lower partial product, we subtract 128 $(128 \cdot 16 = 2048)$. So, to produce the product of S and A, we actually implement $S \cdot A = 16 \cdot (U \cdot A - 128) + L \cdot A + 2048$.

The implementation is diagrammed in Fig. 9. The eight-bit input S is broken into two four-bit quantities U and L. L is multiplied by A and added to 2048 producing a 12-bit quantity. The lower four of these 12-bits are the lower four bits of the 16-bit product. The other eight bits feed one input of an eight-bit adder. The lower eight bits of $U \cdot A - 128$ is the second input to the adder. The eight bits from the adder are the middle eight bits of the final product. The upper four bits of $U \cdot A - 128$ are fed to a four-bit incrementer. The incrementer adds the carry out from the adder to the upper four bits of $U \cdot A - 128$ to produce the upper four bits of the final product.

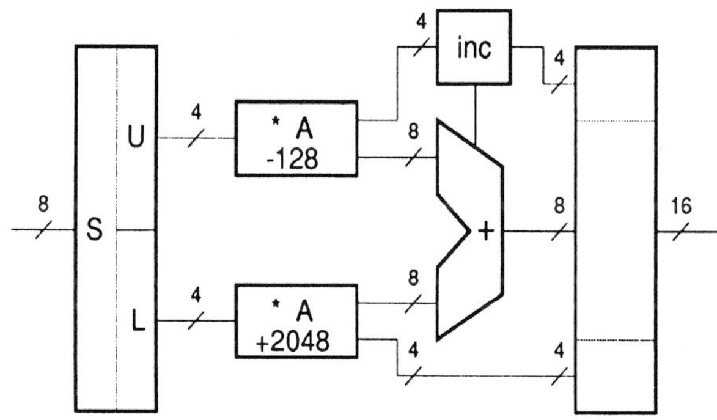

Fig. 9. Basic multiplication scheme.

The four-bit variable by eight-bit constant multiplication can be performed by 12 independent functions of four variables each, i.e. one for each bit in the 12-bit product. This method of multiplication is ideally suited for implementation in the XC3000 family of LCAs from Xilinx. Recall that the basic logic unit of the LCA, the CLB, can perform two arbitrary logic functions of four bits each. Hence, one CLB can be used to produce two bits of the product: the twelve bits of the partial product $L \cdot A + 2048$ (or $U \cdot A - 128$) can be produced using only 6 CLBs.

Summation. The second task performed by the nodes is the summation of the partial products into a single 20-bit result. The big expense in building any adder is that of carry propagation. The carry may be rippled across the sum cheaply in terms of logic, but with great expense in time. Alternatively, carry lookahead techniques may be employed to generate the sum quickly, but at considerable expense in logic. Our machine vision application for GANGLION dictates very high throughput, but places few requirements on latency. We take advantage of this by using a highly pipelined adder network to sum the products within the nodes.

Each unit in the hidden layer sums 12 16-bit products and a 16-bit bias value into a single 20-bit sum. Since we split the multiplications in half, the hidden layer units actually sum 24 partial products and the bias value together. The output units sum 28 partial products and the bias value. We take advantage of the fact that we are summing a large number of values together to defer the expense of carry propagation to the generation of the final sum. We use two techniques to avoid the cost in time or in logic of propagating carries across the sum: carry save adders, and three to two reduction adders.

In carry save adders, the carries are propagated as far across the sum as possible in a single clock cycle and then a pipeline register is inserted into the carry chain. Since the adders are implemented inside an LCA, this pipeline register is free. Each CLB contains two flip flops, one for each logic function. The flip flops are either used or bypassed, and if bypassed cannot be used for something else. This pipelined carry must be added to the rest of the sum to produce the final sum. Alternatively, the saved carries can be considered to form a second number that must be added to the first to produce the final sum.

The second method of reducing the carry propagation that we use is the application of three to two reduction adders. A three to two adder cell is simply a full adder cell with a storage element at the carry output. Again, using an LCA, there is no cost for adding the flip flop to the carry output. The three to two adders take three operands in and produce two operands as output: there are no carries propagated between bits.

These two techniques can be combined to make a logic efficient, fast adder. Consider the case of adding six numbers together to form a single sum (see Fig. 10). Call the six numbers A, B, C, D, E, and F. First, the six numbers are passed to two three to two reduction adders. The first takes A, B, and C as inputs and produces G and H, while the second produces I and J from D, E, and F. Next, two carry save adders are employed. The first takes G and H and produces K. K is a number plus some saved carries that need to be added in to complete the addition. The second adder takes I and J and produces L. The two adders are designed such that none of the saved carries from L occupy the same bit positions as any of the saved carries from K. The saved carries from K and L are combined with implicit zeroes to form a new number M. That number M and K and L are fed to another three to two reduction adder that produces N and O. The task of adding A, B, C, D, E, and F together has now been reduced to one of adding N and O together. These two numbers can be added using carry save techniques and multiple stages or carry lookahead techniques.

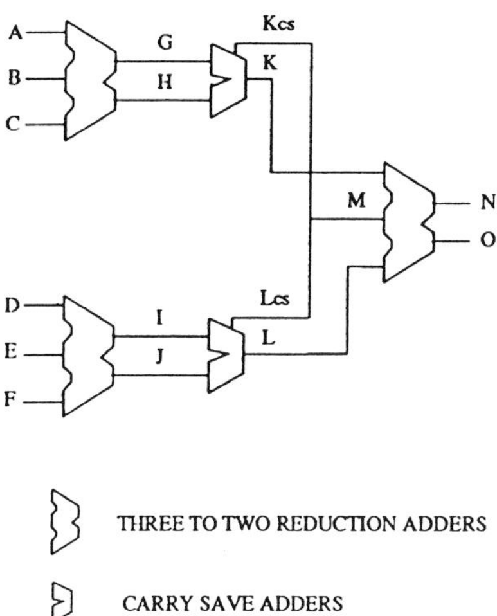

Fig. 10. Adder tree.

Scaling. The final task performed by the units of the hidden and output layers is the scaling of the sum of products and the application of the activation function. The final result of adding all the partial products and the unit bias value together is a 20-bit sum. This sum is exact as no arithmetic overflow could have occurred in the processing up to this point. This 20-bit sum is converted to a ten-bit value. Our hardware provides for a linear scale operation by shifting the sum left or right some number of bits. The scaled sum is then truncated to ten bits. If the scaled sum cannot be represented in ten bits, then a saturation flag is generated. In Section 4.4 we will demonstrate that no precision is lost by these operations. For now it suffices to mention that since we use an eight-bit approximation of the activation function, we hit the minimum and maximum values before we exceed the realm of ten-bit inputs. The ten-bit converted sum and the saturation flag address a 2K by eight-bit PROM programmed with the activation function. All PROM locations where the saturation bit is active are programmed with either the minimum or maximum output value depending on the sign bit of the saturated input.

To save logic resources within the LCA, the shift is actually performed by routing the appropriate bits to pads on the LCA much like the multiplications by a constant are hard wired into the LCA. We have a base design for every shift amount and the proper one is selected when generating a configuration bit stream for a new application.

Output Processing. From an architectural standpoint, there is no meaning in terms of class assignments to the values of the output nodes of GANGLION. Within the range of the general mathematical possibilities of the given connectionist architecture, GANGLION can, for a given input, produce any output at the four output nodes. In other words, what output GANGLION produces for a given input is determined during the adaptation procedure, and hence the meaning of the values of the output nodes and their relation to the class assignment, the ultimate goal, is also determined during adaptation. Typically, one would pick one out of a set of common class assignment schemes during the adaptation, and then use the same scheme on any output that GANGLION produces to determine the proper class assignment for each set of input features.

Since the relation between class assignments and the values of the output nodes is basically arbitrary, one implemented option to deal with these values is to pass them out as four-byte wide fields and leave the final interpretation to subsequent building blocks. Nevertheless, two interpretations of the values of the four output nodes are very common and particularly useful, and therefore GANGLION has built in interpretation capabilities to deal with those two interpretation schemes.

For applications with four or fewer classes, one unit in the output node is assigned to each class. The states of the four units in the output layer are compared and the object is assigned the class label of the output unit with the largest state value. The hardware compares the four values and outputs a two-bit code that is used as the class label.

For applications with five to sixteen classes, a different interpretation model has to be used. Each unit in the output layer is assigned to one bit of a four-bit field. Each of the four units in the output layer is compared against a fixed threshold value. If the unit's state is greater than the threshold, then its bit in the four-bit field is set. If the unit's state is less than the threshold, then its bit is reset. The four-bit field is output by the hardware and is interpreted as the object's class label.

Partitioning. Each of the twelve hidden units on the card is built from two XC3090 LCAs and a 2K × 8 PROM. The two LCAs compute the weighted sum of their 12 eight-bit inputs and the 16-bit bias value, scale the result to ten bits, and generate the saturation flag. The PROM holds the activation function for the node. The output units contain two XC3090 arrays, one XC3042 array, and a 2K × 8 PROM. The two XC3090 designs in the output units are identical (except for the embedded weights and bias value) to one of the designs used in the hidden units. Together, the three LCAs compute the scaled weighted sum of their 14 inputs that is passed through the activation function in the PROM. The XC3090 is the largest member of the 3000 series LCA from Xilinx, containing 320 CLBs. The XC3042 contains 144 CLBs. The 70MHz toggle rate Xilinx parts are used throughout the design since they are sufficient to keep up with our 20MHz system clock.

4. Adaptation of a Neural Net Based Segmentation Engine

The complete adaptation of any neural net based segmentation system to a given task is a rather complex undertaking. Depending on the flexibility that was originally designed into the system, certain steps that are described in this section can be skipped for certain systems, since these systems do not allow the particular parameters to be modified.

Figure 11 depicts parameter adaptation in a general neural net based segmentation engine. A clear distinction between training phase and run phase is typical for these systems, where all application specific parameters are determined during the training phase.

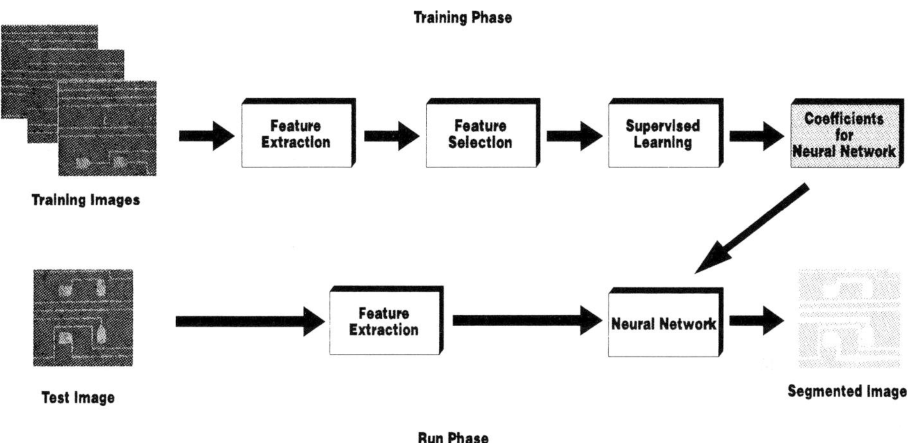

Fig. 11. Training procedure for segmentation system.

In the following subsections we describe how these parameter adaptation steps are done in our system.

4.1. *Feature Selection*

To provide a segmentation system which does not require users to be experts in image processing, our system exhibits a primarily automated adaptation process. To begin the process, a user working only with a monitor and a mouse encircles the objects of interest in a certain number of characteristic scenes. The system then can label all pixels in the training scenes according to the scene region or object to which each pixel belongs. The result of this process is the creation of mask images in which each pixel carries only the object identification code for the object to which it belongs. These mask images can also be viewed as the ideal segmentation results which become the goal for our supervised adaptation procedures.

In the next step we compute a huge number of features for each pixel in each training scene using our feature extraction unit to accelerate the process. We have defined a set of "standard" features which we have found empirically to be useful in a large variety of applications. However, if for a given problem enough *a priori* information exists to define a more powerful feature than the "standard" feature set, our system allows the inclusion of this feature as well (within the computational limits of our feature extraction architecture).

We next construct a random subset of pixels (typically in the tens of thousands in size) from all of the labeled pixels we have created. Using that subset, we determine the most powerful measurements or features for a given application using an information theoretic utility measure. In its simplest form this measure can be computed as

$$Q = \frac{H(f_i) - \sum_c p(c) \cdot H(f|c)}{H(c)}$$

where $H(f_i)$ is the Shannon entropy [25] of feature f_i over all classes, $p(c)$ is the prior for a certain class c (typically the frequency of samples of class c in the training set), $H(f|c)$ is the entropy of feature f_i for class c only, and $H(c)$ is a formal class entropy. This measure is computed for all features for the entire training set and the ten features (12 for multiband systems) with the highest value of that measure are selected for this particular application. A more elaborate procedure for feature selection also using this measure is detailed in [1].

The maximum number of most powerful features we can use in our system is 12 due to the constraints of our GANGLION hardware implementation. If we have only a single band system, i.e. we use only one feature extraction module, the maximum number of features is ten, since this is the maximum number that our feature extraction module can produce.

No hardware other than standard von Neumann type computers exists to accelerate the lengthy process of feature selection, but this process is used only once for each given application of the segmentation engine. This random subset of labeled pixels, each of which is now described by a set of features with high discriminatory power for classification, will be used as a training data set for adaptation of the parameters in the connectionist classifier architecture. The remaining subset of labeled pixels is used as a test data set for evaluation of the classifier performance. In a typical application the number of pixels in the test data set is at least an order of magnitude higher than in the training data set.

4.2. *Modified Backpropagation*

As mentioned earlier, there exists no closed form solution for training of neural network classifiers. This is because training such a network is a nonlinear optimization problem in the space of all weights and biases. These problems are known to be hard and general efficient and reliable solutions do not exist.

For training neural networks, most authors use a heuristically modified hill climbing technique called backpropagation [22]. Standard backpropagation is a supervised learning procedure in which sets of feature vector/class membership pairs are presented to a network. Adaptation of the network is via an error-correction method; weights within the network are changed according to the calculation of each weighted connection's "contribution" to an error signal (a function of the difference between the target output and the actual output produced by the network) which is propagated backwards through the network. The rule for changing weights, called the *Generalized Delta Rule*, employs gradient descent in order to find a point in weight space where the global error is at a minimum. The specific rule for changing a weight is

$$\Delta a_{ij}{}^{(l)((n+1))} = \eta(\delta_j s_i^{(l)}) + \alpha\Delta a_{ij}{}^{(l)((n))}$$

where the superscript $((n))$ is an index to a pattern in the training set of data, η and α are constants typically used in an attempt to influence the convergence of this procedure, and δ_j is the mean square error measure calculated at layer l. Luckily, with our modifications to standard backpropagation the values of α and η are not very critical. We used values of $\alpha = 0.9$ and $\eta = 0.05$ in all of our experiments.

We term a *trial* to be a presentation of every member of the training data set; we update weights and biases after the presentation of each feature vector/class membership pair during a trial. The ordering of the pairs in the training data set is randomized after every trial. A network is considered converged when two separate measurements (misclassification rate for the training data set, and the average difference between the network output and the target output over the training data set) reach a minimum.

Unfortunately, standard backpropagation does not converge to a useful extremum in the weight space for our eight-bit unsigned feature values in most cases. However, it was found empirically [24] that the standard backpropagation training scheme worked significantly better when all features in the feature vector had mean 0 and variance 1. We verified this finding experimentally. Therefore, in our training scheme, we transform all of our feature vectors in the training set such that all components of the feature vector have mean 0 and variance 1. Obviously, this can be done by computing the transformed feature $\hat{f}_i$ as

$$\hat{f}_i = \frac{f_i - \overline{f_i}}{\sigma i}$$

where $\overline{f_i}$ and σ_i are the mean and variance of the original feature f_i, respectively.

After we have trained a net on these transformed features, we would have to use transformed features from there on to do segmentation. From an architectural point of view this is very undesirable, since it would require that another piece of hardware be built to transform the features before they enter the classification block. Fortunately, when we look at the particular architecture of a feed-forward neural network, we realize that the first active layer of such a net can implicitly perform the same transformation on the test vectors that we performed explicitly on the training vectors. This is because we can view this transformation as a multiplication of the incoming feature with the term $1/\sigma_i$ and the addition of the term $-\overline{f_i}/\sigma i$ to the product. All nodes in the hidden layer have the resources to perform exactly these operations. Therefore, we can slightly modify the parameters of each net that was trained on normalized feature vectors such that it performs the normalization implicitly.

Each hidden unit in the trained net initially computes

$$\hat{x}_j = \sum_i \hat{f}_i \hat{a}_{ij} + \hat{b}_j \tag{4.1}$$

with $\hat{x}_j$ being the value that enters the activation function in node j, $\hat{f}_i$ the input of the transformed feature to node i, $\hat{a}_{ij}$ the weight assigned to the edge between node i and node j during the training process, and $\hat{b}_j$ the node-specific bias added at node j, also adjusted during the training on transformed feature vectors. Note, that node i is a member of the input layer, whereas node j is a member of the hidden layer. Hence, the sum extends over all nodes of the input layer. Note further that all entities denoted with a hat ($\hat{\ }$) only exist during the training with transformed feature values. After the transformation described in this subsection, the net operates on untransformed features.

If we rewrite Eq. (4.1) with untransformed feature values we get

$$\hat{x}_j = \sum_i \frac{f_i - \overline{f_i}}{\sigma_i} \hat{a}_{ij} + \hat{b}_j \, . \tag{4.2}$$

If we slightly rewrite Eq. (4.2) we get

$$\hat{x}_j = \sum_i f_i \frac{\hat{a}_{ij}}{\sigma_i} + \left(\hat{b}_j - \sum_i \frac{\overline{f_i}\hat{a}_{ij}}{\sigma_i} \right) \, . \tag{4.3}$$

During the application of the net to untransformed test samples the net computes

$$x_j = \sum_i f_i a_{ij} + b_j \, . \tag{4.4}$$

The net operates correctly if the inputs to the activation functions for an untransformed feature are the same as they were for the transformed features during the training. We obtain $x_j = \hat{x}_j$, i.e. the correct feature transformation *and* correct net operation for test features, iff the new weights and biases are constructed as

$$a_{ij} = \frac{\hat{a}_{ij}}{\sigma_i} \tag{4.5}$$

and

$$b_j = \hat{b}_j - \sum_i \frac{\overline{f_i}\hat{a}_{ij}}{\sigma i} \tag{4.6}$$

which can be easily obtained by coefficient comparison of Eqs. (4.3) and (4.4).

Therefore, if we change the weights and biases according to Eqs. (4.5) and (4.6), we have created a net that automatically performs a transformation of all the input vectors to mean 0 and variance 1.

4.3. *Adaptation of GANGLION*

The adaptation of GANGLION to a specific application is performed on a workstation. During adaptation or training, a representative set of objects described by their features for which the proper class assignments are known, an adaptation set, is presented to the net. The performance of the architecture for a given application depends to a high degree on how well the problem was represented in the training set, and on the training procedure itself. From an architectural point of view it is irrelevant what training procedure was used, as long as the parameters derived during the adaptation phase can perform the classification task sufficiently well.

In our experiments we found that standard backpropagation works much better on real-valued coefficients than on the fixed-point limitations imposed by the hardware. Therefore we use floating point arithmetic and state values between zero and one during our adaptation, and then apply a more sophisticated scaling procedure (see Section 4.4) to transform the obtained coefficients with minimal precision loss to fixed-point coefficients that can be implemented in GANGLION.

The training yields a set of weights, biases, and scaling parameters that need to be mapped to the logic of the LCAs. Our design of the fixed value multipliers allows us to change the constant to any value without altering routing inside the LCA: only the contents of the look-up table function generators within the CLBs need to be modified. The same is true for including the bias value into the adder tree. Rather than using the design tools to customize the field programmable gate arrays for each application of the architecture, we developed a set of base LCA designs for the architecture and then developed code to directly manipulate the LCA configuration files to embed the adjustable parameters into those designs. The scaling parameters are included by selecting the proper base design for modification.

After training the network and modifying the configuration files for the LCAs, the configuration information is loaded into a RAM on the card over the VMEbus. The Xilinx chips on the card are configured from the RAM on command from the VMEbus.

4.4. *Computation of Scaling Parameters*

This subsection describes the scaling of the parameters derived during the adaptation procedure to fit into GANGLION's fixed point arithmetic architecture. Unfortunately, the determination of proper scaling factors for weights and biases is not as straightforward as it might seem at first glance. For instance, we cannot take all the weights in the net and scale them such that the largest still fits the given weight precision, because this would lead to intolerable precision loss for nodes with only small weights incident to them. On the other hand, we cannot do the scaling for each node individually irrespective of all other nodes, because in that case we would have to reload the look-up tables for the activation function for each application differently.

What we want is a hardware realization where the look-up tables for the activation function are the same for all applications, and application specific scaling factors are kept in the Xilinx chips. Therefore, the scaling factors have to be partitioned into an application specific part and a general part that only consists of fixed hardware parameters and that can be molded into the activation function look-up table.

4.4.1. *Determination of scaling factors for weights and biases*

If the states of each node do not range from 0 to 1 anymore we have to rewrite Eq. (2.2) as

$$f(x_j^{(l)}) = \frac{\Delta}{1 + e^{-x_j^{(l)}}} \tag{4.7}$$

where Δ is the maximum value a state can take.

The following transformations of the right hand side of Eq. (2.1) do not change the argument of our activation function and hence do not change the value of the activation function either:

$$\sum_i a_{ij}^{(l)} s_i^{(l-1)} + b_j^{(l)} = \left(\sum_i (a_{ij}^{(l)} \cdot s_i^{(l-1)} \nu^{(l)}) + b_j^{(l)} \nu^{(l)} \right) \cdot \frac{1}{\nu^{(l)}} \,.$$

In other words we can scale the weights and states by choosing $\nu^{(l)}$ appropriately if we just scale the bias and introduce an additional scaling factor $(1/\nu^{(l)})$. The superscript index (l) indicates that we want to use different scaling factors ν for different layers.

We can now construct our hardware such that we implement

$$f(\xi_j^{(l)}) = \frac{\Delta}{1 + e^{-\gamma_j^{(l)} \beta \cdot \xi_j^{(l)}}} \tag{4.8}$$

where β is some global constant factor that we use to construct the look-up table for the activation function, and $\gamma_j^{(l)}$ is an additional factor that we implement by shifting the argument for each node individually before entering the activation function (see Section 3.3.3). This is to partition the scaling parameters into an application independent part β, and an application specific part γ. Because γ is realized as a shift operator we can write $\gamma_j^{(l)}$ as

$$\gamma_j^{(l)} = 2^{k_j^{(l)}} \tag{4.9}$$

with $k_j^{(l)}$ being an integer. $k_j^{(l)}$ is the shift amount applied to the argument of the activation function in node j in layer l before entering the activation function look-up table. Comparing Eq. (4.7) and Eq. (4.8), we find that ξ and x are related as

$$x_j^{(l)} = \gamma_j^{(l)} \; \beta \cdot \xi_j^{(l)}$$

or

$$\begin{aligned}
\xi_j^{(l)} &= \left(\sum_i \left(a_{ij}^{(l)} \cdot s_i^{(l-1)} \nu^{(l)} \right) + b_j^{(l)} \nu^{(l)} \right) \cdot \frac{1}{\nu^{(l)} \beta \gamma_j^{(l)}} \\
&= \sum_i \left(a_{ij}^{(l)} \frac{\Theta_0}{\nu^{(l)} \beta \gamma_j^{(l)}} \cdot s_i^{(l-1)} \nu^{(l)} \right) + \frac{b_j^{(l)}}{\beta \gamma_j^{(l)}} \,. \tag{4.10}
\end{aligned}$$

At this point we have to remember that our hardware actually implements

$$\xi_j^{(l)} = X_j^{(l)} = \sum_i A_{ij}^{(l)} \cdot S_i^{(l-1)} + B_j^{(l)} \tag{4.11}$$

with $A_{ij}^{(l)}$, $S_i^{(l-1)}$, and $B_j^{(l)}$ being the integer representations of the weights, states, and biases (see Section 3.3.1).

With this we can now compute the scaling factors, which is basically done by coefficient comparison of Eq. (4.10) and Eq. (4.11). The simplest scaling is done for the states. We know that the new range of the states is $[0 \ldots \Delta]$. If we denote the maximum state value that we encountered in layer $l-1$ in our unrestricted training environment with $s_{i_{\max}}^{(l-1)}$ we simply set

$$\nu^{(l)} = \frac{\Delta}{s_{i_{\max}}^{(l-1)}}. \tag{4.12}$$

In doing so, we can accommodate a training situation in which the states in all but the input nodes are within $[0 \ldots 1]$ (the standard configuration used by other authors) but the inputs are the actual features with arbitrary bounds. This is actually the reason why we chose $\nu^{(l)}$ to be different for each layer.

Next we determine β. Since we want to have the same application independent look-up table for all nodes we do not want to have any dependencies on l, i, or j in β. To simplify the computation and reduce the shift amount (see below) we set β arbitrarily to

$$\beta = \frac{1}{\Delta \Lambda} \tag{4.13}$$

where Δ is again the maximum value a state can take (i.e. the $s_i^{(l-1)}$ are within $[0 \ldots \Delta]$), and Λ is related to the maximum absolute value a weight can take. Since with ordinary two's complement arithmetic the absolute value of the smallest value a number can take is always one larger than the greatest positive value, we chose Λ to be the greatest positive value the weights can take, not to cause any overflow, i.e. the new weights are within $[-(\Lambda+1) \ldots \Lambda]$.

Since $\gamma_j^{(l)}$ appears as a scaling coefficient for both A and B, we compute an appropriate factor for each (i.e. we compute the factor for the least information loss for both), and restrict ourselves then to the smaller scaling factor so that we do not loose any significant information through overflow.

First we compute the scaling factor for A. From coefficient comparison of Eq. (4.10) with Eq. (4.11) we see that

$$A_{ij}^{(l)} = \frac{a_{ij}^{(l)}}{\nu^{(l)} \beta \gamma_j^{(l)}}.$$

If we insert Eq. (4.12) and Eq. (4.13) there we get

$$A_{ij}^{(l)} = \frac{a_{ij}^{(l)} s_{i_{\max}}^{(l-1)} \Lambda}{\gamma_j^{(l)}}.$$

Since $\gamma_j^{(l)}$ is local to each node we have only to look at all the weights attached to the arcs entering that node, and we define

$$a_{ij_{\max}}^{(l)} = \max_i \left\{ |a_{ij}^{(l)}| \right\} .$$

Since we want to represent the greatest value within the given precision (i.e. $[-(\Lambda+1)\ldots\Lambda]$) for each weight with as little precision loss as possible, we have to make

$$|a_{ij_{\max}}^{(l)} \cdot \frac{s_{i_{\max}}^{(l-1)}\Lambda}{\gamma_j^{(l)}} - \Lambda| \overset{!}{=} \text{Min} . \tag{4.14}$$

As Λ is a positive integer we can divide Eq. (4.14) by Λ and get

$$|a_{ij_{\max}}^{(l)} \cdot \frac{s_{i_{\max}}^{(l-1)}}{\gamma_j^{(l)}} - 1| \overset{!}{=} \text{Min} .$$

Substituting from Eq. (4.9) gives

$$|a_{ij_{\max}}^{(l)} \cdot \frac{s_{i_{\max}}^{(l-1)}}{2^{k_{jA}^{(l)}}} - 1| \overset{!}{=} \text{Min} ,$$

i.e. the shift amount to scale A is

$$k_{jA}^{(l)} = \lceil \log_2(a_{ij_{\max}}^{(l)} s_{i_{\max}}^{(l-1)}) \rceil .$$

The computation of the scaling factor to obtain optimal precision for B, $k_{jB}^{(l)}$, is very similar to the computation for $k_{jA}^{(l)}$. Since the precision for the biases is different from the precision that we spend for the weights, we denote the biases to be within $[-(\Gamma+1)\ldots\Gamma]$. For a given bias $b_j^{(l)}$ we get therefore again from coefficient comparison of Eq. (4.10) and Eq. (4.11)

$$|\frac{b_j^{(l)}}{\beta\gamma_j^{(l)}} - \Gamma| \overset{!}{=} \text{Min} .$$

So we get again with Eq. (4.9)

$$|\frac{b_j^{(l)}}{\beta 2^{k_{jB}^{(l)}}} - \Gamma| \overset{!}{=} \text{Min}$$

which yields

$$k_{jB}^{(l)} = \left\lceil \log_2\left(\frac{b_j^{(l)}}{\beta\Gamma}\right) \right\rceil$$

or with β from Eq. (4.13)

$$k_{jB}^{(l)} = \left\lceil \log_2\left(\frac{b_j^{(l)}\Delta\Lambda}{\Gamma}\right) \right\rceil$$

or

$$k_{j_B}^{(l)} = \left\lceil \log_2 \left(\frac{\Delta \Lambda}{\Gamma} \right) + \log_2(b_j^{(l)}) \right\rceil .$$

With $k_{j_A}^{(l)}$ and $k_{j_B}^{(l)}$ given we can now compute the final shift amount $k_j^{(l)}$ that does not lead to any loss of high order bit information caused by overflow:

$$k_j^{(l)} = \min \left\{ k_{j_A}^{(l)}, \ k_{j_B}^{(l)} \right\} . \tag{4.15}$$

4.4.2. *Implementation of the activation function*

Since we want to minimize the cost of the activation function look-up table we restrict ourselves to a table with N bits input and M bits output ($N > M$). Obviously $\Delta = 2^M$. In our case N is less bits than we allow for the multiply-accumulate register which holds the full precision of all multiply-accumulate operations.

Due to the special shape of the activation function it makes sense to determine an *active range* of that function. Since this function approaches 0 and Δ asymptotically for $x \to -\infty$ and $x \to \infty$ respectively, we define the active range where this function differs from 0 and Δ by more than a certain ϵ, where $\epsilon < 1$ so as not to lose any precision in an integer representation.

We can write the final number that enters the activation function look-up table as an address

$$\eta = \gamma \xi$$

and hence the activation function becomes

$$f(\eta) = \frac{\Delta}{1 + e^{-\beta \eta}} .$$

For a given ϵ we get

$$\Delta - \epsilon = \frac{\Delta}{1 + e^{-\beta \eta_{\max}}} .$$

Because of the symmetry of the activation function $\pm \eta_{\max}$ are the values where the difference between $f(\xi)$ and its asymptotic extrema is smaller than what can be represented with the given precision. From this we get

$$1 + e^{-\beta \eta_{\max}} = \frac{\Delta}{\Delta - \epsilon}$$

$$e^{-\beta \eta_{\max}} = \frac{\epsilon}{\Delta - \epsilon}$$

$$\beta \cdot \eta_{\max} = \ln(\Delta - \epsilon) - \ln \epsilon$$

$$\eta_{\max} = \frac{\ln(\Delta - \epsilon) - \ln \epsilon}{\beta}$$

$$\eta_{\max} = (\ln(\Delta - \epsilon) - \ln \epsilon) \cdot \Gamma \cdot \Delta$$

where we again used Eq. (4.13).

Since η is an integer we can represent η by $\lceil \log_2 \eta_{\max} \rceil$ bits without loosing any precision. If we now have to enter $f(\eta)$ with an N-bit number (where typically $N < \lceil \log_2 \eta_{\max} \rceil$) then we have to shift η by the difference between N and $\lceil \log_2 \eta_{\max} \rceil$, i.e. we have to shift by

$$k_0 = -(\lceil \log_2 \eta_{\max} \rceil - N) \tag{4.16}$$

bits (the minus sign indicates a shift to the right) to obtain an N-bit integer representation of η. We just have to keep in mind that the true value of η is by a factor of 2^{-k_0} bigger than the address that is used to enter the activation function look-up table.

This is the bias shift amount that gets applied to all η, i.e. to all products $\gamma \cdot \xi$. This means, that any shift amount k which was computed according to the considerations in the previous subsection gets added to this basic shift amount k_0.

5. Experimental Results

We performed image segmentation using our segmentation engine on several different sequences of scenes from "real world" applications. One application is taken from combustion research, one is from texture recognition, and the others are taken from industrial inspection within the semiconductor manufacturing industry. We show here only a limited set of images from different applications to demonstrate the flexibility of the pixel classification approach. However, since the engine has been built, millions of frames have been processed by the system with sustained performance. Other experiments have been conducted to show the influence of the fixed point arithmetic used in the hardware implementation of GANGLION, versus the floating point arithmetic used in a software implementation [8].

Combustion chamber images. The combustion chamber images are three images out of a series of images taken with a high speed camera from the inflammation process of a gas/air mixture in a combustion chamber. The segmentation task is to determine the area of inflamed gas in the image; therefore, pixels in a scene are classified into three different classes: cylinder, uninflamed gas, and inflamed gas. In the original images in Fig. 12, the area of inflamed gas is the highly textured and slightly brighter area in the lower right corner of the chamber.

The features used for this problem are f_1 which is programmed as median, f_3, f_4, f_5, f_6 programmed as local maximum, f_7, f_8, and f_{10}, f_{11}, and f_{12} programmed as different gradient operators (refer to Table 1 for a description of the features). Ten units in the input layer, only 12 units in the hidden layer, and three units in the output layer were used in this experiment. Weights entering the unused units were set to zero.

Exact determination of the area of inflamed gas is not possible from pixel classification alone; subsequent processing of a segmented image based on pixel classification is required in order to complete the segmentation task [26]. However, successful completion of the pixel classification step is critical for the successful completion of

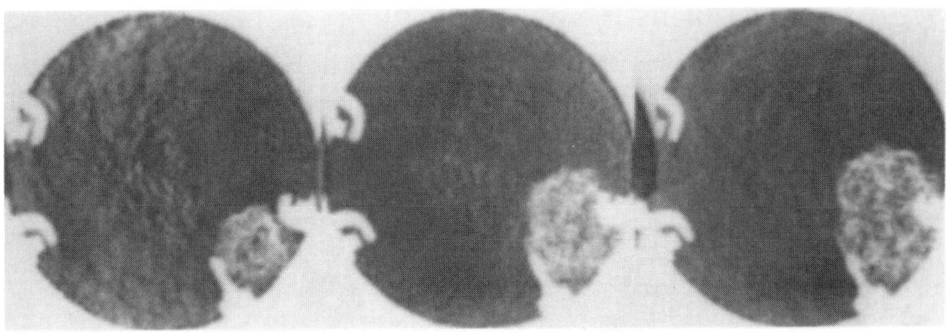

Fig. 12. Original gray level images of turbulent combustion process.

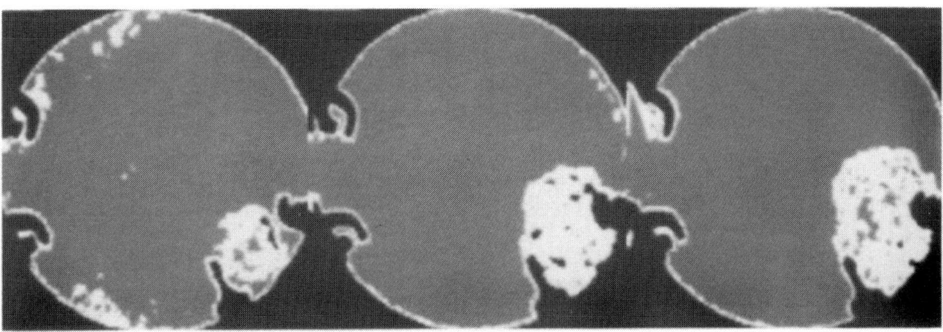

Fig. 13. Result of the pixel classification obtained by a connectionist classifier.

the task; the better the pixel classification step, the more successful the completion of the task will be.

Figure 13 shows the pixel classification results achieved by the neural network classifier for the three combustion chamber scenes in Fig. 12. These results are considerably better than results from several classical statistical methods (linear, quadratic, and cubic polynomial, Gaussian maximum likelihood) applied to the identical training and test data [16].

Printed circuit board images. These are two images taken from an industrial inspection application. The segmentation task is to segment the copper conductors from the board in order to enable the detection of defects such as *opens*, *shorts*, and *mousebytes*. Although the segmentation task looks much simpler than in the first case, it is not possible to determine a simple threshold that works on all images.

The features used for this problem are f_1 which is programmed as median, f_3, f_4, f_5, f_6 programmed as local maximum, f_7, f_8, and f_{10}, f_{11}, and f_{12} programmed as different gradient operators (refer to Table 1 for a description of the features). Ten units in the input layer, 12 units in the hidden layer, and two units in the output layer were used in this experiment. Again, weights entering unused nodes were set to zero.

Figures 14 and 15 show two original printed circuit board scenes and the pixel classification results achieved by the connectionist classifier. These results are comparable with the ones reported in [4].

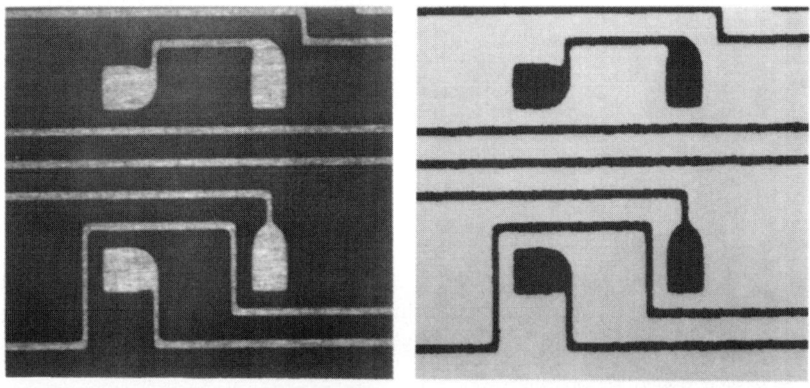

Fig. 14. Original gray level image and segmentation result of printed circuit board.

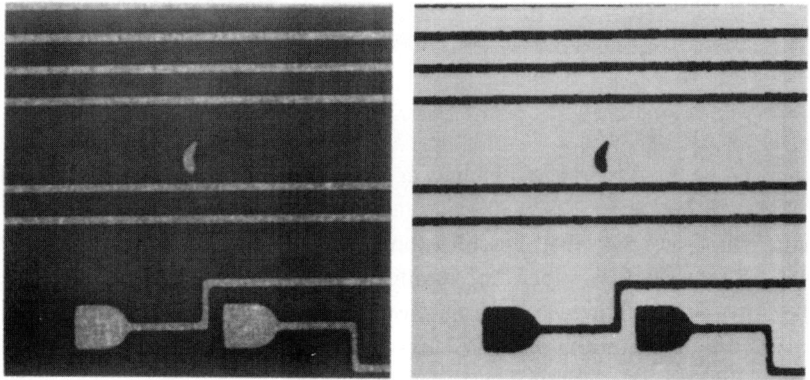

Fig. 15. Original gray level image and segmentation result of printed circuit board.

Thin film images. Just like printed circuit boards which are used to electrically interconnect ordinary electronic components on a larger scale, thin film circuits are used at a smaller scale to interconnect multiple chips on a ceramic substrate. Figure 16 shows microscopic images of such a thin film circuitry. In this case we used a red and a blue channel in a brightfield microscopy set-up and a green

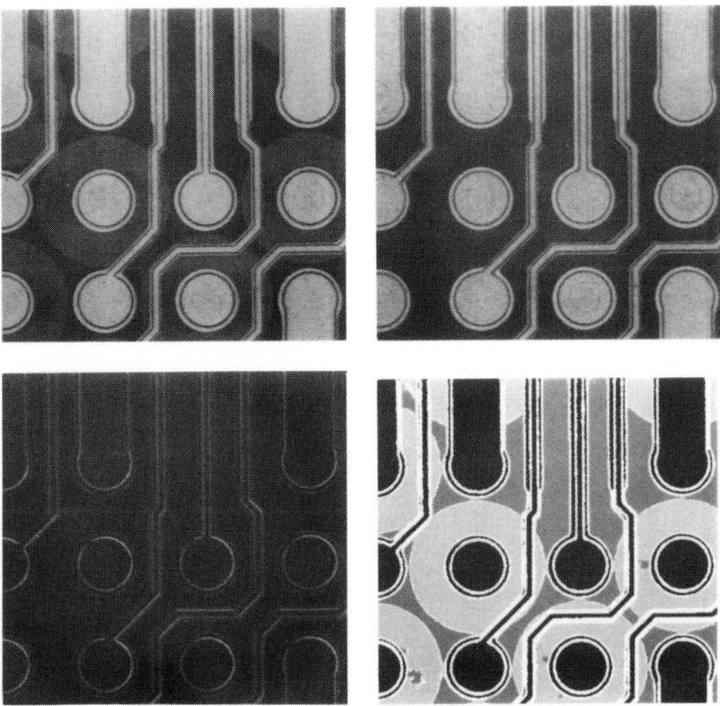

Fig. 16. Original gray level images of thin film circuitry—brightfield red (upper left), brightfield blue (upper right), darkfield green (lower left), and segmentation result (lower right).

channel in a darkfield set-up to compute eight features. In particular, the features were f_1 which is programmed as a local minimum piped into a local maximum, f_3 which is programmed as a local mean, f_5 programmed as the mean of squares, and f_9 with f_{10} through f_{13} is programmed as gradients in different directions from the red channel. Furthermore, f_3 is programmed as the local mean and f_5 as the mean of squares from the blue channel, and f_3 is programmed as the local mean and f_7 from the green darkfield channel. Here we used all 14 nodes in the hidden layer and all four nodes in the output layer. Figures 16 through 19 show the the different bands of the original images and their segmentation results.

C4 images. IBM's packaging technology of interconnecting the above mentioned chips to the ceramic substrate is known as controlled collapse chip connection, or C4 for short. Little solder balls are used to connect the chips to their substrate. The volume of these solder balls is critical for the successful performance of the entire package and therefore is also subject to visual inspection. The complex process of the visual inspection of these solder ball volumes is described in [3]. Therefore we do not elaborate on the inspection process but rather report only the images and the segmentation results here. For further details, refer to [3].

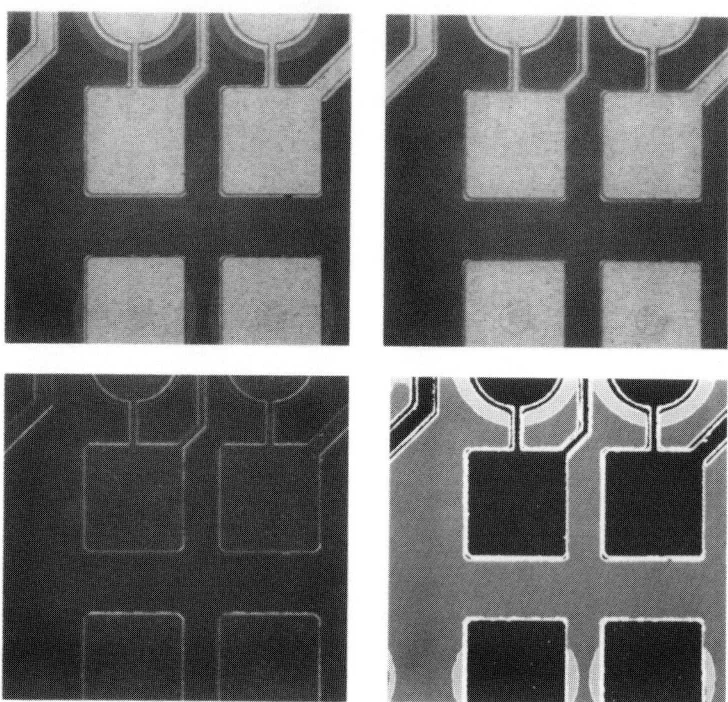

Fig. 17. Original gray level images of thin film circuitry—brightfield red (upper left), brightfield blue (upper right), darkfield green (lower left), and segmentation result (lower right).

The features used in this experiment were f_1 which is programmed as the local minimum, f_3, f_4 programmed as the variance, f_5, f_6 programmed as the local median, f_7, f_9 with f_{10} through f_{13} programmed as gradients in different directions, and f_{14} programmed as the squared gray value.

Figures 18 and 19 show the original images and the segmentation results obtained from a net with all 14 nodes in the hidden layer and two nodes in the output layer. The results are comparable to the ones reported in [3].

Texture images. In this experiment we used textures out of a texture collection book [6]. In particular, we used textures D16 (herringbone weave), D19 (woolen cloth), and D57 (handmade paper), all in front of a background of black foam. The textures were copied onto sheets of paper and the entire sheets and the black foam background were used as training images. Then random shapes were cut out of the paper and tossed onto the foam; this was used as a test scene.

Seven features were used in this experiment: f_1 programmed as the local maximum piped into the local minimum, f_2 programmed as the local maximum, f_3, f_4 programmed as variance, f_6 programmed as the median, f_7 and f_9 with f_{10} through f_{13} programmed as gradients in different directions. All 14 nodes in the hidden layer, and all four nodes in the output layer were used in this experiment.

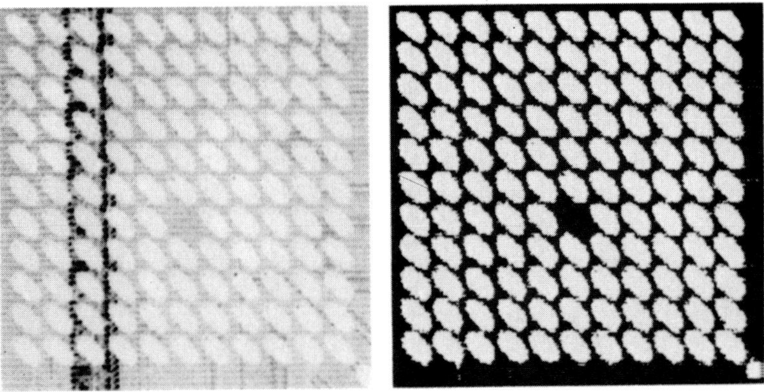

Fig. 18. Original gray level images of solder ball shadow image and segmentation result.

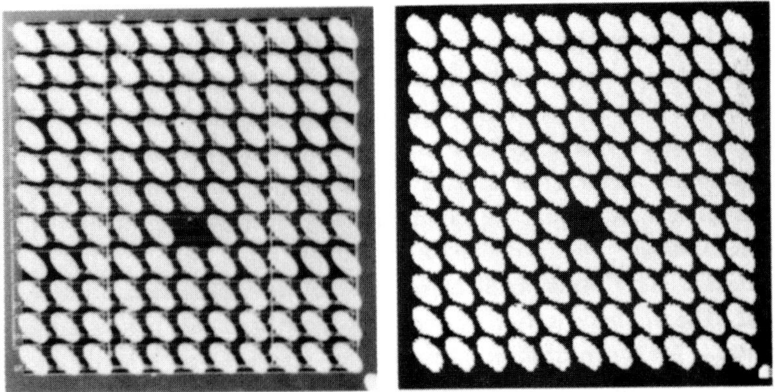

Fig. 19. Original gray level images of solder ball shadow image and segmentation result.

Figure 20 shows the training scene and segmentation result. Although the segmentation results are not a hundred per cent correct, especially along the edges of certain textures, we feel that this is a very good result since we trained on full images and therefore no edges between textures were present in our training set. Also recall that, as in all other cases, the decision for each pixel of these 512×480 pixel images was based on the information obtained from a 7×7 pixel window only, and a correct decision was made for a vast majority of the pixels.

6. Conclusions

Neural network based image segmentation has received increasing interest in the literature, but only very few systems have matured to a hardware implementation for real-world applications. We have shown that an image segmentation engine which represents a generalized solution for real world real-time image segmentation problems is feasible. We have addressed the issue of solution dependence on specific problem characteristics by designing programmability into our feature extraction

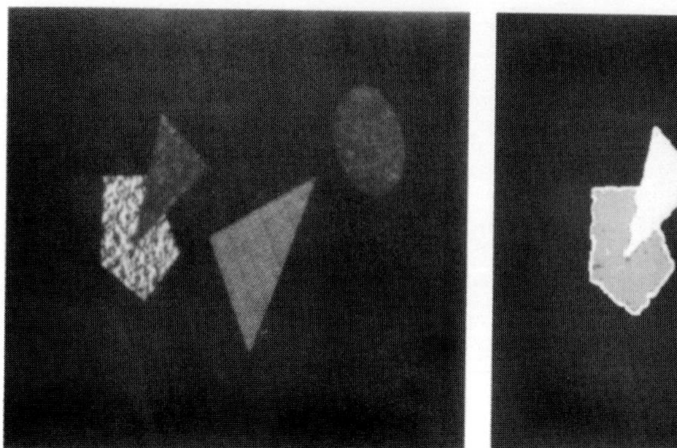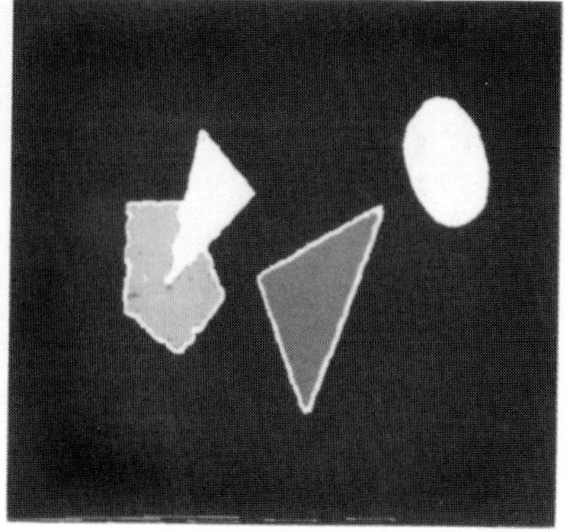

Fig. 20. Original gray level image of texture scene and segmentation result.

process, and by our design choice of viewing image segmentation as a decision analysis task. That design choice allows us to exploit the inherent trainability in decision analysis systems [11]. To insure that a segmentation engine can be used in real world environments where vision systems must be adapted to changing applications by operators who are application domain experts rather than machine vision experts, an adaptation scheme should be based on solely quantitative factors. This design choice eliminates the qualitative factors which are often part of explicit definitions of segmentation algorithms [4,26]. Also, most of the adaptation process should be automated. The implementation of special purpose hardware makes a segmentation engine suitable for incorporation into real-time machine vision applications.

The use of a connectionist architecture for the classifier component of a segmentation engine allows the architectures to meet both the flexibility requirements of such a design approach as well as the constraints of the implementation of special purpose hardware so that image segmentation can be performed in real time. Several authors have demonstrated that, in terms of performance, a connectionist classifier is a viable alternative decision analysis method to classical statistical methods for a set of classification problems of various complexity [15,20]. In the current chapter we also have demonstrated that the connectionist architecture is a good choice for efficient implementation in digital VLSI. Image segmentation in real time is a problem which requires a solution implemented in hardware; once a hardware solution is chosen, the cost of implementation is a major constraint on the design of any solution architecture. A connectionist classifier architecture makes hardware implementation of a robust image segmentation system feasible for real world image segmentation problems because unlike conventional approaches it only requires multiplications of a variable by a constant.

Despite the fact that connectionist classifier architectures represent a new processing alternative in machine vision, the use of these architectures is consistent with the implementation of the decision analysis paradigm. For most authors the connectionist architecture performs the role of a pattern classifier within their segmentation engine. Nevertheless, most research reported to date in which neural networks have been applied to machine vision focuses on explicit maps of the scene pixels "drawn" onto layers of network nodes so that each pixel in the scene corresponds to a separate node in the network layer (see [17,14] for more examples of that type of approach). However, if "real world" image segmentation problems are addressed with connectionist classifiers one has to deal with images of 512 pixels by 512 pixels in size or even 2048 pixels per row and tens of thousands of pixels in a column for line scanning operations. This precludes the use of "neuron-per-pixel" architectures for economical reasons. The connectionist component in a pixel classification based segmentation engine places no such restrictions on system performance. Therefore we feel that this is the way to implement an efficient, flexible segmentation engine which can be used to solve a variety of application scale problems in real time.

References

[1] W. E. Blanz, Non-parameteric feature selection for multiple class processes, in *Proc. 9th Int. Conf. on Pattern Recognition*, Rome, Italy, Nov. 1988.

[2] W. E. Blanz, VLSI-oriented architectures for real-time image processing, in *1990 SPIE/SPSE Symposium on Electronic Imaging Science and Technology*, Santa Clara, CA, Feb. 1990.

[3] W. E. Blanz, J. L. C. Sanz and E. B. Hinkle, Image analysis methods for solder-ball inspection in integrated circuit manufacturing, *IEEE Trans. Robotics and Automation* 4, 2 (1988) 129–139.

[4] W. E. Blanz, J. L. C. Sanz and D. Petković, Control-free low-level image segmentation: Theory, architecture, and experimentation, in J. L. C. Sanz (ed.), *Advances of Machine Vision, Applications and Architectures* (Springer-Verlag, 1988).

[5] W. E. Blanz, B. Shung, C. Cox, W. Greiner, B. Dom and D. Petković, Design and implementation of a low-level image segmentation architecture — LISA, in *Proc. 10th Int. Conf. on Pattern Recognition*, Atlantic City, NJ, Jun. 1990.

[6] P. Brodatz, *Textures: A Photographic Album for Artists and Designers* (Dover Publications, New York, 1966).

[7] C. Cortes and J. A. Hertz, A network system for image segmentation, in *Proc. Int. Joint Conf. on Neural Networks*, Washington, D.C., Jun. 1989, 121–125.

[8] C. E. Cox and W. E. Blanz, GANGLION — fast field programmable gate array implementation of a connectionist classifier, *IEEE J. Solid-State Circuits* 27, 3 (1992) 288–299.

[9] J. Desmouceaux and N. Derycke, Infrared image segmentation by texture analysis using neural works, *Revue Technique Thomson-CSF* 22, 4 (1990) 637–648.

[10] W. Doyle, Operations useful for similarity-invariant pattern recognition, *J. ACM* 9 (1962) 259–267.

[11] R. O. Duda and P. E. Hart, *Pattern Classification and Scene Analysis* (Wiley, New York, 1973).

[12] N. R. Dupaguntla and V. Vemuri, A neural network architecture for texture segmentation and labelling, in *Proc. Int. Joint Conf. on Neural Networks*, Washington, D.C., Jun. 1989, 127–131.

[13] R. A. Fisher, The use of multiple measurements, *Annals Eugen.* **7**, II (1989) 179–188.

[14] K. Fukushima, S. Mikyake and T. Ito, Neocognition: A neural network model for a mechanism of visual pattern recognition, *IEEE Trans. Syst. Man Cybern.* **13**, 5 (1983) 826–834.

[15] S. L. Gish and W. E. Blanz, Comparing a connectionist trainable classifier with classical statistical decision analysis methods, Research Report RJ 6891 (65717), IBM, Jun. 1989.

[16] S. L. Gish and W. E. Blanz, Comparing the performance of a connectionist and statistical classifier on an image segmentation problem, in D. S. Touretzky (ed.), *Neural Information Processing Systems 2* (Morgan Kaufmann Publishers, San Mateo, CA, 1990) 614–621.

[17] Y. Hirai, A model of human associative processor, *IEEE Trans. Syst. Man Cybern.* **13**, 5 (1983) 851–857.

[18] J. Hopfield, Neural networks and physical systems with emergent collective computational abilities, in *Proc. National Academy of Sciences* **79** (1982) 2554–2558.

[19] E. Mesrobian and J. Skrzypek, A connectionist architecture for computing textual segmentation, in *Proc. SPIE Conf. on Image Understanding and Man-Machine Interface*, Los Angeles, CA, Jan. 1987, 123–131.

[20] M. Özkan, H. G. Sprenkels and B. M. Dawant, Multispectral magnetic resonance image segmentation using neural networks, in *Proc. IEEE Int. Joint Conf. on Neural Networks*, San Diego, CA, Jun. 1990, 429–434.

[21] Y. H. Pao, *Adaptive Pattern Recognition and Neutral Networks* (Addison-Wesley, Reading, MA, 1989).

[22] D. E. Rumelhart, G. E. Hinton and R. J. Williams, Learning internal representations by error propagation, in D. E. Rumelhart, J. L. McClelland et al. (eds.), *Parallel Distributed Processing*, vol. 1 (MIT Press, Cambridge, MA, 1986) chapter 8.

[23] D. E. Rumelhart, J. L. McClelland et al. (eds.), *Parallel Distributed Processing* (MIT Press, Cambridge, MA, 1986).

[24] A. V. Scherf and G. A. Roberts, Segmentation using neural networks for automatic thresholding, in *Proc. SPIE Conf. on Applications of Artificial Neural Networks*, Orlando, FL, Apr. 1990, 118–124.

[25] C. E. Shannon and W. Weaver, *The Mathematical Theory of Communication* (The University of Illinois Press, Urbana, IL, 1949).

[26] B. Straub and W. E. Blanz, Combined decision theoretic and syntactic approach to image segmentation, *Mach. Vision Appl.* **2**, 1 (1989) 17–30.

[27] A. Tabatabai and T. P. Troudet, A neural net based architecture for the segmentation of mixed gray-level and binary pictures, *IEEE Trans. Circuits and Systems* **38**, 1 (1991) 66–77.

Handbook of Pattern Recognition and Computer Vision, pp. 921–939
Eds. C. H. Chen, L. F. Pau and P. S. P. Wang
© 1993 World Scientific Publishing Company

CHAPTER 5.6

ARCHITECTURES FOR IMAGE PROCESSING AND COMPUTER VISION

GIOVANNI GARIBOTTO

Research and Development, Elsag Bailey spa, Via G. Puccini, 2, 16154 Genoa, Italy

12.1. Introduction

The main objective of this chapter is to provide a critical analysis of image processing architectures for computer vision with major emphasis on robotic applications.

As such, the wide range of powerful stand-alone image processing workstations, primarily designed for computer graphics and interactive operations, as well as video coding systems for telecommunications will not be considered here. This analysis focuses on hardware and software requirements and solutions of machine vision, as they appear in industrial robotics, service, and advanced robotics for unstructured environments. The more general methodologies and architectures of computer vision are examined and commented upon in the framework of practical machine vision applications.

Conventional computers are unable to fully meet these requirements, so that a number of special-purpose architectures have been developed for the analysis of static and time-varying images. So far no universal solution exists to cover all needs of computer vision. The "optimal" solutions may differ quite a lot, depending on specific constraints and the selected technology. The major drawback is the need to conceive and design new solutions for any new problem. However, a certain degree of flexibility is desirable, at least from the integration viewpoint, to avoid useless duplication of effort. As such, it is necessary to have an efficient hardware and software environment, with suitable tools, to include different modules as required by the application, without altering the basic architecture of the processing system. Some of these architectures for computer vision integration are discussed in Section 12.5, where high level processing is considered.

Reprinted with permission of McGraw-Hill, Inc. from *Computer Engineering Handbook*, ed. C. Chen, 1992, Chapter 12, pp. 12.1–12.17.

921

This chapter begins with a short survey on some issues of image acquisition units and trends of the market. Then the rest is arranged according to the logical scheme of Chap. 11, pointing out the most promising architectural solutions corresponding to the three levels of computer vision system. This classification will be supported by references to commercial systems as well as to advanced prototypes, based on the direct experience of the author.

Sections 12.1, 12.2, and 12.3 will each include a quick analysis of major requirements and expected performance, which is used as reference evaluation criteria of the different possible solutions. Real-time constraints are considered as well as data size for local computation, to establish how much local or temporary storage a single processing unit must have and if independent processing may be performed on different subsets of the input data. Regular or random addressing requirements and data types involved are additional parameters considered in this analysis.

Of course the most demanding level from the computational viewpoint is that of iconic processing where it is necessary also to deal with severe communication and memory addressing problems. Anyway, an increasing role in computer vision is played by more flexible processing on features and structured lists of elements (geometric reasoning and matching). Improved addressing capabilities, higher level abstractions (linked lists and floating point), feedback and feedforward paths, adaptive processing are just a few of the major requirements for intermediate-level processing, and cannot be ignored in this architecture analysis. Other promising areas of development are symbolic processing and logic programming whose application is difficult to generalize since it is highly task-dependent.

To avoid the risk of making too generic an investigation of computer vision systems, a final section is devoted to briefly describe an example of an advanced front-end unit for real-time processing. It consists of a powerful and versatile architecture, for stereovision and motion tracking, suitable for heterogeneous environment, which has been developed under a European ESPRIT project by a highly qualified research team. Some concluding remarks are made about the present efforts towards standardization and the foreseen major trends of the research.

12.2. Image Acquisition Units

This is the first stage of the system to get all necessary pictorial information from the scene, and its relevance to the success of the full machine vision process is well known. The main components of an acquisition unit are summarized in the block diagram of Fig. 12.1.

There are *lookup tables* (LUTs) on the video input and output, where an input signal or byte configuration is used as an address into a stored array of values, so that it can approximate any function of one or more variables. The input LUT adjusts the signal range (normalization or equalization), and the output LUT is mostly used for pseudo-color display purposes.

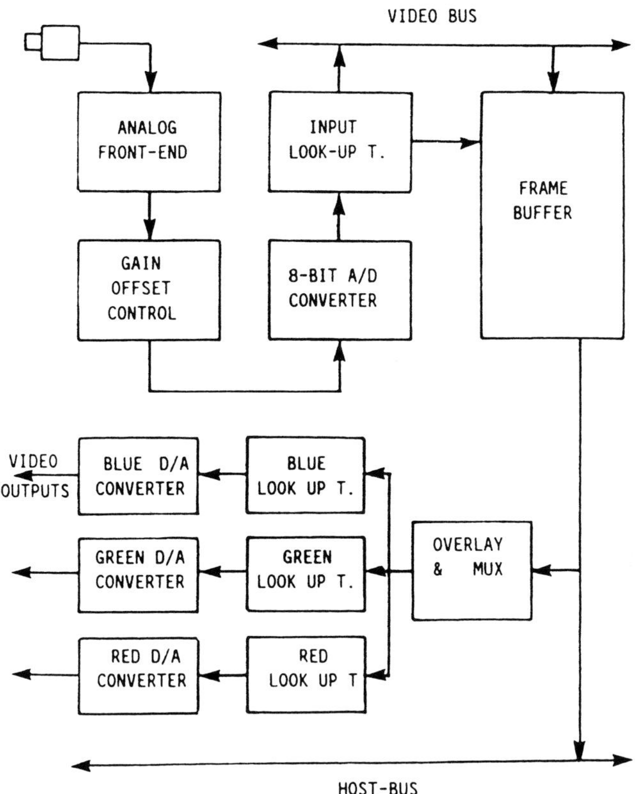

Fig. 12.1. Block diagram of a general video frame grabber digitizer board; sometimes the frame grabber is located into another independent board, connected through the video bus.

The input signal from a TV camera is digitized and stored in a frame buffer. The most common image processing standards are RS-170, Committee on Colorimetry and Illumination Research (CCIR), and RS-343, all producing 2:1 interlaced images with different resolution [17]. Anyway, there are special applications (like optical character readers for mail sorting and document reading) where dedicated solutions are required to achieve higher speed and resolution. In these cases customized reading heads are realized, by using linear arrays of sensors and a special circuitry for preprocessing (enhancement, binarization) and sampling.

Conventional video digitization occurs in time to get a frame which is sampled in space (typical size is 512 × 512 pixels) and quantized in intensity (8 bits), to obtain a two-dimensional array of integer values representing image intensities in the memory. Depending on the buffer size or the availability of a fast communication link to powerful processing modules, time sampling can be performed at the maximum rate of 25 frames per second in the European standard (30 frames, National Television System Committee (NTSC) standard) or 50 interlaced half-size fields each one every 20 ms.

Due to the spatial distribution of the sensory cells in the camera and the sampling frequency of the digitizer, the resulting image matrix has different spacings between horizontal and vertical pixels. This represents a strong limitation in some computer vision applications, expecially in dimensional measuring, and alternative solutions are under development, although not yet widely used, for costs and nonstandard reasons. They use equally spaced camera sensors either with digital interface, to avoid the double step of D/A and A/D conversion, or connected to suitable digitization boards, using appropriate sampling frequencies. High-resolution sensors (for instance 570 lines with 768 pixels) are already commercially available. They provide external synchronization to achieve a correct sampling of the square pixels (11 μm × 11 μm, CCIR version).

It is worthwhile to mention also the emerging new standards for high-definition TV. Another, fully nonstandard solution, which is tightly related to the computer vision task, is the design and realization of special space-variant "retinal" sensors [21], to mimic human perception.

There are different suppliers on the market for image acquisition modules (Data Translation, Matrox, Imaging Technology, Datacube, etc.), and the differences are mainly due to video bus characteristics for video data transfer to other processing modules. Most of these video buses provide three levels of synchronization (pixel timing, horizontal timing and vertical timing) and sometimes a bus to support data transfer of arbitrarily sized windows, or regions of interest in the image plane.

The existence of such different solutions to video bus communication actually prevents a wider interchange of modules for an integration, at least at the very low level of iconic video rate processing, although some standards are emerging de facto on the market. Additional problems come from the need of custom-designed optics and dedicated illumination systems for almost every application. Moreover, the speed of industrial processes is constantly increasing, which means that visual sensors are fast enough to supply the system with the required information.

In general, most technological efforts are now devoted to extend spatial resolution and increase the radiometric sensitivity and the dynamic range of advanced visual sensors.

12.3. Low-Level Image Processing Architectures

The main purpose of this stage of early processing is feature extraction and iconic-to-symbolic transformation to recover geometrical parameters of shape, edges, physical and pictorial contours, textures, colour blobs and regions, etc. The result is a strong compression of information to keep the most relevant description of the scene for the following processing steps of matching, representation, recognition and understanding. The algorithms involved at the low-level stage are almost well defined, data-driven, and their flexibility is limited to the tuning and adaptation of parameters. A quite representative processing tool of this class is given by local neighbourhood computation, as convolution, correlation, clustering or growing and the input data consist of one or more matrices of bytes or words. Many tasks require "real-time" computation, which means something in between video rate processing (25 or 30 Hz, according to video standards) and 1-s delay (1 Hz). General-purpose sequential processors are not adequate to provide the required computational power and data transfer rate.

In fact, in a video sequence the time interval between two consecutive pixels is about 100 ns. To perform a machine vision task of 100 or more operations per pixel, a sequential processor should have a cycle time of less than 1 ns, which is not affordable with present technology. This kind of performance may be achieved by dedicated hardware or parallel computing.

In particular, different kinds of parallelism are possible: parallelism of instructions [multiple-instruction single-data (MISD)], vector processing and parallelism of data (single-instruction multiple-data (SIMD)), and full multiprocessing [multiple-instruction multiple-data (MIMD)]. Some of these solutions are mentioned in the following with examples from existing vision machines.

12.3.1. *Dedicated Hardware Boards and VLSI Technology*

Advances in technology and the evolution of discrete logic into *very large-scale integrated circuits* (VLSI) have enabled cost-effective implementation of processing hardware chips and modules, particularly suited for intense computational tasks. These architectures are usually limited to the level of well-defined fixed-image operations, such as convolution or correlation, edge detection, and linear and nonlinear filtering.

In this case the approach is to map algorithms directly into silicon, to provide a set of chips as a building block for more specialized image processing boards [15].

This is the case of convolution chips from LSI logic for programmable one-dimensional finite impulse response (FIR) filtering, with coefficients up to 64 taps and video rate performance. A separable 2D convolution board may be easily designed and realized around this chip [14]. Recursive filtering chips are now becoming available to implement more general linear filtering, independent of the mask size. Another interesting class of VLSI chip is the programmable linear and non-linear histogram filtering chip, which allows both median and min-max filtering [13]. Many vendors supply high-performance *digital signal processor* (DSP) boards as generic, programmable modules for intense computation; some now support IEEE floating-point standard operations (32 and 64 bits).

Sometimes VLSI technology is used to design a few different types of cells interconnected in a regular pattern where several datastreams flow synchronously through the network, interacting at the cells where they meet. A typical example of this approach is *systolic processing*, pioneered by H. T. Kung at Carnegie Mellon University [12]. The basic idea of this approach is to match the computation rate to the I/O bandwidth of the system, making extensive use of pipelining and parallel processing.

Systolic designs for two-dimensional convolution and template matching have been developed, using either a linear array or a two-dimensional mesh of connected cells. This solution is particularly suitable for those low-level functions where the operations to be performed are quite well defined and repetitive, and their flow is independent of the data.

Sternberg [19] has proposed a serial array processor called the *cytocomputer*, based on neighborhood transformations. The heart of this structure is a *processing element* (PE) which performs a fixed function on a local neighborhood of the sample pixel. It is used as a basis for morphological filtering on binary images as well as gray-level erosion or dilation [20].

12.3.2. *Parallelism of Instruction (Pipeline Implementation)*

To achieve parallelism in instructions it is possible to pipeline data. A *pipeline* is a stream of data that flow at a constant rate through a sequence of processors. Each processor in the pipeline may take as long as it needs to process the data, provided its input and output data rate are synchronous.

The final output is time-shifted from the input, but it flows at the same rate. In this way processing is expanded in space, to provide more computation time. This approach is the most widely used in commercial architectures for image processing. Examples are the Imaging Technology Inc. series 150 processors as well as the Datacube Maxvideo 20 product line. In both cases the integrator is provided with a set of boards, specialized to perform different tasks of image processing, for real-time convolution, linear and nonlinear filtering, histogram processing, morphology, etc. They can operate on subimages or region of interest, at a rate proportionately faster than the entire image size.

Third-party vendors offer other boards, interfaced to standard VME bus, to support high-speed disk control, a large variety of frame storage, and other general-purpose parallel or vector processing. Thus it is very easy to use these modules as building blocks for the realization of a *front-end image processing* (FIP) system, where each board, or a group of boards, can be seen as an element of the pipeline, with its own memory and processing capabilities. Moreover, this architecture can be easily expanded, by adding other boards, according to specific requirements. However, pipeline processing is often limited in local storage, has poor flexibility in addressing capabilities, and has requirements to operate with a single data type (integer or fixed-point representation).

The host communication is usually performed through registers and mailbox protocols. On the host side a "manager" software accepts calls from a program and sends a message to the FIP system, which contains the function to be performed and its arguments. Typically the FIP system has a simple dispatcher or supervisor that interprets this message and initiates processing. Return values are sent back to the host manager and from there to the user's program. The host and the FIP system can operate asynchronously in a parallel concurrent way. To have an idea of the processing speed available in commercial systems, see Preston [16]. For instance, a 512×512 fast-Fourier transform (FFT) takes about 4 s or less depending on the computational power of special-purpose array processors. Geometric warping operations can be performed much faster, in less than 1 s. Unfortunately, more complex functions, such as image enhancement, edge detection, and linking or feature token tracking and stereo matching, cannot be implemented in a single step, and many boards have to be connected, with processing times of tens of seconds, in the best case. Thus the real-time requirements of computer vision are not always satisfied by commercially available pipeline systems.

12.3.3. *Parallelism of Data (SIMD)*

An alternative for real-time implementation is provided by data parallel image processing hardware, where the same instruction is applied in parallel to a block of data. Most common examples of this class are the array processors, often used to efficiently execute a wide variety of DSP algorithms including one- and two-dimensional fast Fourier transforms, digital filters, vector and matrix operations, and other high-speed numeric processing. The local storage of array processors is limited by the number of processors available, and the addressing pattern is usually determined by how the array is loaded. Data types are fixed and may be integers or floating-point values.

Much research effort has been devoted to the development of 2D processing arrays with fixed interconnections, as in the cellular logic image processor (CLIP) program at University College [8] dealing with very simple processing units. In this approach, the structure and the operation of a two-dimensional array of PE modules are matched to the structure of the image data, and different interconnections are possible as in quad trees and pyramids. A pyramid machine [23] is realized by stacking progressively smaller two-dimensional arrays of processing elements, to allow a multiresolution analysis of an input image array. Image data are loaded into the base of the array, and results propagate up to the top of the pyramid. This approach enables an efficient processing at different levels of abstraction and resolution, which, in principle, are important factors for both low-level and middle-level vision. Presently the fine-grained nature of these architectures restricts the controllability of each layer in an SIMD mode of operation. Of course, the increase in the number of connections is the key factor which limits the construction of large systems.

In Cantoni et al. [5] a bin pyramid is adopted, instead of the more common quad pyramid, with the resultant reduction in the total number of connections, at the expense of an increase in the number of planes and layers. A still controversial issue is the tradeoff between the number of processors and the computing power of each individual PE. Improved flexibility for middle and high-level operations seems to suggest a different trend toward coarse-grained systems with increased computational capabilities.

Most SIMD machines have been used primarily for low-level processing or pixel-based transformations, although they are well suited also for certain middle- and high-level processing (consistent labeling and Hough transform). A well-known example of this potential application is given by the connection machine [11], briefly mentioned in Sec. 12.5.

12.3.4. *Multiprocessing MIMD*

These architectures consist of several processors applying different instruction sets to different datastreams. The individual processors may be quite powerful and programmable so that the granularity of the system is necessarily limited. Parallelism may be achieved by simple data partitioning or by concurrent processing. Such extreme versatility of the system may be excessive for low-level processing. But it represents an interesting alternative for a class of algorithms which are the bridge between iconic and symbolic processing. For instance, edge contour linking or pixel grouping or growing, as in region feature extraction, are typical functions where the input is represented by image data (on the video bus) and the output is a list of edge pixels or region features to be further analyzed and interpreted. Still real-time processing at video rate is a heavy constraint of such implementations.

DSP technology now offers some interesting solutions in terms of integer processing of various word lengths (16 and 24 bits) [14], and suitable board architectures may be designed, by integrating multiple DSPs, to do these tasks in an efficient manner.

12.4. Intermediate List Processing

This stage of processing is primarily oriented to perform feature clustering, matching and ordering into higher-level structures. Examples are polygonal approximation of edge contour lists, token tracking, where tokens are already geometric features such as segments or corners, stereo matching, 3D computation and 3D geometric reasoning, and 3D interpolation.

The common property of this stage is the need for adaptive and parameterized processing, the unavailability of an established control flow, different data types and structures, and a large variety of addressing modes. The module architecture should be flexible enough to allow modification and different algorithm implementation and should deal with heterogeneous development environments.

According to the amount of computation needed, some general-purpose *reduced instruction set computer* (RISC) processors or DSP boards may be appropriate to perform geometric processing at a rate greater than 1 Hz. Some relatively simple algorithms such as segment token tracking may be performed at the rate of 10 Hz with a single DSP board [6]. Multiple DSPs boards are necessary for more complex operations such as stereo matching or polygonal approximation at a fast rate (greater than 5 Hz) [9]. An alternative solution is provided by general-purpose powerful MIMD machines which may provide adequate computational power and a reasonable partitioning of data and code. An example of this approach is given by the transputer array which is used in many research laboratories, at both university sites and industrial groups [4], and as an alternative to DSPs and dedicated hardware for low-level processing. In this case the bottleneck is represented by image data transmission to the individual processors, and efficient video bus interfaces have to be provided.

12.5. High Level Processing and System Supervision

This level of processing is most heavily conditioned by the application. It includes system coordination and task-oriented data processing, with scene interpretation and sensory feedback for actuators. At this level it is possible to identify different modules and functions requiring less computational power, but an intensive, though not always predictable, data exchange and interprocessor communications.

The driving criterion is the control architecture of the system. There are bottom-up strategies starting from low-level processing up to feature extraction, object recognition, and decision. Sometimes hierarchical schemes with feedback control are more appropriate to coordinate different machine vision operations. A distributed control system is probably the most flexible solution to address complex tasks, which may be split into a series of subtasks, to be performed independently in parallel. Unfortunately there is not yet a commonly agreed upon solution to process synchronization and activation which is solved in different ways for different machine architectures. Finally we may recall the subsumption architecture, arranged in layers of competencies, [3], particularly attractive for robotics applications.

The most promising candidates for this task are MIMD machines. Among the various solutions currently proposed for computer vision applications, a few examples of different classes of control and integration systems have been selected. The discussion is based on the characteristics of the communication network system starting from an architecture based on a hierarchy of busses, another one with a ring bus topology, and a third one with a regular, fully connected mesh of high-level processing elements. We conclude with some comments on the fine-grain parallelism of the connection machine.

12.5.1. *Hierarchical Distributed System*

Both single-global-bus and multiple-bus structures have been used for connecting groups of processors and memory units. Information or message routing is very simple and is commonly accomplished through a memory-mapped scheme. An improved solution may be obtained by arranging a series of hierarchical levels of busses with reconfigurable clusters of processors, according to the application needs.

Figure 12.2 shows a block diagram for a hierarchical architecture, named EMMA2 [1], an MIMD, shared-memory parallel computer, which has been de-

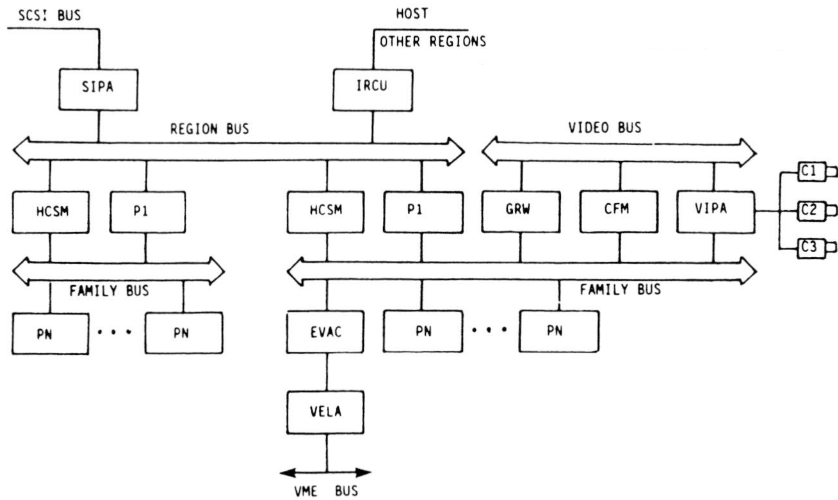

Fig. 12.2. The structure of a region of multiprocessor architecture EMMA2; P1 is a single processor supervisor board in the "family"; PN is a three-processor board which may be equipped with a VLSI integer vector processor (low-level family) or a floating-point accelerator (high-level family); HCSM is a high-capacity system memory; VIPA is a video digitizer board; CFM is a real-time 2D FIR separable convolution filter (31 taps); GRW is a programmable pixel-grouping operator, based on a local (3 x 3) neighborhood. EVAc-VELA is a large-bandwidth communication channel to a standard VME environment.

veloped by Elsag to satisfy both intensive computation constraints and real-time requirements.

This machine is already in use in industrial applications, for mail sorting and document processing, including address localization and character recognition in real time, satellite image acquisition and reconstruction, speech understanding, artificial intelligence and expert systems, with integration of sequential and logic programming.

The efficiency of this hierarchical structure comes from partitioning the whole application into parallel independent subsystems, optimizing the large linear bus bandwidth at two levels of computation: the lower level, an array of processing elements called *families*, and the upper level, consisting of an array of such lower-level cooperant multiprocessor machines named *regions*, interconnected by point-to-point high-speed parallel links, as shown in Fig. 12.2.

The innermost level of this hierarchy is the processing element, an INTELiAPX 286/386 CPU, possibly coupled with an arithmetic standard coprocessor or a proprietary, application-oriented gate array custom chip (*arithmetic logical accelerator*, or ALA), for elementary vector processing operations.

The communication protocol is *message passing* and the network topology is unconstrained and adaptable to application requirements. One of the "region" nodes may be replaced by a standard host computer of DEC VAX/micro VAX family, for software development and machine supervision.

The local busses support 32-bit-wide, 10-Mbytes/s data transfer with fault tolerance, *interrupt program counter* (ipc), interrupt, and memory broadcasting mechanisms.

This general purpose multiprocessor architecture provides the necessary flexibility for realization of high-level computer vision tasks, by exploiting parallel processing. However, most image processing functions, at the iconic level, do not require such flexibility, being essentially data-driven, repetitive processes aimed to achieve data compression from images to features.

For that reason a front-end image processing subsystem has been integrated into a low-level family of processors, including an acquisition board, a 2D separable convolver, and a programmable pixel grouping module, on a dedicated video bus. There is also a large-bandwidth interface to standard VME environments, but an integrated solution is always more efficient than heterogeneous and distributed processing.

Another hierarchical architecture applied to computer vision is discussed by Dickmanns and Graefe [7] where real-time computation is deferred to different clusters of processors for robotics applications. Examples are shown in the precise position control for planar docking between 3D vehicles and in high-speed road vehicle guidance.

12.5.2. *Pipeline Connection*

We have already discussed the wide use of this interconnection of modules for image processing. Multiprocessors can be realized through many different fixed communication links arranged with various topology schemes.

An example of this architecture is shown in Fig. 12.3, corresponding to the CAPITAN machine from MS2i, which was first designed for space and military applications. It is an MIMD distributed computer built around VME bus nodes, which may support a variety of general-purpose CPU boards, as well as DSP and multi-DSP boards, array processors, memory boards, etc. The interconnection network is composed of two ring busses which appear as a series of synchronously rotating slots, each one to convey elementary information.

To provide sufficient reliability of the implementation a double ring bus is used [25], to be able to cope with almost any kind of failure of one element. This reconfiguration property is also useful to obtain a dedicated architecture according to traffic requirements, by splitting the ring bus into three or more subrings, with a smaller number of processing nodes. Again, the resulting architecture provides the necessary flexibility with individual nodes acting as specialized processors for low-level, intermediate-level, and high-level vision. The pipeline interconnection is quite appropriate for a bottom-up processing scheme, but the software reconfigurability of the machine allows also a promising environment for distributed processing. The

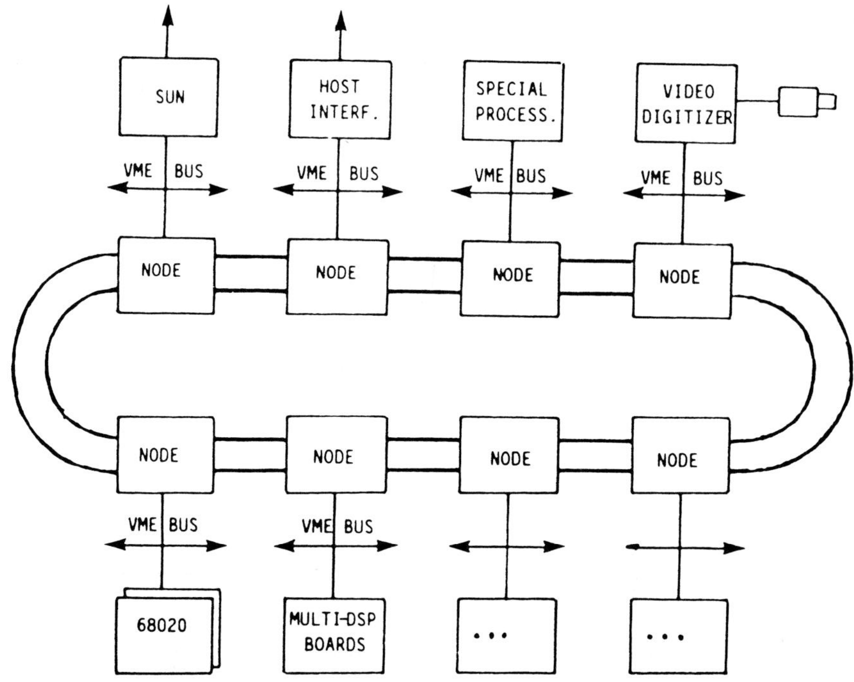

Fig. 12.3. Block diagram of the MIMD processor CAPITAN, built around VME nodes connected through two ring busses, which may be split to create subring sections, each one with the original throughput.

selected standard environment allows an easy introduction of new advances in CPU and VLSI technology.

Yet the resulting configuration is not always the optimal compromise of cost versus performance for specific computer vision applications. The results of 3D vision experiments reported by Vaillant et al. [24] demonstrate that such flexible architecture is more appropriate for high-level processing than for low-level and middle-level image operations, such as gradient computation, edge detection, linking, and polygonal approximation.

12.5.3. *Regular Mesh of High-Level Processors*

Another approach to multiprocessing is based on the use of a regular grid of processors connected together. An example of this scheme is given by the MAR-VIN multiprocessor [18] which has been designed and realized as a fully connected mesh of Transputers T800 and an extension to the root transputer, as shown in Fig. 12.4. One row of processors consists of specially developed transputer cards, named TMAX [4], to provide fast video bus communication, mainly for image data, minimizing data transit time. The adopted model of parallelism is based upon *communicating sequential processes* (CSPs), where the system comprises a number of sequential processes executing concurrently and communicating via channels.

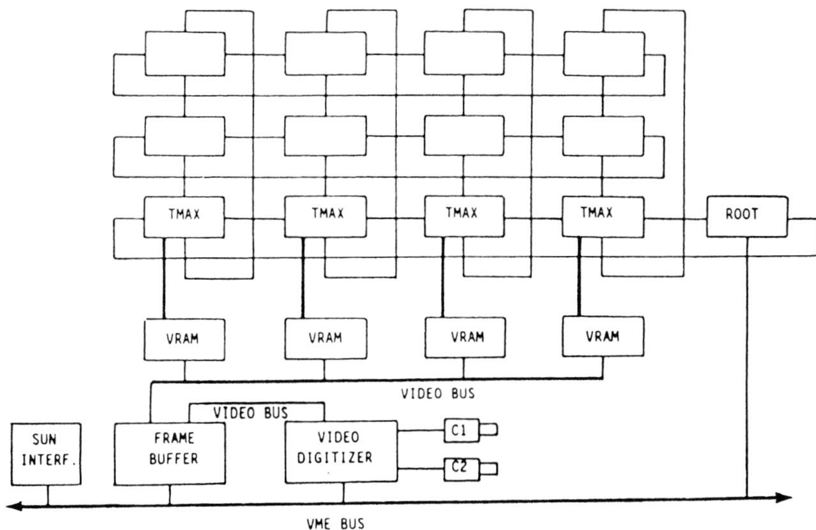

Fig. 12.4. Block diagram of the MARVIN system architecture based on a regular mesh of transputer boards.

The individual processors provide a varied repertoire of resources, as requested, in a client-server model. Vision processing is broken down into a number of tasks, each of which may itself be multithreaded, with dynamic changes of operation in the system. Due to the flexibility of high-level programming and computational power of the TRAMs module, best performances are obtained for intermediate- and high-level vision tasks where feature parallelism may be exploited. Although video bus interconnection is provided by TMAX modules, low-level processing, heavily based on spatial data parallelism, is not optimally performed in this configuration. For instance, Canny edge detection takes about 5.5 s as opposed to 1.6 s for model matching [18].

12.5.4. *Fine-Grain Parallel Machines*

Different comments can be made about the connection machine which fully exploits the connectionist approach. It combines a very large number of physical processors (65,536), but may be configured for a much larger number of logical processors [11]. Each physical processor has 4096 bits of memory, corresponding to 32 Mbytes for the machine as a whole. Memory is bit-addressable, and all data fields are of arbitrary length. Individual processors are quite simple so they do not really permit high-level processing of data, and the primary characteristic of this architecture is the communication system. The simplest way of communication between connection machine processors is between nearest neighbors, to north, east, west, and south. General intercommunication and dynamic reconfiguration are performed by a much more powerful communication system, the connection machine router, which allows full messages to be sent from any processor to any other. Each of the physical processors is in fact connected to 16 other physical units in a special organization (a 16-dimensional hypercube) that provides large numbers of direct paths through the system. It takes a maximum of 12 steps to move from any chip to any other chip.

The connection machine is extremely powerful and appropriate for expensive simulation tasks where other experiments and tests would require days of computation on general-purpose computers. It is particularly suited for computer graphics 3D simulation by matching data topologies exactly.

Moreover sophisticated new approaches for image processing and vision algorithms can be tested and verified on large amounts of data with a relatively small programming effort [22]. For instance, to compute depth maps from binocular stereo, a difference of gaussian filters is applied to both right and left images to detect edge points. Disparity is then computed by sliding one image over the other and producing a new image with incremental values for overlapping edge patterns. The same approach is used to efficiently compute the Hough transform for 2D recognition and labeling of objects in the scene.

From the practical viewpoint of an industrial cost-effective computer vision system for robotic applications, it is not yet an affordable solution.

12.6. A Reference Example: Real-Time 3D Vision System

To avoid the vagueness of a chapter that summarizes computer vision technologies and architectures, an example of real-time implementation is now given. It is the result of development and integration of an ESPRIT program [14], aimed to realize a 3D vision system for robotic inspection and manipulation and mobile robot autonomous navigation. The adopted data representation is based on 2D edge segments, coming from minor modifications of Canny's edge detector, to obtain a strong data compression from input images. A trinocular stereo algorithm has been selected, including an accurate camera calibration and suitable epipolar transformation to simplify segment matching in the three images.

To support the implementation of these algorithms, a real-time vision system has been realized for low and intermediate levels of processing, up to 3D stereo reconstruction and token tracking.

This hardware front end, called *depth and motion analysis* (DMA), is an "open" architecture, which can be interfaced with different standard environments (VAX, SUN, PC) as well as integrated with additional boards from the market. Figure 12.5 shows the DMA chain for a reconfigurable pipeline structure, including one or more acquisition boards.

To solve communication problems, three different links have been selected:

- The VME for control and data transfer of features, such as edge chains or segments, for system start-up and monitoring
- The video bus MAXBUS (from Datacube) for TV-rate image transmission
- Some private interboard links for local communications

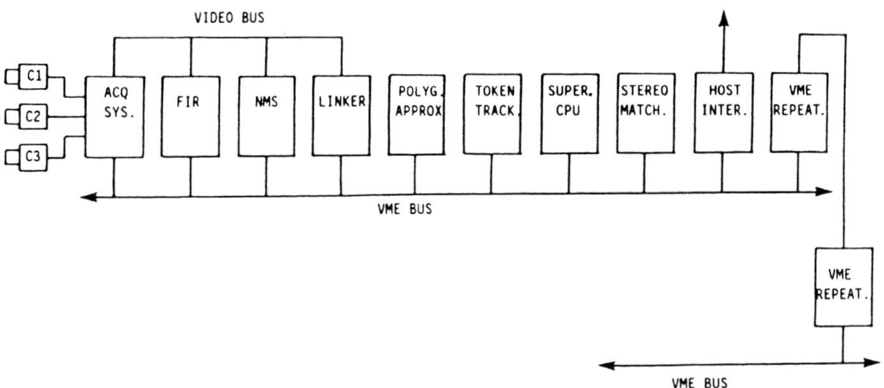

Fig. 12.5. Block diagram of the 3D front-end DMA machine; the functions implemented by the different boards are explained in the text.

Besides standard modules for image acquisition and the supervisor CPU, the DMA machine has some dedicated hardware modules to perform well-defined operations with number crunching requirements, as 2D separable filtering (up to 64 filter taps using the LSI Logic L64240 MFIR chip) and edge detection (non-maxima suppression). Other boards are based on fixed-point DSPs (ADSP2100) for edge linking and token tracking. General-purpose fixed-point multi-DSP boards (Motorola 56000) are available also for polygonal approximation and stereo matching, as well as a floating-point multi-DSP (Motorola 96000) for 3D reconstruction and uncertainty computation. Table 12.1 summarizes the performances of individual boards which have been integrated into the system.

The corresponding implementation may achieve a real-time processing rate at the expense of an overall input/output delay, related to the number of the stages in the pipeline. Particular attention has been paid, during the second phase of the project, to creating an efficient software environment for integration. A standard CPU supervisor on the VME bus has in charge the start-up initialization of all modules, their synchronization, and parameter modification. All DMA modules are VME slaves with interrupt capabilities, excluding FIR and *nonmaxima suppression* (NMS) boards. Communications among the CPU supervisor, the host computer, and the SUN graphic workstation are implemented by message exchange through mailboxes. A powerful software environment has been realized for human-machine interaction through a set of graphic facilities, on the SUN workstation, which allow

- Single-step commands for each individual module activation
- Global commands to run the whole chain or a subpart of it
- Different operating modes such as single shot, n times or continuous
- Debugging facilities such as graphic and testing tools
- I/O files of off-line commands for each module
- Easy control and modification of parameters

Table 12.1. Main Characteristics and Performance of Individual Modules Integrated into Real-Time 3D Vision Machine DMA.

Hardware performance			
Module	Input	Output worst case	Hardware implementation
Finite impulse response (FIR) filtering	Gray-level image 512 × 512 × 8	Gradient components G_x, G_y 2 × (512 × 512 × 8)	Dedicated hardware 40 ms
Nonmaxima suppression	Gradient components 2 × (512 × 512 × 8)	Gradient module + binary edge image 10% edge points	Dedicated hardware 40 ms
Edge linking	Gradient module + binary edge image + $G_x + G_y$	Linked chain lists 250 edge chains 10 kpixels	4 ADSP 2100 + coprocessor 120 ms[†]
Polygonal approximation	Linked edge chain lists	Segments less than 1000	4 Motorola DSP 56000D 200 ms[†]
Stereo matching	Segments + average gradient	Segment triples matched and validated hypothesis, worst case 1000, normal case 200	4 Motorola DSP 56000D 300 ms[†]
Token tracking	Segments + average gradient	Tracked segment list, max. 250 tokens	ADSP 2100 100 ms

[†]Expected computation time with typical configuration. Larger and faster configurations are allowed.

The higher levels of the system, such as symbolic processing or task-oriented control, are implemented on flexible and powerful general-purpose host environments, like the SUN workstation or parallel machines already available in the P940 consortium.

12.7. Conclusions

This chapter provides an overview of machine vision architectures, without any claim to cover the extremely challenging issue of advanced parallel processing systems. The only attempt has been directed to achieve a reference classification scheme for an integration engineer, to better understand the quickly evolving area of image processing for computer vision. The requirements of real-time processing and the need to match also control architectures more oriented to robotics represent strong limitations to possible solutions. As such the proposed scheme is somewhat different from classical reports, which are more oriented to general-purpose image processing machines.

The resulting architecture is actually a heterogeneous solution where a sufficiently powerful and flexible host processor (possibly an MIMD machine) is supposed to provide the integration environment to control and implement the high-level tasks. Different local architectures are possible, to implement low-level iconic processing and image-to-feature transformation (SIMD and pipeline solutions have been presented). Similar comments can be extended also to middle-level processing modules, where multi-DSP boards as well as SIMD or MIMD configurations are often proposed and have proved quite promising.

Standardization. In the last few years there has been a large effort towards standardization. In fact it represents a key point to widen and consolidate the computer vision market and, as a consequence, to push greater investment in the realization of "standard" modules from a much larger number of vendors.

This subject of standardization is very relevant in telecommunications (video compression standards like CCITT M.261, JPEG, MPEG, and HDTV) but some initiatives have been recently reported also in the computer vision community [2]. Anyway, standardization is often contrary to optimization, because the increased generality, flexibility, and redundancy sometimes prevent the achievement of a specifically tailored solution to the current problem.

Hence, a full standardization of processing architectures for computer vision is unlikely to be achieved in the next few years. On the other hand, such standard solutions will definitely appear for the most established processing levels, such as histograms, convolution, mathematical morphology, edge and feature extraction, etc. Many hardware modules on the market are already quite similar, and there is some kind of consensus from the computer vision community on such low-level operations, so that standard solutions seem to be quite possible soon.

Actually, this could be extremely important for the evolution of vision research towards high-level application tasks, by minimizing the time spent to redesign quite established low-level functions.

Performance evaluation. Any effort of classification has to be based on some criteria of evaluation, which should be general enough to cover most practical situations. Unfortunately this is not an easy task for computer vision. Actually some efforts have been reported in the literature, to evaluate image processing computers, where conventional benchmarking techniques are not readily applicable.

A widely accepted tool for evaluation of image processing architectures is the Abingdon cross benchmark, where the task is to find the medial axis of a cross in a noisy background [16]. These results have been used to rate the quality factor against the price performance factor for many commercial systems, although they are limited to a set of very simple geometric functions and point or matrix computations. So far no similar tools are available for more complex machine vision systems belonging to different robotics applications. A possible solution consists of exploiting a systems engineering approach with a thorough evaluation of the full system as well as its individual components. Such an experimental method aims to stress the algorithms and the subsystems to ensure a sufficiently robust behavior. A robust machine vision technology should be almost invariant to sensing and illumination constraints. It needs adaptive mechanisms in the selection of the processing parameters (for instance, in image segmentation, classification, etc.) and should include geometric reasoning tools to deal with 3D scene transformations. Another essential component is an effective hardware and software environment for system control and integration. There are already promising display environments which permit iconic or "visual" programming and simplify the task of the operator, without the need to be expert at the image processing algorithms. Systems engineering criteria will remove the ad hoc nature of present solutions and provide the basis for the new generation of computer vision systems.

References

[1] E. Appiani, B. Conterno, V. Luperini, and L. Roncarolo, EMMA2, a High-Performance Hierarchical Multiprocessor, *IEEE MICRO*, February 1989, pp. 42–56.

[2] ARVISA, Advanced Real-time Vision System Architecture, ESPRIT Project P5225, Technical Annex, February 1991.

[3] R. A. Brooks, A Robust, Layered Control System for a Mobile Robot, *IEEE Journal of Robotics and Automation*, 2:14, 1986.

[4] C. Brown and M. Rygol, MARVIN: Multiprocessor Architecture for Vision, *Proceedings of the 10th Occam User Group Technical Meeting*, 1989.

[5] V. Cantoni, V. Di Gesu', M. Ferretti, S. Levialdi, R. Negrini, and R. Stefanelli, The PAPIA System, *Journal of VLSI Signal Processing*, 2:195–217, 1991.

[6] S. De Paoli, A. Chehikian, and P. Stelmaszyk, Real Time Token Tracker, *Proceedings of EUSIPCO'90*, Barcelona, Spain, 1990.

[7] E. D. Dickmanns and V. Graefe, Applications of Dynamic Monocular Machine Vision, *Machine Vision and Applications*, 1988, pp. 241–261.

[8] M. J. B. Duff, Review of the CLIP Image Processing System, *Proceedings of the National Computer Conference*, 1978, pp. 1055–1060.

[9] O. Faugeras, R. Deriche, N. Ayache, F. Lustman, and E. Giuliano, Depth and Motion Analysis: The Machine Being Developed Within ESPRIT Project P940, *IAPR Workshop on Computer Vision, Special Hardware and Industrial Applications*, October 12–14, 1988, Tokyo, Japan.

[10] G. Gaillat, Le calculateur parallele CAPITAN: 600 MIPS pour l'imagerie temps reel, *Revue Traitement du Signal*, 1(1):19–30, 1984.

[11] D. Hillis, *The Connection Machine*, Cambridge, Mass.: M.I.T. Press, 1985.

[12] H. T. Kung, Let's Design Algorithms for VLSI Systems, *Proceedings of the Caltech Conference in VLSI*, California Institute of Technology, Pasadena, CA, 1979, pp. 65–90.

[13] LSI Logic Co., L64220 Rank-Value Filter RVF, November 1987.

[14] G. Musso, Depth and Motion Analysis: The ESPRIT Project P940, *ESPRIT '89 Conference Proceedings*, November 1989, pp. 10–30.

[15] G. R. Nudd, Image Understanding Architectures, *Proceedings of the National Computer Conference*, 1980, pp. 377–390.

[16] K. Preston, The Abingdon Cross Benchmark Survey, *Computer*, July 1989, pp. 9–18.

[17] J. M. Raynor and P. Seitz, The Technology and Practical Problems of Pixel-Synchronous CCD Data Acquisition for Optical Metrology Applications, *Proceedings of SPIE*, vol. 1395, *Close-Range Photogrammetry Meets Machine Vision*, 1990.

[18] M. Rygol, S. Pollard, and C. Brown, A Multiprocessor 3D Vision System for Pick and Place, *Proceedings of the British Machine Conference*, Oxford, September 1990, pp.169–174.

[19] S. R. Sternberg, Architecture for Neighborhood Processing, *Proceedings of Pattern Recognition and Image Processing Conference*, Dallas, 1981, pp. 374–380.

[20] S. R. Sternberg, Grayscale Morphology, *Computer Vision, Graphics and Image Processing*, 35:333–335, 1986.

[21] M. Tistarelli and G. Sandini, On the Estimation of Depth from Motion Using an Anthropomorphic Visual Sensor, *Proceedings of the European Conference on Computer Vision '90*, Antibes, France, 1990.

[22] L. W. Tucker and G. G. Robertson, Architecture and Applications of the Connection Machine, *Computer*, August 1988, pp. 26–38.

[23] L. Uhr, Pyramid Multi-Computer Structures, and Augmented Pyramids, in M. J. B. Duff (ed.), *Computing Structures for Image Processing*, London: Academic Press, 1983.

[24] R. Valliant, R. Deriche, and O. Faugeras, 3D Vision on the Parallel Machine CAPITAN, *International Workshop on Industrial Applications of Machine Intelligence and Vision* (MIV-89), Tokyo, April 10–12, 1989.

[25] C. Weitzman, *Distributed Micro/minicomputer Systems*, Englewood Cliffs, N.J.: Prentice-Hall, 1980.

[26] S. Yalamanchili, Image Processing Architectures: A Taxonomy and Survey, in L. N. Kanal and A. Rosenfeld (eds.), *Progress in Pattern Recognition*, vol. 2. Amsterdam: Elsevier, 1985.

Handbook of Pattern Recognition and Computer Vision, pp. 941–965
Eds. C. H. Chen, L. F. Pau and P. S. P. Wang
© 1993 World Scientific Publishing Company

CHAPTER 5.7

IMAGE INFORMATION SYSTEMS: WHERE DO WE GO FROM HERE?

SHI-KUO CHANG

Department of Computer Science, University of Pittsburgh, Pittsburgh, PA 15260, USA

and

ARDING HSU

Siemens Corporate Research, Princeton, NJ 08540, USA

A conceptual framework for image information systems is presented. Current research topics are surveyed, and application examples presented, followed by a discussion on the design issues for the next generation of image information systems. It is our view that the next generation of active image information systems should be designed based upon the notions of generalized icons and active indexes, resulting in smart images.

Index Terms: Image information systems, image databases, image data models, feature-based indexing, active index, generalized icons, smart images.

I. Introduction

Recently, advances in image storage technologies have made the creation of very large image databases feasible. Wideband multimedia communications also greatly facilitate the distribution of images across communication networks. Parallel computers lead to faster image processing systems. High resolution graphics and dedicated coprocessors enable the design of image output subsystems with superior image quality. Image information systems have found their way into many application areas, including geographical information systems (GIS's), office automation (OA), medical picture archiving and communications systems (PACS's), computer-aided design (CAD), computer-aided manufacturing (CAM), computer-aided engineering (CAE), robotics, and scientific databases (SD) applications.

An image information system typically has the following five components: (1) an image input subsystem, (2) an image processing system, (3) an image output subsystem, (4) an image database system, and (5) an image communications subsystem [7]. A schematic is illustrated in Fig. 1.

Manuscript received April 15, 1992; revised May 19, 1992.
This work was supported in part by NSF Grant "Visual Reasoning for Information Retrieval."
Reprinted with permission from *IEEE Transactions on Knowledge and Data Engineering*, Vol. 4, No. 5, October 1992, pp. 431–442. © IEEE.

941

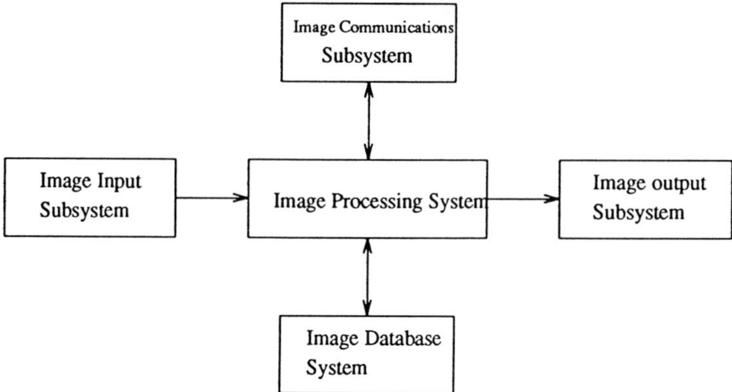

Fig. 1. Components of an image information system.

Image information systems are often integrated with other information systems. For example, a medical PACS is often integrated with the radiology information system (RIS) and the hospital information system (HIS) [43]. Such integration increases the usefulness and applicability of image information systems. Wider applications also lead to more sophisticated end users. Image information systems, like other types of information systems, have increasingly become knowledge-based systems, with capabilities to perform many sophisticated tasks by accessing and manipulating domain knowledge.

So far, image information systems are designed on an *ad hoc* basis. The previously mentioned technological advances dictate a better methodology to design knowledge-based user-specific image information systems. The design methodology, taking into consideration the diversified application requirements and users' needs, should provide a unified framework for image representation, indexing, image structuring, and spatial reasoning.

This paper is organized as follows. In Section II, we present a conceptual framework for image information systems. Current research issues are surveyed in Section III. Application examples and target application areas are described in Section IV. Current commercial database systems capable of supporting image information systems are briefly reviewed in Section V. Finally, in Section VI, we discuss design issues for the next generation of active image information systems.

II. Conceptual Framework

As discussed in Section I, an image information system typically consists of an image input subsystem, an image output subsystem, an image processing system, an image database system, and an image communications subsystem. We will now concentrate on the image processing system and image database system, which constitute the heart of the image information system.

A traditional image processing system primarily performs the tasks of image analysis, image enhancement, and pattern recognition. Within the context of an

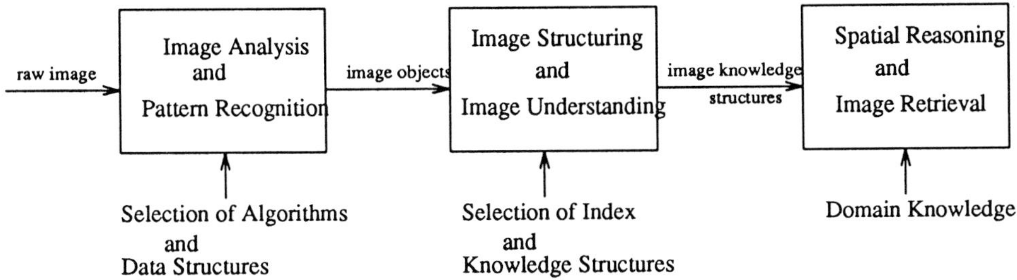

Fig. 2. Stages in knowledge-based image processing.

image information system, the image processing system and image database system must perform the following three functions, which can also be regarded as three stages in knowledge-based image processing. The three stages are illustrated in Fig. 2.

A. *Image Analysis and Pattern Recognition*

The raw image is analyzed, and the image objects recognized. This stage is almost always present in any image processing system. Extensive techniques are available for image enhancement, normalization, segmentation, and pattern recognition. The end result is a collection of recognized image objects. These image objects are usually encoded in some data structures for ease of access and further manipulation. For example, the image objects may be encoded in runlength codes, polygonal contour codes, quad-trees, oct-trees, etc. In general, the image objects are objects with attributes including coordinates, geometric properties, etc. The unanalyzed or unprocessed parts of the image can be regarded as image entities which will be analyzed later if needed. Therefore, the system input to this stage includes the selection of various image processing algorithms, and the selection of data structures.

B. *Image Structuring and Understanding*

For some applications, it may be sufficient to access and manipulate the image objects, and there is no need for further structuring. However, for many applications, the image objects must be converted into image knowledge structures, so that spatial reasoning and image information retrieval can be supported. The particular image knowledge structure depends upon the application domain knowledge on the one hand, and the features to be indexed on the other hand. For example, keywords may be useful for a wide variety of applications. Other indexes, including shape descriptors, color descriptors, and spatial relations such as hypergraphs or 2-D strings, can be used. The indexes can be used to access various data structures, or embedded into hierarchical image knowledge structures. However, it may be desirable to use other image knowledge structures, such as directed graphs of spatial relations, semantic networks, etc. Therefore, the system input to this stage includes the selection of knowledge structures.

C. *Spatial Reasoning and Image Information Retrieval*

An image information system supports the information gathering needs and problem solving activities of the end users. Some applications require spatial reasoning (see Section IV). Other applications are primarily concerned with image information retrieval. In medical imaging applications, for instance, the clinician may want to retrieve CT images of all patients having a tumor similar to the shape present in a specific CT image. Generally speaking, both spatial reasoning and image information retrieval are needed and may complement each other. To solve specific problems in a domain, a domain knowledge base is needed. It may also be necessary to perform various transformations upon the image knowledge structure, so that the desired image knowledge can be easily accessed, visualized, and/or manipulated. The transformations include: rotation, translation, change of point-of-view, projection from 3- to 2-D views, addition/deletion of symbolic image objects, etc. Finally, the result of this stage is a user-specific knowledge structure, such as a navigation plan, a path, a set of retrieved images, an image index or indexes, etc.

In the conceptual framework presented above, the three stages can be regarded as three generalized transformations, to transform a raw image first into an image data structure, then into an image knowledge structure, and finally into a user-specific knowledge structure.

We can express the image knowledge structure as a *generalized icon* [7] (x_i, x_m), where x_i is the "raw image" and x_m is the "assigned meaning." Thus the raw image is (x_i, nil) where the "meaning" is yet undetermined. After the meaning is assigned, the image knowledge structure becomes (x_i, x_m). In other words, the generalized icon acquires more "meaning" as it passes through the various stages in the image information system. On the one hand, this viewpoint is object-oriented. On the other hand, it also implies that a generalized icon, i.e., a pair of raw images (or image object) and its associated knowledge structure, is the minimal unit of communication among different information systems, or between the workstation and the system.

The above conceptual framework is from the image processing viewpoint, which necessarily is process oriented. Based upon the above conceptual framework, a five-level architecture for the image database system is illustrated in Table I. This viewpoint emphasizes the hierarchical structuring of information.

The user provides the information on how an image database could be used regarding high level events. Typically, the user view requires the performance of spatial reasoning tasks. The semantic feature view describes a specific domain view, from the user's perspective, of certain image features. For example, a "wheel" at

Table I. Five-level architecture of the image database system.

Level	Tasks	Example
User View	Spatial Reasoning	Find all motor vehicles with wheels
Semantic Feature View	Image Knowledge Structuring	Find icons, such as (image_object, wheel)
Image Feature View	Image Understanding	Find icons, such as (image_object, circle)
Feature Representation	Image Data Structuring	Find icons, such as (image_object, contour_of_circle)
Feature Organization	Image Data Storage/Retrieval	Store/access icons (image_object, contour_data_structure)

the semantic view level corresponds to a "circle" at the image feature view level. With this separation, an image information system can support different usage of image objects (i.e., icons) and avoid the information loss problem. For example, if we only index on "wheels" and discard information about "circles," later on we cannot process queries regarding "circles" or composite objects containing "circles."

The image feature view is based on image contents, e.g., spatial relationships, shape, etc. Since there is no unique representation for many features, the feature representation level should support multiple representations of the same feature. For example, a "circle" can be represented by its contour, or by its center and radius, etc. The feature organization level is equivalent to the physical storage structure level in traditional database systems (B-tree, hashing, etc.) The software environment for image database research described in [15] adopts a representation pyramid which reflects some of the characteristics of this five-level architecture.

The user should be allowed to query the first three levels, i.e., to express queries at the levels of user view, semantic feature view or image feature view. This five-level architecture also implies that the image data model should accommodate different views on image data. Last, but not least, feature-based indexing must be supported. Current approaches regarding these issues will be discussed in Section III.

III. Current Research Issues

A. *Query Language and User Interface*

Although image information systems primarily deal with image data, many query languages developed for image information systems are command languages, or commands plus expressions [25]. Some of them follow a SQL-like syntax. For example, a PSQL query is given in the following [39]:

```
SELECT STATE_NAME, STATE_REGION,
    AREA (STATE_REGION)
FROM STATE
WHERE POPULATION > 500 000.
```

The GRIM_DBMS graphical image database management system supports a query language with fuzzy measures [38]:

```
RETRIEVE IMAGES (hospital_building/0.9)
CONTAINING
((double_bedroom/1.0) AND (number_of_door ≥ 2)).
```

On the other hand, in one of the early image information systems, the advantage in expressing queries by pictorial examples was already recognized. IMAID supports query-by-pictorial-example (QPE), but the queries are specified using tables, in the style of query-by-example (QBE) [4].

Since then, considerable progress has been made in the QBE approach. In IIDMS, a pictorial query can be expressed directly as a picture, which is then converted into 2-D strings for matching against the iconic index of the image database [6]. An example will be presented in Section IV.

The QBE approach, combined with a direct manipulation interface, should support querying by image content in 2 D or even 3 D [1]. The user can point at an image object and ask for all images "like this", i.e., all images having similar features. Therefore, the user interface must be supported by algorithms for similarity retrieval.

In many applications, there is also a growing need for querying and visualizing images of different modality. The user should also be allowed to switch between interaction paradigms, and/or combine interaction paradigms. For example, the user can use an iconic approach to specify "like this" queries, a tabular approach to specify simple queries, and graphs such as the E-R diagram to specify more complicated queries [9]. How does one design a unified interface supporting multiple paradigm interaction and multiple visualization modalities? How does one design a single-point-of-contact (SPOC) workstation capable of multiple paradigm querying, multiple modality visualization, direct manipulation, data compression, and decompression? These are the research issues to be addressed.

B. Data Models

A data model is a collection of mathematically well-defined concepts to express both static and dynamic properties of data intensive applications [2]. Static properties are objects, attributes, and relationships among objects. Dynamic properties are operations on objects, operations on properties, and relationships among operations. Static properties are expressed using database schema (DDL), and dynamic properties are specifications for transactions (DML) and queries (QL). Integrity rules over objects (i.e., data states) and operations (state transitions) are sometimes also included into the data model.

From hierarchical, network, to relational data models, traditional applications in a business environment with formatted data have enjoyed many successful cases in information management. Even for nontraditional applications such as engineering information management, with extensions on the relational data model (e.g., long field, complex object, etc.) and the advances in object-oriented and semantic data models [14], some successes have also been claimed. With a growing list of new applications based on image information handling, little success has been achieved on the direct management of image information. The standard approach for image data modeling is to model image data and text data separately, and the image is usually stored in its entirety [7,45,12]. All the commercial image information systems are treating images as black boxes (e.g., Binary Large OBjects (BLOB's)). Special functions are provided to access the contents of images (e.g., find_wheel (vehicle)).

Traditionally, a database system could be considered having three basic levels: external models that support individual user views, a single conceptual model which defines an abstract representation of the database in its entirety, and an internal model which defines the database storage structures and cannot be seen by users. Generally speaking, a modeling technique provides a set of type constructs for users to model entities and relationships which exist in application domains. It also provides mechanisms to construct external models from the conceptual model. The relational data model provides a single construct, relation. The (extended) E-R model provides constructs for entity, aggregation, generalization, and general user named relationships.

Compared to alphanumeric data, image information carries some special characteristics as follows.

(1) The content of an image cannot be precisely described. The content of an image could be considered as a group of spatial objects (e.g., line, contour, point, etc.) with spatial relationships (e.g., adjacency, orientation, relative position, etc.) among them. In general, there are no precise ways to represent these objects and relationships. They can only be described by some approximate representations. For example, a closed contour could be represented as a set of vertexes of an inside polygon. On the other hand, alphanumeric data can always be precisely represented with basic data types such as integer, string, etc., or even complex data types formed from basic data types. In either case, whenever a data type is assigned to an object or a relationship, it will not be changed. Therefore, a modeling technique with basic data types and the support of user defined data types is usually sufficient. However, this is not enough to support the modeling of image data. Since a representation is approximate, it is not unique where new and better representations may be adopted in the future. Furthermore, multiple representations are possible and the selection

of the best representation cannot be fixed in the data model. For example, a closed contour could also be represented as a set of rectangles covering the inside of the contour.

From the above discussion, an image modeling technique needs to hide the underlying data representations (data types) of spatial objects and relationships from users and provide mechanisms to map and select the proper representation dynamically. Many interesting issues need to be considered. Is the mapping one to many, many to one, or many to many? How should the consistency issue be considered? For multiple representations, should the equivalence issue be considered?

(2) Spatial entities (objects) and relationships (we will call them image features) in images do not carry any semantic meanings by themselves. With alphanumeric information, entities and relationships carry semantic meanings through their given names. For example, the E-R diagram:

$$\text{manager} - \text{manages} - \text{employee}$$

clearly states that there are two entities, "manager" and "employee," with a relationship "manages" in between. Associating semantic meanings by naming will cause some problems with image information. First, the same image could be interpreted in different ways. Second, the same image could be used in different ways during different time periods. Third, since the image interpretation is an approximation in many cases, it may be changed due to better recognition techniques. In any of the above cases, directly associating semantic meanings to image entities and relationships will severely limit the usage of image information. A more feasible approach is to model the image with spatial meanings, i.e., image features, and then associate semantic meanings, i.e., semantic features, to image features for different usages.

Without associating semantic meanings to spatial entities and relationships, different users may interpret them very differently. For example, one person's definition of relative position may be very different from others. Therefore, in addition to traditional modeling constructs, spatial modeling constructs need to be defined for image modeling. Furthermore, since it is impossible to provide a complete set of image constructs for general applications, the modeling technique needs to provide mechanisms to support user defined image constructs and treat them as first class constructs. It should also support the building of complex image features from simple features.

The mapping between semantic features and image features raises further interesting research issues. Since computer vision technology has not matured, the above mapping cannot be automated. Therefore, the mapping is part of the image schema design. To facilitate database designers and to avoid mistakes, mapping constructs need to be provided by an image modeling technique. Of course, it should also support the evolution of mapping constructs.

(3) Image-based information could be queried by pictures. We always say that a picture is worth a thousand words. However, on the other side, pictures may

cause multiple or imprecise interpretations. Therefore, an image information system needs to provide some domain knowledge to help users incrementally refine their intentions. A user's intention could be a single query or it could be a complicated set of interrelated queries. One approach is to provide a knowledge-based module to guide users and give suggestions. The debate on whether semantics should be described in data models or by integrity constraints in traditional data modeling could be applied here. Many interesting research issues are raised here. First, what should be in data models and what should be in knowledge-based modules? Second, how should this information be represented? Third, how do these two parts interact?

In recent years, researchers have begun to address some of these issues. Researchers from the image processing community generally prefer generalized graph models as data models. For example, GRIM_DBMS uses attributed relational graphs as a data model [38], and RDS promotes the relational data structure as the data model [40]. Researchers from the database camp advocate the use of extensible relational DBMS. Others have begun to explore how to extend the database schema to define conceptual and external schemas for images and associated procedures [33]. VIMSYS is probably the most extensive data model developed for image information management [19]. Based upon the object-oriented approach, this four-level model supports: (a) image representation and relations, (b) image objects and relations, (c) domain objects and relations, and (d) domain events and relations. More recently, the object-oriented approach has become a favorite [20,23,41], although adopting the object-oriented approach alone does not necessarily solve the data modeling problem.

C. *Indexing Techniques and Data Structures*

The discussion of indexing techniques could proceed in three directions: index representation, index organization, and index extraction. The extraction of indexes could be manual, automatic, or something in between (hybrid). For image information systems, index extraction is heavily dependent on the progress in image processing technology. In this section, we will concentrate on index representation and index organization.

In conventional database systems, keyword-based indexing techniques are sufficient to support user needs. In image information systems, there are many applications that cannot be properly supported by keyword-based techniques. In addition to keywords, users often want to retrieve images by shape, texture, spatial relationships, etc. [10,17,18,22,34,44]. That is, image features are used as indexes (called image indexes), and in many cases, they cannot be represented as keywords. The representations of these image indexes possess some special characteristics.

(1) Image indexes are approximately represented.

(2) Image indexes do not have embedded order; in the sense that if a, b and c are three index values and $a < b < c$, it does not mean that image (b) is more similar to image (a) than image (c) is.

(3) Image index representations may have interrelated multiple attributes. That is, if $a1$ and $a2$ are two attributes of an index, result $(a1, a2) \neq$ result $(a1)$ inter result $(a2)$.

With these characteristics, the conventional indexing structures like B-tree, hashing, etc., cannot be used for the organization of image indexes. Visual structures must be explored [29]. The visual structures should also support similarity retrieval [24].

The above considerations lead to the following three dimensions in classifying different approaches to image indexing. (1) First dimension: how to structure the image data? Image data structures include the B-tree, the K-D-tree, the Quad-tree, etc. (2) Second dimension: how to select the image indexes? The choices are the keywords, the shape descriptors, the signatures, and the 2-D strings, etc. (3) Third dimension: how to acquire the image index? We may distinguish between automatic, hybrid or manual means of index construction.

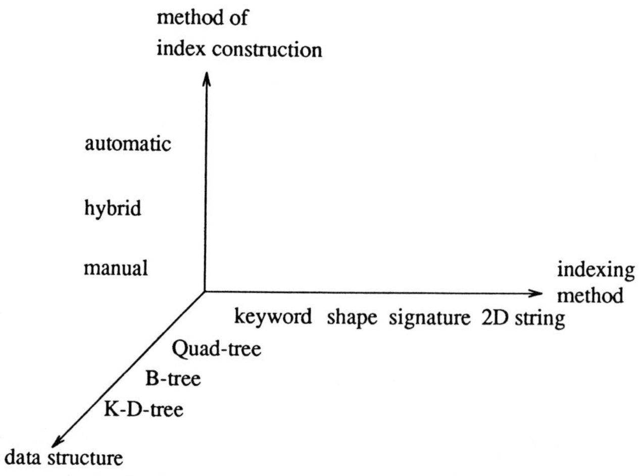

Fig. 3. Three dimensions of image indexing.

The three dimensions are illustrated in Fig. 3. An application area corresponds to a shaded region in this 3-D space. These applications share some common methods of data collection, indexing approach, and data structuring. The combination of indexing and data structures provides the support for an image database system.

A classification of some typical image information systems is given in Table II. This table is not meant to be a comprehensive survey. Some of the systems are chosen for historical reasons, and the recent ones are chosen to illustrate the new approaches. Considered as a whole, Table II illustrates the general trends in current image database research.

Table II. A classification of image information systems.

System Description	Query	Data Model	Index Method	Index Extraction	Data Structure	Application
IMAID: Integrates image and text data interfaced with image processing	query-by-pictorial-example by filling tables	relational	—	—		image processing
PSQL: Integrates image and text data but process them separately	command language SELECT STATE_NAME FROM STATE WHERE POPUL > 50 000	relational	attributes	predefined or manual	R-tree or $R+$ tree	cartography
PICDMS: Picture DBMS using dynamic stacked images and gridded data	command language ADD (IMAGE FIDD FIX (8,0)) DIFF = BAND4-BANDS	stacked image	field name with current location	predefined or manual	flat file (3-D matrix of stacked images)	image processing
IIDMS: Intelligent image database system using 2-D string as an iconic index	iconic query-by pictorial-example by drawing pictorial query	relational	2-D strings	automatic or manual (hybrid)	sigma-tree	image processing
Visual Structure Database	symbolic query Car in front of house	entity-relationship diagram	attributes	manual	quad-tree and entity-relationship records	cartography
GRIM_DBMS: Automatic extraction of objects and semantics using pattern recognition and image processing with fuzzy measure	command language RETRIEVE IMAGES (hospital/0.9) CONTAINING (double_bedroom/1.0)	attributed relational graphs	predefined attributes as cluster indexes	automatic	tree with cluster indexes	CAD/CAM
I-See Software environment emphasizes precompilation and query by image content	(a) Iconic query as guide to search. (b) symbolic query SHOW cities WEST-OF city name = "Pittsburg"	object oriented	—	automatic using image analysis and AI technique		image processing
IDB: Image Archiving by Content	matched example image by similarity retrieval	object oriented	attributes	automatic using image analysis and AI techniques		medical image database

Note: Blank entries mean "do not know" and "—" entries "none".

IMAID, PICDMS, PSQL, GRIM_DBMS, and IIDMS have been discussed earlier. The visual structure database has some nice features by combining the E-R data model and the quad-tree [29]. I-See is a software environment for image database research, emphasizing object-oriented approach, precompilation, and query-by-image content [15]. IDB is an object-oriented image database system emphasizing content-based archiving and retrieval with applications in PACS [30].

IV. Application Examples

We now present three examples to explicate the conceptual framework presented in Section II. The first example is primarily a path finding problem. The second example involves more complex image information processing. The third example is from medical image processing.

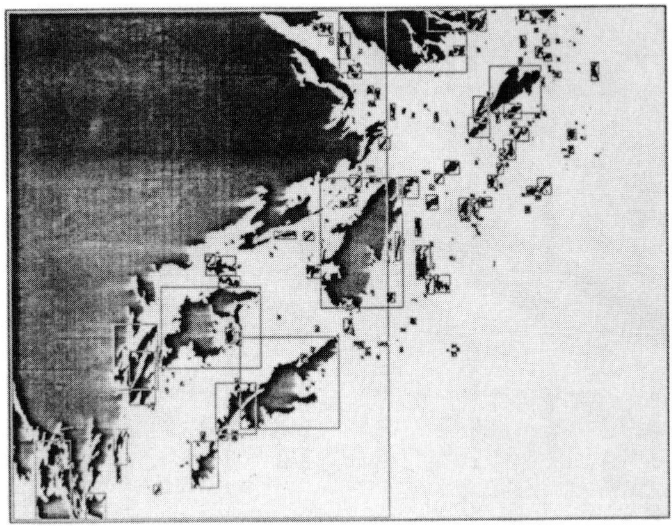

Fig. 4. A coastal region and results of locating the island objects.

Example 1: Fig. 4 illustrates a raw image of a coastal region. The specific problem for this application, is to find a path for navigating a ship from point A to point B. At the image analysis and pattern recognition (IAPR) stage, minimal enclosing rectangles for each island object are constructed, as also shown in Fig. 4. The image objects are runlength encoded and stored in the image database. This is the basic image data structure created by the IAPR stage. At the image structuring and image understanding (ISIU) stage, the runlength encoded data structure is processed, so that a connectivity graph for the "tiles" (the "runs" of white pixels) can be constructed. This is part of the resultant image knowledge structure created by the ISIU stage. A small symbolic image extracted from the image of Fig. 4 is

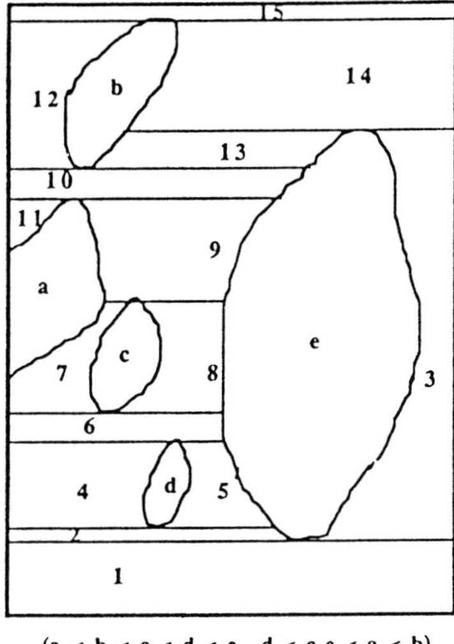

Fig. 5. A small symbolic image extracted from the image of Fig. 4.

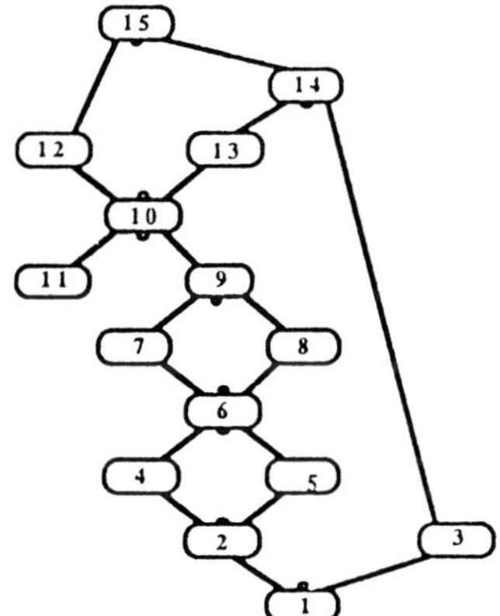

Fig. 6. The tile graph corresponding to the image of Fig. 5. The direction/context of some of the tiles are as follows: 7: no direction; 6: south-north/left turn; 8: north/double-sp-left; 9: north/double-up-sp-left; 10: north/low-left-up-left-sp; 13: north/X-inflection. 14: north-south/right turn; 3: no direction.

shown in Fig. 5. A tile graph is illustrated in Fig. 6. The spatial knowledge structure can be expressed by the 2-D strings as follows [5]:

$$(a < b < c < d < e, d < ce < a < b) \, .$$

Intuitively, the first strings says that "a is to the left of b, which is to the left of c, which is to the left of d, which is to the left of e," and the second string says that "d is below c and e, which are below a, which is below b." Therefore, the 2-D strings express the approximate spatial relations among image objects.

The spatial relations can be expressed even more precisely, if the image objects are segmented, as also illustrated in Fig. 5. After segmentation, the generalized 2-D strings are as follows [26]:

$$(a|ab|cab|cb|dcb|db|d < e\ ,$$
$$(e|de|e|ace|ae|e|be|b)\ .$$

In the above expression, the "edge-to-edge" operator "$|$" is used to connect two adjacent pieces of objects. The tile graph and the generalized 2-D strings are equivalent image knowledge structures, and there are transformations to convert from one representation into another [8].

Suppose the user wants to find a navigation path from the region of tile 7, to the region of tile 3. At the spatial reasoning and image retrieval (SRIR) stage, the tile graph is examined by a path finding algorithm so that different navigation plans can be generated. The resultant, user-specific knowledge structure is a plan, or a number of alternate plans. An example of a plan is 7-6-8-9-10-13-14-3, indicating the tiles successively visited by the ship.

We can summarize the knowledge-based image processing activities for this path-finding example as follows:

Activities	Results
Image analysis and pattern recognition	Identify image objects (islands) and produce runlength encoded image data structure
Image structuring and image understanding	Produce tile graph as the image knowledge structure
Spatial reasoning and image retrieval	Produce navigation plans as the final output

The above example illustrates the transformations from raw images to image data structures, image knowledge structures, and finally navigation plans (user-specific knowledge structures). For a more complicated planning problem, the transformations are more complex.

Example 2: Fig. 7 illustrates a map which can be displayed on the screen of the Forest Fire Crisis Management system [13]. The raw images, which are the maps, are either manually digitized or automatically digitized. The map objects, such as towns, cities, forests, rivers, roads, etc., are stored in the image database. The image data structure could again be the runlength code.

This image database for maps, with its runlength encoded data structure, can be used to answer many map related queries, such as "find the roads within the city boundary of city A". However, to support the planning and problem solving activities for a system such as the Forest Fire Crisis Management system, it will be too time consuming to process the image database to answer some queries. Therefore, a symbolic spatial data structure called the sigma-tree, which is a hierarchical

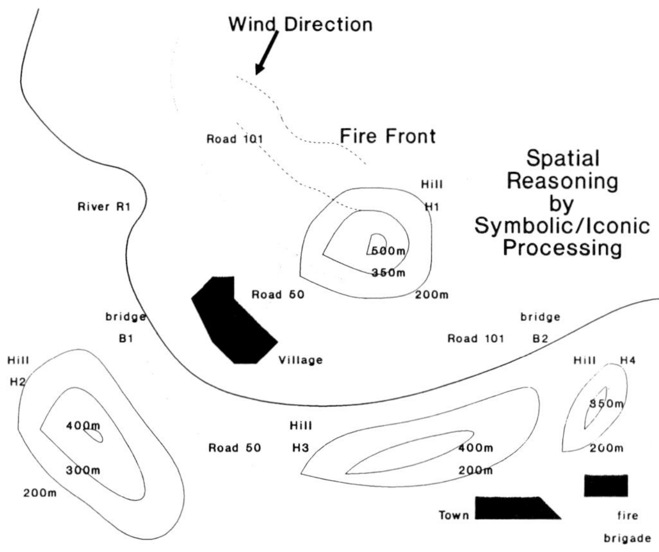

Fig. 7. Spatial reasoning by two-level symbolic/iconic processing.

structure with embedded 2-D strings, can be created by the ISIU stage. From this spatial knowledge structure, an efficient 3-D model can be generated and displayed [11].

We now have two image structures: a runlength encoded image data structure for the maps, which will be regarded as the low level image structure; and a spatial knowledge structure called the sigma-tree, which will be regarded as the high-level image structure. In what follows, we illustrate a scenario where the user's problem solving activities are supported by the image information system, which performs both high and low-level image processing activities.

Suppose the user poses the following query: "From the current fire front, compute fire fronts 1 h, 2 h, 3 h, etc., from the present time."

This query can be answered first by high level processing of the symbolic spatial data structure as follows. From the symbolic structure, compute the fire fronts in areas other than the hill $H1$. Since all objects and their locations are stored in the symbolic structure, this computation can be done quickly.

However, insufficient information is carried by the symbolic structure as far as $H1$ is concerned. Therefore, low level processing of the image data structure is necessary, to find out the areas in $H1$ covered by forest. After such processing, we can also compute the fire front in the $H1$ area. It is worth noting that the high and the low level processing tasks can be carried out simultaneously by parallel processes, so that the user will first receive a quick but incomplete (and less accurate) reply, while more detailed information will be supplied later.

The second query is as follows. The user would place a cross on the symbolic image, indicating the approximate location of the fire corridor to be constructed by the firefighters, and ask "what is the estimated time needed to deploy the firefighters?"

Again, both high and low-level processing are necessary. At high level processing, we can estimate the approximate times needed to travel from town T to bridge $B1$ and bridge $B2$. These are the two alternate paths that the firefighters may take. Again, since object locations are known, the travel times can be estimated from the symbolic structure. At the low-level processing, the approximate times of travel between T and $B1$ or $B2$ are replaced by more accurate results, by taking into consideration road types, road conditions, terrain conditions, etc. Similarly, we can first do high level processing to estimate the travel times from $B1$ and $B2$ to the cross X, and at the same time do low level processing to recompute the travel times. The refined results are supplied to the user when available.

This second example illustrates the desirability of having two levels of knowledge structures, the high level image knowledge structure for quick computation and spatial reasoning, and the low level image data structure for more elaborate accurate computation. However, we must be able to efficiently switch between the two levels of processing, by quickly relating image knowledge structure and image data structure.

Example 3: Fig. 8 is a chest x-ray image showing an abnormality in the right lung [16]. This particular abnormality is an example of a homogeneous nonsegmental infiltrate. The diagnosis is Hodgkins disease.

The flowchart for the physician to make decisions is illustrated in Fig. 9, and the accompanying image queries are as follows:

Box 2:
- Is the image clear?
- Can all desired organs be seen?

Box 3:
- Does an abnormality exist?

Box 4:
- Has the abnormality changed? *
- Is the abnormality new? *

Box 5:
- How big is the abnormality?
- If the abnormality is a nodule, then:
    Is there calcification?
    Is it solid?
    Is it cystic?
    Is it regular in shape? #
    Is it irregular in shape? #
    Is it single?
    Is it multiple?

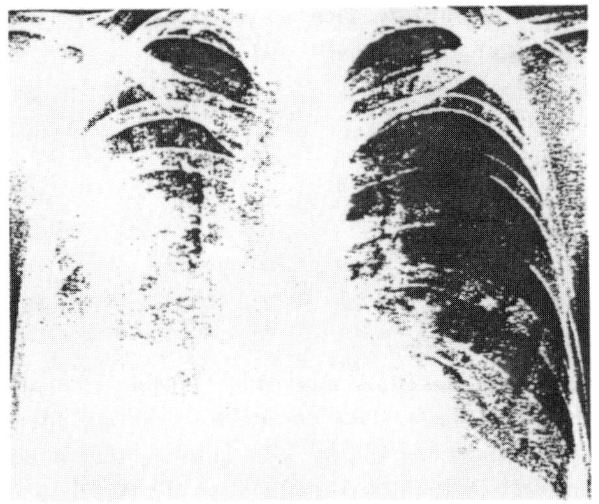

Fig. 8. Chest x-ray image.

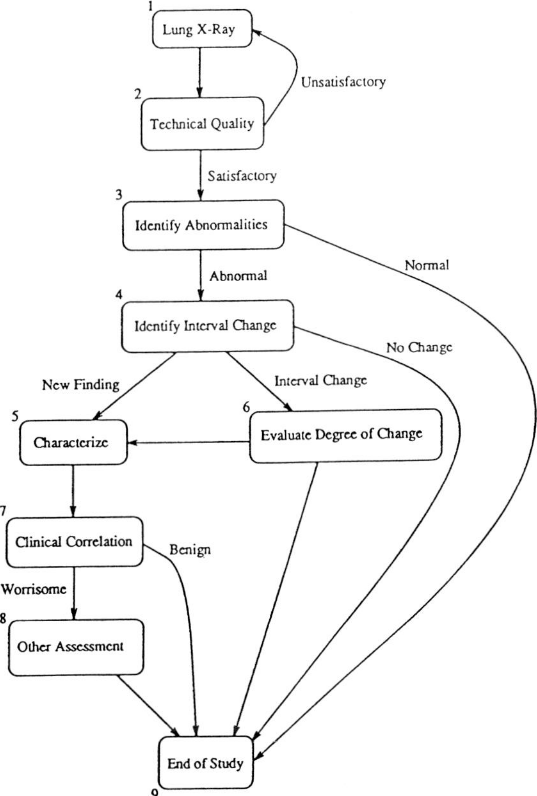

Fig. 9. Decision flowchart.

- If the abnormality is infiltrate, then:
    Is is homogeneous?
    Is it inhomogeneous?
    Is it segmental?
    Is it nonsegmental?
    Is it single?
    Is it multiple?
  Box 7:
- Is the abnormality benign?
- Is the abnormality worrisome?

Notice some image queries (those marked by *) require comparison with previous x-ray images. In other words, these are queries requiring interimage processing. Some image queries (those marked by #) require contour analysis. Finally, the benign/worrisome decision requires a combination of image data and patient/family history. Some of the issues in accessing images by content in the PACS environment are discussed in [30], which uses an object-oriented approach as the data model.

Target application areas for image information systems are diverse and may include: office, library, printing, publishing and advertising, security and identification, medicine, geographic information systems, remote sensing, education and training, science, fine arts, entertainment, and others.

It is clear that not all these application areas share the same requirements. However, timely delivery of information and easy accessibility seem to be the key requirements for many of these applications.

V. Commercial Products

As we discussed in the previous sections, to provide image information management in advanced applications, an image information management system should support:

(1) "like-this" visual query processing;
(2) multilevel image data models;
(3) content-based indexing;
(4) tertiary memory management;
(5) knowledge-based reasoning.

The support of image information in commercial database systems is still at its infancy. There are two approaches. One is to extend the relational data model with a new data type Binary Large OBjects (BLOB's) to store images. Some systems also provide an abstract data type (ADT) facilities for users to define new image information management functions. The other is the object-oriented approach in which users could define data types and related methods for image information. In both approaches images are treated as black boxes and text-based technologies are used to handle image information.

In Table III, we present a brief survey of a few commercial database systems for both approaches. These are: Informix-OnLine [42], UniSQL [47], GemStone [3], and Ontos [36]. This is not a comprehensive list and the information is based on published material.

Table III. Survey of commercial database systems.

Features	Informix	UNISQL	GemStone	Ontos
Query Language	SQL	SQL	OPAL	SQL(C++)
Data Model	Relational	Extended Relational	Object Oriented	Object Oriented
Image Data	BLOB's	BLOB's+ADT	ADT	ADT
Indexing	B+	B+, Extended Hashing	B	B*, Hashing
Tertiary Memory Management	NO	NO	NO	NO
Knowledge-based reasoning	NO	YES	NO	NO

VI. Design Issues for the Next Generation of Image Information Systems

An active image information system should meet the following general requirement from the user: *timely delivery and easy accessibility of image and associated information for the user, at a resolution appropriate for the intended task(s).*

This single yet comprehensive requirement implies an active image information system supporting user interface with multiple modalities, multilevel query processing, extensible and evolutionary image data models, flexible indexing methods and appropriate image data structures. In what follows, we argue that such an active image information system should be designed based upon the notions of generalized icons and active indexes. The result is a system capable of supporting **smart images**, which are images with associated knowledge structures.

A. *Generalized Icons*

In an active image information system, the minimal unit of communication is a generalized icon, which is an object consisting of a pair made of the image (physical part) and its logical interpretation (logical part). The logical part may be, in the simplest case, the label of the image. It may contain nonimage attributes and features extracted from the image.

The various subsystems of an image information system exchange generalized icons, or iconic data structures. The image information system exchanges information with another information system by exchanging generalized icons. They may exchange image as well as nonimage information. Icons can be transmitted progressively over the communications network: first the icon's label, then the nonimage attributes (if any), followed by the image features and the indexes and a crude (low resolution) image, then a more refined image, and finally the image in its full resolution.

Icons allow partial, distributed, and personalized indexing. Some icons may have built-in indexes. Finally, the various icons are sent to the workstation, which integrates the icons, fuses the images, resolves the logical interpretations, and presents the resulting images and nonimage data to the user.

Generalized icons imply an object-oriented viewpoint [28,27]. However, both the extended relational approach and the object-oriented approach may be used in the actual implementation. How much object orientedness is enough? Do we still require an extensive data model, or will a "minimalist" approach, based upon the notion of icons, be preferable? Such issues require careful consideration.

B. *Active Indexes*

Currently, many image information systems are being implemented, but they typically do not employ new data models, nor do they support image indexing. The unavailability of content-based indexing leads to the user's claim that they do not need content-based indexing. However, this may be due to the user's inability to perceive usefulness of indexing.

We can find evidence from experimental psychology, where indexing is the identification of the particular image "chunk", or feature, to function as a starting point of a given cognitive visual routine. According to such studies, indexing (problem of initial access) accounts for a large percentage of the variance in human performance on information extraction tasks [32]. Symbolic operations (such as searching for an item in memory) are in the order of 1200 ms [35], while indexing operations are around 100–300 ms [46]. Direct indexing is indexing a visual item directly without the need for searching the rest of the contents of an image. This is possible, when the target is specified by a combination of local features such as color, curvature, line terminations, etc., and shares only one such feature in common with the other (irrelevant) items in the image. The time required for direct indexing is independent of the rest of the image contents and is on the order of approximately 30 ms [46].

Our goal should be to fully exploit the potential of computer vision and feature-based indexing, so that we can push such technologies to the limit, to support image information systems. We can use supercomputers to do the computer vision and feature extraction work. Massively parallel architecture should also be exploited to support active indexing.

One central research issue for image information systems is how to construct feature-based indexes automatically or at least semi-automatically. The indexes should be highly flexible, with the following characteristics:

(1) An active index instead of a passive index: the index can be used to initiate actions.

(2) A partial index instead of a total index: only a few objects or images are indexed.

(3) A dynamic index instead of a static index: the index can evolve, grow, and shrink.

(4) A visible index instead of a transparent index: the user is aware of the existence of the index, perhaps as part of the knowledge structure. So the index is not necessarily transparent.

(5) An imprecise index instead of a precise index: the index can be used to answer imprecise or approximate queries.

With active index, we can have smart images that can respond to accessing, probing, and other actions. Image integrity constraints will enable the smart images to behave according to the user's specifications [37]. Conceptually, the image integrity rules are input (as part of the domain knowledge) to the spatial reasoning stage of the three-stage model illustrated in Fig. 2. In reality, they may be part of the multilevel image data model discussed previously.

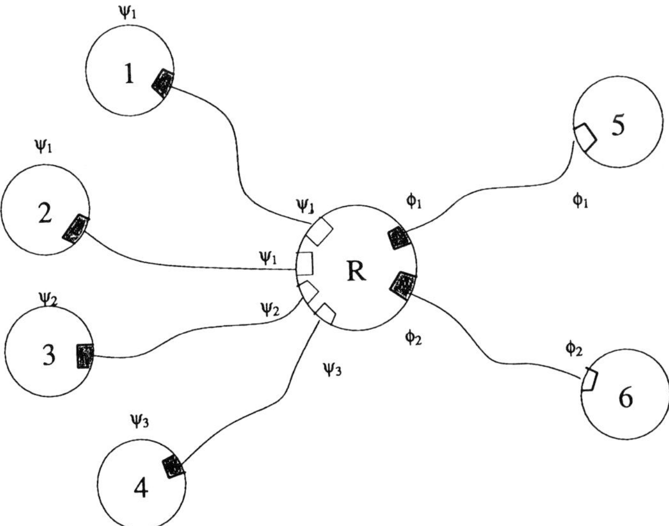

Fig. 10. Active index cell.

Figure 10 illustrates an active index cell. Each cell has a number of input slots and output slots. Each input slot (white slots) is connected to the output slot (black slots) of another cell, and each output slot is connected to an input slot of another cell. The connected pair of input and output slots must have the same predicate. A cell R is enabled if a token satisfying the input predicate flows into the cell. When the cell R is fired, one token each will flow to the input slot of another cell provided that the token satisfies the output predicate.

When several input slots have identical predicates, then they must all have tokens satisfying the predicate, before R is enabled. The equivalent Petri-net structure is shown in Fig. 11.

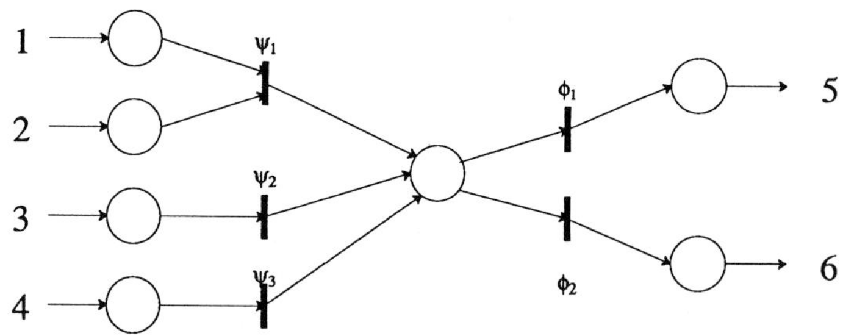

Fig. 11. Equivalent Petri-net structure.

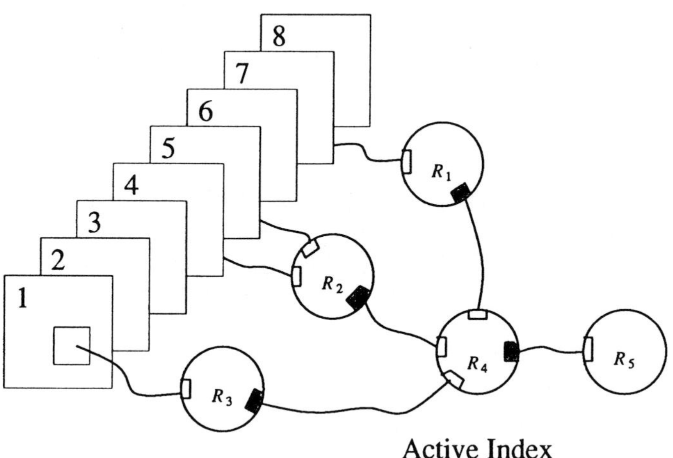

Fig. 12. Image database with active index.

Fig. 12 shows an image database with an active index, where R1 is an index on image 7, $R2$ is index on images 4 and 5, and $R3$ is an index on objects in image 1.

Feature extraction algorithms are needed to extract features from the images and these become input tokens to the cells $R1$, $R2$, and $R3$. The active index can then activate other cells, leading to the firing of the primary cell (maybe an icon in the user's window). Using this approach, "hot spots" in images can be defined, which are then connected to the first level active index cells. A latent query can be defined for a hot spot so that, for example, an alarm message is generated when the fire front reaches the city. Since the active index can be changed into a passive one, by input/output reversal, we can also use the index structure to perform normal search operations.

VII. Conclusion: Toward Smart Images

Generalized icons and active indexes, considered together, lead to smart images. Smart images can behave differently in different environments. They become crisper when the user needs better resolution, and become more blurry when there is no such requirement. Supported by semantic progressive transmission algorithms [31], smart images of multiple modalities can be visualized at different resolutions based upon user needs, through image fusion and image superposition. Supported by active indexing, smart images can initiate appropriate actions or react to user manipulation. Smart images can point to other images as an index. In other words, images can be used to depict other images.

In conclusion, to develop the next generation of active image information systems, we envision the confluence of active database, Petri nets, neural nets, image processing, artificial intelligence, data modeling, and object-oriented systems. Many research issues need to be explored.

Acknowledgment

The authors gratefully acknowledge the permission of Dr. Jungert to use Fig. 4. Figs. 5 and 6 are from [21]. Fig. 8 is from [16]. Fig. 9 was prepared by Brent Baxter.

References

[1] A. D. Bimbo, M. Campanai and P Nesi, Using 3D spatial relationships for image retrieval by contents, Tech. Rep., Univ. of Florence, Italy 1992.

[2] M. L. Brodie, On the development of data models, in *On Conceptual Modeling*, M. L. Brodie, J. Mylopoulos, and J. W. Schmidt, eds. (Springer-Verlag, New York, 1984) 19–48.

[3] P. Butterworth, A. Otis and J. Stein, The GemsStone object management system, *Commun. ACM* Oct. (1991) 64–77.

[4] N. S. Chang and K. S. Fu, Query-by-pictorial example, *IEEE Trans. Software Eng.* **6** (1980) 519–524.

[5] S. K. Chang, Q. Shi and C. Yan, Iconic indexing by 2-D strings, *IEEE Trans. Patt. Anal. Mach. Intell.* **9** May (1987) 413–428.

[6] S. K. Chang, C. W. Yan, T. Arndt and D. Dimitroff, An intelligent image database system, *IEEE Trans. Software Eng.* May (1988) 681–688.

[7] S. K. Chang, *Principles of Pictorial Information Systems Design* (Prentice-Hall, Englewood Cliffs, NJ, 1990).

[8] S. K. Chang and E. Jungert, Pictorial data management based upon the theory of symbolic projections, *J. Visual Lang. Comput.* **2**, 3 (1991) 195–215.

[9] S. K. Chang, M. F. Costabile and S. Levialdi, A framework for intelligent visual interface design for database systems, in *Proc. Int. Workshop on Interfaces to Database Systems*, Scotland, July 1–3, 1992.

[10] S. K. Chang, Active index for smart images, Tech. Rep., Univ. of Pittsburgh, May 1992.

[11] S. K. Chang and E. Jungert, The sigma-tree — A symbolic spatial data structure, in *Proc. Int. Conf. on Pattern Recognition*, The Hague, The Netherlands, Aug. 29–31, 1992.

[12] M. Chock, A. F. Cardenas and A. Klinger, Database structure and manipulation capabilities of a picture data base management system (PICDMS), *IEEE Trans. Patt. Anal. Mach. Intell.* **5** (1984) 484–492.

[13] P. R. Cohen, M. L. Greenberg, D. M. Hart and A. E. Howe, Trial by fire: Understanding the design requirements for agents in complex environments, *Al Mag.* (1989) 32–48.

[14] D. B. Farmer, R. King and D. A. Myers, The semantic database constructor, *IEEE Trans. Software Eng.* **11** (1985) 583–591.

[15] F. Fierens, J. Van Cleynenbreugle, P. Suetens and A. Oosterlinck, A software environment for image database research, *J. Visual Lang. Comput.* **3** (1992) 49–68.

[16] R. G. Fraser and J. A. P. Pare, *Diagnosis of Diseases of the Chest* (W. B. Saunders, Philadelphia, PA, 1970) 381.

[17] W. L. Gosky, Iconic indexing using generalized pattern matching techniques, in *Computer Vision, Graphics, and Image Processing* (Academic, New York 1986) 308–403.

[18] W. L. Gosky and Z. Jiang, A hierarchical approach to feature indexing, in *SPIE/IS&T Conf. on Image Storage and Retrieval System*, Feb. 1992, 9–20.

[19] A. Gupta, T. Weymouth and R. Jain, Semantic queries with pictures: The VIMSYS model, in *Proc. VLDB'91*, Spain, 1991, 69–79.

[20] R. Gupta and E. Horowitz, *Object-Oriented Database with Applications to CASE, Networks and VLSI CAD* (Prentice-Hall, Englewood Cliffs, NJ, 1991).

[21] P. D. Holmes, Using connectivity graphs to support map-related reasoning, M. S. thesis, Dept. Comput. Inform. Sci., Linköping Univ., 1991.

[22] T. Y. Hou *et al.*, A contact-based indexing technique using relative geometry features, in *Proc. SPIE/IS&T Symp. on Electronic Imaging Science and Technology*, San Jose, CA, 1992, 59–68.

[23] H. V. Jagadish and L. O'Gorman, An object-oriented model for image recognition, *IEEE Comput.* **22** (1989) 33–41.

[24] H. V. Jagadish, A retrieval technique for similar shapes, in *Proc. 1991 ACM SIGMOD Int. Conf. on Management of Data* **20**, 2 (1991) 208–217.

[25] T. Joseph and A. F. Cardenas, Picquery: A high level query language for pictorial database management, *IEEE Trans. Software Eng.* **14**, May (1988) 630–638.

[26] E. Jungert and S. K. Chang, An algebra for symbolic image manipulation and transformation, in *Visual Database Systems* (North-Holland, Amsterdam, 1989) 301–317.

[27] W. Kim and F. Lochovsky, eds., *Object-Oriented Concepts, Databases, and Applications* (Addison-Wesley, Reading, MA, 1989).

[28] W. Kim, Object-oriented databases: Definition and research directions, *IEEE Trans. Knowl. Data Eng.* **2**, Sept. (1990) 327–341.

[29] A. Klinger and A. Pizano, Visual structures and data bases, in *Visual Database Systems* (North-Holland, Amsterdam, 1989) 3–25.

[30] P. Kofkis, A. Karmirantzos, Y. Kavaklis and S. Orphasnoudakis, Image archiving by content: An object-oriented approach, in *Proc. SPIE Medical Imaging IV: PACS System Design and Evaluation*, vol. 1234, 1990.

[31] P. Liu, T. Hou, A. Hsu and M. Chiu, Semantic-based progressive image transmission, private communications, 1992.

[32] J. Lohse, A cognitive model for the perception and understanding of graphs, in *Proc. CHI91*, New Orleans, 1991, 137–144.

[33] R. Mehrotra and W. I. Grosky, REMINDS: A relational model-based integrated image and test database management system, in *Proc. IEEE Workshop on Computer Architecture for Pattern Analysis and Image Database Management*, Miami Beach, FL, 1985, 348–354.

[34] ______, Shape matching utilizing indexed hypotheses generation and testing, *IEEE Trans. Robot. Automat.* **5**, Feb. (1989) 70–77.

[35] J. R. Olson and G. M. Olson, The growth of cognitive modeling in human–computer interaction since GOMS, *Human Comput. Interaction* (1990).

[36] "Ontos," in *Ontos System Documentation*, Burlington, MA, 1991.

[37] A. Pizano, A. Klinger and A. F. Cardenas, Specification of spatial integrity constraints in pictorial databases, *IEEE Comput.* Dec. (1989) 59–71.

[38] F. Rabitti and P. Stanchev, GRIM_DBMS: A GRaphical IMage DataBase Management System, in *Visual Database Systems* (North-Holland, Amsterdam, 1989) 415–430.

[39] N. Rossoupoulos *et al.*, An efficient pictorial database system for PSQL, *IEEE Trans. Software Eng.* **14**, May (1988) 639–650.

[40] L. G. Shapiro and R. M. Haralick, Organization of relational models for scene analysis, *IEEE Trans. Patt. Anal. Mach. Intell.* **4** (1982) 595–602.

[41] O. R. L. Sheng and C.-P. Wei, Object-oriented modeling and design of knowledge-base/database system, in *Proc. Eighth Int. Conf. on Data Engineering*, Tempe, AZ, 1992, 87–102.

[42] *Informix Products for Document Imaging*, Informix Software, Lenexa, KS, Jan. 1991.

[43] H. D. Tagare, C. C. Jaffe and J. S. Duncan, Requirements for medical image databases, Tech. Rep., School of Medicine, Yale Univ., Jan. 1992.

[44] H. D. Tagare, G. R. Gindi, J. S. Duncan and C. C. Jaffe, A geometric indexing schema for an image library, *Computer Assisted Radiology* (1991) 513–518.

[45] G. Y. Tang, A management system for an integrated database of pictures and alphanumeric data, *Comput. Graphics Image Process.* **16** (1981) 270–286.

[46] A. Treisman, Search asymmetry: A diagnostic for preattentive processing of separable features, *J. Experiment. Psychol. General* **114** (1985) 285–310.

[47] "UniSQL", *UniSQL System Documentation*, Austin, TX, 1991.

SUBJECT INDEX

f. — following page, *ff.* — following pages